# Technology, Globalization, and Sustainable Development

# TECHNOLOGY, GLOBALIZATION, AND SUSTAINABLE DEVELOPMENT

## Transforming the Industrial State

**NICHOLAS A. ASHFORD**

**RALPH P. HALL**

Yale UNIVERSITY PRESS

New Haven & London

Yale University Press books may be purchased in quantity for educational, business, or promotional use. For information, please e-mail sales.press@yale.edu (U.S. office) or sales@yaleup.co.uk (U.K. office).

Set in Times 10 and Scala Sans type by Westchester Book Group, Danbury, CT
Printed in the United States of America

Library of Congress Control Number: 2011927542
ISBN 978-0-300-16972-0 (alk. paper)

A catalogue record for this book is available from the British Library.

This paper meets the requirements of ANSI/NISO Z39.48-1992 (Permanence of Paper).

10 9 8 7 6 5 4 3 2 1

*To those who seek to understand and meet the sustainable development challenge ahead.*

# Contents

# Detailed Table of Contents

# Illustrations

**Tables**

**Boxes**

# Preface

Technology, Globalization, and Sustainable Development explores the rich and multidimensional elements of sustainable development. This book grew out of courses taught over the past decade at the Massachusetts Institute of Technology, Cambridge University, and the Harvard-Cyprus International Institute for the Environment and Public Health, now associated with the Cyprus University of Technology. More recently, the course was offered at Virginia Tech.

During the first decade of the twenty-first century, there has been a significant increase in academic and societal interest in sustainable development, which has been accompanied by important political and legal changes. Although some scholars continue to insist that the concept is vague and unwieldy, this writing seeks to explore the rich and multidimensional elements of sustainability and, further, to offer an integrative, transdisciplinary approach to policy design for its attainment. Sustainability and the related concepts of development, globalization, and economic and environmental justice are interwoven with technological, organizational, institutional, and social changes and with trade as drivers of the transformation of industrial and industrializing societies.

The Schumpeterian notion of technological innovation as "the engine of growth" is being challenged as the globalization of trade is increasingly recognized to be an additional and different driving force for growth of industrial economies. With the establishment of the World Trade Organization (WTO) implementing the General Agreement on Tariffs and Trade (GATT), the North American Free Trade Agreement (NAFTA), and other trading regimes, serious questions have been raised concerning the effects of global trade on sustainability. These effects must be viewed broadly to include not only a healthy economic base but also a sound environment, stable employment with adequate purchasing power, distributional equity, national self-reliance, maintenance of cultural integrity, and social inclusion.

Different trading regimes treat environment and labor standards differently, sometimes regarding more stringent regulatory requirements as illegal nontariff trade barriers. This book explores the many dimensions of sustainability and the use of national, multinational, and international political and legal mechanisms to further sustainable development. The interrelationship of technological change, economic growth, industrial development, employment, and the environment is examined in the context of theories of trade, employment, and regulation and of the importance of networks and organizational innovation and learning. Policies for resolving the apparent conflicts among development, the environment, and employment are explored in generating a different vision for the future.

This book draws extensively on both American and European writings on social and political theory; management science; industrial, labor, and environmental economics; ecological economics; and environmental and international law. Students from a variety of courses of study in three countries have taken the courses on which this work has been developed, and it is hoped that this book can be taught in programs of schools of engineering, management and economics, industrial relations, law, science, public health, and international relations and political science beyond the American venue.

This work can serve both as a comprehensive reference book on the many aspects of sustainable development and as a textbook that would ideally be taught on a multidisciplinary team basis. However, parts of the book could also be incorporated into existing conventional curricula. For example, Chapter 2 (in Part I and in its expanded form on the website accompanying this text), "The Emergence of Sustainable Development," is relevant for courses in history, sociology, and political science. Chapters 3, 4, and 5 (Part II) would be valuable in courses on economic growth and development in economics departments, schools of management, and international relations programs. Chapters 6, 7, and 8 ideally fit into courses on innovation and industrial policy in both engineering and management schools. Chapters 9 and 10 (Part IV) and Chapter 11 are dedicated to national, regional, and international environmental law and could be taught in law schools, international relations programs, political science, and schools of public health. Chapter 12 is an expansive treatment of international finance for development and the environment suitable for schools of management and departments of economics and political science.

Thus a number of selected chapters from this work could easily fill several traditional courses in different departments, but the entire book offers an opportunity for a transdisciplinary course that cuts across departments and schools, which is the trend in many forward-looking programs.

# Acknowledgments

We wish not only to acknowledge the support of our families during this challenging effort but also to thank the students, scholars, writers, and public servants from whom we have learned so much. We also thank our colleagues at the Massachusetts Institute of Technology, Cambridge University, the Cyprus University of Technology, and Virginia Tech who understood the importance of crossing disciplinary lines and engaging in transdisciplinary thinking.

This work has been in development for more than a decade and has benefited from the keen insight and inquisitive minds of hundreds of students and numerous colleagues. We are indebted to all those who have played a part in enriching the writing of this work. In particular, we would like to thank Charlotte Neve De Mevergnies, Kate Parrot, Claire Lunn, and Mark Venema and Georgios Triantafyllou for their early but significant contributions to Chapters 5, 7, 10, and 12, respectively, and Kyriakos Pierrakakis for his contributions to Chapters 3 and 4. We are also grateful to Professor Robert H. Ashford of Syracuse Law School, who contributed original writing and thinking on binary economics found in Chapter 12. Finally, we thank Ambuj Sagar and Mark Stoughton for their assistance in organizing a course on sustainability, trade, and the environment from which this published book ultimately emerged.

Financial support to accommodate a face-to-face meeting of the authors during the preparation of the finished draft was provided by the Ridenour Fellowship Fund in the School of Public and International Affairs at Virginia Tech.

# Overview

## 0.1 INTRODUCTION

Like other books with the word "sustainability" in the title, the motivation of this work stems from a dissatisfaction with the current state of the world and from a desire to identify those policies and strategies that will transform firms, institutions, governments, and societies in a more positive direction. We will argue that the main driving forces that have sent us in the wrong direction are the same forces, but differently fashioned and designed, that could be used to reverse course and improve the state of the world. These forces fall under the broad heading of technology and trade or, more strictly speaking, technology and globalization. We hope that the prescriptions discussed in this work will not be regarded as utopian. Indeed, it may be difficult to decide precisely on the right course of action, but a major accomplishment would be to deepen our understanding of, and refrain from continuing, those policies and strategies that are clearly wrongheaded. It is also important to acknowledge that there are many more ways to do it wrong than to get it right. But understanding the history, mistakes, and successes of industrialization, economic change, and policy formulation and implementation is an essential step in getting it right.

There are those who argue that the economic system and the political system are the things that primarily need fixing, and, to a certain extent, they are right. But, as will be shown, there is much more that needs fixing. Systemic difficulties are central to understanding the unsustainable industrial state, and both economic and political dynamics affect the extent and direction of technological advance and social change. But it is also true that social and cultural attitudes influence the direction of policy, both through markets and through the political choices we make. Because there are important interacting elements that need to be put in place to achieve more sustainable transformations, we will argue that holistic and integrated policy design, as distinct from mere coordination of policies, is essential. As Costanza and Daly (1991) argue, achieving a more sustainable world requires transdisciplinary approaches involving democratic, participatory governance. A transdisciplinary perspective is what characterizes the analysis and recommendations emanating from this work.

## 0.2 THE MULTIDIMENSIONAL CHARACTER OF SUSTAINABILITY

The concept of sustainability and, indeed, most of the writings on sustainable development most often conjure up *environmental* sustainability. We will argue that the three essential pillars of sustainable development must necessarily focus on a broader set of policies for improving *competitiveness;*\* *the environment and public and worker health and safety*; and *meaningful and well-paid employment and earning capacity.*

The relationship between industrialization and its effects on the environment has captured the serious attention of national governments and international organizations, especially in light of increasing international trade and globalization. Sustainability in products, processes, and services has been increasingly emphasized by placing the environment (or at least climate change) at the center of some industrial transformations or on a par with competitiveness. The key to *environmental* sustainability was recognized early as involving the design and implementation of environmentally sound products, processes, and services rather than addressing environmental concerns as an afterthought in industrial systems. At the same time at which the environment has become more important in economic policy, European as well as American industrial economies have also begun to pay attention to the restructuring of labor markets to reflect changes brought about by or anticipated from new and emerging technologies, new environmental

priorities, particularly global climate change, and globalization. However, unlike recent initiatives addressing environmental issues, these policies have been largely reactive rather than proactive toward new job creation and better organization of work.

In addition to the environment, work and the workplace are essential elements of industrial and industrializing economies. Human effort (work) is combined with physical and natural capital to produce goods and services. The workplace is the marketplace where workers and owners or managers exchange their contributions, with the transfer of financial capital as wages providing purchasing power for those workers. Beyond markets, work provides both a means of engagement of people in society and an important social environment and mechanism for enhancing self-esteem. Finally, work is the main means of distributing wealth and generating purchasing power in dynamic national economic systems. There is a complex relationship between employment and the increasingly environmentally unsustainable and globalizing economy. The changing nature of industrial economies presents new challenges and opportunities for the organization of work, as well as for the environment, in both industrialized and industrializing countries.

Just as thinking about the environment before industrial development is planned and implemented is necessary to optimize environmental quality, consideration of labor concerns also requires deliberate and intelligent actions before embarking on (re)industrialization efforts in guiding industrial transformations. The recent downturn of the extraordinarily long economic boom and the financial crisis that began in 2008 might be expected to reveal fundamental structural employment problems in the industrialized world that were not previously appreciated. It is likely that employment considerations will be the central issue in the coming decade for countries in the expanding European Union, as well as for the United States and the developing world, and employment concerns will influence the nature and direction of (re)industrialization and the growth of the manufacturing and service economies. It is therefore timely to explore options and opportunities for co-optimizing economic development, environmental quality, and labor and employment concerns.[†]

---

\*     Competitiveness can have two different meanings: (1) improvements in "competition" that yield higher national or corporate revenues and market share, or (2) the ability of the nation-state to provide the necessary goods and services to the largest possible segment of its populations. As the remainder of this book will reveal, policies directed at these two different formulations of competitiveness can be very different and have different consequences.

---

†     Co-optimization will be a central theme throughout this book and describes the fashioning and implementation of policies and initiatives that achieve multiple goals without sacrificing one for another, that is, reaching an optimum described as achieving "a proper balance," that is, a compromise among goals.

## 0.3 THE UNSUSTAINABLE INDUSTRIAL STATE

Those who argue that the industrialized state, whether developed or developing, is currently unsustainable emphasize a number of problems. These are depicted schematically in Figure 0.1. A key problem is the failure of government to provide—either directly or indirectly through the private sector—an adequate supply of, and access to, essential goods and services for all its citizens. Here the term "adequate" can be considered to mean the ability of citizens to enjoy a decent standard of living. This, of course, constitutes what is agreed to be acceptable minimum welfare and is likely to differ among countries and over time, but which can be determined for a specific context. Goods and services include manufactured goods, food, housing, transportation, and information and communication technology (ICT), among others. The environmental problems include toxic pollution (which directly affects public and worker health and safety), climate change, resource depletion, and problems related to the loss of biodiversity and ecosystem integrity. The environmental burdens—and efforts to ameliorate them—are felt unequally within nations, among nations, and among generations, giving rise

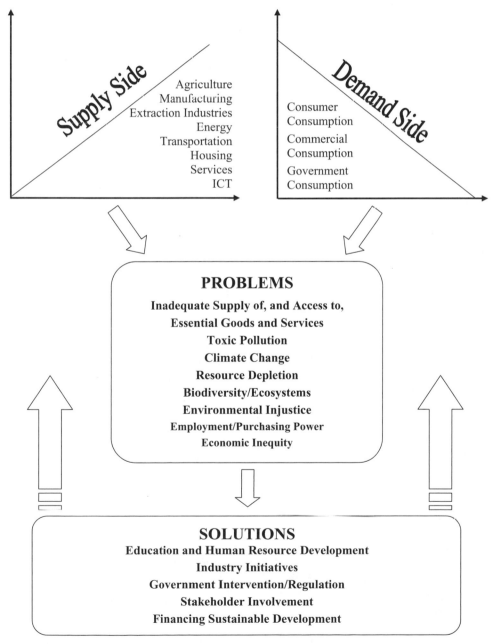

FIGURE 0.1: THE ORIGINS OF UNSUSTAINABILITY PROBLEMS IN THE INDUSTRIAL STATE AND POSSIBLE SOLUTIONS

to international, intranational, and intergenerational equity concerns that are often expressed as "environmental injustice." All three kinds of maldistributions are important.

The environmental problems stem from activities concerned with agriculture, manufacturing, extraction, transportation, housing, energy, and services—all driven by the demands of consumers, commercial entities, and government. In addition, there are effects of these activities on the amount, security, and skill of employment, the nature and conditions of work, and purchasing power associated with wages. An increasing concern is economic inequity stemming from inadequate and unequal purchasing power and earning capacity within and among nations and for the workers and citizens of the future.

Whether solutions involving education and human resource development, industry initiatives, government intervention, stakeholder involvement, and financing can resolve these unsustainability problems depends on their potential for correcting a number of fundamental flaws (the systemic problems mentioned earlier) in the characteristics of the industrial state:

1.  *The fragmentation and inadequacy of the knowledge base*, resulting in a lack of understanding of the complex origin and interrelatedness of problems and the need for integrated solutions rather than unidisciplinarily designed and/or single-purpose solutions

2.  *The inequality of access to economic and political power* among people and nations and between individuals and corporations or business organizations

3.  *The tendency toward gerontocracy*, whereby there is technological and political lock-in, usually, but not always, accompanied by concentration of economic and political power

4.  *The failure of markets* and of the policies that shape market transactions to price correctly the adverse human and environmental consequences of industrial activity

5.  *The limitations of perfectly working markets* due to (a) *disparate time horizons*, whereby costs must be incurred now to solve problems whose solutions yield benefits later, sometimes in generations to come, which are discounted in value in present terms and therefore receive inadequate attention, and (b) *the delay in recognizing problems* with current industrialization and consumption, such that responses come very late (for example, the failure to perceive limits to growth), both of which cause inappropriate production and consumption patterns to persist

6.  *The failure to engage individuals (workers and citizens) in society* to realize their human potential, resulting in social exclusion

7.  *A high-throughput industrial system*, driven by ever-increasing material and energy consumption

8.  *An addiction to growth and productivity*

9.  *Corruption**

## 0.4 GLOBALIZATION

Globalization affects four major areas important for sustainable development: (1) the production of goods and services (which we will call industrial globalization), (2) the mobility of knowledge and information, (3) capital mobility, and (4) the international movement of labor and human resources, and migration. All these present opportunities and challenges for sustainable development.

The mobility of knowledge and information is facilitated both through changes in the locus of production and services (otherwise known as the international division of labor) and through advances in ICT, such as the Internet and wireless technologies. Capital mobility has in turn been greatly enhanced by ICT. Both financial and knowledge mobility allow almost instantaneous transfer of money and information, a radical departure from the industrial system of twenty years ago.

In the context of industrial and commercial production, the term "globalization" has at least three distinct meanings (Gordon 1995), with different implications for the environment and for workers and working life. First, "internationalization" is the expansion of product and service markets abroad, facilitated by ICT and e-commerce, with the locus of production remaining within the parent country. Second, "multinationalization" occurs when a (multinational) company establishes production or service facilities abroad to be nearer to foreign markets and/or to take advantage of more industry-friendly labor, environmental, and tax policies while maintaining research-and-development (R&D) and innovation-centered activities in the parent country. The third meaning of industrial globalization is the creation of strategic

---

*      Corruption is more than the misappropriation of funds or unjustifiably favoring a firm or person in government dealings. We argue that it includes the perversion of governmental responsibility implicit in the social contract, such as failing to enact, monitor, or enforce environmental, public health, antitrust, banking, economic, labor, social, and other regulations or legislation that protects or promotes the public welfare. In the United States, the 2008 financial and mortgage industry breakdown stands out as the most recent example.

alliances, what might be called "transnationalization," in which two different foreign enterprises merge or share their R&D and other capabilities to create a new entity or product line or service. Those concerned with enhancing trade are especially worried about barriers to internationalization, while those concerned with possible erosion of labor and environmental standards bemoan the consequences of multinationalization. Multinationalization and transnationalization may lead to industrial restructuring, with unpredictable consequences for national economies. Indeed, some corporations doing business in the global marketplace have larger annual cash flows than many small countries. All three kinds of globalization raise questions of excessive market, and hence political, power where concerns for profits overwhelm democratic and ethical values, even if international nongovernmental organizations, such as Greenpeace, or international institutions, such as the International Labour Organization (ILO), challenge their activities.

Globalization raises new challenges for governance, especially vis-à-vis the roles of government, workers, and citizens in the new economic order. Within nation-states, the extent to which the externalities of production—adverse health, safety, and environmental effects—are internalized differs according to the differential success of regulation and compensation regimes and the extent to which economies incorporate the ethics of fair play into their practices. There has been a constant struggle to establish good environmental and labor standards and practices within nations. With the advent of globalized, competition-driven markets, attention has now shifted to the harmonization of standards through multilateral environmental agreements and ILO conventions, with only a modicum of success. Countries are slow to give up national autonomy, and only where there is a trend toward significant economic integration (as in the European Union [EU]) are there successes at harmonization. But globalization has brought an even more complex set of challenges through the creation of trade regimes—such as the World Trade Organization (WTO), the Association of Southeast Asian Nations (ASEAN), and the North American Free Trade Agreement (NAFTA)—where the term "free trade" means the elimination (or equalization) of tariffs and so-called nontariff trade barriers, which, in practice, place environmental and labor standards at odds with trade objectives. Free trade may not be fair trade.

The trade regimes promote international laissez-faire commerce; and rights-based laws and protections and market economics have become competing paradigms for public policy and governance. Government plays very different roles when it acts as a facilitator or arbitrator to resolve competing interests than when it acts as a trustee of citizen and worker interests to ensure a fair outcome of industrial transformations (N. A. Ashford 2002). The differences are pronounced when stakeholders have significantly disparate power, or when some are not represented in the political process, as in the case of emerging or new technology-based firms.

John Rawls argues that no transformation in a society should occur unless those who are worse off are made relatively better off (Rawls 1971). Operationalizing a Rawlsian world has its difficulties, but law operates to create certain essential rights that enable just and sustainable transformations.* These include the right to a healthy and safe environment, products, and workplace; citizen and worker right to know; the right to participate in decisions affecting one's working and nonworking life; and the right to benefit from the transformation of the state or global economy. Struggles won at the national level are now being eroded by a shift in the locus of commerce. Without consensus about fair play and the trustee institutions to ensure fair distributions from, and practices in, the new global economy, equity and justice cannot be achieved. It is now agreed that future development must be "sustainable," but that means different things to different commentators.

## 0.5 DRIVERS OF ECONOMIC GROWTH AND DEVELOPMENT

### 0.5.1 Strategies to Enhance Competitiveness

We have already argued that sustainable development must be seen as a broad concept, incorporating concerns for the economy, the environment, and employment. All three are driven or affected both by technological innovation (Schumpeter 1939) and by globalized trade (Diwan and Walton 1997; Ekins, Folke, et al. 1994). They are also in a fragile balance, are interrelated, and need to be addressed together in a coherent and mutually reinforcing way (N. A. Ashford 2001).

Technological innovation and trade drive national economies in different ways (Charles and Lehner 1998). The former exploits a nation's innovative potential, the latter its excess production capacity. Innovation-based performance is enhanced by technological innovation and changing product markets,

---

* For an argument that law is essential for achieving just transformations, see Dernbach (2008).

characterized by fluid, competitive production, often with the upskilling of labor. Innovation-based strategies have positive impacts in both domestic and international markets. In contrast, cost-reduction strategies are enhanced by increased scales of production and/or automation, usually characterized by rigid, mature monopolistic production, the shedding and deskilling of labor, the saturation of domestic markets, increased reliance on trade, and the location of production where wages and health, safety, and environmental costs are minimized. Economies seeking to exploit new international markets may enjoy short-term benefits from revenues gained as a result of production using existing excess capacity, but they may ultimately find themselves behind the technological curve. In contrast, performance-driven markets, which capitalize on first-mover advantages, may be slower to gain profits but may outlast markets driven by cost-reduction strategies that are unable to compete with emergent and disrupting innovations.*

### 0.5.2 The Consequences of Different Industrial Strategy Options for Workers

Increasing labor productivity, defined as output per unit of labor input, is a concern in nations pursuing either strategy to encourage economic growth. But labor productivity can be improved in different ways: (1) by utilizing better tools, hardware, software, and manufacturing systems; (2) by increasing workers' skills; and (3) by a better matching of labor with physical and natural capital and with ICT. Theoretically, increasing worker productivity lowers the costs of goods and services, thereby lowering prices and ultimately increasing the demand for and sale of goods and services. It can be argued that at least in some markets, more workers may be subsequently hired than displaced as a consequence of needing fewer workers to produce a given quantity of goods and services.[†] This optimistic scenario assumes a continual throughput society with increasing consumption. However, the drive toward increased consumption may

have dire consequences for the environment (Daly 1991). In addition, questions arise whether, in practice, (1) labor is valued and paid more or less after productivity improvements, (2) there are positive or negative effects on job tenure and security, and (3) more workers are hired than displaced. The answers depend on the sources of the increases in worker productivity and the basis of a nation's competitiveness. Giving workers better technologies to work with may increase their productivity, but not their *productiveness*; that is, the labor content of, and contribution to, the product or service may have actually decreased. Here it is *capital* productiveness that has increased. Increasing workers' skills, even if the technologies of production remain unchanged, can increase both worker productivity and worker productiveness, the latter reflecting an increase in the contribution that labor makes to the production of goods or services. Better matching of skills to technology artifacts may yield synergistic effects, increasing labor productivity and both labor and capital productiveness.

A sector or national economy that increases its competitiveness through innovation-based performance presents opportunities for skill enhancement and higher-paying jobs, whereas pursuing competitiveness through cost-reduction strategies focuses on lean production (with worker displacement), flexible labor markets, and knowledge increasingly embodied in hardware and software rather than in human capital. The consequences of these two strategies for workers are different. The former strategy rewards and encourages skill acquisition for many, with appropriate financial benefits for those workers. The latter creates a division between workers: some are necessarily upskilled, but the skill content of many is reduced. Different national strategies might be pursued, reflecting different domestic preferences and culture, but there are further implications, depending on the extent to which trade drives the economy. Interestingly, while the United States was globalizing and focusing on expanding markets abroad, the EU was selling a smaller amount and percentage of goods and services outside its borders and was focusing instead on integrating its internal markets in which its various members compete on performance (Kleinknecht and ter Wengel 1998). In the United States, wage disparities are large and increasing, while in some parts of the EU, notably the Netherlands, wage disparities are much smaller and decreasing. The economic crisis of 2008 has exacerbated disparities in income throughout the world.

Even before the crisis of 2008, the changing global economy presented challenges for all nations as con-

---

*        See the discussion later in this chapter of the important distinction between sustaining and disrupting innovation.

†        Robert Ayres (2006) observes, "Information technology has exemplified the feedback cycle and the rebound effect. Costs have fallen, prices have followed and demand has risen in consequence. But IT [information technology] is not the panacea for the economy as a whole, unless it results in dramatically lower costs and increased demand for all other tangible goods and services the society needs. Up to now the applications of IT outside its own sector seem to be eliminating more jobs than it creates, but without significant corresponding impacts on consumer demand for products and services that would create more jobs" (ibid., p. 1194)

cerns about the number of jobs, job security, wages, and occupational health and safety increased. In the private sector, labor needs a role in choosing and implementing information-based and labor-affecting technologies. In the public sector, there is a need to integrate industrial development policies with those of employment, occupational health and safety, and the environment. The following strategic changes are expected to influence firms to use labor more effectively:

- Distinguishing productiveness from productivity
- Striving for an innovation-enhancing rather than a cost-reduction strategy
- Investing in increasing the capacity of human resources rather than replacing labor with capital
- Paying attention to the human/technology interface
- Advancing beneficial industrial relations in the nation, sector, or firm
- Investing in education and training
- Using economic incentives to maximize human resource use and improvement
- Taxing pollution and carbon content of energy sources rather than labor

From the perspective of labor, the success of these strategies requires implementation of the right to know, the right to participate, and the right to benefit from industrial transformations.

The right to know has been described elsewhere (N. A. Ashford and Caldart 2008, chap. 10) and includes citizens' and workers' right to know and have access to scientific, technological, and legal information and manufacturers' and employers' corresponding duty to inform and warn workers about this information. Scientific information includes chemical or physical hazards or risk information related to product or material ingredients, exposure, health effects, and individual or group susceptibility (N. A. Ashford, Spadafor, et al. 1990). As important as information about hazards is, information about technology is key to enable citizens and workers to play a role in reducing risks. This kind of information includes not only knowledge about pollution and accident control and prevention technology, but also technology options for industrial, agricultural, and other kinds of commercial activity. Knowing how production and services might be changed to make them inherently cleaner, safer, and healthier and the source of more rewarding, meaningful work is a sine qua non of being able to participate meaningfully in firm-based decisions. Finally, information about legal rights and obligations is crucial for using legal and political avenues for environmental and workplace improvement and redress from harm.

Workers' right to know is made operational through the right of workers to participate in (1) the technology choices of the firm (through technology bargaining and system design) (N. A. Ashford and Ayers 1987); (2) firm-based training, education, and skill enhancement; (3) the formation of national and international labor-market policies; and (4) the setting of national and international labor standards. Although national unions enable workers to work with employers through industrial relations systems, and the ILO uses a tripartite system that includes labor, management, and government, the trade regimes mentioned earlier give few or no participatory rights to labor (or environmentalists) in global economic activities that have potentially significant effects on wages and working conditions. As trade becomes an important part of national economies, this omission needs to be corrected (EC 2003, 2006). Ironically, under the WTO trade rules, importing countries can restrict imports or place countervailing duties on items that harm their environment, but it is unclear whether there is any equalizing action that can be taken if the exporting countries produce those goods unsafely or with adverse environmental effects within their own borders (see the discussion in Chapter 11). This reinforces nonenactment or nonenforcement of national health, safety, or environmental laws in the exporting countries, to the detriment of their own citizens and workers. Further, countries may be reluctant to ratify or adopt international accords, including multilateral environmental agreements or ILO conventions, in hopes of maintaining or gaining short-term competitive advantage (see the discussion in Chapter 10).

Finally, and at the core of justice in the global work life, is the right of working people to benefit from industrial transformations. The right to know and the right to participate are essential, but the ultimate rights are those of a fair division of the fruits of the industrial or industrializing state, as well as a safe and healthful workplace. This translates into sufficient job opportunities, job security, and purchasing power, as well as rewarding, meaningful, and safe employment. This cannot be left to chance or serendipitous job creation. In formulating policies for environmental sustainability, economic growth and environmental quality should be simultaneously optimized rather than having environmental interventions occur after harmful technologies are in place. Instead, we need to design and implement cleaner and inherently safer production. Employment concerns deserve no less a place in center stage; competitiveness, environment, and employment must be *co-optimized*. Systemic changes must be pursued and selected that intentionally benefit both the environment and employment. Even with better prospects for employment, in an industrial system that continues to replace labor with physical capital, increasing worker capital ownership and access to credit (R. Ashford 1998) that turns workers into owners may be an additional and necessary long-term option if disparities of wealth and income prevail.

## 0.6 CONCEPTUALIZATIONS OF SUSTAINABLE DEVELOPMENT

### 0.6.1 The Interrelatedness of the Economy, of the Environment, Health, and Safety, and of Employment and the Need to Address Them Together

It makes quite a difference whether one looks at sustainable development as just an environmental issue or as a multidimensional challenge in three dimensions: economic, environmental, and social.* We argue that competitiveness, the environment, and employment are the *operationally important* dimensions of sustainability, and these three dimensions together drive sustainable development along different pathways and go to different places than environmentally driven concerns alone, which may otherwise require trade-offs, for example, between environmental improvements and jobs. The interrelatedness of competitiveness, the environment, and employment is depicted in Figure 0.2. (In Section 12.11 in Chapter 12, we address the broader issue of enhancing

---

* The sustainability triangle is often depicted as the economy, the environment, and *social concerns*, or the economy, the environment, and *equity*. Because all policies that affect the economy and environment have social effects and because the distributional consequences of differential access to necessary goods and services and different environmental burdens have significant equity consequences, we do not relegate the third corner of the triangle to either. Instead, we argue that *employment* should occupy the third corner of the triangle because employment is the enabling activity that allows workers and citizens to achieve economic, environmental, and social well-being and because employment is the focus of traditional government concerns and policies, along with economic and environmental policies. Because an important aspect of this book focuses on changes in current government policies, the depiction of a triangle that is consistent with policy areas better serves our purposes. We argue for attention to equity within each corner and further acknowledge the importance of culture in interpreting the triangle. What is an acceptable distributional disparity in one culture is different in another, and the importance work and environment have in one system may be very different in another. Broad, participatory mechanisms of affected stakeholders are needed to account for the acceptability of different policy mixes and outcomes.

earning capacity by changes in capital ownership which can supplement or even supplant wages.)

A *sustainable development* agenda is, almost by definition, one of systems change. This is not to be confused with a (*health, safety, and) environmental policy* agenda (depicted in Table 0.1), which is explicitly effect based, and derived from that, a program of policies and legislation directed toward environmental improvements, relying on specific goals and conditions.

The *environmentally* sustainable development policy agenda focuses at least on processes (for example, related to extraction, manufacturing, transport, agriculture, energy, and construction) and may extend to more cross-cutting technological and social systems changes, but an all-encompassing sustainable development agenda deals with more than health, safety, and the environment.

In Table 0.2, note that *current strategy agendas*, even those that go beyond environmental goals, are defined as those that are focused on those policies that (1) improve profit and market share by improving performance and efficiency in current technologies or by cutting costs; (2) control pollution, make simple substitutions and changes to products and processes, conserve energy and resources, and find new energy sources; and (3) ensure an adequate supply of appropriately skilled labor, confer with workers, and provide safer and healthier workplaces. We describe these strategies as reactive vis-à-vis technological change, rather than proactive. They are usually pursued separately and by different sets of government ministries and private-sector stakeholders. At best, policies affecting competitiveness, the environment, and employment are coordinated but not integrated.

In contrast, *sustainable agendas* are those policies that focus on (1) technological changes that alter the ways goods and services are provided, (2) the prevention of pollution and the decreased use of energy and resources through more far-reaching system changes, and (3) the development of novel sociotechnical systems—involving both technological and organizational elements—that enhance the many dimensions of meaningful and rewarding employment through the integration rather than the coordination of policy design and implementation.

### 0.6.2 Sustaining and Disrupting Innovation Distinguished

The kind of innovation likely to be managed successfully by industrial corporations is relevant to the differences between current and sustainable technology agendas. We argue that the needed major product,

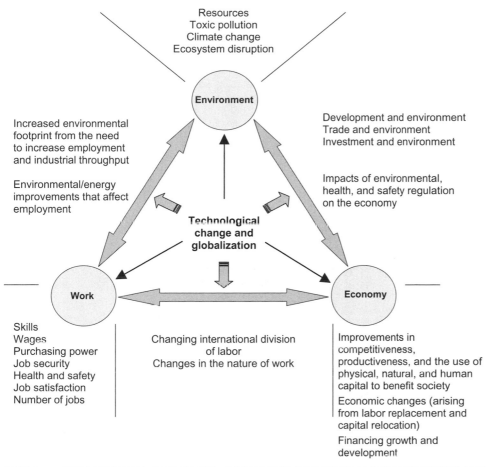

Resources
Toxic pollution
Climate change
Ecosystem disruption

Environment

Increased environmental
footprint from the need
to increase employment
and industrial throughput

Environmental/energy
improvements that affect
employment

Technological
change and
globalization

Development and environment
Trade and environment
Investment and environment

Impacts of environmental,
health, and safety regulation
on the economy

Work

Skills
Wages
Purchasing power
Job security
Health and safety
Job satisfaction
Number of jobs

Changing international division
of labor
Changes in the nature of work

Economy

Improvements in
competitiveness,
productiveness, and the use of
physical, natural, and human
capital to benefit society

Economic changes (arising
from labor replacement and
capital relocation)

Financing growth and
development

**FIGURE 0.2: TECHNOLOGICAL CHANGE AND GLOBALIZATION AS DRIVERS OF CHANGE WITHIN AND BETWEEN THREE OPERATIONALLY-IMPORTANT DIMENSIONS OF SUSTAINABILITY**

**TABLE 0.1: EVOLUTION OF APPROACHES TO HEALTH, SAFETY, AND ENVIRONMENTAL PROBLEMS**

| APPROACH | OBSERVATIONS |
|---|---|
| Dispersion of pollution and waste | The solution to pollution is dilution (ultimately leading to trans-boundary pollution) |
| End-of-pipe pollution control | Collecting wastes; workplace ventilation and protective equipment |
| | No fundamental changes in inputs, final products, or production technology |
| | Media shifting: air and water pollution → waste and workplace exposures |
| | Problem shifting: toxicity → accident potential |
| Industrial ecology: waste and material exchange and consolidation | No fundamental changes in inputs, final products, or production technology |
| Pollution prevention and cleaner technology | Improvements in eco-efficiency and energy efficiency; fundamental changes in inputs, final products, or production technology |
| Shifts to product services, system changes, and sustainable development | Restructuring of industrial, agricultural, and service industry actors and relationships involving new collaborations and actors; changes in the nature of consumer and business demand |

**TABLE 0.2: COMPARISON OF CURRENT AND SUSTAINABLE POLICY AGENDAS**

| AGENDA | COMPETITIVENESS (Economic development) | ENVIRONMENT | EMPLOYMENT |
|---|---|---|---|
| **Current** | Improve performance and efficiency | Control pollution | Reduce worker hazards |
| | Cut costs | Make simple substitutions or changes to products and processes | Maintain dialogue with workers on working conditions and terms of employment |
| | | Conserve energy and resources; find new energy sources | Ensure supply of adequately trained people |
| **Sustainable** | Change the nature of meeting market needs through radical or disrupting innovation (a systems change) | Prevent pollution through system changes | Radical improvement in human-technology interfaces (a systems change) |
| | Transition toward product services | Design environmentally-sound products and processes | Design inherently safe products and processes |
| | Change the nature of demand by cultural transformation | Decrease resource and energy dependence | Create meaningful and rewarding jobs |

process, and system transformations may be beyond those that the dominant industries and firms are capable of developing easily, at least by themselves. Further, industry and other sectors may not have the intellectual capacity and trained human resources to do what is necessary.

This argument is centered on the idea of "the winds of creative destruction" developed by Joseph Schumpeter (1939) in explaining technological advance. The distinction between incremental and radical innovations—be they technological, organizational, institutional, or social—is not simply line drawing along points on a continuum. Incremental innovation generally involves continuous improvements, while radical innovations are discontinuous (Freeman 1992), possibly involving *displacement* of dominant firms, institutions, and ideas rather than evolutionary transformations. In semantic contrast, Christensen (2000) distinguishes continuous improvements as "sustaining innovation" and uses the term "disrupting innovation" rather than radical innovation, arguing that both sustaining and disrupting innovations can be either incremental or radical, where the term "radical" is reserved for rapid or significant performance changes *within* a particular technological trajectory.

Thus in Christensen's terminology, radical sustaining innovation is a major change in technology along the lines which technology has been changing historically—for example, a much more efficient air-pollution scrubber—and is often pioneered by incumbent firms. A major innovation that represents an entirely new approach, even if it synthesizes previously invented artifacts, is termed "disrupting," and in product markets, it usually is developed by firms not in the prior markets or business. This is consistent with the important role of outsiders—both to existing firms and as new competitors—in bringing forth new concepts and ideas (van de Poel 2000).

Counting only or mainly on existing industries or traditionally trained technical expertise for a sustainable transformation ignores increasing evidence that not just willingness, opportunity, and motivation are required for needed change, but a third crucial condition—the ability or capacity of firms and people to change—is essential (N. A. Ashford 2000). Incumbent firms may develop disrupting innovations in response to a strong signal from society or the market, but such occurrences appear to be uncommon.

We argue here that the same holds true for government and societal institutions faced by the triple challenge emanating from new demands in the areas of competitiveness, the environment, and employment. Intelligent government policy is an essential part of encouraging appropriate responses of the system under challenge, and of assisting in educational transformations as well.

An essential concept in fostering innovative technical responses is that of "design space." As originally introduced by Allen, Utterback, et al. (1978) of MIT, design space is a cognitive concept that refers to the dimensions along which the designers of technical systems concern themselves. Especially in industrial organizations that limit themselves to current or traditional strategies or agendas, there is a one-sided use of the available design space. Solutions to design problems are sought only along traditional engineering lines. In many cases, unconventional solutions—which may or may not be high-tech—are ignored. For that reason, radical, disrupting innovations are often produced by industry mavericks or as a result of some disruptive outside influence (such as a radically different or more stringent environmental regulation, foreign competition, or the influence of an outsider on the organization).

### 0.6.3  A Capsule Definition of Sustainable Development

To summarize the discussion so far, sustainable development decries a simplistic definition and rather is a multidimensional concept characterizing development that seeks to

- meet needs and avoid adverse effects of industrialization within and among nations and on subsequent generations;

- provide an adequate supply and fair distribution of essential goods and services;

- provide for good health, safety, and an environment without environmental injustices;

- provide for fair working conditions and occupational health and safety;

- provide for fair and meaningful employment;

- provide for adequate and fair purchasing power;

- meet and expand the potential for a nation's self-reliance, capacity for innovation, and participation in the global economy; and

- engage individuals in society to realize their human potential (that is, social inclusion).

## 0.7  GOVERNANCE OPTIONS FOR ACHIEVING A TRANSFORMATION TO A MORE SUSTAINABLE STATE

Various commentators offer a range of strategies to improve the sustainability of the world's economies. These include (1) collaborative approaches among stakeholders, locally, nationally, and internationally; (2) mobilization of public opinion, especially at the grassroots level, to provide pressure on government and the private sector and to shift the nature of the demand for goods and services; and (3) government intervention in areas from environmental protection to energy supply, antimonopoly action, and job creation.

Government action has not been particularly popular among free-market advocates, although recent events have increased the demand for more government involvement.

Although we are strong advocates of civic engagement and participatory democracy, we contend that their power is seriously compromised by vested financial and political interests, the power of the corporate sector, the influence of advertising and ideological broadcast and electronic media, and the buying of elected officials through campaign contributions. One needs only to examine the results of negotiated regulation in U.S. environmental and safety areas to be convinced of the inadequacy of the collaborative approach at the national level (N. A. Ashford and Caldart 2005).* The unimpressive commitments made at Copenhagen speak for themselves in the international climate-change debate.† The U.S. national health-care and climate-change debates continue to be so fraught with misinformation and so influenced by vested private-sector money that the public remains confused and suspicious, especially of government. The intended outcome of these orchestrated and well-funded misinformation campaigns is to weaken the case for strong government oversight and action.

Although the recent election of a new U.S. president was accomplished by grassroots, Internet-aided communication and fund-raising, this success is now challenged by so-called grassroots rebellions in elections and town-hall meetings that are encouraged, if not funded, by an opposition exploiting an angry, uninformed, and/or manipulated polity. The facts and details of private-sector malfeasance are there to be found, but they are so overwhelmed by propaganda that hopes for public enlightenment fade quickly. The recent U.S. Supreme Court decision in *Citizens United* (*Citizens United v. Federal Election Commission*, S. Ct. 2010) establishing almost unlimited constitutional protection that "money is speech" does not bode well for the democratic process.

Although stakeholder involvement and enhancing public awareness are essential elements of a needed transformation, these vehicles move too slowly and ineffectively to address the challenges brought on by

---

\*        Collaboration and negotiation may well be successful at the local level, where public concern about local pollution or economic issues makes political accountability more visible and important.

†        At the international level, because supranational governmental authority rarely exists, collaboration and negotiation among stakeholders may be valuable, but whether voluntary or mandatory agreements are negotiated, national governmental action must follow lest those agreements remain a paper tiger.

the tipping points immediately ahead. National health care, environmental protection, the creation of needed jobs, the saving of people's homes, and the creation of real incentives to stem financial manipulation cannot wait for enlightenment and public involvement processes. In the end, even strong leadership from the executive branch of government, in combination with public participation and increased awareness, may not come quickly enough to avoid serious consequences, but strong and deliberate executive leadership and aggressive initiatives by the administrative agencies of government already legally empowered to act are certainly necessary components worthy of resurrection in the political process.

Further, industrial policy, environmental law and policy, and trade initiatives must be "opened up" by expanding the practice of multipurpose policy design and that these policies must be integrated as well. Sustainable development requires stimulating revolutionary technological innovation through environmental, health, safety, economic, and labor market regulation. Greater support for these changes must be reinforced by "opening up the participatory and political space" to enable new voices to contribute to integrated thinking and solutions. This may require political, institutional, and social innovation as well.

## 0.8 THE ROLE OF GOVERNMENT

In this book, we will argue that national government support and intervention are essential for achieving the kinds of industrial transformations that are desirable from an economic perspective, but that are also fair and just in their production and delivery of essential goods and services. Among the suggested general functions of government are the following:

- To provide the necessary physical/legal infrastructure
- To support basic education and skills acquisition (human resource development)
- To invest in pathbreaking science and technology development to enhance competitiveness, environmental improvement, and job design
- To sustain a healthy economy that creates rewarding and meaningful employment with sufficient purchasing power, reduces poverty, and provides the opportunity for a high quality of life for all
- To protect the environment and ensure that every person benefits from clean air, clean water, and a healthy home, work, and leisure environment
- To regulate deceptive and inaccurate advertising, as well as to provide counteracting government messaging to discourage unsustainable consumption

- To act as a facilitator or arbitrator of competing stakeholder interests to ensure a fair process
- To act as a trustee of (underrepresented) present and future worker and citizen interests to ensure a fair outcome in transformations of the economy
- To act as a trustee of new technologies
- To act as a force to integrate, not just coordinate, policies;
- To ensure a democratic political process, free from corruption and undue influence of vested interests which act to the detriment of the rest of society.

More specifically, depending on the specific transformation desired, there is a role for government from the direct support of R&D and incentives for innovation through appropriate tax treatment of investment to the creation and dissemination of knowledge through experimentation and demonstration projects; the creation of markets through government purchasing; the removal of perverse incentives of regulations in some instances and the deliberate design and use of regulation to stimulate change in others; training of owners, workers, and entrepreneurs; and education of consumers. The role of government should be considered beyond simply creating a favorable climate for investment. Although it is true that the government may not be competent to choose winners, it can create winning forces and provide an enabling and facilitating role by creating visions and scenarios for sustainable transformations.

There is continuing debate about the appropriate role of government in encouraging industrial transformations (N. A. Ashford 2000). Major differences revolve about two competing philosophical traditions: the dominance of unfettered market approaches and a more interventionist, directive role for government through laws and regulation. Market approaches concentrate on "getting the prices right," ensuring competition in capital and labor markets, and increasing demand for a clean environment, product safety, and good working conditions through providing information and education. In contrast, government-intervention approaches focus on establishing minimum environmental, product-safety, and labor standards and practices; requiring full disclosure by employers and producers of information needed by consumers, citizens, and workers to make informed choices and demands; encouraging technology development, transfer, and infrastructure through a deliberate industrial policy; and requiring decision bargaining in industrial relations.

Alternative roles for government in promoting sustainable development accomplish different things:

- *Correcting market failures* by regulating pollution and by addressing inadequate prices, monopoly power, uncompetitive labor markets, and lack of information *achieves static efficiency* through better working markets.

- Acting as a *mediator or facilitator of environmental and labor* disputes and conflicts among the stakeholders *achieves static efficiency* through reducing transaction costs.

- Facilitating an industrial transformation by *encouraging organizational learning, pollution prevention, and dialogue with stakeholders* leading to win-win outcomes—based on the concepts of *ecological modernization* (Jänicke and Jacob 2005; Mol 2001) or *reflexive law* (Teubner 1983)—relies on *rational choice and evolutionary change* that moves toward a more *dynamic efficiency*, usually over many decades.

- Moving beyond markets and *acting as a trustee for minority interests, subsequent generations, and new technologies* by forcing and encouraging innovation through coordinated regulatory, industrial, employment, and trade policy transcend markets, *moving toward dynamic efficiency* within a shorter time horizon.

These options are listed in increasing order of intervention, and different stakeholders will, of course, have different preferences according to their ideology and self-interests. As a practical matter, we will argue in this book that extensive intervention is needed to address the nine systemic problems discussed in Section 0.3. Some of the specific interventions that are needed are, respectively:

1. adopting a transdisciplinary approach to sustainable development;*

2. establishing mechanisms for democratic, participatory governance; reducing channels of influence by concentrated sources of power and wealth;

3. stimulating technological, institutional, organizational, and social innovation;

4. getting prices right—or least not wrong—through effective corrective tax and other policies;

5. transcending markets and implementing farsighted and integrated policies;

6. instituting deliberate policies and strategies for the development and utilization of human resources, that is, education (for both skills and citizenship), training, and job creation;

7. enforcing anti-corruption, anti-monopoly, fair-trade, and advertising law; undertaking serious campaign finance reform and disclosure legislation; considering term limits for elected officials; establishing accountability and whistle-blower protection measures; reforming the chartering of corporations;

8. encouraging innovation in material and energy use; taxing unsustainable extraction, production, products, and services; educating citizens and consumers; and

9. replacing GDP, labor productivity, and other inappropriate measures of progress with more sustainability-relevant metrics; reforming the reward structure that encourages unsustainable growth.

In addition to national responsibilities in a world of increasingly globalized commerce, information, finance, and interconnectedness, national governments also have a responsibility to

- reform institutions at the global level to ensure that developing nations have equitable access to international markets, technology, and information;

- establish trade and foreign policies that further the achievement of sustainable development;

- ratify, implement, and enforce international treaties and accords designed to protect the environment, workers, and human rights; and

- ensure peace and tranquility.

These and other interventions will be explored throughout this book, but especially in the last chapter where our policy recommendations are organized and discussed in greater depth.

---

* Appreciating the distinctions among inter-, multi-, and transdisciplinary approaches is essential to understanding why well-meaning efforts to solve complex problems by assembling professionals from different disciplines or to expand traditional education in a particular direction often lead to disappointing results.

Interdisciplinary research (and teaching)—literally "between disciplines"—often precedes the creation of a new, well-defined field. Thus biochemistry begins with a focus on traditional chemistry principles and knowledge applied to understanding biological systems; it adapts and grows; and the intellectual boundaries are refocused and redrawn. Finally, biochemistry becomes a field of its own, different from but not necessarily broader or narrower than the parent disciplines that spawned it.

Multidisciplinary research (and teaching)—literally "several or many disciplines"—brings together several disciplinary foci and thus deals with more than one traditional concern. For example, costing out different energy options necessarily involves knowledge of both energy technology and economics. Multidisciplinary research and teaching can be carried out by multidisciplinary teams or by one individual who has been trained in more than one discipline.

Transdisciplinary research (and teaching)—literally "across disciplines"—transcends the narrow focus of one or more disciplines and is not constrained to adopt preexisting models for problem definition or solution. Boundaries might necessarily have to be drawn as a practical matter, but they are not dictated by limitations of the analyst or designer. Where broad system changes are desirable, transdisciplinary approaches are essential. Transdisciplinary approaches open up the problem space of the engineer. By their nature, transdisciplinary approaches synthesize and integrate concepts whose origins are found in different disciplines, and system innovation requires synthesis.

## 0.9 THE WAY FORWARD

If we recall that a sustainable future requires technological, organizational, institutional, and, social changes, it is likely that an evolutionary pathway is insufficient to achieve the needed factor ten or greater improvements in ecological and energy efficiency and reductions in the production and use of, and exposure to, toxic substances. Nor are fundamental changes in the organization of work likely to emerge through evolutionary change. Such improvements require more systemic, multidimensional, and disruptive changes. We have already asserted that the capacity to change can be the limiting factor. This is often a crucial missing factor in optimistic scenarios.

Such significant industrial transformations occur less often from dominant technology firms—or in the case of unsustainable practices, problem firms' capacity-enhancing strategies—than from new firms that displace existing products, processes, and technologies. This can be seen in examples of significant technological innovations over the last fifty years, including transistors, computers, and polychlorinated biphenyl (PCB) replacements.

Successful management of disruptive product innovation requires initiatives from outsiders to produce the expansion of the design space that limits the dominant technology firms (van de Poel 2000). Especially in sectors with an important public or collective involvement, such as construction and agriculture, this means that intelligent government policies are required to bring about necessary change.

Rigid industries whose processes have remained stagnant also face considerable difficulties in becoming significantly more sustainable. Shifts from products to product-services rely on changes in the use, location, and ownership of products in which mature product manufacturers may participate, but this requires significant changes involving managerial, institutional, organizational, and social (customer) innovations. Changes in sociotechnical systems, such as transportation or agriculture, are even more difficult. This suggests that the creative use of government intervention is a more promising strategic approach for achieving sustainable industrial transformations than the reliance of the more neoliberal policies relying on firms' more short-term economic self-interest.

This is not to say that enhanced analytic and technical capabilities on the part of firms; cooperative efforts and improved communication with suppliers, customers, workers, and other industries; and environmental, consumer, and community groups are not valuable adjuncts in the transformation process. But in most cases these means and strategies are unlikely to be sufficient by themselves for significant transformations, and they will not work without clear mandated targets to enhance the triple goals of economic development, environmental quality, and enhancement of employment and earning capacity.

The history of innovation has amply demonstrated that disruptive innovations are feasible, and they may bring substantial payoffs in terms of triple sustainability. They are within the available but unused design space. However, the general political environment, governmental dedication, and the incentive structure have to be right for the needed changes to occur.

We have already argued that government has a significant role to play, but the government cannot simply serve as a referee or arbiter of existing competing interests, because neither future generations nor future technologies are adequately represented by the existing stakeholders. Government should work with stakeholders to define far-future targets—but without allowing the agenda to be captured by the incumbents—and then use its position as trustee to represent the future generations and the future technologies to backcast what specific policies are necessary to produce the required technical, organizational, and social transformations. Backcasting enables policy makers to look back from a desirable future to create strategies that will, it is hoped, enable the future visions to materialize. This approach is in contrast to current planning processes that develop strategies based on forecasts. The backcasting approach adopted will have to be of a next-generation variety. It has to go beyond its historical focus on coordinating public- and private-sector policies. It must be multidimensional and directly address the present fragmentation of governmental functions, not only at the national level but also among national, regional, and local governmental entities. In this book, we will argue that what is needed is stronger and smarter government. However, this does not necessarily mean bigger government if integration and coordination of the functions that government can provide are achieved. (For a concise treatment of the role that government might play, based on this book, see Ashford and Hall 2011.)

There is a great deal of serendipity and uncertainty in the transformation process, and the long-term prospects may not always be sufficiently definable to suggest obvious pathways or trajectories for the needed transformations. Thus it may be unreasonable to expect that government can always play a definitive futures-making role. What follows from this is that rather than attempting tight management of the pathways for the transformations that are sustainable in the broad sense in which we define that term in this work, the government's role might be better conceived as one of enabling or facilitating change while at the same time lending visionary leadership to co-optimize competitiveness, the environment, and employment and earning capacity. This means that the various policies must be mutually reinforcing. This newly conceptualized leadership role—focused on opening up the problem space of the engineer, designer, or policy maker—is likely to require participation of more than one ministry or department. In parallel with this, the "participatory and political space" needs to be opened up to enable new voices to contribute to integrated thinking and solutions.

Increasingly, ministries or departments of commerce and economic affairs and of the environment are working together to fashion a vision of *environmental* sustainability. What has been missing is a similar proactive role of ministries or departments of labor to interface and integrate *employment-related policies* into the national and global policy agendas. Finally, in an increasingly global marketplace, the integration of trade, industrial, employment, and environmental policies has to receive major attention lest strictly national efforts are undercut by global economic and political forces.

Readers should frequently consult the website associated with this work (www.yalebooks.com) to access an extended Primer on Sustainable Development and to view any updates to the text. The website will also provide educators with access to book-related teaching materials.

## 0.10 REFERENCES

Allen, T. J., J. M. Utterback, et al. (1978). "Government Influence on the Process of Innovation in Europe and Japan." *Research Policy* **7**(2): 124–149.

Ashford, N. A. (2000). An Innovation-Based Strategy for a Sustainable Environment. *Innovation-Oriented Environmental Regulation: Theoretical Approach and Empirical Analysis*. J. Hemmelskamp, K. Rennings, and F. Leone. New York, Physica-Verlag Heidelberg: 67–107.

Ashford, N. A. (2001). Innovation—The Pathway to Threefold Sustainability. *The Steilmann Report: The Wealth of People; An Intelligent Economy for the 21st Century*. F. Lehner, A. Charles, S. Bieri, and Y. Paleocrassas. (eds.) Bochum, Germany, Brainduct: 233–274.

Ashford, N. A. (2002). "Government and Environmental Innovation in Europe and North America." *American Behavioral Scientist* **45**(9): 1417–1434.

Ashford, N. A., and C. Ayers (1987). "Changes and Opportunities in the Environment for Technology Bargaining." *Notre Dame Law Review* **62**: 810–858.

Ashford, N. A., and C. C. Caldart (2005). Negotiated Regulation, Implementation and Compliance in the United States. *The Handbook of Environmental Voluntary Agreements*. E. Croci. Dordrecht, Springer—Environmental and Policy Series (43): 135–159.

Ashford, N. A., and C. C. Caldart (2008). *Environmental Law, Policy, and Economics: Reclaiming the Environmental Agenda*. Cambridge, MA, MIT Press.

Ashford, N. A. and R. P. Hall (2011). "The Importance of Regulation-Induced Innovation for Sustainable Development" *Sustainability* **3**(1): 270–292. Available at www.mdpi.com/2071-1050/3/1/270/pdf (accessed January 20, 2011).

Ashford, N. A., C. J. Spadafor, et al. (1990). *Monitoring the Worker for Exposure and Disease: Scientific, Legal, and Ethical Considerations in the Use of Biomarkers*. Baltimore, John Hopkins University Press.

Ashford, R. (1998). "A New Market Paradigm for Sustainable Growth: Financing Broader Capital Ownership with Louis Kelso's Binary Economics." *Praxis: The Fletcher Journal of Development Studies* **14**: 25–59.

Ayres, R. U. (2006). "Turning Point: The End of Exponential Growth?" *Technological Forecasting and Social Change* **73**: 1188–1203.

Charles, T., and F. Lehner (1998). "Competitiveness and Employment: A Strategic Dilemma for Economic Policy." *Competition and Change* **3**(1/2): 207–236.

Christensen, C. (1997). *The Innovator's Dilemma: When New Technologies Cause Great Firms to Fail*. Cambridge, MA, Harvard Business School Press.

Costanza, R., and H. Daly (1991). Goals, Agenda, and Policy Recommendations for Ecological Economics. *Ecological Economics*. R. Costanza. New York, Columbia University Press.

Daly, H. E. (1991). *Steady-State Economics*. Washington, DC, Island Press.

Dernbach, J. C. (2008). "Navigating the U.S. Transition to Sustainability: Matching National Governance Challenges with Appropriate Legal Tools." *Tulsa Law Review* **44**: 93–120.

Diwan, I., and M. Walton (1997). "How International Exchange, Technology and Institutions Affect Workers: An Introduction." *World Bank Economic Review* **11**(1): 1–15.

Ekins, P., C. Folke, et al. (1994). "Trade, Environment and Development: The Issues in Perspective." *Ecological Economics* **9**(1): 1–12.

European Commission (EC) (2003). "European Commission Welcomes Council Conclusions on Promoting Core Labour Standards." Press Release, IP/03/1054 Brussels, July 21. Available at http://europa.eu/rapid/pressReleasesAction.do?reference=IP/03/1054&format=HTML&aged=0&language=EN&guiLanguage=en (accessed January 12, 2011).

EC (2006). Trade Policy and Decent Work. Speech by the EU Trade Commissionor Peter Mandelson at the EU Decent Work Conference on Globalisation, Brussels, December 5. Available at http://europa.eu/rapid/press

ReleasesAction.do?reference=SPEECH/06/779&format=HTML&aged=0&language=EN&guiLanguage=en (accessed January 12, 2011).

Freeman, C. (1992). *The Economics of Hope*. London, Pinter.

Gordon, R. (1995). Globalization, New Production Systems, and the Spatial Division of Labor. *The New Division of Labor: Emerging Forms of Work Organization in International Perspective*. W. Littek and C. Tony. New York, Walter de Gruyter: 161–207.

Jänicke, M., and K. Jacob (2005). Ecological Modernisation and the Creation of Lead Markets. *Towards Environmental Innovation Systems*. M. Weber and J. Hemmelskamp. Heidelberg, Springer: 175–193.

Kleinknecht, A., and J. ter Wengel (1998). "The Myth of Economic Globalisation." *Cambridge Journal of Economics* **22**: 637–647.

Mol, A. (2001). *The Ecological Modernization of the Global Economy*. Cambridge, MA, MIT Press.

Rawls, J. (1971). *A Theory of Justice*. Cambridge, MA, Harvard University Press.

Schumpeter, J. A. (1939). *Business Cycles: A Theoretical, Historical, and Statistical Analysis of the Capitalist Process*. New York, McGraw-Hill.

Teubner, G. (1983). "Substantive and Reflexive Elements in Modern Law." *Law and Society Review* **17**: 239–285.

van de Poel, I. R. (2000). "On the Role of Outsiders in Technical Development." *Technology Analysis and Strategic Management* **12**(3): 383–397.

# I

# The Multidimensional Concept of Sustainability

In Part I of this book we discuss the nature (Chapter 1) and evolution (Chapter 2) of the multidimensional concepts of sustainability and sustainable development.

Chapter 1 begins by exploring two central components of sustainable development—meeting basic human needs and equality, which are discussed in the context of governance. We then consider the current economic growth model and the importance given to technological innovation as the key to solving the sustainability challenge. The chapter ends by highlighting several critical issues that we argue must be included in future development strategies. A narrow focus on one issue, such as climate change, or even a small group of concerns will limit options and ignore opportunities to develop cross-cutting approaches to address unsustainable trends in a comprehensive manner.

Chapter 2 provides a brief historical context for the ideas and themes discussed in Chapter 1. It identifies a number of important texts, national and international events, and U.S. regulations from 1951 to 2009 that helped shape the current and continually evolving notion of sustainable development. An expanded version of Chapter 2 is provided in the Primer on the Emergence of Sustainable Development found on the website associated with this work.

# 1

# Concern for a Global Future

At the beginning of the twenty-first century, the world might have been described as one of significant technological progress, industrialization, and globalization. Our current standard of living is based on many drivers of modern progress. In developed nations, energy systems supply power to our homes, places of work, and general environment. When we become ill, we find an abundance of modern drugs that can ease or cure our suffering, maintaining or improving our physical and emotional well-being. Global financial and commodity markets provide trillions of dollars a day to supply our investment and consumption needs. The agricultural sector, through mechanization and other technological and biological advances, has been able to supply our growing sustenance requirements. Telecommunications systems have enabled friends, families, businesses, organizations, and governments to communicate verbally and visually across thousands of miles. Combine these technologies with our modern transportation systems, and we remove the notion of the frontier.

Having achieved such progress, why should we now be concerned about the future of humankind on a global scale? One answer is that just over 1 billion people have any meaningful access to the resources and quality of life described above. The rest of the world's population—some 5 billion people who live in less developed regions—have only a taste of what this standard of living might be like (Durning 1992, 1994; UNDP 2003). Second, even within the developed countries, many people do not have access to an adequate supply of essential goods, services, housing, health care, and other necessities. As a result of the financial crisis of 2008, a significant number of people in the developed world are losing their homes and/or their jobs. Energy supply and use in the face of both the uncertainty of future availability and global climate disruption are increasingly becoming serious concerns. Inequality is leading toward a world of growing disparity both between industrialized and developing nations and among different segments of the population within those countries. In effect, the communities of less developed regions and poor areas are held captive to the needs and wants of those who are well-off in industrialized (and some in industrializing) nations, whose living and consuming habits are in many ways condemning billions of people to a lower (material) quality of life. Put simply, if each member of the global community were to live the lifestyle of the average U.S. or U.K. citizen, holding technology constant, we would need the resources of somewhere between 1.5 and 8 planet Earths (McLaren, Bullock, et al. 1997; Wilson 2002; WWF 2006). It is clear that a global drive to reach the Westernized view of the good life, without a drastic change in production processes and consumption patterns, will soon bring us up against ecological and physical limits and force us to rethink what we mean by a secure and fulfilling lifestyle.

These introductory paragraphs present a highly simplified view of the world, and there is clearly a continuum of positions between those presented. The central argument of this book is that if we are interested in the well-being of current and future generations, we not only should be concerned for the future of the world but also should be actively searching for new ways to enable individuals, communities, and nations to live a sustainable life, what might be called a sustainable livelihood. If present trends continue and the structural forces driving them remain substantially unchanged, there is a strong possibility that within a few generations the world will be incapable of sustaining the human population at an adequate level of material well-being and health, and that it will lack sufficient and equitable opportunities for the realization of human potential. These trends include persistent (and often growing) inequalities between and within nations (including the United States) and persuasive evidence that we are living beyond our ecological and physical means.

Further, the social and political environment in which policy responses to these trends must be made is a difficult one. It is defined by globalization and rapid technological change, which are mutually reinforcing and create a set of conditions that shortens the necessary response time for policy, restricts national policy options, and possibly exacerbates distributional inequality and ecological damage. This chapter sets out these concerns.

## 1.1 HUMAN NEEDS

The major problems of the world today can be solved only if we improve our understanding of human behavior. Skinner, *About Behaviorism,* 1974

During the mid-1970s, the idea that the purpose of development was to develop *things* (for example, to transform resources into commodities/products) was rejected and redefined to focus development on satisfying the needs of *humankind*.

In 1973, Schumacher published *Small Is Beautiful*, which challenged the prevailing patterns of development and approach to global economics. Schumacher (1999, p. 139) rejected the idea that what "is best for the rich must be best for the poor" and redefined the conventional view of development toward human needs. "Development does not start with goods; it starts with people and their education, organization, and discipline. Without these three, all resources remain latent, untapped, potential" (ibid.).

A year later, the Cocoyoc Declaration built on the ideas of Schumacher and placed basic human needs at the center of development efforts, stating that "any process of growth that does not lead to their fulfilment—or, even worse, disrupts them—is a travesty of the idea of development."[1]* The following year the Dag Hammarskjöld Foundation (1975) articulated a similar position on the objective of development in *What Now: Another Development*. It called for the "development of every man and woman—of

---

* The influence of Schumacher's work is clearly evident throughout the Cocoyoc Declaration. Schumacher's call for a "metaphysical reconstruction" (Schumacher 1999, p. xi)—the need to reconstruct the meaning of ideas such as development, economics, knowledge, wealth, employment, and technology—is present in the Cocoyoc Declaration's redefinition of development in terms of self-reliance. Like Schumacher, the declaration rejects economic development that maintains or increases the disparities between and within countries and argues for economic growth that benefits the poorest sections of each society. Further, the declaration also rejects what might be called the "developed-nation model" in favor of development that supports a nation-state's societal and cultural norms. In this sense, the declaration asks the international community to respect the diversity of each country and to accept that there is more than one type of development trajectory.

the whole man and woman—and not just the growth of things, which are merely means" (ibid., p. 5). Further, the report emphasized the importance of satisfying the basic needs of the poor, as well as the universal "needs for expression, creativity, conviviality, and for deciding . . . [one's] own destiny" (ibid.). It continues, "Development is a whole; it is an integral, value-loaded, cultural process; it encompasses the natural environment, social relations, education, production, consumption and well-being" (ibid.).

In 1987, over a decade later, the World Commission on Environment and Development (WCED) published *Our Common Future*, which again placed "human needs" at the center of concerns for "sustainable" development.

> Sustainable development is development that meets the needs of the present without compromising the ability of future generations to meet their own needs. It contains within it two key concepts:
> * the concept of "needs," in particular the essential needs of the world's poor, to which overriding priority should be given; and
> * the idea of limitations imposed by the state of technology and social organization on the environment's ability to meet present and future needs. (WCED 1987, p. 43)

The WCED's conceptualization of sustainable development, which built on the development vision articulated in *What Now: Another Development*, made an influential case for "the need to integrate economic and ecological considerations in decision making" (WCED 1987, p. 62). The basic notion was that social and economic development must not undermine the natural environment on which they are based. Hence sustainable development "requires views of human needs and well-being that incorporate such non-economic variables as education and health enjoyed for their own sake, clean air and water, and the protection of natural beauty" (ibid., p. 53).

In concert with both the Cocoyoc Declaration and *What Now: Another Development*, *Our Common Future* spoke to the different needs of developed and less developed nations. For developing nations, the "principal development challenge is to meet the needs and aspirations of an expanding . . . population. The most basic of all needs is for a livelihood: that is, employment" (WCED 1987, p. 54). It follows that employment—"the opportunity to satisfy . . . aspirations for a better life" (ibid., p. 44)—will lead to the satisfaction of such basic human needs as food, clothing, and shelter. However, some observers expressed concern that the needs of people in less

developed nations are much broader than employment and must "include the right to preserve their cultural identity, and their right not to be alienated from their own society, and their own community" (ibid., p. 31).

For developed nations, the focus was not on meeting basic human needs for food, clothing, and shelter per se, but instead on the ecological consequences of an overindulgent lifestyle. "Living standards that go beyond the basic minimum are sustainable only if consumption standards everywhere have regard for long-term sustainability. . . . Perceived needs are socially and culturally determined, and sustainable development requires the promotion of values that encourage consumption standards that are within the bounds of the ecologically possible and to which all can reasonably aspire" (WCED 1987, p. 44). Interestingly, both the Cocoyoc Declaration and *What Now: Another Development* expand the WCED's view of human needs (in relation to developed nations) to include the physiological and psychological consequences of overconsumption.

The preceding discussion provides strong evidence that understanding the fundamental needs of humans is essential if we are to develop strategies to transition toward more sustainable forms of development.

As a consequence of influential publications such as *Our Common Future*, the current discourse on sustainable development tends to center on trade-offs among economic development and environmental and social goals. Areas of contention frequently arise during such discussions because the *goals* of each nation, group, or individual—which are based on their *needs*—are often at odds with one another. Hence if we are concerned for humankind, then we need to understand the basic needs that are inherent in human nature and also those that are a product of the socialization of humans.

A key argument of this book is that the satisfaction of essential needs should drive economic and (democratic) political systems. Borrowing the language of modern economics, we understand that a rational person will maximize his or her utility function when making a decision to buy a product or service to satisfy a need. It follows, therefore, that societal demand is the canonical ensemble of everyone's individual utility function.* With regard to the political system,

---

\* In a developed country, a consumer is a very sophisticated concept, but in a developing nation where no markets exist, people cannot be called consumers in an organizational sense.

we satisfy our political needs by voting for the politician or political party that is most likely to support our lifestyle and beliefs. When the votes are aggregated, the candidate or party whose views align more closely with the needs and wants of society should be elected.* Indeed, for many, free markets and democracy are intertwined.[†]

This demand-side notion that our needs drive economic and political systems raises an interesting question about how change is likely to occur in practice. If we make decisions on the basis of our individual needs, then it can be argued that a society is likely to address unsustainable activities only once the individual is negatively affected. Neoclassical economics argues that each person should act in his or her own interest and let the market allocate resources accordingly, but this assumes that each person is receiving perfect or good information and is able to make informed, rational decisions.[‡] It also

assumes that the "invisible hand" of the market will generate outcomes that maximize social welfare.[§] In this framework, the role of government should be to ensure that markets work and, if necessary, to redistribute wealth out of concern for equity through a progressive tax system.

Many have argued that reliance on the market is likely to result in overconsumption and environmental harm due to inadequate consumer information. Manno (2002) argues that the present industrial capitalist system of incentives and disincentives is invariably directed toward increasing levels of consumption. The environmental problems associated with increasing consumption are further compounded by the fact that as commodity chains grow in length and become more complex and more international, the spatial and social distances between production and consumption are widened (Conca 2002; Princen 2002). The result of this *distancing effect* is that consumers lack the information and incentives to behave in a more sustainable manner even if they wish to do so.

The literature on human needs and their fulfillment is extensive and beyond the scope of this work.[2] Here we proceed to the related issue of measuring human progress or development and its relationship to sustainability.

### 1.1.1 The Measurement of (Human) Development

Perhaps the most common measures equated with progress or development (or, more accurately, economic growth) are gross domestic product (GDP), gross national product (GNP), and gross national income (GNI). GDP tries to examine the economy from a macro perspective by measuring the total output produced by a country. It is the value of all final goods and services produced in a particular country in a one-year period.[¶] GDP is the total annual value of all goods and services produced within a nation's borders, whereas GNP is the total annual value of all goods and services produced by a nation's residents (or firms), wherever they are located. GNI adds in-

---

However, satisfaction of needs drives even the most primitive economic systems of exchange and commerce.

\* This statement assumes that there is sufficient diversity between the political candidates to present an individual with a real choice. It also assumes that a large enough proportion of a society will vote that it is possible to gauge societal demand accurately.

† For a critique that challenges this notion, see Soros (1997). Soros (1997, p. 45) argues that "the untrammeled intensification of laissez-faire capitalism and the spread of market values into all areas of life is endangering our open and democratic society." His main concern lies with the assumption that individuals (or consumers) have "perfect knowledge" and that by acting in their own self-interest, they will promote the common (or greater) good. Because our understanding of the world is inherently imperfect, promoting laissez-faire capitalism at the expense of the values and institutions that underlie an open and democratic society is what Soros refers to as the "capitalist threat." His concern is that the free market is changing society's perception of what is right and wrong by, for example, focusing on financial success and overlooking how that success was achieved. Soros (1997, 1998) argues that a better approach would be to create an open society that accepts our fallibility—i.e., that we will never have perfect information—and enables different ideological perspectives to inform and be reconciled in the political and social arena. Thus, put simply, an open society is "a society open to improvement" (Soros 1998, p. 24).

‡ A survey by the American Association of Retired Persons (AARP 2004) asked whether spending power is all that an individual requires to achieve "consumer sovereignty"—i.e., the successful selection of a product or service. The survey concluded that consumers—aged forty-five and over and who represent 52 percent of consumer spending—are finding it increasingly difficult to use their spending power effectively because of (1) "less time and more decisions"; (2) the "increasing complexity of products and services"; and (3) "low levels of financial literacy" (ibid., pp. 2–3). Hence many are unable to exercise consumer sovereignty because they are not receiving good information and, therefore, cannot make informed, rational decisions. To solve this problem, the AARP calls on business and government to improve the quality of consumer information, to increase financial literacy, and to increase options for banking and credit in

---

segmented markets that often suffer from predatory financial practices.

§ One criticism of a utility-oriented system is that it does not incorporate concern for others. People vote their interests in the marketplace, but people do not express (in the market) their valuation of other people, relationships, and global equity and security. The market exists to satisfy individual, not social, wants.

¶ Statisticians count only final products in GDP calculations, not intermediate ones. Counting intermediate products would lead the GDP statistics to account for the same output more than once, which would not capture the true production taking place in the economy.

come received from other countries (principally dividends and interest payments) less similar transfers to other countries. The fundamental equation of GDP is the following:

$$GDP = C + I + G + (X–M),$$

where $C$ is consumption, $I$ is investment, $G$ is government expenditure, $X$ is exports, and $M$ is imports.

In very broad terms, output can be divided into two basic forms of production. The first includes the vast spectrum of goods and services that will be bought by households and individuals for private use, for example, books, haircuts, clothing, and health services. This part of output is what we understand as consumption, and the various goods and services included are consumer goods (Heilbroner and Thurow 1998). There are also certain goods and services that do not end up in the possession of consumers. This category includes roads, machinery, airports, ports, and bridges, but also smaller objects such as office furniture and typewriters (ibid.). These goods are investment or capital goods.

The breakdown of GDP is not limited only to consumption and investment. It also includes government spending and the trade balance. Depending on whether consumption is private or public, that is, depending on whether the final good is consumed by private households or the government, a certain purchase can be counted as consumption or as government spending. The same holds true for investment. Although the GDP equation does not distinguish between government consumption and government investment and counts everything under government expenditure, GDP statistics in some countries actually do use that classification (Heilbroner and Thurow 1998). It is interesting that not all government spending is included in the GDP calculation. Specifically, although transfer payments (such as Social Security payments, health care, unemployment protection, and various subsidies and measures of social protection) account for a significant portion of government spending, they are not considered an "output-producing" activity because "no direct production takes place in exchange for a transfer payment" (ibid., p. 75). This exclusion perhaps creates the first criticism of GDP, because transfer payments increasingly augment the quality of life of the citizenry.

Finally, the GDP metric includes the trade balance. GDP accounts for all domestic production that is sold abroad minus all foreign production purchased domestically. A negative trade balance, for instance, signifies a "net stream of purchasing power that wends its way abroad" and that should be subtracted from

the GDP analytics (Heilbroner and Thurow 1998, p. 76). Furthermore, GDP is a useful tool in the realm of international politics because, apart from being an economic measure, it also constitutes a useful measure of state power.

GNP and GDP were originally developed during the 1940s—with the formation of Systems of National Accounts (SNAs) throughout the world—to measure *total economic output* (Hodge 1997; Neumayer 2004; Vanoli 2004). Because total economic output does not distinguish between "good" and "bad" forms of spending, take forgone opportunities into account (that is, option values), consider nonmarket goods and services, or account for unpaid work and leisure activities, it is arguably not an accurate measure of economic welfare (Glasser and Craig 1994).* Overall, GDP displays a series of limitations as a measure of economic success:

- GDP does not effectively capture the distribution of wealth in an economy. GDP per capita simply divides GDP by the population of the country. The information that this metric conveys, however, for a country with significant income disparities is rather limited. Saudi Arabia and South Korea, for instance, have similar GDPs per capita. Nevertheless, Saudi Arabia is a country with widely disparate personal incomes and whose growth has been fueled by its vast oil reserves, while South Korea's growth model is primarily based on technological innovation, and income disparity is significantly lower.

- Environmental quality is not included in the GDP metric. Environmental issues, however, are central to any measure of quality of life. Broadly, economists classify such issues as "externalities," which are altogether neglected in GDP calculations.

- GDP does not take into account parts of the "black" sectors of the economy. Nevertheless, underground economic transactions can significantly affect the quality of life of the citizens of a country, both positively and negatively.

- GDP does not capture nonmonetary activities, such as unpaid or volunteer work. However, as Putnam, Leonardi, et al. (1993) have prominently described, social capital is central to development and economic success.

---

* Liagouras (2005) raises a more fundamental problem with economic measures such as productivity and growth. As developed nations transition toward the service economy, concepts such as productivity (the number of products produced per unit of input) no longer make sense in a context where quality and variety take precedence over quantity. Thus our current measures of progress/development may not be able to measure the real change that is occurring. See Section 3.3.1.2 in Chapter 3 for a more detailed discussion of Liagouras's (2005) ideas.

- Many economic activities included in GDP calculations do not advance "real" economic development. For instance, increasing costs associated with health care or costs of dealing with human-made or natural disasters or war can significantly boost GDP. Thus an oil spill can increase GDP because the cleanup costs are accounted for in GDP metrics. However, such an incident diminishes well-being and GDP-enhancing activities such as fishing, as seen in the aftermath of the 2010 BP oil spill in the Gulf of Mexico. Costanza, Hart et al. (2009) points out that increased crime, sickness, war, pollution, fires, storms, and pestilence are all positive for GDP because they boost economic activity.

- GDP fails to capture any measure of the quality of goods sold. A higher volume of low-quality products sold can perhaps boost GDP; however, low-quality products are typically less durable and can thus create more waste and inefficiency.

- GDP growth also fails to capture whether a country's growth path can be sustained in the long run. For instance, in 2009, Russia required a $70 per barrel price for oil in order to balance its budget (Briançon 2009). Russia is one of the key examples of an imbalanced growth model, which can be easily disrupted by fluctuations in energy prices.

- GDP includes no measure of societal opportunity costs. For instance, costs associated with the remediation of harm (such as natural disasters) divert funding from wealth-generating activities and investments.

- GDP does not directly capture the essence of product innovation. It does so only indirectly, through the monetary value of products sold. However, pharmaceutical and technological innovations have increased the quality of goods—and perhaps life— drastically. For instance, a person can be reached in almost any part of the globe at minimal cost, and many diseases considered incurable thirty or forty years ago are now treatable. GDP does not convey any information about such advancements, even though they constitute main pillars of development.

- It is also possible that GDP may similarly not reflect improvements in processes, for example, information and communication technology (ICT) increasing the overall quality of services.

It is useful to note how these limitations are met in practice. Ponting (2007, p. 337) notes that "in the 1990s the GDP per head in the United States was 40 percent higher than in Italy but life expectancy was lower by almost two years because of the poor [U.S.] health system." Moreover, as noted earlier, averages tend to hide distributional realities. For instance, "the life expectancy of African Americans is lower than the average in China and infant mortality rate in cities such as Washington, DC, and Baltimore and St. Louis is higher than in cities such as Bangkok and Cairo" (Ponting 2007, p. 337). Furthermore, Ponting (2007, pp. 337–338) underlines that although Sri Lanka had a GDP per capita equal to 20 percent of that of Malaysia, it had a comparable mortality rate, food intake, and number of doctors per capita, and its literacy rate appeared to be significantly better.

Given the limitations of GDP/GNP, there have been a number of attempts to adjust (or "green") the measure to provide a better indication of progress. Two examples are the Index of Sustainable Economic Welfare (ISEW) (Daly and Cobb 1994) and the more recent Genuine Progress Indicator (GPI) (Talberth, Cobb, et al. 2006; Venetoulis and Cobb 2004). Using the principle of weak sustainability as a guide,* the ISEW and the GPI first make adjustments to account for unequal income distribution by using the Gini coefficient (see the discussion in Section 1.1.3.1). They then add or subtract a number of different elements to account for ecological and social benefits or costs.

Over the past decade, the ISEW and the GPI have been developed for a number of nations, including Australia, Austria, Chile, Germany, Italy, the Netherlands, Scotland, Sweden, Thailand, the United Kingdom, and the United States (Neumayer 2004). In each case, the ISEW and the GPI appear to increase until around 1970 or 1980 (depending on the nation), after which they level off or decline. Over the same period, GNP continues to increase, thereby widening the gap between perceived and actual human welfare. Max-Neef (1995, p. 117) referred to these trends as evidence of his "threshold hypothesis": "For every society there seems to be a period in which economic growth (as conventionally measured) brings about an improvement in the quality of life, but only up to a point— the threshold point—beyond which, if there is more economic growth, quality of life may begin to deteriorate."

Although many see the ISEW and the GPI as valuable tools to broaden policy prescriptions beyond a reliance on economic growth (Clarke 2004; C. Hamilton 1999; P. A. Lawn 2003; Patterson and Jollands 2004), others point to its methodological problems and question whether there is in fact a growing gap between ISEW/GPI and GNP (Neumayer 2000). Levett (1998, p. 297) even goes so far to say that "as soon

---

* *Weak sustainability* implies that the total stock of natural, human-made, human, and social capital remains constant over time. For this to happen, it is assumed that human-made capital can replace natural capital and that human and social capital can be maintained by investment in education, health, and other forms of social services.

as we try to modify GDP to bring it closer to some conception of welfare . . . we are back to subjectivity in deciding which things need to be added to and subtracted from GDP, and how they should be measured and weighted." An alternative to the ISEW and the GPI that is not as vulnerable to these types of criticisms is the measure of Genuine Savings (GS).

The notion of Genuine Savings (GS) was developed by K. Hamilton (1994, 2000) while working in the World Bank's Environment Department (K. Hamilton, Atkinson, et al. 1997). GS (also referred to as Adjusted Net Savings) is an annual measurement of *changes* in national wealth, where "national wealth" is defined as the total amount of natural, human-made, and human capital (Bolt, Matete, et al. 2002). Thus GS does not account for changes in social capital, which one could argue that the ISEW and the GPI attempt to consider through measures such as "defensive expenditures" and the cost of divorces, crime, and lost leisure time (Venetoulis and Cobb 2004). Interestingly, the World Bank (WBG 1997) has argued that social capital is the "missing link" in the creation of a more accurate measure of sustainable development. However, difficulty in finding a suitable indicator for social capital has resulted in it not being included in the GS calculation.

A positive GS value indicates that the total stock of capital is increasing.* A zero GS value indicates no change, and a negative value means that total national wealth is in decline. Thus a negative GS provides a signal that a nation's activities are (potentially) unsustainable. Here, "unsustainable" is defined in relation to the Hartwick-Solow weak sustainability principle. A simple formula that clearly describes GS is as follows (Dietz and Neumayer 2004, p. 277):

Genuine Savings = net investment in produced capital
− net depreciation of natural capital
+ investment in human capital (that is, education).

In general, neoclassical economists appear more comfortable with GS than with the ISEW and the GPI because it is based on the already-familiar system of national accounts and avoids the more subjective elements included in the ISEW and the GPI. In addition, Bolt, Matete, et al. (2002, p. 4) argue that "adjusted net savings [or GS] seeks to offer policy-

makers who have committed their countries to a 'sustainable' pathway a badly needed, first-approximation indicator to track their progress in this endeavor."

Those who reject GS as a suitable measure of sustainable development also reject the ISEW and the GPI on the grounds that they violate the principle of strong sustainability. For strong sustainability to be achieved, there can be no depreciation in the stock of natural capital. Thus human-made capital cannot replace natural capital, because the former relies on the latter, and, more important, it is simply not possible for human-made capital to replace the life-support systems of the planet (Hueting and Reijnders 1998). Strong sustainability also implies that nonrenewable resources cannot be depleted. If such a constraint were applied to modern production systems, it would most likely force a drastic reconceptualization of what is meant by "manufacturing" and "industrialization." Therefore, its advocates have weakened this constraint somewhat to allow for systems that *minimize* the use of finite terrestrial resources (that is, low-entropy matter and energy) as part of a "steady-state economy" (Daly 1991b).

Hueting and Reijnders (2004) recognize that it is "theoretically" possible to increase production and consumption and maintain natural capital. However, such a scenario would require the creation of technologies that are

(i)   sufficiently clean,
(ii)  do not deplete renewable natural resources,
(iii) find substitutes for nonrenewable resources,
(iv)  leave the soil intact,
(v)   leave sufficient space for the survival of plant and animal species and
(vi)  are cheaper in real terms than current available technologies, because if they are more expensive in real terms, growth will be checked. (Hueting and Reijnders 2004, p. 252)

Given the stringency of these requirements, they conclude that "meeting all these six conditions is scarcely conceivable for the whole spectrum of human activities" (Hueting and Reijnders 2004, p. 252).

An alternative to the ISEW and the GPI and to GS that attempts to integrate economic and environmental data through a nation's system of national accounts (SNA) is the System of Integrated Environmental and Economic Accounting (SEEA) (UN, EC, et al. 2003). The SEEA was developed by the United Nations Statistical Commission with support from the International Monetary Fund, the World Bank, the European Commission, and the Organisation for Economic Co-operation and Development (OECD).

---

* Hueting and Reijnders (2004) list a number of conditions that must hold for a positive GS to signal a weak form of sustainable development. Possibly one of the most important conditions is that GS ≥ 0 for the entire time series and not just for the year of the analysis. Another important condition is that technology can only substitute *nonrenewable* resources and cannot replace nature (Hueting and Reijnders 1998).

Although the system was not created specifically to address sustainable development—for example, it is currently unable to account for the social and institutional dimensions of sustainability (UNDESA 2007)—it does provides a platform to combine economic and environmental data using consistent classifications and definitions.

The SEEA extends the SNA to include environmental aspects through a system of satellite accounts.* By providing guidance on how environment-related statistical accounts can be compiled, the SEEA provides a mechanism to study interactions between the economy and the environment. For example, the impact of different production and consumption patterns on the environment can be considered. Conversely, the economic impact of environmental standards designed to keep economic activity within ecological limits can be explored.

Because the system is based on the SNA, it is believed that the use of the SEEA will improve the availability of environment-related data and provide a foundation for further development of integrated indicators (UN, EC, et al. 2003). Although, in theory, the SEEA can be used to evaluate economic activity through a lens of weak or strong sustainability, the system's grounding in economics is likely to promote the former approach through its attraction to neoclassical economists.

With the growing interest in preserving the integrity of the environment, some measures of progress/development focus on the *condition* of the environment (along with trends). In contrast, others attempt to measure whether development activities/trends are likely to be sustainable into the *future*. The Living Planet Index (LPI) is a good example of the former (WWF, ZSL, et al. 2010). It measures changes in the population of some eight thousand vertebrate species, providing an indication of the impact of human activity on their habitats. The Environmental Sustainability Index (ESI) provides a good example of the latter type of index (Esty, Levy, et al. 2005). By combining a wide range of national-level socioeconomic, environmental, and institutional indicators, the ESI calculates the relative likelihood that a nation will be able to maintain or enhance its environmental condition over the next several generations.[3]

Another well-known metric created to measure the environmental burden of human activity is the Ecological Footprint (EF).† Developed by Wackernagel and Rees (1995, 1997), this metric attempts to translate human activity into the corresponding ecological area required to sustain that activity (Wackernagel 2001; Wackernagel, White, et al. 2004). More specifically, an ecological footprint "represent[s] the biologically productive area required to produce the food and wood people consume, to supply space for infrastructure, and to absorb the greenhouse gas carbon dioxide ($CO_2$) emitted from burning fossil fuels" (Wackernagel, Monfreda, et al. 2002). Thus the EF is based on the idea of environmental carrying capacity—that is, the total rate at which renewable resources can be produced (or regenerated) and waste (such as $CO_2$) can be absorbed in sinks.

The problem with using the EF as a measure of "sustainable" development is that it does not consider the interactions between the various system components and thereby ignores important processes that can dramatically affect carrying capacity (Becker 1997; Hueting and Reijnders 2004). In addition, van den Bergh and Verbruggen (1999) argue that the EF fails to reveal the underlying causes of environmental overshoot or provide adequate policy solutions to problems. Further, the EF ignores international and regional trade, thereby making an implicit assumption that national and regional self-reliance is a desired objective.

---

* The SEEA consists of four categories of accounts (UN, EC, et al. 2003). The first considers industry-level physical data on the flows of materials and energy through the economy. More specifically, the category focuses on the energy and materials used in production and the subsequent creation of pollutants and solid waste. The category also combines physical and monetary flows into hybrid accounts that are able to provide information on, for example, the impacts of greenhouse gas emissions.

The second category focuses on the existing elements of the SNA that relate to the effective management of the environment. For example, accounts could track the expenditures of businesses, governments, and households on activities intended to protect the environment.

The third category of accounts considers environmental assets in physical and momentary terms. For example, the accounts document the stocks and changes in stocks of natural resources, such as forests, water, and minerals.

The final category of SEEA accounts considers how the existing SNA could be adjusted to account for the impact of the economy on the environment. The approaches used to create these accounts are similar to those used in the creation of the ISEW, the GPI, and GS. In this category, three types of adjustments can be made to existing SNA accounts to consider (1) the costs of resource depletion, (2) defensive expenditures (e.g., money spent on environmental protection or remediation), and (3) environmental degradation (or decline in environmental health).

---

† A similar type of holistic indicator not discussed here is maximum suitable yield (MSY). MSY provides a measure of the maximum long-term average yield that can be taken from a renewable resource (such as a fishery or forest). If the maximum yield is exceeded, the ability of the resource to renew itself through natural growth/replenishment is affected, reducing its ability to "carry" human activities.

Notwithstanding these alternative measures of progress/development, the reliance of governments on GDP/GNP as a gauge of progress led the United Nations Development Programme (UNDP) to create an alternative measure of *human* development—the Human Development Index (HDI) (Moldan 1997).

The UNDP (1995, p. 11) defined human development as a "process of enlarging people's choices." In particular, it identified three core choices (or opportunities) for people: (1) to lead a long and healthy life, (2) to acquire knowledge, and (3) to have access to sufficient resources to be able to obtain a decent standard of living (ibid.). Other opportunities it described as being highly valued by society include economic, social, and political freedom and opportunities for creativity, productivity, enjoying personal self-respect, and guaranteed human rights. Hence human development was seen to have two sides. The first was the establishment of human *capabilities*, such as improved health, skills, and knowledge. The second was how people put these acquired capabilities to use, for example, by being active in cultural, social, and political affairs. The UNDP's use of the term "choices" in defining human development was deliberate because it raised the question whether a person has the opportunity to improve his or her current situation.*

Although the UNDP created the HDI in 1975, it was not published until the (somewhat controversial) Human Development Report (HDR) of 1990 (UNDP 1990). Since then, the HDI has undergone several iterations over the past two decades, but the three main components of the index have remained intact: (1) life expectancy at birth; (2) educational attainment; and (3) income (UNDP 1995; UNDP 2010). During its existence, the HDI has served as an important measure of development in contrast to GDP/GNP. Its role was reaffirmed in the UNDP's 2010 HDR which argued that "the evidence [presented in the report] does cast doubt on whether economywide income growth is instrumental in furthering health and education at low and medium levels of human development. . . . Using a new dataset and analysis, our results also confirm a central contention of the *Human Development Reports* (*HDRs*) from the outset: that

human development is different from economic growth and that great achievements are possible even without fast growth" (UNDP 2010, p. 49).†

The 2010 HDI and its sister indexes—the Inequality-adjusted HDI, the Gender Inequality Index, and the Multidimensional Poverty Index—represent the latest evolution in the human development indexes. The 2010 HDR addresses many of the criticisms levied at the indexes included in previous reports (Raworth and Stewart 2002; UNDP 2010). The most significant changes in the 2010 HDR are to the calculation of the HDI, the ability to compare HDI values over time—a problem which the UNDP and others had recognized (Morse 2003; UNDP 2005)—and the development of new sister indexes that have replaced their predecessors. With regards to the HDI, in addition to adjusting the education and income indices that form part of the index, the index is now calculated using the geometric mean of its three health, education, and income indices. A change that measures how well rounded a country's performance is across the three indices, avoiding the pitfalls of using a simple average that allowed for perfect substitution across indices (UNDP 2010).

When looking at the HDI values in Table 1.1, those countries that have higher HDI values also tend to have a high level of Gross National Income (GNI) per capita. Conversely, those countries with a low HDI value face severe poverty.

The majority of EU member states have a relatively high HDI rank. Within this group of twenty-seven countries, with the exception of Portugal, it is the newer EU member states from the Czech Republic to Bulgaria that have the lowest HDI values.

A look at several countries in the Middle East reveals a wide range in HDI values. Israel, the UAE, Qatar, Kuwait, and Saudi Arabia have HDI values comparable to those of several EU states, whereas Yemen, for example, falls within the bottom quarter of all HDI rankings. A similar range of HDI values exists for the selected Latin American and Caribbean states, although a comparison of the GNI per capita values reveals that these countries tend to be poorer than a similarly ranked middle east countries—for example, compare Kuwait with Argentina.

Finally, the selected African countries embody a significant proportion of the lowest HDI values. At face value, the best place to live from a human

---

* Section 1.2.3 will take a more detailed look at Amartya Sen's (1992) discussion of inequality. In particular, it will focus on the difference between *achievement* and *freedom* to achieve, and on the concept that one's capability to achieve represents the opportunity to pursue his or her objectives.

† See Section 3.4 in Chapter 3 for a discussion of alternatives to the northern growth model, especially Section 3.4.2 that discusses the case studies of the state of Kerala—which has one of the highest HDI values of any state in India—and Costa Rica.

**TABLE 1.1: THE UNDP DEVELOPMENT INDEXES FOR SELECTED COUNTRIES INCLUDING THEIR HAPPY PLANET INDEX (HPI) RANKING**

| HDI RANK[a] | Country | POPULATION (Millions; 2010)[a] | HUMAN DEVELOPMENT INDEX (HDI) (2010)[a] | INEQUALITY-ADJUSTED HDI (Change in HDI rank; 2010)[a,b] | GENDER INEQUALITY INDEX (Rank; 2008)[a] (out of 138 countries) | MULTIDIMENSIONAL POVERTY INDEX (% of population suffering multiple deprivations) (2000–2008)[a] | GROSS NATIONAL INCOME (GNI) PER CAPITA (PPP U.S.$ 2008) (2010)[a] | ECOLOGICAL FOOTPRINT OF CONSUMPTION (Hectares per capita) (2006)[a] | OVERALL LIFE SATISFACTION (2006–2009) (0–least satisfied, 10–most satisfied)[a] | HAPPY PLANET INDEX (HPI) RANK (2009)[c] (Out of 143 countries) |
|---|---|---|---|---|---|---|---|---|---|---|
| **Top Ten Countries by HDI** | | | | | | | | | | |
| 1 | Norway | 4.9 | 0.938 | 0 | 5 | .. | 58,810 | 4.2 | 8.1 | 88 |
| 2 | Australia | 21.5 | 0.937 | 0 | 18 | .. | 38,692 | .. | 7.9 | 102 |
| 3 | New Zealand | 4.3 | 0.907 | .. | 25 | .. | 25,438 | 7.6 | 7.8 | 103 |
| 4 | United States | 317.6 | 0.902 | -9 | 37 | .. | 47,094 | 9.0 | 7.9 | 114 |
| 5 | Ireland | 4.6 | 0.895 | -3 | 29 | .. | 33,078 | 8.2 | 8.1 | 78 |
| 6 | Liechtenstein | 0.0 | 0.891 | .. | .. | .. | 81,011 | .. | .. | .. |
| 7 | Netherlands | 16.7 | 0.890 | 1 | 1 | .. | 40,658 | 4.6 | 7.8 | 43 |
| 8 | Canada | 33.9 | 0.888 | -2 | 16 | .. | 38,668 | 5.8 | 8.0 | 89 |
| 9 | Sweden | 9.3 | 0.885 | 4 | 3 | .. | 36,936 | .. | 7.9 | 53 |
| 10 | Germany | 82.1 | 0.885 | 3 | 7 | .. | 35,308 | 4.0 | 7.2 | 51 |
| **Selected European Countries** | | | | | | | | | | |
| 1 | Norway[d] | 4.9 | 0.938 | 0 | 5 | .. | 58,810 | 4.2 | 8.1 | 88 |
| 5 | Ireland | 4.6 | 0.895 | -3 | 29 | .. | 33,078 | 8.2 | 8.1 | 78 |
| 6 | Liechtenstein[d] | 0.0 | 0.891 | .. | .. | .. | 81,011 | .. | .. | .. |
| 7 | Netherlands | 16.7 | 0.890 | 1 | 1 | .. | 40,658 | 4.6 | 7.8 | 43 |
| 9 | Sweden | 9.3 | 0.885 | 4 | 3 | .. | 36,936 | .. | 7.9 | 53 |
| 10 | Germany | 82.1 | 0.885 | 3 | 7 | .. | 35,308 | 4.0 | 7.2 | 51 |
| 13 | Switzerland[d] | 7.6 | 0.874 | 4 | 4 | .. | 39,849 | 5.6 | 8.0 | 52 |
| 14 | France | 62.6 | 0.872 | -3 | 11 | .. | 34,341 | 4.6 | 7.1 | 71 |
| 16 | Finland | 5.3 | 0.871 | 2 | 8 | .. | 33,872 | 5.5 | 8.0 | 59 |
| 18 | Belgium | 10.7 | 0.867 | 2 | 6 | .. | 34,873 | 5.7 | 7.3 | 64 |
| 19 | Denmark | 5.5 | 0.866 | 6 | 2 | .. | 36,404 | 7.2 | 8.2 | 105 |
| 20 | Spain | 45.3 | 0.863 | 0 | 14 | .. | 29,661 | 5.6 | 7.6 | 76 |
| 22 | Greece | 11.2 | 0.855 | -2 | 23 | .. | 27,580 | 5.8 | 6.8 | 97 |
| 23 | Italy | 60.1 | 0.854 | -5 | 9 | .. | 29,619 | 4.9 | 6.7 | 122 |
| 24 | Luxembourg | 0.5 | 0.852 | 2 | 24 | .. | 51,109 | .. | 7.7 | 69 |
| 25 | Austria | 8.4 | 0.851 | 5 | 19 | .. | 37,056 | 4.9 | 7.8 | 57 |
| 26 | United Kingdom | 61.9 | 0.849 | 1 | 32 | .. | 35,087 | 6.1 | 7.4 | 74 |
| 28 | Czech Republic | 10.4 | 0.841 | 8 | 27 | 0 | 22,678 | 5.3 | 6.9 | 92 |
| 29 | Slovenia | 2.0 | 0.828 | 5 | 17 | 0 | 25,857 | 3.9 | 7.1 | 66 |
| 31 | Slovakia | 5.4 | 0.818 | 3 | 31 | 0 | 21,658 | 4.9 | 5.8 | 73 |
| 33 | Malta | 0.4 | 0.815 | .. | 35 | .. | 21,004 | .. | 7.1 | 44 |
| 34 | Estonia | 1.3 | 0.812 | 0 | 39 | 7 | 17,168 | 6.4 | 5.6 | 131 |
| 35 | Cyprus | 0.9 | 0.810 | -1 | 15 | .. | 21,962 | .. | 7.1 | 62 |

| | | | | | | | | | | |
|---|---|---|---|---|---|---|---|---|---|---|
| 36 | Hungary | 10.0 | 0.805 | 3 | 34 | 1 | 17,472 | 3.2 | 5.7 | 90 |
| 40 | Portugal | 10.7 | 0.795 | −1 | 21 | : | 22,105 | 4.4 | 5.9 | 98 |
| 41 | Poland | 38.0 | 0.795 | 1 | 26 | : | 17,803 | 3.9 | 6.5 | 77 |
| 44 | Lithuania | 3.3 | 0.783 | 1 | 33 | : | 14,824 | 3.3 | 5.8 | 86 |
| 48 | Latvia | 2.2 | 0.769 | 2 | 22 | 0 | 12,944 | 4.6 | 5.4 | 101 |
| 50 | Romania | 21.2 | 0.767 | 3 | 49 | : | 12,844 | 2.7 | 5.9 | 70 |
| 58 | Bulgaria | 7.5 | 0.743 | 5 | 36 | : | 11,139 | 3.3 | 4.4 | 82 |
| | **Selected Asian Countries** | | | | | | | | | |
| 27 | Singapore | 4.8 | 0.846 | : | 10 | : | 48,893 | 4.5 | 6.7 | 49 |
| 57 | Malaysia | 27.9 | 0.744 | : | 50 | : | 13,927 | : | 6.6 | 33 |
| 89 | China | 1,354.1 | 0.663 | 0 | 38 | 12 | 7,258 | 1.8 | 6.4 | 20 |
| 92 | Thailand | 68.1 | 0.654 | 5 | 69 | 2 | 8,001 | 1.7 | 6.3 | 41 |
| 108 | Indonesia | 232.5 | 0.600 | 9 | 100 | 21 | 3,957 | : | 5.7 | 16 |
| 119 | India | 1,214.5 | 0.519 | 0 | 122 | 55 | 3,337 | 0.8 | 5.5 | 35 |
| 125 | Pakistan | 184.8 | 0.490 | 1 | 112 | 51 | 2,678 | 0.7 | 5.4 | 24 |
| | **Selected Middle East Countries** | | | | | | | | | |
| 15 | Israel | 7.3 | 0.872 | −11 | 28 | : | 27,831 | 5.4 | 7.1 | 67 |
| 32 | United Arab Emirates | 4.7 | 0.815 | : | 45 | 1 | 58,006 | 10.3 | 7.3 | 123 |
| 38 | Qatar | 1.5 | 0.803 | : | 94 | : | 79,426 | 9.7 | 6.7 | .. |
| 47 | Kuwait | 3.1 | 0.771 | : | 43 | : | 55,719 | 7.9 | 6.6 | 128 |
| 55 | Saudi Arabia | 26.2 | 0.752 | : | 128 | : | 24,726 | 3.5 | 7.7 | 13 |
| 70 | Iran | 75.1 | 0.702 | : | 98 | : | 11,764 | 2.7 | 5.6 | 81 |
| 83 | Turkey | 75.7 | 0.679 | 1 | 77 | 8 | 13,359 | 2.8 | 5.5 | 83 |
| 133 | Yemen | 24.3 | 0.439 | −2 | 138 | 53 | 2,387 | 1.0 | 4.8 | 50 |
| | **Selected Latin American and Caribbean Countries** | | | | | | | | | |
| 45 | Chile | 17.1 | 0.783 | −10 | 53 | : | 13,561 | 3.1 | 6.3 | 46 |
| 46 | Argentina | 40.7 | 0.775 | −11 | 60 | 3 | 14,603 | 3.0 | 7.1 | 15 |
| 54 | Panama | 3.5 | 0.755 | −20 | 81 | : | 13,347 | 3.2 | 7.8 | 18 |
| 56 | Mexico | 110.6 | 0.750 | −8 | 68 | 4 | 13,971 | 3.2 | 7.7 | 23 |
| 62 | Costa Rica | 4.6 | 0.725 | −6 | 51 | : | 10,870 | 2.7 | 8.5 | 1 |
| 73 | Brazil | 195.4 | 0.699 | −15 | 80 | 9 | 10,607 | : | 7.6 | 9 |
| 75 | Venezuela | 29.0 | 0.696 | −1 | 64 | : | 11,846 | 2.3 | 7.8 | 36 |
| 77 | Ecuador | 13.8 | 0.695 | 3 | 86 | 2 | 7,931 | 1.9 | 6.4 | 25 |
| 79 | Colombia | 46.3 | 0.689 | −18 | 90 | 9 | 8,589 | 1.9 | 7.3 | 6 |
| 95 | Bolivia | 10.0 | 0.643 | −17 | 96 | 36 | 4,357 | 2.4 | 6.5 | 47 |

(continued)

**TABLE 1.1:** (continued)

| HDI RANK[a] | Country | POPULATION (Millions; 2010)[a] | HUMAN DEVELOPMENT INDEX (HDI) (2010)[a] | INEQUALITY-ADJUSTED HDI (Change in HDI rank; 2010)[a,b] | GENDER INEQUALITY INDEX (Rank; 2008) (out of 138 countries)[a] | MULTIDIMENSIONAL POVERTY INDEX (% of population suffering multiple deprivations) (2000–2008)[a] | GROSS NATIONAL INCOME (GNI) PER CAPITA (PPP U.S.$ 2008) (2010)[a] | ECOLOGICAL FOOTPRINT OF CONSUMPTION (Hectares per capita) (2006)[a] | OVERALL LIFE SATISFACTION (2006–2009) (0—least satisfied, 10—most satisfied)[a] | HAPPY PLANET INDEX (HPI) RANK (2009)[c] (Out of 143 countries) |
|---|---|---|---|---|---|---|---|---|---|---|
| | **Selected African Countries** | | | | | | | | | |
| 101 | Egypt | 84.5 | 0.620 | −7 | 108 | 6 | 5,889 | 1.4 | 5.8 | 12 |
| 110 | South Africa | 50.5 | 0.597 | −1 | 82 | 3 | 9,812 | 2.7 | 5.0 | 118 |
| 128 | Kenya | 40.9 | 0.470 | −1 | 117 | 60 | 1,628 | .. | 3.7 | 125 |
| 130 | Ghana | 24.3 | 0.467 | 7 | 114 | 30 | 1,385 | 1.6 | 4.7 | 100 |
| 144 | Senegal | 12.9 | 0.411 | 0 | 113 | 67 | 1,816 | 1.2 | 4.5 | 96 |
| 148 | Tanzania | 45.0 | 0.398 | 9 | .. | 65 | 1,344 | 1.0 | 2.4 | 142 |
| 152 | Rwanda | 10.3 | 0.385 | 3 | 83 | 81 | 1,190 | .. | 4.2 | 119 |
| 153 | Malawi | 15.7 | 0.385 | 8 | 126 | 72 | 911 | .. | 6.2 | 107 |
| 157 | Ethiopia | 85.0 | 0.328 | 1 | .. | 90 | 992 | .. | 4.2 | 124 |
| 158 | Sierra Leone | 5.8 | 0.317 | −1 | 125 | 81 | 809 | 0.8 | 3.6 | 136 |
| 159 | Central African Republic | 4.5 | 0.315 | −3 | 132 | 86 | 758 | 1.4 | 4.6 | 137 |
| 160 | Mali | 13.3 | 0.309 | 0 | 135 | 87 | 1,171 | 1.9 | 3.8 | 132 |
| 165 | Mozambique | 23.4 | 0.284 | −2 | 111 | 80 | 854 | .. | 3.8 | 133 |
| 167 | Niger | 15.9 | 0.261 | 2 | 136 | 93 | 675 | 1.7 | 3.8 | 129 |
| 168 | Congo | 67.8 | 0.239 | 0 | 137 | 73 | 291 | 0.7 | 4.4 | 120 |
| 169 | Zimbabwe | 12.6 | 0.140 | 0 | 105 | 38 | 176 | 1.0 | 2.8 | 143 |

[a] Source: UNDP (2010).
[b] Change in rank is based on countries for which IHDI is calculated.
[c] Source: Abdalla, Thompson, et al. (2009).
[d] Non-EU member state.

development perspective would appear to be Norway and the worst place would be Zimbabwe.

In addition to the main headline indexes, 2010 HDR provides a suite of supplementary indicators that reveal the complexity of human development. A close review of these data—covering areas such as infrastructure, energy usage, ecological footprint, subjective-welling and happiness, employment, empowerment, freedom, community safety, and financial flows—shows that a country with a high HDI might have less freedoms and be on a unsustainable pathway, whereas the opposite might be true for a country with a low HDI. Hence, a broad viewing of the data is essential.

Table 1.1 presents (where applicable) country data relating to the HDI, the Inequality-adjusted HDI (IHDI), the Gender Inequality Index (GII), the Multidimensional Poverty Index (MPI), and several other measures such as ecological footprint, the overall life satisfaction of a country's people, and the New Economics Foundation's Happy Planet Index (HPI), which is discussed later in this section.

Since the HDI does not reveal disparities in measures of human development that may exist across people within a nation, the IHDI adjusts the HDI to take these inequalities into account. The IHDI effectively discounts each of the three dimensions of the HDI based upon the extent of inequality experienced in a dimension—for example, significant income inequality within a nation would reduce the value of the HDI's "income" index. If no inequalities existed within a nation, the HDI and IHDI would be the same. Thus, the HDI can be considered as a measure of "potential" human development, whereas the IHDI measures the "actual" level of human development (UNDP 2010). The IHDI-related data in Table 1.1 shows the number of positions a country would move up or down the HDI ranking once inequalities have been taken into account. For example, the U.S. HDI rank (column 5) falls by nine positions once inequalities have been taken into account. The main reason for this decline in rank is income inequality, which reduces the income index for the HDI by 24 percent.* Table 1.1 also shows that the IHDI rank of Israel, Chile, Argentina, Panama, Brazil, Colombia, and Bolivia drop by more than ten positions, primarily as a result of significant income inequality within these countries. The latter three countries also have high education and health inequalities among their people.

The GII (column 6) measures women's disadvantage in terms of (1) reproductive health (using a maternal mortality rate and adolescent fertility rate); (2) empowerment (using parliamentary representation and attainment at secondary and higher education); and (3) the labor market (using a labor market participation rate). The GII replaced the Gender Development Index (GEM) and Gender Empowerment Measure (GEM) that were in use since 1995. Table 1.1 shows that nine of the top ten nations in terms of the GII are located in Europe; Singapore is ranked 10th. Perhaps somewhat surprisingly, the United States is ranked 37th.

Finally, the MPI (column 7) measures multiple (and overlapping) deprivations at the household level in the dimensions of health, education, and standard of living. The ten component indicators used in the MPI have equal weights within their dimension, and each dimension is given an equal weight of one third. A household is considered to be multidimensionally poor if it is deprived in two of the ten component indicators. The MPI replaced the Human Poverty Index (HPI) that was in use since 1997. Table 1.1 shows the percentage of the population in each country that is classified as being multidimensionally poor. As might be expected, the extent of multidimensional poverty is the greatest in developing regions, especially in sub-Saharan Africa where around 65 percent of the population falls into this classification (UNDP 2010).

The ecological footprint and overall life satisfaction data (columns 9 and 10) in Table 1.1 further enrich the picture of human development in the countries shown. It is evident that nations with higher HDI values also have larger ecological footprints, whereas nations with lower HDIs values have smaller ecological footprints. This is primarily because countries with low HDI values are typically emerging or developing economies that have yet to create significant industrial sectors and domestic consumer demand. It also highlights the burden developed nations place on the environment through their production systems and consuming habits. With regards to the overall life satisfaction measure, countries with the lowest HDI values also have the lowest levels of overall life satisfaction; however, the difference in life satisfaction between countries with medium to high HDI values is harder to distinguish. For example, people within Costa Rica, which is ranked 62nd in terms of its HDI value, have a greater level of overall life satisfaction than people in any other nation. In Colombia, which is ranked 79th in terms of its HDI value, people have the same level of overall life satisfaction than people in Germany, which is ranked 10th in terms of its HDI

---

*      See Section 1.1.3.1 for a detailed discussion of the growing income inequality in the United States and other regions and its major causes.

value. Thus, a broad perspective of human development is essential when viewing progress through the lens of sustainable development. After all, sustainable development is a multidimensional concept and will therefore require multiple measures to capture its many-sidedness.

The UNDP's (2010) HDR reflects this view in the breadth of all emasures it presents for comparison. For example the inclusion of subjective well-being and happiness measures is a step forward, one that is perhaps overdue (Diener and Suh 2000).

The measurement of subjective well-being (SWB) and happiness and their relationship to income have been the focus of a substantial amount of research by psychologists and social scientists over the past thirty years (Argyle 2002; Diener and Oishi 2000; Diener and Suh 1997; Diener, Suh, et al. 1997; Inglehart and Klingemann 2000; Kenny 1999; Layard 2005; Oishi, Diener, et al. 1999).* In the context of sustainable development, measuring whether people feel *happy* and *satisfied* with life is also seen as a good proxy for assessing whether they are living in accord with *human nature* (Kellert and Wilson 1993). In general, the relationship between income and SWB tends to follow the same trend observed for income and life expectancy. First, there is a dramatic increase in well-being up to a certain income (which is around $10,000 per capita for SWB), after which increases in income have only a limited effect on improving a person's well-being, although there is a slight increase (Inglehart 2000; Inglehart and Klingemann 2000). A note of caution is added here: this outcome does not mean that unlimited wealth will not affect an individual's well-being. There is a substantial amount of research that shows that if an individual focuses on materialistic pursuits, his or her well-being is likely to decrease (Kasser 2002). However, there appears to be a general consensus that poor people are less happy than wealthy people and that wealthy nations tend to be the happiest, although wealthy societies have not grown in SWB (Diener and Oishi 2000; Kenny 1999).

A new measure of development that combines subjective well-being (that is, self-reported life satisfaction), life expectancy, and the EF is the Happy Planet Index (HPI) (Abdallah, Thompson, et al. 2009); see the last column in Table 1.1:

$$\text{Happy Planet Index (HPI)} = (\text{Life Satisfaction} \times \text{Life Expectancy})/\text{Ecological Footprint}$$

Rather than attempting to revise existing measures such as GDP/GNI or the HDI, the HPI was created to combine fundamental inputs (that is, planetary resource consumption) and ultimate ends (that is, a long and happy life) to measure the ecological efficiency of delivering human well-being (Abdallah, Thompson, et al. 2009). The index rejects GDP/GNI as a measure of development/progress and shifts the focus to human well-being and environmental sustainability.

The comparison of a country's HDI and HPI rankings in Table 1.1 highlights some interesting points. For example, Norway has the highest HDI ranking, but it is ranked 88th by the HPI. Similarly, the United States has an HDI rank of 4, but an HPI rank of 114. The reason for this dramatic difference in their rankings on these two indexes is the large ecological footprint of these (consumer or industrialized) societies. Indeed, a closer look at those nations with a high GNI per capita and a HDI ranking show that these countries all have relatively low HPI rankings. Conversely, those nations with a more modest GNI per capita (and hence a smaller ecological footprint)—such as many Latin American and Caribbean states—where life expectancy fluctuates around the mid seventies and people tend to be quite satisfied with life have high HPI rankings. The top 10 countries in the HPI ranking (ordered from 1 to 10) are Costa Rica, the Dominican Republic, Jamaica, Guatemala, Vietnam, Colombia, Cuba, El Salvador, Brazil, and Honduras. The low GNI per capita (and ecological footprints) of many African countries, combined with low life expectancy and levels of life satisfaction, mean that these nations tend to rank poorly in the HPI. The bottom ten countries in the HPI ranking are all found in sub-Saharan Africa.

When the HPI is considered alongside measures such as the HDI, it reveals the poor environmental performance of industrialized nations. It indicates that the (typically) long and happy lives of people in these regions are grounded on an environmentally

---

* Diener and Suh (2000) highlight a few important methodological issues relating to the measurement of SWB that are worth mentioning. First, initial measurements of SWB do seem to be comparable across individuals and societies. Second, the translation of the questions used to measure SWB into different languages does not seem to affect the research results. However, further research is called for. Third, even though there have been some positive results, there are still many methodological problems associated with measuring well-being across cultures. For example, the numeric scales used in the questionnaires might be interpreted differently by different cultures. The selection of an indicator (or index) to measure predictor variables such as freedom or equality is extremely difficult. Also, it is not yet clear what type of information each culture is using when it is responding to the questions. Although there are clearly problems with measuring SWB, the initial results presented by Diener and Suh (2000) are informative.

unsustainable lifestyle. It also reveals those nations, such as Costa Rica, that provide an example of what a more sustainable lifestyle might look like (see the discussion of Costa Rica in Section 3.4.2 in Chapter 3).

For each of the measures or indexes discussed here, it is possible to find supporting or discrediting arguments. On the one hand, proponents argue that the informative power of indexes outweighs any potential methodological or subjectivity problems embedded in their calculation. The political support given to GDP/GNI as *the* measure of progress (and human welfare) is often cited as an example of the need to present countermeasures that measure real progress toward sustainable development. On the other hand, opponents of indexes argue that the subjective selection of indicators (from one or more domains of sustainable development) that are adjusted and aggregated into a single value makes the final output difficult to use in a meaningful way (Becker 1997). Further, combining indicators that measure both short- and long-term concerns and processes hides difficult decisions associated with intergenerational equity. "There is undeniably a serious conflict between the wishes regarding production in the short term and the wishes not to jeopardize the living conditions of future generations. By adding elements reflecting these conflicting goals together in a sustainability indicator, the danger arises that inevitable choices are concealed. This hampers an open decision-making process in the course of which the inevitable sacrifice of either less sustainability or—more likely—less production in the short run is not hidden" (Hueting and Reijnders 2004, p. 254).

It seems clear that although all the indexes relating to development have some form of shortcoming, they serve a valuable role in raising public awareness about unsustainable development patterns. However, because indexes do not reveal the *processes* that are driving unsustainable trends, it would seem unwise to base a decision-making process solely on them.

Having introduced several indexes that can be used to measure (human) development, we now turn to the challenges raised by the predominant laissez-faire (that is, market-oriented) approach to development and how this approach can affect human well-being.

### 1.1.2 Consumption and Well-Being

As globalization proceeds, one could argue that feelings of deprivation are creating a motivation for better material standards of living. Until we reached the era of global media, people did not feel deprived in relation to other nations. Now that the differences in consumption are conspicuously visible, poverty and its effect on culture become important issues—that is, people "feel" economically and materially poor. If we assume that the satisfaction of needs drives economic and political systems, one quickly realizes that if basic human needs become confused with materialistic wants on a global scale, the rapid expansion of the throughput society could lead to serious environmental consequences.

A throughput (or high-waste) society, by definition, depends on increasing rates of consumption (or throughput) (Daly 1996; Princen, Maniates, et al. 2002). To the extent to which we are losing jobs as a result of production efficiencies (or innovation), the only way to create more jobs is to expand the economy and increase throughput. A critical question, therefore, is whether basic human needs drive our throughput society, or whether this drive stems from a *conditioned* response.

In neoclassical economics, human needs/wants drive systems of exchange and markets. Although many economists might argue that consumer demand—derived from the purchasing habits of consumers—is an accurate representation of what people desire, they often forget to mention the $277 billion (2006 data) that corporations spend annually on advertising with the sole purpose of creating demand (U.S. Census Bureau 2010, Table 737). Hence a concern is that the world of industrialization and commerce has made the distinction between basic human needs and wants unclear (Michaelis 2000). Indeed, one could argue, as Galbraith (1958) did, that if a want is to be urgent, it should be the result of a need that originates within the individual. This position was later supported by economist Nicholas Georgescu-Roegen (1971, p. 324), who argued that "only those goods and services an individual can enjoy personally influence his satisfaction." If a want is externally contrived, it cannot be an urgent (or basic) need. Hence satisfying that want will occur only through behavior that is led by extrinsic motivation, which is not likely to result in the enhancement of an individual's well-being.*

---

* The idea that capitalist economies have been successful in achieving intermediate goals of increasing material wealth, but that this has been accomplished at the expense of underlying human values [and the environment], is becoming more widely accepted by economists (Ackerman, Kiron, et al. 1997). Indeed, the emerging field of ecological economics is a good example of a branch of economics that is attempting to integrate human values into economic analysis (Krishnan, Harris, and Goodwin 1995).

The inference from these remarks is that in promoting economic growth, companies entice people to buy their services or products. The primary way for the value or benefit of a product or service to be conveyed to the consumer is through advertising. M. R. Smith (1994, p. 13) describes how American advertising "became the instrument by which big business, in need of ever-expanding markets for its mass-produced products, imprinted instrumental values—and with them, the ethos of mass consumption—on the populace." Hence it can be argued that advertising leads to *producer-created demand*—that is, what we need/want is conditioned by advertising. Galbraith (1967) provides a succinct example of this idea: "Were there but one manufacturer of automobiles in the United States, it would still be essential that it enter extensively on the management of its demand. Otherwise consumers, exercising the sovereignty that would be inconsistent with the company's planning, might resort to other forms of transportation and other ways of spending their income" (p. 207). Further, Soros (1997) argues that the notion of producer-created demand has established money as *the* measure that identifies a product or an individual's value: "Advertising, marketing, even packaging aim at shaping people's preferences rather than, as laissez-faire theory holds, merely responding to them. Unsure of what they stand for, people increasingly rely on money as the criterion of value. What is more expensive is considered better. The value of a work of art can be judged by the price it fetches. People deserve respect and admiration because they are rich. What used to be a medium of exchange has usurped the place of the fundamental values, revising the relationship postulated by economic theory" (ibid., p. 52).

Michaelis (2000) takes the concept of producer-created demand one step further by extrapolating it to other areas. In particular, she asks whether a government's failure to regulate advertising may inhibit our ability to satisfy our intrinsic need for autonomy. "The market economy contains structural incentives for businesses to market conceptions of the good life that support sales of their own products. Many other circumstances, including social norms, work culture, and infrastructure constraints, provide strong pressures for individuals to adopt particular conceptions of the good life. Hence, by adopting a hands-off approach, governments may actually be failing to protect an important freedom" (Michaelis 2000, p. 26). A major problem with the current form of advertising is that people start to live their lives believing that a high level of income and material wealth are essential to their happiness (Jacobson and Mazur 1995).

Similarly, Sanne (2002) argues that a focus on the social and psychological factors of consumer behavior neglects to consider how producers and businesses *create* consumption to satisfy their own interests.[4] It also neglects the role of the state and how business has a tendency to co-opt or lobby government for market conditions that favor consumption. This latter issue creates what Sanne (2002, p. 282) calls "structural lock-in effects." These effects are the following (in order of impact):

1. the pattern of work-and-spend promoted by naturalising paid work as "full time" with continuous, life-long occupation supported by a legal structure of social insurance, eligibility to social benefits, etc.

2. the making of a consumer culture where marketable goods are forwarded as the means to satisfy not only material needs but also needs of social stratification* and cultural identification†

3. the promotion of individual means of transport, in particular cars, which presuppose heavy investments in road infrastructure, a classical aim of much business lobbying

4. new communication infrastructures which force a technology shift on consumers. (Sanne 2002, p. 282)

Sanne (2002) argues that governments and businesses tend to counter incentives to curb consumption with deference to consumer sovereignty. This position passes the responsibility to the consumer, whose purchasing behavior then becomes subject to moral inquiry. The basic argument is that firms would provide environmentally friendly products if consumers demanded them. Hence we must first address the values that support present lifestyles by educating consumers about the effects of their behavior. The problem is that there is a fine line between education and persuasion or coercion; the latter is an

---

\* The differentialist view of consumption is that of social stratification, i.e., the use of wealth to *conspicuously consume*, to display artifacts of taste or expense commensurate with one's position in society (Sanne 2002). See also Thorstein Veblen's (1994 [1902]) classic work *The Theory of the Leisure Class*, which introduced the phrase "conspicuous consumption."

† The culturalist view of consumption connects the individual to her own self-understanding (Sanne 2002). Consumption is seen as a reflection of the self; what you buy supports your understanding of who you are. Both differentialist and culturalist views are part of utilitarianism because in both cases the objective is to increase overall well-being.

infringement on an individual's freedom to choose. But one could argue that an individual's freedom to choose is affected by advertising targeted directly at our insecurities. A reliance on consumer sovereignty is further complicated by the fact that a growing number of consumers in America seem paralyzed by an inability to speak out against materialistic tendencies because this would go against our core belief that people should have the freedom to make their own decisions (Harwood Group 1995). Hence people turn away from questioning their behavior and that of others, undermining any argument that society will act responsibly if it is provided with sufficient information about the problems associated with its consumption. Thus one pathway to a sustainable future may be to counter the pattern of work-and-spend by establishing shorter working hours or building in work arrangements that anticipate more holidays and leisure time (Kenny 1999; Sanne 2002).* The notion here is that with less income and fewer working hours, we will consume less and be able to enjoy more leisure time. However, there are those who question whether more leisure time would lead to a better quality of life: "The psychological underpinnings of capitalism have enabled the leisure time which technology affords us to be converted into yet another opportunity for the consumption of unnecessary goods. Inasmuch as capitalism has 'freed' the worker from the worst excesses of the labour process, it has sought to occupy his free time with 'compensatory needs' that bring neither happiness nor personal fulfillment" (M. Redclift 1984, p. 53).

---

* In 1998, France's ruling left-wing coalition introduced a law to reduce the legal workweek from thirty-nine to thirty-five hours for most employees, effective January 1, 2000. The objectives of the law were to create jobs, enhance competitiveness, and establish a better balance between work and personal life (Ministère de l'emploi, de la cohésion sociale et du logement 2002). The basic idea was that capping working hours would force employers to hire more workers to cover any loss in productivity. However, since the law was enacted, it has failed to deliver on its promises: unemployment remains high and productivity has declined. A study by Estevão and Sá (2006) concluded that the law also caused an overall decline in welfare. Their conclusion was based on subjective measures of satisfaction with work hours, an increase in the number of workers holding two jobs, and data indicating that workers tried to circumvent the law by transitioning from large to small firms with fewer than twenty people. These small firms were required to implement the thirty-five-hour week by January 1, 2002. There was also concern that the law would reduce working conditions by, for example, increasing the amount of staggered hours worked, with a corresponding increase in task-splitting and hand-over procedures (Bulard 1999). Given concerns such as those mentioned here, the current administration has introduced greater flexibility into the laws to (effectively) re-establish a thirty-nine-hour workweek in the private sector.

The psychological and environmental problems associated with advertising and the throughput (or consumer) society have been well documented (Brown 1981; de Graaf, Wann, et al. 2002; Diener and Suh 2000; Durning 1992, 1994; Goodwin, Ackerman, et al. 1997; Kasser 2002; Layard 2005; Princen, Maniates, et al. 2002; J. C. Ryan and Durning 1997; Schlosser 2002; P. C. Stern, Dietz, et al. 1997). However, calls for public recognition of the potential problems with a market economy have failed to materialize. One possible reason for this is that we are so entrenched in the current economic paradigm that we are unable to recognize that we are in some way addicted to consuming (Ehrenfeld 2004). Although the consumption of products and services clearly improves our quality of life, we should be aware that our perception of the good life has been and is being manipulated by market actors whose primary incentive is profit. Hence the line between consumption that satisfies intrinsic and extrinsic needs is becoming blurred.

In conclusion, this section asks whether focusing on industrialization and commerce is likely to enhance overall human well-being. It seems clear that relying solely on economic growth (and consumption) to advance human well-being is too simplistic and that government has an important role to play in shaping the institutional structure of the economy to better accommodate nonconsumption solutions to human needs (Kenny 1999; Manno 2002; Michaelis 2000; Sanne 2002). Thus there is a need to consider innovative public policies to ensure that noncommercial values—such as the benefits received from family and community life—form an integral part of modern society.

### 1.1.3 Employment

Work and the workplace are essential elements of industrialized and industrializing economies. Work is combined with physical and natural capital to produce goods and services. The workplace is where the comparative advantages of workers and owners/managers create a market for exchange of talents and assets. Significantly, work is the main means of distributing wealth and generating purchasing power in dynamic national economic systems. Beyond markets, work provides both a means of engagement of people in the society and an important social environment and mechanism for enhancing self-esteem and satisfaction with life.[5]

The following two sections address the issues of income inequality—both between and within nations (specifically within the United States)—and the importance of employment beyond the creation of purchasing power.

### 1.1.3.1 Income and Wage Inequality

Since the early 1990s, the *Human Development Report* and development indexes have highlighted the disparities between the developed and developing regions of the world. As the reports and indexes make clear, the record is mixed: spectacular development successes in the years since World War II coexist with persistent human suffering and wasted potential.

Although many nations have experienced substantial economic growth since the 1960s, it is unclear whether this growth has increased or reduced between-nation income inequality. The confusion lies in how *national incomes*—measured using gross domestic product (GDP) or gross national product (GNP)—are compared.*

Two common ways to convert GDP or GNP into a single currency are to use foreign exchange rates (the FX method) or PPP comparisons (based on the Penn World Table) (Firebaugh 2003).[6] In general, it appears that the FX method tends to reveal increasing inequality (UNDP 1999), whereas PPP comparisons show no discernible trends (or a decline in inequality depending on the period of analysis) (Dowrick and Akmal 2005; McGillivray and Shorrocks 2005). In addition, the measure of inequality (such as the Gini, Theil, or Mean Logarithmic Deviation [MLD] indexes) and whether this measure has been weighted by population[†] also affect the

assessment of between-nation income inequality (Wade 2001).

Although more research is needed to identify better ways to adequately compare the income of different nations, Firebaugh (2003) and Ghose (2003) provide informative analyses of how the spread of industrialization and trade liberalization during the last part of the twentieth century has led to a corresponding decrease in inequality between nations during this period. Their analyses are based on nations that are weighted by population, which both authors argue is a more accurate way to measure global income inequality.

In contrast to the debate on between-nation income inequality, there is more agreement on the trends of within-nation income and wage inequality or wage dispersion. For example, there is a strong consensus that since the 1970s both income inequality and wage inequality have increased in the United States (Barnet 1993; Bernstein and Mishel 1997; Cornia, Addison, et al. 2004; Firebaugh 2003; R. B. Freeman 1996; Gottschalk and Danziger 2005; Grubb and Wilson 1992; Head 1996; Hyclak 2000; Ilg and Haugen 2000; Johnson, Smeeding, et al. 2005; Katz and Autor 1999; Katz and Murphy 1992; Levy, Bluestone, et al. 1986; Madden 2000; Madrick 1999; Morris and Western 1999), reversing trends of equalization that occurred following the Great Depression.[‡] Outside the United States, similar trends have been observed in many advanced industrialized economies since the 1980s (R. B. Freeman and Katz 1994, 1995; Ghose 2003; ILO 2008; Kahai and Simmons 2005). Further, Cornia, Addison, et al. (2004) show that over the past two decades income inequality within a significant number of developing, transitional, and de-

---

\*        The debate whether between-nation income inequality has increased is more concerned with how national income is converted to a common currency than with the selection of GDP or GNP.

†        The decision whether to weight a measure of inequality by population depends on the purpose of the analysis. As Firebaugh (2003, pp. 126–127) remarks, "If the goal is to test a theory of how national economies work—so each nation can be viewed as a separate realization of some underlying economic processes—then each nation would be weighted the same. But if the goal is to calculate the average disproportionality of individuals' income ratios—that is, to make inferences about global income inequality—there is no reason why citizens of large countries should carry less weight than citizens of small countries, as an unweighted index gives us. People in China and Chad should have equal value in the analysis."

A proportional share, or equality, implies that an income ratio equals 1.0 (i.e., $r = X / \overline{X} = 1.0$, where $r$ denotes income ratio, $X$ denotes income, and $\overline{X}$ denotes the mean of $X$). Hence the greater the distance that a given unit ($X_j$) lies from the proportional share ($\overline{X}$), the greater the inequality or disproportionality (ibid.). The summary indexes (such as the Gini or Theil indexes) measure the average disproportionality across all units—i.e., they measure the average distance of the $r_j$ from 1.0, where distance is a function $f$ such that $f(1.0) = 0$ (ibid.).

---

‡        For a contrasting view, see Fogel (2000). Fogel (2000, p. 143) argues that the increase in income inequality in the United States during the 1970s and 1980s can be explained by lifestyle choices, primarily by the decision of how to use one's free (or leisure) time. His argument is based on the notion that two people in the same occupation can choose two very different work schedules that enable one to retire earlier than the other. The basic idea is that the person who retires early is able to do so because he or she opted to work more hours per week than his or her colleague who chose a more leisurely workweek and a longer career. Although their cumulative lifetime wages might be the same, the differences in their yearly incomes would put them in different income distributions. Fogel argues that such differences in the hours worked by heads of households and spouses account for some 54 percent of the rise in income inequality between the top and bottom 10 percent of household incomes. This means that more than half of the growth in income inequality that occurred during the 1970s and 1980s can be attributed to the changing pattern of labor supply. In addition, Fogel presents data showing that changes in wages accounted for less than 6 percent of the growth in income inequality.

veloped nations has increased (to varying degrees), slowing development efforts and poverty alleviation.* More generally, the ILO (2005, 2006) has found that between 1990 and 2000 wages in high-skilled occupations increased faster than in low-skilled occupations globally, resulting in growing inequality.

Although understanding the trends and potential causes of inequality within different nations is of value, we will focus our discussion on the United States, where wage and income disparity seem to be accompanied by policies of wage liberalization (that is, wage flexibility)† and a relatively low concern for the welfare of workers. Thus calls for emulating the U.S. approach could portend serious social problems if it is adopted in Europe and other regions.

With regard to U.S. wages, the trends over the past quarter century indicate a decline in median weekly earnings of full-time workers (R. B. Freeman 1996; Madrick 1999; Morris and Western 1999). During this period there was also a persistent growth in wage inequality as those at the top of the wage distribution pulled away from middle- and low-wage workers (Bernstein and Mishel 1997; Mishel, Bernstein, et al. 2005, 2009).‡ For example, Figure 1.1 shows that the hourly wages of both men and women in the bottom 10 percent (P10) of the wage distribution fell significantly between 1975 and the late 1980s, after which the decline stabilized. In 2002 the hourly wages of both genders within this group were some 20 percent lower (in real terms) than they were in 1975. In contrast, the hourly wages for both men and women in the top 10 percent (P90) of the wage distribution

grew continuously during the same period. This growth in wage inequality was also accompanied by an increase in the number of hours worked by both men and women (Gottschalk and Danziger 2005) and a recent decline in the benefits employers provide, such as health insurance and pensions (R. B. Freeman 1996; Krugman 2006). Thus the evidence points to a growing divide (or wedge) between high-paid and low-wage workers that is creating an "apartheid economy" of haves and have-nots (R. B. Freeman 1996).§

The growth in wage inequality has been accompanied by a growth in inequality of household incomes.¶ For example, between 1979 and 2000, the real income of the lowest fifth of U.S. households grew by 6.4 percent, for the top fifth it grew by 70 percent, and for the top 1 percent it grew by 184 percent (Mishel, Bernstein, et al. 2005, p. 2). Figure 1.2 shows how family income and male wage inequality (measured by dividing the incomes of the top 10 percent of the income distribution by the incomes of the bottom 10 percent for each group—that is, the P90/P10 ratio) grew significantly from 1975 to 2002. It also shows how the growth in income experienced during the economic recovery in the later 1990s was insufficient to offset the inequality that occurred in the previous two decades (Gottschalk and Danziger 2005). Low-income families are not the only ones that have lost ground. Since the late 1970s, the gap between middle-income families and high-income families has widened in forty-four states across America (Bernstein, Boushey, et al. 2002). To compound the problem

---

\* In a somewhat contradictory study, Kahai and Simmons (2005) found that the process of globalization—measured using a comprehensive globalization index—tends to reduce income inequality in developing nations. Further, their analysis did not find any systematic relationship between globalization and income inequality in developed nations. Factors considered in the creation of their globalization index included the volume of international travel and phone calls, cross-border remittances and other transfers, the number of Internet hosts within a nation, and a nation's economic integration and share of international trade. The fact that Kahai and Simmons were comparing a general index of globalization with income inequality (measured using the Gini Index) might help explain the differences in their findings.

† The idea of allowing the market to determine wages is parallel to the U.S. approach to trade (i.e., the Washington Consensus), which promotes market-liberalizing policies and a limited role for government in the economy.

‡ Wright and Dwyer (2003) examined the quality of jobs generated during periods of job expansion from the 1960s through to the 1990s in the United States. The long 1990s boom produced polarized job expansion characterized by a slower growth of middle-level jobs due to the decline of manufacturing, and stronger growth in bottom-end jobs in retail trade and personal services, and very strong growth in high tech sectors.

§ R. B. Freeman (1996, p. 121) argues that although some 25 million jobs were created during the Reagan, George Bush, and Clinton administrations, the nation needs to recognize that it "has an inequality problem based on falling real earnings for low-paid workers that is unparalleled at least since the Great Depression." In making his case, he states that the problem with the economy is not the nation's strong track record of productivity, technological leadership, or rate of economic growth; instead, it is the manner in which the economy distributes the economic benefits from this progress. Mishel, Bernstein, et al. (2005, p. 5) reinforce Freeman's arguments by stating that between 2000 and 2003, "income shifted extremely rapidly and extensively from labor compensation to capital income (profits and interest), so the benefits of faster productivity went disproportionately, in fact completely, to capital."

¶ In the United States, wages and salaries for the bottom four-fifths of families by income account for approximately 70 percent of total household income (Mishel, Bernstein, et al. 2009). Approximately, 7 percent of their income is from business and capital sources with the remainder coming from other sources such as social security benefits and tax deferred retirement accounts. In contrast, the top fifth of families by income obtain 60 percent of their income from wages and salaries, 26 percent from business and capital sources, and 14 percent from other sources (ibid.).

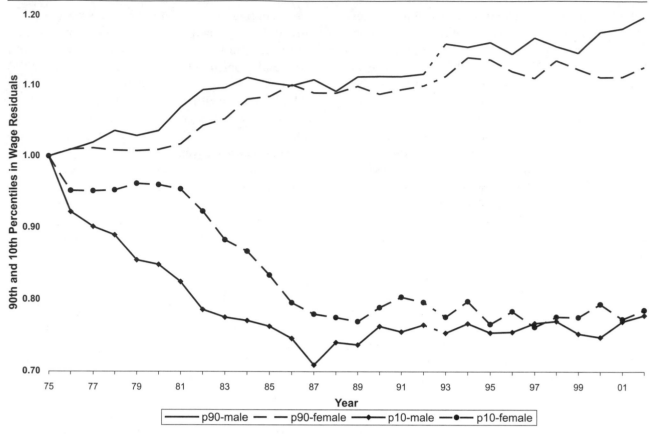

**FIGURE 1.1: RESIDUAL WAGE INEQUALITY: 90TH AND 10TH PERCENTILES IN HOURLY WAGES (1975 = 1.0)**
Source: Gottschalk and Danziger (2005, p. 243).

further, recent trends in fuel-price inflation in the United States—four times the inflation of the general consumer price index from 1999 to 2007—have reduced the relative purchasing power of the poorest 20 percent of households, which spend a larger proportion of their income on fuel and food (ILO 2008).

Figure 1.3 displays the actual P90/P10 ratios for several developed nations, including the United States, from 1990 to 2006. The growth in income inequality is steadily increasing in the United States, the United Kingdom, and Germany, but not in Canada and Ireland.

Because of factors such as the decline in hourly pay for middle- and low-wage workers, the reduction in employee benefits, increasing health-care costs, and a decline in purchasing power, the only ways for households to maintain or enhance their income and well-being (without further developing their skills) are to increase the number of hours worked, to increase the number of workers in the household, or both. Since the 1970s, this is exactly what has happened. A significant number of women now provide important additional household income, and be-

tween 1973 and 2002 the average worker's annual hours increased from 1,679 to 1,851 (Mishel, Bernstein, et al. 2005). However, between 2000 and 2006, the annual hours worked by men and women declined due to the longest jobless recovery on record (Mishel, Bernstein, et al. 2009). During this period, the income from women played an important role in limiting the decline of family income for the top 40 percent of earners and dampened the decline to the bottom 60 percent (ibid.). Interestingly, the growing number of women who have entered the workforce has had the effect of narrowing gender wage differentials for all age and education groups (Autor, Katz, et al. 2005; Gottschalk and Danziger 2005; Yun 2006).

Those who support the U.S. economic model generally cite income mobility, the fact that overall household incomes have risen in real terms, and the employment opportunities that the American dream provides to downplay the current growth in inequality. However, the empirical evidence undermines these arguments. First, income mobility—that is, the movement of individuals or households between income quintiles—has fallen over the past several decades

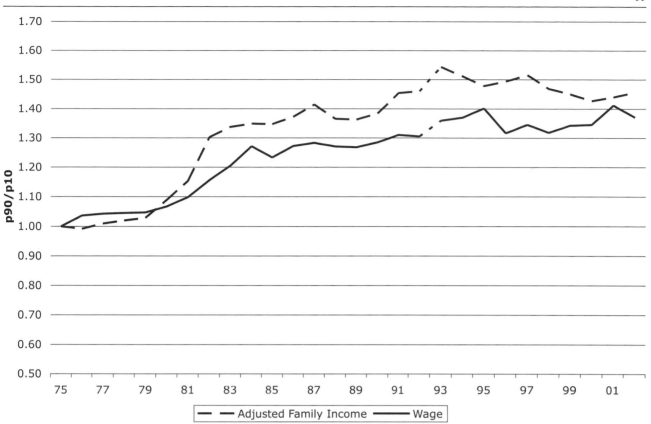

**FIGURE 1.2: INEQUALITY OF ADJUSTED FAMILY INCOME AND INEQUALITY OF MALE HOURLY WAGE RATES, 1975–2002 (1975 = 1.0)**
Note: The hourly wage rates are for male workers aged between twenty-two and sixty-two. Family income is adjusted for family size with heads of households falling within the same age range.
Source: Gottschalk and Danziger (2005, p. 232).

(Bradbury and Katz 2002; Mishel, Bernstein, et al. 2005, 2009). The situation is particularly stark for those who fall at the bottom of the low-income distribution (Theodos and Bednarzik 2006). During the 1990s, 36.3 percent of people who began in the second quintile remained there, compared with 27.8 percent and 31.5 percent in the 1970s and 1980s, respectively (EPI 2005). This fall in income mobility means that families at the bottom of the income ladder are more likely to remain there than they were three decades ago. In fact, when compared with other nations in the OECD, the United States had the highest percentage (9.5 percent) of people who were "always poor" (Mishel, Bernstein, et al. 2005, p. 409), creating the foundation for a permanent underclass.* Further, in Europe, low-income persons are much more likely to

be upwardly mobile than their U.S. counterparts (Gangl 2005). This is partly due to the fact that income trends in Europe have been positive in the bottom of the income distribution and negative in the top deciles, which is the opposite of what has been happening in the United States (ibid.). Thus "the typical European income distribution shows evidence of regression-to-the-mean effects in individual incomes over time, whereas the U.S. distribution does not" (ibid., p. 159). Mishel, Bernstein, et al. (2009, p. 14) make the following observations about the differences between the United States and its European counterparts with regard to income inequality and productivity:

> First, while the United States is a very rich country—second only to Norway in per capita income—much less of the vast income of the United States is reaching the lower end of the income distribution. The United States has the highest level of inequality of its peers, whether measured in terms of Gini coefficients or the ratio of earnings of high earners (90th percentile) to low earners (10th percentile) . . . . Second, it is far from

---

\* Although much attention has been given to the digital divide between developed and developing nations, the creation of an "apartheid economy" within many developed nations (such as the United States and the United Kingdom) highlights a different kind of divide that threatens the very fabric of communities. Identifying ways to reduce inequality and strengthen communities must lie at the center of development strategies. See Section 1.2.2 for a discussion of how to operationalize a Rawlsian approach to decision making, whereby government policies are

designed to make the most disadvantaged members of society relatively better off under new social arrangements.

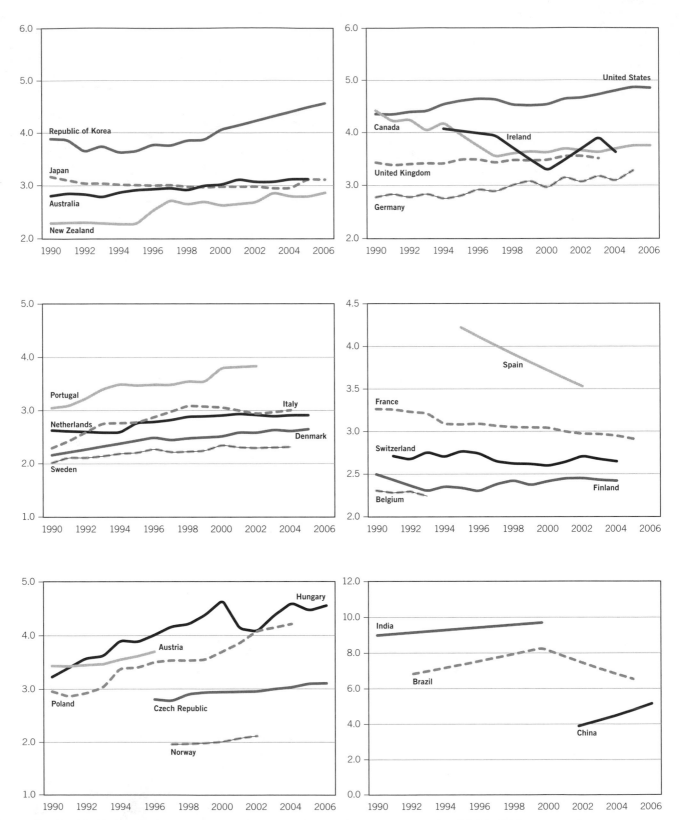

**FIGURE 1.3: RATIO OF EARNINGS OF TOP 10 PERCENT EARNERS VIS-À-VIS BOTTOM 10 PERCENT EARNERS, 1990–2006**
Source: ILO (2008, p. 13).

a foregone conclusion that economies that have strong welfare states and labor protection are also necessarily less productive, less-employment-generating, and less "flexible" than the U.S. economy. Many peer countries with strong unions, high minimum wages, generous social benefits, and high taxes have caught up with, and in many cases, surpassed U.S. productivity while achieving low unemployment levels. Both Norway and the Netherlands, for example, have higher productivity than the United States and lower unemployment rates. It is an important point that so many peer countries have been successful and productive within different economic models.

Second, although household incomes have risen in real terms since the 1970s (albeit at a much slower rate than that experienced from the mid-1940s to the 1970s), the significant growth in income for those households near the top of the income ladder has given them much greater ability to withstand income shocks (caused by unemployment or ill health) than poorer families (Mishel, Bernstein, et al. 2005, p. 360).* This growing divide between the rich and poor not only reduces income mobility but has the additional effect of making the poor feel poorer (see Section 1.1.2 for a related discussion). Thus the American dream may be only a dream for those who begin at the bottom of the income ladder, undermining a central pillar of the American way of life (Judt 2005; Rifkin 2004b).[†]

Finally, the dynamics that underlie the recent growth in U.S. income and wage inequality are likely to continue to affect future employment opportunities, incomes, and wages in both positive and negative ways. The main factors shaping trends in inequality include the following (Barnet 1993; R. B. Freeman 1996; ILO 2008; Mishel, Bernstein, et al. 2005, 2009; Morris and Western 1999; O'Rourke 2001; Osterman, Kochan, et al. 2001):

1. Technological change (with consequential changes in the skills required of workers) that displaces workers in *traditional* industries (including the impacts of automation and productivity gains and enabling effects of information communication technology [ICT])

2. Demand for skilled/educated workers and a shift in the types of skills demanded (that is, structural changes in the mixture of the types of skills required to make/use new products, processes, and services)

3. Trade liberalization and the loss of national jobs to the international economy through *multinationalization*—that is, the relocation of a firm's production facilities or services outside its home country (see Section 5.2.1)

4. Shifts in the mixture of lower-paid service jobs and higher-paid manufacturing jobs (that is, deindustrialization) due to the single and combined effects of factors 1, 2, and 3[7]

5. Supply-side shifts in the demographics of the labor market—that is, changes in the number and type of workers due to (a) immigration and the associated influx of unskilled workers, (b) the increased participation of women in the workforce, and (c) the entrance (and pending exit) of the baby boomers into (and out of) the labor market

6. Changes in (a) the organization of work (including an increase in the number of contingent or temporary workers, who are much less likely than regular employees to receive benefits) (see Chapter 7 for a discussion of organizational innovation and learning), (b) the sources of compensation of employees (that is, shifts in the proportion of income derived from wages and benefits), and (c) the broader political and institutional environments that affect factors such as the minimum wage and the strength of trade unions (whose decline over the past several decades has reduced the ability of employees to address low pay and benefits)

The challenge facing U.S. policy makers is that the combined impacts of these factors are complex. Both the mechanism by which each factor can affect inequality and the time period over which the impact occurs can vary significantly. It is possible to reveal some of this complexity (1) by exploring how technological change (the first factor above) can affect wages and (2) by looking at the debate surrounding the skill-based technological change (SBTC) hypothesis and how this debate points to other influential factors. Even if the relative contribution of each of the various factors is not known, policies to correct or lessen inequalities can nonetheless be fashioned (see the discussions in Chapters 7 and 8).

---

* From 1979 to 2006, the bottom 90 percent of wage earners saw their annual earnings increase by 16 percent. In contrast, during the same period, wage earners in the 95th to 99th percentile saw their earnings grow by 52 percent, and the top 1 percent experienced an increase of 144 percent. The wage earners in the top 0.1 percent saw their earnings increase by an astonishing 324 percent—increasing their wages from $525,000 in 1979 to $2,224,000 in 2006 (Mishel, Bernstein, et al. 2011, p. 29). Similarly, in corporate America in 2007, CEOs earned 521 times more than the average employee; this figure was 370 four years earlier (ILO 2008, p. 18).

† As concern has risen over the future of the American way of life, a number of commentators have pointed to the European Union as embodying an alternative development model—one that relies less on capitalism and more on multistate cooperation, justice, community, harmony, and the creation of meaningful employment (Reid 2004; Rifkin 2004b). For a thoughtful critique of these publications, see Judt (2005).

**1.1.3.1.1 The Impact of Technological Change on Wages and Employment**  Technological change (or innovation) can create both up- and downskill jobs and (perhaps) displace workers' jobs that existed before the introduction of a new technology, all of which can affect wages (see Section 7.6.3 for a discussion of technological change and employment). For example, the introduction of a more advanced computer or automated process could have the effect of increasing the skills of the fewer workers needed to operate the work-saving technologies, while other applications of advanced technologies could reduce the skill level required because the new technology embodies knowledge previously held by workers (for example, manufacturing knowledge is incorporated into automation equipment, or the knowledge of service workers is transferred into, or embodied in, menus or repair manuals). Further, if the total number of new jobs created that demand higher-skilled workers is less than the number of new jobs created for lower-skilled workers, then the wages of the latter group of workers could be depressed. The total effect on the average or median wage rate could be negative. (The Dutch policy of educating people for work with skills that are more than those thought to be needed in the jobs envisioned by industry has resulted in a counteracting effect whereby workers initially viewed to hold "lower skills" are more highly valued by the firm than originally anticipated. The result is that firms have increased the wages of lower-skilled workers, which has led to a reduction in wage dispersion in Holland [ter Weel and Kemp 2000]. The Dutch model highlights the value of an educational policy that is not tightly coupled to market demand and focuses on communication skills, teamwork, and learning abilities that are essential in the knowledge economy [ibid.].)*

In this scenario, an existing worker who previously used a firm's older technology faces the option of upgrading his or her skills or accepting a lower-paid position if suitable compensation or retraining mechanisms are not in place.† Beyond the individual firm, the benefits received by employees who decide to retrain for higher-skilled jobs rest on the number of these jobs created by the economy. Government policies designed to increase the number of skilled workers—whom Robert Reich (1992, p. 177) refers to as the providers of "symbolic analytic services"—without a strategy to increase the size of the skilled job market will have the effect of flooding this section of the labor pool and lowering wages there. (The main criticism of Reich's formula of addressing employment problems by creating more high-skilled workers, such as computer programmers or technicians [IPR 2005], is that many high-skilled workers, especially those in information technology occupations, are now experiencing growing unemployment rates because of offshoring and outsourcing [Herbert 2003; Mishel, Bernstein, et al. 2005, p. 236].‡ Further, the task of increasing the number of high-skilled jobs is also undermined by the growing movement of high-skilled manufacturing operations to China [Bronfenbrenner and Luce 2004; Manufacturing News 2003]. Hence low-skilled manufacturing workers are not the only ones who are being affected by the relocation of production facilities overseas.)

Although we have discussed technological change in general terms, it is possible to classify technological change into four broad categories (see Section 6.2.1):

1. *Product changes* (for example, the creation of a new product/technology/service)

2. *Process changes* (for example, improvements or efficiency gains in the process of manufacturing a product or delivering a service)§

3. Shifts from products to *product-services* (for example, purchasing a photocopying service rather than a photocopying machine)

4. More far-reaching *system changes* (for example, a dramatic realignment of producers, service providers, and other actors to create entirely new ways of delivering a product or service)

The first two categories have received the most attention in the literature on job displacement and

---

* The OECD (2001, p. 19) adopted a similar "jobs strategy" based on "measures that promote broad-based upskilling and lifelong learning [that] can help . . . raise the mobility and employability of workers and mitigate the costs of job displacement resulting from rapid technological change." See the discussion below on the 2010 OECD initiatives to link innovation policy with increases in employment.

† The implementation of a new technology requires a period of transition (or gearing up) within the firm during which the skills of existing workers might be enhanced. However, the demand for workers with these higher skills required for the new technology may be transient and reach saturation or a plateau once the technology has been implemented. Thus volatility in wages and the availability of jobs might be high.

‡ It is important to recognize that some skills are specialized, while others are more *enabling capacities* that make workers more broadly educated/trained and more adaptable, such as having interpersonal skills or data-researching skills, as distinct from specialized knowledge of, for example, how to repair electronic equipment using vacuum tubes, which become obsolete.

§ Process innovations can occur as a result of technological as well as organizational change (Edquist, Hommen, et al. 2001).

wage inequality (Vivarelli and Pianta 2000). In particular, process changes—productivity gains that occur because of the improved productiveness of capital (such as the use of more efficient technology)*—are often cited as the main cause of job displacement. The writer Jeremy Rifkin (2004a) is perhaps the most visible critic of the negative impact of advances in capital productivity, especially those that relate to gains in information and communication technology (ICT). In his book *The End of Work*, Rifkin (2004a, p. xvii) argues that "the old logic that technology gains and advances in productivity destroy old jobs but create as many new ones is no longer true."[8] Further, he argues that it is not only the low-skilled workers who are being displaced; high-skilled workers are also becoming increasingly vulnerable to technological displacement.[9] From the perspective of declining real wages, a diminishing number of jobs, and the recent unsustainable growth in consumer credit in the United States, Rifkin raises a fundamental question about where the consumer demand (and necessary purchasing power) will come from to buy the new and better products and services made available through productivity gains. His answer lies in rejuvenating the trade-union movement and extending its geographic reach across financial markets to ensure that the benefits of technological change reach the workers—not just the CEOs and shareholders.

It should be noted that although Rifkin's ideas have received much attention in the popular press, his arguments have not been well received by some academics who view his work as alarmist and based on weak and incoherent empirical claims (Castells 1999; V. Smith 2006). Further, Vivarelli (1996) and Spiezia and Vivarelli (2000) argue that the "end-of-work" literature has a tendency to overemphasize the labor-saving impacts of process innovation and neglects to consider the compensation effects of technological change (discussed later) and the positive impacts of product innovations (see also Economist 1995). A more general criticism of the work of Rifkin and others (King 1991; Aronowitz and Di Fazio 1994) is that although these studies announce the emergence of a jobless society due (primarily) to ICT, they fail to take a broader look at the economy-wide growth in jobs that occurred, for instance, in the United States and Japan and in the manufacturing industries in East and Southeast Asia during periods of ICT expansion (Castells 1999). Further, although there has been a decline in the global employment-to-population ratio (which is the share of the world's working-age population aged fifteen years or older that is in work) over the past decade, the total number of people employed increased from 2.45 billion in 1995 to 2.85 billion in 2005 (an increase of 16 percent) (ILO 2006).

In his writings on what he calls "the new, ruthless economy," the journalist Simon Head (1996, 2003) paints as stark a picture as Rifkin of how *lean production*, *reengineering*, and *enterprise resource planning*—enabled by advances in ICT and software and hardware packages—are negatively affecting the workplace. His central argument is that these technologies have allowed the manufacturing principles of Henry Ford and Frederick W. Taylor to survive in the modern manufacturing industry and also to cross over to the service economy. Head (2003, p. 188) concludes that "the link between higher productivity and higher real wages and benefits breaks down when technology is used in ways that deskill most workers, undermine their security in the workplace, and leave them vulnerable to employers possessed of overwhelming power. . . . In such an economy one would expect the figures for the growth of labor productivity and figures for the growth of real wages and benefits to grow far apart, and that is exactly what the statistics do show." Indeed, between 2000 and 2005, worker productivity in the United States grew by 16.6 percent, while total compensation for the median worker increased 7.2 percent (Greenhouse and Leonhardt 2006).

C. Freeman and Soete (1994) provide a contrasting view on the impacts of ICT-related product and process innovations. Although they acknowledge that productivity-enhancing ICT innovations can reduce employment, they are optimistic that new products and services will create a "virtuous circle of high output growth, high employment growth and high labour productivity growth [that] tend to go together and to reinforce each other" (ibid., p. 59).[†] Their

---

*       There are three different ways to improve productivity: (1) improve the productiveness of capital (through modernization); (2) improve the productiveness of labor (through enhancing worker skills); or (3) improve the interface between the factors of labor and capital (i.e., technological artifacts). The problem with using productivity to measure performance is that it is a ratio (or a statistic) and provides no information on what is driving efficiency improvements.

†       B. Davis and Wessel (1998, p. 5) provide a similar optimistic view, arguing that the prosperity of middle-class Americans will be enhanced over the coming decades by a combination of (1) future productivity gains made possible by better use of ICT, (2) improved levels of education, and (3) growing levels of trade, especially with the emerging consumer class in developing nations. In critiquing Rifkin's ideas on mass unemployment, the authors argue that "nothing about the computer suggests that its

belief that ICT advances will be accompanied by a growth in employment is based on the assumption that the diffusion of ICT will be rapid because of the vast number of applications of ICT, such as tele-working. In contrast to Head's views, Freeman and Soete (1994, p. 170) state that "nightmare scenarios of total dehumanising computerisation are . . . often misconceived. . . . ICT-based services will not (indeed cannot) replace personal caring services, including most health and education. What they can do is to improve and enhance these services and in some cases to make them more accessible to people who otherwise could not enjoy them." To avoid the creation of a permanent underclass of low-paid, low-skilled workers, the authors promote policies for training/education and high-quality services—based on an extensive ICT infrastructure—to increase the proportion of ICT-related employment.*

A more balanced view of the impact of ICT on employment is provided by Castells (1999). After reviewing a wide body of literature, he concludes "that there is no systematic structural relationship between the diffusion of information technologies and the evolution of employment levels in the economy as a whole. Jobs are being displaced and new jobs are being created, but the quantitative relationship between the losses and the gains varies among firms, industries, sectors, regions, and countries, depending upon competitiveness, firms' strategies, government policies, institutional environments, and relative position in the global economy" (ibid., p. 263). Although he is not as optimistic as C. Freeman and Soete (1994), Castells does believe that ICT will lead to the creation of more jobs over the long run.†

A study by van Ark, Inklaar, et al. (2003) provides a more nuanced look at the impacts of ICT on employment and productivity in the United States and Europe. The authors focus on three groups of industries—industries that produce ICT products and services, industries that invest heavily in ICT, and industries that make less intensive use of ICT. The results of their study are informative: "First, we find that the inverse relationship between productivity and employment growth is mostly stronger in manufacturing than in services. Second, as a result of increased use of ICT, this relationship has turned positive during the second half of the 1990s, in particular in ICT-using services. Finally, Europe fell behind the US in most industry groups because of slow productivity growth and/or limited employment expansion. Indeed the employment-reducing effects of productivity growth have remained much more persistent in Europe than in the US" (ibid., p. 93).

Van Ark, Inklaar, et al. (2003) argue that the U.S. experience provides some evidence that ICT is an important factor in stimulating innovations in ICT-using services industries that create productivity gains. The OECD (2003, 2010a, 2010b) also supports the notion that ICT may increase the efficiency of innovation, enhancing the potential for long-term economic growth. Further, van Ark, Inklaar, et al. (2003) argue that organizational innovation—the subject of Chapter 7—may be just as important for strong productivity growth as ICT investment. Although ICT-related innovation can displace employment and affect employment opportunities (Edquist, Hommen, et al. 2001), van Ark, Inklaar, et al. (2003) note that the growth in demand for ICT-using services during the 1990s offset any employment-reducing effects in the United States. With regard to Europe, the authors suggest that the national systems of innovation in European countries have so far been unable to generate the type of product and organizational innovations needed to strengthen employment and productivity growth simultaneously.

In contrast to the "end-of-work" literature, most economists tend to view technological change as beneficial to employment (at least over the long run) (Economist 1995; Spiezia and Vivarelli 2000; Vivarelli 1996). Their support for technological advancement is grounded on Schumpeter's (1962 [1942], p. 84) idea of "creative destruction." Schumpeter viewed the economy as a dynamic environment in which new firms and industries continually emerge and displace existing market players that are either unprofitable or offer outdated (or unwanted) products and services. The process of creative destruction can be rather dra-

---

effects will be different from those of other powerful technologies since the Industrial Revolution—steam power, railroads, electricity, automobiles—that produced more jobs than they destroyed" (ibid., p. 245).

*        On a related subject, the idea that investing in ICT (or high-tech) research will lead to significant economic growth (and job creation) has been questioned by Havas (2006). His main concern is that focusing R&D efforts mainly on high-tech (ICT-based) industries ignores the fact that the OECD has a sizeable number of low- and medium-tech industries. Because these industries have significant growth potential and tend to be knowledge intensive, Havas (2006) suggests that a better strategy would be to invest in a well-functioning knowledge infrastructure that can support technological upgrading in all sectors. In this regard, his views are similar to those of C. Freeman and Soete (1994) in that the full potential of the ICT infrastructure has yet to be realized.

†        In contrast, Drucker (1999) argues that it is not ICT and computers that have revolutionized work, but e-commerce. See the discussion of Drucker's ideas in the following section titled "Skill-Based Technological Change and the Relative Importance of Other Factors in Inequality."

matic for employees of displaced firms. However, the same process also creates new employment opportunities, although these may not arise in the same market and may demand new sets of skills.

The OECD is a proponent of the view that technological change is beneficial to employment. In a study, *Technology, Productivity and Job Creation*, it concluded that "technological change, even in the form of new labour-saving production processes, does not reduce aggregate employment but generates more growth and jobs" (OECD 1996, p. 4). This position is also embodied in the OECD's 2001 jobs strategy: "New technologies destroy jobs in some industries, especially among the low-skilled, while creating jobs which are often in different industries and require different skills. Historically, this process has led to net job creation, as new industries replace old ones and workers adapt their skills to changing and expanding demand" (OECD 2001, p. 3).*

In May 2010, the OECD (2010a) released its "Innovation Strategy" in which it stated: "Human capital is the essence of innovation. Empowering people to innovate relies on broad and relevant education as well as on the development of wide-ranging skills that complement formal education." The same sentiments are reflected in the OECD Development Agenda released later that same year (OECD 2010b).

The views of economists differ, however, on the mechanisms by which technology-based efficiency gains affect new employment opportunities (Addison, Fox, et al. 2000; Cyert and Mowery 1987). Vivarelli and Pianta (2000) provide a useful summary of the main compensation theories developed by economists to explain the *positive* relationship between technological change and employment (see Table 1.2). The basic premise behind the mechanisms described in Table 1.2 is that economic forces will compensate for the labor-saving effects of technological change.

The most effective compensation mechanism in Table 1.2 is seen by Vivarelli and Pianta (2000) to be the development of "new products." Their position is reinforced by several recent empirical studies that all concluded that product innovation is associated with employment growth (García, Jaumandreu, et

al. 2005; Harrison, Jaumandreu, et al. 2008; Jaumandreu 2003; Peters 2004). However, these studies also found that process innovation may not displace employment, as is commonly suggested (Head 1996, 2003; Rifkin 2004a). For example, in a study of Spanish manufacturing firms, García, Jaumandreu, et al. (2005, p. 1) found that "the potential employment compensation effect of process innovations surpasses the displacement effect, both in the short and long run (when competitors react)." However, Pianta (2000) found that the long-run trends in process-innovation-based industries in Germany, France, the United Kingdom, and Italy show a pattern of technological unemployment over the past two decades. He also argues that the dominant impact of technological change in Europe's manufacturing industry has been labor displacing. Notwithstanding these studies, the general consensus is that process innovation causes job displacement† and that product innovation leads to job creation (Edquist, Hommen, et al. 2001).

The concern that Europe is displacing jobs through specialization in process innovation provides a useful link to the emerging European interest in *product-service innovation/systems* (Mont and Tukker 2006; Tukker and Tischner 2006). This interest is driven by the realization that European manufacturing industries are unable to compete with low-wage countries such as China in labor-intensive, mass-consumption products (EC 2003). Therefore, a new approach to business is needed that builds on the core competencies of the European industry. Tukker and Tischner (2006) explain how the convergence of two strands of research focused on business management and sustainability have created a new business model for product-services or integrated solutions. The idea is to improve the position of companies in the value chain by focusing on ways to sell "need fulfillment" rather than products that the customer must then use to satisfy his or her own needs. For example, the decision of Xerox to sell a photocopying service rather than photocopying machines means that customers no longer need to worry about owning and operating equipment. This new form of business model also means that Xerox must rethink the design of its

---

*     A background paper for the conference of the European Foundation for the Improvement of Living and Working Conditions (in Dublin) titled *Competitive Europe—Social Europe: Partners or Rivals?* discusses the uncertainty in fulfilling the EU's Lisbon Strategy to make Europe "the most competitive and dynamic knowledge-based economy in the world, capable of sustainable economic growth with more and better jobs and greater social cohesion" (Eurofound 2006a, p. 1). See Section 1.5 for a discussion of Europe 2020, the successor to the Lisbon Strategy.

†     A possible exception to this general rule is "organizational" process innovations, particularly capital-saving (as opposed to labor-saving) organization innovations that can have (potentially) neutral impacts on employment (Edquist, Hommen, et al. 2001). By definition, capital-saving organizational innovations reduce the amount of capital engaged in work-in-progress. This type of innovation is associated with ideas such as just-in-time production. In contrast, labor-saving organizational innovation consistently has a negative impact on employment that is, in effect, designed out of a process.

**TABLE 1.2: KEY ELEMENTS OF COMPENSATION THEORY**

| IMPORTANT COMPENSATION MECHANISMS[a] | COMMENTS[b] |
|---|---|
| *Compensation "via new machines."* The same process innovations which displace workers in the user industries create new jobs in the capital sectors where the new machines are produced. | Mechanism offers limited benefits to employment. No longer used much by economists. |
| *Compensation "via decrease in prices."* On the one hand, process innovations involve the displacement of workers; on the other hand, these very innovations lead to a decrease in unit costs and prices and so to an increase in demand, production and employment[, either in the modernized sector or in other sectors where consumption of new goods and services increases.] | The effectiveness of mechanism relies on the idea of perfect competition. Thus an oligopolistic regime is likely to undermine expected compensation by maintaining higher prices. Productivity increases may simply be appropriated through increased profits or dividends to shareholders. Does not take into account the fact that demand constraints may occur. |
| *Compensation "via new investments."* If the reduction of costs due to technological progress is not completely translated into prices, innovative firms will accumulate extra profits: to the extent these profits are invested, they raise production and generate new jobs. | Compensation depends on the decision to invest profits. Capital-intensive investments may not produce significant employment opportunities. |
| *Compensation "via decrease in wages."* As for other forms of unemployment, the direct effect of labour-saving technologies may be compensated by a decrease in wages which induces the adoption of more labour-intensive techniques of production. | Lower wages can induce firms to hire additional workers, but a decrease in aggregate demand can also lower employers' expectations, resulting in the hiring of fewer workers. |
| *Compensation "via increase in incomes."* Directly in contrast with the previous mechanism, this compensation channel has been put forward by the Keynesian and Kaldorian tradition. To the extent the increase in productivity due to technological change is translated into higher wages, it stimulates consumption and leads to an increase in employment which may compensate the initial job losses due to process innovations. | Flexible wages and the decline in the median earnings of full-time workers in the U.S., undermine this Fordist approach to compensation. |
| *Compensation "via new products."* Technological change is not always equivalent to process innovation, but it can also assume the form of creation and commercialisation of new products; in this case, new economic branches develop and additional jobs are created. | Product innovations remain the most effective mechanism to counterbalance labour-saving process innovations. However, the impact of product innovations varies significantly depending on the type of product and the prevailing institutional framework. |

[a] The text shown in this column is extracted from Vivarelli and Pianta (2000, pp. 16–17).

[b] The comments shown in this column are adapted from Vivarelli and Pianta's (2000, pp. 16–17) discussion of each of the compensation mechanisms.

Source: Vivarelli and Pianta (2000, pp. 16–17).

machines for ease of recyclability and longevity—two factors that are critical to reduce the ecological footprint of products.

Because the transition from products to product-services is a recent phenomenon, there is a lack of empirical evidence assessing how this new type of innovation might affect employment and wages. However, we believe that product-service innovation can provide significant and rewarding employment opportunities. For example, the frontline employees at Xerox are now required to visit customers regularly to maintain their equipment. This mobility provides its employees with work variety and an opportunity for social engagement, both of which are essential aspects of meaningful work (see Section 1.1.3.2). Further, the specific skills held by the Xerox employee are likely to be highly valued by his or her customers, which could enhance wages.

A critical aspect of product-service innovation is that labor can be essential to integrate technology (a product) and its associated service(s). In this context, the current emphasis on how product-services can contribute to competitiveness and to more sustainable production and consumption patterns (Tukker and Tischner 2006) should be extended to explicitly include employment. In fact, research is needed to identify how meaningful employment can be designed into product-service innovations.

Finally, given the nature of *system innovations*, it is difficult to know how a structural change in the way products, services, or product-services are manufactured and delivered will affect employment and wage inequality. Thus system innovations should be considered on a case-by-case basis, and the outcomes of such studies are likely to depend on the types of innovation that are driving a system transformation (see Section 6.2.1).

What is evident from the preceding discussion is that (1) the type of technological change—that is, process, product, product-services, or system innovation—can have differing impacts on the skills demanded and on wages, and (2) it is important to look not only at the firm or industry level but also at the entire economy to identify the broader impacts of technological change. The challenge facing policy makers is to try to understand the complex interrelationship among technological innovation, job displacement, reemployment opportunities, and economy-wide job growth when developing technology and employment policy.

**1.1.3.1.2 Skill-Based Technological Change and the Relative Importance of Other Factors on Inequality** Having discussed the interconnections between technological change and employment, we now shift our focus to the skill-based technological change (SBTC) debate. The SBTC hypothesis has been put forward to explain the growth in inequality between the wages of skilled and unskilled workers in the United States and other industrialized nations during the 1970s, 1980s, and 1990s (Acemoglu 2002b; Katz and Autor 1999; Katz and Murphy 1992; Machin, Ryan, et al. 1996).* The SBTC hypothesis states that production technology has evolved to favor skilled over unskilled labor by increasing its relative productivity and, therefore, its demand. Thus the growth in inequality reflects a technology-based increase in demand for educated or skilled workers (measured using wage premiums) combined with a simultaneous decline in the supply of these workers.† However, there are those who criticize the emphasis given to SBTC as the leading factor behind the increase in inequality (Howell 1994, 2000; Singh and Dhumale 2004).‡

For example, Card and DiNardo (2002, p. 735) argue that "contrary to the impression conveyed by most of the recent literature, the SBTC hypothesis falls short as a unicausal explanation for the evolution of the U.S. wage structure in the 1980s and 1990s. Indeed, we find puzzles and problems for the theory in nearly every dimension of the wage structure." Similarly, Beaudry and Green (2002, p. i) "do not find much empirical support for the view that ongoing (factor-augmenting) skill-biased technological progress has been an important driving force" in the growth of income inequality between 1976 and 2000. Mishel, Bernstein, et al. (2005, p. 111) argue that "skill demand and technology have little relationship to the growth of wage inequality within the same group (i.e., workers with similar levels of experience and education), and this within-group inequality was responsible for half of the overall growth of wage inequality in the 1980s and 1990s. Technology has been and continues to be an important force, but there was no 'technology shock' in the 1980s or 1990s and no ensuing demand for 'skill' that was not satisfied by the continuing expansion of the educational attainment of the workforce." A main point of many opponents of the SBTC hypothesis is the fact that the growth in wage inequality in the early 1980s began before the mass introduction of computers, which means that other factors were involved.

The debate surrounding the likely impact of SBTC on wage and income inequality provides a useful bridge to other factors that might underlie the growth in inequality. For example, a study by Singh and Dhumale (2004) questions the emphasis the inequality literature has given to the impact of technological change and trade on wages and income in the recent period. Instead, they argue that "there is robust empirical evidence to indicate that the concentration on these two factors to the exclusion of others [—such as the role of social norms, economic institutions, and growth in output and employment—] is not justified" (ibid., p. 161).

A brief digression on the arguments about the impacts of trade on wage inequality is informative. The inequality literature addressing trade liberalization is grounded on the Heckscher-Ohlin model of trade that incorporates the Stopler-Samuelson theorem (Anderton and Brenton 2006; Bhagwati and Dehejia

---

\* In contrast to the United States, wage inequality in continental Europe "has been much lower and stable" (Devillanova 2004, p. 231). There are several potential explanations for this difference, which include the theories that (1) the supply of skilled workers increased faster in Europe than in the United States over the past several decades (Kranz 2006); (2) the stronger labor unions and social assistance programs in Europe protected the wages of low-/semi-skilled workers at the expense of higher unemployment (Blank 1998; Mahler 2004; Morris and Western 1999); and (3) technological change was less skill based in Europe than in the United States (Acemoglu 2002a, 2002b).

† Another way to consider SBTC is that an initial growth in the supply of skilled workers induces faster technological change that in turn leads to an increase in the demand for skilled labor (Greiner, Rubart, et al. 2001).

‡ A new strand of research that builds on the SBTC hypothesis looks at the potential impact of skill-based *organizational* change (SBOC) (Piva, Santarelli, et al. 2003). The SBOC hypothesis states that skill upgrading occurs as a direct result of a firm's reorganizational strategies rather than the introduction of new technologies. Indeed, in a study of some four hundred

Italian manufacturing firms, Piva, Santarelli, et al. (2003) show that upskilling is more a function of SBOC than of SBTC. However, they also find some evidence of a combined, coevolutionary impact of technological and organizational change on upskilling.

1994; Cornia 2004; Guscina 2006; Wood 1994).* The basic theory is that countries should specialize in the production of commodities for which they have an advantage in resource endowments and/or productive capabilities (such as labor skills) and should exchange any surplus home-produced commodities for those more easily produced by others. Because high-skilled workers are more abundant in developed nations and low-skilled workers are prevalent in developing and transitional economies, it follows that developing nations should focus on the production of low-skill- or labor-intensive commodities (such as agricultural goods, raw materials, and minerals) and export any surplus in exchange for imports of high-skill- or capital-intensive commodities produced (mainly) in developed nations. With regard to developed nations such as the United States, the importation of labor-intensive goods is seen to reduce the demand for low- and semiskilled workers, depressing their wages and increasing income inequality (Mahler 2004; Wood 1994). The reverse occurs in developing nations (exporting labor-intensive goods), which are seen to experience a decline in income inequality.†

The mechanism by which trade can affect employment is captured quite succinctly by Castells (1999, p. 254): "The more the process of economic globalization deepens, the more the interpenetration of networks of production and management expands across borders, and the closer become the links between the conditions of the labor force in different countries, placed at different levels of wages and social protection, but decreasingly distinct in terms of skills and technology." According to Castells (1999), it is more

useful to focus on the indirect impacts of production and management techniques—such as lean production, downsizing, and restructuring—on employment than to try to measure the impacts of international trade or cross-border direct employment.

Notwithstanding Castells's (1999) remarks, a study by Kletzer (2000) on the impacts of trade on job losses in U.S. manufacturing concluded that there was a strong positive relationship between increasing foreign competition and job displacement (between 1979 and 1994) for import-competing industries, although the scale of job displacement caused by increasing foreign competition was found to be relatively small when it was considered next to the turnover of jobs in the U.S. economy. Similarly, Scott (2003) finds that the North American Free Trade Agreement (NAFTA) eliminated some 879,000 U.S. jobs between 1993 (when NAFTA was signed) and 2004 because of the rapid growth in the net U.S. export deficit with Mexico and Canada.‡ More generally, he argues that the process of trade liberalization has led to growing structural trade deficits that have put downward pressure on the wages of low-skilled workers in the United States (Scott 2001).§

More recent studies of the decline in labor's share of national income—that is, the share of income accruing to labor compared with that accruing to capital—as a result of trade and other factors reveal some interesting findings. Guscina (2006) finds that since the mid-1980s, the decline in labor's share of income in industrialized countries has been equally driven by openness to trade and by technological progress. Similarly, Jaumotte and Tytell (2007) show that trade has played an important role, but that rapid technological change, particularly in ICT, has had a more significant (negative) impact. Workers in low-skilled sectors are more adversely affected than those in high-skilled sectors. Both studies identify employment-protection policies as an important factor in moving income toward labor, although the

---

* See Section 4.4.1 in Chapter 4 for a discussion of the Heckscher-Ohlin model of trade and Stopler-Samuelson theorem.

† The impact of trade on employment and wages in the manufacturing sector of developing nations differs among countries (WCSDG 2004). For example, it is apparent that manufacturing workers in Asian economies have generally benefited from growth in trade (Jaumotte and Tytell 2007), but unskilled workers in Latin American countries such as Brazil and Mexico have seen their real wages decline, while those of skilled workers have increased (WCSDG 2004). Further, the relative size of a nation's labor pool is also likely to affect wage inequality. For example, it is estimated that China has some 200 million underemployed workers in rural areas who could move into industry over the next two decades (Economist 2004a). This surplus of cheap labor is likely to hold down the wages of low-skilled workers, enabling China to sustain its competitive advantage in labor and resulting in a growth in wage inequality between low- and high-skilled workers. However, it is also important to recognize that although developing nations such as China do have a significant pool of unskilled labor, if the majority of this labor does not have an education, then this limits a nation's potential comparative advantage in labor-intensive manufacturing (Wood 1994).

‡ More generally, NAFTA has been described as a failure for working people in the United States, Mexico, and Canada (Faux, Scott, et al. 2001). A study by economists at the Economic Policy Institute found that since the signing of NAFTA, each nation has experienced a decline in real wages combined with an upward redistribution of income and a significant expansion in the number of informal jobs offering low security, low pay, and no bargaining power (ibid.).

§ Bivens (2006) argues that when trade imbalances in manufacturing are properly accounted for, they caused over a fifth of the job losses in this sector between 2000 and 2003. To stem the loss of manufacturing jobs, Bivens (2004) recommends that the U.S. trade account should be balanced by depreciating the U.S. dollar to make domestically produced goods more competitive in global and domestic markets.

impact of such measures is undermined by globalization.

Another important factor depressing wages is the threat levied by firms that unless workers accept their terms of employment, their jobs will be relocated to nations where wages are cheaper and labor regulations are less stringent or more difficult to enforce (Bluestone and Harrison 1982; Bronfenbrenner 1997). Bronfenbrenner (2000, p. 53) argues, "Capital mobility and the threat of capital mobility have had a profound impact on the ability of American workers to exercise their rights to freedom of association and collective bargaining." This view is also held by Jeff Faux, the founding president of the Economic Policy Institute in Washington, DC. In a speech at the 2002 World Social Forum in Brazil, Faux (2002) argued that "the fundamental purpose of neo-liberal policies of the past 20 years has been to discipline labor in every country in order to free capital from having to bargain with workers over the gains from rising productivity. Such bargaining is the essence of a democratic market system." See Section 5.2.3 for a discussion of the impacts of *technology-enabled* capital mobility on development.

In taking a closer look at the impacts of trade on displaced U.S. manufacturing workers in import-competing markets, Kletzer (2000) found that these workers suffered the largest average earnings loss of any industrial group, which was particularly acute for those reemployed in the service sector (see also Kletzer 1998).* This finding highlights the growth of the service sector (or deindustrialization) as a factor behind the decline in wages.† The basic argument is that service-sector jobs are, on average, less well paid than manufacturing jobs. Thus the growth of the service sector represents an overall decline in wages and income for those workers who might previously have found employment in manufacturing. This view is supported by Drucker (1994), who argues that the problem with the service economy is that displaced industrial workers cannot simply move into knowledge-based or service employment because they lack the formal education and qualifications necessary to do so. Hence the challenge of upgrading one's skills and general approach to employment (such as embracing continuous learning) may simply be too much for displaced industrial workers, who may have no choice but to accept low-wage employment in the service sector.

Although many commentators view computers as revolutionizing work (and contributing to wage inequality), Drucker (1999) makes a strong case that the computer has simply transformed processes that already existed during the Industrial Revolution.‡ He argues that it is the Internet and, more specifically, e-commerce (both of which rely on computers) that will transform the global economy. His main point is that e-commerce will change the *mental* geography of commerce by eliminating distance—there will be "only one economy and only one market" (ibid., p. 50). Competition will know no boundaries, but the products and sectors that are affected will be eclectic and unexpected. "New distribution channels [will] change not only *how* customers behave, but also *what* they buy" (ibid., p. 52). Thus Drucker provides an alternative view of how trade, or, more accurately, the *systems* supporting trade, can affect the global economy and employment:

---

\* Similarly, in their classic work *The Deindustrialization of America*, Bluestone and Harrison (1982, p. 10) argue that "studies of workers who lose their jobs as the result of a plant closing show that a large proportion of the unemployed take years to recover their lost earnings and many never find comparable work at all." Further, they argue that the whole society suffers when workers from high-productivity jobs have no option but to accept low-productivity (and service-oriented) jobs such as washing cars. Their concern is that deindustrialization can result in serious physical and emotional health problems for displaced workers and their families and can lead to a decline in tax revenue that undermines essential public services. In effect, what Bluestone and Harrison (1982) are describing is the other (negative) side of the coin of Schumpeter's (1939) notion of "creative destruction."

† The so-called service sector, unlike manufacturing, is composed of very different types of activities. These activities include (1) retail trade; (2) repair of products, appliances, and automobiles, trucks, and buses; (3) delivery of health care; (4) transport services; (5) banking and financial services; (6) educational services; (7) activities related to the response to natural hazards such as drought, hurricanes, and blizzards; and (8) security and defense expenditures. A growth in these activities is not always an index of progress. For example, a growth in (1) might

---

signal a rise in the consumerism, with a corresponding growth in the associated negative environmental and social impacts. A growth in (2) might mean that the quality of manufactured goods has diminished and they need to be repaired more often. Increases in (3) might highlight a rise in poverty and environmental or occupational disease, and increases in (4) might highlight poor urban planning or a failure to internalize the true social costs of transportation. A growth in (5) might portend corruption in financial markets, and (6) might point toward the failure of traditional education, increases in attention-deficit/hyperactivity disorder (ADHD) related to environmental exposures or poor diet, or problems of social exclusion creating problem youth. Finally, increases in (7) may highlight the growing impacts of global climate change, and increases in (8) an increase in international conflict or crime within communities.

‡ This view is reinforced by Gordon (1999, 2000) and Petras (2002), who argue that technological changes during the early and mid-twentieth century had a much greater impact on economy-wide productivity growth than the introduction of computers in the later twentieth century.

The truly revolutionary impact of the Information Revolution is just beginning to be felt. But it is not "information" that fuels this impact. . . . It is not the effect of computers and data processing on decision-making, policymaking, or strategy. It is something that practically no one foresaw or, indeed, even talked about ten or fifteen years ago: *e-commerce*— that is, the explosive emergence of the Internet as a major, perhaps eventually *the* major, worldwide distribution channel for goods, for services, and, surprisingly, for managerial and professional jobs. This is profoundly changing economies, markets, and industry structures; products and services and their flow; consumer segmentation, consumer values, and consumer behavior; jobs and labor markets. . . . E-commence is to the Information Revolution what the railroads were to the Industrial Revolution—a totally new, totally unprecedented, totally unexpected development. And like the railroad . . . , e-commerce is creating a new and distinct boom, rapidly changing the economy, society, and politics. (Drucker 1999, pp. 47, 50)

To return to the opponents of the SBTC hypothesis, Howell (1994, 2000) rejects the theory, arguing that labor's declining bargaining power and increasingly global and deregulated labor markets—which dramatically increase the number of available low-skilled workers—are the primary causes behind the collapse of wages at the bottom of the wage distribution. Beaudry and Green (2002) argue that the declining ratio of human to physical capital is more useful for explaining the change in wages since 1976 than the SBTC hypothesis. Finally, in acknowledging that some of the rise in inequality during the early 1980s was due to rapid technological change, Card and DiNardo (2002) point to the decline in the real value of the minimum wage as being the primary cause of inequality.

A neglected source of wage dispersion, exacerbating especially gender and racial inequality, was studied by Dwyer (2010) who analyzed job polarization in the United States since 1980 and concluded that rather than increases in high-paying technology jobs (due to skill-biased technological change), wage dispersion (or job polarization) might better be explained by the increase in lower-skilled jobs in "carework." Carework is defined as "labor that maintains health or well-being or involves the capabilities of people" (ibid). "Reproductive labor jobs" involve more of the physical labor of care and are distinguished from "nurturant carework" such as teaching, social services, etc., which tend to be more highly paid. The distinction between nuturant and reproductive carework parallels the distinction between non-routine cognitive and manual carework occupations. The great increase in the creation of jobs in the latter category accounts for the increased job polarization.

Drucker's (1994) notion of the "knowledge-based" worker seems to fall into the category of nuturant carework. Note that the monetization of previously uncompensated work discussed by Ayers (2006) is consistent with Dwyer's (2010) analysis, but Ayres argues that the contribution of this work to total wages paid is now saturated, one factor contributing to reaching a plateau in growth of GDP. Dwyer's focus on routinization might offer a new lens through which to view wage dispersion. If routinization of both manufacturing and service jobs, facilitated by technological change and computerization, indeed characterizes employment trends, one could expect a significant fall in wages in both contexts.

Note, further, that technological displacement in any category of work caused by the replacement of labor by capital, will put downward pressure on wages, reflecting the diminishing contribution of any kind of labor to production and the provision of services, compared to the contribution of capital. The extent to which wages go up or down in any category of jobs will also depend on the existence of labor surpluses or shortages, but that is a different matter and should not be confused with technological displacement and consideration of policies that would minimize or even reverse that trend.

The different and competing perspectives on which factors are the most important determinants of income and wage inequality highlight the complexity that accompanies empirical studies. It seems that any attempt to isolate the effects of factors such as rapid technological change, the available skills in the labor market, the monetization of previously uncompensated work (e.g., carework), trade, or institutional and organizational arrangements must be cognizant of how other factors might be driving or influencing any observable trends. Further, the impact of such factors on low-, middle-, and high-wage workers is likely to be different. Mishel, Bernstein, et al. (2005, p. 5), however, offer a rough assessment of the likely impact of several different factors on wage inequality that provides a useful rule of thumb. In particular, they attribute one-third of wage inequality to *shifts in the labor market* (for example, the decline of trade unions and the drop in the real value of the minimum wage), one-third to the combined effects of *economic globalization* (for example, growth in trade, immigration, and capital mobility) and the *shift toward a service economy* (with lower-paying jobs),* and one-third to *macroeconomic factors* (such as the impacts of high unemployment).†

**1.1.3.1.3 Addressing Wage and Income Inequality in the United States**  The manner in which wage and income inequality is addressed in the United States will depend on the degree to which the nation leans toward "human development" and away from a "neoliberal" view of development (see Section 1.2.3 for a discussion of both views of development). The former view is more likely to distribute economic gains through taxes or a higher minimum wage, for example. The latter view is more likely to adopt the view that economic growth will eventually improve everyone's well-being and is less concerned with economic inequalities in the near term. Another critical factor is the extent to which employment is included in innovation-driven strategies designed to enhance national competitiveness. Charles and Lehner (1998) argue that if government and industry approach national competitiveness and international productivity using a "cost-driven strategy," the end result is likely to be a reduction in mass wealth (through the lowering of wages) and an increase in unemployment (through the introduction of lean-production processes). In essence, competitiveness is traded off against employment. To address this problem, they suggest that an alternative approach would be to adopt an "innovation-driven strategy" for competitiveness (that is, for a competitive advantage).‡ They argue that such an approach focuses on increasing wealth and welfare.

The objective of innovation-driven strategies is to reduce the relevance of prices and costs for competitive advantage and shift the focus to the creation of *new* products, services, and markets. Thus *innovation* becomes the mechanism through which a nation can sustain or improve its international share of production and profit. The idea is that if a large enough group of firms adopt such a strategy, it will create a "leading-edge" economy that is less concerned about price competition and generates more opportunities for long-term competitiveness and employment.§ Innovation-driven strategies rely on what Charles and Lehner (1998, p. 218) call "intelligent production systems," which exploit the potential for creativity that exists at the interfaces of an organization's production system (physical capital) where different knowledge and experience (human capital) intertwine. This approach is the opposite of lean-production strategies that seek to minimize the interfaces in a production system to save costs.

Kleinknecht (1998) argues that liberalizing wages (downward) discourages innovation by rewarding firms that do not use labor effectively, thus dampening Schumpeterian displacement of suboptimal firms and industries by more innovative entities. He notes that relaxing environmental standards similarly rewards firms that do not deal most effectively with environmental challenges.

In summary, although the debate over the trend in *between-nation* income inequality has yet to be resolved, there is consensus that *within-nation* wage and income inequality in many developed, transitional, and developing nations has steadily increased over the past several decades. There is also a growing consensus that no one factor or theory can adequately explain the trends in inequality. Instead, a combination of factors is more likely to explain the trends in inequality. These factors include (1) technological change that displaces workers in *traditional* industries; (2) the changing demand for skilled/educated workers and shifts in the type of skills demanded; (3) trade liberalization and the loss of national jobs to the international economy through multinationalization; (4) shifts in the mixture of lower-paid service jobs and higher-paid manufacturing jobs because of the single and combined effects of factors 1, 2, and 3; (5) supply-side shifts in the demographics of the labor market due to (a) immigration and the associated influx of unskilled workers, (b) the increased participation of women in

---

* This figure is comparable to that given by the U.S. Trade Deficit Review Commission (2000, p. 111), which concluded that trade is responsible for at least 15 to 25 percent of the growth in wage inequality.

† Although the impact of technological change on *wage inequality* may not be significant (see the discussion of SBTC), the fact that the real median value of wages has declined over the past quarter century indicates that wages have not kept up with technological progress (i.e., productivity gains). The evidence points to the fact that between 1966 and 2001, only the top 10 percent of the income distribution experienced a growth rate of real wage and salary income that matched or exceeded the average rate of economy-wide productivity growth (Dew-Becker and Gordon 2005). Thus the real wage of the average worker has not grown with advances in technology, indicating that the financial benefits of productivity gains are not trickling down to the vast majority of the U.S. workforce.

‡ It is important to recognize that cost-driven strategies also rely on innovation. However, rather than focusing on the creation of products and new markets, cost-driven strategies rely on *process* innovation to cut costs (Charles and Lehner 1998). If product innovation does occur under a cost-driven strategy, it is likely to arise within existing product lines and markets (ibid.).

§ A leading-edge economy does not rely solely on high-tech industries. Rather, such an economy will consist of low-, medium-, and high-tech industries that are focused on delivering products and services with better market-relevant qualities than the majority of their competitors (Charles and Lehner 1998).

the workforce, and (c) the entrance (and pending exit) of the baby boomers into (and out of) the labor market; and (6) changes in (a) the organization of work, (b) the sources of compensation of employees, and (c) the broader political and institutional environment that affect factors such as the minimum wage and the strength of trade unions.

In the United States, there is a clear need to identify strategies that can begin to close the wage and income inequality gap. It seems that identifying ways to combine national competitiveness with employment opportunities—for example, through the creation of intelligent production systems or new product-services—is one approach that would not only strengthen the economy but also improve the quality and (potentially) the availability of well-paid employment.

As this book goes to press, the 2008 financial crisis has led to serious repercussions on employment. Reported levels of unemployment are among the highest, and periods of unemployment are the most protracted, since the Great Depression. Those who have found jobs often receive less than their previous compensation. Some people are losing their homes. Not only is the purchasing power of ordinary citizens diminishing, but wage inequality is further exacerbated as well. Although global climate change and other environmental issues may be the focus of those scholars and social activists who are promoting sustainability, it may be that unemployment, underemployment, and personal economic insecurity become the main driving forces behind public anger and frustration and as a result drive political change,

which may or may not focus on *environmental* sustainability.

### 1.1.3.2 The Importance of Employment beyond the Creation of Purchasing Power

Section 1.1.3.1 focused primarily on the factors behind the growing trends in income and wage inequality in the United States and other developed nations. However, income and wages are only part of the overall benefit or satisfaction derived from employment. Beyond the creation of purchasing power and economic status, meaningful employment can provide social contacts/inclusion, enhance self-esteem, and lead to a better quality of life (Eurofound 2004). Further, our occupations and professions inform "our conception of self" and play an important role in shaping human character (Bertram and Sharpe 2000, p. 44).

European studies of living and working conditions point to the critical importance of income and employment in life satisfaction (Eurofound 2002, 2004, 2005a). These studies also stress that life satisfaction improves when high levels of employment coexist with high-quality jobs. A number of factors combine to influence the quality of jobs and employment. These include career and employment security, skills development, issues relating to work-life balance, and worker health and safety (see Figure 1.4).

During the turbulent period of social unrest in the 1960s, more highly educated industrial workers began to reject the routinization of jobs and the lack of creativity they represented and to call for more humane working conditions (Ashford 1976; Ashford

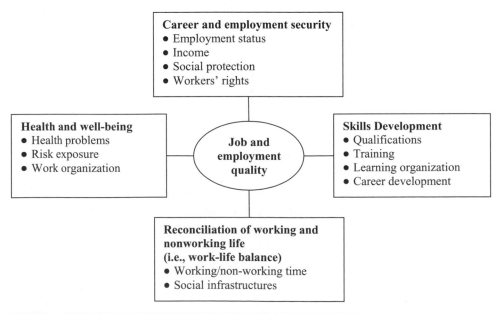

**FIGURE 1.4: FACTORS THAT INFLUENCE JOB AND EMPLOYMENT QUALITY**
Source: Eurofound (2002, p. 6).

and Caldart 1996; HEW 1973).[10] At the center of their concerns lay the need for more autonomous and engaging work that enables the potential and capabilities of workers to flourish (Green 1980; Heckscher 1996; Walton 1985). Today, concerns about worker autonomy, working hours, the intensification of work, physical and psychological working conditions, and the growth in contingent/temporary workers are important factors in the debate on life satisfaction. For example, a survey of workers in twenty-eight European countries, including the acceding and candidate countries as well as the current member states of the European Union, found that individuals with low levels of work autonomy are less satisfied with their lives than those with high levels of work autonomy (Eurofound 2005b).

Both Hochschild's (1997) and Schor's (1991) studies of work patterns in America point to the negative impacts that the increase in daily working hours since the 1970s has had on many working families, especially on neglected children. Further, Boisard, Cartron, et al. (2003a) find that increased working time is clearly linked by employees to increasing health and safety risks. The perception of these employees is reinforced by the empirical evidence that links growing incidences of headaches, muscular pains, fatigue, anxiety, and insomnia to increasing daily working hours (ibid.). Although policies designed to reduce daily hours worked might appear to be the logical way to enhance well-being—such as the French thirty-five-hour week—the European survey mentioned in the preceding paragraph (preliminarily) concluded that "reduced working time only has a minor impact on overall life satisfaction" (Eurofound 2005b, p. 54). This finding highlights the need to identify those factors that play a more significant role in enhancing the benefits of employment. The same European study found that long-term unemployment was the most significant factor affecting subjective quality of life, followed by physical and psychological working conditions and low work autonomy. The number of hours worked and the intensification of work—that is, work carried out at a faster pace (see Boisard, Cartron, et al. 2003b)—were statistically significant but had a lower relative impact.*

It should be no surprise that long-term unemployment is the most important work-related factor affecting an individual's overall well-being. In addition to the obvious financial implications, extended periods of unemployment can damage self-esteem (Goldsmith, Veum, et al. 1997), worsen symptoms of somatization, depression, and anxiety (Linn, Sandifer, et al. 1985), and lead to social exclusion (Eurofound 2005a). More generally, people who have been unemployed for prolonged periods report lower levels of satisfaction with family life, social life, and health than those who have had continuous employment (Eurofound 2004). All these findings reinforce the view of many sociologists that work is an anchor point in life (between learning and retirement), and involuntary unemployment is detrimental to individual and family well-being. The negative impacts of unemployment also highlight the important benefits that meaningful employment can provide.

Although the significance of unemployment points to the dilemma that a "bad" job is better than no access to a job over a prolonged period (Eurofound 2005a), adopting policies simply to create jobs with little concern for the value they provide workers seems unwise. The idea of designing meaningful jobs that enrich lives is not new. For example, in *Design of Jobs*, L. E. Davis and Taylor (1972, p. 9) recognize that "we are faced with a new and serious responsibility for appropriately developing jobs and organizations, and linking them to the larger society. The requirement now is to design jobs and roles in a context having few external referents and in which all must be designed: the jobs, roles, and the technological and social systems that will provide meaning for individuals and institutions in the larger society."

With the nature of work continually changing, primarily in response to global competition (Ackerman, Goodwin, et al. 1998; Carr and Chen 2004; Dougherty 1998), creating jobs that provide workers with value beyond income becomes increasingly challenging. In the continual drive for competitive advantage, firms can search for improved performance by enhancing the skills and ability of their internal workforce to respond to rapid change or search for ways to cut costs by reducing their commitment to the workforce in favor of contingent workers who can be hired as needed (Cappelli 1998). These two strategies for competitiveness lie at opposite ends of a continuum, where the former approach tends to reinforce job security and meaningful employment and the latter approach tends to undermine it.

The recent growth in the number of contingent workers and in the rate at which workers move between firms (reducing job tenure) creates a number of problems. First, temporary workers are unlikely

---

* Although these two last factors are found to be relatively less important, work intensity has been linked to stress (Dhondt 1997; Kompier and Levy 1994) and musculoskeletal disorders (Eurofound 2002), and the growing number of hours worked is commonly associated with the breakdown of family life (Hochschild 1997; Schor 1991).

to form bonds of friendship, trust, and commitment if they are employed for a short period of time (Bertram and Sharpe 2000). This situation not only undermines these key elements of human character (Sennett 1998) but also reduces opportunities for social inclusion. Second, the growing mobility of workers and the transferability of skills discourage firms from investing in training because they may not see a return on their investment. If a large proportion of firms adopted a poaching rather than a nurturing approach to the acquisition of worker skills, workers would become more responsible for their own training and career development (Cappelli 1998). This development might also raise distributive justice concerns, because firms (that is, executives and shareholders) would reap the benefits of the additional educational burden put on society as a whole (ibid.). Further, those workers who might not see the value of education and skill development would face increased social exclusion due to reduced ability for participation.

The strain that the changing nature of work has placed on employees and their families and friends has elevated the debate on work-life balance (Woolley 2006). For example, improving living and working conditions in Europe is the primary mission of the European Foundation for the Improvement of Living and Working Conditions (Eurofound).[11] In the United States, the concept of work-life balance has been adopted by many firms that are keen to create a working environment more conducive to family life. For example, in 2006, IBM had over fifty programs to promote work-life balance, and Bank of America had more than thirty (Economist 2006). More generally, companies in the United States are being recognized for their family-friendly policies. For example, *Working Mother* magazine annually compiles a list of the top one hundred companies in America that offer the best work-life-balance programs.[12] With the growing number of women in the workforce, the need for more flexible but secure working arrangements is becoming more evident. Indeed, Eurofound (2006b, p. 110) argues that "issues of flexitime and flexicurity should be systematically integrated with those of equal opportunity, and with those of good quality and affordable child and frail elderly care." It also argues that "family-friendly employment policies might be defined as the basis for a new family policy, in which not only income, but time (time to care, to develop relationships) is conceptualised as a crucial resource" (ibid.).

In summary, although paid employment provides an essential resource to help satisfy basic human needs

for safety, security, and sustenance, employment (both paid and unpaid) is also a critical factor in the satisfaction of our human needs relating to competence, efficacy, and self-esteem; autonomy and authenticity; and connectedness. This section emphasizes the importance of thinking beyond policies that focus only on job creation to strategies that encourage the creation of *meaningful* jobs that ultimately enhance our general well-being and satisfaction with life. The growing interest in work-life balance in many firms and institutions across the world is encouraging, but the real challenge lies in developing jobs that enhance competitiveness without undermining the value employees derive from workforce participation (see Section 7.6.4 in Chapter 7 for a related discussion of values for sustainable employment).

### 1.1.4 Human Needs and Sustainability

There is convincing evidence to suggest that understanding the fundamental needs of humans is essential if we are to develop strategies to transition society toward more sustainable forms of development. Put simply, human needs motivate behavior, and developing a better understanding of this relationship is needed to enhance economic, social, and political decision making.

It is well documented that individuals, groups, and cultures develop the *actions* and *value systems* that are used to realize their needs. This is especially important when one is considering differences in the needs of people in developed versus developing nations, where livelihoods vary significantly. It also means that the satisfiers of needs will change over time and across cultures with socioeconomic change. Further, if societal and cultural values nurture basic psychological needs, it is likely that the social fabric of a community will strengthen, which in turn will facilitate the well-being and integrity of individuals within that community (R. M. Ryan 1995). If not, then the reverse is likely to occur.

A growing concern in Western culture is that our view of the good life has been affected (or put out of balance) by the forces of the market economy (through advertising, as well as social competition for conspicuous consumption). The result of this imbalance is that an individual's behavior is being *externally regulated*—that is, it is aimed at obtaining the approval of others. For example, we buy a certain type of product or strive for a high income to ensure that we gain the approval of our friends or maintain our perceived status in society. Such behavior is not likely to result in our ability to satisfy our intrinsic needs for competence, autonomy, and connectedness.

A neoclassical economics solution to this concern might be that each person should act in his or her own interests and let the market allocate resources accordingly. This solution assumes that each person is receiving good information and is able to make informed, rational decisions. However, this does not appear to be the case for consumers aged forty-five and over in the United States, who are finding it increasingly difficult to use their spending power effectively (AARP 2004). It also assumes that even if a person had perfect information, he or she would act in a socially responsible (and rational) manner—an assumption that is likely to be challenged by the communitarian movement.* An additional problem is that today's youth have become the most targeted audience for advertising in history, primarily because of their future spending power.[13] It is well established that alcohol (Center on Alcohol Marketing and Youth 2002, 2005; Jones and Donovan 2001)[14] and tobacco (Cummings, Morley, et al. 2002) companies have targeted products at youth with the intention of creating lifelong consumers. But beyond these arguably harmful products, encouraging youth to buy music, sports equipment, automobiles, electronics, and other products is also a major force for consumption. The "burgeoning youth marketing industry" not only is raising important ethical questions (Kasser and Linn 2004, p. 1) but also is reinforcing producer-created demand and the throughput economy. These two outcomes have the potential to lead to significant negative psychological and environmental impacts, respectively. Reconceptualizing advertizing to provide (less intrusive) "information" on products and services rather than messages designed to encourage lifestyles geared to consumption is one solution (Victor 2008), although achieving such a shift in the approach of the advertising industry would be no simple feat.

---

* The objective of communitarianism is to identify ways to restore social and moral consensus to communities without imposing a set of behaviors and values on them. The movement is based on the concern that in the United States the relationships between individuals and groups, between rights and responsibilities, and among the institutions of state, market, and civil society are out of balance. This imbalance means that personal and social ethics are also out of balance, resulting in a preoccupation with individualism. Thus if a large segment of society exhibits individualistic tendencies, it is questionable whether its members would act in a more socially responsible manner if they were provided with perfect information about the impacts of their (economic and social) behavior.

Further, relying solely on the market to ensure that basic human needs are met is clearly not a viable option if sustainability is to be achieved—who would provide education and primary health care for the poor? Hence government has an important role to play in ensuring that markets function for the benefit of society and intervening where they fall short. To enable an acceptable balance of responsibility to be achieved, there needs to be a willingness on the part of governments, society, and industry to engage in discussion and the analysis of the connection between freedom, regulation, and control—and its relationship to overall societal good—if and when radical changes to our social and physical systems become necessary (Haland 1999). Further, reliance on social influence (or goodwill) to initiate change ignores evidence that unless the right environment and resources are made available, society will be asked to act beyond its capacity (Schmuck and Schultz 2002). In many ways, what is needed is a coevolutionary approach to change, in which the values held by government, society, and industry evolve to support human needs and the objectives of sustainable development.

Although markets do provide the goods and services that can help meet human needs, the industries that operate within the market economy also provide another essential and often overlooked function: the provision of *employment*. Holding a well-paid and meaningful job not only enables an individual to purchase goods and services but also provides opportunities to enhance psychological well-being. The problem, however, is that the growing trends of within-nation wage and income inequality in the United States and many other developed nations, combined with low income mobility, are undermining the ability of the poor to access important services, such as health care. Further, the changing nature of work—for example, the growing number of contingent workers—is reducing the potential value derived from employment. If these two trends are left unchecked, they could lead to growing feelings of deprivation and a declining satisfaction with life among the workforce.

These concerns present a significant challenge to creating a more sustainable society. Determining the root causes of diverse issues such as consumerism, growing inequalities, and changing employment opportunities is extremely difficult. However, what is clear is that human needs and behavior are common to all these issues. As Pol (2002, p. x) argues, "The sustainability problem is a result of individual and collective human behaviour. It cannot be treated as an economic or technical problem, without considering the mechanics that intervene on the behavioral side of it."

Placing human needs at the center of sustainable development strategies is likely to be a positive step forward. Such strategies would mean that government, society (that is, communities and individuals), and industry would need to promote values that center on innate human needs. In the context of employment, this is already recognized in the use of the term "anthropocentric production" (Brödner 1990; Lehner 1992), which distinguishes people-centered employment from the use of human resources in the most profitable or efficient production schemes, to the detriment of workers.

Equally important is the promotion of levels of consumption and manufacturing processes that do not exceed ecological limits. Ultimately, turning our focus to meeting human needs is likely to "make fewer demands on our environmental resources, but much greater demands on our moral resources" (Brown 1981, p. 359). A term such as "anthropocentric consumption" as an analogue to anthropocentric production sounds inappropriate because almost all consumption is intended for human consumption. "Sustainable consumption" is a better term.

Because the single-purpose design of policies is unlikely to address multidimensional sustainable development problems adequately, a better approach would be to search for ways to co-optimize (or even better, integrate) policies that can address multiple concerns. For example, identifying ways to combine national competitiveness with employment opportunities—for example, through the creation of intelligent production systems or new product-services—is one approach that would not only strengthen the economy but also improve the quality and (potentially) the availability of well-paid employment. In the end, the challenge facing society is how to reconcile the void between individual human needs, on the one hand, and the sustainable development of social and physical systems at local, national, and global levels, on the other. It seems that a good way forward would be to accept the complexity of sustainable development and focus on the design of policies that bring together competitiveness, employment, and environmental protection.*

## 1.2 SOCIAL JUSTICE, INEQUALITY, AND THE SOCIAL CONTRACT BETWEEN THE GOVERNED AND THE GOVERNMENT

The test of our progress is not whether we add more to the abundance of those who have much; it is whether we provide enough for those who have too little. Franklin Delano Roosevelt, Second Inaugural Address, January 20, 1937

An important conclusion drawn previously is that government should act as a trustee to ensure that basic human needs are met in an equitable and just manner. However, governments cannot provide the whole answer; competitive markets will also continue to play a vital role in meeting human needs. The challenge is to find a tolerable balance between government regulation and economic (and other forms of) freedom.†

In general, economists tend to reject the notion that the government should interfere with the market and argue that we should let people express their utility in the marketplace. However, as discussed in the previous section, consumers are finding it increasingly difficult to use their spending power effectively. Hence it appears that there are two predominant views: (1) there are basic needs, and that is why we need *markets*; and (2) there are basic needs, and that is why we need *government*.

The focus of this section will be on the problems of equity within a country or region, equity between developed and developing nations, and intergenerational equity. The critical questions addressed here are what is fair *within* society and what role government should play. If the state is to play a role in needs satisfaction, we should have some understanding of the relative roles of the governed and the government. In this regard, we begin this section with a look at the *social contract*.

### 1.2.1 The Social Contract and the Theory of Justice

Man is born free; and everywhere he is in chains. One thinks himself the master of others, and still remains a greater slave than they. Jean-Jacques Rousseau, 1762

---

\* For example, enhancing purchasing power by increasing commercial activity may inadvertently create environmental problems. Thus in this situation a physical standard of living needs to be co-optimized with environmental quality and employment.

---

† A reliance on markets is not likely to be sufficient, because if there is *producer-created demand*, then businesses influence both the supply and the demand side of the economy. Although such influence may not result in monopoly prices, it has the potential to reduce our ability to fulfill our basic human needs. Hence government has a role to play in ensuring that a full range of products and services is provided for society.

The modern notion of the social contract can be traced back to the political and moral theories of Thomas Hobbes (1985 [1651]), John Locke (1988 [1690]), Jean-Jacques Rousseau (1968 [1762]), and Immanuel Kant (1989 [1785]), but the present-day interpretation rests most heavily on the work of John Rawls (1971).

The basic premise of the social contract is that an individual, in accepting that the pursuit of self-interest is ultimately self-defeating, relinquishes certain freedoms and rights to a system of collectively enforced social arrangements in exchange for peace and security (Friend 2004). Hence he or she agrees to follow the "general will" of society and be held accountable if his or her "individual will" motivates behavior that breaks the social contract—that is, the law of the land (Rousseau 1968 [1762]). Whatever freedoms an individual loses in the transition from the state of nature* to the civil state are more than compensated for by belonging to a civil society that ensures liberties and property rights. Hence the social contract tries to balance individual freedom with being a member of a civil society that limits freedoms for the greater good.

During the nineteenth century, interest in the social contract declined as the utilitarian movement took hold (Rawls 1971). Utilitarianism argues that all moral judgments should aim to achieve the greatest good for the greatest number (Bentham 1970 [1781]; Mill 2002 [1863]). Hence the objective of social institutions and human actions under a utilitarian frame-work is to develop and enforce laws that maximize the well-being and happiness of society. But utilitarianism suffers from two major problems (Brock 1973). First, the theory raises moral conflicts, particularly in regard to justice. For example, although reducing taxes might maximize the happiness (or material well-being) of society, it might also have the effect of reducing the availability of basic health or educational services for the disadvantaged. The aggregative character of utilitarianism means that it is not concerned about the pattern of distribution of welfare,[†] and therefore it provides no justification for inequality in its distribution (Cohen 1993). Further, "It would not only be morally right to sacrifice the interests of individuals or minority groups if this would serve to maximize common utility, but those who are sacrificed would even have a moral duty of benevolence to let this happen" (Wetlesen 1999, p. 42). Second, utilitarianism fails to support the more liberal nature of Western societies that emphasize liberty and individual rights. For example, slavery was a useful institution in the United States for promoting the success of agricultural advance, but it was ultimately rejected on moral and sociopolitical grounds. Similar arguments apply to the elimination of child labor in industrialization.

In an effort to address the shortcomings of utilitarianism, as well as those of intuitionism (that is, systems of philosophy that consider intuition the fundamental process of our knowledge), John Rawls published his seminal work in 1971, *A Theory of Justice*, which renewed the notion of the social contract by arguing that political and moral positions can be determined by using impartiality.

The traditional social contract (envisioned in its various forms by Hobbes, Locke, Rousseau, and Kant) revolved around the agreement of people in a state of

---

* The "state of nature" refers to a hypothetical state of living that occurred before the establishment of society and the introduction of any form of government or social arrangements. Hence in the state of nature there are no restraints on how one can behave. The manner in which one defines the state of nature has implications for how the social contract is subsequently envisioned. For example, Hobbes's (1985 [1651]) political philosophy was based on the idea that men in a state of nature (i.e., in a state without civil government) are in a state of constant war, which any rational and self-motivated individual would want to end. Hence the solution is to establish a social contract to ensure peace and order and to enable individuals to live in a civil society, which suits their own interest. Hobbes's hypothetical view of the state of nature was extreme in that he envisioned a world in which man would constantly fear for his life. Locke (1988 [1690]) built on Hobbes's notion of the social contract but constructed his theories on a different view of the state of nature. Locke (1988 [1690]) argued that without government to enforce social arrangements and laws, man is not free to do anything he pleases because he is constrained by a sense of morality. In this regard, the "State of Nature is pre-political, but it is not pre-moral. . . . It is therefore both the view of human nature, and the nature of morality itself, which account for the differences between Hobbes' and Locke's views of the social contract" (C. Friend [2004], "The Social Contract," *The Internet Encyclopedia of Philosophy*, www.iep.utm.edu/soc-cont/ [accessed June 8, 2010]).

---

† The Brundtland report, *Our Common Future*, interprets "welfare" as the "satisfaction of human needs and aspirations" (WCED 1987, p. 43). This interpretation rests on fundamental human needs for "primary goods," such as food, shelter, clothing, and employment, and the legitimate expectations for a better life. Wetlesen (1999) argues that we can reasonably interpret the Brundtland Commission's view of welfare in an *objective* and a *subjective* sense. The former is concerned with conditions and standards of living, and the latter with the perceived quality of life that an individual is able to achieve. The Brundtland report is also concerned about the equitable distribution of welfare. "The essential needs of vast numbers of people in developing countries—for food, clothing, shelter, jobs—are not being met, and beyond their basic needs these people have legitimate aspirations for an improved quality of life. A world in which poverty and inequality are endemic will always be prone to ecological and other crises. Sustainable development requires meeting the basic needs of all and extending to all the opportunity to satisfy their aspirations for a better life" (WCED 1987, pp. 43–44).

nature to form a society and government that they will be obligated to obey (Brock 1973). In this regard, the social contract is "primarily a theory of political obligation" (ibid., p. 488). In contrast, Rawls developed a version of the contract in which the relevant agreement revolves around moral principles, the principles of justice (ibid.). These principles can be considered a set of game rules that must be followed in designing new social arrangements, such as policies and programs. Central to Rawls's theory is the hypothetical situation, the "original position," in which an individual's knowledge is constrained by a "veil of ignorance." Behind the veil of ignorance, "No one knows his place in society, his class position or social status; nor does he know his fortune in the distribution of natural assets and abilities, his intelligence and strength, and the like. Nor, again, does anyone know his conception of the good, the particulars of his rational plan of life, or even the special features of his psychology such as his aversion to risk or liability to optimism or pessimism. . . . The parties do not know the particular circumstances of their own society, . . . its economic or political situation, or the level of civilization and culture it has been able to achieve" (Rawls 1971, p. 137). Rawls argues that decisions made for society should be made as if the participants do not know in advance what their lot in life will be.

In essence, Rawls's original position is an abstract version of the state of nature. It follows that from the original position people are able to identify what they must do individually and collectively (through social institutions) to realize the nature of justice. The simplicity of the veil of ignorance is its strength. By denying contracting parties the knowledge of their own characteristics or circumstances, they are forced to adopt the moral point of view and are unable to develop principles or policies that favor themselves. Rawls also states that contracting parties are assumed to be "rational and mutually disinterested" (Rawls 1971, p. 13): "rational" in the sense that the contracting party makes the most effective decision to reach a given end, and "mutually disinterested" in the sense that each person does not take "an interest in one another's interests" (ibid.). Thus the "rational" choice is to develop principles and strategies for a just society from initial conditions that are inherently fair. Justice, therefore, proceeds out of fairness, giving rise to Rawls's formulation of "justice as fairness" (ibid., p. 17). Further, as Brock (1973, p. 489) notes, in Rawls's theory there is no historical agreement, which means that contracting

parties are able to adopt "the standpoint of someone in the original position, and so the moral point of view, at any time." In theory, an individual in the original position will adopt the same principles for justice as any other person, thereby establishing a robust set of principles and arrangements to regulate a just society.

A problem identified by Rawls when he is considering the design of the social institutions that form the basic structure of society is that individuals are born into the world with a wide range of circumstances and characteristics. Although it is not possible to alter many of the human characteristics that form our personalities and physical ability, Rawls argues that it is possible to adjust the social institutions to favor those who are disadvantaged. Hence Rawls develops two principles of justice that he argues contracting parties would select in the original position—behind the veil of ignorance—to establish a just society:

*First Principle:* "Each person is to have an equal right to the most extensive total system of equal basic liberties compatible with a similar system of liberty for all."

*Second Principle:* "Social and economic inequalities are to be arranged so that they are both (a) to the greatest benefit of the least advantaged, consistent with the just savings principle, and (b) attached to offices and positions open to all under conditions of fair equality of opportunities" (Rawls 1971, p. 302).

The first principle determines the distribution of civil liberties. It states that each member of a society is to receive as much liberty (or personal freedom) as possible, as long as every other member of society receives the same. The principle "implies that one person's good can never be considered a good if it constitutes an obstacle to someone else's pursuit of *their* good, even if that someone else comes a generation or two later" (Voorthuis and Gijbels 2010, p. 376). The second principle states that social and economic inequalities are justified only if the most disadvantaged members of society are made relatively better off under new arrangements. As Friend (2004) notes, "Only if a rising tide truly does carry all boats upward, can economic inequalities be allowed for in a just society."

Rawls (1971) developed the second principle (known as the *difference principle*) using the *maximin rule*—that is, the best outcome is one that minimizes the maximum loss. He argued that since people do not know their position in society when they are behind the veil of ignorance, they will select the difference principle because it will be to their benefit if they end up in the most disadvantaged section of society.

In the latter part of principle 2(a), Rawls introduces the notion of "just savings," which is the first comprehensive treatment of intergenerational equity (or justice). The basic idea is that when individuals are in the original position, behind the veil of ignorance, they do not know which generation or in what stage of socioeconomic development they might live and must, therefore, select "savings" principles that do not favor earlier generations over later ones.* In *A Theory of Justice*, Rawls's formulation of the just savings principle was based on a "motivational assumption" that contracting parties would want to save for their successors, regardless of whether their ancestors saved for them.[15] This formulation runs counter to the notion of "mutually disinterested" contracting parties and has been criticized as being sexist and arbitrary (Barry 1978; Okin 1989).

In *Political Liberalism*, Rawls (1993) revised his notion of the just savings principle to address these inconsistencies. His revised assumption is that *generations* are mutually disinterested. Therefore, contracting parties in the original position, behind the veil of ignorance, should "agree to a savings principle subject to the further condition that they must want all previous generations to have followed it. Thus the correct principle is that which the members of any generation (and so all generations) would adopt as the one their generation is to follow and as the principle they would want preceding generations to have followed (and later generations to follow), no matter how far back (or forward) in time" (ibid., p. 274). In this formulation, the principle of just savings is considered as binding for all previous and future generations. A problem, however, with Rawls's restatement is that he does not consider the implications of an increasing number of people in the future,[†] or that the current generation has a larger population than the previous generation—a fact that will clearly change how much society should save (Barry 1999; Casal and Williams 1995; P. Dasgupta 1994; Heyd 1992). Nevertheless, Rawls's ideas provide a useful starting point for discussions about intergenerational equity.

The two principles of justice are to be considered in a specific order. The first principle must be considered before the second principle because "liberty can only be restricted for the sake of liberty, not for other social and economic advantages" (Brock 1973, p. 490).[‡] This ranking implies that society would rank the determination of civil liberties above that of economic advantage. Also, within the second principle, equality of opportunity (2b) is to be considered before the difference principle (2a), using the same rationale.

Before we progress further, it is worth mentioning that there are those who question these basic principles of justice. For example, Brock (1973) argues that people in the original position are likely to tolerate minor sacrifices in liberty for substantial economic gain, especially in situations of severe economic underdevelopment. Further, the difference principle assumes that all risk taking in the original position is irrational: "It allows no possible gain in one's life prospects, should one turn out to be among the better off members of society" (ibid., p. 491). This latter point reflects a common criticism of Rawls's decision to use a maximin rule (Harsanyi 1975). Rawls (1974) counters such arguments by stating that the original position masks the probabilities of outcomes, making alternative decision rules too risky. In addition, the difference principle acknowledges the fact that any good circumstances into which a person is born are "unearned and undeserved" (Brock 1973, p. 491). The benefits that are derived from these circumstances should therefore benefit all of society. Thus whether a person is for or against Rawls's theory of justice will depend, to a certain extent, on that person's perceived position in society.

---

* In the words of Rawls (1971, p. 287): "The parties do not know to which generation they belong or, what comes to the same thing, the stage of civilization of their society. They have no way of telling whether it is poor or relatively wealthy, largely agricultural or already industrialized, and so on. The veil of ignorance is complete in these respects. Thus the persons in the original position are to ask themselves how much they would be willing to save at each stage on the assumption that all other generations are to save at the same rates. That is, they are to consider their willingness to save at any given phase of civilization with the understanding that the rates they propose are to regulate the whole span of accumulation. In effect, then, they must choose a just savings principle that assigns an appropriate rate of accumulation to each level of advance."

† In contrast, in Northern industrialized societies there are implications of decreasing populations that can not provide sufficient amenities for those retiring (International Economy 2004).

‡ It is possible to envisage a situation where liberty is constrained to protect liberty—i.e., "restrictions to individual freedoms are justified when the unfettered exercise of these freedoms conflicts with other freedoms" (Beatley 1994, p. 156). For example, the speed at which vehicles are allowed to drive is constrained to protect broader public freedoms such as individual safety.

Rawls argues that his notion of justice as fairness begins with the adoption of the principles of a just society, which will guide all subsequent actions, including the reform of institutions. "Having chosen a conception of justice, we can suppose that . . . [the contracting parties] are to choose a constitution and a legislature to enact laws, and so on, all in accordance with the principles of justice initially agreed upon. . . . Moreover, assuming that the original position does determine a set of principles (that is, that a particular conception of justice would be chosen), it will then be true that whenever social institutions satisfy these principles those engaged in them can say to one another that they are cooperating on terms to which they would agree if they were free and equal persons whose relations with respect to one another were fair" (Rawls 1971, p. 13).

Rawls argues that the challenge raised by the difference principle is how to choose a social system (that is, a basic structure of government) that will ensure *distributive justice* in a capitalist market economy. From the premise that the basic structure of government and its actions are regulated by a constitution protecting the liberties of equal citizenship, Rawls outlines four branches of government (Rawls 1971, pp. 274–284). The first is the *allocation branch*, required to keep markets competitive, prevent the formation of unreasonable market power, and correct for externalities. The second is the *stabilization branch*, needed to bring about strong effective demand (through the deployment of finance) and to maintain full employment and choice of occupation (that is, those who desire work can find it). The third is the *transfer branch*, essential to the formation and maintenance of a social minimum. By considering basic human needs, this branch determines the level of guaranteed minimum income that maximizes the long-term expectations of the least advantaged. Finally, there is the *distribution branch*, needed to enforce inheritance and gift taxes, in addition to general income or expenditure taxes. It follows that the allocation and stabilization branches are required to maintain an efficient economy; the transfer branch is designed to ensure that basic human needs are identified and met; and the distribution branch is needed to prevent the concentration of economic power.

As stated in the introduction to Section 1.2, we argue that government has an important role as a trustee to ensure that basic human needs are met in an equitable and just manner. The preceding discussion of the social contract and Rawls's theory of justice indicates how government could be structured to enable it to achieve this goal. But establishing a philosophy of government that ensures that basic human needs are met is a complex task.

Basic human needs are categorized under the headings of *sustenance, competence, autonomy,* and *connectedness* (Kasser 2002). However, this formulation does not provide government with a clear directive on what actions are required to satisfy our basic needs. In this regard, Max-Neef, Elizalde, et al's (1989) theory of human needs and satisfiers is of value in that it identifies the *qualities, things, actions,* and *settings* that are associated with fundamental needs such as protection, participation, and freedom. Further, because *satisfiers* are ultimately defined by society—an essential characteristic of the social contract—an interesting experiment would be for a representative group of contracting parties to complete Max-Neef, Elizalde, et al's (1989) matrix of needs and satisfiers while behind the veil of ignorance . In theory, this action would develop the satisfiers of human needs that are culturally defined and impartial.

Once the basic human needs of a society are agreed on, the role of government (in a Rawlsian sense) is to develop laws, policies, and programs to assist those members of society who are unable to satisfy their basic needs. Opponents to the formation of such a welfare state argue that the only way to meet the needs of the disadvantaged is through economic regulation and taxation, which results in a loss of civil liberties (Nozick 1974).* Hence civil liberty and social welfare stand in constant tension with each other.†

---

\* In 1974 the late Robert Nozick—a professor of philosophy at Harvard and a colleague of John Rawls—published *Anarchy, State, and Utopia* in opposition to the *nonminimal welfare state* proposed in *A Theory of Justice.* Nozick (1974, p. ix) defined the minimal state as follows: "Our main conclusions about the state are that a minimal state, limited to the narrow functions of protection against force, theft, fraud, enforcement of contracts, and so on, is justified; that any more extensive state will violate persons' rights not to be forced to do certain things, and is unjustified; and that the minimal state is inspiring as well as right. Two noteworthy implications are that the state may not use its coercive apparatus for the purpose of getting some citizens to aid others, or in order to prohibit activities to people for their own good or protection." Interestingly, although Nozick's and Rawls's philosophies of government were opposed, they both agreed that individual rights are more important than utilitarian considerations and that government should be neutral in respect to people's right to choose and pursue their own vision of a good life (Sandel 1996).

† "The extent to which the needs theory dominates the philosophy of government . . . can be measured by the levels of taxation and regulation of economic activity. Government takes money out of the hands of individuals and spends it on what it considers are the needs priorities of the people. The more an individual is taxed, the greater the loss of his freedom to determine

One might question, however, whether a laissez-faire market is able to operate free from government intervention and supply the products and services that society needs. In particular, Brulle (2000, p. 37) expresses concern that government is not able to operationalize the social contract, arguing that "there is little public policy about policy."

Brulle (2000) describes how since the Great Depression, the U.S. government has become an active participant in economic activity, primarily to stabilize the economic system and to compensate for the adverse effects of capital accumulation. This involvement in the economy means that the government assumes a level of responsibility to ensure the legitimacy of the market. Because economic growth is based on investment and consumption, the government plays an important role in furthering these two drivers of economic development. Brulle (2000, pp. 34–35) argues that the "inability of the market to maintain itself creates a politically maintained private market in which socialized production and private appropriation of production exist in a system legitimized by formal democratic rules. This creates a conflict between the normative justifications for collective decisions. Market outcomes are legitimized as the outcomes of democratic will formation. This leads to a series of contradictions and crises in Western society."

Brulle's (2000) major concern is that the public sphere—"an arena in which the common good was debated and a democratic consensus was reached" (p. 37)—has been undermined by the insulation of government action from public input.* This situation

has had the effect of exposing the public sphere to "the manipulative deployment of media power to procure mass loyalty, consumer demand, and compliance with systemic imperatives" (Habermas 1992, p. 452, quoted in Brulle 2000, p. 37). In such an environment, it is difficult to envision how society can be an effective part of the decision-making process. Thus the social contract between the governed and the government is undermined, thwarting efforts to establish a social order that enables "the communicative generation of legitimate power" (ibid.).

### 1.2.2 Operationalizing the Social Contract

Given the preceding discussion, a critical question remains: how should we operationalize the social contract? Further, if government is to act as a trustee, how should it interact with the public?

Ashford and Rest (2001) provide some useful answers to these questions. In particular, they argue that the perceived and actual role of government in public participation is crucial, as is the role adopted by the stakeholders:

> Specifically, what is important is whether the government sees itself and is seen as (1) a trustee of community/stakeholder interests, or alternatively (2) as a mediator or arbitrator of conflicting interests in the community or stakeholder group. The roles adopted by the participants of community and stakeholder involvement processes are likewise important, specifically the participant dynamics that foster majoritarian or utilitarian outcomes, versus communitarian outcomes.[†] Both sets of roles can affect the process and outcomes of public participation efforts. In other words, the role of government and the tenor of community or stakeholder participation are codeterminative of success—which we define, in large measure, as enhancing fairness, justice, and empowerment for the most [adversely] affected.

> In order for the government to act in a trusteeship capacity, it must be committed to justice and fairness in the Rawlsian sense—i.e., it must first and foremost

---

his own priorities and to satisfy his individual needs. In short, through taxation and regulation, government decides how a person should spend his money. Rather than leave a person's resources to himself and permit him to make his own arrangements for the satisfaction of his needs, the government expropriates his wealth and in return seeks to provide him the necessities of life as determined by government.... It is clear that a needs based theory of human rights can be pursued only at the expense of the gradual loss of freedom and a gradual movement towards totalitarianism" (M. Cooray [1985], "Human Rights in Australia," *The Basic Human Rights and the Needs Based Human Rights*, www.ourcivilisation.com/cooray/rights/chap5.htm [accessed June 8, 2010]).

* Brulle (2000, pp. 36–37) puts forward a number of ways in which government policy is insulated from the public. For example, the use of scientific discourse in the development and analysis of state policy has the effect of limiting the public's access to institutional policies. The management of political demand through the selective involvement of certain groups in negotiations presents clear barriers to public participation. Also, public demands are insulated by increasing the decision-making authority of the executive agencies of the state. Korten (2001) and Nader (2004) also argue that the power of commercial enterprises has grown to such an extent that they are able to exert a

strong influence over government, thereby undermining the ability of society to express its views through the democratic process.

† "The . . . communitarian approach to conflict resolution is a process wherein the various community members or stakeholders strive to achieve the greater social good rather than maximize their own benefit, thereby transcending individual interests. We emphasized the distinction between a consensus reached by majoritarian processes (where the political majority gets what it wants, thereby approximating maximum collective utility), and a communitarian approach using normative processes, in which citizens and other stakeholders are willing to sacrifice self-interest on behalf of longer-term and more far-reaching societal goals" (Ashford and Rest 2001, p. VII-9).

**TABLE 1.3: TYPES AND OUTCOMES OF INTERACTIONS BETWEEN THE GOVERNMENT AND STAKEHOLDERS**

| GOVERNMENT'S ROLE | STAKEHOLDER POSTURE | |
| --- | --- | --- |
| | UTILITARIAN (Maximizing individual/social benefit) | COMMUNITARIAN (Promoting the greater social good) |
| **As a trustee for the affected stakeholders** | 1. Decision is made by government in a trusteeship role on behalf of all the *participating stakeholders*. | 2. Decision is made by government in a trusteeship role on behalf of the stakeholders (mirroring a *normative* consensus, possibly expanding to benefit the larger nonparticipating public as well). |
| **As a facilitator of utilitarian or majoritarian consensus, or alternative dispute resolution among the stakeholders** | 3. Stakeholder involvement processes reach a *consensus* or *compromise* among the *participating* stakeholders. | 4. Idealized stakeholder involvement processes reach *normative* consensus, possibly expanding to benefit the larger nonparticipating public as well. |

Source: Adapted from Ashford and Rest (2001, p. VII-14).

encourage or allow those activities that provide relatively greater advantage to those individual members or groups who are relatively worse off to begin with. . . . In a political climate where stakeholder involvement is encouraged to legitimize conflict resolution or the parceling out of scarce agency resources, government can easily abdicate its trusteeship role in favor of a more utilitarian approach to problem solving. The result is often a continued polarization of various community groups and members. . . .

To the extent that government sees and presents itself as a convener or mediator of opposing interests, government itself may foster utilitarian, rather than communitarian values and outcomes. Conversely, where government presents itself as a guardian of the disadvantaged, community participation mechanisms that protect minority views and interests by addressing imbalances of power are encouraged. The community members themselves may step out of their roles as representatives of narrow community interests, and address issues of fairness on a broader scale. Thus, vehicles for public participation and stakeholder involvement must be seen within this broader perspective in order to gauge their accomplishments. (Ashford and Rest 2001, p. VII-9)

The research undertaken by Ashford and Rest (2001) indicates that the outcome of discourse between government agencies and the public depends on the roles adopted by each. To help visualize the interactions between government and society, they developed a matrix that presents the likely outcomes under the different government/stakeholder positions (Table 1.3).*

In the left column of Table 1.3, the two roles of government are indicated: (1) the government acts as a *trustee* of stakeholder interests, and (2) the government acts as a *mediator* of conflicting interests between or among stakeholders. For the stakeholders, two (somewhat idealized) positions are presented: (1) *utilitarianism*, in which stakeholders seek to maximize their own utility; and (2) *communitarianism*, in which stakeholders act for what they perceive as the greater social good. Further, a distinction is made between the *participating* stakeholders—that is, those actively involved in public participation efforts—and the nonparticipating public who are also stakeholders.

If we consider the first row in Table 1.3 where the government adopts the role of *trustee*, two situations can arise (Ashford and Rest 2001, p. VII-13). First, government acts on behalf of the participating stakeholders to promote utilitarian solutions (cell 1). Second, government acts on behalf of all stakeholders, including those who are not present, to promote communitarian solutions (cell 2). Likewise, if we consider the second row in Table 1.3 where the government adopts the role of *facilitator* of compromise or consensus, we see two different situations (ibid.). First, government acts to implement the compromise or consensus reached by the participating stakeholders (cell 3). Second, government acts to implement the normative consensus achieved by stakeholders on behalf of the larger nonparticipating public (cell 4).

---

* Although Ashford and Rest (2001) use two matrices to distinguish the community from the wider group of stakeholders, only the second matrix is discussed here. Those interested in the difference between community involvement mechanisms and stakeholder involvement mechanisms are directed to Ashford and Rest (2001).

As before, the former promotes utilitarian solutions and the latter communitarian ones.

Ashford and Rest (2001, p. VII-15) draw the following conclusions from the matrix:

> If what is desired is reaching decisions that benefit the larger group of stakeholders (both participating and non-participating), this can be achieved either by government adopting a role as a trustee/decision-maker for the larger group of stakeholders . . . [cell 2] or through an idealized stakeholder involvement process facilitated by government . . . [cell 4]. This is especially appropriate in environmental justice communities.
>
> On the other hand, if the participating stakeholders are able or not [able] . . . to think beyond their narrow self-interests, stakeholder involvement processes will leave them most satisfied if either the government facilitates giving them what they want through meaningful participation in reaching compromises or resolving disputes . . . [cell 3] or if the government serves as a trustee for their interests . . . [cell 1].

Hence the public participation mechanism should be chosen with care, "paying special attention to the best way to achieve procedural fairness, procedural competence, and optimal outcome. . . . This will necessarily involve a variety of complementary mechanisms, utilizing both community and stakeholder involvement processes" (Ashford and Rest 2001, p. VII-14).

To help visualize the implications of Ashford and Rest's (2001) framework, we have created Table 1.4 to show whether the (idealized) roles of government and stakeholder postures are likely to result in a Rawlsian outcome. As in Table 1.3, the stakeholders' posture in the decision process is idealized as being either utilitarian or communitarian. Table 1.4 uses the terms "Rawlsian outcome," "Rawlsian government," and "non-Rawlsian government," which require some clarification.

A *Rawlsian outcome* is where new legislation, policies, or programs support initiatives that offer greater advantage to individuals or groups who are relatively worse off to begin with.

A *Rawlsian government* refers to a government that is willing and has the capacity to either impose or endorse Rawlsian outcomes. If the stakeholders hold a predominantly utilitarian posture, it is likely that the Rawlsian outcomes will need to be *imposed* on the stakeholders, which a Rawlsian government may be willing to do. Although this situation appears autocratic, it should be recognized that utilitarian solutions can result in unjust outcomes that could infringe on an individual's liberty and rights. Here the fundamental assumption is that Rawlsian outcomes are more likely to be just and fair for all members of society. Hence if the stakeholders hold a predominantly communitarian posture—which promotes the (perceived) greater societal good—the government is likely simply to *endorse* the solutions agreed on by stakeholders.

It follows that a *non-Rawlsian government* is either unwilling or does not have the capacity to impose Rawlsian outcomes on the stakeholders. Instead, it adopts the position of mediator of stakeholder interests. Under this arrangement, the responsibility for achieving a just and fair society is left to the stakeholders. A non-Rawlsian government does not mean that a Rawlsian outcome cannot be achieved; it simply means that the government does not act as a trustee for stakeholder interests, and it would take a strong communitarian group of stakeholders to press for a Rawlsian outcome.

The ideas presented in Table 1.4 present some useful insights that can help guide decision making toward a just and fair society. In effect, the table shows two important outcomes: (1) a Rawlsian-sympathetic government may not be sufficient to achieve a Rawlsian outcome if the stakeholders adopt a utilitarian posture and the government accedes to their wishes; and (2) a non-Rawlsian government can arrive at a Rawlsian outcome, but only if stakeholders adopt a

**TABLE 1.4: LIKELIHOOD OF ACHIEVING A *REVISED* RAWLSIAN OUTCOME WITH A RAWLSIAN/ NON-RAWLSIAN GOVERNMENT *AND* UTILITARIAN/COMMUNITARIAN STAKEHOLDERS**

| GOVERNMENT | STAKEHOLDER POSTURE IN THE DECISION-MAKING PROCESS | |
| --- | --- | --- |
| | UTILITARIAN (Maximizing individual/social benefit) | COMMUNITARIAN (Promoting the greater social good) |
| **Rawlsian government** (government acts as trustee for stakeholders) | Revised Rawlsian outcome **possible** | Revised Rawlsian outcome **highly likely** |
| **Non-Rawlsian government** (government acts as facilitator for utilitarian/ majoritarian consensus) | Revised Rawlsian outcome **unlikely** | Revised Rawlsian outcome **likely** |

communitarian posture* and the government accedes to their wishes.†

If stakeholders adopt a communitarian posture, the likelihood of a Rawlsian outcome being reached is good but variable, depending on whether the government is a trustee or mediator of stakeholder interests. If there is a Rawlsian government, a Rawlsian outcome will be more likely (see the upper right cell). In contrast, if stakeholders adopt a utilitarian posture, it is less likely that a Rawlsian outcome will be reached. If there is a Rawlsian government and stakeholders adopt a utilitarian posture, a Rawlsian outcome is possible, although its achievement may not satisfy the winning party as a result of hard-won compromises. In many respects, the United States is a good example of this situation, where government tends to facilitate utilitarian consensus (Ashford and Rest 2001).

The strength of the decision-making philosophy just described can be illustrated by a simple example. In a typical policy setting, if one were to adopt a Rawlsian approach to decision making—that is, any new social arrangement should preferentially advantage the least advantaged—analysts would likely ask by how much the least advantaged should be made better off, Because the Rawlsian approach talks only about *movement* toward justice (or fairness), there is no unique answer to how much to preferentially advantage the least advantaged as long as significant maldistributions remain. In contrast, if we were to adopt a utilitarian approach, it would be possible to identify the optimum level of safety or income transfer, for example. Therefore, the Rawlsian approach should be seen as a movement (a process) and not a final state, but it is nonetheless possible to operationalize Rawls's theory of justice by "bounding" the acceptable moves and rejecting the clearly utilitarian moves that are not Rawlsian.

If we consider the risks that workers are willing to accept to take a dangerous job, it is possible to illustrate the concept of *bounding acceptable moves.* It has been observed that workers coming from a poor socioeconomic class are willing to accept a dangerous job at a lower level of pay than workers who come from a more affluent socioeconomic class—for example, the sons or daughters of the executives of the firm that is offering employment (Ackerman and Heinzerling 2004; Ashford 1981; Ashford and Caldart 1996). In this case, the sons or daughters of the executives are likely to demand higher pay to accept the risks associated with the work. Therefore, *consciously* setting the pay at a level that only workers from a poor socioeconomic class would accept is wrong from a moral standpoint. This outcome is what economic efficiency and utilitarianism dictate. Clearly, a Rawlsian solution is not to provide a level of pay that only workers from a poor socioeconomic class would accept but something much more toward what the most advantaged would be willing to accept, given the associated level of risk. Although the Rawlsian outcome is not calculable in the absolute sense, it can certainly be bounded. Further, the solution should arrive at "a well-grounded and situationally determined feeling of fairness" (Voorthuis and Gijbels 2010, p. 376). At the upper bound, if the executives paid their workers as much as the richest portions of society would require to assume the job, it would not be anti-Rawlsian. Thus the final solution will lie between the upper and lower bounds at a point that the stakeholders believe is fair, economically feasible, and in line with the interests of society as a whole. The idea of bounding the acceptable moves and rejecting the clearly utilitarian moves that are not Rawlsian is explored later in this section.

The preceding illustration shows that Rawls's original position is essentially a voting tool. It is a way of getting society to agree on what is fair for society. In this sense, it has a communitarian weighting—it helps individuals instill in social arrangements what they perceive as the greater social good. Thus asking society to "vote" about what is fair from the original position can be seen as a way of operationalizing the communitarian choice process.

If we consider the concept of sustainable development, an interesting question is whether Rawls's

---

* It should be understood that communitarian stakeholders will not develop a Rawlsian outcome based on Rawls's (1971) theory of justice; rather, they are likely to approximate a Rawlsian outcome by pursuing the greater social good (or common purpose or goal). Thus communitarians are likely to arrive at a Rawlsian outcome from the perspective of shared moral values that stem from the traditions of a community. Although it is not possible to know whether, and to what extent, communitarian stakeholders will develop Rawlsian outcomes—because the perception of a "fair outcome" is likely to differ between communities—one would imagine that their strong emphasis on the "community" is likely to prevent or minimize the marginalization of disadvantaged groups. For an insightful discussion of the differences between views of liberals (i.e., Rawlsians) and communitarians, see Etzioni (1990).

† It is important to realize that this framework does not attempt to achieve a single state of utopia; Rawls does not define such a state. This fact highlights an important difference between Rawlsian thinking and utilitarianism—utilitarian outcomes *can* be defined by an end state (i.e., efficiency). In contrast, Rawlsian outcomes should be seen as a *movement* toward equality, not equality per se. If a society were to continually advantage the least advantaged, it is conceivable that it would eventually achieve equality, but this is not necessarily the case. If a society continually allowed concentrations of wealth in an effort to make the economic pie bigger, it might never reach total egalitarianism (i.e., social equity).

theory of justice can ensure that human activity does not degrade the environment to a state where it is unable to recover. The reason for asking this question is simple. It stems from the belief that the ultimate rationale of governance is to support and encourage a way of life that recognizes and values human (economic and social) needs and the natural environment, is just and fair, and continually strives to achieve an acceptable balance between civil liberty and regulation. Hence the philosophy of government and the stakeholder posture adopted by society will have a significant influence on whether it is able to move toward sustainability.

The four major environmental factors that underlie the concern for sustainable development (to be discussed further in Section 1.4) are the following:

1. The disruption of ecosystems and loss of biological diversity and the indirect effects these have on human health and well-being

2. The rapid use of finite resources and energy supplies

3. The direct impacts of toxic pollution on human health and the health of other species

4. The disruption of the global climate

All four of these factors occur as a result of *human action* and the *technology* we have at our disposal. Therefore, it will be possible to address these problems only if there are social arrangements that enable us to do so in an effective manner. The growing interest in *environmental justice*[16] provides some evidence that society is willing to ensure that development does not adversely affect the disadvantaged by protecting the environment in which they live. However, as a practical matter, environmental justice is primarily concerned with the protection of people. Hence in addition to searching for Rawlsian solutions to social problems (which include economic and indirect environmental considerations), government and stakeholders also need to search for solutions that take environmental protection into consideration.

In *A Theory of Justice*, Rawls provides little discussion of the environment. His rationale for this omission is given in one lengthy paragraph in which he raises the notion of justice to nature (in contrast to justice to humans). Rawls begins the paragraph by recalling the limits to his theory of justice:

> Not only are many aspects of morality left aside, but *no account is given of right conduct in regard to animals and the rest of nature*. A conception of justice is but one part of a moral view. While I have not

maintained that the capacity for a sense of justice is necessary in order to be owed the duties of justice, it does seem that we are not required to give strict justice anyway to creatures lacking this capacity. But it does not follow that there are no requirements at all in regard to them, nor in our relations with the natural order. Certainly it is wrong to be cruel to animals and the destruction of a whole species can be a great evil. The capacity for feelings of pleasure and pain and for the forms of life of which animals are capable clearly imposes duties of compassion and humanity in their case. I shall not attempt to explain these considered beliefs. *They are outside the scope of the theory of justice, and it does not seem possible to extend the contract doctrine so as to include them in a natural way. A correct conception of our relations to animals and to nature would seem to depend upon a theory of the natural order and our place in it.* One of the tasks of metaphysics is to work out a view of the world which is suited for this purpose; it should identify and systematize the truths decisive for these questions. *How far justice as fairness will have to be revised to fit into this larger theory it is impossible to say.* But it seems reasonable to hope that if it is sound as an account of justice among persons, it cannot be too far wrong when these broader relationships are taken into consideration. (Rawls 1971, p. 512; emphases added)

Several interesting points can be gleaned from Rawls's comments (D. R. Bell 2006; Partridge 1976). First, Rawls adopts the position that because creatures "lack the capacity for a sense of justice," they should not be considered moral agents within the community afforded justice. Thus rather than extending "duties of justice" to individual animals or entire species, Rawls states that society has an obligation to impose "duties of compassion and humanity in their case." Rawls does not extend his thoughts on what these "duties of compassion and humanity" might be because he believes that they are not commensurate with the "contract doctrine" on which *A Theory of Justice* is based. D. R. Bell (2006, p. 210) makes an interesting argument that although Rawls excludes sentient animals from the community afforded "justice," this does not mean that he intended to exclude them "from the community of moral subjects." As Rawls comments, "A conception of justice is but one part of a moral view."

Second, Rawls appears to view humans (or social systems) as separate from nature. The impression he gives is that a theory of justice is separate from "a theory of the natural order." Adopting this position leads Rawls to several conclusions that seem "to be at considerable variance with key components of the ecological point of view" (Partridge 1976, p. 209). For example, Rawls (1971, p. 287) states that "a society meets its duty of justice by maintaining just institutions and preserving their material base," with no recognition that such a position might be constrained by the availability of natural resources or by ecological limits. In addition, Rawls tends to adopt a reductionist view of systems* and does not include environmental goods in his list of "just savings" (Partridge 1976, p. 210).[†]

Finally, Rawls ends his paragraph by recognizing that his theory of justice "will have to be revised" to account adequately for "animals and the rest of nature." In many ways, his decision not to extend his theory represents a missed opportunity. The recognition that his theory of justice needs to be amended or incorporated into a "larger theory" has encouraged many to take up this challenge (Dobson 1998; Lehman 1995; Miller 1999; Partridge 1976). The most common recommendations for changing Rawls's theory are to make the "environment" or "ecosystems" into "primary goods" and to consider these forms of natural capital under the just savings principle. Environmental justice advocates have also argued that "the ability to live in a safe environment is a primary good" (Chapman 2001, p. 16). In contrast, Voorthuis and Gijbels (2010) combine Rawls's principles of liberty and fairness with McDonough and Braungart's (1998) "cradle-to-cradle" design concept. Although this combination is an effective way to guide the *design* of new products, process, and services, it is less applicable to the design of policies to transition the actions of society toward sustainability. Hence our focus is to consider how Rawls's theory might be adapted to integrate the social and natural realms into a set of simple game rules for decision making and policy formulation.

Rawls (1971, p. 62) defines "social" primary goods as "things that every rational man is presumed to want," such as rights and liberties, powers and opportunities, income and wealth, and self-respect.[‡] These goods are seen to be essential to human development and to the realization of one's life plan. Because the "basic structure of society" (ibid.) is the main conduit through which these primary goods are distributed, creating a structure that fosters justice and fairness is of paramount importance. This objective forms the bases for Rawls's theory of justice.

Although making the environment into a "primary good" is an elegant solution, it does not make explicit the relative importance of the environment compared with the "social" primary goods. If we are concerned about sustainable development, then social systems need to be considered within the broader context of the natural environment within which they exist. When the environment is viewed in this manner, it becomes a "metaprimary good"—that is, without it none of the "social" primary goods could exist. One interesting way to give the environment a much more prominent role in Rawls's theory of justice is to include it in a third principle of justice. Because protecting and preserving the environment are essential for the longevity of the human race, one can envisage the following principle of justice that could be considered in the original position:

> *Third Principle*: Social arrangements are to be organized so that they (a) protect and continually improve the environment, especially for those individuals and species most heavily affected by environmental degradation or pollution, and (b) do not result in activities that exceed ecological carrying capacity.

The intent of the third principle—the *environmental principle*—is (1) to ensure that society continually strives to protect and improve the environment and the lives of people negatively affected by pollution (broadly defined), and (2) to keep human activity within ecological limits.[§] The basic premise of this principle is twofold. First, protecting human health

---

\*      Such a view stands in contrast to an "ecological ethic" that values each part of a system in the context of the whole (Partridge 1976, p. 210).

†      Rawls (1971) argues that each generation has a responsibility to pass on to the next a certain amount of "capital" that is to be agreed on using his just savings principle. The purpose of the just savings principle is to achieve a fair distribution of capital between the most disadvantaged members of the current and future generations. Rawls (1971, p. 288) defines "capital" as "not only factories and machines, and so on [i.e., human-made capital and possibly financial capital], but also the knowledge and culture [i.e., social capital], as well as the techniques and skills [i.e., human capital], that make possible just institutions and the fair value of liberty." What is most apparent from this statement is that "natural capital" is clearly not part of Rawls's notion of capital.

‡      Interestingly, Rawls (1971, p. 62) does refer to "natural" primary goods, but these are described as health and vigor and intelligence and imagination—i.e., they are not concerned with the "natural environment." Because these natural primary goods are not *directly* affected by the "basic structure of society," Rawls considers them to fall outside his theory of justice.

§      A significant work that focuses on the links between environmental *quality* and human *equality* and those between sustainability and environmental justice more generally is Agyeman, Bullard, et al.'s (2003) *Just Sustainabilities: Development in an Unequal World*. This publication, which consists of a selection of essays, focuses specifically on the linkages between the political and policy processes surrounding environmental justice and sustainability. *Just Sustainabilities* highlights "an important and emerging realization that a sustainable society must also be a just society, locally, nationally and internationally, both within and between generations and species" (ibid., p. 3).

is believed to be of paramount importance. Second, the natural environment is believed to be good in and of itself and should be protected and regenerated if it is being degraded by human activity. In reality, part (a) of this principle is likely to be the most useful because defining and agreeing on the ecological carrying capacity of the environment to implement part (b) is still a major work in progress. In addition, part (a) of the principle aligns well with the idea of *movement toward justice* (or *fairness*) and does not attempt to define an end state or goal.

We believed that the environmental principle is consistent with the just savings principle because it can be argued that past, current, and future generations would select it. First, let us consider the present generation. When contracting parties are in the original position, behind the veil of ignorance, they do not know whether they live in an area of high pollution and low environmental quality. Therefore, it can be argued that a rational and mutually disinterested individual would select the environmental principle on the grounds that it would improve his or her quality of life—especially if he or she ended up living in an area bearing a disproportionate amount of pollution. The same argument also applies across generations. Because contracting parties do not know whether they live in a generation that is negatively affected by poor environmental quality, it is in their own interests to adopt a principle "that they must want all previous generations to have followed" (Rawls 1993, p. 274). Thus the third principle of justice should be selected because any rational individual would want the previous generation to have applied it.

If we consider future generations, a potential problem does arise. If each generation continually improves the environment, then subsequent generations are likely to be better off from an environmental quality and health standpoint. However, if each subsequent generation happens to gain from an improved environment, surely this outcome is desirable from a human perspective. Indeed, one might argue that society has a duty to preserve and improve the environment for the well-being of future generations—a fundamental principle of sustainable development.*

---

\* The third principle of justice is designed to "protect and continually improve the environment, especially for those individuals and species most heavily affected by environmental degradation or pollution." The principle is in keeping with Rawls's general formulation that any new social arrangement should advance (i.e., improve) the well-being of the least advantaged. Thus the third principle of justice should be considered as more than a conservation principle. In addition to conservation, it aims to replenish or restore environmental capacity that has been lost to industrialization.

Another argument one could make that deviates from the just savings principle is that because each generation is mutually disinterested in one another, the critical point is that the environmental principle improves the quality of the environment *within* each generation. Thus it seems plausible that past and future generations would choose the environmental principle because it would be in their own rational interests to protect and improve their environment.

The third principle follows the lexicographical structure of Rawls's two principles of justice (that is, it is to be considered third). This ordering means that human considerations are put before the natural environment, which means that the framework could be labeled one of "liberal ecologism" (D. R. Bell 2006, p. 215). Although some might argue that the environmental principle is of paramount importance and should be put first, if Rawls's theory of justice is used as a basis, then the environmental principle should build on his theory. In addition, placing the environmental principle first would undermine the stability of Rawls's theory of justice. As it is, only the first principle of justice achieves relative stability (or "overlapping consensus") when it is compared with other comprehensive theories on the political conception of justice (Barry 1995). Thus placing the environment first would undermine the stability and elegance of Rawls's theory.

A final point is that the environmental principle does not make species into "formal" stakeholders that are part of the community afforded justice. This outcome is in keeping with Rawls's (1971) argument that we have "duties of compassion and humanity" to animals (and the natural world). One can argue that society's "duty" toward the natural environment is to act as trustee on its behalf. Therefore, because species (other than humans) are not represented in the original position, individuals or groups must act on their behalf. Perhaps ecologists are the only group that has the capacity to adopt such a role. However, it is possible that other groups might want to act as trustee for species and the environment on the basis of different belief systems.

An important objective of the third principle of justice is to focus attention on *movement toward environmental justice (broadly conceived)*. Given the inherent complexity of intergenerational issues and the fact that it is problemmatic to allocate resources fairly within current generations, we believe that the environmental principle will be a useful guide for decision making and policy formulation. Wells (1996, p. 195) argues that Rawls's "two principles of justice are extremely important for an ethic suitable to a global ecology. Their implications for environmental policy are pervasive and so important that they should be the objective of much careful thought." We believe that adding the environmental principle to Rawls's theory of justice will show how his ideas can form a central pillar of our thinking about sustainable development. While Rawls's two principles of justice focus on the social world, the third principle is designed to require decision makers and stakeholders to consider how their decisions might affect the natural world.*

By bounding decisions using the Rawlsian/utilitarian decision-making philosophy,† we have developed what Petrinovich (1999, p. 5) refers to as a "pluralistic moral philosophy" that considers "both utilitarian concerns and basic rights and freedoms of individuals" rather than relying on a single philosophical view for decision making (also see Beatley 1994). The argument put forward in this section is that outcomes that lean toward Rawlsian solutions are more likely than purely utilitarian ones to move a society toward sustainable development through the reduction of inequality.

The value of the bounded Rawlsian/utilitarian decision-making philosophy is that it is not applicable only to social outcomes. It can also be used to consider decisions that affect *trade* and *technological development*—two factors that have a significant influence on whether society moves toward or away from sustainable development.

One can argue that government is, in fact, the trustee of trade because trade is currently the province of government—for example, government negotiates trade agreements and engages in designing the rules of international commerce. It can also be argued that an equal province of a Rawlsian government is the trusteeship of technology.

The importance of technological development becomes apparent when we consider a shift from an outcome focus (identified using the Rawlsian framework) to the mechanistic, pragmatic question of *who* guides the pathway to realizing that outcome. For example, if technology is central to achieving a larger economy that can be divided in a more equitable way, then someone needs to be a trustee for the birth of that technology. If government acts as a trustee for society, it should by default assume this role. If not, then it is left either to industry or to society to adopt this role. However, from a Schumpeterian perspective,‡

---

\* The integration of environmental and social (e.g., employment) concerns is vital for making progress toward sustainable development, but the major international declarations that address development do not explicitly link these concerns. For example, the 1972 Stockholm and 1992 Rio declarations focus on improving the human *living* environment, but they do not address the human *working* environment. The topic of human welfare—which includes the protection of workers in all occupations—and development is addressed separately by the 1994 Declaration of Philadelphia. Hence there is a need to establish a fundamental framework that encourages the integration of both the natural and the social worlds in decision making. By revisiting Rawls's notion of the social contract from the perspective of the environment, we have been able to develop a framework that tries to achieve this objective. See the later discussion of the 1972 Stockholm Declaration and the 1994 Declaration of Philadelphia in the context of the critical environmental and social (e.g., employment) factors that underlie the concern for sustainable development. Finally, for an interesting application of a Rawlsian approach to trade and development, see Stiglitz and Charlton (2005).

† When one is deciding on a new social arrangement, the range of potential outcomes (the decision space) can be "bounded" by identifying those outcomes that are purely Rawlsian and those that are purely utilitarian. These two sets of outcomes mark opposite ends of a continuum. As one moves from the utilitarian to the Rawlsian end of the continuum, the potential outcomes will transition from focusing on maximizing societal welfare (without concern for the distributional impacts of a new social arrangement) to identifying the best (or fair) outcome for all individuals in a society. In the latter case, the distributional impacts of a new social arrangement are of paramount importance.

‡ Joseph Schumpeter, born in Austria, was an influential Harvard economist of the mid-twentieth century who is best known for describing the process of competition and monopoly in a capitalist market as "the process of creative destruction" (Schumpeter 1962 [1942], p. 82). Schumpeter believed that the main principle of capitalism was *innovation* and the development of new technologies rather than the "entirely imaginary" notion of perfect competition (ibid.). He saw the process of *innovation* as being distinct from an *invention*. An invention is conceived as an idea, a sketch, or model for a new or improved device. An innovation occurs when the invention is put into use/practice. Schumpeter argued that innovations either passed or failed the "market test." Schumpeter's central idea was that innovation leads to economic growth and is, therefore, the engine of capitalism. However, the success of one firm's innovations will ultimately lead to the destruction of another firm's market share. Schumpeter's idea of creative destruction can also work in the opposite direction toward monopolies. The Schumpeterian perspective is thus the process of creative destruction, where "innovators out-compete non-innovators" (Kleinknecht 1998, p. 392). In the words of Schumpeter, "The essential point to grasp is that in dealing with capitalism we are dealing with an evolutionary process.... Capitalism...is by nature a form or method of economic change and not only never is but never can be stationary.... The fundamental impulse that sets and keeps the capitalist engine in motion comes from the new consumers, goods, the new methods of production or transportation, the new markets, the new forms of industrial organization that capitalist enterprise creates.... The opening up of new markets, foreign or domestic, and the organizational development from the craft shop and factory to such concerns as U.S. Steel illustrate the same process of industrial mutation...that incessantly revolutionizes the economic structure from within, incessantly destroying the old one, incessantly creating a new one. This process of Creative Destruction is the essential fact about capitalism. It is what capitalism consists in and what every capitalist concern has got to live in" (Schumpeter 1962 [1942], pp. 82–83).

it is unlikely that industry will displace itself by encouraging the development of technologies that undermine its existing products/services. Also, it is unlikely that the "diffuse society" will have the institutional capacity to assume this role. Thus government—whether acting as a trustee for society or not—has an important role to play in guiding the development of new technology.

By focusing on the social outcomes of justice and fairness (and environmental protection), it is possible to identify the various pathways that must be taken to achieve these outcomes. Because Rawlsian outcomes and sustainable development are really processes, we should feel comfortable using trade and technological development as instruments through which social (and environmental) objectives can be achieved.

Hence the pathway to achieving sustainable development is not just a matter of developing the right social arrangements. It is also a matter of trade (which affects distribution) and technological development. With regard to technological development, what is needed is a combination of a Schumpeterian and a Rawlsian vision if technology is to advance at a rate necessary to realize the objectives of sustainable development. Implicit in this statement is the notion that current rates of technological progress, if left to the market, are unlikely to adequately address social and environmental problems in a fair and just manner. To achieve the desired rate of change will require "waves of creative destruction" in order to obtain the best technology, and this may require disruptive forms of technological change (see Section 6.2 in Chapter 6).

The value of the framework proposed in this section is that it can be applied to any situation in which government is needed to change or implement new social arrangements (that is, rules, regulations, laws, or policies) to improve the well-being of society. By introducing the idea of *bounding the acceptable moves* when one is behind the veil of ignorance, it has been possible to discuss how Rawls's theory of "justice as fairness" can be operationalized by explicitly relating it to utilitarianism. Bounding the acceptable moves enables stakeholders to move away from a purely utilitarian approach to problem solving, which can be unfair to disadvantaged members of society. Justice does not stem from unfair practices.

The third principle of justice—the environmental principle—has been added to Rawls's framework in an effort to link the social and natural worlds in decision making. The significance of the revised Rawlsian/utilitarian decision-making philosophy is that it supports decision making that can move society toward sustainable development. First and foremost, it places *social equity* at the center of decision making. Second, it supports the notion of *economic growth* so long as the benefits from this growth are distributed fairly among society. Social and economic inequalities are tolerated only if the most disadvantaged members of society are made better off under new arrangements. Finally, it makes movement toward a better *environment* a critical component of any new social arrangements. Hence the framework provides a valuable tool through which movement toward sustainable development becomes a real possibility.

### 1.2.3 Equality of What?

The manner in which equality is defined and evaluated is directly linked to the types of inequalities one is trying to right. This section takes a brief look at the various ways in which equality is considered and how these considerations relate to the broader picture of sustainable development.

The major philosophies of government (or social arrangements), some of which are discussed in the previous section, all support the notion of *equality* in terms of a "focal variable" such as income, wealth, happiness, opportunities, rights, or needs fulfillment (Sen 1992, p. 2). The basic premise of these theories is that each individual should have *equality of opportunities* in regard to the variable(s) selected (see Rawls's second principle of justice). For example, everyone should have an equal opportunity to gain employment or to have an education. In a world in which everyone's circumstances and abilities are the same, focusing on *equality of opportunity* would suffice. But this is not the world in which we live, and adopting such a posture in decision making often results in unequal treatment of the disadvantaged.

In the book *Inequality Reexamined*, Nobel Prize–winning economist Amartya Sen (1992) raises the question "equality of what?" and links it directly to the consideration of human diversity. In particular, he argues that social arrangements (for example, government policies and laws) should be assessed in relation to a person's capability to achieve functionings.

Sen's (1992) idea of *functionings* is Aristotelian in origin.* He defines *functionings* as the various things

---

\*        Aristotle believed that the attainment of the good life or happiness was the result of *self-realizationism*—i.e., the ability to realize one's potentialities, character, or personality. To Aristotle, the person who has the greatest potentialities and is able to actualize this potential has the brightest prospect of happiness. Conversely, the person whose potential remains unfulfilled will ultimately be frustrated and unhappy.

that a person has "reason to value," from being well nourished or avoiding escapable morbidity to more complex realizations, such as having self-respect or being a valued member of a community (ibid., p. 5). Alkire (2003, p. 5) describes Sen's idea of functionings as "an umbrella term for the resources and activities and attitudes people spontaneously recognize to be important—such as poise, knowledge, a warm friendship, an educated mind, a good job. What is centrally important varies in different places, which is why there is no rigid and inflexible set of specific capabilities—the priorities will have to be set and reset again and again in different ways."

It follows that an individual's *achieved functionings* are those that the individual has successfully pursued and realized. However, Sen (1992) argues that focusing on achieved functionings (or focal variables) alone is not sufficient. The inherent diversity of external circumstances and psychological and physiological makeup among individuals means that the characteristics of inequality tend to diverge within the variable under analysis. In other words, differences in the circumstances and abilities of people mean that *equality of opportunity* will not lead to *equal* wealth or happiness, for example. In addition, "equality in terms of one variable may not coincide with equality in the scale of another. Equal opportunities can lead to very unequal incomes. Equal incomes can go with significant differences in wealth. Equal wealth can coexist with very unequal happiness. Equal happiness can go with widely divergent fulfilment of needs. Equal fulfilment of needs can be associated with very different freedoms of choice. And so on" (ibid., p. 2). Hence Sen's core argument is that "the basic heterogeneity of human beings" and "the multiplicity of variables in terms of which equality can be judged" are two factors that complicate the idea of equality (ibid., p. 1). This means that a focus on individual functionings (or focal variables) does not necessarily incorporate an individual's *freedom*\* to achieve. Hence Sen intro-

duces the concept of *capability* to describe an individual's freedom to achieve "valuable" functionings. "It represents the various combinations of functionings (beings and doings) that the person can achieve. Capability is, thus, a set of vectors of functionings, reflecting the person's freedom to lead one type of life or another . . . to choose from possible livings" (ibid., p. 40).[†]

Sen's focus on functionings and on the *capability* to achieve functionings differs from the traditional views of equality that tend to focus on variables such as income, wealth, or happiness (1992, p. 7). Instead of measuring equality using such focal variables, Sen argues that a "more adequate way of considering 'real' equality of opportunities must be through equality of capabilities (or through the elimination of unambiguous inequalities in capabilities, since capability comparisons are typically incomplete)" (ibid.).

A major difference between Sen's capabilities-based assessment of equality and Rawls's theory of "justice as fairness" lies in their assessment of the holdings of "primary goods"—that is, goods that are considered essential for the survival and self-respect of individuals (Rawls 1971).

Rawls's theory is that in the original position— behind the veil of ignorance —most people will be able to agree on a set of primary goods that are considered important regardless of an individual's circumstances. Rawls argues that social primary goods are "things that every rational man is presumed to want," such as "rights and liberties, powers and opportuni-

---

\* The freedom Sen (1992, p. 31) refers to is "the *real opportunity* that we have to accomplish what we value." Sen (1999, p. 36) also described development as the "process of expanding real freedoms." Sen views the expansion of freedom as both "(1) the *primary end* and (2) the *principal means* of development" (ibid.). The former is referred to as the "constitutive role" and the latter as the "instrumental role." The "constitutive role" refers to the basic premise that freedom must be regarded as a primary objective of the development process. The "instrumental role" refers to the various ways in which freedom can act as an "instrument" of development. Sen identifies five types of instrumental freedoms that tend to enhance the capability of an individual to live more freely (ibid., pp. 38–40): (1) *political freedoms* (the opportunities that individuals have to be a part of democratic pro-

cesses); (2) *economic facilities* (the opportunities that individuals have to "utilize economic resources for the purposes of consumption, or production, or exchange"); (3) *social opportunities* (the access that individuals have to facilities such as basic education and health care, which are essential if a person is to have an effective role in economic and political activities); (4) *transparency guarantees* ("the freedom to deal with one another under guarantees of disclosure and lucidity"); and (5) *protective security* (the need to provide a social safety net to assist those individuals who face abject misery and possibly even starvation and death).

† Although Sen does not formally list *capabilities*, this has not prevented others from doing so. The most comprehensive attempt is presented by Nussbaum (2000), who developed a set of "central human functional capabilities." The major headings of Nussbaum's list of capabilities include the following: life; bodily health; bodily integrity; senses, imagination, thought; emotions; practical reason; affiliation; other species; and control over one's environment (ibid., pp. 78–80). Under each heading, Nussbaum defines the "combined" capabilities that a person should be able to achieve. For example, the capabilities for bodily health are defined as "being able to have good health, including reproductive health; to be adequately nourished; to have adequate shelter" (ibid., p. 78).

ties, income and wealth[, and] . . . self-respect" (Rawls 1971, p. 62).* Hence Rawls's general conception is that "all social primary goods . . . are to be distributed equally unless an unequal distribution of any or all of these goods is to the advantage of the least favored" (ibid., p. 303). The focus of Rawls's formulation is "equality of opportunity," which is captured within the difference principle (see Section 1.2.1).

Sen identified a fundamental problem with Rawls's formulation of the difference principle: "Two persons holding the same bundle of primary goods can have very different freedoms to pursue their respective conceptions of the [greater] good (whether or not these conceptions coincide). To judge equality—or for that matter efficiency—in the space of primary goods amounts to giving priority to the means of freedom over any assessment of the extents of freedom, and this can be a drawback in many contexts" (Sen 1992, pp. 8–9). Thus Sen argues that equality in the holdings of primary goods or resources ignores the fact that disadvantaged members of society may not have the capability or freedom to convert these goods/resources into the things that they value. Therefore, if a government were to use primary goods as a measure of well-being for purposes of justice, there is a concern that disadvantaged members of society might suffer from unjust (or unequal) treatment. To put it another way, these people are likely to have an unfair share of opportunity. Thus Sen's capability-based assessment of equality forms the foundation for affirmative action, for empowering the powerless, and for positive discrimination (Bidwai 1998).

Sen's theories of capabilities and functionings and Rawls's theory of "justice as fairness" have had a significant impact on how governments have shaped social arrangements to establish equitable and just societies.† Sen's theories have also provided a strong conceptual foundation for the UN's work on human development (Fukuda-Parr 2002, 2003). In particular, his ideas have shaped the UN *Human Development Reports* (*HDRs*) and the Human Development Index (HDI), including its extensions.

The essence of Sen's conception of equality is that "a person's capability to achieve does indeed stand for the opportunity to pursue his or her objectives" (Sen 1992, p. 7). From this premise, the UN defined human development as the "process of enlarging people's choices" (UNDP 1995, p. 11) and sought the removal of obstacles—"such as illiteracy, ill health, lack of access to resources, or lack of civil and political freedoms" (Fukuda-Parr 2003, p. 303)—that prevent an individual from achieving his or her valued objectives in life. Thus the intention of the UN HDI was to shift international attention to the expansion of basic human capabilities, especially the capability to (1) have a healthy life, (2) acquire knowledge, and (3) reach a decent standard of living.‡ Because the purpose of the *HDRs* is the "global evaluation of development," these three indexes were selected for their universal value since they form the basis on which many choices in life depend (Fukuda-Parr 2002, p. 6). The notion of investing in health and education in particular maps closely with *physical health* and *learning*, two essential attributes an individual requires to attain a high level of well-being.

To provide a context for the preceding discussion, Table 1.5 compares and contrasts the human development approach with the neoliberal (utilitarian) alternative and its precursor, the basic-needs approach (first espoused by Paul Streeten [1982] and Frances Stewart [1985]).§ Table 1.5 also presents an idealized framework from which public policy formulation can be considered. For example, by looking at the "evaluative" and "agency" aspects of a set of policies, it should be possible to determine whether the government supports a *human development* approach (that is, its policies are just and fair and consider human capabilities) or a *neoliberal* approach (that is, its policies are utilitarian in nature) to the process of development. It is interesting to note that none of the approaches contain an explicit concern for the environment, on which human activity and development

---

*     Rawls (1971, p. 62) states that other primary goods, such as health and vigor or intelligence and imagination, are "natural" primary goods. Although natural primary goods can be influenced by social arrangements, they are not directly under their control.

†     Incidentally, it was Sen (1993, p. 43) who once said that "it is significant that no democratic country with a relatively free press has ever experienced a major famine." That is, there are no famines in democracies.

‡     Although the HDI's focus is on "evaluating" human development, Sen (2003) argues that the human development perspective also contains an "agency perspective" that is often overlooked. When one has identified where improvement to human lives can be made though the HDI, it is necessary to turn to the agency perspective to develop policy and political strategies to realize the necessary changes.

§     It is worth noting that Sen's theories on capabilities and functionings grew from the basic-needs approach to international development (Alkire 2005). Sen's main reason for rethinking the basic-needs approach was to introduce a greater role for individual freedom. His concern was that the basic-needs approach tended to focus on commodities, as opposed to human beings and their functionings.

**TABLE 1.5: COMPARISON OF KEY FEATURES OF THE HUMAN DEVELOPMENT APPROACH WITH THE NEOLIBERAL ALTERNATIVE AND THE BASIC-NEEDS ANTECEDENT**

| | HUMAN DEVELOPMENT[a] | NEOLIBERALISM | BASIC NEEDS |
|---|---|---|---|
| **Philosophical underpinnings** | | | |
| Normative assumptions | Explicit | Implicit | Not fully specified |
| Concept of well-being | Functionings and capabilities | Utility | Meeting basic needs |
| **Evaluative aspect** | | | |
| Leading criterion for evaluating development progress | Human capabilities; equality of outcomes; fairness and justice in institutional arrangements | Economic well-being; economic growth; efficiency | Poverty reduction in terms of income; access to basic social services |
| Measurement tools favored | Human outcomes, deprivational and distributional measures | Economic activity and condition, averages and aggregate measures | Access to material means; deprivational measures |
| **Agency aspect** | | | |
| People in development as ends and/or means | Ends and means: beneficiaries and agents | Means: human resources for economic activity | Ends: beneficiaries |
| Mobilizing agency | Individual action and collective action | Individual action | Concern with political will and political base |
| **Development strategy** | | | |
| Key operational goals | Expanding people's choices (social, economic, and political) | Economic growth | Expanding basic social services |
| **Policy concerns** | | | |
| Distribution of benefits and costs | Emphasis on equality and human rights of all individuals | Concern with poverty | Concern with poverty |
| Links between development and human rights and freedoms | Human rights and freedoms have intrinsic value and are development objectives; current research on their instrumental role through links to economic and social progress | No explicit connection; current search for link between political and civil freedoms and economic growth | No explicit connection |

[a] This perspective is specifically and especially concerned with distributional equity. Neoliberalism and basic needs are not. For example, a neoliberal approach might focus on raising people above a poverty level, but it will still tolerate enormous levels of disparity.

Source: Adapted from Fukuda-Parr (2002, 2003).

depend.* It is clear that if we are to transition toward sustainable development, the need to protect the environment must be added to the need to ensure that we live in an equitable and just society that recognizes human capabilities.

Sen's work has also had an important influence on the formulation on the concept of sustainable development, which he defines as "development that promotes the capabilities of present people without compromising capabilities of future generations" (Sen 2000, p. 5). Sen believes that the Brundtland (need-centered) view of development is "illuminating" but "incomplete" (ibid., p. 2). He argues that individuals must be seen as "agents who can think and act, not just as patients who have needs that require catering" (ibid.). His basic premise is that by treating people as

agents, they will—given the opportunity—be able to "think, assess, evaluate, resolve, inspire, agitate, and through these means, reshape the world" (ibid., p. 1). Hence Sen advocates a capability-centered approach to sustainable development. The objective of Sen's ideas is to "integrate the idea of sustainability with the perspective of freedom, so that we see human beings not merely as creatures who have needs but primarily as people whose freedoms really matter" (ibid., p. 6). (See Section 1.2.1 for a discussion of how Rawls's theory of justice combines individual freedom with sustainable development.) Sen's contribution to our understanding of equality and his more recent notion of development as "a momentous engagement with freedom's possibilities" (Sen 1999, p. 298) provide one of the few credible challenges to the neoliberal (or utilitarian) orthodoxy that has guided development efforts since the 1980s (Saha 2002).

As mentioned earlier, one of Sen's major contributions to sustainable development is his influence on the UN's conceptualization of human develop-

---

* However, they do implicitly incorporate employment and purchasing power. This highlights the two different strands of sustainability scholarship, one focusing on the environment and the other on economic empowerment.

ment that formed the basis for the *HDR*s and the HDI. Fukuda-Parr (2002), the director of the *HDR*s since 1995, argues that it is possible to describe the UN's general human development agenda using five core elements. Fukuda-Parr calls these five elements the "New York Consensus"* because they are reflected in many of the UN agreements. It is interesting to note the similarities between Sen's ideas on human development and the ideas presented in the New York Consensus. The five elements of the UN's general human development agenda (or the New York Consensus) are as follows:

- Priority to "social development" with the goals of expansion of education and health opportunities;
- Economic growth that generates resources for human development in its many dimensions;
- Political and social reforms for democratic governance that secure human rights so that people can live in freedom and dignity, expanding . . . [collective] agency, participation and autonomy;
- Equity in above three elements with a concern with all individuals. Special attention to the downtrodden and the poor whose interests are often neglected in public policy;
- Policy and institutional reforms at the global level that create a more conducive economic environment for poor countries to have access to global markets, technology, information. (Fukuda-Parr 2002, p. 10)

The preceding list presents a robust agenda (or paradigm) for *human* development, but human development is only a part—although an extremely vital part—of the broader notion of sustainable development. If we take a holistic look at all the UN agreements, it is possible to identify several elements that, if added to the New York Consensus, would transform it into a consensus of sustainable development. It is possible to describe the international community's notion of sustainable development as consisting of five critical components: (1) peace and security, (2) economic development, (3) social development, (4) national governance that ensures peace and development, and (5) environmental protection (Dernbach 1998, 2004). A comparison of these five components with the five elements listed previously reveals that

national governance that ensures peace and security, environmental protection, and employment (an important objective of economic and social development) are not explicitly mentioned in Fukuda-Parr's New York Consensus. Hence if we are to integrate human development with the broader notion of sustainable development, the following elements need to be added:

- Environmental protection at local, regional, national, and global levels constitutes an integral part of the social and economic development process and is not to be considered in isolation from it.
- Extending equity considerations to future generations.
- National governance that ensures peace and security.
- The creation of secure, satisfying, and safe employment with adequate purchasing power.

The first three additional elements might be called the "Rio elements" because they stem from the 1992 Rio Declaration on Environment and Development. A significant challenge posed by these new elements lies not so much in the need to protect the environment or in peace and security (although achieving these objectives has proved far from easy) as in the idea of intergenerational equity. Put simply, it is apparent that we are unable to allocate resources equitably in the present, let alone across generations. Hence we do not have a *near future* that is properly allocated. Further, the ability of governments to develop equitable social arrangements that also transition societies toward more sustainable forms of development will depend on how they, and society, view the purpose of development—either to establish a fair and just society (Rawlsianism) or to maximize the well-being of society in the neoclassical sense (utilitarianism).

### 1.3 LIVING BEYOND OUR ECOLOGICAL MEANS: THE TECHNOLOGY DEBATE

A central question in the sustainable development discourse is how inflexible but fragile *ecological limits* are with respect to human activity—especially activity supporting economic growth.[17] With all else remaining constant, the more rigid the limits, the more radical and painful the changes necessary for sustainability become. Therefore, the debate has traditionally centered on the potential and ability of technology to substitute one resource for another, reduce material

---

* The New York Consensus stands in stark contrast to the Washington Consensus, which promotes market-liberalizing policies and a reduction in big government (ul Hague 2004). "Washington Consensus policies are sometimes referred to as 'neo-liberal,' based on 'market fundamentalism,' a resuscitation of the laissez-faire policies that were popular in some circles in the nineteenth century" (Stiglitz 2002, p. 74).

and energy content/intensity, or otherwise render these limits less relevant.*

Building on the growth theories of Adam Smith and David Ricardo, Thomas Malthus provided one of the earliest predictions of how population growth is likely to be constrained to a "stationary state" by the availability and productivity of agricultural land.† More recently, during the emergence of the environmental movement in the 1960s and 1970s, the issue of limits to growth arose again. However, this time it was debated from a number of different perspectives. The predominant views linked the prevailing and perceived future ecological crisis to the failure to internalize environmental externalities (Pigou 1932);‡ the use of pesticides/chemicals (Carson 1962); inadequate property rights (Coase 1960; Hardin

1968);§¶ population growth (Ehrlich 1968).**†† flawed technology (Commoner 1971); the exploitation of nonrenewable energy (R. U. Ayres 1978; Georgescu-Roegen 1971); the fixation on economic growth (Ecologist 1972); and prevailing world trends in population growth, capital investment, resource usage, agricultural productivity, and pollution rates

---

* During the 1980s, the most salient example of human society living outside its ecological means could be found in sub-Saharan Africa. Long before the problem of global climate change had been recognized, sub-Saharan Africa experienced periods of rapid growth with no consideration (or banking) for harder conditions in the future, and in future years when a prolonged drought struck, the result was mass starvation. The cause of the crisis was perceived to be "natural variation" in the weather. Less than a decade later, it was as if global climate change was waiting in the wings to be formulated as an "ecological issue" as opposed to a "natural variation." It now seems that industrialized societies exceeded the limits of natural variations in the climate long before they linked them to ecological damage.

† A central theme of Malthus's work was that once all the available agricultural land was used, a population could no longer continue to grow and would arrive at a "stationary state." Although Malthus recognized that the stationary state could be postponed by technological progress or a halt in population growth, his model has since been regarded as too pessimistic (M. R. Redclift 2000). It underestimated the ability of technology to extend ecological limits and did not account for the fact that rising per capita incomes, education, and urbanization can lead to a reduction in birth rates (OECD 1995). "What the years since Malthus have shown incontrovertibly is that high living standards do not engender population growth; that population growth can be reduced and halted; and that the productive power of technology is enormous. It is as clear today as it was to Malthus, that the stationary state is not an inevitability" (M. R. Redclift 2000, p. 37). See New School University, *Classical Growth Theory*, www.newschool.edu/nssr/het/essays/growth/growthcont .htm (accessed February 8, 2011).

‡ Pigou (1932) argued that an externality occurs when an individual's decision to buy a product/service results in costs or benefits to other individuals or groups who are not part of the transaction. Thus the individual does not bear all the costs or receive all the benefits from his or her action. To address this problem, Pigou argued that the costs of "negative" externalities need to be "internalized" in the end price of a product/service to reflect its true social costs. This internalization of costs could be achieved by matching a firm's marginal cost of environmental damage with the marginal benefit received from the product/service provided. One mechanism for doing this is to use a Pigouvian tax to correct for the negative effects of externalities. Pigou's notion of internalizing external costs is also commonly known as the "polluter-pays principle."

§ Coase (1960) rejected the idea that externalities can be addressed by internalizing external costs and argued that a close-to-optimal outcome could be achieved through private bargaining. Coase's theorem states that if there are zero transaction costs and legal rights (land rights in particular) are well defined, then the socially efficient solution to negative externalities will occur regardless of legal entitlement. Hence under these assumptions, environmental disputes, for example, will be resolved through *private* negotiations. The problem with Coase's theory, however, is that transaction costs are almost never zero, property rights may be difficult to define, and identifying who is responsible for certain externalities can be complicated. Thus one inference from Coase's theorem is that government has a role in minimizing transaction costs to enable the market to function efficiently.

¶ Garrett Hardin's "Tragedy of the Commons" popularized the effect of different regimes of property rights on the exploitation of public-domain resources. The basic premise of this article is that without the private ownership of land or the governmental allocation of usage rights (i.e., regulation), the *free* commons creates an economic incentive for each user to exploit the resource to his or her advantage. The example Hardin uses is the overgrazing of a public common by cattle. Because there are no (grazing) costs to the farmer for adding one additional cow to his herd, the more cows that are added, the wealthier the farmer is likely to become through the produce from, and the eventual sale of, his livestock. The inherent problem with these activities is that the eventual overgrazing of a growing number of cattle will destroy the public common and bring ruin to all the farmers. In essence, Hardin saw the problem as overpopulation, a point often not mentioned in recitation of his work.

** Paul Ehrlich's book *The Population Bomb*, as indicated by its title, also saw the problem of the commons in terms of too many people. Ehrlich's argument was the modern exposition of Malthus's concern that living conditions in nineteenth-century England were likely to decline as a result of overpopulation. Ehrlich predicted that by the 1970s and 1980s hundreds of millions of people would starve to death as a result of overpopulation and a fixed amount of resources. Although Ehrlich's predictions have yet to materialize, his book was influential for the antigrowth movement.

†† One of the most famous examples of how population growth can lead to environmental destruction and the eventual collapse of a civilization is the history of Easter Island. See Clive Ponting's (1991) discussion of the lessons of Easter Island for an informative account of how sustained population growth, combined with limited resources, led to the overshoot and collapse of ecological systems (as a result of deforestation) on which the island's inhabitants depended. Research has shown that once the island's forests were depleted, the advanced Polynesian society that had successfully survived on the island for centuries (between the fifth and fifteenth centuries A.D.) was gradually forced into primitive living conditions, tribal warfare, and cannibalism. The story of Easter Island also supports the argument made in *Limits to Growth* (D. H. Meadows, D. L. Meadows, et al. 1972), that once human activity exceeds (or overshoots) the ecological limits of the earth, humanity will face a rapid decline in population and industrial capacity.

(D. H. Meadows, D. L. Meadows, et al. 1972). (See the Primer on Sustainable Development at this book's website for a discussion of these theories.) It is not only the increase in the volume of chemicals used and the consequential pollution that are of concern. New understanding has refined the picture. The nature of chemical production, use, and disposal has shifted toward halogenated synthetic chemicals that are particularly hazardous (Commoner 1979). We have a growing appreciation that increases in environmental degradation and infectious diseases are related, and that both antibiotic and pesticide resistance have increased (Pimentel, Cooperstein, et al. 2007), that cancers that are chemically caused are on the increase globally (Sasco 2008), and that hormone (endocrine) disruption is increasingly leading to reproductive damage in all species (Colborn, Dumanowski, et al. 1996). Each of these concerns gives rise to particularized perspectives on environmental damage, and each suggests that "tipping points" not only exist with respect to global climate change but also are to be expected with regard to chemically caused cancer, reproductive health, neurological and autoimmune diseases, and contagion.

According to *World Resources, 2000–2001: People and Ecosystems*, prepared by the UNDP, the United Nations Environment Programme (UNEP), the World Bank, and the World Resources Institute, half of the world's wetlands have been lost in the past century, nearly half of the world's forests have been cut down, 70 percent of the world's major marine fisheries have been depleted, and all of the world's coral reefs are at risk. The next report in the series, *World Resources, 2002–2004*, pointed out that one out of every six humans is dependent primarily on fish for protein, but 75 percent of the world's fisheries are overfished or fished at their biological limit. A more recent study in *Science* warns that global fisheries might actually collapse as early as 2050 if current trends persist (Worm, Barbier, et al. 2006). Already, 20 percent of the world's river flows are extracted for human use, and 40 percent of the world's people live in water-stressed river basins. Both of the *World Resources* reports conclude that the capacity of ecosystems to deliver goods and services is declining, while our demand on ecosystem products, such as food, water, and timber, is increasing.

In his book *Collapse,* Diamond (2004) examined a series of old civilizations and societies and attempted to identify why they collapsed or survived in a significantly reduced form. This work came after the publication of his previous book, in which he attributed historical differences in economic and social development to environmental and ecological variations (Diamond 1997). In considering the collapse of a society, Diamond (2004) employs a framework that consists of five sets of factors that may affect what happens to a society:

- Environmental damage
- Climatic change
- Hostile neighbors
- Loss of trading partners
- Society's responses to environmental problems

Using this prism, Diamond (2004) manages to explain the collapse of societies as diverse as the Maya of Central America (environmental damage, climate change, and hostile neighbors), the Rapa Nui of Polynesia (environmental damage), and the Greenland Norse (climate change, environmental damage, loss of trading partners, hostile neighbors, and unwillingness to adapt). Scholars have also cited the case of Easter Island, which Diamond singles out as the best historical example of societal collapse in isolation (Diamond 2004; Ponting 2007).

Expanding on the preceding list, Diamond (2004) lists eight specific factors that have historically contributed to the collapse of past social structures:

- Deforestation and habitat destruction
- Soil erosion, salinization, and fertility losses
- Water-management problems
- Overhunting
- Overfishing
- Effects of introduced species on native species
- Population growth
- Increased per capita impact of people

However, apart from these "historical factors," Diamond (2004) also identifies a series of new factors that are highly likely to contribute to the reduction or collapse of contemporary or future societies:

- Global climate change
- Buildup of toxins in the environment
- Energy shortages
- Full human utilization of the earth's photosynthetic capacity

Most, if not all, of these factors, however, constitute main consequences of contemporary economic growth and the Northern growth model. Furthermore, there is an additional element that makes Diamond's (2004) analysis all the more worrisome. In the distant past, societies were significantly isolated, and societal collapses appeared to be rather isolated, without systemic spillover effects on other societies. Today's societies, however, are significantly interconnected, and the international economy reaches even the most distant regions of the world. As the economic crises of the past decades have shown, a simple economic crisis that occurs in some regional financial markets can spill over to other nations with unimaginable speed. Although this is a consequence that could potentially be mitigated by returning to a more highly regulated international financial regime, ecological collapse will need far more effort than a new Bretton Woods—it will require unprecedented international cooperation despite a significant rift between the interests of developed and developing nations.

Unfortunately, global ecological collapse is not an unimaginable scenario. Ponting (2007) notes:

> The increase in the amount of carbon dioxide in the atmosphere in the last 250 years reflects the second great transition in human history—the exploitation of fossil fuels and the development of societies dependent on high energy use. Coal production is now 350 times higher than in 1800 and oil production is 350 times higher than in 1900. The number of vehicles in the world rose from almost nil in 1900 to 775 million in 2000. In parallel, forests—particularly tropical forests—have been destroyed on an unprecedented scale in the last two hundred years. All these forces have had an impact on the earth's atmosphere. Since 1750 about 300 billion tonnes of carbon dioxide has been added to the atmosphere through human actions—but half of that total has been added since 1975. The result has been a rise in the amount of carbon dioxide in the atmosphere (p. 386).
>
> Concentrations are measured in parts per million (ppm) and in 1750, before the widespread use of fossil fuels, there were about 270 ppm of carbon dioxide in the atmosphere. This is the baseline against which additions are measured. The slow pace of industrialization in the nineteenth century can be judged from the fact that concentrations had only risen to 280 ppm by 1850 and 295 ppm by 1900. By 1950 this had still only risen to 310 ppm—a roughly 15 per cent rise in 200 years. . . . In 1959 the figure was 316 ppm, by 1985 it was 345 ppm and by 2005 it was 381 ppm—a 20 per cent rise in forty-five years, reflecting the huge increase in carbon dioxide output in the second half of the twentieth century. . . . The rate of increase is also rising—it was about 1.5 ppm a year in the mid-twentieth century but reached a record 2.6 ppm in 2005 (pp. 386–387).

In general, carbon dioxide is not the most powerful greenhouse gas, but because of the huge volumes that have been released, it accounts for about two-thirds of the total effect of greenhouse gas emissions (Ponting 2007, p. 387). However, other gases, such as methane and nitrous oxide, have also been released into the atmosphere in significant volumes, thus exacerbating the ecological disequilibrium. Finally, the air pollutants black carbon and ozone constitute 30 percent of the sources of global warming, linking concerns of public health with global climate change (Moore 2009). Table 1.6 provides some indication of the growth of industrial activities during the twentieth century.

The fact that a collapse or breakdown has not occurred so far does not signify that it will not happen in the years to come. Many of the societies that collapsed in the past also believed that they were in a sustainable societal equilibrium, only to discover later that they were mistaken. Ponting (2007, p. 423) notes: "By the time they had to face the crisis, they were unable to make the social, economic and political changes necessary for survival. The problem for all human societies has been to find a way of extracting from the environment their food, clothing, shelter and other goods in a way that does not render it incapable of supporting them."

In *The Limits to Growth*, D. H. Meadows, D. L. Meadows, et al. (1972, pp. 23–24) listed three conclusions:

- If the present growth trends in world population, industrialization, pollution, food production, and resource depletion continue unchanged, the limits to growth on this planet will be reached sometime within the next one hundred years. The most probable result will be a rather sudden and uncontrollable decline in both population and industrial capacity.

- It is possible to alter these trends and to establish a condition of ecological and economic stability that is sustainable far into the future.

**TABLE 1.6: SUSTAINABILITY AND THE WORLD IN THE TWENTIETH CENTURY**

| FACTOR | INCREASE, 1900–2000 |
|---|---|
| World population | ×3.8 |
| World urban population | ×12.8 |
| World industrial output | ×35 |
| World energy use | ×12.5 |
| World oil production | ×300 |
| World water use | ×9 |
| World irrigated area | ×6.8 |
| World fertilizer use | ×342 |
| World fish catch | ×65 |
| World organic chemical production | ×1,000 |
| World car ownership | ×7,750 |
| Carbon dioxide in atmosphere | 30% up |

Source: Ponting (2007, p. 412).

- The sooner the world's people decide to strive for this stability, the greater will be their chance for success.

In a subsequent article, D. L. Meadows (2007, p. 405) underlined an important change that had occurred since the publication of *The Limits to Growth*: "In 1972 we concluded that global population and industrial activity were still below the levels that could be supported indefinitely on earth. By 2004, it was clear to us that they had grown above sustainable levels. So in 1972 the main objective seemed to us to be finding ways of slowing down physical expansion on the planet. In 2004 the main objective had become getting physical flows that are propelled by population and industry back down below the carrying capacity of the planet."

This point is corroborated by the *Millennium Ecosystem Assessment Synthesis Report* (MEA 2005), which summarized the work of approximately 1,360 experts from ninety-five countries who tried to assess the consequences of ecosystem change for human well-being and to establish the scientific basis for actions needed to enhance the conservation and sustainable use of ecosystems (D. L. Meadows 2007). As D. L. Meadows (2007) notes, in the MEA report, among the five drivers of change in ecosystems and their services, population change and change in economic activity were the first two to be mentioned. Furthermore, the notion of collapse was also put forward as a possible or even likely scenario (MEA 2005, p. 1): "Approximately 60% (15 out of 24) of the ecosystem services examined during the Millennium Ecosystem Assessment are being degraded or used unsustainably, including fresh water, capture fisheries, air and water purification, and the regulation of regional and local climate, natural hazards, and pests. . . . The challenge of reversing the degradation of ecosystems while meeting increasing demands for their services can be partially met under some scenarios that the . . . [MEA] has considered but these involve significant changes in policies, institutions and practices that are not currently under way." Thus the goal of modern societies should be none other than to anticipate the point at which the environment is being harmed by contemporary societal demands and to find the optimal systemic (economic, social, political) measures to respond accordingly (Ponting 2007, p. 423).

The consequences of increased ecological damage as a result of growth have led to four optimistic scenarios. The first is that the ecological impacts of growth (whether from population growth or increases in per capita consumption) can be countered by the substitution of available existing technologies. The second is that increasing levels of wealth will be accompanied by environmental improvement because firms, individuals, and society will be increasingly willing to pay for more environmentally sound technology, products, and services. The central idea is that the perceived value of the environment increases with rising affluence. This implies that the solution to environmental degradation is economic growth that enhances per capita income—perhaps the faster the better. Third, some believe that *new* technology can and will emerge to address even the most difficult environmental problems. Finally, there are those who argue that both the social and the technological responses will arise *in time* to prevent irreversible ecological damage. These four manifestations of optimism are related to the concepts of (1) substitution of alternatives (Section 1.3.1), (2) the environmental Kuznets curve (EKC) (discussed in Section 1.3.2), (3) technological optimism (discussed in Section 1.3.3), and (4) the absence of tipping points beyond which no solution will be found to be adequate because of its late realization and response (see the discussion of *The Limits to Growth* in Section 1.3.2).

### 1.3.1 Growth, Technology, and Substitution versus a Steady-State Economy

The dominant neoclassical economic paradigm assumes the existence of utility functions, which constitute the foundation of production and consumption functions. These functions act as simplified abstractions of economic decisions. In the consumption-production framework, every material product in the system is produced by other products made within the system, plus exogenous capital and labor (R. Ayres and Warr 2009). A particularly interesting observation made by R. Ayres and Warr (2009), but also by Georgescu-Roegen (1971), is that this model of the economy displays a characteristic neglect of energy and material flows. In addition, there is an obvious need to relate changes in the economy and technology to environmental impacts.

One of the earliest, most intuitive approaches to understanding environmental problems came from the "$I = PAT$" formula (Ehrlich and Holdren 1971):

Impact (environmental) = Population × Affluence (GDP per capita) × Technology (environmental impact per dollar of GDP).

Since its publication, a number of revisions have been suggested. For example, Holdren, Daily, et al. (1995) adjusted the formula to disaggregate affluence from resource use and to separate measures of the "stress" that technology imposes on the environment from measures of actual damage, which depend on stress and "susceptibility." The measurement of susceptibility is predominantly a function of cumulative damage from previous environmental stress. Thus the revised formula is

Damage (environmental) = Population × Economic activity per person (affluence) × Resource use per economic activity (resources) × Stress on the environment per resource use (technology) × Damage per stress (susceptibility).

It is important to acknowledge that formulas such as these are a simple representation of a highly complex system. They are informative and can help stimulate discussions about the causes of environmental degradation, but to argue whether they are "right" is unwise (Holdren, Daily, et al. 1995). What they indicate is that the magnitudes of all the factors need to be considered because these factors have multiplicative effects on environmental damage. However, we should also recognize the limitations of these formulas. They do not take into account the interdependencies or nonlinearity that might exist between the factors, there is no explicit consideration of societal factors and how they can influence each variable, and they do not consider how each of the variables can change over time, which is especially critical for technological change (ibid.).

Given the political difficulty inherent in developing measures to curtail population growth or limit/reduce affluence and the associated levels of consumption, it seems that the easiest way to achieve a less environmentally destructive society is to focus on technological innovation. Indeed, the "technological fix" has become a major or integral aspect of many theories put forward on how society can live within its ecological means.

Two interesting (somewhat academic) developments in economics that treat technology differently are the ideas of *substitutability* (Solow 1993) and the *steady-state economy* (Czech and Daly 2004; Daly 1991b, 1996, 2008),[18] which is part of the much broader view of *ecological/green/natural/sustainability economics* (R. U. Ayres 2008; Costanza 1991; Lawson 2006; Ruth 2006; Söderbaum 2008).*

Solow's (1993) approach to sustainability is rooted in the idea that technology can create high degrees of substitutability between one resource and another and, implicitly, that natural and human-made capital are in some sense "fungible." This is what R. U. Ayres (2007) describes as the "weak" sustainability position, which essentially argues that all kinds of natural capital can be substituted by human-made capital.† If resources are fungible, society has no obligation to save a resource for future generations as long as an alternative resource is made available. Solow (1993, p. 182) argues that "what we are obligated to leave behind is a generalized capacity to create well-being, not any particular thing or any particular resource." It follows that

---

The human economy is seen as part of a larger whole. Its domain is the entire web of interactions between economic and ecological sectors. Ecological economics defines sustainability in terms of natural capital—the ability of natural systems to provide goods and services, including clean air and water and climatic stability. Ecological economists propose that the vital role of natural capital (e.g., mineral deposits, aquifers, and stratospheric ozone) should be made explicit in commodity production (Daly 1994b). Thus consumption should not deplete natural capital at a faster rate than it can be replaced by human capital. Daly's notion of the steady-state economy views natural ecosystems as being finite and, therefore, focuses on the scale of human activity (i.e., the economy) that can be supported. Living (and producing) within ecological limits is the major focus of ecological economics. *Green economics* (Lawson 2006) and *natural economics* (Ruth 2006) build on ecological economics but focus more explicitly on informing/shaping political views and policy for sustainable economic development.

† Neoclassical economics views *technological innovation* and *reproducible human-made capital* as providing "substitutes" for natural capital (Hartwick 1977, 1978a, 1978b; Solow 1974). Under these assumptions of *weak sustainability*, consumption can be sustained, environmental externalities can be overcome, and resource scarcity problems can be solved. Neoclassical economists argue that as prices increase because of scarcity, investment in technological innovation creates substitutes to replace the scarce resources. The idea that technological innovation will free society from concerns of resource scarcity, enabling economies to become less reliant on natural resources, has been rejected by some. R. U. Ayres (1978) presented a convincing case that the laws of thermodynamics place limits on the ability of human-made resources to replace or substitute natural capital. The basic argument is that human-made capital is built and maintained using natural capital. Thus both forms of capital are complementary and cannot be substituted for one another. It follows that the maintenance of natural capital stock is *essential* for the economic process. A reduction in the availability of natural capital will reduce the productivity of human-made capital, which depends on ecosystem goods and services. The same argument is also made by Georgescu- Roegen (1993). Similarly, R. U. Ayres (1997) argues that the neoclassical view of externalities as exceptional occurrences in a larger economic context is incorrect. He considers environmental externalities *pervasive* because the real economy depends on extracting, processing, and converting materials (and energy), which create waste residuals that can have negative environmental and economic consequences. Because these consequences are not priced in the real economy, the environment is treated as a free good and medium for disposal.

---

* In general, the emerging field of *ecological* (or *sustainability*) *economics*, which combines both the economy and technology with ecology, provides a holistic perspective of sustainable development (R. U. Ayres 2008; Costanza 1991; Söderbaum 2008). It studies the relationships between ecosystems and economic systems, encompassing both biological and cultural change.

resources should be assessed as if they were savings and investments (that is, we have a choice between current consumption and providing for the future through the investment of nonrenewable resource rents).*

In contrast, Daly (1991b) holds what R. U. Ayres (2007) calls a "strong" sustainability position, which entails that many of the most fundamental services provided by nature cannot be replaced by services produced by humans or human-made capital. Daly (1991b) provides what is probably the best-developed vision of an economy that functions within ecological limits. Arguing from the first principle of thermodynamics, Daly describes a steady-state economy (SSE) as one in which births replace deaths and production replaces depreciation. The objective of the SSE is to keep the throughput of raw materials (low entropy) and waste (high entropy) at levels within the regenerative and assimilative capacity of the ecosystem. Whereas neoclassical economics views the growth economy as a continual expansion of production and consumption (Figure 1.5), the SSE considers these cycles to be in equilibrium with the ecosystem (Figure 1.6).†

Within the SSE, technology, knowledge, the distribution of income, and the allocation of resources are fluid.‡ Because a fixed amount of resources will yield constant flows of goods and services (all else being equal), technological progress is one way in which more (or more highly valued) goods and services can be produced (Czech 2003; Czech and Daly 2004). However, given the laws of thermodynamics, there are limits to what is technologically feasible. Thus there is a theoretical maximum size (an ecological carrying capacity) at which a steady-state economy may exist. This constraint implies that high-quality, long-lasting, and repairable goods are preferable to low-quality, short-lived, and disposable goods.§

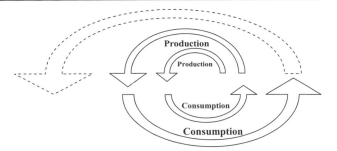

**FIGURE 1.5: NEOCLASSICAL ECONOMICS VIEW OF GROWING CYCLES OF PRODUCTION AND CONSUMPTION**
Source: Adapted from Daly (1991b, p. 181).

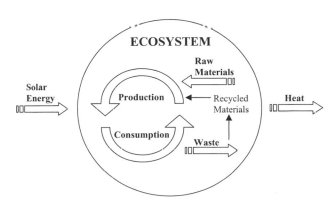

**FIGURE 1.6: STEADY-STATE ECONOMICS VIEW OF PRODUCTION AND CONSUMPTION CYCLES IN EQUILIBRIUM WITH THE ECOSYSTEM**
Source: Adapted from Daly (1991b, p. 181).

To help describe the SSE, Daly (1991b) compares it to a steady-state library, where the addition of a new book would mean the removal of an old book. Thus, although the quantitative physical scale remains constant, the library would continue to improve in a qualitative sense. In this regard, Daly's view of the necessary technological fixes for environmental degradation is more conservative than Solow's. Rather than continuing business as usual and investing in future alternatives, Daly's focus is to develop new science/technology that reduces the environmental burden to rates within ecosystem limits and also extends human lives. Daly's and Solow's viewpoints are quite different and represent contrasting views of the role that technology plays in development.

R. U. Ayres (2007) offers a critique of proponents of both strong and weak sustainability. In his view, although the mathematics of Solow's argument are "impeccable," the underlying assumptions, or what

---

* Solow (1993) describes resource rents as the investment of the pure return on a nonrenewable resource. For example, in using up a natural resource such as oil in the North Sea oil field, the revenues that are intrinsic to the oil itself should be invested in new technologies that will eventually replace oil. Hence investing the "rent" from the nonrenewable resource is seen as an effective way to continue the current levels of consumption while providing for future generations.

† See Rees (1995a) for a useful review of the expansionist (neoclassical economic) and steady-state (ecological economic) views of development.

‡ In general, ecological economists, especially those who focus on steady-state economics, are concerned with the size of the economy relative to the ecosystem. The efficient allocation of resources is a concern, but it is not the primary focus, as in neoclassical economics.

§ Although one could argue that an effective recycling process reduces the need to extend the lifespan of goods, this argument is weakened by the fact that (1) recycling processes use

energy that reduce the available stock of terrestrial resources (assuming that the recycling process is not powered by solar energy), and (2) most recycling involves the degradation of material, which means that it is suitable only for poorer-quality goods. The latter point is often referred to as "downcycling."

Ayres calls "the physics," are not. R. U. Ayres (2007, p. 116) believes that proponents of strong sustainability are right to point out the relevance of entropy law, the second law of thermodynamics, and the impossibility of perpetual-motion machines; however, they are wrong to assert that human civilization is totally dependent on a finite stock of high-quality (low-entropy) resources stored in the earth's crust. As R. U. Ayres (ibid.) points out, "The fact that much of our industrial base currently utilizes fossil fuels and high quality metal ores is merely due to the ready availability of these resources at low cost. It does not follow from the entropy law that there are not substitutes." Nonetheless, R. U. Ayres (2007, p. 126) concludes, "I have to reiterate that, while there is plenty of room for substitution and some possibility of major breakthroughs (e.g., in manufacturing room temperature super-conductors or carbon nanotubes) the pessimists—those who espouse the notion of 'strong sustainability' appear to be closer to the truth than the optimists who believe in more or less unlimited substitution possibilities."

In general, in this time of growing ecological and economic crisis, it becomes increasingly apparent that questions of ecology cannot be separated from questions of economics, and that building a truly sustainable future will necessarily involve new theories, new paradigms, and new policies. Ecological and steady-state economics provide the first step in thinking about the economy and the environment in different terms. As old theories become obsolete in light of events with real consequences and a political economy that is both unsustainable and immoral, new paradigms will emerge.

The financial crisis that began in 2008 is connected to the issue of ecological limits to growth. In tandem with the significant economic and financial disturbances, the ecological situation is particularly problematic and is a direct consequence of the workings of our industrial systems. Kallis, Martinez-Alier, et al. (2009) put forward an alternative framework for studying the financial crisis of 2008. According to their analysis, the economy must be analyzed at three levels (from top to bottom):

- The financial level
- The real economy
- The "real-real" economy

Kallis, Martinez-Alier, et al. (2009, p. 16) note:

> At the top there is the financial level that can grow by loans made to the private sector or to the state, sometimes without any assurance of repayment as in

the present crisis. The financial system borrows against the future, on the expectation that indefinite economic growth will give the means to repay the interests and the debts. Then there is what the economists describe as the real economy, the GDP at constant prices. When it grows, it indeed allows for paying back . . . some or all the debt, when it does not grow enough, debts are defaulted. Increasing the debts forces the economy to grow, up to some limits. Then, down below underneath the economists' real economy, there is what the ecological economists call the "real-real" economy, the flows of energy and materials whose growth depends partly on economic factors (types of markets, prices) and in part from physical and biological limits. The "real-real" economy also includes land and capacity of humans to do work.

The ecological approach to the present crisis states that the level of finance grew too large and too fast for the real economy to adapt. The financial system also increased debts too much, in the absence of coherent regulation, and this expansion of credit lines was mistaken for real wealth (Kallis, Martinez-Alier, et al. 2009). At the same time, the economy is not a closed system but operates within certain ecological limits and biophysical constraints, which condition the rate at which real wealth can increase. This analysis resembles that of Polanyi (1944), who placed markets within social systems rather than regarding them as independent "value-neutral" entities.

In general, energy resources appear to be of increasingly pivotal importance around the world. As Klare (2001, p. 13) notes, ever since the end of the Cold War, political analysts of different persuasions have attempted to identify the "defining principle of the new international environment." Although there have been many competing theories about this new defining paradigm, such as Samuel Huntington's "clash of civilizations," Robert Kaplan's return to Malthusian dynamics, and Tom Friedman's "flat world," Klare is correct to note that "the fervent pursuit of resource plenty in total disregard of any civilizational loyalties" appears to have much more significant explanatory power with regard to contemporary international dynamics (ibid.).

### 1.3.2 The Environment and Affluence: The Environmental Kuznets Curve

A somewhat academic idea—but one that seems to persist in many development/policy dialogues*—that

---

\* For example, the WTO promotes an environmental Kuznets curve approach to development in its discussion of how trade liberalization and stable and predictable trade conditions support the environment. "An important element of the WTO's

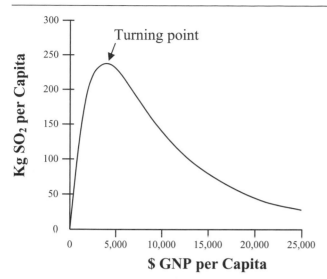

FIGURE 1.7: ENVIRONMENTAL KUZNETS CURVE FOR SULFUR
DIOXIDE EMISSIONS
Source: Panayotou (1993) from Stern, Common et al. (1996, p. 1152).

focuses on the relationship between economic growth
and environmental impact is the environmental
Kuznets curve (EKC). The EKC hypothesis postulates that the relationship between a specific environmental pollutant (such as sulfur dioxide) and per
capita income follows an inverted-U shape (Figure
1.7).* This relationship implies that as a nation's GDP
per capita increases, environmental degradation will
first increase up to a turning point that varies by pollutant (Barbier 1997a; Yandle, Bhattarai, et al. 2004),
after which it will begin to fall.

Since the early 1990s, a significant number of studies have tried to identify whether an inverted-U-shaped
relationship (or an EKC) exists between different indicators of environmental degradation and per capita
income (Barbier 1997b; M. A. Cole, Rayner, et al.
1997; de Groot, Withagen, et al. 2004; Grossman and
Krueger 1993, 1995; Hettige, Lucas, et al. 1992; List
and Gallet 1999; Panayotou 1993; Selden and Song
1994; Shafik and Bandyopadhyay 1992).* In general,

these empirical studies suggest that an EKC exists for
production-based, relatively short-lived pollutants
that have a regional/local impact, such as sulfur dioxide ($SO_2$), oxides of nitrogen ($NO_x$), carbon monoxide (CO), suspended particulates (SPM), and fecal
coliforms. However, many authors of these studies
are careful to state that their findings should be
treated with caution. For example, Grossman and
Krueger (1995, p. 372) stress that "there is nothing at
all inevitable about the relationships that have been
observed in the past. These patterns reflect the technological, political and economic conditions that existed at the time." See Box 1.1 for a summary of key
points related to the EKC.

The EKC hypothesis effectively challenged the
idea that the process of industrialization and economic development "inevitably hurts the environment" (IBRD 1992, p. 38). For example, Beckerman
(1992, p. 482) claimed that "there is clear evidence
that, although economic growth usually leads to environmental deterioration in the early stages of the process, in the end the best—and probably the only—way
to attain a decent environment in most countries is
to become rich." Bartlett (1994, p. 18) even suggested
that "existing environmental regulation, by reducing
economic growth, may actually be reducing environmental quality." The clear focus of these "income-
deterministic" arguments was that economic growth
is the best way to alleviate poverty and (eventually)
address environmental degradation.

In a critique of the environmental Kuznets curve
that is traditionally focused on a few specific pollutants as measures of total environmental pressure,
Spangenberg (2001) finds no indication of an environmental Kuznets curve can be found for the total resource throughput in several advanced countries. The
vast majority of man-made emissions of suspended

---

contribution to sustainable development and protection of the
environment comes in the form of furthering trade opening in
goods and services to promote economic development, and by
providing stable and predictable conditions that enhance the
possibility of innovation. This promotes the efficient allocation
of resources, economic growth and increased income levels that
in turn provide additional possibilities for protecting the environment." WTO, "An Introduction to Trade and Environment in
the WTO," www.wto.org/english/tratop_e/envir_e/envt_intro_e
.htm (accessed June 8, 2010). The WTO's statement implies that
negative environmental impacts that result from economic
growth can be addressed once income levels increase, which is
clearly the opposite of a precautionary approach to development.
*          The first empirical EKC study is attributed to Grossman and Krueger (1993), who investigated whether the North
American Free Trade Agreement (NAFTA) would lead to envi-

---

ronmental degradation. Their results identified an inverted-
U-shaped relationship between $SO_2$, dark matter (fine smoke),
and suspended particles and income per capita. In addition, the
World Bank's 1992 *World Development Report* (IBRD 1992;
Shafik and Bandyopadhyay 1992) and research by Panayotou
(1993) and Selden and Song (1994) are often associated with the
early development of the EKC hypothesis. Interestingly, there
appears to be some confusion over whether Panayotou or Selden
and Song coined the term "environmental Kuznets curve"; see
Dinda (2004), Gawande, Berrens, et al. (2001), and Tisdell (2001).
Others have applied the EKC concept to consider the relationship between per capita income and specific concerns, such as
the percentage of threatened bird and mammal species in a country (McPherson and Nieswiadomy 2005), the rate of deforestation of natural tropical forests (Bhattarai and Hammig 2004), the
intensity of material consumption (Canas, Ferrao, et al. 2003),
and consumption-based measures such as ecological footprint or
number of hazardous-waste sites (Gawande, Berrens, et al. 2001;
Rothman 1998).

---

### BOX 1.1: KEY POINTS RELATING TO THE ENVIRONMENTAL KUZNETS CURVE (EKC)

#### THE EKC HYPOTHESIS

The EKC hypothesis states that the relationship between a specific environmental pollutant—such as sulfur dioxide ($SO_2$)—and per capita income follows an inverted-U shape. This relationship implies that environmental degradation will first increase with rising income per capita up to a turning point, after which it will start to fall with higher levels of income. If one accepts the EKC hypothesis, the solution to global environmental degradation would appear to be rapid economic growth.

#### POINTS OF CONCERN

1. The EKC does not seem to hold for $CO_2$ or for toxics associated with increasing industrialization and especially increasing consumption.
2. The EKC may not even hold for regular pollutants like $SO_2$.
3. The adoption of pollution-prevention and cleaner technology reflecting sustainable practices may explain Kuznets-type behavior, but such behavior depends on the constant application of these sustainable practices that are promoted by regulation, not laissez-faire policies.
4. Late developers and those that decide to adopt cleaner technology late may seem to provide evidence for Kuznets-type behavior, but this action highlights a cultural shift in the importance of protecting a community's livelihood and not an income effect.
5. The adoption of more efficient technology that initially reduces environmental degradation, resource usage, and overall costs might eventually lead to higher levels of environmental impact through the Jevons paradox or rebound effect—that is, the lower cost of using a more efficient technology increases its demand and (potentially) offsets the original efficiency gains.
6. Even if per capita production of pollution declines, population increases could swamp any environmental gains.

---

particulate matter, $SO_2$ and $CO_2$ all originate from the use of fossil fuels for which environmental laws eventually limit emissions through end-of-pipe abatement technologies. The modernization of pollution sources more generally requires substitution and more fundamental technological change than end-of-pipe traditional pollution control. Otherwise, increased wealth associated with economic growth increases the production of other kinds of pollution that can only be offset by technology modernization and improvements in resource productivity that lead to an absolute reduction in resource consumption. Commenting that "wealth is not green," Spangenberg (2001) argues that the emphasis of ecological economics must be that resource productivity needs to improve well beyond the economic growth rate for there to be a future positive effect of growth on pollution reduction.

The EKC hypothesis stood in stark contrast to the "limits-to-growth" debate of the early 1970s (see the Primer on Sustainable Development at this book's website for a discussion of *The Limits to Growth* and other influential publications released before the 1972 UN Conference on the Human Environment in Stockholm). This debate centered on the notion that sustained economic growth would eventually lead to the "overshoot and collapse" of critical ecosystems—that is, human activity moves beyond a "tipping point."

Using system dynamics techniques developed by Jay Forrester at MIT,* the 1972 *Limits to Growth* report

---

\* In 1971 the book *World Dynamics* presented the results of a computer model developed by Professor Forrester and his colleagues at MIT, called "World 2." Forrester describes how the model was created to support a two-week workshop at MIT in 1970 during which the Executive Committee from the Club of Rome was invited to learn the process of model formulation and computer simulation. The World 2 model was designed to analyze the problems facing the "world system," which was defined as incorporating humankind, humankind's social systems, humankind's technology, and the natural environment. Using five key variables—population, capital investment, natural resources, the fraction of capital devoted to agriculture, and pollution—the model provided evidence that within the next one hundred years "man may face choices from a four-pronged dilemma—suppression of modern industrial society by a natural-resource shortage; decline of world population from changes wrought by pollution; population limitation by food shortage; or pollution collapse from war, disease, and social stresses caused by physical and psychological crowding" (Forrester 1971, p. 11).

In addition, the simulations indicated that the high standard of living in developed countries is likely to fall as industrialization reaches a "natural-resource limit," and that developing countries might have "no realistic hope" of reaching the standard of living experienced in developed nations (Forrester 1971, p. 12). These predictions fueled the debate in developed and developing countries about the sovereign right to, and best process of, development. Following the workshop at MIT, the Club of Rome, convinced that Forrester's model had identified many of the factors behind the "world problematique," decided to launch Phase One of its study of the predicament of humankind. This phase, headed by Dennis Meadows, led to the creation of the World 3 model, on which the *Limits to Growth* report was based. The

discussed the results of a computer model (called "World 3") designed to predict the future if current trends of increasing population, industrialization, pollution, food production, and resource depletion continued unabated. The report reached three salient conclusions:

1.  If the present growth trends in world population, industrialization, pollution, food production, and resource depletion continue unchanged, the limits to growth on this planet will be reached sometime within the next one hundred years. The most probable result will be a rather sudden and uncontrollable decline in both population and industrial capacity.

2.  It is possible to alter these growth trends and to establish a condition of ecological and economic stability that is sustainable far into the future. The state of global equilibrium could be designed so that the basic material needs of each person on earth are satisfied and each person has an equal opportunity to realize his individual human potential.

3.  If the world's people decide to strive for this second outcome rather than the first, the sooner they begin working to attain it, the greater will be their chances of success. (D. H. Meadows, D. L. Meadows, et al. 1972, pp. 23–24)

*The Limits to Growth* raised the important idea of "overshoot and collapse"—that is, to go inadvertently beyond a system's limits, creating a situation that is nearly impossible to reverse (D. H. Meadows, D. L. Meadows, et al. 1972, p. 144). Overshoot can occur, the study's authors opined, because (1) growth can lead to rapid change within the system; (2) there is a limit to the system beyond which it becomes unstable; and (3) delays in feedback mechanisms mean that the system's limits are exceeded before the problems are identified. For example, "Pollution generated

in exponentially increasing amounts can rise past the danger point, because the danger point is first perceived years after the offending pollution was released. A rapidly growing industrial system can build up a capital base dependent on a given resource and then discover that the exponentially shrinking resources reserves cannot support it" (ibid., p. 145).*

In 1992, the authors of *The Limits to Growth* published *Beyond the Limits*, which argued that the conclusions they had reached in 1972 were still valid, but the underlying logic needed to be strengthened (D. H. Meadows, D. L. Meadows, et al. 1992).† The 1992 book painted an even more convincing picture of

---

World 3 model contained about three times as many mathematical equations as its predecessor and used empirical data for many of its numerical relationships (H. S. D. Cole 1973). (The phrase "world problematique" was created by the Club of Rome to describe the set of crucial problems—political, social, economic, technological, environmental, psychological, and cultural—facing humanity.) The most common criticism of the first World 3 model was that it underestimated the influence of technology and did not adequately represent the adaptive nature of the market. Some twenty years later, D. H. Meadows, D. L. Meadows, et al. (1992) designed a new version of the model that did not rely solely on technology or solely on the market, but instead on a smooth interaction between the two. The outcome from the new model showed that in many cases, resource and pollution flows had already surpassed levels that are physically sustainable.

---

\*     For a recent study that explores whether it is possible to achieve a low- or no-growth economy, see Victor (2008). Victor developed an interactive model of the Canadian economy, called "LowGrow," which he used to explore different assumptions, objectives, and policy measures designed to transition the economy toward zero economic growth. To avoid the criticisms levied at the World 3 systems model supporting the work of *The Limits to Growth*, the LowGrow model was based firmly on standard economic theory. Victor concluded that the careless implementation of a "no-growth" strategy can be disastrous, bringing about significant hardship. However, if a low-growth strategy, followed by a no-growth strategy, is pursued with high investment, it is possible (in theory) to achieve (by 2035) a future of full employment with low levels of poverty, increased leisure time, reduced greenhouse gas emissions, and fiscal balance. Although the LowGrow model has limitations, such as its high level of aggregation, its value lies in its ability to enable analysts and decision makers to explore potential pathways toward a "no economic growth" future. What is evident from Victor's (2008) work is that there are several pathways to achieving such a goal.

†     The revised conclusions are as follows: "[1] Human use of many essential resources and generation of many kinds of pollutants have already surpassed rates that are physically sustainable. Without significant reductions in material and energy flows, there will be in the coming decades an uncontrolled decline in per capita food output, energy use, and industrial production; . . . [2] This decline is not inevitable. To avoid it two changes are necessary. The first is a comprehensive revision of policies and practices that perpetuate growth in material consumption and in population. The second is a rapid, drastic increase in the efficiency with which materials and energy are used; . . . [3] A sustainable society is still technically and economically possible. It could be much more desirable than a society that tries to solve its problems by constant expansion. The transition to a sustainable society requires a careful balance between long-term and short-term goals and an emphasis on sufficiency, equity, and quality of life rather than on quantity of output. It requires more than productivity and more than technology; it also requires maturity, compassion, and wisdom" (D. H. Meadows, D. L. Meadows, et al. 1992, pp. xv–xvi). In 2004, the thirty-year update of *The Limits to Growth* was published (Meadows, Randers, et al. 2004a). "Now, three decades later, we are into the 21st century within 20 years of the time when our scenarios suggest that growth will near its end. The basic conclusions are still the same. . . . The world's use of materials and energy has grown past the levels that can be supported indefinitely. Pressures are mounting from the environment that will force a reduction. Rising oil prices, climate change, declining forests, falling ground water levels—all of

system collapse.* This newer work argues that the limits to growth are not physical limits, such as limits to population growth or to the number of automobiles on the road. Rather, they are limits to *throughput*, that is, limits to the flows of energy and materials required to keep people alive, to build more automobiles, and the like. By this they mean that the limits to growth are not only the limits to the earth's ability to provide the *resource streams* of energy and materials necessary to meet predicted consumption levels, but also limits to its ability to absorb the *pollution and waste streams* in natural sinks such as forests and oceans.

Although the legitimacy of D. H. Meadows, D. L. Meadows, et al.'s (1972) limits-to-growth argument was criticized (H. S. D. Cole, Freeman, et al. 1973; Kaysen 1972; Maddox 1972), the intellectual debate surrounding the topic clearly informed Daly's (1991b, 1996) notion of the SSE.

When *The Limits to Growth* was published in 1972, the general consensus of the international community was that economic growth was a major cause of environmental harm (see Chapter 2). However, toward the end of the 1970s, following two oil shocks and amid a global recession, this perspective began to change. The emerging view of economic growth and its impact on the environment was perhaps most clearly articulated in a United Nations Environment Programme (UNEP) report titled *The Environment in 1982: Retrospect and Prospect*: "A decade ago the desirability of further economic growth was questioned in some quarters but the negative effects of the recent slow-down in economic growth have reinforced the view that it is an essential instrument in achieving social goals. In developing countries particularly, economic growth is vitally important and remains a major force for improving the health and welfare of people. It is now perceived that economic growth can often be managed not only to avoid environmental degradation but also, in many cases, to improve the environment" (UNEP 1982, p. 37).

The idea that economic development and environmental protection could advance in unison became central to the vision of sustainable development articulated by the World Commission on Environment and Development (WCED 1987) (see Chapter 2). In the classic text *Our Common Future*, the WCED (1987, p. 43), also known as the Brundtland Commission, defined sustainable development as development that meets present needs without damaging the environment or compromising the ability of future generations to meet their own needs. It viewed the environment and development as being "inexorably linked," stating that "development cannot subsist upon a deteriorating environmental resource base; the environment cannot be protected when growth leaves out of account the costs of environmental destruction" (ibid., p. 37). Sanders (2006, p. 386) aptly describes the WCED (or Brundtland) approach as "growth within limits."

This formulation of sustainable development meant that it could be incorporated into the conventional economic paradigm through ideas such as "balancing social, economic, and environmental objectives," the "triple bottom line," "getting the process right," "dematerialization," and "ecological modernization." Sanders (2006) argues that formulating sustainable development in such a politically palatable, rather than scientific, manner has severely limited progress toward sustainability.

It is important to recognize that the Brundtland Commission's view of development is quite different from that envisioned by proponents of the EKC hypothesis. The EKC hypothesis implies that environmental degradation is an unavoidable part of the early stages of economic development/growth. The purely empirical nature of the hypothesis means that it is not concerned with whether environmental degradation exceeds critical ecological limits (K. Arrow, Bolin, et al. 1995; Munasinghe 1999; Tisdell 2001). In this regard, great care must be taken not to confuse the growth- and trade-liberalization (or "business-as-usual") approach of the EKC hypothesis with a more "sustainable" approach to development. The former adopts a laissez-faire view (that is, the market will efficiently respond to problems as they arise), whereas the latter takes explicit (interventionist) steps through regulation, policies, and/or programs to protect important natural and social systems.

What is perhaps most interesting about the EKC hypothesis is that its proponents point to many aspects of the sustainable approach to development when they are describing the underlying dynamics behind the empirical relationship. In general, the logic

---

these are simply symptoms of the overshoot" (Meadows, Randers, et al. 2004b).

* Oddly enough, even though there is evidence that limits are in fact now being surpassed—as shown by the destruction of the ozone layer, global warming, widespread contamination of drinking-water systems, and the possibility of widespread species harm through endocrine disruption—*Beyond the Limits* did not receive serious attention. In the closing chapter of *Beyond the Limits*, the authors argue that an environmental ethic backed by love is required to prevent system collapse. Given the tremendous challenge of living within ecological limits, it seems that the authors hope that moral rectitude will one day save the environment.

behind the EKC goes as follows. At very low levels of economic activity (that is, in a preindustrial and agricultural society), environmental degradation is relatively low.* As industrialization proceeds, the growing use of raw materials and relatively "dirty" (less efficient) technologies leads to increasing levels of pollution/waste and environmental degradation. The objective of the industrial (or "adolescent") phase of development is to maximize economic growth by expanding throughput with little consideration for the environmental consequences. Finally, as an economy matures and transitions into the postindustrial phase (also known as the service or information economy), there is a gradual leveling off and decline in environmental degradation. As Panayotou (1993, p. 1) explains, environmental quality begins to improve because of "increased environmental awareness, enforcement of environmental regulations, better technology, and higher environmental expenditures." The growing societal demand and "willingness to pay" for a healthy environment mean that governments are able to establish initiatives to protect and enhance the environment. Such initiatives can be influential in promoting the adoption (or creation) of technologies to enhance production efficiency and/or reduce emissions. If these initiatives are designed in an integrated manner, they can also encourage a transition toward a less environmentally destructive "input mix" to the economy—that is, environmentally damaging inputs are gradually replaced with less damaging inputs (D. I. Stern 2003, 2004). In the absence of government intervention, a firm's desire to lower costs (through efficiency gains), combined with consumer pressure for greener products and services, can directly promote less environmentally destructive practices. However, without capping total emissions or constraining resource usage to sustainable levels,

the "rebound effect" or Jevons paradox (described in the following section) can potentially overwhelm any environmental benefits achieved through technological improvements.

The creation of environmental regulation that reduces and caps pollution levels, the promotion of highly efficient technologies, and the reduction in use of raw materials and shifts to renewable resources are all critical elements of a sustainable approach to development. The difference, however, between proponents of the EKC hypothesis and those of the sustainable approach to development is that the former do not actively promote these structural/technological changes in the economy. Instead, they tend to treat them as an inevitable part of economic growth/development, viewing laissez-faire capitalism as the most effective development pathway.† In contrast, proponents of the sustainable approach tend to be more interventionist and to seek opportunities to halt and/or reverse clearly unsustainable activities. In their opinion, although pollution prevention and cleaner technologies may explain the EKC relationship, in many cases these sustainable practices are the result of regulation that needs to be constantly revised as the economy evolves.

The validity and implications of the EKC hypothesis have been the subject of much critical debate (K. Arrow, Bolin, et al. 1995; Barbier 1997a; Cavlovic, Baker, et al. 2000; de Bruyn, van den Bergh, et al. 1998; Dinda 2004; D. I. Stern 1998, 2003, 2004; D. I. Stern, Common, et al. 1996; Unruh and Moomaw 1998). Although the empirical support for the EKC relationship and its very existence have been disputed (Harbaugh, Levinson, et al. 2002; P. Lawn 2006; Perman and Stern 2003), a more general criticism is that EKCs have been shown to exist only for local air pollutants and not for long-lived measures such as carbon dioxide ($CO_2$), municipal waste, and persistent toxic

---

\*       The statement that low economic activity equates with low environmental degradation should be treated with care. For example, ten years after the 1972 Stockholm Conference on the Human Environment, the UNEP's Governing Council reached "agreement on the need to make a direct attack on poverty, which was the main source of environmental degradation in the third world[;] breaking the vicious circle of extreme poverty would help to unravel the tangled interrelationships between population, resources, development and the environment" (UNEP, *Report of the Governing Council on Its Tenth Session*, *General Debate*, 51, www.unep.org/Documents.multilingual/Default.asp ?DocumentID=70&ArticleID=702 [accessed June 8, 2010]). In addition to the idea of the "poverty trap," the argument that agricultural societies do not degrade the environment is also debatable. Throughout the history of civilization, great societies such as the Polynesian cultures on Easter Island and the American civilizations of the Anasazi and the Maya have fallen because of the degradation of their productive capacities (Diamond 2004).

---

†       The reader should be aware that this discussion attempts to draw a clear distinction between proponents of the EKC hypothesis and proponents of the sustainable approach to development. However, in reality, there is a clear spectrum of opinions that fall between these two extremes. The majority of academics who support the existence of EKC curves are very careful when they are interpreting the results from their research. For example, M. A. Cole (2003, p. 575) states that improvement in air quality with increasing income per capita "is not an automatic procedure. Growth does not reduce pollution. Rather, the evidence suggests that growth *can* facilitate the required legislation and investment to help reduce *per capita* emissions of *some* pollutants." Thus the proponents of an EKC-hypothesis approach to development—referred to in the main text—are those who take the inverted-U relationship at face value and are not concerned about whether the theory holds true for all environmental indicators.

chemicals (M. A. Cole, Rayner, et al. 1997; S. Dasgupta, Laplante, et al. 2002; Hettige, Lucas, et al. 1992; Holtz-Eakin and Selden 1995; Rothman 1998). These mainly consumption-based measures are shown to increase monotonically with per capita income.

Another important criticism is that EKCs are generated by a composition effect, whereby developed nations improve their environmental performance by exporting energy- and pollution-intensive activities to developing nations (K. Arrow, Bolin, et al. 1995; M. A. Cole and Neumayer 2005; Rothman 1998; D. I. Stern, Common, et al. 1996).* This criticism raises the question whether developing nations will be able to replicate the environmental improvements achieved by developed nations. As their economies grow, their options for exporting energy- and pollution-intensive activities are limited. A related problem mentioned earlier is that international trade creates a "distancing effect" (Conca 2002; Princen 2002), where consumers are spatially and temporally separated from industrial processes and their environmental impacts. Because consumers (primarily in developed nations) are not directly confronted by the impacts of their purchasing habits, their willingness to address the problems experienced elsewhere is limited. Thus to keep the process of economic globalization from deteriorating the global environment, the international community has a vital role to play in halting and reversing unsustainable development (Tisdell 2001).

Other criticisms are that the EKC hypothesis is not directly concerned with the total impact of economic growth on the environment and whether this may (in some cases) be irreversible; that the earth's stock of resources may not be able to support indefinite economic growth (K. Arrow, Bolin, et al. 1995; Rothman 1998); and that the focus on economic growth ignores the more important issue of human well-being (Daly and Cobb 1994; Max-Neef 1995).

Even if one accepts that an EKC relationship may exist for specific pollutants such as local air pollutants, the vast majority of the world's population lies on the upward slope of EKC curves, which means that considerable environmental damage is likely to occur before any environmental improvement becomes visible (Ekins 1997). Similarly, any environ-

mental improvements gained through production efficiencies can be overwhelmed by growing levels of consumption in both developed and developing economies. The deterministic nature of the EKC hypothesis raises the question whether developing nations can learn from developed nations and adopt initiatives to "tunnel through" or "flatten" the inverted-U relationship (S. Dasgupta, Laplante, et al. 2002; Munasinghe 1999; Panayotou 1997). These initiatives include the establishment and enforcement of sophisticated and anticipative environmental regulation and the adoption of cleaner technologies that allow developing nations to leapfrog over older, dirty technologies.† In general, the idea that developing nations could "escape the pattern of the EKC" is becoming more widely supported (M. A. Cole and Neumayer 2005, p. 316).

In conclusion, one can argue that (1) technological change is critical to enabling society to live within ecological limits, and (2) governments have a vital role in creating an innovative regulatory environment that protects critical ecological systems and spurs the necessary technological change.

### 1.3.3 Technological Optimism

During the emergence of sustainable development, the environmental discourse was strongest between the technological optimists,‡ on one side, and the self-proclaimed Malthusians, on the other, who could foresee no technological solution to the pending problems of pollution and scarcity (Krier and Gillette 1985). Although the technological optimists were concerned about the environment, they believed that human scientific and technological ingenuity would be able to extend any limits faced by society.

As discussed in Chapter 3, the growth of new (and successful) technology tends to follow an S-curve.

---

* An issue closely related to the composition effect is the "pollution-haven hypothesis": dirty industries relocate to developing nations to take advantage of their lower environmental standards (Ekins, Folke, et al. 1994; Hettige, Lucas, et al. 1992). In practice, the pollution-haven hypothesis is not seen to be a significant factor behind the EKC relationship (Grossman and Krueger 1995; Rothman 1998).

† Interestingly, the decision of developing nations to adopt cleaner technologies may not be due to an income effect but rather to a cultural shift in the importance of protecting a community's livelihood.

‡ Krier and Gillette (1985, p. 406) describe technological optimism as "a term of art, an article of faith, and a theory of politics." They argue that technological optimism obtained its precise meaning as a result of the limits-to-growth model, which assumed that factors such as population, industrial production, and pollution would continue to grow exponentially. Thus it follows that the position of a technological optimist is "that *exponential technological* growth will allow us to expand resources ahead of exponentially increasing demands. This is the precise meaning of technological optimism as a term of art" (ibid., p. 407). There is also the implicit assumption that technological innovation will not cause any further pollution or social problems.

Therefore, if we consider the entire field of technological advance, it follows that it will be composed of a series of such curves. The question is, however, what shape will this series of S-curves follow? Technological optimists responded to this question by arguing that technological innovation will continue to advance at an exponential rate, thereby establishing a world of utopia as opposed to disaster (Boyd 1972; Kaysen 1972; Starr and Rudman 1973). Others, however, were not as convinced (K. J. Arrow 1969). Indeed, as Krier and Gillette (1985) argue, if the S-curve holds for a single technology, why should it not be true for a set of technologies (Figure 1.8)? And if it holds for a set, should it not also be true for the entire field of technology? Thus if we are experiencing rapid growth in technological performance, it might simply be due to the fact that we are in the center of a series of S-curves that together also form an S-curve (Figure 1.8).

The problem with this type of debate, as recognized by Krier and Gillette (1985), is that the assertions made are most likely unprovable. Although it is possible to assess individual technologies, it is extremely difficult to assess (in any rigorous manner) whether technology as a whole is progressing at a faster or slower rate than before and whether this means that we are reaching a plateau in performance (however "performance" is defined).

With the publication of the World Commission on Environment and Development's report *Our Common Future* (WCED 1987), it was clear to many that technological optimism had prevailed (Moser 1999). The WCED had chosen science and technological innovation—two mainstays of economic growth in industrial (expansionist) societies—as central pillars of the notion of sustainable development.* As Dryzek (1997, p. 136) notes, the concept of sustainable

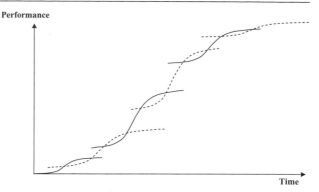

**FIGURE 1.8: THE ACCUMULATION OF S-CURVES FOR A TECHNOLOGY SET**

development would surely have been lost "unless it could be demonstrated that environmental conservation were obviously good for business profitability and economic growth everywhere, not just that these competing values can be reconciled."

As a result of the decision to focus more heavily on science and technology—as opposed to market reforms and/or government policy to guide development—there has been a strong (European and Japanese) research interest in what has been termed "factor X" (Reijnders 1998). The idea of factor X is similar to that of dematerialization, ecoefficiency, and enhanced natural resource productivity, but whereas these measures of environmental impact tend to be more open ended, the factor X debate attempts to put an exact number on the level of efficiency to be achieved (ibid., p. 14). This willingness to quantify implies that (1) the environmental problem is in fact quantifiable, and (2) that technological improvements are required beyond what current technology is able to achieve.[†] The current set of factor X values ranges from 4 to 50 (Factor 10 Club 1995, 1997; Jansen and Vergragt 1992; Reijnders 1996; von Weizsäcker, Hargroves, et al. 2010; von Weizsäcker, Lovins, et al. 1997); however, there is no overall agreement on the environmental impact to which factor X relates (Reijnders 1998). This fact, combined with differences in the perceived severity of the environmental threat, explains the wide range of factor X values.

It is helpful to connect the factor X debate to the $I = PAT$ formula because they are closely interlinked. The factor X approach is clearly a technologically

---

*     A retrospective analysis of *Our Common Future* concluded that the economic and environmental objectives put forward by the Brundtland Commission "cannot be achieved simultaneously" (Duchin and Lange 1994, p. 8). To address this problem, Duchin and Lange (1994) put forward two paths of action. First, much broader technological and social changes are needed than those espoused in *Our Common Future* if sustainable development is to be brought within reach. Second, "development economics" (which includes factors such as international lending and advisory practices) need to focus on specific situations and move away from the conviction that there is only one development path—that of liberalized markets that situate all factors of production in the most privately profitable location for their exploitation. Duchin and Lange (1994) argue that a failure to consider national circumstances is likely to affect traditional social relationships in a way that (indirectly) leads to the rise of "both religious fundamentalism and urban misery in the developing world" (ibid., p. 9).

---

†     It is important to recognize that although the notion of a factor X economy recognizes the inherent unsustainability of prevailing human activities, its proponents' conceptualization of development remains firmly grounded in the "growth ethic and technological fix paradigm" (Rees 1995a, p. 355). An alternative view of development is based on the idea of a steady-state economy (SSE), whereby economic (human) activity remains within fixed ecological limits.

optimistic view of development. But technology is only one factor that affects the environment. It is quite plausible that the environmental benefits achieved by technological innovation will be countered by growth in population and/or affluence leading to greater total consumption of materials and energy (Herman, Ardekani, et al. 1989; Reijnders 1998; W. Sachs 1993).* In addition, there is also the problem that although technological improvements increase the efficiency with which resources are used, the total consumption of these resources might increase rather than decrease. This phenomenon is known as the *rebound effect* (Berkhout, Muskens, et al. 2000) or the *Jevons paradox* (Clark and Foster 2001; Jevons 1965 [1865]). William Stanley Jevons was a nineteenth-century economist who observed that efficiency gains in the use of coal did not necessarily lead to a reduction in its overall use.† More recently it has been observed that increases in the fuel efficiency of vehicles have been accompanied by an increase in vehicle-miles traveled and by an increase in sales of larger vehicles (Goldberg 1998). Therefore, the implementation of factor X (or highly efficient) technology needs to be part of a more comprehensive process of environmental improvement or *ecological modernization* (Ashford, Ayers, et al. 1985; Kemp 1995; York, Rosa, et al. 2003).

When one is considering factor X targets, it is possible to focus on individual products/technologies or the economy as a whole. Although factor X advocates support the notion of setting informed and modifiable

targets, it is recognized that the pace of rapid technological change and the presence of the Jevons paradox complicate the management of such a schema (Reijnders 1998). In this regard, *movement in a more sustainable direction* might provide an alternative. However, the problem here is what instrument will be used to encourage such movement. Examples of types of mechanisms that can be used to encourage the adoption of factor X technology are demonstration projects (for social learning), government-driven technology forcing (using legislation), financial incentives, ecotaxation,‡ and market mechanisms (such as tradable emissions permits) (ibid.). The role of government in stimulating technological change is discussed in Chapter 8.

## 1.4  A CONCEPTUAL FRAMEWORK FOR SUSTAINABLE DEVELOPMENT

The literature relating to sustainability has produced an extensive array of definitions, principles, and conceptual frameworks to describe the concept (Hall 2006; Holdren, Daily, et al. 1995; Murcott 1997; Rees 1995a). Box 1.2 provides a selection of some of the better-known definitions that have arisen since 1980.

The most widely quoted definition of sustainable development—the Brundtland definition (Box 1.2)—centers on the concept of meeting human needs. This chapter began with an anthropocentric look at sustainable development in an attempt to understand what meeting human needs entails. Perhaps the most widely accepted notion of human development—though not ideal—is put forward by the UN's Human Development Index (HDI; see the discussion in Section 1.1.1). The HDI measures human development by looking at health, education, and income. However, if we are to begin to address the problems that confront sustainable development, understanding human needs and how these motivate behavior is essential.

In 1992, the National Research Council (NRC) undertook an assessment of research focused on ecological degradation and concluded that "the quality

---

\*        Here we should recognize that whereas the connection between *population* growth and ecological decline is widely understood, the same cannot be said for increasing levels of *affluence* and consumption and their associated impacts on the environment. Indeed, consumption "is almost universally seen as good, . . . [and] increasing it is the primary goal of national economic policy" (Durning 1994, p. 41). Although the environmental and psychological problems associated with consumption are well documented (de Graaf, Wann, et al. 2002; Durning 1992, 1994; Goodwin, Ackerman, et al. 1997; Kasser 2002; Princen, Maniates, et al. 2002; J. C. Ryan and Durning 1997; Schlosser 2002; P. C. Stern, Dietz, et al. 1997), they have yet to gain traction in mainstream political and economic decision making. For an insightful debate on the effects of economic growth and consumption on the environment, see Sagoff's (1997) article in the *Atlantic Monthly* and its rebuttal by Ehrlich, Daily, et al. (1997).

†        Jevons (2001 [1865]) observed that the consumption of coal in England increased significantly when the efficiency of the steam engine was improved by James Watt. Watt's innovations, the condenser and the expansive mode of working, reduced the amount of coal needed to fuel the steam engine's furnace, making the engine a cost-effective power source that was soon adopted by industry. As the number of industries using steam engines grew, so too did the amount of coal required to fuel these engines, thereby increasing the overall usage of coal.

‡        See Daly (1994a) and Rees (1995b) for a discussion of how taxing the *bads* (such as resource extraction/depletion or pollution) and not the *goods* (such as labor and income) provides a good example of considering both the environment and employment in one macroeconomic framework. The basic idea is to shift the tax burden away from the goods and onto the bads in a revenue-neutral manner. In addition to promoting a more sustainable form of industrialization, ecotaxation would also reduce the price of labor, making it more attractive to retain existing workers or employ more workers. See also Green Innovations Inc., *Ecotaxation*, www.green-innovations.asn.au/ecotax.htm (accessed June 8, 2010).

## BOX 1.2: SOME DEFINITIONS OF SUSTAINABLE DEVELOPMENT

Development is defined . . . as: the modification of the biosphere and the application of human, financial, living and non-living resources to satisfy human needs and improve the quality of human life. For development to be sustainable it must take account of social and ecological factors, as well as economic ones; of the living and non-living resource base; and of the long term as well as short term advantages and disadvantages of alternative actions. (IUCN, UNEP, et al. 1980, p. 1)

Sustainable development is development that meets the needs of the present without compromising the ability of future generations to meet their own needs. It contains within it two key concepts:

- the concept of "needs", in particular the essential needs of the world's poor, to which overriding priority should be given; and
- the idea of limitations imposed by the state of technology and social organization on the environment's ability to meet present and future needs. (Brundtland definition; WCED 1987, p. 43)

Improving the quality of human life while living within the carrying capacity of supporting ecosystems. (IUCN, UNEP, et al. 1991, p. 10)

Economic growth that provides fairness and opportunity for all the world's people, not just the privileged few, without further destroying the world's finite natural resources and carrying capacity. (Pronk and ul Haq 1992)

1. The main principle [of sustainable development] is to limit the human scale (throughput) to a level which, if not optimal, is at least within carrying capacity and therefore sustainable. . . .
2. Technological progress for sustainable development should be efficiency-increasing rather than throughput-increasing. . . .
3. Renewable resources, in both their source and sink functions, should be exploited on a profit-maximizing sustained yield basis and in general not driven to extinction (regardless of the dictates of present value maximization), since they will become ever more important as nonrenewables run out. . . . Specifically this means that: (a) harvesting rates should not exceed regeneration rates; and (b) waste emissions should not exceed the renewable assimilative capacity of the environment.
4. Nonrenewable resources should be exploited, but at a rate equal to the creation of renewable substitutes. (Daly 1991, pp. 44–45).

Sustainable development "is an obligation to conduct ourselves so that we leave to the future the option or the capacity to be as well off as we are" (Solow 1993, p. 181).

Sustainability is a strategy for improving the quality of life while preserving the environmental potential for the future, of living off interest rather than consuming natural capital. Sustainable development mandates that the present generation must not narrow the choices of future generations but must strive to expand them by passing on an environment and an accumulation of resources that will allow its children to live at least as well as, and preferably better than, people today. Sustainable development is premised on living within Earth's means. (National Commission on the Environment 1993, p. 2)

**Necessary Conditions for Global Sustainability:**
Ecological stability requires that:

- consumption by the economy of the products and services of nature be compatible with rates of production by the ecosphere.
- the production of wastes by the economy remain within the assimilative capacity of the ecosphere.
- economic activity protect the essential life-support functions of the ecosphere and preserve the biodiversity and resilience of Earth's ecological systems.

Geopolitical security requires that:

- society satisfy basic standards of material equity and social justice.
- governance mechanisms be in place to enable an informed citizenry to have an effective participatory role in decision-making.
- people share a positive sense of community cohesion (local and global) and a sense of collective responsibility for the future. (Rees 1995a, p. 356)

An expanded set of principles for sustainable development

| Sustainability | Development |
|---|---|
| $S_a$—preserving natural resources for future generations | $D_a$—improving quality of life for individuals |
| $S_b$—preserving the option value of human and man-made capital for future generations | $D_b$—ensuring a fair distribution of life-quality (Gudmundsson and Hojer 1996, p. 273) |

The *possibility* that human and other forms of life will *flourish* on the Earth *forever*. (Ehrenfeld 2004, p. 8)

Sustainable development is the process of meeting the needs of current and future generations without undermining the resilience of life-supporting properties or the integrity & cohesion of social systems.

Extending this definition further, we differentiate among four dimensions of sustainability:

1. Ecological configuration
2. Economic production & consumption
3. Governance & politics
4. Institutions & performance

(continued)

BOX 1.2 (continued)

To become sustainable, a system must meet four conditions:
(a) Ecological systems exhibit balance and resilience,
(b) Economic production & consumption do not threaten ecological systems,
(c) Governance modes reflect participation and responsiveness,
(d) Institutions demonstrate adaptation and feedback.
If, and only if, these conditions hold will a system dispose toward sustainability. (GSSD, 2004)[a]

[a]Global System for Sustainable Development (GSSD), http://gssd.mit.edu (accessed June 8, 2010).

of environmental analyses is limited by the quality of the behavioral analysis that it includes" (P. C. Stern, Young, et al. 1992, p. 21). The NRC report also suggested that there is a "need to build stronger links between the natural sciences and the social sciences in efforts to understand global environmental changes and to devise public policies to respond to them in an effective manner" (ibid.). With this in mind, Figure 1.9 attempts to present a holistic view of the drivers, challenges, and solutions for globalization within a context of human needs.

In Section 1.1.2, the argument is made that our perspective of human needs and our view of a fulfilling life is being affected (or put out of balance) by the forces of the market economy (that is, advertising, as well as social competition for conspicuous consumption). As a result, Western society is increasingly becoming a throughput society in which the consumption of products and services (to satisfy needs and wants) supports the growth of the economy. Putting aside the question whether the current forms of consumption are satisfying fundamental physiological and psychological needs, it is possible to identify the social and environmental challenges that are often associated with the unsustainable industrial state (see Figure 1.9).

The first challenge is the need to provide society with adequate and high-quality goods and services—for example, food, health care, transportation, and security. The second, third, fourth, and fifth challenges (discussed below) relate to four environmentally different concerns: (1) ecosystem integrity and the loss of biodiversity; (2) resource depletion; (3) toxic pollution; and (4) climate change. The burden of these environmental problems is felt unequally within nations, among nations, and among generations, leading to concerns for intranational, international, and intergenerational equity. These concerns for equity are often expressed under the heading of "environmental justice." The final two challenges relate to economic and social concerns associated with employment, wages, and economic inequality.

Over the past forty years, the *drivers* of sustainable development have incorporated—to varying degrees and at different times—four environmentally different concerns (see the challenges in Figure 1.9). The first is the disruption of ecosystems and the loss of biological diversity and the indirect effects these have on human health and well-being. This concern was initially raised in the early 1960s when industrial processes and the use of pesticides led to environmental degradation and a loss of wildlife (Carson 1962), and again more recently in the context of endocrine disrupters that affect reproductive health in all species (Colborn, Dumanowski, et al. 1996; Solomon and Schettler 1999). Significant progress has been made in improving industrial and agricultural practices; however, the negative impacts of these sectors still present a problem in both developed and developing countries.*

The second concern relates to the world's finite resources and energy supplies and asks whether there are sufficient resources to fuel the economy in its current form (R. U. Ayres 1978; R. Ayres and Warr 2009; Georgescu-Roegen 1971; D. H. Meadows, D. L. Meadows, et al. 1972). A corollary concern is what the environmental impact will be from using a significant proportion of the existing resources.

The third concern is that toxic pollution directly affects human health and the health of other species (Ashford and Miller 1998; Baskin, Himes, et al. 2001; Chivian, McCally, et al. 1993; Colborn, Dumanowski, et al. 1996; Commoner, Bartlett, et al. 2000; Fagin and Lavelle 1996; Geiser 2001; McCally 1999; Schettler, Solomon, et al. 1999). As scientists began to understand how ecosystems, humans, and other organisms were affected by industrial and agricultural processes, the issue of how toxic chemicals interact with biological systems grew in importance.

---

* Poor environmental standards and underresourced or nonexistent environmental agencies in developing countries mean that environmental problems from industrial processes and the mechanization of agriculture more frequently go unchecked in these regions.

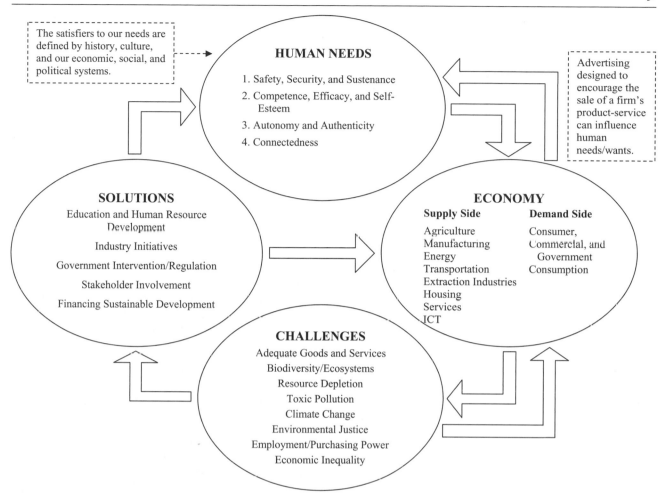

The satisfiers to our needs are defined by history, culture, and our economic, social, and political systems.

**HUMAN NEEDS**

1. Safety, Security, and Sustenance
2. Competence, Efficacy, and Self-Esteem
3. Autonomy and Authenticity
4. Connectedness

Advertising designed to encourage the sale of a firm's product-service can influence human needs/wants.

**SOLUTIONS**

Education and Human Resource Development

Industry Initiatives

Government Intervention/Regulation

Stakeholder Involvement

Financing Sustainable Development

**ECONOMY**

**Supply Side**
Agriculture
Manufacturing
Energy
Transportation
Extraction Industries
Housing
Services
ICT

**Demand Side**
Consumer,
Commercial, and
Government
Consumption

**CHALLENGES**

Adequate Goods and Services
Biodiversity/Ecosystems
Resource Depletion
Toxic Pollution
Climate Change
Environmental Justice
Employment/Purchasing Power
Economic Inequality

FIGURE 1.9: DRIVERS, CHALLENGES, AND SOLUTIONS FOR GLOBALIZATION WITHIN A CONTEXT OF HUMAN NEEDS

The final concern is that greenhouse gases from anthropocentric (human-driven) sources are leading to a disruption of the global climate (International Climate Change Task Force 2005; IPCC 2001; Schmidheiny 1992). Scientists predict that these gases will cause the globally averaged surface air temperature to increase 1.8°C to 4.0°C by 2090–2099 relative to 1990–1999, and the globally averaged sea level to rise 1.1–2.9m to 2.4–6.4m by 2090–2099, respectively (IPCC 2007), with consequent dramatic changes in weather, droughts, and floods. Such scenarios have led to the acknowledgment that immediate action must be taken to minimize the significant long-term financial and social impacts of climate change (N. Stern 2007).

The first, third, and fourth environmental concerns are connected with the unintended effects of human development/growth, while the second deals with increasing shortages of resources needed to fuel development/growth.

It is noteworthy that the seeds of each of the four environmental concerns seem to have been planted during the 1960s and 1970s. The 1960s decade was the era when the destruction of ecosystems was recognized as a significant problem in the United States. The other three environmental concerns began to emerge to varying degrees during the 1970s.* In the 1980s, chemical toxicity began to be downplayed as the chemical industry itself started to point the finger at climate change as the most important environmental problem, almost to the exclusion of toxicity. The 1980s also mark a turning point when nations

---

* The Stockholm Conference on the Human Environment in 1972 brought the topics of ecosystem integrity, biological diversity, and human health and the issue of ecological and resource limits to growth to the attention of the international community. Although the conference did raise the potential problem of toxic substances in its Action Plan, this third environmental concern remained the focus of national legislation during the 1970s. The passage of the 1976 Toxic Substances Control Act in the United States is a prime example. Toward the end of the 1970s, the international community began to discuss the related concerns of ozone depletion and greenhouse gas emissions—the fourth environmental concern. However, it was not until the second half of the 1980s and the 1990s that international action was taken to address ozone depletion and global climate change, respectively.

began to recognize that their environmental problems extended beyond national boundaries and were having impacts on a global scale. This realization spurred the formation of an international environmental agenda, and the actions taken in the following two decades as a result of this agenda can be considered the first attempt at global environmental governance (Speth 2003).

A detailed discussion of the historical evolution of the four environmental concerns reveals that different environmental groups and nations have prioritized the concerns at different times (see Chapter 2). Political agendas are almost always focused on one or two of the four major environmental concerns to the exclusion of the others. Such a nonintegrated planning approach means that nation-states and the international community have been able to create only partial solutions to growing environmental problems.* This situation is further exacerbated by the fact that each nation is at a different level of development and therefore has different needs, resulting in different political agendas. In addition, even if two nations are alike from a development perspective, their values and beliefs might lead to disagreement over what constitutes an *appropriate* solution.

What is perhaps most striking about the current conceptualization of sustainable development is the inadequate treatment of employment. For example, McEntire (2005) provides a succinct review of many of the publications and events that are commonly associated with environmental sustainability; however, like many commentators on the subject, he does not identify employment as an important aspect. The reason for this is the strong emphasis given to environmental challenges at the 1972 Stockholm and 1992 Rio conferences, which effectively locked sustainability thinking into an environment and development (that is, economic) framework. Early expressions of sustainability in terms of working conditions and economic welfare do exist—for example, in the 1944 Declaration of Philadelphia developed at the creation of the International Labour Organization (ILO)—but these have yet to be formally integrated into the environmental sustainability perspective. The separation and isolation of these approaches to development must obviously be bridged for a successful modern approach to sustainable development. One step toward this objective is to highlight several connec-

tions between the 1972 Stockholm Declaration and the 1944 Declaration of Philadelphia.

The Stockholm Declaration focuses on the preservation and improvement of the human *living* environment. Several of the key principles of the declaration are shown in Table 1.7, which organizes them according to Dernbach's (1998, 2004) five components of sustainable development: peace and security; economic development; social development; national governance that ensures peace and development; and environmental protection measures. In contrast, the Declaration of Philadelphia, developed by the ILO more than twenty years earlier, was adopted to enhance the condition of the human *working* environment. These two declarations provide the major intellectual underpinnings of the concept of sustainable development.

The Declaration of Philadelphia expands the aims and purposes of the ILO "based on the relationship between labor and social, and economic and financial problems" and outlines the principles that should guide the national policies of its members (Bartolomei de la Cruz, von Potobsky, et al. 1996, p. 5).† A core belief behind the Declaration of Philadelphia is that peace can be achieved only if it is based on "social justice," a concept that is much broader than "human rights" and focuses on human aspirations as a struggle between the individual and the state (Bartolomei de la Cruz, von Potobsky, et al. 1996). Social justice is defined in terms of human values and aspirations: "All human beings, irrespective of race, creed or sex, have the right to pursue both their material well-being and their spiritual development in conditions of freedom and dignity, of economic security and equal opportunity."[19] In addition, achieving these conditions "must constitute the central aim of national and international policy," and these "policies and measures, in particular those of an economic and financial character," should be assessed against the fundamental objective of social justice.[20]

The notion of social justice supports the fundamental principles on which the ILO was based, namely, that

(a) labour is not a commodity;
(b) freedom of expression and of association are essential to sustained progress;

---

* Indeed, all "environmental" problems are related. Large transformations of materials and use of energy create resource shortages, toxic pollution, and greenhouse gases that lead to climate change and the destruction of ecosystems and biodiversity.

† On November 1, 1945, all members of the UN automatically became members of the International Labour Organization (ILO). In addition, any nation-state that subsequently joined the UN could also become a member of the ILO if it accepted the obligations under the ILO's Constitution. States that were not members of the UN could join the ILO by a majority vote of the ILO Conference (Bartolomei de la Cruz, von Potobsky, et al. 1996).

**TABLE 1.7: DERNBACH'S (1998) FIVE COMPONENTS OF SUSTAINABLE DEVELOPMENT AND THE PRINCIPLES OF THE STOCKHOLM AND RIO DECLARATIONS**

| COMPONENT OF SUSTAINABLE DEVELOPMENT | PRINCIPLES OF THE STOCKHOLM DECLARATION[a] | PRINCIPLES OF THE RIO DECLARATION[b] |
|---|---|---|
| Peace and security | Principle 26—Man and his environment must be spared the effects of nuclear weapons and all other means of mass destruction. States must strive to reach prompt agreement, in the relevant international organs, on the elimination and complete destruction of such weapons. | Principle 24—Warfare is inherently destructive of sustainable development. States shall therefore respect international law providing protection for the environment in times of armed conflict and cooperate in its further development, as necessary. Principle 25—Peace, development and environmental protection are interdependent and indivisible. Principle 26—States shall resolve all their environmental disputes peacefully and by appropriate means in accordance with the Charter of the United Nations. |
| Economic development | Principle 8—Economic and social development is essential for ensuring a favorable living and working environment for man and for creating conditions on earth that are necessary for the improvement of the quality of life. Principle 18—Science and technology, as part of their contribution to economic and social development, must be applied to the identification, avoidance and control of environmental risks and the solution of environmental problems and for the common good of mankind. | Principle 5—All States and all people shall cooperate in the essential task of eradicating poverty as an indispensable requirement for sustainable development, in order to decrease the disparities in standards of living and better meet the needs of the majority of the people of the world. Principle 12—States should cooperate to promote a supportive and open international economic system that would lead to economic growth and sustainable development in all countries, to better address the problems of environmental degradation. Trade policy measures for environmental purposes should not constitute a means of arbitrary or unjustifiable discrimination or a disguised restriction on international trade. . . . Principle 25—see above. |
| Social development | Principle 1—Man has the fundamental right to freedom, equality and adequate conditions of life, in an environment of a quality that permits a life of dignity and well-being, and he bears a solemn responsibility to protect and improve the environment for present and future generations. In this respect, policies promoting or perpetuating apartheid, racial segregation, discrimination, colonial and other forms of oppression and foreign domination stand condemned and must be eliminated. Principle 16—Demographic policies which are without prejudice to basic human rights and which are deemed appropriate by Governments concerned should be applied in those regions where the rate of population growth or excessive population concentrations are likely to have adverse effects on . . . the human environment and impede development. Principles 8 and 18—see above. | Principle 1—Human beings are at the centre of concerns for sustainable development. They are entitled to a healthy and productive life in harmony with nature. Principle 8—To achieve sustainable development and a higher quality of life for all people, States should reduce and eliminate unsustainable patterns of production and consumption and promote appropriate demographic policies. Principle 20—Women have a vital role in environmental management and development. Their full participation is therefore essential to achieve sustainable development. Principle 21—The creativity, ideals and courage of the youth of the world should be mobilized to forge a global partnership in order to achieve sustainable development and ensure a better future for all. Principle 25—see above. |
| National governance that ensures peace and development | Principle 13—In order to achieve a more rational management of resources and thus to improve the environment, States should adopt an integrated and coordinated approach to their development planning so as to ensure that development is compatible with the need to protect and improve [the] environment for the benefit of their population. Principle 14—Rational planning constitutes an essential tool for reconciling any conflict between the needs of development and the need to protect and improve the environment. | Principle 3—The right to development must be fulfilled so as to equitably meet developmental and environmental needs of present and future generations. Principle 10—Environmental issues are best handled with participation of all concerned citizens, at the relevant level. At the national level, each individual shall have appropriate access to information concerning the environment that is held by public authorities, including information on hazardous materials and activities in their communities, and the opportunity to |

(continued)

**TABLE 1.7** (continued)

| COMPONENT OF SUSTAINABLE DEVELOPMENT | PRINCIPLES OF THE STOCKHOLM DECLARATION[a] | PRINCIPLES OF THE RIO DECLARATION[b] |
|---|---|---|
| | **Principle 15**—Planning must be applied to human settlements and urbanization with a view to avoiding adverse effects on the environment and obtaining maximum social, economic and environmental benefits for all. In this respect projects which are designed for colonialist and racist domination must be abandoned.<br><br>**Principle 17**—Appropriate national institutions must be entrusted with the task of planning, managing or controlling the environmental resources of States with a view to enhancing environmental quality.<br><br>**Principles 16 and 26**—see above. The preamble to the declaration also reinforces the importance of national governance. | participate in decision-making processes. States shall facilitate and encourage public awareness and participation by making information widely available. Effective access to judicial and administrative proceedings, including redress and remedy, shall be provided.<br><br>**Principle 11**—States shall enact effective environmental legislation. Environmental standards, management objectives and priorities should reflect the environmental and development context to which they apply. Standards applied by some countries may be inappropriate and of unwarranted economic and social cost to other countries, in particular developing countries.<br><br>**Principle 13**—States shall develop national law regarding liability and compensation for the victims of pollution and other environmental damage. States shall also cooperate in an expeditious and more determined manner to develop further international law regarding liability and compensation for adverse effects of environmental damage caused by activities within their jurisdiction or control to areas beyond their jurisdiction.<br><br>**Principle 22**—Indigenous people and their communities and other local communities have a vital role in environmental management and development because of their knowledge and traditional practices. States should recognize and duly support their identity, culture and interests and enable their effective participation in the achievement of sustainable development. |
| **Environmental protection measures** | **Principle 2**—The natural resources of the earth, including the air, water, land, flora and fauna and especially representative samples of natural ecosystems, must be safeguarded for the benefit of present and future generations through careful planning or management, as appropriate.<br><br>**Principle 3**—The capacity of the earth to produce vital renewable resources must be maintained and, wherever practicable, restored or improved.<br><br>**Principle 4**—Man has a special responsibility to safeguard and wisely manage the heritage of wildlife and its habitat, which are now gravely imperilled by a combination of adverse factors. Nature conservation, including wildlife, must therefore receive importance in planning for economic development.<br><br>**Principle 5**—The non-renewable resources of the earth must be employed in such a way as to guard against the danger of their future exhaustion and to ensure that benefits from such employment are shared by all mankind.<br><br>**Principle 6**—The discharge of toxic substances or of other substances and the release of heat, in such quantities or concentrations as to exceed the capacity of the environment to render them harmless, must be halted in order to ensure that serious or irreversible damage is not inflicted upon ecosystems. The just struggle of the peoples of ill[-affected] countries against pollution should be supported. | **Principle 4**—In order to achieve sustainable development, environmental protection shall constitute an integral part of the development process and cannot be considered in isolation from it.<br><br>**Principle 7**—States shall cooperate in a spirit of global partnership to conserve, protect and restore the health and integrity of the Earth's ecosystem. In view of the different contributions to global environmental degradation, States have common but differentiated responsibilities. The developed countries acknowledge the responsibility that they bear in the international pursuit of sustainable development in view of the pressures their societies place on the global environment and of the technologies and financial resources they command.<br><br>**Principles 8, 11, and 13**—see above.<br><br>**Principle 14**—States should effectively cooperate to discourage or prevent the relocation and transfer to other States of any activities and substances that cause severe environmental degradation or are found to be harmful to human health.<br><br>**Principle 15**—In order to protect the environment, the precautionary approach shall be widely applied by States according to their capabilities. Where there are threats of serious or irreversible damage, lack of full scientific certainty shall not be used as a reason for postponing cost-effective measures to prevent environmental degradation. |

| COMPONENT OF SUSTAINABLE DEVELOPMENT | PRINCIPLES OF THE STOCKHOLM DECLARATION[a] | PRINCIPLES OF THE RIO DECLARATION[b] |
| --- | --- | --- |
| | **Principle 7**—States shall take all possible steps to prevent pollution of the seas by substances that are liable to create hazards to human health, to harm living resources and marine life, to damage amenities or to interfere with other legitimate uses of the sea. | **Principle 16**—National authorities should endeavour to promote the internalization of environmental costs and the use of economic instruments, taking into account the approach that the polluter should, in principle, bear the cost of pollution, with due regard to the public interest and without distorting international trade and investment. |
| | | **Principle 17**—Environmental impact assessment, as a national instrument, shall be undertaken for proposed activities that are likely to have a significant adverse impact on the environment and are subject to a decision of a competent national authority. |
| | | **Principle 18**—States shall immediately notify other States of any natural disasters or other emergencies that are likely to produce sudden harmful effects on the environment of those States. Every effort shall be made by the international community to help States so afflicted. |
| | | **Principle 19**—States shall provide prior and timely notification and relevant information to potentially affected States on activities that may have a significant adverse transboundary environmental effect and shall consult with those States at an early stage and in good faith. |
| | | **Principle 23**—The environment and natural resources of people under oppression, domination and occupation shall be protected. |
| | | **Principles 25 and 26**—see above. |

[a] Principles 9, 10, 11, 12, 19, 20, 21, 22, 23, 24, and 25 of the Stockholm Declaration are not included in the table because they do not fit within any of the categories listed.

[b] Principles 2, 6, 9, and 27 of the Rio Declaration are not included in the table because they do not fit within any of the categories listed.

(c)  poverty anywhere constitutes a danger to prosperity everywhere,

(d)  the war against want requires to be carried on with unrelenting vigor within each nation, and by continuous and concerted international effort in which the representatives of workers and employers, enjoying equal status with those of governments, join with them in free discussion and democratic decision with a view to the promotion of the common welfare.[21]

In concert with the Stockholm Declaration, the Declaration of Philadelphia supports economic and social development and the creation of a stable international market. In particular, it calls for international and national "measures to expand production and consumption, to avoid severe economic fluctuations to promote the economic and social advancement of the less developed regions of the world [see Principle 8 from the Stockholm Declaration], to assure greater stability in world prices of primary products [see Principle 10 from the Stockholm Declaration[22]], and to promote a high and steady volume of international trade."[23] However, whereas the Declaration of Philadelphia explicitly links development concerns to human welfare, including the protection of workers in all occupations, the Stockholm Declaration links such concerns to the protection and improvement of the natural environment. Hence, taken together, the declarations protect both aspects of the human environment—that in which we *live* and that in which we *work*.

There is also a positive tension between the two declarations with regard to economic growth. The Declaration of Philadelphia calls for the expansion of the international economy to improve human welfare and to create more jobs,* but the Stockholm

---

*       This position was recently reaffirmed in a report by the ILO, which suggests that globalization's "potential for good is immense. . . . Wisely managed, [the global market economy] can deliver unprecedented material progress, generate more productive

Declaration qualifies this by stating that economic development should occur in such a way that the environment is protected. In many ways it is surprising that it took the international community so long to connect these two different strains of human welfare—employment and a healthy environment—with economic development.

The 1992 Rio Declaration reaffirmed and built on the 1972 Stockholm Declaration. Although some of the principles included in these two declarations cover the same subject matter—compare the principles in Table 1.7—the Rio Declaration effectively broadened the notion of "conventional development" or "ecodevelopment"* to "sustainable development" by integrating environmental protection into the development process. Principles 3 and 4 of the declaration speak directly to this end. For a critical discussion of the Rio Declaration, see Box 2.1 in Chapter 2.

If one considers the 1972 Stockholm and 1992 Rio declarations alongside the 1944 Declaration of Philadelphia and other relevant documents such as Agenda 21, the positive tensions generated between these instruments begin to provide a more robust and comprehensive formulation of the notion of sustainable development.[†]

More recently, the most significant effort to integrate employment into a development strategy has been occurring within the European Union (EU). In 2010, the EU launched Europe 2020, the next step or successor of the EU Lisbon Strategy that was created to make "growth" and "employment" the main development objectives of the European community within the context of a sustainable environment. Europe 2020 is the next evolution of the strategy that

focuses on making Europe a smart (knowledge-based), sustainable, and inclusive economy. See Section 1.5 below for a discussion of Europe 2020 and how this is likely to impact the EU's progress toward sustainable development.

To return to Figure 1.9, the environmental problems discussed in detail above occur from activities within the supply side of the economy that are driven by consumer, commercial, and governmental demands (or needs).[‡] In addition to these problems, there are social problems that result from industrial activities—in particular, from rapid technological change and globalization (see Chapter 5). For example, the creation of global communication networks and the spread of industrial capacity are changing the international division of labor, affecting the amount, security, and skill of employment and also the conditions of work and purchasing power. In addition, economic inequality that arises through inadequate and unequal purchasing power within and between nations remains an important problem of our time.

The solutions to these environmental and social problems are likely to be found in education and human resource development, industry initiatives, government intervention/regulation, stakeholder involvement, and financing for sustainable development, and through changes in the (culturally defined) satisfiers of our basic needs. However, if solutions within these categories are to be successful, they must address a number of fundamental problems within the industrial state (Ashford 2004). Some of these problems are presented in Table 1.8 along with recommended solutions.

In addition to the industrial state, as the international economy continues to expand and reach deeper into untapped/underdeveloped regions of the

---

and better jobs for all, and contribute significantly to reducing world poverty" (WCSDG 2004, p. x). For a discussion of how globalization affects employment, see Section 5.2 in Chapter 5.

* The concept of ecodevelopment was a precursor to sustainable development. Its objective was to achieve sustainability at the local or regional scale by responding to the potentials of the area involved, using available natural resources in a rational/ecologically sound manner, and working with indigenous technology styles (UNEP 1975). An important idea central to ecodevelopment was *self-reliance* (I. Sachs 1976, 1984), which ran counter to the forces of rapid technological change and globalization that ultimately redefined ecodevelopment as sustainable development during the 1980s. Today, many scholars argue that economic globalization is producing the exact opposite results of those promised (IFG 2002; Mander and Goldsmith 2000). As an alternative, these opponents of trade liberalization call for a return to forms of development that revitalize democracy, basic human rights, local self-sufficiency, and ecological sustainability—arguably the core principles of ecodevelopment.

† See Chapter 2 for a discussion of the Stockholm, Rio, and Philadelphia declarations and important documents such as Agenda 21.

---

‡ In economics, the term "demand" refers to *effective demand*, or the *ability to pay*, and not to human needs, however urgent and acute (Gilpin 2000). Thus the 2.5 to 3 billion people on earth with virtually no purchasing power (less than $2 per day PPP; WBG 2002) are not represented by the "economy" depicted in Figure 1.9. Because these people have no real role in the "economy," it follows that they cannot have played a direct role in causing the environmental impacts that result from economic activity. However, with the possible exception of toxic pollution, it is understood that poverty (like economic activity) can also affect biodiversity/ecosystem health and resource availability and contribute to climate change (all of which are listed in Figure 1.9), although the mechanisms through which the impacts occur are likely to be considerably different. Therefore, it is important to recognize the difference between the environmental impacts caused by *economic activity* and those caused by *poverty*. It can be argued that the former occur as a result of the aggregate choices made by consumers, whereas the latter occur through the actions taken by individuals struggling to survive (i.e., to satisfy their most fundamental human needs).

world, *international institutions* will have an increasingly important role in promoting progress toward sustainable development (see Chapter 10).

Although this chapter has introduced many important ideas incorporated into the concept of sustainable development, what is missing is the historical evolution of how these ideas became central pillars of the concept. This shortcoming is addressed in Chapter 2. By tracking key events, publications, U.S. legislation, and international conventions from the 1960s until 2002, it has been possible to trace the concept of sustainable development from the formation of the U.S. environmental movement in the 1960s to the rise of international concern for the environment (and ecodevelopment) in the 1970s and its final emergence in the 1980s and 1990s. What is perhaps most important is that the concept is still evolving today. We hope that this book will contribute to a better understanding of the concept of sustainable development and shape its future evolution.

## 1.5 THE EUROPEAN UNION'S STRATEGY FOR SUSTAINABLE DEVELOPMENT: THE LISBON STRATEGY AND EUROPE 2020

In March 2000, the Council of the European Union established the goal of making Europe by 2010 "the most competitive and dynamic knowledge-based economy in the world, capable of sustainable economic growth with more and better jobs and greater social cohesion" (Eurofound 2006a, p. 1).[24] The Lisbon Strategy, as it was known, is of particular interest because it represents perhaps one of the most serious attempts to create a strategy for sustainable development. Although the initial intention of the strategy was clear, its ability to initiate change within Europe was found wanting. A midpoint review of progress toward achieving the strategy's objectives concluded that the "disappointing delivery is due to an overloaded agenda, poor coordination and conflicting priorities" (European Commission High Level Group 2004, p. 6). The lack of urgency given to the strategy by EU member states was also seen as a major barrier to progress.

Against the backdrop of continued growth in the United States and Asia, in 2005 a new urgency was placed on a more streamlined Lisbon Strategy as a model for "growth and employment." The rationale behind the new approach was that "improved economic growth and increased employment provide the means to sustain social cohesion and environmental sustainability. In their turn, social cohesion and environmental sustainability can contribute to a higher growth and employment" (European Commission High Level Group 2004, p. 6). To achieve its objectives, the revised Lisbon Strategy promoted two types of structural reform. The first was to create a liberalized internal European market. The second focused on developing factors that promote endogenous growth—that is, R&D that can enhance scientific, technological, and intellectual capital and

**TABLE 1.8: FUNDAMENTAL PROBLEMS WITH THE INDUSTRIAL STATE AND THEIR SOLUTIONS**

| PROBLEMS WITH THE INDUSTRIAL STATE | SOLUTION |
|---|---|
| The fragmentation and inadequacy of the knowledge base leads to a myopic understanding of problems and the creation of insufficient single-purpose or narrowly-focused solutions by technical and political decision-makers. | Adopt an integrative (or transdisciplinary) approach to problem framing and to the creation of solutions to environmental and social problems and apply the precautionary principle when the negative impacts of a human activity are uncertain. |
| There is inequality of access to economic and political power. | Establish mechanisms for democratic, participatory governance. |
| There is a tendency to govern industrial systems using old ideas—that is, "gerontocracy" | Stimulate technological, organizational, institutional, and social innovation.[a] |
| Markets fail to price the adverse consequences of industrial activity correctly. | Internalize as far as possible the external environmental and social costs. |
| Markets fail to deal sensibly with social and environmental problems that span long time horizons, which pricing and markets are inherently incapable of solving. | Transcend markets and implement far-sighted and integrated government policies. |

[a] These four types of innovation can be defined in the following manner (Ashford 2005; Rennings 2000). *Technological innovation* is defined as the first commercially successful application of a new technical idea (or an invention). *Organizational innovation* is defined as changes in and among various organizational aspects of a firm's *functions*, such as R&D and product development, marketing, environmental and governmental affairs, industrial relations, worker health and safety, and customer and community relations. *Institutional innovation* is defined as changes in and among various legal norms, as well as institutions/departments within a government, with regard to their *functions* and *goals* and the working relationships and shared visions among them. *Social innovation* is defined as changes in the *preferences* of consumers, citizens, and workers for the types of products, services, environmental quality, leisure activities, and work they require, and changes in the *processes* by which the new preferences are selected. Social innovations can alter both the *supply* and *demand* for products/services.

Source: Adapted from Ashford (2004).

improved levels of education. The revised strategy also established two headline targets: (1) an annual total (public and private) investment of 3 percent of Europe's GDP in R&D by 2010, and (2) an overall employment rate (that is, the proportion of Europe's working-age population in employment) of 70 percent by the same time (Blanke 2006). In addition to the emphasis on growth and employment, the Lisbon Strategy also anticipated a revision of the rules that govern the EU's twenty-seven members, rules that were previously designed for the EU 15. In December 2007, the revised Treaty of Lisbon (not to be confused with the Lisbon Strategy) was signed by EU leaders. It then needed to be ratified by all twenty-seven member states by the deadline of January 1, 2009. After an initial setback when Ireland rejected the treaty in a public referendum in 2008, a revised treaty was ratified by a 2:1 margin by Ireland in October 2009. The treaty was signed by the requisite number of Member States on November 3, 2009.

The emphasis the Lisbon Strategy gives to "growth" (via industrial competitiveness) and "employment" raises some important questions about sustainable development. In 2001, the EU's Strategy for Sustainable Development was adopted in Gothenburg. The SSD adopted a long-term perspective to development and included a wider array of issues such as pandemic diseases, whereas the Lisbon Strategy had a more medium-term focus of ten years and was EU centric. The formulation of the SSD added an environmental dimension to the initial Lisbon commitments, creating a framework to address environmental, social, and economic concerns in an integrated way.

This expansion of the Lisbon Strategy agenda also began to blur the distinction between the two strategies. The reformulation of the Lisbon Strategy toward "competitiveness" in 2005 raised some concerns that social and environmental policies could be weakened if they are found to hinder this objective (Hochfeld, Schmitt, et al. 2006; Wolff, Schmitt, et al. 2006). Others similarly question whether social and competitive policies designed to create a "competitive social market economy" would actually support or conflict with each other (Eurofound 2006a). It seems that a high degree of competitiveness can coexist with extensive and expensive social models, but this situation is limited to the Nordic countries within the EU (ibid.). The critical question is whether the Nordic model—which is based on high levels of civic responsibility and institutional trust—can be transferred to other EU nations.

The ability of the original Lisbon Strategy, and its successor Europe 2020, to promote sustainable development will ultimately depend on how EU countries approach competitiveness. Clearly, any weakening of environmental and social policies in the name of industrial competitiveness would be a step backward. Therefore, what is needed is an approach to policy design (and development more broadly) that seeks "substantive" (or simultaneous) improvements in environmental, social, and economic performance (Dernbach 2003). One approach that has significant potential is the creative use of government policy as a mechanism to encouraging disrupting or radical technological (as well as political and social) changes. We explore this idea in detail in Chapters 8 and 9.

The formulation of Europe 2020 occurred within the aftermath of the 2008 financial crisis, which highlighted the fact that the Lisbon Strategy had "been too inward-looking, focusing on preparing the EU for globalization rather than trying to shape it" (EC 2010a, p. 7). As a result, the EU has taken a proactive stance within the G20 in an effort to shape the new post-crisis financial architecture under development. This new role for the EU, to shape the future through leadership and example, is also reflected in the European Commission's consultation document on the future Europe 2020 strategy:

> Europe needs a strengthened and competitive industrial base, a modern service sector and a thriving agriculture, rural economy, and maritime sector. As "first mover" in building this society of the future, Europe can derive important benefits by developing competitive, innovative products, rolling out the infrastructures of the future, entering new markets and creating new, high-quality jobs. But the benefits go much wider. A Europe that is open to the world will continue to be a model for others to follow, projecting its values and fostering stronger labour, environmental, and safety standards around the globe" (EC 2009, p. 4).

We believe such a vision of a future Europe could be achieved by following the strategies discussed and promoted throughout this text (see especially Chapter 13).

Europe 2020 retains the growth and jobs focus of the Lisbon Strategy. The growth dimension is divided into two priority areas of Smart and Sustainable Growth. The Smart Growth priority focuses on (1) education, (2) research and innovation to create products and services that create jobs and address major social challenges, and (3) laying the foundation for a digital society. The Sustainable Growth priority focuses on creating a resource efficient, greener, and more competitive economy. A critical component of this priority is the EU's Industrial Policy for the Globalization Era (EC 2010b). The policy centers around creating a competitive economy—which nurtures small businesses—that delivers on the promise of sustainability. The policy calls for a broad evaluation of the competitiveness effects of all other policy initiatives in sectors such as transportation and energy, and single-market and trade policies. It is likely that such an approach will promote the co-optimization (or integration) of policy between economic sectors, but care must be taken not to compromise labor in the pursuit of competiveness.*

The third priority of Europe 2020 is Inclusive Growth, described as promoting a high-employment economy delivering economic, social, and territorial cohesion. The first initiative in this priority area is directed at developing new worker skills and jobs through education/training and modernizing labor markets, respectively. The modernization of labor markets, embodied in the term "flexicurity," is discussed in more detail below. The second initiative is to establish an EU platform against poverty that ensures a social safety net is provided for those people experiencing poverty and social exclusion.

Europe 2020 incorporates a more nuanced approach to EU-level performance targets; moving away from the one-size fits all indicators of the Lisbon Strategy (EC 2010a). The significant differences in starting positions and capabilities of EU member states (as evidenced by the range of HDI values shown in Table 1.1 in Section 1.1.1) means that any development agenda needs to account for what is realistic and fair in any given context. This approach should also promote greater national ownership of Europe 2020, which was a problem with the Lisbon Strategy. Europe 2020 has established five targets (below) that are to be translated into national targets in each EU country, reflecting their different situations and circumstances.[25]

1. Employment
   — 75% of the 20–64-year-olds to be employed
2. R&D/innovation
   — 3% of the EU's GDP (public and private combined) to be invested in R&D/innovation
3. Climate change/energy
   — greenhouse gas emissions 20% (or even 30%, if a satisfactory international agreement can be achieved to follow Kyoto) lower than 1990
   — 20% of energy from renewables
   — 20% increase in energy efficiency
4. Education
   — Reducing school drop-out rates below 10%
   — at least 40% of 30–34-year-olds completing third level education (or equivalent)
5. Poverty/social exclusion
   — at least 20 million fewer people in or at risk of poverty and social exclusion

An important policy development under the Lisbon Strategy that will be continued in Europe 2020, is the notion of "flexicurity":

Flexicurity represents a new way of looking at flexibility and security in the labour market. The concept recognises that globalisation and technological progress are rapidly changing the needs of workers and enterprises. Companies are under increasing pressure to adapt and develop their products and services more quickly; while workers are aware that company restructurings no longer occur incidentally but are becoming a fact of everyday life. Rather than protecting a job, which will ultimately disappear, flexicurity starts from the assumption that it is the worker who needs protection and assistance to either transition successfully in his/her existing job or move to a new job. Flexicurity therefore provides the right reform agenda to help create more adaptable labour markets and in particular to tackle often substantial labour market segmentation (EC 2010a, pp. 16–17).

The modernization of the labor market to promote the notion of flexicurity is one component of Europe 2020 that could seriously undermine the ability of the EU economy to sustain well-paid, meaningful, and secure employment. Rather than flexicurity, we advocate "flex-capacity," which means that workers have a broader set of training and skills to enable them to adapt and to innovate—in a technological and organization sense (see Chapter 7)—to allow a firm to remain completive in a dynamic global economy without shedding its workers. In this approach, workers have broadly applicable skills and capabilities and comprise *the* competitive advantage of firms operating at the leading edge of an economy. While some workers may require assistance to transition between employment, a European workforce that is formed upon the notion of flex-capacity should have a *natural* ability to adjust to changing circumstances in innovative ways. This has serious implications for how we educate people for work.

---

* See Section 1.9 for a discussion of the need to think holistically when designing policy to promote sustainable development.

The dynamic forces of rapid technological change and globalization (that is, the integration of markets for goods, services, and finance both within and outside the EU) are likely to present challenges for increasing and maintaining employment levels. As production relocates to areas of comparative advantage and innovative and efficient companies gain market share, the pressure on companies to become competitive increases. The way in which the EU defines or approaches the idea of competitiveness is, therefore, important. There is a significant difference between the idea of competitiveness that supports the effective delivery of essential goods and services to most or all of its citizens, and competitiveness as "competition" that is focused on achieving greater profits, revenues, and market share, often accompanied by unemployment or underutilization of human capital on a wide scale. A focus on competition, rather than economic welfare of a nation's citizens, is likely to promote economies of scale and greater throughput and be less concerned with the nature of the goods and services that are being provided—and to whom. It also relies more on the market economy for the provision of these goods and services, which may fall beyond the reach of many who are unable to afford them.

The growing levels of competition faced by EU-based companies from economic globalization are likely to result in job losses in those industries unable to complete. Although public opinion within the EU about the promise of globalization was once positive, this position has now reversed, with many becoming increasingly concerned as EU jobs are exported overseas (Eurofound 2008). The challenge facing the EU will be whether these concerns will limit policies designed to liberalize the internal market and open it to global competition. A critical factor in the success of the Europe 2020 Strategy will be whether the promotion of competitiveness in the sense of providing domestically-needed goods and services and employment will create new forms of employment that are less susceptible to global competition.

## 1.6 THE REFORMULATION OF SUSTAINABLE DEVELOPMENT AS A PROBLEM OF GLOBAL CLIMATE CHANGE

Anyone new to the concept of sustainable development might be led to believe that the only major environmental concern related to the concept is *global climate change*. In recent years, starting with the Kyoto Protocol in 1997, there has been a dramatic increase in the international visibility of the climate problem. The release of Al Gore's documentary *An Inconvenient Truth*, followed by the award of the 2007 Nobel Peace Prize to him and the International Panel on Climate Change "for their efforts to build up and disseminate greater knowledge about man-made climate change,"[26] did much to raise global concern about the issue. Equally important was the publication of the *Stern Review on the Economics of Climate Change* (known as the *Stern Review*) by the U.K. Treasury on October 30, 2006 (N. Stern 2007). Although the review was not the first economic analysis of climate change (Cline 1992; Mendelsohn, Morrison, et al. 1998; Nordhaus and Boyer 2000), its status as an official government document significantly raised its importance and made it one of the most widely known and debated studies of its kind.

The *Stern Review* focuses on the impact of global climate change on the world economy. More specifically, it argues that if governments fail to take action today, "the overall costs and risks of climate change will be equivalent to losing at least 5 percent of global GDP each year, now and forever. If a wider range of risks and impacts is taken into account, the estimates of damage could rise to 20 percent of GDP or more" (N. Stern 2007, p. vi). The study finds that the potential future impacts of inaction on social and economic systems will be "on a scale similar to those associated with the great wars and the economic depression of the first half of the 20th century" (ibid.). The study concludes by arguing that these impacts could be significantly reduced if 1 percent of global GDP is invested each year in mitigation activities. Such activities include the pricing of carbon (via taxes, carbon trading, and/or regulation), mechanisms to support innovation for low-carbon technologies, and actions to remove perverse incentives or barriers to energy efficiency gains.

The enthusiastic response by many politicians and environmental groups to the *Stern Review* has been tempered somewhat by heavy criticism of the study from several well-known economists (P. Dasgupta 2006; Mendelsohn 2006–2007; Nordhaus 2006; Tol 2006; Tol and Yohe 2006; Yohe 2006; Yohe and Tol 2007). Others, while critical of the study's basic assumptions and analysis, gave more positive commentaries (K. J. Arrow 2007; Neumayer 2007; Weitzman 2007). The concerns with the study tend to center on several key issues. First, the review relies on existing data sources and does not develop any new estimates of the impacts or costs of climate change. Thus it is surprising to some that the review develops numbers that lie far outside the range of estimates found in previously published literature (Mendelsohn 2006–2007; Tol and Yohe 2006).

Second, a dual critique of the science and economic aspects of the *Stern Review* concluded that the study "greatly understates the extent of uncertainty, for there are strict limits to what can be said with assurance about the evolution of complex systems that are not well understood" (Carter, de Freitas, et al. 2007, p. 168). These authors were also greatly concerned about the treatment of sources and evidence, which they perceived as "persistently selective and biased" (ibid., p. 224). Their general opinion of the *Stern Review* is that it is "a vehicle for speculative alarmism" (ibid.).

A final criticism worth mentioning, which is perhaps the most controversial issue, was the *Stern Review*'s selection of a low discount rate.* The study selected a rate that was 0.1 percent above the global rate of growth of consumption. Because the rate of consumption is assumed to increase at 1.3 percent per year, the chosen discount rate was 1.4 percent. This value falls below the conventional range used by many economists when considering measures to mitigate climate change (Weitzman 2001). It is also lower than the discount rates used by HM Treasury, which decline from 3.5 percent (for years 0 to 30) to 1 percent (after 300 years) (HM Treasury 2003). The *Stern Review* argued that selecting a higher discount rate would be unethical because it would reduce the importance given to the welfare of future generations who are likely to bear the brunt of climate change. A higher discount rate would also reduce the pressure for immediate and aggressive action to reduce greenhouse gas emissions. As Mendelsohn (2006–2007, p. 43) comments, "The low discount rate implies far future events are important in the near term."

Although there are clearly reasons to treat the recommendations of the *Stern Review* with caution, this does not detract from the impact the study has had on refocusing government agendas and the actions of environmental and social organizations toward the mitigation of climate change. The problem with the growing momentum behind climate change, however, is that other critical environmental concerns are at risk of being excluded from sustainable development strategies, marginalized, or even exacerbated.† An important argument made in Section 1.4 is that the concern for sustainable development is based on four broad environment-related concerns. The first concern relates to the disruption of ecosystems and the loss of biological diversity and the indirect effects these have on human health and well-being. The second highlights the world's finite resources and energy supplies and raises the question whether there are sufficient resources to fuel the economy in its current form. A corollary concern is what the environmental impact will be from using a significant proportion of the remaining resources. The third concern is that toxic pollution directly affects human health and the health of other species. The final concern is that greenhouse gases from anthropocentric (human-driven) sources are leading to a disruption of the global climate. In this context, it is worrisome that the concern for climate change appears to be dominating the sustainable development debate. That preoccupation also makes it much more difficult to develop coordinated (or, at best, integrated) environmental and social policies to address the four environmental problems.

The point here is not to devalue the significant progress that has been made in raising concern about climate change. It is to make the argument that climate change is one of several critical environmental challenges that must be addressed simultaneously to prevent the unforeseen occurrence of a non-climate-related tipping point (the focus of the next section).

## 1.7 BROADENING OUR AWARENESS OF TIPPING POINTS

A "tipping point" can be described as the point beyond which it becomes extremely difficult (if not impossible) to reverse a negative trend. An alternative way to think about tipping points is to consider the idea of "overshoot"—that is, to inadvertently go beyond a system's limits, creating a situation that is nearly impossible to reverse (see Section 1.3.2 for a discussion of limits to growth and the concept of "overshooting").

The key argument articulated in the previous section is that the current discourse on sustainable development is becoming dominated by concerns about

---

* A discount rate is used to translate future benefits/costs into present-day values. The choice of the discount rate can have a dramatic effect on the benefit/cost estimates used to evaluate the desirability of a policy. Because many government initiatives involve an investment of resources in early periods that generate benefits/costs in later periods, the major effect of discounting is to reduce the magnitude of future benefits/costs. The larger the discount rate, the larger the reduction in future benefits/costs, and vice versa.

---

† Consider, for example, the increased concerns that ethanol and other biofuels are expected to produce toxic air pollutants and also result in a reallocation of food-growing land to growing energy-producing crops.

global climate change. Within the climate-change debate, several possible tipping points have emerged. These include the sudden disintegration of the Greenland and Antarctic ice sheets (Alley, Clark, et al. 2005), the collapse of coral reefs due to "coral bleaching" caused by rising sea temperatures (Knowlton 2001), and the shutting down of the Atlantic thermohaline circulation that conveys warm surface water to northern Europe and returns cold, deep-ocean water south (Vellinga and Wood 2004). Although these potential system collapses are of great concern, there are other tipping points not far on the horizon that deserve equal attention. Examples of these other modes of collapse include the following:

- Limits on the ability of conventional antibiotics and pesticides (through antibiotic and pesticide resistance) to prevent virulent disease and pestilence, leading to a rapid decline in population and food crops

- Damage to reproductive health (through endocrine disruption) to the extent that all species (including humans) no longer reproduce or reproduce with reproductive anomalies, such as sterility and hermaphroditism (Colborn, Dumanowski, et al. 1996; Cordier 2008; Saey 2008)

- The widespread decline of human health due to increasing levels of toxic chemical exposures that cause cancer, autoimmune diseases, neurological harm such as autism, attention-deficit/hyperactivity disorder, and general toxic-induced loss of tolerance (Ashford and Miller 1998; Sasco 2008)

- Significant growth in the incidence of human disease and deaths in regions experiencing rapid population growth, worsening levels of malnutrition, and environmental degradation (D. H. Meadows, Randers, et al. 2004; Pimentel, Cooperstein, et al. 2007)

Supporting or driving these modes of collapse are the processes of rapid technological change and economic globalization. For example, more efficient and affordable transportation systems are increasing the ease with which diseases can be transmitted between populations. The significant growth in trade between regions has also exposed previously healthy populations to new health risk factors (Yach and Bettcher 1998a, 1998b). Indigenous societies that are becoming interconnected with the global economy are now exposed to modern diets, additive products, pharmaceuticals, and toxic products that significantly increase cancer risks (Sasco 2008). In this context, the historic debate between economic development and environmental degradation (questioning the logic of the environmental Kuznets curve—see Section 1.3.2) must be expanded to include the impacts of economic development on human health. This new dimension is different from the impacts of environmental degradation on human health, which could be considered as a negative side effect of industrialization. The concern is that the products and services associated with the current form of industrialization are themselves directly causing harm.

A final mode of possible collapse relates to social systems, such as the global financial system or the ability of the nation-state to provide gainful employment.* Although these tipping points are influenced by external environmental factors, the modes of failure are firmly embedded within social networks. Another example of a "social tipping point" could be increasing social tensions that lead to persistent regional/global conflicts due to increasing shortages of resources such as fresh water or oil (Myers 1993).

## 1.8 THE 2008 FINANCIAL CRISIS AND OPPORTUNITIES FOR RECONCEPTUALIZATION OF THE GROWTH PARADIGM

As this book is being written, the world is experiencing the worst economic crisis since the 1930s. In essence, what the world is facing today is what some would describe as a "Minsky" moment. The late economist Hyman Minsky asserted in his 1986 book *Stabilizing an Unstable Economy* that an extended period of rapid growth, low inflation, low interest rates, and macroeconomic stability did not constitute an equilibrium but bred complacency and an increased willingness to bear risks (Minsky 1986). Instability, in his view, was a hidden element of stability, and an undue faith in unregulated markets, along with securitization, off-balance-sheet financing, and other financial innovations, would create a particularly dangerous and disruptive mix.

Galbraith observed in *A Short History of Financial Euphoria* that "the more obvious features of the speculative episode are manifestly clear to anyone open to understanding . . . and especially so after the fact" (Galbraith 1990, p. 4). On July 19, 2007, the Dow Jones Industrial Average rose above 14,000 points for the first time in its history. Less than a month later, however, the French bank BNP Paribas suspended withdrawals from three of its funds. Accord-

---

* Lester Brown of the Earth Policy Institute also discusses the tipping points related to the world's political system, such as population growth, leading to "failing states" (Brown 2008, pp. 5–6, 18–20).

ing to Krugman, this was the moment "the first great financial crisis of the twenty-first century had begun" (Krugman 2009, p. 165).

The exact characteristics of the 2008 crisis can potentially tempt one to observe that this crisis is like nothing we have ever seen before. This is, after all, what expert figures such as George Soros seem to assert (Soros 2008). Perhaps more accurate observation, however, would lead us to the conclusion that this crisis is exactly like everything we have seen before, only this time simultaneously: a real estate bubble, reminiscent of Japan at the end of the 1980s; a wave of bank runs similar to those of the Great Depression in the early 1930s (but which now mainly involved the "shadow" banking system of derivatives, hedge funds, and the like rather than conventional banking organizations); a liquidity trap in the United States, again similar to what happened in Japan; and finally, a disruption of international capital flows and a wave of currency crises, comparable to what happened in East Asia in the late 1990s (Krugman 2009).

It is important, however, to underline that more than anything else, the 2008 crisis is the outcome of a culmination of problems inherent in the unsustainable nature of the economic system (see especially Stiglitz 2010). Some facts are particularly elucidating. Between 1951 and 1983, consumption as a proportion of GDP remained within the range of 60–64 percent (Walker 2009). However, after 1983, consumption grew to 66 percent in 1990, 68 percent in 1998, 70 percent in 2001, and 71 percent by the end of 2007 (ibid.). It is particularly interesting to observe the evolution of the savings rate and the trade deficit as consumption was increasing. Walker (2009) cites an analysis by Wen and Shimek (2007) that explains that the trade deficit was at a maximum of 1 percent of GDP until 1983, moved to 3 percent in 1986, decreased again during the recession of 1991–1992, and then rose to 5 percent in 2004, where it has remained. At the same time, savings fell from 10 percent of GDP in 1980 to 0.4 percent in 2006, household consumption's share of disposable income grew from 87.5 percent to 95.8 percent, and revolving credit (mainly credit cards) grew from about 2.7 percent of personal income to 9.8 percent of personal income (Walker 2009; Wen and Shimek 2007).

As Wen and Shimek (2007) note, the increase in the trade deficit ($762 billion), the increase in consumption's share of personal income ($802 billion), and the increase in revolving credit outstanding ($800 billion) are strikingly similar to earlier problem periods. The 2008 crisis has, of course, had an effect on these figures; consumption declined by 3.7

percent in the third quarter of 2008, while savings have started moving upward (Walker 2009).* However, contrary to Walker's interpretation, it is not necessary for this short-term response to the crisis to constitute a significant cultural shift, one that would be essential for a transition to a more sustainable economic model.

Apart from the structural shift in consumption, savings, and trade, the U.S. economy has also experienced a growing imbalance in the relationship between business and government, especially during the past thirty years. In the 1950s, Galbraith (1952) coined the term "countervailing power" to describe the idea that in market economies, both government and organized labor must be strong in order to balance the power of large corporations. Galbraith's analysis dictated that economic life was not governed by small firms battling one another through price competition to serve consumers, but by large corporations in oligopolistic markets that had the power to dictate the terms of their engagement with both buyers and suppliers (Auerswald and Acs 2009). Galbraith believed that the dominance of large corporations in the economy would lead to a countervailing response from workers and consumers that would decrease their influence. At the same time, government would be the force responsible for balancing interests in markets and moderating the adverse effects of business cycles (ibid.).

This balance was termed by some policy scholars an "iron triangle." However, it was not meant to last, because the organizational realities of the mid-twentieth century were going to change in the coming decades. In the mid-1970s, rising inflation and unemployment, high energy prices, increasing international competition, and the fall in innovation and productivity were forces that undermined the profitability of large corporations and started changing the balance of the "iron triangle" (Auerswald and Acs 2009). The deregulatory measures of the Reagan administration were the beginning of the end for countervailing power. In the financial industry, deregulation, along with the emergence of information technologies, drove new innovative business models. Although these models had certain positive effects in the short run, their complexity increased, while government supervision eroded.

---

* This element corroborates the fears of those commentators who have a structural preference for infrastructure spending instead of tax cuts. A central irony of the crisis is that the consumption vice becomes a virtue in the Keynesian space because more spending is necessary to come out of the crisis. Increased savings, on the other hand, will be a sine qua non of sustainable development, but this is an "equilibrium" condition, under a different growth regime.

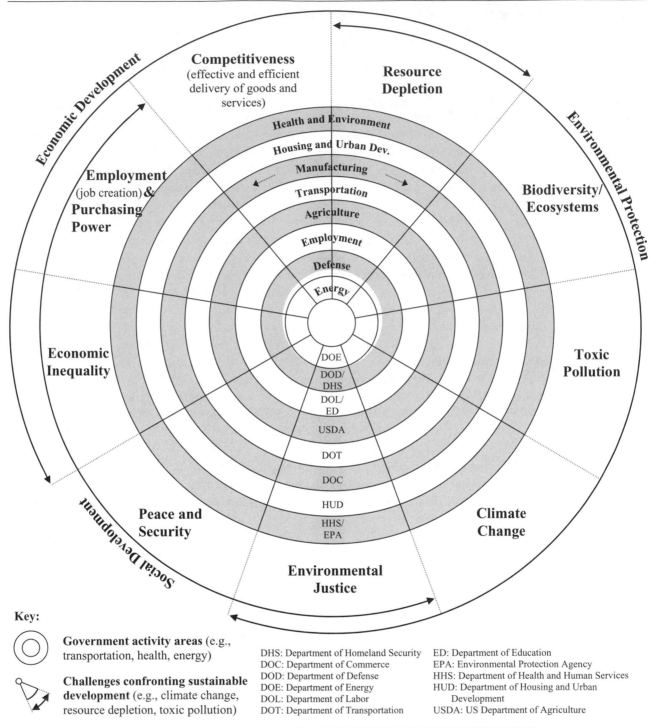

Key:

○ **Government activity areas** (e.g., transportation, health, energy)

▽ **Challenges confronting sustainable development** (e.g., climate change, resource depletion, toxic pollution)

DHS: Department of Homeland Security
DOC: Department of Commerce
DOD: Department of Defense
DOE: Department of Energy
DOL: Department of Labor
DOT: Department of Transportation

ED: Department of Education
EPA: Environmental Protection Agency
HHS: Department of Health and Human Services
HUD: Department of Housing and Urban Development
USDA: US Department of Agriculture

**FIGURE 1.10: GOVERNMENT ACTIVITY AREAS AND CHALLENGES CONFRONTING SUSTAINABLE DEVELOPMENT**

The consequences of that trend have never been more pronounced than in today's financial crisis.*

The 2008 financial crisis presents a challenge to rethink the growth paradigm within the context of

* Of course, the "iron triangle" was probably destined to collapse despite government policy. Galbraith's observation was particularly valid in the 1950s, when large corporations were indeed dominant. However, despite the fact that some corporations are still large today, the economy of the twenty-first century is highly networked and distributed. In most cases, large corpora-

tions are no longer sufficiently economically dominant to dictate the terms of engagement with buyers and suppliers (Auerswald and Acs 2009). As Auerswald and Acs point out, this is most obvious in the fact that government's greatest challenge at the moment is not restraining the biggest firms but keeping them afloat.

environmental and social sustainability. It is toward this goal that the present book is dedicated.*

## 1.9 THE NECESSITY OF SOLVING PROBLEMS ON A COMPREHENSIVE BASIS

Figure 1.10 has been created to help visualize the need to broaden the current discourse on sustainable development to include concerns in addition to global climate change. The figure highlights all four of the critical environmental concerns related to sustainable development. In addition, it captures important social concerns such as the need for peace and security and equality, both in terms of environmental justice and of income. Employment is also placed alongside these concerns, given its critical role in raising purchasing power and providing sufficient income to make essential goods and services accessible to all. The "competitiveness" wedge was included in the diagram to account for the economic challenge of delivering effective and efficient goods and services†—a challenge that is central to the Lisbon Strategy. The rationale is that competitiveness is a critical factor of economic growth and one that is closely related to technological innovation—an issue of direct interest to virtually all government activity areas.

The three arrows that follow the circumference of the outer circle in Figure 1.10 identify which challenges relate to environmental protection, social development, and economic development. Figure 1.10 also highlights the critical need for *integrated decision making* by representing several U.S. federal government activity areas (that is, those areas where government provides basic goods and services) with the major challenges confronting sustainable development. There is no hierarchy to the activity areas shown. Thus those located near the center of the circle are not necessarily more or less important than those located near the edge.

Figure 1.10 shows that focusing on climate change as the major challenge confronting sustainable development ignores the importance of other environ-

mental, social, and economic challenges. In addition, single-purpose policies designed to confront climate change may inadvertently worsen problems in other areas. For example, increasing the percentage of ethanol in gasoline to reduce $CO_2$ emissions might lead to the production of additional toxic air pollutants and to an increased use of pesticides, worsening the toxics problem, as well as raising the cost of food and actually increasing greenhouse emissions through additional land use (Searchinger, Heimlich, et al. 2008). Thus a major advance in confronting sustainable development would be the integration of government decision making to address environmental, social, and economic problems that are not constrained by institutional missions or the fragmentation of activities within government agencies (Hall 2006). Specific recommendations for achieving integration are addressed in the last chapter.

## 1.10 NOTES

1. The Cocoyoc Declaration can be viewed at www.jstor.org/stable/2706353 (accessed June 8, 2010).

2. To gain some insight into the various theories on—or approaches to considering—human needs, see Doyal and Gough (1991); Erikson (1963); Kasser (2002); Maslow (1943); Max-Neef, Elizalde, et al. (1989); R. M. Ryan (1995); and R. M. Ryan and Deci (2000a, 2000b). In addition, see the following websites: University of Rochester, Department of Clinical and Social Sciences in Psychology, *Self Determination Theory, an Approach to Human Motivation and Personality*, www.psych.rochester.edu/SDT/ (accessed June 8, 2010); and George Boeree, *The Ultimate Theory of Personality*, http://webspace.ship.edu/cgboer/conclusions.html (accessed June 8, 2010).

3. See Jha and Murthy (2003) for a critique of the 2002 ESI and Appendix H, "Critiques and Responses," of Esty, Levy, et al. (2005) for a discussion of the strengths and weaknesses of the 2005 ESI.

4. For an insightful discussion of the historical and theoretical foundations of the consumer society and consumerism, see Firat and Dholakia (1998); Krishnan, Harris, et al. (1995); Miles (1998); Miles, Anderson, et al. (2002); and Stearns (2001).

5. See the programs of the European Foundation for the Improvement of Working and Living Conditions (Eurofound) for linkages between work and other life activities, www.eurofound.europa.eu/ (accessed June 8, 2010).

6. The Penn World Table can be accessed from the Center for International Comparisons of Production, University of Pennsylvania, http://pwt.econ.upenn.edu/php_site/pwt_index.php (accessed June 8, 2010).

7. Two classic texts that address the topic of deindustrialization are *The Deindustrialization of America* by Bluestone and Harrison (1982) and *The Second Industrial Divide* by Piore and Sable (1984).

8. For a similar (historical) discussion of whether we are "inventing ourselves out of jobs," see Bix (2000).

9. The data presented by Mishel, Bernstein, et al. (2005) seem to support this position.

10. For critiques of the Department of Health, Education, and Welfare's (HEW) influential report *Work in America*, see Karsh (1974) and Koo (1973).

---

\* See Section 3.6 in Chapter 3 for a discussion of the "new economics."

† The decision to highlight competitiveness as an important issue rather than economic growth is intentional. The basic argument is that focusing on the competitive delivery of goods and services is more likely to lead to long-term economic benefits than a focus on short-term economic growth. See Chapter 7 for a discussion of how technological innovation can enhance competitiveness and lead to economic growth.

11. For more information, see European Foundation for the Improvement of Living and Working Conditions, www.eurofound.europa.eu/ (accessed June 8, 2010).

12. See Working Mother Media, *Working Mothers 100 Best Companies, 2010*, www.workingmother.com/?service=vpage/106 (accessed June 8, 2010).

13. Media Awareness Network, *Marketing and Consumerism—Overview*, www.media-awareness.ca/english/parents/marketing/ (accessed June 8, 2010).

14. Center on Alcohol Marketing and Youth, http://camy.org/ (accessed June 8, 2010).

15. Stanford Encyclopedia of Philosophy, "Intergenerational Justice, Rawls's Just Savings Principle," http://plato.stanford.edu/entries/justice-intergenerational/#RawJusSavPri (accessed June 8, 2010).

16. See U.S. Presidential Executive Order 12898, *Federal Actions to Address Environmental Justice in Minority Populations and Low-Income Populations*, February 11, 1994, www.archives.gov/federal-register/executive-orders/pdf/12898.pdf (accessed June 8, 2010).

17. For a somewhat outdated but important treatment of the environmental effects of technology and globalization, see the classic work of Grübler (1998).

18. See the Center for the Advancement of the Steady State Economy, http://steadystate.org/ (accessed February 10, 2011).

19. The Declaration of Philadelphia, Annex II, (a), www.ilo.org/ilolex/english/iloconst.htm (accessed February 11, 2011).

20. The Declaration of Philadelphia, Section II, (b) and (c).

21. The Declaration of Philadelphia, Section I.

22. Principle 10 of the Stockholm Declaration: "For the developing countries, stability of prices and adequate earnings for primary commodities and raw materials are essential to environmental management, since economic factors as well as ecological processes must be taken into account."

23. The Declaration of Philadelphia, Section IV.

24. See the European Commission's website on the Lisbon Strategy, http://ec.europa.eu/archives/growthandjobs_2009/ (accessed June 3, 2010).

25. Europe 2020, EU-wide targets, http://ec.europa.eu/europe2020/targets/eu-targets/index_en.htm (accessed February 11, 2011).

26. Nobel Foundation, The Nobel Peace Prize 2007, http://nobelprize.org/nobel_prizes/peace/laureates/2007/ (accessed January 14, 2011).

## 1.11 ADDITIONAL READINGS

Bertram, Eva, and Kenneth Sharpe (2000). "Capitalism, Work, and Character." *American Prospect* **11**(20): 44–48.

Daly, Herman (1991). The Steady-State Economy: Alternative to Growthmania. *Steady-State Economics*. Washington, DC, Island Press: 180–194.

Economist (2007). "The End of Cheap Food." *Economist*, December 6.

Pollan, Michael (2007). "Our Decrepit Food Factories." *New York Times*, December 16.

Solow, R. M. (1993). Sustainability: An Economist's Perspective. *Economics of the Environment: Selected Readings*. R. Dorfman and N. S. Dorfman. New York, W. W. Norton: 179–187.

Soros, Gorge (1998). "Toward a Global Open Society." *Atlantic Monthly* **281**(1): 20, 22, 24, 32.

Tukker, Arnold, and Bart Jansen (2006). "Environmental Impact of Products: A Detailed Review of Studies." *Journal of Industrial Ecology* **10**(3): 159–170.

## 1.12 REFERENCES

AARP (2004). *Beyond 50.04: A Report to the Nation on Consumers in the Marketplace*. Washington, DC, AARP.

Abdallah, S., S. Thompson, et al. (2009). The (un)Happy Planet Index 2.0. Why Good Lives Don't Have to Cost the Earth. New Economics Foundation, London.

Acemoglu, D. (2002a). Cross-Country Inequality Trends. NBER Working Paper 8832. National Bureau of Economic Research, Cambridge, MA.

Acemoglu, D. (2002b). "Technical Change, Inequality, and the Labor Market." *Journal of Economic Literature* **40**(1): 7–72.

Ackerman, F., N. R. Goodwin, et al., Eds. (1998). *The Changing Nature of Work*. Washington, DC, Island Press.

Ackerman, F., and L. Heinzerling (2004). *Priceless: On Knowing the Price of Everything and the Value of Nothing*. New York, New Press.

Ackerman, F., D. Kiron, et al., Eds. (1997). *Human Well-Being and Economic Goals*. Frontier Issues in Economic Thought. Washington, DC, Island Press.

Addison, J. T., D. A. Fox, et al. (2000). "Trade Sensitivity, Technology, and Labor Displacement." *Southern Economic Journal* **66**(3): 682–699.

Agyeman, J., R. D. Bullard, et al., Eds. (2003). *Just Sustainabilities: Development in an Unequal World*. Cambridge, MA, MIT Press.

Alkire, S. (2003). The Capability Approach as a Development Paradigm? Material for the training session preceding the 3rd International Conference on the Capability Approach, Pavia, September 7. Available at www.capabilityapproach.com/pubs/461CAtraining_Alkire.pdf (accessed February 11, 2011).

Alkire, S. (2005). Needs and Capabilities. *The Philosophy of Need*. S. Reader. Cambridge, Cambridge University Press: 229–252.

Alley, R. B., P. U. Clark, et al. (2005). "Ice-Sheet and Sea-Level Changes." *Science* **310**(5747): 456–460.

Anderton, R., and P. Brenton (2006). Globalisation and the Labour Market. *Globalisation and the Labour Market: Trade, Technology, and Less-Skilled Workers in Europe and the United States*. R. Anderton, P. Brenton, and J. Whalley. London, Routledge: 1–10.

Archibugi, D., and J. Michie (1997). The Globalisation of Technology: A New Taxonomy. *Technology, Globalisation and Economic Performance*. D. Archibugi and J. Michie. Cambridge, Cambridge University Press: 172–197.

Argyle, M. (2002). *The Psychology of Happiness*. 2nd ed. London, Routledge and Kegan Paul.

Aronowitz, S., and W. Di Fazio (1994). *The Jobless Future" Sci-tech and the Dogma of Work*. Minneapolis, University of Minnesota Press.

Arrow, K., B. Bolin, et al. (1995). "Economic Growth, Carrying Capacity, and the Environment." *Ecological Economics* **15**: 91–95.

Arrow, K. J. (1969). "Classificatory Notes on the Production and Transmission of Technological Knowledge." *American Economic Review* **59**(2): 29–35.

Arrow, K. J. (2007). "Global Climate Change: A Challenge to Policy." *Economists' Voice* **4**(3, Article 2).

Available at www.bepress.com/ev/vol4/iss3/art2/ (accessed February 11, 2011).

Ashford, N. A. (1976). *Crisis in the Workplace: Occupational Disease and Injury*. Cambridge, MA, MIT Press.

Ashford, N. A. (1981). "Alternatives to Cost-Benefit Analysis in Regulatory Decisions." *Annals of the New York Academy of Science* **363**(1): 129–137.

Ashford, N. A. (2004). "Major Challenges to Engineering Education for Sustainable Development: What Has to Change to Make It Creative, Effective, and Acceptable to the Established Disciplines?" *International Journal of Sustainability in Higher Education* **5**(3): 239–250.

Ashford, N. A. (2005). Government and Environmental Innovation in Europe and North America. *Towards Environmental Innovation Systems*. M. Weber and J. Hemmelskamp. Heidelberg, Springer: 159–174. Available at http://dspace.mit.edu/handle/1721.1/41850 (accessed February 11, 2011).

Ashford, N. A., C. Ayers, et al. (1985). "Using Regulation to Change the Market for Innovation." *Harvard Environmental Law Review* **9**(2): 419–466.

Ashford, N. A., and C. C. Caldart (1996). *Technology, Law, and the Working Environment*. Washington, DC, Island Press.

Ashford, N. A., and C. S. Miller (1998). *Chemical Exposures: Low Levels and High Stakes*. New York, Van Nostrand Reinhold.

Ashford, N. A., and K. M. Rest (2001). Public Participation in Contaminated Communities. Cambridge, Center for Technology, Policy, and Industrial Development, Massachusetts Institute of Technology. Available at http://web.mit.edu/ctpid/www/tl/ (accessed February 11, 2011).

Auerswald, P., and Z. Acs (2009). "Defining Prosperity." *American Interest* **4**(5): 4–13.

Autor, D. H., L. F. Katz, et al. (2005). Trends in U.S. Wage Inequality: Re-assessing the Revisionists. NBER Working Paper 11627. Cambridge, MA, National Bureau of Economic Research.

Ayres, R., and B. Warr (2009). *The Economic Growth Engine: How Energy and Work Drive Material Prosperity*. Williston, VT, Edward Elgar.

Ayres, R. U. (1978). Application of Physical Principles to Economics. *Resources, Environment and Economics: Applications of the Materials/Energy Balance Principle*. R. U. Ayres, Ed. New York, Wiley: 37–71.

Ayres, R. U. (1997). "Environmental Market Failures: Are There Any Local Market-Based Corrective Mechanisms for Global Problems?" *Mitigation and Adaptation Strategies for Global Change* **1**: 289–309.

Ayres, R. U. (2006). "Turning Point: The End of Exponential Growth?" *Technological Forecasting and Social Change* **73**: 1188–1203.

Ayres, R. U. (2007). "On the Practical Limits to Substitution." *Ecological Economics* **61**(1): 115–128.

Ayres, R. U. (2008). "Sustainability Economics: Where Do We Stand?" *Ecological Economics* **67**(2): 281–310.

Barbier, E. B. (1997a). "Environmental Kuznets Curve Special Issue: Introduction to the Environmental Kuznets Curve Special Issue." *Environment and Development Economics* **2**(4): 369–381.

Barbier, E. B. (1997b). "Summaries: Introduction to the Environmental Kuznets Curve Special Issue." *Environment and Development Economics* **2**(4): 357–367.

Barnet, R. J. (1993). "The End of Jobs: Employment Is One Thing the Global Economy Is Not Creating." *Harper's Magazine* **287**: 47–52.

Barry, B. (1978). Circumstances of Justice and Future Generations. *Obligations to Future Generations*. R. I. Sikora and B. Barry. Philadelphia, Temple University Press.

Barry, B. (1995). "John Rawls and the Search for Stability." *Ethics* **105**(4): 874–915.

Barry, B. (1999). Sustainability and Intergenerational Justice. *Fairness and Futurity: Essays on Environmental Sustainability and Social Justice*. A. Dobson. Oxford, Oxford University Press: 93–117.

Bartlett, B. (1994). "The High Cost of Turning Green." *Wall Street Journal*, September 14, sec. A, p. 18, col. 13.

Bartolomei de la Cruz, H., G. von Potobsky, et al. (1996). *The International Labour Organization: The International Standards System and Basic Human Rights*. Boulder, CO, Westview Press.

Baskin, L. S., K. Himes, et al. (2001). "Hypospadias and Endocrine Disruption: Is There a Connection?" *Environmental Health Perspectives* **109**(11): 1175–1183.

Beatley, T. (1994). *Ethical Land Use: Principles of Policy and Planning*. Baltimore, Johns Hopkins University Press.

Beaudry, P., and D. A. Green (2002). Changes in U.S. Wages, 1976–2000: Ongoing Skill Bias or Major Technological Change? NBER Working Paper 8787. Cambridge, MA, National Bureau of Economic Research.

Becker, B. (1997). *Sustainability Assessment: A Review of Values, Concepts and Methodological Approaches*. Washington, DC, World Bank.

Beckerman, W. (1992). "Economic Growth and the Environment: Whose Growth? Whose Environment?" *World Development* **20**: 481–496.

Bell, D. (1999). *The Coming of Post-industrial Society: A Venture in Social Forecasting*. New York, Basic Books.

Bell, D. R. (2006). "Political Liberalism and Ecological Justice." *Analyse & Kritik* **28**: 206–222.

Bentham, J. (1970 [1781]). *An Introduction to the Principles of Morals and Legislation*. London, Athlone Press.

Berkhout, P. H. G., J. C. Muskens, et al. (2000). "Defining the Rebound Effect." *Energy Policy* **28**: 425–432.

Bernstein, J., H. Boushey, et al. (2002). *Pulling Apart: A State-by-State Analysis of Income Trends*. Washington, DC, Economic Policy Institute.

Bernstein, J., and L. Mishel (1997). "Has Wage Inequality Stopped Growing?" *Monthly Labor Review* **120**(12): 3–16.

Bertram, E., and K. Sharpe (2000). "Capitalism, Work, and Character." *American Prospect* **11**(20): 44–48.

Bhagwati, J., and V. H. Dehejia (1994). Freer Trade and Wages of the Unskilled—Is Marx Striking Again? *Trade and Wages: Leveling Wages Down?* J. Bhagwati and M. H. Kosters. Washington, DC, AEI Press: 36–75.

Bhattarai, M., and M. Hammig (2004). "Governance, Economic Policy, and the Environmental Kuznets Curve for Natural Tropical Forests." *Environment and Development Economics* **9**: 367–382.

Bidwai, P. (1998). "Triumph of Humanist Reason." *Frontline* **15** (22). Available at www.hinduonnet.com/fline/fl1522/15220120.htm (accessed February 11, 2011).

Bivens, J. L. (2004). Shifting Blame for Manufacturing Job Loss: Effect of Rising Trade Deficit Shouldn't Be Ignored. Briefing Paper 149. Washington, DC, Economic Policy Institute.

Bivens, J. L. (2006). Trade Deficits and Manufacturing Job Loss: Correlation and Causality. Briefing Paper 171. Washington, DC, Economic Policy Institute.

Bix, A. S. (2000). *Inventing Ourselves out of Jobs? America's Debate over Technological Unemployment: 1929–1981.* Baltimore, Johns Hopkins University Press.

Blank, R. M. (1998). Is There a Trade-off between Unemployment and Inequality? No Easy Answers: Labor Market Problems in the United States versus Europe. Public Policy Brief 33. Levy Economics Institute.

Blanke, J. (2006). *The Lisbon Review 2006: Measuring Europe's Progress in Reform.* Geneva, World Economic Forum.

Bleijenberg, A. N. (1995). "Fiscal Measures as Part of a European Policy on Freight Transport." *World Transport Policy and Practice* **1**(2): 40–45.

Bluestone, B. A., and B. Harrison (1982). *The Deindustrialization of America: Plant Closings, Community Abandonment, and the Dismantling of Basic Industry.* New York, Basic Books.

Board on Science Technology and Economic Policy (STEP) (1994). *Investing for Productivity and Prosperity.* Washington, DC, National Research Council.

Bognanno, M. F., M. P. Keane, et al. (2005). "The Influence of Wages and Industrial Relations Environments on the Production Location Decisions of U.S. Multinational Corporations." *Industrial and Labor Relations Review* **58**(2): 171–200.

Boisard, P., D. Cartron, et al. (2003a). *Time and Work: Duration of Work.* Dublin, European Foundation for the Improvement of Living and Working Conditions.

Boisard, P., D. Cartron, et al. (2003b). *Time and Work: Work Intensity.* Dublin, European Foundation for the Improvement of Living and Working Conditions.

Bolt, K., M. Matete, et al. (2002). *Manual for Calculating Adjusted Net Savings.* Washington, DC, World Bank, Environment Department.

Boughton, J. M. (2001). *Silent Revolution: The International Monetary Fund, 1979–1989.* Washington, DC, International Monetary Fund.

Boyd, R. (1972). "World Dynamics: A Note." *Science* **177**: 516–519.

Bradbury, K., and J. Katz (2002). "Issues in Economics: Are Lifetime Incomes Growing More Unequal? Looking at New Evidence on Family Income Mobility." *Regional Review* **12**(4): 2–5.

Briançon, P. (2009). "Oil Surge Is Mixed Blessing for Russian Economy." *Telegraph*, June 18.

Brock, D. W. (1973). "The Theory of Justice." *University of Chicago Law Review* **40**: 486–499.

Brödner, P. (1990). *The Shape of Future Technology: The Anthropocentric Alternative.* London, Springer-Verlag.

Bronfenbrenner, K. (1997). "We'll Close! Plant Closings, Plant-Closing Threats, Union Organizing, and NAFTA." *Multinational Monitor* **18**(3): 8–13.

Bronfenbrenner, K. (2000). Uneasy Terrain: The Impact of Capital Mobility on Workers, Wages, and Union Organizing. Commissioned research paper for the U.S. Trade Deficit Review Commission.

Bronfenbrenner, K., and S. Luce (2004). *The Changing Nature of Corporate Global Restructuring: The Impact of Production Shifts on Jobs in the U.S., China, and around the Globe.* Washington, DC, US-China Economic and Security Review Commission.

Brown, L. R. (1981). *Building a Sustainable Society.* New York, W. W. Norton.

Brown, L. R. (2008). *Plan B 3.0: Mobilizing to Save Civilization.* New York, W. W. Norton.

Brulle, R. B. (2000). *Agency, Democracy, and Nature: The U.S. Environmental Movement from a Critical Theory Perspective.* Cambridge, MA, MIT Press.

Bulard, M. (1999). "Missed Opportunity for Job Creation: What Price the 35-Hour Week?" *Le Monde Diplomatique*, English Edition September 1999. Available at http://mondediplo.com/1999/09/12hours (accessed February 11, 2011).

Canas, A., P. Ferrao, et al. (2003). "A New Environmental Kuznets Curve? Relationship between Direct Material Input and Income per Capita: Evidence from Industrialised Countries." *Ecological Economics* **46**: 217–229.

Cappelli, P. (1998). Rethinking Employment. *The Changing Nature of Work.* F. Ackerman, N. R. Goodwin, L. Dougherty, and K. Gallagher. Washington, DC, Island Press: 189–192.

Card, D., and J. E. DiNardo (2002). "Skill-Biased Technological Change and Rising Wage Inequality: Some Problems and Puzzles." *Journal of Labor Economics* **20**(4): 733–783.

Carr, M., and M. Chen (2004). Globalization, Social Exclusion and Work: With Special Reference to Informal Employment and Gender. Working Paper 20. Geneva, International Labour Office.

Carson, R. (1962). *Silent Spring.* Boston, Houghton Mifflin.

Carter, R. M., C. R. de Freitas, et al. (2007). "The Stern Review: A Dual Critique." *World Economics* **7**(4): 165–232.

Casal, P., and A. Williams (1995). "Rights, Equality and Procreation." *Analyse und Kritik* **17**: 93–116.

Castells, M. (1999). *The Rise of the Network Society.* Oxford, Blackwell Publishers.

Cavlovic, T. A., K. H. Baker, et al. (2000). "A Meta-analysis of Environmental Kuznets Curve Studies." *Agriculture and Resource Economics Review* **29**(1): 32–42.

Center on Alcohol Marketing and Youth (2002). *Overexposed: Youth a Target of Alcohol Advertising in Magazines.* Washington, DC, Georgetown University.

Center on Alcohol Marketing and Youth (2005). *Youth Overexposed: Alcohol Advertising in Magazines, 2001 to 2003.* Washington, DC, Georgetown University.

Chapman, G. (2001). The Intersection of Environmental Planning and Social Justice: Denver's Platte River Greenway.Cambridge, Massachusetts Institute of Technology. Available at http://dspace.mit.edu/handle/1721.1/8686 (accessed February 11, 2011)

Charles, T., and F. Lehner (1998). "Competitiveness and Employment: A Strategic Dilemma for Economic Policy." *Competition and Change* **3**(1/2): 207–236.

Chivian E., M. McCally, et al., Eds. (1993). *Critical Condition: Human Health and the Environment.* Cambridge, MA, MIT Press.

Clark, B., and J. B. Foster (2001). "William Stanley Jevons and the Question of Coal: An Introduction to Jevons's 'Of the Economy of Fuel.'" *Organization and Environment* **14**(1): 93–98.

Clarke, M. (2004). "Widening Development Prescriptions: Policy Implications of an Index of Sustainable Economic Welfare (ISEW) for Thailand." *International Journal of Sustainable Development* **3**(3/4): 262–275.

Cline, W. R. (1992). *Optimal Carbon Emissions over Time: Experiments with the Nordhaus DICE Model.* Washington, DC, Institute for International Economics.

Coase, R. H. (1960). "The Problem of Social Cost." *Journal of Law and Economics* **3**: 1–44.

Cohen, G. A. (1993). "Equality of What? On Welfare, Goods, and Capabilities" in M. Nussbaum and A. Sen. *The Quality of Life.* Oxford, Clarendon Press: 9–29.

Colborn, T., D. Dumanowski, et al. (1996). *Our Stolen Future: Are We Threatening Our Own Fertility, Intelligence, and Survival? A Scientific Detective Story.* New York, Dutton Press.

Cole, H. S. D. (1973). The Structure of the World Models. *Thinking About the Future: A Critique of "The Limits to Growth."* H. S. D. Cole, C. Freeman, M. Jahoda and K. L. R. Pavitt. London, Sussex University Press: 14–22.

Cole, H. S. D., C. Freeman, et al., Eds. (1973). *Thinking About the Future: A Critique of "The Limits to Growth."* London, Sussex University Press.

Cole, M. A. (2003). "Theory and Applications: Development, Trade, and the Environment; How Robust Is the Environmental Kuznets Curve?" *Environment and Development Economics* **8**: 557–580.

Cole, M. A., and E. Neumayer (2005). Economic Growth and the Environment in Developing Countries: "What Are the Implications of the Environmental Kuznets Curve?" *International Handbook of Environmental Politics.* P. Dauvergne. Cheltenham and Northampton, Edward Elgar: 298–318.

Cole, M. A., A. J. Rayner, et al. (1997). "The Environmental Kuznets Curve: An Empirical Analysis." *Environment and Development Economics* **2**(4): 401–416.

Commoner, B. (1971). "The Closing Circle: Nature, Man, and Technology." *Thinking about the Environment.* M. A. Cahn and R. O'Brien. New York, M. E. Sharpe: 161–166.

Commoner, B. (1979). Chemical Carcinogens in the Environment. *Identification and Analysis of Organic Pollutants in Water.* L. H. Keith. Ann Arbor, MI, Ann Arbor Science Publishers: 49–71.

Commoner, B., P. W. Bartlett, et al. (2000). Long-Range Air Transport of Dioxin from North American Sources to Ecologically Vulnerable Receptors in Nunavut, Arctic Canada. New York, Center for the Biology of Natural Systems (CBNS), Queens College.

Compaine, B. M. (2001). *The Digital Divide: Facing a Crisis or Creating a Myth?* Cambridge, MA, MIT Press.

Conca, K. (2002). Consumption and Environment in a Global Economy. *Confronting Consumption.* T. Princen, M. Maniates, and K. Conca. Cambridge, MA, MIT Press: 133–153.

Cordier, S. (2008). "Evidence for a Role of Paternal Exposures in Developmental Toxicity." *Basic and Clinical Pharmacology and Toxicology* **102**: 176–181.

Cornia, G. A. (2004). Inequality, Growth, and Poverty: An Overview of Changes over the Last Two Decades. *Inequality, Growth, and Poverty in an Era of Liberalization and Globalization.* G. A. Cornia. Oxford, Oxford University Press: 3–25.

Cornia, G. A., T. Addison, et al. (2004). Income Distribution Changes and Their Impact in the Post–Second World War Period. *Inequality, Growth, and Poverty in an Era of Liberalization and Globalization.* G. A. Cornia. Oxford, Oxford University Press: 26–54.

Costanza, R., Ed. (1991). *Ecological Economics: The Science and Management of Sustainability.* New York, Columbia University Press.

Costanza, R., M. Hart, et al. (2009). Beyond GDP: The Need for New Measures of Progress. The Pardee Papers 4. Boston, Boston University. Available at www.oecd.org/dataoecd/29/6/42613423.pdf (accessed February 11, 2011).

Cummings, K. M., C. P. Morley, et al. (2002). "Marketing to America's Youth: Evidence from Corporate Documents." *Tobacco Control* **11**: i5–i17.

Cyert, R. M., and D. C. Mowery, Eds. (1987). *Technology and Employment: Innovation and Growth in the U.S. Economy.* Washington, DC, National Academy Press.

Czech, B. (2003). "Technological Progress and Biodiversity Conservation: A Dollar Spent, a Dollar Burned." *Conservation Biology* **17**(5): 1455–1457.

Czech, B., and H. E. Daly (2004). "In My Opinion: The Steady State Economy—What It Is, Entails, and Connotes." *Wildlife Society Bulletin* **32**(2): 598–605.

Dag Hammarskjöld Foundation (1975). *The 1975 Dag Hammarskjöld Report—What Now: Another Development.* Uppsala, Dag Hammarskjöld Foundation.

Daly, H. E. (1991a). Elements of Environmental Macroeconomics. *Ecological Economics: The Science and Management of Sustainability.* R. Costanza and L. Wainger. New York, Columbia University Press: 32–46.

Daly, H. E. (1991b). *Steady-State Economics.* Washington, DC, Island Press.

Daly, H. E. (1994a). "Fostering Environmentally Sustainable Development: Four Parting Suggestions for the World Bank." *Ecological Economics* **10**: 183–187.

Daly, H. E. (1994b). Operationalizing Sustainable Development by Investing in Natural Capital. *Investing in Natural Capital.* A. Jansson, M. Hammer, C. Folke, and R. Costanza. Washington, DC, Island Press: 22–37.

Daly, H. E. (1996). *Beyond Growth: The Economics of Sustainable Development.* Boston, Beacon Press.

Daly, H. E. (2008). A Steady-State Economy: A Failed Growth Economy and a Steady-State Economy Are Not the Same Thing; They Are the Very Different Alternatives We Face. Paper written for the Sustainable Development Commission, United Kingdom, April 24. Available at www.sd-commission.org.uk/publications/downloads/Herman_Daly_thinkpiece.pdf (accessed February 10, 2011).

Daly, H. E., and J. B. Cobb (1994). *For the Common Good: Redirecting the Economy toward Community, the Environment, and a Sustainable Future.* Boston, Beacon Press.

Dasgupta, P. (1994). "Savings and Fertility." *Philosophy and Public Affairs* **23**: 99–127.

Dasgupta, P. (2006). "Commentary: The Stern Review's Economics of Climate Change." *National Institute Economic Review* **199**: 4–7.

Dasgupta, S., B. Laplante, et al. (2002). "Confronting the Environmental Kuznets Curve." *Journal of Economic Perspectives* **16**(1): 147–168.

Davis, B., and D. Wessel (1998). *Prosperity: The Coming Twenty-Year Boom and What It Means to You.* New York, Random House.

Davis, L. E., and J. C. Taylor, Eds. (1972). *Design of Jobs.* Harmondsworth, Penguin Books.

de Bruyn, S. M., J. C. J. M. van den Bergh, et al. (1998). "Economic Growth and Emissions: Reconsidering the Empirical Basis of Environmental Kuznets Curves." *Ecological Economics* **25**: 161–175.

de Graaf, J., D. Wann, et al. (2002). *Affluenza: The All-Consuming Epidemic.* San Francisco, Berrett-Koehler Publishers.

de Groot, H. L. F., C. A. Withagen, et al. (2004). "Dynamics of China's Regional Development and Pollution: An Investigation into the Environmental Kuznets Curve." *Environment and Development Economics* **9**: 507–537.

Dernbach, J. C. (1998). "Sustainable Development as a Framework for National Governance." *Case Western Reserve Law Review* **49**(1): 1–103.

Dernbach, J. C. (2003). "Achieving Sustainable Development: The Centrality and Multiple Facets of Integrated Decisionmaking." *Indiana Journal of Global Legal Studies* **10**(1): 247–285.

Dernbach, J. C. (2004). "Making Sustainable Development Happen: From Johannesburg to Albany." *Albany Law Environmental Outlook* **8**: 173–186.

Devillanova, C. (2004). "Interregional Migration and Labor Market Imbalances." *Journal of Population Economics* **17**(2): 229–247.

Dew-Becker, I., and R. J. Gordon (2005). Where Did the Productivity Growth Go? Inflation Dynamics and the Distribution of Income. NBER Working Paper 11842. Cambridge, MA, National Bureau of Economic Research.

Dhondt, S. (1997). *Time Constraints and Autonomy at Work in the European Union.* Dublin, European Foundation for the Improvement of Living and Working Conditions.

Diamond, J. (1997). *Guns, Germs, and Steel: The Fate of Human Societies.* New York, W. W. Norton.

Diamond, J. (2004). *Collapse: How Societies Choose to Fail or Succeed.* New York, Viking Adult.

Diener, E., and S. Oishi (2000). Money and Happiness: Income and Subjective Well-Being across Nations. *Culture and Subjective Well-being.* E. Diener and E. M. Suh., Cambridge, MA, MIT Press: 185–218.

Diener, E., and E. M. Suh (1997). "Measuring Quality of Life: Economic, Social, and Subjective Indicators." *Social Indicators Research* **40**: 189–216.

Diener, E., and E. M. Suh, Eds. (2000). *Culture and Subjective Well-Being.* Cambridge, MA, MIT Press.

Diener, E., E. M. Suh, et al. (1997). "Recent Findings on Subjective Well-Being." *Indian Journal of Clinical Psychology* **24**(1): 25–41.

Dietz, S., and E. Neumayer (2004). "Genuine Savings: A Critical Analysis of Its Policy-Guiding Value." *International Journal of Sustainable Development* **3**(3/4): 276–292.

Dinda, S. (2004). "Environmental Kuznets Curve Hypothesis: A Survey." *Ecological Economics* **49**: 431–455.

Dobson, A. (1998). *Justice and the Environment: Conceptions of Environmental Sustainability and Dimensions of Social Justice.* Oxford, Oxford University Press.

Dougherty, L. (1998). Restructuring Employment: Flexibility versus Security; Overview Essay. *The Changing Nature of Work.* F. Ackerman, N. R. Goodwin, L. Dougherty, and K. Gallagher. Washington, DC, Island Press: 171–177.

Dowrick, S., and M. Akmal (2005). "Contradictory Trends in Global Income Inequality: A Tale of Two Biases." *Review of Income and Wealth* **51**(2): 201–229.

Doyal, L., and I. Gough (1991). *A Theory of Human Need.* New York, Guilford Press.

Drucker, P. F. (1994). "The Age of Social Transformation." *Atlantic Monthly* **274**(5): 53–80.

Drucker, P. F. (1999). "Beyond the Information Revolution." *Atlantic Monthly* **284**(4): 47–57.

Dryzek, J. S. (1997). *The Politics of the Earth: Environmental Discourses.* New York, Oxford University Press.

Duchin, F., and G. M. Lange (1994). *The Future of the Environment: Ecological Economics and Technological Change.* New York, Oxford University Press.

Durning, A. T. (1992). *How Much Is Enough?* New York, W. W. Norton.

Durning, A. T. (1994). The Conundrum of Consumption. *Beyond Numbers: A Reader on Population, Consumption, and the Environment.* L. A. Mazur. Washington, DC, Island Press: 40–47.

Dwyer, R. E. (2010). The Care Economy? Job Polarization and Job Growth in the U.S. Labor Market. Paper presented at MIT, November 9.

Ecologist (1972). *Blueprint for Survival.* Boston, Houghton Mifflin.

Economic Policy Institute (EPI) (2005). *State of Working America 2004/2005. Facts & Figures: Inequality.* Washington, DC, Economic Policy Institute. Available at www.epi.org/page/-/old/books/swa2004/news/swafacts_inequality.pdf (accessed February 11, 2011).

Economist (1995). "Technology and Unemployment." *Economist*, February 11, pp. 21–23.

Economist (2004a). "The Halo Effect: How China's Expansion Will Affect Growth and Jobs Elsewhere." *Economist*, September 30.

Economist (2004b). "Pushing a Different Sort of Button: The Changed Nature of Work." *Economist*, October 28.

Economist (2006). "Work-Life Balance: Life beyond Pay." *Economist.* June 15.

Edquist, C., L. Hommen, et al. (2001). *Innovation and Employment: Process versus Product Innovation.* Cheltenham, Edward Elgar.

Ehrenfeld, J. R. (2004). "Searching for Sustainability: No Quick Fix." *Reflections: The SoL Journal* **5**(8): 1–13.

Ehrlich, P. R. (1968). *The Population Bomb.* New York, Ballantine Books.

Ehrlich, P. R., G. C. Daily, et al. (1997). "No Middle Way on the Environment." *Atlantic Monthly* **280**(6): 98–104.

Ehrlich, P. R., and J. P. Holdren (1971). "Impact of Population Growth." *Science* **171**: 1212–1217.

Ekins, P. (1997). "The Kuznets Curve for the Environment and Economic Growth: Examining the Evidence." *Environment and Planning A* **29**: 805–830.

Ekins, P., C. Folke, et al. (1994). "Trade, Environment and Development: The Issues in Perspective." *Ecological Economics* **9**(1): 1–12.

Erikson, E. H. (1963). *Childhood and Society.* New York, W. W. Norton.

Estevão, M. M., and F. Sá (2006). Are the French Happy with the 35-Hours Workweek? Paper presented at the 9th IZA European Summer School in Labor Economics, April 3–9.

Esty, D. C., M. Levy, et al. (2005). *2005 Environmental Sustainability Index: Benchmarking National Environmental Stewardship.* New Haven, CT, Yale Center for Environmental Law and Policy.

Etzioni, A. (1990). "Liberals and Communitarians." *Partisan Review* **57**(2): 215–227.

European Foundation for the Improvement of Living and Working Conditions (Eurofound) (2002). *Quality of Work and Employment in Europe: Issues and Challenges.* Luxembourg, Office for Official Publications of the European Communities.

Eurofound (2004). *Quality of Life in Europe: First European Quality of Life Survey, 2003.* Luxembourg, Office for Official Publications of the European Communities.

Eurofound (2005a). *Perceptions of Living Conditions in an Enlarged Europe: Resume.* Luxembourg, Office for Official Publications of the European Communities.

Eurofound (2005b). *Quality of Life in Europe: Working and Living in an Enlarged Europe.* Luxembourg, Office for Official Publications of the European Communities.

Eurofound (2006a). Competitive Europe—Social Europe: Partners or Rivals? Foundation Forum 2006. Background paper EF/06/56/EN. Dublin, European Foundation for the Improvement of Living and Working Conditions.

Eurofound (2006b). *First European Quality of Life Survey: Families, Work and Social Networks.* Luxembourg, Office for Official Publications of the European Communities.

Eurofound (2008). *Perceptions of Globalisation: Attitudes and Responses in the EU.* Dublin, European Foundation for the Improvement of Living and Working Conditions.

European Commission (EC) (2003). Working Document for the MANUFUTURE 2003 Conference. MANUFUTURE 2003 Conference: European Manufacturing of the Future; Role of Research and Education for European Leadership, Milan, December 1–2.

EC (2009). Consultation on the Future "EU 2020" Strategy, COM(2009)647 final. Brussels, Commission of the European Communities.

EC (2010a). Lisbon Strategy evaluation document, SEC(2010) 114 final. Brussels, EC.

EC (2010b). An Integrated Industrial Policy for the Globalisation Era Putting Competitiveness and Sustainability at Centre Stage, COM(2010) 614. Brussels, EC.

European Commission High Level Group (2004). *Facing the Challenge: The Lisbon Strategy for Growth and Employment.* Report from the High Level Group chaired by Wim Kok. Luxembourg, Office for Official Publications of the European Communities.

Factor 10 Club (1995). *Carnoules Declaration.* Wuppertal, Wuppertal Institute.

Factor 10 Club (1997). *The International Factor 10 Club's Statement to Government and Business Leaders: A Tenfold Leap in Energy and Resource Efficiency.* Wuppertal, Wuppertal Institute.

Fagin, D., and M. Lavelle (1996). *Toxic Deception: How the Chemical Industry Manipulates Science, Bends the Law, and Endangers Your Health.* Secaucus, NJ, Carol Publishing Group.

Faux, J. (2002). A Global Strategy for Labor. Speech given at the 2002 World Social Forum in Porto Alegre, Brazil, January 30–February 2. Washington, DC, Economic Policy Institute.

Faux, J., R. E. Scott, et al. (2001). *NAFTA at Seven: Its Impact on Workers in All Three Nations.* Washington, DC, Economic Policy Institute.

Firat, F. A., and N. Dholakia (1998). *Consuming People: From Political Economy to Theaters of Consumption.* New York, Routledge.

Firebaugh, G. (2003). *The New Geography of Global Income Inequality.* Cambridge, MA, Harvard University Press.

Fogel, R. W. (2000). *The Fourth Great Awakening and the Future of Egalitarianism.* Chicago, University of Chicago Press.

Forrester, J. W. (1971). *World Dynamics.* Cambridge, MA, Wright-Allen Press.

Freeman, C., and L. Soete (1994). *Work for All or Mass Unemployment? Computerised Technical Change into the 21st Century.* London, Pinter Publishers.

Freeman, R. B. (1996). "Toward an Apartheid Economy." *Harvard Business Review* **74**(5): 114–121.

Freeman, R. B. (2003). The World of Work in the New Millennium. *What the Future Holds: Insights from Social Science.* R. N. Cooper and R. Layard. Cambridge, MA, MIT Press: 157–178.

Freeman, R. B., and L. F. Katz (1994). Rising Wage Inequality: The United States vs. Other Advanced Countries. *Working under Different Rules.* R. B. Freeman. New York, Russell Sage Foundation: 29–62.

Freeman, R. B., and L. F. Katz (1995). Introduction and Summary. *Differences and Changes in Wage Structures.* R. B. Freeman and L. F. Katz. Chicago, University of Chicago Press: 1–24.

Friend, C. (2004). The Social Contract. The Internet Encyclopedia of Philosophy, The Social Contract, www.iep.utm.edu/soc-cont/ (accessed February 10, 2011).

Fukuda-Parr, S. (2002). Operationalising Amartya Sen's Ideas on Capabilities, Development, Freedom and Human Rights—The Shifting Policy Focus of the Human Development Approach. New York, UNDP.

Fukuda-Parr, S. (2003). "The Human Development Paradigm: Operationalizing Sen's Ideas on Capabilities." *Feminist Economics* **9**(2–3): 301–317.

Galbraith, J. K. (1952). *American Capitalism: The Concept of Countervailing Power.* Boston, Houghton Mifflin.

Galbraith, J. K. (1958). *The Affluent Society.* Boston, Houghton Mifflin.

Galbraith, J. K. (1967). *The New Industrial State*. Boston, Houghton Mifflin.

Galbraith, J. K. (1990). *A Short History of Financial Euphoria*. New York, Penguin Books.

Gangl, M. (2005). "Income Inequality, Permanent Incomes, and Income Dynamics." *Work and Occupations* **32**(2): 140–162.

García, A., J. Jaumandreu, et al. (2005). Innovation and Jobs: Evidence from Manufacturing Firms. Paper prepared for the European project "Innovation and Employment in European Firms: Microeconometric Evidence." Available at http://128.197.153.21/jordij/papers/innovationc.pdf (accessed February 11, 2011).

Gawande, K., R. P. Berrens, et al. (2001). "A Consumption-Based Theory of the Environmental Kuznets Curve." *Ecological Economics* **37**: 101–112.

Geiser, K. (2001). *Materials Matter: Toward a Sustainable Materials Policy*. Cambridge, MA, MIT Press.

Georgescu-Roegen, N. (1971). *The Entropy Law and the Economic Process*. Cambridge, MA, Harvard University Press.

Georgescu-Roegen, N. (1993). Energy and Economic Myths. *Valuing the Earth: Economics, Ecology, Ethics*. H. E. Daly and K. N. Townsend. Cambridge, MA, MIT Press: 89–112.

Ghose, A. K. (2003). *Jobs and Incomes in a Globalizing World*. Geneva, International Labour Organization.

Gilpin, A. (2000). *Environmental Economics: A Critical Overview*. New York, John Wiley and Sons.

Glasser, H., and P. P. Craig (1994). "Towards Biogeophysically Based 'Green Accounts.'" *Trumpeter* **11** (2). Available at http://trumpeter.athabascau.ca/index.php/trumpet/article/view/331/510 (accessed February 11, 2011).

Goldberg, P. K. (1998). "The Effects of the Corporate Average Fuel Efficiency Standards in the US." *Journal of Industrial Economics* **46**(1): 1–33.

Goldsmith, A. H., J. R. Veum, et al. (1997). "Unemployment, Joblessness, Psychological Well-Being and Self-Esteem: Theory and Evidence." *Journal of Socio-economics* **26**(2): 133–158.

Goodwin, N. R., F. Ackerman, et al., Eds. (1997). *The Consumer Society*. Frontier Issues in Economic Thought. Washington, DC, Island Press.

Gordon, R. (2000). "Does the 'New Economy' Measure Up to the Great Inventions of the Past?" *Journal of Economic Perspectives* **14**: 49–74.

Gordon, R. J. (1999). "U.S. Economic Growth since 1870: One Big Wave?" *American Economic Review* **89**(2): 123–128.

Gottschalk, P., and S. Danziger (2005). "Inequality of Wage Rates, Earnings and Family Income in the United States, 1975–2002." *Review of Income and Wealth* **51**(2): 231–254.

Green, J. R. (1980). *The World of the Worker: Labor in Twentieth-Century America*. New York, Hill and Wang.

Greenhouse, S., and D. Leonhardt (2006). "Real Wages Fail to Match a Rise in Productivity." *New York Times*, August 28.

Greiner, A., J. Rubart, et al. (2001). Economic Growth, Skill-Biased Technical Change and Wage Inequality: A Model and Estimations for the U.S. and Europe. Working Paper 7. Bielefeld, University of Bielefeld, Department of Business Administration and Economics.

Grossman, G. M. and A. B. Krueger (1993). *Environmental Impacts of the North American Free Trade Agreement. The U.S.-Mexico Free Trade Agreement*. P. Garber, Ed. Cambridge, MIT Press: 13–56.

Grossman, G. M., and A. B. Krueger (1995). "Economic Growth and the Environment." *Quarterly Journal of Economics* **110**(2): 353–377.

Grubb, W. N., and R. W. Wilson (1992). "Trends in Wage and Salary Inequality, 1967–88." *Monthly Labor Review* **115**(6): 23–39.

Grübler, A. (1998). *Technology and Global Change*. Cambridge, Cambridge University Press.

Gudmundsson, H., and M. Hojer (1996). "Sustainable Development Principles and Their Implications for Transport." *Ecological Economics* **19**: 269–282.

Guscina, A. (2006). Effects of Globalization on Labor's Share in National Income. IMF Working Paper 06/294.

Habermas, J. (1992). Further Reflections on the Public Sphere. *Habermas and the Public Sphere*. C. Calhoun. Cambridge, MA, MIT Press.

Haland, W. (1999). On Needs—A Central Concept of the Brundtland Report. *Towards Sustainable Development: On the Goals of Development—and the Conditions of Sustainability*. W. M. Lafferty and O. Langhelle. New York, St. Martin's Press: 48–69.

Hall, R. P. (2006). Understanding and Applying the Concept of Sustainable Development to Transportation Planning and Decision-Making in the U.S. PhD dissertation, Engineering Systems Division, Massachusetts Institute of Technology. Available at http://esd.mit.edu/students/esdphd/dissertations/hall_ralph.pdf (accessed January 14, 2011).

Hamilton, C. (1999). "The Genuine Progress Indicator: Methodological Developments and Results from Australia." *Ecological Economics* **30**(1): 13–28.

Hamilton, K. (1994). "Green Adjustments to GDP." *Resources Policy* **20**(3): 155–168.

Hamilton, K. (2000). *Genuine Savings as a Sustainability Indicator*. Washington, DC, World Bank, Environment Department.

Hamilton, K., G. Atkinson, et al. (1997). *Genuine Savings as an Indicator of Sustainability*. Washington, DC, World Bank, Environment Department.

Harbaugh, W. T., A. Levinson, et al. (2002). "Reexamining the Empirical Evidence for an Environmental Kuznets Curve." *Review of Economics and Statistics* **84**(3): 541–551.

Hardin, G. (1968). "The Tragedy of the Commons." *Science* **162**: 1243–1248.

Harrison, R., J. Jaumandreu, et al. (2008). Does Innovation Stimulate Employment? A Firm-Level Analysis Using Comparable Micro Data from Four European Countries. Discussion Paper 08-111. Mannheim, ZEW—Centre for European Economic Research. Available at http://papers.ssrn.com/sol3/papers.cfm?abstract_id=1338697 (accessed February 11, 2011).

Harsanyi, J. C. (1975). "Can the Maximin Principle Serve as a Basis for Morality? A Critique of John Rawls' Theory." *American Political Science Review* **69**(2): 594–606.

Hartwick, J. M. (1977). "Intergenerational Equity and the Investing of Rents from Exhaustible Resources." *American Economic Review* **67**(5): 972–974.

Hartwick, J. M. (1978a). "Investing Returns from Depleting Renewable Resource Stock and Intergenerational Equity." *Economics Letters* **1**: 85–88.

Hartwick, J. M. (1978b). "Substitution among Exhaustible Resources and Intergenerational Equity." *Review of Economic Studies* **45**(2): 347–354.

Harwood Group (1995). *Yearning for Balance: Views of Americans on Consumption, Materialism, and the Environment*. Bethesda, MD, Harwood Institute.

Havas, A. (2006). Knowledge-Intensive Activities vs. High-Tech Sectors: Policy Challenges and Options for the Central European Countries in the Enlarged European Union. *The Knowledge-Based Economy in Central and East European Countries: Countries and Industries in a Process of Change*. K. Piech and S. Radosevic. Basingstoke, Palgrave Macmillan.

Head, S. (1996). "The New, Ruthless Economy." *New York Review of Books* **43**(4): 47–52.

Head, S. (2003). *The New Ruthless Economy: Work and Power in the Digital Age*. Oxford, Oxford University Press.

Heckscher, C. C. (1996). *The New Unionism: Employee Involvement in the Changing Corporation*. Ithaca, NY, ILR Press.

Heilbroner, R., and L. Thurow (1998). *Economics Explained: Everything You Need to Know about How the Economy Works and Where It's Going*. New York, Touchstone.

Held, D., and A. McGrew, Eds. (2002). *The Global Transformations Reader: An Introduction to the Globalization Debate*. Malden, MA, Polity Press.

Herbert, B. (2003). "Sending America's Best Jobs Offshore." *New York Times*, December 27–28, p. 6.

Herman, R., S. Ardekani, et al. (1989). Dematerialization. *Technology and Environment*. J. Ausubel and H. Sladovich. Washington, DC, National Academy Press: 50–69.

Hettige, H., R. E. B. Lucas, et al. (1992). "The Toxic Intensity of Industrial Production: Global Patterns, Trends, and Trade Policy." *American Economic Review* **82**(2): 478–481.

HEW (1973). *Work in America: Report of a Special Task Force to the Secretary of Health, Education, and Welfare*. Cambridge, MA, MIT Press.

Heyd, D. (1992). *Genethics: Moral Issues in the Creation of People*. Berkeley, University of California Press.

HM Treasury (2003). *The Green Book—Appraisal and Evaluation in Central Government*. London, HM Treasury.

Hobbes, T. (1985 [1651]). *Leviathan*. London, Penguin Books.

Hochfeld, C., K. Schmitt, et al. (2006). *Competitiveness for Sustainability—Positions and Perspectives*. Berlin, Oko-Institut e.V.

Hochschild, A. R. (1997). *The Time Bind: When Work Becomes Home and Home Becomes Work*. New York, Metropolitan Books.

Hodge, T. (1997). "Toward a Conceptual Framework for Assessing Progress toward Sustainability." *Social Indicators Research* **40**: 5–98.

Holdren, J. P., C. Daily, et al. (1995). The Meaning of Sustainability: Biogeophysical Aspects. *Defining and Measuring Sustainability: The Biogeophysical Foundations*. M. Munasinghe and W. Shearer. Washington, DC, World Bank, distributed for the United Nations University.

Holtz-Eakin, D., and T. M. Selden (1995). "Stoking the Fires? $CO_2$ Emissions and Economic Growth." *Journal of Public Economics* **57**(1): 85–101.

Howell, D. (1994). The Collapse of Low-Skill Male Earnings in the 1980s: Skill Mismatch or Shifting Wage Norms? Levy Economics Institute Working Paper 105. Available at http://papers.ssrn.com/sol3/papers.cfm?abstract-id137429 (accessed January 14, 2011).

Howell, D. (2000). "Skills and the Wage Collapse." *American Prospect* **11**(15): 74–77.

Hueting, R., and L. Reijnders (1998). "Sustainability Is an Objective Concept." *Ecological Economics* **27**(2): 139–147.

Hueting, R., and L. Reijnders (2004). "Broad Sustainability contra Sustainability: The Proper Construction of Sustainability Indicators." *Ecological Economics* **50**(3–4): 249–260.

Hyclak, T. (2000). *Rising Wage Inequality: The 1980s Experience in Urban Labor Markets*. Kalamazoo, MI, Upjohn Institute for Employment Research.

Ilg, R. E., and S. E. Haugen (2000). "Earnings and Employment Trends in the 1990s." *Monthly Labor Review* **123**(3): 21–33.

Inglehart, R. (2000). "Globalization and Postmodern Values." *Washington Quarterly* **23**(1): 215–228.

Inglehart, R., and H. Klingemann (2000). Genes, Culture, Democracy, and Happiness. *Culture and Subjective Well-Being*. E. Diener and E. M. Suh. Cambridge, MA, MIT Press: 166–183.

Institute for Policy Research (IPR) (2005). "2004–05 IPR Distinguished Public Policy Lecture: Education Key to Solving America's 'Real Jobs Problem.'" *Institute for Policy Research, Newsletter* **27**(1): 11.

Intergovernmental Panel on Climate Change (IPCC) (2001). *Climate Change, 2001: Synthesis Report, Summary for Policymakers*. New York, Cambridge University Press.

IPCC (2007). *Climate Change, 2007: Synthesis Report*. Geneva, IPCC.

International Bank for Reconstruction and Development (IBRD) (1992). *World Development Report 1992: Development and the Environment*. New York, Oxford University Press.

International Climate Change Task Force (2005). *Meeting the Climate Change Challenge: Recommendations of the International Climate Change Taskforce*. London, Institute for Public Policy Research.

International Economy (2004). "Is the Aging of the Developed World a Ticking Time Bomb?" *International Economy* **18**(1): 6–19.

International Forum on Globalization (IFG) (2002). *Alternatives to Economic Globalization: A Better World Is Possible*. San Francisco, Berrett-Koehler Publishers.

International Labour Organization (ILO) (2005). *Key Indicators of the Labour Market (KILM)*. 4th ed. Geneva, International Labour Organization.

ILO (2006). Global Employment Trends Brief, January 2006. Geneva, International Labour Organization. Available at www.ilo.org/empelm/what/pubs/lang–en/WCMS_114294/index.htm (accessed February 11, 2011).

ILO (2008). *World of Work Report, 2008: Income Inequalities in the Age of Financial Globalization*. Geneva, International Labour Organization.

International Union for Conservation and Nature and Natural Resources (IUCN), United Nations Environment Programme (UNEP), et al. (1980). *World Conservation Strategy*. Gland, IUCN.

IUCN, UNEP, et al. (1991). *Caring for the Earth: A Strategy for Sustainable Living*. Gland, IUCN, UNEP, and WWF.

Jacobson, M. F., and L. A. Mazur (1995). *Marketing Madness*. Boulder, CO, Westview Press.

Jansen, L., and P. Vergragt (1992). *Sustainable Development: A Challenge to Technology*. Leidschendam, Ministry of Housing, Physical Planning, and Environment.

Jaumandreu, J. (2003). Does Innovation Spur Employment? A Firm-Level Analysis Using Spanish CIS Data. Paper prepared for the European project "Innovation and Employment in European Firms: Microeconometric Evidence." Available at www.diw.de/sixcms/detail.php/42063 (accessed February 11, 2011).

Jaumotte, F., and I. Tytell (2007). How Has the Globalization of Labor Affected the Labor Income Share in Advanced Countries? IMF Working Paper 07/298.

Jevons, W. S. (1965 [1865]). *The Coal Question: An Inquiry Concerning the Progress of the Nation, and the Probable Exhaustion of Our Coal-Mines*. New York, A. M. Kelley.

Jha, R., and K. V. B. Murthy (2003). A Critique of the Environmental Sustainability Index. Departmental Working Papers 2003–08. Canberra, Australian National University, Economics RSPAS.

Johnson, D. S., T. M. Smeeding, et al. (2005). "Economic Inequality through the Prisms of Income and Consumption." *Monthly Labor Review* **128**(4): 11–24.

Jones, S. C., and R. J. Donovan (2001). "Messages in Alcohol Advertising Targeted to Youth." **25**(2): 126–131.

Judt, T. (2005). "Europe vs. America." *New York Review of Books* **52**(2): 37–41.

Kahai, S., and W. Simmons (2005). "The Impact of Globalisation on Income Inequality." *Global Business and Economics Review* **7**(1): 1–15.

Kallis, G., J. Martinez-Alier, et al. (2009). "Paper Assets, Real Debts: An Ecological-Economic Exploration of the Global Economic Crisis." *Critical Perspectives on International Business* **5**(1/2): 14–25.

Kant, I. (1989 [1785]). *Foundations of the Metaphysics of Morals*. 2nd ed. New York, Prentice Hall.

Karsh, B. (1974). "Work in America." *Journal of Business* **47**(4): 577–579.

Kasser, T. (2002). *The High Price of Materialism*. Cambridge, MA, MIT Press.

Kasser, T., and S. Linn (2004). Public Attitudes toward the Youth Marketing Industry and Its Impact on Children. Boston, Judge Baker Children's Center, www.jbcc.harvard.edu/publications/05_youthmarketingsurvey.pdf (accessed October 7, 2006).

Katz, L. F., and D. H. Autor (1999). Changes in the Wage Structure and Earnings Inequality. *Handbook of Labor Economics*, vol. 3A. O. Ashenfelter and D. Card. Amsterdam, North-Holland: 1463–1555.

Katz, L. F., and K. Murphy (1992). "Changes in Relative Wages, 1963–1987: Supply and Demand Factors." *Quarterly Journal of Economics* **107**(1): 35–78.

Kaysen, C. (1972). "The Computer That Printed Out W*O*L*F*." *Foreign Affairs* **50**: 660–668.

Kellert, S. R., and E. O. Wilson, Eds. (1993). *The Biophilia Hypothesis*. Washington, DC, Island Press.

Kemp, R. (1995). *Environmental Policy and Technical Change*. Maastricht, Datawyse.

Kenny, C. (1999). "Does Growth Cause Happiness, or Does Happiness Cause Growth?" *Kyklos* **52**(1): 3–26.

King, A. (1991). *The First Global Revolution: A Report by the Council of the Club of Rome*. New York, Pantheon Books.

Klare, M. (2001). *Resource Wars: The New Landscape of Global Conflict*. New York, Owl Books.

Kleinknecht, A. (1998). "Commentary: Is Labour Market Flexibility Harmful to Innovation?" *Cambridge Journal of Economics* **22**: 387–396.

Kletzer, L. G. (1998). "Job Displacement." *Journal of Economic Perspectives* **12**(1): 115–136.

Kletzer, L. G. (2000). Trade and Job Loss in U.S. Manufacturing, 1979–94. *The Impact of International Trade on Wages*. R. C. Feenstra. Chicago, University of Chicago Press: 349–393.

Knowlton, N. (2001). "The Future of Coral Reefs." *Proceedings of the National Academy* of Sciences **98**(10): 5419–5425.

Kompier, M., and L. Levy (1994). *Stress at Work: Causes, Effects and Prevention*. Dublin, European Foundation for the Improvement of Living and Working Conditions.

Koo, P. (1973). "Work in America: Attack and Rebuttal." *American Vocational Journal* **48**(5): 79–82.

Korten, D. C. (2001). *When Corporations Rule the World*. San Francisco, Berrett-Koehler Publishers.

Kranz, D. F. (2006). "Why Has Wage Inequality Increased More in the USA Than in Europe? An Empirical Investigation of the Demand and Supply of Skill." *Applied Economics* **38**(7): 771–788.

Krier, J. E., and C. P. Gillette (1985). "The Uneasy Case for Technological Optimism." *Michigan Law Review* **84**: 405–429.

Krishnan, R., J. M. Harris, et al., Eds. (1995). *A Survey of Ecological Economics*. Frontier Issues in Economic Thought. Washington, DC, Island Press.

Krugman, P. (2006). "The Big Disconnect." *New York Times*. September 1.

Krugman, P. (2009). *The Return of Depression Economics and the Crisis of 2008*. New York, W. W. Norton.

Kuznets, S. (1955). "Economic Growth and Income Inequality." *American Economic Review* **45**(1): 1–28.

Lakshmanan, T. R., and W. P. Anderson (2002). Transportation Infrastructure, Freight Services Sector and Economic Growth. White Paper prepared for the U.S. Department of Transportation Federal Highway Administration. Boston, Center for Transportation Studies, Boston University. Available at http://ops.fhwa.dot.gov/freight/freight_analysis/improve_econ/appb.htm (accessed January 14, 2011).

Lawn, P. (2006). "A Theoretical Investigation into the Likely Existence of the Environmental Kuznets Curve."

*International Journal of Green Economics* **1**(1/2): 121–138.

Lawn, P. A. (2003). "A Theoretical Foundation to Support the Index of Sustainable Economic Welfare (ISEW), Genuine Progress Indicator (GPI), and other Related Indexes." *Ecological Economics* **44**(1): 105–118.

Lawson, R. (2006). "An Overview of Green Economics." *International Journal of Green Economics* **1**(1/2): 23–36.

Layard, R. (2005). *Happiness: Lessons from a New Science*. New York, Penguin Press.

Lehman, G. (1995). "A Legitmate Concern for Environmental Accounting." *Critical Perspectives on Accounting* **6**: 393–412.

Lehner, F. (1992). *Anthropocentric Production Systems: The European Response to the Advanced Manufacturing and Globalization; Synthesis Report*. EUR report, vol. 13969. Luxembourg, European Commission, Directorate-General Telecommunications, Information Market and Exploitation of Research.

Levett, R. (1998). "Sustainability Indicators—Integrating Quality of Life and Environmental Protection." *Journal of the Royal Statistical Society* **162**(3): 291–302.

Levy, F., B. Bluestone, et al. (1986). *Declining American Income and Living Standards*. Washington, DC, Economic Policy Institute.

Levy, F., and R. J. Murnane (2004). *The New Division of Labor: How Computers Are Creating the Next Job Market*. New York, Russell Sage Foundation.

Liagouras, G. (2005). "The Political Economy of Postindustrial Capitalism." *Thesis Eleven* **81**: 20–35.

Linn, M. W., R. Sandifer, et al. (1985). "Effects of Unemployment on Mental and Physical Health." *American Journal of Public Health* **75**(5): 502–506.

List, J. A., and C. A. Gallet (1999). "The Environmental Kuznets Curve: Does One Size Fit All?" *Ecological Economics* **31**: 409–423.

Locke, J. (1988 [1690]). *Two Treatises of Government*. Cambridge, Cambridge University Press.

Machin, S., A. Ryan, et al. (1996). Technology and Changes in Skill Structure: Evidence from an International Panel of Industries. CEPR Discussion Paper Series 1434. London, Centre for Economic Policy Reseach: 1–42.

Madden, J. F. (2000). *Changes in Income Inequality within U.S. Metropolitan Areas*. Kalamazoo, MI, Upjohn Institute for Employment Research.

Maddox, J. (1972). *The Doomsday Syndrome—An Attack on Pessimism*. New York, McGraw-Hill.

Madrick, J. (1999). "How New Is the New Economy?" *New York Review of Books* **46**(14): 42–50.

Mahler, V. A. (2004). "Economic Globalization, Domestic Politics, and Income Inequality in the Developed Countries: A Cross-National Study." *Comparative Political Studies* **37**(9): 1025–1053.

Mander, J., and E. Goldsmith (2000). *The Case against the Global Economy and for a Turn towards Localization*. London, Earthscan.

Manno, J. (2002). Commoditization: Consumption Efficiency and an Economy of Care and Connection. *Confronting Consumption*. T. Princen, M. Maniates, and K. Conca. Cambridge, MA, MIT Press: 67–99.

Manufacturing News (2003). "Shift of Manufacturing to China Impacts Highest Value-Added Goods and Jobs." *Manufacturing News* **10**(2): 3–4.

Maslow, A. H. (1943). "A Theory of Human Motivation." *Psychological Review* **50**: 370–396.

Max-Neef, M. (1995). "Economic Growth and Quality of Life: A Threshold Hypothesis." *Ecological Economics* **15**: 115–118.

Max-Neef, M., A. Elizalde, et al. (1989). "Human Scale Development: An Option for the Future." *Development Dialogue* **1**: 5–81.

McCally, M. (1999). *Life Support: The Environment and Human Health*. Cambridge, MA, MIT Press.

McDonough, W., and M. Braungart (1998). "The NEXT Industrial Revolution." *Atlantic Monthly* **282**(4): 82–92.

McEntire, David A. (2005). "The History, Meaning and Policy Recommendations of Sustainable Development: A Review Essay." *International Journal of Environment and Sustainable Development* **4**(2): 106–118.

McGillivray, M., and A. Shorrocks (2005). "Inequality and Multidimensional Well-Being." *Review of Income and Wealth* **51**(2): 193–199.

McLaren, D., S. Bullock, et al. (1997). *Tomorrow's World—Britain's Share in a Sustainable Future*. London, Earthscan.

McPherson, M. A., and M. L. Nieswiadomy (2005). "Environmental Kuznets Curve: Threatened Species and Spatial Effects." *Ecological Economics* **55**: 395–407.

Meadows, D. H., D. L. Meadows, et al. (1972). *The Limits to Growth*. New York, Potomac Associates.

Meadows, D. H., D. L. Meadows, et al. (1992). *Beyond the Limits: Confronting Global Collapse, Envisioning a Sustainable Future*. Post Mills, VT, Chelsea Green Publishing Co.

Meadows, D. H., J. Randers, et al. (2004a). *Limits to Growth: The 30-Year Update*. White River Junction, VT, Chelsea Green Publishing Co.

Meadows, D. H., J. Randers, and D. Meadows (2004b). *Facing the Limits to Growth*, AlterNet www.alternet.org/story/18978/ (accessed June 8, 2010)

Meadows, D. L. (2007). *Evaluating Past Forecasts: Reflections on One Critique of the* The Limits to Growth. *Sustainability or Collapse? An Integrated History and Future of People on Earth*. R. Costanza, L. Graumllich and W. Steffen. Cambridge, MA, MIT Press: 399–415.

Mendelsohn, R. O. (2006–2007). "A Critique of the Stern Report." *Regulation* (Winter). Available at http://environment.yale.edu/files/biblio/YaleFES-00000260.pdf (accessed February 11, 2011).

Mendelsohn, R. O., W. Morrison, et al. (1998). "Country-Specific Market Impacts of Climate Change." *Climatic Change* **54**: 553–569.

Michaelis, L. (2000). *Ethics of Consumption*. Oxford, Oxford Centre for the Environment, Ethics, and Society.

Miles, S. (1998). *Consumerism—as a Way of Life*. London, Sage Publications.

Miles, S., A. Anderson, et al., Eds. (2002). *The Changing Consumer: Markets and Meanings*. New York, Routledge.

Mill, J. S. (2002 [1863]). *Utilitarianism*. Indianapolis, Hackett Pub. Co.

Millennium Ecosystem Assessment (MEA) (2005). *Millennium Ecosystem Assessment Synthesis Report.* Washington, DC, Island Press.

Miller, D. (1999). Social Justice and Environmental Goods. *Fairness and Futurity: Essays on Environmental Sustainability and Social Justice.* A. Dobson. Oxford, Oxford University Press.

Ministère de l'emploi, de la cohésion sociale et du logement (2002). The Law on a Negotiated Shorter Working Week in France: The Bill Relating to Pay, the Working Week and Job Creation (Currently Discussed at the Assemblée Nationale on October 15, 2002). Paris, Ministère de l'emploi, de la cohésion sociale et du logement. Available at www.35h.travail.gouv.fr/index.htm (accessed July 21, 2006).

Minsky, H. (1986). *Stabilizing an Unstable Economy.* New Haven, CT, Yale University Press.

Mishel, L., J. Bernstein, et al. (2005). *The State of Working America, 2004/2005.* Ithaca, NY, Cornell University Press.

Mishel, L., J. Bernstein, et al. (2009). *The State of Working America, 2008/2009.* Ithaca, NY, Cornell University Press.

Moldan, B. (1997). The Human Development Index. *Sustainability Indicators: A Report on the Project on Indicators of Sustainable Development.* B. Moldan, S. Billharz, and R. Matravers. Chichester, Wiley: 242–252.

Mont, O., and A. Tukker (2006). "Product-Service Systems: Reviewing Achievements and Refining the Research Agenda." *Journal of Cleaner Production* **14**(17): 1451–1454.

Moore, F. C. (2009). "Climate Change and Air Pollution: Exploring the Synergies and Potential for Mitigation in Industrializing Countries." *Sustainability* **1**: 43–54.

Morris, M., and B. Western (1999). "Inequality in Earnings at the Close of the Twentieth Century." *Annual Review of Sociology* **25**: 623–657.

Morse, S. (2003). "For Better or for Worse, Till the Human Development Index Do Us Part?" *Ecological Economics* **45**: 281–296.

Moser, I. (1999). The "Technology Factor" in Sustainable Development. *Towards Sustainable Development: On the Goals of Development—and the Conditions of Sustainability.* W. M. Lafferty and O. Langhelle. New York, St. Martin's Press: 193–212.

Munasinghe, M. (1999). "Is Environmental Degradation an Inevitable Consequence of Economic Growth: Tunneling through the Environmental Kuznets Curve." *Ecological Economics* **29**: 89–109.

Munck, R. (2002). *Globalisation and Labour: The New "Great Transformation."* London, Zed Books.

Murcott, S. (1997). Sustainable Development: A Meta-review of Definitions, Principles, Criteria Indicators, Conceptual Frameworks and Information Systems. Paper presented at the Annual Conference of the American Association for the Advancement of Science, Seattle, WA, February 13–18.

Myers, N. (1993). *Ultimate Security: The Environmental Basis of Political Stability.* New York, W. W. Norton.

Nader, R. (2004). *The Good Fight: Declare Your Independence and Close the Democracy Gap.* New York, Regan Books.

National Commission on the Environment (1993). *Choosing a Sustainable Future.* Washington, DC, Island Press.

Neumayer, E. (2000). "On the Methodology of ISEW, GPI and Related Measures: Some Constructive Suggestions and Some Doubt on the 'Threshold' Hypothesis." *Ecological Economics* **34**(3): 347–361.

Neumayer, E. (2004). *Sustainability and Well-Being Indicators.* Helsinki, United Nations University, World Institute for Development Economics Research (WIDER).

Neumayer, E. (2007). "A Missed Opportunity: The Stern Review on Climate Change Fails to Tackle the Issue of Non-substitutable Loss of Natural Capital." *Global Environmental Change* **17**(3–4): 297–301.

New Economics Foundation (NEF) (2009). *The (Un) Happy Planet Index 2.0.* London, NEF.

Nordhaus, W. D. (2006). The Stern Review on the Economics of Climate Change. NBER Working Paper W12741. Available at http://papers.ssrn.com/sol3/papers.cfm?abstract_id=948654 (accessed February 11, 2011).

Nordhaus, W. D., and J. G. Boyer (2000). *Warming the World: Economic Models of Global Warming.* Cambridge, MA, MIT Press.

Norris, P. (2001). *Digital Divide: Civic Engagement, Iinformation Poverty, and the Internet Worldwide.* Cambridge, Cambridge University Press.

Nozick, R. (1974). *Anarchy, State, and Utopia.* New York, Basic Books.

Nussbaum, M. (2000). *Women and Human Development: The Capabilities Approach.* Cambridge, Cambridge University Press.

Oishi, S., E. Diener, et al. (1999). "Cross-Cultural Variations in Predictors of Life Satisfaction: Perspectives from Needs and Values." *Personality and Social Psychology Bulletin* **28**(8): 980–990.

Okin, S. M. (1989). *Justice, Gender, and the Family.* New York, Basic Books.

Organisation for Economic Co-operation and Development (OECD) (1995). *Sustainable Agriculture: Concepts, Issues and Policies in OECD Countries.* Paris, OECD.

OECD (1996). *Technology, Productivity and Job Creation: Analytical Report.* Paris, OECD.

OECD (2001). *The OECD Jobs Strategy: Technology, Productivity, and Job Creation; Best Policy Practices; Highlights.* Paris, OECD.

OECD (2003). *The Sources of Economic Growth in OECD Countries.* Paris, OECD.

OECD (2010a). The OECD Innovation Strategy: Getting a Head Start on Tomorrow. Paris, OECD.

OECD (2010b). The OECD Development Agenda. Paris, OECD.

O'Rourke, K. H. (2001). Globalization and Inequality: Historical Trends. NBER Working Paper 8339. Cambridge, MA, National Bureau of Economic Research.

Osterman, P., T. A. Kochan, et al. (2001). *Working in America: A Blueprint for the New Labor Market.* Cambridge, MA, MIT Press.

Panayotou, T. (1993). Empirical Tests and Policy Analysis of Environmental Degradation at Different Stages of Economic Development. Working Paper WP238. Geneva, ILO, Technology and Employment Programme.

Panayotou, T. (1997). "Demystifying the Environmental Kuznets Curve: Turning a Black Box into a Policy

Tool." *Environmental and Development Economics* **2**: 465–484.

Partridge, E. (1976). Rawls and the Duty to Posterity. PhD dissertation, University of Utah.

Patterson, M., and N. Jollands (2004). "The Power of One: Developing a Headline Indicator for Tracking Progress to Sustainability in New Zealand." *International Journal of Environment and Sustainable Development* **3**(3/4): 316–338.

Perman, R., and D. I. Stern (2003). "Evidence from Panel Unit Root and Cointegration Tests That the Environmental Kuznets Curve Does Not Exist." *Australian Journal of Agricultural and Resource Economics* **47**(3): 325–347.

Peters, B. (2004). Employment Effects of Different Innovation Activities: Microeconometric Evidence. Discussion Paper 04-73. Mannheim, Centre for European Economic Research (ZEW). Available at http://econstor.eu/bitstream/10419/24697/1/dp0473.pdf (accessed February 11, 2011).

Petras, J. (2002). "The Myth of the Third." *Latin American Perspectives* **29**(127): 44–58.

Petrinovich, L. (1999). *Darwinian Dominion: Animal Welfare and Human Interests.* Cambridge, MA, MIT Press.

Pianta, M. (2000). The Employment Impact of Product and Process Innovations. *The Employment Impact of Innovation: Evidence and Policy.* M. Vivarelli and M. Pianta. London, Routledge: 77–95.

Pigou, A. C. (1932). *The Economics of Welfare.* 4th ed. London, Macmillan.

Pimentel, D., S. Cooperstein, et al. (2007). "Ecology of Increasing Diseases: Population Growth and Environmental Degradation." *Human Ecology* **35**: 653–668.

Piore, M. J., and C. Sable (1984). *The Second Industrial Divide: Possibilities for Prosperity.* New York, Basic Books.

Piva, M., E. Santarelli, et al. (2003). The Skill Bias Effect of Technological and Organizational Change: Evidence and Policy Implications. Discussion Paper 934. Bonn, Institute for the Study of Labor.

Pol, E. (2002). Preface. *Psychology of Sustainable Development.* P. Schmuck and W. P. Schultz. Boston, Kluwer Academic Publishers: ix–x.

Polanyi, K. (1944). *The Great Transformation.* Boston, Beacon Press.

Ponting, C. (1991). *A Green History of the World: The Environment and the Collapse of Great Civilizations.* New York, Penguin Books.

Ponting, C. (2007). *A New Green History of the World: The Environment and the Collapse of Great Civilizations.* New York, Penguin Books.

Porter, M. E. (1986). Competition in Global Industries: A Conceptual Framework. *Competition in Global Industries.* M. E. Porter. Cambridge, MA, Harvard Business School Press: 15–60.

Princen, T. (2002). Distancing: Consumption and the Severing of Feedback. *Confronting Consumption.* T. Princen, M. Maniates, and K. Conca. Cambridge, MA, MIT Press: 103–131.

Princen, T., M. Maniates, et al., Eds. (2002). *Confronting Consumption.* Cambridge, MA, MIT Press.

Pronk, J., and M. ul Haq, Eds. (1992). *Sustainable Development: From Concept to Action; The Hague Report.* New York, United Nations Development Programme.

Putnam, R. D., R. Leonardi, et al. (1993). *Making Democracy Work: Civic Traditions in Modern Italy.* Princeton, Princeton University Press.

Rawls, J. (1971). *A Theory of Justice.* Cambridge, MA, Harvard University Press.

Rawls, J. (1974). "Some Reasons for the Maximin Criterion." *American Economic Review* **64**(2): 141–146.

Rawls, J. (1993). *Political Liberalism.* New York, Columbia University Press.

Raworth, K. and D. Stewart (2002). *Critiques of the Human Development Index: A Review. Readings in Human Development, Concepts, Measures and Policies for a Development Paradigm.* S. Fukuda-Parr and A. K. Shiva Kumar. New York, Oxford University Press.

Redclift, M. (1984). *Development and the Environmental Crisis: Red or Green Alternatives?* London, Methuen.

Redclift, M. R., Ed. (2000). *Sustainability: Life Chances and Livelihoods.* New York, Routledge.

Rees, W. E. (1995a). "Achieving Sustainability: Reform or Transformation?" *Journal of Planning Literature* **9**(4): 343–361.

Rees, W. E. (1995b). "More Jobs, Less Damage: A Framework for Sustainability, Growth and Employment." *Alternatives* **21**(4): 24–30.

Reich, R. B. (1992). *The Work of Nations: Preparing Ourselves for 21st-Century Capitalism.* New York, Vintage Books.

Reid, T. R. (2004). *The United States of Europe: The New Superpower and the End of American Supremacy.* New York, Penguin.

Reijnders, L. (1996). *Environmentally Improved Production Processes and Products: An Introduction.* Dordrecht, Kluwer Publishing.

Reijnders, L. (1998). "The Factor X Debate: Setting Targets for Eco-efficiency." *Journal of Industrial Ecology* **2**(1): 13–22.

Rennings, K. (2000). "Redefining Innovation—Eco-innovation Research and the Contribution from Ecological Economics." *Ecological Economics* **32**: 319–332.

Riesenhuber, E. (2001). *The International Monetary Fund under Constraint: Legitimacy of Its Crisis Management.* The Hague, Kluwer Law International.

Rifkin, J. (2004a). *The End of Work: The Decline of the Global Labor Force and the Dawn of the Post-market Era.* New York, G. P. Putnam's Sons.

Rifkin, J. (2004b). *The European Dream: How Europe's Vision of the Future Is Quietly Eclipsing the American Dream.* New York, Tarcher/Penguin.

Rothman, D. S. (1998). "Environmental Kuznets Curves—Real Progress or Passing the Buck? A Case for Consumption-Based Approaches." *Ecological Economics* **25**: 177–194.

Rousseau, J.-J. (1968 [1762]). *The Social Contract.* London, Penguin Books.

Ruth, M. (2006). "A Quest for the Economics of Sustainability and the Sustainability of Economics." *Ecological Economics* **56**(3): 332–342.

Ryan, J. C., and A. T. Durning (1997). *Stuff: The Secret Lives of Everyday Things*. Seattle, Northwest Environmental Watch.

Ryan, R. M. (1995). "Psychological Needs and the Facilitation of Integrative Processes." *Journal of Personality* **63**(3): 397–427.

Ryan, R. M., and E. L. Deci (2000a). "The Darker and Brighter sides of Human Existence: Basic Psychological Needs as a Unifying Concept." *Psychological Inquiry* **11**: 319–338.

Ryan, R. M., and E. L. Deci (2000b). "Self-Determination Theory and the Facilitation of Intrinsic Motivation, Social Development, and Well-Being." *American Psychologist* **55**: 68–78.

Sachs, I. (1976). Environment and Styles of Development. *Outer Limits and Human Needs*. W. H. Matthews. Uppsala, Dag Hammarskjöld Foundation: 41–65.

Sachs, I. (1984). "The Strategies of Ecodevelopment." *Cerrs* **17**(4): 17–24.

Sachs, W. (1993). "Die vier E's: Merkposten für einen mass-vollen Wirtschaftsstil" [The Fours Es: Indicators for a Sustainable Economy]. *Politische Oekologie* (September/October): 69–72.

Saey, T. H. (2008). "Dad's Hidden Influence: A Father's Legacy to a Child's Health May Start before Conception and Last Generations." *Science News* **173**(13): 200.

Sagoff, M. (1997). "Do We Consume Too Much?" *Atlantic Monthly* **279**(6): 80–96.

Saha, S. K. (2002). Theorising Globalisation and Sustainable Development. *Globalisation and Sustainable Development in Latin America: Perspectives on the New Economic Order*. S. K. Saha and D. Parker. Cheltenham, Edward Elgar: 13–50.

Sandel, M. J. (1996). *Democracy's Discontent: America in Search of a Public Philosophy*. Cambridge, MA, Harvard University Press.

Sanders, R. (2006). "Sustainability: Implications for Growth, Employment, and Consumption." *International Journal of Environment, Workplace and Employment* **2**(4): 385–401.

Sanne, C. (2002). "Willing Consumers—or Locked-In? Policies for a Sustainable Consumption." *Ecological Economics* **42**: 273–287.

Sasco, A. J. (2008). "Cancer and Globalization." *Biomedicine and Pharmacotherapy* **62**(2): 110–121.

Schettler, T., G. M. Solomon, et al. (1999). *Generation at Risk*. Cambridge, MA, MIT Press.

Schlosser, E. (2002). *Fast Food Nation: The Dark Side of the All-American Meal*. New York, HarperCollins.

Schmidheiny, S. (1992). *Changing Course: A Global Business Perspective on Development and the Environment*. Cambridge, MA, MIT Press.

Schmuck, P., and W. P. Schultz, Eds. (2002). *Psychology of Sustainable Development*. Boston, Kluwer Academic Publishers.

Schor, J. B. (1991). *The Overworked American: The Unexpected Decline of Leisure*. New York, Basic Books.

Schumacher, E. F. (1999). *Small Is Beautiful: Economics as If People Mattered, 25 Years Later . . . with Commentaries*. Point Roberts, WA, Hartley and Marks Publishers.

Schumpeter, J. A. (1962 [1942]). *Capitalism, Socialism, and Democracy*. New York, Harper Torchbooks.

Scott, R. E. (2001). NAFTA's Hidden Costs: Trade Agreement Results in Job Losses, Growing Inequality, and Wage Suppression for the United States. *NAFTA at Seven: Its Impact on Workers in All Three Nations; Briefing Paper*. Washington, DC, Economic Policy Institute: 3–11.

Scott, R. E. (2003). The High Price of "Free" Trade: NAFTA's Failure Has Cost the United States Jobs across the Nation. EPI Briefing Paper 147, November 17. Washington, DC, Economic Policy Institute. Available at http://epi.3cdn.net/bd3621354eb363cc30_9um6be9q0.pdf (accessed February 11, 2011).

Searchinger, T., R. Heimlich, et al. (2008). "Use of U.S. Croplands for Fuels Increases Greenhouse Gases through Emissions from Land-Use Change." *Science* **319**: 1238–1240.

Selden, T. M., and D. Song (1994). "Environmental Quality and Development: Is There a Kuznets Curve for Air Pollution Emissions?" *Journal of Environmental Economics and Management* **27**: 147–162.

Sen, A. K. (1992). *Inequality Reexamined*. Cambridge, MA, Harvard University Press.

Sen, A. K. (1993). "The Economics of Life and Death." *Scientific American* **268**(5): 40–47.

Sen, A. K. (1999). *Development as Freedom*. New York, Alfred A. Knopf.

Sen, A. K. (2000). The Ends and the Means of Sustainability. Keynote address at the International Conference on Transition to Sustainability, Tokyo, May.

Sen, A. K. (2003). Foreword. *Readings in Human Development: Concepts, Measures, and Policies for a Development Paradigm*. S. Fukuda-Parr and A. K. Shiva Kumar. Oxford, Oxford University Press.

Sennett, R. (1998). *The Corrosion of Character: The Personal Consequences of Work in the New Capitalism*. New York, W. W. Norton.

Shafik, N., and S. Bandyopadhyay (1992). Economic Growth and Environmental Quality: Time Series and Cross-Country Evidence. Background paper for the *World Development Report*. Washington, DC, World Bank.

Singh, A., and R. Dhumale (2004). Globalization, Technology, and Income Inequality: A Critical Analysis. *Inequality, Growth, and Poverty in an Era of Liberalization and Globalization*. G. A. Cornia. Oxford, Oxford University Press: 145–165.

Skinner, B. F. (1974). *About Behaviorism*. New York, Random House.

Smith, M. R. (1994). Technological Determinism in American Culture. *Does Technology Drive History? The Dilemma of Technological Determinism*. L. Marx and M. R. Smith. Cambridge, MA, MIT Press: 1–35.

Smith, V. (2006). "It's the End of Work as We Know It . . . but Maybe Not." *Work and Occupations* **33**(3): 303–306.

Söderbaum, P. (2008). *Understanding Sustainability Economics: Towards Pluralism in Economics*. London, Earthscan.

Solomon, G. M., and T. Schettler (1999). Environmental Endocrine Disruption. *Life Support: The Environment and Human Health*. M. McCally. Cambridge, MA, MIT Press: 147–162.

Solow, R. M. (1974). "Intergenerational Equity and Exhaustible Resources." *Review of Economic Studies* **41**: 29–46.

Solow, R. M. (1993). *Sustainability: An Economist's Perspective. Economics of the Environment: Selected Readings*. R. Dorfman and N. S. Dorfman. New York, W. W. Norton: 179–187.

Soros, G. (1997). "The Capitalist Threat." *Atlantic Monthly* **279**(2): 45–58.

Soros, G. (1998). "Toward a Global Open Society." *Atlantic Monthly* **281**(1): 20, 22, 24, and 32.

Soros, G. (2008). "The Crisis and What to Do about it." *New York Review of Books* **55**(19): 63–65.

Spangenberg, J. H. (2001). "The Environmental Kuznets Curve: A Methodological Artifact?" *Population and Environment* **23**(2): 175–191.

Speth, J. G. (2003). Two Perspectives on Globalization and the Environment. *Worlds Apart: Globalization and the Environment*. J. G. Speth. Washington, DC, Island Press: 1–18.

Spiezia, V., and M. Vivarelli (2000). The Analysis of Technological Change and Employment. *The Employment Impact of Innovation: Evidence and Policy*. M. Valenti and M. Pianta. London, Routledge: 12–25.

Starr, C., and R. Rudman (1973). "Parameters of Technological Growth." *Science* **182**: 358–364.

Stearns, P. N. (2001). *Consumerism in World History: The Global Transformation of Desire*. New York, Routledge.

Stern, D. I. (1998). "Progress on the Environmental Kuznets Curve?" *Environment and Development Economics* **3**: 173–196.

Stern, D. I. (2003). The Environmental Kuznets Curve. International Society for Ecological Economics, *Internet Encyclopaedia of Ecological Economics,* www.ecoeco.org/pdf/stern.pdf (accessed March 20, 2008).

Stern, D. I. (2004). "The Rise and Fall of the Environmental Kuznets Curve." *World Development* **32**(8): 1419–1439.

Stern, D. I., M. S. Common, et al. (1996). "Economic Growth and Environmental Degradation: The Environmental Kuznets Curve and Sustainable Development." *World Development* **24**(7): 1151–1160.

Stern, N. (2007). *Stern Review on the Economics of Climate Change*. Cambridge, Cambridge University Press.

Stern, P. C., T. Dietz, et al. (1997). *Environmentally Significant Consumption*. Washington, DC, National Academy Press.

Stern, P. C., O. R. Young, et al. (1992). *Global Environmental Change: Understanding the Human Dimensions*. Washington, DC, National Research Council.

Stewart , F. (1985). *Planning to Meet Basic Needs*. London, Macmillan.

Stiglitz, J. (2002). *Globalization and Its Discontents*. New York, W. W. Norton.

Stiglitz, J. (2010). *Freefall: America, Free Markets, and the Sinking of the World Economy*. New York, W. W. Norton.

Stiglitz, J., and A. Charlton (2005). *Fair Trade for All: How Trade Can Promote Development*. Oxford, Oxford University Press.

Streeten, P. P. (1982). *First Things First: Meeting Basic Human Needs in the Developing Countries*. Oxford, Oxford University Press.

Talberth, J., C. Cobb, et al. (2006). *The Genuine Progress Indicator, 2006: A Tool for Sustainable Development*. Oakland, Redefining Progress.

ter Weel, B., and R. Kemp (2000). The Dutch Labour Market and the New Economy. Report for the project "Pathways to Sustainable Industrial Transformations: Co-optimising Competitiveness, Employment, and Environment." Maastricht, MERIT.

Theodos, B., and R. Bednarzik (2006). "Earnings Mobility and Low-Wage Workers in the United States." *Monthly Labor Review* **129**(7): 34–46.

Tisdell, C. (2001). "Globalisation and Sustainability: Environmental Kuznets Curve and the WTO." *Ecological Economics* **39**: 185–196.

Tol, R. S. J. (2006). "The Stern Review of the Economics of Climate Change: A Comment." *Energy and Environment* **17**: 977–981.

Tol, R. S. J., and G. W. Yohe (2006). "A Review of the Stern Review." *World Economics* **7**(4): 233–250.

Tukker, A., and U. Tischner, Eds. (2006). *New Business for Old Europe: Product-Service Development, Competitiveness and Sustainability*. Sheffield, U.K., Greenleaf Publishing.

ul Hague, I. (2004). Globalization, Neoliberalism and Labour—Discussion Paper. Geneva, United Nations Conference on Trade and Development (UNCTAD).

United Nations (UN), European Commission (EC), et al. (2003). *Handbook of National Accounting: Integrated Environmental and Economic Accounting, 2003*. New York, United Nations Statistics Division.

United Nations Department of Economic and Social Affairs (UNDESA) (2007). *Indicators of Sustainable Development: Guidelines and Methodologies*. New York, UN.

United Nations Development Programme (UNDP) (1990). *Human Development Report 1990*. New York, Oxford University Press.

UNDP (1995). *Human Development Report 1995*. New York, Oxford University Press.

UNDP (1999). *Human Development Report, 1999*. New York, Oxford University Press.

UNDP (2003). *Human Development Report 2003: Millennium Development Goals; A Compact among Nations to End Human Poverty*. New York, Oxford University Press.

UNDP (2005). *Human Development Report, 2005: International Cooperation at a Crossroads; Aid, Trade and Security in an Unequal World*. New York, UNDP.

UNDP (2010). *Human Development Report 2010—20th Anniversary Edition. The Real Wealth of Nations: Pathways to Human Development*. New York, UNDP.

UNDP, United Nations Environment Program (UNEP), et al. (2000). A Guide to World Resources 2000–2001: People and Ecosystems: The Fraying Web of Life. Washington, DC, World Resources Institute. Available at http://pdf.wri.org/world_resources_2000-2001_people_and_ecosystems.pdf (accessed February 10, 2011).

UNDP, UNEP, et al. (2003). World Resources 2002–2004: Decisions for the Earth: Balance, Voice, and Power. Washington, DC, World Resources Institute. Available at http://pdf.wri.org/wr2002_fullreport.pdf (accessed February 10, 2011).

UNEP (1975). *The Proposed Programme*. Nairobi, UNEP.

UNEP (1982). *The Environment in 1982: Retrospect and Prospect*. Nairobi, UNEP.

Unruh, G. C., and W. R. Moomaw (1998). "An Alternative Analysis of Apparent EKC-Type Transitions." *Ecological Economics* **25**: 221–229.

U.S. Census Bureau (2010). *Statistical Abstract of the United States: 2010*. Washington, DC, U.S. Census Bureau. Available at www.census.gov/prod/2009pubs/10statab/business.pdf (accessed February 11, 2011).

U.S. Trade Deficit Review Commission (2000). *The U.S.Trade Deficit: Causes, Consequences and Recommendations for Action*. Washington, DC, U.S. Trade Deficit Review Commission.

van Ark, B., R. Inklaar, et al. (2003). "The Employment Effects of the 'New Economy': A Comparison of the European Union and the United States." *National Institute Economic Review* **184**: 86–98.

van den Bergh, J. C. J. M., and H. Verbruggen (1999). "Spatial Sustainability, Trade and Indicators: An Evaluation of the 'Ecological Footprint.'" *Ecological Economics* **29**(1): 61–72.

Vanoli, A. (2004). *A History of National Accounting*. Amsterdam, ISO Press.

Veblen, T. (1994 [1902]). *The Theory of the Leisure Class*. New York, Dover Publications.

Vellinga, M., and R. A. Wood (2004). "Global Climatic Impacts of a Collapse of the Atlantic Thermohaline Circulation." *Climatic Change* **54**(3): 251–267.

Venetoulis, J., and C. Cobb (2004). *The Genuine Progress Indicator, 1950–2002 (2004 Update)*. Oakland, Redefining Progress.

Victor, P. A. (2008). *Managing without Growth: Slow by Design, Not Disaster*. Cheltenham, Edward Elgar.

Vivarelli, M. (1996). Technical Change and Employment: A Twofold Critique. Paper presented at the TSER Conference on Technology, Economic Integration and Social Cohesion, Paris, November 22–23.

Vivarelli, M., and M. Pianta, Eds. (2000). *The Employment Impact of Innovation: Evidence and Policy*. London, Routledge.

Voisey, H., and T. O'Riordan (2001). Globalization and Localization. *Globalism, Localism and Identity*. T. O'Riordan. London, Earthscan: 25–42.

von Weizsäcker, E. U., K. C. Hargroves, et al. (2010). *Factor Five: Transforming the Global Economy through 80% Improvements in Resource Productivity*. London, Earthscan.

von Weizsäcker, E. U., A. B. Lovins, et al. (1997). *The Factor Four*. London, Earthscan.

Voorthuis, J., and C. Gijbels (2010). "A Fair Accord: Cradle to Cradle as a Design Theory Measured against John Rawls' Theory of Justice and Immanuel Kant's Categorical Imperative." *Sustainability* **2**(1): 371–382.

Wackernagel, M. (2001). *Advancing Sustainable Resource Management: Using Ecological Footprint Analysis for Problem Formulation, Policy Development, and Communication*. Oakland, Redefining Progress.

Wackernagel, M., C. Monfreda, et al. (2002). Ecological Footprint of Nations: November 2002 Update; How Much Nature Do They Use? How Much Nature Do They Have? Sustainability Issue Brief. Oakland, Redefining Progress.

Wackernagel, M., and W. E. Rees (1995). *Our Ecological Footprint: Reducing Human Impact on the Earth*. Gabriola Island, British Columbia, Canada, New Society Publishers.

Wackernagel, M., and W. E. Rees (1997). "Perceptual and Structural Barriers to Investing in Natural Capital: Economics from an Ecological Footprint Perspective." *Ecological Economics* **20**(1): 3–29.

Wackernagel, M., S. White, et al. (2004). "Using Ecological Footprint Accounts: From Analysis to Applications." *International Journal of Environment and Sustainable Development* **3**(3/4): 293–315.

Wade, R. H. (2001). "The Rising Inequality of World Income Distribution." *Finance and Development* **38**: 37–39.

Walker, M. (2009). "Silver Lining: How the Financial Crisis Can Make Us Healthier, Wealthier and Wiser." *American Interest* **4**(4): 7–12.

Walton, R. (1985). "From Control to Commitment in the Workplace." *Harvard Business Review* **63**(2): 77–84.

Weitzman, M. L. (2001). "Gamma Discounting." *American Economic Review* **91**: 260–271.

Weitzman, M. L. (2007). "A Review of the Stern Review on the Economics of Climate Change." *Journal of Economic Literature* **45**(3): 703–724.

Wells, D. T. (1996). *Environmental Policy: A Global Perspective for the Twenty-first Century*. Upper Saddle River, NJ, Prentice Hall.

Wen, Y., and L. M. Shimek (2007). "The U.S. Consumption Boom and Trade Deficit." *National Economic Trends*. October. Available at http://econpapers.repec.org/article/fipfedlne/y_3a2007_3ai_3aoct.htm (accessed January 14, 2011).

Wetlesen, J. (1999). A Global Ethic of Sustainability? *Towards Sustainable Development: On the Goals of Development—and the Conditions of Sustainability*. W. M. Lafferty and O. Langhelle. New York, St. Martin's Press: 30–47.

Wilson, E. O. (2002). *The Future of Life*. New York, Alfred A. Knopf.

Wolff, F., K. Schmitt, et al. (2006). *Competitiveness, Innovation and Sustainability—Clarifying the Concepts and Their Interrelations*. Berlin, Oko-Institut e.V.

Wood, A. (1994). *North-South Trade, Employment and Inequality: Changing Fortunes in a Skill-Driven World*. Oxford, Clarendon Press.

Woolley, J. (2006). Can Work and Life Be friends? *Above the Clouds: A Guide to Trends Changing the Way We Work*. H. Legenvre, L. Mallinder, and J. Woolley. Sheffield, U.K., Greenleaf Publishing: 158–164.

World Bank Group (WBG) (1997). *Expanding the Measure of Wealth: Indicators of Environmentally Sustainable Development*. Washington, DC, World Bank.

WBG (2002). *World Development Report 2003: Sustainable Development in a Dynamic World: Transforming Institutions, Growth, and Quality of Life*. Washington DC, World Bank.

World Commission on Environment and Development (WCED) (1987). *Our Common Future*. Oxford, Oxford University Press.

World Commission on the Social Dimension of Globalization (WCSDG) (2004). *A Fair Globalization: Creating Opportunities for All*. Geneva, ILO Publications.

World Wildlife Fund (WWF), Zoological Society of London, et al. (2010). *Living Planet Report 2010. Biodiversity, Biocapacity and Development.* Gland, WWF.

Worm, B., E. B. Barbier, et al. (2006). "Impacts of Biodiversity Loss on Ocean Ecosystem Services." *Science* **314**(5800): 787–790.

Wright, E. and Dwyer, R. (2003) "The Patterns of Job Expansion in the USA: A Comparison of the 1960s and 1990s." *Socio-Economic Review* **1**: 289–325.

Yach, D., and D. Bettcher (1998a). "The Globalization of Public Health, I: Threats and Opportunities." *American Journal of Public Health* **88**(5): 735–738.

Yach, D., and D. Bettcher (1998b). "The Globalization of Public Health, II: The Convergence of Self-Interest and Altruism." *American Journal of Public Health* **88**(5): 738–741.

Yandle, B., M. Bhattarai, et al. (2004). Environmental Kuznets Curves: A Review of Findings, Methods, and Policy Implications. PERC Research Study 02–1 Update. Bozeman, MT, Property and Environment Research Center (PERC).

Yohe, G. W. (2006). "Some Thoughts on the Damage Estimates Presented in the Stern Review—An Editorial." *Integrated Assessment Journal* **6**: 65–72.

Yohe, G. W., and R. S. J. Tol (2007). "The Stern Review: Implications for Climate Change." *Environment* **49**: 36–42.

York, R., E. A. Rosa, et al. (2003). "Footprints on the Earth: The Environmental Consequences of Modernity." *American Sociological Review* **68**(2): 279–300.

Yun, M. (2006). "Earnings Inequality in USA, 1969–99: Comparing Inequality Using Earnings Equations." *Review of Income and Wealth* **52**(1): 127–144.

# 2

# The Emergence of Sustainable Development

This chapter provides an abbreviated overview of the emergence of the concept of sustainable development during the latter part of the twentieth century. For a more detailed discussion, see the extended Primer on Sustainable Development found at the website associated with this book.

The concept of sustainable development obtained formal international recognition at the 1992 United Nations Conference on Environment and Development (UNCED) in Rio de Janeiro, Brazil. However, it is possible to trace the modern environmental movement back to the 1950s, when developed nations—for example, the United States, Japan, and several nations in what is now the European Union—became increasingly aware that the *local* or *regional* environment was being stressed by rapid industrialization. Here, we focus our attention on the United States because the environmental policy and laws enacted during the early environmental movement (of the 1960s and 1970s) played an influential role in shaping the actions of other nations.*

The U.S. environmental movement began when the nation's communities became increasingly aware that the industrial and agricultural processes that contributed to the nation's economic growth were simultaneously distressing ecosystem integrity and biological diversity (Table 2.1). In essence, as large-scale productive capacities in industry and agriculture increased, so did the rates at which these sectors discharged pollution and waste into the environment. Once the environment surrounding the industrial and agricultural land was no longer able to assimilate or store this waste, negative impacts soon began to emerge. In some cases, the pollution was clearly visible; in others, its manifestation occurred through the gradual loss or deterioration of wildlife. Hence the concern for the environment was driven primarily by local issues, such as air, water, and noise pollution, toxic-waste disposal sites, oil spills, highway construction, and suburban sprawl, and by a concern for the integrity of ecosystems.

Before the 1960s, communities had turned somewhat of a blind eye to pollution from industrial activities because of the perception that economic

---

* Other countries in the European Union may now have advanced beyond the United States in certain areas with regard to innovative environmental policy and law designed to promote sustainable development (Vogel 2003). See Chapter 10 for a discussion of regional and international regimes to protect health, safety, and the environment.

**TABLE 2.1: THE CREATION OF A NATIONAL ENVIRONMENT AND DEVELOPMENT AGENDA—1951 TO 1970**

| YEAR | EVENTS | PUBLICATIONS | U.S. LEGISLATION |
|---|---|---|---|
| 1951 | President Truman appoints the *Paley Commission* to study the long-range aspects of the national resource base. | | |
| 1952 | *Resources for the Future* is established. | *Resources for Freedom*—The President's Material Policy Commission | |
| 1954 | | *The Nation Looks at Its Resources: Report of the Mid-century Conference on Resources for the Future*—Resources for the Future | |
| 1960 | *World population—3 billion.* The World Bank creates the International Development Association (IDA). | *Energy in the American Economy, 1850–1975: An Economic Study of Its History and Prospects*—S. H. Schurr and B. C. Netschert | |
| 1961 | The OECD (Organisation for Economic Co-operation and Development) is created from the OEEC (Organisation for European Economic Co-operation). The World Wildlife Fund (WWF) is established. | | |
| 1962 | | *Silent Spring*—R. Carson<br>*Resources in America's: Future patterns of requirements and availabilities, 1960–2000*—H. H. Landsberg, L. L. Fischman, and J. L. Fisher | |
| 1963 | | *Scarcity and Growth: The Economics of Natural Resource Availability*—H. J. Barnett and C. Morse | |
| 1964 | The UN Conference on Trade and Development (UNCTAD) is established. | | |
| 1965 | | *Unsafe at Any Speed: The Designed-in Dangers of the American Automobile*—R. Nader | |
| 1966 | | *Environmental Quality in a Growing Economy: Essays from the Sixth RFF Forum*—K. E. Boulding, H. J. Barnett, R. Dubos, L. J. Duhl, R. Turvey, R. N. McKean, A. V. Kneese, M. M. Gaffney, G. F. White, D. Lowenthal, N. E. Long, J. H. Beuscher, and J. Jarrett (eds.) | The Freedom of Information Act (FOIA) |
| 1967 | The Environmental Defense Fund (EDF) is created. | | |
| 1968 | The Biosphere Conference is held in Paris under the auspices of the UN Educational, Scientific, and Cultural Organization (UNESCO).<br><br>The topic of "the human environment" is addressed by the UN Economic and Social Council (ECOSOC). ECOSOC Resolution 1364 (XLV) eventually leads to the 1972 Stockholm Conference.<br><br>An explosion occurs at a mine in Farmington, West Virginia, killing seventy-eight people. | *The Tragedy of the Commons*—G. Hardin<br>*The Population Bomb*—P. Ehrlich | |
| 1969 | An oil spill on the Cuyahoga River in Ohio catches fire.<br><br>An oil spill occurs off the coast of Santa Barbara, California, discharging some 200,000 gallons of crude oil into the sea.<br><br>United Mine Workers strike over coal workers' pneumoconiosis, or "black lung."<br><br>Friends of the Earth is formed. | *Partners in Development*—Report prepared by the Commission on International Development | The Coal Mine Health and Safety Act<br><br>The National Environmental Policy Act (NEPA) |
| 1970 | First Earth Day—April 22.<br>The Natural Resources Defense Council (NRDC) is formed.<br><br>President Nixon creates the Environmental Protection Agency (EPA) in the United States by executive order. | *Economics and the Environment: A Materials Balance Approach*—R. U. Ayres, R. C. D'Arge, and A. V. Kneese<br><br>*Man's Impact on the Global Environment*—Report prepared by a scientific group assembled at MIT | The Clean Air Act (CAA)<br><br>The Occupational and Safety Health Act (OSH Act) |

gains were considered to outweigh the environmental and health costs. This perception began to change in 1962 with the publication of Rachel Carson's book *Silent Spring*. Carson described the potential dangers of the pesticide DDT (dichlorodiphenyl trichloroethane) and argued that its development and continued use served the interests of chemical companies, industrial agriculture, the military, and universities. The fierce opposition to her book by the chemical industry had the effect of strengthening the public resolve behind her work. "*Silent Spring* altered a balance of power in the world. No one since would be able to sell pollution as the necessary underside of progress so easily or uncritically" (Hynes 1989, p. 3).

The growing concern about the adverse effects on the environment was paralleled by an increasing concern that available national resources might not be sufficient to sustain economic growth into the future. Although this concern was tempered by several influential studies (Barnett and Morse 1963; President's Material Policy Commission 1952; RFF 1954), the issue returned with a vengeance in 1972 with the publication of *The Limits to Growth* (Meadows, Meadows, et al. 1972).

Accompanied by a growing distrust of government-industrial coziness during the 1960s, arguments warning of the environmental problems associated with the prevailing development model of rapid industrialization and economic growth began to surface. Two classic publications which supported this movement were "The Tragedy of the Commons" by Garrett Hardin and *The Population Bomb* by Paul Ehrlich, both written in 1968. In addition to these publications, the late 1960s experienced two environmental disasters—the Santa Barbara oil spill and the oil fire on the Cuyahoga River—that increased the pressure on the U.S. government for action.

In response to the growing public concern, the U.S. Congress passed the National Environmental Policy Act (NEPA), which was signed by President Nixon in 1970. This act was followed by other key environmental and worker health and safety regulations, such as the following:

- The 1970 Clean Air Act (CAA)
- The 1970 Occupational Safety and Health Act (OSH Act)
- The 1972 Federal Water Pollution Control Act
- The 1972 Federal Environmental Pesticide Control Act (now known as the Federal Insecticide, Fungicide, and Rodenticide Act)
- The 1973 Endangered Species Act (ESA)

- The 1974 Safe Drinking Water Act (SDWA)
- The 1976 Resource Conservation and Recovery Act (RCRA)
- The 1976 Toxic Substances Control Act (TSCA)
- The 1977 Clean Air Act Amendments (CAAA)
- The 1980 Superfund legislation.

These pieces of legislation directly reflect three of four environmental concerns that can be associated with sustainable development—(1) that industrialization negatively affects ecosystem integrity and biological diversity and indirectly affects human health; (2) that the world's resources and energy supplies are finite; and (3) that toxic pollution directly affects human health and the health of other species. The fourth environmental concern—that greenhouse gases from anthropocentric sources are leading to the disruption of the global climate—is somewhat loosely connected to the CAAA of 1977 and 1990.*

On April 22, 1970, almost four months after the signing of the NEPA, the first Earth Day was held. Some 20 million Americans peacefully demonstrated in streets, parks, and auditoriums for a healthy environment and in support of environmental reform.[1] The event crystallized the views of those who had been protesting against harm to the environment and to humans and enabled them to articulate a shared set of common values.

It has been argued that the 1960s' influence on modern environmentalism is what the 1970s were to the formulation of sustainable development (Speth 2002, 2003). As national environmental agendas began to be established throughout the world, the 1970s witnessed the emergence of a concern for the human environment in the international arena (Table 2.2).

---

* In the mid-1970s, scientists concluded that chlorofluorocarbons (CFCs) had the potential to deplete stratospheric ozone that provides an essential barrier to the damaging UV-B radiation emitted from the sun (Molina and Rowland 1974). In response to this research, the CAAA of 1977 included a congressional directive to undertake further research on ozone depletion, and the later CAAA of 1990 called for a reduction in the amount of CFCs that were being used. The recognition that human activity could change the thermal radiative process of the atmosphere led scientists to consider the potential impact of the vast amount of carbon dioxide ($CO_2$) that had entered (and continues to enter) the atmosphere since the start of the Industrial Revolution. A 2007 Supreme Court decision found that greenhouse gases such as $CO_2$ could be regulated under the Clean Air Act (Ashford and Caldart 2008), and in December 2009 (at the beginning of the UN climate-change conference in Copenhagen, COP-15), the Environmental Protection Agency (EPA) issued a final ruling that greenhouse gases were a danger to human health and the environment, paving the way for regulation of carbon dioxide emissions.

**TABLE 2.2: THE CREATION OF AN INTERNATIONAL ENVIRONMENTAL AGENDA—1971 TO 1980**

| YEAR | EVENTS | PUBLICATIONS | U.S. LEGISLATION |
|---|---|---|---|
| 1971 | The Man and the Biosphere program (MAB) is founded by UNESCO (UN Educational, Scientific, and Cultural Organization). Greenpeace starts in Canada. The OECD creates the Environment Committee (now the Environment Policy Committee—EPOC) and the Environment Directorate. President Nixon closes the gold window and unilaterally terminates the international gold exchange standard established by the Bretton Woods agreements. Thus the dollar is no longer effectively linked—directly or indirectly—to gold. | *Founex Report*—Report by the Preparatory Committee for the United Nations Conference on the Human Environment *Only One Earth*—B. Ward and R. Dubos *The Closing Circle: Nature, Man, and Technology*—B. Commoner *The Entropy Law and the Economic Process*—N. Georgescu-Roegen | |
| 1972 | The UN Conference on the Human Environment is held in Stockholm, Sweden (known as the Stockholm Conference). The United Nations Environment Programme (UNEP) is formed following the Stockholm Conference. | *The Limits to Growth: A Report for the Club of Rome's Project on the Predicament of Mankind*—D.H. Meadows, D.L. Meadows, J. Randers, and W.W. Behrens III *Blueprint for Survival*—The Ecologist *Exploring New Ethics for Survival: The Voyage of the Spaceship Beagle*—G. J. Hardin *Only One Earth: The Care and Maintenance of a Small Planet*—B. Ward | The Federal Water Pollution Control Act Amendments (this law is amended in 1977 and becomes known as the Clean Water Act—CWA) The Federal Environmental Pesticide Control Act, which amended the 1947 Federal Insecticide, Fungicide, and Rodenticide Act (FIFRA) |
| 1973 | OPEC oil embargo begins. | *Small Is Beautiful*—E. F. Schumacher | The Endangered Species Act (ESA) |
| 1974 | *World population—4 billion.* The World Food Council is formed and a reconstituted World Food Programme (WFP) is established following the World Food Conference in Rome. | *Cocoyoc Declaration*—Prepared by a UN-sponsored meeting in Cocoyoc, Mexico, called to discuss how development can be focused on achieving basic human needs *Stratospheric Sink for Chlorofluoromethanes: Chlorine Atom-Catalysed Destruction of Ozone*—F. S. Rowland and M. J. Molina | The Safe Drinking Water Act (SDWA) |
| 1975 | The Worldwatch Institute is established. | What Now: Another Development—Report by the Dag Hammarskjöld Foundation, Sweden | |
| 1976 | The UN Habitat program is created following the UN Conference on Human Settlements (Habitat I) in Vancouver, Canada. | *Crisis in the Workplace: Occupational Disease and Injury*—N. A. Ashford | The Resource Conservation and Recovery Act (RCRA) The Toxic Substances Control Act (TSCA) |
| 1977 | The UN adopts a Plan of Action to Combat Desertification (PACD) following the UN Conference on Desertification in Nairobi, Kenya. | | |
| 1978 | | *World Development Report (WDR)*—The WDR is first published by the World Bank *The Human Future Revisited*—H. Brown *The Twenty-Ninth Day*—L. Brown | |
| 1979 | The World Meteorological Organization (WMO) sponsors the first World Climate Conference held in Geneva, Switzerland. Three Mile Island nuclear accident occurs in Pennsylvania. Second oil shock occurs as the Iranian oil sector reduces its oil exports. | *Banking on the Biosphere*—International Institute of Environment and Development (IIED) *Progress for a Small Planet*—B. Ward *Scarcity and Growth Reconsidered*—V. K. Smith (ed.) | |
| 1980 | | *World Conservation Strategy*—Published by the IUCN (International Union for Conservation of Nature and Natural Resources), the UNEP, and the WWF North-South: A Program for Survival—Report by the Independent Commission on International Development Issues The Global 2000 Report to the President—Report by the U.S. Council on Environmental Quality and the Department of State | The Comprehensive Environmental Response, Compensation, and Liability Act (CERCLA)—also known as Superfund |

The impetus for this development was the UN Conference on the Human Environment that was held in Stockholm on June 5–16, 1972 (McEntire 2005). Caldwell and Weiland (1996) attribute such importance to the Stockholm Conference for two reasons. First, it legitimized the critical need for all nation-states to establish environmental policy at the national level. Second, it informed the world society of the vital role that a healthy biosphere plays in sustaining life, and hence it placed a concern for the environment on national agendas. Both of these developments were deemed necessary for the international community to address environmental concerns legitimately (ibid.).

Although the Stockholm Conference and its agreements were influential in advancing concerns for the human environment, many suggest that the conference's major impact came from the intense preconference deliberations and the explosion of literature that raised the world's consciousness about the natural environment (Emmelin 1972; Dernbach 1998; Strong 1972; UNEP 1982b, 1982c). One notable example was the preconference deliberation that occurred at Founex, Switzerland (UN 1972), on the relationship between the environment and development. The meeting recognized that because almost all nations needed to undergo some form of development, sound approaches to environmental planning needed to be established (UNEP 1982c). The meeting broadened the dialogue beyond environmental concerns in industrialized regions by making an explicit link between poverty and environmental degradation, highlighting the need for economic growth in developing regions. This latter recognition is considered a key reason that many developing nations participated in the Stockholm Conference (UNEP 1982d).

From the deliberations at Founex and the debates that ensued during the Stockholm Conference, the term "ecodevelopment" emerged to describe the process of "ecologically sound development," which included the "positive management of the environment for human benefit" (UNEP 1982c, p. 7). The prefix "eco" is used to signify both "economic" and "ecological" because both words stem from the Greek root *oikos*, meaning house or home (Colby 1991). The term "ecodevelopment" was subsequently adopted and advocated by the UNEP during the 1970s.* In a

sense, ecodevelopment could be described as the predecessor to sustainable development. The UNEP defined ecodevelopment as "development at regional and local levels . . . consistent with the potentials of the area involved, with attention given to the adequate and rational use of the natural resources, and to applications of technological styles" (UNEP 1975, quoted in Redclift 1987, p. 34). Hence ecodevelopment focused on satisfying basic human needs in an "environmentally sound [regional] production system" (Nayar 1994, p. 1327).

Although the Stockholm Conference placed a concern for the environment on the international agenda, its official agreements sidestepped a number of important issues raised by developing nations. A notable case is the call by developed nations for global economic reforms to address the declining terms of trade faced by many raw-commodity exporters in developing economies (Clapp and Dauvergne 2005). By enabling developing nations to realize higher returns on their exports, poverty and the related environmental degradation could be addressed. The issue of global economic reforms continued to be debated during the 1970s, but calls for a new international economic order did not lead to substantive changes.

Ten years after Stockholm, the UN held a meeting in Nairobi to review progress in implementing the Stockholm Action Plan and to make recommendations with respect to prevailing environmental trends for the future actions of the UNEP. The preconference reports prepared by the UNEP (1982b, 1982d) and the Nairobi Declaration presented a clear message that although nation-states had made progress toward environmental protection, their actions were insufficient to reverse the rate of environmental degradation occurring throughout the world.

The Nairobi meeting raised several important issues that warrant discussion. First, the negative impacts of overpopulation were formally recognized as a growing problem. Whereas population had been largely overlooked at the Stockholm Conference, it played a much more prominent role at the Nairobi meeting. In particular, the Nairobi Declaration made an explicit connection between population, resources, and the health of the environment: "During the last decade, new perceptions have emerged: the need for environmental management and assessment, the [proposition of a] . . . complex interrelationship between environment, development, population and resources and the strain on the environment generated,

* Although the UNEP was an advocate of ecodevelopment, Colby (1991, p. 200) argues that its predominant practices were still locked in the realm of environmental protection that focused on "*damage control*: on repairing and setting limits to harmful activity. Rather than focusing on ways to *improve* both

development actions and ecological resilience, this approach was inherently *remedial* in practice."

particularly in urban areas, by increasing population have become widely recognized" (UNEP 1982a).

Second, during the decade since Stockholm, developing countries that had previously rejected the imposition of strict environmental standards had now become worried about the damage that was being done to their environment (Redclift 1984, p. 49). Their concern was that this environmental damage was affecting both the health of their people and their future development prospects. This transition in opinion is most clearly reflected in the report of the Governing Council of the UNEP on the general debate at the Nairobi meeting: "Differences of views between developed and developing countries with regard to environmental perceptions had to a large extent faded over the last 10 years, and the concepts of sustainable development and rational management of natural resources were now widely accepted as the cornerstones of environmental policies."[2] Hence it was unlikely that developing nations would continue to disagree in principle with the creation of standards to protect the environment on which their livelihoods depended.

Finally and most important, the Nairobi meeting highlighted a reversal of the perceived impacts of economic growth. The UNEP report titled *The Environment in 1982: Retrospect and Prospect* provides a succinct description of the turnaround in opinion: "A decade ago the desirability of further economic growth was questioned in some quarters, but the negative effects of the recent slow-down in economic growth have reinforced the view that it is an essential instrument in achieving social goals. In developing countries particularly, economic growth is vitally important and remains a major force for improving the health and welfare of people. It is now perceived that economic growth can often be managed not only to avoid environmental degradation but also, in many cases, to improve the environment" (UNEP 1982b, p. 37).*

Because the initial concerns for the human environment grew from the negative impacts of industrialization in developed countries, the shift in the international focus toward the environmental problems faced by developing nations is significant. The identification of poverty as a major contributor to environmental degradation increased the importance of economic growth because it was the only pragmatic way to alleviate poverty. Developing countries argued that if poverty and underdevelopment were made a priority, this would enable them to break free from the poverty trap in which poverty and environmental degradation were continually worsening. However, because no progress had been made during the 1970s in creating a new form of environmentally sound development, the only way to grow the economy was to follow the path of conventional development. This meant a reliance on technology that was fueled by nonrenewable resources and generated a significant amount of pollution, which would likely damage ecosystems and human health. Whereas developing nations made the case in the 1971 Founex report that because their environment had not been burdened by industrial pollution they could carry a certain amount of industrial activity (UN 1972), their position changed during the next decade as studies revealed the worsening condition of their environment (UNEP 1982c, 1982d). Thus developing countries faced a paradox. They needed to develop to protect and improve their environment—on which their future depended—but in doing so, they would ultimately damage the very environment they wished to safeguard. This contradiction led to the birth of sustainable development, the idea that development and environmental protection could advance in unison. Hence sustainable development would be able not only to meet the needs of the present but also to do so in a manner that did not damage the environment and compromise the ability of future generations to meet their needs (WCED 1987, p. 43). The WCED (Brundtland) definition of sustainable development is discussed in more detail later.

The 1980s marked a turning point when nations began to recognize that their environmental problems extended beyond national boundaries and were having impacts on a global scale (Table 2.3). This realization further spurred the development of an international environmental agenda, and the actions taken in the following two decades as a result of this agenda can be considered the first attempt at global environmental governance (Speth 2003).

---

* The slow growth of the world economy during the early 1980s, combined with rising debt-service obligations and a reduction in the inflow of finance, meant that many developing nations faced severe economic crises and were forced to reduce social spending and curtail environmental protection efforts (Redclift 1996; WCED 1987). The 1991 UNEP report *The State of the World Environment* described the 1980s as being the "lost decade" (UNEP 1991, p. 2). The report criticized the structural adjustment policies of developing nations that were designed to dampen demand, devalue currencies, remove subsidies from fuel and foodstuffs, and reduce government spending (ibid., p. 3). In particular, it stated that the poor tended to bear the brunt of such policies, which had the result of increasing malnutrition and reducing health services and school enrollment rates. It concluded that these negative effects of structural adjustment were "inhuman

and ultimately inefficient" and that future adjustment policies must have a "human face—which protects the poor" (ibid., p. 4).

**TABLE 2.3: THE EMERGENCE OF SUSTAINABLE DEVELOPMENT—1981 TO 2010**

| YEAR | EVENTS | PUBLICATIONS | U.S. LEGISLATION |
|---|---|---|---|
| 1981 | | *Global Strategy for Health for All by the Year 2000*—Prepared by the World Health Organization | |
| 1982 | The International debt crisis erupts and threatens the world financial system. World Resource Institute (WRI) is established. | *The Environment in 1982: Retrospect and Prospect*—UNEP<br>*The World Environment: 1972–1982*—UNEP<br>*World Charter for Nature*—Adopted by the UN General Assembly | |
| 1983 | The World Commission on Environment and Development (WCED) is formed. | *Environmental Research and Management Priorities for the 1980s*—Report prepared by an international group of scientists on behalf of the Royal Swedish Academy of Sciences | |
| 1984 | Drought in Ethiopia—between 250,000 and 1 million people die from starvation.<br>Bhopal incident—a leak of deadly methyl isocyanate at a Union Carbide pesticide plant in Bhopal, India, kills thousands of people.<br>The OECD International Conference on Environment and Economics is held in Paris, France. | | |
| 1985 | British scientists discover an ozone hole over the Antarctic.<br>The World Meteorological Society, the UNEP, and the International Council of Scientific Unions meet in Villach, Austria, to report on the build-up of $CO_2$ and other greenhouse gases in the atmosphere. | | |
| 1986 | A nuclear reactor meltdown at the Chernobyl power station releases radioactive material throughout the Northern Hemisphere.<br>The IUCN (International Union for Conservation of Nature and Natural Resources) Conference on Environment and Development is held in Ottawa, Canada.<br>The Uruguay Round of the General Agreement on Tariffs and Trade (GATT) lays the foundation for the establishment of the World Trade Organization (WTO) in 1995. | | The Superfund Amendments and Reauthorization Act (SARA), which amended CERCLA<br>The Emergency Planning and Community Right-to-Know Act (EPCRA) |
| 1987 | *World population*—5 billion.<br>The IMF (International Monetary Fund) establishes the Enhanced Structural Adjustment Facility (ESAF). | *Our Common Future*—WCED | |
| 1988 | The Intergovernmental Panel on Climate Change (IPCC) is established. | | |
| 1989 | The Exxon Valdez oil tanker runs aground spilling 11 million gallons of oil into Alaska's Prince William Sound. | *Valdez Principles* (later renamed the *CERES Principles*)—CERES | |
| 1990 | The International Institute for Sustainable Development (IISD) is established in Canada. | | The Oil Pollution Act (OPA)<br>The Pollution Prevention Act (PPA) |
| 1991 | The Global Environmental Facility (GEF) is established.<br>The European Bank for Reconstruction and Development (EBRD) is established. | *Caring for the Earth: A Strategy for Sustainable Living*—Published by the IUCN, the UNEP, and the WWF<br>*Ecological Economics: The Science and Management of Sustainability*—R. Costanza | The Intermodal Surface Transportation Efficiency Act (ISTEA) |
| 1992 | The UN Conference on Environment and Development (UNCED) is held in Rio de Janeiro, Brazil.<br>The Earth Council is established in Costa Rica. | *Agenda 21*—UN Department of Economic and Social Affairs (DESA)<br>*Changing Course*—S. Schmidheiny | |
| 1993 | The UN World Conference on Human Rights is held in Vienna, Austria.<br>The UN Commission on Sustainable Development that was created at the UNCED holds its first meeting.<br>The North American Free Trade Agreement (NAFTA) is signed by Canada, Mexico, and the United States.<br>President Bill Clinton announces the creation of the President's Council for Sustainable Development (PCSD). | *Beyond the Limits: Confronting Global Collapse, Envisioning a Sustainable Future*— D. H. Meadows, D. L. Meadows, and J. Randers | |
| 1994 | The UN International Conference on Population and Development is held in Cairo, Egypt. | | |

| YEAR | EVENTS | PUBLICATIONS | U.S. LEGISLATION |
|---|---|---|---|
| 1995 | The UN World Summit for Social Development is held in Copenhagen, Denmark.<br>The UN Fourth World Conference for Women is held in Beijing, China.<br>The WTO is established.<br>The World Business Council for Sustainable Development (WBCSD) is established in Geneva, Switzerland. | | |
| 1996 | The Summit of the Americas on Sustainable Development is held in Santa Cruz, Bolivia.<br>ISO 14001 is formally adopted as the voluntary international standard for corporate environmental management systems.<br>The Second United Nations Conference on Human Settlements (Habitat II) is held in Istanbul, Turkey. | *Sustainable America: A New Consensus for Prosperity, Opportunity, and a Healthy Environment for the Future*—Report by the President's Council for Sustainable Development<br>*Beyond Growth*—H. E. Daly<br>*How Much Is Enough?*—A. T. Durning<br>*Our Stolen Future: Are We Threatening Our Fertility, Intelligence, and Survival? A Scientific Detective Story*—T. Colburn, D. Dumanoski, and J. P. Myers | The Food Quality Protection Act (FQPA) |
| 1997 | The IMF establishes the Supplemental Reserve Facility (SRF).<br>The Special Session of the UN General Assembly to Review and Appraise the Implementation of Agenda 21 is held. | *Do We Consume Too Much?*—M. Sagoff<br><br>*No Middle Way on the Environment*—P. R. Ehrlich, G. C. Daily, S. C. Daily, and J. Salzman | |
| 1998 | *World population—6 billion.*<br>The IMF activates General Arrangements to Borrow for the first time in twenty years. | *Cradle to Cradle: Remaking the Way We Make Things*—W. McDonough and M. Braungart | The Transportation Equity Act for the 21st Century (TEA-21) |
| 1999 | The first Dow Jones global sustainability index is launched. | *Our Common Journey*—National Research Council<br><br>*Natural Capitalism: Creating the Next Industrial Revolution*—P. Hawken, A. Lovins, and L. H. Lovins | The Chemical Safety Information, Site Security, and Fuels Act |
| 2000 | The UN Millennium Summit is held in New York<br>The EU establishes the Lisbon Strategy to promote sustainable economic growth (via competitiveness) and employment while respecting the environment. | | |
| 2001 | The IMF announces that it will establish the International Capital Markets Department to enhance its surveillance, crisis-prevention, and crisis-management activities. | | |
| 2002 | The UN World Summit on Sustainable Development (WSSD) is held in Johannesburg, South Africa. | | |
| 2004 | | *Limits to Growth: The 30-Year Update*—D. H. Meadows, J. Randers, and D. L. Meadows | |
| 2005 | | *Scarcity and Growth Revisited: Natural Resources and the Environment in the New Millennium*—R. D. Simpson, M. A. Toman, and R. U. Ayres (eds.) | |
| 2006 | | *Stern Review on the Economics of Climate Change*—N. Stern | |
| 2008 | | *The Bridge at the Edge of the World: Capitalism, the Environment, and Crossing from Crisis to Sustainability*—J. G. Speth<br>*Managing without Growth: Slow by Design, Not Disaster*—P. A. Victor | |
| 2009 | Treaty of Lisbon is signed by the requisite number of EU member states. | | |
| 2010 | The European Commission established the Europe 2020 Strategy to promote sustainable growth and employment. | *Cents and Sustainability: Securing Our Common Future by Decoupling Economic Growth from Environmental Pressure*—M. H. Smith, K. C. Hargroves, C. Desha | |
| 2010 | The Preparatory Committee for the UN Conference on Sustainable Development held its first meeting in preparation for the Rio+20 Earth Summit in 2012. | | |
| 2010 | The BP Gulf oil spill occurs. | | |

One of the foundational texts on sustainable development, which was published two years before the Nairobi meeting, was the International Union for Conservation of Nature and Natural Resources (IUCN), UNEP, et al.'s (1980) *World Conservation Strategy* (*WCS*). The *WCS* is an eloquent synthesis of a decade of intense debate in the international community over the need to protect the environment while continuing the process of development. The *WCS* used the term "sustainable" to describe development that takes "account of social and ecological factors, as well as economic ones; of the living and non-living resource base; and of the long term as well as short term advantages and disadvantages of alternative actions" (IUCN, UNEP, et al. 1980, p. 18). Acknowledging that "conservation and development have so seldom been combined that they often appear—and are sometimes represented as being—incompatible" (ibid.), the *WCS* proceeds to develop its case why conservation and economic and social development are mutually supportive endeavors. In using the word "sustainable" to describe the development process, the *WCS* effectively rechristened "ecodevelopment" (the term previously used to describe ecologically sound socioeconomic development) as "sustainable development" (Caldwell and Weiland 1996, p. 243). However, this rechristening was more than simply a name change.

A central aspect of ecodevelopment was *national self-reliance*, which focused on local and regional development to meet human needs. National self-reliance also implied that nation-states should be able to detach themselves from the international economic system temporarily if they were adversely affected by, for example, fluctuations in the world commodity market.* However, the oil shocks of the 1970s led to economic recessions throughout the world, drastically reducing trade and the availability of aid for developing nations. During this period, environmental degradation in developing nations worsened, highlighting the essential role that the international economy plays in national development (UNEP 1982b). Recognizing that conservation and development are closely interlinked, the *WCS* highlighted the importance of a "New International Development Strategy." The purpose of this strategy was "(a) to redress the inequalities in the relations between richer and poorer nations; (b) to establish a more dynamic, more stable and less vulnerable world economy, in which all countries have opportunities to participate on a fuller and more equal basis; (c) to stimulate accelerated economic growth in the poorer countries of the world; and (d) to reduce and eventually overcome the worst aspects of poverty by improving the lot of the hundreds of millions of people now living in abject poverty and despair" (IUCN, UNEP, et al. 1980, p. 62). To achieve this strategy, the *WCS* called for the liberalization of trade and the removal of all trade barriers to goods from developing countries. In addition, it recommended that economic and social growth be accelerated in developing nations.† Hence the *WCS* did more than simply rename ecodevelopment as sustainable development; it connected local, regional, and national economic and social development with the conservation of living resources and the need for a stable, equitable, and more liberalized (that is, less regulated or subsidized) international economic system in which developing countries could participate on a more equal footing.

The *WCS*'s notion of sustainable development—the idea that economic and social development can occur in unison with the conservation of living resources—presented a different perspective on global problems. Although the *WCS* did not fully integrate development and environmental considerations (Clapp and Dauvergne 2005), their use of the term "sustainable development" gave it greater recognition and increased its use in the international arena. The term became the central theme of the World Commission on Environment and Development's report *Our Common Future* and was the integrating theme of the 1992 UN Conference on Environment and Development (Caldwell and Weiland 1996).

In light of the evidence that environmental conditions around the world were deteriorating (Brandt 1980; CEQ 1980; IUNC, UNEP, et al. 1980; UNEP 1982b) and population and economic growth—two critical factors affecting the environment—were continuing to increase (Strong 2003), the Governing Council of the UNEP called for the creation of a "global strategy for sustainable development."[3] The

---

*   Such fluctuations might occur because of the dumping of a heavily subsidized agricultural product onto the international market. This action reduces the price of the commodity, making it impossible for the farmers of nations that do not (or are unable to) subsidize the agricultural sector to compete.

†   This recommendation can be traced back to the 1974 Declaration on the Establishment of a New International Economic Order (NIEO), which states that the purpose of the new international economic order is to "ensure steadily accelerating economic and social development." *Declaration on the Establishment of a New International Economic Order*, Resolution 3201 (S-VI), May 1, 1974, www.un.org/Depts/dhl/resguide/resins .htm (accessed May 13, 2010). The declaration was released in 1974, the year the first oil crisis ended.

following year, the UN General Assembly passed Resolution 38/161, approving the creation of a special independent commission on the environment to propose "long-term environmental strategies for achieving sustainable development to the year 2000 and beyond."[4] As part of its terms of reference, the commission was required to consider the interrelationships between developed and developing nations and between people, resources, the environment, and development. In short, the commission was required to do nothing less than rethink and articulate a new vision of development.

Under the chairmanship of then Prime Minister Gro Harlem Brundtland of Norway, the World Commission on Environment and Development (WCED, also known as the Brundtland Commission) was subsequently formed and held its first meeting in Geneva, Switzerland, in October 1984. The commission consisted of twenty-three members: four from central European countries, seven from developed nations (including Maurice Strong, the chairman of the 1972 Stockholm Conference), and twelve from developing nations (WCED 1987).

Between 1984 and 1987, the Brundtland Commission received advice and support from thousands of individuals, institutions, and organizations from all over the world (WCED 1987, p. 359). The commission also visited each world region to obtain a firsthand view of environment and development issues and to hold deliberative meetings and open public hearings. On December 11, 1987, the commission's report, *Environmental Perspective to the Year 2000 and Beyond*, was submitted to, and adopted by, the UN General Assembly via Resolution 42/186 as a "broad framework to guide national action and international co-operation on policies and programmes aimed at achieving environmentally sound development."[5] That same year, the commission's report was published as *Our Common Future*.

Benefiting from more than a decade of debate over the notion of ecodevelopment and then of sustainable development, the Brundtland Commission sought to effectively integrate social and economic development with the need for environmental protection. By combining these elements with the important notion of intergenerational equity, the commission created what has become the first widely accepted definition of sustainable development.

Sustainable development is development that meets the needs of the present without compromising the ability of future generations to meet their own needs. It contains within it two key concepts:

- the concept of "needs," in particular the essential needs of the world's poor, to which overriding priority should be given; and
- the idea of limitations imposed by the state of technology and social organization on the environment's ability to meet present and future needs.

Thus the goals of economic and social development must be defined in terms of sustainability in all countries—developed or developing, market-orientated or centrally planned. Interpretations will vary, but must share certain general features and must flow from a consensus on the basic concept of sustainable development and on a broad strategic framework for achieving it. (WCED 1987, p. 43)

This definition highlights what has since become one of the major issues of contention about sustainable development: the *interpretation* of sustainable development by one nation might be seen as leading to "unsustainable" development by another. The ongoing debate between developed and developing nations reveals that the commission's objective to find middle ground between developed and developing nations' positions was largely unsuccessful (Cock 2002).

In keeping with the approach to development articulated by the 1974 Cocoyoc Declaration and influential publications such as *Small Is Beautiful* (Schumacher 1999)* and *What Now: Another Development* (Dag Hammarskjöld Foundation 1975),† *Our Common Future* defined the major objective of development as the "satisfaction of human needs and aspirations" (WCED 1987, p. 43). Further, it saw sustainable

---

*     Schumacher (1999, p. 139) rejected the idea that what "is best for the rich must be best for the poor" and redefined the conventional view of development toward human needs. "Development does not start with goods; it starts with people and their education, organization, and discipline. Without these three, all resources remain latent, untapped, potential" (ibid.). Schumacher's ideas are clearly reflected by the Cocoyoc Declaration, which establishes human needs as the focus of development efforts.

†     The Cocoyoc Declaration, *Small Is Beautiful*, and *What Now: Another Development* all present a consistent message of the need to redefine the whole purpose of development. They reject development that is focused on economic growth in favor of development that aims to satisfy the basic physiological and psychological needs of humankind. Although the primary focus is on meeting the basic needs of the poorest sections of each society, there is recognition that the needs of affluent sections of society are also not being satisfied. Free trade is rejected in favor of an international economic system that allows nation-states to enter and exit the economic system in concert with their own development strategies. Such an economic system is also seen to promote a more equitable distribution of economic gains and respond to concerns about environmental justice. In parallel, national sovereignty, the right to diversity, self-reliance, and endogenous development are all recognized as essential components of the satisfaction of human needs. Finally, there is a unanimous recognition that development must be in harmony with the environment.

development not as an end state but rather as "a process of change in which the exploitation of resources, the direction of investments, the orientation of technological development, and institutional change are made consistent with future as well as present needs" (ibid., p. 9). The Brundtland Commission adopted a highly political agenda by viewing "sustainable development as a policy objective, rather than a methodology. It is an over-arching concept. . . . Such an approach is unapologetically normative, and places both the responsibility for problems, and the political will to overcome them, in the hands of human actors" (ibid., p. 37).

The Brundtland Commission made a convincing argument that the environment and development are "inexorably linked" and cannot be treated as separate challenges (WCED 1987, p. 37). It concluded: "Development cannot subsist upon a deteriorating environmental resource base; the environment cannot be protected when growth leaves out of account the costs of environmental destruction" (ibid.). This recognition that the "costs of environmental destruction" need to be considered in the development equation provided the field of environmental economics with a strong endorsement. Further, the commission highlighted the role public policy could play in using "incentives and disincentives" to guide commercial organizations to develop environmentally sound technologies (ibid., p. 60). Redclift (1996, p. 18) argues that the endorsement of economic mechanisms as valid policy tools to protect the environment "effectively opened the door to environmental economics which sought to fill the policy vacuum."

*Our Common Future* appeared at a time when the political climate was beginning to become more receptive to the issues raised by the report. Future prospects for economic growth in industrialized nations were beginning to look positive, while global ecosystems were beginning to show signs of distress (Engfeldt 2002). Hence there was an international audience eager to learn how to embrace economic growth while reducing pressure on ecosystems. The commission's insistence that science and technology could be used to meet human needs and solve environmental problems was the answer many were looking for. Toward the end of the 1980s, many governments were committed to market liberalization as a means of solving their economic problems. They saw trade as a way of stimulating ordinary (and unsustainable) economic growth. Therefore, by focusing on technological improvements that could support economic growth, conserve natural resources, and protect the environment, the commission gained the

support of both developed and developing nations. As Dryzek (1997, p. 136) notes, "Sustainable development would surely lose unless it could be demonstrated that environmental conservation . . . [was] obviously good for business profitability and economic growth everywhere, not just that these competing values can be reconciled." Hence unless science and technological innovation—two mainstays of economic growth in industrial societies—were a central theme of sustainable development, national governments (primarily of the North) would most likely have rejected the concept as another radical and politically unrealistic form of environmentalism.

By explicitly bringing science and technology into the development equation, the technologically optimistic Brundtland Commission sought to articulate a new era of economic growth where policies were designed to release human ingenuity to expand and increase the natural resource base. Hence economic growth could continue, and the environment could be protected. The commission stipulated, however, that for this to be achieved, the protection of ecosystems "must be guaranteed," and all "economic partners must be satisfied that the basis of exchange is equitable" (WCED 1987, p. 17).

Having articulated a bold new development agenda, the Brundtland Commission highlighted a major problem with the institutional frameworks that would implement the new era of economic and social development. It argued that most governmental environment agencies, especially those in developing nations, "tend to be independent, fragmented, [and] working to relatively narrow mandates with closed decision processes" (WCED 1987, p. 9). It stated that the same was true for many international agencies responsible for areas such as development lending, trade regulation, and agricultural development. The commission believed that the solution to these problems lay in ensuring that national and international institutions consider the ecological dimensions of policy together with economic, social, trade, energy, agricultural, and other dimensions. Such integration would close "institutional gaps" and bring environmental concerns into the center of decision making. The idea was to develop a more proactive approach to environmental protection, rather than the more expensive "react-and-cure" approach that was typical of many government policies in the post-Stockholm era (Runnalls 2008). In parallel with this approach, the commission called for the strengthening of international law and conventions and for better implementation of these mechanisms for change.

*Our Common Future* was the first rigorous attempt to formulate the concept of sustainable development. A major part of its success was due to the commission's efforts to base its recommendations on institutional and political realities and on what needed to be accomplished in the short term. The endorsement of an equitable and liberal international economy, fueled by scientific advance and technological progress that conserved resources and minimized environmental harm, resonated well with those who were struggling to reconcile development with the environment. Developed nations could continue along their development paths guided by economic incentives encouraging sustainable development. Simultaneously, developing nations could look forward to rapid economic growth by joining a more equitable international economic system.

However, even before the report's publication, some commentators remained skeptical whether nation-states could implement the recommendations put forward (Redclift 1987). See also Runnalls (2008), who argues that the failure to dramatically reform domestic institutions and establish an international framework to address sustainability concerns is the core reason for the persistent worsening global threats.

In response mainly to the Brundtland Commission's call for an international conference to "review progress made, and to promote follow-up arrangements . . . [to *Our Common Future*] to set benchmarks and to maintain human progress within the guidelines of human needs and natural laws" (WCED 1987, p. 343), the UN General Assembly decided to "convene the United Nations Conference on Environment and Development"[6] (UNCED) in Brazil in 1992.* The decision to hold the conference

in a developing nation—especially one that had made significant progress on environmental issues since the 1972 Stockholm Conference—"had enormous political relevance and symbolism" (McCormick 1995, p. 254). In addition, the importance of the UNCED was reinforced when it was decided that the conference should be held at the "summit level," meaning that heads of state should be present. This decision had the effect of renaming the UNCED in the media as the Earth Summit (Strong 2003).

The UNCED was subsequently held in Rio de Janerio on June 3–14, 1992, and attracted some 178 nation-states, including 110 heads of state who attended the final two-day meeting (UN 1993b, 1993c, 1993d). The Earth Summit (also known as the Rio Summit) was much larger than the Stockholm Conference and was the first time in history that so many influential people had gathered in one place.

The main objectives of the UNCED were to review the progress that had been made since the Stockholm Conference and to identify strategies, programs, legal mechanisms, financial resources, and regional/national/global institutional frameworks that could protect and enhance the environment in the socioeconomic development process of all nation states.[7] Its purpose was nothing less than to develop ways to protect the planet and ensure the welfare and future of humankind. Further, the UNCED planned to bridge the major conflicts between developed and developing nations in order to increase the likelihood that its outcomes would be implemented (Linner and Selin 2003). For this objective to be achieved, the impact that both poverty and affluence, individually and together, have on the environment needed to be addressed in the search for sustainable forms of economic development (South Centre 2002a).

The UNCED produced three official agreements: (1) the Rio Declaration on Environment and Development; (2) Agenda 21; and (3) the Statement on Forest Principles.[8] In keeping with the Stockholm format, the Rio Declaration provided a statement of principles that was supported by an action plan (Agenda 21) for its implementation. In addition, two conventions were opened for signature—the Convention on Biological Diversity and the Framework Convention on Climate Change. These conventions were a response

---

* Although the 1980s had witnessed a rise in the use of the term "sustainable development," it was not used in the title of the conference because influential developing countries feared that doing so would reduce their freedom of action. Their position was that the title "Environment and Development" provided a level of ambiguity that strengthened their case that the environmental destruction witnessed during the latter part of the twentieth century was caused primarily by developed countries. Hence developed nations should take the lead in rectifying the environmental destruction experienced around the world (Engfeldt 2002). In a similar context, Sachs (2001) argues that the word "development" in the title of the conference was a code word used by developing countries to express their desire for "recognition and justice" (ibid., p. 5). Following the aborted negotiations for a new international economic order in the 1970s and the international debt crisis of the 1980s, developing nations had a strong case for placing their "right to development" at the forefront of discussion (ibid.). Principle 3 of the Rio Declaration—"the right to development must be fulfilled so as to equitably meet developmental and environmental needs of present and fu-

ture generations"—speaks directly to these concerns. Notwithstanding the politics behind the official title of the Earth Summit, Dernbach (1998) argues that the international community's efforts to "synthesize and integrate environment and development issues" (ibid., p. 21) provided a strong endorsement to the notion of sustainable development.

to events of the late 1980s that raised concerns about the continuing extinction of species and depletion of biodiversity (the first environmental concern underlying sustainable development in our framework) and about ozone depletion and global climate change* (the fourth environmental concern).

The UNCED agreements highlight a transition in the international community's conceptualization of development. The notion that prevailing economic policies were deepening economic divisions between developed and developing nations was widely understood by the Earth Summit delegates (UN 1993a). Therefore, the UNCED agreements sought to manage and protect ecosystems so as to establish a *prosperous* future for humankind. Further, it was widely accepted that no nation-state could achieve the objective of sustainable development on its own. As Caldwell and Weiland (1996, p. 107) note, the recognition that global international action would be required to address issues such as climate change meant that "Only One Earth"—the title of the Stockholm Conference—"became an operational reality at Rio."

Continuing the Brundtland Commission's conception of sustainable development, the Rio Declaration and Agenda 21 did not supplant prior approaches to development; rather, they revised (in fundamental ways) the *conventional development* approach. Before the 1990s, the conventional development model (promoted by the international community) incorporated four related concepts: (1) peace and security; (2) economic development; (3) social development; and (4) national governance that secures peace and development (Dernbach 1998, 2004). The Brundtland Commission and the UNCED agreements called for environmental concerns to be *integrated* into the conventional development model. Principles 3 and 4 of the Rio Declaration speak directly to this aim:[9]

> Principle 3: The right to development must be fulfilled so as to equitably meet developmental and environmental needs of present and future generations.

> Principle 4: In order to achieve sustainable development, environmental protection shall constitute an integral part of the development process and cannot be considered in isolation from it.

The recognition of the need to protect the environment—on which the development process depends—can be considered the "fifth element" of the international notion of development (Dernbach 1998, p. 21).

Whereas the Rio Declaration provided a vision of sustainable development, Agenda 21 provided a comprehensive plan of action that was created to guide and coordinate the work of the UN, governments, and other major groups in their efforts to transition society toward sustainable development. In this regard, Agenda 21 is often described as the first blueprint for sustainable development. The preamble to Agenda 21 states that national strategies, plans, policies, and processes are crucial to achieving its successful implementation, and the responsibility for sustainable development consequently lies with national governments. With the emergence of globalization and regional integration over the past two decades, the idea of making national governments responsible for achieving sustainable development is open to debate. For example, the formation of the European Union (EU) provides an alternative regional model for international engagement. The EU Lisbon Strategy—not to be confused with the Lisbon Treaty—is briefly discussed later (also see Section 1.5 in Chapter 1).

Although the UNCED is considered a watershed event in the formation of sustainable development, Box 2.1 provides a discussion of several important dissenting views.

In 1997, five years after the Earth Summit, the UN held a General Assembly Special Session (otherwise known as the Earth Summit II or Earth Summit +5) to review and appraise the implementation of Agenda 21. The evidence presented indicated that the condition of the global environment had continued to deteriorate and looked set to worsen (UNCSD 1997). Although some nations had been able to reduce pollution levels and the degradation of resources through institutional change and capacity-building efforts (involving both public participation and private-sector actions), these actions were not sufficient to counteract the sheer scale of human activity that fed negative environment and development trends (ibid., p. 5).

The 2002 Johannesburg Summit (or the Earth Summit III) was held to review progress since the UNCED. During the ten years since Rio, the world had experienced a new phase of economic growth that was largely based on patterns of development, consumption, and lifestyles that had the effect of widening the gap between affluent and poor nations (South Centre 2002b). Although many developed nations had experienced enhancements in their overall quality of life, the direct or indirect effects of globalization led

---

* The decision to develop the Convention on Climate Change was made at the first meeting of the Intergovernmental Panel on Climate Change (IPCC), established by the World Meteorological Organization (WMO) and the UNEP, in 1988.

## BOX 2.1: CRITIQUES OF THE EARTH SUMMIT AND THE RIO DECLARATION

The 1992 United Nations Conference on Environment and Development (UNCED), commonly known as the Earth Summit, is seen as a seminal event, when the international community gathered to recognize and articulate the concept of sustainable development. Indeed, the summit was unprecedented in its scale and scope. Its mission was to revolutionize the way we think and live so as to protect the planet and ensure the welfare and future of humankind. A major part of this vision was to bridge the conflicts between developed and developing nations that had preoccupied many of the "development" discussions of the previous twenty years. However, although the Earth Summit was perceived by many to have addressed these issues successfully (given the challenge of achieving consensus among so many nation-states), there were those who argued that the summit had sidestepped vitally important and politically volatile questions.

In their review of the Rio Declaration, Grubb, Koch et al. (1993) argue that the principles reveal weaknesses in the compromises that were agreed on to make the declaration politically palatable. "Far from a timeless ethic, it was . . . a snapshot of history" (ibid., p. 85). A significant turning point in the negotiations of the declaration was the success of developing nations in placing their "right to development" at the forefront of considerations (Sachs 2001). The recognition that less developed nations needed to "develop" meant that the Rio Declaration effectively turned into a "declaration on development, rather than on environment" (ibid., p. 5). Further, because "development" can be defined in multiple ways, it can be argued that the Rio Declaration supports a business-as-usual approach to development where the environment is more of an afterthought.

On the eve of the UNCED, David Korten, founder and president of the People-Centered Development Forum, published a column that highlighted three questions that he argued had not been asked in the pre-summit discussions:

1. "Is sustained economic growth possible within a finite ecosystem?"
2. "Is the removal of barriers to the free international flow of trade and capital consistent with the essential need for community and environmental stewardship?"
3. "Is official international assistance part of the solution or part of the problem?"[a]

The first two questions addressed the conviction that economic growth would be sufficient to alleviate the world's problems of poverty and environmental degradation. Korten argued that even a smarter (more environmentally sound) approach to sustained economic growth ignores data that indicate that the earth cannot support the scale of economic (that is, industrial) expansion envisioned by its proponents. Second, a reliance on free trade is likely to enable goods and capital to move freely across national borders, weakening the ability of governments to regulate their own economies and protect their citizens against fluctuations in the international economy. "Where corporate globalists tell of the spread of democracy and vibrant market economies, civil society tells of the power to govern shifting away from people and communities to financial speculators and global corporations dedicated to the blind pursuit of short-term profit in disregard of human and natural concerns."[b] Korten saw the UNCED process as being dominated by nation-states whose political power and social systems were grounded in market capitalism. Hence there was no incentive for them to consider alternative forms of development that moved away from economic growth through industrialization.[c] Those nations, groups, or individuals who questioned the economic belief that a "rising tide will raise all boats" faced ridicule for being insensitive to the needs of the poor.

Korten's third question was based on the fact that although the amount of aid given to developing nations had increased over the previous four decades, environmental conditions in these nations had consistently worsened. Therefore, it seemed only logical to ask whether there were alternative international mechanisms through which developing nations could be assisted.

In response to Korten's column, Herman Daly (1992) suggested that the first question was becoming impossible to ignore because of an increasing volume of data on the declining vitality of the earth's ecosystems. He also suggested that Korten's second and third questions were vitally important and would be the most challenging to address. Rather than attempting to tackle them at Rio, he recommended that they be resolved through further research after the summit and that the UNCED focus its attention on the first question. A look at both the Rio Declaration and Agenda 21 provides some evidence that the UNCED did attempt to address the first question directly. For example, Rio Principle 8 calls for nation-states to try to "reduce and eliminate unsustainable patterns of production and consumption." In support of this principle, Agenda 21 dedicates an entire section to promoting "patterns of consumption and production that reduce environmental stress" (UN 1993a, p. 31).

(continued)

**BOX 2.1** (continued)

One year after the Earth Summit, the *Ecologist* magazine published *Whose Common Future?* (1993), which addressed questions similar to those raised by Korten. However, its critique of the summit was rather more scathing. A main conclusion of *Whose Common Future?* is that communities should be reinstated as sources of social and political authority, and the idea that the modern CEO faces the same common future as the peasant in Bihar should be rejected. A critical question raised by the book is, who will manage the environment for whose interest? It argues that how the environment should be managed is known through past experience and indigenous/local knowledge—both of which are becoming lost in the international economy. Further, the book's arguments highlight the importance of balancing the role of national/local government with the role of the market, both of which must be held accountable to the people's interests by the legal/institutional frameworks of civil society.

Finally, Michael Redclift (1996) provides a valuable retrospective on the Earth Summit. His main criticism is that its spectators might have been convinced that the principal environmental problems facing the world were "climate change, a loss of forests and, with them, biodiversity" (ibid., p. 19). Redclift argues that the UNCED neglected to address important questions relating to population, trade, poverty, the debt crisis (faced by many oil-importing developing nations), and distributional inequality more generally. In addition, he raises the important question whether the "development" of industrialized nations is what the developing world should be aspiring to achieve.

[a] D. Korten (1991), People-Centered Development Forum, "The UN Conference on Environment and Development: Unasked Questions," Column no. 12, April 15, http://livingeconomiesforum.org/1991/12KORTEN (accessed January 13, 2011).

[b] D. Korten (2003), Global Economics, Environmental Integrity, and Justice: Reflections of an "Economic Missionary," National Council of Churches, Enough for All: Sustainable Living in a Global World, Seattle University, June 20–23, www.pcdf.org/2003/NCC.htm (accessed May 13, 2010).

[c] In a speech to the World Business Council on Sustainable Development (WBCSD) on November 4, 1999, Gro Harlem Brundtland admitted that markets are not always right. To provide an example, she quoted a former prime minister of India who "saw no multinational companies willing to invest in educating the children of India, or immunising them and helping them to grow up" (Saha 2002, p. 23).

to the gradual degradation of the social, economic, political, and natural environment in many developing nations (ibid., pp. 6–7). Further, the international economic system was still far from being equitable. Differing levels of development and bargaining power throughout the world meant that the international economy tended to be dominated by those with excessive economic and political power.

Although there was a clear high-level commitment to make progress at Johannesburg, the intractable problems identified at the time of the 1997 Earth Summit II continued to be a problem during the Johannesburg plenary sessions (see Section 2.10 in the Primer on Sustainable Development). The final meeting of the Preparatory Committee for the Johannesburg Summit, held in Bali, Indonesia, from May 27 to June 7, 2002,[10] failed to break the deadlock between developed and developing nations on how to reconcile the conflicting goals of economic development, poverty reduction, and environmental protection (New Scientist 2002a, 2002c).

An important development at the Johannesburg Summit was the recognition that the new era of economic globalization had changed the approaches

considered necessary to transition the world toward sustainable development. The Johannesburg Declaration states that "the rapid integration of markets, mobility of capital and significant increases in investment flows around the world have opened new challenges and opportunities for the pursuit of sustainable development" (UN 2002). In addition to reaffirming a commitment to sustainable development, the declaration specifically urges developed nations to provide the internationally agreed-on levels of official development assistance (ODA) to developing nations. Further, and for the first time in such a declaration, the private sector is called on to recognize its role in achieving sustainable development. Finally, the declaration states that the goals of sustainable development will be achieved through "effective, democratic and accountable international and multilateral institutions," putting multilateralism at the center of sustainable development efforts (ibid.).

A significant outcome from the Johannesburg process was the international community's commitment to market mechanisms and capacity building (or capacity development) as critical measures to achieve sustainable development. Developing nations, however, were concerned about the nature of this transition because it reduced the pressure on (and responsibility of) developed nations to provide their agreed-on share of overseas development assistance since "the market" would make up for any shortfall.* Although the creation of a fair (or equitable) trade regime is essential for development in less developed regions, the assistance that industrialized nations provide to less developed nations is likely to remain an important aspect to their early progress. Further, the transition toward reliance on the market reflects a continuing ideological shift away from the role of the government as a policy driver.[†] In effect, the trend to greater trade liberalization allows industry (in theory) to escape or minimize the social costs of production by locating its operations in places where national laws of environmental protection are weak and good health and the environment are less valued.

The decisions by the United States to withdraw from many multilateral agreements and, instead, focus on voluntary partnerships, is a signal to many environmental organizations that the United States is attempting to redefine sustainable development away from environment and development issues toward trade liberalization (James 2002). The fact that the Johannesburg delegates were able to reject a sentence from the summit's final resolution that would have given the WTO a judicial role in trade and environment disputes, indicates that the lines are drawn for a future battle on economic globalization (New Scientist 2002b).

Two other notable documents that contribute to an understanding of sustainable development are the Earth Charter (launched by the Earth Charter Commission in 2000) and the United Nations Millennium Declaration. Interestingly, the structures of both the Earth Charter[11] and the Millennium Declaration[‡] align closely with the five components of sustainable development: peace and security; economic development; social development; national governance that ensures peace and development; and environmental protection. Because the two publications are produced by different sources (the UN and a nongovernmental organization [NGO]), it provides additional support for the notion that "sustainable" development can be broadly defined using these five critical elements.

As should be evident from this brief overview chapter, the concept of sustainable development is not static and continues to be shaped by key events, new knowledge, and the actions of nations, regions, and the international community. One example of a new dynamic that could further shape the concept is the European Union's efforts to address sustainable development. More specifically, the Europe 2020 Strategy provides the foundation for a regional—as opposed to a national or international—approach to sustainable development (see Section 1.5 in Chapter 1 for a discussion of Europe 2020). The strategy is focused on establishing a competitive and greener economy that creates employment.[12] In this regard, the strategy aligns well with the ideas discussed throughout this text and the argument that employment considerations are as central to sustainability as environmental concerns.

Although there are some concerns that the focus on "competitiveness" could undermine social and environmental policies (Hochfeld, Schmitt, et al. 2006; Wolff, Schmitt, et al. 2006), the regional focus of the Lisbon Strategy provides an example of how other world regions could work together to create strategies for moving toward sustainable development. The EU strategy will also reveal whether it is possible—in the

---

\* Given the fact that few developed nations have been able to meet their commitments to provide 0.7 percent of their GNP for official development assistance (Martens 2001; UNCSD 1997), developing nations have had no real option but to compete for "private capital" to assist with their development. This transition to a reliance on transnational corporations for capital has undermined the notion of the social contract between developed and developing nations (Sachs 2001). There is also a parallel concern that in order to secure private capital, recipient businesses, organizations, and institutions within nation-states might be forced to accept unfavorable terms of agreement. Alternatively, governments might be coerced into adjusting regulations to lower the financial risk of investing in their nation compared with other nation-states. If such regulatory adjustments have the effect of lowering environmental and worker health and safety standards, this outcome would clearly be a shift away from the objectives of sustainable development. The need to look to the international economy for development assistance further reinforces the international economy as *the* mechanism through which nation-states should follow their "right to development." In this regard, Sachs (2001) suggests that a more accurate name for the 1992 Earth Summit would have been "Environment, Development, and the Global Economy" (ibid., p. 11).

† See the discussion of the so-called Washington Consensus in Section 3.4.1 of Chapter 3.

‡ The major headings of the United Nations Millennium Declaration are the following: (1) values and principles (specifically: freedom; equality; solidarity; tolerance; respect for nature; and shared responsibility); (2) peace, security, and disarmament; (3) development and poverty eradication; (4) protecting our common environment; (5) human rights, democracy, and good governance; (6) protecting the vulnerable; (7) meeting the special needs of Africa; and (8) strengthening the United Nations. United Nations, *United Nations Millennium Declaration*, www.un.org/millennium/declaration/ares552e.htm (accessed May 13, 2010).

context of economic globalization and rapid technological change—to create a competitive (regional) economy that provides good job opportunities without degrading the environment, or, conversely, that maintains a good environment without compromising employment and economic opportunity.

Although sustainable development emerged as a concept acknowledging the nexus between economic development (loosely defined) and the environment, there were other more international expressions that focused explicitly on employment as a major concern related to achieving social justice.* The earliest notable event was the 1944 Declaration of Philadelphia creating the International Labour Organization[†] that emphasized the essential need to obtain agreement on policies to address the terms and conditions of employment, safe and satisfying employment, purchasing power, and unfair exploitation of human capital, such as child labor. As a result of the recent global economic upheaval, fair employment with adequate purchasing power has emerged as an essential third pillar of the concept of sustainable development.

Finally, some critics associated with ecological economics go so far as to state that sustainable development cannot be achieved unless the current Northern model of economic development is abandoned (Sanders 2006).

During May 2010, the Preparatory Committee for the UN Conference on Sustainable Development held its first meeting in preparation for the Rio+20 Earth Summit in 2012.[13] The focus of Rio+20 is on a green economy in the context of sustainable development and poverty eradication, and on creating an international framework for sustainable development.[14] The stark realities brought about by the financial meltdown in 2008 are sure to influence a reexamination of the neoliberal Washington Consensus and question whether the largely unregulated control of economic development by financial institutions and powerful corporations can be reconciled with sustainable development.[‡]

As this work goes to press, the twenty-year update to *Our Common Future*, entitled *Cents and*

*Sustainability* (Smith, Hargroves, et al. 2010), has been released. The principal argument of *Cents and Sustainability* is that economic growth can be significantly decoupled from environmental pressures—continuing the message of *Our Common Future* that economic growth and environmental protection can advance in unison while reducing poverty. The premise of the book is that progress toward decoupling can and has been made and that since there is currently no political commitment to "slow" economic growth, a decoupling agenda presents the most viable pathway toward sustainable development.[§] We would argue that *Cents and Sustainability* falls within the realm of evolutionary change. A critical question therefore, is how can a *revolutionary*, rather than evolutionary, decoupling agenda be achieved.

While *Cents and Sustainability* is an important text that promotes some of the policy instruments discussed throughout this work, we believe more is needed. In this text, we have argued that a sustainable development approach must be fashioned to create a competitive and green economy that creates safe, meaningful, and well-paid employment and sufficient earning capacity within the context of rapid technological change and globalization. This approach is grounded upon the belief that current rates of change are too slow to make serious inroads into the environmental and social challenges discussed in this chapter. What is needed is revolutionary change—both of a technical and strategic nature, and of a political and social nature—and it is to this end that this work is directed.

## 2.1 NOTES

1. Earth Day Network, www.earthday.net/about/default .aspx (accessed April 8, 2006).

2. UNEP, *Report of the Governing Council on Its Tenth Session*, *General Debate*, 36, www.unep.org/Documents.multilingual/ Default.asp?DocumentID=70&ArticleID=702 (accessed May 13, 2010).

3. UNEP, *Report of the Governing Council on Its Tenth Session*, *General Debate*, 49, www.unep.org/Documents.multilingual/Default.asp?DocumentID=70&ArticleID=702 (accessed May 13, 2010).

4. UN General Assembly, *Resolution 38/161*, *Process of Preparation of the Environmental Perspective to the Year 2000 and Beyond*, December 19, 1983, sec. 8(a), www.un.org/documents/ga/res/38/a38r161.htm (accessed May 13, 2010).

5. UN General Assembly, *Resolution 42/186*, *Environmental Perspective to the Year 2000 and Beyond*, December 11, 1987, p. 2, http://www.un.org/documents/ga/res/42/a42r186.htm (accessed May 13, 2010).

---

* Indeed, Principle 8 of the Stockholm Declaration clearly recognizes that "economic and social development is essential for ensuring a favorable living and working environment for man."

† See the discussion in the extended Primer on the Emergence of Sustainable Development at the website associated with this book.

‡ See especially the discussion of the "new economics" in Section 3.6 in Chapter 3.

---

§ See Section 3.6 in Chapter 3 for a discussion of the "new economics" and whether continuous economic growth is possible.

6. UN General Assembly, *Resolution 44/228, United Nations Conference on Environment and Development*, December 22, 1989, p. 1, www.un.org/documents/ga/res/44/a44r228.htm (accessed May 13, 2010).

7. UN General Assembly, *Resolution 44/228, United Nations Conference on Environment and Development*, December 22, 1989, secs. 15(a)–15(w), www.un.org/documents/ga/res/44/a44r228 .htm (accessed May 13, 2010).

8. For an informative discussion of the UNCED agreements, see Grubb, Koch et al. (1993).

9. *UNCED Declaration on Environment and Development*, www.un.org/documents/ga/conf151/aconf15126–1annex1.htm (accessed May 13, 2010).

10. See the Fourth Summit Preparatory Committee (PREPCOM 4) reports, www.johannesburgsummit.org/html/documents/prepcom4.html (accessed May 13, 2010).

11. The Earth Charter Initiative, The Earth Charter, www .earthcharterinaction.org/content/pages/Read-the-Charter.html (accessed Janruary12, 2011)

12. See the European Commission's website on the Europe 2020 Strategy, http://ec.europa.eu/europe2020/index_en.htm (accessed January 12, 2011).

13. Co-Chairs' Summary, First Preparatory Committee Meeting for the UN Conference on Sustainable Development, 2012, May 20, 2010, www.uncsd2012.org/files/other_pdfs/prep com1/CoChairsSummary.pdf (accessed on January 7, 2011).

14. Co-Chairs' Summary, First Preparatory Committee Meeting for the UN Conference on Sustainable Development, 2012, May 20, 2010, www.uncsd2012.org/files/other_pdfs/prep com1/CoChairsSummary.pdf (accessed January 7, 2011).

## 2.2 ADDITIONAL READINGS

Ashford, N. A., and R. P. Hall (2011). *Primer on Sustainable Development*, found at the website associated with this book.

Jackson, T. (2009). *Prosperity Without Growth*. London and Sterling, VA, Earthscan.

McEntire, David A. (2005). "The History, Meaning and Policy Recommendations of Sustainable Development: A Review Essay." *International Journal of Environment and Sustainable Development* 4(2): 106–118.

Sanders, Richard (2006). "Sustainability: Implications for Growth, Consumption, and Employment." *International Journal of Environment, Workplace and Employment* 2(4): 385–401.

Smith, M. H., K. C. Hargroves, et al. (2010). *Cents and Sustainability: Securing Our Common Future by Decoupling Economic Growth from Environmental Pressure*. London, Earthscan.

Speth, J. G. (2008). *The Bridge at the Edge of the World: Capitalism, the Environment, and Crossing from Crisis to Sustainability*. New Haven, CT, Yale University Press.

Victor, P. A. (2008). *Managing without Growth: Slow by Design, Not Disaster*. Cheltenham, Edward Elgar.

## 2.3 REFERENCES

Ashford, N. A., and C. C. Caldart (2008). *Environmental Law, Policy, and Economics: Reclaiming the Environmental Agenda*. Cambridge, MA, MIT Press.

Barnett, H. J., and C. Morse (1963). *Scarcity and Growth: The Economics of Natural Resource Availability*. Baltimore, Johns Hopkins University Press for Resources for the Future.

Brandt, W. (1980). *North-South: A Programme for Survival; Report by the Independent Commission on International Development Issues*. Cambridge, MA, MIT Press.

Caldwell, L. K., and P. S. Weiland (1996). *International Environmental Policy: From the Twentieth to the Twenty-first Century*. 3rd ed. Durham, Duke University Press.

Carson, R. (1962). *Silent Spring*. New York, Houghton Mifflin Company.

Clapp, J., and P. Dauvergne (2005). *Paths to a Green World: The Political Economy of the Global Environment*. Cambridge, MA, MIT Press.

Cock, P. H. (2002). Psychology for Ecology. *Psychology of Sustainable Development*. P. Schmuck and W. P. Schultz. Boston, Kluwer Academic Publishers: 175–195.

Colby, M. E. (1991). "Environmental Management in Development: The Evolution of Paradigms." *Ecological Economics* 3(3): 193–213.

Council on Environmental Quality (CEQ) (1980). *The Global 2000 Report to the President: Entering the Twenty-first Century*. Vol. 1. Washington, DC, U.S. Government Printing Office.

Dag Hammarskjöld Foundation (1975). *The 1975 Dag Hammarskjöld Report—What Now: Another Development*. Uppsala, Dag Hammarskjöld Foundation.

Daly, H. E. (1992). "UN Conferences on Environment and Development: Retrospect on Stockholm and Prospects for Rio." *Ecological Economics* 5(1): 9–14.

Dernbach, J. C. (1998). "Sustainable Development as a Framework for National Governance." *Case Western Reserve Law Review* 49(1): 1–103.

Dernbach, J. C. (2004). "Making Sustainable Development Happen: From Johannesburg to Albany." *Albany Law Environmental Outlook* 8: 173–186.

Dryzek, J. S. (1997). *The Politics of the Earth: Environmental Discourses*. New York, Oxford University Press.

Ecologist (1993). *Whose Common Future? Reclaiming the Commons*. London, Earthscan Publications.

Ehrlich, P. R. (1968). *The Population Bomb*. New York, Ballantine Books.

Emmelin, L. (1972). "The Stockholm Conferences." *Ambio* 1(4): 135–140.

Engfeldt, L. G. (2002). "The Road from Stockholm to Johannesburg." *United Nations Chronicle* 29(3).

Grubb, M., M. Koch, et al. (1993). *The "Earth Summit" Agreements: A Guide and Assessment: An Analysis of the Rio '92 UN Conference on Environment and Development*. London, Earthscan Publications.

Hardin, G. (1968). "The Tragedy of the Commons." *Science* 162: 1243–1248.

Hochfeld, C., K. Schmitt, et al. (2006). *Competitiveness for Sustainability—Positions and Perspectives*. Berlin, Oko-Institut e.V.

Hynes, P. H. (1989). *The Recurring Silent Spring*. New York, Pergamon Press.

International Union for Conservation of Nature and Natural Resources (IUCN), United Nations Environment Programme (UNEP), et al. (1980). *World Conservation Strategy*. Gland, IUCN.

James, B. (2002). Growth versus Environment. *International Herald Tribune,* August 8, pp. 1, 8–9.

Linner, B., and H. Selin (2003). How It All Began: Global Efforts on Sustainable Development from Stockholm to Rio. 6th Nordic Conference on Environmental Social Sciences, Åbo, Finland.

Martens, J. (2001). Rethinking the Relevance of ODA: Current Trends in the Debate on the Future of Official Development Assistance. Background paper for the United Nations Financing for Development Process. Berlin, World Economy, Ecology and Development Association (WEED), Heinrich Böell Foundation, and the Global Policy Forum.

McCormick, J. (1995). *The Global Environmental Movement.* 2nd ed. New York, John Wiley and Sons.

McEntire, D. A. (2005). "The History, Meaning and Policy Recommendations of Sustainable Development: A Review Essay." *International Journal of Environment and Sustainable Development* **4**(2): 106–118.

Meadows, D. H., D. L. Meadows, et al. (1972). *The Limits to Growth.* New York, Potomac Associates.

Molina, M., and F. S. Rowland (1974). "Stratospheric Sink for Chlorofluoromethanes: Chlorine Atom-Catalysed Destruction of Ozone." *Nature* **249**: 810–812.

Nayar, K. R. (1994). "Politics of 'Sustainable Development.'" *Economic and Political Weekly* **29**(22): 1327–1329.

New Scientist (2002a). "Development Talks Falter." *New Scientist* **174**(2347): 7.

New Scientist (2002b). "Editorial: The Party's Over. Have We Got What It Takes to Deliver on the Promises Made at Joburg?" *New Scientist* **175**(2359): 3.

New Scientist (2002c). "Joburg or Bust." *New Scientist* **175**(2356): 37.

President's Material Policy Commission (1952). *Resources for Freedom.* Washington, DC, U.S. Government Printing Office.

Redclift, M. (1984). *Development and the Environmental Crisis: Red or Green Alternatives?* London, Methuen.

Redclift, M. (1987). *Sustainable Development: Exploring the Contradictions.* London, Methuen.

Redclift, M. (1996). *Wasted: Counting the Costs of Global Consumption.* London, Earthscan.

Resources for the Future (RFF) (1954). *The Nation Looks at Its Resources: Report of the Mid-century Conference on Resources for the Future.* Washington, DC, Resources for the Future.

Runnalls, D. (2008). "Our Common Inaction: Meeting the Call for Institutional Change." *Environment Magazine* **50**(6): 18–28.

Sachs, W. (2001). *Rio + 10 and the North-South Divide.* Berlin, Heinrich Böell Foundation.

Saha, S. K. (2002). Theorising Globalisation and Sustainable Development. *Globalisation and Sustainable Development in Latin America: Perspectives on the New Economic Order.* S. K. a. P. D. Saha. Cheltenham, Edward Elgar: 13–50.

Sanders, R. (2006). "Sustainability: Implications for Growth, Employment, and Consumption." *International Journal of Environment, Workplace and Employment* **2**(4): 385–401.

Schumacher, E. F. (1999). *Small Is Beautiful: Economics as If People Mattered, 25 Years Later . . . with Commentaries.* Point Roberts, WA, Hartley and Marks Publishers.

Smith, M. H., K. C. Hargroves, et al. (2010). *Cents and Sustainability: Securing Our Common Future by Decoupling Economic Growth from Environmental Pressure.* London, Earthscan.

South Centre (2002a). Environment and Development—Towards a Common Strategy of the South in the UNCED Negotiations and Beyond. *The South and Sustainable Development Conundrum: From Stockholm 1972 to Rio 1992 to Johannesburg 2002.* Geneva, South Centre: 105–133.

South Centre (2002b). The South, the North and Sustainable Development: The Continuity of Basic Issues. *The South and Sustainable Development Conundrum: From Stockholm 1972 to Rio 1992 to Johannesburg 2002.* Geneva, South Centre: 4–30.

Speth, J. G. (2002). The Global Environmental Agenda: Origins and Prospects. *Global Environmental Governance: Options and Opportunities.* D. C. Esty and M. H. Ivanova. New Haven, CT, Yale F&ES Publications: 11–30.

Speth, J. G. (2003). Two Perspectives on Globalization and the Environment. *Worlds Apart: Globalization and the Environment.* J. G. Speth. Washington, DC, Island Press: 1–18.

Strong, M. F. (1972). "The Stockholm Conference—Where Science and Politics Meet." *Ambio* **1**(3): 73–78.

Strong, M. F. (2003). Global Sustainable Development. *Globalization, Globalism, Environments, and Environmentalism: Consciousness of Connections.* S. Vertovec and D. A. Posey. Oxford, Oxford University Press: 103–122.

United Nations (UN) (1972). *Development and Environment: Report and Working Papers of a Panel of Experts Convened by the Secretary-General of the United Nations Conference on the Human Environment (Founex, Switzerland, June 4–12, 1971).* Paris, Mouton.

UN (1993a). *Earth Summit: Agenda 21, the United Nations Programme of Action from Rio.* New York, UN.

UN (1993b). *Report of the United Nations Conference on Environment and Development.* Vol. 1, *Resolutions Adopted by the Conference.* New York, UN.

UN (1993c). *Report of the United Nations Conference on Environment and Development.* Vol. 2, *Proceedings of the Conference.* New York, UN.

UN (1993d). *Report of the United Nations Conference on Environment and Development.* Vol. 3, *Statements Made by Heads of State or Government at the Summit Segment of the Conference.* New York, UN.

UN (2002). Johannesburg Declaration on Sustainable Development, Adopted at the 17th plenary meeting of the World Summit on Sustainable Development, September 4. Available at www.un.org/esa/sustdev/documents/ WSSD_POI_PD/English/POI_PD.htm (accessed January 12, 2011).

United Nations Commission on Sustainable Development (UNCSD) (1997). *Report of the Ad Hoc Open-Ended Inter-sessional Working Group of the Commission on Sustainable Development, 17 March 1997.* New York, United Nations Economic and Social Council, UN.

United Nations Environment Programme (UNEP) (1975). *The Proposed Programme.* Nairobi, UNEP.

UNEP (1982a). Nairobi Declaration on the State of World-wide Environment, UNEP/GC.10/INF.5, May 19. Available at www.unep.org/Documents.multilingual/Default.asp?DocumentID=70&ArticleID=737&l=en (accessed January 12, 2010).

UNEP (1982b). *The Environment in 1982: Retrospect and Prospect.* Nairobi, UNEP.

UNEP (1982c). *The State of the Environment, 1972–1982.* Nairobi, UNEP.

UNEP (1982d). *The World Environment, 1972–1982: A Report by the United Nations Environment Programme.* Dublin, Tycooly International Publishing.

UNEP (1991). *The State of the World Environment.* Nairobi, UNEP.

Vogel, D. (2003). "The Hare and the Tortoise Revisited: The New Politics of Consumer and Environmental Regulation in Europe." *British Journal of Political Science* **33**(4): 557–580.

Wolff, F., K. Schmitt, et al. (2006). *Competitiveness, Innovation and Sustainability—Clarifying the Concepts and Their Interrelations.* Berlin, Oko-Institut e.V.

World Commission on Environment and Development (WCED) (1987). *Our Common Future.* Oxford, Oxford University Press.

# II

# Economic Development, Globalization, and Sustainability

In Part I of this book, we discussed the nature (Chapter 1) and evolution (Chapter 2) of the multidimensional concepts of sustainability and sustainable development. In Part II, we discuss economic development within the context of (domestic supply and demand) forces operating more or less within the nation-state (Chapter 3), how the nation-state develops in an environment increasingly influenced by forces (for example, globalized trade, information, and finance) operating in the global economy (Chapter 4), and the effects that both technological change and globalization have, or are expected to have, on the three pillars of sustainability (Chapter 5).

As we shall see, technological change is both a vehicle for the improvement of the workings of the industrial state and a cause of unsustainability. Therefore, understanding the technological change process (Chapter 6) and the possible roles of the private sector (Chapter 7) and the government (Chapter 8) in promoting economic development is essential to the design of industrial policy, which is the focus of Part III.

# 3

# Economic Development and Prosperity: Current Theory and Debate

Coauthored with KYRIAKOS PIERRAKAKIS

## 3.1 THE MEANING OF ECONOMIC DEVELOPMENT

### 3.1.1 Growth and Development Distinguished

In Chapter 1, we discussed fundamental concepts of economic growth and the metrics that might be used to measure that growth in terms of increased GNP and GDP. We also argued that not all increases in these metrics were necessarily good. For example, the GDP of a region might go up as a result of activities related to digging out of a blizzard or rescuing people in a flood, but no one would argue that more of this kind of increase in GDP was good, even if some firms and people bene-fited or profited from the activity. Increased economic activity (involving expenditures for goods and services) necessitated by natural or human-made disasters are not part of any deliberate growth strategy of government in its trusteeship role for its people. Thus there are "good GDP" and "bad GDP." On the other hand, other positive attributes of development are not captured by GNP and GDP.* For this reason, other indexes of human development† have also re-

---

\*   See Section 3.3.1.2 for a deeper discussion of problems of measurement in a postindustrial society.

†   See Daly (1994) for a discussion of the distinction between growth and development that applies to developed as well as developing countries.

ceived attention (see Section 1.1.1 in Chapter 1). Nonetheless, many contributions to GNP and GDP growth are desirable and concern a government's economic or industrial policy. In this chapter, we first focus on understanding the historical patterns and determinants of economic growth in the positive sense, ignoring for the moment the undesirable externalities that might flow from that growth. We then summarize critiques of what has come to be called "the Northern model" of development.

Long-run economic growth has been at the heart of economic analysis since the first founding documents of economic theory. Economic growth was, in essence, the topic of Adam Smith's treatise *The Wealth of Nations*. Growth, however, should not be considered as an end in itself. Economists have focused their efforts on analyzing the causes of growth for centuries because it has the potential to decrease poverty, increase the standard of living, support goals such as education and health care, and substantially affect the quality of life of the citizenry.

It is essential to note that as an area of study of national economies, *development* is generally distinguished from *economic growth*. Economic growth is measured in "economic" terms—for example, GNP, GDP, and other economic metrics—and does not account for nontraded goods, services, and cultural attributes. Development is not a purely economic phenomenon. According to Todaro and Smith (2009, p. 16), "Development must . . . be conceived of as a multidimensional process involving major changes in social structures, popular attitudes, and national institutions, as well as the acceleration of economic growth, the reduction of inequality, and the eradication of poverty. Development, in its essence, must represent the whole gamut of change by which an entire social system, tuned to the diverse basic needs and desires of individuals and social groups within that system, moves away from a condition of life widely perceived as unsatisfactory toward a situation or condition of life regarded as materially and spiritually better."

According to Todaro and Smith (2009, p. 22), economic and social development in all societies should have at least the following three objectives:*

- To increase the availability and widen the distribution of basic life-sustaining goods such as food, shelter, health, and protection

- To raise the quality of life (securing more meaningful jobs and enhancing cultural and human values)

- To expand the range of economic and social choices available to individuals and nations by freeing them from dependence on other nations, but also from the forces of ignorance and human misery

The role of national governments in the context of economic development is essential. Contrary to the view of many economists of the neoclassical mainstream, we argue that this role should not be limited to ensuring the proper functioning of markets and the correction of market failures.

Traditional economics focuses on the efficient, least-cost allocation of scarce resources and the optimal growth of these resources over time in order to produce an expanding range of goods and services (Todaro and Smith 2009). Furthermore, traditional economics also focuses on neoclassical economics as taught in introductory and intermediate economics textbooks in universities (Söderbaum 2008). Markets, in that context, are considered to be "perfect," while the consumer is perceived as a rational utility maximizer.

On the other hand, development economics has a more extensive scope. Apart from being concerned with the optimal allocation of scarce resources and with their sustained growth over time, development economics also deals with the economic, social, political, and institutional mechanisms necessary to bring about rapid, large-scale improvements for developing countries (Todaro and Smith 2009). In this context, market imperfections are the rule rather than the exception, and limited consumer rationality is taken as a given, while disequilibriums often prevail in the economy.

Formal economic thinking remains essentially confined to static equilibrium instead of examining the dynamics of the economy (Niehans 1990). The historical perspective and the empirical observations of the first classical economists (Adam Smith, David Ricardo, and Karl Marx, among others) led to some key intuitions about the growth process but not to coherent theories of economic growth (ibid.). However, this was something that was destined to change in the era of model building, through the contributions of a series of scholars who dramatically shifted the way their contemporaries ended up viewing the process of economic growth.

### 3.1.2 Factor Endowments and the Classification of Capital

Economic historians speak in terms of "factor endowments" that nations might possess to explain their economic growth. Early lists included land, material

---

* See Section 3.4 for the contributions of Seers (1979) and Sen (1999) to the discussion of development.

resources, energy, and a physically strong labor force. When nations were essentially agricultural, land was the most highly valued factor—and thus the driving force behind colonialism—and only after the Industrial Revolution did material resources, energy, and more skilled labor take on importance.

Advanced nations are often described now as being in the postindustrial era, in which services, rather than manufacturing, become increasingly important and "knowledge-based" work replaces physical work. Today an expanded list of factor endowments might include the following:

- Land
- Material Resources (natural and physical capital)
- Energy
- Labor capable of performing physical work
- Know-how (intellectual human capital)
- [Innovation systems]*
- Built capital (that is, infrastructure, such as railways, bridges, roads, ports, airports, and dams)
- Information and communication technology (ICT)
- (Health and the environment)†
- Structural capital (knowledge and productive routines held by organizations)
- Networks and outsiders (linking organizations, people, and entrepreneurs)
- Social capital (knowledge held by consumers and citizens)

Although these factors are not listed in order of importance nor in strictly chronological order of their emergence as important for growth, this list does describe an unfolding of factor endowments and characteristics that more or less parallels the phases

of successive industrial development that have occurred and are discussed later in this chapter.

## 3.2 THEORIES AND PERSPECTIVES ON ECONOMIC GROWTH

The relationship between different factor endowments or types of capital and economic growth has been the subject of volumes of analysis, predictions, and reinterpretations. It is beyond the scope of this book to provide a comprehensive review of that literature. What we do provide is the salient evolution of major thinking that has guided economic and industrial policy from Adam Smith to David Ricardo to current innovation-based perspectives, including the so-called knowledge-based economy. This section draws heavily on the scholarship of R. Ayres and Warr (2009), Drucker (1994, 1999), Niehans (1990), Schumpeter (1939), and Todaro and Smith (2009).

### 3.2.1 Rostow's Stages-of-Growth Model

After the end of World War II, concern with theories of growth became particularly prevalent, especially in the case of poor or underdeveloped countries. Western economists, however, only had one economic growth paradigm to draw conclusions from—that of the economic development of the Western world. Their rationale lay in the fact that all developed Western societies were in essence agrarian at some point of their histories, but industrialized through a series of steps or stages.

Out of this intellectual environment came the stages-of-growth model of development, the most outspoken proponent of which was the American economist Walter Rostow (Todaro and Smith 2009). The rationale of this model was fairly obvious. All industrialized countries, Rostow argued, had already completed a stage of "takeoff" and had moved toward "self-sustaining growth." The underdeveloped world, according to this mind-set, was still in either the traditional society or the "preconditions" stage and thus had to follow a particular set of prescriptive policies in order to move to the next stage (ibid.).

Generally, the success in rebuilding Europe through massive financial aid in the Marshall Plan suggested that a similar influx of capital was needed to advance the faltering economies of Asia, Africa, and Latin America. Thus particular emphasis was placed on accelerated capital accumulation (Todaro and Smith 2009), which is also known as "capital fundamentalism." Furthermore, the fundamental strategy of development necessary for economic takeoff had to be

---

*     Innovation systems are discussed in Chapter 6 in the context of the institutions that foster technological innovation. We place this asset in square brackets to serve as a reminder that unlike other factors that can be easily acquired, this describes a complex *system* of interacting determinants that reflect different political, social, and economic development cultures and traditions. In general, industrialized nations have highly developed innovation systems, while developing countries differ markedly in their infrastructure, legal institutions, and political systems that could enhance more optimal use of the other factor endowments that they possess. See Rodrik (2007), who argues for more "self-discovery," coordination of government policies, and government–private-sector communication in developing nations.

†     Good human health (both physical and mental) and an unpolluted and preserved environment (what could be called "environmental capital") are increasingly regarded as essential for maintaining the productiveness of human and natural/physical capital even if they are not factors of production per se. For this reason we place them in parentheses.

rooted in the mobilization of domestic and foreign saving, which would then generate sufficient investment to increase economic growth (ibid.).

### 3.2.2 Linear Stages-of-Growth Models: The Harrod-Domar Model

In the context of the stages-of-growth analysis, the mobilization of foreign investment and domestic saving was also deemed necessary for economic growth. The Harrod-Domar model offers a description of the economic mechanism by which increases in saving and investing would lead to accelerated growth.

The Harrod-Domar model—today often cited as the AK model because of the employment of a linear production function with output of the economy ($Y$) defined as the product of the capital stock ($K$) times a constant ($A$)—was one of the first models to suggest that the economy could grow in perpetuity (Todaro and Smith 2009).* The main point of the model is that if actual growth is above the warranted (expected or achievable) growth, the existing production of capital goods is below the required (that is, demanded) level of capital goods; hence growth will be stimulated through increases in orders. If growth, on the other hand, appears to be sluggish, the capital stock will appear to be underutilized, and growth will be further slowed (Niehans 1990). Hence the growth path appears to be on a knife's edge, with significant centrifugal forces at work.

Furthermore, the stability problem of the model also relates to the full employment of labor. For given rates of population growth and technical progress, continued full employment will result in a certain rate of output growth, or a "natural rate." If the warranted rate appears to be less than the natural rate, the implication of the model is that there is no reason that the economy should not enjoy boom conditions, which can also be potentially inflationary (Niehans 1990). Nevertheless, if the warranted rate

surpasses the natural rate, actual growth must fall short of warranted growth most of the time, with the consequence that depressions will be long and considerable, while booms will be ephemeral.

Aside from its potentially inadequate descriptive capacities, the model appeared to have other limitations. Labor-force growth and technological progress constitute two other components of economic growth, apart from savings and investment. Labor-force growth is omitted from the Harrod-Domar model, and labor is assumed to be abundant, an assumption that can be valid in the developing-country context, though not always (Todaro and Smith 2009). Technological progress can be expressed in the context of the Harrod-Domar model as a decrease in the required capital/output ratio for a specific growth-rate target. Nevertheless, the fixed capital/output ratio does not allow for the most efficient use of each factor of production. However, this limitation of the Harrod-Domar model was one of the driving forces behind the introduction of Solow's model, which is examined later.

Although the linear stages-of-growth model may be incomplete, it could be argued that high domestic savings and/or the injection of foreign capital are necessary, though not sufficient, conditions for economic growth in an underdeveloped economy.

### 3.2.3 Structural-Change Models

Structural-change models focus on the mechanism by which poor or underdeveloped economies manage to transform their domestic economic structures from agrarian to more modern and industrially diverse manufacturing and service economies (Todaro and Smith 2009). The best-known and most representative example of the structural-change approach is the "two-sector surplus labor" theoretical model of W. Arthur Lewis. Lewis's model focused on the structural transformation of a primarily subsistence economy and became the general theory of the development process in surplus-labor developing nations during most of the 1960s and 1970s; it still has many adherents today (ibid.).

According to Todaro and Smith's (2009, p. 115) analysis, "In the Lewis model, the underdeveloped economy consists of two sectors: a traditional, overpopulated rural subsistence sector characterized by zero marginal labor productivity—a situation that permits Lewis to classify this as surplus labor in the sense that it can be withdrawn from the traditional agricultural sector without any loss of output—and a high-productivity modern urban industrial sector

---

\*    The equation $\frac{\Delta Y}{Y} = \frac{s}{k}$ is a simplified version of the famous equation in the Harrod-Domar model of economic growth. The equation states that the GDP growth rate ($\Delta Y/Y$) is determined by the net national savings ratio $s$ and the national capital/output ratio $k$, which is fixed in the Harrod-Domar model. In fact, this equation can be interpreted simply as determining the savings necessary to achieve a certain growth rate depending on the capital/output ratio. One of the fundamental intuitions of the model was that doubling the savings rate would double the rate of economic growth for a given capital/output ratio. An increase in the propensity to save and in the average productivity of capital appeared to be a sine qua non of rapid economic growth (Niehans 1990). For a given $k$, the corresponding growth rate is the warranted or justified rate of growth.

into which labor from the subsistence sector is gradually transferred. The primary focus of the model is on both the process of labor transfer and the growth of output and employment in the modern sector."

The key point of the model is that the process of self-sustaining growth of the modern sector, along with employment expansion, will continue until all surplus rural labor is absorbed into the new industrial sector. After that point, additional workers can be withdrawn from the agricultural sector only at the cost of lost food production. This process shifts the balance of economic activity from traditional rural agriculture to modern industries (Todaro and Smith 2009).

However, even though the Lewis model reflects the historical experience of economic growth in industrialized nations, a series of concerns have been voiced about the descriptive capacity of the model in the context of contemporary developing countries. Todaro and Smith (2009, pp. 118–120) focus on four different points of criticism:

1. The model implicitly assumes that the rate of labor transfer and employment creation in the modern sector is proportional to the rate of modern-sector capital accumulation. However, Todaro and Smith note that if capitalist profits are reinvested in more sophisticated labor-saving capital equipment rather than just duplicating the existing capital, then, even though output does increase, wages and employment rates remain unchanged, and all the extra output accrues to capitalists in the form of profits. This is a process that some have described as "antidevelopmental economic growth," with all the extra input and output growth distributed to the owners of capital rather than the working classes.*

2. The assumption of the Lewis model that surplus labor exists in rural areas while there is full employment in the urban areas is contradicted by the latest research, which indicates that there is little surplus labor in rural locations.

3. An additional questionable assumption is linked to the notion of a competitive modern-sector labor market that can guarantee the continued existence of constant real urban wages up to the point where the supply of rural surplus labor is exhausted. Todaro and Smith (2009, p. 120) note that until the 1980s, "a striking feature of urban labor markets and wage determination in almost all developing countries was the tendency for these wages to rise substantially over time (both in real and nominal terms), even in the presence of rising

levels of open modern-sector unemployment and low or zero marginal productivity in agriculture." This was due to a series of institutional factors, such as unionization and civil service wage scales.

4. Finally, Lewis made the assumption of diminishing returns in the modern industrial sector. However, evidence suggests that increasing rather than diminishing returns prevail in that sector.

Technological displacement (or the tendency of technology transfer to be biased toward labor-saving changes) may offset technology gains that accrue to workers. Finally, this model, as well as others, may not apply uniformly in all developing countries (Rodrik 2007).

### 3.2.4 The International-Dependence Perspective

International-dependence models gained increasing support during the 1970s as a result of increasing disenchantment with the linear stages-of-growth and the structural-change models (Todaro and Smith 2009). Even though this theory became less mainstream in the 1980s and 1990s, it has resurfaced in various versions in the past decade and has been adopted by proponents of the antiglobalization movement. The main intuition of these models is that developing countries are "beset by institutional, political and economic rigidities, both domestic and international, and caught up in a dependence and dominance relationship with rich countries" (ibid., p. 122). There are three major streams of thought in the context of the international dependence models:

- The neocolonial-dependence model
- The false-paradigm model
- The dualistic-development thesis

The neocolonial-dependence model is a direct by-product of Marxist analysis. Its basic thesis is that the existence of underdeveloped countries is a direct consequence of the highly unequal capitalist system. Even though it might not be the case that rich countries intentionally exploit poor and less developed countries, the very structure of the system, which is dominated by unequal power relationships between the center and the periphery (the developed and the underdeveloped nations), makes any attempt of poor nations to be self-reliant and independent difficult or even unattainable (Todaro and Smith 2009).

On the other hand, the false-paradigm model does not attribute underdevelopment to the inherent structure of the global economic system, but rather to "faulty and inappropriate advice provided

---

\* For an alternative model of capital accumulation, see Section 12.11 in Chapter 12 for a discussion of binary economics.

by well-meaning but often uninformed, biased and ethnocentric international 'expert' advisers from developed-country assistance agencies and multinational donor organizations" (Todaro and Smith 2009, p. 124). These experts are considered to offer complex and theoretically sound but often faulty and misleading models of development that often lead to inappropriate or incorrect policy approaches.

Central to the understanding of the dualistic-development thesis is the notion of dualism. Dualism is "a concept widely discussed in development economics. It represents the existence and persistence of substantial and even increasing divergence between rich and poor nations and rich and poor peoples on various levels" (Todaro and Smith 2009, p. 124). This notion underlines that different sets of conditions—some superior and some inferior—can coexist in a given space. Wealthy, educated elites, for instance, can coexist with poor, uneducated masses. According to the dualistic-development thesis, this coexistence is not a mere systemic transition but is actually chronic and hardwired in underdeveloped societies.

In developed nations, the growth of an "underclass" parallels this dualism, with one part of a nation's economy linking producers, workers, and consumers (even across borders), and another part of the nation's economy consisting of low-wage workers or the unemployed, possibly but not necessarily subsidized by welfare programs of the state.

### 3.2.5 Neoclassical Growth Theory: The Solow Model

The Solow neoclassical growth model, for which Robert Solow received the Nobel Prize in economics in 1987, encapsulates the main features of the neoclassical growth theory and is probably the most famous model of economic growth to date.* Solow's basic innovation was to construct his model of pro-

duction in a different way from that of the Harrod-Domar model, which did not allow for the substitution of labor for capital in production. The labor/capital ratio was fixed in the Harrod-Domar model, and steady growth occurred only under certain specific conditions. Solow substituted the fixed labor/capital ratio with a production function in which both capital and labor could vary. This had significant advantages. First, it allowed the producer to switch from capital to labor when capital became too expensive, and vice versa (Warsh 2006). Furthermore, the model also allowed for an exogenous parameter that described the rate of technical change. Because the rate of technological progress is given exogenously, the Solow neoclassical model is sometimes called an exogenous growth model. Thus the model has no explanatory power with respect to the source of technical change.

The key implication of the Solow model is that unlike the Harrod-Domar model, an increase in savings in the Solow model will not by itself increase growth in the long run. In fact, according to the model, growth depends only on population and technology. An increase as a result of increased savings will occur, but it will be only temporary, and the economy will eventually return to the level of steady-state growth. An increase in savings, on the other hand, will increase only the equilibrium level of capital (Todaro and Smith 2009). However, Mankiw, Romer, et al. (1992), from analysis of cross-national data, note that it appears that if the rate of savings is increased, then the economy may not return even halfway to its former lower steady state for decades. Furthermore, even though the model predicts that an increase in savings does not change the equilibrium rate of growth, it does increase the equilibrium output per person. Hence from an empirical standpoint, even if the Solow model does depict the economy accurately, Mankiw, Romer, et al. (1992) argue that an increase in the savings rate can boost the rate of economic growth for decades. This expectation, however, remains controversial for some developmental economists (see Todaro and Smith 2009).

Another key point in Solow's analysis was the estimated contribution of technical change to the rate of U.S. GDP growth over the period 1909–1949. Through the use of a modified production function $Y = f(K, L, t)$, where $K$ is capital, $L$ is labor, and $t$ represents technical change over time, Solow found that technical change accounted for approximately 50

---

* The equation $\Delta k = sf(k) - (\delta + n)k$ is the fundamental equation of the Solow model. The intuition behind this equation is that the change in the capital/labor ratio $k$ (or growth in capital intensity in the course of time) depends on aggregate savings $sf(k)$ (savings rate $s$ times $f(k)$, which is the output of the economy) after allowing for the amount of capital required to service depreciation, $\delta k$, and after providing the existing amount of capital per worker to new workers joining the labor force, $nk$ (Todaro and Smith 2009). If $sf(k^*) = (\delta + n)k^*$, then the capital intensity remains unchanged, and the economy grows without any change in its structure. This, according to the model, is the path of balanced growth (Niehans 1990).

The notation $k^*$ denotes the level of capital per worker when the economy is in steady state. Solow deemed this equilibrium level of capital to be stable. If $k < k^*$, then $(n + \delta)k < sf(k)$. But from the equation we see that when $(n + \delta)k < sf(k)$, $\Delta k > 0$. As a

result, $k$ in the economy will grow toward the equilibrium level $k^*$ (Todaro and Smith 2009). Similar reasoning applies when $k > k^*$.

percent of the increase in output per capita, which corresponded to a contribution to GNP growth of the nonfarm sector of about 1.5 percent a year (Todaro and Smith 2009). Solow's finding underlined the importance and provided a means of including technical change explicitly (even though only as a residual) in the mathematical modeling of economic growth.

### 3.2.6 New Growth Theory: Romer's Model

New or endogenous growth theory was developed during the late 1980s by Paul Romer, but many of its basic elements and intuitions were already present in the work of Joseph Schumpeter. The motivation behind the introduction of this new theory originated from the limitations of the neoclassical theories in illuminating the sources of long-term economic growth (Todaro and Smith 2009). In these models, technological change is treated as mostly exogenous. In contrast, Romer's (1990) model treats technical change as endogenous.

Endogenous growth simply means technological change generated from within a system, as opposed to technological change that is treated as a "black box" in exogenous growth models. In the 1990s, output was much higher than it was in the 1890s. Economics needed some economic theory to account for that level of growth. In 1990, output per hour worked in the United States was calculated as ten times as valuable as output per hour worked one hundred years before (Romer 1990). Technological progress provided a good-quality explanation for that level of growth, along with the growth in human capital, or the development of an effective labor force.

Romer's (1986) and (1990) articles, which some regard as the centerpieces of the new growth theory, emanated from a main contradiction lying at the heart of economic theory since Adam Smith's *Wealth of Nations* was published in 1776, (see Box 3.1). Smith's central point was the increases in productivity that could be achieved both through competition among economic actors and through the division of labor, which was illustrated by the now-famous example of

---

### BOX 3.1: ADAM SMITH (1723–1790)

Adam Smith is regarded as the patriarch of classical economic growth theory. In his magnum opus, *An Inquiry into the Nature and Causes of the Wealth of Nations*, which is considered the founding document of the science of economics, Smith linked the division of labor and the pursuit of self-interest to the general welfare of society and outlined the guiding principles behind the allocation of resources in a growing economy.

Perhaps the most famous phrase that emerges from his book is Smith's "invisible hand," a term that describes a process that advances the interests of a society through the individual's search of self-interest and self-advantage. Thus what Smith essentially argued was that greed will drive actors to socially beneficial behavior. This is nothing different from the process of "competition," working though the interdependent system of prices and quantities that is known today as the price system.

Smith's central message with respect to growth was that the division of labor increases labor productivity. In his analysis, Smith used the examples of workers in several different disciplines to make the case that under an optimal division of labor, they would end up producing more output than they would produce if they worked independently to satisfy their various needs. In Smith's view, this was the locomotive behind increasing productivity and improving standards of living.

At its core, Smith's growth model is an optimistic one. In Smith's viewpoint, an increased division of labor will lead to increases in productivity, incomes, and consequent increases in demand that will increase the size of markets and, through this virtuous spiral, cause further increases in the division of labor, productivity, and so on. However, this process was neither automatic nor inevitable. "Good government" was necessary in order to maintain a competitive environment and avoid the emergence of monopolies, which would restrict output in order to increase prices and, consequently, their profits. Even though the role of the government was not needed for the functioning of the market for Smith, except to maintain a competitive economy and avoid monopoly, it played a central role in other areas such as defense, administration of justice, and the consolidation of public institutions. He also made a forceful case for the mutual benefits of free trade among nations, introducing the principle of comparative advantage. For him, it was better to buy a cheaper commodity from another country and pay for it with the resources obtained from a local industry with some advantage in comparison to other countries. The concept of comparative advantage was later further developed by David Ricardo.

**BOX 3.2: DAVID RICARDO (1772–1823)**

David Ricardo's most famous contribution to economics is the theory of comparative advantage.* Ricardo's theory argues that a nation is economically best off if it does whatever it is best at, even if others are better at it. According to that perspective, if two countries specialize in the production of those goods for which they have a comparative advantage, and trade ensues, there is an absolute gain in welfare for both economies (Gill and Law 1988).

This theory, however, appears to have significant limitations. In globalization, foreign direct investment is the rule rather than the exception. Hence the export sector of one nation can be owned by capitalists from another, and nothing prevents these foreign owners from repatriating most of their profits (Gill and Law 1988). This was exactly the case for countries like India, most of whose resources were depleted by England. In general, relying on trade for economic growth can be problematic, especially in the case of developing countries. This does not mean that growth cannot be achieved in that scenario. However, it can be achieved only at the cost of escalating international, North-South, and internal inequalities, along with increasing dependence on transnational firms (ibid.).

Unlike Smith, Ricardo did not offer a new model of economic growth. While Smith had tried to explain the growth of wealth, Ricardo deemed that the proper task of an economist was to study the distribution of wealth among the three major classes of society: the workers, the landowners, and the capitalists (Warsh 2006). However, Ricardo did modify Smith's existing model of economic growth to include diminishing returns to land.

According to his analysis, unlike labor, the output of which could be increased through increases in productivity, Ricardo deemed land to be "variable in quality and fixed in supply." Hence as growth increases, more land is necessary, but land cannot just be created, because it already exists in limited supply. This significantly affects growth. First, the limited supply of land will lead to increases in rents and consequently decrease entrepreneurial profits. Furthermore, the prices of agricultural goods will increase over time, and this will lead to workers requiring wage increases. This leads to a quicker barrier to growth than Smith allowed for, but Ricardo also claimed that this decline can be happily checked by technological improvements in machinery and the specialization brought by trade.

* See also see Section 4.4.1 in Chapter 4 for a discussion of comparative advantage in the context of a barter economy.

the pin factory, whose employees, by focusing on narrow tasks, end up producing more output than they could if each worked independently. This point, however, hid a contradiction. The example of the pin factory describes the reality of an increasing return to scale: more workers produce a bigger factory and consequently more pins. Moreover, increasing returns to scale are associated with the emergence of natural monopolies because a larger business can achieve lower costs through the advantages of scale. This is the opposite of Adam Smith's description of the "invisible hand," which requires a large number of competitors and the absence of monopoly power. In the theory of perfect competition, the idea that free markets operate smoothly and optimally largely depends on the assumption of diminishing returns to scale. Even if the emergence of a natural monopoly were possible, the scale advantages of a natural monopoly could be offset by greater incentives for profit-seeking competitors who try harder (this assumes that there are low barriers to entry). Also, neoclassical economics predicts that competitive prices are generally lower and output greater than under monopoly conditions. The most important fact assumed by the new endogenous growth theory

is the expectation of increasing returns on capital because of technological change (Warsh 2006).

This model fills the gap unexplained by the neoclassical theory that considers technological progress as being independent of decisions of economic agents. Neoclassical theory also fails to explain big differences in growth among countries with similar technologies. Furthermore, at the core of endogenous growth theory lies a criticism of globalized trade. In traditional neoclassical models, growth emanates from trade. Neoliberal economists have interpreted the association between higher growth rates and a larger volume of trade as one where causality flows from the second to the first rather than the other way around (Gill and Law 1988). However, as the criticisms of Ricardo's theory of comparative advantage (see Box 3.2) suggest, an increasing volume of trade does not necessarily lead to sustainable growth. What endogenous growth theory did was to show how countries can work in the context of a globalizing economy to focus on complementary activities, such as education and retraining, and coherent regulatory frameworks, which can facilitate their economic development.

In his 1986 article "Increasing Returns and Long-Run Growth," Paul Romer essentially laid the foundations of endogenous growth theory. In that article, he proposed a model where economic growth is driven by the accumulation of knowledge, which is the really important form of capital (Romer 1986). Romer essentially tried to discard the neoclassical hypothesis of diminishing marginal returns in capital investments, permitting increasing returns in aggregate production and focusing on the role of externalities (specifically, knowledge spillover effects) in determining the rate of return on capital investments (Todaro and Smith 2009). According to Romer, investment in knowledge leads to *increasing* returns in marginal products because technological innovation can lead to the deployment of new technologies, which can reduce the cost of production and put one company ahead of its competition. Romer's last point in his 1986 article was that knowledge has what he described as a "natural externality" because it cannot be perfectly patented or kept secret. Hence new knowledge has a spillover effect on the production possibilities of other firms as well.

In his 1990 article "Endogenous Technological Change," Romer (1990) set out the preconditions for the deployment of endogenous growth. His model has four basic inputs: capital, labor, human capital (education, training) and an index of the level of technology. Romer's key intuition is that the most important precondition of growth lies not in population dynamics but in human capital dynamics. Hence it is investments in new research, education, and human capital rather than investments in physical capital accumulation that should be fostered.

In general, endogenous growth theory, by focusing on knowledge and externalities, provides a way for countries to enter the new knowledge economy by making the best use of their available resources. The main weakness of this model, however, is that it overlooks inefficiencies that arise in developing countries (poor infrastructure and poor capital and goods markets) that can significantly affect one country's growth prospects.

### 3.2.7 The Ayres-Warr Analysis

Although new growth theory has been widely considered to complement the fundamental weakness of the Solow model—that is, that Solow merely assumes growth rather than explains it—a series of scholars believe that Romer's analysis still displays significant weaknesses.

As elaborated earlier, Solow's model entails that capital displays diminishing returns. Fundamentally, this implies that developing economies will grow faster than developed economies, and that economic convergence will be the realistic result. Nonetheless, this fact is widely disputed because most scholars believe that convergence has not been observed in reality (R. Ayres and Warr 2009; Clark 2007). Romer's model essentially tried to build on Solow while endogenizing the standard theory—without, however, making fundamentally drastic alterations. As R. Ayres and Warr (2009, pp. 162–163) explain: "Although not emphasized in neoclassical growth theory, there is an endogenous mechanism that can explain a part of this residual, that is, beyond that which is accounted for by labor and capital accumulation. The part that can be explained without radical (structure-changing) technological innovations is due to learning, economies of scale and the accumulation of general knowledge (for example, computer literacy) that leads to cost savings and product improvements."

Romer puts forward a trade-off between current consumption and investment in knowledge. He further makes the assumption that knowledge can be monopolized long enough to be profitable to the discoverer, but it is also possible that the knowledge becomes available as a free good (R. Ayres and Warr 2009). The central point of Romer's analysis lies in the fact that positive returns to scale constitute the main explanation behind economic growth. Romer, however, puts forward an additional point. He postulates that economic growth essentially takes place when people take resources and rearrange them in ways that are more valuable, thus creating new economic "recipes." From his analysis, as R. Ayres and Warr (2009) underline, Romer seems to believe that the magnitude of knowledge capital and the rate of growth depend on the number of new "recipes" discovered instead of the quality or sector of application. However, knowledge capital does not constitute a homogeneous entity, because some ideas and some sectors are fundamentally more productive than others (ibid.).

R. Ayres and Warr (2009) opine that growth without energy (or with less of it) is not possible. They argue that past growth was driven not by globalization or consumer spending but by the ever-declining price of energy or energy services (performing useful work) since the start of the Industrial Revolution. They also suppose that it is the technology of energy conversion and utilization, rather than technology in general, that drives growth. This approach portends serious impediments to growth for the near future. Neoclassical economists argue that energy is not an important factor of growth because its cost share is so small, but this is based on the questionable assumption that there are no real constraints on substitution between capital, labor, and energy (see Mankiw, Romer, et al. 1992). The output elasticity of energy, or of useful work, can be—and eventually is—much larger than the cost share.

Thus R. Ayres and Warr (2009) have put forward an alternative model of economic growth that manages to account for useful work or exergy (energy accounting for efficiency) as a factor of production. As they note (ibid., p. 218):

> A strong implication of our main results is that future economic growth depends either on continued declines in the cost of primary exergy or on an accelerated increase in the output of useful work from a decreasing exergy input, that is, increasing exergy-to-work conversion efficiency. Energy prices have increased significantly in the last few years and are almost certain to increase further, both because of increased demand and because of the need to cut greenhouse gas emissions. If the rate of technological progress in conversion efficiency slows down, we believe that economic growth will necessarily slow down as well. Hence, it can no longer be assumed, without question or doubt, that growth along the "trend" will continue indefinitely and that "our grandchildren will be much richer than we are" as some economists have asserted.

It is interesting to note that their perspective is consistent with the effect of energy price spikes on economic growth and with job losses through process innovations on behalf of big firms, which manage to sustain output with fewer employees.

### 3.2.8 Implicit Assumptions about Technological Innovation in Neoclassical Environmental and Ecological Economics

Environmental and ecological economics implicitly adopt or assume contrasting views on the ability of technology to overcome social and environmental problems stemming from economic (or human) activity. Whereas neoclassical economics leans toward technological optimism, ecological economics is more pessimistic about the ability of new technology to address negative externalities (or spillovers) without extensive government intervention.

In neoclassical economics, technology is treated as an exogenous factor in the economy (Huber 2004), and the price of resources is determined using static rather than dynamic efficiency (see Section 9.3 in Chapter 9). As resources become scarce, prices will rise until they reach a level (an *upper limit*) that will enable a substitute to enter the market—this idea follows Solow's (1993) notion of resource *fungibility*. If

technological innovation (either in the realm of resource-extraction technology or product/material development) is not able to provide a substitute—and the incumbent resource is essential—then the resource is likely to be used until an ecological limit is reached, after which the environment will be irreparably damaged. This point highlights the major difference between neoclassical and ecological economics. Neoclassical economics is not directly concerned about ecological limits per se, whereas identifying these limits and living within them are primary foci of ecological economics.

Like neoclassical economics, ecological economics does not explicitly address the process of technological (or system) innovation. It assumes that if it is possible to set ecological limits, then technology will somehow adjust (using pricing or other economic or legal instruments) to operate within these limits. One approach that ecological economists might use to address the problem of global warming is capping global $CO_2$ emissions and establishing a mechanism to trade emission rights. However, there is evidence to suggest that emission-trading schemes do not encourage technological innovation, but rather the diffusion of existing technology (N. A. Ashford and Caldart 2008; Driesen 2004; Kemp 2000). If improvement in efficiency by a factor of ten or more is what is required to transition toward sustainable development, then simply diffusing existing technology is not likely to be sufficient (see Section 1.3.3 in Chapter 1 for a discussion of the "factor X" debate).

A tenuous argument—based on the notion of a Faustian pact—against the idea of living within ecological limits is that given the societal benefit received from a particular sociotechnical system (such as the transportation or energy systems), societies around the world might be willing to tolerate a certain amount of environmental degradation (for example, global climate change) to continue receiving an important service (such as mobility or electricity). One way to avoid the debate over whether we should stress ecological limits is to ask how much we can make technology into a driver for sustainable development. Focusing on technology as a driver raises several important questions. Do we need incremental, revolutionary, or disrupting forms of change? Are marginal changes to large-scale sociotechnical systems adequate? For the most part, disrupting technology was originally discussed in the realm of products displacing other products (Christensen 1997); how can disrupting technology lead to a process change or further to a system innovation? The answers to such questions are explored in Chapters 6, 7, and 8.

### 3.2.9 Peak Oil and Economic Growth

Despite the fact that most models of economic growth omit energy from their analysis, some analysts describe growth as being increasingly energy dependent (R. Ayres and Warr 2009). An interesting empirical observation is the fact that significant recessions have taken place following past oil crises. Even in the context of the 2008–2009 financial crisis, many experts have argued that the spike in energy prices, and especially that of oil, contributed significantly to the recent recession, augmenting the effects of the burst of the housing bubble.

How long will oil last? This fairly simple question has generated an extremely heated debate for decades. Nonetheless, Smil (2008) notes that most of the debate does not occur because of this question as such, because we certainly know that commercial production of crude oil will persist throughout the twenty-first century. The central issue lies in what is widely known as "peak oil theory." Peak oil is the point when the maximum rate of global petroleum extraction is reached. After this point, according to the theory, the rate of production will enter a phase of terminal long-term decline. The basic assumption of the proponents of the peak oil theory states that when we compare the total volume of the estimated ultimate recovery (EUR) of oil with the worldwide cumulative production, half of the EUR has already been extracted or will be in a matter of years (Smil 2008).

The decline in oil production has been treated by many theorists as extremely important—some have gone so far as to describe it as the "doomsday" of modern civilization—while others have merely treated it as a relatively minor issue, given the rate of technological innovation. The peak oil alarmists, as they are called, have their detractors. Among them, Vaclav Smil paints a more optimistic picture, referring to similar false alarms levied at coal. His critique is rooted in the following observations (Smil 2008, p. 165):

- The values of EUR are anything but certain and tend to rise with better understanding of petroleum geology, with frontier exploration, and with enhanced recovery techniques.

- The proponents of an imminent peak of global oil extraction disregard the role of prices, ignore historical perspectives, and presuppose the end of human inventiveness and adaptability.

- Recent peak oil worries are only the latest installment in a long history of failed peak forecasts. The proponents claim that this time the circumstances are not the same and their forecasts will not miss the mark, which "mixes correct observations with untenable assumptions."

- Finally, when one contemplates a world with little or no oil, a gradual decline of global oil production does not have to translate into economic and social catastrophes.

Thus Smil's (2008) principal arguments are that estimates of EUR are just that—estimates—and they have been systematically revised upward historically. No one really knows what the real EUR is. In addition, there is no fundamental reason that the recovery curve should be bell shaped over time. We may very well decline to a plateau—rather than experiencing a steep decline—as technology advances, energy-relevant efficiency increases, and the demand for oil decreases. Although Smil (ibid., pp. 176–177) admits that the occurrence of an oil peak, along with major energy transitions, would wreak havoc on current energy producers and could lead to severe socioeconomic dislocations, he still does not believe that serious concern is justified. Smil (ibid., p. 182) offers that "with the exception of flying and long-distance land and maritime transport . . . everything that is done with liquid fuels can be done with gases." He argues, "The combination of non-conventional oil, natural gas, and gas-to-liquid conversions means that hydrocarbons should be with us as major sources of global energy supply far beyond the middle of the century" (ibid., p. 186).

Should peak oil simply be dismissed as a nonissue, raised by alarmists who have a skewed view of reality? Not quite. The increasing use of cheap energy and particularly fossil fuels was the catalyst of the Industrial Revolution and historically has been one of the most important factors behind economic growth and prosperity. The impact of peak oil on economic growth will generally depend on the exact rate of decline and on the development and speed of adoption of viable alternatives (or backstop technologies).

In 2005, the U.S. Department of Energy published a report titled *Peaking of World Oil Production*. This report, known as the Hirsch report (Hirsch, Bezdek, et al. 2005), noted that "the peaking of world oil production presents the United States and the world with an unprecedented risk management problem. As peaking is approached, liquid fuel prices and price volatility will increase dramatically, and, without timely mitigation, the economic, social, and political costs will be unprecedented. Viable mitigation options exist on both the supply and demand sides, but to have substantial impact, they must be initiated more than a decade in advance of peaking."

In general, the economic growth of the past decades has been fueled by cheap energy prices. In that context, peak oil, when met with increased energy demand from industrializing countries, will quite possibly create a situation that, depending on the speed of deployment of viable alternatives, will create significant limits to growth. As the Hirsch report underlines, oil is going to peak at some point (or already has). Thus the main issue lies in the mitigation effort that will need to take place in order for the world to experience the least possible impact.

The reader may want to read R. Ayres and Warr (2009), Hirsch, Bezdek, et al. (2005), and Smil (2008) in order to have a firmer base for judging. Technological optimism clearly underlies Smil's analysis. Whether R. Ayres and Warr are unnecessarily pessimistic remains to be seen. As with other potential impending crises, the precautionary principle needs to be brought into the policy choices in this area of substantial future uncertainty.

## 3.3 TECHNOLOGICAL DEVELOPMENT AND GROWTH THEORY

### 3.3.1 Technological Change

Technology and society are forces that together shape the world in which we live, shifting its contours and rearranging its parts, just as oceans move sand dunes. . . . To thrive amidst these waves of change requires both a sense of direction and an ability to understand how change works. Westrum, *Technologies and Society: The Shaping of People and Things*, 1991, p. 4

For almost three centuries, societies have experienced the transformative power of technological innovation. This section looks at why technological innovation has been and is such an important driver of progress, especially during the last one hundred years, which has been an era of unprecedented technological change. Technology—defined here as the application of science for the achievement of practical purposes (Dorf 2001)—is considered in the context of society, the economy, employment, the environment, and national governance.

The characteristics and capabilities of modern technology far surpass any forms of technology that supported earlier societies. One major point of distinction between the technologies of the Industrial

Revolution and those used by hunter-gatherer and agricultural societies concerns the energy sources on which technologies depend. Modern technology is predominantly dependent on fossil fuels and other sources of nonrenewable energy (oil, coal, gas, and nuclear), whereas the more primitive technologies were powered by the three Ws—wind, water, and wood (Wetlesen 1999).* In this regard, the first industrial revolution was primarily an *energy* revolution. Perhaps a future industrial transformation will be characterized by a shift to renewable energy sources and away from a reliance on nonrenewable supplies (Jänicke and Jacob 2008).

#### 3.3.1.1 The Long Waves

The first person to identify the occurrence of major technological transitions during the nineteenth and twentieth centuries was the Russian economist Nikolai Kondratieff (Kondratieff 1935 [1925]). Kondratieff's notion of a long-wave cycle (known as a Kondratieff wave, or K-wave) was originally used to describe long-wave economic cycles, or structural changes in the world economy.[1] By observing the behavior of prices and interest rates in the United Kingdom and the United States between 1789 and 1925, Kondratieff identified long-wave cycles of S-shaped growth (that is, initial slow growth that is followed by a period of rapid growth toward saturation) that occurred over a period of fifty to sixty years. His ideas were later adopted and further elaborated by the Austrian economist Joseph Schumpeter (1939), who argued that K-waves were caused by the clustering of innovations that led to rapid technology-based economic growth, which either opened up new markets or disrupted existing ones (see the discussion in Section 3.3.2).[†]

---

\*    However, the muscle power of humans and domestic animals also played an important role in helping these societies achieve their objectives (Wetlesen 1999).

†    Schumpeter (1934 [1912]) was the first person to distinguish diffusion from invention and innovation by describing technological innovation as the linear process of *invention-innovation-diffusion*. His theory was that entrepreneurs innovate not only by taking an invention to market but also by creating new manufacturing processes (for example, Eli Whitney's "American system" of manufacture of interchangeable parts), identifying products for new consumer markets, and developing new forms of industrial organization. However, a limitation of Schumpeter's theories is that he was preoccupied "with the individual entrepreneur and the individual innovation" and was reluctant to "conceptualize invention, innovation, and technology accumulation as a social process" (Freeman 1990, p. 24). Schumpeter (1934 [1912], p. 228) explained clustering by stating that "the appearance of one or a few entrepreneurs facilitates the appearance of others," and he provided no real explanation of what caused clustering or why Kondratieff's long-wave cycles occurred in nonuniform but necessarily periodic intervals (Ruttan 1959). Today it is

Kaplinsky (2005, pp. 225–228) describes the work of Perez (2002) which offers an alternative explanation to innovation clusters causing surges in growth and emphasizing a "rejuvenation of all economic activities" by across-the-board deepening and broadening of those activities by new technology, for example, ICT technology. Perez's conceptualization involves four phases: (1) "irruption," which offers the possibility of dramatic changes in otherwise mature industries with market saturation; (2) a "frenzy" of investment leading to the creation of a financial bubble (with the potential to create excess productive capacity), followed by its collapse; (3) diffusion of the technology; and (4) maturation and saturation of markets, creating vulnerability to subsequent technological displacement and disruption. Perez argues that the disjuncture between financial capital and production capital (the latter is important in moving from phase 2 to phase 3) resulted in structural overcapacity and falling prices that explain, for example, price and profit squeezes, default on investment loans, and the ultimate collapse of the dot.com industry. Although Perez's conceptualization may well explain historical surges in the growth of industrial economies, and her ideas may well describe the pathology of the "dot.com surge," it has little to do with the financial crisis of 2008, which was fed by both the circulation of illusory financial instruments and the unjustified expansion of credit markets.*

Within the modern era of technological development, there have been four distinct sixty- to seventy-year K-waves (or periods) of technology-driven economic development (Grübler and Nowotny 1990). Each of these waves can be characterized by growth sectors, emerging technologies, and new concepts of management and industrial organization (Table 3.1). In each case, the emergence of new technologies resulted in a technological transition that tended to follow a sigmoid curve (S-curve) (Figure 3.1). Although the fifth technological cycle of development (1985–2050) is in the process of being defined, the items/characteristics identified are those emerging in many industrial societies today, with the possible exception of the nuclear sector being a growth sector.† A poten-

tial growth sector that has been added to Table 3.1 is the *NBIC convergence* (that is, the convergence of nanotechnology, biotechnology, information and communication technology, and cognitive sciences into major new areas of research and development). Important emerging technologies that have been added to the list in Table 3.1 are nanotechnology and ubiquitous computing—that is, computers/technologies that are embedded and networked into all aspects of our lives to such an extent that we are not fully aware of their existence or simply take them for granted.

Perhaps what is most striking about the waves of economic development (represented by the pace of innovation) is how the scientific and technological breakthroughs that fueled them have also shaped the modern era by improving public health and changing the fabric of modern society (Langford 2004). From the steam engine to the combustion engine and from the telegraph to satellite and laser communications, each transition has provided new opportunities to improve our quality of life. These transitions in technology have been paralleled by major scientific advances in such areas as medicine and genetic engineering, which have improved the health of those societies with access to the new medicines or knowledge.

With each transition, the complexity of new technological systems is increasing and is placing greater demands on our ability to understand how these new systems interact and behave. The task of defining and understanding the dynamic and evolving nature of technological systems will be a major undertaking of the twenty-first century. One might argue that our inability to understand or predict, and then to counteract or respond to, the behavior of these systems is the main reason that there exists so much concern about the future prospects of developed societies on the part of those analysts concerned with safety.‡ We need not look far to see numerous events that have devastated communities and the natural world as a result of technological and scientific advances.§ Nonetheless, the

---

widely recognized that the institutional or legislative framework within which businesses operate (what might be called "institutional capital") plays an influential role in the formation of innovation clusters (Freeman 1990; Kingston 2004).

\* For an in-depth explanation of the 2008 financial crisis and its aftermath, see especially Stiglitz (2010).

† Public unease about the safety of nuclear technology, nuclear proliferation, long-term waste-management requirements, and life-cycle costs are four important factors limiting the growth of the nuclear sector. However, if greater emphasis is placed on electricity production that does not produce $CO_2$ and

these four factors are adequately addressed, the nuclear sector might experience a resurgence (Deutch, Moniz, et al. 2003; Nuttall 2004). In any event, nuclear power is likely to remain a highly controversial energy option.

‡ See the discussion in the next section of the information revolution, which raises the question whether its advances can be measured by the metrics developed for the first and second industrial revolutions.

§ A few salient examples include the 1969 oil spills and subsequent fire on the Cuyahoga River in Ohio and off the coast of Santa Barbara, California; the 1979 Three Mile Island nuclear accident in Pennsylvania; the 1984 incident where a leak of deadly methyl isocyanate at a Union Carbide pesticide plant in Bhopal, India, killed some 3,800 people; the 1986 nuclear reactor meltdown at the Chernobyl power station that released radioactive material

**TABLE 3.1: CHARACTERISTICS OF MAJOR TECHNOLOGICAL COMPLEXES**

| | First Wave 1770–1830 | Second Wave 1820–1890 | Third Wave 1880–1945 | Fourth Wave 1935–1995 | Fifth Wave 1985–2050 |
|---|---|---|---|---|---|
| **Growth sectors** | Water power Ships Canals | Coal Railroads Steam power Mechanical equipment | Cars Trucks Trolleys Chemical industry Metallurgical processes | Electric power Oil Airplanes Radio and Television Instruments and controls | Gas Nuclear Information Telecommunications Satellite and laser communications [NBIC] |
| **Emerging technologies** | Mechanical equipment Coal Stationary steam power | Electricity Internal combustion Telegraph Steam shipping | Electronics Jet engines Air transport | Nuclear Computers Gas Telecommunications | Biotechnology Artificial intelligence Space communication and transport [Nanotechnology Ubiquitous computing] |
| **Management** | | Economy of scale Interchangeable parts | Administrative management | Professional management | Participatory and interconnected systems management |
| **Industrial organization** | Concept of the industrial firm Division of labor | Concept of mass production Interchangeable parts | Concept of management structure and delegation | Concept of decentralization | Concept of systems structure |

Source: Grübler and Nowotny (1990), reproduced in NRC (2002, p. 73).

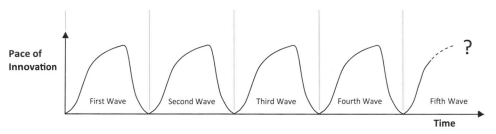

**FIGURE 3.1: STYLIZED GRAPH OF SCHUMPETER'S WAVES OF TECHNOLOGY-BASED ECONOMIC DEVELOPMENT**
Note: This figure is based on a similar diagram presented in Jowitt (2004, p. 81). However, an important difference is that Jowitt's graph depicts a reduction in the duration of each subsequent wave of innovation (i.e., the first wave is sixty years in length, the second wave is fifty-five years in length, and so on until the fifth wave, which is predicted to be thirty years in length). If we look at specific technologies there is evidence to suggest that the rate at which society adopts new technology is increasing. See, for example, Christensen's book *The Innovator's Dilemma* (1997), in which he charts the rapid advance of disk-drive technology that occurred over a contracted time period.
Source: Adapted from Jowitt (2004, p. 81).

idea that technology has played, and will continue to play, an influential role in shaping modern industrial societies predominates. This idea of *technological determinism*—a *technology-led* theory of social change—can be traced back to the early stages of the Industrial Revolution.*

---

throughout the Northern Hemisphere; the 1989 *Exxon Valdez* oil spill that released 11 million gallons of oil into Alaska's Prince William Sound; and the 2010 BP Gulf oil spill. Although preventing such disasters is a primary objective of systems engineering, some argue that no matter how many warnings and safeguards are designed into our modern large-scale technological systems (such as a nuclear power or petrochemical plant), growing systems complexity means that failures are inevitable (Perrow 1999). Of course, what are missing from the preceding list are incidents that occurred through the intentional use of nuclear, chemical, biological, and conventional weapons.

* Smith (1994) provides an insightful discussion of how technological determinism, initially conceived in Europe, found a fertile ground in the newly independent United States as a result of its desire for progress. He argues that Benjamin Franklin and Thomas Jefferson were the "nation's prophets of progress" who sought new mechanical technologies as a means to realize the vision of a "virtuous and prosperous republican society" (ibid., p. 3). Smith suggests that to Franklin and Jefferson, "progress meant the pursuit of technology and science in the interest of human betterment (intellectual, moral, spiritual) and material prosperity" (ibid.). However, Smith (1994) describes how, at the turn

### 3.3.1.2 The Information or Postindustrial Revolution

It is now apparent, at the turn of the twenty-first century, that developed economies are transitioning toward a postindustrial, or information-based, society (Castells 1999). Bell (1999) describes a postindustrial society as one that relies on the economics of information (or intellectual capital) as opposed to the economics of goods (from manufacturing) or reliance on the services sector of production versus the manufacturing sector of production. Where the steam engine was argued to be the catalyst for the Industrial Revolution, global information technology is argued to be the catalyst for the information revolution. Therefore, the signs of an emerging postindustrial society are a growing services sector and an increasing reliance on information technology. However, the postindustrial society will not displace the older one; instead, it will overlie some of the previous layers, just as the industrial society did not eliminate the agricultural sectors of society (ibid.). People will still rely on agriculture and manufacturing to survive. The development of new technological forms for the postindustrial society will need to respond to this new era of human development, where information and products and services become intertwined.

In the insightful article "The Age of Social Transformations," Drucker (1994) charts the major changes that have occurred in the structure of society from the early agricultural to the new knowledge-based societies. In particular, he describes how two technology-based shifts in the nature of employment have occurred.

It is evident that before World War I, the single largest group in every country consisted of traditional farmers, followed in developed nations by live-in domestic servants (Drucker 1994, p. 54). By the 1950s, the Industrial Revolution—triggered by emerging technologies such as the steam engine—had gathered full momentum, and industrial workers now formed the single largest group in developed nations (ibid., p. 56). The core tasks of these workers were manufacturing and serving the products of manufacturing (such as car and appliance repair). Interestingly, the skills that agricultural workers and domestic servants brought to their new "industrial" positions meant that they were often overskilled for their jobs. At the turn of the millennium, the traditional industrial worker began to be replaced by the technologist—"someone who works both with hands and with theoretical knowledge" (ibid.). Good examples of technologists are dentists and computer and X-ray technicians. More generally, Drucker (ibid., p. 62) refers to the newly emerging dominant group as "knowledge workers." He argues that although the foundation of the knowledge worker is a formal education, this is only the beginning. If the new comparative advantage lies in the application of knowledge, this means that the knowledge worker must be able to learn continuously to bring value to his or her firm or business (ibid., pp. 62–63). Modern-day knowledge-based workers form what is now termed the "service industry," which includes (1) health-care services (such as dentistry and medicine), (2) knowledge-based services (such as banking and information management), and (3) food and retail services. However, it should be recognized that the first two job categories are likely to require higher levels of educational achievement than the third category.

Drucker (1994) argues that the problem with this latest transition is that displaced industrial workers cannot simply move into knowledge-based or service employment because they lack the education necessary to do such tasks. Hence if industrial workers are to succeed in knowledge-based employment, they must "change their basic attitudes, values, and beliefs" (ibid., p. 62). The transition also means that good education and a capacity for lifelong learning become paramount.

What Drucker fails to acknowledge, though, is that displaced industrial workers may have no choice but to accept low-wage employment in the service sector (Berger 2005) (see Section 1.1.3.1). Although working in a fast-food establishment, for instance, will bring in some income, it is debatable whether such employment is fulfilling to the worker, given his training and preferences (see Section 1.1.3.2). Hence the future does not look particularly promising for those industrial workers caught in the transition between the industrial economy and the service economy,

---

of the nineteenth century, Franklin and Jefferson's views failed to prevail because of the emergence of a more technocratic vision of progress espoused by Alexander Hamilton and Tench Coxe. This technocratic view grew from the belief that America's political independence rested on economic independence. The early success of machine-based manufacturing convinced Hamilton and Coxe that technology would be the means by which economic independence could be achieved. In addition, with the nation's abundant resources and a limited populace to exploit them, if America was to surpass Britain and Europe in technological prowess, then new technology and machines would be required (Pursell 1996). During the following century and a half, America's decision to focus on technological advance laid the groundwork for major advances in manufacturing that had a significant influence on American culture (Pursell 1996; Smith and Marx 1994). An example of two influential innovations produced during this period were Eli Whitney's "American system" of manufacture of interchangeable parts (Smith 1994) and Henry Ford's triumph of the automobile (Flink 2001). See Pursell (1996) for an insightful discussion of influential technologies from America.

although the economy as a whole showed great promise at the time.

Productivity growth in the United States in the second half of the 1990s had been attributed to the information revolution, and Europe adopted its famous Lisbon Strategy in 2000 to emulate the ICT-driven knowledge-based economy as explaining the apparent cause of the U.S. economic success (Hagemann 2008). However, there have been many disappointments associated with the performance of the information revolution. The tech bubble burst in 2001 and the ICT productivity "miracle" may have imploded at the same time. Solow (1987) famously said, "You can see the computer age everywhere but in the productivity statistics," giving rise to the productivity or Solow paradox. In 1997 in the *Financial Times*, Stephen Roach, chief economist for Morgan Stanley, opined: "The productivity gains of the Information Age are just a myth" (Griffith 1997). Acknowledging the greater productivity growth in the United States than in Europe, Roach attributed greater output to longer working hours in the United States.

Lynch (2008) argues that investments in human capital, information technology, R&D, and physical capital appear to be complementary to investments in organizational innovation. She observes that "even after accounting for capital deepening, total productivity growth has been a very important determinant of the growth of average labor productivity." Citing her earlier work (Black and Lynch 2004, 2005), she repeats her argument that during the 1990s, changes in organizational innovation may have accounted for as much as 30 percent of output growth in U.S. manufacturing.*

In examining the relationship between ICT and trends in labor productivity and employment in the 1990s in Europe and the United States, van Ark, Inklaar, et al. (2003, p. 86) found: "The inverse relationship between employment and productivity growth has been much more prominent in manufacturing industries than in service industries. Secondly, during the 1990's, the relationship has turned positive in many industries, in particular ICT-using industries in the service sector. Finally, the employment-reducing effects of productivity growth have remained considerably stronger in Europe than in the U.S."

Commenting on the sources of economic growth in the 1990s, in 2003 the OECD (2003, p. 14) nonetheless voiced optimism about the new economy,

saying, "The use of ICT may be increasing the efficiency of innovation, further contributing to long-term growth potential." The OECD's optimism has not waned, even in the light of the 2008 financial crisis OECD (2010a, 2010b).

ICT is identified as a general-purpose technology (GPT) that may take a long time to become manifest in macroeconomic growth and productivity data. Alan Greenspan's characterization of the large price-to-earnings ratio in the late 1990s as "irrational exuberance" following Robert J. Shiller's analysis in his book of the same title (Shiller 2000), published just before the 2000 stock-market crash,[†] represented further doubt about ICT as a source of significant economic growth. Another doubt stemmed from a failure to find rises in multifactor productivity (MFP) that varied across countries and could have been attributed to increases in R&D and organizational innovations rather than directly to ICT (Hagemann 2008).

Hagemann (2008, p. 61) offers three possible explanations for the Solow paradox:

1. Some of the benefits of ICT may not be picked up by the productivity statistics, such as improvements in the quality and diversity of services.

2. The benefits of ICT, such as organizational change and the upskilling of workers, may be slow to emerge.

3. The creation and expansion of networks take time to occur and may not show up in the statistics.

Liagouras (2005), on the other hand, raises more fundamental questions about the usefulness of metrics of progress that had been developed for industrial societies in "postindustrial capitalism":

Perhaps the most serious difficulty is to find convenient indicators in order to measure what is intangible or invisible. . . . This is a more general problem, which concerns not only investment but also all basic concepts, such as product, productivity, growth, etc., which we inherited from the industrial era. (ibid., p. 24)

The essentials of business organization in industrial capitalism can . . . be found in the writings of classical economists: the long-term performance of the enterprise is identified with productivity. And productivity is obtained in three correlated ways: the deepening of the (technical) division of labour, the mechanization of the labour process, and economies of scale. (ibid., p. 23)

---

\* See Chapter 7 for a discussion or organizational innovation and learning.

---

† The 2008 global stock-market crash and financial crisis are generally acknowledged to have stemmed from excessive borrowing driven by unjustifiable optimism in continual high growth of both housing and financial markets.

The notion of productivity no longer makes sense in an economic context where quality and variety take precedence over quantity. Investment in intangible capital (R&D, training, software, and long-term marketing positioning) becomes more important than the mechanization of labour processes. Last, but not least, the secular tendencies towards specialization and de-qualification of labour—and the vertical-horizontal expansion of the firm—are clearly reversed. (ibid.)

In commenting on the currency of the need to resolve the Solow paradox, in which large investments in ICT have not shown up in the productivity statistics, Liagouras (2005) asks:

> If the inventions in ICTs and in biotechnologies are so revolutionary as it is said, why after two decades of unprecedented technical progress is this not reflected in output and productivity statistics? (ibid., p. 29)
>
> The first explanation concerns the incapacity of national account systems, constructed within and for industrial capitalism, to measure the economic performance of post-industrial societies. In industrial societies, the wealth of individuals and nations takes the form of an accumulation of standardized commodity goods. The production of the latter is achieved through the use of other goods like machines and materials. In this schema of "production of commodities by means of commodities," even work is reduced to unqualified (simple) labour and then to the goods required for its reproduction. Thus, increases in the wealth of individuals and nations are identified with increases in the quantities of goods that they produce and sell. However, given that the value of the total product also depends on the evolution of prices of different goods, the elaboration of cost-of-living indexes—like the Consumer Price Index (CPI)—permits the isolation of the quantity-effect from the price-effect, and thus the measurement of the real growth of output. Still, the above framework becomes problematic when (a) there are important and/or continuous changes in the quality, variety, and convenience of the goods, (b) new goods are introduced very often, (c) investment in different forms of intangible capital becomes important, and (d) service relationships become dominant in the whole economy (and not only in the service sector). This means that what exactly characterizes postindustrial capitalism cannot be easily measured, and by consequence, contemporary national accounts overstate inflation and understate growth in output and in productivity. (ibid.)
>
> In activities like healthcare, education, culture, insurance, knowledge-intensive business services and environmental services, the objective is not to accumulate commodities, but to maintain and ameliorate the state of a human or a natural system in the long run. This implies first of all that long-run outcomes cannot be reduced to a measurable immediate output—as is the case with manufacturing and agricultural goods. (ibid., p. 30)

> In conclusion, the more we move towards post-industrial society, the more the notions of growth, output, and productivity that we inherited from industrial capitalism will become obsolete. This means also that, with time, it will be necessary to invent a new national accounts system, and not simply improve on the existing one. Note however that the elaboration of new conventions for post-industrial economic performance go far beyond measurement issues. The ultimate question is what kind of (post-materialist) development do we want, and in what kind of (post-industrial) society do we want to live? (ibid.)

These observations bring into question whether all the attempts to develop sustainability metrics may, in the end, be inadequate to track failures and successes in transformational initiatives. (See Section 3.4.2 for a related discussion of the measures used to track development in Kerala, India, and in Costa Rica.)

An important metric relevant to employment is *inherent lower cost*, which measures the cost savings that can be attributed to enhanced capital, labor, and labor-capital-interface* productiveness. Here productiveness should not be confused with productivity. *Productivity* is found by dividing an output by a factor of input—that is, it is the amount of output per unit of input. *Productiveness* is a measure of the quality of being productive or the capacity for producing. Examples are a more productive machine that is capable of faster output and a more productive worker who is capable of more creative or faster work and higher-quality outputs if his or her skills have been enhanced. Therefore, labor productivity can be enhanced by the use of more productive capital (such as a smarter machine) or more productive workers. As a result, it is important to measure the productiveness of labor, capital, and the labor-capital interface because this provides a more accurate measure of where a company's/nation's competitiveness lies—in its capital, its labor, the interface between the two, or a mixture of two or more of these elements. The problem with conventional measures of labor productivity—such as that included in the 2006 United Nations Commission on Sustainable Development (UNCSD) framework (Ekins and Medhurst 2006) (which divides output by a labor factor input, such as number of hours worked or wages paid)—is that it fails to identify who or what is responsible for the production/competitiveness.

---

* The labor-capital interface is the match between a particular technology and a person for a given production scenario. For example, ergonomically designed workstations are a better match than poorly designed ones.

Another interesting indicator or metric is the cost savings *derived from environmental and social factors* that can be attributed not to production efficiencies, but rather to improvements in environmental, social, and/or employment factors that yield positive financial benefits in terms of reduced costs or even positive social benefits such as more satisfied workers. Using the current situation as a baseline, new initiatives/programs can be assessed by how much future expenditure they *save*. A "lower-cost" analysis takes a broad view of the problem being addressed. For example, the use of a new process/initiative that reduces accidents and lowers pollution levels is likely to avoid health costs associated with injured or ill workers/bystanders and lower any potential environmental cleanup/remediation costs.

Finally, it would be valuable to measure how the *performance*—which is similar to the quality and variety of outputs discussed by Liagouras—of an industry sector or products has improved over time. This indicator may reflect changes in the rate of innovation, which is a central determinant of competitiveness.

The meaning, sources, and measurement of competitiveness continues to draw attention of those scholars, organizations, and institutions concerned mainly with economic growth. The Washington-based European-American Business Council addressed this issue in a 2009 report (Atkinson and Andes 2009). Noting that capital accumulation and economies of scale were the important drivers in the old economy and asserting that "in the United States ... virtually all the increase in productivity after 1995 has been due to the use of IT by organizations" and that better use of IT explains faster growth in the United States than in Europe, the report argues that:

> many nations no longer compete principally on low costs, but instead compete on the basis of innovation and knowledge as they seek to create, grow and attract high value-added firms. This report assesses nations' innovation-based, global competitiveness. . . .
>
> The 16 indicators used in this study to assess global competitiveness fall into six broad categories: (1) human capital; (2) innovation capacity; (3) entrepreneurship; (4) IT infrastructure; (5) economic policy; and (6) economic performance.
>
> Unlike several recent studies that find that the United States is the global leader in innovation and competitiveness . . . [we find] that the United States ranks sixth overall among the 40 nations/regions (with a global competitiveness score of 63.9 that is 15 percent below the leader Singapore's score of 73.4).

The EU-15 region ranks 18th in global competitiveness among the 40 nations/regions (with a global competitiveness score of just 52.5, 40 percent below Singapore's score). Thus, our analysis indicates that the United States is not the runaway leader in global competitiveness that some believe it to be, but still leads Europe.

Moreover, strikingly ITIF finds that all of the 39 other countries and regions studied have made faster progress toward the new knowledge-based innovation economy in recent years than the United States. As indicated by the change score, the United States has made the least progress of the 40 nations/regions in improvement in international competitiveness and innovation capacity over the last decade. The EU-15 region has made some improvements over the last decade, but slower than the overall average and as a result, ranks 29th among the 40 nations/regions. But this is still considerably higher than the United States. If the EU-15 region as a whole continues to improve at this faster rate than the United States, it would surpass the United States in innovation-based competitiveness by 2020.

These findings have significant implications for Europe and the United States. First, the rise of global economic competition means that the United States and Europe need to . . . put in place national or continental economic development strategies. This particularly applies to the United States, where the prevailing view among many Washington policymakers is that the United States has been number 1 for so long that it will continue to be number 1. Given this situation, the thinking goes, there is no need for the United States to develop and implement a national economic development or competitiveness strategy. . . . Likewise, the European Commission needs to expand its efforts to spur economic development, particularly by increasing its support for science and innovation

and ensuring that its regulatory framework supports innovation.

. . . Nations or regions should:

1. **Put in place incentives for firms to innovate within their borders.** These should include robust R&D tax incentives; incentives, such as accelerated depreciation, to invest in new equipment, particularly IT; and other policies that spur investment in the building blocks of growth, such as workforce development tax credits.

2. **Be open to high-skill immigration.** High skill immigrants are the source of many new ideas and innovations. Countries that are open to high skill immigration will be able to better succeed.

3. **Foster a digital economy.** Nations should not only expand public investments in IT in areas such as health care, energy systems, transporta-

tion, government, and education, but also put in place the right regulatory frameworks to spur, not limit, digital investment. Nations need to also consider how existing regulatory and public procurement policies can be redesigned to intentionally spur digital transformation.

4. **Support the kinds of institutions that are critical to innovation.** Nations need to expand funding not just for university research, but for the kinds of mechanisms and institutions that help foster commercialization of research. In addition, they need to boost support for a host of efforts such as local economic development, entrepreneurship development, and workforce training.

5. **Ensure that regulations and other related government policies support, not retard, innovation.** Too often, powerful interest groups (business, civic, and labor) fight against change and innovation, often under the guise of the public interest, but all too often the result is that progressive and positive innovation is slowed. Nations should ensure that their regulations, procurement, and other related policies tilt toward innovation."

### 3.3.2 Joseph Schumpeter's "Creative Destruction"

The now-famous term "creative destruction" was coined by Austrian economist Joseph A. Schumpeter to describe how innovative products and processes displace old ones in the context of a dynamic market economy (McCraw 2007). Contrary to the Smithian/Marshallian description of the economy as being in a state of equilibrium, Schumpeter described capitalism as being "by nature a form or method of economic change . . . [that] not only never is but never can be stationary" (Schumpeter 1962 [1942], p. 82).

Schumpeter's description of the process of creative destruction challenged the fundamental premise of neoclassical economics with respect to the notion of price competition at the epicenter of the capitalist process. In *Capitalism, Socialism, and Democracy*, Schumpeter argued that the new products and processes that result from technological competition and product and process innovation are more important in understanding the essence of capitalism than the standard model of price competition that places emphasis on decentralized markets as the means to lowering prices for a given set of goods and technologies (Diamond 2006). Capitalism, according to Schumpeter, could be better understood as an

evolutionary rather than a static process, whose basic drivers of change were not social and natural transformations but the introduction of new goods, new methods of production and processes, new markets, and new forms of industrial organization inherent in the capitalist process.

Schumpeter considered the forces of creative destruction to be the locomotive of the capitalist process and the driving force behind economic growth. To disregard creative destruction would be, in Schumpeter's (1962, p. 86) words, similar to having "Hamlet without the Danish prince." An increasing number of economists are arguing that it is conceivable that policies that would make a national economy more open to creative destruction would promote a higher rate of economic growth (Diamond 2006).

Figure 3.2 provides supportive evidence of Schumpeter's conceptual framework of the economy. As Clark (2007, p. 1) notes: "Before 1800, income per person—the food, clothing, heat, light, and housing available per head—varied across societies and epochs. But there was no upward trend. A simple but powerful mechanism, [ . . . ] the *Malthusian Trap*, ensured that short-term gains in income through technological advances were inevitably lost in population growth."

Clark (2007) argues that the average person of 1800 was essentially as well-off as the average person of 100,000 B.C. Although this assumption might initially seem to be mistaken, it is corroborated by the facts. In essence, the median citizen of the 1800 world was actually worse off than her remote ancestors. Life expectancy in the 1800s was as high as it was for hunter-gatherers (thirty to thirty-five years), while average stature, a measure of health, was actually higher in the Stone Age (ibid.).

Clark (2007) notes that this lack of progress was due to a mechanism he calls "the Malthusian Trap,"

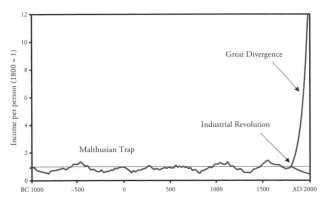

**FIGURE 3.2: WORLD ECONOMIC HISTORY IN ONE PICTURE**
Source: Clark (2007, p. 2). Reprinted with permission. Copyright © 2007 Princeton University Press.

---

**BOX 3.3: THOMAS ROBERT MALTHUS (1766–1834)**

Malthus's central contribution to the early discussions of the causes and effects of economic growth was his much-debated 1798 work *An Essay on the Principle of Population, as It Affects the Future Improvement of Society, with Remarks on the Speculations of Mr. Goodwin, M. Condorcet, and Other Writers*. The historical context sheds significant light on Malthus's insights. In the 1800s, the population of London had increased from 200,000 to 900,000 people, and most of the new residents were underprivileged (Warsh 2006).

Both Malthus and Ricardo focused on the principle of diminishing returns. The central argument of Malthus's analysis, however, relied on a single comparison between arithmetic and geometric growth rates. Malthus argued that population increases could be stopped only by misery and vice in the long run. He based his arguments on two variables: *population* and *food*. The central claim of his theory, however, was that these two variables had two fundamentally different potential growth rates: geometric and arithmetic.

Malthus declared that there was empirical evidence that populations grew with a fixed amount of time to double. He noted, especially, the resource-rich United States, where he claimed that the population doubled every twenty-five years. This fixed doubling time is called geometric growth. In contrast to population growth, he asserted that food resources could, at best, exhibit arithmetic growth, which means food increasing by a fixed absolute amount in a fixed amount of time.

In general, Malthus's analysis made the case that the actual population has the propensity to push above the food supply. Because of this propensity, any effort to improve the quality of life of the lower classes by increasing their incomes or improving agricultural productivity would be futile, because the extra resources would be entirely absorbed by an induced increase in population.

Malthus later proposed a series of practical policies commensurate with his analysis of demographics. His goal was to instill middle-class virtues in the lower classes, which were responsible for boosting the birth rate. His proposed policies included the introduction of universal voting rights, state-run education for the poor, the abolition of the Poor Laws, and the creation of a free nationwide labor market. In his view, once the poor developed a taste for comfort, they would require a better standard of living for themselves before starting a family. Hence Malthus suggested that sufficiently high incomes might be enough by themselves to reduce the average national birth rate.

---

named after the person who first described this economic logic, the Reverend Thomas Robert Malthus (see Box 3.3). The Malthusian model had three main assumptions about the economy (ibid., p. 20):

1. Each society has a *birth rate*, determined by customs regulating fertility, but increasing with material living standards.
2. The *death rate* in each society declines as living standards increase.
3. *Material living standards* decline as population increases.

Hence the main intuition of the model is that any benefits from technological increases before the 1800s were absorbed by population increases and were thus not reflected in the per capita standard-of-living analytics. However, at some point between 1770 and 1860, something occurred. The English population tripled; however, real incomes, instead of collapsing, increased (Clark 2007). There exist many competing explanations of why the Industrial Revolution occurred, why it took place in the given time frame, or

why it began in England. However, most explanations contain a central element of technological innovation (with the notable exception of R. Ayres and Warr 2009) and lend credence to Schumpeter's perspective that technology and innovation lie at the epicenter of economic growth.

### 3.3.3 Market Structure and Innovation

In *Capitalism, Socialism, and Democracy* (1962 [1942]), Joseph A. Schumpeter outlined that large firms operating in concentrated markets, often enjoying monopoly power, are the main engine of technological progress and innovation. An important element of the Schumpeterian paradigm was the monopolist's ability to bear risks, attract the best workforce, and enjoy a superior financial position (Scherer 1992). Schumpeter argued that giant firms could afford to gamble on new techniques and were willing to absorb losses in some of their new ventures because they could be confident of profits in others (McCraw 2007). This position contrasted with the one that he had previously outlined in his *Theory of Economic Development* (1934 [1912]), in which he insisted that innovations emanate from new and characteristically small firms.* These firms would eventually grow large; however, they would start as "outsiders" in Schumpeter's analysis.

Schumpeter, partially influenced by the German historical school's approach to economics, which consisted of detailed histories of various industries and institutions, was not trying to devise elaborate mathematical theories on paper, but rather to observe his surroundings in order to derive tangible conclusions. He cited the United States as his most favored example. Indeed, at the beginning of the twentieth century, firms such as General Electric, Eastman Kodak, and DuPont founded research departments explicitly for the purpose of developing new technologies and products. In that way, innovation was made part of their normal business routine, which constituted a profound change in business structures. However, at the same time, new companies continued to bud and innovate alongside the large-scale establishments, which lent support to what Schumpeter had predicted in 1912 but contradicted his stated thesis in *Capitalism, Socialism, and Democracy*, published in 1942.

This latter view was particularly radical given the mainstream economic thought of the era, which was encapsulated in Adam Smith's treatise on the merits of competitive markets and of the invisible hand as heralds of affluence and prosperity. The Schumpeterian hypothesis was making exactly the opposite assumption: that innovation, which was the cornerstone of economic progress and prosperity, directly relied on the expectation of a monopoly position or the possession of it.

Economists appear to be split on the issue. Kenneth Arrow and William Fellner have argued that the incentives to innovate are greater in a framework of competitive market pricing (Scherer 1992). On the other hand, John Kenneth Galbraith suggested that it is in a strategic interactions environment among few oligopolists that innovation is optimally fostered (ibid.). Moreover, some found evidence for the original Schumpeterian assumption of a linear relationship between firm size and R&D, while others, such as F. M. Scherer, Morton Kamien, and Nancy Schwartz, found an inverted-U relationship, with diseconomies of scale after a certain point (ibid.).

On the whole, there is little empirical support for the view that large firm size or concentration is directly associated with a higher degree of innovative activity. Even when such a correlation is present, we are not in a position to be sure about the direction of causality. In specific industries that are research intensive, such as pharmaceuticals, a high degree of concentration or monopoly power may be unavoidable because of the significant fixed costs and indivisibility of research that are associated with the characteristics of the specific industries in question. In the pharmaceutical industry's case, monopoly power is provided through comprehensive patent rights on specific drugs. Alternatively, Rodrik (2007) argues, the results may be context specific, reflecting differences in the entirety of governmental policies in different countries. See also the work of van Ark, Inklaar, et al. (2003), where the growth experience in the "new economy" vis-à-vis large versus small firms is different in the United States from that in the EU.

The Schumpeterian "more-is-better" hypothesis, as a "one-size-fits all" approach, does not display a significant level of descriptive capacity in the case of industries such as computer software and semiconductors. Industry behavior is better explained in those cases by the following scenario: Firms with dominant market positions maximize their profit margins by choosing a "leisurely" and inexpensive level of R&D. If smaller rivals or potential entrants threaten profit making through innovation, dominant firms are then provided with incentives to innovate and accelerate their development efforts further (Scherer 1992). The theory of "the fast second" relies on this logic. In that theory, dominant incumbents permit smaller rivals to be the technological pioneers at the beginning. IBM exploited this strategy by repeatedly announcing a new product in advance of actual deliveries. This allowed IBM, as the dominant incumbent, to retain its existing customers despite the fact that it marginally lagged behind rivals in product deliveries. Another example of this is the extensive leapfrogging activity by industry leaders such as IBM and Microsoft. The "browser wars" between Microsoft and Netscape and the operating-system competition between Microsoft and Apple easily come to mind as cases where Microsoft's rivals had the initial technological advantage, but where Microsoft managed to emulate them effectively by "leapfrogging" the first mover's technology.[†]

---

* See the discussion in Chapters 6 and 7 of whether radical innovation is more likely to arise in small firms.

† See also the discussion of the computer hard-drive industry by Christensen (1997), where there was constant displacement of the dominant technological firm by a new entrant.

On the other hand, the Schumpeterian hypothesis seems to have increasing explanatory power in the case of Japanese and European industries. Japan's national industrial strategy appears to be very close to the Schumpeterian paradigm in the formation of large enterprises that undertake collaborative R&D efforts. At the same time, Japan's high-technology start-up sector was limited by the beginning of the 1990s. However, the European and particularly the Japanese cases could be attributed to a series of reasons, such as the increasing scale pressure from globalization, the possible increases in the cost of conducting R&D, the existence of cultural differences that facilitate such industry structures, and the technical problem in question that the specific organizational structures aim to address (Scherer 1992).

It is useful to note, however, that although Schumpeter wrote about innovation in general, not all innovations are qualitatively the same. Christensen (1997) distinguishes between two types of innovative activities in the product context: (1) sustaining innovations and (2) disruptive innovations (see the discussion in Chapter 6). Sustaining innovations are innovations that will be generally valued by the incumbent firm's customer base (Diamond 2006). This is the sort of innovations that the incumbent firm is expected to pursue generally by engaging in evolutionary transformations. On the other hand, disruptive innovations are generally discontinuous and possibly involve the displacement of dominant firms and institutions, with new firms catering to a different customer base (N. A. Ashford, Hafkamp, et al. 2002; Luiten 2001; Moors 2000; Partidario 2003).

The most recent body of literature has focused on modeling the desire of firms to innovate. Aghion and Howitt (2005) studied the relation between innovation and competition, trying to address the question whether increased competition stimulates innovation. Their analysis concludes that the effect of competition on innovation decisively depends on where firms are situated relative to the technological frontier. For instance, in sectors where competition is significant for firms that are close to the technological frontier, an increase in competition will induce firms with additional incentives to innovate in order to move ahead and reap some monopoly profits. However, if firms are far from the technological frontier, competition discourages innovation because there is little profit to be made from catching up with the front-runners.

In sum, empirical evidence on the correlation between market size and innovative activity has provided us with mixed results so far, and thus the validity of the Schumpeterian hypothesis will need to be questioned empirically.

## 3.4 CRITIQUES OF, AND ALTERNATIVES TO, THE NORTHERN GROWTH MODEL

### 3.4.1 Growth in Developing Economies and the Washington Consensus

Challenging economic orthodoxy, Seers (1997) questions some of its fundamental precepts in single-mindedly promoting economic growth in developing countries:

> We can, after all, fall back on the supposition that increases in national income, if they are faster than population growth, sooner or later lead to the solution of social and political problems. . . . Economic growth may not merely fail to solve social and political difficulties; certain types of growth can actually cause them. (ibid., p. 39) [Seers argues that increases in per capita income may occur with adverse distributional inequities.]
>
> Inequality cannot really be reduced so long as property ownership is concentrated. (ibid., p. 41)
>
> In a highly unequal society, personal savings often flow abroad or go into luxury housing and other investment projects of low or zero priority for development. (ibid.)

Further, he notes that "national income measures published for most developing countries have very little meaning" (Seers 1997, p. 40). Seers argues that the purpose of economic development is the reduction of poverty, inequality, and unemployment.

According to Nafziger (2006), Amartya Sen (1999) adopts a different definition, stating that freedom of choice to determine one's future and pathways to that future, instead of development, is the ultimate goal of economic life and the most efficient means of realizing general welfare. Actually, Seers (1997) is close to Sen when he states: "What are the necessary conditions for a universally acceptable aim [of development]?—the realization of the human personality" (ibid., p. 40).

Sen's definition of freedom differs greatly from that of neoclassical economics. For Sen, "unfreedoms" include hunger, famine, ignorance, unsustainable economic life, unemployment and underemployment,* barriers to economic fulfillment by women of minority communities, premature death, violation of political freedom and basic liberty, threats to the environment, and little access to health, sanitation, or clean water

---

*     Again, Seers's (1997, p. 41) views are complementary: "To reduce unemployment is to remove one of the main causes of poverty and inequality."

(Nafziger 2006). According to this analysis, freedom of exchange, labor contract, social opportunities, and protective security are not just ends of development but also the means to it. In general, economic development constitutes the most powerful instrument for reducing poverty. Although this issue is highly important for every society, it is, of course, more relevant for the developing world.

The characteristics of development policy have changed drastically in the past decades. During the 1950s and 1960s, "big-push, planning and import-substitution" policies dominated the development agenda of reformers in poor nations (Rodrik 2007, p. 16). These ideas started losing prominence in the 1970s, when more market-oriented approaches started being adopted. By the late 1980s, views had converged around a set of policies that John Williamson dubbed "the Washington Consensus."[2] As Rodrik notes, these policies (see Table 3.2) remain at the heart of the conventional understanding of a desirable policy framework (possibly now rejected), even though they have been augmented and expanded in recent years.

The original list of Williamson was augmented by a series of second-generation reform policies of a more institutional nature than those targeted on good governance. As Rodrik notes, these second-generation reforms arose from the growing recognition that market-oriented policies might be inadequate without a more fundamental institutional transformation.

Nevertheless, contemporary growth experiences do not corroborate the widespread adoption of the Washington Consensus as the orthodox growth paradigm. The region that made the most determined attempt to remake itself through the adoption of the Washington Consensus was none other than Latin America, which reaped minimal growth benefits from these policy choices. In fact, countries such as

Mexico, Brazil, and Argentina did more liberalization, deregulation, and privatization in a few years than the East Asian countries did in four decades (Rodrik 2007). A similar case could be made for Africa, where decline persists even though Washington Consensus policies have been adopted in different states. South Korea's and Taiwan's growth policies were significantly different from the Washington paradigm. Instead of privatizations, both countries invested in public enterprises. It is interesting to note that South Korea also did not permit foreign direct investment (FDI) inflows (ibid.).

China and India, the two locomotives of Asian growth, also constitute interesting cases in that respect. It is true, of course, that both countries during their growth path departed from previous policy choices and decided to adopt policy frameworks based on markets and private enterprise. However, China never adopted a private-property-rights regime and "merely appended a market system to the scaffolding of a planned economy" (Rodrik 2007, p. 20). At the same time, India deregulated at a particularly slow pace, had significant trade restrictions until recently, and undertook minimal privatization (Rodrik 2007).

The picture that emerges from this analysis is quite clear. Although some key elements of success are the same in all growth strategies (sustainable government finances and sound money, a healthy institutional environment, some degree of market orientation), different regions require a different set of policies. Key to this claim is the central message of Hernando de Soto's book *The Mystery of Capital* (2000) that most of the world's potential capital assets outside the Western world and Japan are unusable under the legal property system and inaccessible as collateral for loans or to secure bonds. For Seers (1997), the greatest error of neoclassical economics

## TABLE 3.2: RULES OF GOOD BEHAVIOR FOR PROMOTING ECONOMIC GROWTH

| ORIGINAL WASHINGTON CONSENSUS | AUGMENTED WASHINGTON CONSENSUS |
| --- | --- |
| 1. Fiscal discipline | 11. Corporate governance |
| 2. Reorientation of public expenditures | 12. Anticorruption |
| 3. Tax reform | 13. Flexible labor markets |
| 4. Interest-rate liberalization | 14. Adherence to WTO disciplines |
| 5. Unified and competitive exchange rates | 15. Adherence to international financial codes and standards |
| 6. Trade liberalization | 16. "Prudent" capital account opening |
| 7. Openness to foreign direct investment | 17. Non-intermediate exchange-rate regimes |
| 8. Privatization | 18. Independent central banks and inflation targeting |
| 9. Deregulation | 19. Social safety nets |
| 10. Secure property rights | 20. Targeted poverty reduction |

Source: Rodrik (2007, p. 17).

was the universalization of the West's development experience.[3] The Washington Consensus, in particular, has been catastrophic for the developing world. It is not accidental that those countries that decided to embark on different growth strategies were the ones that showed the highest growth rates and the most significant poverty reduction.

As this work goes to press, we are in the aftermath of the 2008 financial crisis and the unraveling of the global financial system. In a provocative essay in the *Guardian* titled "The Death of the Washington Consensus? Paul Krugman's Nobel Prize for Economics Signals the Intellectual Tide Is Turning against Unrestricted Free Trade," Kevin Gallagher (2008) recites Krugman's and others' argument that "tariffs and subsidies to domestic industries can divert profits away from foreign firms and increase a nation's income," challenging the orthodoxy of market fundamentalism in the context of the benefits of trade to developing countries. Although this is certainly not the last word in the debate, the 2008 financial crisis compels a reexamination of neoliberal doctrine.[4]

### 3.4.2 Sustainability in Practice: The Cases of Kerala and Costa Rica

The Indian state of Kerala, on the southern Indian coast, has been one of the most widely cited cases of successfully practicing sustainable development (Franke and Chasin 1990; Parayil 1996). Kerala is one of the twenty-five constituent states of India, with a population of 32 million people, occupying about 1 percent of the total land area of the country. A series of statistics make Kerala one of the most interesting case studies in sustainable development and of alternative paths to social and economic development. Life expectancy for the average Keralite is seventy-four years, eleven years more than the average Indian life expectancy of sixty-three years and approaching the average U.S. life expectancy of seventy-seven years (Deparle 2007). Furthermore, Kerala has a literacy rate of 91 percent, compared with an Indian average of 65 percent (ibid..). This number is not too far from that in the United States, where 99 percent of the population is literate.

According to Parayil (1996, p. 952), "Though Kerala has a low throughput, the indicators of social progress have not suffered because of sustained efforts to limit population growth and social inequality, to conserve resources frugally and to use them on a shared basis." A particularly interesting facet of Kerala's development is that it is completely hidden

from the GDP per capita statistics. As Parayil (1996) notes, states with per capita incomes higher than that of Kerala fared much worse than Kerala in social indicators of development. In 1991–1992, Punjab, which had a GDP per capita twice that of Kerala, had a Physical Quality of Life (PQLI) rating 33 points lower than that of Kerala, underscoring the limitations of the GDP and the GDP per capita statistics with respect to economic and social development (ibid.).

None of these outcomes occurred by chance. On the contrary, they are the direct result of a set of policy choices by Kerala's liberal administrations, which have a policy priority of investing in a welfare state. Kerala spends 46 percent more on health and 36 percent more on education than the average Indian state (Deparle 2007). Hence if there is one point to be made about the Kerala model, it is that it constitutes a clear example of how the quality of life of the citizenry can be improved through government intervention in the economy, without a primary focus on encouraging economic growth.

The model, however, appears to have limitations. Kerala has been suffering from elevated rates of sustained unemployment, with many Keralites preferring to work in jobs in the Persian Gulf, where salaries are understandably higher. Unemployment is presently 20 percent, with one out of six workers working abroad, mostly in the Arab emirates. These workers augment the state's economic output by 25 percent. With all its achievements with respect to the welfare state, Kerala has a per capita income of $675, while India's nationwide per capita income is $730 (Deparle 2007). But more important, the disparity of income (and wealth) is much less than in other Indian states.

Although Kerala appears to be poor from an Indian comparison, the average income statistics do not take into account the socially important nonmonetizables, such as average life expectancy, education, and health care. Nor do the average figures reveal the disparity of wages or wealth in other Indian states. A more complete set of criteria of success should include not only environmental stewardship but also political, social, and economic justice, along with the improvement in the quality of life of the most vulnerable section of the population and the improvement of women's rights in society (Parayil 1996).

In light of Kerala's huge successes in education and health care, one must be careful in criticizing the model and must draw the appropriate lessons from Kerala for sustainable development. If there exists one conclusion that seems indisputable, it is that widespread poverty does not exist, giving one pause to think about whether concentrated wealth can exist without pockets of manifest poverty in a growth-oriented economy. Parayil (1996) observes that "the 'Kerala model' is not based on any one of the existing theories or models of development and modernization" and that it "should be studied earnestly for improvements and possible replication." The view that perhaps best encapsulates the success of Kerala is that of Samir Amin (1991, p. 29), who notes that "Kerala's achievements are the best way to prepare for the next stage, if only because they result in strong popular organization, and give reasons for hope, and something to guard." While otherwise positive about Kerala, Parayil (1996, p. 952) is realistic in noting that "the fact that industrial and agricultural growth has to be achieved to improve the material standards of living for all Keralans is undeniable; but the high indicators of social development and a highly literate populace are conducive to rapid industrialization of the state which is essential for creating more jobs and material outputs to meet local needs."

More recently, Costa Rica has been gaining publicity for the sustainable character of its policies. More than 25 percent of the country's landscape is a protected area because of a set of policies meant to preserve and protect its cornucopia (Friedman 2009). Friedman (2009, p. WK8) notes the following with respect to the Costa Rican model of development:

[Costa Rica] has created a holistic strategy to think about growth, one that demands that everything gets counted. So if a chemical factory sells tons of fertilizer but pollutes a river—or a farm sells bananas but destroys a carbon-absorbing and species-preserving forest—this is not honest growth. You have to pay for using nature. It is called "payment for environmental services"—nobody gets to treat climate, water, coral, fish and forests as free anymore.

The process began in the 1990s when Costa Rica, which sits at the intersection of two continents and two oceans, came to fully appreciate its incredible bounty of biodiversity—and that its economic future lay in protecting it. So it did something no country has ever done: It put energy, environment, mines and water all under one minister.

"In Costa Rica, the minister of environment sets the policy for energy, mines, water and natural resources," explained Carlos M. Rodríguez, who served in that post from 2002 to 2006. In most countries, he noted, "ministers of environment are marginalized." They are viewed as people who try to lock things away, not as people who create value.

Their job is to fight energy ministers who just want to drill for cheap oil.

But when Costa Rica put one minister in charge of energy and environment, "it created a very different way of thinking about how to solve problems," said Rodríguez, now a regional vice president for Conservation International. "The environment sector was able to influence the energy choices by saying: 'Look, if you want cheap energy, the cheapest energy in the long-run is renewable energy. So let's not think just about the next six months; let's think out 25 years.'"

As a result, Costa Rica hugely invested in hydro-electric power, wind and geo-thermal, and today it gets more than 95 percent of its energy from these renewables. In 1985, it was 50 percent hydro, 50 percent oil. More interesting, Costa Rica discovered its own oil five years ago but decided to ban drilling—so as not to pollute its politics or environment! What country bans oil drilling?

Rodríguez also helped to pioneer the idea that in a country like Costa Rica, dependent on tourism and agriculture, the services provided by ecosystems were important drivers of growth and had to be paid for. Right now, most countries fail to account for the "externalities" of various economic activities. So when a factory, farmer or power plant pollutes the air or the river, destroys a wetland, depletes a fish stock or silts a river—making the water no longer usable—that cost is never added to your electric bill or to the price of your shoes.

Costa Rica took the view that landowners who keep their forests intact and their rivers clean should be paid, because the forests maintained the watersheds and kept the rivers free of silt—and that benefited dam owners, fishermen, farmers and eco-tour companies downstream. The forests also absorbed carbon.

To pay for these environmental services, in 1997 Costa Rica imposed a tax on carbon emissions—3.5 percent of the market value of fossil fuels—which goes into a national forest fund to pay indigenous communities for protecting the forests around them. And the country imposed a water tax whereby major water users—hydro-electric dams, farmers and drinking water providers—had to pay villagers upstream to keep their rivers pristine. "We now have 7,000 beneficiaries of water and carbon taxes," said Rodríguez. "It has become a major source of income for poor people. It has also enabled Costa Rica to actually reverse deforestation. We now have twice the amount of forest as 20 years ago."

As we debate a new energy future, we need to remember that nature provides this incredible range of economic services—from carbon-fixation to water filtration to natural beauty for tourism. If government policies don't recognize those services and pay the people who sustain nature's ability to provide them, things go haywire. We end up impoverishing both nature and people. Worse, we start racking up a bill in the form of climate-changing greenhouse gases, petro-dictatorships and bio-diversity loss that gets charged on our kids' Visa cards to be paid by them later. Well, later is over. Later is when it will be too late.

Although the two models presented here have significant differences, both have important characteristics of sustainability in the policies that they have chosen to pursue. The Kerala model focuses on a series of parameters other than GDP growth, such as literacy rates, education, and health. At the same time, the Costa Rican model places any growth considerations inside the context of environmental protection and preservation. In general, could a growth model that would combine the positive aspects of Kerala and Costa Rica, without the increased unemployment of Kerala, and that would be applicable to states with less biodiversity than Costa Rica, be realistic? Whatever the case might be, both Kerala and Costa Rica deserve to be studied and monitored closely.

## 3.5 WHAT LIES AHEAD FOR ECONOMIC GROWTH AND DEVELOPMENT IN INDUSTRIALIZED AND DEVELOPING ECONOMIES?

### 3.5.1 The End of Sustainable Growth?

Perpetual economic growth does not constitute a law of nature, but rather an extrapolation of past trends. Writing before the economic crisis that began in 2008, Robert Ayres (2006, p. 1188) noted that although "the economy has a lot of inertia, whence the future is more likely to be a continuation of past trends than otherwise," a continuation of exponential growth until 2100 is not to be taken for granted.

This point of view is vastly different from that of the economic "optimists" who make the case that the pace of technological growth will continue in a series of industries, especially those related to the so-called converging technologies. Converging technologies represent a movement focused on the unification of science and technology and can be defined by interactions among nanotechnology, biotechnology, information technology, and pharmaceutical technologies. It is argued that, in general, converging technologies hold tremendous potential for improvements in health care, the production of clean water and energy, and increasing advances in information technology and telecommunications. The convergence of these profoundly transformative technologies and technology-enabling scientific fields can potentially

constitute one of the central research initiatives of the twenty-first century.

According to R. U. Ayres (2006), a series of drivers of past growth in industrialized countries now indicate signs of saturation or exhaustion:

1. Division of labor (job specialization)
2. International trade (globalization)
3. Monetization of formerly unpaid domestic and agricultural labor as a consequence of urbanization
4. Saving and investing
5. Borrowing from the future, which also tends to increase consumption in the present without added value
6. Extraction of high-quality and irreplaceable natural resources and destruction of the waste-assimilation capacity of nature
7. Increasing technological efficiency of converting resource (especially fossil fuel) inputs to useful work and power

Ayres deemed that the first four trends have largely completed their full effect in the industrial world, even though they have just started making their impact in the developing world. According to Ayres, the benefits of scale from division of labor and international trade have probably peaked already, while the monetization of formerly unpaid domestic labor is now fulfilled in the OECD countries (R. U. Ayres 2006). Perhaps the most interesting case is that of saving and investing. According to Ayres, the United States essentially stopped saving in the 1990s and actually started living on capital and on money borrowed from others, or even by borrowing from the future. In the same manner, exploiting nonrenewable natural resources resembles borrowing from nature. This form of converting long-term assets into current income is also meeting its limits (ibid.).

Hence this leaves technological efficiency of converting resource inputs to useful work and power, along with unrealized technological progress from newer technologies, as the sole determinants of economic growth. Technological efficiency emanating from the conversion of raw materials into useful work boomed during the end of the nineteenth century and the first half of the twentieth century, resulting to the substitution of labor by machines powered by fossil fuels. This led to significant increases in efficiency. In the past, increases in efficiency led to lower costs, which in their turn led to lower prices and higher demand. The increase in demand was a driver for increases in investment and, ultimately, increases in supply and even lower costs.

This "positive feedback cycle" is none other than the engine of economic growth and has been the primary driver of productivity gains in the last two centuries (R. U. Ayres 2006). Nevertheless, sources of primary energy are getting more expensive instead of cheaper, and the rate of increase in efficiency of energy conversion in industrial societies has decreased.

In the words of Robert Ayres (2006, p. 1195), "All of these [seven] phenomena taken together . . . suggest that US economic growth is almost certainly decelerating and could soon cease altogether," a pattern already visible in a series of other countries in the developed world. (See Section 3.2.7 for a discussion of R. Ayres and Warr's [2009] alternate model of economic growth that includes useful work or exergy [energy accounting for efficiency] as a factor of production.)

Jay Forrester, the father of system dynamics, which formed the basis of the work on limits to growth,* addressed the question whether crises in sustainability would lead to new opportunities for needed technological change. Forrester argues that seeing the real opportunities in "the no-growth, no-population rise, no increase-in-industrialization areas" (quoted in Hopkins 2009, p. 10) would require a major (perhaps fundamental) change in our culture, which assumes that "technology can solve all problems," that "growth is good and can go on forever," and that controlling population is "too treacherous a debating area" (ibid., p. 11). Although Forrester does not explicitly say so, his analysis underscores the need to engage ourselves not only in technological innovation but in organizational, institutional, and societal change as well.

Finally, echoing the perspective of ecological economics,† some critics go so far as to state that sustainable development cannot be achieved unless the current Northern model of economic development is abandoned (Sanders 2006). Again, note that this writing preceded the economic crisis that began in 2008. Others are less pessimistic and argue that (1)

technological advance has not reached any kind of natural limit, and (2) a future shift to ecologically sustainable technologies will loosen nascent creativity and that the basis of (post)industrial activity will change. Still others have challenged how growth and development are measured and argue that the metrics we use are not measuring the actual development that is occurring (see Section 3.3.1.2.).‡

### 3.5.2 The Impact of Economic Growth on Employment in the Developed World

Although there has been much discussion about the link between increases in productivity and economic growth, the effects of innovation and economic growth on employment have been discussed far less. In fact, perhaps the most central question about the consequences of economic growth from a societal perspective is the issue of increasing unemployment and underemployment.

Rifkin (2004) states that the old logic that technology gains and advances in productivity destroy old jobs but create new ones does not appear to be true anymore. Productivity has traditionally been considered an engine of job creation and economic prosperity. The economic intuition behind this is that productivity allows firms to produce goods at declining costs, which leads to cheaper goods. These cheaper goods increase demand in the market, which leads to even more production and productivity, which further simulates demand, and so on. According to Schumpeter's specification, innovation and specifically the process of creative destruction constitute the locomotive of capitalist economic growth through the introduction of new technologies, processes, and ideas that displace old ones. Thus it is argued that even if creative destruction displaces labor in the short run, the increase in demand for cheaper products, along with the new industries created through technological innovation, will ensure that additional people will be hired in the medium to long run. However, this is only theory. In reality, productivity increases, at least in the United States, have been associated with increasing numbers of unemployed workers and/or lower wages, especially in the manufacturing industries.

A case in point in the positive feedback cycle of economic growth is information and communication technologies (ICT). In fact, the acceleration of

---

\* See the discussion of limits to growth in the extended Primer on Sustainable Development at this book's website. Also see Kleiner (2009).

† The European Society of Ecological Economics held its First Conference on Socially Sustainable Economic Degrowth for Ecological Sustainability and Social Equity in April 2008 in Paris, in which "de-growth" was explicitly addressed in a series of thoughtful papers (see the *Journal of Cleaner Production* 2010, 18: 511–606) and presentations culminating in a declaration on growth (see www.degrowth.eu/v1/index.php?id=56, accessed May 17, 2010). Also see the discussion of degrowth in the context of the "new economics" in Section 3.6.

---

‡ See also Section 3.5.4, which addresses the idea of broadening capital ownership in order to increase society's consumption of goods and services.

productivity growth in the United States during the 1990s has been widely attributed to the rapid increases in investment in the ICT industry. Advances in ICT allegedly have led to decreasing costs, falling prices, and increasing demand.* However, according to Robert Ayres (2006), the applications of information technology outside its own sector seem to have led to the elimination of more jobs than the ones created, without corresponding impacts on consumer demand on products and service that would end up creating more jobs.

In their study of the employment effects of the new economy, van Ark, Inklaar, et al. (2003) found that this inverse relationship between productivity and employment growth was much stronger in manufacturing than in services. This result is intuitive and largely depends on whether the labor force of a specific industry has skills transferable to other industries. To a large degree, the process of creative destruction is actually inevitable. The point is to acknowledge the effects of increases in productivity on the average worker of the economy and to implement policies that will alleviate those effects by social safety nets, labor retraining, and a variety of other options discussed in Section 13.8.3 in Chapter 13.[†]

Commenting on the "digital divide," Liagouras (2005, p. 27) notes:

> If the vicious cycle of social exclusion is not stopped in the near future, social polarization risks becoming a structural feature of post-industrial economy and society. . . .
>
> Inequality depends above all on what organizational and institutional innovations are linked to digital technologies. On the one hand, the capacities required in order to cope with ICTs at a basic level are rather overestimated. As the objective of producers is to sell more and more, most of the new software hardware combinations have become so user-friendly that what is primarily required for basic applications is non-computer-specific skills like reading, writing, counting, communicating and, first of all, motivation. The above skills, on the other hand, are clearly underestimated by digital divide analysts. Indeed, the 21st century risks being characterized by the expansion of illiteracy in the middle of knowledge abundance. Of course this is a complex social phenomenon, which defeats monocausal approaches. From an economic point of view, the main responsible agent for social exclusion has been national and international neoliberal economic policies. That is why the digital divide discourse proposed by prestigious international organizations sounds like a nice excuse for the economic policies they have applied for two decades. If it is an inherent characteristic of digital technologies to divide societies, neoliberal policies are then beyond doubt, and the only solution for governments is to spend a bit more on education and training.

### 3.5.3 The Next Industrial Revolution?

In an article titled "The NEXT Industrial Revolution," environmentalists McDonough and Braungart (1998) argued that the greater use of natural capital and ecologically sound sources and uses of energy would spawn a new era of industrial activity to satisfy human needs, but they ignored the role of government in achieving this goal. A full decade later, reflecting a Schumpeterian perspective, two established scholars identified with ecological modernization who see a central role for government, Jänicke and Jacob (2009 pp. 2–3), described their vision for the future:

> we assume that after a long phase of technological innovation towards the substitution of fossil energy and exhaustible raw materials, which started with the first oil crisis (1973), a phase of radically accelerated transformation now lies ahead. We expect that the starting point will be in Europe. In addition to the technological competence and the necessary capital available here, there is also a relatively demanding regulative environment which is simultaneously open to innovation. Those are three conditions necessary for rapid change to occur, but unfortunately they are not sufficient to guarantee success. There is a risk that conventional structures could weaken the dynamic, thereby only allowing for limited or marginal improvements to the status quo. Finally, such a disruptive development has the risk of devaluing investments and related skills in currently dominating sectors and regions. In order to assure that the imminent Third Industrial Revolution will not be accompanied by distortions and social conflicts similar to those experienced during the First Industrial Revolution, there is a need for broad steering and decisive action. The relationship between economic markets and the state, which was for a long time characterized by the withdrawal of the state from the economic process, needs to be reassessed.

Unlike proponents of market fundamentalism, Jänicke and Jacob (2008) see an important steering mechanism for government (see Chapter 8 for an extensive discussion of government's role in industrial policy).

---

\* Much has been written about the "ICT productivity paradox" that little productivity growth has actually occurred from the adoption of the computer. See Griffith (1997).

† Also see the discussion of degrowth in the context of the "new economics" in Section 3.6.

### 3.5.4 Broadening Capital Ownership and Its Effects on Consumption-Led Growth, Sustainable Livelihoods, and the Environment*

Building on the ideas of Louis Kelso, Robert Ashford has argued that poor and middle-class people can more fully participate in the so-called labor productivity gains stemming from increasingly capital-intensive production of goods and services if the broadening of capital ownership is included among the strategies intended to maintain and enhance the more widespread distribution of earning capacity.†

Although many people are familiar with capital ownership-broadening programs such as employee stock ownership plans (ESOPs), 401(k) plans, and other "ownership-society" approaches, the economic analysis that gave rise to ESOPs is much deeper and more ambitious. Observing that almost all capital is acquired with the earnings of capital and relatively little capital is acquired with the earnings of labor, Ashford maintains that the most efficient way to preserve individual earning capacity is to broaden capital ownership by opening to poor and middle-class people the same financial institutions that presently enable wealthy people to acquire capital with the earnings of capital. These are the institutions of corporate finance, capital credit, capital credit insurance, and monetary policy.

According to Ashford, because present demand for investment in capital and labor depends on anticipated demand for consumer goods and services in a future period, and because poor and middle-class people spend a greater portion of their earnings on consumption, a voluntary pattern of steadily broadening capital acquisition promises more consumer demand for goods and services in future years and therefore more demand for the employment of labor and capital in earlier years. In other words, broadening ownership promises more economic growth. The broader distribution of capital acquisition, ownership, and income strengthens the promise of capital to pay for itself out of its future earnings and makes more investment profitable and less risky. With funds borrowed through investment trusts (not qualitatively different from those that borrow and invest for the wealthy), after the capital-acquisition debt obligations of the trusts have been satisfied, the distributed earnings of capital acquired by members of the poor and middle class will create more consumer demand for goods and services than if that capital had been acquired by the wealthy. In contrast, if capital is acquired by the wealthy, most of the capital earnings will, of course, seek investment opportunities, but in the context of creating weaker consumer demand.

Thus by increasing their capital-earning capacity, this new class of owner-buyers may be expected to consume much more than equivalent well-capitalized buyers whose needs to purchase basic and goods and services have already been largely satisfied. In other words, the increased purchasing power leading to consumer spending that is likely to result from more broadly distributed capital-earning capacity of the economy would be expected to be positively correlated with economic activity and growth in both goods and services. In effect, by way of voluntary capital acquisition transactions, the binary approach links productivity gains from advancing technology with increasing consumer demand resulting from more broadly distributed capital earning capacity.

By broadening the strategies intended to preserve and enhance earning capacity to include not only labor employment but also broadening capital ownership, society can more comprehensively address the practical difficulties that are presented by the long-term trend of replacing and supplementing labor-intensive production increasingly with capital-intensive production. In other words, less work is accomplished by labor and more by capital, but individual earning capacity is preserved and enhanced because capital ownership is broadened or "democratized."

Finally, Ashford argues that the growth stimulated by the broadening of capital acquisition is likely to be relatively greener growth—a view that is supported by the widely held belief that environmental degradation is linked to poverty. Nevertheless, the increased threats to the environment that might result from the increased growth from broadening ownership might require governmental policies that link the increased production and consumption to environmentally sustainable goods and services.

## 3.6 THE NEW ECONOMICS

Since the economic meltdown in 2008, economists (and others) have been trying to develop new insights into the causes of the crisis and a new theory of economics for the industrial state upon which to build future policy interventions. Of course, the two are connected, but understanding the causes is easier than fashioning effective future policy.

---

* These ideas are developed more fully by Robert Ashford in Section 12.11 of Chapter 12, "Financing Sustainable Development." See also R. Ashford (2009).

† Earning capacity is often included in the term "sustainable livelihoods" to connote more than wage income.

Beyond the optimism associated with the enhancement of ICT innovation in traditional economic systems expressed by the OECD and the ICT industry groups, there are a number of contrasting views of the "end of exponential growth" (Ayres 2006) and the nature of future growth* offered by various scholars and commentators that are concerned with sustainable growth (although some academics—such as Georgescu-Roegen—believe that the term "sustainable growth" is an oxymoron[5]). These alternative schemes might be characterized as promoting a "new economy" based on the "new economics."

A variety of names are offered for the new economics: "greener growth," "selective growth" (popular in the Netherlands in the 1970s), "conditioned growth," "sustainable de-growth" (Harris 2010; Jackson 2009; Kallis, Martinez-Alier, et al. 2009; Martinez-Alier, Pascual, et al. 2010; Schor 2010; Victor 2008), "post growth" (Goodwin 2010; Speth 2008, 2010a, 2010b, 2010c), "agrowth" (van den Bergh 2011), and "policy integration" (Spangenberg 2007). They focus on promoting environmentally and socially sustainable development through differing combinations of technological progress in dematerialization and energy-efficiency, decreased overall consumption of products and services that are environmentally destructive, reduction of the workweek, and redistribution of wealth or income through a basic income guarantee and/or the reduction of individual working time accompanied by no decrease in purchasing power, thereby retaining existing wages for current employees while adding others to the employment rolls.

Neva Goodwin (2010), co-director of the Global Development and Environment Institute at Tufts University[6] analyzes the core problems of a nation being guided by standard economic theory as having a preoccupation with wealth creation, as opposed to well-being, a bias toward monetary evaluation of non-monetary goods and amenities, discounting, Pareto optimality rather than distributional equity, a preference for markets rather than government intervention, and the dominance of economists in the political process (issues that have been fully addressed in this work). While acknowledging the need for increased production and consumption in the short-run, she rejects Keynesian spending advocated by Paul Krugman in a non-growth economy (Krugman 2009). Curiously, she asserts that "in a non-

growing global economy, there is only one way for the poor to have more: that is for the rich to have less" (Goodwin 2010). This contrasts with Robert Ashford's rejection of the notion of a zero sum game with his advocacy for broadening growth-enhancing ownership via binary economics, by which the poor also have the effective right to acquire capital with the future earnings of capital.[†]

In addition, Goodwin (2009) states "if labor productivity continues to increase . . . in a post-growth world one result could be even greater unemployment." Of course, this may be true if the source of increased labor productivity continues to be due to increased *capital* productiveness leading to less earning capacity on the part of labor, with resulting increases in unemployment in terms of the number of jobs and/or lower wage rates. In contrast, if labor productivity increases as a result of increased *labor* productiveness, workers need not earn less, even if they work less hours. Increasing labor productiveness would require increasing the value of labor in production and services by deliberate design. Goodwin has argued for a re-conceptualization of economic theory which she calls "contextual economics" to describe a possible future pathway for industrial economies involving a different and more appropriate balance between the private sector, government, non-profits, communities, and people. Just how this pathway is to be achieved remains unspecified.

Harris (2010), also at Tufts University, argues specifically for an eco-Keynesian approach focusing on fostering human-capital-intensive services, investment in energy-conserving capital, and investment in natural and human capital leading to increases in wellbeing without growth in throughput, a major concern of Herman Daly (1996) who long ago advocated a steady-state economy as the basis for ecological economics. Harris advocates policies geared toward achieving dynamic, rather than static efficiency through innovation, and also argues for more labor-intensive production, recurrent themes emphasized throughout the present work. Focusing on environmentally-friendly technology and social investment [which can bring about disruptive innovation] results in growth of a different kind of economic activity, without growth in resource throughput and harmful ecological consequences.

The Canadian Peter Victor (2008, 2010b), a self-described ecological economist, in his book *Managing Without Growth: Slower By Design, Not Disaster*

---

* Victor (2010a) distinguishes green growth, brown growth, black growth, and green de-growth according to whether GNP is increasing or decreasing, alongside changes in greenhouse gas intensity and overall emissions.

† See the discussion of binary economics in Section 3.5.4 and Section 12.11 in Chapter 12.

presents detailed models purporting to show how a good environment, shorter work weeks, greater spending, and wealth accumulation on the part of ordinary citizens are possible in a economy that is not growing by judicious choices ranging from population control to tax policies. In a similar vein, Tim Jackson (2009) in *Prosperity without Growth: Economics for a Finite Planet*, argues for doing more with less, but also asserts that striving for labor productivity at the expense of workers is the most important defect of the present economic system in need of attention. While concentrating on dematerialization and eco-efficiency, Jackson focuses almost entirely on energy, and not on other environmental problems, such as toxic pollution and eco-system deterioration. Like Schor (2010), he joins the cadre of others calling for "spreading out the work"—which may result in more employment of people working less hours for the time being—but without really addressing an essential flaw in the current industrial state, that of a continuing decline in labor hours needed in production and services (see the discussion of structural unemployment below). Without increasing labor content and its value in production and services, labor cannot demand an overall increase in its share of profit and thereby increase its purchasing power. More people working with smaller wages does not help those with diminishing purchasing power, although it spreads out the diminished purchasing power—and the resulting pain.

Greener growth or "sustainable de-growth"—as some call it—is one thing, but deliberate redistribution of the spoils of the industrial state is another. Redistribution options necessitate tax-based transfers of wealth and income from more well-endowed parts of a developed nation's economy (both well-off persons and business entities) to working families (Spangenberg 2007). Neither (1) the legal (or market-based) tools that mandate the internalization of environmental damage costs (such as taxing resource consumption, placing caps on $CO_2$ emissions, or establishing a carbon tax) nor (2) wealth or income transfers to create more purchasing power in working families through "spreading the work out," but *with fully compensated reduced working time that maintains wage parity* is likely to be greeted enthusiastically by profit- and traditional growth-oriented enterprises, at least initially.* However, reflecting on

the observation that labor costs make up about 20 percent of business costs, while material and energy costs represent over half and 2 percent of business costs, respectively, Spangenberg (2007, p.32) argues that by "stimulating resource productivity gains over labor productivity increases" a reorientation of the economy is possible.

Of course, dematerialization and reduction of energy in production and the provision of services not only have the potential to decrease the environmental footprint, they also offer some possibility of decreasing the capital and energy content relative to labor inputs, *providing* labor is not shed at the same time. It is well-established that whenever modernization of production and services occurs, management seeks every opportunity to shed and deskill labor as well, except in a minority of cutting edge, emerging high-tech enterprises. The much heralded opportunities for significant net job creation through "green jobs" may be more grounded in wishful thinking than in reality.† Sustainable employment requires both increasing the overall claim, through wages, of workers on the profits of the enterprises in a nation and achieving a fairer distribution of job and earning opportunities. Increasing the wages of some (higher skilled or supply-constrained workers) can lead to increasing wage disparities and result in decreases in the total wages paid. Unless wages are subsidized, increasing the total wages paid requires increasing the labor content and value of all those that desire to be employed, hopefully in meaningful and rewarding work, but this approach requires rethinking the role of labor in the industrial state.

Many commentators (e.g., Jackson 2009; Schor 2010; Speth 2010a, 2010b, 2010c) advocate spreading out the work without addressing the question of the level of overall wages paid. Increasing the number of workers employed can effectively redistribute wages among the working and potentially working population, but it does nothing or little to redistribute the share of profits of industrial production or the provision of services from capital or business owners to workers. Jackson's (2009) and Schor's (2010) focus on labor productivity sets their contributions apart from many others who ignore not only the importance of work for a sustainable society, but also the impacts of policy changes on employment. However,

---

* The European Commission (2010, p. 1) recognizes this explicitly in its discussion of sustainable de-growth. An EC news alert—which carefully states that the opinions expressed therein "do not necessarily represent those of the Commission"—states

that "sustainable de-growth has at its core a downscaling of economy and believes that economic growth, even if disguised as sustainable development, will lead to social and ecological collapse" and "has an obvious disadvantage in that it confronts powers in society."

† See Section 5.3.2 in Chapter 5 on green employment.

they assume that most improvements in labor productivity will follow the historical patterns that come from increases in capital, rather than from labor *productiveness*, resulting in fewer hours worked. As emphasized in this work, productivity and productiveness are not the same. Labor productivity can be increased by either capital productiveness, or by labor productiveness, or by some combination of both. Other ways to increase labor productivity through increases in *labor* productiveness of course exist: better training, improved skills, and the redesign of jobs and work. Whether or not the total hours worked fall or not, *ceterus parabus*, labor would be more highly valued and paid as a result.

Technological advance is only one means to improve labor productivity; increasing the contribution of labor as a factor of production (and services) is another. Not only are we addicted to GDP and growth as a source of improved welfare—what some describe as a GDP fetish (Stiglitz 2009)—we are also addicted to the idea that only improvements in technology can advance our development. General Electric, Siemans, and Toyota sell products, not the services of people. Corporations own capital; people own their own labor, an unfortunately diminishing factor in how economies grow and are measured. Jackson describes the contributions of labor to labor productivity as "dismal" in economics parlance. But labor *productiveness* in the provision of non-material, non-energy-intensive services can be high, depending on the nature of the activity. Jackson appropriately suggests that more community-based activities, rather than the production of "stuff" might employ increasingly numbers of people. Not only do we need to abandon or at least refine our measures of well-being in terms of GNP, we also need to assign value to labor productiveness. The only reason that the business enterprise does not care about labor productiveness in this context is they cannot profit from its deployment or sale, as much as they can from improving the productiveness of capital which they own. Business creates demand through advertising. Who will create the demand for community-based services such as education? This requires a cultural transformation.

The creation of temporary increases in purchasing power (and consequential consumer demand) through traditional Keynesian spending to "get the economy moving" (Krugman 2009) is not a permanent fix. Further Keynes's "paradox of thrift" encouraging people to save, rather than to spend newly acquired increases in income, may blunt its effect (see Jackson 2009, p. 106).

Robert Ashford's (2009) proposal to achieve more broadly distributed capital earning capacity (and thereby create more consumer purchasing power by effectively extending to all individuals the right to acquire capital with the future earnings of capital through voluntary binary economics financing) avoids the pitfalls of both continued wealth or income redistribution, and the temporary solutions offered by traditional Keynesian spending. However, the basic binary proposition (that the broader distribution of capital acquisition with the earnings of capital will both broaden the distribution of earning capacity *and* promote growth) is yet to be embraced conceptually by mainstream economists. In light of environmental concerns, Robert Ashford acknowledges that the facilitation of ownership-broadening binary-financing may need to be complemented with other governmental policies to ensure that the resulting increased purchasing power is not spent in an environmentally destructive way. Increasing purchasing power and changing the nature of what is demanded by aggregate increases in disposable income needs to be factored into a coherent policy.

The 2009 Nobel Prize in economics was given to three economists who demonstrated that some unemployment is inevitable, even in economies that are in equilibrium because of "search friction"—also known as "structural unemployment" or "equilibrium unemployment"—because of the mismatch between the skills of the current workforce and the needs of employers (Cho 2010, p. 330). Unemployment exists alongside vacancies in jobs. While 2–3 percent unemployment was at one time considered structural, equilibrium unemployment seems to have now approached a number two or three-fold that historical measure.

An analysis by van Zandweghe (2010) of the 1981–1982, 1990–1991, and 2007–2008 recessions attempts to explain "the jobless recovery" in terms of the structural changes (and a dampening of cyclicality) in the labor supply during booms and busts, rather than "supply shocks" related to the business cycle. Structural changes are brought about by (1) a reduction in "labor hoarding" (as a result of decreases in labor adjustment costs and labor protection) whereby labor is used less intensely, but retained, by employers during busts and (2) technological changes brought about by ICT that have allowed work previously done by moderately-educated workers to be done by computers ("skill-biased technical change"). While van Zandweghe (2010, p. 19) concedes that "it is difficult to find direct evidence of the role of structural change" supply shocks do not explain the nature of recovery in the last two recessions.

Changes in the recovery time after recessions may also reflect mismatches between job skills demanded and workers available to fill them. Goodman (2010) reports that before 1990, it took an average of twenty-one months for the economy to regain the jobs shed during a recession. After the recessions in 1990 and 2001, thirty-one and forty-six months respectively passed before employment returned. The length of the recovery after the 2008 economic crisis has yet to be revealed.

Is the continued increase in structural unemployment necessary and inevitable or does it suggest that we must find a way to change the nature of work and the consequential skills required and also increase the value to work relative to capital in productive and service activities? Engineering and management schools have contributed mechanisms and strategies for decreasing the labor content of production. Can they now be redirected to increasing labor content? More than technical changes may be needed. Societal evolution as to both what kinds of goods and services are demanded in the future could be shifted toward more labor intensive activities, such as the provision of extra-mural education in languages, music, art, money management, etc., that is, in activities in which the environmental and energy footprint is necessarily negligible and labor, rather than capital and energy, constitutes the vast content of production and services.

Jackson (2009, p. 109), while acknowledging that "meaningful employment is itself a key constituent in prosperity," just hints at this by suggesting disposable income could be spent on "yoga lessons" (ibid., p. 129), but he otherwise does not explore how the demand for labor-focused activities can arise in a new economy. Instead, he focuses on the need to create green jobs in re-designed dematerialized and less energy-intensive production and services which only change the kinds of products and product-related services that the society provides, but does not address the more difficult challenge of shifting demand to labor-intensive services.

The 2008 financial crisis has brought forth a stark reality that consumption-led growth may never be able to return to what it once was. With the end to borrowing from the future, there is simply not enough purchasing power (i.e., demand)—nor can there be enough—to (re)fuel the decades-old former high rate of economic growth. Thus, out of necessity, perhaps more than some moral or practical awakening, rethinking consumption—especially material and energy consumption—has taken on new importance. Not really "doing more with less" but rather "doing with less" and changing the very nature, not just the amount, of consumption is now on the table.[7] As opposed to a "revolution from below" to change the nature of governance that some hope for or predict (Speth 2008), an evolution of necessity may more accurately characterize the cultural transformation that may come upon us.

Achieving dematerialization and eco-efficiency of traditionally-demanded products, production, and services can result in the deployment of increased disposable income elsewhere that "boomerangs" into more total consumption. Individuals spending more money on people serving people, unmediated by heavy environmental and energy footprints, could not only change the equation by bypassing economic activities that convert materials and energy, but also bypasses interests promoted by the entrenched corporations and established businesses that lock-in the present economic system. But will they allow this to happen? Remember the often-omitted question raised in this work: who is standing in the way of sustainable transformations?

While some might balk at the concept of "degrowth"—partly intended to shock—the movement does have some cache. The second International Conference on Economic Degrowth for Ecological Sustainability and Social Equity held in Barcelona on March 26–29, 2010, issued the Barcelona Degrowth Declaration in which it was stated:[8]

> We assert that these proposals are not utopian: new redistributive taxes will address income inequality and finance social investments and discourage consumption and environmental damage, while reduced working hours with a reinforced social security system will manage unemployment. As the economy of wealthy parts of the world quietly contracts and our damage to the environment through new infrastructures and extraction activities is constrained, well-being will increase through public investments in low-cost social and relational goods.

At that conference, van den Bergh (2011, p. 881) categorized and critiqued five types of degrowth:

1. GDP degrowth;
2. Consumption degrowth;
3. Work-time degrowth;
4. Radical degrowth; and
5. Physical degrowth.

Van der Bergh (2011, p. 286) opines that degrowth is too imprecise and ambiguous a term, that focusing on

GDP per capita ("the largest information failure in the world" [van den Bergh 2009, p. 127]) is too imperfect an indicator of social welfare to be the target of policy, and that the likely resistance to degrowth from various quarters will make degrowth—especially 1, 2, 4 and 5—hard to sell. He (ibid., p. 889) instead offers a vision of "agrowth" focusing on getting democratic and political support for (1) stringent and serious environmental regulation which may or may not reduce GDP growth, (2) encouraging people to work less hours, earn less income, and consume less, (3) regulate advertising, especially of status goods, (4) work on changing environmentally-relevant consumption, (5) give less importance to GDP changes, and (6) develop and redirect alternative technological options and scenarios.* In his view, focusing on consumption degrowth may result in rebound effects that can exacerbate environmental problems for a variety of reasons.† Reducing working time and radical degrowth, while requiring cultural and social change, *per se*, may not result in significant environmental improvements. Van den Bergh would focus heavily on using regulatory and economic instruments directly to reduce environmental hazards and redirect technology development. His prescriptions do not address directly improving *economic* welfare or disparities, although he would probably argue that an improved environment would positively impact economic welfare. Finally, he does not directly advocate for redistribution of income or wealth, or for a replacement of the current market economy system (the latter being in contrast with the views of Sanders 2006).

Kallis (2011, p. 874), siding with Herman Daly's steady-state economics which assumes a robust relationship between throughput and GDP and the need to reduce GDP, offers a rejoinder to van den Bergh's critique by asserting that "big social change does not take place by appealing to those in power, but by bottom-up movements that challenge established paradigms" and that "scientists have a role to play as partners in these movements . . ." Kallis calls for "a bit more belief on our collective capacity to plan a change." He argues that sustainable or selective degrowth deserves to be considered, not dismissed as a vague concept. Kallis (2011, p. 875) calls for a:

> recognition that there is a possible incompatibility between foundational institutions of market economies and the goal of degrowth to a steady-state . . . It is

in this sense that some people writing on degrowth recognize the need for systemic political, institutional and cultural change (what van den Bergh frames and dismisses as "radical degrowth") in order to create a different system where expansion will no longer be a necessity and where economic rationality and goals of efficiency and maximization will not dominate all other social rationalities and goals . . .

> . . . the crucial question here is whether the capitalist, market economies in which the majority of us live today can conceivably degrow and stabilise into a steady-state. . . . More than likely this will only be possible with such a radical change in the basic institutions of property, work, credit and allocation, that the system will no longer be identifiable as capitalism. . . . There is indeed a problematic vagueness in so far as this post-capitalist alternative is not specified. However this is not a reason for discarding the diagnosis: i.e. that growth is unsustainable and that the institutions of what came to be known as "capitalism" that mandate it, have to change. In fact, it might be better to remain agnostic and pluralistic at this stage about what such an alternative could look like and let it emerge organically from the ground, rather than dictate it from any intellectual or political height.

In addition to taxing international capital movement and environmental damage, restricting advertising, and instituting both emission and salary caps, Kallis (2010) call for a basic income guarantee, redistributive taxation, and more employment of human capital where human contact adds value (e.g., health care and education). Addressing directly van den Bergh's description of a GDP fetish, Kallis asserts that GNP is a manifestation, rather than the cause, of a growth fetishism. Finally, Kallis (2011, p. 878) argues that growth is not a "policy" but rather a political alternative seeking a popular mandate for radical changes. The two articles by Kallis and van der Bergh discussed above sharpen the emerging ideological debate about how, or if, market-based economies can become sustainable.

Finally, Bergmann (2010) has offered a short but insightful essay on rethinking capitalist economies by melding the ideas of no growth with the new economics. Citing the contributions of Jackson (2009), Schor (2010), and Victor (2008), but without any reference to the degrowth literature, Bergmann (2010, pp. 51–52) acknowledges that there might be a need for a limitation of growth, especially in the already wealthy countries, but adds "we would not want to label as prosperous an economy without growth unless all residents had their basic needs met in a fairly generous way." She adds, "designing a no-growth economy that would be labeled "prosperous" would involve making societal arrangements that guaranteed

---

\*     Activities 2 and 4 would be accomplished through communication and information provision to motivate changes in preferences, attitudes, and voluntary actions.

†     See Owen 2010 for a recent discussion of Jevons paradox.

a quite high standard of living as a minimal level" (ibid., p. 52). Four policies would be needed: (1) a reduction in work hours per week with no decrease in pay per week as productivity advances; (2) some regulation of new products and services; (3) redistribution of certain vital services (paralleling what we in this book have characterized as essential goods and services); and (4) control of immigration. Bergmann acknowledges the need to encourage environmentally sustainable products and services but falls short of specifying just how, except to propose a "cap-and-trade" system for labor use as a modulating mechanism on commercial activity. Unlike many others advocating the "new economics" and "degrowth" while dodging the need for a redistribution of wealth, she explicitly acknowledges the need for maintaining parity in wage income, the need to limit the kinds of products and services an economy provides, and the need for minimum welfare. Her ideas of "prosperity without growth" are premised on the requirement that the state finds a way for the economy to meet people's basic needs; this is close to the concept of "competitiveness" introduced in this book that is not synonymous with "competition," but rather is defined as providing an adequate supply of, and access to, essential goods and services.

## 3.7 NOTES

1. G. Modelski, The Evolutionary World of Politics, *Kondratieff Waves*, http://faculty.washington.edu/modelski/IPEKWAVE .html (accessed May 17, 2010).

2. See A Guide to John Williamson's Writing, www.piie .com/staff/jwguide.cfm (accessed January 17, 2011).

3. See also Mehmet's (1995) critique of the "Eurocentricity of economic development theories."

4. See especially Stiglitz (2010).

5. See Martinez-Alier, Pascual, et al.'s (2010) discussion of Georgescu-Roegen.

6. See The Global Development And Environment Institute, Tufts University, www.ase.tufts.edu/gdae/publications/ theorybooks.htm (accessed December 17, 2010).

7. See the Sustainable Consumption Research and Action initiative begun by the Boston-based Tellus Institute (Cohen et al. 2010). See www.scorai.org (accessed December 17, 2010).

8. See the Degrowth Declaration Barcelona 2010, available at: www.degrowth.eu/v1/fileadmin/content/documents/ Degrowth_Declaration_Barcelona_2010.pdf (accessed December 17, 2010).

## 3.8 ADDITIONAL READINGS

Ayres, Robert (2006). "Turning Point: The End of Exponential Growth?" *Technological Forecasting and Social Change* 73: 1188–1203.

Ayres, R., and B. Warr (2009). *The Economic Growth Engine: How Energy and Work Drive Material Prosperity*. Williston, VT, Edward Elgar.

Drucker, P. (1994). "The Age of Social Transformation." *Atlantic Monthly* **274**(5): 53–80.

Drucker, P. (1999). "Beyond the Information Revolution." *Atlantic Monthly* **284**(4): 47–57.

Kallis, G., J. (2011). "In Defence of Degrowth." *Ecological Economics* 70(5): 873–880.

Martinez-Alier, J., U. Pascual, et al. (2010). "Sustainable De-growth: Mapping the Context, Criticisms, and Future Prospects of an Emergent Paradigm." *Ecological Economics* **69**(9): 1741–1747.

Nafziger, E. W. (2006). From Seers to Sen: The Meaning of Economic Development, Research Paper RP2006/20. World Institute for Development Economic Research (UNU-WIDER). Available at www.wider.unu.edu/pub lications/working-papers/research-papers/2006/en_GB/ rp2006-20/ (accessed January 17, 2011).

Speth, J. G. (2008). *The Bridge at the Edge of the World: Capitalism, the Environment, and Crossing from Crisis to Sustainability*. New Haven, CT, Yale University Press.

Speth, J. G. (2010). A New Environmentalism and the New Economy. The 10th Annual John H. Chafee Memorial Lecture, National Council for Science and the Environment, Washington, DC, January 21.

Speth, J. G. (2010). "Towards a New Economy and a New Politics." *Solutions* **1**(5): 33–41.

Stiglitz, J. (2010). *Freefall: America, Free Markets, and the Sinking of the World Economy*. New York, W. W. Norton.

van Ark, Bart, R. Inklaar, et al. (2003). "The Employment Effects of the 'New Economy': A Comparison of the European Union and the United States." *National Institute Economic Review* 184(2003): 86–98. Available at http://ner.sagepub.com/content/184/1/86.full.pdf+html (accessed January 17, 2011).

van den Bergh, J. C. J. M. (2011). "Environment vs. Growth—A criticism of 'Degrowth' and a Plea for 'Agrowth'." *Ecological Economics* **70**(5): 881–890.

## 3.9 REFERENCES

Atkinson, R. D. and S. M. Andes (2009). The Atlantic Century: Benchmarking EU & US Innovation and Competitiveness. Washington, DC, The Information Technology and Innovation Foundation.

Aghion, P., and P. Howitt (2005). Appropriate Growth Policy: A Unifying Framework. Mimeo, Harvard University.

Amin, S. (1991). "Four Comments on Kerala." *Monthly Review* **42**(8): 28–32.

Ashford, N. A., and C. C. Caldart (2008). "Alternative Forms of Government Intervention to Promote Pollution and Waste Reduction." *Environmental Law, Policy and Economics: Reclaiming the Environmental Agenda*. Cambridge, MA, MIT Press.

Ashford, N. A., W. Hafkamp, et al. (2002). *Pathways to Sustainable Industrial Transformations: Cooptimising Competitiveness, Employment, and Environment*. Cambridge, MA, Ashford Associates.

Ashford, R. (2009). "Broadening the Right to Acquire Capital with the Earnings of Capital: The Missing Link to Sustainable Economic Recovery and Growth." *Forum for Social Economics* **39**: 89–100. Available at www.springerlink.com/.

Ayres, R., and B. Warr (2009). *The Economic Growth Engine: How Energy and Work Drive Material Prosperity.* Williston, VT, Edward Elgar.

Ayres, R. U. (2006). "Turning Point: The End of Exponential Growth?" *Technological Forecasting and Social Change* **73**: 1188–1203.

Bell, D. (1999). *The Coming of Post-industrial Society: A Venture in Social Forecasting.* New York, Basic Books.

Berger, S. (2005). *How We Compete: What Companies around the World Are Doing to Make It in Today's Global Economy.* Cambridge, MA, MIT Press.

Bergmann, B. (2010). "Is Prosperity Possible Without Growth" *Challenge* **53**(5): 49–56.

Black, S. E., and L. M. Lynch (2004). "What's Driving the New Economy? The Benefits of Workplace Innovation." *Economic Journal* **114**: 97–116.

Black, S. E., and L. M. Lynch (2005). Measuring Organizational Capital in the New Economy. *Measuring Capital in the New Economy.* C. Corrado, J. Haltiwanger, and D. Sichel. Chicago, University of Chicago Press.

Castells, M. (1999). *The Rise of the Network Society.* Oxford, Blackwell Publishers.

Cho, A. (2010). "Three Laureates Explained Why Unemployment Is Inevitable." *Science* **330**(6002): 303.

Christensen, C. M. (1997). *The Innovator's Dilemma: When New Technologies Cause Great Firms to Fail.* Cambridge, MA, Harvard Business School Press.

Clark, G. (2007). *A Farewell to Alms: A Brief Economic History of the World.* Princeton, NJ, Princeton University Press.

Cohen, M. J., H. S. Brown, et al. (2010). "Individual Consumption and Systemic Societal Transformation: Introduction to the Special Issue." *Sustainability: Science, Practice, & Policy* **6**(2): 6–12.

Daly, H. E. (1994). "Fostering Environmentally Sustainable Development: Four Parting Suggestions for the World Bank." *Ecological Economics* **10**: 183–187.

Deparle, J. (2007). "In India, Even Cared-for Populace Leaves for Work." *International Herald Tribune*, September 6.

De Soto, H. (2000), *The Mystery of Capital: Why Capitalism Triumphs in the West and Fails Everywhere Else.* New York, Basic Books.

Deutch, J., E. Moniz, et al. (2003). *The Future of Nuclear Power: An Interdisciplinary MIT Study.* Cambridge, MA, MIT Press.

Diamond, A. (2006). "Schumpeter's Creative Destruction: A Review of the Evidence." *Journal of Private Enterprise* **22**(1): 120–146.

Dorf, R. C. (2001). *Technology, Humans, and Society: Toward a Sustainable World.* New York, Academic Press.

Driesen, D. M. (2004). "The Economic Dynamics of Environmental Law: Cost-Benefit Analysis, Emissions Trading, and Priority-Setting." *Boston College Environmental Affairs Law Review* **31**(3): 501–528.

Drucker, P. F. (1994). "The Age of Social Transformation." *Atlantic Monthly* **274**(5): 53–80.

Drucker, P. F. (1999). "Beyond the Information Revolution." *Atlantic Monthly* **284**(4): 47–57.

Ekins, P and J. Medhurst (2006). "The European Structural Funds and Sustainable Development: A Methodology and Indicator Framework for Evaluation." *Evaluation* **12**: 474–495.

European Commission (EC) (2010). "Sustainable-De-Growth: An Alternative to Sustainable Development?" *Science for Environment Policy, DG Environment News Alert*, September 16.

Flink, J. F. (1988) *The Automobile Age.* Cambridge, MA, MIT Press.

Franke, R. W., and B. H. Chasin (1990). "The Kerala Experiment: Development without Growth." *Technology Review* **95**(3): 42–51.

Freeman, C. (1990). Schumpeter's Business Cycles Revisited. *Evolving Technology and Market Structure: Studies in Schumpeterian Economics.* A. Heertje and M. Perlman. Ann Arbor, University of Michigan Press: 17–38.

Friedman, T. (2009). "(No) Drill, Baby, Drill." *New York Times*, April 12, p. WK8.

Gallagher, K. P. (2008). "The Death of the Washington Consensus? Paul Krugman's Nobel Prize for Economics Signals the Intellectual Tide Is Turning against Unrestricted Free Trade." *Guardian*, October 14.

Gill, S., and D. Law (1988). *The Global Political Economy: Perspectives, Problems, and Policies.* Baltimore, Johns Hopkins University Press.

Goodman, P. S. (2010). "The New Poor: Millions of Unemployed Face Years Without Jobs." *New York Times*, February 21.

Goodwin, N. (2010). "A New Economics for the 21st Century." Forthcoming in World Futures Review. Available at http://neweconomicsinstitute.org/content/new-economics-21st-century (accessed February 11, 2011).

Griffith, V. (1997). "IT 'Has Failed to Fulfill Its Promise.'" *Financial Times*, August 13.

Grübler, A., and H. Nowotny (1990). "Towards the Fifth Kondratiev Upswing: Elements of an Emerging New Growth Phase and Possible Development Trajectories." *International Journal of Technology and Management* **5**(4): 431–471.

Hagemann, H. (2008). "Consequences of the New Information and Communication Technologies for Growth, Productivity and Employment." *Competetivenss Review: An International Business Journal* **18**(1/2): 57–69.

Harris, J. M. (2010). The Macroeconomics of Development without Throughput Growth. Working Paper 10-05, Medford, MA, Global Development and Environment Institute, Tufts University, September.

Hirsch, R. L., R. Bezdek, et al. (2005). Peaking of World Oil Production: Impacts, Mitigation, and Risk Management. Available at www.netl.doe.gov/publications/others/pdf/Oil_Peaking_NETL.pdf (accessed Janaury 16, 2011).

Hopkins, M. S. (2009). "The Loop You Can't Get Out Of: An Interview with Jay Forrester." *Sloan Management Review* **50**(2): 9–12. Available at http://sloanreview.mit.edu/the-magazine/articles/2009/winter/50201/the-loop-you-cant-get-out-of/ (accessed January 16, 2011).

Huber, J. (2004). *New Technologies and Environmental Innovation.* Cheltenham, Edward Elgar.

Jackson, T. (2009). *Prosperity without Growth.* London and Sterling, VA, Earthscan.

Jänicke, M., and K. Jacob (2009). "The Third Industrial Revolution? Solutions to the Crisis of Resource-intensive Growth Free University of Berlin, FFU-report 02-2009. Available at http://edocs.fu-berlin.de/docs/servlets/MCRFileNodeServlet/FUDOCS_derivate_000000001522/FFU_rep_02_2009.pdf?hosts= (accessed January 17, 2011).

Jowitt, P. W. (2004). "Sustainability and the Formation of the Civil Engineer." *Engineering and Sustainability* **157**(ES2): 79–88.

Kallis, G. (2011 forthcoming). "In Defence of Degrowth." *Ecological Economics* 70(5): 873–880.

Kallis, G., J. Martinez-Alier, et al. (2009). "Paper Assets, Real Debts: An Ecological-Economic Exploration of the Global Economic Crisis." *Critical Perspectives on International Business* **5**(1/2): 14–25.

Kaplinsky, R. (2005). *Globalization, Poverty, and Inequality: Between a Rock and a Hard Place.* Cambridge, United Kingdom, Polity Press.

Kemp, R. (2000). Technology and Environmental Policy: Innovation Effects of Past Policies and Suggestions for Improvement. Paper presented at the Workshop on Innovation and the Environment, Organisation for Economic Cooperation and Development (OECD), pp. 35–61.

Kingston, W. (2004). Schumpeter and Institutions: Does His "Business Cycles" Give Enough Weight to Legislation? Paper presented at the International J. A. Schumpeter Society 10th ISS Conference, Innovation, Industrial Dynamics and Structural Transformation: Schumpeterian Legacies, Università Bocconi, Milan, June 9–12.

Kleiner, A. (2009). "Jay Forrester's Shock to the System." *Sloan Management Review*, February 4. Available at: http://sloanreview.mit.edu/beyond-green/jay-forrester-shock-to-the-system/ (accessed on January 16, 2011).

Kondratieff, N. D. (1935 [1925]). "The Long Waves in Economic Life." *Review of Economic Statistics* **17**(6): 105–115.

Krugman, P. (2009). "How Did Economists Get It So Wrong?" *New York Times*, September 2.

Langford, P. (2004). "Engineering to Shape a Better World." *Engineering Sustainability* **157**(ES2): 69–78.

Liagouras, G. (2005). "The Political Economy of Post-industrial Capitalism." *Thesis Eleven* **81**: 20–35.

Luiten, E. E. M. (2001). Beyond Energy Efficiency: Actors, Networks and Government Intervention in the Development of Industrial Process Technologies. PhD dissertation, Utrecht, Utrecht University.

Lynch, L. (2008). The Adoption and Diffusion of Organizational Innovation: Evidence for the U.S. Economy. Paper presented at the IWER seminar at MIT, October 7.

Mankiw, G., D. Romer, et al. (1992). A Contribution to the Empirics of Economic Growth. NBER Working Papers 3541. Cambridge, MA, National Bureau of Economic Research. Also published in *The Quarterly Journal of Economics* 107(2)(May): 407–437.

Martinez-Alier, J., U. Pascual, et al. (2010). "Sustainable De-growth: Mapping the Context, Criticisms, and Future Prospects of an Emergent Paradigm." *Ecological Economics* **69**(9): 1741–1747.

McCraw, T. (2007). *Prophet of Innovation: Joseph Schumpeter and Creative Destruction.* Cambridge, MA, Belknap Press of Harvard University Press.

McDonough, W., and M. Braungart (1998). "The NEXT Industrial Revolution." *Atlantic Monthly* **282**(4): 82–92.

Mehmet, O. (1995). *Westernizing the Third World: The Eurocentricity of Economic Development Theories.* New York, Routledge.

Moors, E. H. M. (2000). Metal Making in Motion: Technology Choices for Sustainable Metals Production. PhD dissertation, Delft, Delft University of Technology.

Nafziger, E. W. (2006). From Seers to Sen: The Meaning of Economic Development. Research Paper 2006/20, UNU-WIDER.

National Research Council (NRC) (2002). *Our Common Journey: A Transition toward Sustainability.* Washington, DC, National Academy Press.

Niehans, J. (1990). *A History of Economic Theory: Classic Contributions, 1720–1980.* Baltimore, Johns Hopkins University Press.

Nuttall, W. J. (2004). *Nuclear Renaissance: Technologies and Policies for the Future of Nuclear Power.* Bristol, IOP/CRC Press, Taylor and Francis.

Organisation for Economic Co-operation and Development (OECD) (2003). *The Sources of Economic Growth in OECD Countries.* Paris, OECD.

OECD (2010a). *The OECD Innovation Strategy: Getting a Head Start on Tomorrow.* Paris, OECD.

OECD (2010b). *The OECD Development Agenda.* Paris, OECD.

Owen, D. (2010). "The Efficiency Dilemma" *The New Yorker,* December 20 and 27, pp. 78–80, 82, 84–85.

Parayil, G. (1996). "The 'Kerala Model' of Development: Development and Sustainability in the Third World." *Third World Quarterly* **17**(3): 941–957.

Partidario, P. J. (2003). "What-If": From Path Dependency to Path Creation in a Coatings Chain: A Methodology for Strategies towards Sustainable Innovation. PhD dissertation, Delft, Delft University of Technology.

Perez, C. (2002). *Technological Revolutions and Financial Capital: The Dynamics of Bubbles and Golden Ages.* Cheltenham, Edward Elgar.

Perrow, C. (1984). *Normal Accidents: Living with High Risk Technologies.* 1st ed. New York, Basic Books.

Purcell, C. W. Ed. (1996). *Technology in America: A History of Individuals and Ideas,* Cambridge, MA, MIT Press.

Rifkin, J. (2004). *The End of Work: The Decline of the Global Labor Force and the Dawn of the Post-market Era.* New York, G. P. Putnam's Sons.

Rodrik, D. (2005). "Growth Strategies." *Handbook of Economic Growth*, vol. 1, part II, pp. 967–1014.

Rodrik, D. (2007). *One Economics, Many Recipes: Globalization, Institutions, and Economic Growth.* Princeton, NJ, Princeton University Press.

Romer, P. M. (1986). "Increasing Returns and Long-Run Growth." *Journal of Political Economy* **94**(5): 1002–1037.

Romer, P. M. (1990). "Endogenous Technological Change." *Journal of Political Economy* **98**: S71–S101.

Ruttan, V. (1959). "Usher and Schumpeter on Invention, Innovation, and Technological Change." *Quarterly Journal of Economics* **73**: 596–606.

Sanders, R. (2006). "Sustainability: Implications for Growth, Employment, and Consumption." *International Journal of Environment, Workplace and Employment* **2**(4): 385–401.

Scherer, F. M. (1992). "Schumpeter and Plausible Capitalism." *Journal of Economic Literature* **30**: 1416–1433.

Schor, J. B. (2010). *Penitude: The New Economics of True Wealth.* New York, Penguin.

Schumpeter, J. A. (1934 [1912]). *The Theory of Economic Development.* Cambridge, MA, Harvard University Press.

Schumpeter, J. A. (1939). *Business Cycles: A Theoretical, Historical, and Statistical Analysis of the Capitalist Process.* New York, McGraw-Hill.

Schumpeter, J. A. (1962 [1942]). *Capitalism, Socialism, and Democracy.* New York, Harper Torchbooks.

Seers, D. (1997). "The Meaning of Development." *Development* **40**(1): 39–45. [Originally published as Seers, D. (1979). "The Meaning of Development, with a Postscript." *Development Theory: Four Critical Studies.* D. Seers, E. W. Nafziger, D. C. O'Brien, and H. Bernstein. London, Frank Cass.]

Sen, A. K. (1999). *Development as Freedom.* New York, Alfred A. Knopf.

Shiller, R. J. (2000), *Irrational Exuberance.* Princeton, NJ, Princeton University Press.

Smil, V. (2008). *Oil: A Beginner's Guide.* Oxford, One World Publications.

Smith, M. R. (1994). "Technological Determinism in American Culture." *Does Technology Drive History? The Dilemma of Technological Determinism.* Cambridge, MA, MIT Press: 1–35.

Smith, M. R. and L. Marx, Eds. (1994). *Does Technology Drive History? The Dilemma of Technological Determinism.* Cambridge, MA, MIT Press.

Söderbaum, P. (2008). *Understanding Sustainability Economics: Towards Pluralism in Economics.* London, Earthscan.

Solow, R. (1987). "We'd Better Watch Out." *New York Times Book Review*, July 12, p. 36.

Solow, R. M. (1993). Sustainability: An Economist's Perspective. *Economics of the Environment: Selected Readings.* R. Dorfman and N. S. Dorfman. New York, W. W. Norton: 179–187.

Spangenberg, J. H. (2007). Defining Sustainable Growth: The Inequality of Sustainability and Its Applications. *Frontiers in Ecology Research.* S. D. Antonello. New York, Nova Science Publishers.

Speth, J. G. (2008). *The Bridge at the Edge of the World: Capitalism, the Environment, and Crossing from Crisis to Sustainability.* New Haven, CT, Yale University Press.

Speth, J. G. (2010a). A New Environmentalism and the New Economy. The 10th Annual John H. Chafee Memorial Lecture, National Council for Science and the Environment, Washington, DC, January 21.

Speth, J. G. (2010b). "Towards a New Economy and a New Politics." *Solutions* **1**(5): 33–41.

Speth, J. G. (2010c). Letter to Liberals: Liberalism, Environmentalism, and Economic Growth. 13th Annual E. F. Schumacher Lecures, New York City, November 20.

Stiglitz, J. (2009). "GDP Fettishism: The Economists." *Voice* **6**(8): Article 5.

Stiglitz, J. (2010). *Freefall: America, Free Markets, and the Sinking of the World Economy.* New York, W. W. Norton.

Todaro, M. P., and S. C. Smith (2009). *Economic Development.* 10th ed. Boston, Addison-Wesley.

van Ark, B., R. Inklaar, et al. (2003). "The Employment Effects of the 'New Economy': A Comparison of the European Union and the United States." *National Institute Economic Review* **184**: 86–98. Available at http://ner.sagepub.com/content/184/1/86.full.pdf+html (accessed January 17, 2011).

van den Bergh, J. C. J. M. (2009). "The GDP Paradox" *Economic Psychology* **30**(2): 117–135.

van den Bergh, J. C. J. M. (2011). "Environment vs. Growth—A Criticism of "Degrowth" and a Plea for 'Agrowth'." *Ecological Economics* **70**(5): 881–890.

van Zandweghe, W. (2010). "Why Have the Dynamics of Labor Productivity Changed?" *Economic Review* **95**(3): 5–30.

Victor, P. (2010a). Macroeconomics for Sustainability. Presentation at Tufts University, February 16 (contact author at York University, Toronto, Canada).

Victor, P. (2010b). "Questioning Economic Growth." *Nature* **468**: 370–371.

Victor, P. A. (2008). *Managing without Growth: Slow by Design, Not Disaster.* Cheltenham, Edward Elgar.

Warsh, D. (2006). *Knowledge and the Wealth of Nations: A Story of Economic Discovery.* New York, W. W. Norton.

Westrum, R. (1991). *Technologies and Society: The Shaping of People and Things.* Belmont, CA, Wadsworth Publishing Company.

Wetlesen, J. (1999). A Global Ethic of Sustainability? *Towards Sustainable Development: On the Goals of Development—And the Conditions of Sustainability.* W. M. Lafferty and O. Langhelle. New York, St. Martin's Press: 30–47.

# 4

# Globalization: Technology, Trade Regimes, Capital Flows, and the International Economy

Coauthored with KYRIAKOS PIERRAKAKIS

## 4.1 INTRODUCTION

Globalization and trade create new opportunities, alliances, and relationships among technology-based firms and nations. They also create new problems and challenges:

- There are opportunities to expand existing domestic production/services to international markets, but the international marketplace may present additional competitive challenges as well.

- There are opportunities to benefit from lower factors of production by locating facilities abroad, but the advantages of doing so may be undercut by currency fluctuations, political instability, inadequate infrastructure, and lower worker productiveness

- There are opportunities to avoid costly domestic financial, environmental, or tax regulation by operating abroad, but future foreign regulatory systems may be uncertain, and foreign governments may be subject to unanticipated corruption.

Operating in the international marketplace may change the access of potential consumers to credit for purchasing products and services, and of entrepreneurs to investment capital, with mixed results. In addition, different tax treatment of investment and profits and different rules for the expatriation of capital and requirements for domestic content can undermine the profitability of operating internationally. Nonetheless, globalization of markets is proceeding at an unprecedented pace.*

---

\*   See Kleinknecht and ter Wengel (1998) for the observation that Europe (even before the recent addition of new accession countries) was actually deglobalizing as an economic unit/region, i.e., the percentage and level of trade outside the European Union was decreasing relative to the trade associated with the integration of its internal market.

In this chapter, we explore the several dimensions of globalization (Section 4.2), introduce the major emerging international trade regimes (Section 4.3), explore the relationship between trade and economic development (Section 4.4), examine the role of MNEs in the international economy (Section 4.5), and discuss the evolving world financial system (Section 4.6). Both Todaro and Smith's (2009) work on trade and the Bhagwati (1993)/Daly (1993) debate on the merits of free trade are addressed. Finally, a cautious prognosis for future stabilization and the restoration of consumer and producer confidence is offered (Section 4.7).

Chapter 5, which follows, discusses the adverse affects of globalization on the environment and employment (including purchasing power) as a result of (1) shifting the locus and nature of production (the international division of labor) and (2) the opportunity to *externalize* the social consequences of production resulting from differences in the willingness of trading nations to address issues such as environmental degradation, worker safety, and the need to provide a living wage.

## 4.2 GLOBALIZATION

We take the international economy to be composed of the following five highly interrelated aspects:

1. Trade in goods and services*
2. International distribution of production† (more commonly called the international division of labor)
3. Flows of capital across national borders
4. Flows of information and knowledge
5. Flows of labor across national borders

The interrelatedness of the first three features of the international economy is quickly apparent. Trade in goods and services reflects the geographic distribution of production/generation of services—that is, inputs must go to production/service centers. The finished products/services (which may also be used as inputs) subsequently go to consumption centers/consumers. Capital flows across national borders as a consequence of production/service-system investments and because of speculation on the future value of produced goods and services and currencies.

In the age of the so-called knowledge-based economy and information systems using sophisticated information and communication technology (ICT), information/knowledge transfer is crucial not only for optimizing industrial activity but also for the transfer of financial information and assets.

Labor mobility has two important but different dimensions: (1) the flow of intellectual capital (the "brain drain") to places where it is most highly valued; and (2) labor migration to areas with shortages of people to perform physical or so-called low-skilled work (see Chapter 5, Sections 5.2 and 5.3.3, for further discussion).

Not all aspects of globalization are seen to be positive. Nobel Prize economist J. Stiglitz (2002, p. 248) notes: "Globalization has helped hundreds of millions of people attain higher standards of living, beyond what they, or most economists, thought imaginable but a short while ago. . . . But for millions of people globalization has not worked. Many have actually been made worse off, as they have seen their jobs destroyed and their lives become more insecure. They have felt increasingly powerless against forces beyond their control. They have seen their democracies undermined, their cultures eroded." The legendary investor George Soros (1997, p. 45) cautioned as early as 1997: "Although I have made a fortune in the financial markets, I now fear that the untrammeled intensification of laissez-faire capitalism and the spread of market values into all areas of life is endangering our open and democratic society. The main enemy of the open society, I believe, is no longer the communist but the capitalist threat." When Stiglitz (2002) and Soros (1997, 2002) expressed such concerns about economic globalization, it sent a strong message that the current trajectory of economic development is flawed. Six years later, in 2008, we saw the beginning of the worst world economic crisis since the 1930s.

In contrast to the early international debates about the environment and development, which focused mainly on national issues, today's discourse places sustainable development within the much broader concept of globalization. Indeed, globalization was described as adding a "new dimension" to sustainable development in the Johannesburg Declaration (2002).

Globalization can be conceived as a process by which the world is becoming more interconnected, both in economic relations—encompassing trade, investment, finance, and the organization of global production systems—and in social and political interactions among organizations, communities, and

---

\*     As explored later in this section, this kind of industrial globalization is known as "internationalization."
†     As explored later in this section, the location of production/assembly/service operations outside the parent country is a form of industrial globalization known as "multinationalization."

individuals across the world (WCSDG 2004). There is no universally agreed-on definition of globalization, and the concept is still being formulated (Held and McGrew 2002; Saha 2002).* Thus the discourse on globalization can be described as representing an area for discussion rather than an established mode of thought. Three main theories are often used to frame the process of globalization: (1) the world-system theory (the spread of the capitalist system across the globe); (2) the world polity theory (the theory that "a rationalized world institutional and cultural order has crystallized that consists of universally applicable models that shape states, organizations, and individual identities"); and (3) the world culture theory (the formation of a "world consciousness" that gives meaning to living in the world as a single place).[1]

An important element of the globalization discourse is its links to discussions on the "nature and existence of the nation state, economically, politically and culturally" (Voisey and O'Riordan 2001, p. 34). Because the nation-state has a responsibility to move toward the objectives of sustainable development (see the Stockholm, Rio, and Johannesburg[†] declarations and Agenda 21), any forces that might influence the effectiveness of government in this task will have important implications for the design of national and/or international strategies to address sustainable development. Hence it is important to understand how globalization could enhance, undermine, or provide new opportunities for government action (see Section 5.4 in Chapter 5).

The OECD (1997, p. 19) viewed globalization "as a process in which economic markets, technologies, and communication patterns gradually exhibit more 'global' characteristics and less 'national' or 'local'

ones."[‡] More useful definitions -characterize globalization as a linked set of trends in the international economy and elaborate on these trends by identifying their likely cause. Lee (1996, p. 485) comments: "The rapid growth in world trade, foreign direct investment, and cross-border financial flows over the past decade has been the main manifestation of the increasing 'globalization' of the world economy. This phenomenon has been driven primarily by a worldwide wave of economic liberalization—the lowering of tariff and non-tariff barriers to international trade, the encouragement of foreign investment, and the deregulation of financial markets. At the same time technological developments have magnified the effects of this liberalization by reducing the costs of transportation and communications, hence expanding the scope and volume of goods and services that are internationally tradable."

In contrast to Lee's remarks, Judt (2005) argues that globalization is not about trade liberalization or expanding communication networks, but rather

---

* For a useful list of definitions of globalization, see Streeten (2001, pp. 167–173). For a review and critique of the earlier globalization scholarship, see Marshall (1996). Marshall analyzes the *ideological* content of globalization commentary and rhetoric and provides a useful counterpoint to the proponents of globalization.

† The 2002 Johannesburg Declaration called on the private sector to recognize its role in achieving sustainable development. This evolution in strategy broadened the responsibility for action to effectively incorporate all stakeholders working to achieve sustainable development. However, governments—which have retained the sovereign right to use national resources as they see fit within certain international constraints—remain central to any transition toward sustainable development because they define the economic and regulatory environment within which the private sector operates. The major debate with the current process of globalization is that it holds the potential to undermine the ability of governments to establish this environment by transferring political and economic power to corporate interests. This concern is discussed throughout this section.

‡ The OECD's (1997) four "effects" of globalization are the following:

- *Scale effects:* increased world output, thought to arise from the increase in economic efficiency that results as resources are freed to flow to uses that reflect their greatest marginal contribution (a very neoclassical argument).

- *Structural effects:* shifts in the composition and location of production and consumption activities. Note that these shifts in production are *required* to realize scale effects. In general, "Market structures [become] *deeper* (more geographic specialization in production; more contracting-out to independent, but related firms) and *wider*" (more countries participating actively in the global economy). Further, as foreign investment flows become larger, there is "an increase in overseas commercial transactions (especially for primary and intermediate products), and a greater tendency to export final goods. Expansion may also be expected in the number and extend to international co-operative agreements between firms, notably in the fields of R&D, product supply, distribution, and marketing."

- *Technology effects:* promotion of different technology paths and increases in the rate of technological change. (This is difficult because technological change is seen both as an *enabler* of globalization—for example, modern capital markets would be impossible without sophisticated information and communication technology—and as a *consequence* of globalization. For example, free trade increases direct competition between manufacturing industries in Northern and Southern economies. Pressures toward continuous innovation as a means of maintaining comparative advantage thus become more intense in the North.)

- *Product effects:* production and consumption of different product mixes; "globalization might lead to more uniform consumer tastes, influenced by transnational mass media and advertising."

Interestingly, one effect that is not articulated is the effect on financial systems that are affected by, as well as affect, economic welfare.

"about the disappearance of boundaries—cultural and economic boundaries, physical boundaries, linguistic boundaries—and the challenge of organizing our world in their absence." In addition, the disappearance of boundaries has placed limitations on the ability of national governments to address problems adequately and has enhanced the importance of international law and institutions.

Although consensus on a definition of globalization has not yet been reached, there appears to be some agreement on its core drivers (Held and McGrew 2002; Lall 2002; Saha 2002; Stiglitz 2002). These drivers are (1) the gradual removal of barriers to trade and to the movement of capital, services, knowledge, and (to a lesser extent) people between nations; (2) the rapid reduction in the costs of transportation (due to energy efficiency gains and logistical improvements)* and communication; and (3) the creation of new institutions to supplement existing ones to formulate and oversee normative rules of engagement (especially for trade, but also increasingly for the environment) at the international level. The first driver highlights an interesting observation. Although the mobility of goods, firms, and capital has grown significantly over the past two decades, the ability of people to crisscross national borders has not, which is an important difference from previous episodes of globalization (Bordo, Eichengreen, et al. 1999; ECLAC 2002; WCSDG 2004).

These drivers have the effect of bringing nations, people, societies, cultures, economies, and markets closer together, affecting them "in different ways through space and time" (Voisey and O'Riordan 2001, p. 34). A concise description of the wide range of elements that form the process of globalization is put forward by Held and McGrew (2002, p. 3, emphases added):

> Globalization has been variously conceived as *action at a distance* (whereby the actions of social agents in one locale can come to have significant consequences for "distant others"); *time-space compression* (referring to the way in which instantaneous electronic communication erodes the constraints of distance and time on social organization and interaction); *accelerating interdependence* (understood as the intensification of enmeshment among national economies and societies such that events in one country impact directly on others); *a shrinking world* (the erosion of borders and geographical barriers to socio-economic activity); and, among

other concepts, *global integration*, the *reordering of interregional power relations, consciousness of the global condition* and the *intensification of interregional interconnectedness.*

Like the sustainable development discourse, the globalization debate is somewhat polarized by those who are skeptical that such a phenomenon exists and those who believe that it is an integral and unavoidable aspect of our lives. Held and McGrew (2002) provide a useful summary of the perceptions of those who believe in the existence of the globalization process and those who are skeptical (Table 4.1). It is important to recognize that the perceptions presented do not necessarily represent the views of all skeptics and all globalists. By the very nature of the subject, it is highly likely that views on certain issues may begin to diverge within the skeptic and globalist camps.

A relatively skeptical view of economic globalization is presented by Hirst and Thompson (2002, pp. 2–3), who provide a convincing set of evidence to show the following:

1. "The present highly internationalized economy is not unprecedented. . . . In some respects, the current international economy is less open and integrated than the regime that prevailed from 1870 to 1914.

2. Genuinely transnational companies appear to be relatively rare. . . . [†]

3. Capital mobility is not producing a massive shift of investment and employment from the advanced to the developing countries. . . .

4. As some of the extreme advocates of globalization recognize, the world economy is far from being genuinely "global." Rather trade, investment and financial flows are concentrated in the Triad of Europe, Japan and North America and this dominance seems set to continue.

5. These major economic powers, the G3, thus have the capacity, especially if they coordinate policy, to exert powerful governance pressures over financial markets and other economic tendencies. Global markets are thus by no means beyond regulation and control, even though the current scope and objectives of economic

---

* Internalizing the environmental costs (pollution and global climate change) may very well offset or even reverse the trends toward the reduction of transportation costs.

† A transnational company or corporation is "an economic entity operating in more than one country or a cluster of economic entities operating in two or more countries—whatever their legal form, whether in their home country or country of activity, and whether taken individually or collectively" (United Nations Economic and Social Council [ECOSOC] 2003, p. 7). See Section 4.5.

**TABLE 4.1: THE GREAT GLOBALIZATION DEBATE**

|  | SKEPTICS | GLOBALISTS |
|---|---|---|
| **Concepts** | Internationalization, not globalization<br>Regionalization | One world, shaped by highly extensive, intensive, and rapid flows, movements, and networks across regions and continents |
| **Power** | Rule by the nation-state<br>Intergovernmentalism | Erosion of state sovereignty, autonomy, and legitimacy<br>Decline of the nation-state<br>Rise of multilateralism |
| **Culture** | Resurgence of nationalism and national identity | Emergence of global popular culture<br>Erosion of fixed political identities<br>Hybridization |
| **Economy** | Development of regional blocs<br>Triadization<br>New imperialism | Global informational capitalism<br>The transnational economy<br>A new global division of labor |
| **Inequality** | Growing North-South divide<br>Irreconcilable conflicts of interest | Growing inequality within and across societies<br>Erosion of old hierarchies |
| **Order** | International society of states<br>Inevitable persistence of political conflict between states<br>International governance and geopolitics<br>Communitarianism | Multilayered global governance<br>Global civil society<br>Global polity<br>Cosmopolitanism |

Source: Adapted from Held and McGrew (2002, p. 37).

governance are limited by the divergent interests of the great powers and the economic doctrines prevalent among their elites.

Held and McGrew (2002, p. 20) support the notion of the "triadization of the world economy" but argue that economic integration has occurred between the broader group of Europe, Asia-Pacific, and the Americas. This broader grouping incorporates the formation of the NAFTA, MERCOSUR (involving Argentina, Brazil, Paraguay, and Uruguay), APEC (Asia-Pacific Economic Cooperation), and ASEAN (the Association of Southeast Asian Nations) multilateral agreements and the recent economic integration of the EU. It also suggests that reducing globalization to a purely economic or technological discourse is misleading because it does not take into account other important forces shaping modern societies.

The notion of the triad may need to be reconsidered, however, if countries such as China and India, previously considered "peripheral" economies, continue to emerge as the "new core" of the world economy (Muradain 2004). See Section 4.4.4 for a discussion of how the dominance of manufacturing and services by China and India and the consolidation of retailing power in developed countries are reshaping the structure of markets.

One additional aspect of globalization that has important challenges for sustainability, and an issue often neglected in discussions focusing on technology and industrialization, is the movement of labor/human resources in response to pressures for migration. This is discussed more fully in Section 5.3.3 of Chapter 5.

### 4.2.1 Industrial Globalization

Globalization connects the world through the transfer and sharing of knowledge/information, financial systems, labor, and the production and consumption of goods and services. The last is termed "industrialization." It is possible to identify three main types of industrial globalization—*internationalization, multinationalization*, and *transnationalization* (Gordon 1995)*—the first two of which can have a direct impact on environmental degradation.

*Internationalization* is the expansion of product/service markets abroad while the locus of production remains within the parent country. The process of internationalization is primarily facilitated by cheap transportation services, with information and communication technology (ICT) and e-commerce taking a secondary—but, nevertheless, increasingly important—role. Technology or products that are

---

* For an insightful (early) discussion of how competition in global industries drives the geographic configuration and co-ordination activities of firms/industries, see M. E. Porter (1986).

produced in industrial nations and exported over-seas can provide significant benefits to governments, firms, communities, and individuals in the importing nations.* However, these technologies and products can also introduce new problems or worsen existing problems in these nations. For example, the sale of pesticides to a nation that previously had never used such chemicals can result in negative environmental and human health impacts. These problems are exac-erbated by improper or uncontrolled use that can oc-cur as a result of inadequate warnings, training, or monitoring. Of course, the impacts of such products need to be considered against the conditions that likely would exist had they not been introduced.

*Multinationalization* is where a (multinational) company establishes production/service facilities abroad to be nearer to foreign markets and/or to take advantage of more industry-friendly labor and envi-ronment and tax policies while maintaining research-and-development (R&D) and innovation-centered activities in the parent country. In this situation, the parent company is no longer *sending* products over-seas but is *manufacturing* or *assembling* its products overseas. However, it is important to recognize that very few companies actually operate branches abroad that are a direct extension of the parent company itself. As Clegg (1996, p. 104) comments, "The pre-ponderance of firms work through foreign affiliates incorporated according to local law. The parent firm in the home country will normally own significant eq-uity in the foreign affiliate." Clegg (1996) argues that the increased turbulence of the international business environment, combined with cheap and effective com-munication and transportation services, provides the incentive for parent firms to coordinate with foreign affiliates.

In a study of the U.S. manufacturing industry, Whitford (2006) provides a more nuanced descrip-tion of how firms have outsourced much of their pro-ductive capacity to other firms in the United States and abroad. He observes that "most of what matters to manufacturing firms no longer happens under roofs they own or control. This has made the quality of relationships between firms much more important and their structure much more complex. . . . How (and where) these large firms choose and direct their armies of suppliers has tremendous consequences

for the regional economies in which they are embed-ded, because firms selling in the more profitable markets where competition depends as much on in-novation and quality as it does on price are more likely to use skilled and better-paid workers" (ibid., p. 3). Whitford (2006) also argues that the structure of manufacturing networks has more to do with how a firm is embedded in a particular historical and in-stitutional context than with factors such as trade policy or international regulatory arbitrage.

As with internationalization, the process of multi-nationalization has provided significant benefits to societies outside a multinational enterprise's (MNE's) home nation. However, MNEs are also responsible for some of the world's worst industrial accidents.† The more industrial globalization occurs in this sec-ond category, the more concerned we should become because the impacts on other nations can be exten-sive.‡

Benton and Redclift (1994) present another way to consider multinationalization by discussing how the spatial relocation of the Japanese car-manufacturing industry has led to both positive and negative envi-ronmental impacts. On the one hand, the relocation of car-manufacturing plants in other nations is seen to have reduced the environmental pollution prob-lem in Tokyo. On the other hand, the creation of new consumer markets for Japanese cars is seen to have increased the per capita consumption of energy and material at the global level, with a corresponding in-crease in the amounts of total pollution and waste. Hence the authors argue that this second type of in-dustrial globalization has the effect of redistributing environmental costs and benefits.

What is evident from these first two types of industrial globalization is that when technology is

---

* The idea of the developed countries selling inexpen-sive products to millions of people in the developing world is known as "trading from the bottom of the pyramid"—see Hart and Milstein (1999), London and Hart (2004), and Prahalad and Hart (2002).

† An example of an MNE's operation that had devastat-ing consequences for society in the recipient nation was the Bho-pal incident in India. In 1984, a leak of deadly intermediate methyl isocyanate at a Union Carbide pesticide plant killed some four thousand people and affected the health of tens of thou-sands more in the city of Bhopal. Although Union Carbide batch processing plants in the United States are subject to strict health and safety and environmental controls, the state of Madhya Pradesh in India did not have the motivation to deploy a similar monitoring/control regime. Indeed, it has been argued that health and safety violations at the Bhopal plant were overlooked in the name of industrialization and agricultural self-sufficiency. In this case, the problem was not due to the sale of products or equip-ment but to the transfer of manufacturing capacity—see Lopatin (2004).

‡ Note, however, that MNEs have come under greater scrutiny by NGOs and stockholders and have increasingly re-sponded to these concerns by adopting "at-home practices" abroad. See the codes of conduct and principles developed in the context of foreign investment discussed in Chapter 12.

transferred between nations—primarily by MNEs (see Section 5.1.2 in Chapter 5)*—both the positive and negative aspects of the technology are transferred with the equipment and products. If the receiving nation's ability to control the new technology or industrial processes is limited, then what might well be an environmentally sound technology in an industrialized nation can become environmentally destructive if it is used in an uncontrolled manner.

The third type of industrial globalization, which we will call *transnationalization*, is the creation of strategic alliances in which two different foreign enterprises merge/share their R&D and other capabilities to create a new entity or product line, reduce expenditures, and open up new markets (Gordon 1995; Mowery and Rosenberg 1989). An example of a strategic alliance was the ultimately unsuccessful Daimler-Chrysler merger, where different technological and managerial capacities were combined, ostensibly to create a whole that was expected to be greater and more efficient than the sum of its parts. This form of industrial globalization is not as common as the first two and is most likely to occur between developed nations, as opposed to between developed and developing nations.

## 4.3 TRADE REGIMES

The most significant trade regimes are the World Trade Organization (WTO), the North American Free Trade Agreement (NAFTA), the Association of Southeast Asian Nations (ASEAN), and various agreements involving countries in Central and South America. A detailed examination of the WTO is provided in Chapter 11. The exploration of ASEAN and trade agreements involving South America is beyond the scope of this text. The WTO and NAFTA are briefly discussed in the following sections.

### 4.3.1 The World Trade Organization

The WTO describes its agreements as follows:[2] "The WTO agreements cover goods, services and intellectual property. They spell out the principles of liberalization, and the permitted exceptions. They include individual countries' commitments to lower customs

tariffs and other trade barriers, to minimize or eliminate subsidies, to open and keep open services markets, and to respect intellectual property. They set procedures for settling disputes. They prescribe special treatment for developing countries. They require governments to make their trade policies transparent by notifying the WTO about laws in force and measures adopted, and through regular reports by the secretariat on countries' trade policies."

The agreements are often called the WTO's trade rules, and the WTO is often described as "rules based." The "rules" are agreements that governments negotiated, which can be renegotiated or further clarified though the resolution of trade disputes. The legal texts consist of about sixty agreements, annexes, decisions, and understandings. The main agreements fall into a simple structure with six main parts: an umbrella agreement (the Agreement Establishing the WTO); agreements for each of the three broad areas of trade that the WTO covers (goods, services, and intellectual property); dispute settlement; and reviews of governments' trade policies.

### 4.3.2 The North American Free Trade Agreement

NAFTA differs from the WTO in that, like the ASEAN, it is a regional trade agreement involving the United States, Canada, and Mexico. It is also unique in that in order to get the support—or at least lessen the resistance to its adoption—of environmental groups and organized labor, it contains two side agreements on the environment and labor. Unlike the WTO, which speaks directly to environmental agreements but obliquely to labor issues, NAFTA does not address either, which necessitated the side agreements. In contrast to multilateral environmental agreements (MEAs) and conventions of the International Labour Organization (ILO)[†] and to the preference for uniformity among trading partners of environmental safeguards expressed by the WTO, the NAFTA side agreements do not encourage uniformity but rather adherence of each separate country's requirements to its own laws and standards. Two separate institutional dispute-resolution mechanisms that operate outside other traditional (economic) trade-dispute mechanisms are established for environmental and labor issue disputes.[3]

Interestingly, although NAFTA was originally intended to expand its membership to Central and South America, the Bush administration's resistance

---

* The recent growth inflows of foreign direct investment (FDI) have been primarily driven by global production systems that are made up of some 65,000 MNEs with around 850,000 foreign affiliates (WCSDG 2004). Within these production systems, high-tech industries (e.g., electronics, semiconductors) and labor-intensive industries (e.g., textiles, garments, footwear) have experienced the most pronounced growth (ibid.).

---

† See Chapter 10 for a discussion of regional and international regimes to protect health, safety, and the environment.

to including side agreements caused the United States to attempt to negotiate an entirely separate agreement under a Free Trade Agreement of the Americas (FTAA) banner, but this ultimately failed. The United States then resorted to negotiating separate bilateral agreements with selected South American countries, undermining the likelihood of a regional approach to trade.

## 4.4 TRADE AND ECONOMIC DEVELOPMENT

Trade consists of the flow of goods and services between nations. These flows are heavily mediated by the international division of labor (that is, the location of production versus consumption) and by the institutional organization of that labor (for example, MNEs, which conduct significant interfirm transfers of goods and services). But the international trading system is also founded on *theoretical beliefs* about the gains from trade, and the international agreements that codify and regulate the conduct of trade reflect both these beliefs or ideology and a process of historical evolution. This section is therefore designed to provide an introduction to trade theory and its relationship to development/economic prosperity and to the practice of trade as embodied in trade agreements. We provide an evaluation of the implications of trade for work and the environment in the next chapter.

### 4.4.1 Free Trade: Winners and Losers

Although modern development theory emphasizes technological innovation as the "engine of economic growth," trade also contributed to advancing industrializing nations during the nineteenth and twentieth centuries. Now trade is increasingly described as a major engine of economic growth, both for advanced economies with "excess productive capacity" and saturated domestic markets and for less industrialized countries with unutilized natural resources increasingly needed by the industrialized economies. For both, outward-looking strategies are being fashioned for more participation in world markets.*

_____

*　　See Schmidheiny (1992, pp. 69–81) for an insightful discussion of "trade and sustainable development." Schmidheiny (1992, p. 79) makes the observation that "traditionally, the industrial nations of North America and Europe have championed free trade, against the resistance of most developing nations and centrally planned economies. Today, it is the former that tend to question the benefits of liberalized trade, while developing nations and the newly emerged democracies of Eastern Europe see

The purpose of this section is to articulate why trade is seen as an important driver of development.

Since the time of Adam Smith, most economists have considered free trade to be a beneficial activity toward which societies should strive. The most fundamental argument for free trade lies in the existence of efficiency losses associated with the enforcement of protectionist policies, such as tariffs, quotas, and subsidies, which do not take advantage of lower factor costs elsewhere and which could be avoided through the imposition of a free-trade policy regime.

It is becoming increasingly apparent that developed nations (the United States in particular) believe that trade is critical to achieving sustainable development. It is seen as the mechanism through which poverty will be reduced, human well-being will increase, and environmental problems will be addressed. However, focusing on trade as a driver of sustainable development has its supporters and critics.

Economists have identified a series of additional gains associated with free trade. One such gain involves the emergence of so-called spillover effects. By providing entrepreneurs with an incentive to devise new ways to export or to compete with imports, free trade results in innovation and increased learning opportunities. An additional gain involves the surfacing of economies of scale in production (Krugman and Obstfeld 2003). An expected consequence of protected markets is that they decrease production internationally; however, they also lead to a reduction in competition and an increase in profits for industry in the protected economy. On the other hand, low barriers to entry can lead too many firms to enter the protected industry, making the scale of production of each firm inefficient. A good example is the Argentine automobile industry, which owes its emergence to import restrictions. Although an efficient assembly plant should be making 80,000 to 200,000 automobiles per year, in 1964 the Argentine industry was producing only 166,000 cars per year in a market of thirteen firms (ibid., p. 219).

The proponents of trade generally ground their arguments in the notion that free trade will enhance the welfare of humans by increasing prosperity. The basic economic theory is that international trade that is free from protectionist barriers will reduce

_____

it as their main hope for economic development." To address the inherent conflicts associated with the expansion of trade and environmental protection, Schmidheiny (1992) calls for the harmonization of environmental regulations throughout the world.

prices and increase the amount of goods and services available (Driesen 2001). Because free trade enables corporations (predominantly based in developed nations) to become global in their operations, proponents argue that less developed nations will benefit from job creation and the spread of advanced technology; health, safety, and environmental standards; and environmental management techniques (OECD 1997). In addition, as individual prosperity increases, so does the tax base for environmental and social programs that governments can implement in response to increasing demands for a healthier environment (Bhagwati 1993; Speth 2003).* In effect, proponents argue that international trade is opening up new opportunities to protect and enhance the environment through the reorientation of economic policies (OECD 1997). Further, as governments' ability to manage their economic affairs is enhanced, there are likely to be spillover effects that will enable them to address environmental concerns (Speth 2003).

Although free trade is a preferred policy measure in theory, it does not uniformly advance all social interests. It is important to ask who wins from free trade and who loses.

David Ricardo's theory of comparative advantage remains the most central formulation of the theory of the benefits of international trade. The idea of comparative advantage states that countries can better their financial position by specializing in what they do best.† In the 1920s, the Swedes Eli Heckscher and Bertil Ohlin showed that even when technologies could be copied, as in manufacturing, countries' differing endowments of factors of production could explain different countries' gains from trade. Capital-rich countries would specialize in goods whose production required an abundance of capital, while labor-rich countries would specialize in labor-intensive goods and land-rich countries in land-intensive (that is, agricultural) goods. Instead of making goods that would primarily require the factors they possessed the least, countries could trade for them and acquire more goods overall.‡ The Hecksher-Ohlin theory recognizes that trade will not benefit everyone uniformly. For instance, capital in labor-rich countries will lose from imports of capital-intensive goods. This helps explain why capitalists in low-wage countries, such as Brazil, opposed trade with capital-rich countries for capital-intensive goods, because this threatened their scarce premium. On the other hand, capitalists in capital-intensive Britain were among the primary proponents of free trade. Symmetrically, labor in capital-rich countries will lose from imports of labor-intensive goods, which explains why labor unions in rich countries are usually antitrade, and also why the United States and Europe have been reluctant to reduce subsidies of agricultural production.

Furthermore, by understanding which productive factors are required to manufacture commodities and relating this information to the relative endowments and factors of production of each country, factor-endowment trade theory encourages countries to *specialize* in commodities in which they have a comparative advantage. Hence the most efficient (worldwide) allocation of resources will be achieved if all countries specialize in their relative strengths and trade their surplus for needed commodities that are more easily produced by others. This view of trade ultimately leads to the integration of regional and national markets, increasing the importance of transnational corporations (TNCs) and the need to transport resources and commodities between nations (Korten 2001).

In an article published in 1941, twenty years after the Heckscher-Ohlin contribution, Harvard

---

*     This type of argument is often put forward by those who believe in inverted-U-shaped or environmental Kuznets curve relationships—i.e., environmental quality falls during the initial stages of economic growth and industrial expansion but later improves with increasing GDP. See the discussion in Sections 1.3.2 and 5.1.1.3 of Chapters 1 and 5, respectively.

†     In a self-contained economy, an example of this theory is bartering between a dentist and a carpenter. The carpenter needs his teeth fixed, and the dentist needs shelves in his study. They agree freely on an exchange of services, and it sounds like a marriage made in heaven. Both are made better off by the exchange. The dentist fixes two teeth, and the carpenter builds three shelves. Five years later the carpenter needs four teeth fixed, but the dentist has enough shelves and wants a tool shed built in his garden. At that particular time, the exchange still looks like a marriage made in heaven. Both are benefiting from the exchange. Ten years later the bargain is six teeth fixed in exchange for a garage. It is still a mutually advantageous exchange, but note that one party to the bargain (the carpenter) is increasingly impoverished relative to the other (the dentist). The dentist is further advantaged by the greater technological advances in dentistry compared with carpentry. Although at any one time welfare is maximized, examination over time reveals a problem. The analogy to first-world economies (providing advanced

goods) trading with third-world countries (providing basic commodities) is obvious.

‡     The early theories of comparative advantage were based on a set of *static* (endowment/core) factors, namely, labor, natural resources, land, and population size. However, comparative advantage is now understood to be more of a dynamic process (Dicken 1994). Possibly the best-known description of the factors that determine a nation's competitiveness is M. E. Porter's (1990) "diamond of competitive advantage," discussed later in this section.

classmates Wolfgang Stopler and Paul Samuelson explored who benefits and who loses from trade. The authors began with the assumption that trade is beneficial for producers of exports and harmful for producers who compete with imports, with Heckscher and Ohlin predicting that export producers have the factor that is abundant in their country (Frieden 2006). In accordance with this analysis, an increase in exports will lead to an increase in demand for the factors employed in their production. For instance, as a labor-rich country exports labor-intensive products, the demand for labor increases, which leads to a corresponding increase in wages—at least in theory. At the same time, the demand for the products of import-competing producers will decrease, thus pushing them out of the market. In summary, the Stopler-Samuelson scheme constitutes a central theory of the politics of trade, making the case that trade makes the national owners of an abundant factor of production better off and the owners of a scarce factor of production worse off.

Indeed, in the late nineteenth and early twentieth centuries, farmers in land-rich countries were free traders in almost all cases, whether they were cattle ranchers in Australia or wheat farmers in Canada (Frieden 2006). The same held true for owners of capital in capital-rich countries, such as Britain and other countries of northwestern Europe. Stopler and Samuelson's analysis also appeared to hold for the enemies of free trade as well. In labor-poor Australia, Canada and the United States, labor was protectionist, while in capital-poor Russia and Brazil, it was the owners of capital who primarily opposed free trade (ibid.). Finally, farmers in land-poor Europe are still protectionist today, with countries such as France and Greece known for the subsidization of their respective national agricultural activities.

Nevertheless, although international differences in factor costs and endowments have been important in the determination of the international division of labor and the patterns of international trade, Ricardo's comparative advantage does not have sufficient explanatory power (Coffey 1996). In fact, most world trade seems to be taking place between countries with similar factor endowments and costs. According to Porter (1990), the notion of *competitive* advantage constitutes a much more elaborate scheme for understanding international trade. Competitive advantage is a much broader concept than comparative advantage. Four attributes or interacting factors constitute Porter's diamond of competitive advantage (ibid.):

- Factor conditions (such as resources, labor, and infrastructure)*

- Demand conditions (characteristics of consumers in domestic markets)

- Related and supporting industries (suppliers, collaborators, competitors)

- Firm strategy, structure, and rivalry (market conditions, competitive structure, and company organization, that is, the factors that influence an industry's/firm's attitude toward competition and innovation)

These factors can combine to generate new advanced factor endowments (such as a high-technology sector or a large pool of skilled labor) that determine a nation's comparative advantage. A clear omission from Porter's (1990) theory, however, is the failure to include government as a factor (Dicken 1994). Instead, government is described as having a proactive "influence" on the four core endowment factors.†

Daly (1993), in a comprehensive critique of free trade, underlines that even the term "free trade" is fallacious because it creates the erroneous impression that people who support some set of trade restrictions are against "freedom." In that context, the real debate is not over being for or against "free trade" (because there is no such thing as purely free trade), but over what sets of regulations and restrictions should be put in place and what goals are legitimate. Hence, according to Daly (1993), a more accurate name than "free trade" would be "deregulated international trade."

Greider (1997) agrees with this analysis. A passage from his 1997 book *One World, Ready or Not* is particularly elucidating: "Lawrence B. Krause, international relations professor at the University of California at San Diego, aggregated all of the different ways in which trade was managed—openly and covertly—and concluded that only about 15 per cent of global trade was genuinely conducted in free-market circumstances. Other scholars have calculated that governments directly managed 25 to 30 per cent of trade through their various non-tariff [trade] barriers. Multinational corporations themselves managed about 40 percent of global trade through the intrafirm trade among their own subsidiaries. Further, Krause noted that the top ten trade

---

* Even though this may sound similar to Ricardo's notion of comparative advantage, Porter does not limit his analysis to factor endowments. Porter believes that the key factors of production are actually created (i.e., skilled labor, capital, and infrastructure).

† See also Section 3.1.2 in Chapter 3 on factor endowments necessary for economic development.

sectors, from aircraft to petroleum, were managed by governments or concentrated firms, with the single exception of paper. These accounted for 22 percent of world trade" (ibid., pp. 137–138). More than ten years have passed since the publication of Greider's book, but these observations remain relevant today.

Informed by Daly's and Greider's analyses, an extension of Porter's model of competitive advantage would contribute the insight that government has an important regulatory role to play. Governments can affect all four elements of Porter's diamond through subsidies, the creation of infrastructure, tax policy, education policy, standardization, regulations, and other measures

Daly (1993, 1999) however, makes an additional observation, often disregarded by some economic theorists. According to Ricardo's specification, following trade liberalization, countries can specialize on the basis of comparative advantage, with the possibility of investing all of a country's capital in a single product. However, the hidden assumption of the theory of comparative advantage, according to Daly (1993, 1999), is that capital earned from trade cannot cross borders, as was the case in the pre-1970 Bretton Woods world, and will be invested in the country in which the product was produced. If capital is mobile as well, then it can follow *absolute advantage* rather than *comparative advantage*, and one country could conceptually end up producing everything because it could have lower costs, better infrastructure, larger or better markets, and other advantages and attract foreign capital.*

Morris (2001) extends Daly's critique by offering a reassessment of some of free trade's assumptions. In his view, prices do not provide accurate measures of real efficiency, because they are the outcome of a series of variables, such as market structure and subsidization. Furthermore, Morris (2001, p. 121) cites Howard Wachtel, who notes that "differences in product cost that are due to totalitarian political institutions or restrictions on economic rights reflect no natural or entrepreneurial advantage. Free trade has nothing to do with incomparable political economic institutions that protect individual rights in one country and deny them in another."

Furthermore, a significant set of additional arguments against free trade needs to be examined. For instance, labor used in a sector that would be harmed by import competition might otherwise be unemployed or underemployed. Also, the assertion that labor and capital markets clear perfectly is not corroborated by the evidence in all cases.[†] In fact, defects often exist in the capital and labor markets that prevent resources from being transferred as rapidly as they should be to sectors that yield high returns. There is also a significant argument to be made about the protection of nascent domestic industries that can be particularly innovative and produce technological spillover effects.[‡]

In general, the proponents of free trade claim that it lowers import prices, a case that becomes all the more clear when one thinks of cheap Wal-Mart products. However, this is not what theory claims to be the case. In fact, comparative advantage theory states that free trade affects relative rather than absolute prices. Absolute prices are actually determined by monetary and macroeconomic policies. The effect of a country's liberalization of its trade regime is that the relative price of imports decreases relative to exports, or, inversely, that the relative price of exports increases relative to imports. The determinant of whether consumers will be better or worse off will be the extent to which their consumption basket is dominated by imports, after accounting for the net change in the amount of jobs. However, one cannot argue from first principles that this relationship will always be positive, especially in countries that seem to be running significant trade surpluses.

Nevertheless, on many occasions, trade restrictions, such as tariffs and import quotas, are undertaken not in the context of an elaborate and well-planned industrial policy but in order to protect the income of particular interest groups. Given the fact that trade restrictions are associated with efficiency losses, one would automatically make the case that such trade restrictions would reduce national welfare. However, there are theoretical grounds to believe that activist trade policies can in some instances, apart from protecting the income of certain segments of society, increase the welfare of a nation as a whole.

Contributing to this view involves the "Olsonian" nature of the debate of free trade. The term "Olsonian" connotes the presence of concentrated losses from trade in specific segments of the society and diffused benefits from lower consumer prices from

---

\* See Section 4.4.4 on the emergence of China and India as major economic powerhouses.

† See Section 4.4.4 on the creation of a "reserve army of labor."

‡ See Amsden (1994) for an explanation of the success of the so-called Asian tigers as being the result of promoting national champions under a cloak of protectionism.

import competition. Olson's (1982) "logic of collective action" has long been invoked by economists in order to explain seemingly irrational trade policies as a result of small concentrated groups capturing the political process. This is highly relevant for countries where the harmed interest groups can closely influence the policy-making process through their linkages to specific party interests. Organized labor was the natural base of the British Labour Party in the 1970s and 1980s, while the policies of the Tories in the late 1970s and early 1980s reflected their proximity to capital owners and City financiers.

### 4.4.2 The Effects of Trade in the Developed World

In general, the established consensus among most members of the economic profession appears to be that trade constitutes "an important stimulus to economic growth" (Todaro and Smith 2009, p. 603). Trade increases a country's consumption capacities, expands world output, and provides access to scarce resources and global markets for products, without which poor countries would not have been able to develop (ibid.).

However, although agreements such as NAFTA are generally considered by economists to have been beneficial for the United States, the population of the United States appears to be particularly divided on the issue (Warf and Kull 2002). How can Americans be that divided when NAFTA has purportedly been beneficial for the majority of the population through lower consumer prices? One answer attractive to the proponents of the mainstream view has to do with the relative visibility of NAFTA's effects. In general, job losses are more obvious and concentrated than lower prices* and are more easily attributable. Therefore, even though one might have gained personally from free trade, the adverse effects of trade liberalization through the associated job losses in sectors like manufacturing can increase insecurity in the working population and create hostility toward free trade (see Section 4.4.4).

Nevertheless, other commentators seem to disagree with this "established" view. Scott (2002) states that NAFTA was eventually harmful for the U.S. economy, costing 766,030 jobs and job opportunities in the period 1993–2002, while the total U.S. trade deficit cost approximately 3 million jobs in the period

1994–2002. Furthermore, according to Berger (2006, pp. 20–21), "More than two million jobs disappeared from the U.S. workforce between 2001 and 2004. By one calculation, a half-million of them were in high-tech industries like electronics, components, and telecoms. The layoff rate has risen, and while many of those who lose jobs get hired again fairly soon, two-thirds of the jobs they get pay less than the jobs lost."

Hence apart from the impact of trade on employment statistics, trade has also significantly affected wages. According to Scott (2002), trade's indirect effects on wages through the elimination of good job opportunities and the possibility of relocation as a threat in wage negotiations have led to a series of effects on wages:

- A 5.4 percent decrease in real production worker wages between 1978 and 2000
- Growing wage inequality since the late 1970s
- Increasing income inequality since 1979
- Flat incomes for the bottom 60 percent despite a 7.6 percent increase in working hours

Scott (2002) notes that trade explains at least 15 to 25 percent of the increase in income inequality, along with other factors, including deregulation, liberalization, and weak macroeconomic policies. Furthermore, Charles and Lehner (1998) argue that trade might actually facilitate rigidity and lack of innovation and actually contribute to a long-term decline in competitiveness.

Faux's (2007) analysis moves along similar lines, but the picture that he paints is even more bleak. Although he deems globalization to be a force that can potentially be beneficial and enhance living standards for workers around the world, he argues that it has been "tragically mismanaged," entailing an accumulation of international trade and investment agreements that are "increasingly unaccountable to any country's citizens" (ibid., p. 1). Faux's (2007) calculations are dire. According to his analysis, between 1979 and 2007, 7 million jobs were displaced in the United States because of the expansion of trade. Further, real wages have not declined. In fact, the wages of nonsupervisory employees (accounting for 80 percent of U.S. workers) increased by a marginal 4 percent; however, this increase did not remotely match the corresponding 71 percent increase in the productivity of the U.S. economy, as traditional economic theory would have us believe. Furthermore, the 4 percent increase includes the increasing participation of female workers in the workplace. In fact, among

---

* It is also not clear that the location of production abroad inures to the benefit of domestic consumers. Monopoly wholesalers or retailers could very well retain saved costs and increase profits.

working males, real hourly wages have remained at the 1973 level (ibid., p. 3; see the related discussion in Section 1.1.3.1 in Chapter 1).

The proponents of free trade underline that these costs are inflated. However, they also note that even if such costs are inflated, they should be expected to some degree, given the lack of skills of the unskilled workers of the manufacturing sector. According to mainstream economic thinking, these workers, as they obtain portable skills and become better trained, will be channeled to other productive activities. Scott (2002) seems to agree that college-educated workers, who account for 20 to 40 percent of U.S. households, constitute the second category of winners from globalization in the United States, apart from MNEs. Nevertheless, Faux (2007) does not come to the same conclusion. Americans are working longer hours and are increasingly educated. The percentage of workers with college degrees has doubled from 15 percent in 1973 to 30 percent today, while the share of high-school dropouts has fallen from 29 percent to 10 percent. Nevertheless, the U.S. economy, in this process of Schumpeterian creative destruction, does not seem to be fulfilling the "creative" part. Faux (2007) cites projections from the Bureau of Labor Statistics that conclude that by 2014, the number of occupations filled by people with college degrees will rise by only 1 percent—from 28 percent to 29 percent—while the share of jobs for which a college degree is required is projected to be only 21 percent.

However, some level of costs that emanate from increasing trade openness is to be expected even from the most fervent advocate of trade. The point is whether these costs, as accounted from the preceding analysis, are less than the projected benefits. In theory, free trade creates losers in the domestic economy in those industries that are not able to compete in the international spectrum; however, it also entails cheaper imports and products, which can increase the standard of living of the domestic population, providing lower costs are passed on to consumers.

But is this the case? Are lower prices that prevalent? Faux (2007, p. 6) again offers compelling evidence to the contrary. He notes: "Comparing the price change of domestic and imported goods... yields a savings from imports to the average American of about $36 a year. A gain, but hardly substantial enough to justify any costs." Faux (2007) does note that other authors are led to conclude that there are higher benefits; however, most of these studies seem to be based on unrealistic assumptions and simulation rather than being grounded in facts. The

reality of the benefits of free trade for the United States thus seems unclear.

### 4.4.3 The Effects of Trade in the Developing World

Although there appears to be a consensus among many economists that free trade produces net gains for developing societies, and that countries should unambiguously adopt trade-liberalization policies, reality paints a more complex picture. Rodrik (2007) cites the particularly elucidating case of two different countries, Vietnam and Haiti. Vietnam still engages in state trading, maintains import monopolies, retains quotas and tariffs (in the range of 30 to 50 percent) on imports of agricultural and industrial products, and is not a member of the WTO. On the other hand, Haiti undertook significant trade liberalization in 1994–1995, joined the WTO, diminished import tariffs to a maximum of 15 percent, and removed all quotas. The result? Vietnam experienced annual GDP growth rates in the area of 8 percent, reduced poverty, expanded trade significantly, and attracted significant foreign direct investment. On the other hand, even before the recent earthquake, Haiti stagnated and suffered from significant poverty and unemployment rates, having made little progress in integrating into the world economy.

Rodrik (2007) is right that trade should not be viewed as a goal in itself but rather as a means toward the goal of increasing economic development. As he notes, "A leadership committed to development and standing behind a coherent growth strategy counts for a lot more than trade liberalization, even when the strategy departs sharply from the enlightened view of reform" (ibid., p. 217). His view is corroborated by the facts. The cross-national evidence on the relationship between open trade policies and higher economic growth and poverty reduction has shown no systematic relationship between a country's average level of tariff and nontariff restrictions and its subsequent economic growth rate. In fact, if anything, the evidence from the 1990s suggests a positive (but statistically insignificant) relationship between tariffs and economic growth, with the only systematic relationship being that as countries get richer, they tend to liberalize trade.

Hence integration into the world economy through trade liberalization should be viewed as an outcome rather than a prerequisite of a successful growth strategy. As Stiglitz (2002) and Rodrik (2007) note, the fact that all of today's advanced countries embarked on their growth under trade restrictions and some protection should be viewed as a lesson. Finally, almost all the outstanding success stories, such as China, India, and the East Asian countries, involved partial and gradual trade and capital liberalization. A country's trade policy should be eclectic and should take into account a series of national and external variables, such as the industries that will be harmed from trade openness and the capacity of the domestic market to reallocate workers.

Although international trade has some positive effects on developing regions and can potentially help protect/enhance the environment, it is also seen to have negative environmental (OECD 1994) and social (welfare) impacts (Rees and Westra 2003). Among the main arguments against the international integration of economies are the following:

- Free trade is accompanied by environmental degradation and growing economic inequality (Borghesi and Vercelli 2003; Held and McGrew 2002).

- Free trade weakens the democratic accountability of governments through the transfer of power from people (and society in general) to global financial institutions and corporations (Korten 2001). This transfer of power is mirrored by "a corresponding shift in economic priorities from the production of goods and services to meet human needs to a wholly different agenda centered on extracting wealth from the larger society to increase the financial assets and power of the wealthiest among us."[4]

- Free trade is not proceeding in a fair and equitable manner. A main contention is that industrialized nations have pressured developing nations to eliminate their trade barriers while keeping their own intact. This has the effect of opening up the markets of developing nations to capital-intensive products from developed nations, but has prevented them from exporting their labor-intensive products, depriving them of vital export income (Stiglitz 2002).

- Free trade encourages economically rational corporations to invest capital in countries with the lowest environmental and health and safety standards. Such action reduces the cost of producing commodities and might also lead countries to specialize in those sectors where regulations are weakest (Cole 2000). Alternatively, the pressure to produce commodities at or below the price dictated by the international market creates a perverse incentive to lower health and safety and environmental standards to improve the competitiveness of national sectors (Daly 1993).

- Free trade creates a situation in which capital from developed nations is invested only in nations that offer the potential for a high rate of return. This means that it is more profitable to invest in the inefficient and polluting industries of Eastern Europe, for example, than in the less attractive markets of developing nations (Reid 1995). Hence economic "logic" is reducing the already-limited financial flows reaching developing nations.

- Free trade leads to the "spatial and temporal separation of action and impact from responsibility" (Speth 2003, p. 13). The spatial and social distance between production and consumption is widened as commodity chains grow in length and become more complex and more international, (Conca 2002; Princen 2002). Consumers lack the information and incentives to behave in a more sustainable manner even if they wished to do so as a result of this *distancing effect*. To put it another way, as trade increases and countries continue to specialize, the transaction costs (linked to externalities) become hidden by the distancing effect. Therefore, it becomes increasingly difficult for communities in different nations to communicate and agree on collective solutions to externality problems (Costanza, Cumberland, et al. 1997). Further, the growing movement of resources between nations in response to *market demands* is reducing the effectiveness of traditional local controls over resource use (Speth 2003). This loss of indigenous control can lead to the exploitation of resources as a result of unsustainable rates of extraction.

The preceding concerns have led a series of scholars to move their point of reference, asking for trade to become part of a larger development scheme. Najam and Robins (2001) note that it is in the interest of the developing world ("the South") to shift the terms of the debate from "trade and environment" to "trade and sustainable development." Furthermore, in their view (ibid., p. 68), "If sustainable development is to become the organizing focus of the international trade regime, then at some point, 'sustainable trade' will have to replace 'free trade' as the grand rationale for our efforts. For the early advocates of GATT, the ultimate and non-negotiable goal—to be reached through small steps—was to create a world in which all trade was 'free.' The new goal, equally non-negotiable at its core, must be the creation of a world where all trade is seen as a part of the larger sustainable development enterprise."

### 4.4.4 Current Structural Changes Stemming from Manufacturing and Services Dominated by China and India, and from the Consolidation of Retailing Power in the Developed Countries

Aside from economic effects accruing to an individual nation from trade—which provides new markets for exports and new opportunities to acquire cheaper and/or better imports used to promote export-bound production or domestic consumption—the structure of markets may change appreciably for the better or for the worse. Ricardo's theory of comparative advantage (see Section 3.2.6 in Chapter 3) argues that trade promotes win-win scenarios among the trading partners, while others have argued that there are also win-lose scenarios (Kaplinsky 2005; Kaplinsky and Messner 2007; Kaplinsky and Morris 2007).

In the context of win-win opportunities in international trade, Ricardo's theory of the benefits of specialization and exchange between countries (the theory of comparative advantage) depends on three crucial assumptions (Kaplinsky 2005, p. 209):

1. The existence of full employment in both exporting and importing economies

2. The mobility of capital and skilled entrepreneurship*

3. Implicitly, that income transfers must be easily made to facilitate producers moving from one economic activity to another

These assumptions may not hold in the real world. Perhaps the most succinct observations are offered by Raphael Kaplinsky and colleagues (Kaplinsky 2005; Kaplinsky and Messner 2007; Kaplinsky and Morris 2007). Found in the writings of Malthus and Marx, an alternative perspective to the clearing of labor markets is that there is a systematic tendency toward structural unemployment consisting of a "reserve army of labour" that can depress the wage rate (Kaplinsky 2005, p. 210). Thus Kaplinsky (p. 230) argues that "there is a structural excess in the global economy, not just in productive capacity, but also in the labour market." W. A. Lewis (1954) observed that "in most developing countries there was a dual economy—one segment composed of a modern sector with near-full employment, and the second comprised of a sector characterized by heavily disguised unemployment, where people undertook all kinds of work at very low (and often zero) productivity" (quoted in ibid., p. 211).

Tectonic changes in both developed and developing nations have occurred in the past ten to fifteen years that threaten global economic and financial stability. These involve not the theoretical benefits of competition brought on by international trade, but rather monopoly/oligopoly in manufacturing and services (predominantly in China and India, respectively), which, combined with monopsony in retailing (for example, Wal-Mart and Tesco), have squeezed out competition through concentration of both producers and (mostly) corporate buyers and price reductions. The result is that there are a few national winners and many national losers. On the supply side, the tendency toward a concentration of large producers is enhanced by the fact that the costs of advancing technological progress may require large markets to sustain profitability and an attractive return on investment (Kaplinsky 2005, p. 11). The easing of financial flows following the globalization of finance has largely facilitated the creation of most of the profitable large centers of production, moving world production from undercapacity to overcapacity in what Kaplinsky terms "the 'outward-inward' breath of the global economy" (ibid., p. 23). The ideology that fanned an uncritical endorsement of free trade also concentrated developed-nation currency holdings in the hands of those few nations to the extent that geopolitical stability may be threatened.

Kaplinsky (2005, p. 196) argues that the worst price squeezing (that is, the price falls) occurs in products embodying low technological content and in low-income economies and that "a significant degree of poverty and inequality are relational outcomes of globalization [arising from] excess global capacity and constrained global consumption, . . . [leading] to a race to the bottom in real incomes" (ibid., p. 197). The key relationships of falling prices involve (1) the extent to which prices of the *nation's* exports fall relative to the prices of the products it imports, (2) the extent of price falls received by *producers* relative to the prices of the inputs into their production processes, and (3) the extent of price falls received by *producers* relative to the cost reductions enabled by productivity improvements (ibid., p. 199). Productivity improvements derived from replacing labor with capital adversely affect workers, depressing wages, unless they are accompanied by sufficiently larger revenues from greater sales derived from lower prices, whatever the source. Whether serious structural unemployment in manufacturing is caused by technological displacement or by the import of labor-intensive goods, it is now acknowledged in both developed and developing countries, including China and Brazil (ibid.). Structural unemployment is also evident in services, especially those that can be outsourced, such as ICT and banking. To

---

* It has been argued that a critical (but little-noticed) assumption of Ricardo's theory of comparative advantage is that capital is *immobile* between nations (Daly 1999). If capital can move freely between nations, the idea of comparative capital advantage becomes less important because capital can move in search of absolute advantage. See the discussions in Section 4.4.1 and in Section 5.1.2.4 in Chapter 5.

the extent that a country builds up a large trade deficit, fueling a buying spree supported by credit-driven purchases, structural unemployment may be delayed and may not be currently visible. The 2008 financial crisis can be seen as a rude awakening in this regard.

China not only has greatly increased its share of manufacturing markets but also has become a very large market for the exports of other (especially Asian developing) countries (Kaplinsky 2005, p. 206). Paradoxically, the massive expansion of industrial capacity in China is destroying jobs (ibid., p. 208). It has also squeezed out many developing-country producers, especially in Latin America, the Caribbean, and sub-Saharan Africa (ibid., p. 167). Global capital has also shifted to Asia and, in particular, to China (ibid., p. 209). Kaplinsky and Messner (2007, p. 197) opine that "China is likely to become the second biggest economy in the world by 2016, and India the third largest by 2035.... The economic processes they engender are likely to radically transform regional and global economic, political, and social interactions and to have a major impact on the environment."*

Kaplinsky (2005, p. 240) concludes that "market forces alone, as the Washington Consensus proposes, will neither solve the problem of absolute poverty nor result in a more equal world. On the contrary, they are likely to exacerbate both.... Thus to achieve a different outcome requires policies to promote and sustain innovation." For further policy discussions related to technological, organizational, institutional, and social innovation, see Chapters 8 and 13 of this work.

In summary, there are two perspectives on globalization, poverty, and inequality: (1) global poverty is the result of the failure of producers and nations to engage in globalized commerce, and (2) the global economy deepens global poverty for many producers who are unable to compete effectively in a world of growing surplus capacity (Kaplinsky 2005, p. 208). Add to the latter the artificial expansion of demand by credit promotion and debt that encourages borrowing from the future that is not likely to be better

than the present, and we have a global economic disaster.

Finally, to return to the geopolitical arena, whenever a country holds a very large reserve of another country's currency, mischievous political actions may ensue, leading to interference in the other country's internal affairs, straining international relations and agreements, or even to economic subjugation and war. Globalized trade needs to be evaluated along many dimensions.

## 4.5 THE ROLE OF MULTINATIONAL ENTERPRISES IN THE INTERNATIONAL ECONOMY

A discussion of globalized commerce would be incomplete without a discussion of the role of multinational enterprises (MNEs), also referred to as multinational corporations (MNCs). The most straightforward and least technical definition is perhaps that of Gilpin (2001, p. 278), who defines the MNE as "simply, a firm of a particular nationality with partially or wholly owned subsidiaries within at least one other national economy."

### 4.5.1 MNEs and Neoclassical Economics

Gilpin (2001) offers an extensive overview of the different schools of thought with respect to the role of MNEs in the international economy. One key point he makes is that despite the central role of MNEs in the international economy, mainstream economists have chosen to focus elsewhere. Gilpin (2001) provides the reasons behind this observation. In his view, economists

- have a strong belief in the primacy of markets and not in the importance of institutions;

- believe that a firm's behavior is determined primarily by market variables, thus making its location selection of secondary importance;

- assert (through the Mundell equivalency)[†] that trade and investment constitute perfect substitutes for one another, with trade preceding investment;

- expect that production will be located where it is most efficient, in line with the theory of location and Ricardo's theory of comparative advantage; and

---

* Lee (2008) reinforces the views of Kaplinsky (2005) by arguing that the successful integration of China and India into the global economy leaves little space for other developing nations to enter and succeed. While several developing nations could successfully pursue an export-led development strategy, if many developing nations followed suit, the same success is unlikely to be realized. Foreign direct investment (FDI) flows are unlikely to be diverted from the two Asian giants now playing such a large role in the global economy. The problem is compounded by the fact that there are potential limits to the growth of consumer demand in developed countries (Lee 2008).

---

† The Mundell equivalency argues that trade in factors of production, such as labor and capital, has essentially the same effect as trade in goods. Hence exporting labor-intensive goods and importing capital-intensive goods is exactly the same as the labor-abundant country exporting labor directly for capital (Gilpin 2001).

- have chosen not to focus on MNEs because of methodological obstacles in the analysis of oligopolistic firms in imperfect markets.

The last point is a crucial one. MNEs arise in the context of market distortions. International manufacturers, such as IBM, for instance, elect to invest in many countries for reasons other than economics, such as good public relations. An interesting point that Gilpin (2001, p. 280) raises is that "some market [distortions] are created by national governments through such policies as trade protection and industrial policy; in fact, a government sometimes creates market imperfections to encourage foreign [MNEs] to invest in their economies. A notable example is the erection of trade barriers and the provisions of tax breaks to encourage FDI. Without such [distortions], a firm might find it more efficient to export its products from its home economy[*], or to license its technology to a foreign firm."

However, unlike most neoclassical economists, business economists, beginning from the 1960s, have attempted to put forward alternative theories of the MNE. Gilpin (2001) focuses on three theoretical contributions:

- Vernon's product cycle theory
- The Reading school's eclectic theory
- Porter's strategic theory.

The main idea of Vernon's product cycle theory is that every product follows a certain life cycle from innovation through maturity to decline and to final obsolescence (Gilpin 2001). According to Vernon (1971), American firms had a comparative advantage in product innovation because of the significant size of the American market on the demand side and the American superiority in R&D on the supply side. As Gilpin (2001, p. 282) notes, "During the initial phase of the product cycle, firms export new products from their home industrial base, but in time, a number of changes associated with the maturing of the product—such as standardization of production techniques—diffusion abroad of industrial know-how, and creation of significant foreign demand for the product ultimately stimulate the entry of foreign imitators into the market. To deter foreign firms from entering the market and undercutting their monopoly position, the original firms establish production facilities in other economies." Thus, according to Vernon's product cy-

cle theory, "Foreign direct investment is principally a device used by firms to preempt foreign competition and to maintain their monopoly rents." However, this theory was largely a product of the 1960s, which saw the primacy and overseas expansion of the American corporation. It did not account for a series of other variables, such as the erection of trade barriers, market proximity, falling transportation costs, and currency risks (Gilpin 2001).

The eclectic school was developed by John Dunning and carries the name of the University of Reading in the United Kingdom. The central tenet of this theory is to emphasize the role of technology as a factor in MNE development (Gilpin 2001). Gilpin (p. 284) notes that "according to [the Reading school's] eclectic theory, the unique nature and extraordinary economic success of the [MNE] are due to particular characteristics that give the [MNE] . . . important advantages over purely domestic corporations. These advantages are ownership, location, and, most importantly, internalization. . . . These oligopolistic firms usually possess some proprietary or firm-specific advantage that they want to exploit rather than lose to a rival firm; such an internal advantage may be a trademark or possession of a particular technology. Although some of the most important [MNEs] are not high-tech, it is not coincidental that many [MNEs] predominate in industries characterized by extensive and expensive research and development activities."

Porter's (1990) analysis largely departed from the analyses conducted by Vernon and by the Reading school. According to Porter, it is the firm's strategy that actually determines its structure and its location of economic activities. According to Gilpin (2001, p. 285):

Porter assumes that international business is characterized by a value chain of activities ranging from extraction to production to marketing. The individual firm must decide which and how many of these activities it wishes to pursue and in what locations around the globe. These decisions in turn depend on the overall competitive strategy of the firm. . . . The essence of strategic management is that the transnational firm has available to it more extensive options and techniques than do even the largest domestic firms. These mechanisms include not only FDI, but also strategic alliances, outsourcing component production, and licensing technologies. These corporate activities create international complexes or networks of corporate relations with the parent MNC in its home economy. Through modern information technologies and monopoly of information resources, the multinational corporation can become dominant

---

* Note, however, that this holds true only up to some level of transportation costs, because proximity to suppliers can be an important consideration.

over both its domestic and international competitors. Needless to say, such a depiction of a firm's strategy, structure, and activities has evolved far beyond that portrayed in Vernon's product cycle model or even in [the Reading school's] eclectic theory. [MNEs] have become worldwide institutions coordinating economic activities that are located in many countries.

### 4.5.2 The Centrality of Foreign Direct Investment for Development

MNEs expand outside the reality of the nation-state mainly through foreign direct investment (FDI). In general, FDI occurs when the residents of one country acquire control over, or create, a business enterprise in another country. This acquisition may involve buying enough stock in an existing enterprise to become a controlling shareholder (10 percent of ownership), taking over the enterprise outright, or building a new factory or enterprise from scratch, including the purchase of real estate (Caves, Frankel, et al. 2006).

There are two major types of FDI: (1) greenfield FDI and (2) mergers and acquisitions (M&A) FDI. Greenfield FDI refers to direct investment in new facilities or in the expansion of existing facilities, whereas M&A FDI is investment that takes the form of acquisition of existing assets. Cross-border mergers take place when resources and management of firms from different countries are assembled in order to create a new legal entity.* Cross-border acquisitions refer to the transfer of control from a local company to an MNE, with the local company becoming an affiliate or branch of the MNE.

Dunning (1993) distinguishes four distinct types of FDI on the basis of the motives of the investing firm:

- Resource-seeking (RS) investment, in which TNCs focus on the exploitation of physical resources and labor differentials

- Market-seeking (MS) investment, which usually takes place in order to penetrate new markets or defend existing markets (Georgopoulos and Preusse 2006)

- Efficiency-seeking (ES) investment, which builds on existing firm activity (RS or MS) and aims at rationalizing the firm's activities by optimizing the intrafirm division of labor (Georgopoulos and Preusse 2006) and taking advantage of economies of scale and scope and of the benefits of common ownership

- Strategic-asset-seeking (SAS) investment, which aims to augment the existing set of assets through merger and acquisition activities

The effects of FDI, as studied in the literature, vary and include productivity spillover effects, cluster formation, and innovation, as well as a positive degree of correlation between FDI and real GDP growth rates. However, it proves to be significantly difficult to measure and quantify these effects.

As mentioned, one of the most studied and frequently cited effects of FDI is the *efficiency spillovers* from MNEs to domestic firms in the host country (Barrios, Dimelis, et al. 2002). MNEs are usually characterized by the employment of a level of technology higher than that of domestic firms. Furthermore, knowledge displays some characteristics representative of those of public goods (Markusen 1995). This signifies that there is a broad scope of potential positive externalities that flow from multinationals to domestic firms. Blomstrom and Kokko (1998) identify three main channels of spillovers:

1. Movements of highly skilled staff from multinational to domestic firms

2. "Demonstration effects" through complementary production relationships between domestic and foreign firms

3. Competition between multinationals and domestic firms, which provides the firms with efficiency and productivity incentives

However, these spillover effects are not omnipresent in each economy in question and mainly depend on the sector and country under consideration. In their analysis, Blomstrom and Kokko (1998, p. 247) note that "the positive effects of foreign investment are likely to increase with the level of local capability and competition." The internalization of spillovers from multinational firms thus largely depends on the absorptive capacity of local firms. Hence only firms with the technological abilities to absorb spillovers are expected to profit from multinational operation in the context of their sectors (Barrios, Dimelis, et al. 2002). Additionally, it is crucial to define when a firm is considered to be foreign in terms of measuring spillovers. An interesting example of this can be found in the analysis of Barrios, Dimelis, et al. (ibid., p. 9), who, when estimating the effects of foreign presence in the productivity levels of the Greek market, found that "majority-held foreign firms [with more than 50 percent foreign ownership] may be more independent and hence more isolated from the host country environment, causing less technology

---

\* This constitutes what we have defined as "transnationalization" in contrast to "multinationalization."

transfer." In contrast, minority-held foreign firms (with less than 50 percent foreign ownership) are likely to have more interaction with foreign and domestic firms, increasing spillover effects.

Hence foreign ownership should not be considered merely a "relabeling" of firms but rather a "potential transformation of the economy" (Barrell and Pain 1997, p. 1778), because these technological spillovers will affect not only productivity rates but also innovation, R&D, and many other technologically critical variables.

Furthermore, governments can employ *clusters*\* both to become more successful in attracting FDI and to increase the economic value that FDI generates for their economies (Porter 1998). FDI flows seem to target existing or emerging cluster locations instead of avoiding them (Ketels 2004). Empirical evidence suggests that attracting foreign companies through the existence of clusters at a national and/ or regional level not only generates direct benefits through job creation and wage increases but also improves the quality of the location for the companies that already participate in the cluster by improving the overall cluster business environment, which will further attract foreign companies. This strategy boosts continuous FDI attraction and helps avoid short-term arbitrage opportunities that destabilize the economy.

Nevertheless, although there is consensus that inward FDI has increased the growth rates of many developing countries (Blomstrom, Lipsey, et al. 1994), less research has been conducted about the impact of FDI on the economic performance of developed countries, and specifically of those of the European Union. An interesting study of the issue conducted by the OECD (2002, p. 5) notes that "given the appropriate

host country policies and a basic level of development...FDI triggers technology spillovers, assists human capital formation, contributes to international trade integration, helps create a more competitive business environment, and enhances enterprise development." The authors conclude that all these effects contribute to higher levels of economic growth. On the whole, one can be quite confident that causality between FDI and growth rates flows in both directions, with countries that grow quickly attracting increasing volumes of FDI, and FDI leading to increasing real GDP growth rates.

### 4.5.3 MNEs: Blessing or Peril?

In Section 4.5.1, we noted that mainstream economists have mainly omitted MNEs from their analysis because of modeling difficulties and a different methodological focus. However, this has recently started to change, mainly because of advances in industrial organization and in strategic trade theory (Gilpin 2001). In this growing area in the economic literature, MNEs have increasingly been considered a means to reduce transaction costs, because vertical organization through FDI might be less costly than market transactions (ibid.).

Many critics of globalization consider the role of MNEs highly controversial, especially in the case of developing countries. Korten (2001) notes that the international integration of economies through free trade has weakened the democratic accountability of governments through a transfer of power from society to global financial institutions and corporations. Gilpin (2001, p. 286) cites Stephen Hymer's radical theories, according to which "FDI was fundamentally different from portfolio investment and could be explained as part of a firm's expansionist strategy and by its desire to control productive or other facilities in foreign countries." Hymer considered what he called "monopoly capitalism" to be driven by two fundamental laws (Gilpin 2001):

- The law of increasing firm size: as firms grow in size and scope, they should be expected to expand within and across national borders, creating a hierarchical core/periphery structure and international division of labor around the world.

- The law of uneven development: because of their large size, mobility, and power, MNEs exercise control over and exploit the world to their own advantage.

Indeed, MNEs today appear to be richer than most countries in the developing world. As Stiglitz

---

\* According to Porter (1998, pp. 215–216), "A cluster is a geographically proximate group of interconnected companies and associated institutions in a particular field, linked by commonalities and complementarities. The geographic scope of a cluster can range from a single city or state to a country or even a network of neighboring countries. Clusters take varying forms depending on their depth and sophistication, but most include end-product or service companies; suppliers of specialized inputs, components, machinery, and services; financial institutions; and firms in related industries. Clusters also often include firms in downstream industries (that is, channels or customers); producers of complementary products; specialized infrastructure providers; government and other institutions providing specialized training, education, information, research, and technical support (such as universities, think tanks, [and] vocational training providers); and standards setting agencies. Government agencies that significantly influence a cluster can be considered part of it. Finally, many clusters include trade associations and other collective private sector bodies that support cluster members."

(2006, pp. 187–188) notes, in 2004, the revenues of General Motors ($191.4 billion) surpassed the GDP of more than 148 countries, while in 2005, the revenues of Wal-Mart ($285.2 billion) surpassed the GDP of sub-Saharan Africa. As their sizes suggest, these behemoths exert significant political power. If governments attempt to significantly regulate their activities or tax them, they threaten to relocate because "there is always another country that will welcome their tax revenues, jobs, and [FDI]" (ibid., p. 188). Furthermore, on many occasions, MNEs have acted in ways of disputed legality, undermining societal priorities in their quest for lower costs and higher profits. Stiglitz (2006) cites a series of such cases, such as Nestlé's campaign to persuade third-world mothers to use infant formula instead of breast milk to feed their children, Bechtel's attempt to privatize Bolivia's water, and Monsanto's development of seeds that grew into plants that produced seeds that could not be replanted, thus forcing farmers to buy new seeds each year.

Indeed, Coffey (1996, p. 58) notes that "the international division of labor has been largely regulated by the MNE through its decisions to invest or not invest in particular countries." This assertion is debatable in the context of a series of countries, such as South Korea or Japan, for example, which permitted little equity ownership by foreign firms. However, it does point to the fact that the evolution of the international economy is closely related to the changing nature of MNEs.

However, although both of Hymer's "laws" raise important points, they seem exaggerated to some degree and disregard a series of positive effects emanating from FDI, which we discussed in Section 4.5.2. Because of increasing scrutiny of the activities of MNEs by stakeholders, they are increasingly adopting "at-home" environmental and labor practices in their foreign locations. For instance, Wallace (1996, p. 73) sees that there is "much the [MNEs] can do to contribute to sustainable patterns of industrialization in developing countries. In financial terms, direct investment in developing countries [generally] exceeds official development assistance. Investors can bring industry-specific and more general skills, and can potentially have a profound influence on development. This potential can be realized if it becomes the norm for (MNEs) to transfer knowledge and skills, with an emphasis upon environmental issues, and to engage with wider society."

Along similar lines, Stiglitz (2006, p. 188), a famous critic of present-day globalization, notes:

[MNEs] have been at the center of bringing the benefits of globalization to the developing countries, helping to raise standards of living throughout much of the world. They have enabled the goods of developing countries to reach the markets of the advanced industrial countries; modern corporations' ability to let producers know almost instantly what international consumers want has been of enormous benefit to both. Corporations have been the agents for the transfer of technology from advanced industrial countries to developing countries, helping to bridge the knowledge gap between the two. The almost $200 billion they channel each year in [FDI] to developing countries has narrowed the resource gap. Corporations have brought jobs and economic growth to the developing nations, and inexpensive goods of increasingly high quality to the developed ones, lowering the cost of living and so contributing to an era of low inflation and low interest rates.

Ultimately, Gilpin (2001, 299) argues that "both extreme positions are exaggerations. Critics exaggerate the evils of the MNEs and their role in the world economy. Although some MNEs do exploit and damage the world, the MNE as an institution is beneficial to many peoples worldwide; it is, for example, a major source of capital and technology for economic development. On the other hand, the proponents of the MNEs exaggerate their importance and overstate the internationalization of services and production. The nation-state remains the predominant actor in international economic affairs, and domestic economies are still the most important feature of the world economy."

The financial crisis of 2008 brought new attention to the dominant position of MNEs in developing countries, especially in the least developed countries (LDCs) where local firms are at a competitive disadvantage as a result of MNE's better access to advanced technologies, better technical flexibility and faster adaptive capacity to market changes, more available skilled labor and organizational capabilities and experience, operation at larger economies of scale, production sharing with their other subsidiaries, and additional features of modernization (South Centre 2010).

In spite of the mixed critiques, MNEs continue to come under great criticism for exploiting the environment and workers. Accidents such as the explosion at Bhopal, India, and the use of child labor in Asia are memorable examples. The effects of their great financial power have been recognized as being in need of oversight, and in the financial realm, codes of good practice for projects financed by MNEs have emerged to address this concern (see Chapter

12 for a fuller discussion of the Equator Principles and other vehicles for checking finance-related activities in developing countries).

Beyond the harmful effects related to their investment activities, MNEs have come under direct scrutiny by the United Nations. More specifically, questions have been raised whether corporations have human rights obligations under national and international law (Cernic 2008). A 2003 attempt by the UN to adopt the UN Norms on the Responsibilities of Transnational Corporations and Other Business Enterprises with Regard to Human Rights[5] was not successful. In an interim report by John Ruggie, a special representative of the UN secretary general on the issue of human rights and transnational corporations and other business enterprises, it was concluded that "states have a duty to protect against human rights abuses by third parties," and "evidence suggests that corporations operating in only one country, and state-owned corporations, are often worse offenders than their highly visible private sector transnational counterparts" (ibid., pp. 4–5). The final report to the UN Human Rights Council concludes that "the corporate responsibility to respect [human rights] exists independently of States' duties," recommended "due diligence," and noted the commonplace inadequacy of judicial mechanisms and remedies to address human rights abuses (Ruggie 2008, p. 1).

## 4.6 EVOLUTION OF FINANCIAL INSTITUTIONS

### 4.6.1 Bretton Woods and Its Aftermath

In the aftermath of World War II, a new system of financial architecture was created. The pillars of this system were initially put in place in 1944 during a conference in Bretton Woods, New Hampshire. The head of the State Department's delegation at Bretton Woods and subsequent secretary of state, Dean Acheson, described his participation at the 1944 conference as "being present at the creation." It was in Bretton Woods that the International Monetary Fund (IMF) and the World Bank were created in the context of a new international financial system, where "never again" would a great depression occur.

Relevant to this discussion is the notion of the Mundell-Fleming "unholy" trinity (Obstfeld and Taylor 2002): fixed exchange rates, capital mobility, and monetary independence. A country can choose to have any two of these attributes, but it cannot choose

all three.* The financial architecture of Bretton Woods constructed a world of fixed exchange rates and low capital mobility. In that era, the IMF sanctioned capital controls as a means to prevent currency crises and bank runs, which lent some level of autonomy to governments by providing more power to monetary policy (Obstfeld and Taylor 2002). Nonetheless, by the late 1960s, it was difficult to contain global capital in the confines of the nation-state.

Key countries in the Bretton Woods system, such as the United States and Germany, fearful of sluggish growth and increased inflation, respectively, proved unwilling to accept the domestic policy implications of maintaining a fixed-exchange-rate regime. Even in the pre-1970s world of low capital mobility, furious speculative attacks on the major currencies led to the collapse of fixed exchange rates. The "adjustable-peg" system of fixed exchange rates was, to a large extent, unstable. If a specific country faced economic difficulties and it started to look as if the country would consider a devaluation of its currency, speculators would start selling its currency in anticipation. This would force the central bank of the country to raise interest rates (which would worsen the slump), to devalue the currency, or to impose capital controls (Krugman 2009). After the system of fixed exchange rates was abandoned in March 1973, several major countries no longer needed the capital controls that had been put in place in order to protect their monetary policy independence. That, along with the emergence of enhanced communication technologies, made the removal of capital controls imminent.[†]

In general, we can distinguish between two broad types of capital controls. One category aims to control capital inflows, while the other aims to control capital outflows. In West Germany, the controls in place by the early 1970s were designed to discourage the acquisition of assets by foreign residents. The German government prohibited the payment of

---

\*    Fabella (2008) writes "China devalued the yuan by 40% in January 1994 and stayed with the old-fangled regime of fixed exchange-rates and capital controls to maintain an undervalued Yuan. That effectively burned portfolio investors and cooled off the then-simmering asset-price bubble. That set of policies, known otherwise as the 'East Asian model' and declared dead and buried by the braintrusts of Western banks, effectively kept the Mundell-Fleming 'Unholy Trinity' from making a beachhead and saved China from the Asian Crisis contagion."

†    See also the discussion in Section 11.5 in Chapter 11 on the limits of countries to use capital controls to restrict capital inflows, if they have signed on to certain sections of the WTO's Agreement on Trade in Services (GATS) relating to financial services.

interest from large bank deposits to nonresidents, taxed new credits by nonresidents to German banks, and prohibited nonresidents from buying German bonds (Caves, Frankel, et al. 2006). The German government was essentially trying to limit the flow of capital from the United States to Germany, which was putting upward pressure on the mark as it put downward pressure on the dollar. The other reason behind the imposition of such controls was that in the fixed-exchange-rate world of Bretton Woods, foreign capital inflow could result in the possible loss of control of the money supply, because if a large volume of foreign reserves flowed in, the central bank of the capital-receiving country might not be able to counter the effects on the money supply, which could lead to inflation.

Gallagher (2010) has advocated for an expansion of vehicles to facilitate capital controls, even for those countries that are somewhat restrained to do so (unless sanctioned by the IMF) by virtue of their signing on to sections of the General Agreement on Trade in Services that liberalize certain financial services affecting inflows of capital (see Section 11.5 in Chapter 11).

### 4.6.2 The Benefits and Perils of Increased Capital Mobility

In general, in a rapidly growing economy with a high return to domestic capital, investment can be financed more cheaply by borrowing from abroad than from domestic savings alone. This is perhaps the most significant argument for financial integration and increased capital mobility. Symmetrically, investors in wealthier countries can sometimes earn higher rates of return (for a variety of reasons) by investing in emerging markets rather than investing domestically. Arguably, this process of openness can further lead to everyone benefiting from the opportunity to diversify risks and dampen volatility.

An additional argument in favor of capital inflows is that letting foreign financial institutions into a country with an underdeveloped financial system improves the efficiency of domestic financial markets. Internationalized financial markets foster a competitive environment, making it more difficult for overregulated and potentially inefficient domestic institutions to operate as they did previously. Finally, governments face the discipline of international capital markets in the event they make substantial policy missteps in their domestic regulatory duties.

Nevertheless, recent crises underline that financial markets do not work as perfectly as economic theorists seem to predict. Practice does not corroborate the argument that investors have punished countries only when governments are following mistaken macroeconomic policies. In many cases, large capital inflows are succeeded by large capital outflows, with no significant reasons appearing in the interim that could justify such a shift (Caves, Frankel, et al. 2006). In addition, if international capital controls are removed prematurely, massive capital inflows might occur internally. For instance, liberalization in Chile resulted in a large trade deficit financed by a large increase in domestic borrowing, thus leaving the country with an excessive level of debt throughout the 1980s.

As with free trade, capital mobility has clear winners and losers. Investors are generally better off because they are offered an expanded portfolio of investment options. On the other hand, increasing options for capital reduce those of labor, making it less costly for capital to move than to comply with labor demands (Frieden 1991). Furthermore, according to Heckscher and Ohlin, increased capital mobility will benefit capital where it is abundant and hurt capital where it is scarce. It is argued that, as a rule, capital flows out of capital-rich countries, raising the return to (now-scarcer) local capital, and flows toward capital-poor countries, lowering the return to local capital there. Hence capitalists in capital-rich countries in the developed world arguably have gained from increased capital mobility, while the opposite probably holds true for capitalists in capital-poor countries.

However, despite the theoretical prediction that capital will move from more to less developed countries, empirical observation suggests the opposite. According to Raja (2008, p. 1):

> The capital-poor developing world is lately exporting more capital to developed countries than it receives. . . . In its Trade and Development Report 2008 (http://www.unctad.org/en/docs/tdr2008_en.pdf), UNCTAD said that the puzzle is all the more intriguing because many of these capital-exporting countries have been achieving higher rates of investment and growth than those that rely on the standard economic model of net capital imports. . . . The beginning of the millennium saw the shift of developing countries as a group from net capital importers to net capital exporters. Indeed, since the Asian financial crisis in 1997–1998, capital has increasingly been flowing "uphill"—from poor to rich countries. The magnitude of this new phenomenon has caused some observers to conclude that some developing countries have been creating a global savings glut. The emergence of developing countries as net capital exporters contrasts

with expectations derived from standard growth theories. These theories postulate that with open capital markets, capital will flow from rich to poor countries in order to exploit the higher expected rates of return on capital and bridge the "savings gap" in capital-scarce countries. The theories also predict that capital inflows will spur economic growth.

However, . . . these predictions are not supported by developments over the past few years. Not only is capital flowing "uphill," but net capital-exporting developing countries also tend to grow faster and invest more than those developing countries that receive net capital inflows. Thus, higher rates of investment for diversification and structural change do not always require current-account deficits or net capital inflows, as suggested by standard economic models. Indeed, many developing countries, particularly in Latin America, failed to achieve higher productive investment under the mainstream approach because the monetary and financial policies that attracted waves of capital inflows also led to high domestic financing costs and to currency appreciation. [Finally], these developments also call into question another hypothesis of standard economic theory, namely that there is a close and positive relationship between capital account liberalization and economic growth.

In a provocative essay, Rodrik and Subramanian (2008) argue:

Financial globalization has not generated increased investment or higher growth in emerging markets. (ibid., p. 18)

Countries that grow more rapidly are those that rely less and not more on foreign capital; and in turn foreign capital tends to go to countries that experience not high, but low productivity growth. (ibid., p. 2)

While some nations may be severely constrained by inadequate access to finance, others—and perhaps a majority—are constrained primarily by inadequate investment demand, due either to low social returns or to low private appropriability. (ibid., pp. 2–3)

In this case, the effect of financial liberalization is to boost consumption, not investment. If the goal of aid is to boost consumption of essential goods, like food, drugs, and shelter, that is all well and good, but financial flows are not thereby likely to boost self-reliance or transform the domestic economic system.

Furthermore, the authors observe: "There is a crucial difference between domestic and foreign finance: improvements in the former depreciate the real exchange rate [making export-oriented activities more profitable], while improvements in the latter appreciate it [placing domestic producers of tradable goods at more of a disadvantage relative

to imports of tradable goods, thus dampening domestic growth]" (Rodrik and Subramanian 2008, p. 17).

Although FDI generally involves the transfer of skills and technology, it "may or may not be accompanied by a capital inflow" (Rodrik and Subramanian 2008, p. 16). In fact, depending on the extent of constraints on expatriation of capital by MNCs, capital outflows may well occur, giving rise to the criticism that foreign investment causes money to flow from the South to the North rather than fulfilling the promise of the reverse.

A theoretical assertion similar to the one made about capital in capital-rich countries could be made for labor in capital-poor countries—that in fact, capital mobility empowers them by increasing investment in labor-intensive activities—but Frieden (1991) argues that this argument is not clear-cut. Although the Heckscher-Ohlin model might be useful with respect to identifying long-term economic trends, it might not be the best tool for analyzing the near-term distributional effects of international capital movements. Frieden (1991) identifies a different conceptual model for analyzing the winners and losers of financial integration. His model follows a sectoral approach to political economy rather than a class-based approach like that of Heckscher and Ohlin. The model predicts that in the developed world, winners (and thus supporters) of financial openness include the owners and managers of financial assets and multinational firms with internationally diversified investments. On the other hand, participants in "specific" industries, especially those tied to a particular national market, are among the losers from increased capital mobility. In broad terms, the model indeed predicts the patterns of political activity on the issues in question. In the United States, for instance, the country's financial centers and its internationally oriented nonfinancial corporations were among the major proponents of financial deregulation. On the contrary, domestic manufacturing and farm interests have either been ambivalent or even hostile (ibid.).

It is not only the outflow of capital from developing economies, lowering available capital for investment, that causes concern. High volatility of capital flows makes it difficult, if not impossible, to engage in longer-term industrial planning and investment (Gallagher 2010). Capital controls have been found to stabilize short-term volatility and give government a chance to use other policies to improve the investment picture and discourage capital outflows (Ostry, Ghosh, et al. 2010).

### 4.6.3 Toward a New Bretton Woods?

The mainstream belief in financial integration/liberalization seems to have been shaken by recent events. The 2008 financial crisis has led to an increasing number of voices demanding a more "fair" and "stable" international financial system. We have reached a point where, as Wolf (2008a) emphasizes ambitious leaders call for a new Bretton Woods. However, is a new Bretton Woods attainable? Perhaps it is, but probably not under the "fierce urgency of now." The original Bretton Woods agreement, despite having been achieved during a period when the outcome of World War II was far from certain, was a product of two years of extensive preparation. It is not clear that an agreement could actually be reached today on the exact nature of a novel financial architecture. The Europeans, through the statements of their national governments, are pushing for the creation of new global regulators for the international financial system. The Americans and the Chinese, however, despite a change in administration in the first case, should still be expected to be cautious about such a development (Rachman 2008). In addition, it is very unclear whether a country like China would accept changing its reserve accumulation policy to fit the needs of the United States or the United Kingdom.

Another point is that multilateral institutions such as the IMF, the World Bank, and the UN were the product of America's strength in 1944–1945. Gideon Rachman (2008, p. 22) suggests that "one of the reasons Bretton Woods worked was that the U.S. was clearly the most powerful country at the table, and so ultimately was able to impose its will on others, including an often-dismayed Britain." Contrary to Rachman's (2008) view that unlike the situation in 1944, the United States "lacks the power and the inclination to impose a new set of arrangements on the rest of the world," the 2008 election of the Obama administration perhaps represents a defining moment, where the realm of possibility appears significantly expanded, and the "soft power" of the United States seems augmented. However, the interim election of 2010 throws doubt on the possibility that the Obama administration can come to the table with sufficiently increased authority to forge a politically difficult agreement. This, of course, also depends on the political preferences of other advanced economies which are in flux.

For a frank and critical description of the responses of the developed countries and international financing institutions to the plight of the poor countries see Gurtner (2010), who places the G20 over the G8 in the driver's seat, with Brazil, China, India, and South Africa demanding more influence. While developing countries and NGOs are happier with the responses of the UN (World Bank) institutions—which are regarded as advocating for their situation, but also still regarded as not sufficiently democratized—they are not at all satisfied with the IMF which is regarded as having gained influence over the UN (World Bank) institutions. In recognition of the demands from developing economies for the IMF to modernize its governance system, in 2009 it committed to a shift of 5 percent or more of quota shares from over- to under-represented countries (G20 2009).* The long-term legitimacy of the IMF will likely depend on whether developing nations feel they have been given a fair voice in decision making. Interestingly, if the shift in quota shares to emerging and developing countries is closer to seven percent, it would give this group a majority share of the quotas and perhaps signal a major change in IMF governance (see Carrasco 2011). The 2008 financial crisis has provided an opening for developing nations to obtain a greater voice in formulating global economic and financial policy (ibid.). However, the extent to which their voices are heard will depend upon how willing multilateral organizations and key economic and financial entities are to fully democratizing their governance systems. There is also the question of whose interests will really be promoted by emerging economies such as China and India—those of developing or developed nations (ibid.).

What could a Bretton Woods II agreement consist of? First, one needs to approach the subject with a certain degree of humility. As the *Economist* (2008) readily points out, "International finance cannot just be 'fixed,' because the system is a tug-of-war between the global capital markets and national sovereignty." In general, the most "globalized" component of the international economy—finance—appears to be its weakest link. Some analysts have argued that the crisis we are facing is essentially the outcome of the mismatch of international financial markets and national regulation and control measures (Frieden 2006). Hence if a new comprehensive architecture were to be proposed, some version of a global financial regulator, or a global lender of last resort, would be vital.

---

* The IMF generates most of its financial resources through its quota subscriptions. Each IMF member country is assigned a quota based on its relative position in the world economy. The quota allocated to a member determines its level of financial commitment to the IMF as well as its voting power and access to IMF financing.

Today, noncoordinated national supervisors, in some cases even state based, oversee regulated financial firms, while the "shadow" financial system* is largely unregulated. International differences in regulation led to what the *Economist* (2008) calls "regulatory arbitrage." The big lesson of the crisis is that policy makers did not understand the nature of the financial system when they were engaging in extensive deregulation. Hence instead of just reregulating domestically, the new administration should propose reforms of financial structure and regulation at both the domestic and the international level, with less speculation and more real investment.

### 4.6.4 Steps toward a New Financial Architecture

It is difficult to distinguish between the purely domestic and the purely international in the policies that will need to be adopted on behalf of the United States. In fact, in a world of free trade and low or nonexistent capital controls, a domestic fiscal expansion can, among other things, increase demand for imports, which can significantly help the prospects of other economies. According to Frankel (2007), it was the 1967–1972 U.S. fiscal expansion that led to, or at least accelerated, the crash of the Bretton Woods system in 1973. If monetary policy is essentially noncoordinated, then investors and speculators can move their capital to the countries with the highest interest rates for a given level of risk. Hence a certain level of coordination, especially during times of crisis, needs to characterize both fiscal and monetary policies.

In this discussion, one needs to pay greater attention to the specifics. The world, indeed, appears to have run out of creditworthy private borrowers. Governments, through increased fiscal deficits, can play this role in the short run by replacing private-sector borrowers. However, this does not constitute a sustainable policy prescription. As Wolf (2008b, p. 3) notes, "If [current-account] surplus countries do not expand domestic demand relative to potential output, the open world economy may even break down."

The emergence of significant current-account imbalances constitutes an important variable of the crisis that needs to be taken into account in any policy prescription. In 2009, the aggregate excess of savings over investment in surplus countries was over $1.2 trillion (IMF 2010b). The countries with the highest savings were China ($297 billion), Germany ($163 billion), and Japan ($142 billion) (ibid.). These three countries have one-half of the world's savings. At the same time, the big current-account deficit countries were the United States (–$378 billion), Spain (–$81 billion), Italy (–$67 billion), France (–$51 billion), Australia (–$43 billion), Canada (–$38 billion), Greece (–$37 billion), and India (–$35 billion) (ibid.). These seven countries represent around three quarters of the world's deficits (ibid.).

The sum of net foreign lending (gross savings less domestic investment) and the government and private-sector financial balances must be zero. In the case of the United States, the counterparts of net foreign lending were mainly fiscal deficits, along with government and household deficits (Wolf 2008b). During recessions, the government deficit increases and the private-sector deficit retracts, with the existence of a housing boom making huge household deficits possible in many of the deficit countries mentioned (the United States, the United Kingdom, Spain, Australia, and others). However, at this point of crisis, with households and businesses cutting back, government deficits are expected to explode. So, as Wolf (ibid., p. 3a) underlines, "This is the endgame for the global imbalances" because deficits aimed at sustaining aggregate demand at a time of crisis will be added to the fiscal costs of rescuing bankrupt banking systems.

Sooner or later, the willingness of surplus countries to absorb government paper and the liabilities of central banks will reach a plateau. The probability of facing a crisis will be particularly elevated. For crisis to be averted, the private sector of the deficit countries will need to be able and willing to borrow, or the economy must be rebalanced with stronger external balances and smaller domestic deficits (Wolf 2008b). Given the characteristics of the current crisis, an increase in private debt seems not only unrealistic but also lethal. Hence a U.S. expansion in net exports, which took place during recent years, must continue, a scenario that is not overly realistic, given the recent dollar appreciation and the nature of the global financial downturn.

The preceding analysis makes the case that the current financial crisis is, to some extent, a by-product of increasing current-account deficits on behalf of

---

* This is a term coined by Krugman (2009, p. 158). The shadow banking system consists of non-depository banks and other financial entities (such as investment banks and hedge funds) that provide finance/credit to the business sector. In 2007, the credit provided by the traditional depository banking system (~$12 trillion) was less than that provided by market-based institutions (~$16 trillion) (Tobias and Shin 2009, p. 1). In 2008, the shadow banking system experienced a collapse in its lending activities, primarily due to the subprime mortgage crisis (ibid).

the United States. Hence this significant imbalance will need to be alleviated in some way in order to avert further global financial turmoil. Unfortunately, the probability that a country like the United States will significantly rebalance its current account does not seem particularly realistic. Hence attention needs to shift on the other side of the equation. In normal times, current-account surpluses of countries that follow mercantilist policies (for example, China, which keeps its currency artificially low through foreign-currency intervention policies) or that are structurally mercantilist (for example, Germany and Japan, which have a chronic excess of output over spending) can perhaps even be useful (Wolf 2008a). However, in times of recession and insufficient aggregate demand, these policies are perilous and contractionary.

It becomes more obvious, therefore, that surplus countries must expand domestic demand relative to potential output, or, in other words, spend more at home in order to stabilize the global economy. Global imbalances are hurting the international financial system, and it is in the interest of the surplus countries to be accommodating in their policy approach. After all, if the surplus countries do not act, they should not be surprised if the deficit countries resort to protectionist measures in order to alleviate their troubles. The expansion program announced by the Chinese government in early November 2008 is exactly in that spirit (Wolf 2008c). Hence the immediate way to deal with this challenge is to demand and coordinate a global fiscal stimulus in which the surplus countries will implement the biggest packages (ibid.).

In addition to the aforementioned remedies, the fundamental reform of additional elements that made this crisis possible is essential. Krugman (2008, p. 1) notes that "growing international capital flows set the stage for devastating currency crises in the 1990s and for a globalized financial crisis in 2008. The growth of the shadow banking system, without any corresponding extension of regulation, set the stage for latter-day bank runs on a massive scale. These runs involved frantic mouse clicks rather than frantic mobs outside locked bank doors, but they were no less devastating."

Therefore, a higher level of transparency in the financial sector, and specifically in the shadow banking sector, should be among the first steps. Transparency should be understood as the better provision of financial information in a manner similar to the requirement that corporations in the United States provide accurate public reports of their financial po-

sitions. Increased transparency has the potential to reduce the tendency of very elevated levels of capital rushing into a country under favorable financial conditions and flowing out in times of stress.

Stronger banking systems are also essential. The severity of the Asian financial crisis of the 1990s was due to the fact that the currency crisis was associated with bank runs (Krugman and Obstfeld 2003). Had the banking institutions been stronger, it is quite possible that the situation would have been milder. A stronger banking system denotes a more closely regulated banking system with increased capital requirements in order to alleviate moral hazard on behalf of the bank owners. As Gao Xiqing, president of the China Investment Corporation, underlines, "Thirty years ago, the leverage of investment banks was like 4-to-1, 5-to-1. Today it's 30-to-1. This is not just a change of numbers. It's a change of fundamental thinking" (Fallows 2008, p. 27). Since the 1930s, commercial banks in the United States have been required to possess adequate capital, hold reserves of liquid assets that can be quickly converted into cash, and limit the types of investments they make, all in return for federal guarantees in case of a crisis (Krugman 2008). Comparable regulation will need to be put in place for the shadow banking system as well.

This point is also made by Soros (2008), who makes the case that variable margin requirements and minimal capital requirements that are meant to control the amount of leverage market participants can employ should also be instituted. He notes, "Central banks even used to issue guidance to banks about how they should allocate loans to specific sectors of the economy. Such directives may be preferable to the blunt instruments of monetary policy in combating irrational exuberance in particular sectors, such as information technology or real estate" (ibid., p. 2). However, in order to employ such requirements, financial engineering should also be regulated,* and new products should be registered and approved by the appropriate authorities before they can be used.

Finally, enhanced credit lines that nations could draw from in the event of a credit crisis, adding to their foreign-exchange reserves, would also help moderate the likelihood of having a credit crisis, along with diminishing its potential effects in case such a crisis becomes unavoidable.

Returning to a world of low capital mobility neither constitutes a political reality nor is a develop-

---

*      Financial engineering refers to the creation of new financial instruments, such as derivatives.

ment that nations should seek. The most realistic and effective option would be the adoption of coordinated policies that would modify the composition of capital inflows rather than completely discouraging them. In general, the higher the reliance on foreign-currency borrowing that is short term or intermediated through banks, the higher the probability of having a crisis, because short-term flows are prone to moral hazard and asset mismatch (Krugman and Obstfeld 2003). On the other hand, policies that would seek to shift the composition of capital inflows, instead of affecting their total level, would be significantly beneficial. These policies would include taxes or restrictions on short-term inflows, along with a set of measures that would create incentives for foreign direct investment and longer maturities.

A success story in this regard is Chile. Chile imposed a tax on inflows in 1991. This tax took the form of a requirement that a percentage of any foreign borrowing be left in a non-interest-bearing deposit maintained at the central bank for up to one year. Additionally, a requirement was put in place that all FDI must remain in the country for at least one year. These controls were successful in changing the composition of the capital inflows to Chile in the 1990s in the direction of longer-term maturities while having a minimal effect on the total magnitude of capital inflows (Edwards 2000). Hence countries should aim for increased foreign direct investment and long-term inflows relative to debt and portfolio capital inflows. Nevertheless, if such a policy is implemented on a country-by-country basis, this will do little to avert a future crisis—it will only better protect the set of countries that adopt such measures, and only up to a certain degree. Policy coordination again appears to be at the epicenter.

Another possibility that should be explored is the adoption of a measure similar to what is now called the "Tobin tax." The Tobin tax, which was proposed by the late Nobel laureate James Tobin, essentially entailed a very low tax imposed on each individual foreign currency transaction* This measure would have two fundamental effects: first, it would reduce currency speculation by "throwing sand in the wheels" of the financial system and perhaps make it easier for governments to pursue their own monetary and fiscal policies without excessive concern about the exchange rate; second, it would also raise significant amounts of revenue, which could be used for activities such as financing development assistance or alleviating the debt of the developing world (Wolf 2004). Another use of the tax revenue could be to provide insurance in the form of, for example, a resolution fund that could be drawn upon in the time of a future financial crisis (IMF 2010a). Whether a form of Tobin Tax would indeed be beneficial is still debated (Crouse 2009). Economists such as Martin Wolf think that it would actually be a bad idea because, in his view, the tax would not prevent big jumps in exchange rates and, by reducing hedging activity, might eventually increase volatility (Wolf 2004). Others, such as investor George Soros, do not share this view and believe that some variation of tax would actually be significantly beneficial (Soros 2001). In any case, "throwing sand in the wheels" is exactly one of the things that the financial system seems to need right now, so any measure that proposes to do so should be thoroughly examined.

## 4.7 NOTES

1. Emory University, The Globalization Website, *Globalization Theories*, www.emory.edu/SOC/globalization/theories.html (accessed May 17, 2010).

2. WTO, www.wto.org/english/docs_e/legal_e/legal_e.htm #GATT94 (accessed May 11, 2010).

3. See Deere and Esty (2002), Hufbauer and Goodrich (2004), and Hufbauer and Schott (2007).

4. People-Centered Development Forum, *History*, www.pcdf.org/About_PCDF/history.htm (accessed May 17, 2010).

5. U.N. Doc. E/CN.4/Sub.2/2003/12/Rev.2 (2003).

## 4.8 ADDITIONAL READINGS

Kaplinsky, R. (2005). *Globalization, Poverty, and Inequality: Between a Rock and a Hard Place*. Cambridge, Polity Press.

Rodrik, Dani (2007). *Globalization for Whom? One Economics: Many Recipes*. Princeton, NJ, Princeton University Press: 237–255.

---

* In August 2009, the President of the British Financial Services Authority, Adair Turner proposed to the G20 the introduction of a financial transactions tax that was not limited to *foreign* financial transactions. It was not seriously considered (cited in Gurtner 2010, paragraph 75). However, a year later, sixty nations proposed a tax on international currency transactions during the UN MDG Summit (September 20–22, 2010) (The Leading Group on Innovative Financing for Development, www.leadinggroup.org, accessed January 8, 2011). While the merits and structure of a financial transactions tax (FTT) continues to be debated by the international community, the idea is gaining traction within the EU where the European Commission has supported the idea of a financial transactions and a financial activities tax (Europa, Commission Outlines Vision for Taxing the Financial Sector, IP/10/1298, Brussels, October 7, 2010). Some argue, however, that an international FTT system is necessary since a regional system would be inefficient and may force trading outside of the covered area (Crouse 2009; UN Advisory Group on Finance 2010).

## 4.9 REFERENCES

Amsden, A. H. (1994). "Why Isn't the Whole World Experimenting with the East Asian Model to Develop? Review of 'The East Asian Miracle'." *World Development* **22**(4): 627–633.

Barrell, R., and N. Pain (1997). "Foreign Direct Investment, Technological Change and Economic Growth within Europe." *Economic Journal* **107**: 1770–1786.

Barrios, S., S. Dimelis, et al. (2002). Efficiency Spillovers from Foreign Direct Investment in the EU Periphery: A Comparative Study of Greece, Ireland and Spain. FEDEA Discussion Paper 2002-02.

Benton, T., and M. Redclift (1994). Introduction. *Social Theory and the Global Environment*. M. Redclift and T. Benton (Eds.) London, Routledge: 1–27.

Berger, S. (2006). *How We Compete: What Companies around the World Are Doing to Make It in Today's Global Economy*. Cambridge, MA, MIT Press.

Bhagwati, J. (1993). "The Case for Free Trade." *Scientific American* **269**(5): 42–49.

Blomstrom, M., and A. Kokko (1998). "Multinational Corporations and Spillovers." *Journal of Economic Surveys* **12**(3): 247–277. Available at http://onlinelibrary.wiley.com/doi/10.1111/1467-6419.00056/pdf (accessed January 17, 2011).

Blomstrom, M., R. E. Lipsey, et al. (1994). What Explains the Growth of Developing Countries? *Convergence of Productivity: Cross-National Studies and Historical Evidence*. W. J. Baumol, R. R. Nelson, and E. N. Wolff. New York, Oxford University Press.

Bordo, M. D., B. Eichengreen, et al. (1999). Is Globalization Today Really Different than Globalization a Hundred Years Ago? NBER Working Paper 7195. Cambridge, MA, National Bureau of Economic Research.

Borghesi, S., and A. Vercelli (2003). "Sustainable Globalisation." *Ecological Economics* **44**: 77–89.

Carrasco, E. R. (2011). An Opening for Voice in the Global Economic Order: The Global Financial Crisis and Emerging Economies. University of Iowa Legal Studies Research Paper 11-05. Available at http://papers.ssrn.com/sol3/papers.cfm?abstract_id=1754690# (accessed March 3, 2011).

Caves, R., J. Frankel, et al. (2006). *World Trade and Payments*. Boston, Addison Wesley Longman.

Cernic, J. L. (2008). Corporate Responsibility for Human Rights: A Critical Analysis of the OECD Guidelines for Multinational Enterprises. Libertas Working Paper 1/2008. Ljubljana, Slovenia, Pravni Institute for European, Constitutional International Law and Law of Economics.

Charles, T., and F. Lehner (1998). "Competitiveness and Employment: A Strategic Dilemma for Economic Policy." *Competition and Change* **3**(1/2): 207–236.

Clegg, J. (1996). The Development of Multinational Enterprises. *The Global Economy in Transition*. P. W. Daniels and W. F. Lever. London, Addison Wesley Longman: 103–134.

Coffey, W. J. (1996). The "Newer" International Division of Labour. *The Global Economy in Transition*. P. W. Daniels and W. F. Lever. London, Addison Wesley Longman: 40–61.

Cole, M. A. (2000). *Trade Liberalisation, Economic Growth and the Environment*. Cheltenham, Edward Elgar.

Conca, K. (2002). Consumption and Environment in a Global Economy. *Confronting Consumption*. T. Princen, M. Maniates, and K. Conca. Cambridge, MA, MIT Press: 133–153.

Costanza, R., J. Cumberland, et al. (1997). *An Introduction to Ecological Economics*. Boca Raton, FL, St. Lucie Press.

Crouse, E. C. (2009). Look! Up in the Sky! It's a Bird . . . It's a Plane . . . It's the Tobin Tax! Is a Global Financial Transactions Tax the World's Next Economic Superhero? Available at SSRN: http://ssrn.com/abstract=1649572 (accessed Janruary 8, 2011).

Daly, H. E. (1993). "The Perils of Free Trade." *Scientific American* **269**(5): 50–54.

Daly, H. E. (1999). "Globalization versus Internationalisation—Some Implications." *Ecological Economics* **31**: 31–37.

Deere, C., and D. C. Esty (2002). *Greening the Americas: NAFTA's Lesson for Hemispheric Trade*. Cambridge, MA, MIT Press.

Dicken, P. (1994). "The Roepke Lecture in Economic Geography. Global-Local Tensions: Firms and States in the Global Space-Economy." *Economic Geography* **70**(2): 101–128.

Driesen, M. (2001). "What Is Free Trade? The Real Issue Lurking behind the Trade and Environment Debate." *Virginia Journal of International Law* **41**(Winter): 279–369.

Dunning, J. (1993). *Multinational Enterprises and the Global Economy*. Reading, MA, Addison-Wesley.

Economic Commission for Latin America and the Caribbean (ECLAC) (2002). *Globalization and Development*. Santiago, United Nations.

Economist (2008). "Redesigning Global Finance." *Economist*, November 15.

Edwards, S. (2000). *Capital Flows and the Emerging Economies*. Chicago, University of Chicago Press.

Fabella, R. (2008). The Peso Appreciation and the Sustainability of Philippine Growth: Need We Worry? Discussion Paper 0803, Manila, the University of the Philippines. Available at www.econ.upd.edu.ph/respub/dp/pdf/DP2008-03.pdf (accessed January 17, 2011).

Fallows, J. (2008). "Be Nice to the Countries That Lend You Money: Interview of Gao Xiqing." *Atlantic Monthly*, December, p. 27. Available at http://bassimalim.com/pictures/pdf/s_s_cfc9c96d-d742-46df-8c8b-1c1260891904.pdf (accessed February 13, 2011).

Faux, J. (2007). Globalization That Works for Working Americans. Briefing Paper 179. Washington, DC, Economic Policy Institute.

Frankel, J. (2007). "Responding to Crises: Federal Reserve Policy in the Face of Crises." *Cato Journal* **27**(2): 165–178.

Frieden, J. (1991). "Invested Interests: The Politics of National Economic Policies in a World of Global Finance." *International Organization* **45**(4): 425–451.

Frieden, J. (2006). *Global Capitalism: Its Fall and Rise in the Twentieth Century*. New York, W. W. Norton.

G20 (2009). *Leaders' Statement: The Pittsburgh Summit.* The Pittsburg Summit, September 24–25, Pittsburg. Available at www.pittsburghsummit.gov/mediacenter/129639.htm (accessed March 5, 2011).

Gallagher, K. P. (2010). Policy Space to Prevent and Mitigate Financial Crises in Trade and Investment Agreements, G-24 Discussion Paper Series 58, May 2010. Intergovernmental Group of Twenty-four, United Nations Conference on Trade and Development.

Georgopoulos, A., and H. Preusse (2006). "European Integration and the Dynamic Process of Investments and Divestments of Foreign TNCs in Greece." *European Business Review* **18**(1): 50–59.

Gilpin, R. (2001). *Global Political Economy: Understanding the International Economic Order.* Princeton, NJ, Princeton University Press.

Gordon, R. (1995). Globalization, New Production Systems, and the Spatial Division of Labor. *The New Division of Labor: Emerging Forms of Work Organization in International Perspective.* W. Littek and C. Tony. New York, Walter de Gruyter: 161–207.

Greider, W. (1997). *One World, Ready or Not: The Manic Logic of Global Capitalism.* New York, Simon and Schuster.

Gurtner, B. (2010). The Financial and Economic Crisis and Developing Countries. International Policy Development Series. Available at http://poldev.revues.org/144 (accessed December 21, 2010).

Hart, S., and M. B. Milstein (1999). "Global Sustainability and the Creative Destruction of Industries." *Sloan Management Review* **41**(1): 23–33.

Held, D., and A. McGrew, Eds. (2002). *The Global Transformations Reader: An Introduction to the Globalization Debate.* Malden, MA, Polity Press.

Hirst, P., and G. Thompson (2002). *Globalization in Question*, 2nd ed. Cambridge, Polity Press.

Hufbauer, G. C., and B. Goodrich (2004). *Free Trade Agreements: US Strategies and Priorities.* Washington, DC, Peterson Institute.

Hufbauer, G. C. and J. Schott, J. (2007). "NAFTA Revisited." *Policy Options*: 83–88.

International Monetary Fund (IMF) (2010a). A Fair and Substantial Contribution by the Financial Sector. Final Report for the G-20. Washington, DC, International Monetary Fund.

IMF (2010b). World Economic Outlook (WEO) Database. Washington, DC, IMF. Available at www.imf.org/external/pubs/ft/weo/2010/02/weodata/index.aspx (accessed February 12, 2011).

Judt, T. (2005). "Europe vs. America." *New York Review of Books* **52**(2): 37–41.

Kaplinsky, R. (2005). *Globalization, Poverty, and Inequality: Between a Rock and a Hard Place.* Cambridge, Polity Press.

Kaplinsky, R., and D. Messner (2007). "Introduction: The Impact of Asian Drivers on the Developing World." *World Development* **36**(2): 197–209.

Kaplinsky, R., and M. Morris (2007). "Do the Asian Drivers Undermine Export-Oriented Industrialization in SSA [Sub-Saharan Africa]?" *World Development* **36**(2): 254–273.

Ketels, C. (2004). Interview. *FDI Magazine*, June 2.

Kleinknecht, A., and J. ter Wengel (1998). "The Myth of Economic Globalisation." *Cambridge Journal of Economics* **22**: 637–647.

Korten, D. C. (2001). *When Corporations Rule the World.* San Francisco, Berrett-Koehler Publishers.

Krugman, P. (2008). "What to Do?" *The New York Review of Books* **55**(20): 1–2 (electronic version). Available at www.nybooks.com/articles/archives/2008/dec/18/what-to-do/ (accessed February 13, 2011).

Krugman, P. (2009). *The Return of Depression Economics and the Crisis of 2008.* New York, W. W. Norton.

Krugman, P., and M. Obstfeld (2003). *International Economics: Theory and Policy.* Boston, Addison-Wesley, World Student Series. Available at www.scribd.com/doc/7258029/Krugman-and-Obstfeld-International-Economics-Theory-and-Policy (accessed February 13, 2011).

Lall, S. (2002). The Employment Impact of Globalisation in Developing Countries. QEH Working Paper Series. Geneva, International Policy Group (IPG) unit of the International Labour Office (ILO).

Lee, E. (1996). "Globalization and Employment: Is the Anxiety Justified?" *International Labour Review* **135**(5): 485–497.

Lee, E. (2008). Harnessing Globalization for Development: Opportunities and Obstacles. Geneva, International Institute for Labour Studies, International Labour Organization.

Lewis, W. A. (1954). Economic Development with Unlimited Supplies of Labour. *The Economics of Underdevelopment (1958).* A. N. Agarwala and S. P. Singh. Oxford, Oxford University Press.

London, T., and S. L. Hart (2004). "Reinventing Strategies for Emerging Markets: Beyond the Transnational Model." *Journal of International Business Studies* **35**: 350–370.

Lopatin, J. (2004). Environmental Justice Case Study: Union Carbide Gas Release in Bhopal, India. Available at www.umich.edu/%7Esnre492/lopatin.html (accessed April 8, 2006).

Markusen, J. R. (1995). "The Boundaries of Multinational Enterprises and the Theory of International Trade." *Journal of Economic Perspectives* **9**: 169–189.

Marshall, D. D. (1996). "National Development and the Globalisation Discourse: Confronting 'Imperative' and 'Convergence' Notions." *Third World Quarterly* **17**(5): 875–901.

Morris, D. (2001). *Free Trade: The Great Destroyer. The Case against the Global Economy: And for a Turn towards the Local.* J. Mander and E. Goldsmith. London, Earthscan: 115–124.

Mowery, D. C., and N. Rosenberg (1989). *Technology and the Pursuit of Economic Growth.* Cambridge, Cambridge University Press.

Muradain, R. (2004). Economic Globalisation and the Environment. *Internet Encyclopaedia of Ecological Economics.* International Society for Ecological Economics.

Najam, A., and N. Robins (2001). "Seizing the Future: The South, Sustainable Development and International Trade." *International Affairs* **77**: 49–67.

Obstfeld, M., and A. Taylor (2002). Globalization and Capital Markets. NBER Working Paper 8846. Cambridge, MA, National Bureau of Economic Research.

Olson, M. (1982). *The Rise and Decline of Nations: Economic Growth, Stagflation, and Social Rigidities.* New Haven, CT, Yale University Press.

Organisation for Economic Co-operation and Development (OECD) (1994). *The Environmental Effects of Trade.* Paris, OECD.

OECD (1997). *Economic Globalization and the Environment.* Paris, OECD.

OECD (2002). *Foreign Direct Investment for Development: Maximizing Benefits, Minimizing Costs.* Committee on International Investments and International Enterprises (CIME). Paris, OECD. Available at www.oecd.org/dataoecd/47/51/1959815.pdf (accessed February 13, 2011).

Ostry, J. D., A. R. Ghosh, et al. (2010). Capital Inflows: The Role of Controls. IMF Staff Position Note, SPN/10/04. Washington, DC, International Monetary Fund.

Pierrakakis, Kyriakos (2009). The Sustainable Growth Paradigm: Implications for Technology and Policy. Masters thesis, Technology and Policy Program. Cambridge, MA, MIT.

Porter, M. E. (1986). Competition in Global Industries: A Conceptual Framework. *Competition in Global Industries.* M. E. Porter. Cambridge, MA, Harvard Business School Press: 15–60.

Porter, M. E. (1990). *The Competitive Advantage of Nations.* New York, Free Press.

Porter, M. E. (1998). *On Competition.* Boston, Harvard Business School Press.

Prahalad, C. K., and S. L. Hart (2002). "The Fortune at the Bottom of the Pyramid." *Strategy + Business* (26): 2–14.

Princen, T. (2002). Distancing: Consumption and the Severing of Feedback. *Confronting Consumption.* T. Princen, M. Maniates, and K. Conca. Cambridge, MA, MIT Press: 103–131.

Rachman, G. (2008). "The Bretton Woods Sequel Will Flop." *Financial TimesI* 19(November 11): 22.

Raja, K. (2008). "The Paradox of Capital Flows from South to North." The second part of a two-part article on the Trade and Development Report 2008. See United Nations Conference on Trade and the Environment, Trade and Development Report, 2008: Commodity Prices, Capital Flows and the Financing of Investment. Available at www.unctad.org/en/docs/tdr2008_en.pdf (accessed February 13, 2011).

Rees, W. E., and L. Westra (2003). When Consumption Does Violence: Can There Be Sustainability and Environmental Justice in a Resource-Limited World? *Just Sustainabilities: Development in an Unequal World.* J. Agyeman, R. D. Bullard, and B. Evans. Cambridge, MA, MIT Press: 99–124.

Reid, D. (1995). *Sustainable Development: An Introductory Guide.* London, Earthscan.

Rodrik, D. (2007). *One Economics, Many Recipes: Globalization, Institutions, and Economic Growth.* Princeton, NJ, Princeton University Press.

Rodrik, D., and A. Subramanian (2008). Why Did Financial Globalization Disappoint? Unpublished manuscript, Cambridge, MA, Harvard University.

Ruggie, J. (2008). Promotion and Protection of All Human Rights, Civil, Political, Economic, Social and Cultural Rights, Including the Right to Development: Protect, Respect and Remedy; a Framework for Business and Human Rights. Report of the Special Representative of the Secretary-General on the issue of human rights and transnational corporations and other business enterprises. New York, UN Human Rights Council.

Saha, S. K. (2002). Theorising Globalisation and Sustainable Development. *Globalisation and Sustainable Development in Latin America: Perspectives on the New Economic Order.* S. K. Saha and D. Parker (Eds.). Cheltenham, Edward Elgar: 13–50.

Schmidheiny, S. (1992). *Changing Course: A Global Business Perspective on Development and the Environment.* Cambridge, MA, MIT Press.

Scott, R. (2002). "Globalization and Employment" Paper presented at the MIT Symposium on Exploring the Many Dimensions of Sustainable Development, Cambridge, MA, MIT.

Soros, G. (1997). "The Capitalist Threat." *Atlantic Monthly* **279**(2): 45–58.

Soros, G. (2001). Keynote Address, Asia Society Hong Kong Center, 11th Annual Dinner.

Soros, G. (2002). *George Soros on Globalization.* New York, Public Affairs.

Soros, G. (2008). "The Crisis and What to Do about It." *New York Review of Books* **55**(19): 1–4 (electronic version). Available at www.nybooks.com/articles/archives/2008/dec/04/the-crisis-what-to-do-about-it/ (accessed February 13, 2011).

South Centre (2010). The Impact of the Global Economic Crisis on the Industrial Development of the Least Developed Countries. Research Paper 28, May. Available at http://citeseerx.ist.psu.edu/viewdoc/download?doi=10.1.1.168.3265&rep=rep1&type=pdf (accessed December 21, 2010).

Speth, J. G. (2003). Two Perspectives on Globalization and the Environment. *Worlds Apart: Globalization and the Environment.* J. G. Speth. Washington, DC, Island Press: 1–18.

Stiglitz, J. (2002). *Globalization and Its Discontents.* New York, W. W. Norton.

Stiglitz, J. (2006). *Making Globalization Work.* New York, W. W. Norton.

Streeten, P. (2001). *Globalisation: Threat or Opportunity?* Handelshojskolens Forlag, Copenhagen, Copenhagen Business School Press.

Tobias, A. and H. S. Shin (2009). The Shadow Banking System: Implications for Financial Regulation. Staff Report 382. New York, Federal Reserve Bank of New York.

Todaro, M. P., and S. C. Smith (2009). *Economic Development.* 10th ed. Boston, Addison-Wesley.

United Nations Advisory Group on Finance (2010). Work Stream 5 on Financial Transaction Tax (FTT). New York, UN Advisory Group on Finance.

United Nations Economic and Social Council (ECOSOC) (2003). Norms on the Responsibilities of Transnational Corporations and Other Business Enterprises with Regard to Human Rights. Doc. E/CN.4/Sub.2/2003/12/Rev.2. Geneva, Office of the United Nations High Commissioner for Human Rights, United Nations. Available

at www.unhchr.ch/huridocda/huridoca.nsf/%28Symbol
%29/E.CN.4.Sub.2.2003.12.Rev.2.En (accessed February 31, 2011).

Vernon, R. (1971). *Sovereignty at Bay*. New York, Basic Books.

Voisey, H., and T. O'Riordan (2001). Globalization and Localization. *Globalism, Localism and Identity*. T. O'Riordan. London, Earthscan: 25–42.

Wallace, David. (1996) *Sustainable Industrialization*. London, Earthscan Publications/Royal Institute of International Affairs.

Warf, P., and S. Kull (2002). Tepid Traders: US Public Attitudes on NAFTA and Free Trade Expansion. *NAFTA in the New Millennium*. E. J. Chambers and P. H. Smith. Edmonton, University of Alberta Press: 214–238.

Whitford, J. (2006). *The New Old Economy: Networks, Institutions, and the Organizational Transformation of American Manufacturing*. Oxford, Oxford University Press.

Wolf, M. (2004). *In Defense of Globalization*. New Haven, CT, Yale Nota Bene Books.

Wolf, M. (2008a). *Fixing Global Finance*. Baltimore, Johns Hopkins University Press.

Wolf, M. (2008b). "Global Imbalances Threaten the Survival of Liberal Trade." *Financial Times*, December 2, p. 3.

Wolf, M. (2008c). "Obama's Economic Challenges." *Financial Times*, November 11.

World Commission on the Social Dimension of Globalization (WCSDG) (2004). *A Fair Globalization: Creating Opportunities for All*. Geneva, ILO Publications.

# 5

# Globalization and Sustainability

In previous chapters, we have introduced three dimensions of sustainability—the economy, work, and the environment—that we argue are continually influenced by the dynamic forces of both technological change and globalization. What has so far been avoided is putting the pieces together—that is, attempting to articulate the effects of both technological innovation and important trends in the international economy on national economies, work, and the environment. This chapter focuses on "globalization" and its impact on sustainability. Part III, which consists of Chapters 6, 7, and 8, takes a detailed look at the impact of technological change on sustainability. Chapter 6 articulates the theories behind technological innovation, Chapter 7 explores technological change from the perspective of the business firm, and Chapter 8 considers the role of government in promoting technological change for sustainability.

For this chapter, combining the terms "globalization" and "sustainability"—two of the most overused, overly glib, and underdefined neologisms currently afflicting the popular and academic environmental, labor, and political economy literatures—presents certain inherent hazards to the integrity of scholarship. We have attempted to avoid the pitfalls of vagueness and fuzzy thinking in discussing "globalization and sustainability" by prefacing this chapter with a systematic survey of the issues and clear statements of what aspects of "sustainability" we are and are not addressing. Further, we have tried to avoid the tempting but problematic approach of formulating narrow, analytically convenient (but conceptually deficient) definitions of either "sustainability" or "globalization." Overly simple definitions lead to oversimplified discussion, especially when a large part of the debate concerns definitional and conceptual issues.

Before we consider the impacts of globalization on sustainability, it is useful to restate the important models and perspectives that structure our approach to sustainable development.

We argue that a *technological perspective* can make a particular contribution to three aspects of the sustainability debate.

- Technology is the medium through which an economy (the production of goods and services that satisfy needs and wants) interacts with the environment. The scale, mix, and management of the technologies of production within an economy are significant determinants of anthropogenic environmental change.

- Technology is the medium through which labor and capital are combined in production. Technology is thus an important determinant of the nature of *work* (the provision of employment, the conditions under which individuals earn their livelihoods, and the distribution of remuneration).

- Competitiveness*—in the long run, equivalent to an economy's ability to deliver an adequate level of material well-being to its citizens—is substantially dependent on technology. Achieving and maintaining competitiveness (or, in a developing-economy context, succeeding at economic development) are, in an important sense, processes of technological change within the economy as a whole and within particular industries and firms.

More generally, we have argued that a sustainable society can be characterized by at least the following:

- *Economy*—The economy provides goods and services adequate to satisfy the basic material needs of all members of society and provides abundant and equitable opportunities for the realization of human potential.

- *Work*—Livelihoods are secure and available that provide satisfying engagement in work and equitable reward for labor, permit the maintenance of a decent standard of living, and are conducted in a safe working environment.

- *Environment*—Long-run flows of environmental services are provided at a level sufficient to maintain a stable ecosystem and to support human health and welfare.

---

* Competitiveness is not to be confused with the term "competition." In one sense, "competitiveness" is an unfortunate word to describe economic goals because it suggests winners and losers among nations. The EU's Europe 2020 Strategy (see Section 1.5) unfortunately is couched in terms of enhancing the EU's competitive position vis-à-vis other trading regimes while attempting to engage in sustainable development. For reasons that will become apparent, this may be an unrealistic expectation.

We contend that to move toward these goals on a worldwide basis, sustainability policy must be made in a dynamic environment in which economic linkages between nations are increasingly deep and pervasive, and changes in technology and these economic linkages are becoming more rapid and interconnected. The implication of attempting to pursue sustainable development in such an environment is the challenge to which we now turn.

The structure of this chapter follows Figure 5.1 that was first introduced as Figure 0.2 in the Overview. The first three sections of the chapter move systematically through interactions that occur between *the economy and the environment* (Sector II on Figure 5.1; Section 5.1), between *the economy and work* (Sector IV on Figure 5.1; Section 5.2), and between *work and the environment* (Sector VI on Figure 5.1; Section 5.3). In each section, a version of Figure 5.1 is provided in which the relevant issues that will be discussed are highlighted. Note that to the extent possible, we exclude the analysis of policy responses and options, as well as a discussion of constraints on national policy options. Section 5.4 concludes the chapter with a discussion of the impacts of globalization on governance.

## 5.1 EFFECTS OF GLOBALIZATION ON ECONOMY/ENVIRONMENT INTERACTIONS: SECTOR II

In this section, we analyze Sector II of Figure 5.2. (In Figure 5.2, and in subsequent versions of Figure 5.1, the focus of each section is presented in boldface text). Sector II represents the interactions between the economy and the environment in a globalized and rapidly changing world. Thus the following subsections will attempt to answer the following questions:

- How does globalization affect the environment?

- What is the effect of globalization on environmental regulation?

- How does environmental, health, and safety regulation affect the economy?

The first question addresses direct environmental impacts through changes in economic and industrial activity. The second question addresses instrumental impacts operating through the legal and political system. The third question addresses impacts in the opposite direction—the effects of regulation on economic activity.

As introduced in Chapter 1 (Section 1.4) and developed in Chapter 2, the environmental consequences

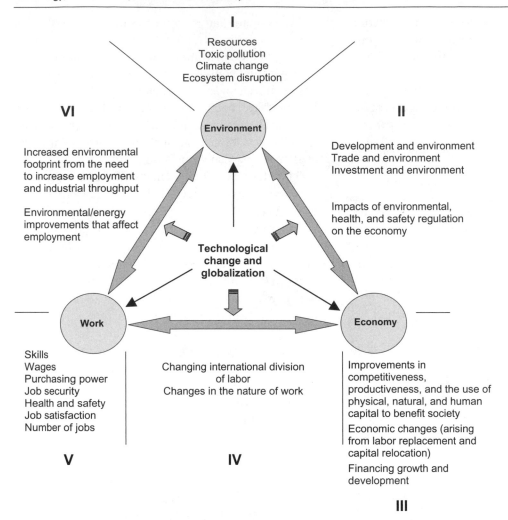

**I**

Resources
Toxic pollution
Climate change
Ecosystem disruption

**VI**

**Environment**

**II**

Increased environmental
footprint from the need
to increase employment
and industrial throughput

Environmental/energy
improvements that affect
employment

Development and environment
Trade and environment
Investment and environment

Impacts of environmental,
health, and safety regulation
on the economy

**Technological
change and
globalization**

**Work**

**Economy**

Skills
Wages
Purchasing power
Job security
Health and safety
Job satisfaction
Number of jobs

Changing international division
of labor
Changes in the nature of work

Improvements in
competitiveness,
productiveness, and the use of
physical, natural, and human
capital to benefit society

Economic changes (arising
from labor replacement and
capital relocation)

Financing growth and
development

**V**

**IV**

**III**

FIGURE 5.1: TECHNOLOGICAL CHANGE AND GLOBALIZATION AS DRIVERS OF CHANGE WITHIN AND
BETWEEN THREE OPERATIONALLY-IMPORTANT DIMENSIONS OF SUSTAINABILITY

that underlie the concern for sustainable development (Sector I in Figure 5.1) incorporate what have been identified as four different environmental concerns: (1) the disruption of ecosystems and the loss of biological diversity (which relates to environmental degradation and the loss of wildlife and fauna) and the indirect effects these have on human health and well-being; (2) resource depletion (from the use of finite stocks of material resources and energy); (3) toxic pollution (and its impact on human health and other species); and (4) global climate change (the impacts of global air warming, climate disruption, and the rise of the sea level). Therefore, throughout the following subsections, we will focus on understanding the interactions between the economy and these four environmental concerns in a globalized world.

Three avenues of impacts on the environment (identified in Sector II) will be considered successively in assessing the effects of globalization on the environment: *development (industrialization) and*

*the environment* (Section 5.1.1.), *trade and the environment* (Section 5.1.2), and *investment and the environment* (Section 5.1.3). Because these aspects can be considered essential contributors to more globalization—and to loss of control over the national economy—they form the basic structure of this section.

Section 5.1.1, on development and the environment, focuses on the way the environment is transformed by technological change and industrialization. Section 5.1.2 addresses the trade and environment debate or, more precisely, the effects of trade liberalization or protectionism on the environment. Finally, Section 5.1.3 addresses the role of investment decisions and how they affect the environment. In addition, the impacts of environmental, health, and safety regulation on (1) economic development/growth, (2) trade and competitiveness, and (3) investment decisions will be addressed in each subsection.

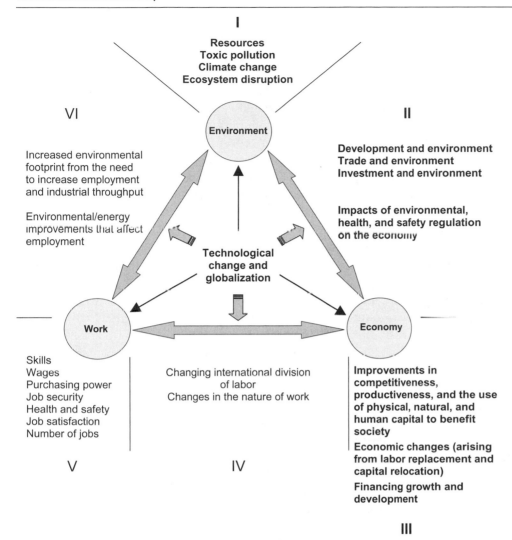

I
Resources
Toxic pollution
Climate change
Ecosystem disruption

Environment

VI

Increased environmental
footprint from the need
to increase employment
and industrial throughput

Environmental/energy
improvements that affect
employment

Technological
change and
globalization

II

Development and environment
Trade and environment
Investment and environment

Impacts of environmental,
health, and safety regulation
on the economy

Work

Skills
Wages
Purchasing power
Job security
Health and safety
Job satisfaction
Number of jobs

V

Changing international division
of labor
Changes in the nature of work

IV

Economy

Improvements in
competitiveness,
productivity, and the use
of physical, natural, and
human capital to benefit
society

Economic changes (arising
from labor replacement and
capital relocation)

Financing growth and
development

III

FIGURE 5.2: TECHNOLOGICAL CHANGE AND GLOBALIZATION AS DRIVERS OF CHANGE THAT
AFFECTS THE ENVIRONMENT AND THE ECONOMY (SECTORS I, II, AND III)

## 5.1.1 Development (Industrialization) and the Environment

*How is the environment transformed or affected as countries advance technologically or industrialize?*

Economic development has traditionally been measured by growth of the gross national product (GNP). Typically, a country is regarded as "developing" as long as its GNP grows at a rate of 5 percent to 7 percent a year and outpaces the population growth of the country, which implies that per capita income increases (Todaro and Smith 2009, p. 14). Development has also traditionally been associated with the alteration of the structures of production and employment so that the share of agriculture in the economy decreases as the manufacturing and service industries grow; such structural changes are typical outcomes of industrialization. Since the 1970s, the concept of development has evolved tremendously to

incorporate not only dimensions of distributional equity but also changes in social structures and national institutions, the eradication of poverty, and the creation of opportunities (Todaro and Smith 2009).[1]

Bearing in mind a more expansive conceptualization of development, we review the impacts of economic growth on the environment—specifically, the four environmental concerns we mentioned above: ecosystem health, resource depletion, toxic pollution, and global climate change—across the centuries, from the Industrial Revolution until today.

### 5.1.1.1 From Early Industrialization to *Silent Spring*

Industrialization started more than two centuries ago in Britain, at a time when natural resources seemed limitless compared with the workforce, which was considered the scarce factor of production. The density of population was low compared with the immensity of the land, the air, and the seas, and that context strengthened the belief in the regenerative and absorptive capacity of the ecosystem. More recently, Hardin (1968, p. 1245) quotes his grandfather saying that "flowing water purifies itself every 10 miles," which was probably not far from being true in the nineteenth century.

In *Essay on the Principle of Population* (1798), Thomas Malthus was one of the first to recognize that human activity could potentially be constrained by nature. In the nineteenth century, John Stuart Mill voiced concern about the social and environmental impacts of continued industrialization, conceived as ever-increasing production and consumption. Although most neoclassical economists tend to ignore the environmental impacts of economic growth, in 1920, Arthur Pigou defined what would later be called externalities by considering the full social costs (of production) as the sum of the production costs (for example, raw materials, workforce, and plant) and the external costs that arise, for example, from pollution.

As discussed in Chapter 2, the environmental movement began to gain momentum in the United States in the 1960s. Publications such as Rachel Carson's *Silent Spring* raised public awareness of the environmental impacts of the unrestricted use of certain chemicals in pesticides and insecticides. In "The Tragedy of the Commons," Hardin (1968) stated the negative effects of (population-driven) economic growth on the commons—that is, that pollution of the air and the water, exploitation of the land, and resource depletion are direct effects of the activity of rational individuals striving to maximize their own utility functions. At the global level, it seemed that the rational actions of governments and corporations since the dawn of the industrial era were creating a situation where the regenerative and absorptive capacities of important ecosystems were being exceeded. The limitless availability of natural resources was also called into question (the subject of the following section).

### 5.1.1.2 Growthmania and Its Discontents

In 1951, President Truman appointed the Materials Policy Commission (known as the Paley Commission) to consider whether sufficient resources would be available to fuel the U.S. economy into the foreseeable future ("to 1975—and beyond"). Although the commission's report did recognize the problem of resource depletion, its general message was that saving resources for the future might be unnecessary because of technological innovation and new re-

source discoveries (RFF 1954). Notwithstanding this optimistic perspective, the report can be seen as one of the first significant works to raise the question of "resource limits/depletion." It would take some two decades before the question of limits to economic growth would capture the attention of the international community.

In their report titled *The Limits to Growth*, Donella and Dennis Meadows (Meadows, Meadows, et al. 1972) concluded that the limits to the use of materials and energy would lie somewhere in the coming decades.[*] Furthermore, even though they insisted that their model was unable to provide exact predictions, they estimated that the limits to growth on this planet would be reached within the next one hundred years, mainly because of the exhaustion of nonrenewable resources. Although their conclusions were controversial, their report highlighted the important need to find ways "to bring about a society that is materially sufficient, socially equitable, and ecologically sustainable, and one that is more satisfying in human terms than the growth-obsessed society of today" (Meadows, Meadows, et al. 1992a, p. xiv).

Since the early 1960s, many individuals, groups, and agencies have worked on this challenge, and the concept of sustainable development has evolved, as discussed in Chapter 2. Nevertheless, when Meadows, Meadows, et al. updated their report in 1992, they titled it *Beyond the Limits* and prefaced it with the following words: "In spite of the world's improved technologies, the greater awareness, the stronger environment policies, many resource and pollution flows had grown beyond their sustainable limits. . . . The human world is beyond its limits. The present way of doing things is unsustainable" (Meadows, Meadows, et al. 1992a, pp. xiv–xv).

In *Limits to Growth: The 30-Year Update*, Meadows, Randers, et al. (2004, p. 176) consider falling resource stocks and rising pollution as indicators that society is in advanced stages of "overshoot": "a condition in which the delayed signals from [adverse impacts on] the environment are not yet strong enough to force an end to growth." According to the authors, a sustainability revolution is needed to reverse the tendencies. Although they say that it is impossible to depict what society will look like after such a revolution, they identify two key properties of complex systems that are related to this profound transformation: the importance of information flows and the strong resistance of systems to change.[2]

---

[*] See Chapter 1, Section 1.3.2, for a more detailed treatment of *The Limits to Growth*.

Herman Daly also challenges the view of growth as the centerpiece of economic development. As an alternative to standard economics, which "promotes an ever-expanding scale of resource use by appealing to growth as the cure for all economic and social ills," he proposes steady-state (or stationary) economics, stressing the importance of "the optimal scale of total resource use relative to the ecosystem" (Daly 1991, p. 180). Believing in the existence of limits to growth, he criticizes the "growthmania" or "growth dogma" that prevails in the modern world. Redclift (1987) adds that it is important to recognize that a system has not only natural limits but also structural ones. By structural limits, he suggests that political impediments to achieving sustainable development exist.

As discussed in Section 3.4.2 in Chapter 3, the state of Kerala in southern India provides an interesting example of development without growth. Although the per capita income in the state is very low (below India's average) and unemployment is high, economic redistribution has allowed sufficient essential goals to reach relatively high scores on important development indicators compared with other developing countries. Kerala has achieved remarkably high levels of adult literacy, life expectancy, and basic services (such as health, education, transportation, and shops) and has controlled infant mortality and the birth rate much better than the rest of India. According to Franke and Chasin (1990), who conducted a two-year study in Kerala, the keys to achieving a high level of development under limited growth were radical reform aiming at making poor people the main beneficiaries of development through redistribution of income and income-producing assets such as land.*

A similar contestation of growth as the primary objective of development was expressed by many people in the developing world after the Brundtland Commission defined sustainable development. In 1993, Nagpal and Foltz solicited a diverse group of people—the majority originating from the South—to write their views on a sustainable future.† In the article published by Nagpal in 1995, it appears that the focus on economic growth and the Western definition of sustainable development are contested by many people in the South: "Those in developing countries argue that Western proponents of sustainable development 'just don't get it.' They point out that the debate on sustainability closely mirrors those on development. By using terms of economic growth and efficiency, important issues are ignored: the urgency of nurturing human life and ecosystem health and the primacy of people, their communities, and the environment they depend on for their livelihood" (Nagpal 1995, p. 13).

For many participants in the project, "Coexistence with nature is the crux of a desirable future" (Nagpal 1995, p. 34). But with economic growth as the primary objective under Western dominance, the environment is not sufficiently integrated into development plans. The lack of importance given to the environment is reflected, according to many essayists, in attaching contradictory words such as "sustainable" and "development": "Equating development with growth and growth with increases in wealth are at the heart of the struggle between development and sustainability" (ibid.). Paralleling Daly's view on a form of development with an emphasis not on growth but on wealth redistribution and population control, essayists argue for the restructuring of economies and consumption patterns.

Wagle (1993) studied the critiques of and alternative perspectives to the World Commission on Environment and Development's (WCED's) concept of sustainable development.[3] Although Wagle considered the main theme of the WCED to be economic growth,‡ she reminds us that development is much more than growth and should include dimensions of equity, self-respect, and harmony (that is, social

---

* It is important to note that our point here is not about considering Kerala as a new model of development that should universally be applied in all developing countries (and neither is it the objective of Franke and Chasin, who rather propose lessons from Kerala). We are aware of the problems that the state of Kerala faces (especially its high unemployment rate) and the potential "unsustainability" of the welfare system because of declining fiscal support. For more details, see critiques by Omvedt (1998) and Tharamangalam (1998). However, the Kerala experiment illustrates that it is possible to achieve high levels of social development without economic growth. Conversely, it can be argued that high per capita income can hide maldistribution and poor scores on indicators of development. See also Parayil (1996) and Deparle (2007) for updates on Kerala and pressures on the population to migrate to other parts of India in search of work.

---

† The objective of Nagpal and Foltz's (1995) "2050 Project" was to identify the common elements and the differences among people's views on sustainability. To obtain these views, they solicited written essays from fifty-two individuals from thirty-four countries and conducted nineteen interviews with people from fourteen countries.

‡ Wagle (1993, p. 314) notes that following the WCED report, under the United Nations Conference on Environment and Development, "'development' is rehabilitated as a commendable objective and desirable process—if a few of its accompanying problems, mainly environmental and social, are resolved by the application of a progressive, forward-looking principle like 'sustainability'."

harmony and harmony with nature): "Development thinking that mainly emphasizes economic growth, even for satisfaction of basic needs, will necessarily lead to social and environmental conflicts. Capitalism or state-capitalism [is] antithetical to sustainable development because neither the market mechanism nor the state bureaucracy are geared to integrate equity and justice as priorities. However, in both of these systems it is possible to satisfy basic needs through economic growth" (ibid., p. 319).

Wagle states that Lele (1991) goes even further by arguing that "economic growth by itself cannot lead to environmental sustainability nor to the removal of poverty" (Wagle 1995, p. 319) Although Robert McNamara, the former president of the World Bank, admitted in 1978 that despite unprecedented increases in GNP in many developing countries, "800 million people continue to be trapped in . . . absolute poverty" (cited in Ackerman, Kiron, et al. 1997, p. 379), the Western model of development with economic growth as its centerpiece has not been abandoned.

Wagle (1993) also stresses the political problems with the WCED concept of sustainable development: the risk that the Northern definition will be imposed on the rest of the world. For example, she points out that the 1992 United Nations Conference on Environment and Development (UNCED) meetings reinforced the role of the World Bank in the development-environment conflicts, where the North has near-monopolistic control (as in many other international institutions). Finally, Wagle (1993) fears that with many Southern resources being controlled by dominant interests, sustainability could be used to distract attention from unequal access to natural resources.

The growth dogma has its intended policy effect: encouraging consumption.* Increased customer spending, through economic growth, is seen as the miracle cure to solve society's problems; it illustrates that development is taking place and that people are better off. International trade and globalization of information tend to foster this trend. However, there is no doubt that increased consumption means increased waste, and this relationship feeds the heart of our four environmental concerns: ecosystem health, resource depletion, toxic pollution, and global climate change.[†] Wagle (1993) regrets that the WCED report fails to address wasteful consumption and instead concentrates on stopping poverty in order to reduce ecological harm. The suggestion that progress implies increased consumption is also attacked by many participants in the 2050 Project. Essayists hope for a future in which no one has more or less than needed for basic survival, luxury becomes a pejorative term, consumption and production are dematerialized, and everything is resacralized, from community and nature to consumption and technology (Nagpal 1995).[‡] As Nagpal (p. 35) states: "The debate on the nonsustainability of growth and increased consumption illustrates the ideological divide between groups that appear to be equally concerned about the future generations."

The debate about the virtues of limiting growth versus increased economic expansion may soon be answered if the recent work by Ayres and Warr (2009) holds true. By developing a new economic theory that is grounded on the relationship between the laws of physics (thermodynamics) and economics, the authors recast the debate on "limits to (economic) growth" as one of limits on our ability to realize significant energy efficiency gains in the future. In contrast to mainstream economic thinking, Ayres and Warr (2009) argue that the majority of economic growth experienced during the Industrial Revolution was not driven by the exogenous "black box" of innovation but rather by the continual improvement in energy efficiency—that is, in the conversion of raw materials to final products and of raw fuels to finished fuels and electricity. The problem, they argue, is that the "opportunities for further technological improvements in the energy- and materials-conversion stages of the economic system are simultaneously approaching exhaustion" (ibid., p. xviii). Therefore, the dependency of the current economic system on nonrenewable and limited energy supplies makes it vulnerable to sustained energy price increases. On the basis of their theory and analysis, Ayres and Warr (ibid., p. 297) reach the following conclusion:

> The most important implication of the new theory . . . is that future economic growth is not guaranteed

---

* One suggested pathway to break the vicious circle of poor and unsustainable societies, where increased consumption leads to environmental degradation and therefore unsustainability, is to replace products with product-services—where products such as washing machines are shared—so as to satisfy the needs of the developing world. See Section 6.2 in Chapter 6.

† Section 5.1.2 on trade and the environment (and globalization) will further examine the impacts of increased consumption on the environment.

‡ As one of the participants from the Philippines puts it, referring to the unprecedented economic growth in East Asia and its environmental problems: "In time, perhaps, the Asia which the West converted to a non-sustainable lifestyle will repay the West by teaching it the ways of sustainability" (Nagpal 1995, p. 35).

because the efficiency gains that have driven growth in the past may not continue. Economic growth depends on producing continuously greater quantities of useful work. This depends, in turn, upon finding lower-cost sources of exergy [the useful component of energy, for example, oil, coal, and gas] inputs or more efficient ways of converting higher cost inputs into low-cost work outputs. In a world where the cheapest sources of exergy seem to be approaching exhaustion, the key to continued growth must be to accelerate the development of lower-cost alternative technologies, and policies, that increase conversion efficiency.

Meanwhile, if the rate of technological advance fails to compensate for the combination of approaching resource (notably cheap oil) exhaustion and policies needed to cut back on carbon dioxide emissions, we have to anticipate the possibility that economic growth will slow down or even turn negative. Global depression in the coming decades seems to us to be a serious risk.

An innovation of Ayres and Warr (2009) is to consider *exergy* as the third independent factor of production alongside capital and labor, and, more specifically, how improvements in *exergy efficiency*—a measure of the difference between the theoretical and actual amount of work performed for a given amount of energy—can reinforce or undermine economic growth. An important conclusion of their work that relates directly to this book is how government and industry can craft policies and strategies to encourage the radical innovation needed to stay ahead of the potential slowdown in exergy efficiency gains.

### 5.1.1.3 The Relationship between Economic Development/Growth and the Environment: An Analytic Approach

In the past decade, various studies have attempted to analyze the relationship between economic growth and the environment (Antweiler, Copeland, et al. 2001; S. Chua 1999; Feridun, Ayadi, et al. 2006; Grossman and Krueger 1993, 1995; Lopez 1994). These studies typically focus on three factors that help explain how economic development/growth, trade, and foreign direct investment (FDI) affect the environment: (1) the *scale* of production/consumption; (2) the *composition* of production/consumption; and (3) the *technique* or method of production. The common view is that as economies grow, and as trade and FDI encourage increased production possibilities,* the *scale* effect affects the environ-

ment. Further, trade and FDI can alter the *production composition* in a nation to the detriment of the environment. This gives rise to the "pollution-haven" hypothesis whereby trade and FDI favor the relocation of polluting activities to regions that have less stringent environmental regulation (Neumayer 2001).† Finally, *technique* effects have to be considered because, by altering the method of production, they can have either a positive or a negative impact on the environment.

Grossman and Krueger (1995) examined empirically the relationship between economic growth (national GDP) and various indicators of environmental conditions.‡ They found that there was no clear evidence that economic growth was deteriorating the environment. "Rather, for most indicators, economic growth brings an initial phase of deterioration followed by a subsequent phase of improvement" (ibid., p. 353). This relationship can be represented by an inverted-U shape between the income level and the environmental indicator.§ Although the turning point varies for the indicators they observe, they agree that most of them should come before a country reaches a per capita income of $8,000. However, Grossman and Krueger (ibid., p. 371) stress that "there is no reason to believe that the process has been an automatic one." A policy response induced by demand of citizens for greater environmental quality seems to be "the strongest link between income and pollution" (ibid., p. 372). Finally, Holtz-Eakin and Selden (1995) observed that in the case of per capita municipal waste and emissions of carbon dioxide, environmental conditions appear to be worsening even in countries with high income levels.

O'Connor (1994) analyzed the environmental effects of "rapid and largely unregulated industrialisation" and policy focus on economic growth in five Asian countries (Japan, Korea, Taiwan, Thailand, and Indonesia). He found that an inverted-U-shaped curve between economic growth and pollutant levels or indicators of water quality seems to be observed

---

† The pollution-haven hypothesis will be analyzed in Section 5.1.2.6.

‡ It is worth noting that the indicators used in their study relate to air pollution and contamination in water basins, which, as the authors admit, cover few dimensions of environmental quality. However, similar results relative to concentrations of sulfur dioxide and suspended particles in city air, total and annual deforestation, and per capita national emissions of sulfur dioxide, particulates, oxides of nitrogen, and carbon monoxide were obtained beforehand (and were published in Selden and Song 1994; Shafik and Bandyopadhyay 1992; WBG 1992).

§ The inverted-U-shaped relationships are also referred to as environmental Kuznets curves (EKCs). For a detailed discussion of the EKC, see Section 1.3.2 in Chapter 1.

---

* An analysis of the impacts of trade and FDI on the environment will be presented in the next two subsections.

in these economies:* as per capita income increases, these levels and indicators rise and then level off before declining as GDP continues to rise. The rise of pollution levels in the first stages of industrialization is easy to understand: the increase in the scale of production depletes more resources and produces more waste—toxic or not—and more effluents. O'Connor (1994) also noted that the structural shift from agriculture to industry and services led to increased pollution problems in the agricultural sector due to crop intensification and the heavy use of fertilizers and pesticides in response to rapidly growing population. Finally, he added that the growth of urban population (with rising incomes) also creates environmental problems: increased consumption leads to increased waste production, the rising number of motor vehicles exacerbates air pollution, and the rising demand for energy also has environmental impacts, depending on the energy mix of the country. Therefore, after a disastrous initial impact of industrialization on the environment, one could wonder how the leveling off of the inverted-U-shaped curve occurs. Why and how is a change brought about? O'Connor (1994) provides an explanation of the leveling off: with the increase of income, people are more willing to pay for a cleaner environment, governments respond to pollution problems with stricter environmental policy, and finally, technological innovation occurs in response to stringent environmental regulation and standards, which favor less polluting industries.

The relationships between the economy and the environment are in fact much more complex than what the inverted-U-shaped curve shows (S. Chua 1999). In many cases, empirical evidence fails to demonstrate that indicators of environmental degradation increase before decreasing as GDP rises. Furthermore, such analysis strengthens the belief that environmental problems will be solved by themselves as income rises, which is not the case (ibid.).

S. Chua (1999) inspected the empirical results of studies of the relationship between growth and environmental indicators. By adapting a critique by Ekins (1997), shown in Table 5.1, he shows that results from different studies are ambiguous (sometimes even inconsistent) and far from presenting inverted-U shapes in all cases. He concludes that "there is no consistent, unequivocal inverted-U relationship between environmental degradation and economic growth. . . . The results suggest that inter-

actions between economic growth and environmental quality are too complex to be satisfactorily captured by income differences alone" (ibid., pp. 395–396).[†] As S. Chua (1999) suggests, a closer look at the "composition" and "technique" effects is needed in order to understand these interactions better. In particular, "Technological changes can outweigh the scale effects and are fundamental in determining the relation between growth and environmental quality" (ibid., p. 399).[‡] S. Chua's (1999) findings show that there is no reason to believe that growth will be the solution to environmental degradation, and that countries will naturally grow out of their environmental problems.[§] To the contrary, he suggests that well-designed environmental policies, coordinated with economic policies, can encourage technological innovation in order for technical effects to outweigh the negative scale effects of economic growth on the environment.

Using state-level data from the United States, Aslanidis and Xepapadeas (2006, p. 182) show that "sulfur dioxide emissions are found to smoothly peak at a relatively late stage of economic development and then smoothly decrease at high levels of income. However, for the nitrogen oxide emissions, environmental pressure tends to rise with economic growth, then slows down but does not decline with further growth."

In a subsequent article focusing on a large number of countries, Aslanidis and Xepapadeas (2008) demonstrate a "turning point" for $SO_2$ and smoke on the basis of a "regime-switching model" for countries that adopt more stringent environmental controls leading to decreases in emissions, in agreement with S. Chua's (1999) expectations. Using material flows as a proxy for environmental degradation, Vehmas, Luukkanen, et al. (2007, p. 1162) find a "weak de-linking" of material flows and economic growth in the EU during

---

* However, O'Connor (1994) admits that different patterns are observed among countries and pollutants.

† The limited amount of empirical data on the link between growth and the environment is primarily focused on developed nations. However, a study by Feridun, Ayadi, et al. (2006) of Nigeria reached conclusions similar to those of S. Chua (1999). Feridun, Ayadi, et al. (2006, p. 39) found evidence that "trade intensity, real GDP per square kilometer and GNP are positively related to environmental degradation indicating that the technique, scale, and total effects of liberalization are detrimental to the environment."

‡ Commoner (1979) makes the same point in arguing that it is the nature rather than the volume of chemicals produced that threatens the biosphere and human health.

§ S. Chua (1999) suggests that the observation of inverted-U-shaped curves could lead to that conclusion. Nevertheless, it is worth remembering that previous authors who have shown such a relationship insisted that the leveling off was not an automatic process and necessitated a policy response, as we have seen earlier.

**TABLE 5.1: SUMMARY OF ENVIRONMENTAL-INCOME RELATIONSHIP FOR DIFFERENT INDICATORS[a]**

| STUDY (REFERENCE) (TYPE) | ENVIRONMENTAL INDICATOR[b] | SHAPE | 1ST TP (U.S. $) | 2ND TP (U.S. $) |
|---|---|---|---|---|
| **Sulfur dioxide** | | | | |
| Grossman and Krueger (7) (RE) | Urban concentration | R5 | 4,100 | 14,000 |
| Grossman and Krueger (7) (FE) | Urban concentration | R5 | ~4,300 | na |
| Shafik (6) | Urban concentration | R3 | 3,700 | |
| Grossman (2) | Urban concentration | R5 | 4,100 | 14,000 |
| Grossman (2) | Urban concentration (U.S.) | R5 | 13,400 | 24,000 |
| Grossman and Krueger (8) | Urban concentration | R5 | 4,100 | 14,000 |
| Selden and Song (5) (FE) | Emission per capita | R3 | 8,900[c] | |
| Selden and Song (5) (RE) | Emission per capita | R3 | 10,700 | |
| Panayotou (4) | Emission per capita | R3 | 3,000 | |
| **Suspended particulates** | | | | |
| Grossman and Krueger (7) (RE) | Urban concentration | R1 | – | |
| Grossman and Krueger (7) (FE) | Urban concentration | R2 | – | |
| Shafik (6) | Urban concentration | R3 | 3,300 | |
| Grossman (2) | Urban concentration (U.S.) | R3 | 16,000 | |
| Grossman and Krueger (8) | Urban concentration | R1 | – | |
| Selden and Song (5) (FE) | Emission per capita | R3 | 9,800 | |
| Selden & Song (5) (RE) | Emission per capita | R3 | 9,600 | |
| Panayotou (4) | Emission per capita | R3 | 4,500 | |
| **Dark matter (smoke)** | | | | |
| Grossman and Krueger (7) (RE) | Urban concentration | R5 | 5,000 | 10,000 |
| Grossman and Krueger (7) (FE) | Urban concentration | R5 | ~4,000 | 10,500 |
| Grossman (2) | Urban concentration | R5 | 4,700 | 10,000 |
| Grossman and Krueger (8) | Urban concentration | R5 | 6,200 | na |
| **Nitrogen oxide** | | | | |
| Grossman (2) | Urban concentration | R3 | 18,500 | |
| Selden and Song (5) (FE) | Emission per capita | R3 | 12,000 | |
| Selden and Song (5) (RE) | Emission per capita | R3 | 21,800 | |
| Panayotou (4) | Emission per capita | R3 | 5,500 | |
| **Carbon monoxide** | | | | |
| Grossman (2) | Urban concentration | R3 | 22,800 | |
| Selden and Song (5) (FE) | Emission per capita | R3 | 6,200 | |
| Selden and Song (5) (RE) | Emission per capita | R3 | 19,100 | |
| **Carbon dioxide** | | | | |
| Shafik (6) | Emission per capita | R2 | – | |
| Holtz-Eakin and Selden (3) | | | | |
|   Level of emissions per capita | Emission per capita | R3 | 35,400 | |
|   Log of emissions per capita | | R3 | >8 million | |
| **Dissolved oxygen (water pollution)** | | | | |
| Shafik (6) | Concentration | R1[d] | – | |
| Grossman (2) | Concentration | R4[e] | 8,500 | |
| Grossman and Krueger (8) | Concentration | R4[e] | 2,703 | |
| **Fecal coliform (water pollution)** | | | | |
| Shafik (6) | Concentration | R5 | 1,400 | 11,400 |
| Grossman (2) | Concentration | R3 | 8,500 | |
| Grossman and Krueger (8) | Concentration | R3 | 8,000 | |
| **Total coliform (water pollution)** | | | | |
| Grossman (2) | Concentration | R5 | No downturn[c] | |
| Grossman and Krueger (8) | Concentration | R5 | 3,043 | 8,000 |

[a] Table adapted from Ekins (10:808). Key; R1, linear, downward-sloping; R2, linear, upward-sloping; R3, quadratic, inverted-U; R4, quadratic, U; R5, cubic; TP, turning points for the quadratic and cubic functions; na, not available; RE, random-effects estimation; FE, fixed-effects estimation.

[b] Unless indicated, global data from different countries are used.

[c] The cubic function continuously rose with income.

[d] Because this is an indicator of environmental quality rather than degradation, this shape indicates continually worsening environmental quality with income.

[e] Because this is an indicator of environmental quality rather than degradation, this shape indicates continually improving environmental quality after the turning point income.

2. Grossman G. 1993. *Pollution and growth: what do we know? CEPR DP-848.* Cent. Econ. Policy Res., London.

3. Holtz-Eakin D., Selden T. 1992. *Stoking the fires? CO2 emissions and economic growth. WP-4248.* Natl. Bur. Econ. Res., Cambridge, MA.

4. Panayotou T. 1993. *Empirical tests and policy analysis of environmental degradation at different stages of development.* World Employment Programme Res. Work. Pap., WEP 2-22/WP 238. Int. Labour Off., Geneva.

(continued)

**TABLE 5.1** (continued)

5. Selden TM, Song D. 1994. Environmental quality and development: Is there a Kuznets curve for air pollution emissions? *J. Environ. Econ. Manage.* 27:147–62.

6. Shafik N. 1994. Economic development and environmental quality: an econometric analysis. *Oxford Econ. Pap.* 46:757–73.

7. Grossman GM, Krueger AB. 1993. Environmental impacts of a North American Free Trade Agreement. In *The Mexico-U.S. Free Trade Agreement*, ed. PM Garber, pp. 13–56. Cambridge, MA: MIT Press.

8. Grossman GM, Krueger AB. 1995. Economic growth and the environment. *Q. J. Econ.* 110:353–78.

Source: S. Chua (1999, pp. 397–398). Reproduced with permission.

the period 1980–2000 and conclude that "the material intensity of the economy has generally decreased due to increased efficiency, but the absolute amount of material use has increased."

In general, the existing empirical studies point to an increasing level of environmental impact—when one considers types of pollution—from economic development/growth. This finding calls into question the adequacy of the present emphasis on dematerialization, efficiency improvements, and environmental regimes for decreasing environmental impacts as a whole (see the later discussions of environmental policy and technological changes in Chapters 6, 7, and 8).

### 5.1.1.4 The Conflict between Economic Growth and the Environment

Typical opponents of the hypothesis that economic growth harms the environment include world-renowned economist Jagdish Bhagwati (1993). Bhagwati states that growth enables governments to raise tax money in order to protect the environment, and growth can increase the demand for high environmental quality. This view is consistent with one of the explanations given for the inverted-U-shaped or environmental Kuznets curves: environmental quality is considered a luxury good, and therefore, once a certain level of income has been reached, the demand for a better environment increases. As part of his argument in favor of free trade, Bhagwati (1993) argues that rising income and freer trade enable countries to import pollution-fighting technologies. We will discuss Bhagwati's arguments in more detail in Section 5.1.2 when we analyze the impacts of trade on the environment.

Ekins (1995) and Daly (1993, 1999) both vigorously disagree with Bhagwati's claims. In particular, Ekins contests the assertion that economic growth increases the demand for a better environment and provides more resources to fund environmental protection, for four reasons:

1. Economic growth creates more absolute environmental damage.

2. The resources that could be spent on environmental protection are not in fact allocated in this way.

3. Much environmental damage cannot be repaired.

4. Countries with stringent environmental regulations are being increasingly pressured by competitiveness to relax them.

Daly (1993) adds that the environmental degradation caused by economic growth (the environmental costs of growth) increases at a faster rate than the benefits. Again, these views are part of counterarguments by Daly (1993, 1999) and Ekins (1995) on the perils of free trade.

### 5.1.1.5 The Relationship between Environmental Regulation and Economic Growth

Having considered the impacts of economic growth on environmental quality, we now reverse the question and discuss the potential impacts of environmental protection on economic growth. We are interested in answering this question: how do activities that aim at preserving environmental quality (environmental regulation) affect economic growth?*

The common perception of the factual basis for the antagonism between economists and environmentalists is that environmental regulation hurts the economy,† affects productivity, and leads to a slowdown of economic growth. It is also traditionally believed that environmental regulation affects international competitiveness by increasing the costs of production. Therefore, in a world of free movement of capital, it is argued that investments tend to relocate to regions with lax environmental regulation (the pollution-haven hypothesis).‡

In his article on economic growth, liberalization, and the environment, S. Chua (1999) reviews the lit-

---

\* The corollary of this question is, does environmental regulation affect the employment outlook of a country? The debate on the interactions between the environment and employment will be our focus in Section 5.3.

† This opinion is shared by Bhagwati (1993).

‡ The effects of stringent environmental regulation on trade, international competitiveness, and FDI will be analyzed in Section 5.1.2.6.

erature that attempts to answer this question. In particular, he analyzes the results of studies of the costs of abatement of carbon emissions, criticizes the methodologies used, and arrives at three important conclusions:

1. Most of the studies do not take into account the technique effect in their models, which neglect both the importance of technological innovation in reducing emissions and the fact that innovation can be enhanced by environmental policy.*

2. None of the studies integrates into its model the potential beneficial feedback of a better environment on the whole system. Examples of such benefits include better worker health that in turn enhances productivity and better soil/water quality that improves ecosystem health.

3. Most of the studies come up with relatively low costs of reductions in carbon emissions, with an average annual growth rate decline of the order of 0.1 percent.

Therefore, S. Chua (1999, p. 404) concludes "that environmental control does not incur excessive economic costs nor significantly retard economic growth. Furthermore, the costs of pollution control are often offset by economic benefits from higher productivity of resources, including labor."

### 5.1.2 Trade (Globalization) and the Environment

Even more heated and passionate than the debate on economic development/growth and the environment is the debate on trade and the environment. As we have seen in the previous section, the mere concept of economic growth is somewhat contested by some scholars, nongovernmental organizations, and representatives of the South, but this opposition is relatively limited. In the political arena, almost everywhere, the centerpiece of concern focuses on economic growth. The belief that economic growth is the cure to all problems remains predominant. On the other hand, the opposition to free trade is embraced by a much larger audience, including not only nongovernmental organizations but also numerous politicians and representatives of the economic sector. Free trade is far from being considered by all actors and thinkers as something necessary to achieve (sustainable) development. This view is en-

hanced by the perceived negative impacts of free trade on the environment by environmentalists, effects that are strongly contested by free-trade advocates. (More recently, concern has been increasingly voiced that free trade accelerates job losses in developed nations.) Therefore, we start our discussion by asking: what are the possible environmental impacts of trade liberalization or protectionism?

At the center of the debate about the impacts of free trade on the environment lies the existence of externalities. As we defined them earlier, externalities are costs that arise from an activity but are not integrated into the total cost of the activity. For example, an unregulated factory that is polluting the air is creating an environmental and potentially public health externality. An advertising campaign to promote a beer brand creates a social externality by increasing the risk of car accidents due to alcohol consumption. These are examples of market failures: the environmental or social costs associated with the activity are externalized. When the externality is integrated into the total cost of the activity, it is said that the externality is internalized. For example, a factory can be forced by environmental regulation to bear the cost of polluting the air by having to comply with pollution standards or to pay a tax for the environmental harm caused by pollution. In this case, public intervention attempts to internalize externalities.

Some authors (Cole 2000) argue that trade by itself does not have a negative impact on the environment.[†] Environmental harm is caused by the following failures:

- Market failures: the market fails to internalize externalities or "to properly value and allocate environmental goods, with the result that prices do not cover the full social costs of production" (ibid., p. 23). Cole recalls the three reasons for market failure that were first outlined by the OECD (1994, pp. 23–24): (1) the costs of environmental harm are not being included in the price of goods and services; (2) the market fails to take into account the full value that society places on an environmental asset; and (3) there is a lack of property rights for certain environmental assets (the resource is considered "free of charge").

- Intervention failures and distortions: these "occur when government policy creates, exacerbates or fails to remove market failures" (Cole 2000, p. 24).

---

* As we will see in Section 5.1.2.6, Ashford, Ayers, et al. (1985), Ashford, Heaton, et al. (1979), and Porter and van der Linde (1995) argue that technological innovation is encouraged by environmental regulation, and this improves both sectoral and international competitiveness.

---

† This perspective reflects the view that some environmental harm is acceptable so long as the marginal benefits of an economic activity are equal to or greater than its environmental costs.

### 5.1.2.1 The Rationale for Free Trade

The rationale for free trade comes from the early nineteenth century and Ricardo's theory of comparative advantage. Countries are encouraged to specialize in those sectors that make use of the resources that they have in abundance.* Theoretically, the specialization of each country in those industries in which it is the most productive and efficient (that is, in which it has a comparative advantage over other countries) ensures the best allocation of resources. Therefore, through free trade and specialization, the amount, variety, and quality of the goods produced are supposedly superior. Continuing this logic, "if trade maximises allocative efficiency in this manner, then economic activity should be allocated in accordance with the environmental capacities and conditions of different countries, thus, theoretically, keeping environmental stress to a minimum" (Cole 2000, pp. 25–26).

Therefore, free-trade advocates call for a liberalization of all world trade exchanges. In order to solve environmental problems, they consider that externalities should be tackled directly, rather than by changing the world trade system. Although the principle of internalizing all externalities is attractive (in a perfect world, it means that the polluter-pays principle is always enforced and that "dirty goods" are priced higher than environmentally sound products, which favors the production and consumption of cleaner goods), the reality is much more complex. Externalities cannot always easily be internalized, especially when their scope is global (Cole 2000).†

On the basis of the rationale for free trade and the need to internalize externalities, the OECD (1997b) considers that free trade has positive aspects by improving allocation of resources (and therefore promoting growth and welfare), provided appropriate environmental policy is enforced. Depending on the environmental policy and the extent of government intervention, the OECD recognizes that the net effect is uncertain. Estimations of this net effect are probably at the source of the passionate debate between environmentalists and free-trade advocates.

### 5.1.2.2 Criticism of the Rationale

Before we review the respective arguments of free-trade advocates and environmentalists about the net effects of liberalized trade on the environment, it is worth mentioning that the rationale for free trade is not universally accepted. Ekins, Folke, et al. (1994) consider that the assumptions on which the theory of comparative advantage is based do not prevail in our modern society:

- *Absence of externalities*: If part of the cost of production is externalized, the apparent low price does not reflect a true comparative advantage. However, as we have seen earlier, the presence of externalities is exactly at the center of the debate between advocates of free trade and environmentalists.

- *Stable prices*: When the demand for a good is inelastic, an increase in supply may lower the price of the good, changing the distribution of comparative advantage.

- *Equally dynamic comparative advantage*: The theory assumes that the relative comparative advantage of trading parties remains more or less the same, whereas in reality, countries specializing in high technology will grow faster than others and thus increase their comparative advantage.‡

- *International immobility of factors of production*: The theory assumes that capital and labor will remain within the country "to produce according to the country's comparative advantage" (ibid., p. 5). Otherwise, if capital and labor become mobile, which is especially the case today for capital, trade tends to become based more on absolute rather than comparative advantage, and countries experience pressures on wages, working conditions, and environmental laws in order to be competitive (see also Daly 1999).

---

\* The term "resource" is to be understood in its broadest sense: it includes not only physical and natural resources but also resources such as talents and experience of the workforce, technologies, customs, and geographic location. Ricardo's theory considered these resources (or factors of production) to be immobile between nations. However, the recent and rapid increase in capital mobility and the transportation of raw and semiprocessed materials and, to a lesser extent, people between nations means that modern comparative advantages may no longer be anchored to resources available within national boarders (Daly 1993, 1999). The implications of these changes are discussed in the following section.

† Local externalities cannot always be easily internalized because the governments that impose them face the risk of loss of competitiveness. This relates to the interrelation of stringent environmental regulation and international competitiveness, a topic we will explore later in this chapter. Internalization of global externalities is even more complicated. First, internalizing global externalities necessitates estimating the effects of the global problem (its distribution and severity, in particular) (Cole 2000). Second, all parties involved need to accept this estimation before an environmental agreement can be concluded and enforced; this is never a simple task, as we will see in Chapter 10.

‡ Although trade may continue to benefit both trading partners, the partner with the lesser-valued comparative advantage becomes increasingly impoverished relative to the partner with the greater-valued advantage. See Section 4.4.1 in Chapter 4 on winners and losers from free trade.

Furthermore, Ekins, Folke, et al. (1994) contest certain benefits of free trade. First, they state that when a shift of subsistence production to production for trade occurs, a false amount of gain is considered: while production for trade is accounted for in economic accounts, subsistence production is not. In calculating the gain from trade, the loss of subsistence product should therefore be deducted from the traded good. Second, they argue that specialization can have perverse effects by increasing the dependency of the country on the international demand for the good it produces,* as well as on external financing (which is often needed for export-led production). Daly (1993) adds that the local community suffers from specialization because diversity is lost (for example, in occupational choices). Third, Ekins, Folke, et al. (1994) contend that increased consumption does not necessarily increase social welfare and raises the question of equity, because the gains from trade might not be equally shared. In their opinion, the supposed superiority of free trade is therefore more dogmatic than scientific. Also, instead of comparative advantage, competitive advantage prevails in the modern world, with the following result: "Instead of prosperity, the . . . experience of increased trade has often been low commodity prices, poor terms of trade, high debt service, protected Northern markets, and an increasingly degraded environment. The North is also affected as unemployment and underemployment in the South put pressure on wages worldwide. There is a danger that trade will increasingly become a 'zero sum game' rather than the 'positive sum game' of traditional trade theory" (Ekins 1995, p. 309).

Similarly, Ernst and O'Connor (1989) affirm that the assertion that comparative advantage drives international competition is a reductionist concept. In their opinion, international competition is rather characterized by oligopolistic competition and strategic interaction. Soros (1998) also comments that the outcome of international competition, when it is combined with limited/weak international regulations, will be a natural tendency toward monopolies and oligopolies as corporations seek to preserve global market position.†

Finally, Daly (1993) considers an additional argument: that the subsidies of the energy-intensive transportation costs associated with international trade should be deducted from the so-called benefits of trade, and that doing so will undoubtedly reduce the overall gains of international trade.

### 5.1.2.3 The Positive Impacts of Free Trade on Environmental Quality

Free-trade advocates generally argue that the net effects of liberalized international exchange on the environment are positive. Their arguments are as follows:

- Free trade favors economic growth, and the growth of income has positive effects on the environment because of the increased demands for a clean environment and the ability to pay for them.

- Free trade favors the international exchange of technology and environmentally sound products and services.

- Free trade induces the removal of trade-distorting and environment-harming policies.

As we have seen in Section 5.1.1 on development and the environment, free-trade advocates oppose the argument that economic growth harms the environment. To the contrary, they believe in inverted-U-shaped relationships or environmental Kuznets curves.‡ Bhagwati (1993) argues that economic growth enables governments to raise taxes to protect the environment and increases the demand for higher environmental quality. Similarly, according to Cole (2000), the expansion of the scale of economic activity through liberalized trade increases the financial resources available to improve environmental quality. He states that in developing countries, growth in income is essential if they are to improve the quality of their environment. He recalls the example of Mexico, given by Voigt (1993), where the lack of financial resources has limited the ability of the government to control the environmental effects of development.

A second argument used by free-trade advocates to promote international liberalized exchange emphasizes the benefits of the free trade of environmentally cleaner technologies, products, and services. For Bhagwati (1993), freer trade and rising income enhance the exchange of pollution-fighting and resource-efficient technologies: trade liberalization plays a role in expanding the potential market for environmentally cleaner products, services, and technologies, and, in turn, this market expansion boosts technological innovation and trade (OECD 1994). Cole (2000) concurs

---

* Daly (1993) says that countries "become locked into free trade" once they specialize because they lose the option not to trade.

† See Section 4.4.4 in Chapter 4 for a discussion of how the dominance of manufacturing and services by China and India and the consolidation of retailing power in developed countries are reshaping the structure of markets.

---

‡ For a discussion of the evidence against environmental Kuznets curves, see Sections 1.3.2 and 5.1.1.3.

that free trade can be beneficial to the environment through the technique effect: by allowing the expansion of markets, free trade increases access of countries to cleaner technologies, products, and services, but also to more efficient production methods. Therefore, output might be produced in a much cleaner and more efficient way following trade liberalization.

It appears that proponents of free trade consider a kind of "natural virtuous circle" between trade liberalization (market expansion) and technological innovation, so that environmental quality eventually benefits from increased international exchanges. However, the OECD (1994) recognizes that environmental quality suffers from the scale effects of trade and that, overall, the total burden for the environment could possibly be higher.

Finally, another advantage of trade liberalization is the removal of trade-distorting and environment-damaging policies. As Cole (2000, p. 27) states: "The very existence of such measures means that resources are not being allocated as efficiently as they could be, and thus both the location and intensity of technology, production and consumption are distorted." In particular, Cole (2000) gives the example of the Common Agricultural Policy (CAP) of the European Union. The CAP system, which guarantees prices to farmers, has resulted in production of food considerably in excess of the market's requirements. Besides not enhancing an effective allocation of resources, the CAP system has adverse impacts on the environment. Not only does it create an incentive for farmers to produce more using more intensive methods of production (and more artificial inputs), but the excess foodstuffs also represent a huge waste that needs to be disposed of. Similarly, Reijnders (2003) states that subsidies distort the efficient use of physical inputs. In particular, he argues that the removal of subsidies of energy and water would improve energy and water efficiency. He also adds that subsidies of pesticides and fertilizers, road and air transport, and raw materials have disfavored cleaner production programs.

One of the reasons for defending vehemently the environmental benefits of free trade is that above all, free-trade advocates fear "green protectionism," where environmental standards would be used as barriers to trade and limit the efficiency gains from world trade (Cole 2000). Bhagwati (1993) stresses that countries have the right to prioritize the environmental problems they want to tackle in their own way. Furthermore, he rejects what he recalls the "eco-imperialism" of countries that try to impose their values on other countries, when northern countries

have the most adverse environmental impacts (ibid., p. 45). According to Bhagwati (1993), the tuna-dolphin case (see Chapter 11 for a discussion of environment-related trade disputes) provides an example of eco-imperialism of the United States over Mexico. In his opinion, "the simultaneous pursuit of the two causes of free trade and a protected environment often raises problems .... But none of these conflicts is beyond resolution with goodwill and ... imaginative institutional innovation" (ibid., p. 49).

Rather than restricting liberalized international exchanges, free-trade advocates believe that externalities should be tackled directly.* They also urge environmentalists to use methods such as lobbying countries with poor standards and boycotting certain commodities, rather than attacking free trade (Bhagwati 1993). Finally, they believe in the potential of voluntary approaches to promote both free trade and the quality of the environment.

### 5.1.2.4 The Adverse Effects of Free Trade on the Environment

The optimistic picture painted above is contested by many—for example, environmentalists, numerous scholars, opponents of globalization, some nongovernmental organizations, and many people in developing countries. In their opinion, Bhagwati's (1993) position that free trade favors the efficient allocation of resources and a better environment is purely theoretical. In the absence of internalization of externalities, it appears that trade is rather conducted on the "back of the environment" (as well as by exploiting workers). By encouraging trade with nations that do not internalize their externalities, free trade leads to inefficient allocation of resources and harms the environment (Daly 1993).

> The prevalence of externalities, due in part to the difficulty of internalisation, means that trade liberalisation may exacerbate environmental damage. One reason for this is the scale effect associated with free trade. It was stated ... that perfectly free trade will ensure that resources are utilized in the most efficient manner possible, thus minimising inputs per unit of output. Indeed, this is the case in a static framework. However, once we enter a dynamic framework then it is likely that liberalised trade will lead to an expansion of markets and hence economic growth. The increase in income associated with such growth may mean that nations now find themselves with greater resources to protect the environment, but the environmental

---

\* Bhagwati (1993) sees nothing wrong with countries "trading on externalities," e.g., choosing to suffer environmental damage to gain economically.

impact of such an expansion in the scale of production may be considerable. (Cole 2000, p. 27)

Similarly, Daly (1993) argues that the environmental costs of growth increase faster than its potential benefits, dampening the argument that growth generates wealth that can be used to protect the environment.

A second reason for questioning the supposedly more efficient allocation of resources and the better environment brought by free trade relates to the different environmental (and labor) standards among nations. First, comparative advantage arises from differences in environmental standards. Countries are likely to specialize in those sectors where their country has the weakest environmental regulation, and, as a result, the production *composition* effect of trade liberalization will lead to a decrease of environmental quality (Cole 2000).* Second, international competition arising from free trade can lower costs by keeping environmental standards low in developing countries and providing pressure to lower, or at least not to raise, those standards in the industrialized nations,† rather than through increasing efficiency (Daly 1993). Further, the ease with which capital can move between nations creates an additional force to lower standards in an effort to retain or attract capital (Daly 1999). The idea that free trade and increased competition among nations will lead to a lowering of environmental standards is usually referred to as the "race to the bottom."

---

\* The rationale for trade is, in fact, to exploit differences between nations; if there were no differences, trade would be worthless. Although the comparative advantage of nations is typically based on natural resource endowments and the skills and availability of labor, it can also be extended to include differences in national environmental and labor standards (Sinden 2007). From an economic perspective, it can be argued that if the standards in each nation were *efficient*—that is, they reflected the true *preferences* of citizens—then trade that exploits a comparative advantage in lower standards would actually be welfare enhancing for all trading parties. Such an argument that favors free trade without the need to raise/harmonize standards fails to acknowledge the reality that regulations in developing (and developed) regions are often inefficient—that is, the "wealth effect" lowers the stringency of standards because there is less willingness/ability to pay for better working/environmental conditions, and there are political/market failures that lower the actual standards beyond those differences and hence contribute to inefficient standards (Gitterman 2002; Sinden 2007). The result of inefficient standards is a welfare loss in the host nation. Therefore, increasing the volume of trade will further promote a loss of welfare. Sinden (2007) argues that the solution to this problem is the upward harmonization of standards. However, harmonizing standards to the most stringent *existing* standard may not be sufficient to address many critical environmental problems and ignores changes in technology that lead to new dynamic efficiency.

† This may also be true for employment standards.

Some authors, and free-trade advocates in particular, contest the existence of the "race to the bottom." Vogel (2000) defends the existence of the opposite effect: he believes that under certain circumstances, global economic integration can lead to the strengthening of consumer and environmental standards, resulting in a "race to the top." However, even though he contends that the "race to the bottom" is not observed in practice, he mentions Esty and Geradin's (2000) supposition that international competitiveness and differences in environmental regulation can have a "political drag" effect. This means that developed countries become reluctant to enforce higher environmental standards, while rapidly industrializing countries remain "stuck at the bottom" of environmental regulation (Porter 1990), "dragging down" standards in other poor countries.

Gitterman (2004) argues that the harmonization or convergence of standards is not driven by Vogel's notion of internationally oriented producers, but by political and institutional factors. In particular, Gitterman (ibid., pp. 340–341) contends that the stringency of standards depends on "the national *preferences* of the member states or trading partners (and political parties with control); the formal institutional and *decision rules* for aggregating policy preferences; and the *collective action* problem of joint decision making among many governments." Gitterman (ibid., p. 333) concludes that the expansion of trade has not resulted in a race to the top or bottom, and that "integration appears to result in an incremental march toward common regional and international minimum rules and norms."

The level of corruption in a given country also has to be taken into account in evaluating the effects of trade liberalization on the stringency of environmental (and labor) regulation (Damania, Fredriksson, et al. 2003; Cole 2007). In particular, Damania, Fredriksson, et al. (2003) show that corruption reduces environmental policy stringency.

Besides claiming that free trade leads to the inefficient allocation of resources and environmental harm, Daly (1993, p. 53) adds that free trade is problematic for the goal of a "sustainable scale of total resource use." As we have discussed in Section 1.3.1 in Chapter 1, Daly (ibid., p. 56) advocates the steady-state economic paradigm, which means that "the economy is . . . [an] open subsystem in a finite, non-growing and materially closed ecosystem." He considers that there are limits to economic growth because there is an optimal level of throughput for an economy. Therefore, free trade, by favoring increase in growth and throughput and allowing countries to exceed their regenerative and absorptive capacities by "importing" these capacities, will result in economies overshooting their optimal scales (ibid., p. 57). The fact that the benefits and the costs of environmental exploitation tend to be separated in time (that is, there are "divergent time horizons") increases this tendency. In addition, the efficiency of modern transportation systems creates a "distancing effect," whereby consumers are unable to know how their purchasing habits are affecting the environment in another country (Princen 2002).

Finally, the question of free trade and transportation deserves some attention. Daly (1993) states that the gains from free trade would be highly reduced if the subsidies of the energy-intensive transportation costs associated with increased global trade were to be deducted. Moreover, Cole (2000) argues that trade liberalization and the subsequent expanding volume of trade directly affect the environment by favoring increased transportation, because fuel prices do not fully internalize environmental costs associated with transportation. Thus an unsustainable transportation system is linked to unsustainable consumption (Hall 2006).

It seems that environmentalists and some economists tend not to believe in the voluntary approaches and the "natural virtuous circle" that promote free trade and protect the environment simultaneously. But the opposition of economists and environmentalists in favor or disfavor of free trade is not the real issue, according to Daly (1993). What really matters is what regulations and goals are legitimate. For example, he argues that countries that internalize their externalities should have the right to impose trade tariffs on those that do not.* Similarly, he favors a regionalization of trade among like partners.

### 5.1.2.5  The Relationship between Trade and the Environment: An Analytic Approach

Just as the relationship between growth (traditional development) and the environment has been an important topic of research in the past decades, so too has the relationship between trade and the environment.

As mentioned in Section 5.1.1.3, the three factors driving pollution emissions are the *scale* of produc-

tion/consumption, the *composition* of production/consumption, and the *technique* or method of production. The common view is that as economies grow, and as trade and FDI encourage increased production possibilities,

- the *scale* of economic activities affects the environment;

- the *composition* effect will cause increased pollution because comparative advantage might arise from differences in environmental regulations, and dirty industries will tend to relocate to regions that have less stringent environmental regulation (the "pollution-haven" hypothesis); and

- the *technique* effect might affect the environment, although this type of impact is less predictable.

S. Chua (1999) compiled the results of empirical research conducted in the late 1990s on the impacts of trade liberalization on pollution levels, mainly in North and South America. The results are shown in Table 5.2, with a decomposition of the *scale*, *composition*, and *technique* effects.

It appears that the *scale* effect is constantly associated with an increase in the pollution level. On the other hand, the impacts of the *composition* effect on the environment show more conflicting results. S. Chua (1999) argues that comparative advantage and trade patterns are mostly determined by factor intensities rather than by differences in environmental regulations, as one might have expected. This means that developing countries tend to specialize in the low-skilled labor-intensive sectors, while developed countries favor industries that require high-skilled labor and are capital intensive. Furthermore, S. Chua (1999) shows that there is no evidence that labor-intensive industries are the most polluting.[†] On the contrary, on the basis of the results of a study conducted by the World Bank (WBG 1998), S. Chua (1999, p. 405) argues that the *composition* effect "tend[s] to shift [production] towards cleaner goods in developing countries and dirtier goods in developed countries." Finally, the *technique* effect has been neglected in many studies. Nevertheless, from one of the studies (see Beghin, Bowland, et al. [1998]), it appears that the trade-liberalization regime plays an important role by affecting prices of inputs and therefore influ-

---

\*     Not all such tariffs comport with current WTO rules (see Chapter 11).

---

†     S. Chua (1999) uses the results of a study by Mani and Wheeler (1998) to make this argument. Mani and Wheeler found that the five most polluting industries (iron and steel, nonferrous metals, industrial chemicals, pulp and paper, and nonmetallic-mineral products) are more capital and energy intensive and less labor intensive than the five less polluting, or cleaner, sectors (textiles, nonelectrical machinery, electrical machinery, transport equipment, and instruments).

**TABLE 5.2: SUMMARY OF ESTIMATES OF THE IMPACT OF TRADE LIBERALIZATION ON POLLUTION[a]**

| COUNTRY AND TRADE REFORM | SCALE | COMPOSITION | TECHNIQUE | TOTAL POLLUTION |
|---|---|---|---|---|
| Grossman and Krueger (7)[b] (hazardous waste) Liberalization under NAFTA | | | | |
|     Mexico | + | − | na | Small decrease |
|     United States | + | + | na | Increase |
|     Canada | + | + | na | Increase |
| Grossman and Krueger (7) (hazardous waste) NAFTA with investment liberalization | | | | |
|     Mexico | + | + | na | Increase |
|     United States | + | + | na | Increase |
|     Canada | + | + | na | Increase |
| Beghin et al. (84) (various pollutants) Liberalization with better TOT with United States and Canada | | | | |
|     Mexico | 2.8%–3.7% | −4.3%–2.6% | −0.7%–3.5% | −0.2%–6.4% |
| Lee and Roland-Holst (85) (various pollutants) Trade liberalization between Japan and Indonesia | | | | |
|     Indonesia | 0.87% | −0.36%–2.86% | na | 0.51%–3.73% |
|     Japan | 0.00% | (−0.09%)–(−0.02%) | na | (−0.09%)–(−0.02%) |
| Strutt and Anderson (86)[c] (various pollutants) Trade reform in Indonesia | | | | |
|     Uruguay Round reforms (2010) | 1.6%–7.6% | (−6.6%)–(−1.3%) | na[d] | −2.5%–5% |
|     APEC (2020) | 0.3%–4.1% | −8.4%–3.4% | na | −4.2%–7.9% |
| Madrid-Aris (87) (hazardous wastes) Trade liberalization under NAFTA | | | | |
|     Mexico | No decomposition between scale and composition effects | na | 4.683% | |
|     California | | | na | 0.083% |
|     Rest of United States | | | na | 0.086% |
| Madrid-Aris (87) (hazardous wastes) NAFTA + investment liberalization | | | | |
|     Mexico | No decomposition between scale and composition effects | na | 4.895% | |
|     California | | | na | 0.0818% |
|     Rest of United States | | | na | 0.0867% |
| Beghin et al. (33) (various pollutants) Trade reform in Chile | | | | |
|     Unilateral liberalization | No decomposition between scale, composition, and technique effects[d] | | | 2.8%–19.9% |
|     Accession to NAFTA | | | | 4.8%–3.6% |
|     MERCOSUR | | | | −1.2%–8.1% |

[a] . . . Where emission changes are estimated for individual pollutants, only the highest and lowest changes are summarized in this table. The ranges reported here do not refer to estimated intervals of changes. Abbreviations: TOT, terms of trade; APEC, Asia-Pacific Economic Cooperation; NAFTA, North American Free Trade Agreement; MERCOSUR, Mercado Commun del Sur [Southern Common Market . . . ].

[b] Percentages were not available; only absolute values were reported.

[c] Results reported here are percentage changes compared with the baseline case of forecasted absolute changes in emissions from growth and structural change from 1992-2010 (for the Uruguay round case) and from 1992-2020 (for the APEC case).

[d] When estimating the changes in emissions caused solely by growth and structural change (without trade reform), a technology effect was imposed, assuming linear changes in pollution/output ratios. However, when the effects of trade reform were compared with this baseline case, no further technology effect from trade was allowed for.

7. Grossman GM, Krueger AB. 1993. Environmental impacts of a North American Free Trade Agreement. In *The Mexico-U.S. Free Trade Agreement*, ed. PM Garber, pp. 13–56. Cambridge, MA: MIT Press.

33. Beghin J, Bowland B, Dessus S, Roland-Holst D, van der Mensbrugghe D. 1998. *Trade, environment and public health in Chile: evidence from an economywide model*. Presented at World Bank Conf. Trade, Glob. Policy Environ. Washington, DC.

84. Beghin J, Roland-Holst D, van der Mensbrugghe D. 1995. Trade liberalization and the environment in the Pacific Basin: coordinated approaches to Mexican trade and environment policy. *Am. J. Agric. Econ.* 77: 778–85.

85. Lee H, Roland-Holst D. 1997. The environment and welfare implications of trade and tax policy. *J. Dev. Econ.* 52:65–82.

86. Strutt A, Anderson K. 1998. *Will trade liberalisation harm the environment? The case of Indonesia to 2020*. Presented at World Bank Conf. Glob. Policy Environ., Washington, DC.

87. Madrid-Aris ME. 1998. *International trade and the environment: evidence from the North America (NAFTA)*. Presented at 1st World Congr. Environ. Resourc. Econ., Venice, Italy.

Source: S. Chua (1999, pp. 406–407). Reproduced with permission.

encing the choice of the mix of inputs and techniques The lack of analysis of the *technique* effect is a serious omission, according to S. Chua (1999), because it can have a potentially beneficial effect on the environment in developing countries.* On the basis of the conflicting results of these studies, S. Chua (1999) concludes that the effects of trade liberalization on the environment are relatively small compared with the effects of growth and the structural changes that would have taken place anyway.

### 5.1.2.6 The Effects of Stringent Environmental Regulation on Trade and Competition[†]

The general perception of the relationship between environmental policy and international trade is that the international competitiveness of the countries that enforce stringent environmental regulation is affected. On the basis of this hypothesis, countries with a stringent environmental policy feel that they suffer from the unfair competition of their "dirtier" trade partners and require the introduction of the harmonization of environmental standards in international trade arrangements. Moreover, the harmonization of environmental standards is also advocated by those who fear the "race to the bottom" that was mentioned earlier. The following paragraphs will challenge this hypothesis and review the respective arguments of proponents and opponents of the harmonization of environmental standards.[‡] However, it is important to commence by restating the distinction between the two categories of environmental problems that countries face—that is, (1) domestic environmental problems and (2) global environmental problems—because these problems call for different kinds of policy responses.

Both S. Chua (1999) and Cole (2000) dismiss the general perception that stringent environmental policy affects international competitiveness by arguing that research conducted on that topic shows mixed results. According to S. Chua (1999), most studies show an insignificant relationship between stringent environmental requirements and trade patterns.[4] Low (1992) and Low and Yeats (1992) provide an exception: focusing their research work on dirty indus-

tries, they found that between 1965 and 1988, more developing countries gained comparative advantage in those industries than developed countries. Furthermore, Low (1992) shows that in Mexico, between 1981 and 1989, the growth in dirty exports outpaced the growth of total exports. However, as S. Chua (1999) comments, the fact that OECD countries are still responsible for the largest share of total production in dirty industries provides evidence to undermine these findings. Similarly, Cole (2000) uses several studies[5] to argue that the abatement costs are so small compared with the total costs of a firm that their impact on international competitiveness is limited, undermining at the same time the pollution-haven hypothesis. On the other hand, he presents the results of other studies that support the pollution-haven hypothesis,[6] implicitly recognizing the loss of international competitiveness in those countries that enforce stringent environmental regulation. Therefore, as Cole (2000) concludes, the impact of environmental regulation on competition is clearly uncertain.

Nonetheless, there are strong proponents of the harmonization of environmental (and health and safety) regulation (see Esty 1994 and Sinden 2007). Although earlier history may not reveal a strong differential impact on trade or the existence of pollution havens, it has been suggested that recent experience in Asia, particularly China, indicates that lax health, safety, and environmental regulation and enforcement do confer a comparative advantage in trade of goods. However, a paper on the effects of regulation on the structure of bilateral trade between fourteen countries in the EU and China in eighteen manufacturing industries between 1996 and 2006 concludes that China does not enjoy a measureable comparative advantage over the fourteen EU countries (Marconi, 2010).

According to Bhagwati (1993), the request for harmonization of environmental standards is unfair, and he defends the idea that each country has the right to prioritize the environmental problems it decides to tackle. In other words, this means that he recognizes that environmental regulation can affect the international competitiveness of countries, but he disapproves of the claim for the introduction of environmental standards in trade terms. In his opinion, differences of standards between countries are legitimate (he calls them "Cross-Country Intra-Industry differences"), especially those that target domestic environmental problems: countries should have the right to value environmental goods differently and to trade off between pollution and income. Therefore, while the United States and Europe consider differences in environmental regulation ecodumping or un-

---

\* For example, by allowing cheaper access to cleaner inputs and a transfer of cleaner production methods (S. Chua 1999).

† Here we discuss how environmental regulation affects decisions to invest in various economies. The possible positive effects of stringent regulation on technological change with resulting economic benefits that offer a competitive advantage to the innovator are discussed in Part III of this book.

‡ Chapter 11 on trade regimes will delve more deeply into this topic.

fair subsidies, Bhagwati (1997) treats the demands for so-called fair trade (and for inclusion of environmental and labor standards in the World Trade Organization) as "intrusionist" measures from powerful countries that "imagine" threats from elsewhere and wish to impose policy changes on the rest of the world. However, he recognizes that global solutions for global environmental problems are required.

Ashford, Ayers, et al. (1985), Ashford, Heaton, et al. (1979), Porter (1991), and Porter and van der Linde (1995) defend the opposite argument. On the basis of their research, conducted, respectively, in the late 1970s and early 1990s, they argue that stringent environmental regulation can improve the comparative advantage of the sector and country that adopt and enforce them, at least in developed societies. The rationale is that properly designed environmental policy will stimulate technological innovation and offset initial compliance costs through technology modernization.*

### 5.1.3 Global Investment and the Environment

A third subject of discussion in the debate over the economy and the environment relates to investments and the transfer of funds across countries. As we will see in more detail in Chapter 12, funds can originate from either private or public sources. The following discussion outlines the relationships between the environment and both foreign direct investment (FDI), that is, private-sector investment, and official (government) development assistance (ODA). Regarding FDI, it is important to understand the nature of investment decisions and the determinant factors that govern the process. Thus we will address the following questions: (1) What is the effect of globalized investment on the environment? (2) What is the effect of environmental regulation on investment decisions? Because existing data do not appear to provide clear answers to these questions (S. Chua 1999; ECLAC 2002; ECLAC and UNEP 2001), the following discussion will look more qualitatively at the potential links between the environment and private and public investments, respectively.†

Over the past two decades, FDI has grown explosively (WBG 2002, 2006, 2007). This growth in FDI has meant that private capital investment now outstrips public (government) investment in developing regions. In 2005, the net private capital flow to developing countries was $491 billion, compared with $107 billion in development assistance (WBG 2006). This surge in private capital can be of mutual benefit to the developed and the developing worlds. FDI not only injects money into the recipient's economy but also brings with it technology, managerial skills, and market access, thereby accelerating growth and development. It may even upgrade worker skills and create new jobs that might otherwise not have existed (Chesky 1998; Hausmann and Fernández-Arias 2000). To a certain extent, FDI investments are a vote of confidence. They flow into a country because investors are attracted by the country's policies and institutions and its long-term growth prospects.

Proponents of financial globalization point out that over the past decade, tens of thousands of companies have crossed their national boundaries in search of new markets, cheaper labor, and higher profits, resulting in a powerful transfer of advanced technologies, products, and managerial experience to the developing world, as well as a boost of wages, creation of jobs, and improvements in the quality of life for millions of people. Skeptics, on the other hand, point to the various adverse effects of this surge in international investment: the often terrible working conditions and low wages, the damage to the environment, and the widespread corruption, as well as the exposure of weak economies to destructively high volatility shocks (Chesky 1998). All these issues have strong elements of truth in them, and the economic and environmental implications of financial globalization remain controversial (A. S. Miller 2000, p. 1230).

One significant challenge facing governments of developing nations is how to attract private capital while at the same time ensuring that this capital is invested in ways that promote—or at least do not prevent—*sustainable* progress. The problem is that many developing countries often bargain with foreign investors from the industrialized world from a position of weakness. For example, A. S. Miller (2000) explains that the developing world has borne some severe environmental and social costs in order to attract investors and acquire higher levels of private capital it desperately needed for economic growth. For several decades now, developing countries have functioned as the main exporters of natural resources

---

\*     For a more detailed discussion of the *weak* and *strong* forms of the "regulation-induced-innovation hypothesis," see Section 9.4 in Chapter 9. See also the extensive European literature on the strengths and limitations of "ecological modernization" (Ashford 2002; Jänicke 2008).

†     S. Chua (1999) argues that this lack of evidence is due to three factors that have not been considered in the analyses: environmental innovation, international diffusion of clean technologies, and the economic benefits of having a better environment.

whose extraction and preparation for export have a dramatic impact not only on their environment but also on levels of human health and the incidence of many illnesses.

In previous sections, we have discussed the pollution-haven hypothesis or "race to the bottom" (the "Delaware effect") and the "California effect" or "race to the top." Interestingly, the presence of limited amounts of FDI could create a dynamic where environmental standards are strengthened in the developing nations and reduced in the developed nations to attract private capital, resulting in a "race to the middle." The basic rationale is that developed nations, in an effort to remain competitive, face downward pressure on environmental standards, whereas developing nations, in response to international institutions and green consumers, face upward pressure on their environmental and health and safety standards.

The lack of any convincing evidence about the extent to which companies invest through FDI in nations on the basis of regulatory, tax, or wage arbitrage suggests that the presence of a stable regulatory system might be just as important as a weak system in attracting FDI (Gitterman 2004; Rodrik 1996). The ability of foreign firms to secure a return on their investments is linked to their ability to secure legal protection for their activities within a nation. Such legal protection pertains to well-defined property rights and legal codes that are stable (or predictable) and not subject to frequent changes, permitting sound business planning. Thus firms seeking to invest in foreign markets might also push for more stable and stringent regulations, reinforcing the idea of a "race to the middle" described above, or at least not a "race to the bottom."

The Global Sullivan Principles provide a different mechanism through which foreign firms investing private capital in developing nations could create upward pressure, particularly on social regulations. High-standard firms that endorse the principles (see Box 5.1) agree to support far-reaching economic, social, and political justice objectives that have their roots in South Africa's antiapartheid era. The Global Sullivan Principles require firms to extend their domestic standards and procedures to their overseas operations.[7] In effect, the principles require a firm that is investing in a developing nation to extend its corporate social responsibilities to all of its operations and not to apply them only to regions where government and society have a watchful eye on their activities.

One way to enhance the impact of the Global Sullivan Principles would be to require all firms that en-

dorse the principles to extend their practices to their in-country suppliers and subcontractors. Although this extension is likely to be resisted by multinational corporations because of the implementation challenges, such an extended responsibility scheme could have a significant impact on enhancing the social, economic, and environmental performance of firms within a developing nation. For instance, it would potentially affect all firms within a manufacturing supply chain, from resource-extraction companies to the firms responsible for the disposal of consumer products.*

In addition to the Global Sullivan Principles, there are other less ambitious but nevertheless important industry-led initiatives designed to raise standards. For example, Carrefour, Wal-Mart, Tesco, and Migros endorsed the Global Social Compliance Programme (GSCP), which aims to "harmonise their respective efforts in delivering a shared, global and sustainable approach for the improvement of working conditions in the global supply chain" (CIES 2008).

With regard to public funding for development, it is important to consider the impacts of official development assistance (ODA), investments backed by export credit agencies (ECAs), and investments/loans by multilateral development banks (MDBs) on the environment.

Over the past two decades, financing for environmental protection has emerged as an essential component of ODA, at both multilateral and bilateral levels (Franz 1996). A wide range of development organizations, from multilateral institutions to national governments to NGOs, have reconsidered the goals of their programs and projects in order to respond to, and properly incorporate, the growing awareness of environmental concerns. Still, this effort to integrate environmental concerns into development assistance is relatively new, and the results thus far have been far from ideal, primarily because of limited funds for environmental protection (Grieg-Gan, Banuri, et al. 2002; WBG 1997). Further, even if ODA is considered as supporting/promoting "sustainable" development, it is likely that some sizable component of the funding aligns with the donor nation's strategic development or security priorities (Gardner and Lugo 2009).

Notwithstanding the challenges, bringing environmental concerns into the realm of international

---

*       See the discussion in Chapter 10 of "extended producer responsibility" for electronic equipment, products, and waste under the EU's WEEE Directive.

---

**BOX 5.1: THE GLOBAL SULLIVAN PRINCIPLES**

**THE PRINCIPLES**

As a company which endorses the Global Sullivan Principles we will respect the law, and as a responsible member of society we will apply these Principles with integrity consistent with the legitimate role of business. We will develop and implement company policies, procedures, training and internal reporting structures to ensure commitment to these Principles throughout our organization. We believe the application of these Principles will achieve greater tolerance and better understanding among peoples, and advance the culture of peace.

Accordingly, we will:

- Express our support for universal human rights and, particularly, those of our employees, the communities within which we operate and parties with whom we do business.
- Promote equal opportunity for our employees at all levels of the company with respect to issues such as color, race, gender, age, ethnicity or religious beliefs, and operate without unacceptable worker treatment such as the exploitation of children, physical punishment, female abuse, involuntary servitude or other forms of abuse.
- Respect our employees' voluntary freedom of association.
- Compensate our employees to enable them to meet at least their basic needs and provide the opportunity to improve their skill and capability in order to raise their social and economic opportunities.
- Provide a safe and healthy workplace; protect human health and the environment; and promote sustainable development.
- Promote fair competition including respect for intellectual and other property rights, and not offer, pay or accept bribes.
- Work with governments and communities in which we do business to improve the quality of life in those communities—their educational, cultural, economic and social well-being—and seek to provide training and opportunities for workers from disadvantaged backgrounds.
- Promote the application of these Principles by those with whom we do business.

We will be transparent in our implementation of these Principles and provide information which demonstrates publicly our commitment to them.

Source: The Leon H. Sullivan Foundation, The Global Sullivan Principles of Social Responsibility, www.thesullivanfoundation.org/about/global _sullivan_principles (accessed January 13, 2011).

---

development assistance has affected strategies for sustainable development in two important ways (Fairman and Ross 1996). First, it has led to a new range of institutions, projects, and programs devoted to the protection of the environment. Second, it has made conventional development programs more environmentally aware through, for instance, the promotion of environmental impact statements and the restriction of funds for environmentally harmful projects.

Although some progress has been made through ODA, there is concern that this might be undermined by the activities of publicly funded ECAs (Norlen, Cox, et al. 2002).* ECAs provide guaranteed loans/credits to private investors investing in projects that are usually not eligible for funding by international institutions because they have questionable effects on the environment or are otherwise

not seen as sufficiently beneficial. ECAs are now the single largest public financiers of large-scale infrastructure projects (power generation, telecommunications, and transportation) in the developing and emerging economies (ECA-Watch 2003; Rich 2000). These include large dams, coal and nuclear power plants, mining projects, roads, oil pipelines, chemical and other industrial facilities, logging, and plantation schemes. ECAs provide twice as much money to developing countries as the total of all official development assistance worldwide, both bilateral and multilateral, including the UN agencies and the World Bank (Rich 2000).

In contrast to ODA lenders, ECAs are not foreign assistance agencies but domestic assistance agencies, used to boost the sales of a country's multinational corporations undertaking activities that some call the "new Mercantilism" (Rich 2000). ECAs are taxpayer supported but tend not to be politically accountable, having no or very little legislative oversight. In recent years, ECAs have come under increasing scrutiny by civil society and policy makers because of their backing of investments that have had negative environmental, social, and human rights impacts. Of the wide

---

*        ECAs are government or quasi-governmental institutions that provide government-backed loans, guarantees, and insurance to MNEs based in their home country with the purpose of promoting international trade and investment. For a more detailed discussion of ECAs, see Section 12.3.5 in Chapter 12.

range of projects that ECAs have supported in sectors such as oil, gas, coal, and mining, but also nuclear energy, hydropower, and pulp and paper, many have had detrimental effects on the environment, social structures, and human rights (Norlen 2002).

With limited social and environmental guidelines informing their investment decisions, there is concern that the actions of ECAs are fueling a "race to the bottom"—that is, investments flow to those regions with the lowest overheads and standards (Norlen 2002). Further, the lack of public disclosure of their activities is seen to be at odds with the tenets of democracy to which their parent governments aspire (ibid.). In response to such concerns and to the unfair competition that ECAs posed to national import-export banks, in 2001 the OECD agreed to nonbinding guidelines that asked ECAs of member states to incorporate environmental and social considerations into their lending practices (Evans 2005; Evans and Oye 2001; Nakhooda, Seymour, et al. 2009).[8] In 2004, the recommendations—known as "common approaches"–were accepted as binding standards for project support and requirements for ex ante transparency. However, countries could choose between World Bank/International Finance Corporation (IFC) standards and more lax regional bank rules, and thus the goal of harmonization was not achieved. In addition, transparency could be thwarted by a country's ECA invoking confidentiality or proprietary concerns (Schaper 2009). More recently, the OECD Export Credit Group (ECG) was criticized for weakening the environmental policy for ECAs (ECA-Watch 2007). In countries such as the United Kingdom, which is considered to be proactive on addressing the shortcomings of ECAs,[9] there continues to be concern about the role of ECAs in promoting environmentally destructive projects (Appleyard 2008). It seems, therefore, that there is much to be done to green the investment activities of ECAs.

In contrast to ECAs, the investment actions of multilateral development banks (MDBs)—such as the World Bank, the African Development Bank, the Asian Development Bank, the European Bank for Reconstruction and Development, and the Inter-American Development Bank Group—can have a significant impact on furthering sustainable development objectives in developing regions. Guided by the Millennium Development Goals and other international agreements, the investment decisions of MDBs have the potential to limit social and environmental burdens related to large-scale projects (Nakhooda, Seymour, et al. 2009). The actions of MDBs also influence the private banking sector. For example, the

Equator Principles—modeled on the World Bank's environmental principles and the IFC's social policies—shape the investment decisions of some seventy private banks that have adopted the principles (as of January 12, 2011). The Equator Principles try to ensure that the adopting financial institutions support only projects where measures have been taken to mitigate, monitor, and manage any significant social and environmental risks.

In conclusion, the link between global investment activities and the environment is complex. Both private and public investment in developing countries can advance or hinder important social and environmental objectives. With regard to private investment, no clear evidence exists whether FDI harms the environment or whether environmental regulation impedes investment. A dynamic situation exists in which pressure on firms to invest in regions with low wages and standards to reduce costs is countered by pressure from consumers and international organizations to act responsibly. The situation is somewhat different with regard to public investments in development. Because ODA is subject to the rules and regulations of national and international institutions, there are mechanisms that can prevent investments that have significant negative environmental and social impacts. In contrast, because ECAs are not publicly accountable and existing ECA investment principles (or "common approaches") can be circumvented, ECA-backed investments can lead to significant social and environmental impacts. One way to reduce the destructive investment activities of ECAs would be to make them publicly accountable. However, such action is likely to reveal uncomfortable tensions between the need to grow the national economy and protecting the environment and society of foreign regions. Finally, placing sustainable development objectives at the center of MDB investment decisions would raise the profile of social and environmental outcomes in relation to the traditional economic indicators of success. Such progressive actions would set an important precedent for other public and private financial institutions to follow.

## 5.2 EFFECTS OF GLOBALIZATION ON ECONOMY/WORK INTERACTIONS: SECTOR IV

The purpose of this section is to explore how technological change and globalization—or technological change in the context of globalization—might affect development in industrialized and developing regions, and the implications of that development on employment. Technological change and globalization are considered as drivers of change *within* and *between* three operationally important dimensions of sustainable development (Figure 5.3). Although the "sustainability triangle" is often defined as the economy, the environment, and equity (the three Es of sustainability), here we argue that equity is not a separate concern; rather, considerations of "equity" occur in each corner of the triangle. Thus equity is replaced with employment because technological change and globalization have direct implications for employment in both developed and developing nations, and labor-market policies share importance with government policies focusing on improving economic competitiveness and environmental quality. In addition, if we are to meet the basic human needs for such items as food, clothing, and shelter, the only practical way to do this is to satisfy the basic need for a sustainable livelihood by creating employment op-

portunities with adequate purchasing power. "There is no point to a globalization that reduces the price of a child's shoe, but costs the father his job" (anonymous, from WCSDG 2004, p. 13).

It is possible to consider the impact of rapid technological change and globalization on employment through three broad lenses: (1) the international division of labor, (2) the creation of purchasing power, and (3) technology-enabled capital mobility. Although it is recognized that technological innovations in products, industrial processes, and services can enhance our quality of life, these innovations can also bring social and environmental consequences. These consequences are discussed in the following subsection.

### 5.2.1 The International Division of Labor (Resulting from Multinationalization)

*How can technology affect the international division of labor—that is, the distribution of manufacturing/*

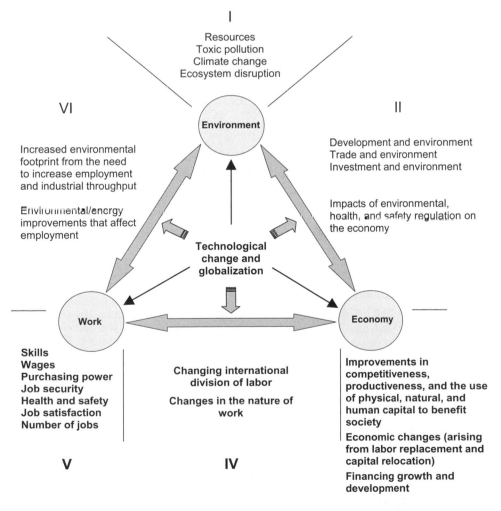

FIGURE 5.3: TECHNOLOGICAL CHANGE AND GLOBALIZATION AS DRIVERS OF CHANGE THAT AFFECTS THE ECONOMY AND WORK (SECTORS III, IV, AND V)

*assembly facilities and service centers among countries?*

In Section 1.1.3.1 in Chapter 1, we introduced the Heckscher-Ohlin model of trade that incorporates the Stopler-Samuelson theorem. This model provides the basic rationale for the international division of labor. It states that countries should specialize in those activities in which they have a comparative advantage and exchange any surplus home-produced commodities (or services) for those more easily produced by others. The model implies that countries endowed with high-skilled workers and capital should focus on the production of high-skill- or capital-intensive commodities and export any surplus in exchange for imports of low-skill- or labor-intensive commodities produced by countries with abundant low-skilled labor. This simple economic logic, which builds on Ricardo's theory of comparative advantage, underlies much of the discussion surrounding international trade.

Although the Heckscher-Ohlin model is useful, it is important to recognize that the composition of labor within nations varies considerably and continually evolves with development. For example, the transition of many developed nations from agricultural to industrial to service economies has been accompanied by technology-based shifts in the skills required of workers (Drucker 1994). Further, although countries such as the United States are described as having a postindustrial, service, or knowledge-based economy, it is important to recognize that the agricultural and industrial sectors have not been replaced (Bell 1999). Rather, the size of these sectors has declined with the growth of the service economy, but they still form an important component of the U.S. economy. Thus understanding a nation's "sectoral composition"—that is, the proportion of an economy attributed to agriculture, manufacturing, services, and other sectors—is important when one is considering the potential impact of technology and globalization on labor (Coffey 1996). Further, unlike the manufacturing sector, which is somewhat homogeneous in character, the service sector varies considerably, from fast food to banking, dentistry, car repair, and teaching.

Two important factors that have shaped the international division of labor are the declining costs of freight transportation[10] and new process technologies that permit "the division, subdivision and standardization of specific tasks which could be easily learned and carried out by unskilled or semi-skilled labour" (Coffey 1996, p. 53). The fall in freight transportation costs has meant that distance has become a less con-straining factor (Glaeser and Kohlhase 2003). Specifically, it has enabled manufacturing firms to rethink the location from which factors of production—such as labor and resources—are obtained and brought together. Further, advances in process technologies have effectively reduced the need for manufacturers to maintain low-skilled operations in industrialized nations where labor tends to be more expensive. The combination of these two factors has meant that a nation's comparative advantages are likely to rest on its "administrative" conditions[*] and the costs of its labor. In industrialized nations, these factors are often associated with *deindustrialization*, where labor-intensive and low-skilled parts of manufacturing processes are relocated (primarily) to developing nations, leaving behind the more highly skilled components in the home nation (Coffey 1996).[†] In addition, as more production capacity is built in low-wage countries, manufacturing companies in industrialized nations employing unskilled and semiskilled labor face growing competition, further promoting the displacement of manufacturing jobs (Kletzer 1998, 2000).[‡] Thus although globalization holds the potential to enhance quality of life through economic development, processes such as multinationalization and deindustrialization are likely to feed the general perception that it can also reduce pay and undermine worker rights (Environics International 2002; Pew Research Center 2003).

In addition to the factors described above, the growth of the global communication network is also shaping the international division of labor. Information and communication technologies (ICT) have enabled companies to outsource jobs, such as those

---

[*]     Although a nation's comparative advantage is (theoretically) determined by its geographic location and its natural and human capital endowment, the administrative conditions within a nation can also influence competitiveness (Bleijenberg 1995). For example, a nation that has low environmental standards and taxes might be "artificially" competitive. However, although wages and the industrial relations environment of a nation are statistically significant factors that influence the location decisions of MNEs, a more important factor appears to be the size of a nation's market (Bognanno, Keane, et al. 2005). Also, Whitford (2006, p. 3) argues that the "particularities of firms' embedding in particular historical and institutional contexts" tends to be more important than factors such as international regulatory arbitrage.

[†]     See the classic book titled *The Deindustrialization of America* (Bluestone and Harrison 1982) for an early discussion of how growing international competition and capital mobility caused a "crisis of competitiveness" and deindustrialization in the United States.

[‡]     See Section 1.1.3.1 for a related discussion of how trade and technological change can displace jobs and affect income and wage inequality.

of programmers and telephone operators, to firms in other nations with seemingly little difficulty.* In 2003, A. T. Kearney predicted that U.S. financial services firms were likely to relocate more than 500,000 jobs (8 percent of the financial services workforce) to other nations over a five-year period (Benjamin and Perry 2003; K. Lee 2003). More generally, it was estimated that by 2015, 3.4 million U.S. service-industry jobs will relocate offshore to countries such as India, Russia, China, and the Philippines (McCarthy 2004; McCarthy, Dash, et al. 2002). The jobs most likely to be relocated are based primarily in the ICT industry and are those that do not require any face-to-face contact.[†]

The recent trends in outsourcing can be seen as a new form of multinationalization, where the jobs of semi- and highly skilled workers in industrialized nations are being displaced by semi- and highly skilled workers in developing nations such as India. The fact that distance is not really a consideration for ICT-based services means that multinational enterprises (MNEs) are likely to focus more on the price and availability of labor than on its location.[‡] Although ICT has facilitated job displacement in developed nations, the broader impacts from such displacement may also have benefits. For example, the tech-support savings achieved by relocating call centers to India can be built into the lower price of new computers that, in turn, can theoretically spur U.S. productivity growth (Akst 2004; Mann 2003). Also, the transfer of software jobs to countries such as India can actually lead to the creation of some new jobs in America if specific high-skilled tasks are outsourced back to the United States (Economist 2004a; T. L. Friedman 2004). Finally, it is important to recognize that the total number of jobs outsourced represents only a small percentage (estimated to be around 2 percent in 2015) of total U.S. employment in a single year (Levine 2004). The limited scale of offshoring is argued to have a negligible impact on U.S. wage levels as a whole (Farrell 2006), although the displaced workers may bear the brunt of the effects of offshoring. Like the threat of capital flight, the specter of an employer outsourcing overseas may do much to dampen employee demand for wage and/or job benefit increases.

A useful way to consider changes in the international division of labor is to look at the flows of FDI from MNEs. Indeed, Coffey (1996) argues that the FDI decisions of MNEs effectively "regulated" the location of jobs through decisions whether to invest in a particular country.[§] Similarly, Castells (1999, p. 235) argues that MNEs, with their international networks, effectively "organize the core labor force in the global economy." In addition to the investment decisions and strategies of MNEs, ECAs and MDBs such as the World Bank—discussed in Section 5.1.3 and in Chapter 12, "Financing Sustainable Development"—also have considerable influence on where companies are able to invest overseas. Therefore, it appears that there are several major forces shaping the international division of labor: (1) the FDI investment decisions of MNEs; (2) the investment decisions of ECAs and MDBs; and (3) the regulatory environments and financial incentives created by governments to attract foreign investment in their home nations.

It is important to consider these forces in the context of the global economy, which is far from being truly "global" in scope (Hirst and Thompson 2002; Stallings 1993, 1995). Flows of FDI and trade tend to concentrate in the triad of Europe, Japan, and North America,[¶] limiting the creation of employment opportunities in other regions of the world. However, the triad may need to be reclassified if China and other "peripheral" economies continue to emerge as the "new core" of the world economy (Muradian 2004).

The transition of industrialized nations toward service or knowledge-based societies adds a new dimension to the problems discussed above. A knowledge-based society reduces the need for unskilled or semiskilled workers in developed nations—who form the largest proportion of the working population—and increases the importance of a well-trained and educated labor force (Drucker 1994; Levy and Murnane

---

* See R. B. Freeman (2003) for a valuable discussion of the world of work in the new millennium. In addition to discussing such factors as the feminization of work and the shift in the world labor force to less developed countries, Freeman argues that the rapid growth of computers and information and communication technology are important factors shaping the nature of employment, particularly in developed nations.

† The global spread of ICT is mirrored by a reduction in the scale and power of "traditional" trade unions (Munck 2002). This trend has led trade unions to consider ways to reinvent themselves. It seems that their future now lies in finding ways to pull together workers with common interests from a diffuse global labor network that transcends national boundaries (ibid.).

‡ Although manufacturing/assembly plants might be located abroad to be nearer to markets, services may be located abroad because location is not relevant. In both cases, jobs may be relocated.

---

§ This assertion is debatable in the context of South Korea or Japan, for example, which permitted little equity ownership by foreign firms. However, it does point to the fact that the evolution of the international economy is closely related to the changing nature of MNEs.

¶ See the related discussion in Section 4.2 in Chapter 4.

2004; M. Miller 1995; WCSDG 2004).* In effect, it is argued that in knowledge-based societies, unskilled labor is being replaced by (computer-powered) technology that requires a smaller amount of skilled labor to maintain and operate (Rifkin 2004). These skilled laborers are what Drucker (1994) refers to as the "technologists." The growing differential in wages between educated/skilled workers and unskilled workers and the higher unemployment rates in the latter group all point to the formation of a knowledge-based society and the reduction of manufacturing (and now servicing-producing) capacity (Firebaugh 2003; M. Miller 1995).

In developing nations, the emergence of technology-enabled, knowledge-based societies is widening the educational/informational gap and extending the digital divide.† In addition, the problem of high unemployment is worsened by the fact that over the next fifty years, the vast majority of population growth is predicted to occur in urban areas in developing nations (UNPD 2003). The constant flow of new entrants into the labor force in these countries is argued to result in "jobless growth," meaning that the rise in unemployment is a structural phenomenon (M. Miller 1995). In this situation, it seems that the

formation of high-tech industries in developing nations will be sustained only if a reliable stream of well-educated workers can be established. But the provision of basic education is a luxury for the vast majority who struggle daily against the poverty trap. Even if an adequate supply of educated workers could be provided, there is concern that the sheer scale of technology-displaced workers is likely to overshadow any growth in high-tech industries (Rifkin 2004).

However, there are those who question whether the predicted technological changes will result in the formation of a "jobless economy" due to an increasing demand for highly skilled and trained workers (Drucker 1954; C. Freeman and Soete 1994; Levy and Murnane 2004; Simon 1960). Again, the problem with these more optimistic views is the failure to address the fact that the level of education required for high-technology jobs is likely to be unattainable for the vast majority of people in developing nations. Education aside, the impact that rapid technological change in industrialized (or information-based) nations is having on developing nations is put quite succinctly by M. Miller (1995, p. 128): "Rapid changes are stressful enough, but when the spearheading technologies are 'high-tech,' labour-saving and involve extremely mobile intangible assets, the social impact is magnified. Unable to keep up with the rapidly and profoundly changing nature of technology, most developing countries are falling further and further behind the industrialized nations in the acquisition and deployment of these technologies that are opening the way to new modes of production, distribution and, in effect, new modes of economic and social life."‡

Given that reducing inequality is central to achieving sustainable development, understanding how rapid technological change and globalization can affect the international division of labor is of critical importance. Although it seems that workers with advanced technology-related (and transferable) skills and a high level of education are well positioned in the in-

---

*     In *The New Divisions of Labor*, Levy and Murnane (2004, p. 54) argue that the introduction of the computer has raised the demand for people who are able to perform jobs requiring expert thinking and complex communication—i.e., "tasks that computers cannot do." It follows that those jobs that consist of routine cognitive and manual work are susceptible to being displaced by computer programs, and advances in computerization only increase the likelihood of such substitution. Levy and Murnane (ibid., p. 9) define expert thinking as "solving new problems for which there are no routine solutions," and complex communication as "persuading, explaining, and in other ways conveying a particular interpretation of information." In both cases, computers provide an essential support function but are unable to replace a human's ability to think creatively in difficult and unpredictable circumstances. The "ability to develop, produce, and market new products relies on the human ability to manage and solve analytic problems and communicate new information, and so it keeps expert thinking and complex communication in strong demand" (ibid., p. 54). The objective of Levy and Murnane's (2004) work is to outline what constitutes a good, well-paid job in a rapidly computerizing economy. See Economist (2004b) for a discussion of how computers have changed the nature of work.

†     Norris (2001) describes how the Internet is creating a global information divide between industrialized nations and developing societies, a social divide between the information-rich and the information-poor within nations, and a democratic divide between individuals who do and do not have access to the Internet for political purposes. See Compaine (2001) for an insightful discussion of the digital-divide discourse, from those who believe that societies without access to the Internet are at a social and economic disadvantage to those who argue that it is a nonissue and that the digital divide is rapidly closing without government intervention.

‡     Since the eighteenth century, agricultural societies (in the now-developed nations) have transformed themselves into industrial societies and are currently in the midst of a new transformation into postindustrial, or information-based, societies (Castells 1999; Drucker 1994). The rate of change in these nations is placing significant pressure on developing nations that by and large remain agricultural societies in a state of transformation. Although nations such as Malaysia, South Africa, and Brazil are progressing along the industrialization pathway, a significant number of people in developing nations either rely on subsistence farming for their survival or are migrating to cities in search of unskilled or low-skilled (in a technological sense) employment.

ternational economy, workers with a less flexible skill set and a lower level of education—who constitute the vast majority of people in the world—appear most at risk of unemployment with every move of the international economy's invisible hand.

Daly (1994, p. 186) argues that one potential way to protect labor markets is to "move away from the ideology of global economic integration by free trade, free capital mobility, and export-led growth and toward a more nationalist orientation that seeks to develop domestic production for internal markets as the first option, having recourse to international trade only when clearly much more efficient."* This strategy would put the control of a country's labor markets in the hands of the national government and industry, avoiding pressures to lower standards and wages and externalize environmental and social costs, which are some of the perils of global economic integration (Daly 1993).† However, such an approach to protecting labor markets runs directly against the predominant economic view of trade and wage liberalization. Rather than establish antiglobalization measures, Brenton (2006) argues that income-redistribution policies that preserve the gains from trade are a more effective way to address problems of growing income inequality and social exclusion (that is, unemployment) caused by trade and investment liberalization. His basic argument is that although the process of globalization will inevitably create some losers, if these groups are compensated (by national governments and international institutions), the benefits from more rapid economic development are likely to outweigh the costs. However, creating effective compensation mechanisms is a complex task, especially in the international arena.

Regardless of one's view on the effects of globalization, the importance of national governments in shaping the structure and dynamics of the international economy should not be overlooked. As Castells (1999, p. 98) argues, "There is not, and there will not be in the foreseeable future, a fully integrated, open world market for labor, technology, goods, and services, as long as nation states (or associations of nation states, such as the European Union) exist, and as long as governments are there to foster the interests of their citizens and of firms in the territories under their jurisdiction, in the global competition."

It is interesting that while Daly (1994) argues for "renationalization," Castells (1999) suggests that national policies already play a much more influential role in shaping a nation's competitiveness, productivity, and technology than they are often given credit for doing. To support his argument, Castells (ibid., p. 89) documents cases where "some governments [for example, those of Japan, Taiwan, and South Korea or the "Asian tigers"] have restrained as much as possible the penetration of their markets by foreign competition, thus creating competitive advantage for specific industries in their period of nurturing."‡ It is also apparent that those nations that resisted the advice of the Washington Consensus have experienced some of the fastest growth since the early 1980s (Faux 2002b). Beyond policies aimed at competitiveness, productivity, and technology, national governments also play a critical role in shaping employment opportunities. For example, E. Lee (1996, pp. 495–496) argues that "in spite of increasing globalization, national policies are still paramount in determining levels of employment and labour standards. These policies have to be more sensitive to considerations of international competitiveness, but this by no means implies that policy autonomy has ended or that the reduction of wages and labour standards is the only viable response to increasing globalization."

In conclusion, it seems that a useful way to transition toward sustainable development would be to combine the inherent national desire to protect citizen,

---

* Similarly, Stiglitz (2002b) promotes government intervention in situations where the pursuit of free trade is likely to undermine or destroy emerging domestic industries in developing nations that are unable to complete in the global market. He also reminds us that today's industrialized nations did not practice free trade when their industries were developing. Indeed, one can argue that although many industrialized nations now promote trade liberalization (or the Washington Consensus), many still have policies in place that protect their agricultural sectors and domestic industries. To limit the potential negative impacts of free trade, Stiglitz (2002b) promotes a range of government interventions that can stimulate and protect domestic economies; stabilize financial institutions; create, protect, and/or enhance existing employment opportunities; and shoulder some of the financial burdens during periods of unemployment that are caused by factors beyond an individual's control.

† Further, Kleinknecht (1998) argues that a flexible wage policy would reward firms that do not use labor effectively and thus slow the industrial displacement and transformation processes described by Schumpeter.

‡ Although national governments have an incentive to craft policies to promote/protect the interests of their citizens and industries, the same is also true for economic regions such as the triad of Europe, Japan, and North America. Hirst and Thompson (2002, pp. 2–3) argue that "these major economic powers, the G3, . . . have the capacity, especially if they coordinate policy, to exert powerful governance pressures over financial markets and other economic tendencies. Global markets are thus by no means beyond regulation and control, even though the current scope and objectives of economic governance are limited by the divergent interests of the great powers and the economic doctrines prevalent among their elites."

worker, and industry interests with the need to protect critical natural capital (that is, ecological systems and resources).* Such a strategy would make environmental protection and enhancement core objectives that shape national policies for employment, competitiveness, productivity, and technology development. However, the trade-off between establishing an attractive investment environment (with low taxes and a smaller role for government) and protecting social welfare (especially that of displaced or underemployed workers) is likely to continue to cause controversy and force government officials, industry, and civil society to think carefully about the delicate balance between competitiveness and social inclusion/cohesion.

### 5.2.2 The Creation of Purchasing Power

*How does technology facilitate the creation of purchasing power throughout the world?*

In Section 1.1.1 in Chapter 1, we reviewed the Human Development Index (HDI), which measures the level of development achieved by a nation by using three indexes—health, education, and income. The HDI does not explicitly consider the impact of technology. However, it does provide a clear indication of the extent of the gap between the purchasing power of the rich and the poor. For example, almost all of the top twenty nations of the HDI have a GNI per capita (adjusted for purchasing power) that falls between $22,917 and $81,011, whereas the twenty nations ranked lowest have a GNI per capita between $176 and $2,051 (UNDP 2010). Therefore, even if developing nations experienced a significant rate of economic growth, their total relative amount of income would remain substantially lower than that of more developed nations. If we make the additional observation that around 1.2 billion people out of the developing world's 4.8 billion people are living on less than $1 a day, and around 2.8 billion people are living on less than $2 a day (WBG 2002), this provides strong support to Durning's (1992, 1994) argument that just over 1 billion people are part of the market economy (who form the consumer society). The remainder either live on its periphery (around 3 billion people) or have no role in

the economy (1.2 billion people). In addition, although income inequality exists between nations, it is also present within nations (see Section 1.1.3.1). It is in this context that the implications of rapid technological change and globalization should be considered.

The transfer and diffusion of technology from industrialized to developing nations is a powerful mechanism that is creating a new working and purchasing class and reducing income inequality between these nations (Firebaugh 2003). The impact of this mechanism on increasing purchasing power and reducing inequality depends on the changing "technology-geography nexus." Firebaugh (2003) describes how the importance of (geographically fixed) natural resources can change dramatically as new technologies emerge. For example, the invention and diffusion of the internal combustion engine dramatically enhanced the real estate value of oil-rich regions of the world, leading to significant investment in these areas and job creation. In addition, he argues that technological change can also alter the "habitability" of those parts of the world that experience extreme temperatures and/or difficult living environments. For example, installing air-conditioning systems in factories and office buildings can enhance worker productivity by eliminating periods when it is simply too hot to work effectively. Firebaugh (ibid., p. 181) captures these ideas in two simple models that indicate how new technologies can shape the continually evolving pattern of global income inequality:

- Changing technology→changing value of natural resources that vary geographically→changing global income inequality
- Changing technology→changing relative habitability of the world's regions→changing productivity by region→changing global income inequality

A potential problem with these models is that there is no explicit consideration of how changing technology is affecting the sustainability of development pathways. A concern is that the transfer and diffusion of technology from developed to developing nations is fueled by an underlying desire to spread consumerism and expand markets for Westernized products and services (Benton and Redclift 1994). Further, it has been argued that the global agenda is dominated by the industrial globalization plans of the North, which are grounded on conventional economic development theory (Redclift 1992). This idea is perhaps best captured by Daly's (1996, pp. 31–44) notion of "economic growthmania."

---

* Although protecting the environment is directly relevant to a nation's health and well-being, the growing trends of environmental destruction and the decline in global resources (WWF 2006) indicate that the desire to promote national competitiveness, productivity, and technological capacity has yet to be explicitly linked to the environment.

Mehmet (1995, p. 7) provides a political critique of the mainstream Western (or European-centered) view of development economics (for example, trickle-down theory), which he argues is not "culture-friendly and has effectively denied the cultural diversity that exists in non-Western branches of humanity, where group and community rights are often held in higher esteem than individualism, and cooperation rather than competition is prized." Mehmet (1995) goes on to argue that international security will not be achieved without sound population policies in developing nations and the correction of global inequality generated by development economics that continually concentrate capital ownership in the North and support Northern consumerism. Although the alleviation of poverty in developing nations is clearly a desirable goal, Mehmet asks the fundamental question of whom the transfer of technology and the opening up of new markets is really benefiting.

In theory, the installation of production capacity in developing nations increases the purchasing power of those who are employed, enabling them to enjoy many of the products and services widely available in the North. The problem with this optimistic scenario of development is that the world's resources are insufficient to perpetuate the Western lifestyle throughout the world (Goleman 2009; Wilson 2002; WWF 2006). Although technological innovation can extend the availability of resources, the new limits to growth appear to be not resource limits, but limits on the ability of sinks to absorb the externalities (that is, pollution and greenhouse gases) from economic growth (Meadows, Randers, et al. 2004). Therefore, simply relocating manufacturing plants from developed to developing nations without any significant improvements in environmental performance is clearly not sustainable development.

Although considerations of whole life-cycle impacts of products/services and the introduction of "factor X" technology can lead to more sustainable forms of development (see Section 1.3.3), they do not address the question whether the developed-nation model is the one developing nations should be following. With such powerful economic and political forces behind industrial globalization, establishing a viable alternative seems extremely difficult. A more fruitful option might be to search for radically different forms of industrial globalization that can operate within ecological limits and better suit the different needs of societies throughout the world. Unfortunately, the formation of new forms of technology-

enabled development is likely to be hampered by technology-enabled financial capital mobility.

## 5.2.3 Technology-Enabled Capital Mobility

*How does technology-enabled (financial) capital mobility affect government and industry efforts to promote sustainable development?*

The primary driver behind the mobility of financial capital is the rapid global expansion of information and communication technologies (ICT) and networks, specifically the Internet. Further, the decline in capital controls over the past decades has also led to a dramatic increase in international capital mobility. For example, between 1980 and 1997 (the year before the Asian financial crisis), the flows of financial capital to developing nations increased from $1.9 billion to $120.3 billion—an increase of more than 6,000 percent (Weller, Scott, et al. 2001). Further, some 36 percent of these capital flows consisted of short-term portfolio investments (ibid.). Although many commentators and organizations (including the International Monetary Fund [IMF]) consider the benefits of financial globalization to outweigh the costs (Fischer 1997, 2003; Mishkin 2006), there are those who are less convinced (Rodrik 2007; Rodrik and Subramanian 2008). This section discusses several of the challenges posed by the recent trends in technology-enabled capital mobility.

The ease with which technology-enabled capital can flow between markets has led to a shortening of investment horizons as investors speculate on currencies, which can have detrimental impacts on development. For example, Block (1996) makes a convincing case that changes in the international financial regime following the breakdown of the Bretton Woods system in the 1970s have led directly to higher unemployment and slower growth rates. The most important of these changes was the transition to a floating-exchange-rate system. Block (1996) argues that high real interest rates—which occurred in response to the new floating-rate system—have made it difficult for governments to lower domestic rates to stimulate employment. Any attempt to do so would risk large outflows of capital that would move to regions with higher interest rates. As Block (p. 27) explains, "High levels of capital mobility create a strong bias toward restrictive monetary policies in the world economy. Countries that fail to align their interest rates with those of the large economy with the highest interest rate risk substantial capital outflows and intense speculative pressures on their currencies."[*] Thus with the advent of technology-enabled capital mobility, important segments of a nation's tax base are able to invest their capital efficiently in locations where they can avoid or minimize tax payments and obtain a higher return on their investment. This has the effect of increasing the "tax rates disproportionately on labor income" (Rodrik 1997, p. 6) and can lead to a number of "lowest-common-denominator socioeconomic and policy tendencies" (Paehkle 2003, p. 2). Further, evidence from developing nations—for example, Mexico and the East Asian economies—that have exposed themselves to large flows of potentially reversible short-term international capital has not been encouraging (Griffith-Jones, Montes, et al. 2001; Stiglitz 2002a, 2002b). The problem is that the liberalization of short-term capital flows limits a nation's autonomy, leaving it at the mercy of international market forces that can be "fickle and erratic" (Stiglitz 2002a, p. 27). In addition, it is the poor who are most likely to lose during a financial crisis, because higher-income earners have better access to insurance mechanisms that can help limit the impact of financial shocks (Weller, Scott, et al. 2001). Thus a major challenge facing governments is how to create an attractive and competitive market while providing an appropriate level of social welfare.[†]

Swank (2002, p. 4) provides a useful explanation of how increasing capital mobility can negatively affect social policies: "In brief, the economic logic argues that international capital mobility constrains social policies of democratically elected governments through the operation of markets: in a world of high or near perfect capital mobility, mobile asset holders pursue the most profitable rate of return on investment and governments compete to retain and attract that investment. . . . Politically, international capital mobility may constrain the social welfare policies of democratically elected governments through the routines of conventional politics; the credible threat of exit may enhance the conventional political resources of mobile asset holders and their interest associations."

But contrary to this economic logic, Rodrik (1997, 1998, 1999, 2007) argues that as national economies have become more open, their social spending has increased. For example, in small and open economies such as the Netherlands and Belgium, government spending has increased to insulate society against external risks (such as the 1970s oil shocks). Rodrik (1997, 1999) argues, therefore, that the welfare state could be viewed as the other side of the coin to economic globalization. His point is that "the provision of social insurance is an important component of market reforms—it cushions the blow of liberalization among those most severely affected, it helps maintain the legitimacy of these reforms, and it averts backlashes against the distributional and social consequences of integration into the world economy" (Rodrik 1999, p. 98). In this regard, Rodrik (1997) identifies two dangers that arise from complacency about the social consequences of globalization. First, as indicated above, there is the risk of a political backlash against trade.[‡] For example, it is easier for a politician to defend protectionist policies if this action is likely to secure employment for his or her constituents and subdue anxiety about globalization. Second, and potentially more important, globalization that is achieved at the cost of social disintegration would pay a very high price for development. Both of these concerns point to the need for well-conceived government intervention that protects the environment and social stability and cohesion from the downsides of economic globalization (Stiglitz 2002c).[§] In Rodrik's (2007, p. 219) view, those regions and nations that have benefited the most from foreign trade and investment—such as East Asia, China, and India—were able to "com-

---

[*]    In an earlier work, Piore and Sable (1984, p. 174) describe how the floating-rate system contributed to a crisis in mass production: "The unexpected, increasing volatility of exchange rates—due to the hunt for a safe store of value—created two . . . obstacles to a return to business-as-usual under the existing regulatory regime: it discouraged investment in mass production, and it encouraged the formation of major trade blocs." The authors were particularly concerned that the creation of trade blocs—i.e., agreements between nations/regions that protect firms against market fluctuations—would threaten the entire open-trading system by undermining the principles of trade liberalization.

[†]    This challenge is made even greater if one agrees with Soros (2002, p. 14) that "economic development, that is, the production of private goods, has taken precedence over social development, that is, the provision of public goods." His main concern is that although international trade and financial markets are efficient at generating wealth, they are unable to take care of essential social needs "such as the preservation of peace, alleviation of poverty, protection of the environment, labor conditions, or human rights" (ibid.). Thus governments have an important role in establishing regulatory frameworks that nurture both economic development and social welfare.

[‡]    The differences on trade between the two major candidates in the U.S. 2008 presidential campaign reflected very different perspectives on who was benefiting from trade.

[§]    It is important to recognize that the type of government intervention will vary between nations depending on existing labor-market institutions, corporate governance, social and environmental regulation, and other factors (Rodrik 1999, 2007). Further, such variation in legal and social structures makes the notion of a fully integrated global economy with common standards and regulations an unlikely prospect, at least in the foreseeable future (Rodrik 2005).

bine the opportunities offered by world markets with a domestic investment and institution-building strategy to stimulate the animal spirits of domestic entrepreneurs."

Although the benefits from liberalizing capital are clearly questionable, Rodrik and Subramanian (2008) do believe that real gains can be achieved from *domestic* financial liberalization that avoids the costs of external liberalization. On the basis of the work of Prasad, Rajan, et al. (2007), Rodrik and Subramanian (2008, p. 17) argue that "the evidence . . . suggests that for any given level of investment, the more that is financed by domestic savings the greater the long-run growth." Similarly, those countries that relied on foreign capital grew less rapidly than those that did not (ibid.), indicating that governments that retain some control over capital flows are more likely to strengthen their economies and foster economic development.*

To return to the earlier discussion, the shortening of investment horizons has also occurred within corporations at the potential expense of longer-term sustainable industrialization. In a report by the National Research Council's (NRC's) Board on Science, Technology, and Economic Policy (STEP), the structure of U.S. capital markets was described as causing corporate investment to focus on the short run.[†] The problem with shorter investment horizons is that they encourage low-risk and lower-payoff R&D investments that are seen as a considerable source of competitive disadvantage (NAE 1992; Tassey 1999). Firms focusing on short-term investment horizons tend to emphasize incremental inno-

vations and product-line extensions instead of more risky, long-term, and expensive next-generation (radical or disrupting) innovations that are likely to be more profitable (Tassey 2003). The creation of international financial markets has made it possible for an individual (with access to a brokerage) to invest in any market. Therefore, the mobility of financial capital is creating a highly competitive capital market that is reducing the time frames over which return on investment is demanded to the detriment of more long-term and (perhaps) more sustainable industrialization. In addition, capital can easily be expatriated rather than reinvested in countries where production and services centers are located.

Another point to consider is that global competition in technology (including the establishment of product standards and the notion of technological and organizational innovation) is predominantly shaped by competitive actions among the United States, Japan, and Western Europe (Ernst and O'Connor 1989). Within this highly competitive environment, technologies are becoming increasingly reliant on scientific advances supported by techno-nationalism—that is, the creation of domestic high-tech industries and/or the attraction of high-tech foreign firms to supply the domestic consumption of technology (Gibbons 1990; Weiss 1997). Because the vast majority of developing nations do not have their own high-tech industries, their only option (if they wish to be part of the global economy) is to import technologies designed for industrialized nations that inevitably shape (or regulate) the activities of their societies (Winner 1977, 1986).

The various forms of "techno-globalization" (the globalization of technology)[‡] discussed in the previous sections provide an indication of the extent to which Western technology is becoming an integral part of societies throughout the world. As the techno-economic interdependence between nations increases, the issue of technological dominance arises. Further,

---

* As this book goes to press, the world is in the midst of a financial crisis where the global mobility of financial instruments played a key role. Particularly adversely affected were Greece, Portugal, Spain, and Ireland, who purchased U.S. "toxic financial assets" that resulted in the proliferation of ultimately worthless financial assets that have threatened the stability of the euro (see Stiglitz 2010).

† The NRC's Board on Science, Technology, and Economic Policy (STEP 1994, p. 6) argues that "relative to those of most other countries, U.S. capital markets exhibit many characteristics that are worth preserving: liquidity, openness, and fairness with respect to investors in public companies, among other characteristics. As a consequence of our regulatory system requiring openness and fairness, however, there are limits to the amount of proprietary information made available by issuers to financial investors. Information about competitively sensitive longer-term strategic investments of the corporation is most likely to be withheld from investors. For this reason and because financial investment managers as fiduciaries are usually judged on a short-term basis, U.S. capital markets tend to bias the evaluation of corporate performance toward the short run. Short-run performance is certainly not an irrelevant criterion; it is simply overemphasized to the neglect of long-term growth, especially in publicly held companies."

‡ Archibugi and Michie (1997) provide a useful taxonomy for discussions of techno-globalism. In particular, they identify three types of techno-globalism: (1) the "global exploitation of technology," where "an increasing proportion of technological innovations are exploited in international markets" (p. 176); (2) "global technological collaboration," where international collaboration occurs among firms, governments, and academic institutions in the sharing of technological knowledge; and (3) the "global generation of technology," where "firms are increasing the international integration of their R&D and technological activities" (p. 177). Archibugi and Michie (1997) consider the last type of techno-globalism (which is more or less restricted to multinational enterprises) the technological equivalent of foreign direct investment. In general, the term "techno-globalism" is used to describe the increasing diffusion, adoption, and adaptation of technology throughout the world.

because MNEs are the primary mechanism for the diffusion of technology in developing nations, there is also a related issue of their dominance in the global economy (Korten 2001; WCSDG 2004). The blind adoption of technology or products by developing nations can cause significant economic and social follow-on costs. These costs occur as a result of the inability of host nations to manage the adoption (and potential adaptation) and diffusion of advanced technologies in a way that is safe and fits with the culture of their societies. Thus the worldwide diffusion of Western technology is creating a global society that is reliant on technology, the majority of which is designed to meet the needs of industrialized nations but possibly not those of the people in developing nations.*

It is evident from the preceding discussion that the current international financial regime, combined with the drive for the liberalization of short-term capital flows, can (1) undermine the ability of governments to provide public goods and (2) focus corporations on short-term investments to the possible detriment of more sustainable forms of industrialization. The common factor underlying both of these concerns is the ease with which technology-enabled capital can flow across borders at the click of a button. As the international economy continues to expand by incorporating emerging economies, the nations that are likely to gain the most are those that have found ways to protect the welfare of their citizens while remaining attractive to international investors.

### 5.2.4 Interconnections between the International Division of Labor, Purchasing Power, and Capital Mobility

The previous sections have attempted to provide some insight into how the forces of technological change and globalization can shape development and affect employment opportunities. The challenge in considering these two forces of change is that their impacts on nations and societies depend on a wide range of factors, such as a nation's level of industrialization, its administrative environment, and its openness to trade.

We conceive sustainable development through the triad of the economy, work, and the environment (see Figure 5.1). These interconnected dimensions are considered in the context of the international division of labor, the creation of purchasing power, and technology-enabled capital mobility. Although

these three issues are addressed separately in an effort to explore specific trends/concerns, it is evident that they are all highly interconnected, and changes in one will most likely affect the others.

With regard to industrial globalization, it is apparent that internationalization and multinationalization are directly linked to the transfer of technology between nations. In situations where the recipient nation's ability to control the new technology or industrial process is limited, such a transfer might well result in negative environmental[†] and social/worker[‡] impacts. The growth of these forms of industrialization can also shape the international division of labor and enhance purchasing power in regions where MNEs have established operations. Indeed, some commentators argue that the FDI decisions of MNEs actually regulate the location of jobs through decisions whether to invest in certain regions (Castells 1999; Coffey 1996). Although growth in FDI can enhance employment opportunities in developing nations, this same trend can lead to deindustrialization in developed regions that see (particularly) their manufacturing and also some service-industry jobs sent overseas. The actions of ECAs also shape the process of industrial globalization through their support of MNEs based in their home nations, which, in turn, shapes the international division of labor.

Beyond the investment decisions of MNEs and ECAs, the ease with which short-term portfolio capital can flow across borders is placing many nations at the mercy of international market forces. The concern is that the more open a nation becomes to these financial flows, the more difficult it is for governments to provide public goods. For example, a decision to increase the stringency of environmental and worker health and safety standards[§] or to lower interest rates

---

* See Chapter 12, "Financing Sustainable Development," for a related discussion of the role of finance in development.

† The most notorious example, which led to EU directives on chemical plant safety (see Chapter 10), is the building of the Union Carbide plant in Bhopal, India, where a plant explosion involving methyl isocyanate killed some two thousand people outright and caused serious chronic health problems to over twenty thousand people. However, other historical problems predated that incident. Pesticide poisoning of Egyptian farmers and the human consumption of mercurial-pesticide-treated grain not intended for eating also come to mind. See also Yach and Bettcher (1998).

‡ See Frumkin and Pransky (1999) for a general description of occupational hazards resulting from the flow of technologies from developed to developing countries.

§ Those who are concerned about a "race to the bottom" regarding health and safety standards argue that developing countries seek to attract investment by offering a more conducive regulatory environment (or none whatsoever), and at the same time, regulations may be repealed or not enforced in developed countries, or, at best, efforts to strengthen these standards may be discouraged or compromised.

to stimulate employment can reduce the attractiveness of a nation's market to overseas investors or risk capital flight, respectively. A potential solution offered by Daly (1994) is for governments to focus on growing internal markets and then look to expand trade once these have matured sufficiently to be competitive internationally. Although this strategy runs against the Washington Consensus and, indeed, trade theory, it appears that those developing nations and transitional economies that have resisted pressure to be fully integrated into the international economy have experienced significant progress over past decades. Further, if a developing nation is able to nurture its own internal markets, this might also help limit the negative impacts of techno-globalization and reduce concerns about cultural erosion. Of course, the trade-off of such an approach is that the diffusion of Western technologies that could radically improve the well-being of societies may be inhibited. Notwithstanding this concern, it seems that there is sufficient merit in Daly's ideas for them to receive serious consideration before fully opening the markets of developing nations to speculative international investors.

With regard to technology, advances in transportation and information and communication systems, combined with declining user costs, have had profound impacts on the structure of industries, trade, labor, wages/incomes, societies, and the environment. These two forms of technological advance could be described as the core enabling mechanisms of globalization. Other technologies have also been influential. For example, air-conditioning systems have changed the relative habitability of entire regions of the world, increasing worker productivity, reconfiguring the international division of labor, and enhancing purchasing power (Firebaugh 2003). These observations show that technological change and globalization are closely intertwined and should be considered together.

## 5.3 EFFECTS OF GLOBALIZATION ON ENVIRONMENT/WORK INTERACTIONS: SECTOR VI

This section completes the discussion of the sustainability triad by focusing on the effects of globalization on interactions between the environment and work (Figure 5.4). Two effects are discussed: (1) the increased environmental footprint from increased output that results from population-led and/or economic-driven growth, or from an effort to employ more people, and (2) the employment effects of a greener and more energy-efficient economy.

### 5.3.1 Increasing the Environmental Footprint

One response to population and/or economic-driven growth is likely to be an increase in environmental footprint (Thampapillai, Wu, et al. 2007; Wackernagel, Monfreda, et al. 2002; Wackernagel, White et al. 2004). Through a combination of new searches for trade revenues and increases in production/industrial throughput (and consumption) to accommodate the need to employ workers, the demand for resources and the environmental impacts are likely to increase. Although recommendations for advancing dematerialization (Schmidt-Bleek 1998) and ecoefficiency have been offered, far more may be needed (McDonough and Braungart 1998).

Ecological economists have long argued that growth in real GDP is ecologically unsustainable and that society, therefore, needs to transition toward a steady-state economy (Czech and Daly 2004; Daly 1991, 1996).* The challenge, however, is that policies designed to keep economic activity within ecological limits raise difficult questions about how full employment is to be achieved (Lawn 2004b). The current approach to creating employment is based on the assumption that increasing GDP will ultimately lead to job creation through the reinvestment of income/profits—"a rising tide lifts all boats." Thus any effort to constrain growth in GDP on the grounds of ecological sustainability is likely to have negative effects on job creation. The solution, therefore, is considered to lie in the creative design of policies that focus on decoupling the "GDP-employment" link (ibid.).

How to transition toward a steady-state economy while enhancing employment is the focus of the *International Journal of Environment, Workplace and Employment* (Lawn 2004a). This journal provides a forum in which the potential conflict between sustainability and full-employment objectives is considered and solutions are developed that try to "establish sustainable, equitable, and efficient economies" (ibid., p. 4). Since its creation in 2004, a range of strategies have been considered that seek to sever the GDP-employment link and promote steady-state thinking. These strategies include ecological tax reform—for example, taxing the "bads," such as resource depletion and pollution, and not the "goods," such as labor and income (Lawn 2004b, 2006); establishing a "basic income" to remunerate nonpaid household and volunteer work (Lawn 2005); and creating a "job

---

\*       For a discussion of the steady-state economy, see Section 1.3.1.

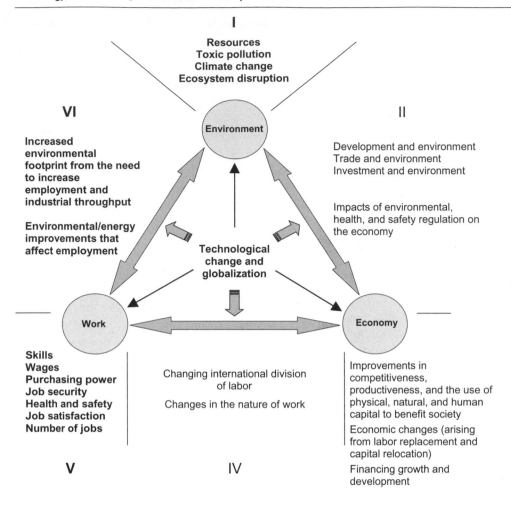

I

Resources
Toxic pollution
Climate change
Ecosystem disruption

**VI**

**Environment**

Increased
environmental
footprint from the need
to increase
employment and
industrial throughput

Environmental/energy
improvements that
affect employment

**Technological
change and
globalization**

**II**

Development and environment
Trade and environment
Investment and environment

Impacts of environmental,
health, and safety regulation on
the economy

**Work**

**Economy**

Skills
Wages
Purchasing power
Job security
Health and safety
Job satisfaction
Number of jobs

Changing international division
of labor

Changes in the nature of work

Improvements in
competitiveness,
productiveness, and the use of
physical, natural, and human
capital to benefit society

Economic changes (arising
from labor replacement and
capital relocation)

Financing growth and
development

V

IV

III

FIGURE 5.4: TECHNOLOGICAL CHANGE AND GLOBALIZATION AS DRIVERS OF CHANGE THAT
AFFECTS WORK AND THE ENVIRONMENT (SECTORS I, V, AND VI)

guarantee" where government provides basic (and ecologically sensitive) employment to labor displaced from the private sector (Forstater 2004; Harvey 2006; Lawn 2005). Of these strategies, ecological tax reform and the job guarantee are considered the most effective, so long as additional quantitative through-put controls are used to keep economic activity within ecological limits (Lawn 2005, 2006).

In addition to the above strategies, Lintott (2004) presents an approach that redefines "full employment." He argues for progressively fewer working hours and the redistribution of *existing* employment and income, rather than increasing the number of jobs. The time that is freed up from employment can then be invested in other life-enhancing activities. In contrast, G. Smith (2005) argues that a vigorous and well-guided approach to public investment in health, education, and infrastructure programs is likely to promote job creation and environmental sustainability (see Chapter 13).

Regardless of the approach one adopts, the preceding discussion highlights the important interaction between work and environment that falls into Sector VI of Figure 5.4.

### 5.3.2  The Effects of a Greener Economy on Employment

Research on the link between efforts to improve an economy's environmental performance and the impacts of these efforts on employment is limited, but those studies that do exist reveal some interesting results.

One strategy for greening the economy, which could result in significant business and employment opportunities, is to delink economic growth (and employment) from environmental degradation via investments that promote new environment-friendly technologies (Somavia 2002). Underlying this vision is the assumption that investing in the environment can create a "double dividend" of a better environment and more jobs. The European Commission (1994) put forward a white paper articulating this strategy, but it has not come to pass. The challenge to this approach is that although the implementation of cleaner technologies and production has created new jobs, it has also destroyed older, dirtier jobs involving end-of-pipe pollution control. Thus the overall impact of clean technology on job creation seems marginal (Getzner 1999, 2004).

Getzner (2004) identified several interesting observations from a study of firms that implemented environmental protection measures such as environmental management systems, waste-management systems, and water- and wastewater-management schemes. Many of these measures also involved environmental innovations (both process and product innovations). Three findings from Getzner's (2004) study are of particular interest. First, although the environmental protection measures were found to have only a slightly positive quantitative effect on employment, they resulted in significant environmental improvements.

Second, the environmental protection measures and innovations had a noticeable positive impact on employment quality. For example, in many firms, employee contact with hazardous materials was reduced, as were smells, noise, heat, and emissions of particulate matter. The more sustainable production methods were also found to change the organization of work through increased labor-market flexibility and new work processes. The extent to which the working environment was improved was found to be correlated with the level of employee involvement in implementing the measures.

Finally, the implementation of environmental protection measures was found to have a positive impact on the skill level of workers, primarily because of in-house training programs. The need for workers to enhance their skills in response to sustainable production initiatives led to a corresponding increase in the demand for skilled workers and a decrease in the demand for less skilled workers. This finding has also been observed by others. In a study of the impact of environmental protection measures on employment in Florida and Michigan, Bezdek, Wendling, et al. (2008, p. 76) reaches the following conclusion: environmental protection "generates jobs that are disproportionately for highly skilled, well-paid, technical and professional workers, who in turn underpin and provide foundation for entrepreneurship and economic growth."

Bezdek, Wendling, et al.'s (2008) findings are important because they challenge the commonly held belief that environmental protection measures are economically negative. Indeed, regions that focus on the development of environmental and environment-related industries could enhance their economy by attracting and retaining high-skilled workers.* Further, Bezdek, Wendling, et al. (2008) argue that many policy makers are unaware of the relative number of jobs created by the environment industry compared with other sectors of the economy. For example, in Florida, it is estimated that there are approximately 220,000 high-skilled environment-related jobs and 540,000 tourism jobs (ibid.).

Although firms could voluntarily adopt environmental protection measures and create high-skilled environmental jobs, the regulatory framework within which firms operate will also have an important role. Indeed, Getzner (2004, p. 392) argues that "without strict regulation, many measures adopted voluntarily by companies would be uneconomic and would, in all probability, not be taken, since businesses are largely motivated by economic advantages. Environmental restrictions (laws, regulations, employee protection legislation and problems with local residents) put a price on pollution, which in turn encourages voluntary efforts." Getzner (2004) also recognizes the importance of creating economic incentives to integrate environmental protection measures into production. When these measures are linked with the regulatory framework, they provide valuable market signals to firms that wish to act.

In the European Union (EU), the broader impact of climate-protection measures on employment is now an emerging issue. It has also become part of the strategic plan for economic recovery by the Obama administration in the United States (discussed later in this section). The European Trade Union Confederation (ETUC, ISTAS, et al. 2007) recently completed a study on the link between both climate change and the EU's policies to reduce $CO_2$ emissions and employment. The impacts on employment were found to vary by region and sector. Under an optimistic scenario of moderate climate change (that is, +2°C at the planetary level), the impacts of climate change on employment were found to be more negative in southern Europe than in northern Europe and more severe in sectors such as

---

*       Bezdek, Wendling, et al. (2008, p. 69) defines environmental industries "as those which, as a result of environmental pressures and concerns, have produced the development of products, processes, and services, which specifically target the reduction of environmental impact." Further, he considers environment-related jobs to be "those created both directly and indirectly by . . . [environmental protection] expenditures" (ibid.).

agriculture, forestry, and fisheries than in others. The study focused specifically on four key sectors: (1) energy-intensive industries (iron and steel, and cement); (2) transportation; (3) energy production; and (4) building/construction. The results of the assessment of these four sectors are briefly discussed below.

The main challenge to energy-intensive industries was considered to be the risk of relocation of production facilities outside the EU and/or freezes on investments, both of which would limit or reduce employment opportunities.

The employment impact in the transportation sector was considered to be positive and significant. By 2030, the number of people employed in railway (related to freight transport) and public transportation operations was expected to quadruple. However, this figure was tempered by reductions in the growth of employment (compared with a reference scenario) in areas such as the road transportation of freight and the automotive sector.

The employment impacts in the energy sector are more complex and depend on factors such as the mix of energy production systems employed (for example, coal, nuclear, and renewable energy systems), potential reductions in the demand for energy, and the potential deployment of carbon-sequestration technology and practices. Despite the variation in future scenarios, the study found the impact of energy savings on employment to be positive.

Finally, the building and construction sector is set to gain significant employment opportunities in the thermal renovation of existing buildings. One interesting aspect of these potential employment gains is that they would tend to be geographically fixed positions for relatively low-skilled workers. Such positions could lead to substantial social benefits through the employment of long-term jobless or socially impaired persons.

In general, the ETUC, ISTAS, et al. (2007) study concludes that there is likely to be a limited positive impact on EU employment from climate change, provided appropriate policies are put in place. It also concludes that the large-scale redistribution of employment resulting from the implementation of climate-change policies will occur within, rather than between, sectors. Finally, the study also reinforced the notion that environmental policies are likely to increase the demand for qualified workers, specifically those who are able to innovate in response to regulatory instruments and competitive forces.

In conclusion, the ETUC study of the impact on employment of strategies designed to address energy and climate-change imperatives is mixed. Employment that is created via environmentally sound products, processes, product-services, and services is tempered by a loss of jobs in those industries that are replaced. Typically, these industries are older, more polluting, and less able to adjust quickly to new operating environments. Further, the relative impact on employment of strategies designed to green the economy is likely to depend on a nation's existing industrial sectors, the extent to which cleaner technologies and processes are deployed within these sectors, the available natural and human resources, and the extent to which significant innovation is stimulated.

Although creative destruction appears to be the engine of economic growth, it is useful and important to examine its effects not only from the perspective of the state or the private sector, but also from the perspective of the labor force. The prospect of creating "green jobs" in the United States provides a particularly interesting case study of certain aspects of innovation and sustainability.

In general, green energy is considered highly labor intensive, at least initially. The Obama administration has proposed a cumulative $150-billion investment in green energy technologies and infrastructure, which is projected to create 5 million jobs in the United States. Green jobs at this moment are estimated at 2.3 million worldwide, a rather conservative estimate, with half that number employed in the biofuel industry (UNEP 2008). Along similar lines, in a report published by the Center for American Progress, Pollin, Garrett-Peltier, et al. (2008) calculated how many jobs would be created by a $100-billion green stimulus program. According to their model, a $100-billion green stimulus is projected to create 2 million jobs in the United States, while a "traditional" stimulus in household consumption would create 1.7 million jobs. Notably, spending $100 billion within the U.S. oil industry would create only around 542,000 jobs (ibid.). Apart from the elevated performance of a green stimulus in job creation, it also entails a series of long-term benefits, including increased consumer savings through the reduction of energy bills; the stabilization of oil, gas, and coal prices through reduced demand and increased energy diversity; and, obviously, a cleaner, low-carbon environment (ibid.).

A green stimulus program would create three kinds of jobs (Pollin, Garrett-Peltier, et al. 2008):

- Direct jobs: construction jobs created by retrofitting buildings to make them more energy efficient or manufacturing jobs created to build energy turbines

- Indirect jobs: manufacturing and service jobs in associated industries that supply intermediate goods for building retrofits or wind turbine manufacturing, such as lumber, steel, and transportation

- Induced jobs: retail and wholesale jobs created by workers in these construction, manufacturing, and service industries when they spend the money they earn on other products of the economy

The first two categories are straightforward, while the third category is an attempt of the model to capture the "Keynesian multiplier" effect. In the breakdown of the 2 million jobs, the model predicts that 935,200 jobs will be direct, 586,000 jobs will be indirect, and 496,000 jobs will be the multiplier effect through increased spending.

Other studies of green jobs have led to different conclusions. Getzner (2002) concluded that although the qualitative impact of green technologies is significant, their quantitative impact through job creation is marginal. Looking specifically at five innovations that promote material efficiency—plastic and paper recycling, increased life span of automobiles, car sharing, and bio-based products—Walz (2010, p. 811) finds the overall net economic impact on employment to be mixed:

> The resulting overall tendency is towards (small) positive employment effects. However, the small overall effects hide [the fact] that there are substantial net changes in the structural composition of the economy. Not surprisingly, the supply of (traditional) basic material is decreasing. On the other hand the winning sectors . . . depend . . . on the case example. In some cases, it is clearly the service-oriented sectors which gain the most, especially in the car related strategies. The investment sectors also gain, however with exception of the car related strategies. Agriculture wins of course in the case example of bio-based products. The sensitivity analysis for a first mover advantage for cars with extended life span leads to a much stronger increase in the total net effects to more than 40,000 jobs. The increasing labor productivity, on the other hand, reduces the total effect substantially and leads to a small net loss of jobs, which can be attributed mainly to the service sector.

Pollin, Garrett-Peltier, et al. (2008) have essentially conducted a classical economic ceteris paribus analysis—that is, investment and job creation is seen as a one-step policy, which disregards significant economic processes outside the focus of the model. There are two main criticisms to be made:

1. The model disregards the 3.5 million workers in the traditional energy industry in the United States, many of whom could be displaced.

2. The model calculates the jobs that will be created in the immediate short run.

The first criticism is fairly straightforward. Green technologies constitute a clear-cut case of innovation in the Schumpeterian sense. However, as Schumpeter elaborated, innovation unleashes powers of creative destruction, and although the creation of green jobs is indeed creative, there is also an element of destruction, which is typically expressed by the dislocation of competitive industries that were deemed to be technologically inferior. In the case of green energy, the potentially disrupted industries are the traditional energy industries (oil, gas, and coal). Hence a truly comprehensive calculation, useful for state policy, would actually focus on the net amount of jobs created and would include a calculation of the amount of jobs that will actually be lost in the process.

Furthermore, the introduction of green energy technologies will most certainly have to be reconciled with a series of regulations and policies that will seek to correct the externalities of pollution in energy prices. Hence these policies (such as $CO_2$ taxes or cap-and-trade) should be expected to increase traditional energy prices. Thus an additional and equally important consideration is that higher energy costs could have an adverse effect on the payrolls of energy-intensive companies, such as manufacturers (Wolgemuth 2009).

An additional issue is average compensation. In general, not all green jobs are equally green, both in compensation and in how environmentally friendly they are (UNEP 2008). In general, it is important that a significant number of new jobs will be created through a green stimulus program; however, the nature, quality, and compensation of these jobs are of equal importance. The $100-billion green stimulus program is projected to generate significant numbers of well-paying jobs, but also a relatively high proportion of lower, entry-level jobs (Pollin, Garrett-Peltier, et al. 2008). According to Pollin, Garrett-Peltier, et al. (2008), the average compensation of employees associated with green investment areas is about 20 percent less than the average of those in the oil industry. Pollin, Garrett-Peltier, et al. (2008) claim that this number is deceptive because the true comparison should be made not with already-existing jobs in the oil industry, but with the jobs that would be created if the stimulus were not spent in green technologies but in alternative ways. This is a valid statement; however, the fact that green jobs are paid less remains and cannot be disregarded, especially given the displacement of jobs in the traditional oil industry, which will also occur and has not been calculated.

A key criticism is that Pollin, Garrett-Peltier, et al.'s (2008) model assumes a certain labor intensity for green jobs, which, while realistic in the short run, is certainly unrealistic in the long and perhaps even the medium run. In general, as new innovations appear in the marketplace, the form in which they are introduced originally tends to be the most labor intensive. However, as new process innovations take place, labor tends to be increasingly replaced by capital, and many jobs are lost in the process. This paradigm is particularly relevant in the case of ICT, for instance. Hence although green jobs are accurately considered labor intensive, more light needs to be shed on the duration of their labor intensiveness. For instance, what fraction of the jobs created will involve the initial installation of the facilities versus the operation of the facilities or green service jobs?

There is no objective answer to such questions a priori. Nonetheless, such questions are key for policy planners, and the considerations that they entail should not be disregarded.

### 5.3.3 Immigration and Population

In Chapters 3 and 4, changes in the economy that have their origins in the nation-state were contrasted with those that are deeply influenced by supranational activities. Globalization occurs in (1) the nature of industrial activity (involving the international sale of national goods and services, the location of facilities that manufacture goods and provide services in foreign venues, and the multinational sharing of technological capabilities and R&D), (2) the internationalization of knowledge and information and improved access to markets through ICT, and (3) the globalization of capital markets. In addition, human resources, the least mobile of the factor endowments important to nations, increasingly present both a challenge to sustainability and an opportunity for its advancement (see Muradian, Neumayer, et al. 2006).

What is perhaps most interesting about the current form of globalization—which stands in contrast to that of the late nineteenth and early twentieth centuries—is that international migration is not a major factor (Tapinos and Delaunay 2000). There also seems to be a growing incompatibility between government actions to liberalize markets, knowledge, and information and policies that restrict immigra-

tion, forcing many who choose to migrate to do so illegally (ECLAC 2002).

Pressures created by immigration and immigrants raise economic, social, ethical, and strategic dilemmas. On the one hand, from an industrialized nation's perspective, immigration alleviates labor shortages (at the prevailing local wage) for lower-paid (and sometimes, but not always, low-skilled) jobs, brings welcomed high-skilled talent to the industrialized North, provides a means to create the financial surplus for a decent retirement for an aging workforce, and enriches the cultural base of a nation. On the other hand, immigration of culturally different peoples looking to improve their situation engenders resentment* and social exclusion, creates more consumption that adds to the ecological/environmental footprint, depresses the salaries of lower-wage jobs, and presents a future retirement burden that portends no end. Interestingly, research on the impacts of immigration finds that such common perceptions of the negative effects of immigration are often unwarranted (ECLAC 2002; Mármora 2001). For example, a study commissioned by the U.S. Congress finds that immigration had only a minor impact on wage and job opportunities of competing local groups (J. P. Smith and Edmonston 1997). The most significant effect was the improvement in the well-being of immigrants, not the reduction in well-being of, or opportunities for, citizens.

Many proponents of sustainable development focus on population—and immigration—control as an important policy tool. However, few have come to grips with the challenge of how to build a society that grows indefinitely but does not create more mouths to feed and more persons to clothe, house, and employ in the face of increasing unemployment and underemployment and falling real wages for many. The immigration of Southern workers to the North allows them to support families back home through remittances, but it does not create economic development and self-sufficiency for the less developed nation. These "social" issues are very much a part of the sustainability challenge. Given the aspirations of those who live in the developing world to increase their standard of living, a future world with 9 billion consumers creates a serious challenge to environmental sustainability. To this group, population control is

---

* Interestingly, culturally distinct groups in a society, even if they are not of recent origin like the Chinese minority in some Asian countries, are experiencing increased violence as a result of their entrepreneurship and higher economic status accelerated by trade (see A. Chua 2004).

seen as a discriminatory and untenable policy approach, especially when the first world consumes an ever-increasing percentage of the world's resources and energy. The globalization of the world's economy contributes to a visible contrast between those who have and those who have not.

## 5.4 GLOBALIZATION AND GOVERNANCE

In a major compendium, *Governing Sustainability*, Adger and Jordan (2009, p. xvii) opine that the "crisis of unsustainability is, first and foremost, a crisis of governance," and "governance of sustainable development is likely to be a hugely complicated and politically contested undertaking." They continue, "What we as a human race lack is the political, and ultimately *societal*, will to establish the necessary governance mechanism and procedures" (ibid., p. xviii), and "Sustainability is elusive because of the nature of global economic forces and the uneven distribution of political power [the 'new imperialism']" (ibid., p. 4).

Globalization presents special problems for governance to achieve sustainable development.* The following are some examples:

- Many economic activities are beyond the reach of national governments, and the ability to internalize the social costs of industrial or commercial activity may be difficult to achieve.

- Not all nations have established mechanisms for full stakeholder participation, and civil-society-based controls are in their infancy, although they are growing in importance.

- National preferences for market fundamentalism, regulation, and the welfare state differ widely.

- The international integration of economies can weaken the democratic accountability of governments (and hence their ability to address sustainability concerns) through the transfer of power from people (and society in general) to global financial institutions and corporations.

- The influence of the nation-state, for example, through regulatory means, on actors acting in the global environment may be lessening.

- There is a classic free-rider problem in getting all nations to agree to sustainability measures because of the weakness of global governance institutions.

- Integrated approaches,† rather than merely coordinated strategies, need to be fashioned among the

many initiatives, activities, and programs to achieve threefold sustainability in enhancing competitiveness, improving employment and working conditions, and maintaining environmental quality, public and worker health and safety, and consumer product safety. This is difficult enough to accomplish within a national context; it is even more difficult at the global level.

- Conflicts over the importance attached to the various elements of sustainable development and different conceptualizations of intergenerational equity, intranational equity, and international equity are difficult to resolve among the key players, such as nations, areas within nations, trade regions encompassing several nations, and different stakeholders.

Further, Dobson (2009) suggests that changing attitudes is harder than changing behavior, which may be short lived, and that governance should be society-centric.

Two key questions related to globalization and governance are the following:

1. What are the effects of globalization on governance?

2. How does globalization modify the balance of power among the actors and institutions involved in governance?

*Governance* (the management of needed change) pertains to different aspects of sustainable development—the economy, employment, and the environment—and it presents a formidable problem because the policies for these different concerns are the province of different branches of government and divisions of industry, as well as different stakeholder groups. Governance involves a variety of actors, organizations, and institutions—for example, national governments, stakeholders (business, consumers, workers, citizens, unions, and nongovernmental organizations such as environmental groups), and international organizations. Thus governance does not imply the existence of any one institution; it is the combination of separate but interconnected bodies that share common objectives and purposes (Halliday 2002). Governance seeks to achieve equity among people within a nation (intranational equity), among present and future generations (intergenerational equity), and among nations (international equity). Governance on a global scale presents considerably greater challenges than governance on a national, regional, or local level. Global governance expands the number of bodies that shape decision making or an activity to include intergovernmental organizations (such as the UN system), multinational or transnational corporations, and nongovernmental organizations that have an international presence.

---

\* See especially Sonnenfeld and Mol (2002).

† Brown (2009, pp. 36–39) suggests that integration involves three activities: (1) linking social and ecological systems; (2) linking different actors, stakeholders, and institutions; and (3) horizontal and vertical policy integration (also see Chapter 13).

The type of governance that exists within a nation is shaped by whether the national government is democratic or autocratic, liberal or authoritarian, and so on; the extent to which citizens and (private/public) stakeholders are able to participate in, and influence, the political process; and other important factors such as the level of corruption.

When one considers the role of government in promoting development, two diverging views emerge (see Section 1.2). The first view is that basic goods and services should be met through the efficient operation of markets, where the role of government is limited to establishing property rights and a stable legal system. The second view holds that markets are incapable of meeting all the basic needs of society and that government has an important role in ensuring access to these goods and services—such as health care for the poor. These two views lie at opposite ends of a continuum from utilitarianism to Rawlsianism.

The extent to which governments promote markets or act as a trustee for society depends not only on their posture in decision making but also on the relative posture of stakeholders (Ashford and Rest 2001). For example, in Section 1.2.2, governments are characterized as Rawlsian or non-Rawlsian and stakeholders as utilitarian or communitarian. These dimensions create four possible combinations that characterize the likely outcome of decision making. This framework is useful when one is considering whether the postures of a government and its stakeholders/society are likely to combine to promote sustainable development.* However, this framework is less useful when it is considered in the context of globalization, where governments and stakeholders can adopt the full complement of positions with regard to development.

This section addresses governance challenges in the context of globalization. A deeper discussion of international institutions and multilateral agreements for addressing environmental and worker health and safety problems is found in Chapter 10, while Chapter 11 addresses trade regimes. Chapter 13 addresses the governance challenges discussed throughout this section and explores specific initiatives for achieving sustainable economies.

Governance plays an essential role in shaping the economy, the employment outlook, and the level of environmental protection in a country or region, which are the pillars of our sustainability triad. Furthermore, as the ILO states, "The results of global-ization are what we make of it. They depend on the policies, rules and institutions which govern its course; the values which inspire its actors; and their capacity to influence the process" (WCSDG 2004, p. 2). Thus at the same time at which the lack of governance can adversely affect sustainability, governance is being transformed by globalization. It seems important, therefore, to start our discussion by analyzing the changing roles of the actors and institutions involved in governance.†

Chapters 8 to 11 develop strategies to strengthen equity-enhancing mechanisms and integrate the existing fragmented national/global governance efforts. National efforts to address economic/employment and health, safety, and environmental problems are the focus of Chapters 8 and 9, respectively. Chapters 10 and 11 address the international regimes.

### 5.4.1 The Role of National and International Governance in Promoting Sustainable Development

International trade and global financial markets are very good at generating wealth, but they cannot take care of other social needs, such as the preservation of peace, alleviation of poverty, protection of the environment, labor conditions, or human rights—what are generally called "public goods." Economic development, that is, the production of private goods, has taken precedence over social development, that is, the provision of public goods. Soros, *George Soros on Globalization*, 2002, p. 14

Sustainable development advocates often use the process of globalization to describe unsustainable pathways of development (Speth 2003). However, it is apparent that sustainable development and globalization are not the polar opposites they are often seen to be. Instead, both discourses see development and efficiency as critical mechanisms for achieving sustainability (Byrne and Glover 2002).

Evidence suggests that economic globalization has benefited those nations that have sought to expand their export markets while encouraging foreign investment (Stiglitz 2002c). Further, within this group of nations, those that have benefited the most recognized that government had an important role to play in addressing the social and environmental costs of economic development.

Each of the most successful globalizing countries determined its own pace of change; each made sure as

---

*        Refer to Section 1.2 for a detailed exploration of these ideas.

†        Organizational innovation in both the private and public sectors is the focus of Chapter 7.

it grew that the benefits were shared equitably; each rejected the basic tenets of the "Washington Consensus," which argued for a minimalist role for government and rapid privatization and liberalization.

In East Asia, government took an active role in managing the economy. The steel industry that the Korean government created was among the most efficient in the world—performing far better than its private-sector rivals in the United States (which, though private, are constantly turning to the government for protection and for subsidies). Financial markets were highly regulated. My research shows that those regulations promoted growth. It was only when these countries stripped away the regulations, under pressure from the U.S. Treasury and the IMF, that they encountered problems. (Stiglitz 2002b, p. 17)

An important argument from Stiglitz's (2002b, 2002c) work is that *globalization is not the problem*; the problem is how a nation chooses to integrate its economy into the international economy.* The more open an economy becomes, the less control the government has over how (mobile) capital should be invested—that is, investment decisions are left to the market. The problem with this dynamic is that foreign investors can speculate on what investments are likely to generate the most return—devoid of any substantive knowledge of such factors as a nation's history, culture, and development objectives—which can lead to decisions that run against the best interests of society. Stiglitz (2002b) describes how once Thailand's restrictive policies on speculative real estate were removed by the IMF, the market supported investments in office buildings that stood empty, wasting valuable capital that could have been invested in schools or industrial plant.

The challenge facing governments, therefore, is how to support a competitive market while advancing important (and often costly) development objectives within its nation. With the liberalization of capital markets, tax revenue can be undermined as citizens look to foreign markets in search of higher returns on their investments. Further, in an effort to retain mobile asset holders, national governments might limit the extent of their social welfare policies to keep their economies competitive (see Section 5.2.3). Factors such as these could reduce the ability

of governments to advance important social aspects of sustainable development. However, contrary to this logic, Rodrik (1998, 2007) points to a different outcome where social spending might actually increase when national economies become more open. He argues that investment in nationally appropriate forms of social insurance can legitimize the market economy by making it "compatible with social stability and cohesion" (Rodrik 2007, p. 160).†

With regard to the United States, during his tenure as chairman of President Clinton's Council of Economic Advisers, Stiglitz fought to develop an economic policy "that viewed the relationship between governments and markets as complementary, both working in partnership, and recognized that while markets were at the center of the economy, there was an important, if limited, role for government" (Stiglitz 2002c, p. xiii). This role for government was to address inequality, unemployment, and pollution, all of which cannot be adequately addressed by markets alone. In his later work, Stiglitz's views moved further to the left (B. M. Friedman 2002). In *Globalization and Its Discontents*, Stiglitz (2002c, p. 218) argues that "government can, and has, played an essential role not only in mitigating . . . market failures, but also in ensuring social justice." His position is that governments can improve the market and the well-being of society by making well-chosen interventions (B. M. Friedman 2002). These interventions include expansionary monetary and fiscal policies to stimulate demand for goods and services, tax policies that encourage investment in more productive industries, trade policies that protect new industries until they are ready to compete in the international economy, and policies/programs that protect workers in times of hardship. However, in the United States, the neoliberalism personified by the Washington Consensus promotes a very different view from that of Stiglitz. By citing the mantra of a "free economy," its proponents mean not only free unfettered markets for goods and services but also the production of goods and services in unregulated or less regulated markets from a social perspective. Thus the neoliberal approach tends to promote minimal health, safety, and environmental regulations and inadequate social protection initiatives such as a minimum wage that is not a living wage, limited unemployment and health insurance, and rollbacks of affirmative action and educational expenditures. In Europe, the so-called social safety net is also eroding.

---

*        Hirst and Thompson (1999) also make the argument that increasing exposure to the international economy is not causing the downward pressures on spending for public welfare. Instead, it is a nation's political response to this exposure that is important: more specifically, the need to develop well-conceived and appropriate policies such as supporting social programs via general taxation rather than from employers' contributions and the capital gains tax.

---

†        See Section 5.2.3 for a discussion of Rodrik's (1997, 1998, 2007) work.

Although national governments can take steps to ensure that markets work for their citizens, there is no equivalent entity at the international level to ensure that markets do not undermine strategies to promote sustainable development (Streeten 2001). As national economies become more open, there is (to a certain extent) a transfer of authority away from national democratic institutions to nondemocratic international institutions (such as the World Trade Organization [WTO], the IMF, and the World Bank) and multinational corporations. The problem is that the missions and capabilities of these international entities align with, and respond to, the financial community, and the voices of other social and environmental organizations are seldom heard in their decision-making processes. Stiglitz (2002b, p. 19) refers to this problem as "global governance without a global government." He argues, "International institutions like the World Trade Organization, the IMF, the World Bank, and others provide an ad hoc system of global governance, but it is a far cry from [a] global government and lacks democratic accountability. Although it is perhaps better than not having any system of global governance, the system is structured not to serve general interests or assure equitable results. This not only raises issues of whether broader values are given short shrift; it does not even promote growth as much as an alternative might" (ibid.). It could be argued that the recent liberalization of markets has occurred at such a rate that it has left considerations of a system of global governance at a standstill.

To prevent the erosion of national social and environmental objectives by economic globalization, governments may need to focus more of their efforts on collective action at the international level (OECD 1997a). The establishment of mechanisms for global governance, if they are designed to ensure the well-being of society and the protection of the environment, are likely to reduce the risks of trade liberalization. However, the establishment of global governance through "enforceable" international law is likely to be politically difficult and time consuming. A major challenge will be to overcome resistance from government and corporate representatives charged with the defense of national and corporate interests (Paehkle 2003). In addition, the scale of global governance is problematic because of its inaccessibility to citizens.

These difficulties are compounded by the three legal frameworks that govern the transnational world: (1) the *economic regime*, led by the WTO and supported by the IMF and the World Bank; (2) the *environmental regimes*, created through conventions and treaties covering such topics as environmental protection, climate change, wildlife, and biodiversity, which are inconsistent and often contain direct contradictions with one another (Sachs 2001); and (3) the *working-conditions regime*, embodied in the International Labour Organization (ILO).

The aggressive advocacy of trade liberalization by powerful countries and MNEs has entrenched the economic regime at the expense of other frameworks designed to protect the environment and social rights (Khor 2001).* This dominance of the "investor class"—embodied in the WTO and the Bretton Woods institutions—has created an international environment where investors enjoy extraordinary protections against financial risks, but labor, the environment, and consumers are left to the mercy of deregulated markets (Faux 2002a, 2002b). The ascendancy of the economic regime also signals a decline of the UN system and its ability to influence national agendas.

Advocates of trade liberalization—the "investor class"—tend to adopt what might be called a "minimal state" approach to international governance, where the role of international institutions is limited to enforcing established contracts and agreements and protecting member nations against crime and aggression. Under such an international regime, nations would retain sovereignty and would not be subject to a coercive apparatus designed to redistribute wealth or enforce standards that are perceived as protectionist. Within this framework, one idea that has received some attention is that of strengthening the role of the WTO. However, placing the WTO at the forefront of development efforts raises several issues in relation to "sustainable" development. In particular, four charges against the WTO have been made (Singer 2002, p. 55):

1. The WTO places economic considerations ahead of concerns for the environment, animal welfare, and even human rights.
2. The WTO erodes national sovereignty.
3. The WTO is undemocratic.
4. The WTO increases inequality; or (a stronger charge) it makes the rich richer and leaves the world's poorest people even worse off than they would otherwise have been.

Although there are signs that the WTO is attempting to address these charges through plans to integrate environmental and development concerns into its core activities, a major problem remains. The core competencies of the WTO lie in trade and economics, not in human health, ecosystem integrity, or human rights. Expertise in the latter areas would be essential if the WTO were to become an arbitrator for environmental and human health disputes. Instead of trying to integrate sustainable development objectives into the WTO's mandate, many argue that although the WTO needs to be made more open and accountable, a more useful outcome would be to establish an equally effective institution to serve environmental and social goals (Cole 2000; Charnovitz 2002; Esty 2000; Esty and Ivanova 2001; Soros 2002; Speth 2003). Indeed, the idea of creating a World Environmental Organization (WEO) or a Global Environmental Organization (GEO) was raised by France and Germany at the 2002 Johannesburg Summit but was heavily opposed by other G8 members. Interestingly, the G77 (including China and India) were also reluctant to support the formation of a WEO/GEO and favored a strengthened United Nations Environment Programme (UNEP). One concern with the creation of a new international agency is the additional layer of bureaucracy that will be added to an already-complex system of international law and organizations (von Moltke 2001).

Whether the WTO succeeds in securing control over environmental disputes, or existing international agencies, programs, and multilateral environmental agreements are centralized into a WEO/GEO, the lines seem to be drawn for an intense and protracted debate. On one side are those who believe in trade liberalization and would like the authority for decisions related to sustainable development to lie with the institutions that oversee the international economy. On the other side are those who believe that giving such authority to trade/economic bodies is fundamentally flawed and argue for the creation of institutions that have a stronger voice for the environment. One particular concern is that in the absence of a global democratic government, international financial institutions will be captured by business interests at the expense of society and the environment (Faux 2002b). In the post-Johannesburg climate, the final outcome will most likely rest on the position of developed nations that currently have the economic and political power to imprint their views on the international community.

If it is accepted that developed nations have largely filled the available global ecological space, it seems unfair to place environmental limits on the progress of developing nations without first dramatically reducing the environmental burden of modern lifestyles. Without such a transformation, the establishment of free trade and/or the provision of international aid to help developing nations develop will simply perpetuate these unsustainable forms of living. There is also a need to balance the power of the market with the role of government. One potential way of achieving this is through international trade and environmental institutions designed to ensure that the process of trade liberalization does not weaken a government's ability to achieve its social and environmental goals. In short, what is needed at the national level are "policies for sustainable, equitable, and democratic growth" (Stiglitz 2002c, p. 251) that are enhanced, not undermined, by the international economy and the wide range of multilateral agreements, treaties, and conventions in existence. Such a grand plan is likely to succeed only if a democratic global forum for negotiation can be established (Faux 2002b). What is not clear, however, is whether the political drive in developed and developing nations will be sufficient for this to occur.*

Hirst and Thompson (2002) present a well-conceived *economic* governance framework—consisting of five levels of governance from the international economy to industrial districts (see Box 5.2)—that could provide a foundation for an effective system of global governance.

The first level of governance focuses on stabilizing the international economy through negotiations among the triad of Europe, Japan, and North America. This aspect of the framework is perhaps the most limiting with regard to sustainable development. As Hirst and Thompson (2002, p. 275) recognize, this level provides a "minimum level of international economic governance, at least to the benefit of the major advanced industrialized nations." One way to address this concern could be to expand the number of political entities included in the financial/economic discussions beyond the triad to include representatives from rapidly emerging economies, such as China and India. Although such an approach is clearly not ideal, it would help balance the negotiations and give developing nations a voice at the table.

The second level of governance recognizes that nation-states, as legitimate representatives of their territories and populations, should collectively develop international regulatory agencies to police economic as well as social (that is, worker health and safety) and environmental standards.

---

\*     The approach and commitment of developed and developing nations to sustainable development is addressed in Chapter 2, "The Emergence of Sustainable Development."

---

### BOX 5.2: FIVE LEVELS OF ECONOMIC GOVERNANCE

The five levels [of economic governance] are:

1. Governance through agreement between the major political entities, particularly the G3 (Europe, Japan and North America), to stabilize exchanges rates, to coordinate fiscal and monetary policies, and to cooperate in limiting speculative short-term financial transactions.
2. Governance through a substantial number of states creating international regulatory agencies for some specific dimension of economic activity, such as the WTO to police the GATT settlement, or possible authorities to police foreign direct investment and common environmental standards.
3. The governance of large economic areas by trade and investment blocs such as the EU, [NAFTA, Greater Arab Free Trade Area (GAFTA), MERCOSUR, ASEAN, South Asian Association for Regional Cooperation (SAARC), Economic Community of West African States (ECOWAS), and so on]. [These blocs] . . . are large enough to pursue social and environmental objectives in the way a medium-sized nation-state may not be able to do independently. [They] . . . are capable of enforcing adequate minimal standards in labour market policies or forms of social protection. The blocs are big enough markets in themselves to stand against global pressures if they so choose.
4. National-level policies that balance cooperation and competition between firms and the major social interests, producing quasi-voluntary economic coordination and assistance in providing key inputs such as R&D, the regulation of industrial finance, international marketing, information and export guarantees, training, etc., thereby enhancing national economic performance and promoting industries located in the national territory.
5. Governance through regional level policies of providing collective services to industrial districts, augmenting their international competitiveness and providing a measure of protection against external shocks.

Source: Hirst and Thompson (2002, pp. 191–192).

---

The third level is a subset of the international level and focuses on the economic governance of trade blocs by member states. Hirst and Thompson (2002) argue that the common interests of these regions provide a strong incentive for the regions to collectively agree on, and enforce, important economic, social, and environmental standards.

The fourth and fifth levels of governance reside within national territories and focus on national and regional strategies, respectively, to promote economic development in the context of the international economy.*

One strength of Hirst and Thompson's (2002) framework is that it provides nation-states with an important role to play in economic governance, both nationally and internationally. This role could also be expanded (as the authors suggest in Box 5.2) to include social and environmental governance (see the related discussion in Chapters 9 and 10). As discussed previously, nation-states have an important role to play in collective action at the international level (OECD 1997a). If nations are able to represent the voice of their citizens adequately, this is one mechanism through which global citizens could have input into global governance. These citizens could also influence the process of global governance by belonging to NGOs that regularly engage with inter-national institutions and national governments, or by owning shares in multinational organizations and exercising their voting rights.

What is evident from the preceding discussion is the need to readdress the lack of effective governance mechanisms to deal with social and environmental concerns. The existence of powerful mechanisms for international economic governance needs to be matched by equally effective social and environmental governance mechanisms. Although there is no clear and simple solution to this challenge, the ideas raised in this section and further explored in Chapters 8 to 11 should help demystify the subject.

In the preceding discussion, the political challenge raised by globalization and sustainable development is described as the need to balance the interests of citizens (or constituents) with the welfare of people throughout the world. Achieving a balance, however, may be the wrong objective because it involves trade-offs, which imply losses and gains.† A more appropriate concept, developed in Chapter 13, is "co-optimization," whereby multiple gains are possible by enlisting innovative solutions in the technological, social, institutional, and organizational realms in an integrated, rather than merely coordinated, fashion.

The relatively brief treatment of the impacts of globalization on governance and sustainable development in this section has covered two dimensions of the

---

* Government policies to foster innovation, economic growth, and employment are the focus of Chapter 8. A closely related subject, the role of the firm in achieving sustainability, is addressed in Chapter 7.

† Brown (2009, p. 47) takes the opposite position, arguing that searching for win-win solutions inhibits the more realistic need to deal with the necessary trade-offs.

**TABLE 5.3: IMPORTANT ELEMENTS OF GLOBALIZATION AND THEIR EFFECTS ON DEVELOPMENT**

| FACTORS LIKELY TO AFFECT DEVELOPMENT | POTENTIAL IMPACTS | MEASURES LIKELY TO AUGMENT DEVELOPMENT |
|---|---|---|
| Internationalization | • Opportunity for firms to expand their consumer base by selling their products/processes overseas | National regulations that protect worker health and safety and the environment |
| | • Potential transfer of negative environmental/ social impacts with products/processes | Proper in-country training and guidance on how to adopt (and adapt) potentially hazardous products and processes |
| Multi-nationalization | • *Deindustrialization* of developed nations and *industrialization* of developing nations | The adoption, within an entire MNE, of the most stringent health and safety and environmental standards used by the enterprise |
| | • Investment decisions of MNEs organizing/ regulating the international division of labor | The adoption of the Sullivan Principles (Box 5.1) by MNEs and the *extension* of these principles to local in-country partners |
| | | Green consumerism |
| | | Pressure on MNEs from international/national environmental and social groups/institutions to adhere to international environmental and labor standards |
| Transnationalization | • Limited because of small number of transnational enterprises | — |
| Economic liberalization | • Significant growth in trade, especially between the triad of the Americas, Europe, and Asia-Pacific | National fiscal policies that develop the demand for essential goods and services |
| | • Significant growth in flows of short-term capital that can depress wages and limit a government's autonomy | The creation of social programs to compensate workers during periods of industrial transformation |
| | | The adoption of policies to protect new industries against foreign competition until they are ready to compete |
| | | The adequate inclusion/consideration of environmental and social factors in decision-making at the international level |
| | | Imposition of trade tariffs on imports from countries that have not taken steps to internalize the negative externalities associated with their products, when such action has been taken by the importing country |
| Falling international transportation costs | • Distance becoming less of a factor | A carbon tax that increases and helps internalize the costs of international transportation |
| | • Enhancement of ability of firms to be competitive in foreign markets | |
| Global expansion of ICT networks | • Facilitation of the movement of financial capital | The adoption of restrictive policies on investment in market segments where speculative investing could undermine a nation's development objectives |
| | • Facilitation of outsourcing/offshoring | |
| National regulations (such as environmental and labor standards) | • Attraction or discouragement of foreign direct investment because of stringency of regulations | National regulations that protect worker health and safety and the environment |
| National financial incentives designed to attract trade | • Distortion of the efficient allocation of capital by creating artificially competitive regions | The delinking of national regulations that protect worker health and safety and the environment from trade policies |
| Actions of export credit agencies (ECAs) | • Ability of MNEs (from an ECA's home nation) to move into high-risk markets with reduced financial risk | Making ECAs more accountable for their actions |
| | • Expansion of market size for MNE and creation of employment opportunities in the recipient nation | |

sustainability triad: Sectors III, IV, and V, *economy-work*; and Sectors I, V, and VI, *work-environment* (see Figure 5.1). In both of these dimensions, two levels of governance—national and international—have been considered.

The *economy-work* dimension is shaped by industrial policies that address competitiveness, wages, job creation, and labor policies. In this context, Chapter 8 will consider government policies for fostering innovation, economic growth, and employment at the national level. Chapter 11 expands this discussion to the international level by focusing on trade regimes and sustainability. At the national level, there are already conceptual differences between nation-states in the way in which externalities are internalized, stakeholders are involved in decision-making, and related issues. As will be seen in Chapter 11, these challenges are compounded at the international level by weak protocols and structures that have the effect of worsening problems relating to the global commons.

The *work-environment* dimension is shaped by social policies that address environmental protection and worker health and safety. In this context, Chapter 9 will consider government policies that protect the environment, worker health and safety, and consumer product safety at the national level. Chapter 10 will build on this discussion by considering the effectiveness of international regimes at protecting the environment and worker health and safety. The lack of strong national and international governance regimes in the field of social policy is reflected by unsustainable practices. The problem is worsened by the lack of harmonization of practices. Both of these challenges will be addressed in Chapters 9 and 10.

To help conclude the discussion in this and the previous sections, we have created Table 5.3 to try to capture (1) some of the main elements of globalization that are likely to affect development, (2) what the impacts of these elements are likely to be, and (3) how any negative outcomes could be offset.

## 5.5 NOTES

1. For a detailed description of the evolution of the definition of development, see Todaro and Smith (2009).

2. Meadows et al., *Facing the Limits to Growth*, www.alternet.org/story/18978 (accessed May 18, 2010).

3. Those include Michael Redclift's book *Sustainable Development: Exploring the Contradictions* (1987), *Beyond the Brundtland Report* by a coalition of Southern and Northern NGOs (by T. De La Court; New York, Zed Books, 1990), and *Energy for a Sustainable World* by Goldemberg et al. (New Delhi, Wiley Eastern, 1988).

4. See Grossman and Krueger (1993), Kalt (1988), Robison (1988), Tobey (1990), and van Beers and van den Bergh (1997).

5. See Dean (1991), Jänicke, Binder, et al. (1997), Tobey (1990), and Walter (1973, 1982).

6. See Birdsall and Wheeler (1992), Esty (1994), and Lucas, Wheeler, et al. (1992).

7. See the Global Sullivan Principles, www.thesullivanfoundation.org/gsp/principles/gsp/default.asp (accessed May 17, 2010).

8. OECD, Recommendations on Common Approaches on Environment and Officially Supported Export Credits, www.oecd.org/dataoecd/26/33/21684464.pdf (accessed May 17, 2010).

9. See the ECA-Watch commentary on the ECA-Watch reform efforts occurring in several developed nations, www.eca-watch.org/ (accessed May 17, 2010).

10. See Lakshmanan and Anderson (2002) for a useful discussion of the factors behind the decline of freight transportation costs in the United States. However, with the rapid increase in the price of oil since 2007, there has been a corresponding increase in the cost of freight transportation; most notably in the cost of freight transported via trucks. Because the costs relating to inefficient transportation and logistical systems have largely been addressed over the past decade, it is unlikely that the high price of oil can be absorbed through additional efficiency gains. Increases in both oil prices and price volatility could very well reshape the international division of labor.

## 5.6 ADDITIONAL READINGS

Kaplinsky, Raphael, and Dirk Messner (2007). "Introduction: The Impact of Asian Drivers on the Developing World." *World Development* **36**(2): 197–209.

Rodrik, Dani (2007). Globalization for Whom? *One Economics: Many Recipes: Globalization, Institutions, and Economic Growth*. Princeton, NJ, Princeton University Press: 237–255.

Sinden, A. (2007). The "Preference for Pollution" and Other Fallacies, or Why Free Trade Isn't "Progress." *Progress in International Law*. R. A. Miller and R. M. Bratspies. Leiden, Martinus Nijhoff Press.

## 5.7 REFERENCES

Ackerman, F., D. Kiron, et al., Eds. (1997). *Human Well-being and Economic Goals*. Frontier Issues in Economic Thought. Washington, DC, Island Press.

Adger, W. N., and A. Jordan, Eds. (2009). *Governing Sustainability*. Cambridge, Cambridge University Press.

Akst, D. (2004). "Job Flight Isn't America's Biggest Problem." *International Herald Tribune*, February 13.

Antweiler, W., R. B. Copeland, et al. (2001). "Is Free Trade Good for the Environment?" *American Economic Review* **4**(2): 877–908.

Appleyard, B. (2008). "Britain's Dirty Business: These Four Projects Are among the Most Environmentally Damaging on the Planet. So Why Is a British Government Department Backing Them?" *Sunday Times* (London), April 6.

Archibugi, D., and J. Michie (1997). The Globalisation of Technology: A New Taxonomy. *Technology, Globalisation and Economic Performance*. D. Archibugi and J. Michie. Cambridge, Cambridge University Press: 172–197.

Ashford, N. A. (2002). Technology-Focused Regulatory Approaches for Encouraging Sustainable Industrial Transformations: Beyond Green, beyond the Dinosaurs, and beyond Evolutionary Theory. Paper presented at the 3rd Blueprint Workshop on Instruments for Integrating Environmental and Innovation Policy, Brussels, September 26–27.

Ashford, N. A., C. Ayers, et al. (1985). "Using Regulation to Change the Market for Innovation." *Harvard Environmental Law Review* **9**(2): 419–466.

Ashford, N. A., G. R. Heaton, et al. (1979). Environmental, Health and Safety Regulations and Technological Innovation. *Technological Innovation for a Dynamic Economy*. C. T. Hill and J. M. Utterback. New York, Pergamon Press: 161–221.

Ashford, N. A., and K. M. Rest (2001). Public Participation in Contaminated Communities. Cambridge, MA, Center for Technology, Policy and Industrial Development, MIT. Available at http://web.mit.edu/ctpid/www/tl/TL-pub-PPCC.html (accessed January 22, 2011).

Aslanidis, N., and A. Xepapadeas (2006). "Smooth Transition Pollution-Income Paths." *Ecological Economics* **57**(2): 182–189.

Aslanidis, N., and A. Xepapadeas (2008). "Regime Switching and the Shape of the Emission-Income Relationship." *Economic Modelling*. Available at www.sciencedirect.com (accessed January 22, 2011).

Ayres, R., and B. Warr (2009). *The Economic Growth Engine: How Energy and Work Drive Material Prosperity*. Williston, VT, Edward Elgar.

Beghin, J., B. Bowland, et al. (1998). Trade, Environment, and Public Health in Chile: Evidence from an Economywide Model. Available at http://are.berkeley.edu/~dwrh/Docs/BBDRHM_Chile.pdf (accessed January 22, 2011).

Bell, D. (1999). *The Coming of Post-industrial Society: A Venture in Social Forecasting*. New York, Basic Books.

Benjamin, M., and J. Perry (2003). " The New Job Reality." *U.S. News and World Report* **135**(4): 24–28.

Benton, T., and M. Redclift (1994). Introduction. *Social Theory and the Global Environment*. M. Redclift and T. Benton. London, Routledge: 1–27.

Bezdek, R. H., R. M. Wendling, et al. (2008). "Environmental Protection, the Economy, and Jobs: National and Regional Analyses." *Journal of Environmental Management* **86**: 63–79.

Bhagwati, J. (1993). "The Case for Free Trade." *Scientific American* **269**(5): 42–49.

Bhagwati, J. (1997). "The Global Age: From a Sceptical South to a Fearful North." *World Economy* **20**(3): 259–283.

Birdsall, N., and D. Wheeler (1993). "Trade Policy and Industrial Pollution in Latin America: Where Are the Pollution Havens?" *Journal of Environment and Development* **2**(1): 137–149.

Bleijenberg, A. N. (1995). "Fiscal Measures as Part of a European Policy on Freight Transport." *World Transport Policy and Practice* **1**(2): 40–45.

Block, F. (1996). "Controlling Global Finance." *World Policy Journal* **13**(3): 24–34.

Bluestone, B. A., and B. Harrison (1982). *The Deindustrialization of America: Plant Closings, Community Abandonment, and the Dismantling of Basic Industry*. New York, Basic Books.

Board on Science Technology and Economic Policy (STEP) (1994). *Investing for Productivity and Prosperity*. Washington, DC, National Research Council.

Bognanno, M. F., M. P. Keane, et al. (2005). "The Influence of Wages and Industrial Relations Environments on the Production Location Decisions of U.S. Multinational Corporations." *Industrial and Labor Relations Review* **58**(2): 171–200.

Brenton, P. (2006). Adjusting to Globalisation: Policy Responses in Europe and the US. *Globalisation and the Labour Market: Trade, Technology, and Less-Skilled Workers in Europe and the United States*. R. Anderton, P. Brenton, and J. Whalley. London, Routledge: 143–161.

Brown, K. (2009). Human Development and Environmental Governance: A Reality Check. *Governing Sustainability*. W. N. Adger and A. Jordan. Cambridge, Cambridge University Press: 32–52.

Byrne, J., and L. Glover (2002). "A Common Future or towards a Future Commons: Globalization and Sustainable Development since UNCED." *International Review for Environmental Strategies* **3**(1): 5–25.

Castells, M. (1999). *The Rise of the Network Society*. Oxford, Blackwell Publishers.

Charnovitz, S. (2002). "A World Environment Organization." *Columbia Journal of Environmental Law* **27**(2): 323–362.

Chesky, E. (1998). "International Investment." *Praxis: The Fletcher Journal of Development Studies* **14**: 5–24.

Chua, A. (2004). "Conference: The Profitable and the Powerless; International Accountability of Multinational Corporations. The Sixth Annual Grotius Lecture: World on Fire." *American University International Law Review* **19**(6): 1239–1253.

Chua, S. (1999). "Economic Growth, Liberalization, and the Environment: A Review of the Economic Evidence." *Annual Review of Energy and the Environment* **24**: 391–430.

CIES (The Food Business Forum) (2008). *GSCP Reference Code: Version 1 (September 2008)*. Madrid, CIES.

Coffey, W. J. (1996). The "Newer" International Division of Labour. *The Global Economy in Transition*. P. W. Daniels and W. F. Lever. London, Addison Wesley Longman: 40–61.

Cole, M. A. (2000). *Trade Liberalisation, Economic Growth and the Environment*. Cheltenham, Edward Elgar.

Cole, M. A. (2007). "Corruption, Income and the Environment: An Empirical Analysis." *Ecological Economics* **62**(3–4): 637–647.

Commoner, B. (1979). Chemical Carcinogens in the Environment. *Identification and Analysis of Organic Pollutants in Water*. L. H. Keith. Ann Arbor, MI, Ann Arbor Science Publishers: 49–71.

Compaine, B. M. (2001). *The Digital Divide: Facing a Crisis or Creating a Myth?* Cambridge, MA, MIT Press.

Czech, B., and H. E. Daly (2004). "In My Opinion: The Steady State Economy—What It Is, Entails, and Connotes." *Wildlife Society Bulletin* **32**(2): 598–605.

Daly, H. E. (1991). *Steady-State Economics*. Washington, DC, Island Press.

Daly, H. E. (1993). "The Perils of Free Trade." *Scientific American* **269**(5): 50–54.

Daly, H. E. (1994). "Fostering Environmentally Sustainable Development: Four Parting Suggestions for the World Bank." *Ecological Economics* **10**: 183–187.

Daly, H. E. (1996). *Beyond Growth: The Economics of Sustainable Development*. Boston, Beacon Press.

Daly, H. E. (1999). "Globalization versus Internationalisation—Some Implications." *Ecological Economics* **31**: 31–37.

Damania, R., P. G. Fredriksson, et al. (2003). "Trade Liberalization, Corruption, and Environmental Policy Formation: Theory and Evidence." *Journal of Environmental Economics and Management* **46**(3): 490–512.

Dean, J. M. (1992). Trade and the Environment: A Survey of the Literature. Policy Research Working Paper Series, WSP 966, World Bank.

Deparle, J. (2007). "In India, Even Cared-for Populace Leaves for Work." *International Herald Tribune*, September 6.

Dobson, A. (2009). Citizens, Citizenship and Governance for Sustainability. *Governing Sustainability*. W. N. Adger and A. Jordan. Cambridge, Cambridge University Press: 125–141.

Drucker, P. F. (1954). *The Practice of Management*. New York, Harper.

Drucker, P. F. (1994). "The Age of Social Transformation." *Atlantic Monthly* **274**(5): 53–80.

Durning, A. T. (1992). *How Much Is Enough?* New York, W. W. Norton Company, Inc.

Durning, A. T. (1994). *The Conundrum of Consumption. Beyond Numbers: A Reader on Population, Consumption, and the Environment*. L. A. Mazur. Washington, DC, Island Press: 40–47.

ECA-Watch (2003). Race to the Bottom—Take II: An Assessment of Sustainable Development Achievements of ECA-Supported Project Two Years after OECD Common Approaches Rev 6. Available at www.eca-watch.org/eca/race_bottom_take2.pdf (accessed January 22, 2011).

ECA-Watch (2007). "OECD Approves Weak, Unenforceable Environmental Policy for Export Credit Agencies." *ECA Watch*, Paris, June 29.

Economic Commission for Latin America and the Caribbean (ECLAC) (2002). *Globalization and Development*. Santiago, United Nations.

ECLAC and United Nations Environment Programme (UNEP) (2001). *La sostenibilidad del desarrollo en América Latina y el Caribe: Desafíos y oportunidades*. Santiago, ECLAC.

Economist (2004a). "Jobs in America: The Great Hollowing-out Myth." *Economist*, February 19.

Economist (2004b). "The Changed Nature of Work. Pushing a Different Sort of Button: How Jobs, in the Rich World, Have Become Less Boring (though There's Still Plenty to Whine About)." *Economist, U.S. Edition*, October 28.

Ekins, P. (1995). Trading off the Future: Making World Trade Environmentally Sustainable. *A Survey of Ecological Economics*. R. Krishnan, J. M. Harris, and N. R. Goodwin. Washington, DC, Island Press.

Ekins, P. (1997). "The Kuznets Curve for the Environment and Economic Growth: Examining the Evidence." *Environment and Planning A* **29**: 805–830.

Ekins, P., C. Folke, et al. (1994). "Trade, Environment and Development: The Issues in Perspective." *Ecological Economics* **9**(1): 1–12.

Environics International (2002). *Global Issues Monitor, 2002*. Toronto, Environics International.

Ernst, D., and D. O'Connor (1989). *Technology and Global Competition: The Challenge for Newly Industrialising Economies*. Paris, OECD Development Centre Studies.

Esty, D. C. (1994). *Greening the GATT: Trade, Environment and the Future*. Washington, DC, Institute for International Economics.

Esty, D. C. (2000). "Stepping up to the Global Environmental Challenge." *Fordham Environmental Law Journal* **8**(1): 103–113.

Esty, D. C., and D. Geradin (2000). "Regulatory Co-opetition." *Journal of International Economic Law* **3**(2): 235–255.

Esty, D. C., and M. Ivanova (2001). Making International Environmental Agreements Work: The Case for a Global Environmental Organization. Working Papers Series Working Paper 2/1. New Haven, CT, Yale Center for Environmental Law and Policy.

European Commission (EC) (1994). *Growth, Competitiveness, Employment: The Challenges and Ways Forward into the 21st Century*. Brussels, EC.

European Trade Union Confederation (ETUC), Instituto Sindical de Trabajo, Ambiente y Salud (ISTAS), et al. (2007). *Climate Change and Employment: Impact on Employment in the European Union-25 of Climate Change and $CO_2$ Emission Reduction Measures by 2030*. Brussels, ETUC.

Evans, P. C. (2005). "Export Finance and Sustainable Development: Do Export Credit Subsidy Rules Require Revision?" *Oil, Gas & Energy Law Intelligence* **3**(2): 1–44

Evans, P. C., and K. A. Oye (2001). International Competition: Conflict and Cooperation in Government Export Financing. *The Ex-Im Bank in the 21st Century*. G. C. Hufbauer and R. M. Rodriguez. Washington, DC, Institute for International Economics: 113–158.

Fairman, D., and M. Ross (1996). Old Fads, New Lessons: Learning from Economic Development Assistance. *Institutions for Environmental Aid*. R. O. Keohane and M. A. Levy. Cambridge, MA, MIT Press.

Farrell, D. (2006). "U.S. Offshoring: Small Steps to Make It Win-Win." *Economists' Voice* **3**(3): 1–5.

Faux, J. (2002a). A Global Strategy for Labor. Speech given at the 2002 World Social Forum in Porto Alegre, Brazil, January 30–February 2. Washington, DC, Economic Policy Institute. Available at www.epi.org/publications/entry/webfeatures_viewpoints_global_strat_labor/ (accessed January 22, 2011).

Faux, J. (2002b). Rethinking the Global Political Economy. Speech given at the Asia-Europe-U.S. Progressive Scholar's Forum: Globalization and Innovation of Politics, Japan, April 11–13. Washington, DC, Economic Policy Institute. Available at www.epi.org/publications/entry/webfeatures_viewpoints_global_polit_econ/ (accessed January 22, 2011).

Feridun, M., F. S. Ayadi, et al. (2006). "Impact of Trade Liberalization on the Environment in Developing Countries: The Case of Nigeria." *Journal of Developing Societies* **22**(1): 39–56.

Firebaugh, G. (2003). *The New Geography of Global Income Inequality*. Cambridge, MA, Harvard University Press.

Fischer, S. (1997). Capital Account Liberalization and the Role of the IMF. Speech at the IMF Annual Meeting, September 19. Available at www.imf.org/external/np/speeches/1997/091997.htm (accessed January 22, 2011).

Fischer, S. (2003). "Globalization and Its Challenges." *American Economic Review* **93**(2): 1–30.

Forstater, M. (2004). "Green Jobs: Addressing the Critical Issues Surrounding the Environment, Workplace, and Employment." *International Journal of Environment, Workplace and Employment* **1**(1): 53–61.

Franke, R. W., and B. H. Chasin (1990). "The Kerala Experiment: Development without Growth." *Technology Review* **95**(3): 42–51.

Franz, W. E. (1996). The Scope of Global Environmental Financing—Cases in Context. *Institutions for Environmental Aid.* R. O. Keohane and M. A. Levy. Cambridge, MA, MIT Press.

Freeman, C., and L. Soete (1994). *Work for All or Mass Unemploymet? Computerised Technical Change into the 21st Century.* London, Pinter Publishers.

Freeman, R. B. (2003). The World of Work in the New Millennium. *What the Future Holds: Insights from Social Science.* R. N. Cooper and R. Layard. Cambridge, MA, MIT Press: 157–178.

Friedman, B. M. (2002). "Globalization: Stiglitz's Case." *New York Review of Books* **49**(13): 48–53.

Friedman, T. L. (2004). "What Goes Around . . ." *New York Times*, February 26.

Frumkin, H., and G. Pransky (1999). "Special Populations in Occupational Health." *Occupational Medicine: State of the Art Reviews* **14**(3): 479–484.

Gardner, R. C., and E. Lugo (2009). Official Development Assistance: Toward Funding for Sustainability. *Agenda for a Sustainable America.* J. Dernbach. Washington, DC, Environmental Law Institute: 399–411.

Getzner, M. (1999). "Cleaner Production, Employment Effects and Socio-economic Development." *International Journal of Technology Management* **17**(5): 522–544.

Getzner, M. (2002). "The Quantitative and Qualitative Impacts of Clean Technologies on Employment." *Journal of Cleaner Production* **10**(4): 305–319.

Getzner, M. (2004). "Quantitative and Qualitative Employment Impacts of Environmental Innovations." *International Journal of Environmental Technology and Management* **4**(4): 375–399.

Gibbons, M. (1990). "New Rules of the Globalization Game." *Futures* **22**(9): 973–975.

Gitterman, D. P. (2004). *A Race to the Bottom, a Race to the Top or the March to a Minimum Floor? Economic Integration and Labor Standards in Comparative Perspective. Dynamics of Regulatory Change: How Globalization Affects National Regulatory Policies.* D. Vogel and J. Kaiser. Berkeley, University of California Press: 331–370.

Glaeser, E. L., and J. E. Kohlhase (2003). *Cities, Regions and the Decline of Transport Costs.* Cambridge, MA, Harvard Institute of Economic Research.

Goleman, D. (2009). *Ecological Intelligence: How Knowing the Hidden Impacts of What We Buy Can Change Everything.* New York, Broadway Business.

Grieg-Gan, M., T. Banuri, et al. (2002). The Financial Basis for Strategies. *Sustainable Development Strategies: A Resource Book.* D. B. Dalal-Clayton and S. Bass. London, Earthscan.

Griffith-Jones, S., M. F. Montes, et al., Eds. (2001). *Short-Term Capital Flows and Economic Crises.* WIDER Studies in Development Economics. Oxford, Oxford University Press.

Grossman, G. M., and A. B. Krueger (1993). Environmental Impacts of the North American Free Trade Agreement. *The U.S.-Mexico Free Trade Agreement.* P. Garber. Cambridge, MA, MIT Press.

Grossman, G. M., and A. B. Krueger (1995). "Economic Growth and the Environment." *Quarterly Journal of Economics* **110**(2): 353–377.

Hall, R. P. (2006). Understanding and Applying the Concept of Sustainable Development to Transportation Planning and Decision-Making in the U.S. PhD thesis, Engineering Systems Division. Cambridge, MA, MIT, http://esd.mit.edu/students/esdphd/dissertations/hall_ ralph.pdf (accessed 14 January, 2011).

Halliday, F. (2002). Global Governance: Prospects and Problems. *The Global Transformations Reader.* D. Held and A. McGrew. Cambridge, MA, Polity Press: 431–441.

Hardin, G. (1968). "The Tragedy of the Commons." *Science* **162**: 1243–1248.

Harvey, P. (2006). "Funding a Job Guarantee." *International Journal of Environment, Workplace and Employment* **2**(1): 114–132.

Hausmann, R., and E. Fernández-Arias (2000). "Foreign Direct Investment: Good Cholesterol?" Working Paper 417. New York, Inter-American Development Bank.

Held, D., and A. McGrew, Eds. (2002). *The Global Transformations Reader: An Introduction to the Globalization Debate.* Cambridge, MA, Polity Press.

Hirst, P., and G. Thompson (2002). *Globalization in Question*, 2nd ed. Cambridge, MA, Polity Press.

Holtz-Eakin, D., and T. M. Selden (1995). "Stoking the Fires? $CO_2$ Emissions and Economic Growth." *Journal of Public Economics* **57**(1): 85–101.

Jänicke, M. (2008). "Ecological Modernisation: New Perspectives." *Journal of Cleaner Production* **16**: 557–565.

Jänicke, M., M. Binder, et al. (1997). "'Dirty Industries': Patterns of Change in Industrial Countries." *Environmental and Resource Economics* **9**(4): 467–491.

Kalt, J. P. (1988). The Impact of Domestic Environmental Regulatory Policies on US International Competitiveness. *International Competitiveness.* A. M. Spence and H. A. Flazar. Cambridge, MA, Harper and Row: 221–262.

Khor, M. (2001). "Globalization and Sustainable Development: The Choices before Rio+10." *International Review for Environmental Strategies* **2**(2): 210.

Kleinknecht, A. (1998). "Commentary: Is Labour Market Flexibility Harmful to Innovation?" *Cambridge Journal of Economics* **22**: 387–396.

Kletzer, L. G. (1998). "Job Displacement." *Journal of Economic Perspectives* **12**(1): 115–136.

Kletzer, L. G. (2000). Trade and Job Loss in U.S. Manufacturing, 1979–94. *The Impact of International Trade on Wages.* R. C. Feenstra. Chicago, University of Chicago Press: 349–393.

Korten, D. C. (2001). *When Corporations Rule the World.* San Francisco, Berrett-Koehler Publishers.

Lakshmanan, T. R., and W. P. Anderson (2002). Transportation Infrastructure, Freight Services Sector and Economic Growth. A White Paper prepared for the U.S. Department of Transportation Federal Highway Administration. Boston, Center for Transportation Studies, Boston University. Available at www.ncgia.ucsb.edu/ stella/meetings/20020115/Lakshmanan.pdf (accessed on January 22, 2011.)

Lawn, P. (2004a). "Environment, Workplace and Employment: An Introduction." *International Journal of Environment, Workplace and Employment* **1**(1): 4–39.

Lawn, P. (2004b). "Reconciling the Policy Goals of Full Employment and Ecological Sustainability." *International Journal of Environment, Workplace and Employment* **1**(1): 62–81.

Lawn, P. (2005). "Full Employment and Ecological Sustainability: Comparing the NAIRU, Basic Income, and Job Guarantee Approaches." *International Journal of Environment, Workplace and Employment* **1**(3/4): 336–353.

Lawn, P. (2006). "Ecological Tax Reform and the Double Dividend of Ecological Sustainability and Low Unemployment: An Empirical Assessment." *International Journal of Environment, Workplace and Employment* **2**(4): 332–358.

Lee, E. (1996). "Globalization and Employment: Is the Anxiety Justified?" *International Labour Review* **135**(5): 485–497.

Lee, K. (2003). "Financial Services Companies to Export 500,000 Jobs." *Employee Benefit News* **17**(8): 1, 34.

Lele, S. M. (1991). "Sustainable Development: A Critical Review." *World Development* **19**(6): 607–621.

Levine, L. (2004). *Offshoring (a.k.a. Offshore Outsourcing) and Job Insecurity among U.S. Workers*. CRS Report for Congress. Washington, DC, Congressional Research Service.

Levy, F., and R. J. Murnane (2004). *The New Division of Labor: How Computers Are Creating the Next Job Market*. New York, Russell Sage Foundation.

Lintott, J. (2004). "Work in a Growing and in a Steady-State Economy." *International Journal of Environment, Workplace and Employment* **1**(1): 40–52.

Lopez, R. (1994). "The Environment as a Factor of Production: The Effects of Economic Growth and Trade Liberalization." *Journal of Environmental Economics and Management* **27**: 163–184.

Low, P. (1992). Trade Measures and Environmental Quality: The Implications for Mexico's Export. *International Trade and the Environment*. Discussion Paper 159. Washington, DC, World Bank: 105–120.

Low, P., and A. Yeats (1992). Do "Dirty" Industries Migrate? *International Trade and the Environment*. Discussion Paper 159. Washington, DC, World Bank: 89–104.

Lucas, R. E. B., D. Wheeler, et al. (1992). Economic Development, Environmental Regulation, and the International Migration of Toxic Industrial Pollution, 1960–88. Policy Research Working Paper Series, WSP 1062, World Bank.

Mani, M., and D. Wheeler (1998). "In Search of Pollution Havens? Dirty Industry in the World Economy, 1960 to 1995." *Journal of Environment and Development* **7**(3): 215–247.

Mann, C. L. (2003). Globalization of IT Services and White Collar Jobs: The Next Wave of Productivity Growth. International Economics Policy Briefs, December. Washington, DC, Institute for International Economics.

Marconi, Daniela (2010). Environmental Regulation and Revealed Comparative Advantages in Europe: Is China a Pollution Haven? Bank of Italy Occasional Paper 67, June. Available at http://papers.ssrn.com/sol3/papers.cfm?abstract_id=1721426 (accessed December 16, 2010).

Mármora, L. (2001). "Prejuicios y gobernabilidad." *Encrucijadas* **7**: 8–17.

McCarthy, J. C. (2004). Near-Term Growth of Offshoring Accelerating: Resizing US Services Jobs Going Offshore. Forrester Research, May 14.

McCarthy, J. C., A. Dash, et al. (2002). 3.3 Million US Services Jobs to Go Offshore. Cambridge, Forrester Research, November 11.

McDonough, W., and M. Braungart (1998). "The NEXT Industrial Revolution." *Atlantic Monthly* **282**(4): 82–92.

Meadows, D. H., D. L. Meadows, et al. (1972). *The Limits to Growth*. New York, Potomac Associates.

Meadows, D. H., D. L. Meadows, et al. (1992a). *Beyond the Limits: Confronting Global Collapse, Envisioning a Sustainable Future*. White River Junction, VT, Chelsea Green Publishing Co.

Meadows, D. H., D. L. Meadows, et al. (1992b). "Beyond The Limits to Growth: A New Update to *The Limits to Growth* Reveals That We Are Closer to 'Overshoot and Collapse'—Yet Sustainability Is Still an Achievable Goal." *In Context* **32**: 10–13. Available at www.context.org/ICLIB/IC32/Ozone.htm (accessed January 22, 2011).

Meadows, D. H., J. Randers, et al. (2004). *Limits to Growth: The 30-Year Update*. White River Junction, VT, Chelsea Green Publishing Co.

Mehmet, O. (1995). *Westernizing the Third World: The Eurocentricity of Economic Development Theories*. New York, Routledge.

Miller, A. S. (2000). "The Global Environment Facility and the Search for Financial Strategies to Foster Sustainable Development." *Vermont Law Review* **24**: 1229–1244.

Miller, M. (1995). "Where Is Globalization Taking Us? Why We Need a New 'Bretton Woods.'" *Futures* **27**(2): 125–144.

Mishkin, F. S. (2006). *The Next Great Globalization: How Disadvantaged Nations Can Harness Their Financial Systems to Get Rich*. Princeton, NJ, Princeton University Press.

Munck, R. (2002). *Globalisation and Labour: The New "Great Transformation."* London, Zed Books.

Muradian, R. (2004). Economic Globalisation and the Environment. International Society for Ecological Economics, *Internet Encyclopaedia of Ecological Economics*. Available at www.ecoeco.org/pdf/globalisation_environ ment.pdf (accessed January 22, 2011).

Muradian, R., E. Neumayer, et al. (2006). "Migration, Globalization and the Environment—A Special Issue." *Ecological Economics* **59**(2): 185–241.

Nagpal, T. (1995). "Voices from the Developing World: Progress toward Sustainable Development." *Environment* **37**(8): 10–35.

Nakhooda, S., F. Seymour, et al. (2009). Financing Sustainable Development. *Agenda for a Sustainable America*. J. Dernbach. Washington, DC, Environmental Law Institute: 413–424.

National Academy of Engineering (NAE) (1992). *Time Horizons and Technology Investments*. Washington, DC, NAE.

Neumayer, E. (2001). "Pollution Havens: An Analysis of Policy Options for Dealing with an Elusive Phenomenon." *Journal of Environment and Development* **10**(2): 147–177.

Norlen, D. (2002) Export Credit Agencies Explained. What They Are, How They Impact Development, the Environment and Human Rights, and What the International Reform Campaign Is Doing About It." New York, Global Policy Forum. Availavle at http://globalpolicy .org/socecon/tncs/2002/06ecasexplained.htm (accessed January 22, 2011).

Norlen, D., R. Cox, et al. (2002) "Unusual Suspects: Unearthing the Shadowy World of Export Credit Agencies." *ECA-Watch*. Available at www.eca-watch.org/ ccu/unusualsuspects.pdf (accessed January 22, 2011).

Norris, P. (2001). *Digital Divide: Civic Engagement, Information Poverty, and the Internet Worldwide.* Cambridge, Cambridge University Press.

O'Connor, D. (1994). *Managing the Environment with Rapid Industrialisation: Lessons from the East Asian Experience.* Paris, Development Centre of the Organisation for Economic Co-operation and Development.

Omvedt, G. (1998). "Disturbing Aspects of Kerala Society." *Bulletin of Concerned Asian Scholars* **30**(3): 31–33.

Organisation for Economic Co-operation and Development (OECD) (1994). *The Environmental Effects of Trade.* Paris, OECD.

OECD (1997a). *Economic Globalization and the Environment.* Paris, OECD.

OECD (1997b). *Reforming Environmental Regulation in OECD Countries.* Paris, OECD.

Paehkle, R. C. (2003). *Democracy's Dilemma: Environment, Social Equity, and the Global Economy.* Cambridge, MA, MIT Press.

Parayil, G. (1996). "The 'Kerala Model' of Development: Development and Sustainability in the Third World." *Third World Quarterly* **17**(3): 941–957.

Pew Research Center (2003). *Views of a Changing World.* Washington, DC, Pew Research Center for the People and the Press.

Piore, M. J., and C. Sable (1984). *The Second Industrial Divide: Possibilities for Prosperity.* New York, Basic Books.

Pollin, R., H. Garrett-Peltier, et al. (2008). Green Recovery: A Program to Create Good Jobs and Start Building a Low-Carbon Economy. Washington, DC, Center for American Progress.

Porter, M. E. (1990). *The Competitive Advantage of Nations.* New York, Free Press.

Porter, M. E. (1991). "America's Green Strategy." *Scientific American* **264**(4): 168.

Porter, M. E., and C. van der Linde (1995). "Towards a New Conceptualization of the Environment-Competitiveness Relationship." *Journal of Economic Perspectives* **9**(4): 97–118.

Prasad, E., R. G. Rajan, et al. (2007) "Foreign Capital and Economic Growth." *Brookings Papers on Economic Activity* **1**: 153–209.

Princen, T. (2002). Distancing: Consumption and the Severing of Feedback. *Confronting Consumption.* T. Princen, M. Maniates, and K. Conca. Cambridge, MA, MIT Press: 103–131.

Redclift, M. (1987). *Sustainable Development: Exploring the Contradictions.* London, Methuen.

Redclift, M. (1992). "Sustainable Development and Global Environmental Change: Implications of a Changing Agenda." *Global Environmental Change* **2**(1): 32–42.

Reijnders, L. (2003). "Policies Influencing Cleaner Production: The Role of Prices and Regulation." *Journal of Cleaner Production* **11**: 333–338.

Resources for the Future (RFF) (1954). *The Nation Looks at Its Resources: Report of the Mid-century Conference on Resources for the Future.* Washington, DC, Resources for the Future.

Rich, B. (2000). "Exporting Destruction." *Environmental Forum*, September/October: 32–41.

Rifkin, J. (2004). *The End of Work: The Decline of the Global Labor Force and the Dawn of the Post-market Era.* New York, G. P. Putnam's Sons.

Robison, H. D. (1988). "Industrial Pollution Abatement: The Impact on Balance of Trade." *Canadian Journal of Economics* **21**(1): 187–199.

Rodrik, D. (1996). Labor Standards in International Trade: Do They Matter and What Do We Do about Them? *Emerging Agenda for Global Trade: High Stakes for Developing Countries.* R. Lawrence, D. Rodrik, and J. Whalley. Baltimore, Johns Hopkins University Press.

Rodrik, D. (1997). *Has Globalization Gone Too Far?* Washington, DC, Institute for International Economics.

Rodrik, D. (1998). "Why Do More Open Economies Have Bigger Governments?" *Journal of Political Economy* **106**(5): 997–1032.

Rodrik, D. (1999). *The New Global Economy and Developing Countries: Making Openness Work.* Washington, DC, Overseas Development Council.

Rodrik, D. (2005). Feasible Globalizations. *Globalization: What's New.* M. M. Weinstein. New York, Columbia University Press: 196–213.

Rodrik, D. (2007). *One Economics, Many Recipes: Globalization, Institutions, and Economic Growth.* Princeton, NJ, Princeton University Press.

Rodrik, D., and A. Subramanian (2008). Why Did Financial Globalization Disappoint? Unpublished manuscript, Cambridge, MA, Harvard University.

Sachs, W. (2001). *Rio + 10 and the North-South Divide.* Berlin, Heinrich Boll Foundation.

Schaper, M. (2009). *Export Promotion, Trade and the Environment: Negotiating Environmental Standards for Export Credit Agencies Across the Atlantic. Transatlantic Environment and Energy Politics: Comparative and International Perspectives.* M. Schreurs, H. Selin and S. VanDeveer. Aldershot, Ashgate: 189–208.

Schmidt-Bleek, F. (1998). *Das MIPS-Konzept.* München, Droemer-Knaur-Verlag. .

Selden, T. M., and D. Song (1994). "Environmental Quality and Development: Is There a Kuznets Curve for Air Pollution Emissions?" *Journal of Environmental Economics and Management* **27**: 147–162.

Shafik, N., and S. Bandyopadhyay (1992). Economic Growth and Environmental Quality: Time Series and Cross-Country Evidence. Background Paper for the *World Development Report.* Washington, DC, World Bank.

Simon, H. A. (1960). The Corporation: Will It Be Managed by Machines? *Management and the Corporations,*

*1985.* M. L. Anshen and G. L. Bach. New York, McGraw-Hill: 17–55.

Sinden, A. (2007). The "Preference for Pollution" and Other Fallacies, or Why Free Trade Isn't "Progress." *Progress in International Law.* R. A. Miller and R. M. Bratspies. Leiden, Martinus Nijhoff Press.

Singer, P. (2002). *One World: The Ethics of Globalization.* New Haven, CT, Yale University Press.

Smith, G. (2005). "Creating the Conditions for Public Investment to Deliver Full Employment and Environmental Sustainability." *International Journal of Environment, Workplace and Employment* **1**(3/4): 258–264.

Smith, J. P., and B. Edmonston, Eds. (1997). *The New Americans: Economic, Demographic, and Fiscal Effects of Immigration.* Washington, DC, National Academy Press.

Somavia, J. (2002). "Clothes for the Emperor: The World's People Need Decent Jobs." *International Herald Tribune,* August 27.

Sonnenfeld, D., and A. P. J. Mol (2002). "Globalization and the Transformation of Environmental Governance." *American Behavioral Scientist* **45**(9): 1318–1339.

Soros, G. (1998). "Toward a Global Open Society." *Atlantic Monthly* **281**(1): 20, 22, 24, 32.

Soros, G. (2002). *George Soros on Globalization.* New York, Public Affairs.

Speth, J. G. (2003). Two Perspectives on Globalization and the Environment. *Worlds Apart: Globalization and the Environment.* J. G. Speth. Washington, DC, Island Press: 1–18.

Stallings, B. (1993). New International Context of Development. Working Paper Series on the New International Context of Development, Paper 1. Madison, University of Wisconsin-Madison.

Stallings, B., Ed. (1995). *Global Change, Regional Response: The New International Context of Development.* Cambridge, Cambridge University Press.

Stiglitz, J. (2002a). "A Fair Deal for the World." *New York Review of Books* **49**(9): 24–28.

Stiglitz, J. (2002b). Globalism's Discontents. *American Prospect* **13**(1): 16–21.

Stiglitz, J. (2002c). *Globalization and Its Discontents.* New York, W. W. Norton.

Stiglitz, J. (2010). *Freefall: America, Free Markets, and the Sinking of the World Economy.* New York, W. W. Norton.

Streeten, P. (2001). *Globalisation: Threat or Opportunity?* Copenhagen, Handelshojskolens Forlag, Copenhagen Business School Press.

Swank, D. (2002). *Global Capital, Political Institutions, and Policy Change in Developed Welfare States.* Cambridge, Cambridge University Press.

Tapinos, G., and D. Delaunay (2000). Can One Really Talk of the Globalisation of Migration Flows? *Globalisation, Migration and Development.* OECD Proceedings. Paris, OECD.

Tassey, G. (1999). NIST Briefing Note April 1999—R&D Trends in the U.S. Economy: Strategies and Policy Implications. Gaithersburg, National Institute of Standards and Technology.

Tassey, G. (2003). "R&D Investment Trends: U.S. Needs More High Tech." *Research-Technology Management* **46**(2): 9–11.

Thampapillai, D. J., X. Wu, et al. (2007). "Economic Growth, the Environment and Employment: Challenges for Sustainable Development in China." *International Journal of Environment, Workplace and Employment* **3**(1): 15–27.

Tharamangalam, J. (1998). "The Perils of Social Development without Economic Growth: The Development Debacle of Kerala, India." *Bulletin of Concerned Asian Scholars* **30**(1): 23–33.

Tobey, J. A. (1990). "The Effects of Domestic Environmental Policies on Patterns of World Trade: An Empirical Test." *Kyklos* **43**(2): 191–209.

Todaro, M. P., and S. C. Smith (2009). *Economic Development.* 10th ed. Boston, Addison-Wesley.

United Nations Development Programme (UNDP) (2010). *Human Development Report 2010 - 20th Anniversary Edition. The Real Wealth of Nations: Pathways to Human Development.* New York, UNDP.

United Nations Environment Programme (UNEP) (2008). *Green Jobs: Towards Decent Work in a Sustainable, Low-Carbon World.* Job number DRC/1069/PA. Nairobi, UNEP.

United Nations Population Division (UNPD) (2003). *World Population Prospects: The 2002 Revision; Highlights.* New York, United Nations.

van Beers, C., and J. C. van den Bergh (1997). "An Empirical Multi-country Analysis of the Impact of Environmental Regulations on Foreign Trade Flows." *Kyklos* **50**(1): 29–46.

Vehmas, J., J. Luukkanen, et al. (2007). "Linking Analyes and Environmental Kuznets Curves for Aggregated Material Flows in the EU." *Journal of Cleaner Production* **15**: 1662–1673.

Vogel, D. (2000). "Environmental Regulation and Economic Integration." *Journal of International Economic Law* **3**(2): 265–279.

Voigt, D. (1993). "The Maquiladora Problem in the Age of NAFTA: Where Will We Find Solutions?" *Minnesota Journal of Global Trade* **2**(2): 323–357.

von Moltke, K. (2001). "The Organization of the Impossible." *Global Environmental Politics* **1**(2): 23–28.

Wackernagel, M., C. Monfreda, et al. (2002). Ecological Footprint of Nations: November 2002 Update; How Much Nature Do They Use? How Much Nature Do They Have? Sustainability Issue Brief. Oakland, CA, Redefining Progress.

Wackernagel, M., S. White, et al. (2004). "Using Ecological Footprint Accounts: From Analysis to Applications." *International Journal of Environment and Sustainable Development* **3**(3/4): 293–315.

Wagle, S. (1993). "Sustainable Development: Some Interpretations, Implications, and Uses." *Bulletin of Science, Technology and Society* **13**: 314–323.

Walter, I. (1973). "The Pollution Content of American Trade." *Western Economic Journal* **11**(1): 61–70.

Walter, I. (1982). International Economic Repercussions of Environmental Policy: An Economist's Perspective. *Environment and Trade.* S. J. Rubin and T. R. Graham. Totowa, NJ, Allenheld and Osmun.

Walz, R. (2010). "Employment and Structural Impacts of Material Efficiency Strategies: Results from Five Case Studies." *Journal of Cleaner Production* **19**(8): 805–815.

Weiss, P. (1997). "Techno-globalism and Industrial Policy Responses in the USA and Europe." *Intereconomics* **32**(2): 74–86.

Weller, C. E., R. E. Scott, et al. (2001). The Unremarkable Record of Liberalized Trade: After 20 years of Global Economic Deregulation, Poverty and Inequality Are as Pervasive as Ever. Briefing Paper. Washington, DC, Economic Policy Institute.

Whitford, J. (2006). *The New Old Economy: Networks, Institutions, and the Organizational Transformation of American Manufacturing*. Oxford, Oxford University Press.

Wilson, E. O. (2002). *The Future of Life*. New York, Alfred A. Knopf.

Winner, L. (1977). *Autonomous Technology: Technics-out-of-Control as a Theme in Political Thought*. Cambridge, MA, MIT Press.

Winner, L. (1986). *The Whale and the Reactor*. Chicago, University of Chicago Press.

Wolgemuth, L. (2009). "The Truth about All Those Green Jobs." *U.S. News and World Report,* March 25.

World Bank Group (WBG) (1992). *World Development Report: Development and the Environment*. Washington, DC, World Bank.

WBG (1997). *Five Years after Rio: Innovations in Environmental Policy*. Washington, DC, World Bank.

WBG (1998). *World Development Indicators*. Washington, DC, World Bank.

WBG (2002). *World Development Report, 2003*. Washington, DC, World Bank.

WBG (2006). *Global Development Finance, 2006: The Development Potential of Surging Capital Flows*. Washington, DC, World Bank.

WBG (2007). *Global Development Finance, 2007: The Globalization of Corporate Finance in Developing Countries*. Washington, DC, World Bank.

World Commission on the Social Dimension of Globalization (WCSDG) (2004). *A Fair Globalization: Creating Opportunities for All*. Geneva, ILO Publications.

World Wildlife Fund (WWF) (2006). *Living Planet Report, 2006*. Gland, WWF.

Yach, D., and D. Bettcher (1998). "The Globalization of Public Health, I: Threats and Opportunities." *American Journal of Public Health* **88**(5): 735–738.

# Industrial Policy and the Role of the Firm in Pursuing Sustainable Development

In Part II of this book, we articulated the effects that both technological change and globalization have, or are expected to have, on the three pillars of sustainability. Technological change is both a cause of unsustainability and a vehicle for the improvement of the workings of the industrial state. Therefore, understanding the technological change process and the possible roles of the private sector and the government in influencing that process is essential for the design of policy. A number of questions are suggested in this regard. The reader might wish to address them on the completion of all the chapters in this part of the book.

1. How likely is it that the needed sustainability changes will evolve without government intervention, and over what time period will they evolve?

2. If the government greases the innovation system—that is, improves the climate for innovation—through traditional industrial policy by making it more efficient, for example, by increasing rewards to innovation through better patent or IP policy or tax treatment of investment, will this give rise to more and faster development of sustainable innovation, or will it just generate more profits?

3. Do we need stringent/strong regulatory requirements/sticks instead, or as well? Is the second strategy necessary or sufficient?

4. If we move to a more innovation-interventionist and targeted approach with incentives given for more sustainable versus unsustainable innovations in specific problem areas, for example, in energy, what is the likelihood that incumbents versus new entrants will lead the pack?

5. Who is most likely to respond to regulatory fiats, incumbents or new entrants?

6. Are the answers different for different sectors/problems—for example, toxic chemicals versus energy sources/efficiency?

7. Are the answers different in different nations?

The focus of technology policy can be broad or narrow. Historically, the focus of industrial policy was to improve the utility and profitability of the products of industrial development. This meant an essentially utilitarian approach, focused on improved performance, lower costs to consumers and users, and increases in profit for the technology providers. The emergent scholarship on industrial policy thus quite naturally focused on how innovation occurs in firms and how the general technology business environment could be optimized through strengthening the national (or sectoral) innovation system, that is, strengthening the *determinants* of innovation. Although government might be involved in the actual development of "big science," such as computers and aircraft, for the most part, industrial innovation (especially in the development of salable products) was to be left to the private sector, with government benignly "greasing the wheel" where useful. Chapter 6 explores these ideas, which are probably best characterized as the underpinnings of evolutionary change. Chapter 7 provides a more detailed look into how firms "learn to innovate" and whether evolutionary processes—enhanced by organizational changes in existing firms leading to enhanced learning—can lead to significant innovation. The extent to which evolutionary processes—with a minimal government role—will lead to improving the environment and employment is also examined in this chapter. Beyond picking "the low-hanging fruit" that advantages industry directly by eliminating waste and reducing pollution-control costs, or treating labor better because it *might* enhance profitability, it is concluded that firms engaged in evolutionary processes are *unlikely* to contribute to significant innovation in the time period now thought to be needed to address the serious sustainability challenges ahead.

This brings us quite naturally to the focus of Chapter 8: what form(s) could a more interventionist "industrial policy" take? Both management of evolutionary processes through "transition management" or "strategic niche management" and more directive *industrial policy* options are explored, focusing on changing the incentives for technological change. Their influence on competitiveness; health, safety, and the environment; and employment is also discussed for both developed and developing countries. The effects of globalization, mediated through impacts on technology, also have consequences for employment, and these will also be discussed.

Following our exploration of more interventionist government policies focusing on the economy/competitiveness, Chapter 9 in Part IV of this work explores two different policy models for addressing health, safety, and environmental concerns from the perspective of the nation-state through *environmental policy*. It focuses on (1) controlling pollution in various media (air, water, waste, and the workplace), product content and characteristics, and industrial chemical production, use, and disposal; and (2) developing an "industrial policy for the environment" in which encouraging or requiring environmentally sustainable production and products is the focus primarily through the tools of environmental policy and regulation. Whether and how technology might be employed to improve both the environment and employment is reserved for the concluding Chapter 13.

# 6

# The Importance of Technological Innovation

## 6.1 INTRODUCTION

In Part I of this book, we addressed the dimensions and historical evolution of the concept of sustainability. In Part II, we discussed the concept of industrial development, first in the context of the nation-state and then in the context of the globalized economy. We then linked globalization with sustainability, tracing the current and anticipated effects of development on sustainability.

In this chapter that begins Part III, "Industrial Policy and the Role of the Firm in Pursuing Sustainable Development," we focus on a deeper understanding of technological change and argue that technological innovation is essential for achieving sustainable development. In Chapter 7, we explore the role of the industrial firm in improving production processes, products, and services (that is, competitiveness); in improving the environment (through environmental technology or the prevention of pollution at the source); and in providing employment. In

Chapter 8, we address the role of government through various approaches to industrial policy in improving competitiveness and employment. Part IV addresses other roles for government. In Chapters 9 and 10, we discuss nation-based policies and international regimes, respectively, for achieving environmental sustainability and improving the safety of workplaces and products.

## 6.2 TYPES OF INNOVATION AND THE NATURE OF TECHNOLOGICAL CHANGE

### 6.2.1 Categorizing Technological Change

"Technological change" is a general and imprecise term that encompasses invention, innovation, diffusion, and technology transfer. Technological innovation is the first commercially successful application of a new technical idea. It should be distinguished from invention, which is the development of a new technical idea, and from diffusion, which is the subsequent

**Invention** (the first working prototype)

**Innovation** (the first commercially successful introduction)
- *Sustaining Innovation*—innovation that occurs within the current/dominant technological trajectory
- *Disrupting Innovation*—innovation that occurs outside mainstream development trajectory
  - *Intrinsic Innovation*
  - *Architectural Innovation*

**Diffusion** (wider adoption *within* an industry)

**Technology Transfer** (wider adoption across industries or countries)

\*\*\*\*\*

**Product Changes**
**Product-Services**

\*\*\*\*\*

**Process Changes**

\*\*\*\*\*

**System Changes**

**FIGURE 6.1: THE DYNAMICS OF TECHNOLOGICAL CHANGE**

widespread adoption of an innovation beyond those who developed it (Figure 6.1).\*

As industrial societies mature, the nature and patterns of innovation change (Abernathy and Clark 1985; Utterback 1987). New technologies become old technologies. Many product lines (for example, washing machines or lead batteries) become standardized or increasingly "rigid," and innovation, if there is any, becomes more difficult and incremental rather than radical.

In language that is familiar to traditional innovation scholars, an *incremental innovation* involves a step-by-step coevolutionary process of change, whereas *radical innovations* are discontinuous and possibly involve the *displacement* of dominant firms and institutions rather than evolutionary transformation (Ashford, Hafkamp, et al. 2002; Luiten 2001; Moors 2000; Partidario 2003). Christensen (1997) distinguishes the former as *sustaining innovation* and the latter as *disrupting innovation*, rather than "radical." He argues that both sustaining and disrupting innovation can be incremental, moderate, or radical. Unfortunately, the term "radical" in the literature is used in these two different ways and is a source of con-

---

\* The distinction between innovation and diffusion is sometimes hard to draw, however, because innovations can rarely be adopted by new users without some modification. When modifications are extensive, i.e., when adoption requires significant *adaptation*, the result may be a new innovation.

fusion. The later discussion in this chapter will clarify the use of these terms.

Another issue, however, needs clarification: sustaining or disrupting of what? Christensen (1997) uses the term "disrupting" in the context of a customer base that values certain product attributes, and whose changing desires can change the markets for technological variants in products. The context in which we will use the term throughout this book pertains to the product—and also other technological or system changes—from a *technological* as well as a customer-based desirability-of-attribute perspective. In this regard, our use of the term "disrupting" is more in line with Chris Freeman's (1982a) use of the term "radical" or Nelson and Winter's (1977) idea of shifting "technological regimes" (see below). Because we take Christensen's point that the term "radical" should be reserved to describe the *rate* of change rather than its type, we will generally avoid the term as a synonym for "disrupting."

From a technological perspective, disrupting innovations can be either *intrinsic* or *architectural*. The former is a dramatically different way of achieving functionality, such as the transistor replacing the vacuum tube; the latter may combine technological ideas in a new artifact, such as the hybrid electric and internal combustion engine. Christensen, Utterback, et al. (1998) stress the latter and focus on product technology. Utterback and Acee (2005, pp. 15–16) observe that "innovations that broaden the market create new room for firms to start," and "the true importance of disruptive technology . . . is not that it may displace established products. Rather, it is a powerful means for enlarging and broadening markets and providing new functionality."

The problem with restricting one's analysis to the market determinants of technological change is that this neglects the fact that markets may not respond adequately to sustainability concerns. More is needed than matching the technological capacities of firms with current societal demands. Our inquiry will distinguish between sustaining innovation and disrupting innovation in a broader technological and societal context.

Product lines/sectors that are well developed and have become standardized mainly experience incremental innovation. Changes are focused on cost-reducing production methods—including increasing the scale of production, displacing labor with technology, and exercising more control over workers—rather than on significant changes in products. Process innovation usually gradually declines as manufacturing or production processes are standardized. A useful concept related to individual product lines is that of "technological regimes," which are defined by certain boundaries for technological progress and by directions or trajectories in which progress is possible and worth doing (Nelson and Winter 1977).

Sometimes, however, the dominant technologies (such as the vacuum tube and the mechanical calculator) are challenged and rather abruptly displaced by significant disrupting innovations (such as the transistor and the electronic calculator), but this is relatively rare, although very important (Christensen 1997; Kemp 1994). We will argue that disrupting innovations—involving more than incremental changes in product or process attributes—may be needed to achieve sustainability. As industrial economies mature, innovation in many sectors may become more and more difficult and incremental, and regulatory and governmental policies are increasingly influenced, if not captured, by the purveyors of the dominant technology (regime), which becomes more resistant to change. However, occasionally, traditional sectors can revitalize themselves, as in the case of cotton textiles.*

Even if an existing firm is driven by a desire for greater profits or market share, it faces a dilemma (Christensen 1997) whether to continue developing innovation in its traditional and successful product line or to embark on a different (Schumpeterian) pathway that requires changes in its technology and perhaps even in its markets. In an empirical study of the determinants of successful disrupting innovations requiring a transformation of both core competencies and markets, Herrmann, Gassmann, et al. (2007) put forth the following hypotheses, consistent with the expectations of Christensen (1997):

1.  The greater the capacity to transform competencies, the higher the propensity of a company to introduce radical[†] product innovation.

2.  The greater the ability to transform markets, the higher the propensity of a company to introduce radical product innovation.

3.  The more pronounced the orientation toward technological innovation is in a company, the more likely the company will be in a position to transform its competencies.

4.  The more a company can be described as a learning organization,[‡] the more likely the company will be in a position to transform its (a) competencies and (b) markets.

5.  The greater the willingness of a company to take risks, the more likely the company will be in a position to transform its (a) competencies and (b) markets.

6.  The more a company orients itself on a long-term basis, the more it will be in a position to transform its (a) competencies and (b) markets.

7.  The more a company distinguishes itself through traditional customer orientation (in terms of customer led business), the less likely it will be in a position to transform its markets.

Not surprisingly, willingness to take risks and an orientation toward technological innovation had the biggest statistically significant positive influence on the required transformation capabilities and thereby on radical [i.e., disrupting] product innovation. Citing the literature, Herrmann, Gassmann, et al. (2007, p. 101) note that "most case studies on radical innovations describe the high time requirements: a threshold of 10 years is often reached and in some cases substantially exceeded."

Sartorius (2006) recites the importance of radical innovation and the difficulty and resistance of incumbent firms to depart from their historical pathways (that is, exhibiting path dependency), reflecting not only "lock-in" to continued patterns but also "lockout" from changes necessary to become more sustainable. He also adds a further dimension. He distinguishes first-order sustainability, which focuses on specific innovations to achieve a particular environmental goal (articulated in government regulations or strong social demands), from second-order sustainability, which enables an industry system to

---

*   Under the economic threat of more stringent worker protection standards for cotton dust exposure, the leading U.S. textile firm decided to redesign and modernize its technology to reduce occupational exposure to both cotton dust and noise and to improve production efficiency. It stands out as one of the rare instances where an industry reinvented and replaced itself.

†   Herrmann, Gassmann, et al. (2007) use the term "radical" to mean "disrupting" in the Christensen formulation.

‡   The dynamic nature of the innovation process for discontinuous (i.e., radical or disrupting) product innovation is further developed by a theory of "probe and learn" whereby an iterative process of introducing novel products into nascent markets receives feedback from different and shifting consumers/users of those products that involve different design modalities until a successive market and customer base emerges (Lynn, Morone, et al. 1996). In other words, the "product attributes" valued by the relevant customer base, described as "value networks" by Christensen (1997), are fluid and must be discovered by the innovator, who must use that learning to modify the product. This is reminiscent of a "coevolutionary" process later described by Kemp and Rotmans (2001). "Development of a discontinuous innovation becomes a process of successive approximation, probing and learning again and again, each time striving to take a step closer to a winning combination of product and market" (attributed to Charles Lucy by Lynn, Morone, et al. 1996, p. 19). The process is more empirical than analytic. See Chapter 7 for a discussion of organizational learning.

adapt continually to new and changing challenges. Lock-in refers not only to the routines of a particular firm but also to the system in which it is embedded (for example, markets, economies of scale, governmental rules, and short-term time horizons), which present continuing resistance and barriers to future change that would otherwise allow wider choices among more sustainable trajectories. Sartorius (2006) argues that therein lies the real and most difficult challenge. Firms are driven by short-term cost- and risk-reduction concerns rather than longer-term investments in uncertain futures.* Further, Sartorius (2006) emphasizes that coevolution in the technical, economic, and social spheres is a necessary characteristic of system changes that are capable of achieving second-order sustainability. The most favorable likelihood of achieving system changes representing second-order sustainability is in those industries that have been besieged by first-order sustainability challenges that move them on to second-order changes, such as parts of the chemical industry or, lately, industries with high energy costs. This observation supports the proposition that prevalent stringent regulation is a precondition to achieving second-order, long-term sustainability. Sartorius (p. 278) comments:

> The government typically plays a crucial role in overcoming existing barriers to competitiveness [by forcing the internalization of social costs] in the relevant markets. In doing so the government inevitably faces opposition from those whose interests are negatively affected: the incumbent industry and other groups paying the price for measures taken. Typically, the government or policy makers in general are not inclined to neglect such opposition [giving rise to regulatory capture] unless the promoting forces from other parts of the society are sufficiently strong. More so, major techno-economic changes require a general openness or even a readiness to change (i.e., a period of instability) on the part of the political system. For these reasons, the techno-economic factors will have to be supplemented by both political and social factors.

Lock-in is a problem that affects the extent of the *diffusion* as well as innovation of environmentally superior or energy-efficient technologies. Using reasoning similar to that of Sartorius, Carrillo-Hermosilla (2006) argues that as a result of increasing returns to adoption of energy technologies produced by econo-

mies of scale, "apparently inferior designs can become locked in a historically dependent process in which circumstantial events determine the winning alternative." He opines "that it is relatively unlikely that conventional policy measures, not necessarily focused on technological change, may alone be able to bring about this radical change in technologies and practices" (ibid., p. 718). His recommendations to encourage what he calls "techno-environmental transitions" (focusing on the diffusion of superior technologies) must involve coevolutionary processes, including strategic niche management, market-transformation programs, demand-side management, and voluntary environmental agreements.

Firms may innovate for "main business" purposes or in order to achieve compliance with health, safety, and environmental regulations or demands (Ashford, Heaton, et al. 1979). Focusing on product innovations in the disk-drive industry, Christensen (1997) has argued that incumbents† are unlikely to come up with the next radical (that is, disrupting) innovation. Analyzing a broader set of product innovations in consumer durables and office products, Chandy and Tellis (2000) have challenged the idea of the "incumbent's curse" and also the general proposition that small firms are likely to be disproportionately responsible for radical innovations. On the latter point, it is argued that greater access to capital and knowledge of relevant markets and the financial ability to tolerate losses from failed attempts to innovate, combined with greater organizational tolerance for radical ideas, go a long way toward countering the inherent innovativeness of smaller, more flexible firms. Although "first-mover" advantages are emphasized in the literature (Nehrt 1998), Chandy and Tellis (2000, p. 14) argue that the larger incumbents who delay entry into the market do even better, concluding that "dynamic organizational structures and strong technological capability may keep large, incumbent organizations nimble and innovative, but many managers and academics have tended to focus on inertia-prone incumbents."

Without resolving the apparent contradictions of the commentators concerning what kinds of firms are likely to come up with disrupting innovation for what is essentially main business innovation, innovating for sustainable development purposes involving health, safety, and environmental concerns—which are less likely to be seen as driven by new market op-

---

*       Sartorius cites the work of Porter and van der Linde (1995) in arguing that firms that take environmental externalities into account up front when they are undertaking environmentally sound innovation ultimately benefit financially. Note, however, the discussion of the earlier work of Ashford, Ayers, et al. (1985) and Ashford, Heaton, et al. (1979) that incumbents are likely to undertake incremental rather than radical innovation.

†       Citing others, Chandy and Tellis (2000, p. 2) define an incumbent as "a firm that manufactured or sold products belonging to the product generation that preceded the radical innovation." Christenson's (1997) formulation is essentially the same.

portunities for profit—may present a different dynamic. The evidence from innovations spurred by stringent regulations seems to favor displacement of the incumbents of problematic technologies by new entrants (see generally Ashford, Ayers, et al. 1985; Ashford, Heaton, et al. 1979).

As the work of Chandy and Tellis (2000) demonstrates, not all commentators are convinced of the general proposition that disrupting innovations come from incumbents. In the hard-disk-drive industry, on which Christensen (1997) builds this proposition, Chesbrough (1999) argues that three institutional factors promote or inhibit the formation (and success) of start-up firms differently in Japan and the United States: the technical labor market, the venture-capital market, and the structure of buyer-supplier ties. Especially important is the ability of new firms to lure away high-level and specialized technical manpower, a characteristic found to a much greater extent in the United States. Chesbrough (ibid., p. 457) observes that "most of the architectural shifts in technology documented [by the 'new-entrant' proponents] were led by new organizations, but not new people." The pattern is seen in other industries as well. Chesbrough (p. 458) posits that "rigid labor markets therefore increase the benefit of incumbency over newly entering firms." Venture-capital markets and the structure of buyer-supplier ties combine with labor-market features to provide "institutional factors" that favor new entrants in the United States and incumbents in Japan. This study provides a word of caution about overgeneralizing in predicting where disrupting innovation will originate and what policies work best in a particular national or sectoral context.

Sectors other than the established ones, notably those based on emerging technologies, may experience increased innovation. The overall economic health and employment potential of a nation as a whole is the sum of these diverging trends and is increasingly dependent on international trade. Whether nations seek to increase revenues on the basis of competition in technological performance or, alternatively, cost-driven strategies can have an enormous impact on employment (Charles and Lehner 1998). As will be discussed later, health, safety, and environmental regulation, structured appropriately, as well as new societal demands, can also stimulate significant technological changes that otherwise might not have occurred at the time (Ashford, Ayers, et al. 1985).

A technological innovation can be characterized by its *motivating force*, by its *type*, and by its *nature*. The motivating force behind technological change can be the result of an industry's main business ac-

tivities, or it can evolve from the industry's efforts to comply with or respond to health, safety, or environmental regulations and pressures (Ashford, Heaton, et al. 1979). Historically, about one-third of main business innovations have their origins in "technology push" (innovations looking for application) and about two-thirds from "market pull" (meeting an existing customer/societal demand or a regulatory requirement). Regulation, market signals, and anticipated consumer, societal, or worker demand can affect any of the characteristics of innovation. In the following chapter, we discuss the evidence that the most significant driving force for technological change identified by business managers is environmental legislation and enforcement.

Concerning the *type* of innovation, four different levels of technological change need to be considered: (1) product changes, (2) process changes, (3) shifts from products to product-services, and (4) more far-reaching system changes that not only include technological innovation but also effects on employment, the organization of the firm, and societal demands. Innovation can be product oriented, meaning that it involves changes in the design of the final product or service. It can extend further to include shifts to *product-services*, in which the firm envisions delivering a desired service or benefit to the customer in creative new ways, with the goal of minimizing resources, energy use, and pollution. An example is selling copier *services* to customers—in which the copier company owns the machine and performs all maintenance and service on it while it is in use—instead of selling copy *machines*. This kind of change is described subsequently in more detail. Technological innovation can also be process oriented;* that is, it can occur as part of the *production process* of a product or the delivery of a service.

---

\* In acknowledging the importance of technological innovation for both the environment and employment in hopes of attaining triple sustainability, it may be useful to consider the differential effects that product versus process innovation may have on the environment and employment. Cleff and Rennings (1999) argue that the benefits of product innovation may be more readily recognized and therefore pursued by industrial firms. It has been suggested that product innovations for new markets can result in new net employment, partly because of their greater reliance on demand-pull forces (Brouwer and Kleinknecht 1996; Matzner, Schettkat, et al. 1990), but that this is not true for all product innovations (Charles and Lehner 1998). This, of course, does not justify neglecting policies that promote process change. In fact, product innovation that is more closely linked to process innovation and in which there is more reliance on a learning-based mode than on a scientific breakthrough is argued to create more employment (ibid.). See Section 7.6 in the following chapter for a more in-depth discussion of innovation and employment.

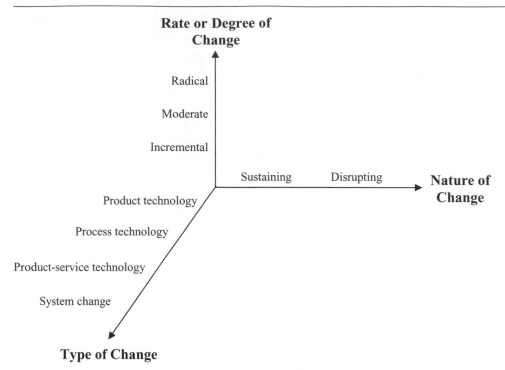

FIGURE 6.2: THE IMPORTANT DIMENSIONS OF TECHNOLOGICAL CHANGE

System changes are the deepest and broadest in scope. They extend outside the boundaries of the firm to include many actors, including suppliers, competitor and collaborator firms, government authorities, and civil society. They involve the reconception and reordering of entire production chains and stakeholder networks, for example, shifting from nonlocal industrial agriculture to locally grown organic food systems, or simultaneously altering production, employment, distribution, and transportation regimes to move people and deliver goods more efficiently, with less energy use and pollution.

As already discussed, in the context of product change, the *nature* of a technological innovation can be evaluated according to whether it serves either to *sustain* or *disrupt* established product lines and value networks of customers with well-defined demands (Christensen 1997). Christensen's (p. 32) concept of a "value network" is "the context within which a firm identifies and responds to customers' needs, solves problems, procures input, reacts to competitors, and strives for profit." In Christensen's formulation, sustaining innovations occur when established firms push the envelope to continue to satisfy existing consumers with improved products within the prior but expanded technological trajectory. Disrupting innovations cater to different, perhaps not yet well-defined customers with product attributes different from those in the established producer-consumer

networks.* Alternatively, the distinction between sustaining and disrupting innovation might be focused on the technological nature of the change, a distinction that invites incentives focused not only on product changes (which may be the main driver in market-pull innovation) but also on changes involving process changes, shifts to product services, and wider system changes. This is not to downplay the importance of consumer demand, but to put it in a proper context, because many desirable technological changes will need to come from more interventionist and regulatory approaches if sustainable development is to be achieved in a timely fashion. We explore these ideas further in Chapters 7, 8, and 9.

The dynamics of technological change were summarized in Figure 6.1. The three dimensions of technological change—the *type* of change, the *rate/degree* of change, and the *nature* of change—are represented in Figure 6.2. It turns out that different kinds of changes affect competitiveness, employment, and the environment differently. This suggests that the emphases of a nation's industrial policy matter for sustainability.

The organizational implications of sustaining versus disrupting innovation by the industrial firm are profound and are addressed in the following chapter.

---

\* The creation of new products in this case is not a wave built on prior waves of technological advance but rather occurs in an entirely new trajectory, often creating a new market.

In the case of sustaining innovation, organizational learning is central; in the case of disrupting innovation, development follows a different path, with learning taking on an entirely different and radical meaning, involving breaking with established patterns and creating new architectures of people and artifacts. Christensen (1997) reviews why established firms might find it difficult to reinvent themselves.

## 6.2.2 Evolutionary versus Revolutionary Change

A further important distinction is the difference between the development of technology—whether product, process, product-service, or system—that proceeds in an evolutionary way (or in a coevolutionary way where technology developers and customers and/or society both change what is produced and demanded, respectively, over time) and what might be termed "revolutionary" development of technology that is driven by influences more exogenous to the firm's immediate sphere of interest, such as government intervention, strong societal pressures, or an energy crisis.

Much innovation scholarship examines evolutionary theory as it relates to *products* (as contrasted with process, product-service, or system-level change). Here the (changing) nature of the customer base is all-important because—ideally—firms innovate with the end customer in mind. Indeed, the survival of the technology and ultimately the firm depends on how well customers take up the innovation.

In the context of encouraging sustainable development transformations, supply-side policies (for example, subsidies, R&D support, and favorable tax treatment of investment) can be general or can focus on encouraging technological changes with certain performance characteristics in mind. Demand-side policies affecting or altering societal preferences (for example, purchasing tax incentives, public-service advertising, counteradvertising, and education) may be useful in implementing or gaining acceptance of sustainable development policies, but they are not nearly as important as they are in evolutionary approaches. Evolutionary approaches may proceed far too slowly to stem sustainability concerns related to global climate change and toxic pollution. These two statements suggest that if one's (political) preference is for evolutionary transformations, changing societal preferences should receive attention, but we argue that supply-side policies, as well as regulation and other interventions, are needed for significant transformations. These ideas are further developed in the next two chapters.

Christensen (1997) does not develop his ideas beyond the product domain or explore how development might be different under strong governmental or societal interventionist policies that supersede evolutionary changes. Process changes and innovation, although important to workers, may not be very important to customers. Producers of products may develop more sustainable processes to make their products, but usually not because customers demand those changes. Thus Christensen's concept of "value networks" and new customer bases may not be relevant in the same way as in the product domain. Distinguishing sustaining and disrupting technologies may be useful, but these "innovations" are not driven by customers of the product, but rather by producers and manufacturers. On the other hand, in shifting from products to product-services, customers may be as important as—or more important than—they are in the product realm, as we argue later. System changes, the most far-reaching changes, involve a number of producers and actors—and perhaps service providers—in a more dramatic realignment of actors.

In Chapter 7, we develop a behavioral model that describes for product, process, product-service, and system changes the influence of incumbent versus new-entrant firms, the likelihood of sustaining versus disrupting technology, and implications for different customer bases. We first examine (for changes involving products, processes, shifts to product-services, and systems) the extent and nature of changes that might be expected under a coevolutionary approach where organizational structure and organizational change (driven by learning and involvement with networks) have a large influence on the extent to which sustainability can be expected to be achieved.

We then turn to interventionist approaches in Chapter 7 (what might be called "revolutionary" approaches in contrast to evolutionary approaches), where organizational characteristics influence the extent to which the incumbent technology firm can or cannot respond with needed significant technological change. Here Christensen's concept of disrupting change is key and is likely to involve new entrants—possibly because they are catering to a new emerging customer base representing strong societal demand (which is unlikely in the short run), but more likely because government is demanding changes in technological performance (on behalf of society, with or without well-formulated demand). Again, in the context of changes involving products, processes, shifts to product-services, and systems, we explore (1) who is—and who is not—likely to develop those technologies under strong government directives or societal demand and (2) the implications for future organizational changes (especially in the context of systems).

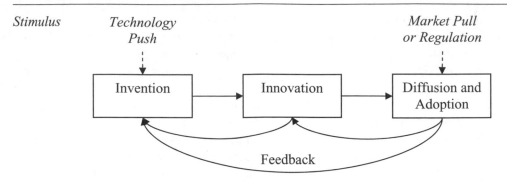

FIGURE 6.3: SIMPLE LINEAR MODEL OF TECHNOLOGICAL INNOVATION WITH FEEDBACK

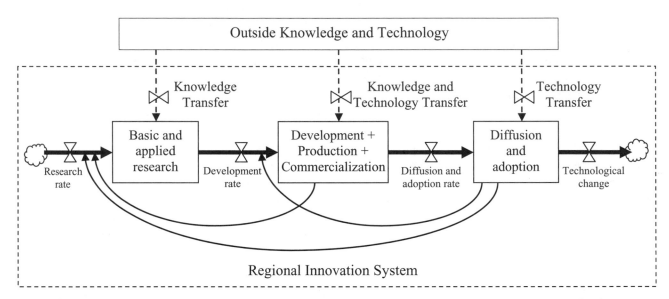

FIGURE 6.4: THE BASIC MODEL OF THE SECTORAL/REGIONAL INNOVATION SYSTEM (EMBEDDED IN SOCIETAL NETWORKS)

Before we turn to these ideas in Chapter 7, we address the so-called innovation process in greater detail.

## 6.3 THE CLASSICAL LINEAR MODEL OF TECHNOLOGICAL INNOVATION

The classical linear model of technological innovation consists of three core components: *invention*, *innovation*, and *diffusion* (Kline and Rosenberg 1986; Schumpeter 1962). An *invention* is an idea, a sketch, or model for a new or improved device, product, process, or system (Freeman 1982a). An *innovation* occurs when the invention is put to use (Moors 2000) or, more specifically, when the first transaction involving the new product, process, or device occurs (Freeman 1982a). Finally, *diffusion* is the widespread adoption (or implementation) of an innovative technology (Luiten 2001). The diffusion of a technology is important from an economic and social perspective because an innovative technology pays off econom-

ically, environmentally, and/or socially only when it is applied and replicated.*

In the classical literature, two main categories of technological innovation are discussed—*product* innovation and *process* innovation (Utterback 1996). A *product innovation* occurs along the lines described above, where a new product is invented and sold in the market, or the composition, design, operation, quality, or function of an existing product is changed in an incremental or radical way. A *process innovation* occurs when an improvement is made in the way a product is manufactured without significantly

---

* Indeed, the preoccupation of scholars with innovation, in contrast to diffusion, may contribute to underdeployment or lack of development of policies needed to promote diffusion. The diffusion of technology is essential for enhancing sectoral and national revenues, as well as promoting more sustainable industrial, agricultural, transportation, and construction practices. See the special issue of the *Journal of Cleaner Production* devoted to strategies for promoting diffusion (Montalvo and Kemp 2008). See also the discussion of the role of government in promoting innovation and diffusion in Chapter 8.

changing the final product. Sometimes a process innovation—such as the polymerization of a plastic or dry painting technology—is sold to industrial users and/or consumers and has most of the market characteristics of a product innovation.

Early criticisms of the linear model of technological innovation focusing on the isolated entrepreneurial firm stemmed from the realization that the process was not unidirectional but rather involved feedback among the three stages (Figure 6.3). Later models of technological innovation recognize the importance of knowledge transfer (Fischer 1999; Kline and Rosenberg 1986) and, more specifically, how learning and feedback are central to the diffusion and adoption of a new technology. Nonetheless, it would be an overstatement to say that the linear model involving three important stages has been rejected; it is now recognized to have more complex temporal and wider stakeholder attributes.

Another depiction of the innovation process within an industrial sector or geographic region using terms familiar to innovation scholars is presented in Figure 6.4. This depiction is useful in discussing the role of different societal stakeholders in the innovation process—in other words, the social embeddedness of innovation (see the discussion in the next chapter).

## 6.4 NATIONAL INNOVATION SYSTEMS

A further refinement of the innovation process places it within a systems context, as described in the following classic essay by Nelson and Rosenberg. Chris Freeman is credited with articulating the first modern version of the idea of "innovation systems" (Freeman 1982b; Freeman and Lundvall 1988). Innovation is "seen as a continuous cumulative process involving not only radical and incremental innovation but also the diffusion, absorption and use of innovation" (Johnson, Edquist, et al. 2003, p. 3).

Excerpt from Richard R. Nelson and Nathan Rosenberg, Chapter 1: Technical Innovation and National Systems, pp. 3–28 in Richard R. Nelson (ed.), *National Innovation Systems: A Comparative Analysis* (New York and Oxford: Oxford University Press, 1993). Excerpted with permission.

### What is This Study About[?]
The project that led to this book was born of the current strong interest in national innovation systems, and came out of a belief on the part of the participants that much of the writing and argument on this subject has been somewhat hyped and rather haphazard. . . .

. . . There is, first the concept of a national innovation system itself. . . . Consider the term "innovation." In this study we interpret the term rather broadly, to encompass the processes by which firms master and get into practice product designs and manufacturing processes that are new to them, if not to the universe or even to the nation. We do so for several reasons. First, the activities and investments associated with becoming the leader in the introduction of a new product or process, and those associated with staying near the head of the pack, or catching up, are much less sharply distinguishable than is commonly presumed. Moreover, the strictly Schumpeterian innovator, the first firm to bring a new product to market, is frequently not the firm that ultimately captures most of the economic rents associated with the innovation. Second, much of the interest in innovative capability is tied to concern about economic performance, and here it is certainly the broader concept rather than the narrower one (the determinants of being first) that matters. This means that our orientation is not limited to the behavior of firms at the forefront of world's technology, or to institutions doing the most advanced scientific research, although in some countries the focus is here, but is more broadly on the factors influencing national technological capabilities.

Then there is the term "system." Although to some the word connotes something that is consciously designed and built, this is far from the orientation here. Rather the concept is of a set of institutions whose interactions determine the innovative performance, in the sense above, of national firms. There is no presumption that the system was, in some sense, consciously designed, or even that the set of institutions involved works together smoothly and coherently. Rather, the "systems" concept is that of a set of institutional actors that, together, plays the major role in influencing innovative performance. . . .

Finally, there is the concept of "national" system. On the one hand, the concept may be too broad. The system of institutions supporting technical innovation in one field, say pharmaceuticals, may have very little overlap with the system of institutions supporting innovations in another field, say aircraft. On the other hand, in many fields of technology, including both pharmaceuticals and aircraft, a number of the institutions are or act transnational. . . .

### Technical Advance: An Overview of the Processes and Institutions Involved
To understand national innovation systems, it is essential to understand how technical advance occurs in the modern world, and the key processes and institutions involved. . . .

### The Intertwining of Science and Technology
Today, R&D facilities, staffed by university trained scientists and engineers attached to business firms, universities, or government agencies, are the principal vehicles through which technological advance

proceeds, in fields such as electrical equipment and systems, chemical products and processes, and aviation.

## Science as Leader and Follower

It is widely believed that new science gives rise to new technology. Although we shall argue that this is at best an oversimplification, the statement is quite true in regard to the rise of the electrical equipment industries. The very existence of these industries is inseparable from the history of theoretical and experimental physics in the nineteenth century. The emergence of electricity as a new source of power, and the wide range of new products that came to be built on it— incandescent light, telephone, gramophone—were the legitimate offspring of a scientific research enterprise that began with Faraday's demonstration of electromagnetic induction in 1831. Several decades later Maxwell's research opened up vast new vistas that led to Hertz's confirmation, in 1887, of the existence of radio waves and the possibility of detecting them at a distance, and then to modern radio and television.

Thus, the discovery of radio waves, which gave birth to radio and television, occurred *not* because scientists were searching for useful applications of their research. Rather, Hertz was pursuing a logic internal to the discipline of science itself, exploring the implications of an earlier theory by searching for empirical evidence that might confirm the theory. Hertz searched for—and found—radio waves because an earlier scientific theory had predicted their existence. Establishing their existence led to the work of Marconi and others in wireless communication.

In contrast with the electrical equipment industries, the industries producing chemical products, or using chemical reactions in the manufacture of other products, long antedated the rise of modern science. Some, such as tanning and dyeing and brewing, are almost as old as civilization itself.

However, in the last four or five decades of the nineteenth century, a systematic body of scientific knowledge about chemistry grew up that laid a new basis for chemical-based innovation. Chemistry became a laboratory discipline in which research could be carried out by trained professionals making use of well-understood methods and experimental procedures. . . .

These stories about advances in physics and chemistry as scientific disciplines appear to show scientific development as autonomous, evolving according to an internal logic of its own, with technology being illuminated as a by-product. But appearances are deceiving. . . .

The advent of new technologies often leads to scientific work aimed at understanding these technologies, so as to enable them to be improved. Sometimes new technology leads to whole new scientific disciplines. Sadi Carnot's work in the early part of the nineteenth century, which led to the new field of thermodynamics, was largely motivated by theoretical interest in the workings of the steam engine. . . .

In addition, the rise of the modern chemical industry led to the rise of a new discipline expressly aimed to service its needs—chemical engineering. . . .

A modern chemical process plant is not a scaled-up version of the laboratory glass tubes and reactors in which scientific discoveries were originally made. Such scaling-up is neither technically nor economically feasible. Rather, entirely different processes have to be invented. . . .

The rise of scientific understanding supporting aircraft design reflects a similar story. Again the technology, or a primitive version of it, came first, and the "science" or engineering discipline developed to support it. . . .

Thus saying that new technologies have given rise to new sciences is at least as true as the other way around. And it is more on the mark to say that with the rise of modern science-based technologies, much of science and much of technology have become intertwined. This is the principal reason why, in the present era, technology is advanced largely through the work of men and women who have university training in science of engineering. This intertwining, rather than serendipity, is the principal reason why, in many fields, university research is an important contributor to technical advance, and universities as well as corporate labs are essential parts of the innovation system. . . .

## The Limits of Science, Learning by Trying, and Cumulative Incremental Technological Advance

It is insufficiently appreciated that successful innovation in high technology industries often is not so much a matter of invention, as a patent examiner would define invention, as it is a matter of design, in the sense of trying to devise a product or process that will achieve a desirable cluster of performance characteristics, subject to certain cost constraints. . . . Moreover, determining where "design" ends and "research" begins is a matter of some real difficulty as soon as one deals with relationships that cannot be optimized by referring to the codified data in the engineering handbooks.

Those aiming for a major design advance almost always are in a position of not knowing whether a design will work or how well it will until they test it out. . . .

. . . Since the technical uncertainties readily translate into huge financial losses if new designs are prematurely introduced into practice, it is prudent to test on a small scale, and to resolve the expensive uncertainties at the technological frontier in a less costly rather than more costly fashion. . . .

Through such vehicles as building and testing pilot plants and prototypes, and testing experimental new drugs, the activities aimed to advance technology generate new knowledge as well as new products and processes. . . . The new device or process that works, sort of, or surprisingly well, stimulates both efforts to explain and understand, and efforts to refine, improve, and variegate. . . .

. . . Most industrial R&D expenditures are on products that have long been in existence—such as aircraft, automobiles, and cameras (which have been in existence fully 150 years). It is these existing products that serve to define the framework within which improvements can be identified and undertaken. Even the transistor, which has so drastically transformed the world in the second half of the twentieth century, has been around for more than 40 years. Its introduction in the late 1940s laid the groundwork for the continuing microelectronics revolution. Yet the original transistor was a fragile, unreliable, and expensive piece of apparatus. It was only the subsequent improvements in that original, primitive device that made the later microelectronics revolution possible.

In this as in other cases, the advance of technology went hand in hand with the advance of science. . . . It is important not to confuse the highly valued autonomy of the individual scientist, in shaping his or her own research agenda, with the determination of research-funding agencies to commit resources to those areas of scientific research that appear to offer the most attractive future returns. Public and private institutions may well be expected to define future returns rather differently, but neither is likely to be indifferent to the size of these returns.

### The Major Institutional Actors

. . . The rise of science based technology did lead to a dramatic change in the nature of the people and institutions involved in technical advance. Through much of the nineteenth century strong formal education in a science provided an inventor with little or no advantage in problem solving, although from time to time inventors would consult with scientists. By 1900 formal training in chemistry was becoming virtually a requirement for successful inventive effort in the chemical products industries. By 1910 or so the days when unschooled geniuses such as Thomas Alva Edison could make major advances in the electrical technologies were coming to an end, and the major electrical companies were busy staffing their laboratories with university trained scientist[s] and engineers.

### Firms and Industrial Research Laboratories

By the beginning of World War I the industrial research laboratory, a facility dedicated to research and the development of new or improved products and processes, and staffed by university trained scientists and engineers, had become the principal locus of technical advance in the chemical and electrical industries, and was beginning to become important more and more widely. . . .

There are several reasons why the industrial research laboratory, rather than university laboratories or government facilities, became the dominant locus of the R&D part of innovation in most (but not all) fields. First, after a technology has been around for a period of time, to orient R&D fruitfully, one needs detailed knowledge of its strengths and weaknesses and areas where improvements would yield big payoffs, and this knowledge tends to reside with those who use the technology, generally firms and their customers and suppliers. . . . Second, profiting from innovation in many cases requires the integration of activity and planning of R&D, production, and marketing, which tends to proceed much more effectively within an organization that itself does all of these. . . .

. . . Many small firms engage in significant design and development work, yet do not have a formally designated R&D department or facility; their design and development work may or may not be accounted and reported as R&D. . . . The lines between R&D, and other activities, such as designing products for particular customers, problem solving on production processes, or monitoring a competitor's new products, are inherently blurry. . . .

. . . In developing countries, what is an innovation for an indigenous firm may largely involve learning to produce a product or employ technology that has been employed for some time by firms in the highly industrialized economies. Learning to make or use a product may require a considerable amount of study as well as the taking apart of products and processes to find out how they work, that is, "reverse engineering." Although generally not so counted, reverse engineering is very much like R&D. . . .

Moreover, even if it is defined quite broadly, R&D usually is only a small part of the resources and problem solving that go into innovation. The amounts that must be invested in new equipment and plant to produce a new product, or embody a new process, generally exceed the R&D costs many fold. New organizations may be called for, or a different division of work, or new skills on the part of the work force, and new approaches in marketing. . . .

### Other Institutional Actors

. . .

Universities in most countries are, first, the places where much of the basic research in fundamental sciences such as physics is undertaken, although the reliance on universities as a locus of basic research, as contrasted with national laboratories, varies across countries. . . .

Many fields of academic science are expressly applications orientated. The very names "material science," "computer science," and "pathology" signal fields of inquiry closely linked to particular practical problems. So too the engineering disciplines, which were expressly established not only to train people for work in industry, but also to develop the scientific foundations of industrial technologies.

In certain cases, university based institutions have been directly oriented toward helping a particular industry or other client advance its technologies. . . .

Government laboratories also are an important part of many national innovation systems. In the United States, government laboratories play important roles in, for example, the fields of agriculture, health, and nuclear energy. However, with only a few exceptions, agriculture being a major one, in the United States government laboratories are tied to public sector missions in contrast to being established to help civilian industry. And, again with a few exceptions, in the United States the universities, rather than government laboratories, are seen as the appropriate sites for fundamental research.

In other countries public laboratories play a significantly larger, or different, role. . . .

Today public monies support not only research at universities and government laboratories, but R&D in industry. For the most part government support of industrial R&D in the United States has been limited to projects of direct governmental interest, principally those involving military and space needs. But as the new Sematech venture shows, even the United States is not averse to using public monies to help the development of industrial technologies that are principally of civilian use, if a strong "public interest" argument can be articulated. . . .

. . . The character and effectiveness of a nation's system of schooling, training, and retraining not only determine the supply of skills from engineer to machine tender, but also influence the attitudes of workers toward technical advance. . . .

## Interindustry Differences

. . . There are important interindustry differences in the nature of technical change, the sources, and how the involved actors are connected to each other, and it is useful to sketch some of these here. Nations differ in the mix of industries and these differences alone strongly influence the shapes of national innovation systems.

A number of industries produce products that can be characterized as complex systems. Much of electrical technology is of this sort. . . .

Technical advance in such fields generally stems from the work of component and material producers, as well as systems designers. In general the larger the system, the greater the role of the component producers. However, the effective incorporation of better components into a system often requires significant R&D work by system assemblers. The integration of component and systems R&D generally involves some combination of independent initiatives mediated by the market, contracting, and express cooperation, with the balance differing from industry to industry and from country to country. In some cases government programs may facilitate coordination.

In some systems technologies users of the system play a major role in inducing technical advance, and they may directly support it. . . .

Technical advance in the industries producing fine chemical products, from synthetic materials to pharmaceutical[s], is different in a number of respects. First, in these industries innovation largely involves the introduction of discrete new products or product classes, such as nylon or valium, that are not in general subject to the continuing incremental improvement that marks systems technologies. . . . Second, since the products do not involve complex systems, input suppliers in general do not play a big role; however, process equipment suppliers may. . . .

Still other industries produce bulk commodities, from steel to milk. Here product innovation is minimal and technical change basically involves new or improved ways to produce or process the product in question. Equipment and input suppliers and processing firms often are the major sources of innovation. Where product producers are large they may do a considerable amount of process R&D on their own or contract for it. Where the product suppliers are small, they may bond together to get work done on production processes or modes of processing products, or on standards for inputs and outputs. Governmental agencies may organize and fund such work. . . .

## Technological Communities, Boundaries, and National Innovation Systems

. . .

The important interactions, the networks, are not the same in all industries or technologies. We have pointed to differences between systems technologies and chemical product technologies in the nature of interindustry interactions. In some technologies universities play a key role, for example, pharmaceuticals and computers. In others they play a more modest one, for example, aircraft and steel. Government funding is important in some industries, such as aircraft and agriculture, and unimportant in others. But although its shape and character differ, in virtually all fields one must understand technical advance as proceeding through the work of a community of actors. . . .

Certainly the policies and programs of national governments, the laws of a nation, and the existence of a common language and a shared culture define an inside and outside that can broadly affect how technical advance proceeds. Put another way, national differences and boundaries tend to define national innovation systems, partly intentionally, partly not. Further, general perceptions about national societies and cultures tend to reify national systems.

Thus for the quarter century after World War II both Americans and citizens of other countries recognized a distinctly American model that had a number of particular features. In the first place, as writers such as Servan Schreiber (1968) pointed out in the late 1960s, in many of the key industries American firms were larger than their European countries, spent more on R&D, and had a distinctive management style. Furthermore the U.S. government spent much more on industrial R&D than did the European governments, principally through defense contracts. The U.S. university research system was stronger. To a very large extent firms situated in America were American owned, and although overseas branches were becoming increasingly important, by far most establishments owned by Americans operated in the United States. Most of the goods produced by American firms were sold overwhelmingly to the domestic market. . . . The monies of the U. S. government were almost exclusively spent in U.S. institutions. . . .

. . . One can argue that the European systems were much less strictly "national" systems than was the American. For one thing, even the largest of the European nations was small compared with the United States, and as a result there was much more importing and exporting as a percentage of GNP. For another, increasingly over the period there was a sense of European community that in some ways eroded the significance of national borders and particular citizenship. Third, and foreshadowing subsequent broader developments, American firms in European countries were playing a significant role in many industries. However, as we shall see, in the early postwar era there was a strong sense that although subject to strong influences from abroad, there [were] distinctive and to a large extent self-contained English, German, and French systems.

Until the 1970s there was no strong competitor to the American system as a broad model of how an innovation system should be designed. . . .

As European productivity and income levels have caught up with American levels, and Japan has emerged as a leading economic and technological power, the attraction of the American model has waned, and Japanese institutions have waxed as targets for emulation. . . .

## National Systems and Transnational Technology

. . .

There is good reason to believe that in recent years, just as the idea of national innovation systems has become widely accepted, technological communities have become transnational as never before. There has been, first, a strong trend for manufacturing business firms to become multinational. . . .

. . . Engineers and applied scientists now are taught pretty much the same thing in schools in different countries. The dramatic lowering of national barriers to trade following the war, and the recent convergence of living standards and factor prices in the major industrial nations, means that, increasingly, firms face roughly the same market environment wherever their home base. . . .

More fundamentally, the internationalization of business and technology erodes the extent to which national borders, and citizenship, define boundaries that are meaningful in analyzing technological capabilities and technical advance. . . .

. . . Although there are many areas of similarity between the systems of countries in comparable economic settings, there still are some striking differences as well. Japanese firms in the semiconductor business tend to be different than American, German, or French firms. The university systems are different and play different roles in the national R&D systems. The development paths of Korea and Taiwan have been very different and so too are their present organization of industry and structure of R&D

And the reasons for these differences reside, to a significant degree, in differences in national histories and cultures including the timing of a country's entry into the industrialization process. These have profoundly shaped national institutions, laws, and policies. . . .

On the other hand, although there certainly are durable and important differences in national characteristics that shape national innovation systems and constrain their evolution, these systems have shown striking adaptability. . . . And countries clearly copy each other. . . . And although important national differences remain, it is not clear how much these matter to "national" firms who often have the opportunity to set up shop in another country when it is advantageous to do so.

There is a tension caused by the attempts of national governments to form and implement national technology policies, in a world where business and technology are increasingly transnational.

Nelson and Rosenberg's (1993) discussion clearly articulates that the innovation process is embedded within an innovation "system" involving both institutional actors and individuals within and outside the firm itself. Johnson, Edquist, et al. (2003, p. 4) observe:

A first common characteristic [of innovation systems] is the assumption that national systems differ in terms of specialization in production, trade and knowledge (Archibugi and Pianta 1992). The focus is here upon the co-evolution between what countries do and what people and firms in these countries know how to do well. This implies that both the production structure and the knowledge structure will change only slowly and that such change involves learning as well as structural change.

A second common assumption behind the different approaches to innovation systems is that elements of knowledge important for economic performance are localized and not easily moved from one place to another. . . . Important elements of knowledge are embodied in the minds and bodies of agents, in

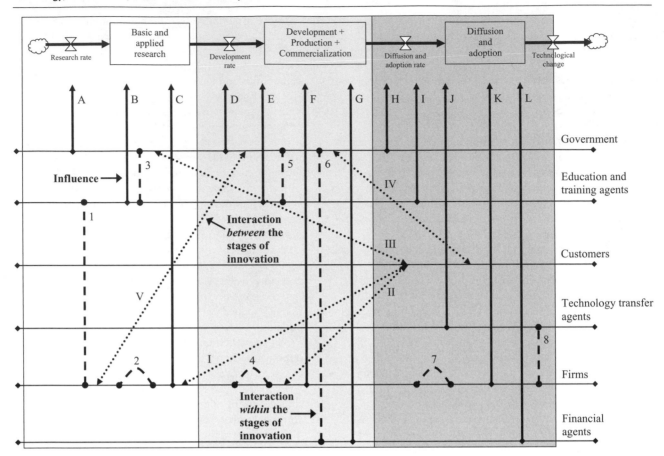

**FIGURE 6.5: DIAGRAM OF A GENERIC INNOVATION SYSTEM**
Source: Adapted from Tsamis (1999, p. 39).

routines of firms and not least in relationships between people and organizations (Dosi 1999).

A third assumption central to the idea of innovation systems is a focus on interactions and relationships. The relationships may be seen as carriers of knowledge and interaction as processes where new knowledge is produced and learnt. This assumption reflects the stylized fact that neither firms and knowledge institutions nor people innovate alone. Perhaps the most basic characteristic of the innovation system approach is that it is "interactionist."

Sometimes characteristics of interaction and relationships have been named "institutions" referring to its sociological sense—institutions[12] are seen as informal and formal norms and rules regulating how people interact (Johnson 1992; Edquist and Johnson 1997). In a terminology emanating from evolutionary economics

and the management literature "routines" are regarded as more or less standardized procedures followed by economic agents and organizations when they act and when they interact with each other (Dosi 1999).

The concept of innovation systems encompasses the *determinants* of innovation and hence provides an enticing framework for policy analysis and design. "The approach emphasizes interdependence and nonlinearity. This is based on the understanding that firms normally do not innovate in isolation but interact more or less closely with other organizations, through complex relations that are often characterized by reciprocity and feedback mechanisms in several loops. This interaction occurs in the context of institutions—e.g., laws, rules, regulations, norms and cultural habits. In fact, the central role of institutions is emphasized in practically all specifications of the concept of innovation systems" (Johnson, Edquist et al. 2003, p. 5).

Tsamis (1999) developed a useful model for a regional innovation system that focuses on the *process* of innovation and the *roles* that each major player has in the process (Figure 6.5). Although it is possible to identify a number of ways to categorize the major players in the innovation process (Braczyk, Cooke, et al. 1998;

---

12     We regard the use of the word "institution" in the literature in this sense as unfortunate and would prefer a term such as "the sociopolitical context." In this book, we reserve the term "institution" for governmental or nongovernmental, nonbusiness organizations, although when we speak of institutional reform, we are addressing both structural changes and changes in norms and rules. This distinction is especially important because one criticism of innovation systems research is said to be that it ignores the role of the state (Johnson, Edquist, et al. 2003).

Padmore, Schuetze, et al. 1998), Tsamis (1999) uses the following in his model: government, education and training institutions, customers, technology transfer and diffusion agencies, firms, and financial services.

The value of Tsamis's qualitative model for a regional (or, equally usefully, for a national or industrial sectoral) innovation system is that it (1) identifies how each player influences different aspects of the innovation process (see the solid-line arrows A to L), (2) indicates the type of interactions that occur among the players *within* each step of the innovation process (see the dashed connectors 1 to 8), and (3) recognizes the interactions that occur among the players *across* the three steps of the innovation process (see the dotted arrows I to V). The model is developed for a traditional industrial innovation process that focuses on improving the general climate for innovation. The dynamics of interactions between these and other key actors are further addressed in the next chapter.

Edquist (1997, p. 14) defines a system of innovation (SI) as "all important economic, social, political, organizational, and other factors that influence the development, diffusion, and use of innovation." An SI is "about the determinants of innovation, not about their consequences," and is thus distinguished from new growth theory (discussed in Chapter 3), which "deals with the effects of innovation and knowledge" (Edquist 2001, p. 2). The SI approach often neglects learning by firms in terms of routines and databases, but also particularly neglects individual learning in terms of education, that is, the building of human capital. Edquist (2005) observes that although "the importance of national systems of innovation has to do with the fact that they capture the importance of the political and policy aspects of processes of innovation," the SI construct neglects the role of the state, including its physical institutions and its system of laws, rules, and infrastructure.

In the next chapter, we examine the role of the industrial firm and its network partners in achieving sustainable development through organizational learning and innovation. In the chapter after that, we take up the role of government in implementing alternative forms of industrial policy to improve competitiveness and employment. In both these subsequent chapters, we explore in greater depth the importance of technological change.

## 6.5 REFERENCES

Abernathy, W. J., and K. B. Clark (1985). "Innovation: Mapping the Winds of Creative Destruction." *Research Policy* **14**(1): 3–22.

Archibugi, D., and M. Pianta (1992). *The Technological Specialization of Advanced Countries*. Dordrecht, Kluwer Academic Publishers.

Ashford, N. A., C. Ayers, et al. (1985). "Using Regulation to Change the Market for Innovation." *Harvard Environmental Law Review* **9**(2): 419–466.

Ashford, N. A., W. Hafkamp, et al. (2002). Pathways to Sustainable Industrial Transformations: Cooptimising Competitiveness, Employment, and Environment. Cambridge, MA, Ashford Associates.

Ashford, N. A., G. R. Heaton, et al. (1979). Environmental, Health and Safety Regulations and Technological Innovation. *Technological Innovation for a Dynamic Economy*. C. T. Hill and J. M. Utterback. New York, Pergamon Press: 161–221.

Braczyk, H. J., P. Cooke, et al. (1998). *Regional Innovation Systems: The Role of Governances in a Globalized World*. London, UCL Press.

Brouwer, E., and A. Kleinknecht (1996). "Firm Size, Small Business Presence and Sales of Innovative Products: A Micro-econometric Analysis." *Small Business Economics* **8**(3): 189–201.

Carrillo-Hermosilla, J. (2006). "A Policy Approach to the Environmental Impacts of Technological Lock-in." *Ecological Economics* **58**: 717–742.

Chandy, R. K., and G. J. Tellis (2000). "The Incumbent's Curse? Incumbency, Size, and Radical Product Innovation." *Journal of Marketing* **64**: 1–17.

Charles, T., and F. Lehner (1998). "Competitiveness and Employment: A Strategic Dilemma for Economic Policy." *Competition and Change* **3**(1/2): 207–236.

Chesbrough, H. W. (1999). "The Organizational Impact of Technological Change: A Comparative Theory of National Institutional Factors." *Industrial and Corporate Change* **8**(3): 447–485.

Christensen, C. M. (1997). *The Innovator's Dilemma: When New Technologies Cause Great Firms to Fail*. Cambridge, MA, Harvard Business School Press.

Christensen, C. M., J. M. Utterback, et al. (1998). "Strategies for Survival in Fast-Changing Industries." *Management Science* **44**(12): S207–S220.

Cleff, T., and K. Rennings (1999). "Determinants of Environmental Product and Process Innovation." *European Environment* **9**: 191–201.

Dosi, G. (1999). Some Notes on National Systems of Innovation and Production and Their Implication for Economic Analysis. *Innovation Policy in a Global Economy*. D. Archibugi, J. Howells, and J. Michie. Cambridge, Cambridge University Press.

Edquist, C. (1997). Systems of Innovation Approaches—Their Emergence and Characteristics. *Systems of Innovation: Technologies, Institutions, and Organizations*. C. Edquist. London and Washington, DC, Pinter/Cassell Academic.

Edquist, C. (2001). The Systems of Innovation Approach and Innovation Policy: An Account of the State of the Art. Paper presented at the DRUID Conference, Aalborg, June 12–15.

Edquist, C. (2005). Systems of Innovation: Perspectives and Challenges. *The Oxford Handbook of Innovation*. J. Fagerberg, D. C. Mowery, and R. R. Nelson. Oxford, Oxford University Press.

Edquist, C., and B. Johnson (1997). Institutions and Organisations in Systems of Innovation. *Systems of Innovation: Technologies, Institutions, and Organizations.* C. Edquist. London and Washington, DC, Pinter/Cassell Academic. Republished in C. Edquist and M. McKelvey, Eds. (2000). *Systems of Innovation: Growth, Competitiveness and Employment.* Cheltenham, Edward Elgar.

Fischer, M. M. (1999). The Innovation Process and Network Activities of Manufacturing Firms. *Innovation, Networks and Localities.* M. M. Fischer, L. Suarez-Villa, and M. Steiner. New York, Springer: 11–26.

Freeman, C. (1982a). *The Economics of Industrial Innovation.* London, Pinter.

Freeman, C. (1982b). Technological Infrastructure and International Competitiveness. Unpublished paper for the OECD Expert Group on Science, Technology, and Competitiveness.

Freeman, C., and B.-A. Lundvall, Eds. (1988). *Small Countries Facing the Technological Revolution.* London, Pinter.

Herrmann, A., O. Gassmann, et al. (2007). "An Empirical Study of the Antecedents for Radical Product Innovations and Capabilities for Transformation." *Journal of Engineering Technology Management* 24: 92–120.

Johnson, B. (1992). Institutional Learning. *National Innovation Systems: Towards a Theory of Innovation and Interactive Learning.* B.-A. Lundvall. London, Pinter.

Johnson, B., C. Edquist, et al. (2003). Economic Development and the National System of Innovation Approach. Paper presented at the first Globelics conference, Rio de Janeiro, November.

Kemp, R. (1994). "Technology and Environmental Sustainability: The Problem of Technological Regime Shift." *Futures* 26(10): 1023–1046.

Kemp, R., and J. Rotmans (2001). The Management of the Co-evolution of Technical, Environmental and Social Systems. Paper for the international conference "Towards Environmental Innovation Systems," Garmisch-Partenkirchen, Germany, September 27–29.

Kline, S. J., and N. Rosenberg (1986). An Overview of Innovation. *The Positive Sum Strategy: Harnessing Technology for Economic Growth.* R. Landau and N. Rosenberg. Washington, DC, National Academy Press: 275–305.

Luiten, E. E. M. (2001). Beyond Energy Efficiency: Actors, Networks and Government Intervention in the Development of Industrial Process Technologies. PhD dissertation, Utrecht, Utrecht University.

Lynn, G. S., J. G. Morone, et al. (1996). "Marketing and Discontinuous Innovation: The Probe and Learn Process." *California Management Review* 38(3): 8–37.

Matzner, E., R. Schettkat, et al. (1990). "Labor Market Effect of New Technology." *Futures* 22(7): 687–709.

Montalvo, C., and R. Kemp, Eds. (2008). "Diffusion of Cleaner Technologies: Modeling, Case Studies and Policy." *Journal of Cleaner Production* 16(1): Supplement 1: S1–S184.

Moors, E. H. M. (2000). Metal Making in Motion: Technology Choices for Sustainable Metals Production. PhD dissertation, Delft, Delft University of Technology.

Nehrt, C. (1998). "Maintainability of First Mover Advantages When Environmental Regulations Differ between Countries." *Academy of Management Review* 23(1): 77–97.

Nelson, R. R., and N. Rosenberg (1993). Technical Innovation and National Systems. *National Innovation Systems: A Comparative Analysis.* R. R. Nelson. Oxford, Oxford University Press: 3–21.

Nelson, R. R., and S. G. Winter (1977). "In Search of Useful Theory of Innovation." *Research Policy* 6: 36–76.

Padmore, T., H. Schuetze, et al. (1998). "Modeling Systems of Innovation: An Enterprise-Centered View." *Research Policy* 26(6): 605–624.

Partidario, P. J. (2003). "What-If": From Path Dependency to Path Creation in a Coatings Chain; A Methodology for Strategies towards Sustainable Innovation. PhD dissertation, Delft, Delft University of Technology.

Porter, M. E., and C. van der Linde (1995). "Green and Competitive: Ending the Stalemate." *Harvard Business Review* 73(5):120–134.

Sartorius, C. (2006). "Second-Order Sustainability—Conditions for the Development of Sustainable Innovation in a Dynamic Environment." *Ecological Economics* 58: 268–286.

Schumpeter, J. A. (1962). *Capitalism, Socialism, and Democracy.* New York, Harper Torchbooks.

Tsamis, A. (1999). Measuring Regional Innovation for Sustainable Development. M.S. dissertation, Technology and Policy Program. Cambridge, MA, MIT.

Utterback, J. M. (1987). Innovation and Industrial Evolution in Manufacturing Industries. *Technology and Global Industry: Companies and Nations in the World Economy.* B. R. Guile and H. Brooks. Washington, DC, National Academy Press: 16–48.

Utterback, J. M. (1996). *Mastering the Dynamics of Innovation.* Cambridge, MA, Harvard Business School Press.

Utterback, J. M., and H. F. Acee (2005). "Disruptive Technologies: An Expanded View." *International Journal of Innovation Management* 9(1): 1–17.

# 7

# Organizational Innovation and Learning: The Role of the Industrial Firm in Achieving Sustainable Development

Coauthored with KATE PARROT

## 7.1 INTRODUCTION

In early chapters, we argued that four types of innovation, technological, organizational, institutional, and social (Ashford 2005; Rennings 2000), were essential in transforming industrialized/industrializing nations into sustainable ones. These distinctions may not always be very sharp (Rennings 1998, 2000). In any event, they are related to one another and are necessary for sustainable development. In this chapter, however, we focus primarily on the intersection between *technological* and *organizational* innovation. Technological innovation is defined as the first commercially successful application of a new technical idea (or an invention). Organizational innovation refers to changes in the private sector, while institutional changes pertain to changes in the organization of government and of nongovernmental organizations (NGOs). Of course, innovations in one domain influence the other domains. The literature is rich on the complex relationship between organization and technological innovation.

We consider organizational innovation to be novel changes in and among various organizational aspects of a firm's *functions*, such as R&D/product development, marketing, environmental and governmental affairs, industrial relations, worker health and safety, and customer and community relations.*

Change in the organizational structure of an industrial firm has long been recognized as both an important determinant and a consequence of technological change (Andreasen, Coriat, et al. 1995). Technological change can proceed gradually in an evolutionary way, or it can advance discontinuously with spurts of changes pioneered by new entrants or by existing firms reinventing themselves. Organizational factors influence, and are affected by, both evolutionary and discontinuous change.†

This chapter discusses the key organizational characteristics of the industrial firm and the nature of organizational change that either inhibits or may generate progress toward sustainable development. As discussed in previous chapters, sustainable development encompasses a process that co-optimizes (1) competitiveness, (2) the environment, and (3) employment.

We first explore organizational features that have positive implications for the general and workplace environment, focusing on energy, toxic pollution, and worker health and safety. We then examine the relationship between the development of new technologies, or the new application of existing technologies, and the skills and capabilities of employees needed at the firm. Finally, we consider how organizational changes can be structured to create or restructure employment as one of several important sustainability goals. The increased globalization of commerce introduces organizational challenges for the business firm beyond those within a national context. We begin our

discussion with a brief review of the dimensions of globalization.

### 7.1.1 Globalization

As discussed in Chapter 5, globalization affects three major areas: production of goods and services, the mobility of knowledge and information, and capital mobility. The mobility of knowledge and information is facilitated both through changes in the locus of production and services (otherwise known as the international division of labor) and through advances in information and communication technologies (ICT), such as the Internet and wireless technologies. Capital mobility has in turn been greatly enhanced by ICT and industrial globalization and will be addressed in Chapter 12 on financing sustainable development.

We begin by giving a brief overview of some of the major trends that characterize the current business climate. The globalizing economy presents new challenges and opportunities for both technology and work in industrialized and industrializing countries. In the context of production and services, "globalization" has several meanings: internationalization, multinationalization, and transnationalization (see Box 7.1 and the discussion in Chapter 5), with different implications for production and services, environment, workers, and working life.

Those concerned with enhancing trade are especially worried about barriers to internationalization or distortions of trade through subsidies or tariffs, while those concerned with possible erosion of labor/environmental standards bemoan the consequences of multinationalization. Transnationalization may lead to industrial restructuring, with unpredictable consequences for national economies. All three kinds of globalization raise questions of excessive market power, and hence political power, where concerns for profits overwhelm democratic and ethical values. See Chapters 5 and 11 for fuller discussions.

Globalization raises new challenges for governance, especially vis-à-vis the roles of government, workers, and citizens in the new economic order. Globalization has brought a complex set of challenges through the creation of trade regimes—such as the WTO, ASEAN, and NAFTA—where the term "free trade" means the elimination (or equalization) of subsidies, tariffs, and so-called nontariff trade barriers (see Chapter 11). Salient features of the current business climate are freer and less encumbered trade across national borders, rapid information transfer, and increasingly fierce global competition from foreign firms.

---

\* An informative study by Lynch (2008) of manufacturing and nonmanufacturing businesses in the United States concluded that the incidence and intensity of organizational innovation—defined as workforce training, employee voice, work design, and shared rewards—were positively associated with past profits and were more likely to occur in young, nonunionized manufacturing plants where management had an external focus. Further, organizational innovation was enhanced by firms belonging to networks that exchanged best practices, but could be constrained by a low-skilled workforce. Hence investment in training (i.e., human capital), as well as other factors such as R&D, physical capital, and ICT, appeared to complement organizational innovation (ibid.). In addition, Hage (1965, 1999) argues that the complexity of the division of labor (and the knowledge it collectively holds) is also a central factor behind organizational innovation because it affords greater adaptiveness or flexibility in meeting external environmental changes.

† For a discussion of defensive planning in reducing vulnerability to shocks (such as an industrial accident or collapse of a key supplier) and maintaining flexibility in the face of changing business environments, see Sheffi (2007).

---

**BOX 7.1: THREE TYPES OF INDUSTRIAL GLOBALIZATION**

**Internationalization** is the expansion of product/service markets abroad, facilitated by information and communication technology (ICT) and e-commerce, with the locus of production remaining within the parent country. Both developed and developing countries engage in this type of globalization, but the nature of the exports may differ as to raw materials and semifinished goods.

**Multinationalization** is where a (multinational) company establishes production/service facilities abroad, to be nearer to foreign markets and/or to take advantage of more industry-friendly labor, environmental, and/or tax policies, while maintaining research-and-development (R&D) and innovation-centered activities in the parent country. Companies engaging in multinationalism sometimes consider the foreign host strictly as an export platform for cheaply produced goods and services. They have little or no interaction with domestic markets and supply chains. The textile factories in China are one such example, where raw materials are supplied to the factories, which employ cheap labor to produce clothing and shoes for sale in developed-country markets. In other cases, the company can become more well-integrated with domestic supply chains and/or produce for domestic markets. Auto manufacturing is such an example.

**Transnationalization**, or the creation of strategic alliances, is where two different foreign enterprises merge or share their R&D and other capabilities to create a new entity or product line.

---

Source: Based on Gordon (1995).

In a world of free trade, countries can create robust environmental regulations and labor laws, but they are then flooded with goods from developing countries that do not adhere to the same standards. Even if it wants to, the importing country may not be able to refuse those goods unless the goods themselves present hazards; under WTO rules, the importer can block goods that harm its own population or environment, but it may have only a limited right to refuse goods that exploit the *exporting* country's workers or damage its domestic environment (see Chapter 11).

Countries are slow to give up national autonomy, and only where there is a trend toward significant economic integration (as in the European Union) is there significant progress toward success at harmonization. Developed nations are fast losing ground on price-sensitive mass-production outputs to industrializing countries like China and India, which draw on large pools of cheap labor and lax environmental standards as sources of competitive advantage. The governments of developed countries are under great pressure to create a more favorable business climate, and they have responded by lowering corporate taxes, allowing the welfare state to erode, tolerating a deteriorating environment, and providing subsidies, tariff protection, and price supports. When all else fails, government may appeal directly to businesses to stop moving production out of the country, as former German chancellor Gerhard Schröder did (Bernstein 2005).

### 7.1.2 Pressures for Corporate Environmental Responsibility

Starting in the 1960s, as scientists and policy makers became more aware of the negative impacts of pollution and the importance of creating a robust environment for economic development and growth, a new era of environmental policy making emerged that has changed the way corporations and businesses view health, safety, and the environment. This policy-making environment has been shaped by multilateral environmental treaties (see Chapters 2 and 10), as well as a host of domestic environmental regulations and programs (see Chapters 9 and 10).

Environmental regulations have gone through cycles of being strengthened and weakened over the past several decades (Vogel 2003). The 1970s were a period of strengthening in the United States with the passage of the Clean Air Act, the Clean Water Act, endangered-species legislation, and the creation of the U.S. Environmental Protection Agency (EPA). In contrast, European legislation was not significantly strengthened until the 1990s. However, the actions taken by the two administrations of George W. Bush have led to a period of weakening in the United States. Gutowski, Murphy, et al. (2005) describe the significant differences in responses to environmental concerns that can now be found among the United States, Europe, and Japan. In Europe, there is a high level of public awareness of environmental issues, which is expressed through elected officials at the national and EU levels. The EU has focused effectively on end-of-life concerns for products and the elimination of hazardous materials (see Chapter 10). It has established product take-back systems, and it is a world leader in the use of life-cycle assessment (LCA). Collaborations among business, government, and academia on environmentally focused projects are more common than in Japan or the United States. In many areas, the EU appears to lead in governmental and educational environmental activities (Vogel 2003).

The Japanese are leaders in the integration of environmental concerns into industrial activities, especially in the areas of water and energy conservation and environmentally benign manufacturing. Japanese firms are engaged in innovation of environmentally friendly technologies, such as lead-free solder, bromine-free printed wiring boards (both in response to the European Waste Electrical and Electronic Equipment [WEEE] directive), and the hybrid-electric car. Japan exhibits a strong alignment of resources, such as public education, government green purchasing, and public development of software tools, such as their national LCA project. The EU appears to lead in waste reduction, but Japan also demonstrates a strong and growing commitment to recycling standards and recycling infrastructure. The EU also has serious initiatives to promote cleaner and inherently safer technologies (see Chapter 10).

Today, the United States is characterized by a fragmented, contentious response to environmental issues, which creates an uncertain environment for domestic firms. Firms are particularly adept at risk mitigation to avoid future liability, but in general, the United States lags behind both Europe and Japan in areas of environmental policy making, education, and integration of environmental concerns into industrial activities (Vogel 2003). Most manufacturing firms focus on materials and processes within the traditional manufacturing environment. In-house environmental performance and supply-chain management are of concern, but less so than in Europe, and are driven more by potential liability or in response to customer demands.

Even though some regions like the United States lag behind others, the tendency in all areas is toward more stringency and comprehensiveness at the level of the nation-state. However, among nations, the extent to which the negative externalities of production—for example, adverse health, safety, and environmental effects—are internalized differs according to the extent to which economies incorporate the ethics of fair play into their practices and the differential success of their regulation/compensation regimes.

Companies routinely engage in practices and sell products in foreign markets that are banned or restricted at home. One salient example of this practice is the export of pesticides to developing countries. In the period 1997–2000, 65 million pounds of pesticide products were exported by U.S. firms that were either forbidden or severely restricted by the United States. Fifty-seven percent of these products were shipped to destinations in the developing world (C. Smith 2001). Nearly half of the remaining 43 percent was shipped to European ports and likely was shipped on to developing countries. By the year 2000, international efforts such as the convention on persistent organic pollutants (POPs) and the convention on prior informed consent (PIC) helped dramatically reduce or eliminate export of banned pesticides (see Chapter 10). (The United States has signed both of these conventions but to date has not ratified them.) However, the reduction in exports of chemicals covered by these conventions is counteracted by high rates of export of pesticides designated "extremely hazardous" (89 million pounds) by the World Health Organization (WHO), pesticides associated with cancer (170 million pounds), and pesticides associated with endocrine-disrupting effects (368 million pounds), mostly to developing countries (ibid.).

Some proposals, such as the UN Global Compact (a group of companies that have committed to advancing ten principles of environmental and social responsibility) would bind their members to behaving abroad according to the laws of their home country, but these initiatives are voluntary and as of this writing have been adopted by only a handful of firms. On the other hand, multinational firms in some cases are obliged to comply with regulations that are more stringent than in the home country. For example, large American firms such as Ford and IBM are responding positively to EU directives like the End-of-Life Vehicle (ELV) and the WEEE directives.*

Although many firms take an active voice in national and international debates—often fighting (successfully) against government action that would hold them more accountable for the environmental impacts of their activities—most firms recognize and expect that regulations will become more stringent in the future. For example, many major oil companies are planning for the eventuality of a "carbon-

---

* The recent shift to increasing trade in manufacturing and goods from China—where health, safety, and environmental standards are either nonexistent or unenforced (Navarro 2008)—ironically has resulted in the export of hazardous and unsafe goods to developed countries.

constrained" world, in which carbon emissions are no longer free and unlimited but are constrained by means of a tax, a permit-trading system, an emissions cap, or some other mechanism.

In general, firms are experiencing a variety of pressures that compel them to pay more attention to the environmental impacts of their activities. H. E. Williams, Medhurst, et al. (1993, p. 118) list some of these pressures:

- Increasingly stringent environmental legislation and enforcement

- Increasing costs associated with pollution control, waste disposal, and effluent disposal

- Increasing commercial pressure from the supply, consumption, and disposal of both intermediate and final products

- Increasing awareness on the part of investors of companies' environmental performance in view of the cost implications associated with liability and the "polluter-pays" principle

- Increasing training and personnel requirements, together with additional information requirements

- Increasing expectations on the part of the local community and the workforce of the environmental performance of firms and their impact on the environment

The study by H. E. Williams, Medhurst, et al. (1993), which surveyed 117 U.K. firms and conducted in-depth interviews with 25, found that of these pressures, government legislation and enforcement was the most tangible and the one that determined the character of company responses.

Another study of nearly sixty major companies, government labs and agencies, and universities aimed to determine why firms were engaging in proactive environmental behavior (Gutowski, Murphy, et al. 2005). The authors found that the motivating factors cited by firms included the pressures listed above, plus additional motivators that could confer a competitive economic (first-mover) advantage such as being first to achieve a cost-effective product take-back system and being first to achieve product compliance.[1] Other motivating factors included corporate image (including avoiding embarrassment by NGOs and others); regulatory flexibility; International Standards Organization (ISO) 14001 certification;[*] market value; and (demand from) green purchasing and ecolabeling.[†]

In addition to possible economic advantages of complying with health, safety, or environmental regulations or social demands, stock value and stockholder responses may drive the firm toward more environmentally sustainable practices (Johnston 2005).

Given the broad range of factors that influence industrial activity, an important question is which of these can guide economic activity toward sustainable development. More important, which *entity* is responsible for promoting these factors? Figure 7.1 attempts to capture the different postures that might be taken by government, corporations, and consumers in the context of citizen, NGO, and shareholder scrutiny. For each key actor, a continuum is shown that ranges from a capitalist/utilitarian to an ecological economic/Rawlsian posture. This continuum implies that governments, corporations, and consumers that adopt an ecological economic/Rawlsian posture are more likely to promote sustainable development than those that adopt a capitalist/utilitarian approach.[‡] For example, a government could act as a trustee for stakeholder interests and advocate—through policy and regulation—a more sustainable approach to development. Alternatively, corporations might take the lead by acting in a socially and environmentally responsible manner and minimize or (even better) eliminate the negative impacts associated with their products and services. Finally, the burden could rest on consumers, whose "green" purchasing habits could shape demand for highly sustainable products and services. It seems clear that all actors have some responsibility. The question is how this responsibility should be distributed. The answer to this question clearly rests on the political and social environment within a nation or region. In this chapter, we focus primarily on the pressures on, and responses of, the

---

* See Sections 10.5.2 and 10.18.7 in Chapter 10 for a discussion of ISO 14001.

† A. A. King, Lenox, et al. (2005) find that ISO 14001 certification, a voluntary standard for environmental manage-

ment systems, provides evidence of an underlying management system, and that such a system is associated with environmental performance improvement. However, ISO 14001 certification is not a signal of superior environmental performance. Rather, firms that pollute more seek certification as a way to manage and reduce their liabilities and to improve their image.

‡ The capitalist/utilitarian posture represents the current approach to development adopted in many industrialized and emerging economies. In this regard, it might be considered the "business-as-usual" approach. Governments, corporations, and consumers that adopt this posture can and are making progress toward sustainable development. However, throughout this text, we view the business-as-usual approach as inadequate to encourage the *rate of change* needed to address some of the most challenging problems facing humanity, such as climate change and resource depletion. Therefore, we advocate an ecological economic/Rawlsian approach because we consider this posture to align more closely with the principles of sustainable development.

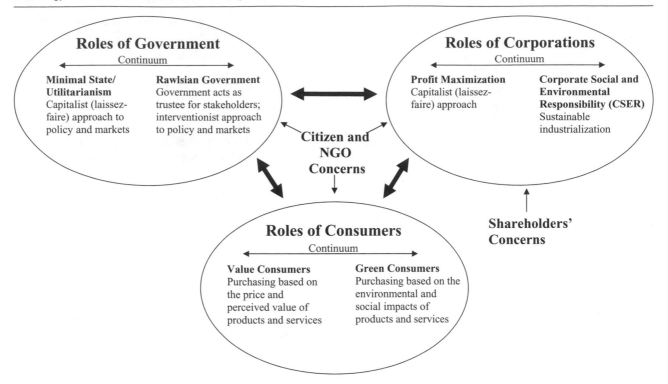

**FIGURE 7.1: DIFFERENT OPERATING POSTURES THAT MIGHT BE ADOPTED BY GOVERNMENT, CORPORATIONS, AND CONSUMERS IN THE CONTEXT OF CITIZEN, NGO, AND SHAREHOLDER SCRUTINY**

business firm to growing concerns about unsustainable forms of industrialization.

### 7.1.3 Responses of Firms to Social Demands

How have firms responded to social demands for less environmentally damaging activities? An important work by Hoffman (2001) on corporate environmentalism in the U.S. chemical and petroleum industries provides some answers to this question. By looking at the responses of corporations to the modern environmental movement (which began in the 1960s; see Section 2.2 of the Primer on Sustainable Development, found at the website associated with this book), Hoffman (2001) identified several distinct phases of corporate activity that changed as the environmental movement grew. During the 1960s, the chemical industry viewed emerging environmental problems as a challenge it could address through management and technology improvements. There was a common belief that "government intervention was . . . unnecessary, and environmentalists' concerns were viewed as exaggerated and not scientifically based" (ibid., p. 12). This view changed dramatically during the 1970s, when the chemical industry was caught off guard by the formation of the EPA and subsequent environmental legislation. Corporations became

defensive in their response to environmental regulations that they perceived as biased toward environmental concerns. Hoffman (2001, p. 80) characterizes corporate environmentalism during this period as externally directed "technical compliance."

Another major shift in corporate attitudes began in the mid-1980s from the dominant response of fighting and resisting adaptation to environmental regulation to accepting regulations and incorporating them into core business strategy and operations (Fischer and Schot 1993; Hoffman 2001). Corporations moved beyond technical compliance and began to develop managerial structures that integrated environmental concerns into their organizational functions. Part of this attitudinal shift can be attributed to global NGOs, which were beginning to hold corporations publicly accountable for their social and environmental impacts. Dramatic accidents, such as the *Exxon Valdez* oil spill off the coast of Alaska, the explosion at Bhopal, India, and careless handling of social and environmental concerns, such as Shell Nigeria's exploitation of the Ogoni people's native lands and the Nike child labor fiasco, outraged world opinion and lent a moral imperative to the growing civil society movement.

At the beginning of the 1990s, the balance of power between the chemical industry, government, and environmentalists began to equalize, and corporations started to adopt a proactive approach to environmental protection (Hoffman 2001). Once again, corporations viewed environmental problems as a challenge they could address, but this time there was a recognition that external stakeholders (such as environmentalists, competitors, government, investors, and insurance companies) had an important role to play.

The history of corporate environmentalism in the chemical industry provides some insight into how firms responded to social demands for less environmentally damaging activities. Their response could be characterized as a complex and dynamic process, influenced by existing institutional and organizational processes and changing social perceptions on what environmental protection really means (Hoffman and Ventresca 2002). For example, environmental NGOs that lobby government and industry for change each have their own conception of the environment and what industry should do to protect it. Thus beyond regulatory compliance, corporations must decide which NGOs present legitimate environmental concerns before addressing these concerns through improvements to their existing services, products, processes, and/or product-services.

At the turn of the twenty-first century, businesses began to realize that "corporate social and environmental responsibility" (CSER) was effectively part of the license to operate in a transparent, globalized world. Those firms that refused to alter their rhetoric and their behavior ran the risk of liability and of attracting unwanted attention to valuable brands and reputations. Hence leading-edge companies began to define new standards for environmental and social best practice. They institutionalized a larger set of environmental concerns in corporate policy and in dedicated staff positions (Tomer 1992). Many found value in "win-win" strategies of reducing wasted energy and resources and fattened the bottom line in the process. An example of a "win-win" approach is the twenty-seven companies that during the late 1990s made pledges to reduce greenhouse gas emissions as part of their participation in the nonprofit Pew Business Environmental Leadership Council.*

As part of this trend, some firms even started to broadcast their environmental commitments as part of a rebranded firm identity, for example BP's and Toyota's "green" product advertising. As of 2008, 79 percent of the Global Fortune 250 companies were publishing some sort of report disclosing their social and environmental impacts (KPMG 2008). In 1990, the number was zero. Business schools have also jumped on board, expanding their offerings to include courses that address environmental and social issues, and some, like the University of Michigan and Yale, even offer dual master's degrees in business and natural resources fields. Clearly, concerns about corporate environmental impacts have graduated from the activist fringe to occupying a place in firms' core strategic considerations. We argue that the shift toward voluntary corporate social and environmental responsibility is not enough to address the massive and widespread social and environmental problems that we face today.[†]

## 7.2 WHAT KINDS OF ENVIRONMENTAL, SKILL, AND EMPLOYMENT CHANGES ARE NEEDED IN THE ECONOMY?

### 7.2.1 Environmental Changes

As described in Chapters 1 and 2, all indications are that human activity is placing unprecedented demands on natural systems to provide energy and raw materials and to absorb pollutants. Such demands are also endangering public and worker health to the point that current industrial, agricultural, and transport systems are becoming unsustainable (Meadows, Meadows, et al. 1992; Meadows, Randers et al. 2004; Schmidt-Bleek 1998; see Sections 1.3 and 1.4

---

* In 1998, BP pledged to reduce greenhouse gas emissions from its operations to 10 percent below 1990 levels by 2010. It achieved its target by 2001, saving $650 million in the process. BP's direct emissions increased slightly from 2001 to 2003, but in 2009 they had dropped by around 20 percent from the 2001 level (www.bp.com, accessed January 28, 2011). DuPont has outperformed BP in terms of greenhouse gases, achieving a reduction of 72 percent below 1990 levels, exceeding the goal of 65 percent by 2010. On hazardous waste, DuPont reduced emissions of substances reported in the U.S. Toxic Release Inventory by nearly 60 percent in 2010 from 1987 levels (www.dupont.com, accessed January 28, 2011).

† Bennear (2007, p. 327) examined fourteen state-based regulatory systems that mandated management-based regulation (MBR), and concluded that MBR had a "measurable positive effect on the environmental performance of manufacturing plants." She found that "plants subject to management-based regulation experienced larger decreases in total pounds of toxic chemicals released and were more likely to engage in source reduction activities" (ibid.). Bennear's (2007) study provides preliminary support for the notion that plants with greater complementarity between planning efforts and pollution reduction will have larger effects from mandated MBR. Greater effects were found for firms that were not members of Responsible Care, the chemical industry's flagship voluntary program, casting doubt on the effectiveness of this program as an industry self-regulatory initiative. Similarly, A. King and Lenox (2000) report that U.S. chemical companies that signed onto Responsible Care improved their environmental performance more slowly than nonparticipating firms. See also Karkkainen (2001).

in Chapter 1 for a discussion of how human activity is affecting the environment).

Our emphasis in this chapter is on the role of business organizations and organizational innovations in stimulating technological change for sustainable development. In the context of environmental sustainability, traditional ways of addressing pollution problems through pollution control or so-called end-of-pipe approaches—after technological systems are designed and implemented—are no longer seen as adequate. Similarly, small advances in the efficiency of energy and resource use can no longer compensate for increased world demand and consumption of resource and energy-intensive technology. Many estimates call for drastic reductions in pollution and energy and resource use, on the order of a factor of ten or more (Reijnders 1998; Schmidt-Bleek 1998). The Intergovernmental Panel on Climate Change (IPCC 2007, pp. 125–126) states that "only in the case of essentially complete elimination of emissions can the atmospheric concentration of $CO_2$ ultimately be stabilised at a constant level," thereby mitigating the expected negative impacts from climate change.) This would require an overwhelming retreat from a dependence on the carbon-based fuels that have powered industrial economies for over a hundred years. Such a retreat is unlikely to be welcomed by countries such as China, which views the use of available carbon-based fuels as essential to its development strategy.

Even if we take comfort from the fact that the eco- or energy efficiency of products and services has improved dramatically over the past decade, the fact is that the rate at which the best technologies are diffused into the world economy is not sufficient to address the rate at which consumption and environmental problems are increasing (Andersen and Massa 2000). Not only are ecosystems seriously endangered by destruction of the ozone layer, global warming, and the global diffusion of pesticides, but new threats are now suggested related to endocrine disruption that compromises the reproductive systems of all species at levels of chemical exposure in the parts-per-billion/trillion rather than parts-per-million range (Colborn, Dumanowski, et al. 1996). Evidence is increasing that diseases heretofore unconnected with chemical exposures, such as autoimmune diseases, attention-deficit/hyperactivity disorder, and childhood cancers, are in fact consequences of chemicals-based industrial production and consumption (Ashford and Miller 1998).

Energy, extraction, production, transportation, and agricultural systems need to be inherently cleaner, safer, and resource conserving—that is, sustainable—

in order to avoid or minimize depletion of resources and pollution. These systems need to be designed with consideration of costs to the environment and consumer and worker health and safety in mind from the beginning,* across every industrial sector, and in every function of the firm. These changes require more than incremental innovation; they present a challenge and opportunity for radical, disrupting technological innovation (see the discussion of different types of innovation in Chapter 6).

### 7.2.2 Changes in Skills and Employment

A cleaner and less resource-intensive environment is only one of several constituents of a sustainable society. Currently, half the people in the world live on less than \$2 a day; of those, 1.2 billion live below the international poverty line of \$1 a day. One-third of children in developing countries are chronically malnourished. Workers in both developing and developed countries put in long hours at menial tasks for pay that is not enough to cover basic living expenses. Secure and meaningful employment that provides workers with adequate purchasing power is an essential ingredient of a sustainable and socially cohesive economy. And a growing economic system, one that increasingly satisfies human needs and wants (that is, increases wealth without enlarging the ecological footprint), needs an adequate supply and quality of human capital, especially if we are to satisfy human needs by more ingenious use of resources and an enhanced service economy.

Incremental labor-saving innovation, which dominates the majority of changes occurring in mature industrial economies, is said to be at the root of creeping unemployment and underemployment involving the deskilling of at least some labor or the "dumbing down" of the workforce (Head 1996; Madrick 1999; Rifkin 2004).† This vernacular expression of deskilling can be seen to be directly relevant to organizational knowledge and learning. Although new higher-skilled or newer-skilled challenging and rewarding work is being created in some firms or sectors, employment is being destroyed in others. It cannot be said that the winners can counterbalance the losers in either the

---

\* See McDonough and Braungart (1998), who argue that more than "ecoefficiency" is required in the sense advocated by Schmidheiny (1992). Fundamental redesign is required. See also the discussion of the boomerang/rebound effect and the Jevons paradox in Section 1.3 in Chapter 1.

† For a discussion of employment concerns, see Section 1.1.3 in Chapter 1.

nature or the amount of employment. Thus in this scenario, net job creation is not an adequate metric of satisfaction with technological change.*

The nature and rewards, both monetary and psychosocial, of work are undergoing structural change and revolution, but these changes are being brought about by new production, transportation, energy, and agricultural technologies that are undergoing innovation without concern or planning for their impact on the nature and level of employment. Although compensatory policies related to education, retraining, and the reorganization of work exist or are being planned, they are *reactive* to technological changes. Here we need to take a lesson from the environmental problems created by rapid and extensive technological change. We recognize that it is not sufficient to consider the effects on the environment as an afterthought. Environmental quality needs to be built in. Similarly, it is likely that thinking about work *after* technologies are planned and disseminated may be far too late to address their possible adverse consequences effectively.

We have argued throughout this book that production, consumption, the environment, and employment ought to be co-optimized and considered simultaneously in an integrated way. This means that technological, organizational, institutional, and social innovation needs to be proactive and anticipatory rather than reactive. A knowledge-based economy potentially allows for more flexibility and new conceptualizations of work, leisure, production, and consumption. Because the private sector is an indispensable partner in sustainable transformations, it is important to examine organizational structures, learning, and innovation in depth.

## 7.3 ORGANIZATIONAL INNOVATION AND LEARNING: THEORY AND BACKGROUND

Much of the literature on organizational innovation is concerned with intrafirm changes in and among various organizational aspects of functions of the firm, such as R&D, marketing, environmental and governmental affairs, industrial relations, worker health and safety, and customer and community relations. The counterpart of organizational innovation in government—what might be called institutional innovation—is also a crucial factor and plays an important role in the policy initiatives for sustainable development addressed in Chapter 13. In this chapter, however, we focus specifically on the firm.

### 7.3.1 Organizational Theory and the Limitations of the Neoclassical Model

The field of organizational theory can be thought of as sociological theory as applied to organizations.[2] Business scholar Thomas Gladwin (1993, p. 47) summarizes the field in this way: "Organizational theory focuses on the basic characteristics of organizational participants, goals, social structure, technology, and external environment, at different levels of analysis. It embodies multiple perspectives or frames of reference, viewing organizations variously as rational, natural, and open systems, using a range of images or metaphors (e.g., organizations as machines, organisms, brains, cultures, political systems, psychic prisons, flux and transformation, and instruments of domination)."

Organizational theory holds more explanatory power for firm behavior than does the conventional economics conception of the firm. The traditional neoclassical view sees the firm—subject to constraints—as a profit-maximizing "black box." Indeed, Friedman (1953) argues that economic models do not need to capture reality; rather, only their forecasts must agree with empirical observations. If one considers the firm as a black box, its internal activities become unimportant because the end result is known—that is, it is defined by economic rationale. But the neoclassical model fails to account for why, when faced with the same set of incentives and regulations, some firms respond minimally, while others consciously choose behavior that is nonopportunistic, long term, and responsible to interests that go beyond their shareholder owners (Tomer 1992).

With regard to technological innovation, the neoclassical model has a number of failings. Neoclassical theory holds that corrections of market failures for factors important to growth should be the extent of government intervention; that is, governments should not intervene to promote or subsidize the development of technologies. Obviously, the government does intervene to support technological development in areas that are important to national

* Although the European Commission white paper titled *Growth, Competitiveness, Employment: The Challenges and Ways Forward into the 21st Century* (European Commission 1994) argues that environmentally sustainable policies will create a "double dividend" of an improved environment and more employment, the evidence so far indicates no significant employment dividend (see Getzner 2002). Although new jobs are indeed created, displaced old polluting industries and practices lose employment. The net effect is unremarkable. See Section 5.3.2 in Chapter 5.

security and economic competitiveness, for example, infrastructure for information and communications, the military, and transportation, including the auto, rail, and aircraft industries. The government also intervenes where the risks of development are too high to entice industry to develop technologies, for example, where the government supports research on cancer therapies and then hands over the research to pharmaceutical companies for commercialization.

The limitations of the standard neoclassical model with regard to organizational learning and technology choice are instructive (Stoughton 1996):

- Continuous process improvement (through the organization of production and fine-tuning of equipment) is as important as new process investment over the long run. This type of continuous improvement is embedded in learning and experience within the firm and cannot be acquired on the market. Thus the ability to use a given technology efficiently is tacit, acquired knowledge. In the context of advanced manufacturing technologies, Zammuto and O'Connor (1992) argue that the benefits gained from technological investment are heavily influenced by organizational design and culture. That is, the greater an organization's emphasis on flexibility-oriented values, the more likely it will benefit from productivity gains following the installation of new process technologies. This argument indicates that organizational design and culture can play a critical role in achieving competitiveness.

- Firms do not have perfect information when they are selecting technologies. At best, technology choice is boundedly rational, and access to technology information is uneven. Firms, particularly in developing countries, are likely to have knowledge of only a fraction of the suite of technologies available to them. Larger firms, which may already have an advantage in technology search activities by virtue of available resources, are also more likely to have a multinational enterprise (MNE) partner and thus have an additional conduit of information. (See the later discussion of the importance of "outsiders" in technological innovation.)

- A firm's ability to switch to more productive/efficient technologies can be limited by previous capital investments—that is, technology choice is "sticky."

- The transfer and adoption of technology are not costless. For example, there are often costs to adapt technologies to local raw-material, scale, and input requirements. Further, there are learning costs (training) and transmission costs associated with technology transfer.

Organizational theory is critical to overcoming the limitations of the neoclassical view of the firm and of technological innovation as they relate to sustainable development. But compared with the attention that has been paid to institutional and market failures, organizational failure within business firms has been given little consideration. This is unfortunate because environmentally undesirable behavior on the part of firms is as much a matter of organizational failure as it is one of markets that do not internalize environmental costs (Gabel and Sinclair-Desgagne 1993). Firms always have a choice of ways to respond to environmental concerns.* They exhibit a wide range of responses, from active evasion or grudging compliance with environmental regulations to innovative behavior that aims for zero net environmental impact from all products, services, and production activities. We explore some of the motivating forces as well as the organizational barriers to environmentally proactive behavior in Section 7.5.

Tomer (1992) proposes a model for understanding the environmental behavior of the firm as the product of additional factors beyond "markets" and "regulators." His socioeconomic (SE) model offers a framework for determining the "human firm's environmental behavior" by (1) the environmental opportunities confronting it; (2) its internal organizational capabilities; (3) the "macro" societal influence; (4) the "micro" social influences of extrafirm institutions and infrastructures; and (5) other regulatory influences.

Other authors have identified stages or typologies of corporate environmental behavior, from ad hoc crisis management to responsible compliance to efforts to go beyond compliance through energy savings and waste-reduction programs and innovations in products and processes (Ehrenfeld and Hoffman 1996; Faucheux, Nicolai, et al. 1998; Fischer and Schot 1993; Hunt and Auster 1990). In Sections 7.5.1 to 7.5.3, we explore variables/determinants that affect a firm's environmental behavior, especially as it relates to technological innovation. These are *willingness*, *opportunity/motivation*, and *capacity/capability* to change/innovate.

### 7.3.2 Organizational Learning

Within the broad field of organizational theory is a well-established subfield called "organizational learning" (Argote and Ophir 2002; Fiol and Lyles 1985; Hedberg 1981; Huber 1991; Lazonick 1998; Levitt and March 1988; J. March 1991; Miller 1996;

---

* Indeed, Michael Porter argues that firms often see "first-mover advantages" by complying early with environmental demands in the development of advanced compliance technologies (Porter and van der Linde 1995a, 1995b).

Schulz 2002; Shrivastava 1983).* In this subfield, the processes by which organizations "learn" are described differently in the literature, and an accepted definition or substantiated theory of organizational learning remains elusive. For example, Levitt and March (1988) view organizational learning as the encoding of history and experience in routines that guide a firm's behavior. Huber's (1991) formulation expands this view by relating organizational learning to four constructs: knowledge acquisition, information distribution, information interpretation, and organizational memory. Lazonick (1998) considers organizational learning in the context of the "skill-based hypothesis" (see Section 1.1.3.1).† Miner, Kim, et al. (1999) consider how organizations learn from failure. Others view a firm's ability to learn—or absorb new information—as a function of its prior related knowledge (Cohen and Levinthal 1990). Akgün, Lynn, et al. (2003, p. 862) view organizational learning through a sociocognitive lens, where learning is the result of "reciprocal interactions of social and cognitive processes embedded in organizational structures, cultures, and interactions." For our purposes, we adopt Miller's (1996) typology of organizational learning. Miller (p. 486) defines organizational learning as "the acquisition of new knowledge by actors who are willing to apply that knowledge in making decisions or influencing others in the organization." Learning is distinct from decision making in the sense

that learning increases organizational knowledge, while decision making need not.

Miller (1996) describes organizational learning theories along two dimensions. The first is *voluntarism* versus *determinism*, or the extent to which firm actors are "relatively free in action versus constrained by cognitive . . . , resource . . . , political . . . , or ideological structures" (p. 487). Global analysis and strategic planning by top managers are given as examples of a relatively unconstrained kind of learning that can expose critical assumptions about a firm's core competencies and its markets and explores a wide range of possible actions. Other scholars view organizational learning as happening more incrementally as the firm conducts small experiments that generate minor modifications in products and processes (Cyert and March 1963; J. G. March and Olsen 1976). An even more constrained kind of learning occurs within existing routines and programs: for example, with experience employees can learn to calibrate and operate a piece of machinery properly. Both of these kinds of learning can be described as "learning by doing," but they are different.

This typology parallels the different kinds of technological change described in greater detail in Section 7.5.4. As the design space expands from (1) *optimizing* existing technologies to (2) *adopting* better, already-established technologies to (3) *creating* new technologies, organizational learning must also expand accordingly, from constrained (or determined) to free (or voluntary). Determinism points to a small design space and the tendency for an organization to become locked in by its own routines and ways of thinking to particular products and processes. Lock-in can happen as product lines develop and mature and firms become more heavily invested in existing technologies (this is one kind of so-called bounded rationality) (Sorensen and Stuart 2000). Firms that are "locked in" can miss important emerging trends and opportunities for radically new technologies, leaving opportunities open for new firms to enter with radical, disrupting innovations (see Section 7.5). Progress made by firms pursuing established avenues for growth is said to exhibit "path dependencies." The paradox that as organizations make sustaining/process innovations, they begin to lose touch with environmental demands (or their customer base—see Section 7.4) can be resolved by the extent to which these organizations shift their learning strategy from one of *exploitation* to *exploration* (J. March 1991).

The second dimension along which Miller (1996) contrasts organizational theories is whether decisions are based on *methodical analyses* and concrete

---

* A closely related field of study is "interorganizational learning," which focuses on learning that occurs through the interaction of two or more organizations (Ingram 2002). An interorganizational learning process can be characterized as one in which the actions of a "sender" organization stimulate learning in a "receiver" organization (ibid.). In this situation, the relationship between the two organizations becomes an important consideration.

† Lazonick (1998) highlights an important difference in the way U.S. and Japanese manufacturing firms involved managers and workers in the process of organizational learning between the 1950s and the 1990s. Whereas Japanese firms utilized the creative potential of their machine operators by involving them in the *development* of technology, U.S. firms tended to confine this task to the managerial level. As a result, new manufacturing technologies in U.S. firms reduced the need for skilled workers on the shop floor. (The deskilling of the workforce is one factor behind the growth of wage inequality between white- and blue-collar workers in U.S. manufacturing firms; see Section 1.1.3.1 in Chapter 1.) The broad skill base of Japanese firms meant that they were able to respond (i.e., innovate) more quickly than U.S. firms to societal demands for new products, a flexibility that enabled them to capture a significant proportion of the U.S. market for manufactured goods. Lazonick (1998) argues that the slowdown in the loss of the U.S. automobile market to Japanese firms during the 1990s was due to investments by U.S. automobile manufacturers in *broader and deeper skill bases*. This argument supports the "skill-based hypothesis"—i.e., that investments in broad and deep skill bases will enable (manufacturing) firms to innovate and achieve sustained prosperity (ibid., p. 205).

**TABLE 7.1: MODES OF LEARNING**

| CONSTRAINTS (Voluntarism to determinism) | MODE OF THOUGHT AND ACTION | |
| --- | --- | --- |
| | METHODICAL | EMERGENT |
| **Few constraints** | **Analytic:** Learning characterized by systematic and objective analysis of available data. Few restrictions are placed on actors. | **Synthetic:** Learning characterized by an instinctive form of pattern formulation that is internal to a manager. Few restrictions are placed on actors. |
| **Action constrained** | **Experimental:** Learning characterized by bounded, problem-driven assessments, incremental experimentation, and satisficing behavior. Experiments can limit action. | **Interactive:** Learning characterized by actors identifying patterns from the contrasting ideas and conflicting objectives facing them as they interact with allies and rivals. Political interactions can limit action. |
| **Action and thought constrained** | **Structural:** Learning characterized by routines that standardize information processing and behavior. Routines constrain both thought and action. | **Institutional:** Learning characterized by institutional forces such as laws, social norms, or personal values that shape actor thinking. Institutional learning constrains both thought and action. |

Source: Adapted from Miller (1996, pp. 488–489).

standards or on *emergent institutions* and subtle values. In the first type of decision, managers are seen as rational actors who use cost-benefit analysis and hard data on competitive options to make decisions. This theory of the firm rests on norms of economic technical rationality. Facts are gathered carefully and methodically, and decisions emerge from rigorous modeling and statistical analysis. Thus organizational learning tends to be deductive and based on objective facts obtained through systematic analyses.

In the second type of decision, organizational actions are more spontaneous and emergent in nature. Firm actors are "driven by subtle normative considerations, fads and rituals, and even personal hunches and motives" (Miller 1996, p. 487). This is an intuitive form of learning that is tacit and inductive and centers on instincts and impressions. When asked, managers operating from this place often cannot explain how they arrive at a particular decision. The source of their knowing is not always clear even to them. See Sections 7.5.1 and 7.5.2 for more discussion of managerial motivation and behavior.

Miller (1996) uses these two dimensions to create a typology of organizational learning. Table 7.1 characterizes the different styles of learning that occur under a *methodical* and *emergent* organizational environment for three different levels of constraint (which range from *voluntaristic* to *deterministic* in nature).

The following subsections consider different ways in which organizational learning can occur within networks. The focus on networks is important because as organizations establish more complex and dynamic relations with other entities, the locus of innovation and learning, which are key determinants of competitiveness, is likely to shift from intra- to interorganiza-

tional collaborative networks (Gray 1989; Huxham and Vangen 2005; Sturgeon 2000).

7.3.2.1 Networks

The networks that comprise firms and in which they are embedded—involving actors inside and outside the company—are an important dimension of organizational theory (W. E. Baker and Faulkner 2002; Borgatti and Foster 2003; Granovetter 1985; Pfeffer 1982; Powell 1990; Uzzi 1997, 2000).* Networks can help stimulate innovation and learning (Bessant, Kaplinsky, et al. 2003); they can also serve to inhibit learning and change. In Chapter 6, we examined the innovation process in firms that are embedded in, and interact with, a variety of network actors. Here we examine different kinds of networks and their contributions in greater depth.

Networks facilitate learning through the dissemination of knowledge and/or skills among their member organizations. The firm participates in networks involving suppliers, consultants, trade associations, geographically close industries, consumers, workers, government, and others. Ashford and Meima (1993) identify several kinds of networks:

1. Those within the organization (units performing planning, production, and innovation functions), which are termed "intraorganizational networks"

2. Those connecting units in the supply chain (suppliers, contractors, and consumers/customers), which are termed "transorganizational networks"

_____

* In discussing the different kinds of capital needed for a society to advance, natural capital, physical capital, and human capital are usually mentioned. Networks are a way of analyzing what is called "structural capital."

3. Those involving other organizations—that is, public interest and community-based groups, competitors, and regulators—which are termed "supraorganizational networks"[3]

The members of supraorganizational networks are not usually tied contractually or commercially to the firm. They are examples of "outsiders." The authors also identify a fourth kind of network whose activities are not related directly to the firm: community-worker networks such as environmental-labor coalitions pressing for better and more coordinated environmental and occupational health and safety programs, policies and laws, and right-to-know coalitions that coordinate toxics information in the workplace and in the environment (Lewis and Henkels 1996).

Ashford and Meima (1993) identify four purposes that networks can serve: (1) to provide *internal* sources of technical ideas and information; (2) to provide technical ideas and information from sources *external* to the firm;[4] (3) to create performance requirements/constraints or provide information about market demand and opportunities; and (4) to provide a means to advance shared decision making with those external to the firm. "Purpose [1] is served by intra-organizational networks. Purposes [2] and [3] are served by both trans- and supra-organizational networks, while purpose [4] is served more specifically by customers, workers, and community-based groups" (ibid., p. 12).

Traditional organizational theory is focused primarily on intraorganizational and transorganizational (that is, within the supply chain) networks, which create the context for the strategic process, management decision making, employee values and attitudes, internal creativity and innovation, resistance to change, and many other phenomena usually considered "organizational" determinants of change. Following this line of thinking, researchers Roome and Clarke (1993) argue that informal networks at the intraorganizational level are "most important for learning related to the application of new technologies; networks on higher levels are weaker, little true collaboration seems to take place, and the deliberate, strategic management of network learning is rare." This may indeed be true in an *evolutionary* context, where the focus of learning is within the *existing* firm for an established customer base. However, change that is more *revolutionary* (that is, disrupting in Christensen's [1997] formulation)* is likely to be stimulated by new configurations and interactions among busi-

ness, government, and civil society networks. This broader network view that focuses on the "sociology of technology" is often referred to in Europe as the "the social shaping of technology" (SST) (MacKenzie and Wajcman 1999).

SST considers "how the design and implementation of technology are patterned by a range of 'social' and 'economic' factors as well as narrowly 'technical' considerations" (R. Williams and Edge 1996, p. 865). Thus SST is a constructivist analysis of technological development. It stands in contrast to the notion of "technological determinism," where technology is viewed as a governing force in society (M. R. Smith and Marx 1994). SST is concerned with how technological innovation and learning are shaped by complex socioeconomic processes within society, and how these are integrated through political, economic, and cultural factors. One of the best-known social shaping models is the "social construction of technology" (SCOT) (Bijker, Hughes, et al. 1987). The SCOT approach considers technological artifacts as having an *interpretive flexibility*—that is, different actors or groups of actors (such as consumers) have different interpretations of the same artifact (Pinch and Bijker 1984). Through processes such as negotiation, rhetoric, and enrollment, the different meanings stabilize around one dominant interpretation, which leads to innovation. What is interesting about the SCOT approach is that not all actors or groups of actors need to accept the dominant interpretation of an artifact. Indeed, those actors whose interpretations fall outside the mainstream view are perhaps more likely to introduce radical or disrupting innovations.

Within the field of SST are several network approaches that try to explain how dynamic systems of actors come together to form networks. These include actor-network theory (Callon, Law, et al. 1986; Latour 1987; Law 1999), techno-economic-network (TEN) theory (Callon, Laredo, et al. 1992), industrial-networks theory (Håkansson 1987, 1989; Håkansson and Snehota 1985), and sociotechnical-networks theory (Elzen, Enserink, et al. 1996). The following two sections take a closer look at the last two approaches. We then look at "learning collaborations" between firms and stakeholders and the potential for these approaches to create more environmentally and socially desirable technologies.

### 7.3.2.2 Industrial-Networks Theory

Industrial-networks theory emphasizes the network character of the firm and its environment (Håkansson 1987, 1989; Håkansson and Snehota 1985). Industrial

---

* See the discussions of disrupting innovation in Sections 6. 2.1 in Chapter 6 and 8.2 in Chapter 8.

networks are considered to be coordinating mechanisms that create a form of economic organization that belongs to "neither market nor hierarchy" (Powell 1990). Network actors are said to be socially "embedded" through exchange relationships (Granovetter 1985). "Embeddedness" describes the process by which social interactions among actors in the value chain shape economic activity (Uzzi 1997, 2000). Embedded networks are created from interactions such as the informal exchange of know-how and joint research and product development ventures. Thus innovation and learning are products of interactions among network actors. Firms seek to maintain networks in order to have direct and indirect access to important resources that they themselves do not possess. Although networks can be based on legal contracts, their stability is derived mainly from the establishment of trust, reliability, and actor reputation and the fact that knowledge and/or skills cannot easily be monopolized by one organization (Luiten 2001; Powell 1990). Noorderhaven, Koen, et al. (2002) describe three key characteristics of embedded relationships: trust, open communication, and joint problem solving.

Networks offer economic opportunities that are not predicted by the neoclassical model, but they produce constraints on technology development as well. Embedded industrial networks rest on particular technologies and established routines, which tend to produce change aimed at *optimization* rather than *transformation*; that is, they are bounded rationally (see the related discussion of types of innovation in Chapter 6). In such networks, the radical character of an innovation can be assessed by the extent to which existing network interactions and structure are displaced by new network formations.

### 7.3.2.3 Sociotechnical Networks

Social network approaches consider technological innovation and learning from a social point of view. These approaches focus on the formation and evolution of social networks that create and support technology. A particular emphasis is given to understanding the characteristics of actor *position* and *relations* within a social network (Burt 1983). For example, negotiations of actor relations can be influenced by an actor's financial resources, technical capabilities, and perceived market power and human factors such as communication skills. Although much emphasis is given to social networks with strong ties (or relations) between actors, Granovetter (1973) points to the value actors obtain from *weak ties* (that

is, short-lived or not very intense relations). More recently, Burt (2004) highlighted how thinking and behavior *within* social groups are more homogeneous than *between* groups. He shows how good ideas are disproportionately held by actors whose networks span groups that have different ways of thinking and behaving. Thus Burt's (2004) conception of a social network emphasizes the importance of between-group brokers whose actions lead to the creation of social capital.

By considering the role of technology in actor relations, Mulder (1992, p. 21) defines a *technology network* as "the ensemble of the relationships, which serve the objective of developing, maintaining and applying a new technology." A technology network is considered to evolve through the creation of new and/or renegotiation of existing relations among actors. This implies that the formation of new technology networks can be influenced by relationships that already exist among actors (Moors 2000). Such influence might explain how firms become locked into the development of sustaining innovations.

Elzen, Enserink, et al. (1996) developed the concept of a sociotechnical-networks (STNs) approach. Like technology-network analysis, STNs describe the interactions among social entities with an explicit focus on the role of technology in these interactions. Their work shows that technological change takes place along two pathways: (1) within existing STNs, which are expected to be conservative, or (2) through the emergence of new STNs, "which produce radical [that is, disrupting] technologies . . . through cooperation between new types of actors" (Moors 2000, p. 66).

Within technology networks or STNs, the evolution of network relations is likely to follow the process of technological development. For example, Lindquist (1996) argues that during the initial development of ideas—the "sensing" stage—a network is broad and dispersed, consisting of many players. Once an idea emerges, the network consolidates during the "response" stage, when product/process/service development occurs. Finally, when the technology is deployed—the "implementation" stage—the network expands as new relations are formed to manufacture, market, and sell the technology. Thus the number of actors involved in a network during the technology development process is considered to follow an hourglass shape. Of course, the evolution of network actors and relations will depend on the type of technology being developed.

Research by Powell, White, et al. (2005) provides a nuanced look at how relationships among network actors in the field of biotechnology have evolved over time. The field of biotechnology is predisposed to the formation of networks, given its complex and expanding knowledge base and the widely dispersed sources of expertise (Powell, Koput, et al. 1996). Powell, White, et al. (2005, p. 1187) found that between 1988 and 1999, "neither money nor market power—not even the sheer force of novel ideas—dominates the field. Rather, those organizations with diverse portfolios of well-connected collaborators are found in the most cohesive, central positions and have the largest hand in shaping the evolution of the field.... The density of the network and the open scientific trajectory combine to enhance the importance of participants' reputation. The pattern of cross-cutting collaborations often results in a partner on one project being a rival on another. The frequent rewiring of attachments means that participants have to learn how to exit from relationships gracefully so as not to damage future prospects for affiliation."

The work by Powell, White, et al. (2005) is part of an emerging body of research that considers how collaborative choices influence the changing dynamics of networks (Ebers 1999; Gulati 1995, 1999; Gulati and Gargiulo 1999; Hagedoorn 2006). More generally, the study of network dynamics is becoming an important research area for sociologists, social psychologists, and network statisticians (Doreian and Stokman 1996, 2003; Stokman and Doreian 2001). See the work of van de Bunt and Groenewegen (2007) for an example of research undertaken on interorganizational network dynamics.*

With regard to the creation of new cooperative alliances among firms, sectors,† and government to address environmental issues, Faucheux, Nicolai, et al. (1998) outline a typology of agreements among network actors for sharing environmental risks and costs: (1) cooperation agreements for the development of *new processes*, such as the partnership between France's Rhône-Poulenc and Sweden's Kenura to look for more efficient and cheaper ways to fight water pollution; (2) cooperative agreements for the development of *new products*, such as Siemens and Bayer's collaboration on catalytic converters; (3) co-

operative agreements for the *recycling of packaging and products*, such as Eco-emballages, founded in France by a group of packaging firms and manufacturers and distributors of packaging materials; and (4) *mergers and acquisitions*, such as Rhône-Poulenc and Sita's acquisition, through their jointly owned subsidiary Teris, of a company called Scori that specializes in the disposal of waste from cement makers.

At the center of these cooperative alliances lies the need for innovation, and by definition, an innovation process is a learning process (O'Sullivan 1998). Although we have considered much on the topic of organizational learning, we have yet to explicitly address the notion of learning for sustainability.

In a discussion of trends and opportunities for innovation for sustainability, Dijkema, Ferrão, et al. (2006, pp. 221–222) argue that the pathway to a sustainable enterprise consists of the following four phases:

- Phase I companies or sectors react to societal pressure to "do something for the environment" through standards, procedures and environmental care systems. Their "leitmotiv" is to "clean-up their act because they must," largely to preserve their license-to-operate.
- Phase II companies consider sustainability on the agenda. They discuss internally: How can we deal with it? What stakeholders are of relevance? What new activities do we envisage? Which innovation activities can be reframed?
- Phase III companies realize and acknowledge that sustainability is crucial for their long-term continuation and extend their value chain, namely through new entrants and adopting new processes.
- Phase IV companies formulate sustainability strategies in interaction with external stakeholders. Sustainability is perceived as a continuous process. The innovation activities repeatedly need redefinition and reformulation, beyond [a] firm's boundaries.

What is perhaps most interesting about these phases is the growing importance given to new entrants, the interaction with *external* stakeholders, and networks. Dijkema, Ferrão, et al. (2006, p. 222) also argue that "the perception of time plays a critical role in the interaction between sustainability and innovation." They maintain that the business-as-usual firm tends to focus on its own organizational structure and near-term problems, whereas sustainable enterprises tend to value extended interorganizational networks and are more concerned with far-reaching life-cycle issues of global importance.

The idea that new entrants (or outsiders) and external stakeholders are likely to play an important

---

* Van de Bunt and Groenewegen (2007) use actor-oriented statistical network models to describe the evolution of a sociotechnical network over time. These models focus on the relational actions of individual actors, who are assumed to maximize their utility functions when making a strategic partner choice. The authors find that in the genome industry, actors have a preference for "high-status" partners that belong to the same group of actors as they do, but with whom they have no prior relations.

† These strategic alliances are referred to as "transnationalization."

role in innovation and learning for sustainability is worth considering further. Van de Poel's (2000) work on outsiders and their role in technical development is of particular relevance to this discussion.[5] Van de Poel (2000, p. 383) defines outsiders as "actors not involved in technical development or decision-making about technology and not sharing the rules that guide the design and further development of a technology." He continues: "The totality of such rules is defined as the technological regime. Outsiders thus do not share the existing technological regime. If outsiders nevertheless become involved in technical development, they may well trigger innovations that depart from the existing technological regime and that possibly transform that regime" (ibid.).

Van de Poel (2000) distinguishes three categories of outsiders: societal pressure groups, professional scientists and engineers, and outsider firms. In his conceptualization, outsiders who both (1) are outside or at least marginal in the relevant system of interaction around technological innovation and (2) do not share some of the relevant rules with respect to technical development can trigger radical (that is, disrupting) technical change if they get involved in technical development in other ways than by adopting the rules of the existing regime. We explore the role of outsiders in technological change in more detail in Section 7.5.6.

The recent development of Web-based communities—such as Innocentive, NineSigma, YourEncore, and Yet2—that match potential innovators with problems facing companies or institutions around the world provides a new dimension to the role of networks and outsiders in learning. In such networks, the identity of the client and innovator can be kept confidential, removing the importance of factors such as status (van de Bunt and Groenewegen 2007) and reputation (Powell, White, et al. 2005) in actor relations. The term "crowdsourcing" is often used to describe the process of harnessing the wisdom and participation of crowds—that is, any individual or group—for commercial purposes.[6] The emergence of Web-based communities has created a new form of learning network in which the best ideas from outsiders are exchanged for financial reward without individuals ever having to meet in person.

An additional group that could be conceived as outside a technology network or STN is consumers. Under certain conditions, societal demand for new and better products and services can be a powerful innovative force. However, the lack of trustworthy and accurate information on the environmental impacts of new technology makes it challenging for consumers to practice green purchasing. Research by Lee, Gemba, et al. (2006) provides some promising evidence that if environmental knowledge and information can flow among firms and societal stakeholders—such as the public/consumers, government, and NGOs—environmentally conscious markets can emerge in which greener products become highly valued and environmentally innovative firms achieve competitive advantage.

In the following section, we consider various mechanisms that attempt to include stakeholders in the learning process to promote sustainability through reducing the impact of environmentally destructive activities.

### 7.3.2.4 Social Networks: Learning Collaborations with Stakeholders

The recent emphasis on sociotechnical networks may be due to the growing influence of stakeholders other than shareholders on the firm (see Figure 7.1). For instance, companies have discovered that since the 1960s, civil society has developed unheard-of power and sophistication to negotiate concessions on environmental and social issues. Waddell (2005) describes how new governance structures were formed by tying together diverse organizations in an intricate network that generates innovation and produces societal learning and change (SLC). SLC is viewed as changing relationships and bridging the differences among the core systems of society—economic, political, and social, represented, respectively, by business, government, and civil society. Waddell's (2005, p. 10) theory emphasizes voluntary cooperation: "By working together voluntarily, each participating organization achieves its own goals by changing its relationship with others to co-ordinate their actions and create synergies. SLC is driven both by each group's goal and by a vision of how to build society's capacity to achieve a jointly valued societal goal."

*Network governance* theories provide a more structured approach to the interaction of public, private, and semiprivate actors in networks (Dewulf, Termeer, et al. 2009; Klijn and Koppenjan 2000).* In particular, network-management strategies are used to improve the interaction between network actors

---

*     Kemp (2008) views networks as important for guiding/influencing transitions toward sustainability. Participation in a network can limit—in a positive sense—the choices available to actors, which provides a collective orientation and reduces uncertainty. Other mechanisms that can be used to coordinate a transition are *markets* (i.e., changes in prices that influence economic decisions) and *hierarchy* (i.e., state or company plans/goals that can influence economic activities) (ibid.).

(process management) and to adjust the institutional characteristics (network constitution) of networks to improve their effectiveness or focus actors on common objectives (Dewulf, Termeer, et al. 2009). Network governance emphasizes less formal and more interactive forms of governance, where stakeholder dialogue and deliberative policy making are viewed as alternatives to state authority and hierarchical government structures.

In their work on social networks, Hall and Ingersoll (1993) focus on how firms can collaboratively learn new knowledge and skills through working with stakeholders.* They find that companies expect all stakeholders (except investors) to become more important in the future. They argue that learning from stakeholders is essential in developing core competence for discovering environmentally focused solution-oriented strategies because it requires changes in a firm's value structure and that the firm develop different skills and attitudes. The firm must shift from a deal-oriented, transactional, and mechanistic approach to a more relational, open, and learning orientation—one that is *voluntary* and *emergent* in Miller's (1996) typology (see the introduction to Section 7.3.2). A profound revision of the current understanding and practice of stakeholder dialogue—as an open-ended learning process rather than an outcome-focused (on growth and profit) "negotiations" process—is necessary. Reciprocal trust is seen as essential in engaging nonbusiness stakeholders in a collaborative effort.

Describing how environmental issues are restructuring markets and redistributing value-creation potential, Hall and Ingersoll (1993) discuss a number of companies, including Arm and Hammer, Wellman, Loblaw's, Electrolux, Werner and Metz, and Conoco. They conclude that "solution-oriented" companies that have moved into a proactive stance on environmental issues are building core competence in a learning collaboration with various stakeholders, which involves completely reenvisioning one's business, consciously developing strategic intent, and finding ways to change the rules of the competitive game. These companies could be considered to fall in Phases III and IV of Dijkema, Ferrão, et al.'s (2006) pathway to becoming a sustainable enterprise.

Supraorganizational networks include nonbusiness stakeholders like community citizens, NGOs, and regulators. In some respects, these stakeholders are "outsiders" ("societal pressure groups" in van de Poel's

formulation). At the community level, social networks embodied in public-based interest groups are potentially important in transforming the firm into a sustainable enterprise, even though the experience to date has not been encouraging. This experience includes (1) company communication about plant-based risk to the surrounding community (Chess 1993), (2) industry-created citizen advisory panels (Lynn 1993), (3) government-mandated emergency planning committees (Rest and Krimsky 1993), and (4) the negotiation of "good-neighbor" agreements between plants and the community (Lewis and Henkels 1996).

Chess (1993) has described two cases of "exemplary" risk-communication efforts by companies that entailed regular communication from the company to the community and involved citizens in reporting offensive odors emanating from the plants, but that did not involve the community in decisions about production or environmental control. Although this experience did involve "two-way" communication, its scope was intentionally limited by the companies. Mutual dialogue in these "exemplary" cases did not extend to other environmental issues between the communities and the companies.

In their investigation of government-mandated emergency planning committees, Rest and Krimsky (1993) reported that the participants on local emergency planning committees (LPECs) focused on emergency response in the event of chemical accidents and were not interested in promoting activities for risk reduction or for either pollution or accident prevention. The jury is still out on community advisory panels (CAPs), which have become integral parts of companies' public relations and community outreach programs but may not be sufficiently representative of community interests or sufficiently empowered to be effective. More specifically, the question is whether CAPs can affect decisions concerning the direction of the enterprise and the technologies used in production (Lynn 1993).

In contrast, about a dozen "good-neighbor" agreements have been signed in the United States that give community representatives access to plant operations and health and safety data (Lewis and Henkels 1996). Community activists behind these initiatives are motivated to encourage pollution prevention and technological change rather than to receive information about plant emissions and respond to accidents. For an evaluation of these agreements in Minnesota, see Murdock and Sexton (2002). Lewis and Henkels's (1996) work distinguishes between voluntary and enforceable, legally binding good-neighbor agreements. Agreements work when

---

*    Here stakeholders may include some members of supraorganizational networks, such as members of the community.

the company fulfills its obligations, but communities have been burned when "nonbinding agreements . . . have been discarded by company officials—for example, when the plant's manager has changed" (ibid., p. 142). At that point, the recourse available to the neighborhood citizen group is limited to adversarial tactics such as launching a negative publicity campaign. Binding good-neighbor agreements, on the other hand, are legally enforceable and are sometimes linked to an environmental permitting process involving a regulatory agency, such as the EPA or state regulators. These agreements provide citizens' groups much greater leverage in dealing with a company.

Realizing both community-based and worker involvement in corporate decisions concerning pollution prevention and technological change may very well require legislation mandating citizen representation or labor-management committees with authority to participate in these decisions (Ashford and Meima 1993). Based on an analysis of the 1991–1992 Toxics Release Inventory (TRI) database—and using the definition of source reduction in the Pollution Prevention Act of 1990 as any practice that "reduces the amount of any hazardous substance, pollutant, or contaminant entering any waste stream or otherwise released into the environment (including fugitive emissions) and reduces the hazards to public health and the environment associated with the release of such substances, pollutants or contaminants," Bunge, Cohen-Rosenthal, et al. (1996) found statistically relevant evidence that manufacturers using a combination of three formal employee participation practices tripled the reduction of emissions over those manufacturers using none of those practices. Source-reduction methods identified for reporting in Section 8.10 on Form R by EPA are listed in Table 7.2. The methods involving employee participation identified by the authors are in boldface type in Table 7.2 and include worker involvement in internal pollution-prevention opportunity audits, participative team management, and employee recommendations. Manufacturers that combined these practices with external pollution-prevention assistance obtained comparable or better results than those that did not.

On a broader scale, green consumers and environmentally minded NGOs (part of a supraorganizational network) may play a part in encouraging green technology development. Hawken, Lovins, et al. (2000) offer the example of Greenpeace's intrepid challenge of Weiss, a Hamburg oil re-refinery that few believed could eliminate its unlicensed discharge into the harbor. Greenpeace activists "got impatient, plugged up the pipe, and announced that the plant had two hours

**TABLE 7.2: TRI FORM R SOURCE-REDUCTION METHODS**

| CODE | SOURCE-REDUCTION METHOD | GROUP |
|------|--------------------------|-------|
| **T01** | **Internal pollution-prevention opportunity audit(s)** | Audits |
| T02 | External pollution-prevention opportunity audit(s) | |
| T03 | Materials balance audits | |
| **T04** | **Participative team management** | Employee-based strategies |
| T05 | Employee recommendation (independent of a formal company program) | |
| **T06** | **Employee recommendation (under a formal company program)** | |
| T07 | State government technical assistance program | External assistance |
| T08 | Federal government technical assistance program | |
| T09 | Trade-association/industry technical assistance program | |
| T10 | Vendor assistance | |
| T11 | Other | – |

Source: Bunge, Cohen-Rosenthal, et al. (1996, p. 11).

to figure out how to clean up before its tanks started overflowing. The plant shut down for half a year, completely redesigning its refining process, and hasn't discharged effluent since" (ibid., p. 65). A more collaborative example is the McDonald's–Environmental Defense Fund partnership, which sought to redesign McDonald's polystyrene food packaging with an environmentally friendly alternative.

Green consumers may be concerned about a number of attributes of a product made by a particular company, including (1) whether the product is manufactured in an environmentally sustainable way, (2) whether its use is energy conserving, (3) whether its disposal is environmentally acceptable, and (4) whether the manufacturing (or disposal) is safe for workers. Directly assessing or verifying claims of being environmentally sustainable or being a green product, however defined, is difficult for consumers (Goleman 2009). Either government or consumers' organizations might have a role to play here by collecting and analyzing appropriate information. Eco-labeling—such as the EnergyStar logo that is placed on energy-efficient appliances—can also be helpful in distinguishing green goods in the marketplace. However, products can be made to look better or worse depending on how the question of environmental impact is framed. For example, the issue of worker impact is often left out of the assessment, resulting in trading better "environmental" performance for worker endangerment.

Government regulators constitute key supraorganizational actors in fostering technological change.

However, whether they interact with the firm in a cooperative manner or act to "force" change makes a difference. The evidence for significant technological change stimulated by cooperative approaches is not impressive. In 1994, the U.S. EPA founded the voluntary Common Sense Initiative (CSI) with the goals of finding "cleaner, cheaper, smarter" ways of reducing pollution and formulating proposed changes in the existing regulatory structure to effectuate them. The CSI succeeded in fostering an ongoing dialogue on issues important to the future development of environmental policy. In this sense, it had a positive impact. But in the end, the bulk of the CSI negotiations reportedly did not focus on pollution-prevention strategies, let alone innovation, and thus fell well below the EPA's original expectations. An independent report issued in 1999 concluded that although there had been a small number of sector-specific modifications, the EPA had made little progress in addressing broad regulatory changes through the CSI, and CSI successes were not being integrated into core EPA programs (Ashford and Caldart 2007). The CSI provides an example of an unsuccessful attempt at institutional innovation.

As mentioned in Section 7.3.2.1, networks can help stimulate innovation and learning but can also serve to inhibit learning and change. An example of the latter in the United States is the Global Climate Coalition, an industry group that has now been disbanded, which actively challenged the science behind climate change and urged U.S. policy makers to oppose the Kyoto Protocol. In the development of EU-level carbon tax regulations, Skea (1993) found great institutional inertia, antagonisms, and paradoxes that led to the design and implementation of suboptimal regulations. One major problem lay within government. Politicians and bureaucrats in Brussels did not communicate; politicians refused to take the initiative, and bureaucrats had little legitimacy with business. As a result, market-based regulation—supposedly in the new spirit of cooperation with business—emerged without the particular features objected to by business, but was met by a confrontation with industry. In this case, established relationships and network inertia hindered organizational innovation and interfered with learning.

At the other end of the spectrum, the cross-sector U.S. Green Building Council (USGBC) is leading a national consensus to produce a new generation of energy-efficient, "green" buildings. The green building standards that the USGBC developed and promulgated are being picked up by local governments; recently they were adopted by the City of Boston for all city-owned buildings. The city sees the standards as a way to stimulate new technology and job creation.[7]

The discussion in this section highlights some of the challenges of creating effective learning collaborations. In the absence of reciprocal trust and open-ended learning processes, it seems that collaborative agreements enforceable by law hold the most potential to achieve significant outcomes.

### 7.3.2.5 Summary

The previous sections have explored the process of innovation and learning in the context of organizations and networks. It is evident that the extent to which networks facilitate firm-based learning that achieves multiple goals through technical and organizational innovation—rather than reinforces prior patterns leading to technological and managerial lock-in and path dependency—depends on a wide range of determinants. This type of learning is not easily programmed and may rely on the competence and strength of participant personalities and network outsiders, as well as the structure of the networks themselves.

The following sections build on several ideas developed throughout Section 7.3 and ask whether organizational learning that leads to evolutionary change is sufficient to make significant progress toward sustainable development. To use the language of Lundvall and Johnson (1994), what is needed is the creation of a "learning economy," where new knowledge continually replaces old and competitive advantage is secured by environmentally innovative and socially conscious firms.

## 7.4 EVOLUTIONARY OR COEVOLUTIONARY TRANSFORMATIONS AND CUSTOMER SATISFACTION AND VALUES

In this section, we examine the importance of organizational factors for evolutionary technological change, driven by customer or social demand. The notion of evolutionary technological change implies that existing rather than new firms or networks are the change agents. In Section 7.5.5, the question whether evolutionary change is sufficient to realize sustainable forms of development is raised. The central issue is the rate at which technological change occurs. In this section, technological change is considered in the context of existing firms and networks that respond to consumer values and demands.

Although Christensen (1997, p. xviii) holds that disrupting technologies "underperform established products in mainstream markets," this may not always be the case for innovations that are disrupting in terms of sustainable development.* For example, hybrid-electric cars like the Toyota Prius—which can be argued to be a disrupting innovation—have performance characteristics similar to those of vehicles in the same class of fuel-efficient sedans. The first hybrid SUV, the Ford Escape Hybrid, which has more than 60 percent greater fuel efficiency than the regular Escape, boasts respectable acceleration performance and has a greater range than its fuel-hungry cousin.[8]

From the perspective of sustainable development and the firm, one could say that the goal is to provide sustainability attributes important to customers through any combination of artifacts (products) and services. Ehrenfeld and Hoffman (1996) write that "sustainability requires paying attention to the nature of . . . artifacts, their creation, use, and what happens to them after their productive lifetime, as well as the context within which they are used."

It is important to clarify the distinction between artifacts (products) that are purchased directly by consumers and those that are purchased indirectly to enable a service to be delivered. The product policy and design community talks about reducing environmental impacts of consumption by shifting from the sale of products to the provision of services. The current literature and policy discussions, including terms like "product as service," often suggest that providing services to customers is generally more sustainable than selling products. This gives the impression that products (generally considered to be material in nature) are substantially different from services (generally considered to be immaterial). But artifacts are always involved, whether a customer owns them or acquires their "services" through other arrangements.†

Given this context, our analysis extends beyond Christensen's definitions to analyze (1) the *means* by which satisfaction is delivered to customers,‡ (2) the *nature* of the satisfaction that is delivered to the customer, and (3) the behavior or values of the customer in relation to the first two factors.

### 7.4.1 The Means of Delivering Satisfaction to Customers

The artifact or service and/or the process by which it is manufactured or delivered can be changed to reduce resources, energy use, and pollution. One could say that this is the *means* by which satisfaction is delivered to customers. As discussed previously, these changes can occur in a way that is technologically disrupting or technologically sustaining. The development of the internal combustion engine, which represents decades of refinement of the same basic concept, provides a good example of sustaining innovation—one that follows the lines along which technology has been developing historically. The hybrid-electric vehicle, which is a break from past technological developments, is an example of one kind of disrupting technological innovation.§

### 7.4.2 The Nature of Customer Satisfaction

Another dimension along which to evaluate a technological innovation is the *nature* of the satisfaction that is delivered to the customer. The innovative new product or service may (1) provide customer satisfac-

---

\* As we discussed in the previous chapter, Christensen uses the term "disrupting" in the context of a customer base that values certain product attributes, and whose changing desires can change the markets for technological variants in products. The context in which we will use the term throughout this book pertains to the product—and also other technological or system changes—from a *technological* as well as a customer-based desirability-of-attribute perspective.

† In a restaurant, a classic *service* provider, the chef uses a stove, food processor, and other tools, just as we might at home, where we purchase and consume food *products* ourselves. The commuter whose car, a *product*, has broken down calls a taxi *service*, which transports the customer using nearly identical technology. Both of these situations contain a mix of artifacts, infrastructure, and an institutional context in which they are em-

ployed. Some services, like airplane transport, require artifacts beyond the means of most consumers, but no one would suggest that they have little environmental impact.

The terms "product" and "service" and related distinctions are ambiguous and mystifying, especially regarding their overall environmental impacts. These two categories are merely different modes of delivering satisfaction, each with its specific set of artifacts, context, and consumer behavior. The conventional terms "products" and "services" have been applied by economists, designers, market researchers, and others to situations where a customer either ends up owning something (a product) or only receives a benefit (a service). It should be clear that sustainability benefits, if they can be found, cannot be associated directly with these distinctions.

‡ Again, *process* changes, while not important to customers, may be demanded by workers and unions.

§ The hybrid-electric car is an example of an "architectural disrupting innovation" involving a new combination of prior advances. Another type of disrupting innovation could be called an "intrinsic disrupting innovation," such as the transistor or the birth control pill, technologies developed along an entirely new and different trajectory from previous market technologies.

tion in essentially the same way, perhaps even without the customer noticing or caring about the innovation; (2) have attributes or qualities that are essentially the same in concept but provide a noticeably different quality or kind of satisfaction; or (3) represent a wholly different way of delivering the desired level of satisfaction. In the first case, the producer does not need to be concerned with significant changes in customer values or behavior. This could involve imperceptible or irrelevant changes in the product, or changes in manufacturing or production processes. In the second and third cases, significant changes in customer behavior and/or values may be required to gain acceptance.

### 7.4.2.1 Innovations That Provide Customer Satisfaction in Essentially the Same Way

An example of the first dimension of change is genetically modified (GM) foods, which confer benefits on farmers through reduced fertilizer and pesticide use, but are indistinguishable to the consumer from non-GM foods. Indeed, in countries like the United States where there are no labeling laws, customers do not even know that they are eating GM foods. Another example of this kind of change is the "green" rubber developed by Nike, which contains 80 percent fewer carcinogens. The outcome of years of product reformulation and testing, green rubber does not even register with customers, despite Nike's attempts to educate them. Even if Nike's customers did know about the company's efforts to green sneaker rubber, they make their purchasing decisions not on environmental considerations but on product performance, which green rubber delivers to the high and exacting specifications of the previous, carcinogen-laden sneaker rubber.

### 7.4.2.2 Innovations That Are the Same in Basic Concept but Differ in Quality of Satisfaction

Ecologically friendly dishwashing soap is an example of an innovation that is the same in basic concept as the original, but differs in the quality of satisfaction. Because of their different product formulations, many ecological dish soaps do not generate the billowy suds that traditional soaps do. Some customers do not mind this difference in product performance, but others do. Recycled-content plastic that is used for decking and park benches is another example. In this case, the products are promoted for their superior attributes compared with wood, for example, low maintenance and durability.

### 7.4.2.3 Innovations That Deliver Customer Satisfaction in a Significantly/Wholly Different Way

A wide range of innovations fall into the third category, where customer satisfaction is provided in a significantly/wholly different manner than before. This involves expanding the design space to include product-service systems rather than incrementally improving existing designs. Here, fresh perspectives on delivering customer satisfaction are explored by inquiring from a fresh perspective how technologies and systems can be designed to deliver products and services with a minimum of resource use and pollution.

For example, bicycle- or car-sharing services are a departure from the privately owned automobile in meeting customers' need to get from one place to another. Likewise, the digital camera is a different way of satisfying customers' desires for photographs. A third example is the new carpet service systems developed by companies like Interface and Milliken. These companies provide service contracts to customers for installing and maintaining their carpets in perpetuity, in theory. The customer's carpets are laid down as carpet tiles. When tiles become worn, they are replaced, and the worn tiles are refurbished or recycled into the original product. This service offering required companies to substitute their traditional carpet products with a new kind of remanufacturable carpet tile and to make changes to their manufacturing processes and customer relations. These changes, in turn, were predicated on a transformation of each company's core business of selling carpet into more of a service model, for which it would be more profitable to eliminate waste from the entire process and to reclaim and reuse the original carpet than simply dispose of it at the end of its life.

Beyond rethinking corporate product-service offerings, entire systems may need to change, for example, substituting rapid public transportation systems and efficient urban layouts for individually operated automobiles and congested highway systems, or changing agricultural growing and distribution systems so that more and better-tasting food is produced locally or regionally without pesticides or herbicides. In the context of carpets, replacing carpets with sustainably-sourced wood flooring would represent a systems change because it would require a radical reconfiguration of raw-materials suppliers, as well as activities related to manufacturing, marketing, sales, maintenance and service provision, and end-of-life treatment.

### 7.4.3 Changes in Customer Behavior and Values

As Christensen has pointed out, disrupting product innovations often appeal to a customer who values a different set of attributes than those the original technology possessed. We argue that for sustainable development innovations, this is true in some instances but not in others. In some cases, if the customer does not or cannot detect (or apparently does not care about) differences in product or service attributes, he or she will adopt technological innovations with little or no change in values or behavior unless costs are significantly greater. This is largely the case for GM foods in the United States. The situation in Europe, on the other hand, is quite different. In the United States, producers of genetically engineered foods were reinforced by their traditional consumer network that these foods would be acceptable, and they therefore ignored a small but vocal and different group of consumers who ultimately became a serious force with which to contend. The values of European consumers have not thus far proved adaptable in the direction of accepting GM foods; in fact, they have gone the other way.

In other cases, a significant change in customer values and/or behavior is required to adopt technological innovations. This is the thesis on which Christensen's definition of disrupting innovation rests: "[Disrupting product technologies] underperform established products in mainstream markets. But they have other features that a few minority (and generally new) customers value. Products based on disrupting technologies are typically cheaper, simpler, smaller, and frequently, more convenient to use" (Christensen 1997, p. xviii). It may be true that disrupting technologies for sustainable development have these positive features, but it is also true that sustainable development innovations can be more expensive, complex, and inconvenient to use, at least at first. This is often because these new products and services internalize negative externalities that would otherwise be borne by the society as a whole. The products and services must either be able to compete on their own merits against traditional competitors or be supported by "minority" customers who value their environmental attributes even if a sacrifice in performance, price, or convenience is required.

What has been said about products can also be said of product-services. However, a shift from satisfying customers by a shift from products to product-services requires much more attention to the marketability and customer acceptance of those changes (Besch 2005).

## 7.5 THE RELATIONSHIP BETWEEN ORGANIZATIONAL LEARNING AND CHANGE AND TECHNOLOGICAL INNOVATION

What do organizational learning and change have to do with technological innovation? In this section, we focus on intraorganizational networks: the firm's organizational structure and the way its groups learn to work together. These factors affect how well the firm can adopt new environmental innovations and generate its own innovations. In order for innovation to occur, actors inside the firm must have the *willingness*, the *opportunity/motivation*, and the *capacity or capability** to innovate (Ashford 1994, 2000). These three elements affect each other, of course, and each is determined by more fundamental factors such as the social and industrial networks in which the firm is embedded and the incentives that are created by government regulation.

### 7.5.1 Willingness

*Willingness* is determined by (1) attitudes toward changes in production in general, (2) an understanding of the problem, (3) knowledge of possible options and solutions, and (4) the ability to evaluate alternatives. Improving factor 3 involves aspects of capacity building by means of the diffusion of information through trade associations, government-sponsored education programs, interfirm contacts, and the like. Changing attitudes toward changes in production (factor 1) often depends on attitudes of managers and on the larger culture and structure of the organization, which may either stifle or encourage innovation and risk taking. Factors 2 and 4 depend on internal intellectual capacities.

In their essay on greening the executive suite, Everett, Mack, et al. (1993) describe the qualities that set "principled risk takers"—that is, people who take unpopular positions on corporate policy in the name of social or environmental values—apart from the "conventional decision makers." The principled risk takers demonstrate (1) behavior that attempts to create harmony between their personal values and business decisions, (2) a high level of personal efficacy, and (3) a greater awareness that they are part of a larger system in which they have an impact. The fol-

---

* Johnson, Edquist, et al. (2003) observe that in the context of third-world development thinking, there is an increased focus on capabilities, rather than resource endowments, as the main instruments and values in development.

lowing story is a demonstration of one manager's high degree of global consciousness.

> Richard, once a rather typical executive in a big construction company, told of enormous change in his life when he began seeing the planet as an integrated whole and consciously considered the meaning of his role as a global manager: "I was called to London to run a division which primarily did overseas work . . . everything from hotels in Jamaica to power stations in Saudi Arabia. . . . A friend in Australia gave me a book called *Limits to Growth*. I had never been involved in any sort of ecological thinking or concerns about the state of the planet. In those days, I traveled first class. I was on a jumbo jet traveling through from Sydney to London, and I went upstairs to the lounge on the jet and for twenty-four hours I just sort of toured the planet. It was a very powerful experience for me, because I realized what I was doing, and what was the whole essence of my life—basically running building projects in the Third World using First World technology—might not be in the best interests of the planet." That realization led Richard to leave the company, spend several years in study and reflection, and finally help create a new business using innovative technologies for solid waste management. (Everett, Mack, et al. 1993, p. 71)

Learning involves not only fact and technique acquisition but also "learning to learn." It is within this framework that new technical and organizational solutions can be found to ensure the future sustainable operation of the firm. Solution-oriented strategies can provide three types of competitive advantage: (1) play the game better by going green and thus enhancing growth; (2) change the rules of the game to the firm's advantage, thus leading to growth and strategic influence; and (3) create an entirely new game (reinvent the corporation), leading to a renewal of the core business. Different managerial mind-sets and corporate cultures characterize companies' responses to environmental challenges, ranging from compliance to pollution prevention to market-based business development. Firms with the last focus tend to be more innovative, solution oriented, and stakeholder based. They also learn how to predict and *lead* the market.

In contrast to the alacrity of principled risk takers and their firms, the syndrome "not in my term of office" describes the lack of enthusiasm of a particular manager (in the firm or government agency) to make changes whose benefits may accrue long after he or she has retired or moved on, and that may require expenditures in the short or near term. This attitude can be prevalent in today's firms oriented to short-term profits, where managers go to great lengths to manipulate quarterly earnings in order to meet expecta-

tions. A study of 401 executives revealed that "80% of survey participants report that they would decrease discretionary spending on R&D, advertising and maintenance[, while] . . . [m]ore than half (55.3%) state that they would delay starting a new project to meet an earnings target, even if such a delay entailed a small sacrifice in value" (J. R. Graham, Harvey, et al. 2005, pp. 15–16). Executives said that they would forgo projects that would boost long-term profitability if it meant missing quarterly earnings estimates; put off equipment maintenance even if it meant costly replacements in the future; and decrease R&D in a potentially down quarter, even if it were adding to the company's net present value (ibid.).

These behaviors are in turn driven by a set of assumptions, including that short-run stock price volatility affects a firm's cost of capital; managers' abilities are judged on the basis of stock price; and they will be fired if the stock price falls and/or they have to answer embarrassing questions from analysts (J. R. Graham, Harvey, et al. 2005). This evidence is consonant with a larger shift in the goal of corporate governance that has been taking place over the past twenty-five years from "retaining and reinvesting" firm wealth to "downsizing and distributing," with a particular emphasis on cutting the size of the labor force in order to increase the return on equity and boost stock prices (O'Sullivan 2000). These trends can be seen as major obstacles to environmental sustainability and sustainable employment goals. One survey of nearly 500 employees at a U.S. Fortune 100 company asked, "What is the most significant constraint to progressing along a sustainable development pathway?" (Zadek 2004). Nearly half the responses were "short-term financial targets." Other responses included "lack of knowledge, lack of technical innovation, competition, and unwillingness to take risks."

The willingness to adopt or create new environmentally sustainable innovations depends on the commitment of management to nurture new approaches that require time and investment and may be at odds with its traditional customer value network. In the current climate, where managers are constrained by system norms that discourage longer-term investments that may not have an overwhelming and immediate business case, it is not surprising that they are rare. Even rarer is the successful development of a disrupting innovation, one that departs from the traditional ways of delivering value to customers and/or threatens to alter fundamental production processes. Often, in instances where firms pursue a dual strategy of supporting a successful product or service line while trying to innovate a new one, the new initiatives are often shortchanged in the allocation of resources and top-flight researchers (Christensen 1997).

## 7.5.2 Opportunity/Motivation

*Opportunity and motivation* involve both supply-side and demand-side factors. On the supply side, technological gaps can exist between the technology currently used in a particular firm and the already-available technology that could be adopted or adapted (known as diffusion or incremental innovation, respectively), or the technology that could be developed (that is, significant sustaining or disrupting innovation). Consciousness of these gaps can prompt firms to change their technology, as can the opportunity for cost savings. Regulatory requirements can also define the changes that will be necessary to remain in the market. On the demand side, three factors can push firms toward technological change, whether through the diffusion of existing technology or through incremental/moderate/radical sustaining innovation: (1) opportunities for cost savings or expansion of sales; (2) public demand for more environmentally sound, ecoefficient, and safer industry; and (3) worker demands and pressures arising from industrial relations concerns. The first factor can result from changes in customer value networks. All these factors, however, may stimulate change too late in the dominant technology firms if new entrants have already seized the opportunity to engage in developing disrupting innovations.

## 7.5.3 Capacity/Capability

Capability or capacity can be enhanced by (1) an understanding of the problem, (2) knowledge of possible options and solutions, (3) the ability to evaluate alternatives, (4) resident/available skills and capabilities to innovate, and (5) access to, and interaction with, outsiders. Knowledge enhancement and learning (2) can be facilitated through deliberate or serendipitous transfer of knowledge from suppliers, customers, trade associations, unions, workers, and other firms, as well from the available literature. The skill base of the firm (4) can be enhanced through educating and training operators, workers, and managers on both a formal and an informal basis, and by deliberate creation of networks and strategic alliances not necessarily confined to a geographic area, nation, or technological regime.

Interaction with outsiders (5) can stimulate more radical and disrupting changes. This last method of enhancing the capacity of firms to undertake tech-

nological change involves new "outsider" firms and stakeholders with which the firm has not traditionally been involved. Capacity to change may also be influenced by the innovativeness (or lack thereof) of the firm as determined by the maturity and technological rigidity of particular product or production lines (Ashford 1994, 2000; Ashford, Ayers, et al. 1985). Some firms find it easier to innovate than others. The heavy, basic industries, which are also sometimes the most polluting, unsafe, and resource-intensive industries, change with great difficulty, especially when core processes are involved. New industries, such as computer manufacturing, can also be polluting, unsafe (for workers), and resource and energy intensive, although conceivably they may find it easier to meet environmental demands.

It has been increasingly argued that *organizational* innovation and learning within the firm, rather than technological innovation per se, is the area most in need of exploitation, especially in Europe (Coriat 1995).* Former Shell executive Arie de Geus, who is widely credited with originating the concept of the "learning organization," has remarked that "the ability to learn faster than your competitors may be the only sustainable competitive advantage" (de Geus 1988, p. 71). In a competitive global context, firms are increasingly finding an underutilized source of competitive advantage in their employees' knowledge and willingness to innovate. Andreasen, Coriat, et al. (1995, pp. 322–323) argue: "The organizational principles and procedures which now underlie the bulk of economic activity follow from past commitments to mass production—to the standardization of product, to the specialization of task, to economies of scale and to a competitive framework narrowly constructed on the basis of price. These competitive attributes have now been supplanted by a new competition in which variety is to the fore, in which product innovation and quality supplement price competition and within which instead of the labor force being seen as a cost to be minimized, it is now recognized as the key competitive asset."

Firms that operate within traditional hierarchical structures find that they are at a disadvantage in capturing the kind of competitive advantage that Andreasen and colleagues and de Geus describe. Some critics point out that corporate culture itself interferes with the learning process. "The prevailing system of management has destroyed our people," said total-

---

* The type of *organizational* innovations that are needed for sustaining innovations may be different from those for disrupting innovations (see later discussion).

quality pioneer W. Edwards Deming. "People are born with intrinsic motivation, self-esteem, dignity, curiosity to learn, joy in learning" (Deming 1990). Deming (1990) claims that the unexamined assumption held by many managers that what cannot be measured cannot be managed has led to an obsession with managing by numbers at the expense of cultivating an organizational environment that stimulates innovation and knowledge creation. Technology, organization, and people combine to influence change. The willingness, opportunity/motivation, and capability/capacity to change all three must be addressed in order to encourage sustainable development. Factor ten (or greater) improvements require radical shifts in production, use, and consumption patterns and are not tied to any particular technological fix. Shifts to product-services, which change the focus from the production of products to the delivery of functions and utility (services), are central to dematerialization, energy deintensification, and the creation of new employment.

The successes of companies like Toyota have inspired many companies to pay more attention to elements such as corporate culture and identity, organizational structure (for example, hierarchical or "flattened"), knowledge creation and circulation within the firm, management style, employee empowerment for decision making, the ability to learn from mistakes, responsiveness to external stimuli, and the capacity to innovate (see Section 7.6 for a detailed discussion of lean-production and "high-performance" work practices). Certainly, changes in management attitudes, capabilities, and incentives are important determinants of the ability of the firm to change and adopt or create new technologies.

With this framing, in the next section we explore three types of environmentally oriented technological changes *within* firms (see Section 7.5.4). These changes are potentially relevant in the context of evolutionary change. In Section 7.5.6, we address more dramatic, disrupting changes that come from *outside* the existing firm or from a firm reinventing itself. We also address the more expansive concept of system changes involving more than a single firm and its supply chain(s). We label these five categories of change types I to V. They are as follows:

Environmentally Oriented Technological Changes within Existing Firms (Section 7.5.4)

I   Changes in internal environmental management practices

II  Adopting and adapting better existing, off-the-shelf technologies (diffusion/ incremental innovation)

III Development of new technologies and new applications of existing technologies by existing firms (mostly involving sustaining innovation)

Environmentally Oriented Technological Changes outside Existing Firms (Section 7.5.6)

IV  Displacement of the problematic technology (product or process) by a new entrant (who mostly develops disrupting innovation)

V   System change necessitating a reorientation or reorganization of industry

## 7.5.4 Environmentally Oriented Evolutionary Technological Changes within Firms

### 7.5.4.1 I—Changes in Internal Environmental Management Practices

The first kind of change occurs when employees adapt to comply with regulations or expected norms using the firm's *existing* organizational structures, routines, products, and processes. This kind of change does not require reconfiguration of the firm's products or processes. In this sense, it is a change that the customer is not aware of because it does not affect the salable product or service. This kind of change often involves better information sharing and knowledge transfer among people *within* the organization, preceded by or following attitudinal changes. An example is building energy commissioning and maintenance, where mechanical and electrical systems are regularly calibrated and maintained to achieve maximum efficient performance. This practice can save 15 to 30 percent of energy use in an average building.[9] This kind of change could be considered tuning or maximizing the use of existing technology. The reporting of toxic chemical emissions required by U.S. community right-to-know legislation has resulted in predominantly good-housekeeping improvements to limit future emissions, rather than fundamental production changes (Ashford and Caldart 2007).

Another example comes from a yogurt-manufacturing plant that was incurring high wastewater-treatment costs. An investigation into the causes of the waste found that a significant source was the small portion of fruit additive that was not extracted from its container by the automated manufacturing system. When workers removed the almost-empty containers to replace them with full ones, they dumped the small remainder portion directly into the wastewater drains in the floor. When the company discovered this, it set up a small collecting bin, which would keep the fruit waste out of the wastewater system. In theory, the fruit waste could be composted as organic waste. It was calculated that this single change would reduce wastewater-treatment costs by up to 50 percent. Unfortunately, the company reportedly was never able to convince its recalcitrant union workers to support the change, and the bin sat empty while employees continued to dump remainder fruit into the floor drains (Parrot 2005). This example underscores the necessity of involving workers, as well as managers, in corporate change.

However, a potential challenge to incorporating employees into the change process is how to overcome bounded rationality—or, to put it another way, how to think outside established ways of doing things. For example, a Dutch chemical firm involved employees from all its activity areas in brainstorming possible solutions to chemical safety problems. The result was the identification of technical approaches easily accessible within the firm, but little diffusion of technologies from outside or innovation was stimulated (Ashford and Zwetsloot 2000; Zwetsloot and Ashford 2003).

### 7.5.4.2 II—Adopting and Adapting Better, Existing Off-the-Shelf Technologies (Diffusion/ Incremental Innovation)

The second kind of innovation involves improving environmental performance by adopting better existing technologies that are proved in the field and are accessible to the firm. In order to make use of such technologies, the firm must change some combination of its products and associated operating or manufacturing processes. This type of change, as in the first type, does not involve any changes in the delivery of customer satisfaction. Many of these changes involve shifting the response of firms from end-of-pipe pollution control to pollution-prevention or clean technologies. In examining the results of mandated requirements to report what pollution-prevention changes firms had made in connection with the reporting of toxic-substances emissions data, the EPA noted that most of those changes involved simple substitutions (EPA 1991).

An example of this kind of change is the automobile industry's switch from traditional wet paint technology to electrostatic powder coating, which both reduced worker exposure and air emissions of volatile organic compounds (VOCs) and saved on material costs. Another example is the installation of sulfur scrubbers on the emissions pipes of coal-fired power plants. The electricity industry is especially cost conscious, and the high price tag of scrubbers, in the

millions of dollars, is a considerable barrier to implementation. Government regulation of air emissions is the primary driver for change in this case, although significant worker or citizen demands could stimulate technological change. Provided that government regulation is not too demanding, the regulated firm often adopts or adapts existing technology to meet new/ existing standards.*

Sometimes, even if a better technology is widely available and carries significant business and environmental benefits, firms resist adopting it because it would require a departure from standard operating practices and/or would trigger higher costs in other areas of the firm. Organizational rigidity and an organizational culture that discourages learning and innovation can prevent the adoption of attractive technologies, even those that are superior in performance and cost. Indeed, a wide range of challenges to technological change can arise throughout the business firm (Ashford 1993, pp. 293–295). They include the following:

1. Technological challenges
   - Skepticism about performance of certain technologies and therefore a reluctance to invest
   - Process inflexibilities

2. Financial challenges
   - Research and development costs of technology
   - Costs related to the risk of process changes with regard to consumer acceptance and product quality
   - Noncomprehensive cost evaluation and cost-benefit analysis, as well as cost calculation methods
   - Lack of understanding and difficulty in predicting future liability costs (for example, the cost of waste disposal)
   - Short-term profitability calculations resulting in low tolerance for longer payback periods of equipment investment
   - Alleged drawback in competitiveness because other companies are not investing in environmentally beneficial technologies
   - Lack of capital investment flexibility due to low profit margin
   - Economies of scale preventing smaller companies from investing in environmentally beneficial technologies

---

* Porter and van der Linde (1995a) tacitly assume that the regulated firm will innovate to comply with regulation and thus gain "first-mover advantage." We term this the "weak" form of the Porter hypothesis. See the discussion in Section 7.5.6.1 of more disruptive/radical change pioneered by others who take over and displace the original product market—the "strong" form of the Porter hypothesis (also see Section 9.4 in Chapter 9).

- Possibilities that investment in process modification can be inefficient for old companies
- Financial (and even technical) commitment of the company to a recent capital investment (such as a wastewater-treatment plant) that limits future investment options
- Actual cost of current technologies masked in operating costs

3. Labor-force-related challenges
   - Inability to manage a technology development program within the company
   - Reluctance to employ trained engineers for the alleged time consuming design of environmentally beneficial technologies
   - Increased management requirements because of implementation of environmentally beneficial technologies

4. Consumer-related challenges
   - Tight product specifications (for example, military purposes)
   - Risk of customer loss if output properties change slightly or if product cannot be delivered for a certain period

5. Supplier-related challenges
   - Lack of supplier support in terms of product/input characteristics, good maintenance service, and expertise in process adjustments

6. Managerial challenges
   - Lack of top management commitment
   - Lack of engineering cooperation to break hierarchical separation of areas of responsibility (for example, production engineers do not cooperate with environmental engineers)
   - Reluctance on principle to initiate change in the company ("Uncle John did it this way; therefore we are doing it the same way!")
   - Lack of education, training, and motivation of employees in good-housekeeping methods or operation and maintenance of environmentally beneficial technologies
   - Lack of expertise of supervisors

This list provides some indication of the organizational inertia that can bound or constrain the actions of a firm even if there is a desire for change.

### 7.5.4.3 III—Development of New Technologies and New Applications of Existing Technologies by Existing Firms (Mostly Involving Sustaining Innovation)

The third kind of innovation is when (1) a firm develops a new technology or (2) applies an existing technology in an innovative way. Sources of innovation include actors in trans- and supraorganizational networks, such as suppliers, consultants, industry asso-

ciations, and academic institutions, among others. This kind of change may implicate one or all three kinds of changes in the delivery of customer satisfaction: (1) where the customer perceives no difference in the product or service; (2) where the customer does perceive a quality difference in what is essentially the same kind of product or service; or (3) where the customer's needs are met in a completely different way.

What would motivate an incumbent firm to make these changes? If the changes are sustaining *product* innovations, the incumbent firm may be motivated to pursue them if there is customer, regulatory, or social demand (see Figure 7.1). However, if the changes required are of the disrupting kind demanded by a nascent customer demand, Christensen (1997) holds that it is doubtful that they will be developed by an incumbent firm. Christensen (1997) provides several factors that could characterize the (rare) successful management of disrupting innovation by the dominant technology firms:

- Managers align the disrupting innovation with the "right" customers.
- The development of those disrupting technologies is placed in an organizational context that is small enough to get excited about small opportunities and small wins, for example, through "spin-offs" or "spin-outs."
- Managers plan to fail early, inexpensively, and perhaps often in the search for the market for a disrupting technology.
- Managers find new markets that value the (new) attributes of the disrupting technologies.

Ensuring that these factors are present makes sense for encouraging the kinds of disrupting innovations described by Christensen (1997) that are outside the core competency of the firm and would otherwise threaten to destroy the market for the firm's main products or services. Christensen uses as examples changes in computer disk size, the evolution of construction equipment from steam shovels to gasoline- and then diesel-powered machines, the impact of hydraulic technology on cable-actuated technology, and leaps in communication technology, such as the development of the telephone.

However, as described in Chapter 6, Christensen's conception of disrupting innovations is different from our definition, which is framed within the context of sustainable development. In our view, demand or requirements for different product or process attributes come not only from evolving customer demand but also from regulation and/or strong societal demand. Examples are regulation-induced changes in the use of bis-phenol A in the plastic liners of canned food and the public demand for a reduction in cell-phone-related traffic accidents by the addition of the attribute of hands-free mobile telephony, not necessarily demanded by cell-phone users themselves.

Disrupting innovations in terms of sustainable development *can* fall inside the core competency of incumbent firms *and* supply the existing customer base. An example given previously is the hybrid-electric vehicle, which was developed and is manufactured by incumbent firms. The vehicle was introduced to the same customers and markets that use the traditional technology; therefore, it is not necessary for firms to develop a new customer base, as Christensen prescribes. In other words, the new "niche market" emerges from the existing customer base.

But what is true for any kind of sustainable development innovation is that it is unlikely to occur for many sustainability goals without either strong social demand or regulation.* Of course, regulatory requirements that are viewed as disruptive by the firm and its managers often require disrupting technological changes. This perception can lead managers of established firms pursuing sustaining innovation to resist regulation and to try to influence the introduction of regulation that can be satisfied by sustaining innovations (if not by diffusion of their existing technologies). This reinforces the view that disrupting innovations are necessary and that the policy instruments chosen to promote sustainable development need to reflect these expectations. This view is discussed further in Section 7.7.

The discussion thus far has been limited largely to consumer products. Changes related to *process* technologies or shifts from products to product-services and system changes may involve a different set of dynamics. Process innovation, which may be invisible to product customers, is likely to occur within existing firms or their suppliers.† In this instance, new product entrants are unlikely to displace the successful incumbent innovator. In addition, workers may be valuable sources of production process

change, as in the case of a large chemical company that sponsored a contest for its workers to submit ideas for energy-saving projects with a return on investment of over 100 percent. Everyone thought that the opportunities for energy savings would be exhausted within a few years, but instead, workers generated more and more project ideas, and the company's annual savings grew from $3 million in 1982 to $37 million at a high point in 1989. People associated with the project now believe that there are "almost an infinite number of projects out there" (Cebon 1993, p. 175).

Two examples of shifts from selling products to selling product-services come to mind: (1) where the original product manufacturer instead sells a service (see the Xerox example below), or (2) where a new entrant sells a service that makes the purchase or lease of a product unnecessary, for example, where the provision of a clothes-cleaning and washing service removes the need to own a washing machine and dryer.

An example of an instance where a major incumbent firm pursued disrupting innovation is the Xerox LAKES program, which in the 1990s set about redefining the industry standard for copy systems. The LAKES goal was to create a multiple-function machine that could copy, print, and scan concurrently, a capability unmatched by the competition. The design also called for remote diagnosis of problems by technicians; units that the customer could replace, reducing downtime; a reduction in parts and the introduction of self-aligning subassemblies, which also reduced the need for mechanical adjustments; and most relevant to our discussion, a self-imposed requirement of "Zero to Landfill"™—a commitment to eliminating waste at every step of the design and to achieve full product recyclability and/or remanufacturability.

> From the beginning, the LAKES program was envisioned as a "clean sheet" design—engineer's jargon for starting, like an artist, with a blank canvas, rather than pursuing progressive refinements of existing products. This meant incorporating new technologies and designs in every major function. Team members would need to be inventors and engineers. They were guided by the idea that this was to be a matrix of hardware, software, facilities, and services—document-based services that would combine to change the way people work, share knowledge, and collaborate. In effect, the mission of the LAKES program was to reinvent copying, transforming it from mere duplication into a true information and knowledge-sharing system. (Hotchkiss, Kelley, et al. 2000, p. 25)

---

* For a more optimistic view that large firms in established product markets can sufficiently transform, see Hamel (2000), Hart and Milstein (1999), and Hart and Sharma (2004). For a further defense of evolutionary transitions, see Rotmans, Kemp, et al. (2001).

† An established supplier may be displaced by a new entrant providing a better process, but the incumbent supplier has every incentive to innovate in order to keep its (privileged) market position.

In the end, the product that Xerox produced is more than 90 percent remanufacturable and 97 percent recyclable.

> Furthermore, the LAKES product continues to be designed in waste-free offices and manufactured in waste-free factories. No part is ever left behind in the customer's office, including packaging. Replaced parts eventually end up with the supplier that produced them, and the assembly is remanufactured according to processes worked out with the supplier as part of the design process. What few parts cannot be remanufactured are recycled. All plastic parts are labeled to facilitate the recycling process. At the end of life, Xerox will take back the entire product. (Hotchkiss, Kelley et al. 2000, p. 29)

Another noteworthy example is the development of formaldehyde-free resin by the resin suppliers to fabric manufacturers making permanent-press fabric to be used in clothing manufacturing.

### 7.5.5 Is Evolutionary Change Enough?

The literature on corporate "sustainability" and corporate social responsibility is replete with examples of proactive environmental behavior of types I, II, and III (discussed above). However, a growing consensus is that although technological and organizational changes like these have produced significant and positive results, they still fall short of sustainable development goals. Many firms put considerable effort into improving or "greening" core business practices and profitable product and service offerings but stop short of completely redesigning or reconfiguring them in line with sustainability goals. Furthermore, even while they have been engaged in greening themselves, firms have continued to oppose regulatory action that would hold them more accountable for their actions. A recent report written in consultation with the UN Global Compact, a group of companies and other groups that have organized around principles for good corporate behavior, summed up the state of corporate responsibility as follows:

> The good news is that many CR [corporate responsibility] initiatives are evolving in the right direction, with a growing variety of companies acknowledging a wider range of stakeholders and acting on an increasing number of key issues. The bad news is that most such initiatives still sit at a distance from the company's core business activities, disengaged from long-term strategy. As a result, even leading companies pursue disjointed and at times conflicting activities, for example lobbying for lower social and environmental standards.

> ... The CR movement has often evolved in the context of weak—or weakening—government leadership. It has made real progress, but is constrained by a lack of appropriate links to wider global, regional and national governance frameworks.

> Equally, few companies have so far sought to create CR-related market opportunities, to evolve relevant new business models or to encourage government policy development and action in line with their stated CR goals. In effect, the current approach to CR may be reaching its system limits. While a small but growing number of bold and visionary companies have made considerable strides and are to be commended for their achievements, their numbers will remain small as long as the business case for getting in front of the corporate pack remains weak.

> So government involvement is going to be crucial. Critically, as some of our respondents noted, and a point we firmly endorse, the challenge is not to get companies to take on the responsibilities of governments but to help ensure governments fulfill their own responsibilities. Our case studies all underscore the crucial roles that governments must play, setting the course, developing incentives and generally helping to create a stronger business case. (SustainAbility 2004, pp. 2–3)

If we recall that a sustainable future requires technological, organizational, institutional, and social/cultural changes, it is likely that an evolutionary pathway is insufficient to achieve the goals of sustainable development. The distinction between incremental and disrupting innovation—be it technological, organizational, institutional, or social—is not simply line drawing along points on a continuum. Incremental innovation generally involves continuous improvements, while radical (that is, disrupting) innovations are discontinuous (C. Freeman 1992), possibly involving displacement of dominant firms and institutions rather than evolutionary transformations (Ashford 1994).

Significant industrial transformations occur less often from dominant technology firms than from new firms that displace existing products, processes, and technologies. This can be seen in examples of significant technological innovations over the last fifty years, including transistors, computers, and polychlorinated biphenyl (PCB) replacements (Ashford 1994, 2000; Ashford and Heaton 1983; Strasser 1997).

It is argued that more disrupting innovation, rather than incremental sustaining innovation, is needed to achieve factor ten (or better) improvements in both resource productivity and pollution reduction (Schmidt-Bleek 1998). Similarly, radical interventions in employment policy may be needed to offset increasing unemployment (for example, in some European countries) and underemployment in the United States. Such improvements require more significant and revolutionary changes (Andersen and Massa 2000; Reijnders 1998). The capacity to change can be the limiting factor—this is often a crucial missing factor in optimistic scenarios. This implies the need for instruments, policies, and targets that are very different from those to foster incremental improvements.

Especially in industries that are "flexible" and always changing their products, we may be justifiably enthusiastic about existing firms' ability to move toward sustainable production. In this case, closer relations with suppliers, customers (or users), and NGOs may be particularly helpful.* But where the product line is "rigid" or mature—as was the case for PCBs, and is the case with other unsustainable technologies—change is not easy, and Schumpeterian revolutionary waves of creative destruction replace the product via new entrants to the market—often necessitated by stringent regulation.

The notion of Schumpeterian creative destruction is aptly expressed in the following passage about BP:

> [Former BP CEO Lord John] Browne . . . [was] trying to prepare BP for the end of the fossil-fuel game—by cutting the emissions of carbon dioxide that it creates while producing oil and gas, by shifting to cleaner fuels like natural gas . . . and ultimately by positioning itself as a producer of alternative and renewable energy: hydrogen, wind, solar.
>
> But whether the company—which made its fortunes in the oil fields of Iran and later on the North Slope of Alaska—can survive the shift to a new energy economy remains an open question. "That's a huge level of wishful thinking," says one American scientist who has advised BP's senior management on climate change and renewable energy. "Of course they say they see themselves that way, and of course they're going to try. But whether they will have any chance of successfully outcompeting newcomers in renewable energy is a very big question. Because historically, once those transformations have happened, the

existing companies have not held the edge. These companies, some of which have existed for a hundred years, are essentially about extracting petroleum. And in a world where you don't extract petroleum anymore, the first order of expectation is that you're dead." (Frey 2002)

The needed transformations may require going beyond product (or process) innovation into the product-service area or may involve system changes. Rigid industries whose processes have remained stagnant also face considerable difficulties in becoming significantly more sustainable. Shifts from products to product-services rely on changes in the use, location, and ownership of products in which mature product manufacturers may participate, but this requires significant changes involving both managerial and social (customer) innovations. Changes in sociotechnological systems, such as transportation or agriculture, are even more difficult (Vellinga and Herb 1999). This suggests that the creative use of law is a more promising strategic instrument for achieving sustainable industrial environmental transformation than the reliance of the more neoliberal forms of ecological modernization on firms' economic self-interest (Andersen and Massa 2000; Mol 1995).

Government has a role to play in providing the opportunity for technological transformation and sustainable development through the setting of clear standards and policy goals while allowing flexible means for industry to achieve those goals—in the spirit of "backcasting" (as opposed to "forecasting" to assess future problems) used in the Netherlands for the Dutch National Environmental Policy Plans (Vergragt and van Grootveld 1994). This approach involves setting long-term goals—as much as fifty years ahead—and putting policies in place to encourage the needed transformations (Keijzers 2000, 2002; Vollenbroek 2002).† Care must be taken to prevent dominant technological regimes from capturing or unduly influencing government regulation or negotiation processes (Ashford, Hafkamp, et al. 2002). New entrants and new technologies must be given a chance to evolve to address environmental problems. Direct support of research and development, tax incentives for investment in sustainable technologies, and other technical assistance initiatives that fall under the rubric of "industrial policy" are

---

* In a study of innovation patterns within existing technological regimes, van de Poel (2003) identifies several mechanisms that can enable and constrain the creation of radical (or disruptive) technology. For example, he finds that firms with *R&D-dependent* innovation patterns are more likely to transform (or disrupt) an existing technological regime than firms that adopt *user-driven* innovation patterns, where the primary focus is to respond to new functional requirements from consumers. On the basis of his analysis, van de Poel (p. 66) argues that the development of radical technological alternatives by incumbent firms (within the existing technological regime) "is an important mechanism in addition to the process of development of alternatives in niches and the introduction of radical innovations by outsiders."

† It has been argued that these transformations or "transitions" can be managed (Rotmans, Kemp, et al. 2001) through "strategic niche management," but others are skeptical about the adequacy of this evolutionary approach (Ashford, Hafkamp, et al. 2002; A. Smith and Kern 2007). See also the discussion in the following chapter.

other areas where government can make a difference (Nelson and Rosenberg 1993). Ideally, an "industrial policy for sustainability" would include provisions relating not only to production and the environment but also to consumption, employment, and trade. Regulatory and other policy design and implementation are largely in the hands of government. The government has to do more than simply serve as a referee or arbiter of competing interests because neither future generations nor future technologies are adequately represented by the existing stakeholders. See Chapter 13 for a fuller discussion.

## 7.5.6 Environmentally Oriented Technological Changes outside Existing Firms

In Section 7.5.4, we discussed three kinds of environmentally oriented technological change within existing firms: (1) when employees adapt or change in order to comply with regulations or expected norms by making the best use of the firm's *existing* organizational structures, routines, and processes; (2) adopting better technologies—those that are already proved elsewhere and in close reach in terms of their availability and the industry's awareness and knowledge of them; and (3) when a firm develops a new technology or applies an existing technology in an innovative way. We also touched on some of the many internal challenges that incumbent firms must overcome to innovate successfully. Challenges are technological, financial, and managerial and also arise from the internal labor force, suppliers, and consumers.

Psychologically and strategically, firms dedicate their talent and resources to established product lines and ways of doing business. Utterback's distinction between competence-enhancing and competence-destroying innovations is useful here (Chandy and Tellis 2000; Tushman and Anderson 1986; Utterback 1987). Firms will invest in innovations that bolster and enhance their core business competency and resist innovations that threaten to destroy it. An automobile firm that is given the right signals from regulators and from social systems will invest in innovation that results in products with better fuel efficiency, fewer toxic chemicals, and enhanced recyclability and reusability at the end of life.

This is sensible for proven and profitable lines of business, but it also means that the incumbent firm has less incentive, financial capital, and managerial and labor commitment to devote to innovation. Automobile firms are unlikely to innovate means of transportation other than the private automobile unless

those innovation centers are housed in a wholly different business unit. Such firms may even resist attempts to move society away from reliance on private auto transportation, such as rail construction and subsidies for mass-transit projects instead of highways. We turn now to the fourth and fifth types of technological change, which involve new actors and new networks of relationships.

### 7.5.6.1 IV—Displacement of a Problematic Technology (Product or Process) by a New Entrant (Who Mostly Develops Disrupting Innovation)

In the fourth kind of technological change, a competing firm or inventor (1) develops a new technology or (2) applies a technology in a different way. For example, the digital camera displaces the traditional camera technology developed by Kodak that relies on film and film developing. Likewise, silicone fluid marketed by Dow-Silicone replaced Monsanto's environmentally regulated and banned PCBs used in transformers.

Van de Poel uses the term "technological regime"—originally coined by Richard Nelson (Nelson and Rosenberg 1993)—to "conceptualize trajectories of technical development and change" (van de Poel 2000, p. 384). In this framework, technical artifacts are understood to have a dual nature, "both a physical object and fulfilling a social [consumer] function." Technical artifacts can be designed to meet requirements and specifications and to achieve certain criteria. These rules are shown to the left of Figure 7.2. Technical artifacts also have a physical structure that can be created by following and using design concepts and tools, respectively. These elements are shown to the right of Figure 7.2. Also, some rules in technological regimes are more general and abstract, while others are specific and explicit. Van de Poel (ibid., p. 386) lists the rules that govern technological regimes as follows:

- Guiding principles are general principles that relate the design of a technology to doctrines and values that are used to legitimate a technological regime and its outcomes.
- Promises and expectations about future technology will, when shared in a technological regime, be translated into more specific requirements for new technology and so guide the development of new artifacts.
- Design criteria define the functions, functional requirements, and boundary conditions to be met by an artifact.
- Design tools are tools used in the design process, like scientific knowledge, design heuristics,

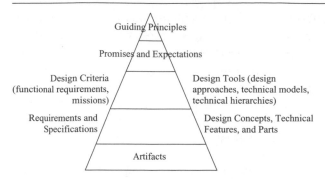

**FIGURE 7.2: THE TRIANGLE OF TECHNICAL DEVELOPMENT**
Source: Adapted from van de Poel (2000, p. 385).

technical models, and design methods and approaches.

- Design concepts are concepts for design of a class of artifacts. Technical features and component parts are characteristics of such artifacts.
- Requirements and specifications are a specification of the more general design criteria.

Firms or inventors that introduce what C. Freeman (1992) and van de Poel (2000) and call "radical" technological changes, which we will call "intrinsic disrupting innovations," deviate from the existing rules of technological regimes. In contrast, insiders usually follow existing rules. Van de Poel (2000) uses the example of the turbojet revolution, where the existing aero-engine community had proposed to exploit the existing aircraft propulsion technology further using piston engines with propellers. It was people outside this community, who held radically different ideas about aircraft propulsion, who in fact initiated the turbojet revolution. This is an example of an *intrinsic* disrupting innovation, not the *architectural* disrupting innovation discussed by Christensen (1997) and Utterback (1987).

As described in Section 7.5.5, gradual, evolutionary change is insufficient for the dramatic reductions in overall resource use and pollution that are needed for the transition to a sustainable economy. Van de Poel's (2000) three types of outsiders—societal pressure groups, engineers and scientists (or entrepreneurs), and outsider firms—all have important roles to play in this transition. Societal pressure groups articulate new functions, design criteria, and requirements. They can encourage the use of technology and promote social experiments that use alternative technologies. Professional engineers and scientists (and entrepreneurs) work on the concept, early prototyping, and design specifications of new technological artifacts, while outsider firms take production to scale in the marketplace.

### 7.5.6.2 V—System Change Necessitating a Reorientation or Reorganization of Industry

Beyond disrupting technological changes that displace product markets, shift the satisfaction of needs from products to providing product-services, or involve process innovation, the approach to meeting a particular societal or consumer demand may involve entire system changes. For example, changes to truly sustainable agriculture may change not only how, where, and by whom crops are grown and transported, but also consumer demand and acceptability. Decentralization of production, crop rotation, changes in pesticide and fertilizer use, and hybridization of crops, both conventional and through bioengineering, may all be involved. Another example of a systems change would be the transformation of industrial systems from reliance on fossil fuels to hydrogen. These kinds of far-reaching changes are discussed by Butter (2002),[10] who considers the role of institutional frameworks, networks, organizations, practices, and guiding principles in stimulating system innovation. His framework is based on evolutionary economics and national innovation systems (NIS)* and focuses on the role government can play in stimulating system change toward sustainable development.

The theories of Butter (2002) and the concept of strategic niche management introduced by Kemp (1994, 1997, 2002; see Section 8.4.2) both rely on the role of government to varying degrees. This raises the critical question: how much government intervention should there be? This issue is addressed in Chapter 8.

Of course, significant technological changes also involve changes in the skills necessary both to develop those changes and to employ new technology in production and services. The next section addresses the relationship between the development of new technologies, or the new application of existing technologies, and the skills and capabilities of employees needed in the firm. We also consider how organizational changes can be structured to create or restructure *employment* as one of several important sustainability goals.

## 7.6 INNOVATION TO STIMULATE EMPLOYMENT

At the core of achieving justice and social inclusion in the globalized economy—an important determi-

---

* See Section 6.4 in Chapter 6 and C. Freeman (1987) and OECD (1996) for a discussion of NIS.

nant of a sustainable economy—is the right of working people and citizens to benefit from industrial transformations. The ultimate governance challenge is to achieve a fair division of the fruits of the industrial or industrializing state, and a safe and healthful environment and workplace. This requires environmental sustainability, but also sufficient job opportunities, job security, and purchasing power, as well as rewarding, meaningful, and safe employment—that is, sustainable employment. Even if concerns of equity were not of paramount importance, inadequate and widely disparate employment opportunities are a source of civil and political instability in both the developed and the industrializing world.

In formulating policies for *environmental* sustainability, economic growth and environmental quality should be optimized simultaneously, rather than having environmental interventions occur after harmful technologies are in place. Employment concerns deserve no less a place in center stage; economic development (competitiveness), environmental quality, and employment must be co-optimized. Systemic changes must be pursued and selected that intentionally benefit employment. In this section, we explore the interrelationship between technology change and organizational changes that can be structured with employment goals in mind. Positive employment goals include work that (1) is safe and gratifying, (2) is adequately remunerative, and (3) meets national employment goals.

### 7.6.1 Wage Inequality and Unemployment

The average worker in the industrialized world has generally suffered from the effects of globalization since about the 1970s. The stylized model of employment trends is that where relative wages are rigid, as in Europe, workers have experienced high unemployment, and where relative wages are flexible, as in the United States, workers have seen a drop in real wages. In wage-flexible countries like the United States and the United Kingdom, income inequality grew throughout the 1980s and 1990s (Diwan and Walton 1997), with the United States earning the distinction of having the third-highest absolute poverty rate among eleven industrialized nations even while it ranked second highest, after Luxembourg, in average annual income (Smeeding, Rainwater, et al. 2001). Even though the U.S. economy expanded during the 1990s, that period was not nearly as strong as past expansions in the 1970s and 1980s. By 1999, average U.S. incomes were only just reaching their 1989 inflation-adjusted levels and were still about 10 per-

cent below the level reached in 1973 (Madrick 1999). The trend of rising inequality is not limited to wage-flexible countries like the United States; research shows that increasing polarization of income distribution has been under way in nearly all advanced industrial economies since the 1980s (R. B. Freeman and Katz 1995; Harrison and Bluestone 1988; Levy 1987).

With regard to levels of employment, unskilled workers have suffered more than skilled workers. In most industrial countries, unemployment rates among unskilled workers have doubled or tripled since the 1970s. The traditional argument is that unemployment is the inevitable outcome when relative wages are not allowed to adjust. But Nickell (1996) points out that Norway, with a rigid labor market, has lower unskilled unemployment than the United States, with a flexible one; and the United Kingdom, with a flexible labor market, has higher unskilled unemployment than most other European economies. His conclusion is that labor-market institutions explain only part of the differential unemployment, and he suggests that countries with low unemployment have better-educated unskilled workers (ibid.).

The causes of rising inequality and unemployment, especially among unskilled workers, are varied, and the relative importance of them is disputed. Most studies make reference to some combination of the use of technology that replaces unskilled labor and requires advanced training and skills; population migration; trade with developing nations; the weakening of unions; and the influx of women and college graduates into the workforce (R. B. Freeman 1996). Most analysts agree that trade, technology, and migration all matter (Diwan and Walton 1997). Research also links inequality with the decline in union membership and power (R. B. Freeman 1996; Katz and Darbishire 2000). See Section 1.1.3.1 for a fuller discussion of the factors that affect wage and income inequality and employment.

### 7.6.2 Working Conditions and Industrial Relations

As discussed in previous sections, companies are realizing that their competitive advantage increasingly depends on harnessing the creativity of their employees. In a globalized world, the uptake of new productivity-enhancing and waste-reducing technologies and the innovation of entirely new technologies depend on a motivated, willing workforce that is flexible, intelligent, and adaptive. Industrial relations has come a long way since the industrial paradigm of the early twentieth century, which saw the rise of Taylorism, with its stark reliance on time and motion studies to determine the "one best method" for performing a given task. In its pure form, which is often associated with the mass Fordist assembly-line production, Taylorism treated with indifference the human being in charge of performing the manual labor. Rather, workers were regarded as impersonal factors of production from whom maximum productivity must be wrung by managers and work system consultants. Turnover was high, but jobs were set up in such a way that workers could learn them quickly, minimizing the costs of replacing people. Absenteeism was high, but temporary replacement workers provided a buffer so production could continue uninterrupted. Motivation was low, but firms relied on close monitoring by supervisors and efficiency wages to stimulate productivity (Macduffie 1995).

Although Taylorism is an extreme form and is not representative of all firms then or now, it is indeed the case that many large organizations, especially until the 1970s, were characterized by hierarchical, authoritarian organizational structures and cultures that left little room for worker creativity and initiative. Workers were not expected to think on the job and were in fact discouraged from doing so (Macduffie 1995). These traditional top-down forms of work organization are now being challenged by the spread of high-performance work systems (HPWSs)—humanistic approaches to work organization that many would consider elements of a good work environment.*

What is exciting firms about HPWSs is that the systems have been associated with higher productivity and improved product quality (see, for example, Ichniowski, Shaw, et al. 1997 and Macduffie 1995). HPWSs are also correlated with superior financial performance, although which is the determinant of the other has not been clearly established (T. Baker 1999). Do firms that are performing better financially adopt HPWSs, or are HPWSs the cause of better financial performance? More research is needed in this area.

In some work settings, HPWSs are combined with changes in the production system itself. "Lean production" is an automated, flexible manufacturing methodology that was originally developed by Toyota.

Lean production encompasses a set of interrelated principles that involve both technology change and innovation in human resources management. Some of these include producing only what the customer needs on the basis of demand pull; reducing inventory and waste; continuous, incremental improvement of the production process; a more flattened organizational structure; and reliance on the ingenuity and initiative of empowered teams of workers, not just those of managers at the top.

A key to the lean-production model is the reduction of buffers like extra inventories and repair space, which are seen as costly for several reasons. First, buffers are a commitment of resources not employed in production. Inventory buffers in particular are costly to store and manage. More important, buffers can hide flaws in the production process. When inventories are large, a defective part can simply be scrapped and replaced, but when inventories are low, as in just-in-time inventory systems, faulty parts draw immediate attention and must be dealt with in order to keep production flowing. In this kind of system, the minimization of buffers serves an information-feedback function, providing valuable information about production problems, which can uncover opportunities to drive errors and waste out of the system. Sophisticated statistical methodologies such as Six Sigma[†] for quality control have been developed for this purpose and are now in widespread use. A big key to making lean production work is worker empowerment and training to handle the quality-control problems that arise in lean production manufacturing.

To summarize, lean-production and other "high-performance" work models, increasingly including those found in the service sector, rely on multiskilled, empowered workers and are "credited both with raising productivity (and thus competitiveness) and with enhancing the quality of workers' daily lives on the job" (Milkman 1998, p. 25).[‡] On the other hand, literature that is critical of these developments has focused primarily on "exposing the exploitative aspects

---

* Jeffrey Pfeffer (1994) offered a set of sixteen practices that characterize a healthy working environment. They include employment security, selectivity in recruiting, high wages, incentive pay, employee ownership, information sharing, participation and empowerment, teams and job redesign, training and skill development, cross-utilization and cross-training, symbolic egalitarianism, wage compression, promotion from within, long-term perspective, measurement of the practices, and the development and communication of an overarching philosophy for the firm and use of the practices.

† Six Sigma is a data-driven, statistically oriented methodology for eliminating defects (driving toward six standard deviations between the mean and the nearest specification limit) in any process—from manufacturing to transactional and from product to service. To achieve Six Sigma, a process must not produce more than 3.4 defects per million opportunities. A "defect" is defined as anything outside customer specifications.

‡ Properly done, lean manufacturing, or the Toyota Production System, has a feedback mechanism that elicits and uses employee-submitted improvement suggestions (innovation) that cut waste. This is argued to be a major strength in this knowledge-driven work system (Betty Barrett, MIT, personal communication, February 2006).

of the changes that have been introduced, arguing that what is touted as workplace democratization is actually a new form of management manipulation and a threat to independent unionism" (ibid., p. 26). Milkman continues:

> The decline in labour's power is an underlying concern in the critical analyses of participation, the "team concept" and "lean production," which have appeared in reaction to the literature advocating such changes. Critics such as Parker and Slaughter (1988) have argued eloquently that what appears as participation is really just a new form of exploitation. (See also Parker and Slaughter (1994); Garrahan and Stewart (1992); Graham (1995); and Babson (1995) for similar critiques.) They stress that innovations like "team concept" sharply increase the pace and pressures of work, despite the rhetoric of worker empowerment. In essence, they argue, such schemes are merely strategies to enhance managerial control, and allow workers to "participate" mainly in the intensification of their own exploitation. "The little influence workers do have over their jobs is that in effect they are organized to time-study themselves," Parker and Slaughter (1988:19) write, noting that participation serves only to mobilize workers' detailed knowledge of the labour process so as to help management speed up production and eliminate wasteful work practices. They label the team concept "management by stress" and emphasize its potential for undermining union power.
>
> This is a trenchant and deservedly influential critique. Yet it overlooks one crucial fact: namely, that workers themselves seem to have a favorable attitude toward the concept of participation. Workers who have experience with both the traditional, authoritarian management approach and with the new, participatory initiative appear to strongly prefer the latter, even if they are critical of it in some respects. (Milkman 1998, p. 31)

Milkman (1998, p. 38) points out that in certain situations, new forms of work organization can have positive benefits for workers, but that in the United States, most firms are following the "low-wage, low-trust, low-skill 'low road'," despite overwhelming evidence that "the 'high road' would serve the long-term interests of both corporations and workers far better." Also, "Most firms continue to employ top-down, authoritarian supervision which constructs workers as objects of suspicion rather than as active contributors to the welfare of the enterprise—a managerial approach that offers fertile soil for downsizing, reducing wages, and avoiding or eliminating unions, but which undermines the possibility of genuine worker participation" (ibid., p. 25). Recall that this is the same participation on which firms are increasingly depending for their global competitive advantage.

Milkman's line of reasoning is related to that of Katz and Darbishire (2000), who argue that the deteriorating situation of workers is linked to the decline of unions and a rise in the variation in employment conditions. Certainly, highly liberalized market economies like the United States and the United Kingdom have seen severe union membership declines, while membership has declined less dramatically in Australia and Italy and even less in Germany and Sweden. But in all countries, there has been a shift to more decentralized forms of bargaining and an accompanying increase in direct communication between employees and managers. During this process, "management has been either circumventing existing union-related negotiation structures or creating alternatives to union representation (such as individual contracts)" (ibid., p. 266).

Table 7.3 summarizes the four patterns of workplace practices, all of which, the authors claim, are becoming more prevalent in industrialized countries. The increased variation in employment systems (a departure from traditional, centralized forms of industrial bargaining) "is directly contributing to the rise in income inequality occurring in most countries" (Katz and Darbishire 2000, p. 280). All four workplace patterns in Table 7.3—"[1] the growth occurring in the relatively low-wage nonunion sector, [2] the low earnings found in the low-wage pattern, [3] the individual pay variation produced by individualized compensation, and [4] the earnings variation produced by contingent compensation schemes"—are argued to be part of the trend of rising income inequality (ibid.). In moving across the four workplace practices (from left to right), there are increasing opportunities to involve employees in organizational learning and involvement to stimulate innovation.

### 7.6.3 Technological Change and Employment

We now turn to the impact of technological change on employment. The specter of "technological unemployment," that is, unemployment caused by labor-saving technology, has haunted workers since the beginning of the Industrial Revolution. The reaction of English workers, led by Ned Ludd, to the new capitalist mode of production in the textile industry was the destruction of machines that threatened their livelihood. Social and economic theorists similarly issue dire evaluations of the impacts of productivity-enhancing technology. Marx warned that by investing in machinery, factory owners would spawn vast numbers of unemployed workers. In the 1940s, Norbert Weiner, a pioneer of computing,

**TABLE 7.3: FOUR PATTERNS OF WORKPLACE PRACTICES**

| | PATTERNS OF WORKPLACE PRACTICES | | | |
|---|---|---|---|---|
| **Industrial Relations Philosophy** | Low wage | Human resource management | Japanese-oriented | Joint team-based |
| **Managerial Prerogatives** | Managerial discretion with informal procedures | Corporate culture and extensive communication | Standardized procedures | Joint decision making |
| **Work Organization** | Hierarchical work relations | Directed teams | Problem-solving teams | Semi-autonomous work groups |
| **Linkage between Work and Pay** | *Low wages with piece rates* | *Above-average wages with contingent pay* | *High pay linked to seniority and performance appraisals* | *High pay with pay-for-knowledge* |
| **Employee Security and Development** | High turnover | Individualized career development | Employment stabilization | Career development |
| **Attitude toward Unions** | Strong anti-union animus | Union substitution | Enterprise unionism | Union and employee involvement |

Source: Adapted from Katz and Darbishire (2000, p. 10); emphasis added.

forecast that computing technology would destroy so many jobs that the Great Depression would pale by comparison. Modern-day economist Jeremy Rifkin, author of *The End of Work*, warns that by the middle of this century, the rich countries will have virtually no need of workers.*

It is true that over the past two hundred years, millions of workers have been replaced by machines. But during the same period, new jobs have grown continuously, as have the real incomes of workers, at least until about the 1970s, when inequality began to grow. Some observers hold that this historical growth in jobs and income occurred as a *result* of technological innovation, not in spite of it (Economist 1995). Many neoliberal economists continue to point to technological change as an engine of economic growth and a source of continually increasing prosperity for the global workforce.

What, then, should we believe? Technological unemployment, or technology as a driver of continual prosperity and employment? On the one hand, the "end-of-work" literature, represented by Jeremy Rifkin's work, focuses on technological innovations that would make workers redundant—the so-called labor-saving effect of technological change. On the other hand, conventional economic thought emphasizes a variety of mechanisms, such as lower prices and cycles of continuous innovation, that spur greater employment prospects and higher standards of living for all workers. Each school of thought carries

threads of the truth, and each undervalues and underestimates the other. Vivarelli (1996, pp. 21–22) summarizes the two poles as follows: "In such a situation, the discussion about the employment consequences of technical change is closer to a stalemate than a fruitful debate. The two positions are extremely apart with respect to their methodologies, aims, and scope; in addition their diffusion is limited to two different pools of people: the 'end of work' literature talk[s] to the general public while the economists talk to academics and policy makers. These two streams of literature do not intercept each other and so we can assert the survival of two opposite orthodoxies: one which is dominant among specialists and policy makers and the other one which is dominant in the general public opinion."

Vivarelli stresses that it is easy to point out the adverse effects of labor-saving innovation, but the indirect effects of technical change and unpredictable job opportunities that can be opened by new products and sectors also have to be taken into account. Piva, Santarelli, et al. (2003) suggest that while skilled workers are generally favored by technological change and workplace reorganization, blue-collar workers are very vulnerable when they are exposed to labor-saving organizational and technological changes. A holistic firm-level strategy (on-the-job training), and extrafirm education and training are prescribed. "In other words," the authors conclude, "only education and training can maximize the joint impact of technological and organizational change on firms' performance and aggregate welfare" (ibid., p. 16).

---

\* See Section 1.1.3.1 in Chapter 1 for a discussion of the impacts of technological change on wages and employment.

There is an attempt to bridge these two different visions of the future in "new growth theory," which asserts that the *combination* of technological, organizational, and social factors more adequately explains growth (and the Solow residual) than R&D, capital, or human investment alone.* This is because greater investment in both physical and human capital may create positive externalities and aggregate economies-of-scale effects rather than simply augment the productivity of labor. Further, it is alleged to lead to more rapid diffusion and adoption of new production methods and techniques.†

In 1992, the OECD was cautious about the conclusiveness of the evidence for new growth theory (OECD 1992, chap. 8). But by 1996, the OECD was enthusiastic about the importance and revolutionary promise of the "knowledge-based economy," arguing that unlike capital investment, the rates of return to investment in education and training seem to increase over time, and further, that industrial networks facilitate the ability of firms to share and combine elements of know-how to even greater advantage (OECD 1996). Thus, through the lens of "knowledge-based" work, the importance of "networks" took on new significance and seemed to provide support for new growth theory. These networks promote interfirm interactive learning and are regarded as important components of "national innovation systems"—the institutions, actors, and practices that influence innovation in general (R. R. Nelson 1996; R. Nelson and Rosenberg 1993). These include not only support for R&D; the training and education of scientists, engineers, entrepreneurs, and managers of technology; more favorable tax treatment of investment; regulations; and support of exports, but also networks involving trade associations, suppliers and other firms, customers, and workers. In the context of new growth theory, these networks are said to effectively compound accumulated knowledge and provide new energy for both growth and employment. To the extent that innovation in the firm involves the increased participation of workers, and those responsible for innovation see workers as more than factors of production, worker know-how and creativity may yield unexpected benefits.[11] Whether "knowledge networks" are important across the board or are useful in a narrower context is an important question to be answered.

An in-depth analysis of technological change and employment undertaken by Edquist, Hommen, et al. (2001) deserves close study. It is generally acknowledged that product innovation usually creates employment and process innovation destroys employment, although there are counteracting forces in both instances. When new products replace old ones, labor-saving processes are usually also used, so net job gains are not certain. Employment opportunities are more likely if the new products are cheaper and consequently (1) command a sufficient increase in demand and units sold or (2) create an increase in disposable income enjoyed by consumers that is spent on other products.

Thus although the immediate effect of new products may be to increase employment, there may be a loss of jobs from the product(s) they replace. Because of the tendency for new production to be more capital intensive (that is, more labor saving), there could easily be a net loss of jobs. Product innovations that neither substitute for an existing product nor are later sold as process innovations have the greatest effect on employment creation.

Sometimes process innovations are commoditized and sold as product innovations. For example, a new polyvinyl chloride (PVC) polymerization process developed in the United States replaced the prior one, which resulted in PVC resin containing too much carcinogenic vinyl chloride monomer. These "new products" are likely to be job destroying.

Process innovation and organizational innovation can have different consequences for employment. The shift to services has a mixed result, depending on whether R&D- intensive manufacturing sectors or knowledge-intensive service sectors are involved. The latter tend to be more employment creating. To quote Edquist, Hommen, et al. (2001, p. 119): "The most important sources of . . . productivity growth [involving fewer workers] are technological or organizational process innovations. While compensation mechanisms can mitigate job losses, they can promote net employment gains only when growth in production (that is, demand) outstrips productivity growth." In sum, "The relation between 'growth' and 'employment' is by no means simple and mechanical. Some kinds of growth create jobs, other kinds destroy jobs, and there is the phenomenon of 'jobless growth.' Economic growth does not automatically or always lead

---

* See Section 3.2.6 in Chapter 3 and the discussion of new growth theory in "Chapter 8: Technology and Economic Growth" in OECD (1992, pp. 167–174). The Solow residual is the part of economic growth that cannot be explained by capital or labor accumulation and is posited by Solow to represent the impact of technological innovation.

† What is missing from this rationalization is the need to reverse the trend of replacing labor with capital, not by merely training and educating workers, but by codesigning work that utilizes both human resources and technological artifacts such that more skilled labor is actually intelligently designed into production and services. This follows the now-old Scandinavian tradition of "socio-technique" of the Tavistock school. See Davis and Taylor (1972). See also Section 7.6.6 for a fuller discussion.

to employment growth and productivity growth normally leads to fewer jobs induced by process innovation. Therefore a general policy of growth will not necessarily create more jobs" (ibid., p. 118).

The analysis offered by Edquist, Hommen, et al. (2001) implies that the most certain pathway to net job creation is to produce more products, with the consequence of more use of materials and energy, which is very likely to increase the environmental footprint of an economy. They do not analyze the possible impact of shifts from products to product-services that could have the effect of both increasing employment and decreasing energy and material use.

### 7.6.4 Values for Sustainable Employment

Now that we have reviewed the global situation of workers and some of the factors that are driving increases in inequality and unemployment, what can be put forth as a set of values and practices that would support a participatory workplace, that would enhance the competitive advantage of firms, and that would satisfy the needs and aspirations of employees as human beings? MIT researchers Osterman, Kochan, Locke, and Piore (2001) led the Task Force on Reconstructing America's Labor Market Institutions, attended by 259 people over three years, which addresses this point directly.

> In our Task Force meetings, we constantly returned to the point that the rhetoric and (to an extent) the practices of the job market have lost their moral grounding. What values reflecting historical values and cultural traditions should we reassert and recommit ourselves to as we update the policies and institutions governing work? We suggest the following for starters:
>
> *Work as a source of dignity:* Work is expected to serve society by providing valued goods and services in an efficient manner. But workers should not be treated merely as commodities. All productive work that improves others' welfare, paid or not, should be accorded respect. Work should be encouraged not only because it is good for the economy but also because it is a manifestation of service to the community for the common good.
>
> *A living wage:* Wages, salaries, and benefits should be sufficient to permit families and individuals to live with dignity and to participate fully in society.
>
> *Diversity and equality of opportunity:* One of the greatest assets of the United States is a diverse population. This diversity should be embraced, not "managed," and all workers, regardless of their origins, must enjoy the same opportunities to develop skills and to gain access to the jobs of their choice.
>
> *Solidarity or social cohesion:* We should focus on achieving the common good for all workers, not just material gain for the individual. A society is only as strong as the solidarity manifest within it. Growing disparities in the incomes of life chances of different members of our society weaken our collective strength and cohesiveness and challenge our sense of fairness. We should take a proactive approach to addressing the needs of the most marginalized workers.
>
> *Voice and participation:* The basic right to freedom of association provides unambiguous support for the right of workers to join unions. We view unions as a positive social and economic institution that helps give workers a voice in regard to their working conditions and a means of achieving their goals at work. But unions are not the only institutions that provide workers with a collective voice. Community and identity groups also play this role in certain contexts. We believe that unions and these other organizations are crucial to enhancing workers' dignity, advancing their interests, and promoting fairness at work (Osterman, Kochan, et al. 2001, pp. 11–12).

These values point to a different way of organizing work than the traditional, hierarchical organizational model or "flattened" models that still view workers as impersonal factors that are to be manipulated for productivity gains. Such a set of principles could guide employers to create workplaces that both value their workers as human beings and tap their creative potential for the competitive edge that is increasingly important for firm survival.

To return for a moment to the HPWS as a potential model for the workplace of the future, the teamwork, job flexibility, and problem-solving orientation of the HPWS potentially provide a richer context for worker gratification than Fordist/Taylorist optimized assembly lines. Human beings are wired for novelty and for learning. Given a challenge, we often rise to meet it, no matter how long our creativity has atrophied from disuse. We are also social creatures who seek out relationships and form complex social structures.

In contrast to neoclassical economists, modern industrial relations theory does assume that workers are more than a labor commodity; they are individual persons who express a desire to engage in meaningful work that involves personal growth and contributes to their self-esteem, as well as providing them with economic and job security. With this in mind, work by the late Alan Fox (1966, 1971, 1974, 1985), a prominent scholar in the field, articulates the difference between a consensus and a power-based model of industrial relations. Workers bring societally shaped expectations and personal needs and goals to the workplace. If managerial behaviors support these needs and goals, the firm can operate on a consensus model. But if employee and managerial interests are at odds with employees' ideas of a legitimate role, work relations will be characterized by power dynamics, necessitating coercion of workers into conforming to managerial orders. Fox's theory of consensus is corroborated by Macduffie's (1995, p. 201) notion that "workers will only contribute their discretionary effort to problem-solving if they believe that their individual interests are aligned with those of the company, and that the company will make a reciprocal investment in their well-being." Macduffie further notes that "flexible production is characterized by . . . 'high commitment' human resource policies [such] as employment security, compensation that is partially contingent on performance, and a reduction of status barriers between managers and workers. The company investment in building worker skills also contributes to this 'psychological contract' of reciprocal commitment" (ibid.).

However, whether HPWSs are on balance good for workers is not entirely clear. On the surface, the HPWS does seem an attractive and humanistic way of organizing work. And clearly, some level of commitment to workers is necessary for the viability of the high-performance work model. But if we remember Milkman (1998), we should note that there is a danger of focusing exclusively on variables like productivity, product quality, machine uptime, and financial performance and ignoring the possibility that a demanding work environment might create additional stress and worker exhaustion. Macduffie (1995, p. 218) himself points out in his study of the success of HPWSs in the auto industry that his research "cannot address the debate about whether flexible production represents 'management by stress.'" He writes, "Critics argue that flexible production plants achieve much of their productivity advantage by 'sweating' workers through a faster work pace, standardized jobs, social control via peer pressure, and stress from a bufferless production system and 'kaizen' efforts that emphasize reductions of labor input. . . . I cannot evaluate the claim that flexible production leads inevitably to 'speedup'—the counterclaim that it requires 'working smarter' more than working harder" (ibid.).

There are few rigorous studies of the impacts of HPWSs. One undertaken by S. Parker (2003) on lean production examined the effects on workers of installing an assembly line in a plant that had never had one before, and introducing lean teams and workflow formalization and standardization. The study showed that employees in all lean-production groups were negatively affected, but those in assembly lines fared the worst, with reduced organizational commitment and role-breadth self-efficacy (a form of proactive behavior) and increased job depression (ibid.). This is an area that requires additional study if the field of industrial relations is to do justice to the "psychological" needs of workers, which scholar Tom Kochan (1980) says should be added to simple economic and job-security needs for consideration by the field of industrial relations.

### 7.6.5 Low-Wage, Cost-Cutting versus Innovation-Driven, Quality Firm Strategy

In Table 7.3, four basic types of firm strategies were presented: low-wage, human resource management, Japanese-oriented, and joint-team-based. In this section, we make an argument against a low-wage strategy and for a quality or innovation-driven strategy at the national macroeconomic level as a means of improving employment prospects and economic competitiveness. Charles and Lehner (1998, p. 222) argue that a "cost-oriented competitiveness policy" is likely to slow down the structural adjustments of advanced economies by motivating companies and whole industries to "remain too long in traditional markets." They write, "Policies aiming at reducing labour costs by means of deregulation, increased labour market flexibility, or cuts in social security systems work in the same direction, as they often remove pressure for productivity growth" (ibid.).

Kleinknecht's (1998) work on the Dutch labor market corroborates that of Charles and Lehner. The Netherlands has achieved reductions in unemployment by focusing on labor-market flexibility, achieving concessions for wage moderation in centralized bargaining, and lowering minimum wages, in particular for young workers. Payroll taxes were also scaled back, especially on low-wage groups. But Kleinknecht argues that lower labor costs may be successful in the short run but harmful to innovation and performance in the long run. The argument for this is that too-modest wage increases, downward wage flexibility, and other attempts to make labor markets more flexible are likely to discourage firms from making investments in productivity-enhancing technology, which will have an overall negative effect on employment and company profits in the global marketplace (ibid.).

There are other features of the Dutch model that deserve emphasis. The Dutch government retained its commitment to providing high levels of education at the high-school level to potential labor-market participants. In addition, wage disparity between high-skilled workers and lower-skilled workers was kept at a minimum through fiscal and tax means. The result was that workers who were better educated than the private sector thought it needed and whose skills were increasingly regarded as valuable by employers were rewarded by higher wages, such that wage disparity actually decreased in the Dutch economy. In contrast, U.S. wage disparity has been much wider historically and has become increasingly so (ter Weel and Kemp 2000).

The Dutch model was seen as the solution to the persistent unemployment in European countries that kept wages and social benefits high. Is there a labor and industrial development policy that can simultaneously keep wages up, unemployment low, and innovation high? Charles and Lehner (1998, p. 223) argue that "the type of innovation which is the key to new employment is one which develops markets in new directions and creates new markets and thus enhances a strong leading-edge economy." As Schumpeter has described, companies in the leading-edge economy can exploit a temporary monopoly resulting from their superior products and services (Schumpeter 1939). As we have already established, advanced-industry economies have already shifted in the last ten to fifteen years from technocentric to anthropocentric production systems—those that capitalize on human intelligence and are designed for continuous improvement and learning. Instead of a cost-driven strategy that calls for reduced labor costs, Charles and Lehner recommend that industrial economies aim for an innovation-driven strategy, which depends on a large number of human interfaces in the company that are likely to produce organizational learning, creativity, new ideas, and well-paying jobs.

At the firm level, Locke and Kochan (1999) differentiate between a cost-based (cutting costs) and a quality strategy for improved competitiveness and argue that the latter has the most positive implications for labor. They also point out that some firms have combined massive layoffs and downsizing with the (later) development of advanced models of labor-management partnership and employee participation. Cost cutting and quality are not mutually exclusive—some firms do them in sequence, and some even try to do them at the same time, although in the process they often destroy and later must try to rebuild the trusting relationships on which a quality strategy depends (ibid., p. 373).

Sisson (1995, pp. 52–53) puts forward a number of interesting hypotheses about the cost-cutting strategy versus the quality strategy that are worthy areas for future research:

- Management in industries with high capital-labor ratios, such as chemicals/pharmaceuticals, is more likely to follow a quality strategy, whereas management in industries with low capital-labor ratios, such as clothing, is more likely to pursue a low-cost strategy.
- Management in companies that have "stuck to their knitting" (to borrow from Peters and Waterman 1982) is more likely to follow a quality strategy, whereas management that is diversified or has become part of diversified companies is more likely to pursue a low-cost strategy.
- Management in companies that practice strategic planning or strategic control from headquarters is more likely to follow a quality strategy, whereas management that relies on financial control is more likely to pursue a low-cost strategy. . . .
- Management in companies belonging to . . . successful clusters of internationally competitive industries is more likely to follow a quality strategy, whereas management in stand-alone companies or companies not part of a successful cluster is more likely to pursue a low-cost strategy. . . .
- Management in general is more likely to be under pressure to adopt a quality strategy in countries where there is a highly centralized trade union movement than where bargaining is decentralized and the power rests in the workplace.
- Management in general is more likely to adopt a quality strategy in countries where there is a high measure of state regulation, especially in the training of workers (e.g., Germany and France), whereas management in relatively unregulated countries such as the United Kingdom and the United States is more likely to follow a low-cost strategy.
- Management in general is more likely to adopt a quality strategy in countries where there is a protected environment (e.g., Germany, France, and Japan), whereas management in countries with a stock market—which puts greater emphasis on short-term profitability and encourages predatorial behavior (e.g., the United States and the United Kingdom)—is more likely to follow a low-cost strategy.

The last point about unions is especially important because firms do not have much control over whether there is a stock market or a high degree of state regulation, but they do have great influence on union formation. Witness the strenuous efforts of one of the most notorious low-wage providers, Wal-Mart, to stifle attempts at union formation. When the meat cutters in one Canadian store began to mobilize for unionization, the company eliminated deli meat products and switched entirely to prepackaged, sliced meat, eliminating all the workers' jobs in one fell swoop. Wal-Mart is also well known and roundly criticized for its rock-bottom wages and meager health insurance coverage, which scholars say transfers health and wage-assistance costs onto taxpayers (Dube and Jacobs 2004).

Wal-Mart's approach is in stark contrast to its cousin Costco, which offers workers an average wage of $17 an hour, over 40 percent higher than its closest competitor, Sam's Club. Costco contributes generously to workers' 401(k) plans and offers workers health insurance after six months on the job (compared with two years at Wal-Mart). Eighty-five percent of Costco's workers have health insurance, compared with less than half at Wal-Mart and Target. Furthermore, Costco has not shut out unions the way Wal-Mart has; the Teamsters Union, for example, represents 14,000 of Costco's 113,000 employees. "They gave us the best agreement of any retailer in the country," said Rome Aloise, the union's chief negotiator with Costco (Greenhouse 2005). Clearly, there are options for treating workers fairly even in the low-wage environment, and unions have an important role to play in compelling firms in that direction. Osterman, Kochan, et al. (2001) sum up the historical role of unions in America and future directions for their growth:

> One of the most important contributions of the American labor movement from the 1930s through much of the postwar period was their success in upgrading the working conditions and living standards of the "unskilled" or "semi-skilled" production workers in the manufacturing sector. That so many auto workers, steel workers, and other workers moved their families into the middle class was no accident of market forces. Econometric studies drawing on national, industry, and company data sets have consistently demonstrated that unions have improved the wages and benefits of workers in entry-level or lower-level jobs and thereby reduced income differentials. Moreover, by negotiating rules governing access to training and internal job ladders (in addition to providing opportunities to take leadership positions in the labor movement), unions helped integrate low-wage workers into the opportunities for upward mobility in the internal labor markets of the time. Therefore, the revival and rebuilding of unions and collective bargaining . . . should be seen as an integral part of a national strategy for addressing both the income and the opportunities that can be created in today's low-income labor markets. However, the strategies unions use to achieve these goals will have to be more varied than in the past, insofar as many low-income workers are scattered in non-standard job

settings, many come from immigrant, racial-minority, and cultural-minority communities, and many lack basic language, social, and behavioral skills needed to succeed in the labor markets. This is one of the reasons we have suggested that unions and community groups work closely together in a variety of political and organizing efforts. (pp. 188–189)

## 7.6.6 Reconceptualizing the Need for Innovation in Approaches to Employment Enhancement

Nations pursuing either performance-driven increases in competitiveness or cost-cutting strategies have articulated a need to increase labor productivity, defined as output per unit (or cost) of labor input.* Labor productivity is only a macroeconomic indicator and hides important details relating to how increases in labor productivity are actually achieved. Labor productivity can be improved in three ways: (1) by utilizing better tools, hardware, software, and manufacturing systems; (2) by increasing workers' skills; and (3) by a better matching of labor with physical and natural capital and with information and communication technologies (ICT).

When strategy 1 is pursued by a firm or a nation, technological unemployment can result, even if skills remain the same, because labor may not be able to demand its former share of production profits since management owns an increased (capital) share of the factors of production. Further, if the adoption of labor-saving technology also involves a deskilling of labor, workers will extract even lower wages. Close analysis of the consequences of pursuing strategy 1 shows that it is not the *productiveness* of labor that has increased, but rather the productiveness of capital.

In contrast, following a national or firm-based strategy that improves the skills of workers, even using the same technological artifacts (strategy 2), will improve both their productiveness and labor productivity. Strategies pursuing skill enhancement should

---

\*      In theory, increasing worker productivity lowers the costs of goods and services, thereby lowering prices and ultimately increasing the demand and sale of goods and services. It can be argued that at least in some markets, more workers may be subsequently hired than displaced as a consequence of needing fewer workers to produce a given quantity of goods and services. If we put aside the potential environmental problems associated with this model of continual throughput and consumption, several important employment-related questions remain. First, are wages increased or reduced following productivity improvements? Second, what are the productivity-related impacts on job tenure and security? Finally, are more jobs created or lost through the productivity gains? The answers to these questions will likely depend on the form of competitiveness—that is, cost-cutting versus innovation driven—pursued by industry.

increase rewards to workers, ceteris paribus, because workers are more valuable to employers. On the other hand, if improvements in technology accompany skill enhancement, these two dynamic factors work in opposite directions. The outcome for wage adjustments may be uncertain. Improvements in workplace technology are inevitable, except perhaps in very low-skilled work, so romanticizing that the pathway to higher wages will be facilitated by skill enhancement alone may not suffice. In addition, labor markets respond to supply and demand dynamics. If no new opportunities for jobs are created, merely increasing the skills of workers may actually lower the wages of skilled workers in some labor markets, because the supply will be increased, but not the opportunities for work.*

Scenario 3—codesigning work that utilizes both human resources and technological artifacts such that more skilled labor is actually intelligently designed into production and services—is not pursued to a significant extent in the United States, Europe, or Asia, although it showed great promise in the 1970s following the Scandinavian tradition of "socio-technique" pioneered by the Tavistock school (see Davis and Taylor 1972). Designing jobs that match labor (that is, human) skills to technology is an area that could yield considerable dividends beyond simply increasing the skills of labor to use technology that was not designed with humans in mind more effectively.

## 7.7 POLICY IMPLICATIONS

The relationship between industrialization and its effects on the environment has captured the serious attention of national governments and international organizations, especially in light of increasing globalization. Sustainability in products, processes, and services has been increasingly emphasized by placing the environment at the center of some industrial transformations—or at least on a par with competitiveness. The key to *environmental* sustainability was recognized early as involving the design and implementation of environmentally sound products, processes, and services, rather than addressing environmental concerns as an afterthought in industrial systems. At the same time at which the environment has become more important in economic policy, European as well as American industrial economies have also begun to pay attention to the restructuring of labor markets to reflect changes brought about by

emerging technologies, new environmental priorities, and globalization. However, policies have been largely reactive rather than proactive toward new job creation and better organization of work.

Just as thinking about the environment before industrial development is planned and implemented is necessary to optimize environmental quality, consideration of labor concerns also requires deliberate and intelligent actions before embarking on industrialization efforts in guiding industrial transformations. We believe that exploring options and opportunities for *co-optimizing* economic development (competitiveness), environmental quality, and labor/employment concerns, all of which have implications for the organization of work, will be one of the most challenging and important issues of the coming decades.

The broad lens of sustainable development needs to refocus on the interrelated concerns of the economy, the environment, and employment. All three are affected by rapid technological change and globalized trade and must be addressed together in a coherent and mutually reinforcing way. In this chapter we have discussed the important difference between a cost-reduction versus an innovation-based strategy for competiveness. While innovation-based markets may take longer to generate sustained economic benefits, they may outlast markets driven by cost-reduction strategies. The consequences for workers may differ as well, with the former approach holding the potential to promote skill enhancement and generate more well-paid and rewording work than the latter. The focus of a nation on trade also has important employment implications. The United States's focus on promoting globalization and expanding markets stands in contrast to the EU approach that focuses more on creating an efficient internal market in which its various members compete on performance. In the United States, wage disparity has grown since the 1970s, whereas in some parts of the EU, notably the Netherlands, wage disparities are much smaller.

The changing global economy, however, presents challenges for all nations as concerns about the number of jobs, job security, wages, and occupational health and safety increase. In the private sector, labor needs a role in choosing and implementing information-based technologies. In the public sector, there is a need to integrate industrial development policies with those of employment, occupational health and safety, and the environment. From the perspective of labor, these require implementation of the *right to know*, the *right to participate*, and the *right to benefit* from industrial transformations. Above all, there needs to be a commitment on the part of government

---

\*　　A failure to appreciate this dynamic can be seen in the work of Robert Reich (1992).

and industry to reconceptualize the relationship between employment and technology, going beyond information-based technological change and redesigning human-technology interfaces that represent new relationships between human capital and technological artifacts. The alternatives are to tolerate increased income and wage inequality and unemployment, implement larger income transfers through expanded welfare, or turn workers into owners by increasing their access to capital for industrial expansion, as suggested by two-factor/binary economics (see Chapter 12).

## 7.8 NOTES

1. See especially the work of Michael Porter and Eric van der Linde (1995a, 1995b).

2. For surveys of organizational theory, see Aldrich and Ruef (2006); Astley and Van de Ven (1983); Baum (2002); Daft (1992); Morgan (1989); Pfeffer (1982); Scott and Davis (2006); and journals such as *Management Science, American Sociological Review, Organization Studies, Journal of Management Studies, Organization Science, International Journal of Organization Theory and Behavior,* and *Annual Review of Sociology.*

3. Ashford and Meima's (1993) framework is similar to the interorganizational-network (ION) model developed by W. E. Baker and Faulkner (2002).

4. See especially Powell (1990) and van de Poel (2000).

5. For an earlier discussion of the role of outsiders in stimulating disrupting (or "competence-destroying") technological change, see Tushman and Anderson (1986).

6. For a good example of a crowdsourcing community, see Cambrian House, www.cambrianhouse.com (accessed May 18, 2010).

7. City of Boston, Office of the Mayor, press release, "Mayor Menino Adopts LEED Green Building Standard for Boston," November 5, 2004.

8. "Road Test: 2005 Toyota RAV4 L vs. 2005 Jeep Liberty CRD 4WD vs. 2005 Ford Escape Hybrid 4WD; In Search of the PC SUV—Hybrid, Turbodiesel, Gas; Which One Will Environmentalists Hate the Least?" *Motor Trend,* March 2005.

9. Western Governors' Association publication on building commissioning, www.westgov.org/wieb/ap2forum/dec2000/commissioning.pdf (accessed May 18, 2010).

10. Also see Butter and Montalvo (2004).

11. For examples of workers assisting their firms in changing technology to meet environmental regulatory requirements, see Kaminski, Bertelli, et al. (1996).

## 7.9 ADDITIONAL READINGS

Edquist, Charles, Leif Hommen, and Maureen McKelvey (2001). *Innovation and Employment: Process versus Product Innovation.* Cheltenham, Edward Elgar.

Faucheux, Sylvie, Isabelle Nicolai, and Martin O'Connor (1998). "Globalization, Competitiveness, Governance and Environment: What Prospects for a Sustainable Development?" *Sustainability and Firms: Technological Change and the Changing Regulatory Environment.* S. Faucheux, J. Gowdy, and I. Nicolai. Cheltenham, Edward Elgar: 13–39.

van de Poel, Ibo (2000). "On the Role of Outsiders in Technical Development." *Technology Analysis and Strategic Management* **12**(3): 383–397.

## 7.10 REFERENCES

Akgün, A. E., G. S. Lynn, et al. (2003). "Organizational Learning: A Socio-cognitive Framework." *Human Relations* **56**(7): 839–868.

Aldrich, H. E., and M. Ruef (2006). *Organizations Evolving.* Thousand Oaks, CA, Sage Publications.

Andersen, M. S., and I. Massa (2000). "Ecological Modernisation: Origins, Dilemmas, and Future Directions." *Journal of Environmental Policy and Planning* **2**(4): 337–345.

Andreasen, L. E., B. Coriat, et al., Eds. (1995). *Europe's Next Step: Organisational Innovation, Competition and Employment.* London, Frank Cass and Co.

Argote, L., and R. Ophir (2002). Intraorganizational Learning. *The Blackwell Companion to Organizations.* J. A. C. Baum. Oxford, Blackwell Publishers: 181–207.

Ashford, N. A. (1993). Understanding Technological Responses of Industrial Firms to Environmental Problems: Implications for Government Policy. *Environmental Strategies for Industry: International Perspectives on Research Needs and Policy Implications.* K. Fischer and J. Schot. Washington, DC, Island Press: 277–307.

Ashford, N. A. (1994). An Innovation-Based Strategy for the Environment. *Worst Things First? The Debate over Risk-Based National Environmental Priorities.* A. M. Finical and D. Golding. Washington, DC, Resources for the Future: 275–314.

Ashford, N. A. (2000). An Innovation-Based Strategy for a Sustainable Environment. *Innovation-Oriented Environmental Regulation: Theoretical Approach and Empirical Analysis.* J. Hemmelskamp, K. Rennings, and F. Leone. New York, Physica-Verlag Heidelberg: 67–107.

Ashford, N. A. (2005). Government and Environmental Innovation in Europe and North America. *Towards Environmental Innovation Systems.* M. Weber and J. Hemmelskamp. Heidelberg, Springer: 159–174. Available at http://dspace.mit.edu/handle/1721.1/41850 (accessed February 11, 2011).

Ashford, N. A., C. Ayers, et al. (1985). "Using Regulation to Change the Market for Innovation." *Harvard Environmental Law Review* **9**(2): 419–466.

Ashford, N. A., and C. C. Caldart (2007). *Environmental Law, Policy, and Economics: Reclaiming the Environmental Agenda.* Cambridge, MA, MIT Press.

Ashford, N. A., W. Hafkamp, et al. (2002). Pathways to Sustainable Industrial Transformations: Cooptimising Competitiveness, Employment, and Environment. Cambridge, MA, Ashford Associates.

Ashford, N. A., and G. R. Heaton (1983). "Regulation and Technological Innovation in the Chemical Industry." *Law and Contemporary Problems* **46**(3): 109–157.

Ashford, N. A., and R. Meima (1993). *Designing the Sustainable Enterprise:* Summary Report of the Second International Research Conference, The Greening of Industry Network, Cambridge, MA, November. Shipley, ERP Environment.

Ashford, N. A., and C. S. Miller (1998). "Low-Level Exposures to Chemicals Challenge Both Science and Regulatory Policy." *Environmental Science and Technology* **32**(21): 508A–509A.

Ashford, N. A., and G. Zwetsloot (2000). "Encouraging Inherently Safer Production in European Firms: A Report from the Field." *Journal of Hazardous Materials* **78**: 123–144.

Astley, W. G., and A. H. Van de Ven (1983). "Central Perspectives and Debates in Organization Theory." *Administrative Science Quarterly* **28**(2): 245–273.

Babson, S., Ed. (1995). *Lean Work: Empowerment and Exploitation in the Global Auto Industry.* Detroit, Wayne State University Press.

Baker, T. (1999). *Doing Well by Doing Good: The Bottom Line on Workplace Practices.* Washington, DC, Economic Policy Institute.

Baker, W. E., and R. R. Faulkner (2002). Interorganizational Networks. *The Blackwell Companion to Organizations.* J. A. C. Baum. Oxford, Blackwell Publishers: 520–540.

Baum, J. A. C., Ed. (2002). *The Blackwell Companion to Organizations.* Oxford, Blackwell Publishers.

Bennear, L. S. (2007). "Are Management-Based Regulations Effective? Evidence from State Pollution Prevention Programs." *Journal of Policy Analysis and Management* **26**(2): 327–348.

Bernstein, R. (2005). "Schröder Calls on Companies to Create Jobs in Germany." *New York Times*, March 28.

Besch, K. (2005). "Product-Service Systems for Office Furniture: Barriers and Opportunities on the European Market." *Journal of Cleaner Production* **13**: 1083–1094.

Bessant, J., R. Kaplinsky, et al. (2003). "Developing Capability through Learning Networks." *Journal of Technology Management and Sustainable Development* **2**(1): 19–38.

Bijker, W. E., T. P. Hughes, et al., Eds. (1987). *The Social Construction of Technological Systems: New Directions in the Sociology and History of Technology.* Cambridge, MA, MIT Press.

Borgatti, S. P., and P. C. Foster (2003). "The Network Paradigm in Organizational Research: A Review and Typology." *Journal of Management* **29**(6): 991–1013.

Bunge, J., E. Cohen-Rosenthal, et al. (1996). "Employee Participation in Pollution Reduction: Preliminary Analysis of the TRI." *Journal of Cleaner Production* **4**(1): 9–16.

Burt, R. S. (1983). *Corporate Profits and Cooptation: Networks of Market Constraints and Directorate Ties in the American Economy.* New York, Academic Press.

Burt, R. S. (2004). "Structural Holes and Good Ideas." *American Journal of Sociology* **110**(2): 349–399.

Butter, M. (2002). A Three Layer Policy Approach for System Innovations. Paper presented at the First Blueprint Workshop, Environmental Innovation Systems, Brussels, January.

Butter, M., and C. Montalvo (2004). Finding Niches in Green Innovation Policy. Paper presented at the Berlin Conference on the Human Dimensions of Global Climate Change, Greening of Policies—Interlinkages and Policy Integration, Berlin, December 3–5.

Callon, M., P. Laredo, et al. (1992). "The Management and Evaluation of Technological Programs and the Dynamics of Techno-economic Networks: The Case of the AFME." *Research Policy* **21**(3): 215–236.

Callon, M., J. Law, et al., Eds. (1986). *Mapping the Dynamics of Science and Technology: Sociology of Science in the Real World.* New York, Macmillan.

Cebon, P. (1993). The Myth of Best Practices: The Context Dependence of Two High-Performing Waste Reduction Programs. *Environmental Strategies for Industry.* K. Fischer and J. Schot. Washington, DC, Island Press: 167–200.

Chandy, R. K., and G. J. Tellis (2000). "The Incumbent's Curse? Incumbency, Size, and Radical Product Innovation." *Journal of Marketing* **64**: 1–17.

Charles, T., and F. Lehner (1998). "Competitiveness and Employment: A Strategic Dilemma for Economic Policy." *Competition and Change* **3**(1/2): 207–236.

Chess, C. (1993). Improving Credibility with Communities: The Organization of Risk Communication Efforts at Two Chemical Plants. Paper presented at the Second International Research Conference of the Greening of Industry Network: Designing the Sustainable Enterprise, Cambridge, MA.

Christensen, C. M. (1997). *The Innovator's Dilemma: When New Technologies Cause Great Fims to Fail.* Cambridge, MA, Harvard Business School Press.

Cohen, W., and D. Levinthal (1990). "Absorptive Capacity: A New Perspective on Learning and Innovation." *Adminstrative Science Quarterly* **35**(1): 128–152.

Colborn, T., D. Dumanowski, et al. (1996). *Our Stolen Future: Are We Threatening Our Own Fertility, Intelligence, and Survival? A Scientific Detective Story.* New York, Dutton Press.

Coriat, B. (1995). Organizational Innovations: The Missing Link in European Competitiveness. *Europe's Next Step: Organisational Innovation, Competition and Employment.* L. E. Andreasen, B. Coriat, F. de Hertog, and R. Kaplinsky. London, Frank Cass and Co.: 3–32.

Cyert, R. M., and J. G. March (1963). *A Behavioral Theory of the Firm.* Englewood Cliffs, NJ, Prentice-Hall.

Daft, R. L. (1992). *Organization Theory and Design.* St. Paul, MN, West Publishing.

Davis, L. E., and J. C. Taylor, Eds. (1972). *Design of Jobs.* Harmondsworth, Penguin Books.

De Geus, A. P. (1988). "Planning as Learning." *Harvard Business Review* **66**(2): 70–74.

Deming, W. E. (1990). *The Fifth Discipline.* P. Senge. New York, Doubleday: Quote from the promotional literature and dust jacket of the book.

Dewulf, A., C. Termeer, et al. (2009). The Value of Theoretical Multiplicity for Steering Transitions towards Sustainability. Paper presented at the First European Conference on Sustainability Transitions, Amsterdam, June 4–6.

Dijkema, G. P. J., P. Ferrão, et al. (2006). "Trends and Opportunities Framing Innovation for Sustainability in the Learning Society." *Technological Forecasting and Social Change* **73**(3): 215–227.

Diwan, I., and M. Walton (1997). "How International Exchange, Technology and Institutions Affect Workers:

An Introduction." *World Bank Economic Review* **11**(1): 1–15.

Doreian, P., and F. N. Stokman, Eds. (1996). "Evolution of Social Networks: Part I. Special Double Issue." *Journal of Mathematical Sociology* **21**(1, 2).

Doreian, P., and F. N. Stokman (2003). "Evolution of Social Networks: Part III. Special Double Issue." *Journal of Mathematical Sociology* **27**(2, 3).

Dube, A., and K. Jacobs (2004). Hidden Cost of Wal-Mart Jobs: Use of Safety Net Programs by Wal-Mart Workers in California. Briefing Paper Series, UC Berkeley Labor Center.

Ebers, M. (1999). The Dynamics of Inter-organizational Relationships. *Research in the Sociology of Organizations, vol. 16, Networks in and around Organizations.* S. B. Andrews and D. Knoke. Stamford, CT, JAI Press: 31–56.

Economist (1995). "A World without Jobs?" *Economist,* February 11, 21–23.

Edquist, C., L. Hommen, et al. (2001). *Innovation and Employment: Process versus Product Innovation.* Cheltenham, Edward Elgar.

Ehrenfeld, J. R., and A. J. Hoffman (1996). Becoming a "Green" Company: Cultural Change and the Learning Process. Working paper. Cambridge, MA, Technology, Business, and Environment Program, MIT.

Ekins, P., C. Folke, et al. (1994). "Trade, Environment and Development: The Issues in Perspective." *Ecological Economics* **9**(1): 1–12.

Elzen, B., B. Enserink, et al. (1996). "Socio-technical Networks: How a Technology Studies Approach May Help to Solve Problems Related to Technical Change." *Social Studies of Science* **26**: 95–141.

Environmental Protection Agency (EPA) (1991). *Pollution Prevention: Progress in Reducing Industrial Pollutants.* EPA 21P-3003. Washington, DC, EPA.

European Commission (EC) (1994). *Growth, Competitiveness, Employment: The Challenges and Ways Forward into the 21st Century.* Brussels, EC.

Everett, M., J. Mack, et al. (1993). Toward Greening in the Executive Suite. *Environmental Strategies for Industry.* K. Fischer and J. Schot. Washington, DC, Island Press: 63–78.

Faucheux, S., I. Nicolai, et al. (1998). Globalization, Competitiveness, Governance, and Environment: What Prospects for a Sustainable Development? *Sustainability and Firms: Technological Change and the Changing Regulatory Environment.* S. Faucheux, J. Gowdy, and I. Nicolai. Cheltenham, Edward Elgar: 13–39.

Fiol, C. M., and M. A. Lyles (1985). "Organizational Learning." *Academy of Management Review* **10**: 803–813.

Fischer, K., and J. Schot, Eds. (1993). *Environmental Strategies for Industry.* Washington, DC, Island Press.

Fox, A. (1966). *Industrial Sociology and Industrial Relations: An Assessment of the Contribution which Industrial Sociology Can Make towards Understanding and Resolving Some of the Problems Now Being Considered by the Royal Commission.* London, Her Majesty's Stationery Office.

Fox, A. (1971). *A Sociology of Work in Industry: Themes and Issues in Modern Sociology.* London, Collier-Macmillan.

Fox, A. (1974). *Beyond Contract: Work, Power and Trust Relations.* London, Faber.

Fox, A. (1985). *History and Heritage: The Social Origins of the British Industrial Relations System.* Winchester, MA, George Allen and Unwin.

Freeman, C. (1987). *Technology Policy and Economic Performance: Lessons from Japan.* London, Pinter.

Freeman, C. (1992). *The Economics of Hope.* London, Pinter.

Freeman, R. B. (1996). "Toward an Apartheid Economy." *Harvard Business Review* **74**(5): 114–121.

Freeman, R. B., and L. F. Katz (1995). Introduction and Summary. *Differences and Changes in Wage Structures.* R. B. Freeman and L. F. Katz. Chicago, University of Chicago Press: 1–24.

Frey, D. (2002). "How Green Is BP?" *New York Times Magazine,* December 8. Available at www.nytimes.com/2002/12/08/magazine/08BP.html (accessed February 1, 2011).

Friedman, M. (1953). *Essays in Positive Economics.* Chicago, University of Chicago Press.

Gabel, H. L., and B. Sinclair-Desgagne (1993). From Market Failure to Organizational Failure. Paper for the Second International Research Conference of the Greening of Industry Network: Designing the Sustainable Enterprise, Cambridge, MA.

Garrahan, P., and P. Stewart (1992). *The Nissan Enigma: Flexibility at Work in a Local Economy.* New York, Mansell Publishing.

Getzner, M. (2002). "The Quantitative and Qualitative Impacts of Clean Technologies on Employment." *Journal of Cleaner Production* **10**(4): 305–319.

Gladwin, T. (1993). Corporate Strategies for a Sustainable Future. *Environmental Strategies for Industry.* K. Fischer and J. Schot. Washington, DC, Island Press: 117–146.

Goleman, D. (2009). *Ecological Intelligence: How Knowing the Hidden Impacts of What We Buy Can Change Everything.* New York, Broadway Business.

Gordon, R. (1995). Globalization, New Production Systems, and the Spatial Division of Labor. *The New Division of Labor: Emerging Forms of Work Organization in International Perspective.* W. Littek and C. Tony. New York, Walter de Gruyter: 161–207.

Graham, J. R., C. R. Harvey, et al. (2005). The Economic Implications of Corporate Financial Reporting. January 11. Available at SSRN, http://papers.ssrn.com/s013/papers.cfm?abstract_id=491627 (accessed January 30, 2011).

Graham, L. (1995). *On the Line at Subaru-Isuzu.* Ithaca, NY, Cornell University Press.

Granovetter, M. (1973). "The Strength of Weak Ties." *American Journal of Sociology* **78**(6): 1360–1380.

Granovetter, M. (1985). "Economic Action and Social Structure: The Problem of Embeddedness." *American Journal of Sociology* **91**(3): 481–510.

Gray, B. (1989). *Collaborating: Finding Common Ground for Multiparty Problems.* San Francisco, Jossey-Bass.

Greenhouse, S. (2005). "How Costco Became the Anti-Wal-Mart." *New York Times,* July 17.

Gulati, R. (1995). "Social Structure and Alliance Formation Patterns: A Longitudinal Analysis." *Administrative Science Quarterly* **40**(4): 619–652.

Gulati, R. (1999). "Network Location and Learning: The Influence of Network Resources and Firm Capabilities on Alliance Formation." *Strategic Management Journal* **20**(5): 397–420.

Gulati, R., and M. Gargiulo (1999). "Where Do Interorganizational Networks Come From?" *American Journal of Sociology* **104**(5): 1439–1493.

Gutowski, T., C. Murphy, et al. (2005). "Environmentally Benign Manufacturing: Observations from Japan, Europe and the United States." *Journal of Cleaner Production* **13**: 1–17.

Hage, J. T. (1965). "An Axiomatic Theory of Organizations." *Administrative Science Quarterly* **10**(3): 289–320.

Hage, J. T. (1999). "Organizational Innovation and Organizational Change." *Annual Review of Sociology* **25**: 597–622.

Hagedoorn, J. (2006). "Understanding the Cross-Level Embededdness of Interfirm Partnership Formation." *Academy of Management Review* **31**(3): 670–680.

Håkansson, H. (1987). *Industrial Technological Development: A Network Approach*. London, Croom Helm.

Håkansson, H. (1989). *Corporate Technological Behaviour: Co-operation and Networks*. London, Routledge.

Håkansson, H., and I. Snehota (1985). *Developing Business Relations in Business Networks*. London, Routledge.

Hall, S., and E. Ingersoll (1993). Leading the Change: Competitive Advantage from Solution-Oriented Strategies. Paper for the Second International Research Conference of the Greening of Industry Network: Designing the Sustainable Enterprise, Cambridge, MA.

Hamel, G. (2000). *Leading the Revolution*. Boston, Harvard Business School Press.

Harrison, B., and B. Bluestone (1988). *The Great U-Turn: Corporate Restructuring and the Polarizing of America*. New York, Basic Books.

Hart, S., and M. B. Milstein (1999). "Global Sustainability and the Creative Destruction of Industries." *Sloan Management Review* **41**(1): 23–33.

Hart, S. L., and S. Sharma (2004). "Engaging Fringe Stakeholders for Competitive Imagination." *Academy of Management Executive* **18**(1): 7–18.

Hawken, P., A. Lovins, et al. (2000). *Natural Capitalism: Creating the Next Industrial Revolution*. Boston, Back Bay Books.

Head, S. (1996). "The New, Ruthless Economy." *New York Review of Books* **43**(4): 47–52.

Hedberg, B. L. T. (1981). How Organizations Learn and Unlearn. *Handbook of Organizational Design*, vol. 1. P. C. Nystrom and W. H. Starbuck. London, Oxford University Press: 8–27.

Hoffman, A. J. (2001). *From Heresy to Dogma: An Institutional History of Corporate Environmentalism*. Stanford, CA, Stanford Business Books.

Hoffman, A. J., and M. J. Ventresca, Eds. (2002). *Organizations, Policy, and the Natural Environment: Institutional and Strategic Perspectives*. Stanford, CA, Stanford University Press.

Hotchkiss, M., C. Kelley, et al. (2000). "The LAKES Story." *Reflections* **1**(4): 24–31.

Huber, G. (1991). "Organizational Learning: The Contributing Processes and the Literatures." *Organization Science* **2**(1): 88–115.

Hunt, C. B., and E. R. Auster (1990). "Proactive Environmental Management: Avoiding the Toxic Trap." *Sloan Management Review* **31**: 7–18.

Huxham, C., and S. Vangen (2005). *Managing to Collaborate*. London, Routledge.

Ichniowski, C., K. Shaw, et al. (1997). "The Effects of Human Resource Management Practices on Productivity: A Study of Steel Finishing Lines." *American Economic Review* **87**(3): 291–313.

Ingram, P. (2002). Interorganizational Learning. *The Blackwell Companion to Organizations*. J. A. C. Baum. Oxford, Blackwell Publishers: 642–663.

Intergovernmental Panel on Climate Change (IPCC) (2007). *Climate Change 2007: The Physical Science Basis. Working Group I Contribution to the Fourth Assessment Report of the Intergovernmental Panel on Climate Change*. Cambridge, Cambridge University Press.

Johnson, B., C. Edquist, et al. (2003). Economic Development and the National System of Innovation Approach. Paper presented at the first Globelics conference, Rio de Janeiro, November.

Johnston, J. S. (2005). Signaling Social Responsibility: On the Law and Economics of Market Incentives for Corporate Environmental Performance. May 11. University of Pennsylvania, Institute for Law & Economic Research Paper 05–16. Available at SSRN, http://ssrn.com/abstract=725103 (accessed January 30, 2011).

Kaminski, M., D. Bertelli, et al. (1996). *Making Change Happen: Six Cases of Companies and Unions Transforming Their Workplaces*. Washington, DC, Work and Technology Institute.

Karkkainen, B. C. (2001). "Information as Environmental Regulation: TRI and Performance Benchmarking, Precursor to a New Paradigm?" *Georgetown Law Journal* **89**: 257–370.

Katz, H. C., and O. Darbishire (2000). *Converging Differences: Worldwide Changes in Employment Systems*. Ithaca, NY, Cornell University Press.

Keijzers, G. (2000). "The Evolution of Dutch Environmental Policy: The Changing Ecological Arena from 1970–2000 and Beyond." *Journal of Cleaner Production* **8**(3): 179–200.

Keijzers, G. (2002). "The Transition to the Sustainable Enterprise." *Journal of Cleaner Production* **10**(4): 349–359.

Kemp, R. (1994). "Technology and Environmental Sustainability: The Problem of Technological Regime Shift." *Futures* **26**(10): 1023–1046.

Kemp, R. (1997). *Environmental Policy and Technical Change: A Comparison of the Technological Impact of Policy Instruments*. Cheltenham, Edward Elgar.

Kemp, R. (2002). Integrating Environmental and Innovation Policies. Paper presented at the International Workshop on Industrial Innovation and Environmental Regulation: Toward an Integrated Approach, Maastricht, September 6–7.

Kemp, R. (2008). Transition Management for Sustainable Consumption and Production. *System Innovation for Sustainability: Perspectives on Radical Changes to Sustainable Consumption and Production*. A. Tukker, M.

Charter, C. Vezzoli, E. Stø, and M. M. Andersen. Sheffield, U.K., Greenleaf Publishing: 369–390.

King, A. and M. Lenox (2000). "Industry Self-Regulation without Sanctions: The Chemical Industry's Responsible Care Program." *Academy of Management Journal* **43**(4): 698–716.

King, A. A., M. J. Lenox, et al. (2005). "The Strategic Use of Decentralized Institutions: Exploring Certification with the ISO 14001 Management Standard." *Academy of Management Journal* **48**(6): 1091–1106.

Kleinknecht, A. (1998). "Commentary: Is Labour Market Flexibility Harmful to Innovation?" *Cambridge Journal of Economics* **22**: 387–396.

Kleinknecht, A., and J. ter Wengel (1998). "The Myth of Economic Globalisation." *Cambridge Journal of Economics* **22**: 637–647.

Klijn, E., and J. Koppenjan (2000). "Public Management and Policy Networks: Foundations of a Network Approach to Governance." *Public Management* **2**(?): 135–158.

Klynveld Peat Marwick Goerdeler (KPMG) (2008). KPMG International Survey of Corporate Responsibility Reporting 2008. Amstelveen, the Netherlands, KPMG International.

Kochan, T. (1980). *Collective Bargaining and Industrial Relations: From Theory to Policy and Practice*. Homewood, IL, Richard Irwin.

Latour, B. (1987). *Science in Action*. Cambridge, MA, Harvard University Press.

Law, J. (1999). *Actor-Network Theory and After*. Oxford, Blackwell Publishers.

Lazonick, W. (1998). Organizational Learning and International Competition. *Globalization, Growth, and Governance: Creating an Innovative Economy*. J. Michie and J. G. Smith. Oxford, Oxford University Press: 204–238.

Lee, J. J., K. Gemba, et al. (2006). "Analyzing the Innovation Process for Environmental Performance Improvement." *Technological Forecasting and Social Change* **73**(3): 290–301.

Levitt, B., and J. March (1988). "Organizational Learning." *Annual Review of Sociology* **14**: 319–340.

Levy, F. (1987). *Dollars and Dreams: The Changing American Income Distribution*. New York, Russell Sage Foundation.

Lewis, S., and D. Henkels (1996). "Good Neighbor Agreements: A Tool for Environmental and Social Justice." *Social Justice* **23**(4): 134–151.

Lindquist, M. (1996). Innovation Networks among Small Firms: The Relative Importance of "Local Environment" over the Innovation Process. 41st ICSB Conference Proceedings, Stockholm, June 17–19.

Locke, R., and T. Kochan (1999). The Transformation of Industrial Relations? A Cross-National Review of the Evidence. *Employment Relations in a Changing World Economy*. R. M. Locke, T. Kochan and M. J. Piore. Cambridge, MA, MIT Press: 359–384.

Luiten, E. E. M. (2001). Beyond Energy Efficiency: Actors, Networks and Government Intervention in the Development of Industrial Process Technologies. PhD dissertation, Utrecht, Utrecht University.

Lundvall, B.-A., and B. Johnson (1994). "The Learning Economy." *Journal of Industry Studies* **1/2**: 23–42.

Lynch, L. (2008). The Adoption and Diffusion of Organizational Innovation: Evidence for the U.S. Economy. Paper presented at the IWER seminar at MIT, October 7.

Lynn, F. M. (1993). Community Advisory Panels: Antecedents and Current Operation within the Chemical Industry. Paper for the Second International Research Conference of the Greening of Industry Network: Designing the Sustainable Enterprise, Cambridge, MA.

Macduffie, J. P. (1995). "Human Resource Bundles and Manufacturing Performance: Organizational Logic and Flexible Production Systems in the World Auto Industry." *Industrial and Labor Relations Review* **48**(2): 197–221.

MacKenzie, D. A., and J. Wajcman, Eds. (1999). *The Social Shaping of Technology*. 2nd ed. Buckingham, Open University Press.

Madrick, J. (1999). "How New Is the New Economy?" *New York Review of Books* **46**(14): 42–50.

March, J. (1991). "Exploration and Exploitation in Organizational Learning." *Organization Science* **2**(1): 71–87.

March, J. G., and J. Olsen (1976). *Ambiguity and Choice in Organizations*. Bergen, Norway, Universitetsforlaget.

McDonough, W., and M. Braungart (1998). "The NEXT Industrial Revolution." *Atlantic Monthly* **282**(4): 82–92.

Meadows, D. H., D. L. Meadows, et al. (1992). *Beyond the Limits: Confronting Global Collapse, Envisioning a Sustainable Future*. Post Mills, VT, Chelsea Green Publishing Co.

Meadows, D. H., J. Randers, et al. (2004). *Limits to Growth: The 30-Year Update*. White River Junction, VT, Chelsea Green Publishing Co.

Milkman, R. (1998). The New American Workplace: High Road or Low Road? *Workplaces of the Future*. P. Thompson and C. Warhurst. London, Macmillan Business: 25–39.

Miller, D. (1996). "A Preliminary Typology of Organizational Learning." *Journal of Management* **22**(3): 485–505.

Miner, A. S., J. Y. Kim, et al. (1999). "Fruits of Failure: Organizational Failure and Population-Level Learning." *Advances in Strategic Management* **16**: 187–220.

Mol, A. P. J. (1995). *The Refinement of Production: Ecological Modernization Theory and the Chemical Industry*. Utrecht, Van Arkel.

Moors, E. H. M. (2000). Metal Making in Motion: Technology Choices for Sustainable Metals Production. PhD dissertation, Delft, Delft University of Technology.

Morgan, G. (1989). *Creative Organization Theory: A Resource Book*. London, Sage Publications.

Mulder, K. F. (1992). Choosing the Corporate Future: Technology Networks and Choice Concerning the Creation of High Performance Fiber Technology. PhD dissertation, University of Groningen, the Netherlands.

Murdock, B. S., and K. Sexton (2002). "Promoting Pollution Prevention through Community-Industry Dialogues: The Good Neighbor Model in Minnesota." *Environmental Science and Technology* **36**(10): 2130–2137.

Navarro, P. (2008). *The Coming China Wars: Where They Will Be Fought, How They Can Be Won*. Rev. and exp. ed. Upper Saddle River, NJ, FT Press.

Nelson, R. R. (1996). *The Sources of Economic Growth*. Cambridge, MA, Harvard University Press.

Nelson, R. R., and N. Rosenberg (1993). Technical Innovation and National Systems. *National Innovation Systems: A Comparative Analysis*. R. R. Nelson. Oxford, Oxford University Press: 3–21.

Nickell, S. J. (1996). Unemployment and Wages in Europe and North America. Leverhulme Trust Programme on the Labour Market Consequences of Technical and Structural Change, Discussion Paper 6, Oxford University.

Noorderhaven, N. G., C. I. Koen, et al. (2002). Organizational Culture and Network Embeddedness. Discussion Paper 91, Tilburg University, Center for Economic Research.

Organisation for Economic Co-operation and Development (OECD) (1992). *Technology and Economy: The Key Relationships*. Paris, OECD.

OECD (1996). *The Knowledge-Based Economy*. Paris, OECD.

Osterman, P., T. A. Kochan, et al. (2001). *Working in America: A Blueprint for the New Labor Market*. Cambridge, MA, MIT Press.

O'Sullivan, M. (1998). Sustainable Prosperity, Coporate Governance, and Innovation in Europe. *Globalization, Growth, and Governance: Creating an Innovative Economy*. J. Michie and J. G. Smith. Oxford, Oxford University Press: 180–203.

O'Sullivan, M. (2000). *Contests for Corporate Control: Corporate Governance and Economic Performance in the United States and Germany*. Oxford, Oxford University Press.

Parker, M., and J. Slaughter (1988). *Choosing Sides: Unions and the Team Concept*. Boston, South End Press.

Parker, M., and J. Slaughter (1994). *Working Smart: A Union Guide to Participation Programs and Reengineering*. Detroit, Labour Notes.

Parker, S. (2003). "Longitudinal Effects of Lean Production on Employee Outcomes and the Mediating Role of Work Characteristics." *Journal of Applied Psychology* **88**(4): 620–634.

Parrot, K. (2005). *Personal Consulting Experience*. Cambridge, MA, MIT Press.

Peters, T. J., and R. H. Waterman (1982). *In Search of Excellence: Lessons from America's Best Run Companies*. New York, Harper and Row.

Pfeffer, J. (1982). *Organizations and Organization Theory*. Boston, Pitman.

Pfeffer, J. (1994). *The Human Equation: Building Profits by Putting People First*. Cambridge, MA, Harvard Business School Press.

Pinch, T. J., and W. E. Bijker (1984). "The Social Construction of Facts and Artefacts: Or How the Sociology of Science and the Sociology of Technology Might Benefit Each Other." *Social Studies of Science* **14**: 399–441.

Piva, M., E. Santarelli, et al. (2003). The Skill Bias Effect of Technological and Organizational Change: Evidence and Policy Implications. Discussion Paper 934, Institute for the Study of Labor, Bonn.

Porter, M. E., and C. van der Linde (1995a). "Green and Competitive: Ending the Stalemate." *Harvard Business Review* **73**(5): 120–134.

Porter, M. E., and C. van der Linde (1995b). "Towards a New Conceptualization of the Environment-Competitiveness Relationship." *Journal of Economic Perspectives* **9**(4): 97–118.

Powell, W. W. (1990). "Neither Market nor Hierarchy: Network Forms of Organization." *Research in Organizational Behavior* **12**: 295–336.

Powell, W. W., K. W. Koput, et al. (1996). "Interorganizational Collaboration and the Locus of Innovation: Networks of Learning in Biotechnology." *Administrative Science Quarterly* **41**: 116–145.

Powell, W. W., D. R. White, et al. (2005). "Network Dynamics and Field Evolution: The Growth of Interorganizational Collaboration in the Life Sciences." *American Journal of Sociology* **110**(4): 1132–1205.

Reich, R. B. (1992). *The Work of Nations: Preparing Ourselves for 21st-Century Capitalism*. New York, Vintage Books.

Reijnders, L. (1998). "The Factor X Debate: Setting Targets for Eco-efficiency." *Journal of Industrial Ecology* **2**(1): 13–22.

Rennings, K. (1998). Towards a Theory and Policy of Eco-innovation: Neoclassical and (Co-)Evolutionary Perspectives. ZEW Discussion Paper 98–24, Centre for European Economic Research (ZEW), Mannheim.

Rennings, K. (2000). "Redefining Innovation—Eco-innovation Research and the Contribution from Ecological Economics." *Ecological Economics* **32**: 319–332.

Rest, K. M., and S. Krimsky (1993). Communicating with the Public at the Local Level: The Role of Local Emergency Planning Committees (LEPCs) in Community Right-to-Know. Paper for the Second International Research Conference of the Greening of Industry Network: Designing the Sustainable Enterprise, Cambridge, MA.

Rifkin, J. (2004). *The End of Work: The Decline of the Global Labor Force and the Dawn of the Post-market Era*. New York, G. P. Putnam's Sons.

Roome, N., and S. Clarke (1993). Towards Management of Environmentally Sensitive Technology: A Typology of Collaboration. Paper for the Second International Research Conference of the Greening of Industry Network: Designing the Sustainable Enterprise, Cambridge, MA.

Rotmans, J., R. Kemp, et al. (2001). "More Evolution than Revolution: Transition Management in Public Policy." *Foresight* **3**(1): 015–031.

Schmidheiny, S. (1992). *Changing Course: A Global Business Perspective on Development and the Environment*. Cambridge, MA, MIT Press.

Schmidt-Bleek, F. (1998). *Das MIPS-Konzept*. München, Droemer-Knaur-Verlag.

Schulz, M. (2002). Organizational Learning. *The Blackwell Companion to Organizations*. J. A. C. Baum. Oxford, Blackwell Publishers: 415–441.

Schumpeter, J. A. (1939). *Business Cycles: A Theoretical, Historical, and Statistical Analysis of the Capitalist Process*. New York, McGraw-Hill.

Scott, R. W., and G. F. Davis (2006). *Organizations and Organizing: Rational, Natural, and Open Systems*. Upper Saddle River, NJ, Prentice Hall.

Sheffi, Y. (2007). *The Resilient Enterprise*. Cambridge, MA, MIT Press.

Shrivastava, P. (1983). "A Typology of Organizational Learning Systems." *Journal of Management Studies* **20**: 1–28.

Sisson, K. (1995). Change and Continuity in British Industrial Relations: "Strategic Choice" or "Muddling Through"? *Employment Relations in a Changing World Economy*. R. M. Locke, T. Kochan, and M. J. Piore. Cambridge, MA, MIT Press: 33–58.

Skea, J. (1993). Business and the Genesis of the European Carbon Tax Proposal. Paper for the Second International Research Conference of the Greening of Industry Network: Designing the Sustainable Enterprise, Cambridge, MA.

Smeeding, T. M., L. Rainwater, et al. (2001). United States Poverty in a Cross-National Context. *Understanding Poverty*. S. H. Danziger and R. H. Haveman. Cambridge, MA, Harvard University Press: 162–189.

Smith, A., and F. Kern (2007). The Transitions Discourse in the Ecological Modernisation of the Netherlands. Working Paper, SPRU (Science and Technology Policy Research), University of Sussex, U.K.

Smith, C. (2001). "Pesticide Exports from U.S. Ports, 1997–2000." *International Journal of Occupational Environmental Health* **7**(4): 266–274.

Smith, M. R., and L. Marx, Eds. (1994). *Does Technology Drive History? The Dilemma of Technological Determinism*. Cambridge, MA, MIT Press.

Sorensen, J., and T. Stuart (2000). "Aging, Obsolescence, and Organizational Innovation." *Adminstrative Science Quarterly* **45**(1): 81–112.

Stokman, F. N., and P. Doreian, Eds. (2001). "Evolution of Social Networks: Part II. Special Issue." *Journal of Mathematical Sociology* **23**(1).

Stoughton, M. (1996). Institutional Development Strategies to Facilitate Technology Transfer and Cooperation. Manuscript, MIT Technology, Management, and Policy Program, Cambridge, MA.

Strasser, K. A. (1997). "Cleaner Technology, Pollution Prevention and Environmental Regulation." *Fordham Environmental Law Journal* **9**(1): 1–106.

Sturgeon, T. J. (2000). Turnkey Production Networks : The Organizational Delinking of Production from Innovation. *New Product Development and Production Networks: Global Industrial Experience*. U. Ju®rgens. Berlin, Springer: 67–85.

SustainAbility (2004). Gearing Up from Corporate Responsibility to Good Governance and Scalable Solutions. London, SustainAbility.

ter Weel, B., and R. Kemp (2000). The Dutch Labour Market and the New Economy. Report for the project Pathways to Sustainable Industrial Transformations: Co-optimising Competitiveness, Employment, and Environment. Maastricht, MERIT.

Tomer, J. F. (1992). "The Human Firm in the Natural Environment: A Socio-economic Analysis of Its Behavior." *Ecological Economics* **6**(2): 119–138.

Tushman, M. L., and P. Anderson (1986). "Technological Discontinuities and Organizational Environments." *Administrative Science Quarterly* **31**: 439–465.

Utterback, J. M. (1987). Innovation and Industrial Evolution in Manufacturing Industries. *Technology and Global Industry: Companies and Nations in the World Economy*. B. R. Guile and H. Brooks. Washington, DC, National Academy Press: 16–48.

Uzzi, B. (1997). "Social Structure and Competition in Interfirm Networks: The Paradox of Embeddedness." *Administrative Science Quarterly* **42**: 35–67.

Uzzi, B. (2000). "The Sources and Consequences of Embeddedness for the Economic Performance of Organizations: The Network Effect." *American Sociological Review* **61**(4): 674–698.

van de Bunt, G. G., and P. Groenewegen (2007). "An Actor-Oriented Dynamic Network Approach: The Case of Interorganizational Network Evolution." *Organizational Research Methods* **10**(3): 463–482.

van de Poel, I. (2000). "On the Role of Outsiders in Technical Development." *Technology Analysis and Strategic Management* **12**(3): 383–397.

van de Poel, I. R. (2003). "The Transformation of Technological Regimes." *Research Policy* **32**: 49–68.

Vellinga, P., and N. Herb (1999). Industrial Transformation Science Plan. IHDP Report 12. Bonn, Germany, International Human Dimensions Programme on Global Environmental Change.

Vergragt, P. J., and G. van Grootveld (1994). "Sustainable Technology Development in the Netherlands: The First Phase of the Dutch STD Programme." *Journal of Cleaner Production* **2**(3–4): 133–139.

Vivarelli, M. (1996). Technical Change and Employment: A Twofold Critique. Paper presented at the TSER Conference on Technology, Economic Integration and Social Cohesion, Paris, November 22–23.

Vogel, D. (2003). "The Hare and the Tortoise Revisited: The New Politics of Consumer and Environmental Regulation in Europe." *British Journal of Political Science* **33**(4): 557–580.

Vollenbroek, F. A. (2002). "Sustainable Development and the Challenge of Innovation." *Journal of Cleaner Production* **10**(3): 215–223.

Waddell, S. (2005). *Societal Learning and Change: How Governments, Business and Civil Society Are Creating Solutions to Complex Multi-stakeholder Problems*. Sheffield, U.K., Greenleaf Publishing.

Williams, H. E., J. Medhurst, et al. (1993). Corporate Strategies for a Sustainable Future. *Environmental Strategies for Industry*. K. Fischer and J. Schot. Washington, DC, Island Press: 117–146.

Williams, R., and D. Edge (1996). "The Social Shaping of Technology." *Research Policy* **25**(6): 865–899.

Zadek, S. (2004). Presentation to MIT Class in Leadership Lab for Corporate Social Responsibility, April.

Zammuto, R. F., and E. J. O'Connor (1992). "Gaining Advanced Manufacturing Technologies' Benefits: The Roles of Organization Design and Culture." *Academy of Management Review* **17**(4): 701–728.

Zwetsloot, G. I. J. M., and N. A. Ashford (2003). "The Feasibility of Encouraging Inherently Safer Production in Industrial Firms." *Safety Science* **41**(2–3): 219–240.

# 8

# Government Policies to Foster Innovation, Economic Growth, and Employment

## 8.1 INTRODUCTION

We have argued earlier that technological innovation is essential for achieving sustainable development. More specifically, that innovation can be focused on improving (1) production processes, products, product-services, and services (that is, competitiveness); (2) the environment (through environmental technology or the prevention of pollution at the source); and (3) employment (through the design of better sociotechnical systems). In Chapter 9, we discuss nation-based policies for achieving environmental sustainability. Here, we address various approaches to industrial policy to improve competitiveness and employment.

Government policy to foster innovation for competitiveness can take various forms:

1. It can provide a suitable business and financial environment through the general support of physical infrastructure (for example, transportation systems) and legal infrastructure (for example, patents) for entrepreneurs and the private sector to flourish.

2. It can inject itself more intrusively into the innovation process by providing federal support for science and new product development (for example, pharmaceuticals, computers, aircraft, nanotechnology, and biotechnology in universities and government research institutions/laboratories and military research), which can then be handed off to the private sector for commercialization.

3. It can actively manage evolutionary change in industrial firms by a series of financial and market incentives.

4. It can create future mandatory targets for performance and operation that may be beyond the current capacity of incumbent firms (for example, by

requiring more efficient internal combustion engines through fuel economy standards).

These alternative approaches are listed in an increasing entente of intervention and discussed in this chapter.

Chapter 5 attempted to provide a broad overview of the challenges to sustainability policy posed by the complex interdependencies among *the environment*, *work*, and *the economy* (the three pillars of sustainability), and the current state of and changes in the international economy (globalization) that, owing to these interdependencies, have strong, linked effects on each of the pillars.

Articulating policy approaches to sustainability, however, requires more than an understanding of the *challenges* to sustainability posed by the international context. Integrated sustainability policies must use, alter, or supplant existing policies (and the institutions that administer them) in the areas of the economy, the environment, and work. Thus knowledge of the existing policy tool set and institutions is necessary.

Therefore, in this and the following chapter, we turn to a comparative examination of *national* policies with regard to each element of the sustainability tripod. In this chapter, we focus on promoting economic prosperity and economic development (emphasizing technological aspects) *and* employment (specifically, the aspect of "work" related to labor as one of an economy's many factor endowments). Hence we here address many aspects of traditional "industrial policy." The next chapter focuses on governmental initiatives to improve workplace conditions—the other half of employment issues—*and* the environment.

Where appropriate, we shall also examine the theoretical models underlying the application of policy. A relevant question is how policy prescriptions change when a different, sustainability-oriented model forms the basis for a policy intervention. In previous chapters, we have stressed that achieving sustainability is an *integrative* process and have explicitly acknowledged the difficulties involved in presenting different elements of the literature separately. Unfortunately, there is little difficulty in separately examining the established policy approaches with regard to the economy, the environment, and work. Historically, these areas have been treated quite separately, and this feature represents a significant obstacle to achieving sustainability.

In Chapter 3, we focused on the importance of technology in achieving economic prosperity and economic development, and that focus is maintained in this chapter. We recall that the focus of the literature on technology is often divided between Northern and Southern economies. In the Northern economies, the focus of policy is on promoting innovation and accelerated diffusion of new technologies. In the Southern economies, the focus is more on the acquisition of technological capabilities to locate, use, and adapt existing technology (that is, diffusion or incremental innovation), and less on moderate or radical innovation. This is consistent with the dominant view that the competitive advantage of "developed" economies lies in innovation and in high-value-added technological "frontier" activities, whereas late-developing countries tend to achieve economic transformation as technological followers, without the benefit of innovative technologies.* However, innovative approaches need not be limited to technological changes. Organizational, institutional, and societal innovations may originate in developing nations. We give significant attention to the impact of globalization on policy making and the policy environment in both types of economies.

## 8.2 TYPES OF TECHNOLOGICAL CHANGE AND SUSTAINING AND DISRUPTING INNOVATION†

The increasing pace at which new technology is being adopted by societies is having the effect of stimulating still more rapid technological change. Today, technological innovation drives high-technology industries in many industrialized nations. The desire to provide customers with new and better products and services—or to reduce/eliminate negative externalities associated with the use or manufacture of products/services—means that companies are pitched in a constant battle to be the first to bring the latest technologies to market. In this environment, companies that rely on incremental innovation can see their markets disappear as new radical (disrupting) innovations enter and displace their products from the marketplace. The purpose of this section is to look at the process of technological change and innovation and ask what types of changes are necessary to transform systems toward sustainable development. Further, this section considers how these changes might be affected by supply- and demand-side policies.

---

* However, see the discussion in Section 8.7 that argues that the developing world suffers more from demand-side failure than from supply-side deficiencies.

† The discussion here somewhat duplicates that found in Chapter 6, but it is reintroduced to allow this chapter to be read on a stand-alone basis.

For policy evaluation and design, we argued in Chapter 6 that it is important to classify technological change and innovation in a functionally useful way. At the outset, we suggested four different kinds of technological change:

- Product changes
- Process changes
- Shifts from products to product-services
- More far-reaching system changes.

All four types of technological change are necessary to achieve sustainable development. However, the impact of each type of change will depend on whether it is incremental, moderate, or radical in nature and on the scale at which the change occurs (regional, national, or international). One way to consider these factors is to look at differences in the processes of technology development. An important distinction is the difference between technology development that proceeds in an *evolutionary* manner (or in a *coevolutionary* manner where technology developers and customers change what is produced and demanded, respectively, over time) and technology development that is driven by *government intervention* or *societal demand*. In both cases, each of the four kinds of technological change presented above can occur.

As discussed in Chapter 6, an *incremental innovation* involves a step-by-step coevolutionary process of change, whereas *radical innovations* are discontinuous and possibly involve the *displacement* of dominant firms and institutions (Ashford, Hafkamp, et al. 2002; Luiten 2001; Moors 2000; Partidario 2003). Christensen (1997) labels the former "sustaining innovation" and the latter "disrupting innovation" (rather than radical innovation) and argues that both sustaining and disrupting innovation can be incremental, moderate, or radical. Unfortunately, the term "radical" is used in the literature in these two different ways and is a source of confusion. The following discussion of product innovation should help clarify its use.

Much of the innovation scholarship relates to evolutionary theory in the context of products, and here the (changing) nature of the customer base is important. In particular, in defining and distinguishing *sustaining* and *disrupting* product innovation, Christensen (1997) relies on the concept of "value networks" made up of different customers. He notes that incumbent firms tend to develop predominantly sustaining product technologies for existing customers, while new entrants pioneer disrupting product technologies for a new customer base. Christensen's (1997) research does not extend beyond the product domain to explore how development might be different under strong governmental or societal interventionist policies that supersede evolutionary changes.

In the context of encouraging sustainable development transformations, supply-side policies (for example, subsidies, R&D support, and favorable tax treatment of investment) can be general or can focus on encouraging technological changes with certain performance characteristics in mind. In contrast, demand-side policies (for example, purchasing tax incentives, public-service advertising, counteradvertising, and education) are designed to change societal preferences and may be useful in implementing or gaining acceptance of sustainable development policies. Although demand-side policies are less interventionist, they can have a significant effect on evolutionary processes of change. The critical question is whether the rate of change toward sustainable development is likely to be sufficient under an evolutionary (laissez-faire) approach to innovation, or whether a more interventionist approach is required. An argument made in this book is that evolutionary approaches may proceed too slowly to stem sustainability concerns related to important problems such as global climate change and toxic pollution (see Sections 2.12 and 2.13 of the extended Primer on Sustainable Development found at the website associated with this book).

We have already mentioned that Christensen's (1997) theories focus on the product domain. Although *process changes* and *innovation* are important to workers, they are not very important to the customers of a product. Producers of products may develop more sustainable processes to make their products, but these actions are not normally driven by customer demand. Hence Christensen's (1997) concepts of "value networks" and new customer bases may not be as useful in the process domain as they are in the product domain. Distinguishing sustaining and disrupting *technologies* may be useful, but these "innovations" are driven by producers and manufacturers who operate within a demanding regulatory environment rather than being influenced by product consumers.

For shifts from products to *product-services*—for example, purchasing a photocopying *service* rather than a photocopying machine—customers may be even more important than they are in the product realm because these shifts may involve behavioral changes on the part of the consumer. Finally, *system changes* involving a number of producers and

**Customer Base/**
**Valued Attributes**

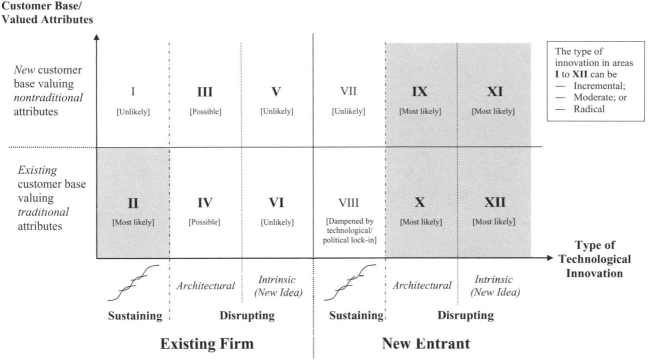

FIGURE 8.1: MATRIX OF POTENTIAL OUTCOMES OF SUSTAINING AND DISRUPTING PRODUCT TECHNOLOGY

actors—and perhaps service providers—involve a more dramatic realignment of actors.

In the discussion that follows, a behavioral model is developed that describes for product changes the influence of incumbent versus new entrants, the likelihood of sustaining versus disrupting technology, and implications for different customer bases.

We have created Figure 8.1 to help explore different types of innovation.* It presents a matrix that can be used to locate an innovation in one of twelve categories. The matrix shows where a sustaining or disrupting innovation originated (that is, from an existing firm or new entrant), its type, and whether the innovation serves existing customers or a new customer base. Although it can be difficult to draw clear boundaries between these descriptors, the framework provides a first-order approximation of whether an emerging technology is of a sustaining or disrupting nature.

An incremental, moderate, or radical *sustaining innovation* is a technological change along the same lines along which technology has been developing historically. The development of the internal com-

bustion engine (ICE) provides a good example of sustaining innovation. Improvements in the performance of an ICE have been incremental, moderate, and radical. Sustaining innovations that originate from an existing firm fall into Category II (which covers the vast majority of sustaining innovations) on Figure 8.1, and those that originate from a new entrant fall into Category VIII. In both of these cases, the existing customer base that values the traditional attributes (or performance) offered by the technology is served.†

Sustaining innovations tend to follow the trajectory of Product A in Figure 8.2. This figure indicates that sustaining innovations may eventually improve the performance of an established technology beyond the actual market demand for the product. To remain competitive in mainstream markets, firms need to continually improve their product to retain

---

\* Although the matrix concept is relevant to product, process, product-service, and system innovations, the focus of this figure is on product innovation. See Figure 8.5 and the accompanying text for other categories of change.

† Category II has been highlighted in Figure 8.1 because the majority of sustaining innovations are likely to originate from existing firms. The presence of technological and political lock-in (or entry barriers) makes it difficult for new firms to enter established markets. In addition, although Categories I and VII have been included in the matrix for completeness, it is unlikely that a sustaining innovation will develop a new customer base that previously did not see the value of the existing technology. However, such a situation might occur where a firm missed an opportunity to sell its product to a consumer base by not perceiving that consumers had a need for its product.

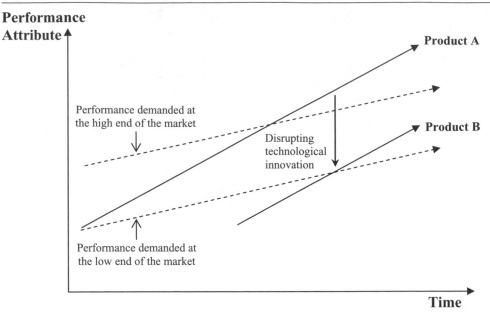

**FIGURE 8.2: INTERSECTING TRAJECTORIES OF PERFORMANCE DEMANDED (DASHED LINES) VERSUS PERFORMANCE SUPPLIED (SOLID LINES) IN A GENERIC PRODUCT MARKET**
Source: Adapted from Christensen (1997, p. xix).

and capture new customers. An improved product can generate higher returns (found in the upper right of Figure 8.2), because firms can charge a premium for their product rather than being forced to compete on price.* However, the further an established technology progresses along a sustaining innovation trajectory, the more vulnerable it becomes (over time) to emerging disrupting technologies that can undermine its customer base. In effect, sustaining innovations can "overshoot" the performance requirements and/or budgets of customers, who will then switch to a cheaper product-service—even one (initially) with somewhat reduced performance—as one becomes available. These more suitable products/services are known as disrupting innovations. They are termed "disrupting" both because the technical development is not within the mainstream development trajectory[†] and because they have attributes that appeal to a new or emerging customer base (in Christensen's conceptualization).

An incremental or radical *disrupting innovation* can take two forms: one that combines two or more prior developments in a new way, creating an "architectural" innovation; or one that stems from a new idea and is an "intrinsic" innovation. The former could be but need not be supported by a significant research and development effort. Disrupting (architectural) innovations tend to be "cheaper, simpler, smaller, and, frequently, more easy to use" (Christensen 1997, p. xviii) and offer a lower level of performance, at least in some ways. Christensen (1997) makes a convincing case that because emerging disrupting technologies (both architectural and intrinsic) are not initially performance competitive (in the context of their traditional attributes) with mainstream technologies, they are initially sold to a niche element of the existing market and/or (more likely) to a new customer base. However, once the performance of a disrupting technology improves (along a sustaining innovation trajectory) to a point at which it becomes competitive with mainstream technologies (because it offers sufficient performance in the traditionally valued attributes and has other attractive attributes as well—see Product B in Figure 8.2)—it can capture the market by displacing the established products/services.

It is important to recognize that the set of attributes valued by the customers of Product B is likely to be different from that valued by the customers of Product A. For example, a desktop computer (Product A) might be valued for its hard-disk capacity, whereas a laptop computer (Product B) might be valued for its sufficient capacity along with its size or portability. As the size, portability, and hard-disk

---

* Firms that compete on price tend to rely on process innovation to reduce production costs and increase profit margins.
† Because the focus is on the technology itself rather than its market appeal, it might be more appropriate to describe disrupting innovations as disrupting *technologies*.

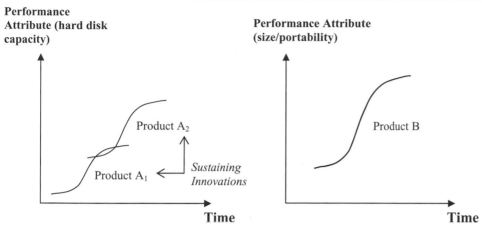

**FIGURE 8.3: DISRUPTING-TECHNOLOGY S-CURVE**

capacity of the laptop computer improve along sustaining innovation trajectories, the laptop may eventually reach a point where it can both compete with desktop computers in hard-disk capacity and offer other attractive features. At this point, the laptop can begin to undermine the market share of desktops. This process of disruption is depicted in Figure 8.3.

The graph on the right of Figure 8.3 shows the home value network for the laptop (Product B), where the size/portability of the computer is assumed to be the important attribute. The rate at which the size of the laptop is reduced is represented by the S-curve. The graph on the left of Figure 8.3 shows the home value network for desktop computers (Product A), where hard-disk capacity is assumed to be the leading attribute. This graph also shows how one model of hard disk used in desktops (Product $A_1$) has been replaced by a more advanced model (Product $A_2$), which provides an example of a sustaining innovation. When the hard-disk capacity of the laptop—a secondary attribute in the home value network for Product B—reaches a level at which it can begin to approach the performance demanded by desktop consumers, it can invade the desktop market and start to capture market share, ultimately displacing the sustaining innovations on the left side of the figure.

An example of a *disrupting "architectural" innovation* is the hybrid electric/internal-combustion engine (ECE) vehicle. This technology combines the ICE with battery technology to develop a new vehicle architecture. Although hybrid vehicles are fuel efficient and offer environmental benefits, they initially provided a lower level of performance

compared with the power and acceleration of ICE vehicles.* Therefore, the majority of customers of ICE vehicles (Product A in Figure 8.2) who value these specific traditional attributes are not likely to purchase a hybrid vehicle (Product B in Figure 8.2). Thus hybrids are initially likely to be sold to customers who value the attributes of a more environmentally sound and fuel-efficient vehicle. However, once the performance and cost of hybrid vehicles approach those of ICE vehicles, they have the potential to disrupt the ICE vehicle technology if power and acceleration remain valued performance attributes.[†] If the hybrid vehicle technology is developed by a new entrant, it falls into Category X; if an existing firm develops the technology, it falls into Category IV (Figure 8.1).

Another way of comparing sustaining and disrupting innovation is to depict three different pathways that innovation could take. In Figure 8.4, the various performance levels of an existing technology regime (for example, various ICEs with different fuel efficiencies) are shown as a function of cost. The most efficient *existing* engine is represented by point *A* at

---

* As sustaining technological advancements occur in hybrid vehicle platforms, their performance is likely to surpass that of comparable ICE vehicles.

† In this example, it is assumed that the hybrid vehicle is competing directly with the ICE vehicle whose customer base values "traditional" performance attributes. However, one might argue that the hybrid vehicle is creating a new customer base that values "nontraditional" (i.e., environmental and efficiency) attributes. In this case, the hybrid vehicle could displace the ICE vehicle market altogether because of an evolution in consumer preferences (which could be stimulated by environmental regulation or evolving consumer preferences). Under this new scenario, if the hybrid vehicle technology was developed by a new entrant, it would fall into Category IX; if an existing firm developed the technology, it would fall into Category III.

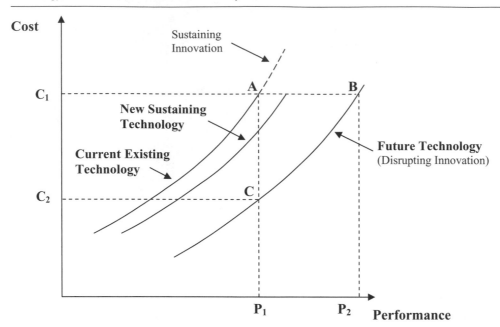

**FIGURE 8.4: THE EFFICIENT FRONTIER FOR CURRENT AND FUTURE TECHNOLOGY, CONTRASTING SUSTAINING AND DISRUPTING INNOVATION**

cost $C_1$. New improvements (sustaining innovations) to internal combustion engines can be developed within the same technological regime in two different ways. First, improvements could be made that extend the capacity of existing technology, but at higher cost, as depicted by the dashed line extending above *A*. Second, a significant innovation could occur within the same technological regime, giving rise to new performance-cost relationships as depicted in the second curve, shifted to the right, in Figure 8.4. Third, a power system based on a different concept of innovation (a disrupting innovation) could be developed, represented by the "future-technology" curve, depicted by the rightmost curve. At some point, fuel-efficient engines can be developed that provide the best efficiency of older engines at a lower cost $C_2$ (represented by point *C*), or better efficiency can be achieved at the same cost $C_1$ (represented by point *B*). Any point between points *C* and *B* on the future-technology curve represents a win-win situation over the sustaining innovations on the dashed line.

An example of a *disrupting "intrinsic" innovation* is Alexander Graham Bell's telephone, which gradually undermined and then supplanted Western Union and its telegraph operators (Christensen, Craig, et al. 2001). In this case, the disrupting technology came from a new entrant, which means that the innovation can be located in Category XI. Another example of a disrupting "intrinsic" innovation is the hydrogen fuel cell vehicle, which holds the potential to displace ICE and hybrid vehicles in the market. In this case, exist-

ing firms are attempting to develop the technology for the U.S. market, placing the hydrogen fuel cell vehicle in Category VI. Whether they succeed remains to be seen.

Christensen (1997) argues that disrupting (product) technologies are almost always developed by firms outside the prior market or business. This is why Categories IX to XII are highlighted in Figure 8.1. Firms in the existing market that develop disrupting technologies (Categories III to VI) might be described as highly innovative, with the capacity and willingness to reinvent themselves, given the opportunity. However, as Christensen's (1997) research reveals, it is questionable whether a firm is able to displace its own product in the market with a new product.

It is important to recognize the evolutionary nature of technological innovation described above. Once an established technology has been displaced by a disrupting innovation, the disrupting innovation then becomes vulnerable to subsequent future disruption as it develops along a sustaining innovation pathway. Thus the process of disruption is unrelenting and continuous. This phenomenon is what Schumpeter (1962, p. 84) famously referred to as the "perennial gale of creative destruction."

Although the preceding discussion focuses on product innovation, we believe that Christensen's ideas can be extended to include process, product-service, and system innovations (Ashford, Hafkamp, et al. 2002). However, relying on existing industries for sustainable transformations ignores evidence

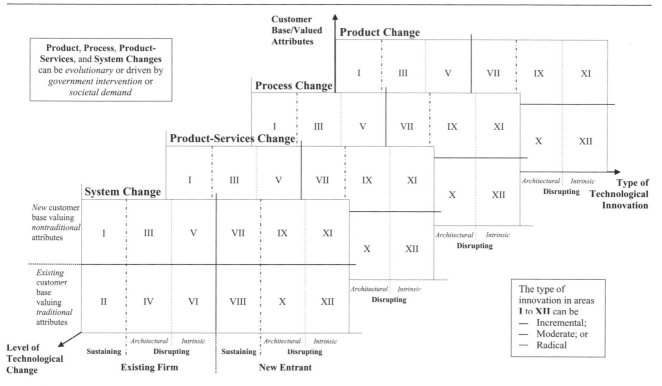

**FIGURE 8.5: MATRIX OF POTENTIAL OUTCOMES OF SUSTAINING AND DISRUPTING TECHNOLOGY FOR FOUR DIFFERENT KINDS OF TECHNOLOGICAL CHANGE OR INNOVATION**

that firms must possess not only the *willingness* and the *opportunity* but also the *capacity* to change (Ashford 2000; see Section 7.5.3 in Chapter 7). It is questionable whether those industries and firms that are responsible for environmental problems are able—through the use of continuous institutional learning, the application of life-cycle analysis, dialogue with stakeholders, and implementation of environmental management systems—to transform themselves into sustainable industries and firms. "It is not marginal or incremental changes that are needed for sustainability but rather major product, process, and system transformations—often beyond the capacity of the dominant industries and firms" (Ashford 2002a, p. 1417). The same problems arise in considering change in government and societal institutions. Therefore, *creative interventionist policies* are seen as essential in encouraging system innovation toward sustainable transformations. Moving from improving pesticide safety and designing bioengineered crops to a reconceptualization of sustainable, perhaps decentralized, agricultural systems is one example where creative government policy would be essential.

It is possible to visualize how Christensen's (1997) ideas can be extended to include process, product-service, and system innovation by expanding Figure 8.1 to reflect these additional kinds of innovation (Figure 8.5). It is important to realize that the dominant mechanisms for change in each kind of innovation are likely to vary, meaning that different categories (I to XII) in the matrix are likely to be shaded. Further, who is—and who is not—likely to develop future technology under strong government directives or societal demand and the implications for *future* organizational changes (especially in the context of systems) are important issues to consider. Although product, process, product-service, and system changes are necessary to achieve sustainable development, it is likely that system innovations will be particularly important when one is focusing on large-scale sociotechnical systems, such as the transportation system or the agriculture/food system.

In conclusion, as a result of sustaining and disrupting innovations, existing technologies are likely to be improved or supplanted over time, provided that new competitors are able to enter existing markets or develop new ones without being held back by entry barriers. If it is possible to influence the dynamics of the evolutionary change process, it might be possible to place development onto a sustainable, potentially radically different trajectory. Thus, as Dorf (2001, p. 70) comments, "For good or ill the contemporary world is and will continue to be substantially shaped by technology."

## 8.3 PREREQUISITES FOR TECHNOLOGICAL CHANGE

The necessary and sufficient prerequisites for technological change are that the innovating entity have the willingness, motivation/opportunity, and capacity to change. For a discussion of these prerequisites for change in the context of the business firm, see Section 7.5 in Chapter 7.

## 8.4 THE ROLE OF GOVERNMENT IN PROMOTING INNOVATION IN DEVELOPED COUNTRIES

We argued earlier that government has a trusteeship role in guiding the development of new technology. This argument becomes particularly important if the long-term development of the next generation of technology lies outside what existing firms are able or willing to pursue. If we consider the factor X concept (Reijnders 1998; see Section 1.3.3 in Chapter 1), the government is seen to have a critical role in assisting the development and adoption of products and processes with factor X improvements. An important point to recognize, though, is that factor X improvements might either result in advances in *existing* technology (the "weak" form of the regulation-induced-innovation—or Porter—hypothesis) or be achieved through *disrupting* technology that displaces existing products, processes, and services from the market (the "strong" form of the regulation-induced-innovation—or MIT—hypothesis.). These waves of creative destruction are not likely to be propagated by the dominant incumbent firms in the market (Christensen 1997), which increases the importance of the role of government in guiding research and development from the initial stages to the final diffusion of the new technologies.*

The critical question, however, is how government should stimulate technological innovation/development to realize the factor X improvements. In the previous section, we focused on more stringent (technology-forcing) regulation. However, regulation and other government initiatives designed to stimulate technological innovation can come in numerous forms.†

In Chapter 6, we addressed the importance of technological innovation in achieving sustainability, and in Chapter 7, we addressed the nexus between organizational and technological innovation. With that understanding, we here undertake an exploration of the tools and mechanisms available to government to influence the nature and direction of technological change in developed countries. From Chapter 6, we learned that the innovation process is embedded within an "innovation system" involving both institutional actors and individuals within and outside the firm itself. There we introduced the work of Tsamis (1999), who developed a useful model that focuses on the *process* of innovation and the *roles* that each major player has in the process in terms of providing an optimal climate for innovation to evolve. Before looking more closely at the role of government in innovation, we first briefly review the various theories of technological innovation, with a specific emphasis on system change/transformation.

### 8.4.1 Review of Government Policy Instruments in the Context of Alternative Theories of Technological Innovation

Luiten (2001) highlights the following government policy instruments that can be used to stimulate the *supply* of and/or the *demand* for technological development and innovation. Going beyond facilitating evolutionary processes, she also indicates whether the instrument is *generic* (designed to maintain basic

---

* The ability of industry to influence government standard setting and regulations often stifles technological innovation, enabling incumbent firms to focus on maximizing the production of existing, but less environmentally sound, technology (Wallace 1995). In such circumstances, firms seek the coercive power of government to establish regulations that restrict market entry, provide subsidies, and/or support prices (Becker 1983; Keohane, Revesz, et al. 1998; Peltzman 1976; Posner 1974; Stigler 1971). Changing the dynamics between government and industry to prevent regulatory capture will be extremely difficult, but not impossible. However, it has been argued that under some circumstances, regulatory capture and environmental performance go hand in hand (Oye and Foster 2002; White 1989).

† Luiten (2001) argues that during the 1960s and 1970s governments tried to stimulate technological development by generating knowledge through investments in R&D in both private firms and national public research institutes. The intention was to use the knowledge generated to improve the competitiveness of industry. In the early 1980s, the focus shifted from R&D funding to the underexploitation of the new knowledge and available technologies. Generating knowledge by itself was not seen as being adequate, and efforts were made to channel technology directly to firms that could use them (e.g., using demonstration projects). In the early 1990s, technological development became a more systemic and interactive process. Thus government measures shifted toward the stimulation of learning and cooperation. Interaction among the actors involved in a research project was seen as being essential. Such action not only had the benefit of sharing the costs and risks of R&D over a greater number of actors but also prevented duplication of efforts and improved the public-sector return on R&D funding by increasing private-sector involvement.

---

### BOX 8.1: THEORIES OF TECHNOLOGICAL INNOVATION AND THE ROLE OF GOVERNMENT

*Neoclassical economic approach:* Technological development is *exogenous*, and technology is treated as a black box. Using this approach, a rational actor will attempt to maximize the production function. Government intervention corrects underinvestment by stimulating fundamental R&D and supporting universities.

*Evolutionary economic approach:* Technological development is *endogenous* and is a path-dependent process of variation and selection. Technology is described as evolving from a firm's knowledge base. Technological development tends to occur along known directions, favoring path dependency and lock-in. The role of the government is to generate variation within an entrepreneurial climate that enhances innovation.

*Systems-of-innovation approach:* Technological development is a process of interactive learning and includes not only R&D and knowledge production but also the transfer, exchange, and use of knowledge and the demand for knowledge. The aim of technological development is to optimize the use of knowledge generated by a system of related and linked actors. The role of the government is to maintain the institutional knowledge infrastructure of universities and research institutes.

*Industrial-networks approach:* Technological development takes place in a process of interactions between actors who perform activities and have access to different resources. Thus technology (innovation) is the result of interactions between firms. No explicit attention is given to directing technological development. The role of the government is to build and renew local knowledge-intensive networks and to stimulate cooperation.

*Social constructivism approaches:* Technological development is led by a process of social interaction that is directed by the values and beliefs of interest groups and actors (including government). The role of the government is to understand and articulate specific positions during negotiations and to develop networks that support social interaction.

*Quasi-evolutionary approach:* Technological development is a process of coevolution at different levels of analysis (micro, meso, and macro). Hence technology is an object in a coevolutionary learning process. The *technological regime*[a] guides, but does not fix, R&D activities. The role of the government is to influence the rules of a technological regime to facilitate learning processes among the various actors, and to establish *niches* of protected learning.

*Large-technical-systems approach:* Technological development is the process of solving critical problems of a technical (or engineering) system. Technology is seen as part of an expanding technical system. Critical problems—or *reverse salients*—of the technical system have to be solved before the system can expand. The role of the government is to avoid causing or strengthening reverse salients and to reinforce the capacities or possibilities of system builders.

---

[a] Rip and Kemp (1998, p. 340) define a technological regime as "the rule-set or grammar embedded in a complex of engineering practices, production process technologies, product characteristics, skills and procedures, ways of handling relevant artifacts and persons, ways of defining problems—all of them embedded in institutions and infrastructures." See also the related concept of "innovation systems" in Chapter 6.

Sources: Luiten (2001), Moors (2000), and Partidario (2003).

---

infrastructure or to enhance the competitiveness of the national industry) or *specific* (designed to address a particular problem or issue).

- Research priorities—matching supply and demand; generic and specific
- Technology standards—demand; specific
- Performance or emission standards—demand; specific
- Technology-forcing standards—demand; specific
- Taxes, fees, and tradable emission permits—demand; specific
- R&D support or subsidies—supply; specific (can also be generic)
- Venture capital—supply; specific (can also be generic)
- Voluntary (R&D) agreements—matching supply and demand; specific
- Technology procurement—femand; specific

- Initiating and stimulating networks*—matching supply and demand; specific or generic

When we move beyond product and process innovation into *system changes*, in addition to the wide range of instruments that can be used to guide technological development (in the product and process contexts), there are a number of theories that describe the process of technological innovation. Box 8.1 shows how the various schools of economic, historical, and sociological thought differ in their approaches to conceptualizing technological development. The description of these approaches draws on the work of Luiten (2001), Moors (2000), and Partidario (2003). In each description, the role of government is identified.

The theories of technological innovation shown in Box 8.1 provide an indication why focusing on

---

\* See the discussion of networks in Section 7.3.2 in Chapter 7.

government intervention in the process of techno-logical innovation is important, even necessary. In addition, although the policy instruments above have been listed in a general form, we should recognize that the success of a particular instrument in directing or stimulating technological development is *context sensitive* (Wallace 1995).

Understanding the role of societal (or cultural) change and how new technology forms can regulate social behavior is essential (Winner 1977, 1986, 1992). If society is unwilling to accept (or buy) a new technology, then that technology will not be diffused sufficiently to affect the overall system (unless it is imposed by regulation). It is also important to consider whether new forms of technology are supporting the satisfaction of fundamental human needs for (1) safety, security, and sustenance; (2) competence, efficacy, and self-esteem; (3) autonomy and authenticity; and (4) connectedness (Kasser 2002). Indeed, because meeting human needs lies at the center of sustainable development (see Section 1.1 in Chapter 1), perhaps greater attention should be paid to the impact of technology on needs fulfillment.

Asking whether a new technology form is likely to be diffused sufficiently to affect the overall system is critical for sustainable development. In Europe, and more specifically in the Netherlands,* there is a growing body of research that looks into how society can transition to (that is, transform) sustainable forms of development through *system innovation* (Elzen 2002; Elzen, Geels, et al. 2004; Kemp and Rotmans 2005). However, the research is not confined to Europe. The U.S. National Research Council (NRC) (2002) undertook an important study that focuses on the "transition toward sustainability."

A "transition" (or transformation) is described as "a long-term change process in an important sub-system encompassing various functional systems (for example, food production and consumption, mobility, energy supply and use, etc.) in which both the technical and the social/cultural dimensions of such systems change drastically" (Elzen 2002, p. 1). A "system innovation" is described as "a set of innovations combined in order to provide a service in a novel way or offering new services. System innova-tions involve a new logic (guiding principle) and new types of practices" (Rennings, Kemp, et al. 2003, p. 14). Geels (2004, pp. 19–20) describes a system innovation as consisting of three important aspects: (1) technological substitution, which includes the emergence and diffusion of new technology that replaces existing technology; (2) the coevolution of technological and social systems, where both types of systems are continually interacting and changing; and (3) the emergence of new functionalities, where a new product or service provides a new functional characteristic. It follows that a "sustainable" system innovation would provide economic, environmental, and social benefits with the offering of new products, processes, or services.

An important characteristic of research focusing on system innovation is the recognition that the relationships among sets of technologies are dynamic, complex, and nonlinear, and that these technologies are socially embedded. This focus supports the idea of dynamic, as opposed to static, efficiency (see Section 9.3 in Chapter 9) and the importance of considering the fourfold coevolution of technology, institutions, organizations, and society. Because the *evolutionary economic* and *quasi-evolutionary* approaches to technological innovation (Box 8.1) make technology and innovation explicit and adopt a system approach, the frameworks developed to assess system innovation are built on these theories. Because neoclassical economic theory treats technology as exogenous, it does not provide fertile ground for considerations of system innovation.

Briefly, *evolutionary economics* focuses on the process of technological innovation from the perspective of the survival of the fittest—that is, its roots are Darwinian and Schumpeterian.[1] Nelson and Winter (1977, 1982) were the first to develop an economic theory in which the evolutionary theory of technological innovation was embedded. Their theory is based on two independent processes: *variation* and *selection*. In addition, because technology is treated as being socially embedded, the ideas of *path dependency* or *lock-in* and *bounded rationality* play important roles in the analysis of technological innovation. The evolutionary model of technological innovation was later extended by focusing on the sociological aspects of the evolutionary approach (Rip 1992; van de Belt and Rip 1987). The so-called quasi-evolutionary approach treats the variation and selection of technology as nonindependent events (Moors 2000). Thus the focus is on how technological variations are influenced by the selection environment.

---

* See the discussion of transition management in the next section. This concept has generated considerable academic and government interest and recently was the subject of a conference in Amsterdam: The First European Conference on Sustainability Transitions: Dynamics and Governance of Transitions to Sustainability, www.ksinetwork.nl/conference2009/ (accessed May 18, 2010).

The field of evolutionary economics is beginning to emerge as an important framework for understanding how modern economies work. Development is conceived as an evolutionary process. In general, evolutionary theory views innovation as a dynamic, interactive process of variation and selection where institutions and actors continually influence and learn from each other.

Evolutionary theory has five important characteristics that differ from the neoclassical economic approach (Butter 2002; OECD 1997). First, because the process of innovation is uncertain and is based on risk taking, there is no rational maximization behavior or optimal solution. Performance objectives can be achieved in many different ways through the creation of entirely new products, processes, or services. Thus the selection of an optimal outcome using a specific form of technology ignores the possible emergence of new, disruptive ideas. Second, because innovation is a state of constant change and is not predictable, there is no one point of equilibrium. Third, technology is made explicit and is treated as a system of interacting subtechnologies designed to achieve an overall objective. Fourth, innovation is made explicit as a dynamic and interactive process of variation and selection. Finally, the technological (or physical) and social (including institutions) structure of a system is made explicit. This enables economic performance to be considered as a function of the facilitating structure—that is, the infrastructure, institutions, financial system, geographic location, and other factors.

There are currently three important frameworks that can be used to develop initiatives to stimulate system innovation for sustainable transformations. Kemp (2002), Kemp, Loorbach, et al. (2007), and Kemp and Rotmans (2005) propose "strategic niche management" and "transition management"—a quasi-evolutionary approach—for achieving system changes necessary for sustainability. Butter (2002) suggests a three-layered approach for "green system innovation," based on a combination of evolutionary theory and national systems of innovation. Ashford (2002b) argues for integrating rather than coordinating government interventions in order to bring about the needed technological, organizational, institutional, and social transformations to achieve significant sustainable system change. A role for government is anticipated by all three of these commentators, but to different degrees and in different ways. The following three sections look at these frameworks more closely.

## 8.4.2 Strategic Niche Management and Transition Management

The concept of strategic niche management (SNM) emerged from the two opposing views of the *technological fix ideology* (or technological optimism) and the *cultural fix paradigm* (Hoogma, Kemp, et al. 2002). The former argues that the benefits associated with technological progress are likely to far outweigh costs, and that a technological solution can be found to all problems. The latter suggests that the technology itself is actually part of the problem and that real solutions will have to come from *social* and *cultural* change. Therefore, SNM was created to "allow for working on both the technical and the social side in a simultaneous and coherent manner" (ibid., p. 3).

Kemp (2002, p. 10) describes SNM as the "creation and management of a niche for an innovation with the aim of promoting processes of co-evolution." The idea is that a new product will be used by *real* users (by society, industry, or government), and its use will promote interactive learning and build a product constituency. The underlying notion is that new technologies will be introduced in a socially embedded manner. It is important to realize that SNM is primarily focused on product innovation, not process innovation. However, its proponents argue that process innovation will be part of technological regime transformations (see the discussion of regime change below). SNM also enables institutions and organizations to adjust the technological development and deployment process to stimulate the adoption and diffusion of a new product.

A key element of the SNM concept is that technological change occurs in a coevolutionary manner—that is, technologies evolve within institutional networks. Saviotti (2005) suggests that two important general points can be made about the co-evolution of technologies and institutions: "First, the emergence of new technologies increases the division of labor in the economy, but in the meantime creates new co-ordination problems. One of the roles of co-evolving institutions is to provide co-ordination. Second, although the firms producing and using the new technologies compete, other co-evolving institutions are in a complementary relationship with the main technology" (ibid., p. 30). Saviotti's comments highlight the complexity that surrounds the introduction of a new technology and provide weight to Kemp's arguments for the creation of protective niches in which promising technology can be tested and developed. The ability to experiment with new technology through demonstration projects that help users and suppliers learn about new possibilities is a vital component of SNM.

The process of experimentation is likely to achieve one of two outcomes: *regime optimization** or *regime shifts.*† These two outcomes can be described as *sustaining* or *disrupting* changes, respectively (see the earlier discussion). A technological regime is defined as "the whole complex of scientific knowledge, engineering practices, production process technologies, product characteristics, skills and procedures, established user needs, regulatory requirements, institutions and infrastructures" (Hoogma, Kemp, et al. 2002, p. 19). In general, the type of technologies that are suitable for experimentation should be ones that hold the potential to bridge the gap between existing and new (sustainable) technological regimes (Kemp 2002). This type of technology is referred to as "pathway technology." In essence, SNM is a bottom-up, initially nondisruptive process where once the niche for experimentation has been established by government policy/regulation, the new technology form *evolves* from interactions among society, government, nongovernmental organizations, and industry. The emphasis is on multistakeholder *governance* rather than on *government* as the dominant actor.

Transition management (TM) is a model of co-evolutionary management of transformative change in societal systems through a process of searching, learning and experimenting (Rotmans and Kemp, 2008).‡ Managing means adjusting, adapting and in-fluencing rather than using a command-and-control approach. There are persistent problems for which there are no immediate solutions. By transforming the persistent problem into a visionary challenge, TM explores a range of possible options and pathways through the carrying out of a diversity of small-scale experiments. Based on what is learned from these, the vision, agenda and pathways are adjusted. Successful experiments are continued and can be scaled up, and failed experiments are abandoned, until convergence is reached. Rather than focusing on a single, available solution, TM explores various options and is aimed at guiding variation-selection processes into more sustainable directions, with the long-term aim of selecting the most sustainable option(s) and paths based on learning experiences. TM is meant to be a mutually supportive vehicle for both sociotechnical and policy changes. It is debatable whether Kemp's description of the latter strategy will result in disrupting innovation. Kemp (2008, p. 374) acknowledges that "faced with sustainability problems, [incumbent] regime actors will opt for change that is non-disruptive from the industry point of view, which leads them to focus their attention on system improvement instead of system innovation." Whether the concept could hold particular merit for system innovation in a specific context remains to be seen. If revolutionary change—or a technological regime shift—can occur via a stepwise system innovation process, SNM can be a useful tool that can be applied to large-scale engineering systems, such as the transportation system (Hoogma, Kemp, et al. 2002; Hoogma, Weber, et al. 2001), but that is a big "if." It depends on the extent to which incumbents dominate the process.

Opponents of SNM argue that one of the shortcomings of the technique is that at some point the "probe and learn" ideology needs to become action and transformation, and Kemp's theory is unclear on how transformation will occur (Smith 2003). Further, if niches grow within or alongside existing regimes, they are unlikely to have radically different practices and rules, which raises the question whether the new products, processes, or services will offer significant benefits. A final point raised by Smith (2003) is the fact that the localization of niches may run against the nationalization or globalization ideology of mainstream government and business institutions. Thus an important question is whether the "transformative potential" of SNM will be inhibited by these powerful forces (ibid.).

---

\*         An example of regime optimization is the development/deployment of highly efficient vehicles that use the improved internal combustion engine as a base.

†         Hoogma, Kemp, et al. (2002) provide the following examples of innovations that have regime-shift potential: battery-powered vehicles, telematics for traffic management, car sharing, smart cards, individualized self-service rental systems, dial-a-ride services, and bicycle pools.

‡         Kemp (2008, p. 375) comments: "The management of institutions can be done through the . . . use of three coordinating mechanisms: markets, hierarchy, and structure." "The basic steering mechanism is *modulation*, not dictatorship or planning and control" (ibid., p. 377), and "The long-term goals for functional systems are chosen by society either through the political process or in a more direct way through a consultative process" (ibid.). Kemp endorses market-based instruments, and although he does not explicitly mention regulation, it is clear that he rejects a regulation as the main steering approach; this is in line with his commitment to evolutionary approaches and strong commitment to markets. This parallels the recent contribution of ecological economists Beddoe, Costanza, et al. (2009, p. 2488), who also ignore regulation as a mechanism to achieve sustainable transformations and instead rely on cultural evolution to "push our society toward the adoption of institutions that best fit the new circumstances." "Creating a sustainable future will require an integrated, systems level redesign of our socio-ecological regime focused explicitly and directly on the goal of sustainable

---

quality of life rather than the proxy of unlimited material growth" (ibid., p. 2483).

Vergragt (2005) raises a slightly different concern from that of Smith (2003). He argues that if the role of government is to legitimize the transition process—including its own reform and the abolition of existing institutional and economic barriers to sustainable development—then a quandary exists because the national government may in fact be part of the problem rather than part of the solution. Therefore, an important question is who will manage the transition process. Quist and Vergragt (2004) also question whether an emerging niche market will survive once its protection mechanisms are removed.

In critiquing the TM approach, Tukker, Charter, et al. (2008) comment that transition management of innovation neglects the role of the consumer and the importance of demand-side policies influencing consumption. It should be noted that regulation is a demand-side policy intervention—it defines the allowable characteristics and places constraints on the nature of products and on their manufacturing, use, and disposal.

Dewulf, Termeer, et al. (2009), in analyzing transition management in the context of other theories of change management—especially intervention by government—question whether transition management is the "only model in town." Dewulf, Termeer, et al. (p. 12) observe that "a distinctive trait of transition management appears to be the assumption of an overarching position of (governmental) transition managers who can apply management tools, niche-building machinery, and engineering devices from a privileged, knowledgeable and external position ... towards a clear and one-dimensional target." The government participates along with other stakeholders, rather than take a more directive role reminiscent of command-and-control regulatory involvement.* The process is characteristically Dutch, using the so-called "polder consensus-seeking model."

Ashford (2002b) argues that although Kemp acknowledges that regulation can be a useful tool to stimulate radical (system) changes, his faith in the formation of strategic niches and stepwise change *within* the original technology regime is not likely to result in disrupting forms of technology that are nec-

essary for sustainable development. The problem is that firms are likely to resist initiatives or regulations that threaten their market position and to focus instead on activities that maintain the status quo. Thus a reliance on evolutionary or even coevolutionary change rather than revolutionary change is not likely to support the emergence of new market entrants who play an important role in introducing radically different (and potentially more sustainable) forms of technology (Reinhardt 1999). Berkhout, Smith, et al. (2004) make a case similar to that of Ashford. They argue that the tendency of critical social groups has been to target the "incumbent regime, rather than its potential successor, ... represents a direct antithesis of the bottom-up niche-based model" (p. 61). The lesson appears to be that attempts at normatively-driven sociotechnical transitions (that is those forms most pertinent to the transition management project) do not follow exclusively that pattern described by the niche-based model, but instead imply much greater attention to macrolevel processes (public opinion, government policy, the structure and scope of markets) and their capacity to influence and induce innovation at the micro- and mesolevel.

Jacob (2005), while generally supportive of decoupling economic growth from environmental degradation through ecological modernization, raises questions similar to those of Ashford and Berkhout, Smith, et al. and asks whether SNM's experimental arena is likely to capture and maintain the necessary political (and financial) support for a real transition. Further, Jacob (2005) argues that although "discourse and persuasion" are useful tools, they are unlikely to resolve any opposing core beliefs held by the actors. Thus bargaining and making trade-offs are likely to play an inevitable role in any decision-making and transition process.

Finally, continuing from Smith's (2003) earlier reservations about the ability of SNM to bring about the needed transformations, Smith and Kern (2007) comment on its limited success in energy policy in the Netherlands. They describe how Kemp and Rotmans persuaded the Dutch government to adopt SNM as a central strategy in its Fourth National Environmental Policy Plan (NMP4) in 2001.† The NMP4 focuses on restructuring production and con-

---

* Dewulf, Termeer, et al. (2009, p. 4) argue that transition management can take a relatively long time—twenty-five to fifty years—whereas collaboration theory in practice focuses on reaching an agreement and effectuating change in a few years' time. Given the existence of relatively short-term "tipping points" in sustainability challenges, e.g., global climate disruption, endocrine disruption, and rapidly changing financial landscapes, the benefits of transition management may come far too late. Collaborative processes, of course, have their own drawbacks.

† It should be noted, however, that the environmental successes of earlier Dutch National Environmental Policy Plans (NEPPs) were premised on the government setting clear future targets but negotiating ways of achieving those targets with stakeholders. The approach later adopted in its NEPP was to negotiate both targets and pathways with stakeholders. Existing industrial stakeholders may not represent the interests or capacity of future technology providers who are likely to displace them.

sumption systems over a thirty-year period to achieve a reduction of one-twentieth in both resource and energy use. Smith and Kern (2007) describe and critique the SNM approach in the context of the Netherlands:

> By creating policies that support niche experiments in sustainability, whilst other policies place incumbent systems under concerted pressure to become sustainable, the transitions approach seeks to facilitate the transformation of systems [citing] Smith, Stirling, et al. 2005). The "S" curve moves the niche "pre-development" phase, through "take off" along an "acceleration" phase, and culminates in "stabilization" around the new structure of sustainable socio-technical practices ([citing] Rotmans[ Kemp, ] et al. 2001). (Smith and Kern 2007, p. 6)
>
> [SNM] offers the prospect of reinvigorating ecological modernization without challenging cherished components. Thus, market-based instruments and win-win regulations, both advocated within ecological modernist discourse, remain key policy tools amongst a portfolio that can help guide transitions. The power of innovation to decouple environmental degradation from economic growth remains as a foundation. The dominant ecological modernization discourse is repackaged in the transitions approach.* (ibid., p. 7)
>
> Many commentators applauded this co-operative, long-term approach. . . . Others were disappointed. The [NMP] plans interpreted ecological modernization technocratically. . . . The plans were weakened by compromises within government and with business that translated into relatively undemanding targets. (ibid., p. 8)
>
> In our view, deeper, more profound envisioning exercise and transition debates will happen in civil society arenas, removed from the messy compromises of government and the economic imperatives of business. What the transitions discourse and ecological modernization lack is an account of how such initiatives become a power base for change. Neither identifies the social agents that can ensure the radical components of a discourse that can carry through to institutionalization. (ibid., pp. 18–19)

A more sympathetic view of transition management is expressed by Meadowcroft (2005, p. 486), who characterizes its proponents as appreciating the "regulatory dimensions" of technological evolution. Although he acknowledges that transitions under transition management may well take more than twenty-five years, that continued economic growth may be possible only at the expense of the environment, and that the role of government in solving environmental prob-

lems has been underestimated, Meadowcroft (2005, p. 492) decries governments being "confined to a top/down and expenditure/regulatory framework" and puts some faith in transition management. More recently, Meadowcroft (2009) comments on the importance of addressing the politics surrounding the implementation TM toward sustainability goals.

Shove and Walker (2007) provide four cautionary concerns:

> Transition managers' efforts to develop and work towards shared societal or environmental goals are all very well but techniques like those of multi-stakeholder involvement in foresight exercises, or methods of public participation and deliberation are never "neutral" and never evacuated of power and strategic behavior. . . . Initiatives of this kind can be experienced as processes of co-option, the effect of which is to neuter rather than embrace dissent. In addition, and in any event, it is important to remember that stakeholders' visions of the future are always and inevitably shaped by the systems and social environments they inhabit today. (ibid., p. 765)
>
> Thoroughly systemic, thoroughly co-evolutionary models of social and environmental change undoubtedly challenge conventional approaches to problems of sustainability. In so far as they embody these ideas, strategies of transition management imply a necessarily radical overhauling of theory and orientation, but our caution is that such techniques can also be incorporated into political business-as-usual, albeit with a little more frequent revisiting of goals and a somewhat longer term horizon. (ibid., p. 767)
>
> How should those concerned with sustainability respond to the increasingly rapid, powerful and expertly orchestrated diffusion of unsustainable technologies, practices and images? Is the subtle modulation of reflexive governance capable of stemming and diverting unforeseen transitions of this kind, or are more robust counter measures required? (ibid.)
>
> [Concerning transitions in practice:] First . . . there is almost no reference to the ways of living or to the patterns of demand implied in what remain largely technological templates for the future. Second, and because large-scale technological examples command so much attention, commentators take it for granted that policy and corporate actors are the key players—even if the involvement of other groups and interests is vital. . . . Third, the transition management literature consequently draws upon a narrow (perhaps necessarily narrow) slice of what is in fact a much wider debate about social systemic change. (ibid., p. 768)

The publication of this critique stimulated a response by Rotmans and Kemp (2008) and a counterresponse by Shove and Walker (2008), illustrating just how important the issue of transition management is becoming in the sustainability debate.

---

* Hey, Jacob, et al. (2007) and Jänicke and Jacob (2005) have been especially critical of relying on market-based instruments for achieving sustainable transformations, advocating, like Ashford, strong regulatory approaches.

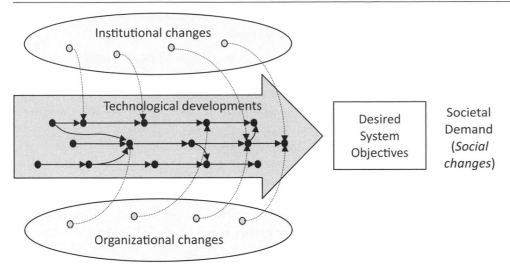

**FIGURE 8.6: THE INTERCONNECTIONS AMONG INSTITUTIONAL, TECHNOLOGICAL, AND ORGANIZATIONAL DEVELOPMENT/CHANGE**
Source: Adapted from Butter (2002, p. 4).

In spite of initial reservations about the success of TM-inspired reincarnation of long-term policy design, some of its critics are cautiously optimistic about its future use (Shove 2010; Voss, Smith et al. 2009). We, however, remain skeptical because (1) the time framework for success is far too long given the challenges of sustainable development, (2) there is too much potential for capture of future agendas by incumbents, even if they change somewhat, and (3) without clear and certain long-term targets characteristic of backcasting, long-term investments by new entrants leading to discontinuous change necessary for radical technological change are unlikely to be made. Backcasting in incremental steps is not long-term backcasting, and while it introduces flexibility and mid-term corrections, it does not provide certain targets toward which to innovate. Again, we find it difficult to be optimistic that step-wise changes made toward uncertain futures involving incumbents will lead to radical, disrupting changes. Ecological modernization or reflexive governance arose historically because governments were not willing to exercise courage at setting long-term goals that challenge incumbent forces and agendas. Second-generation policy design operating under the soft euphemism of accommodation and learning has serious weaknesses.

### 8.4.3 The Three-Layered Approach to System Innovation

Another systemic view of technological development is presented by Butter (2002),[2] who considers the role of institutional frameworks, networks, organizations,

practices, and guiding principles in stimulating system innovation. The framework is based on evolutionary economics and national systems of innovation (NSI)[3] and focuses on the role government can play in stimulating system change toward sustainable development.

Butter (2002) argues that while technological innovation takes place at a micro (or firm) level, *system innovations* (or transformations) occur only as a result of a *combination* of technological, institutional, and organizational innovations (Figure 8.6). The idea is that the alignment of several singular technological innovations, combined with suitable institutional and organizational changes, will result in a system (or *functional*) change toward a desired system objective. "System innovations will lead to changes in organizations, changes of regimes and will be long-term processes of change" (ibid., p. 4).

To formalize the concepts behind Figure 8.6, Butter (2002) describes a three-layered approach to developing a policy for system innovation. (These three layers are different from the three types of innovation shown in Figure 8.6.) The first layer focuses on the alignment of different actors toward a common objective—the *system innovation*. Butter (2002) suggests that by developing stakeholder-endorsed visions of the future (using participatory backcasting; Quist and Vergragt 2004),* establishing cooperation networks (among universities, government, industry, NGOs, and other stakeholders) focused on system change, and reallocating funding to support long-term planning and the creation of niche markets, it is

---

* See Section 8.5 for a discussion of stakeholder participation and participatory backcasting.

possible to stimulate and align singular innovations so that together they will contribute toward a system innovation.

However, a major barrier to system innovation is the financial consequences associated with a systemwide change (Butter 2002). For example, the relatively large research budgets required to develop a new mode of transportation—such as the hydrogen fuel cell vehicle—often exceed the capabilities of a single actor. Hence a normal entrepreneur or firm is unlikely to take the risk of developing a technology capable of radically altering a system. From similar arguments, Butter (2002) draws the conclusion that governments have social legitimacy to intervene in the technological innovation process, especially when there is a focus on solving societal problems.

The second layer addresses *singular innovations* and incorporates the more traditional innovation process of invention, innovation, and diffusion of singular technologies. Butter (2002) argues that government has a role in stimulating innovation, but he stops at negotiation, tax incentives, and financial instruments and ignores the potential gains that can be achieved from more stringent regulation.

The final layer emphasizes the importance of creating an *innovation climate*, in which the vision of sustainable development is clear, financial incentives support sustainable forms of development, and long-term investments and initiatives for sustainable development are nurtured. Butter (2002) states that the largest barrier to the creation of such a climate is the current lack of a long-term vision for the future.

In his guidelines for policy, like the proponents of transition management, Butter (2002) argues that the role of government is not to select winning technologies, but rather to facilitate the process of variation and selection. This role aligns well with the evolutionary economic approach. In addition, he states that technological lock-in effects can be avoided by using outsiders who can initiate system innovations.* However, he does not provide any guidance on how this can be achieved.

In summary, the theories of Butter (2002) and Kemp (2002) both rely on the role of government to varying degrees. This raises a critical question—how much government intervention should there be? Perhaps the role that most deeply involves government in system innovation is put forward by Ashford (2000, 2002b).

### 8.4.4 The Integration of Government Interventions

We endorse Butter's (2002) theory of system innovation and taxonomy of policy approaches, but we argue that it does not go far enough (Ashford 2002b). The multipurpose (rather than single-purpose) design of policy, where government policy is co-optimized, is much more likely to lead to dramatic system changes.

Government has an important role to play in creating winning forces and visions for sustainable transformations (Ashford 2000, 2002b, 2005). Depending on the type of transformation required, the roles of government should encompass the following (Ashford 2002b, pp. 18–19):

- "The direct support of R&D and incentives for innovation through appropriate tax treatment of investment;
- the creation and dissemination of knowledge through experimentation and demonstration projects;
- the creation of markets through government purchasing;
- the removal of perverse incentives of regulations in some instances and the deliberate design and use of regulation to stimulate change in others;
- the training of owners, workers, and entrepreneurs, and educating consumers;" and
- The direct creation of meaningful, rewarding, and satisfying jobs.

It should be clear how these roles relate to the ideas embedded in Kemp's (2002) and Butter's (2002) approaches, but we envision a much stronger role for government in stimulating technological innovation.† Government should go beyond simply creating a favorable investment climate. "Without deliberate design, significant changes—even system changes—are unlikely to improve competitiveness, environment, and employment at the same time" (Ashford 2002b, p. 18). *Stringent regulation* (focusing on environmental issues) is essential to stimulate significant technological changes, and such regulation may in fact be necessary to create niches that facilitate the entry of new firms and organizations into a new market.‡

Others who support the view that stringent (or "properly conceived") regulation is necessary for en-

---

* See van de Poel (2000) for a discussion of the importance of outside involvement in technological development.

† See the detailed discussion of the potential roles for government in Chapter 13 and Ashford and Hall (2011).

‡ See especially the article of Ashford, Ayers, et al. (1985) titled "Using Regulation to Change the Market for Innovation," which appeared considerably earlier than the subsequent formulation of the Porter hypothesis.

**TABLE 8.1: FRAMEWORK OF OPTIONS FOR ANALYSIS**

| | Identify solutions *within* existing legal, institutional, and political system | Identify solutions *outside* existing legal, institutional, and political system—e.g., the creation of a new transportation planning architecture |
|---|---|---|
| Work with *existing stakeholders* | A | B |
| Include *new stakeholders* in the decision-making process | C | D |

vironmental innovation include Foxon, Makuch, et al. (2004), Huber (2004b), and Jänicke (1990). For instance, Huber (2004a, p. 447) comments that "strict environmental performance standards ... [remain] by far the most effective controls instrument for environment and innovation alike (which is not astonishing given the fact that environmental standards are, or immediately translate into, technical standards)."

Ashford, Hafkamp, et al. (2002) argue that an *evolutionary* (or incremental) pathway is insufficient to achieve factor ten or greater improvement in a system's performance. Further, because changes in sociotechnical systems (such as the transportation or energy system) are difficult, the "creative use of government intervention is a more promising strategic approach for achieving sustainable industrial transformations than the reliance on the more neo-liberal policies relying on firms' more short-term economic self-interest" (ibid., p. 10). Hence relying on Christensen's (1997) approach to radical disrupting innovation is seen as being unlikely to result in "system" transitions toward sustainable development (as conceptualized in Section 8.4.1); however, disrupting forms of technological change are likely to continue.

In addition, Ashford, Hafkamp, et al. (2002) state that governments should work with stakeholders to define future targets—while ensuring that their agendas are not captured by incumbent firms—and then use their position as trustee to "represent the future generations and the future technologies to 'backcast' what specific policies are necessary to produce the required technical, organizational, and social transformations" (ibid., p. 10).*

When a system innovation is conceived as integrating policy development, government needs to develop initiatives for change *and* be willing to change its own institutions in the transformation process. Table 8.1 presents a simple matrix that can help decision makers explore whether change is needed within the existing decision-making architecture or whether an entirely new architecture is required.

Cells A and C in Table 8.1 represent situations where the necessary system transformations can be achieved within the existing legal, institutional, and political system. The difference between the two cells is whether it is necessary to bring new stakeholders into the transformation process. Cells B and D in Table 8.1 represent situations where the necessary system transformations cannot be achieved within the existing system. Again, the difference between the two cells is whether it is necessary to bring new stakeholders into the transformation process. If a more radical system innovation is required to move toward sustainable development, it is likely that the necessary solutions will emerge from the right-hand column of the matrix, especially if new stakeholders are included in the analysis (Cell D). The idea of integrating policy for sustainable transformations covers all four of these scenarios.

To return to Butter's (2002) three-layered approach to policy development, different strategies might be used to stimulate singular and system innovations and to establish an innovation climate or policy architecture, depending on the extent to which technological, institutional, organizational, and societal change is contemplated or desired.

In summary, integrated sustainability policies must use, alter, or supplant existing policies (and the institutions that administer them) in the areas of the economy, trade, the environment, and employment.

Recalling that a sustainable future requires technological, organizational, institutional, and societal changes, it is likely that an evolutionary pathway is insufficient to achieve factor ten or greater improvements in eco- and energy efficiency and reductions in the production and use of, and exposure to, toxic

---

* The concept of backcasting was first introduced by Amory Lovins in the 1970s and has since been applied and developed in Sweden and the Netherlands (Quist and Vergragt 2004; Vergragt 2005). The backcasting approach enables policy makers to look back from a desirable future to create strategies that they hope will enable the future visions to materialize. This approach is in contrast to current planning processes that develop strategies based on forecasts. See Section 8.5 for a discussion of backcasting.

substances. Such improvements require more systemic, multidimensional, and disruptive changes. We have already asserted that the capacity to change can be the limiting factor, and that this is often a crucial missing factor in optimistic scenarios.

Successful management of disruptive product innovation requires initiatives and input from outsiders to produce the expansion of the design space that limits the dominant technology firms. Especially in sectors with an important public or collective involvement, like transportation, construction, and agriculture, this means that intelligent government policies are required to bring about necessary change.

Rigid industries whose processes have remained stagnant also face considerable difficulties in becoming significantly more sustainable. Shifts from products to product-services rely on changes in the use, location, and ownership of products in which mature product manufacturers may participate, but this requires significant changes involving both managerial and social (customer) innovations. Changes in sociotechnical systems, such as transportation or agriculture, are even more difficult. This suggests that the creative use of government intervention is a more promising strategic approach for achieving sustainable industrial transformations than an approach that relies on firms' shorter-term economic interests.

This is not to say that enhanced analytic and technical capabilities on the part of firms and cooperative efforts and improved communication with suppliers, customers, workers, other industries, and environmental/consumer/community groups are not valuable adjuncts in the transformation process. But in most cases, these means and strategies are unlikely to be sufficient by themselves for significant transformations, and they will not work without clear mandated targets to enhance the triple goals of competitiveness, environmental quality, and enhancement of employment/labor concerns.

Government has a significant role to play, but the government cannot simply serve as a referee or arbiter of existing competing interests, because neither future generations nor future technologies are adequately represented by the existing stakeholders. Government should work with stakeholders to define far-future targets, but without allowing the incumbents to capture the agenda. It has to go beyond its historical focus on coordinating public- and private-sector policies. It must be multidimensional and directly address the present fragmentation of governmental functions.

There is a great deal of serendipity and uncertainty in the industrial transformation process, and the long-term prospects may not always be sufficiently definable to suggest obvious pathways or trajectories for the needed transformations. Thus it may be unreasonable to expect that government can always play a definitive "futures-making" role. It follows that rather than attempting tight management of sustainable pathways, the government role might be better conceived as one of "enabling" or "facilitating" change while at the same time providing visionary leadership for co-optimizing competitiveness, the environment, and employment. This means that the various policies must be mutually reinforcing. This newly conceptualized leadership role—focused on "opening up the problem space of the engineer/designer/analyst"—is likely to require participation of more than one ministry and more than one division of the industrial firm, with the assistance of professionals trained in a more multidisciplinary way (Ashford 2004; see also Ashford and Hall 2011).

The areas in which governmental programs and initiatives are typically found, especially in industrialized nations, are depicted earlier in Figure 1.10. The idea of integrating policy measures not only applies among sectors and activities associated with, affected by, or affecting competitiveness and employment but also includes health, safety, and the environment. We return to this figure as a mnemonic in devising policies for sustainable transformations involving all three pillars of sustainability in Chapter 13.

## 8.5 THE IMPORTANCE OF DIFFUSION IN ACHIEVING SUSTAINABLE DEVELOPMENT

Although technological innovation is crucial to achieve long-term sustainable development and fosters adaptive transformations, the preoccupation of scholars with innovation, in contrast with diffusion, may contribute to underdeployment or lack of development of policies that promote diffusion. The diffusion of technology is essential for enhancing sectoral and national revenues, as well as promoting more sustainable industrial, agricultural, transportation, and construction practices.[4] There are many existing technologies that could contribute to the reduction of health, safety, and environmental problems and improve labor productiveness, but they either encroach on vested interests in maintaining current practices or may impose costs on firms, on consumers, or on both.

In many cases, "environmental technologies" are process technologies rather than products and may confer proprietary benefits on their designers, who may not want others to have them. Environmental technologies are also difficult to organize into a market.

The slow pace of widespread technology adoption (diffusion) is not due to the fact that the "discovery" of solutions to health, safety, and environmental challenges is lacking, nor is there a need for coevolutionary approaches. Rather, what is missing is political and private-sector will for technology *adoption*. This may be as true for cleaner technologies as for so-called end-of-pipe technologies. After all, if the health, safety, and environmental harms that come from a technology are not internalized in the price of a manufacturer's activities, products, or services, why should he or she care if it is "cleaner"? Technology-diffusion forcing by government and significant demand by consumers, citizens, or workers through the tools of regulation, taxes, legislation, and stakeholder participation (see the next section) represent the driving forces for adoption.* Part IV of this work, which follows this chapter, addresses national, regional, and international governance of activities that improve health, safety, and the environment—and their potential impact on the innovation and diffusion of cleaner technologies.

## 8.6 STAKEHOLDER INVOLVEMENT IN THE CONTEXT OF SUSTAINABLE DEVELOPMENT†

Public and stakeholder participation lies at the heart of the democratic process and has been an important part of decision making for millennia. During the eighteenth century, Jean-Jacques Rousseau introduced the idea of the social contract between the governed and the government, which has since become the cornerstone of many political philosophies of government (see Section 1.2 in Chapter 1).

The rationale for public/stakeholder involvement in decision making has been well documented (Ashford and Rest 2001; NRC 1996; Renn, Webler, et al. 1995; Shepherd and Bowler 1997; Söderbaum 1973, 2004; Yosie and Herbst 1998), along with the mechanisms through which this involvement can occur

(Arnstein 1969; Hale 1993; Nagy, Bowman, et al. 1994; van Gunsteren and van Loon 2000). Not only is public/stakeholder participation likely to lead to more democratic and informed decision making that addresses the needs of citizens and affected stakeholders, but it may be essential if radically new initiatives are to succeed.

In the United States, the demand for public involvement in decision making can be traced back to the social activism and environmental movements of the 1960s and 1970s (Shepherd and Bowler 1997). With the passage of the National Environmental Policy Act (NEPA) in 1969 came the requirement that federal agencies undertake environmental impact assessments (EIAs) for all major projects. In addition to identifying and informing the public of the likely impacts of a project, the NEPA stipulated that the public must be able to participate in the development and review of the EIA. The NEPA also gave the public the right to challenge final rulings in the courts. These requirements have led to the institutionalization of public participation in the federal government's environmental decision-making process (ibid.).

Although the terms "public" and "stakeholder" participation are often used interchangeably, there is an important distinction between them (English, Gibson, et al. 1993). The former does not differentiate between stakeholders, whereas the latter seeks to identify only those groups affected by a specific policy or regulation. Although public participation is necessary to ensure that government is responsive to its citizens, our interest here lies with stakeholder participation (also known as stakeholder "involvement" or "engagement"). Identifying stakeholder groups is important because it can reveal distributive inequalities that occur as a result of government decisions.

Ensuring that stakeholders are included in the decision-making process is critical to sustainable development. As rapid technological change and globalization continue to affect our lives in unforeseen ways, establishing a democratic political philosophy to guide the development of social and technological systems becomes increasingly important.‡ Moreover, governance of sustainable development is a complex process, and the outcome of existing participatory approaches designed to promote or (at a minimum)

---

\* See Ashford and Caldart (2008) for an in-depth discussion of the relative merits of environmental regulation and economic instruments in achieving a reduction in pollution and waste.

† See also Section 5.4 in Chapter 5, "Globalization and Governance."

---

‡ See Section 1.2.2 in Chapter 1 for a discussion of utilitarian versus Rawlsian/communitarian approaches to citizen involvement in governmental decisions.

consider environmental concerns/sustainability is difficult to ascertain (Adger and Jordan 2009). Moving toward sustainability requires technological, organizational, institutional, and social transformations, each of which in turn depends on the willingness, opportunity/motivation, and capacity of key actors and institutions to change (see Chapter 13 for discussion of strategic options).*

In practice, the process of stakeholder involvement can be challenging. For example, decisions about when to involve stakeholders, how to identify and include affected groups, and which engagement mechanism to use are not trivial (Adger and Jordan 2009). However, our intent here is not to explore each and every nuance of stakeholder participation, but to focus on how stakeholders can be involved in identifying desirable *system transformations* (or system innovations) toward sustainable development. Two somewhat related but different techniques that lend themselves to such tasks are *scenario planning* and *backcasting.*[5]

Scenario planning was pioneered during the late 1960s and early 1970s by Royal Dutch Shell as a strategic planning tool (Wack 1985a, 1985b). By using scenarios to create a series of stories about future environments, Shell's strategic planning team was able to inform the perceptions of its managers and key decision makers about how their decisions might play out in the future. Thus the technique goes beyond the provision of scenarios and attempts to change "the image of reality in the heads of critical decision-makers" (Wack 1985b, p. 84). By allowing decision makers to "perceive reality," Shell has been able to respond more effectively to major events such as the oil shocks of the 1970s. The value of scenario planning is that it allows decision makers (1) to anticipate and better understand risk and (2) to develop strategic options that were previously concealed by incomplete perceptions of reality (Wack 1985a).

Hughes (2009a, 2009b) insists that in building images of the future, they must be grounded in reality and therefore in the present, especially with regard to likely technological change. In that sense, it is "evolution" and is relevant to transition or strategic niche management. Although this perspective may garner a stronger basis for consensus in planning, it smacks of technology-push policies and is to be contrasted with an alternative activity, that of

"backcasting," which is much closer to demand- or technology-pull strategies. In our view, backcasting is also more likely to result in radical innovations and avoid lock-in and path dependency. The limitations of scenario planning are acknowledged by Hughes (2009b, p. 13): "With technologies that are still at the research stage, and require radical breakthroughs to bring them into wider use, it is not guaranteed that particular [existing and involved] actor actions will result in such breakthroughs being achieved. . . . In general, it might be argued that what is considered incremental technological change would usually fall under [existing] actor contingent elements whereas radical technological breakthroughs, and unplanned technological failures, would usually fall within non-actor contingent elements [that is, outsiders]." (See also the discussion of the crucial role of outsiders in van de Poel 2000, 2003.)

Like scenario planning, the roots of backcasting can be traced back to the 1970s. The technique was first proposed by Lovins (1976), who suggested that a better approach to predicting energy futures might be to describe a desirable future (or long-term goal) and then work backward to develop a set of policies to realize that future. Figure 8.7 provides a simple example of how a subgoal and a long-term goal could inform the development of policies/strategies a, b, and c and d, e, and f, respectively, to reach the desired future state. The basic idea is that the future is a function of prevailing policies and choices. Thus a strategic change in policy today is likely to influence the future by guiding political, economic, and social systems in a certain direction.

Interestingly, scenario planning and backcasting approach the notion of system transformations/innovation from quite different perspectives. Scenario planning accepts that system transformations are likely to occur, but it does not attempt to influence them directly. Instead, it focuses on developing strategies today that will perform well under a range of potential scenarios (or transformations). Backcasting is more proactive in that it purposefully tries to shape system transformations. Given its focus on guiding change, it can be argued that backcasting is a more useful technique for decision making for sustainable development. To a certain extent, backcasting rejects the "invisible hand" of a laissez-faire economy as an appropriate means through which sustainable development can be achieved (Anderson 2001). Instead, it places importance on the role of government and

---

* See Section 7.5 in Chapter 7 for a discussion of the importance of willingness, opportunity/motivation, and capacity for organizational learning in the context of the industrial firm.

## Target Achievement?

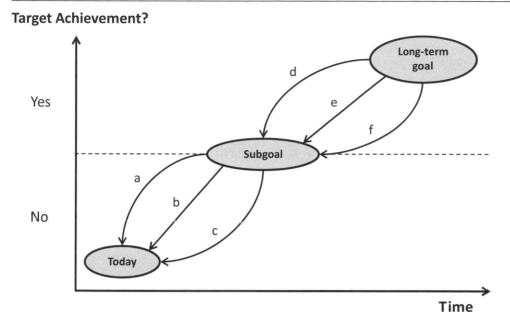

FIGURE 8.7: THE BACKCASTING PROCESS

stakeholders in guiding system transformations. The form of guidance selected will depend on the roles adopted by government and stakeholders and on the expected timescale of the transformation.*

Although the "traditional" use of scenario planning does not directly attempt to influence the future, there is evidence to suggest that if scenarios are developed by a representative group of leaders from within a nation, the scenarios can have a significant influence on how the future of that nation unfolds (Kahane 2001). In addition to creating a series of stories about how their nation might develop, leaders of government, business, and civil society have a direct interest in shaping the future they desire. Thus the process of building a scenario can be an important learning experience where leaders can explore how their actions might support a particular future. The end result is that the collective group of decision makers can take steps to ensure that the more desirable scenarios are supported by their present-day actions. In this regard, the distinction between "participatory" scenario planning and backcasting becomes blurred. Because backcasting focuses explicitly on shaping the future, the following text looks more closely at this technique.

During the 1990s, the idea of backcasting was used in Sweden and the Netherlands to explore potential pathways for achieving more sustainable development (Quist and Vergragt 2004). As Anderson (2001, p. 622) comments, "The structure and characteristics of the backcasting process are, in many respects, a natural complement to the inclusive and conciliatory ethos of sustainable development. While sustainable development provides a strategic framing of environmental reform, backcasting provides the procedural vehicle for translating subsequent objectives into practical policy initiatives. Or, put another way, the objectives arising from sustainable development provide the macro-targets to be achieved through the evolution of micro-policy initiatives developed within the backcast."

Although backcasting was not originally designed as a participatory approach to decision making, Quist and Vergragt (2004, p. 429) make a convincing case that "participatory backcasting . . . [is] a novel, innovative and promising approach for long-term strategizing for sustainability, based on stakeholder involvement, construction of normative sustainable futures, [and] stakeholder learning, in combination with design and analysis activities and construction of follow-up agendas meant for guiding implementation."

Quist (2007, p. 135; 2009b, p. 6) summarizes the findings from the literature regarding backcasting:

- Broad stakeholder participation can help increase legitimacy and accountability, structure

---

* The timescale of a transformation is important because it will indicate whether industry or government should be responsible for guiding the pathway toward sustainable development. It is argued that as the timescale increases, the role of government in guiding the transformation becomes greater—even "indispensable" (Vergragt 2005, p. 313).

complex unstructured problems like sustainability problems, broaden issues with a range of aspects and values and increase support and involvement (also in follow-up).

- New emerging future visions can become guiding images shared by groups of stakeholders that provide guidance and orientation to the supporting stakeholders in line with the future vision in a process of diffusion and further elaboration of the vision.

- Emerging visions face competition from other emerging visions and their supporters, as well as from the regular dominant vision supported by vested interests and actors.

- Visions may have strong normative and ethical assumptions and be generated deliberatively by groups of stakeholders.

- (Higher order) learning may encourage actors to reformulate problem definitions and shift their preferred ways and approaches to dealing with a certain problem. Increased insight into the values and views of other stakeholders may be another result.

- Both the way the backcasting has been applied and the organisational settings of the backcasting experiment are likely to affect the nature and degree of follow-up.

- Network theories[*] provide a promising way for analysing follow-up and spin-off activities.

- Successful networks around follow-up and spin-off activities may lead to instances of institutionalisation in which institutions change, as well as to instances of institutional resistance from vested interests and backing actors who feel threatened.

In a review of ten years of backcasting experience in three case studies in the Netherlands, Quist (2009a) finds that stakeholders had no or very limited influence on the process, although "higher-order learning" could be observed (ibid., p. 12), and that the process "does not automatically lead to follow-up, spin-off, and implementation in line with the vision and the follow-up agenda"—depending on various internal and external factors that could be enabling or constraining (ibid., p. 14). Spin-off or follow-up activities occur within the context of niches in research, business, government, or public interest groups and the general public (ibid., p. 15). He concludes that "careful network management and theories of network management may be more relevant than theories of stakeholder participation in (public) decision-making and science" (ibid.).

The concept of participatory backcasting also provides a way in which technological development can become more responsive to the concerns of stakeholders (or citizens). Some advocates of stakeholder involvement have called for the creation of a democratic decision-making process to guide the development of technological systems (Sclove 1995; Winner 1977, 1986). Their concern is that the rate of technological change is outpacing the ability of government to monitor and guide its progress—meaning that technology is changing without a plan. Further, as technology plays a more dominant role in our lives, it is argued that our freedoms are in some way being inadvertently "regulated" by technology (Lessig 2000; Sclove 1995; Winner 1977, 1986).[†]

The links among democratic decision making for technological development, participatory backcasting, and sustainable development seem relatively clear. Participatory backcasting is one mechanism through which technological development can be democratized by the interaction of decision makers, technology developers, and stakeholder groups. Further, the process of looking back from a shared vision of a sustainable future can be a catalyst for the creation of more sustainable technological systems. "Participatory backcasting has potential for planning in sustainable development, for identification and exploration of promising sustainable technologies, sustainable system innovations and transitions, for guiding technology choices and for generating alternative more sustainable trajectories for present dominant trends and developments" (Quist and Vergragt 2004, p. 429).

In conclusion, public/stakeholder participation is an essential component of sustainable development. Although public/stakeholder participation in the environmental decision-making process is now institutionalized in the U.S. federal government, the philosophy of government and the stakeholder posture adopted by society can have a significant influence on whether it is able to move toward sustainable development. Further, given the ethical and intergenerational importance of protecting species and

---

\* See the discussion of social networks in Section 7.3.2.4 in Chapter 7.

† Sclove (1995) presents a set of recommendations that focus on designing technologies that support democracy in communities, employment, and politics. In addition, he highlights the importance of creating technologies that support sustainable development. Interestingly, Sclove's (1995) focus on developing technologies that support local economic self-reliance, maintain environmental/social harms within political boundaries, and support ecological sustainability leans heavily toward the notion of "ecodevelopment."

the environment, either government or stakeholder groups must represent the interests of these groups in the decision-making process. Finally, participatory backcasting presents a novel way to focus decision making on sustainable development and include stakeholders in the process of technological development.

## 8.7 INNOVATION, INDUSTRIAL, AND TECHNOLOGY POLICY IN THE CONTEXT OF A GLOBALIZED ECONOMY

Earlier we emphasized that the term "competitiveness" as it relates to a national economy has two different meanings: (1) the ability of the nation-state to provide needed goods and services to its people and (2) a synonym for "competition," meaning the extent to which a country (or a sector) is able to garner greater profits and market share. Traditional industrial policy focuses on the second meaning as a goal, often with an inherent "trickle-down" assumption that a rising tide raises all boats, and hence the poorer parts of the society will benefit. In the industrial-nation context, the focus is on increasing trade as a source of revenue, especially if the existing domestic market is "saturated" because either the consumption of a particular good (or service) is already widespread or because the nonconsuming part of society does not have the purchasing power to buy the domestic product. In either case, we speak of "excess capacity" or "overcapacity" in the producing sector.

In both the industrialized world and the developing world, industrial policy has sometimes taken the form of producing "national champions" to compete in world trade. Industrialized nations have attempted this in high-technology sectors, focusing on policies to encourage innovation,* while developing countries have sought to capture larger shares of global markets in areas where they perceive that they have comparative advantages, such as cheaper labor or commodity goods.

In the United States, the issue of cheaper wages in developing countries led to flexible wage policies,

which are partially credited with generating greater labor productivity in the 1990s by allowing wages to fall in line with reduced demand and the isolation of trade unions. Inclinations to emulate this policy in Europe were met with strong resistance, partly because of the greater extent of unionization in many (especially northern) European countries and partly because of objections on theoretical grounds. Kleinknecht (1998), a German-born Dutch economist, argues along Schumpeterian lines that lowering wages should not be adopted as a policy in Europe because it would reward those firms (and industries) that do not know how to use labor effectively. These firms should be allowed to exit the market in favor of firms that do.[†]

Weiss (1997) provides an overview of changes in the industrial policies of the Northern economies over the previous decade. In the context of globalization, he is pessimistic about selective "governmental attempts to foster national high-technology 'champions'" and instead advocates *general* policies for facilitating innovation. This debate between "picking winners" and "general policies" is the central one in the area of industrial policy. He cynically argues that the "winners are good at picking governments," but there are examples where the opposite is the case, such as the Japanese and French high-speed trains and the creation of national champions by the Asian tigers. Mowery and Rosenberg (1989) argue that globalization is driving a convergence of technology and trade issues, although trade policy models and instruments have lagged far behind.

Globalization has indeed changed the economic landscape. It connects national economies in new ways and denationalizes access to information, technology, knowledge, markets, and financial capital. It has also opened up two distinct pathways by which a national sector or economy can compete in international markets: (1) by producing more innovative and superior technology that may or may not be first deployed in niche markets (Kemp 1994, 1997) and (2) by adopting cost-cutting measures that involve increased economies of scale, by shedding labor, and by ignoring health, safety, and environmental hazards. Although some proponents of globalization have argued that globalization also increases the demand for more protective measures worldwide (Bhagwati 1997;

---

* See the discussion of the EU's LisbonStrategy and Europe 2020 in Section 1.5 in Chapter 1. Also see the EU's 1994 white paper *Growth, Competitiveness, Employment: The Challenges and Ways Forward into the 21st Century* (European Commission 1994), in which a multifaceted strategy was suggested in which environmentally sound growth to create jobs promised to deliver a "double dividend." This strategy was never implemented.

---

† Interestingly, Kleinknecht (1998) observes in the same article that environmental standards should also not be relaxed for similar reasons. That would reward firms that do not address environmental problems efficiently.

Vogel 1995), others have cautioned about a "race to the bottom" and an ever-increasing tendency to trade on environmental (and labor) externalities (Ekins, Folke, et al. 1994). Thus we see that not only are there two drivers of economic growth, technology and trade, but that trade itself can take two diametrically opposed directions, innovation-driven competition and traditional cost-cutting competition (Charles and Lehner 1998).

## 8.8 MODERNIZATION, GLOBALIZATION, AND EMPLOYMENT* IN THE NORTH

Charles and Lehner (1998, p. 223) argue that "the type of innovation which is the key to new employment is one which develops markets in new directions and creates new markets and thus enhances a strong leading-edge economy." (One can make the same observation for the enhancement of the environment.) As Schumpeter has pointed out, companies in the leading-edge economy can exploit a temporary monopoly resulting from their superior products and services (Schumpeter 1939, 1962). Charles and Lehner (1998) observed that advanced-industry economies in their innovative sectors had already shifted in the previous ten to fifteen years from technocentric to anthropocentric production systems—those that capitalize on human intelligence and are designed for continuous improvement and learning. Instead of a cost-driven strategy that calls for reduced labor costs, Charles and Lehner recommend that industrial economies aim for an innovation-driven strategy, which depends on a large number of human interfaces in the company that are likely to produce organizational learning, creativity, new ideas, and well-paying jobs. An innovation-driven strategy also affords an opportunity to modernize and improve products, processes, and services.

In Section 7.6.3 in Chapter 7, we discussed the tendency for innovations in products, processes, and services to affect employment in dramatically different ways, with product innovation generally creating employment and process innovation destroying employment (Edquist, Hommen, et al. 2001). When new products replace old ones, because there is a tendency for new production to be more capital intensive (that is, more labor saving), there could easily be a net loss of jobs. Even where the immediate effect of new products may be to increase employment, there may be a loss of jobs from the product(s) they replace. Because globalization seems to be domi-

nated by trade in products, net job gains are at best uncertain. See Hurley Fernández-Macías (2008) for a recent analysis of job gains and losses in different sectors and countries in Europe. Of particular significance is the increase in the length of the working week in the EU, with the exception of Greece and Ireland (Eurofound 2008). See also the discussion in Section 1.1.3 in Chapter 1 of concerns about income and wage inequality and the effects of technological and skill changes on employment.

Job loss of unskilled labor in the North is not new, although with the emergence of China (as a major location for manufacturing jobs) and India (for service jobs), this issue takes on new currency. Without a specific focus on enhancing one kind of technological change over another (for example, more labor-intensive production of products, shifts from products to product-services, or services over products), Wood (1994, p. 347) offered the following policy interventions:

1. Raising barriers against manufactured goods from the South

2. Reducing the relative supply of unskilled labor by education and training (to offset the reduction in demand)

3. Boosting the relative demand for unskilled labor by public works programs or employment subsidies

4. Using taxes and transfers to redistribute income from skilled to unskilled workers

President Barack Obama is committed to economic revitalization that includes concern for employment. He has also promised to reexamine the issue of trade, although it is hard to imagine that he would adopt direct policies to implement the first of Wood's possible policy options. Nor is the fourth redistributive option likely to be implemented. The third option is actually one of his announced strategies. The second option is problematic. Decreasing the share of unskilled labor in favor of increasing training and education of skilled workers does little (in fact, it alone may decrease the wages of skilled workers overall because their supply will be increased) unless high-skilled jobs are actually created as well.[†] In this regard, Obama's policies to create energy-related jobs and increase U.S.-based automobile manufacturing would help, but the devil will be in the details.

---

\* See also the discussion of employment concerns in Section 1.1.3 in Chapter 1.

---

† In this regard, Robert Reich's (1992) now-old suggestion that education alone will solve the U.S. unemployment or underemployment problem is naïve at best.

It is not unlikely that employment, rather than energy or the environment, will be the leading political concern in the next decade at least, especially because the financial-system crisis has left increasing numbers of people without sufficient purchasing power to obtain the necessary goods for a healthy and secure life. If the government wants to create jobs, it must do so with deliberation while focusing on designing specific technological changes that increase the labor content of product manufacturing, shift from products to product-services, and stimulate whole system changes. New industry creation (with new jobs) displaces existing industries (with job losses) with an unjustified optimism based on a "trickle-down" logic that these changes will result in net job gains. Just as it is now accepted that products and processes need to be designed with environmental effects in mind from the beginning, trickle-down improvements in employment are no more likely to succeed than trickle-down approaches to environmental improvement.

## 8.9 INDUSTRIAL AND EMPLOYMENT POLICY IN THE SOUTH

As noted earlier, *innovation* of new technologies is widely seen as the source of competitive advantage for industrialized economies. The corollary of this view is that late-developing economies do not have this advantage. In describing the success of the so-called Asian tigers—Taiwan, South Korea, Singapore, and others—Amsden (1992) articulates this view and argues that even when markets are working, state intervention is required in the industrialization process in the form of subsidies (to keep wages low) and import protectionism. Contrary to the neoclassical economic view, low wages alone do not impart a sufficiently large comparative advantage to developing countries to guarantee economic advance over the productivity advances in the developed nations. In addition to the interventions mentioned above, Amsden (1992) recommends that the government set high performance standards for production volume and keep wage disparity among workers and between managers and workers low to motivate workers.

In a classic article, Lall (1992) argues that the case for market intervention depends on (1) the nature and economic cost of market failures, (2) the availability of market-based solutions, and (3) the ability of the government to design and implement correct solutions. She is less sanguine than Amsden about the ability of the government to adopt the correct

policies and emphasizes the importance of capacity building and organizational learning, especially in product markets, for transformation in developing economies. Lall concludes that success ultimately depends on incentives, capabilities, and institutions and on minimizing both market and government failures, both of which need correcting.

Rodrik (2007, p. 100) takes an intermediate position between those who emphasize market fundamentalism and those who advocate government intervention, arguing that "market forces and private entrepreneurship should be in the driving seat of [the development] agenda, but governments should also perform a strategic and coordinating role in the productive sphere beyond simply ensuring property rights, contract enforcement, and macroeconomic stability. . . . The task of industrial policy is as much about eliciting information from the private sector on significant externalities and their remedies as it is about implementing appropriate policies."

Rodrik (2007) observes that the theory of comparative advantage does not seem to operate to the benefit of the developing world. The challenge government faces is to get the *policy process* right rather than focus on the *outcomes*. What is needed is *institutional innovation*. In this regard, the developing world suffers more from the demand-side faults than the supply-side deficiencies, such as a lack of trained scientists and engineers, R&D institutions, or inadequate protection of intellectual property. Thus the problem is the low demand for schooling—or a low propensity to acquire learning—rather than the failure of the state to provide education.

In Rodrik's (2007) view, the government should focus on addressing *information externalities* rather than on picking winning sectors. Specifically, government needs to (1) engage in a self-discovery process to identify opportunities and deficiencies and (2) coordinate information and learning on the part of strategic actors, and (3) encourage the willingness of government to deploy an industrial policy. The private sector is key to discovering what areas a particular nation should invest in and develop. Government export subsidies should be linked to demanding trade performance requirements.

Rodrik (2007, pp. 114–117) recommends ten design principles:

1. Incentives should be provided only to new activities in order to diversify the economy and establish new areas of comparative advantage (not to be confused with sector promotion).
2. Establish clear benchmarks for success and failure.

3. Establish sunset clauses.

4. Support public activities, not sectors.

5. Subsidize activities that have spill-over and demonstration effects.

6. Vest authority in agencies with demonstrated competence.

7. Insist on politically accountable monitoring.

8. Establish clear channels of communication between agencies and private sector.

9. Tolerate failures.

10. Ensure that activities renew (and rediscover) themselves.

A major goal of state intervention in industrializing economies is argued to be the acquisition of *technological capabilities*. In a classic article, Dahlman, Ross-Larson, et al. (1987) outline what this task entails and what incentives need to be created to achieve it. Ernst and O'Connor (1989) describe policy issues and options facing newly industrializing economies (NIEs), given the need to acquire technological capabilities in a globalizing international economy. Armed with the advantages of a more modern history and the failure of market fundamentalism to deliver on its promise of development for the South—especially in South America, where it had been most extensively embraced—the observations of Rodrik (2007) deserve special attention.

The standard recommendation to improve employment in the South is to focus on supply-side interventions to improve education and skill development. Rodrik (2007) offers a more comprehensive perspective, focusing on developing the needed political and institutional infrastructure to promote, as well, demand-side entrepreneurship appropriate to the specific developing nation.

## 8.10 NOTES

1. See the Association for Evolutionary Economics (AFEE), www.afee.net/ (accessed May 18, 2010).

2. Also see Butter and Montalvo (2004).

3. See Freeman (1987) and OECD (1997) for a discussion of NSI.

4. See the special issue of the *Journal of Cleaner Production* devoted to strategies for promoting diffusion (Montalvo and Kemp 2008).

5. Two alternative, more localized, visioning techniques of interest include PLACE³S (**PLA**nning for **C**ommunity **E**nergy, **E**conomic, and **E**nvironmental **S**ustainability) and CommunityViz. Both techniques use geographic information systems (GIS) and quantitative assessment models to help stakeholders understand the future implications of their current decisions. For more information, see U.S. Department of Energy, *The Energy Yardstick: Using PLACE³S to Create More Sustainable Communities*, www.smartcommunities.ncat.org/pdf/places.pdf (accessed May

18, 2010); and the Orton Family Foundation, *CommunityViz*, www.communityviz.com/ (accessed May 18, 2010).

## 8.11 ADDITIONAL READINGS

Ashford, N. A. and R. P. Hall (2011). "The Importance of Regulation-Induced Innovation for Sustainable Development" *Sustainability* 3(1): 270–292. Available at www.mdpi.com/2071-1050/3/1/270/pdf (accessed January 20, 2011).

Charles, Tony, and Franz Lehner (1998). "Competitiveness and Employment: A Strategic Dilemma for Economic Policy." *Competition and Change* 3(1/2): 207–236.

Edquist, Charles, Leif Hommen, and Maureen McKelvey (2001). *Innovation and Employment: Process versus Product Innovation.* Cheltenham, Edward Elgar.

Kleinknecht, Alfred (1998). "Is Labour Market Flexibility Harmful to Innovation?" *Cambridge Journal of Economics* 22(3): 387–396.

Luiten, Ester E. M. (2001). Beyond Energy Efficiency: Actors, Networks and Government Intervention in the Development of Industrial Process Technologies. PhD dissertation, Utrecht, Utrecht University.

Nehrt, Chad (1998). "Maintainability of First Mover Advantages When Environmental Regulations Differ between Countries." *Academy of Management Review* 23(1): 77–97.

Rodrik, Dani. (2007). *One Economics: Many Recipes: Globalization, Institutions, and Economic Growth.* Princeton, NJ, Princeton University Press.

## 8.12 REFERENCES

Adger, W. N., and A. Jordan, Eds. (2009). *Governing Sustainability.* Cambridge, Cambridge University Press.

Amsden, A. H. (1992). A Theory of Government Intervention in Late Industrialization. *State and Market in Development: Synergy or Rivalry?* L. Putterman and D. Rueschemeyer. Boulder, CO, Lynne Rienner Publishers: 53–84.

Anderson, K. L. (2001). "Reconciling the Electricity Industry with Sustainable Development: Backcasting—A Strategic Alternative." *Futures* 33: 607–623.

Arnstein, S. R. (1969). "A Ladder of Citizen Participation." *Journal of the American Institute of Planners* 35(4): 216–224.

Ashford, N. A. (2000). An Innovation-Based Strategy for a Sustainable Environment. *Innovation-Oriented Environmental Regulation: Theoretical Approach and Empirical Analysis.* J. Hemmelskamp, K. Rennings, and F. Leone. New York, Physica-Verlag Heidelberg: 67–107.

Ashford, N. A. (2002a). "Government and Environmental Innovation in Europe and North America." *American Behavioral Scientist* 45(9): 1417–1434.

Ashford, N. A. (2002b). Technology-Focused Regulatory Approaches for Encouraging Sustainable Industrial Transformations: Beyond Green, beyond the Dinosaurs, and beyond Evolutionary Theory. Paper presented at the 3rd Blueprint Workshop on Instruments for Integrating Environmental and Innovation Policy, Brussels, September 26–27.

Ashford, N. A. (2004). "Major Challenges to Engineering Education for Sustainable Development: What Has to Change to Make It Creative, Effective, and Acceptable to the Established Disciplines?" *International Journal of Sustainability in Higher Education* **5**(3): 239–250.

Ashford, N. A. (2005). Government and Environmental Innovation in Europe and North America. *Towards Environmental Innovation Systems.*M. Weber and J. Hemmelskamp. Heidelberg, Springer: 159–174.

Ashford, N. A. (2009). Environmental Regulation, Globalization, and Innovation. *Handbook on Trade and the Environment.* K. P. Gallagher. Cheltenham and Northampton, MA, Edward Elgar: 297–307.

Ashford, N. A., C. Ayers, et al. (1985). "Using Regulation to Change the Market for Innovation." *Harvard Environmental Law Review* **9**(2): 419–466.

Ashford, N. A., and C. C. Caldart (2008). *Environmental Law, Policy, and Economics: Reclaiming the Environmental Agenda.* Cambridge, MA, MIT Press.

Ashford, N. A., W. Hafkamp, et al. (2002). Pathways to Sustainable Industrial Transformations: Cooptimising Competitiveness, Employment, and Environment. Cambridge, MA, Ashford Associates. Available at http://hdl.handle.net/1721.1/41844 (accessed January 20, 2011).

Ashford, N. A. and R. P. Hall (2011). "The Importance of Regulation-Induced Innovation for Sustainable Development" *Sustainability* **3**(1): 270–292. Available at www.mdpi.com/2071-1050/3/1/270/pdf (accessed January 20, 2011).

Ashford, N. A., and K. M. Rest (2001). Public Participation in Contaminated Communities. Cambridge. Available at Center for Technology, Policy and Industrial Development, MIT. Available at http://web.mit.edu/ctpid/www/tl/ (accessed January 20, 2011).

Beddoe, R., R. Costanza, et al. (2009). "Overcoming Systemic Roadblocks to Sustainability: The Evolutionary Design of Worldviews, Institutions, and Technologies." *Proceedings of the National Academy of Sciences* **106**(8): 2483–2489.

Berkhout, F., A. Smith, et al. (2004). Socio-technological Regimes and Transition Contexts. *System Innovation and the Transition to Sustainability: Theory, Evidence and Policy.* B. Elzen, F. W. Geels, and K. Green. Cheltenham, Edward Elgar: 48–75.

Bhagwati, J. (1997). "The Global Age: From a Sceptical South to a Fearful North." *World Economy* **20**(3): 259–283.

Butter, M. (2002). A Three Layer Policy Approach for System Innovations. Paper presented at the 1st Blueprint Workshop, Environmental Innovation Systems, Brussels, January.

Butter, M., and C. Montalvo (2004). Finding Niches in Green Innovation Policy. Paper presented at the Berlin Conference on the Human Dimensions of Global Climate Change, Greening of Policies—Interlinkages and Policy Integration, Berlin, December 3–5.

Charles, T., and F. Lehner (1998). "Competitiveness and Employment: A Strategic Dilemma for Economic Policy." *Competition and Change* **3**(1/2): 207–236.

Christensen, C. M. (1997). *The Innovator's Dilemma: When New Technologies Cause Great Firms to Fail.* Cambridge, MA, Harvard Business School Press.

Christensen, C. M., T. Craig, et al. (2001). "The Great Disruption." *Foreign Affairs* **80**(2): 80–95.

Dahlman, C. J., B. Ross-Larson, et al. (1987). "Managing Technological Development: Lessons from Newly Industrializing Countries." *World Development* **15**(6): 759–775.

Dewulf, A., C. Termeer, et al. (2009). The Value of Theoretical Multiplicity for Steering Transitions towards Sustainability. Paper presented at the First European Conference on Sustainability Transitions, Amsterdam, June 4–6.

Dorf, R. C. (2001). *Technology, Humans, and Society: Toward a Sustainable World.* New York, Academic Press.

Edquist, C., L. Hommen, et al. (2001). *Innovation and Employment: Process versus Product Innovation.* Cheltenham, Edward Elgar.

Ekins, P., C. Folke, et al. (1994). "Trade, Environment and Development: The Issues in Perspective." *Ecological Economics* **9**(1): 1–12.

Elzen, B. (2002). Transition to Sustainability through System Innovation: Summary Report from Workshop and Follow-up Activities. Forum on Science and Technology for Sustainability. Available at http://sustainability-science.org/content.html?contentid=212&listed=1 (accessed January 20, 2011).

Elzen, B., F. W. Geels, et al., Eds. (2004). *System Innovation and the Transition to Sustainability: Theory, Evidence and Policy.* Cheltenham, Edward Elgar.

English, M., A. K. Gibson, et al. (1993). *Stakeholder Involvement: Open Processes for Reaching Decisions about the Future Uses of Contaminated Sites.* Knoxville, University of Tennessee, Waste Management Research and Education Institute.

Ernst, D., and D. O'Connor (1989). *Technology and Global Competition: The Challenge for Newly Industrialising Economies.* Paris, OECD Development Centre Studies.

European Commission (EC) (1994). *Growth, Competitiveness, Employment: The Challenges and Ways Forward into the 21st Century.* Brussels, EC.

European Foundation for the Improvement of Living and Working Conditions (Eurofound) (2008). "Actual Working Week Is Longer across Europe." Eurofound News Issue 9, 2008. Available at www.eurofound.europa.eu/eiro/studies/tn0903039s/tn0903039s.htm (accessed January 20, 2011).

Foxon, T., Z. Makuch, et al. (2004). Innovation Systems and Policy-Making Processes for the Transition to Sustainability. *Governance for Industrial Transformation: Proceedings of the 2003 Berlin Conference on the Human Dimensions of Global Environmental Change.* K. Jacob, M. Binder, and A. Wieczorek. Berlin, Environmental Policy Research Centre: 96–112.

Freeman, C. (1987). *Technology Policy and Economic Performance: Lessons from Japan.* London, Pinter.

Geels, F. W. (2004). Understanding System Innovations: A Critical Literature Review and a Concept Synthesis. *System Innovation and the Transition to Sustainability: Theory, Evidence and Policy.* B. Elzen, F. W. Geels, and K. Green. Cheltenham, Edward Elgar: 19–47.

Hale, E. O. (1993). "Successful Public Involvement." *Journal of Environmental Health* **55**(4): 17–19.

Hey, C., K. Jacob, et al. (2007). "Better Regulation by New Governance Hybrids? Governance Models and the Reform of European Chemicals Policy." *Journal of Cleaner Production* **15**(18): 1859–1874.

Hoogma, R., R. Kemp, et al. (2002). *Experimenting for Sustainable Transport: The Approach of Strategic Niche Management*. London, Spon Press.

Hoogma, R., M. Weber, et al. (2001). Integrated Long-Term Strategies to Induce Regime Shifts to Sustainability: The Approach of Strategic Niche Management. Paper presented at the conference "Towards Environmental Innovation Systems." Garmisch-Partenkirchen, Germany, September 27–29.

Huber, J. (2004a). Environmental Policy Shift through Technological Innovation. *Governance for Industrial Transformation: Proceedings of the 2003 Berlin Conference on the Human Dimensions of Global Environmental Change*. K. Jacob, M. Binder, and A. Wieczorek. Berlin, Environmental Policy Research Centre: 438–447.

Huber, J. (2004b). *New Technologies and Environmental Innovation*. Cheltenham, Edward Elgar.

Hughes, N. (2009a). A Historical Overview of Strategic Scenario Planning, and Lessons for Undertaking Low Carbon Energy Policy. A joint working paper of the EON/EPSRC Transition Pathways Project (Working Paper 1) and the UKERC. Available at www.ukerc.ac.uk/ResearchProgrammes/EnergySystemsandModelling/ESMUKERCworkingpapers.aspx (accessed January 20, 2011).

Hughes, N. (2009b). Using Scenarios to Bring about Transitions: Lessons from a Broad Scenario Building Tradition. Paper presented at the First European Conference on Sustainability Transitions, Amsterdam, June 4–6.

Hurley, J and E. Fernández-Macías (2008). *More and Better Jobs: Patterns of Employment Expansion in Europe*. Dublin, Eurofound. Available at www.eurofound.europa.eu/publications/htmlfiles/ef0850.htm (accessed January 20, 2011).

Jacob, K. (2005). Management of Industrial Transformation: Potentials and Limits from a Political Science Perspective. *Innovations towards Sustainability: Conditions and Consequences*. M. Lehmann-Waffenschmidt. Berlin, Springer-Verlag: 95–100.

Jänicke, M. (1990). *State Failure: The Impotence of Politics in Industrial Society*. University Park, Pennsylvania State University Press.

Jänicke, M., and K. Jacob (2005). Ecological Modernisation and the Creation of Lead Markets. *Towards Environmental Innovation Systems*. M. Weber and J. Hemmelskamp. Heidelberg, Springer: 175–193.

Kahane, A. (2001). "How to Change the World: Lessons for Entrepreneurs from Activists." *Reflections* **2**(3): 16–29.

Kasser, T. (2002). *The High Price of Materialism*. Cambridge, MA, MIT Press.

Kemp, R. (1994). "Technology and Environmental Sustainability: The Problem of Technological Regime Shift." *Futures* **26**(10): 1023–1046.

Kemp, R. (1997). *Environmental Policy and Technical Change: A Comparison of the Technological Impact of Policy Instruments*. Cheltenham, Edward Elgar.

Kemp, R. (2002). Integrating Environmental and Innovation Policies. Paper presented at the International Workshop on Industrial Innovation and Environmental Regulation: Toward an Integrated Approach, Maastricht, September 6–7.

Kemp, R. (2008). Transition Management for Sustainable Consumption and Production. *System Innovation for Sustainability: Perspectives on Radical Changes to Sustainable Consumption and Production*. A. Tukker, M. Charter, C. Vezzoli, E. Stø, and M. M. Andersen. Sheffield, U.K., Greenleaf Publishing: 369–390.

Kemp, R., D. Loorbach, et al. (2007). "Transition Management as a Model for Managing Processes of Co-evolution towards Sustainable Development." *International Journal of Sustainable Development and World Ecology* **14**: 1–15.

Kemp, R., and J. Rotmans (2005). The Management of the Co-evolution of Technical, Environmental and Social Systems. *Towards Environmental Innovation Systems*. M. Weber and J. Hemmelskamp. Heidelberg, Springer: 33–55.

Keohane, N. O., R. L. Revesz, et al. (1998). "The Choice of Regulatory Instruments in Environmental Policy." *Harvard Environmental Law Review* **22**: 313–368.

Kleinknecht, A. (1998). "Commentary: Is Labour Market Flexibility Harmful to Innovation?" *Cambridge Journal of Economics* **22**: 387–396.

Lall, S. (1992). "Technological Capabilities and the Role of Government in Developing Countries." *Greek Economic Review* **14**(1): 1–36.

Lessig, L. (2000). *Code and Other Laws of Cyberspace*. New York, Basic Books.

Lovins, A. (1976). "Energy Strategy: The Road Not Taken?" *Foreign Affairs* **55**: 65–96.

Luiten, E. E. M. (2001). Beyond Energy Efficiency: Actors, Networks and Government Intervention in the Development of Industrial Process Technologies. PhD dissertation, Utrecht, Utrecht University.

Meadowcroft, J. (2005). "Environmental Political Ecomomy, Technological Transitions, and the State." *New Political Economy* **10**(4): 479–498.

Meadowcroft, J. (2009). "What About the Politics? Sustainable Development, Transition Management, and Long Term Energy Transitions." *Policy Sciences* **42**: 323–340.

Montalvo, C., and R. Kemp, Eds. (2008). "Diffusion of Cleaner Technologies: Modeling, Case Studies and Policy." *Journal of Cleaner Production* **16**(1) Supplement 1: S1–S184.

Moors, E. H. M. (2000). Metal Making in Motion: Technology Choices for Sustainable Metals Production. PhD dissertation, Delft, Delft University of Technology.

Mowery, D. C., and N. Rosenberg (1989). The Merger of Technology and Trade Policies. *Technology and the Pursuit of Economic Growth*. New York, Cambridge University Press: 274–289.

Nagy, M. T., M. Bowman, et al. (1994). *Manual on Public Participation in Environmental Decisionmaking: Current Practice and Future Possibilities in Central and Eastern Europe*. Budapest, Regional Environmental Center for Central and Eastern Europe. Available at www.rec.org/REC/Publications/PPManual/Default.html (accessed January 20, 2011).

National Research Council (NRC) (1996). *Understanding Risk: Informing Decisions in a Democratic Society*. P.

C. Stern and H. V. Fineberg. Washington, DC, NRC, Commission on Behavioral and Social Sciences and Education (CBASSE).

NRC (2002). *Our Common Journey: A Transition toward Sustainability.* Washington, DC, National Academy Press.

Nelson, R. R., and S. G. Winter (1977). "In Search of Useful Theory of Innovation." *Research Policy* **6**: 36–76.

Nelson, R. R., and S. G. Winter (1982). *An Evolutionary Theory of Economic Change.* Cambridge, MA, Harvard University Press.

Organisation for Economic Co-operation and Development (OECD) (1997). *New Rationale and Approaches in Technology and Innovation Policy.* Paris, OECD.

Oye, K., and J. Foster (2002). Public Environmental Regulation and Private Business Risk. Laboratory for Energy and the Environment (LFEE) Working Paper, Cambridge, MA, MIT.

Partidario, P. J. (2003). "What-If": From Path Dependency to Path Creation in a Coatings Chain: A Methodology for Strategies towards Sustainable Innovation. PhD dissertation, Delft, Delft University of Technology.

Peltzman, S. (1976). "Toward a More General Theory of Regulation." *Journal of Law and Economics* **19**(2): 211–240.

Posner, R. A. (1974). "Theories of Economic Regulation." *Bell Journal of Economics and Management Science* **5**(2): 335–358.

Quist, J. (2007). *Backcasting for a Sustainable Future. The Impact after 10 Years.* Delft, Eburon Academic Publishers.

Quist, J. (2009a). The Impact of Backcasting for Sustainability after Ten Years: Linking Stakeholder Involvement to Diffusion and Guidance by Visions. Paper presented at the First European Conference on Sustainability Transitions, Amsterdam, June 4–6.

Quist, J. (2009b). Stakeholder and User Involvement in Backcasting and How This Influences Follow-up and Spin-off. Paper for the conference "Joint Actions on Climate Change," Aalborg, Denmark, June 8–10.

Quist, J., and P. Vergragt (2004). Backcasting for Industrial Transformations and System Innovations towards Sustainability: Relevance for Governance? *Governance for Industrial Transformation: Proceedings of the 2003 Berlin Conference on the Human Dimensions of Global Environmental Change.* K. Jacob, M. Binder, and A. Wieczorek. Berlin, Environmental Policy Research Centre: 409–437.

Reich, R. B. (1992). *The Work of Nations: Preparing Ourselves for 21st-Century Capitalism.* New York, Vintage Books.

Reijnders, L. (1998). "The Factor X Debate: Setting Targets for Eco-efficiency." *Journal of Industrial Ecology* **2**(1): 13–22.

Reinhardt, F. (1999). "Market Failure and the Environmental Policies of Firms: Economic Rationales for 'Beyond Compliance' Behavior." *Journal of Industrial Ecology* **3**(1): 9–21.

Renn, O., T. Webler, et al., Eds. (1995). *Fairness and Competence in Citizen Participation: Evaluating Models for Environmental Discourse.* Dordrecht, Kluwer Academic Publishers.

Rennings, K., R. Kemp, et al. (2003). Blueprints for an Integration of Science, Technology and Environmental Policy (BLUEPRINT). Mannheim, Zentrum für Europäische Wirtschaftsforschung (ZEW). Available at ftp://ftp.zew.de/pub/zew-docs/umwelt/blueprint.pdf (accessed January 20, 2011).

Rip, A. (1992). "A Quasi-evolutionary Model of Technological Development and a Cognitive Approach to Technology Policy." *Rivista di Studi Epistemologici e Sociali sulla Scienza e la Tecnologia* **2**: 69–103.

Rip, A., and R. Kemp (1998). Towards a Theory of Social-Technical Change. *Human Choice and Climate Change*, vol. 2. S. Rayner and E. L. Malone. Columbus, OH, Battelle Press: 329–401.

Rodrik, D. (2007). *One Economics, Many Recipes: Globalization, Institutions, and Economic Growth.* Princeton, NJ, Princeton University Press.

Rotmans, J., and R. Kemp (2008). "Detour Ahead: A Response to Shove and Walker about the Perilous Road of Transition Management." *Environment and Planning A* **40**: 1006–1011.

Rotmans, J., R. Kemp, et al. (2001). Transitions and Transition Management. The Case for a Low Emission Energy Supply. ICIS Working Paper 101-E001, Maastricht.

Saviotti, P. P. (2005). On the Co-evolution of Technologies and Institutions. *Towards Environmental Innovation Systems.* M. Weber and J. Hemmelskamp. Heidelberg, Springer: 9–31.

Schumpeter, J. A. (1939). *Business Cycles: A Theoretical, Historical, and Statistical Analysis of the Capitalist Process.* New York, McGraw-Hill.

Schumpeter, J. A. (1962). *Capitalism, Socialism, and Democracy.* New York, Harper Torchbooks.

Sclove, R. E. (1995). *Democracy and Technology.* New York, Guilford Press.

Shepherd, A., and C. Bowler (1997). "Beyond the Requirements: Improving Public Participation in EIA." *Journal of Environmental Planning and Management* **40**(6): 725–738.

Shove, E. (2010). "Questions Often, Sometimes and Not Yet Asked." *Theory, Culture & Society* **27**(2–3): 288. Available at http://tcs.sagepub.com/content/27/2-3/277.

Shove, E., and G. P. Walker (2007). "Caution! Transitions Ahead: Politics, Practice and Transition Management." *Environment and Planning A* **39**: 763–770.

Shove, E., and G. P. Walker (2008). "Transition Management™ and the Politics of Shape Shifting." *Environment and Planning A* **40**: 1012–1014.

Smith, A. (2003). "Transforming Technological Regimes for Sustainable Development: A Role for Alternative Technology Niches?" *Science and Public Policy* **30**(2): 127–135.

Smith, A., and F. Kern (2007). The Transitions Discourse in the Ecological Modernisation of the Netherlands. Working Paper 160, SPRU (Science and Technology Policy Research), University of Sussex, U.K.

Smith, A., A. Stirling, et al. (2005). "The Governance of Sustainable Socio-technical Transitions." *Research Policy* **34**(10): 1491–1510.

Söderbaum, P. (1973). *Positionsanalys vid beslutsfattande of planering: Ekonomisk analys pa tvarvetenskaplig gr-*

*und* [Positional Analysis for Decision Making and Planning: Economic Analysis on an Interdisciplinary Basis]. Stockholm, Esselte Stadium.

Söderbaum, P. (2004). "Decision Processes and Decision-Making in Relation to Sustainable Development and Democracy—Where Do We Stand?" *Journal of Interdisciplinary Economics* **14**: 41–60.

Stigler, G. J. (1971). "The Theory of Economic Regulation." *Bell Journal of Economics and Management Science* **2**(1): 3–21.

Tsamis, A. (1999). Measuring Regional Innovation for Sustainable Development. M.S. dissertation, Technology and Policy Program. Cambridge, MA, MIT.

Tukker, A., M. Charter, et al. (2008). *System Innovation for Sustainability: Perspectives on Radical Changes to Sustainable Consumption and Production.* Sheffield, U.K., Greenleaf Publishing.

van de Belt, H., and A. Rip (1987). The Nelson-Winter-Dosi Model and Synthetic Dye Chemistry. *The Social Construction of Technological Systems: New Directions in the Sociology and History of Technology.* W. Bijker, T. P. Hughes, and P. Pinch. Cambridge, MA, MIT Press: 135–158.

van de Poel, I. R. (2000). "On the Role of Outsiders in Technical Development." *Technology Analysis and Strategic Management* **12**(3): 383–397.

van de Poel, I. R. (2003). "The Transformation of Technological Regimes." *Research Policy* **32**: 49–68.

van Gunsteren, L. A., and P. P. van Loon (2000). *Open Design: A Collaborative Approach to Architecture.* Delft, Eburon.

Vergragt, P. (2005). Back-casting for Environmental Sustainability: From STD and SusHouse towards Implementation. *Towards Environmental Innovation Systems.* M. Weber and J. Hemmelskamp. Heidelberg, Springer: 301–318.

Vogel, D. (1995). National Regulation in the Global Economy. *Trading Up: Consumer and Environmental Regulation in a Global Economy.* Cambridge, MA, Harvard University Press: 1–23.

Voss, J-P, A. Smith, and J. Grin (2009). "Designing, Long-term Policy: Rethinking Transition Management. *Policy Sciences* **42**: 275–302.

Wack, P. (1985a). "Scenarios: Shooting the Rapids." *Harvard Business Review* **63**(6): 139–150.

Wack, P. (1985b). "Scenarios: Uncharted Waters Ahead." *Harvard Business Review* **63**(5): 72–89.

Wallace, D. (1995). *Environmental Policy and Industrial Innovation: Strategies in Europe, the U.S. and Japan.* London, Earthscan.

Weiss, P. (1997). "Techno-globalism and Industrial Policy Responses in the USA and Europe." *Intereconomics* **32**(2): 74–86.

White, D. L. (1989). "Shaping Antitrust Enforcement: Greater Emphasis on Barriers to Entry." *Brigham Young University Law Review* **3**: 823–851.

Winner, L. (1977). *Autonomous Technology: Technics-out-of-Control as a Theme in Political Thought.* Cambridge, MA, MIT Press.

Winner, L. (1986). *The Whale and the Reactor.* Chicago, University of Chicago Press.

Winner, L., Ed. (1992). *Democracy in a Technological Society.* Dordrecht, Kluwer Academic Publishers.

Wood, A. (1994). Policy Options for the North. *North-South Trade, Employment, and Inequality: Changing Fortunes in a Skill-Driven World.* IDS Development Studies Series. New York, Oxford University Press/Clarendon Press: 346–394.

Yosie, T. F., and T. D. Herbst (1998). *Using Stakeholder Processes in Environmental Decision making: An Evaluation of Lessons Learned, Key Issues, and Future Challenges.* Washington, DC, Ruder Finn.

# IV

# National, Regional, and International Efforts to Advance Health, Safety, and the Environment

There are several types of environmental problems that have been exacerbated by increased industrial throughput (driven by increased consumption) of energy and materials that consume natural and physical resources and energy, and that adversely affect public health and the environment. These problems have already been discussed in prior chapters and include (1) the compromise of ecosystem integrity and the indirect affect this has on human health, (2) the depletion of resources and energy, (3) toxic pollution that directly affects human health and the environment, and (4) global climate change.

In Part III of this work, we explored government intervention to enhance the economy/competitiveness. In Part IV of this work, Chapter 9, "Government Intervention to Protect the Environment, Worker Health and Safety, and Consumer Product Safety," addresses health, safety, and environmental concerns from the perspective of the *nation-state.*

Environmental problems are not bounded by geopolitical borders, but rather have international as well as global consequences that must be managed through both domestic and international legal instruments, agreements, and principles. Inherent in the concept of sustainable development is the necessity to have the fundamental tools and instruments to manage environmental, health, and safety issues effectively for the well-being of both the present generation and future generations. Chapter 10, "Regional and International Regimes to Protect Health, Safety, and the Environment," explores the policy tools and instruments to improve health, safety,

and the environment that function across, as opposed to within, national economies. This includes efforts to harmonize national environmental legislation for nations that are members of a federated entity such as the European Union where member-wide regional law is evolving, and for nations operating independently, but often within the context of multilateral environmental, health, and safety agreements.

There are two different policy models for addressing health, safety, and environmental concerns.

One approach focuses on *environmental policy* controlling pollution in various media (air, water, waste, and the workplace), product safety, and industrial chemical production, use, and disposal. An alternative approach focuses on developing an *industrial policy for the environment* that encourages or requires environmentally sustainable production, products, and energy-related activities through the tools of environmental policy and regulation. Both approaches are explored in Part IV. Whether and how technology might be used to improve both the environment *and* employment are questions reserved for the concluding Chapter 13.

In addition to the four central environmental problems, concerns with environmental justice—the disparate impact of adverse effects on the environment on poorer people and nations, as well as the absence of effective, ameliorating initiatives—will also be discussed, emphasizing the importance of stakeholder representation and participation in the governance of industrial/industrializing economies.

# 9

# Government Intervention to Protect the Environment, Public/Worker Health and Safety, and Consumer Product Safety

## 9.1 INTRODUCTION

Following our exploration of interventionist government policies focusing on the economy/competitiveness and employment in Chapter 8, this chapter, the first of two chapters constituting Part IV of this work,* explores two different policy models for addressing health, safety, and environmental concerns from the perspective of the nation-state. One approach focuses on *environmental policy* controlling pollution in various media (air, water, waste, and the workplace), product safety, and industrial chemical production, use, and disposal. An alternative approach focuses on developing an *industrial policy for the environment* that encourages or requires environmentally sustainable production, products, and energy-related activities through the tools of environmental policy and regulation.[†] Whether and how technology might

---

\*      We recall that environmental concerns encompass four interrelated areas, toxic pollution, climate change, ecosystem degradation, and resource depletion. This chapter focuses mainly on government policies at the level of the nation-state to address the nexus between industrial activity and adverse environmental consequences and damages to public/worker health and safety. Chapter 10, which follows this chapter, addresses regional and international approaches.

---

†      The treatment of regulation in this chapter is necessarily abbreviated. For a fuller treatment of environmental law, see Ashford and Caldart (2008); on occupational health and safety law, see Ashford and Caldart (1996).

be used to improve both the environment *and* employment are questions reserved for the concluding Chapter 13.

The approach to addressing environmental problems is evolving and can be conceptualized as encompassing four stages in the evolution of technological thinking:

- Pollution control—the development of end-of-pipe technologies to capture and reduce emissions/waste.

- Pollution and accident prevention—otherwise known as cleaner and inherently safer production—that involves the creation of better, more environmentally sound products, processes, and services. Gradual pollution, sudden and accidental releases of chemicals by manufacturers and users, and the production of inherently dangerous products are reduced or eliminated.

- Shifts from products to product-services—the establishment of services to replace the need to purchase products. For example, washing services replace the need to buy a washer and dryer; photocopying services replace the need to buy expensive photocopying machinery that instead is loaned and maintained as part of a service contract; and innovative car-sharing programs in cities replace the need to buy an automobile.

- System changes—in contrast to the narrow use of innovation in relation to advances in specific products, processes, and services, it can also be applied in a much broader sense to achieve system innovation. Hence the emphasis is not on technology per se. It is on *functional innovation*—that is, different ways of serving a commercial or social purpose.

A system innovation changes not only technology but also institutional, organizational, and social structures. Because traditional policies focusing on technological, institutional, organizational, and social innovation tend to be somewhat fragmented, there is a need to formally integrate initiatives. This is why government needs to play an active role in encouraging change.* Existing barriers need to be removed, and an integrated systems approach to planning needs to be introduced if we are to realize the "natural capitalism" vision espoused by Hawken, Lovins, et al. (2000).

## 9.2 NATIONAL APPROACHES: REGULATION OF HEALTH, SAFETY, AND THE ENVIRONMENT IN THE UNITED STATES[†]

### 9.2.1 Introduction to the U.S. Regulatory System

The manufacturing, processing, and use of chemicals, materials, tools, machinery, and equipment in industrial, construction, mining, and agricultural workplaces often cause environmental, health, and safety hazards and risks. Occupational and environmental factors cause or exacerbate major diseases of the respiratory, cardiovascular, reproductive, and nervous systems and cause systemic poisoning and some cancers and birth defects. Occupational and environmental diseases and injuries place heavy economic and social burdens on workers, employers, community residents, and taxpayers. In addition, consumer products, pharmaceuticals, and contaminated food present health risks to consumers.

Because voluntary efforts in the unregulated market have not succeeded in reducing the incidence of these diseases and injuries, the public has demanded government intervention into the activities of the private sector. This intervention takes many regulatory forms, including standard setting, government-imposed liability, pollution-reduction markets, and the mandatory disclosure of information. This section addresses the major regulatory systems (or regimes) designed to protect public and worker health from chemicals discharged from sources that pollute the air, water, ground, and/or workplace. The regulation of hazards posed by consumer products, pharmaceuticals, and contaminated food is beyond the scope of this chapter.

The establishment of standards and other legal requirements in these regulatory regimes has occurred over a period of more than forty years that has seen changes in the use of scientific and technical information in regulatory initiatives and in legal doctrine, including the manner in which science, economics, and technological capability are viewed by the courts. The concepts of risk assessment, cost-benefit analysis, and technology forcing have evolved, both through the development of case law and through changes in the political environment. Often, changes in one of

---

\*       See Ashford (2001) and the discussion in Chapter 13.

---

†       This chapter borrows heavily, with permission, from Nicholas A. Ashford and Charles C. Caldart (2008), "Environmental Protection Laws," in *International Encyclopedia of Public Health*, vol. 2, pp. 390–401, Elsevier; and Nicholas A. Ashford and Charles C. Caldart (2008), *Environmental Law, Policy, and Economics: Reclaiming the Environmental Agenda*, MIT Press.

the regulatory regimes have affected the other regulatory regimes as well.

Standards can be classified in a number of ways. A performance standard is one that specifies a particular outcome, such as a specified emission level above which it is illegal to emit a specified air pollutant, but does not specify how that outcome is to be achieved. A design or specification standard, on the other hand, specifies a particular technology, such as a catalytic converter, that must be used. In either case, the standard can be based on (1) a desired level of protection for human health or environmental quality, (2) some level of presumed technological feasibility, (3) some level of presumed economic feasibility, or (4) some balancing of social costs and social benefits. Within each of these options, there is a wide spectrum of possible approaches. A human health-based standard, for example, might choose to protect only the average member of the population, or it might choose to protect the most sensitive individual. A technology-based standard might be based on what is deemed feasible for an entire industry or on what is deemed feasible for each firm within the industry. Moreover, some standards might be based on a combination of these factors. Many standards based on technological feasibility, for example, are also based on some concept of economic feasibility. Beyond standards are a variety of information-based obligations that can also influence industrial behavior, such as (1) the required disclosure of (and retention of or provision of access to) exposure, toxicity, chemical-content, and production data and (2) requirements to conduct testing or screening of chemical products.

Regulation beginning in the United States in the 1970s and continuing through the 1980s created the national model for *controlling* (rather than preventing) pollution in air, water, waste, and the workplace through what is commonly termed an "end-of-pipe" focus. This was largely done under a number of newly passed federal environmental statutes. In the U.S. administrative law tradition, citizens were early given the right to challenge government action in the courts through the Administrative Procedure Act (1946). More specific provisions in the new environmental statutes themselves not only empowered industry, NGOs, and citizens with participatory rights in the setting of standards and other regulations but also provided further particularized avenues for those parties and individuals to challenge both government and industry for violations of those laws and regulations. Eventually, European countries developed similar pollution-control approaches, although less redress was provided to individual citizens through access to the courts. This is slowly changing as the European Union becomes the source of much environmental law for its member states.

As experience with end-of-pipe approaches mounted, it became increasingly clear that *preventing* rather than merely controlling pollution offered advantages for both the environment and industry. Ultimately, in the United States, this found legislative expression in the Pollution Prevention Act of 1990. In the Europe Union, prevention is promoted through specific directives (such as the Integrated Pollution Prevention and Control Directive and the Seveso Directives, discussed in Chapter 10) and in several treaties governing the relationship among the EU member states.

Although the safety of food, drugs, and commercial products in the United States has been a continuing concern in some quarters, recent experiences in the United States with both domestic and imported contaminated food and toothpaste, with drugs whose clearance by the U.S. Food and Drug Administration (FDA) has come under criticism, and with unsafe imported toys and children's items have renewed the call for more vigorous regulation of product safety, both here and abroad. The European Union has followed a similar approach to the safety of food, drugs, and commercial products.

Both the United States and the EU have developed approaches to the problems of testing and clearing the use of industrial chemicals, through the Toxic Substances Control Act (TSCA) and the EU-wide REACH Directive, respectively, although the REACH directive came some thirty years after the TSCA. Table 9.1 lists selected U.S. and EU regulatory initiatives that form the backbone of governmental regulation in their respective venues, showing years of enactment and/or significant amendment. Detailed descriptions of the EU initiatives are found in Chapter 10.

In the United States, exposures to toxic substances in the industrial workplace have been regulated primarily through the Occupational Safety and Health Act (OSH Act) of 1970 and the TSCA of 1976. These federal laws have remained essentially unchanged since their passage, although serious attempts at reform have been made from time to time. Since 1990, sudden and accidental releases of chemicals (chemical accidents), which may affect both workers and community residents, have been regulated under both the Clean Air Act and the OSH Act.

**TABLE 9.1: SELECTED U.S. AND EU ENVIRONMENTAL INITIATIVES**

| THE UNITED STATES | THE EUROPEAN UNION |
| --- | --- |
| The Occupational Safety and Health Act (OSH Act) 1970<br>The Toxic Substances Control Act 1976 | Occupational health directives<br>The REACH Directive 2003 |
| The Clean Air Act (CAA) 1970, 1977, 1990 | The Air Directives 1996, 2008 |
| Water legislation<br>    The Clean Water Act (CWA) 1972, 1977, 1987<br>    The Safe Drinking Water Act 1974, 1986, 1996 | The Water Directive 2000 |
| Hazardous waste<br>    The Resource Conservation and<br>    Recovery Act (part of the Solid<br>    Waste Disposal Act) 1970, 1976, 1984 | The Waste Directive 1975<br>WEEE 1991 |
| Cleanup of contaminated land and water<br>    The Oil Spill Provisions of the CWA 1972<br>    The Comprehensive Environmental<br>    Response, Compensation, and Liability<br>    Act (CERCLA) (the Superfund) 1980, 1986 | The Liability Directive 2004 |
| Pollution prevention and inherent safety<br>    The Pollution Prevention Act 1990<br>    Safety additions to the CAA and the<br>    OSH Act 1990 (workers) and CERCLA 1986 (the community) | The Integrated Pollution<br>Prevention and Control<br>Directive 1996;<br>The Seveso Directives 1982, 1996 |
| The safety of food, drugs, and other consumer products<br>    The Consumer Product Safety Act 1972, 2008<br>    The Federal Hazardous Substances Act 1960, 2008<br>    The Food, Drug, and Cosmetic Act 1938, 1958, 1996 | Product, drug, and food safety<br>directives |
| Worker and community right to know<br>    OSH Act Hazard Communication<br>    Standard 1983<br>    Environmental Planning and Community<br>    Right-to-Know Act (EPCRA) 1986 | Incorporation of the Åarhus<br>Convention into EU law (2006) |

The OSH Act established the Occupational Safety and Health Administration (OSHA) in the Department of Labor to enforce compliance with the act, the National Institute for Occupational Safety and Health (NIOSH) in the Department of Health and Human Services (under the Centers for Disease Control and Prevention) to perform research and conduct health-hazard evaluations, and the independent, quasi-judicial Occupational Safety and Health Review Commission to hear employer and worker appeals of OSHA citations. The evolution of regulatory law under the OSH Act has profoundly influenced other environmental legislation, including the regulation of air, water, and waste, but especially the evolution of the TSCA. The Office of Pollution Prevention and Toxic Substances in the Environmental Protection Agency (EPA) administers the TSCA. The Office of Air, Water, and Solid Waste and the Office of Emergency Response in the EPA regulate media-based pollution. The Office of Chemical Preparedness and Emergency Response in the EPA is responsible for the chemical-safety provisions of the Clean Air Act.

### 9.2.2 Standard Setting and Obligations of the Employer and the Manufacturer or User of Toxic Substances in the United States

9.2.2.1 The Occupational Safety and Health Act of 1970

The OSH Act requires OSHA to (1) encourage employers and employees to reduce hazards in the workplace and to implement new or improved safety and health programs, (2) develop mandatory job safety and health standards and enforce them effectively, (3) establish separate but dependent responsibilities and rights for employers and employees for the achievement of better safety and health conditions, (4) establish reporting and record-keeping procedures to monitor job-related injuries and illnesses, and (5) encourage states to assume the fullest responsibility for establishing and administering their own occupational safety and health programs, which must be "at least as effective" as the federal program.

OSHA can begin standard-setting procedures either on its own or on petition from the secretary of health and human services, NIOSH, state and local governments, any nationally recognized standards-producing organization, employer or labor representatives, or any other interested person. The standard-setting process involves input from advisory committees and from NIOSH. When OSHA develops plans to propose, amend, or delete a standard, it publishes these intentions in the *Federal Register*. Subsequently, interested parties have opportunities to present arguments and pertinent evidence in writing or at public hearings. Under certain conditions, OSHA is authorized to set emergency temporary standards, which take effect immediately, but which are to be followed by the establishment of permanent standards within six months. To set an emergency temporary standard, OSHA must first determine that workers are in grave danger from exposure to toxic substances or new hazards and are not adequately protected by existing standards. Both emergency temporary and permanent standards can be appealed to the federal courts, but filing an appeals petition does not delay the enforcement of the standard unless a court of appeals specifically orders a delay. Employers may make application to OSHA for a temporary variance from a standard or regulation if they lack the means to comply readily with it, or for a permanent variance if they can prove that their facilities or methods of operation provide employee protection that is at least as effective as that required by OSHA.

The OSH Act provides two general means of protection for workers: (1) a general statutory duty of all employers to provide a safe and healthful workplace and (2) promulgation of specific standards to which specified categories of employers must adhere. The act imposes on virtually every employer in the private sector a general duty to "furnish to each of his employees employment and a place of employment which are free from recognized hazards that are causing or are likely to cause death or serious physical harm." A recognized hazard may be a substance for which the likelihood of harm has been the subject of research, giving rise to reasonable suspicion, or a substance for which an OSHA standard may or may not have been promulgated. The burden of proving that a particular substance is a recognized hazard and that industrial exposure to it results in a significant probability of harm is placed on OSHA. Because standard setting is a slow process, protection of workers through the employer's general duty could be especially important, but it is crucially dependent on the existence of reliable health-effects data, as well as on the willingness of a particular OSHA administration to use this statutory duty as a vehicle for protection.

The OSH Act specifically addresses the subject of toxic materials. It states in Section 6(b)(5) that the secretary of labor (through OSHA), in promulgating standards dealing with toxic materials or harmful physical agents, "shall set the standard that most adequately assures, to the extent feasible, on the basis of the best available evidence that no employee will suffer material impairment of health or functional capacity, even if such employee has a regular exposure to the hazard dealt with by such standard for the period of his working life." These words indicate a specific intent to regulate exposure to those hazards, such as chemical carcinogens and reproductive toxicants, whose effects may not be felt for years or decades.

In the 1970s, OSHA set Section 6(b)(5) standards for asbestos, vinyl chloride, arsenic, dibromochloropropane, coke-oven emissions, acrylonitrile, lead, cotton dust, and a group of fourteen carcinogens. In the 1980s, OSHA added standards for benzene, ethylene oxide, and formaldehyde and tightened the standard for asbestos to reflect its status as a carcinogen. In the early 1990s, OSHA set standards for cadmium, blood-borne pathogens, glycol ethers, and confined spaces. The agency also lowered the permissible exposure limit for formaldehyde from 1 to 0.75 parts per million (ppm; averaged over an eight-hour period) and issued a process safety management (PSM) rule (discussed below) designed to reduce the incidence of chemical accidents. Standards for methylene chloride (1997) and hexavalent chromium (2006) were also later established.

Under Section 6(b), the burden of proving the hazardous nature of a substance is placed on OSHA, as is the burden of establishing that the proposed controls are technologically and economically feasible for the regulated industries. The evolution of case law associated with the handful of standards that OSHA promulgated through this section of the OSH Act has been important not only in the implementation of the OSH Act itself, but also in the implementation of environmental law generally. In reviewing OSHA's hazardous-substance standards, the federal circuit courts of appeal squarely addressed the difficult issue of when scientific information is adequate to sustain the statutory requirement that the standards be supported by "substantial evidence" on the record as a whole. They also addressed the extent to which economic factors were permitted or required to be considered in the setting of the standards, the meaning of feasibility, OSHA's technology-forcing authority, the question whether a cost-benefit analysis was required or permitted, and, finally, the extent of the jurisdiction of the OSH Act in addressing different degrees of risk.

### 9.2.2.2 The Toxic Substances Control Act of 1976

The TSCA directs the EPA to require data from industry on the production, use, and health and environmental effects of chemicals. The TSCA also requires the manufacturer of new chemicals, or of existing chemicals put to a significant new use, to file a premanufacturing notification with the EPA detailing known information about the chemical. Further, the TSCA authorizes the EPA to regulate the production and use of those chemicals found to pose an unreasonable risk to human health or the environment. Such regulation may take one or more of a variety of forms, from labeling requirements to tolerance levels to outright bans on chemical use. The EPA may also order a specific change in chemical process technology or require repurchase or recall of banned chemicals. In addition, the TSCA gives aggrieved parties, including consumers and workers, specific rights to sue to enforce the act, with the possibility of awards of attorneys' fees. (This feature was not included in the OSH Act.)

The EPA has issued a worker-protection standard for asbestos at the new OSHA limit of 0.2 fibers/cm$^3$, which applies to state and local government asbestos-abatement workers not covered by OSHA. Although the potential for broader regulation of workplace chemicals exists under the TSCA, the EPA has not been aggressive in this area. Between 1977 and 1990, of the twenty-two TSCA regulatory actions taken on existing chemicals, fifteen addressed polychlorinated biphenyls (PCBs), which the EPA has a specific statutory directive to address under the TSCA. Only three of the regulations (pertaining to asbestos, hexavalent chromium, and metalworking fluids) have a strong occupational exposure component. Although the EPA declared formaldehyde a probable carcinogen and the International Agency for Research on Cancer classified it as a confirmed human carcinogen, the EPA chose not to take regulatory action on this substance, opting instead to defer to OSHA workplace regulations.

Nonetheless, the OSH Act and the TSCA together provide potentially comprehensive and effective information-generation and standard-setting authority to protect workers. In particular, the information-generation activities under the TSCA can provide the necessary data to establish that a substance is a "recognized hazard" that, even in the absence of a specific OSHA standard, must be controlled by the employer to meet the OSH Act's general duty to provide a safe and healthful workplace.

The potentially powerful role of more comprehensive TSCA regulation was seriously challenged by the Fifth Circuit Court of Appeals in 1991 when it overturned an omnibus asbestos phaseout rule issued under the TSCA in 1989. The court held that the EPA could not ban a chemical under the TSCA without having first determined that other regulatory alternatives that would have been less burdensome to industry would not have eliminated the unreasonable risk. This would require the agency to perform a more comprehensive, detailed, and resource-intensive analysis than the one conducted before the promulgation of the asbestos rule. Rightly or wrongly, for more than a decade, the EPA has viewed this case (which was not appealed to the U.S. Supreme Court) as a significant impediment to future TSCA standards, and the agency has generally regarded regulation of chemicals other than PCBs under the TSCA as a nearly impossible task for now. Even so, the TSCA continues to be important because of its surviving authority to require the testing of chemicals and its information-reporting and retaining requirements. Recently, the new administrator of the EPA, Lisa Jackson, has indicated her support of engaging Congress in writing a new chemical risk management law that will fix the weaknesses in TSCA.

### 9.2.3 The Control of Gradual Pollution in Air and Water and Pollution from Waste in the United States

#### 9.2.3.1 The Clean Air Act

The modern Clean Air Act (CAA) came into being in 1970, and although significant changes were made in 1977 and 1990, the basic structure of the act has remained the same, with the addition of provisions for authority over acid rain, chlorofluorocarbons (CFCs), indoor air, and chemical safety, the last of which is discussed in Section 9.2.4. The CAA regulates both stationary and mobile sources of pollution, taking into account the relative contributions of each to specific air-pollution problems and the relative capacity of different kinds of sources within each category to reduce their emissions. The recognition that sources using newer technology might be able to achieve greater emission reductions than older sources with older technology led to the act's distinction in the provisions on both stationary and mobile sources between new and existing sources. Although this approach is driven by equity considerations regarding the relative financial and technical burdens of pollution reduction, it has unwittingly discouraged modernization or replacement of facilities and has resulted in the operation of older (especially energy) facilities beyond their expected useful life. For new sources within each industrial sector, there was recognition of the need for uniformity and also for encouraging technological innovation through the technology-forcing capability inherent in stringent standards. The court decisions recognizing EPA's technology-forcing authority under the CAA were greatly influenced by OSHA's early technology-forcing approach to worker protection.

The 1970 CAA directed the EPA to establish primary ambient air quality standards that would protect public health with an adequate margin of safety (Section 109(b)(1)). As interpreted by the courts and supported by congressional history, these standards are to be established without consideration of economic or technological feasibility. In addition, secondary ambient air quality standards are to be established to protect the public welfare within a reasonable time (Section 109(b)(2)).

Both the federal government and the states have key roles in protecting the ambient air under the CAA. Ambient air quality (concentration) standards are established by the federal government for a small number of "criteria" pollutants designated by the EPA. For each such pollutant, the EPA establishes both primary ambient standards (to protect public health) and secondary ambient standards (to protect public welfare). These ambient standards (identified below) are to be attained through (1) emission limitations placed on individual existing polluters through permits issued by state governments as a part of their state implementation plans (SIPs) (Section 110); (2) nationwide emission limitations for new sources, established by the EPA and known as New Source Performance Standards (Section 111); and (3) a combination of federal and state restrictions on mobile sources. Emission standards, in contrast with ambient concentration standards, are expressed as an emissions rate (milligrams emitted per 100 kg of product, per hour, per day, per week, per quarter, per year, per BTU, per passenger mile, or other unit of measurement).

The CAA does not establish ambient standards for hazardous air pollutants but rather requires compliance with nationwide emission limitations set by the EPA. Hazardous air pollutants are those recognized as extraordinarily toxic and eventually regarded as non- or low-threshold pollutants. Initially, these were to be regulated to protect public health with an ample margin of safety (Section 112), and, as

with the primary ambient standards for criteria pollutants, emission standards for hazardous air pollutants were to be established without consideration of economic burden. These pollutants, Congress determined, were sufficiently dangerous to preclude any reliance on atmospheric dispersion and mixing as a means of reducing their ambient concentrations. The reliance on federal emission standards reflected congressional concern with "hot spots" of localized intense pollution and also with intermittent versus continuous versus sudden and accidental releases of harmful substances. Moreover, ambient concentration standards were considered impractical and of little relevance for the sporadic and idiosyncratic sources of hazardous air pollutants. For all these reasons, uniform federal emission standards were considered necessary. (Note, however, that California did establish an ambient standard as a complement to the federal emission limitation on vinyl chloride.)

In the early stages of the implementation of the stationary-source provisions of the Clean Air Act (approximately 1970–1975), the EPA focused on (1) the ambient air quality standards for criteria pollutants and (2) emission standards for new sources of criteria pollutants and for all sources emitting any of seven regulated hazardous air pollutants (discussed below). Initially, prior advisory ambient standards for criteria pollutants carbon monoxide (CO), sulfur dioxide ($SO_2$), oxides of nitrogen ($NO_X$), large particulate matter, and photochemical oxidants were made mandatory. In 1979, the standard for photochemical oxidants was narrowed to cover only ground-level ozone and was relaxed from 0.08 ppm to 0.12 ppm averaged over a one-hour period. The standard for coarse particulate matter—inhalable particulates up to 10 microns in diameter (PM10)—was adopted in 1987. In 1997, the ozone standard was further revised to 0.08 ppm. At the same time, the particulate standard was altered to place more stringent requirements on smaller (< 2.5 microns) respirable particles (PM2.5), with a twenty-four-hour limit of 65 mg/m$^3$. In 2006, the PM2.5 limit was further lowered to 35 mg/m$^3$. A standard for a sixth criteria pollutant, airborne lead, was promulgated in 1978, and in 2008 the EPA lowered the permissible airborne concentration by one order of magnitude, from 1.5 mg/m$^3$ to 0.15 mg/m$^3$. (Current primary air quality standards set under Section 109 are presented in Table 9.2.) In addition, following a 2007 U.S. Supreme Court decision that the EPA has the authority under the CAA to regulate carbon dioxide, the EPA has indicated its intention to establish national limits on greenhouse emissions from automobiles and to regulate carbon

## TABLE 9.2: NATIONAL AMBIENT AIR QUALITY STANDARDS

| | |
|---|---|
| **Carbon monoxide** | *Primary* (1970)—35 ppm averaged over one hour and 9.0 averaged over eight hours; neither to be exceeded more than once per year. |
| | *Secondary*—none. |
| **Particulate matter:** | (PM$_x$ below refers to particles equal or less than x microns in diameter.) |
| **PM$_{10}$** | *Primary* (1970)—150 μg/m³ averaged over twenty-four hours, with no more than one expected exceedance per calendar year; also, 50 μg/m³or less for the expected annual arithmetic mean concentration. |
| | *Secondary*—same as primary. |
| **PM$_{2.5}$** | *Prior primary* (1997)—65 μg/m³ averaged over twenty-four hours; 15 μg/m³ annual maximum. |
| | *Revised primary* (2006)—35 μg/m³ averaged over twenty-four hours. |
| **Ozone** | *Prior primary* (1979)—235 μg/m³ (0.12 ppm) averaged over one hour; no more than one expected exceedance per calendar year (multiple violations in a day count as one violation). Revoked June 2005. Codified August 2005. |
| | *Secondary*—same as primary. |
| | *Revised primary* (1997)—0.08 ppm averaged over eight hours. |
| | *Revised primary* (2008)—0.075 ppm averaged over eight hours. |
| **Nitrogen dioxide** | *Primary* (1970)—100 μg/m³ (0.053 ppm) as an annual arithmetic mean concentration. |
| | *Secondary*—same as primary. |
| **Sulfur oxides** | *Prior primary* (1970)—365 μg/m³ (0.14 ppm) averaged over twenty-four hours, not to be exceeded more than once per year; 80 μg/m³ (0.03 ppm) annual arithmetic mean. |
| | *Secondary*—1,300 μg/m³ (0.50 ppm) averaged over a three-hour period, not to be exceeded more than once per year. |
| | *Revised primary* (2010)—hourly standard of seventy-five parts per billion; prior daily and annual standards revoked. |
| **Lead** | *Primary* (1977)—1.5 μg/m³ arithmetic average over a calendar quarter. |
| | *Secondary*—same as primary. |
| | *Revised primary* (2008)—0.15 μg/m³ arithmetic average over a calendar quarter. |

dioxide emissions from power plants. In June 2010, the EPA replaced the daily and annual sulfur dioxide standards with an hourly standard of 75 parts per billion (0.075 ppm).

In Section 112 of the CAA, Congress directed the administrator to set emission standards for hazardous air pollutants at a level that protects public health with an ample margin of safety. It is likely that this phraseology reflected an early assumption that although hazardous pollutants were very dangerous, they did exhibit a finite threshold (a nonzero level of exposure below which no harm would occur). As the 1970s progressed, however, there was growing recognition that this assumption might be wrong, and that for many hazardous pollutants there was no level of exposure (at least at levels within the limits of detection) below which one could confidently predict that no harmful or irreversible effects (especially cancer or birth defects) would occur.

This presented an implementation challenge for the EPA. Arguably, given its mandate to protect pub-

lic health with an ample margin of safety, the agency was required to ban the emission of several hazardous substances. This would, as a practical matter, essentially ban the use of these substances in many industries. Seeking to avoid this result, the EPA adopted a policy of setting Section 112 emission standards at the level that could be achieved by technologically feasible technology. (This was the approach followed at the time by OSHA in setting standards for exposure to workplace chemicals. In the case of carcinogens, OSHA considered no levels to be safe and established control requirements at the limit of technological feasibility.) Using this approach, the EPA set finite (nonzero) standards for arsenic, asbestos, benzene, beryllium, coke-oven emissions, mercury, vinyl chloride, and radionuclides. The standard-setting process was slow and had to be forced by litigation; it took four to seven years to establish a final standard for each of these substances. Had the EPA continued to set standards for more substances, and had it used the technological feasibility approach to spur the development of cleaner technology, the environmental groups might well have been content to allow the implementation of Section 112 to proceed in this fashion. When the setting of new Section 112 standards all but stalled during the Reagan administration, however, the National Resources Defense Council (NRDC), an environmental litigation group, decided to press the issue in court.

*NRDC v. EPA*, decided by the District of Columbia Circuit Court of Appeals in 1987, placed new limitations on the EPA's approach to regulating hazardous air pollutants by ruling that the EPA must determine an acceptable (usually nonzero) risk level for a hazardous air pollutant before setting a Section 112 standard for that pollutant. In reaction to this case and to revitalize the moribund standard-setting process, Congress amended Section 112 in 1990 to specify a two-tiered approach: the use of technology-based standards initially, with residual risks to be addressed (at a later date) by health-based standards. In the 1990 CAA Amendments, Congress listed 189 substances as hazardous air pollutants and directed the EPA to add other substances to the list if they "present or may present . . . a threat of adverse human effects (including, but not limited to, substances which are known to be, or may be reasonably anticipated to be, carcinogenic, mutagenic, teratogenic, neurotoxic, which cause reproductive dysfunction, or which are acutely or chronically toxic) or adverse environmental effects whether through ambient concentration, bioaccumulation, deposition or otherwise." The EPA was directed to set maximum achievable control technology (MACT) technology-based standards over a ten-year period for categories of major stationary sources (defined as those emitting more than 10 tons per year of any single hazardous pollutant or more than 25 tons combined). MACT standards must require the maximum feasible degree of reduction (including a prohibition on emissions, where achievable) but must reflect the cost of achieving emissions reduction and any nonair and environmental impact and energy requirements. MACT standards for new sources must be at least as stringent as those met by the best-performing similar source, and MACT standards for existing sources must be at least as stringent as those met by the average of the best-performing 12 percent of similar sources. For categories of smaller (so-called area) stationary sources, the EPA is authorized to set standards that are less restrictive than the MACT standard, based either on generally achievable control technology (GACT) or on the use of specified management practices. For pollutants with an identifi-able health threshold, the EPA is authorized to forgo the technology-based approach and instead to set health-based standards that ensure an ample margin of safety, essentially the original mandate of the 1970 CAA. Finally, the EPA was obligated to issue a report on risk, which it did in 2004. If no new legislation recommended by that report is enacted within eight years, the EPA must issue such additional regulations as are necessary to protect public health with an ample margin of safety in general and, specifically for carcinogens, must ensure that lifetime exposure risks are less than 1 in 1 million. The EPA has made substantial progress on establishing MACT and GACT standards but has just begun the task of developing risk- or health-based approaches. The 1990 amendments to the CAA also placed increased emphasis on toxic air pollutants emitted by mobile sources, and in 2007 the EPA issued a Mobile Source Air Toxics rule designed to lower benzene concentrations in gasoline and to restrict automotive emissions of benzene and a number of other toxic substances.

### 9.2.3.2 Water Legislation

The two most important federal statutes regulating water pollution are the Clean Water Act (CWA) and the Safe Drinking Water Act (SDWA). The CWA regulates the discharge of pollutants into navigable surface waters (and into smaller waterways and wetlands that are hydrologically connected to navigable waters), and the SDWA regulates the level of contaminants in public drinking-water supplies.

**9.2.3.2.1 The Clean Water Act** The modern Clean Water Act has its origins in the Federal Water Pollution Control Act Amendments of 1972. The basic structure of the act was established at that time, although it was refined and refocused by the Clean Water Act Amendments of 1977 (from which it also took its name) and by the Water Quality Act Amendments of 1987. The regulatory focus of the CWA is the discharge of pollutants to surface waters from point sources, principally industrial facilities and municipal sewage treatment plants (known under the act as publicly owned treatment works, or POTWs). The CWA flatly prohibits any discharge of a pollutant from a point source to surface waters unless it is done in conformance with the requirements of the act, and the statute has since 1972 retained as an explicit national goal the elimination of all point-source discharges to surface waters by 1985. Although the no-discharge goal may never be attainable in practical terms, it has helped focus the act's implementation on gradual but inexorable pollution reduction as discharge limits are made more stringent over time.

The centerpiece of this pollution-reduction scheme is the National Pollutant Discharge Elimination System (NPDES) permit. In theory, all point sources must have an NPDES permit before discharging pollutants to surface waters, but some (mostly smaller ones) still do not. The NPDES permit, which is issued after public notice and an opportunity for comment, is to incorporate all the various requirements of the act, including discharge limits that are applicable to the point source in question. Point sources are subjected to both technology-based and water-quality-based limits and to the more stringent of the two when they overlap.

The technology-based limits are established by the EPA as national standards. To set these standards for industrial dischargers, the EPA first divided industries into various industry categories and then established effluent limits for each category based on its assessment of what was technologically and economically feasible for the point sources within that category. Further, as required by the act, the EPA set different standards within each industrial category for conventional pollutants (biochemical oxygen demand, fecal coliforms, oil and grease, pH, and total suspended solids), toxic pollutants (currently a list of 129 designated chemical compounds), and nonconventional pollutants (which simply are other pollutants, such as total phenols, that are listed under neither the conventional nor the toxic designation).

In recognition of the fact that conventional pollutants usually are amenable to treatment by the types of pollution-control equipment that has long been in use at conventional sewage-treatment facilities, the standards for conventional pollutants are set according to what can be obtained through the use of the best conventional pollution control technology (BCT), taking into account the reasonableness of the cost. The standards for toxic and nonconventional pollutants, on the other hand, are set according to the EPA's determination of the level of pollution reduction that can be achieved through the application of the best available technology economically achievable (BAT). Originally, Congress had directed the EPA to set health-based standards for toxic pollutants on a pollutant-by-pollutant basis, but this resulted in only a handful of standards (mostly for pesticide chemicals). The political difficulty of establishing national health-based standards for toxic chemicals led environmental groups, in a suit against the EPA to compel regulation, to agree to a schedule for setting technology-based standards for a list of designated toxic pollutants. Congress formally endorsed this approach in 1977 by amending the act to require the EPA to set BAT standards for all the toxic pollutants on that list.

Under the CWA, the EPA is to consider both control and process technologies in setting BAT standards, which are to result in reasonable further progress toward the national goal of eliminating the discharge of all pollutants and are to require "the elimination of discharges of all pollutants [where] such elimination is technologically and economically achievable." An individual discharger may obtain a cost waiver from BAT standards for nonconventional pollutants if it cannot afford to comply, but no cost waiver is available from the standards for toxic pollutants. For new industrial sources within an industry category, the EPA is to set standards based on best available demonstrated technology (BADT), which can be more stringent than BAT or BCT because of the greater technological flexibility inherent in the design and construction of a new facility. Although the EPA is to consider industry-wide costs in establishing BADT standards, no waivers are available to individual applicants once the standards are set.

The CWA also imposes technology-based standards on POTWs, based on the limitations that can be met through the application of secondary sewage-treatment technology. In essence, this requires an 85 percent reduction in biochemical oxygen demand and total suspended solids. Since 2000, the act has also required POTWs to comply with the EPA's combined sewer overflow (CSO) policy, which is designed to eventually terminate or substantially minimize the discharge of untreated or partially treated sewage during periods of high rain or snow melt.

In addition, the CWA imposes limitations on discharges by industrial sources into POTWs. Such discharges are known under the act as indirect discharges (because the pollutants are not discharged directly to surface waters but rather are discharged indirectly to surface waters through a public sewer system). Limitations on indirect discharges are known under the act as pretreatment standards because they have the effect of requiring the indirect discharger to treat its wastewater before discharging it to the POTW for further treatment. The EPA has set national technology-based limitations (known as the categorical pretreatment standards) on indirect discharges of toxic pollutants by firms in certain industrial categories. The act also requires the POTW to set such additional pretreatment limits and requirements as are necessary both to ensure the integrity of the sewage treatment process and to prevent the indirectly discharged pollutants from passing through the sewer system and causing a violation of the POTW's discharge permit.

For the first fifteen to twenty years of the act's implementation, the primary focus was the establishment and implementation of the technology-based limits discussed above. More recently, however, considerably more attention has been given to the act's system of water-quality-based limits, which is equally applicable to industrial sources and POTWs. Since 1972, the CWA has directed the states to establish and periodically revise ambient water quality standards (in-stream standards) for all lakes, rivers, streams, bays, and other waterways within their borders and has required the EPA to set and revise these standards to the extent that a state declines to do so. Further, the act has required since 1977 that NPDES permits include such additional discharge limits beyond the national technology-based limits as may be necessary to meet the ambient water quality standards of the waterway in question.

To help call attention to these water quality requirements, Congress in 1987 added what became known as the "toxic hot spot" provision of the CWA, which directed the EPA and the states to identify those waters that were in violation of ambient water quality standards because of toxic pollution, to identify those point sources whose discharges of toxic pollutants were contributing to those violations, and to develop an individual control strategy for that source (which almost always meant a revision of the source's NPDES permit to add or tighten limits on toxic pollutants). Another provision of the act that has prompted the addition or tightening of water-quality-based discharge limits has been the requirement that the states (and, if they decline, the EPA) calculate a total maximum daily load (TMDL) for all waters that are in violation of ambient water quality standards. For any particular body of water, the TMDL for a particular pollutant is the total amount of that pollutant that may be discharged to the water body in a day without violating the relevant ambient water quality standard. When a TMDL is set, it often leads inexorably to a tightening of the NPDES permits of those point sources whose discharges are contributing to the particular violation of water quality standards. Although the TMDL requirement has been in the act since 1972, the states and the EPA have been slow to implement it. Over the past fifteen years or so, however, as a result of several successful suits by environmental groups seeking to compel the EPA to set TMDLs in the face of state inaction, the TMDL requirement has come considerably more to the fore. Consequently, the inclusion of water-quality-based limits in NPDES permits has become considerably more commonplace.

**9.2.3.2.2 The Safe Drinking Water Act** Although some sources of drinking water are also regulated as surface waters under the CWA, the legislation specifically designed to protect the safety of the drinking water delivered to the public from public water systems is the SDWA. Passed in 1974 after a series of well-publicized stories about the number of potential carcinogens in the Mississippi River water used as drinking water by the city of New Orleans, it contains very little that is designed to address the sources of drinking-water pollution. Instead, the SDWA directs the EPA to set national health-based goals known as maximum contaminant level goals (MCL goals) for various drinking-water contaminants and to set MCLs that are as close to the MCL goals as is technologically and economically feasible. All public water systems, defined as those with at least fifteen service connections or that serve at least twenty-five people, are required to meet the MCLs.

Over the act's first eight years, the EPA set only twenty-three federal drinking-water standards. Dissatisfied with the pace of implementation, Congress amended the act in 1986 to spur the agency into action. It directed the EPA to set standards (MCLs and MCL goals) for 83 specified contaminants within three years and to set standards for twenty-five additional contaminants every three years thereafter. Ten years later, with scores of MCLs and MCL goals now on the books, Congress scaled back. In a 1996 compromise endorsed by environmental groups and water suppliers alike, Congress eliminated the requirement for twenty-five new standards every three years. At the same time, it added provisions that effectively ensured both that the standards that had been set would largely be allowed to remain in place and that new standards would be far slower in coming (and would likely be relatively weaker because of the addition of a cost-benefit requirement).

Since then, the primary focus of the SDWA program has been bringing public water systems throughout the country into compliance with the existing standards. Although the MCLs are set at a level deemed to be technologically and economically feasible, many water systems have had difficulty affording the cost of meeting and monitoring the MCLs. To attempt to ameliorate the financial burden on municipal water systems, the SDWA has periodically made federal funds available for technology upgrades and infrastructure improvements. The task, however, remains a daunting one. In 2007, the EPA estimated that approximately $335 billion would be needed over the next twenty years to upgrade the nation's 52,000 community water systems and 21,400 non-for-profit noncommunity water systems (that include schools and churches) (EPA 2009).

### 9.2.3.3 The Regulation of Hazardous Waste

Broadly speaking, the generation, handling, and disposal of hazardous wastes are regulated by the interaction of two federal statutes. The primary federal law regulating hazardous wastes is officially known as the Solid Waste Disposal Act. In 1970, Congress amended that statute with the Resource Conservation and Recovery Act (RCRA), and the law has come to be popularly known by that name. The RCRA was given regulatory teeth with a set of 1976 amendments under which the EPA, in 1980, promulgated regulations establishing a cradle-to-grave system for hazardous wastes that tracks the generation, transportation, and disposal of such wastes and establishes standards for their disposal. Initially, however, the EPA's disposal standards were minimal to nonexistent and did little to discourage the landfilling of chemical wastes. This led Congress to pass sweeping amendments to the RCRA in 1984 that (1) established a clear federal policy against the landfilling of hazardous wastes unless they have first been treated to reduce their toxicity and (2) gave the EPA a specific timetable by which it had to either set treatment standards for various categories of waste or ban the landfilling of such waste altogether. Consequently, the EPA has set treatment standards, commonly known as the land disposal restrictions (LDRs), for hundreds of types of hazardous wastes. These standards are based on the EPA's assessment of the best available demonstrated technology for treating the waste in question.

Thus the RCRA directly regulates the handling and disposal of hazardous wastes, and by establishing a set of requirements that must be followed once hazardous waste is generated, it also indirectly regulates the generation of hazardous wastes. RCRA regulations have increased the cost of disposing of most types of waste by two orders of magnitude over the past twenty-five years. In this sense, the RCRA operates as a de facto tax on the generation of hazardous waste.

Another statute that acts as an indirect check on hazardous-waste generation (and that provides additional incentive to ensure that one's waste is safely disposed of) is the Comprehensive Environmental Response, Compensation, and Liability Act (CERCLA, also known as the federal Superfund law). The primary focus of this law is the remediation (cleanup) of hazardous-waste contamination resulting from imprudent handling and disposal practices of the past and the recovery of remediation costs from those designated as responsible parties under the act. CERCLA imposes liability for the costs of remediating a hazardous-waste site both on the owners and operators of the site and on those generators of hazardous waste who sent waste to the site. Because the owners and operators are often business entities that are no longer financially viable, CERCLA liability often falls most heavily on the generators. Also, CERCLA liability is strict liability, meaning that the exercise of reasonable care by the generator is not a defense. Further, unless the generator can establish a convincing factual basis for distinguishing its waste from all or part of the contamination being remediated, CERCLA liability is joint and several, meaning that each responsible party is potentially liable for the full cost of remediation. As a practical matter, this means that the cost of remediation will be borne by those among the responsible parties who are financially solvent unless they can prove that the waste they sent to the site did not contribute to the contamination being remediated.

A prudent business entity, then, has a strong financial incentive to take actions that will minimize the likelihood that it will face CERCLA liability in the future. Because the only certain way to avoid such liability is to refrain from generating the waste in the first place, CERCLA does provide a rationale for pollution prevention. Further, it provides firms with an incentive to meet or perhaps to go beyond RCRA regulations in dealing with wastes they do generate.

This is not to say, of course, that substantial amounts of hazardous waste are no longer generated in the United States, that all hazardous wastes are adequately treated and safely disposed of, or that all instances of hazardous-waste contamination are being adequately addressed (or addressed at all). The RCRA and CERCLA both contain what might reasonably be called loopholes and gaps in coverage, and hazardous-waste contamination remains an ongoing issue. For example, the EPA has not taken an aggressive approach toward "E wastes," the discarded electronic components that have become increasingly common in our computer-dominated society. Further, the most common treatment methodology incorporated into the EPA's RCRA treatment standards is incineration, which has brought with it a release of airborne contaminants that has only recently been meaningfully addressed by regulation. There is no question, however, that the United States has made considerable progress since the late 1970s, when disposal of chemical wastes in unlined landfills at a cost of roughly $15 per ton was common practice.

## 9.2.3.4 The Origins of the Precautionary Approach in U.S. Regulatory Law

The regulation of air, water, waste, and the workplace was aggressively pursued in the 1970s—relying on a precautionary approach—and courts of appeal were deferential to the regulatory agencies in their efforts to advance environmental and public health protection until the Reagan revolution that began in the 1980s adopted cost-benefit analysis as the decision-making rationale for regulatory initiatives, as the following excerpt explains.

**The Legacy of the Precautionary Principle in U.S. Law: The Rise of Cost-Benefit Analysis and Risk Assessment as Undermining Factors in Health, Safety and Environmental Protection**
**Nicholas A. Ashford**
Source: Chapter 19 in Nicolas de Sadeleer (ed.), *Implementing the Precautionary Principle: Approaches from the Nordic Countries, the EU and the United States.* London: Earthscan, 2007. Available at http://hdl.handle.net/1721.1/38470. Excerpted with permission.

### Introduction
Over the last 35 years since the first appearance of federal health, safety and environmental laws in the US, public health and the environment continue to be adversely affected by development[1] and limits to industrial growth are now clearly visible in the examples of global climate disruption, changes in the reproductive health of all species, and shortages of petroleum, freshwater and natural resources. Furthermore, the kinds of risks of concern, and the nature of scientific uncertainty, are changing. These developments have sparked new interest in the concepts of precaution and prevention in many environmental and public policy arenas.

Advances in the understanding of the causes of disease and new damage mechanisms include endocrine disruption[2] and other low-dose effects of chemical exposures[3]; substances, such as nanoparticles, that can cross the blood-brain barrier; antibiotic, drug and pesticide resistance; climate disruption; and interactions between toxic chemicals, nutritional factors, infectious agents and genetics. Advances in scientific risk assessment include green chemistry, green engineering, predictive toxicology, structure activity relationships and rapid *in vitro* screens[4]. Advances in technological approaches include sustainable technology, products and system design.

With advances in science and technology have come changes in the kinds of uncertainty facing government agencies mandated to protect health, safety and the environment. These include classical uncertainty (expressed as probability distributions of dose-response relationships and obscured by the lack of sufficiently definitive information, contradictory evidence, or a deficiency in the knowledge of causal mechanisms and pathways), indeterminacy (where we know what we don't know), and ignorance (where we don't know what we don't know)[5]. The general nature of uncertainty has shifted from classical uncertainty (which itself is now understood to be more complex than originally envisioned and is difficult to apply in many areas of concern), towards indeterminacy (as in the case of the extent of global warming) and ignorance (e.g., of possible risks to ecosystems from deliberately released genetically modified (GM) crops).

Partly because of changing science and partly because of inadequate governmental response, the trust in both government regulators and industry has declined, with a corresponding increased demand for the participation of the public, consumers, nongovernmental organizations (NGOs) and citizens in decision-making related to protection of health, safety and the environment. This increased demand for participation has resulted in a more critical look at the bases for governmental decisions.

Government has approached the problems of risky technologies and products by constructing a two-step exercise: risk assessment followed by risk management[6]. Value judgments pervade both steps[7], and the precautionary principle could be applied in choosing the data and models to inform risk assessment and also in deciding whether, to what extent and how to provide protection[8].

This . . . [text] argues that in the US, the governmental responses to these changes are wrong-headed and hide behind misguided formulaic methodologies of cost-benefit analyses and quantitative risk assessments ostensibly offered to provide more sensible and rational solutions[9] to guide approaches to health, safety and environmental problems, but in actuality motivated by desires to accommodate industrial and producer interests. Reflecting an increasingly anti-regulatory posture on the part of the federal government, the undemocratic use of these methodologies has seriously undermined health, safety and environmental protection in the US and (hopefully temporarily) rendered a precautionary approach to solving health and environmental problems to a historical relic. In the US, the undermining of protection is effectuated through:

- requiring regulations to be based on an increased level of scientific evidence or justification;
- allowing regulations to be delayed because of scientific uncertainty;
- allowing a *de minimis* risk to remain unprotected or requiring a "significant risk" to be present before acting[10]; and
- requiring that the benefits of regulating exceed, or justify, the imposition of costs[11].

These factors, of course, directly impact upon whether and to what extent the precautionary principle can be applied in the US.

The remainder of this [excerpt] provides a brief history of the precautionary principle as developed in the US with comparisons to its evolution in Europe; . . . [and] a capsule history of US chemical regulation and the use of the precautionary principle in US law. . . .

## A Brief History of the Precautionary Principle[*]

The precautionary principle has two distinct formulations[13]:

1. Where there are possibilities of large or irreversible serious effects, scientific uncertainty *should not prevent* protective actions from being taken.
2. Where there are possibilities of large or irreversible serious effects, *action should be taken*, even if there is considerable scientific uncertainty.

The first formulation in the international context appears prominently in the Brundtland formulation agreed to in the United Nations Conference on Environment and Development (UNCED) held in Rio de Janeiro in 1992, and recurs in many multilateral environmental agreements[14]. The second formulation appears in some multilateral agreements and in some European Union (EU) directives on environmental protection[15].

In the US, a precautionary approach has been applied in various ways in decisions about health, safety and the environment for about 30 years, much longer than recent commentaries would have us believe, and earlier than the appearance of the precautionary principle in European law[16]. In interpreting congressional legislation, the US courts have argued that federal regulatory agencies are permitted, and sometimes required, to protect workers even when the evidence is "on the frontiers of scientific knowledge" and to protect public health from emissions to air with "an ample or adequate margin of safety" by "erring on the side of caution." One scholar seeks to make a distinction between a precautionary approach and the precautionary principle, asserting that "with rare exceptions, US law balances precaution against other considerations, most importantly costs" and, hence, is better described as a preference, rather than a principle[17]. I find this distinction superficial, or at least unhelpful, if not often inaccurate; and when understood within the context of Roman/Napoleonic law-based European legal systems preferring "codes" to court-based evolution of common law, this is a semantic rather than a real distinction.

In the US, in a series of industry challenges to regulations, courts acknowledged that even in the case where the scientific basis for a threat to health or the environment is not compelling, regulators have the discretion to "err on the side of caution," often without laying down a specific requirement to do so, although the directive to do so is often found in the enabling legislation of various regulatory regimes. . . . Under [the] *Chevron* [doctrine][18], court deference to agency policy judgments initially not only allowed, but encouraged, agencies to take a precautionary approach under a myriad of legislation, partly by relegating questions of the sufficiency of scientific evidence to the province of discretionary policy-making. In the early environmental decisions, rather than adopting stringent interpretations of statutory language requiring "substantial evidence" in meeting the burden of proof for agencies to act, the courts adopted a deferential stance towards early environmental agency decisions, allowing them to relax the evidentiary showings in furtherance of protective public policy goals.

In the last decade or two, the precautionary inclinations of the American and Anglo-Saxon jurisprudential systems, as well as codified expressions of the precautionary principle in German law, for example, have found their way into multilateral environmental agreements and international law. Principle 15 of the Declaration of the 1992 UNCED (the Rio Declaration) states:

> In order to protect the environment, the precautionary approach shall be widely used by States according to their capabilities. Where there are threats of serious and irreversible damage, lack of full scientific certainty shall not be used as a reason for postponing cost-effective measures to prevent environmental degradation.

This is perhaps the best known, and often cited, statement of the precautionary principle. Note, especially, that the word "approach" rather than "principle" is used, and considerations of cost are certainly present in the phrases "according to their capabilities" and "cost-effective measures." Nonetheless, it is acknowledged to be a principle—but one to be balanced in one way or another against other principles—no different than the situation in US law[19]. Curiously, this statement of the principle is expressed in the negative—uncertainty should not be used to delay protection—rather than a statement that protection should be embraced deliberately even in the face of uncertainty (a subtle but important distinction), a formulation often more positively expressed in US case law[20]. The debate in Europe today is not whether the precautionary principle is a principle, but which formulation should be applied and whether it trumps other international law, particularly the manner in which risk assessment is addressed and is relevant to trade law involving the World Trade Organization (WTO)[21].[†] . . .

---

## A Capsule History of US Chemical Regulation and the Use of the Precautionary Principle in US Law

The history of the use of the precautionary approach in US law contrasts with that in the EU. Whereas in the EU, the precautionary principle appears first in food safety and then moves slowly to develop in environmental regulations and is yet to find full expression in the regulation of occupational health and safety, in the US, it begins strongly and emphatically in worker health and safety, then in the environment, and is weakly expressed in food safety law. In fact, interpretations of what constitutes sufficient scientific evidence and how precautionary agencies should be are given their strongest expression in occupational health and safety law [50], which profoundly affects the development of these considerations in the environmental area.

### The Occupational Safety and Health Act of 1970[51]

The Occupational Safety and Health Act (OSHAct) of 1970 specifically addresses the subject of toxic substances. It states, under Section 6(b)(5) of the act, that the secretary of labor, through the Occupational Safety and Health Administration (OSHA), in promulgating permanent standards dealing with toxic materials or harmful physical agents, shall set the standard that:

> ... most adequately assures, to the extent feasible, on the basis of the best available evidence that no employee will suffer material impairment of health or functional capacity, even if such employee has a regular exposure to the hazard dealt with by such standard for the period of his working life [emphasis added][52].

Standards promulgated under this section of the act are reviewable by the circuit courts of appeal; the standard of judicial review is "substantial evidence on the record as a whole"[53].

The case Industrial Union Department, AFL-CIO v Hodgson[54], promulgated a more stringent regulation for asbestos—at the time regarded as a lung toxin causing asbestosis, but not a carcinogen—and the industry challenged the standard, arguing that there was insufficient evidence to justify lowering the permissible exposure limit. In deferring to the agency's determination that a more protective level was needed, the DC Court of Appeals held that:

> Some of the questions involved in the promulgation of these standards are on the frontiers of scientific knowledge, and consequently ... insufficient data is presently available to make a fully informed factual determination ... it rests, in the final analysis, on an essentially legislative policy judgment, rather than a factual determination, concerning the relative risks of under-protection as opposed to overprotection.

One might regard this as an articulation of the permissive use of the precautionary principle.

In a subsequent case, The Society of Plastics Industry, Inc v Occupational Safety and Health Administration[55] concerning an industry challenge to a very stringent OSHA standard of allowing no more than 1 part per million (ppm) exposure over an eight-hour period to the carcinogen vinyl chloride, the Second Circuit Court of Appeals reiterated the rationale in Industrial Union above, adding: "Under the command of OSHA, it remains the duty of the secretary to act to protect the working man, and to act where existing methodology or research is deficient." Here, applying a precautionary approach appears to be mandatory, rather than permissible, even under industry protests that achieving the standard was not technologically feasible.

These cases profoundly influenced the extent to which the Environmental Protection Agency regulated air pollutants under the 1970 Clean Air Act (amended in 1977 and 1990) and attempted to regulate toxic substances under the 1976 Toxic Substances Control Act.

After industry testing revealed formaldehyde to be an animal carcinogen in 1979, during the 1980s, under President Reagan, the OSHA initially did nothing to follow up on the prior Carter administration's intent to regulate it[56]. Regulatory agency decisions "not to act," while technically reviewable by appellate courts, are notoriously difficult to counter. Ultimately, in 1992, 13 years after the animal study, the OSHA was forced to regulate formaldehyde, but chose to place the most minimal restrictions possible on allowable exposure, permitting lifetime risks of greater than $10^{-3}$ following the directives emanating from the Supreme Court benzene case discussed immediately below.

In a 1980 case involving the industry challenge to an OSHA regulation of the carcinogen benzene at 1 ppm over an eight-hour period, the appellate process reached the Supreme Court. In Industrial Union Department v American Petroleum Institute[57], the Supreme Court added a requirement, with dubious legal justification, to the OSHAct that only "significant risks" could be regulated under the toxic substances provision of the OSHAct. The court remanded the standard to OSHA to determine whether benzene exposure at 1 ppm was "significant," offering guidance that "significance" should lie somewhere between a lifetime risk of $10^{-3}$ (a clearly significant risk) and $10^{-9}$ (a clearly insignificant risk). The OSHA, under President Reagan, chose the "bright line" at the least permissibly protective level of $10^{-3}$. This heralded the end of the precautionary era in toxic substances regulation. Although President Clinton subsequently could have drawn the line differently, he did not change it. The OSHA can also administratively and immediately establish "temporary emergency standards" under the OSHAct; but much discretion is left to the OSHA to determine whether the requirements of a "necessity to prevent grave danger" prevails in a particular case[58]. In addition, there is a provision in the OSHAct that authorizes the OSHA to go to a federal district court (a court of first instance) to restrain or halt an industrial operation in the case of imminent dangers[59].

In addition to complying with specific standards, employers are also under a "general duty" to provide workplaces and work free from "recognized hazards likely to cause death or serious bodily harm"[60]. Again, defining what constitutes a "recognized hazard" is left to the discretion of the OSHA. Thus, what first appears as an emerging mandatory requirement to apply the precautionary principle for worker protection disappears after the benzene case into the abyss of agency discretion dominated by industry interests.

### The 1970 Clean Air Act (CAA) (and Amendments of 1977 and 1990)[61, 62]

The 1970 Clean Air Act (CAA) regulated both criteria pollutants (carbon monoxide, sulfur dioxide, nitrogen oxides, particulates, ozone and lead) under CAA Section 109[63] and so-called hazardous pollutants under CAA Section 112[64], Federal ambient air quality (concentration) standards were established for the former, and federal emission standards were to be established for the latter. The standard of judicial review in the DC Circuit Court of Appeals is "arbitrary or capricious." The ambient air quality standards were to be set by the EPA to protect public health "with an adequate margin of safety" without consideration of economic costs; they were to be achieved through state-imposed emission levels in state permits on existing sources and through state-enforced federal emission limitations on new sources[65], the latter taking economic burdens into account while permitting the standards to be "technology forcing" in stringency.

The leading case interpreting standard-setting for criteria pollutants, *Lead Industries Association, Inc v Environmental Protection Agency*, addressed a new standard for airborne lead compound particulates[66]. There, the DC Circuit Court of Appeals agreed with the EPA that "Congress directed the administrator to *err on the side of caution* in making the necessary decisions" (emphasis added). Furthermore, the court agreed with the EPA that:

- Congress made it abundantly clear that considerations of economic or technological feasibility are to be subordinated to the goal of protecting the public health by prohibiting any consideration of such factors.
- [I]t specified that the air quality standards must also protect individuals who are particularly sensitive to the effects of pollution.
- [I]t required that the standards be set at a level at which there is "an absence of adverse effect" on these sensitive individuals.
- [I]t specifically directed the Administrator to allow an adequate margin of safety in setting primary air quality standards in order to provide some protection against effects that research has not yet uncovered.

It is hard to imagine a stronger endorsement of the precautionary principle. Note the absence of any specific reference to irreversibility of damage or persistence or biomagnifications of the pollutant in the environment or the human body. But do note the specific concern for sensitive individuals, the explicit rejection of cost-benefit balancing, and the endorsement of action "against effects that research has not yet uncovered." But the precautionary approach was not long lived in the agency. Ronald Reagan won a two-term presidency in 1980 and 1984 and dramatically changed the landscape of US environmental regulation.

For hazardous air pollutants, the 1970 CAA similarly directed the EPA to set emission standards "at the level which, in his judgment, provides an ample margin of safety to protect the public health"[67]. Departing from the rationale in *Lead Industries* [addressing a similar directive from Congress to provide an adequate margin of safety to protect the public health], in an industry challenge to the EPA proposed emission standard for vinyl chloride, writing for a three-judge panel of the DC Circuit Court of Appeals, Judge Robert Bork in *Natural Resources Defense Council, Inc v Environmental Protection Agency*[68] opined:

> We find that the congressional mandate to provide "an ample margin of safety" "to protect the public health" requires the Administrator to make an initial determination of what is "safe". . . [T]he administrator's decision does not require a finding that "safe" means "risk free" or a finding that the determination is free from uncertainty. Instead, we find only that the administrator's decision must be based upon an expert judgment with regard to the level of emission that will result in an "acceptable" risk to health. . . . This determination must be based solely upon the risk to health. The administrator cannot under any circumstances consider cost and technological feasibility at this stage of the analysis. . . .

> Congress, however, recognized in Section 112 that the determination of what is "safe" will always be marked by scientific uncertainty and thus exhorted the administrator to set emission standards that will provide an "ample margin" of safety. This language permits the administrator to take into account scientific uncertainty and to use expert discretion to determine what action should be taken in light of that uncertainty. Congress authorized and, indeed, required EPA to protect against dangers before their extent is conclusively ascertained. Under the "ample margin of safety" directive, EPA's standards must protect against incompletely understood dangers to public health and the environment, in addition to well-known risks. . . .

> We wish to reiterate the limited nature of our holding in this case because it is not the court's intention to bind the administrator to any specific method of determining what is "safe" or what constitutes an "ample margin." We hold only that the administrator cannot consider cost and technological feasibility in determining what is "safe."

Unable to shake the clear congressional intent in Section 112 to require standards to be set in the face of considerable scientific uncertainty and without regard to economic or technological feasibility, the three-judge panel of the DC Circuit invented a *de minimis* risk requirement to soften the blow. This case prompted Congress to amend Section 112 of the CAA in the 1990 CAA amendments to allow a technology-based approach to be used, directing the EPA to set technology-based emission standards (based on maximum achievable control technology) established on the level achievable by the "average" performance of the top 12 per cent of the industry[69]. The EPA could establish more stringent emission standards for new sources[70]. Where technology-based standards were not practical, the EPA could resort to a health-based approach, protecting the public health with an ample margin of safety[71], the original mandate of the 1970 CAA. Congress expressly provided that, ultimately, carcinogenic chemicals cannot present a risk greater than a 10–6 lifetime risk[72].

In a later challenge to the EPA's revised standards for the criteria pollutants ozone and particulates, in *Environmental Protection Agency* v *American Trucking Associations, Inc.*[73], the Supreme Court reinforced the correctness of the lead case criteria, with concurring Justice Stephen Breyer echoing Judge Bork's rationale that protecting public health with an "adequate margin of safety" does not mean a world that is "free of all risk." Appellate court deference to the agencies as to what constitutes tolerable *de minimis* risks or significant risks that must be demonstrated in order to be regulated is a "back door" pathway to reducing a precautionary approach by allowing risk assessments that do not clearly show calculable significant risks to justify non-action. Furthermore, by compromising the independence of agency science advisory boards and by eliminating research grants to scientists who do not think "the right way," the federal government has greatly compromised the independence and integrity of science in the political process[74].

### *The 1976 Toxic Substances Control Act* (TSCA)[75]

Under the 1976 Toxics Substances Control Act (TSCA), the EPA must set standards for substances that present or will present "unreasonable risks to health or the environment"[76], taking into account costs, effects on health and the environment, technological innovation and [the availability of] substitutes[77]. The EPA requires industry to test chemicals[78] if there [are] insufficient data and the substance "may present unreasonable risks to health or the environment" *or* if there is a substantial quantity produced or exposure is deemed to be significant. If there may be a reasonable basis to conclude that a chemical presents (or will present) a "significant" risk of cancer, mutation or birth defects, the EPA must either regulate or explain why it has chosen not [to]"—that is, why the risk is not "unreasonable"[79]. Upon challenge, any federal court of appeal can examine the standards to ensure that they are based on "substantial evidence on the record as a whole" (the same standard of judicial review found in the OSHAct)[80]. As with the OSHAct, the TSCA provides for emergency measures[81] and imminent hazards[82]. Under the TSCA, the EPA also requires industry to report "significant adverse reactions" and information about their products' toxicity[83].

Asbestos, the most notorious carcinogen known in the context of workplace, consumer and environmental exposure, did receive EPA attention during the 1980s. The EPA decided to ban the substance under the TSCA for many uses; but the standard was remanded to the agency for reconsideration by the Fifth Circuit Court of Appeals in *Corrosion Proof Fittings* v *EPA*[84]. As stated above, the TSCA requires the EPA to consider, along with the toxic effects on human health and the environment, "the benefits of such substance[s] and mixture[s] and the *availability* of substitutes for such uses" (emphasis added). Because the EPA did not explore regulatory options other than a ban, and, more specifically, because the EPA did not evaluate the toxicity (and costs) of likely substitute products[85] in a search for "least burdensome requirements," the court vacated the proposed standard and remanded it to the EPA for further proceedings. While, arguably, the court incorrectly interpreted the TSCA's requirements regarding mandating substitutes' toxicity (and cost) comparisons (the TSCA mentions only that the "availability" of substitutes must be considered) and [EPA] could have sought to establish [for a different toxic substance a] regulation [likely to be heard] in another circuit court to give a more favorable result concerning what criteria need to be met in order to regulate, the EPA chose not to reinstate the asbestos ban, primarily because of the likely extensive burden on agency resources to perform extensive risk and economic assessments for substitutes. For all intents and purposes, the EPA regards the TSCA as a "dead letter"[86]. The analytic burdens placed by the Fifth Circuit Court of Appeals effectively emasculated the TSCA regulation in the US. . . .

### Notes:

1 This is not to say that some improvements have not also occurred; but the magnitude of problems in other areas has increased, and the nature of risks has also changed.

2 Colborn, T., Dumanowski, D. and Myers, J. P. (1996) *Our Stolen Future*, Dutton Press, New York.

3 Ashford, N. A. and Miller, C. (1998) *Chemical Exposures: Low Levels and High Stakes*, second edition, John Wiley Press, New York.

4 Hoefer, T., Gerner, I., Gundert-Remy, U., Liebsch, M., Schulte, A., Spielmann, H., Vogel, R. and Wettig, K. (2004) "Animal testing and alternative approaches for the human health risk assessment under the proposed new European Chemicals Regulation," *Archives of Toxicology*, vol 78, pp549–564.

5 Wynne, B. (1992) "Uncertainty and environmental learning," *Global Environmental Change*, vol 2, pp111–127.

6 National Academy of Sciences (1983) *Risk Assessment in the Federal Government: Managing the Process*, National Academy Press, Washington, DC.

7 Ashford, N. A. (1988) "Science and values in the regulatory process," *Statistical Science*, vol 3, no 3, pp377–383.

8 See de Sadeleer, N. (2006) "The precautionary principle in EC health and environmental law: Sword or shield for the Nordic countries?"—Chapter 2 in this volume.

9 Indeed, the offered methodologies are based [on] so-called "rational-choice" theory pioneered by the University of Chicago School of Law and Economics. See Ashford, N. and Caldart, C. (2008) "Economics and the environment," in *Environmental Law, Policy, and Economics: Reclaiming the Environmental Agenda*, Cambridge, MIT Press, Chapter 3.

10 Rather than focusing on requiring minimum certainty before acting, agencies sometimes formulate their defense of no regulation by arguing that (conservative) risk assessments yield risks that are too small to justify action—that is, the risks are *de minimis*. See the discussion in the section on "The politics of regulating chemicals in the US." In the context of genetically-modified foods, the then Food and Drug Administration (FDA) Commissioner David Kessler stated that those foods were "substantially equivalent" to foods produced by traditional production, thus glossing over small but possibly important differences vis-à-vis food safety. See Kessler, D. (1984) "Food safety: Revising the statute," *Science*, vol 223, pp1034–1040.

11 There is the increasing tendency of the EU to balance "conflicting interests" rather than costs and benefits. See Chapter 2 in this volume. This turns out to be a major feature of trade-off analysis rather than cost-benefit analysis, as discussed in the section on "A capsule history of US chemical regulation and the use of the precautionary principle in US law." ...

13 For an extensive discussion of these two formulations, see Chapter 2 in this volume. See also de Sadeleer, N. (2002) *Environmental Principles: From Political Slogans to Legal Rules*, Oxford University Press, Oxford.

14 See Chapter 2 in this volume for an in-depth discussion.

15 See Chapter 2 in this volume for an in-depth discussion.

16 de Sadeleer, N. (2000) *Two Approaches of Precaution: A Comparative Review of EU and US Theory and Practice of the Precautionary Principle*, Centre d'Étude du Droit de l'Environnement, Brussels. See also de Sadeleer, N. (2002) *Environmental Principles: From Political Slogans to Legal Rules*, Oxford University Press, Oxford, p139.

17 Applegate, J. S. (2000) "The precautionary preference: An American perspective on the precautionary principle," *Human and Ecological Risk Assessment*, vol 6, no 3, pp413–443.

18 *Chevron, USA, v NRDC*, 467 US 837 (1984).

19 Attempts to distinguish "approaches" from "principles" by arguing that approaches are flexible, but principles are not, fail a logical test. Principles in the law are not without their limits, and they are sometimes in direct conflict. For example, the freedom of speech can be said to be a fundamental principle of U.S. law, but it is not absolute and may be compromised in favor of public safety: "No one has the right to yell fire in a crowded theatre."

20 See Hornstein, D. (1992) "Reclaiming environmental law: A normative critique of comparative risk analysis," *Columbia Law Review*, vol 92, pp562–633.

21 See Chapter 2 in this volume; See also several papers by Majone, G. (2001) *The Precautionary Principle and Regulatory Impact Analysis*, Manuscript, described as an expanded version of a paper submitted at the International Seminar on Regulatory Impact Analysis organized by Progetto AIR, Rome, 15 June 2001; Majone, G. (2002) "What price safety? The precautionary principle and its policy implications," *Journal of Common Market Studies,* vol 40, pp89–106; and Majone, G. and Everson, M. (2001) "Institutional reform: Independent agencies, oversight, coordination and procedural control," in De Schutter, O., Lebessis, N. and Paterson, J. (eds) *Governance in the European Union*, Office for the Official Publications of the European Communities, Luxembourg, pp129–168. ...

50 See Ashford, N. and Caldart, C. (1996) *Technology, Law and the Working Environment,* second edition, Island Press, Washington, DC.

51 29 U.S.C. §§651–683.

52 29 U.S.C. §655(b)(5).

53 29 U.S.C §660.

54 499 F2d 467 (DC Cir. 1974).

55 509 F2d 1301 (2nd Cir 1975).

56 Ashford, N. A., Ryan, W. C. and Caldart, C. C. (1983) "Law and science policy in federal regulation of formaldehyde," *Science*, vol 222, pp894–900, and Ashford, N. A., Ryan, W. C., and Caldart, C. C. (1983) "A hard look at federal regulation of formaldehyde: A departure from reasoned decision-making," *Harvard Environmental Law Review*, vol 7, pp297–370. See also Rest, K. and Ashford, N. A. (1988) "Regulation and technology options: The case of occupational exposure to formaldehyde," *Harvard Journal of Law and Technology*, vol 1, pp63–96.

57 448 U.S. 607 (1980).

58 Temporary emergency standards, which allow the OSHA to put into play immediate restrictions lasting six months without engaging in the long procedural process of promulgating permanent standards, might be compared to the "safeguard principle" in EC environmental law, whereby EU member states reserve the right to address emergency situations without recourse to EC restrictions. Temporary emergency standards also implicitly incorporate the concept of proportionality through the requirement that these standards are "necessary." See Chapter 2 in this volume.

59 29 U.S.C. §662.

60 29 U.S.C. §654.

61 42 U.S.C. §§7401–7671.

62 See Ashford, N. and Caldart, C. (2007) "Limiting exposure to outdoor air contaminants: The Clean Air Act," in *Environmental Law, Policy, and Economics: Reclaiming the Environmental Agenda*, MIT Press, Cambridge, Chapter 7.

63 42 U.S.C. §7409.

64 42 U.S.C. §7412, otherwise known as Section 112 of the CAA.

65 42 U.S.C. §7411. A [Bush-era] ... controversy involve[d] the EPA's relaxation of new source requirements for installing new pollution control equipment where there have been updates to coal-fired power plants ... EPA [had proposed] to replace the mercury hazardous substance emission standard under Section 112 and to establish a cap and trade provision allowing mercury emissions from power plants (and other sources) [to] be traded, thus creating "hot spots." [The Obama administration withdraw that proposal.]

66 647 F.2d 1130 (DC Cir. 1980).

67 §7412(b)(1)(B).

68 824 F.2d 1146 (DC Cir. 1987).

69 §7412(d)(3).

70 §7412(d)(3).

71 §7412(d)(4).

72 §7412(f)(2).

73 531 U.S. 457 (2001).

74 On 18 February 2004, over 60 leading scientists—Nobel laureates, leading medical experts, former federal agency directors, and university chairs and presidents—following up on an initiative organized by the Union of Concerned Scientists (UCS), signed a statement voicing their concern over the misuse of science by the Bush administration. See the UCS website: www.ucsusa.org/scientific_integrity/.

75 15 U.S.C. §§2601–2629.

76 15 U.S.C. §2605a.

77  15 U.S.C. §2605c.

78  15 U.S.C. §2603.

79  15 U.S.C. §2603f. As with OSHA reluctance to take action on formaldehyde, the EPA dragged its feet on formaldehyde, refusing to "either act or explain" as required by this section of the TSCA. For a history of formaldehyde regulation, see Rest, K. and Ashford, N. A. (1988) "Regulation and technology options: The case of occupational exposure to formaldehyde," *Harvard Journal of Law and Technology*, vol 1, pp63–96; and Ashford, N. and Caldart, C. (1996) "The Toxic Substances Control Act," in *Technology, Law, and the Working Environment*, revised edition, Island Press, Washington, DC, Chapter 4.

80  15 U.S.C. §2618.

81  15 U.S.C. §2605d.

82  15 U.S.C. §2606.

83  15 U.S.C. §2607.

84  947 F.2d 1201 (Fifth Cir.1991).

85  Note the contrast with the result reached in the WTO panel's rejection of Canada's argument that France was obligated to assess likely substitutes for asbestos before it should be permitted to ban Canadian asbestos imports under Section XX of the General Agreement on Tariffs and Trade (GATT). Articles 8.218 to 8.223, *European Communities— Measures Affecting Asbestos and Asbestos-Containing Products*, Report of the Panel, WT/DS135/R, 12 March 2001 (00–3353).

86  There is a danger that REACH could suffer the same fate, with the result that regulation (authorization and restrictions) is not often vigorously pursued. Note, as discussed earlier, that comparative assessment of risks and costs [is] not nearly as burdensome as conducting separate risk and cost assessments. Whether using comparative assessment could circumvent the hurdle that the EPA needs to overcome to satisfy the requirements laid out in *Corrosion Proof Fittings* v *EPA* (note 84, *supra*) needs to be explored. Because the issue of alternatives needs to be considered in formulating regulations under the TSCA, this may well be possible.

In contrast, because risk assessment seems to drive the REACH process, and because the consideration of alternatives seems to come in later, whether the use of comparative analysis in the context of REACH can circumvent the need for extensive risk analyses is unclear. See Koch, L. and Ashford, N. A. (2006) *Journal of Cleaner Production*, vol 14, no 1, pp31–46.

## 9.2.4 The Chemical Safety Provisions of the U.S. Clean Air Act: Obligations Imposed by EPA and OSHA to Prevent the Sudden and Accidental Release of Chemicals

Although the first congressional response to the concern generated by the deadly industrial accident in Bhopal, India, was the Emergency Planning and Community Right to Know Act of 1986, the chemical safety provisions of that law are focused almost solely on mitigation and not on accident prevention. A much greater potential for a direct focus on accident prevention can be found in the 1990 Amendments to the Clean Air Act, although that potential has yet to be realized by the EPA and OSHA.

As amended in 1990, Section 112 of the Clean Air Act directs the EPA to develop regulations regarding the prevention and detection of accidental chemical releases and to publish a list of at least 100 chemical substances (with associated threshold quantities) to be covered by the regulations. The regulations must include requirements for the development of risk-management plans (RMPs) by facilities using any of the regulated substances in amounts above the relevant threshold. These RMPs must include a hazard assessment, an accident-prevention program, and an emergency-release program. Similarly, Section 304 of the Clean Air Act Amendments of 1990 directed OSHA to promulgate a Process Safety Management (PSM) standard under the OSH Act. Section 112(r) of the revised Clean Air Act also imposes a general duty on all owners and operators of stationary sources, regardless of the particular identity or quantity of the chemicals used on site. These parties have a duty to

- identify hazards that may result from (accidental chemical) releases using appropriate hazard-assessment techniques,

- design and maintain a safe facility, taking such steps as are necessary to prevent releases, and

- minimize the consequences of accidental releases that do occur.

Thus firms are now under a general duty to anticipate, prevent, and mitigate accidental releases. In defining the nature of this duty, Section 112(r) specifies that it is a general duty in the same manner and to the same extent as that imposed by Section 5 of the OSH Act. Because Section 112(r) specifically ties its general-duty obligation to the general-duty clause of the OSH Act, case law interpreting the OSH Act provision should be directly relevant. In the 1987 *General Dynamics* case, the District of Columbia Circuit Court of Appeals held that OSHA standards and the general-duty obligation are distinct and independent requirements and that compliance with a standard does not discharge an employer's duty to comply with the general-duty obligation. Similarly, compliance with other Clean Air Act chemical-safety requirements should not relieve a firm of the duty to comply with the act's general-duty clause. Further, the requirement that owners and operators design and maintain a safe facility would seem to extend the obligation to the area of primary prevention rather than mere hazard control.

The Clean Air Act also requires each state to establish programs to provide small businesses with technical assistance in addressing chemical safety. These programs could provide information on alternative technologies, process changes, products, and methods of operation that help reduce emissions to the air. However, these state mandates are unfunded and may not be uniformly implemented. Where they are established, linkage with state offices of technical assistance, especially those that provide guidance on pollution prevention, could be particularly beneficial.

Finally, the 1990 CAA Amendments established an independent Chemical Safety and Hazard Investigation Board (CSHIB). The board is to investigate the causes of accidents, conduct research on prevention, and make recommendations for preventive approaches, much as the Air Transportation Safety Board does with regard to airplane safety.

In response to its Clean Air Act mandate, OSHA promulgated a workplace Process Safety Management (PSM) standard in 1992. The PSM standard is designed to protect employees working in facilities that use highly hazardous chemicals, and employees working in facilities with more than 10,000 pounds of flammable liquids or gases present in one location. The list of highly hazardous chemicals in the standard includes acutely toxic, highly flammable, and reactive substances. The PSM standard requires employers to compile safety information (including process-flow information) on chemicals and processes used in the workplace, complete a workplace process hazard analysis every five years, conduct triennial compliance safety audits, develop and implement written operating procedures, conduct extensive worker training, develop and implement plans to maintain the integrity of process equipment, perform pre-start-up reviews of new (and significantly modified) facilities, develop and implement written procedures to manage changes in production methods, establish an emergency action plan, and investigate accidents and near misses at their facilities. In 1996, the EPA promulgated regulations setting forth requirements for the RMPs specified in the Clean Air Act. The RMP rule is modeled after the OSHA PSM standard and is estimated to affect some 66,000 facilities. The rule requires a hazard assessment (involving an off-site consequence analysis including worst-case risk scenarios and compilation of a five-year accident history), a prevention program to address the hazards identified, and an emergency response program.

In 2002, the Chemical Safety and Hazard Investigation Board urged OSHA to amend its 1992 PSM standard and the EPA to amend its 1996 RMP regulation in order to achieve more comprehensive control of reactive hazards that could have catastrophic consequences. The board also asked OSHA to define and record information on reactive chemical incidents that it investigates or is required to investigate. These recommendations have largely been ignored. The board also expressed concern that the material safety data sheets (MSDSs) issued by OSHA do not adequately identify the reactive potential of chemicals. And although the EPA and OSHA signed a memorandum of understanding on the topic in 1996, a 2001 U.S. General Accounting Office (GAO) report called for better coordination between the EPA, OSHA, the CSHIB, and other agencies on chemical safety.

Currently, many aspects of chemical safety are not covered by specific workplace standards. Most OSHA standards that do apply to chemical safety have their origin in the consensus standards adopted under Section 6(a) of the OSH Act in 1971 and hence are greatly out-of-date. Arguably, however, the general-duty obligation of the OSH Act imposes a continuing duty on employers to seek out technological improvements that would improve safety for workers.

### 9.2.5 Pollution Prevention and Inherently Safer Production in the United States

End-of-pipe [pollution] control focuses on reducing or collecting the harmful emissions, effluents, or waste from industrial processes (or, in the case of workers' exposure, on ventilating the workplace or providing personal protective equipment), usually without altering inputs, feedstocks, processes, or final products. Early preoccupation with minimizing air and water pollution often shifted the problem to the hazardous-waste stream and/or increased workplace exposure, resulting in what is popularly known as a "media shift." It also often changed the nature of the hazard by increasing the potential for chemical accidents (sudden and unexpected chemical releases, sometimes with accompanying fires and explosions), thus resulting in what is popularly known as a "problem shift."

Pollution prevention—what the Europeans call "cleaner" production or technology—received its first political push in the United States with the mid-1980s pursuit of "waste minimization," an economically driven movement that grew out of a recognition that the best way to avoid the rising costs of treatment and disposal of hazardous wastes often is simply to generate less waste. Depending on the context and the time period, pollution prevention has also been known as "elimination of pollution at the source," "source reduction," and "toxics use reduction." This approach (whatever its name) entails fundamental changes to the means and/or outputs of production.

Pollution prevention is not a refined version of pollution control. It involves fundamental changes in production technology: substitution of inputs, redesign and reengineering of processes, and/or reformulation of the final product. It may require organizational and institutional changes as well. "Inherent safety"—also known as "primary" accident prevention—is the analogous concept for the prevention of sudden and accidental chemical releases. Inherent safety is a concept similar to—and often is a natural extension of—pollution prevention. The common thread linking the two concepts is that they both attempt to prevent the possibility of harm, rather than to reduce the probability of harm, by eliminating the problem (chemical accidents and chemical pollution, respectively) at its source. The changes necessary for pollution prevention often are associated with improvements in eco-efficiency and energy efficiency. In the context of chemical production, they often involve the exploration of alternative synthetic pathways and green chemistry initiatives. The search for and identification of alternative production methods may also promote the development and use of inherently safer production technology, although the minimization of accident potential may require a somewhat different (though not necessarily inconsistent) set of changes.

The Pollution Prevention Act (PPA) of 1990 endeavors to encourage both pollution prevention and inherent safety. It does this through the rubric of "source reduction," which it defines as any practice that (1) reduces the amount of any hazardous substance, pollutant, or contaminant entering any waste stream or otherwise released into the environment (including fugitive emissions) prior to recycling, treatment, or disposal; and (2) reduces the hazards to public health and the environment associated with the release of such substances, pollutants, or contaminants. Explicitly included within the statutory definition are "equipment or technology modifications, process or procedure modifications, reformulation or redesign of products, substitution of raw materials, and improvements in housekeeping, maintenance, training, or inventory control," while explicitly excluded is any practice that "alters the physical, chemical, or biological characteristics or the volume of a hazardous substance, pollutant, or contaminant through a process or activity which itself is not integral to and necessary for the production of a product or the providing of a service." Thus pollution prevention and primary accident prevention both come within the PPA's definition of "source reduction." On the other hand, recycling or reuse does not meet this definition unless it is done as part of a closed-loop production process (as is often done within the metal-finishing industry, when metals are recovered at the end of the process and immediately returned to the beginning of the process).

The PPA declares, as the "national policy," that pollution is to be addressed in a hierarchical fashion. First, "Pollution should be prevented or reduced at the source whenever feasible." Second, "Pollution that cannot be prevented should be recycled in an environmentally safe manner, whenever feasible." Third, "Disposal or other release into the environment should be employed only as a last resort." The EPA did establish an Office of Pollution Prevention as required by the PPA, but the agency's overall commitment to implementing the PPA has waned considerably since the early 1990s. Neither the Clinton nor the Bush administrations wholeheartedly embraced the potential opportunities for fundamental change that the PPA represents, and the agency's "source-reduction" strategy has largely been allowed to languish.

Nonetheless, many industrial firms have found it in their economic interest to adopt pollution-prevention approaches because they can eliminate the need for waste handling, disposal, and treatment and can reduce pollution-control and abatement costs. However, these incentives may be absent with regard to the prevention of chemical accidents because these events are both rare and not statistically predictable; thus rational behavioral changes premised on cost avoidance are largely absent. As the following excerpt from a letter explains, interventions focusing on information generation may be useful.

> Requiring industry to actually change their technology would be good, but is likely to be resisted. However, one way of providing firms with the right incentives would be to exploit the opportunity to prevent accidents and accidental releases by requiring industry to (1) identify where in the production process changes to inherently safer inputs, processes, and final products could be made and (2) identify the specific inherently safer technologies that could be substituted or developed. The first analysis might be termed an Inherent Safety Opportunity Audit (ISOA). The latter is a Technology Options Analysis (TOA). Unlike a hazard or risk assessment, these practices seek to identify where and what superior technologies could be adopted or developed to eliminate the possibility, or dramatically reduce the probability, of accidents and accidental releases, and promote a culture of real prevention. A risk assessment, such as required by worst-case analysis, is not sufficient. In practice, it is generally limited to an

evaluation of the risks associated with a firm's established production technology and does not include the identification or consideration of alternative inherently safer production technologies. Consequently, risk assessments tend to emphasize secondary accident prevention and mitigation strategies, which impose engineering and administrative controls on an existing production technology, rather than primary accident prevention strategies. Requiring industry to report these options would no doubt encourage more widespread adoption of inherently safer technologies, just as reporting technology options in Massachusetts under its Toxic Use Reduction Act has encouraged pollution prevention. (Ashford 2006)

### 9.2.6 The Right to Know and Information-Based Strategies to Encourage Alternative Technology in the United States

The various media-based environmental laws (regulating air and water pollution and waste) incorporate a number of information-disclosure requirements. Under the Clean Air and Clean Water acts, for example, pollution sources are required to monitor discharges of pollutants and report the results to the EPA or the state. Similarly, those who generate, transfer, treat, store, or dispose of hazardous waste must maintain records of the types and amounts of wastes involved and must supply these records to the appropriate agency. The existence of adequate and accurate information of this nature is essential to the optimal operation of both the command-and-control or regulatory approaches to risk reduction and the so-called market-based approaches. Without such information, neither class of policies can succeed.

Beyond the particular informational requirements attached to the various regulatory regimes, however, there is a class of more broadly based information-disclosure requirements popularly known as "right-to-know" laws. In essence, these laws give workers and citizens a general statutory right to be apprised of the substances to which they are (or may be) exposed, as well as to obtain information about the hazardous nature of those substances. These laws have a twofold risk-reduction purpose. The first is to give potentially exposed persons information that may enable them to take action to avoid or limit such exposure. The second is to encourage those who create such exposures—the manufacturers and users of toxic chemicals—to take actions to reduce or eliminate the exposure.

Many political and legislative initiatives focusing on the right to know emerged in the United States in the early 1980s, a time when the direct regulation of toxic substances was being deemphasized by the federal agencies. Indeed, environmental and worker advocates shifted their attention to information as an area of political action because toxic-substance standard setting and enforcement had slowed significantly.

Workplace information-disclosure and reporting requirements began at state and local levels and were added at the federal level in 1983, when OSHA promulgated a comprehensive Hazard Communication Standard under the OSH Act. These workplace initiatives preceded the more general community right-to-know requirements that were to come a few years later. The worker right-to-know initiatives greatly influenced the evolution of the community right to know. Worker and community right-to-know laws largely focus on scientific information about chemicals: (1) the ingredients of chemical products and the specific composition of pollution in air, water, and waste; (2) the toxicity and safety hazards posed by the related chemicals, materials, and industrial processes; and (3) information related to exposure of various vulnerable groups to harmful substances and processes. The 1976 Toxic Substances Control Act (TSCA) had earlier given statutory authority to the EPA to require industry to test the chemicals it produced or imported—and gave citizens unprecedented access to toxicity and exposure information about industrial chemicals—but barely had the EPA staffed a bureaucracy to implement the TSCA when the Reagan antiregulatory revolution of the 1980s swept government, and the EPA's TSCA budget fell by the wayside. To date, the TSCA's informational initiatives have yet to be fully developed.

In 1986, Congress amended the federal Superfund statute with the Superfund Amendment and Reauthorization Act of 1986 (known as SARA). Beyond strengthening certain provisions governing the cleanup of hazardous-waste sites, Congress took in SARA what it believed to be a significant step toward reducing the likelihood of new hazardous-substance contamination in the future. Title III of SARA created the Emergency Planning and Community Right to Know Act (EPCRA). The EPCRA is a comprehensive federal community right-to-know program implemented by the states under guidelines promulgated by the EPA. The central feature of this federal program is broad public dissemination of information pertaining to the nature and identity of chemicals used at commercial facilities. The EPCRA has four major provisions: emergency planning; emergency release notification; hazardous chemical storage reporting; and the Toxics Release Inventory (TRI). Each of these is summarized in Table 9.3.

The implementation of the EPCRA began with the creation of state and local bodies to implement this community right-to-know program. Section 301 required the governor of each state to appoint a "state emergency response commission" (SERC), to be staffed by "persons who have technical expertise in the emergency response field." In practice, these state commissions have tended to include representatives from the various environmental and public health and safety agencies in the state. Each state commission in turn was required to divide the state into various "local emergency planning districts" and to appoint a "local emergency planning committee" (LEPC) for each of these districts. These state and local entities are responsible for receiving, coordinating, maintaining, and providing access to the various types of information required to be disclosed under the act.

The EPCRA established four principal requirements for reporting information about hazardous chemicals. Section 304 requires all facilities that manufacture, process, use, or store certain "extremely hazardous substances" in excess of certain quantities to provide "emergency" notification to the SERC and the LEPC of an unexpected release of one of these substances. Section 311 requires facilities covered by the OSHA Hazard Communication Standard to prepare and submit to the LEPC and the local fire department material safety data sheets for chemicals covered by the OSHA standard. Under

Section 312, many of these same firms are required to prepare and submit to the LEPC an "emergency and hazardous substance inventory form" that describes the amount and location of certain hazardous chemicals on their premises. Finally, Section 313 requires firms in the manufacturing sector to provide to the EPA an annual report of certain routine releases of hazardous substances. The EPA database containing these hazardous release reports is what is known as the Toxics Release Inventory (TRI), and the underlying reports are known as TRI reports. In addition, Section 303 requires certain commercial facilities to cooperate with their respective LEPCs in preparing emergency response plans for dealing with major accidents involving hazardous chemicals. The applicability of these provisions to any particular facility depends on the amount of the designated chemicals that it uses or stores during any given year.

In 1990, Congress added two more chemical reporting requirements to federal law. The Pollution Prevention Act amended the EPCRA to require firms subject to TRI reporting also to report their "source-reduction" (pollution-prevention) and waste-management practices on an annual basis. Further, as discussed above, the 1990 Clean Air Act Amendments directed the EPA and OSHA to issue regulations governing prevention of chemical accidents. Under these regulations, facilities using certain

## TABLE 9.3: EPCRA CHEMICALS, REPORTABLE ACTIONS, AND REPORTING THRESHOLDS

| | SECTION 302 EMERGENCY PLANNING | SECTION 304 UNEXPECTED RELEASES | SECTIONS 311/312 CHEMICALS IN STORAGE | SECTION 313 (TRI) ROUTINE EMISSIONS |
|---|---|---|---|---|
| Chemicals covered | 356 extremely hazardous substances | > 1,000 substances | 500,000 products with MSDSs* (required under OSHA regulations) | 650 toxic chemicals and categories** |
| Reportable actions and thresholds | Threshold planning quantity, 1–10,000 pounds present on site at any one time; requires notification of the SERC and LEPC within sixty days upon onsite production or receipt of shipment | Reportable quantity, 1–5,000 pounds, released at any time within a twenty-four-hour period; reportable to the SERC and NEPC | TPQ or 500 pounds for Section 302 chemicals; 10,000 pounds present on site at any one time for other chemicals, copy if requested to SERC/LEPC; annual inventory Tier I/Tier II report to SERC/LEPC/ local fire department by March 1 | 25,000 pounds per year manufactured or processed; 10,000 pounds a year used; lower thresholds for certain persistent bioaccumulative toxics; annual report to EPA and the state by July 1 |

* MSDSs on hazardous chemicals are maintained by a number of universities and can be accessed at www.hazard.com
** The TRI reporting requirement applies to all federal facilities that have 10 or more full-time employees, and those that manufacture (including importing), process, or otherwise use a listed toxic chemical above threshold quantities and that are in one of the following sectors: manufacturing (Standard Industrial Classification [SIC] codes 20 through 39), metal mining (SIC code 10, except for SIC codes 1011,1081, and 1094), coal mining (SIC code 12, except for 1241 and extraction activities), electrical utilities that combust coal and/or oil (SIC codes 4911, 4931, and 4939), Resource Conservation and Recovery Act (RCRA), Subtitle C, hazardous-waste-treatment and disposal facilities (SIC code 4953), chemicals and allied products wholesale distributors (SIC code 5169), petroleum bulk plants and terminals (SIC code 5171), and solvent recovery services (SIC code 7389).
Source: The Emergency Planning and Community Right-To-Know Act (EPCRA), EPA 550-F-00-004, March 2000.

chemicals above specified threshold quantities are required to develop a risk-management program to identify, evaluate, and manage chemical safety hazards, to submit a risk-management plan (RMP) summarizing their program to the EPA or the state, and to report accidental chemical releases above specified thresholds. Furthermore, chemical manufacturers and refineries must file start-up, shutdown, and malfunction (SSM) plans with the EPA or state air regulators. Some RMP information is available to the public through RMP*Info, which can be accessed through www.epa.gov/enviro. Worst-case chemical accident scenarios—called "off-site consequence analyses" (OCAs)—are now available for reading, but not for copying, in locally designated reading rooms.

Taken as a whole, these requirements constitute a broad federal declaration that firms choosing to rely heavily on hazardous chemicals in their production processes may not treat information regarding their use of those chemicals as their private domain. Indeed, except for trade secrecy protections (relating to specific chemical identity) that generally parallel those available under the OSHA Hazard Communication Standard, there are no statutory restrictions on the disclosure of EPCRA information to the general public.

Beyond such scientific information, however, disseminating (or providing access to) legal and technological information may be even more important for empowering workers and citizens to facilitate a transformation of hazardous industries and their practices. Legal information, in this context, refers to statements (or explanations) of the rights and obligations of producers, employers, consumers, workers, and the general public with regard to potential or actual chemical exposures. Technological information includes information regarding (1) monitoring technologies; (2) options for controlling or minimizing pollution, waste, or chemical accidents; and (3) available substitutes or alternative inputs, products, and processes that may prevent pollution, waste, and chemical accidents. Dissemination of such technological information tends to have a far greater potential to induce technological change than does simply collecting and disseminating scientific information about chemical risks and exposures.[1]

The excerpt below presents a discussion of the role of different kinds of information in minimizing or eliminating the risks due to the production, use, and disposal of chemical substances. Note the emphasis on the importance of technological information for accident prevention, as well as for pollution *prevention*, as opposed to accident and pollution *control*.

### Rethinking the Role of Information in Chemicals Policy: Implications for TSCA and REACH
### Lars Koch and Nicholas A. Ashford

Source: *Journal of Cleaner Production* 14(1) (2006): 31–46, excerpted with permission.

. . .

The risk management process conventionally includes the three sequential steps of (1) producing or collecting risk-relevant information, (2) performing a risk assessment, followed by (3) risk management practices. The first two steps are necessary to overcome the problem of informational deficits [regarding risk], whereas the third step of risk management refers to the mitigation of the . . . effects [of manufacturing, using, or disposing of a chemical] in terms of hazards and risks. . . .

However, quantitative risk assessment presents major challenges and is—depending on the tests required for risk assessment for several endpoints—costly and time-consuming as well. . . . [Undertaking] a comprehensive risk assessment is problematic.

Uncertainty vis-à-vis hazards and risks of [chemical] substances often cannot be easily overcome by more risk information and risk assessment. It is also questionable whether better future science can reduce uncertainty sufficiently and thereby create a more certain basis for risk management [note 8]. . . . In contrast, an initial rough estimation of potential risks is often possible, based on readily-available fundamental information about certain properties of chemicals. In this case, the analysis of quantitative Structure Activity Relationships (SARs) of substances gains significance, because the information is readily available, is far less expensive, and is predictive of potential hazardousness of substances to some extent.

It should be noted that due to the character of information, its value often cannot be known before having the information. It cannot be determined in advance whether—or to what extent—additional testing significantly increases the knowledge of safety or lack of safety of a substance and thus creates a better decision basis for the risk management process. In general, the more risk information that is required, the longer and more costly the risk assessment is, and the longer it takes before risk reduction measures can be implemented. However, a comprehensive risk assessment is often required in European and American law before regulatory action limiting the production, use, or disposal of the product is justified. But the collection of these data neither reduces risks per se nor stimulates technological innovation. *Thus, we argue that an overly comprehensive and protracted risk assessment process may unjustifiably postpone the implementation of desirable risk reduction measures.*

## Making the case for a more balanced and synchronized process

[It is well known that r]elevant to the consideration of the timing—or the right moment—for undertaking risk reduction measures [i.e., risk management] are two types of risk management errors one might make. A Type I error occurs when a substance is regulated which later on turns out to be either not hazardous or less hazardous than expected, whereas a Type II error occurs when a suspected hazardous substance is not regulated and it turns out to be hazardous or more hazardous than expected. Undertaking a comprehensive risk assessment (and delaying in taking a risk management decision) could substantially minimize Type I errors, whereas risk management at an early stage of knowledge about potential risks minimizes the likelihood of Type II errors.

The avoidance of Type II errors also embodies the precautionary principle. One formulation of the precautionary principle is as follows: "Where there are threats of serious and irreversible damage, lack of full scientific certainty shall not be used as a reason for postponing cost-effective measures to prevent environmental degradation." Thus, essential conditions for applying the precautionary principle are uncertainty and irreversibility. In contrast, avoidance of Type I errors presupposes that a substance is safe, until the opposite has been shown.

Obviously, the relative merits of making a decision between avoiding a Type I error and a Type II error reflect a present trade-off based on currently limited knowledge of the risks of both currently-used technology and alternative technologies, and can hardly be based on strictly quantitatively-rational criteria. The regulatory authorities in the European Union and in the United States historically have acted to avoid Type I as well as Type II errors. The industrial producers of chemicals are more concerned with avoiding Type I errors, especially with regard to existing chemicals. In this context, a central question to consider is whether it is possible to decrease the probability of Type II errors, without significantly increasing Type I errors by appropriate information-enhancing activities. In this regard, we argue that on the one hand a rough *comparative* risk estimation of potential hazards of *alternative technologies (inputs, final products, or processes)* to the technology presenting the putative hazard under scrutiny is possible with relatively low-cost information-enhancing activities, while, on the other hand, a comprehensive and costly risk assessment of the putative hazard alone often does not significantly increase the certainty about risks. Note that *comparative* assessments do not need to entail protracted risk assessments, but rather a comparison of alternatives [that could be adopted or developed] against currently-used technologies. Thus, we argue . . . that imposing a requirement for comparative analyses on the proponents of a particular technology is not necessarily a burdensome one. . . .

Finally, a conventional sequential risk management process postpones risk management measures, but sometimes not by significantly decreasing uncertainty with regard to the risks of chemical substances. Therefore, it is useful to establish the steps of the risk management process in a more synchronized way. Instead of first doing a comprehensive risk assessment of existing chemicals, it may be more reasonable to start the process of comparative risk assessment and risk management earlier and thus encourage the development and adoption of safer (and cheaper) alternatives. Thus, when hazards are expected to exist, the focus does not lie exclusively in revealing all present hazards of a substance, but creating knowledge about future alternatives. This means a shift of focus from scientific information to technological options information.

Unlike a hazard, risk, or technology assessment, technology options analysis seeks to identify where and what superior technologies could be adopted to eliminate the possibility, or to dramatically reduce the probability, of pollution and accidental releases [note 16]. Ashford [ref 5] explains:

In order to facilitate pollution prevention or the shift to cleaner technologies, options for technological change must be articulated and evaluated according to multivariate criteria, including economic, environmental and health/safety factors . . . Trade-off analysis can be used to document the aspects of the different technology options and, further, it can be used to compare improvements that each option might offer over existing technological solutions. The identification of these options and their comparison against the technology in use is what constitutes Technology Options Analysis (TOA). Hornstein [ref 25] points out that "it is against the range of possible solutions that the economist analyzes the efficiency of existing risk levels" and that "to fashion government programs based on a comparison of existing preferences can artificially dampen the decision makers' actual preference for changes were government only creative enough to develop alternative solutions to problems."

At first blush, it might appear that TOA is nothing more than a collection of multivariate impact assessments for existing industrial technology and alternative options. However, it is possible to bypass extensive cost, environmental, health and safety, and other analyses or modeling by performing comparative analyses of these factors (such as comparative technological performance and relative risk and ecological assessment). Comparative analyses are much easier to do than analyses requiring absolute quantification of variables, are likely to be less sensitive to initial assumptions than, for example, cost-benefit analysis, and will enable easier identification of win-win options. Thus, while encompassing a greater number of technological options than simple technology assessment (TA), the actual analysis would be easier and probably more believable.

TOAs can identify technologies used in a majority of firms that might be diffused into greater use, or technologies that might be transferred from one industrial sector to another. In addition, opportunities for technology development (i.e., innovation) can be identified. Government might merely require the firms or industries to undertake a TOA. On the other hand, government might either "force" or assist in the adoption or development of new technologies. If government takes on the role of merely assessing (through TA) new technologies that industry itself decided to put forward, it may miss the opportunity to encourage superior technological options. Only by requiring firms to undertake TOAs, or undertaking TOAs itself, is government likely to facilitate major technological change. Both industry and government have to be sufficiently technologically literate to ensure that the TOAs are sophisticated and comprehensive.

Encouraging technological change may have payoffs, not only with regard to environmental goals, but also to energy, workplace safety, and other such goals. Because many different options might be undertaken, the payoffs are somewhat open-ended. Hence, looking to prioritize different problem areas cannot be the same kind of exercise as a risk-assessment-based approach. A fraction of the amount of money devoted to a single animal study [~$5 million] could instead yield some rather sophisticated knowledge concerning what kinds of technology options exist or are likely in the future. Expert technical talent in engineering design and product development (through green chemistry or green engineering) can no doubt produce valuable information and identify fruitful areas for investment in technology development.

### Informational tools for an orientation towards safer alternatives

For reaching a more synchronized risk management process, risk reduction measures are needed which push firms' efforts towards the search for safer alternatives at an early stage. Where regulatory tools are not implemented or enforceable, it is useful to explore the limits and opportunities of informational tools. As discussed earlier, informational tools can be based on the three types of information—scientific, technological and legal information—with different effects. Questioning the importance of scientific information as a precondition for risk management measures has been discussed above in detail. The availability and the assessment of scientific information alone do not reduce risks, without complementary risk reduction measures. Thus, informational tools useful for risk management should be based on technological information as well. This mainly includes:

(1) Requirements for firms to disclose risk information to the public. Here, the disclosure refers to the exposure profiles of produced substances and to their toxicity, flammability etc. Information disclosure creates the opportunity for the public to react and avoid exposure to existing hazards and risks by, e.g.,

changing consumer behavior or applying pressure on firms. These can be effective parts of the risk management process, without making risk reduction measures obligatory for the firms. Information regulation can help lessen the need for more formal regulatory risk reduction requirements. Information disclosure can motivate firms to search for safer alternatives by public or market pressure. The effectiveness of information disclosure depends on the informational value for different stakeholders, and their reaction [to] the information. . . .

(2) Requirements for the firms to identify and generate technological options to reduce existing risks. This informational requirement obligates firms to go beyond reporting what they have done in the past to reduce risks. A more far-reaching requirement is to require the firms to focus on future options for developing and implementing safer alternatives. This can take place, e.g., by having the firm undertake a technological options analysis. By being required to think about alternatives, firms increase their capacities to undertake changes.

(3) Complementary informational tools include databases of preferred and disfavored technologies, as well as labels for safe or hazardous products (or processes). "Negative" lists can increase the pressure on firms, that use these substances [analogous to (1)], whereas positive lists increase their capacity to substitute hazardous substances or processes [analogous to (2)]. . . .

### References and Notes

. . . Ref 5: Ashford Nicholas A. Implementing the precautionary principle: incorporating science, technology, fairness, and accountability in environmental, health and safety decisions. International Journal of Risk Assessment and Management 2005. Inderscience, UK.

Note 8: This statement reflects the inherent limitations of risk assessment. Of course, conducting toxicological or epidemiological studies where there are little or no prior data does reduce uncertainty to a point.

Note 16: A risk assessment, in practice, is generally limited to an evaluation of the risks associated with the firm's established production technology and does not include the identification or consideration of alternative production technologies that may be environmentally-sounder or inherently-safer than the ones currently being employed. Consequently, risk assessments tend to emphasize pollution control or secondary accident prevention and mitigation strategies, which impose engineering and administrative controls on an existing production technology, rather than primary prevention strategies, which utilize input substitution and process redesign to modify a production technology. In contrast to a risk assessment, a technology options analysis would expand the evaluation to include alternative production technologies and would facilitate the development of primary pollution and accident prevention strategies.

Ref 25: Hornstein David. (1992) Reclaiming environmental law: a normative critique of comparative risk analysis. Columbia Law Review 92:562–633.

In addition to Type I and Type II errors that might be made concerning acting or not acting on uncertain risk information, there is a corresponding set of errors that might be made vis-à-vis technology as a result of regulating too stringently or not regulating stringently enough. It could be said that another Type I error can occur if government regulators regulate too stringently with the result that new technology may not be forthcoming or that society will bear an enormous economic cost for its development. Alternatively, a Type II error can be made by not regulating stringently enough because it may discourage innovative technology from being developed. Historically, we have no examples of government committing a Type I error with regard to technology forcing. Instead, government has been too timid, and there have been significant missed opportunities to advance sustainable technology (EEA 2001).

### 9.2.6.1 Trade-off Analysis

Technology options analysis (TOA), discussed earlier, is an essential component of trade-off analysis. This section provides a description of the trade-off analysis approach.

Trade-off analysis requires decision makers to explore the trade-offs that are often obscured in tools such as cost-benefit analysis (CBA). Instead of aggregating a wide range of heterogeneous factors into a single monetary value, trade-off analysis keeps each factor in its natural units. The trade-off analysis approach can be characterized by a series of six steps outlined below (Ashford 1978, 2007).

**Step 1 Define the problem**: Describe the societal or technical problem in need of attention (for example, unmet needs or technical/institutional failure). Describe why the problem arose. Clarify the problem type (see Table 9.4) and describe why an intervention is required. Identify the key stakeholders.

**Step 2 Describe previous efforts to address the problem**: Describe any prior attempts to resolve/improve the problem and discuss their inadequacy/failures in terms of the following:
- *Economics and markets*
  - Inadequate and/or perverse incentives, prices, markets, institutional/organizational structure and behavior, free-rider problems, and unrecognized/unmet needs and demands
- *Legislation and political process*
  - Inadequacy of existing legislation/regulations, lack of knowledge/enforcement thereof, and inadequate stakeholder involvement
- *Public/private-sector management*
  - lack of adequate incentives or perverse incentives for, or commitment to, management of the problem
- *Technical system capabilities*

**Step 3 Identify instruments to promote change**: Identify the tools, models, techniques, and approaches that could affect the willingness, opportunity/motivation, and capacity of the stakeholders (that is, industry, consumers, workers, citizens, government at all levels) to change (see Section 7.5 in Chapter 7).
*Willingness*
- toward change in general (rigidity)
- influenced by an understanding of the problem
- influenced by knowledge of options or solutions

**TABLE 9.4: EXAMPLES OF PROBLEM TYPES THAT CAN BE ADDRESSED USING TRADE-OFF ANALYSIS**

| PROBLEM TYPES | EXAMPLES |
| --- | --- |
| **Informational**: Problems relating to contradictory or uncertain scientific and technological information | Breast implants; missile defense systems |
| **Technology**: Problems relating to the adverse effects of technology on humans and the environment | Climate change; toxic chemicals |
| **Technology development**: Problems relating to the creation of technology in a socially beneficial way/ direction | Genetically engineered crops |
| **Undeveloped technology**: Problems relating to the lack of technology available to meet unmet human needs | Rapid rail systems; new cancer therapies |
| **Accountability**: Responsibility of scientists and engineers in industry and government | Challenger accidents; FDA clearance of questionable pharmaceuticals |
| **Distributional**: Uneven distributions of the benefits and costs of a technology or policy | Access to healthcare technology |

- influenced by the ability to evaluate alternative courses of action
- other

*Opportunity/motivation*
- presented by gaps in technological/scientific capacity
- possibility of economic cost savings or new/expanded market potential (competitiveness)
- consumer/worker/societal demands
- regulatory/legal requirements
- other

*Capacity*
- influenced by an understanding of the problem
- influenced by knowledge of options or solutions
- influenced by the ability to evaluate alternative courses of action
- resident/available skills and capabilities
- other

**Step 4  Develop alternatives**: Make a creative effort to formulate several alternative futures to address the problem, paying special attention to distributional inequalities. The alternatives should be developed in consultation with the stakeholder groups.* Formulate specific strategies (economic, legal, institutional, firm based, societal based, and so on) for each alternative to affect the willingness, opportunity/motivation, and capacity for change. If technology is an important part of the problem, consider ways to address the problem through technological advancement. The alternatives should consider the following:

- *Economics and markets*
  - Changes in prices, markets, and industry structure
  - Changes in demand
- *Legislation and the political process*
  - Changes in law and political process (legislation, regulation, negotiation, and stakeholder participation)
  - *Public/private-sector management*
  - System changes related to organizational/institutional structure
  - changes in public- and private-sector activity

- *The technical system*
  - Technological/scientific changes (options for R&D, innovation, and diffusion)

**Step 5  Analyze alternatives**: Use the trade-off matrix (represented in its generic form in Table 9.5) to assess qualitatively and quantitatively (in a *comparative* manner) the likely outcomes from each alternative and from the "do-nothing" scenario. Evaluate the likelihood that an alternative will solve the problem under different future scenarios.[†] Particular attention should be paid to whether distributional inequalities are adequately addressed.

**Step 6  Overcoming barriers to change**:[‡] Identify potential barriers (economic, legal, institutional, firm based, technology based, societal based, value based,[§] and so on) to change and identify strategies to overcome them, recognizing that political coalition building is likely to play an important role.

Step 1 of trade-off analysis is describing the societal or technical problem in need of attention. To provide a context to the problem, it is often helpful to document a brief history of why the problem arose and why specific action needs to be taken. Many sociotechnical problems form and develop over time until they reach a point where action becomes necessary. It is also useful to characterize the type of problem because this can inform the development of alternatives—for example, does the problem relate to a lack of information or to undeveloped/missing technology (see Table 9.4)? Finally, the primary stakeholders affected by the problem should be identified.

Step 2 should be undertaken in parallel with step 1. In this step, any prior attempts to address the problem should be identified and documented. To ensure that the problem is considered from multiple perspectives, the analyst should be guided by four broad lenses of inquiry. Each lens focuses on a particular system: economics and markets, legislation and the political process, public/private-sector management, and the technical system. For example, if we consider the poor fuel efficiency of the U.S. vehicle fleet,

---

\*        A complementary step here is not only to consult with stakeholders to identify future positions/states of the world that represent solutions to the current problem, but also to use a participatory backcasting approach (see Section 8.6 in Chapter 8) and work backward from these positions/states to identify a series of policies/choices to achieve this future. Adopting a participatory backcasting approach is recommended if a decision maker, agency, or community is confident of the desirability of future positions or states that are to be achieved (the targets of backcasting). However, if a single desired future is difficult to choose, a portfolio approach may be better because a variety of alternative futures can be investigated.

†        Because the future is uncertain, creating several scenarios against which a policy alternative can be assessed is likely to provide an indication of the *robustness* of the alternative.

‡        Step 6 is to be undertaken by the politician or decision maker, not the analyst. The role of the analyst is to develop and present (in Steps 1 through 5) objective information and to avoid promoting one alternative over another.

§        Value-based conflicts may be characterized as (a) conflicts arising from differences in legitimate interests of different actors/institutions; (b) conflicts in moral and legal duties of each actor/institution; and (c) conflicts among actors/institutions arising from different perceptions of what is right or wrong, fair or unfair (Ashford 1994a, p. 1427).

**TABLE 9.5: GENERIC MATRIX OF POLICY CONSEQUENCES FOR DIFFERENT GROUPS/REGIONS**

| | EFFECTS | | |
|---|---|---|---|
| GROUP | MONETARY/FINANCIAL | HEALTH/SAFETY | ENVIRONMENTAL |
| Group/region A | $C_\$$, $B_\$$ | $C_{H/S}$, $B_{H/S}$ | $C_{Env}$, $B_{Env}$ |
| Group/region B | $C_\$$, $B_\$$ | $C_{H/S}$, $B_{H/S}$ | $C_{Env}$, $B_{Env}$ |
| Group/region C | $C_\$$, $B_\$$ | $C_{H/S}$, $B_{H/S}$ | $C_{Env}$, $B_{Env}$ |
| . . . | . . . | . . . | . . . |

it is possible to characterize the problem as (1) a failure to price fuel correctly, (2) a failure to develop sufficiently stringent corporate average fuel economy (CAFE) standards, (3) a failure of the private sector to invest sufficient R&D funds in the development of more fuel-efficient vehicles/technology, and (4) a lack of readily available technology—such as a hydrogen fuel cell or electric vehicle—to address the problem. In reality, many sociotechnical problems, such as the one described, will be the result of a combination of economic, political, management, and technology failures. If an analyst were to use only an economic lens to view the problem, the alternatives/solutions created might address economic concerns to the exclusion of others. The root cause(s) of the problem may continue to persist in the other systems that were not considered. Thus adopting an approach that seeks to uncover the full complexion of a problem, rather than focusing only on those aspects of a problem that relate to one's area of responsibility/expertise, is essential if society is to make progress on problems relating to sustainable development, which often cross disciplinary boundaries. In this regard, sins of omission are just as important as sins of commission that occur when an alternative is influenced/captured by special interests.

Once any previous attempts to address the problem have been identified and understood, step 3 considers ways to affect the willingness, opportunity/motivation, and capacity of the stakeholders associated with the problem to change (see Section 7.5 in Chapter 7 for a detailed discussion of these factors). Although many stakeholders might have the willingness to act, they may not have the opportunity or capacity to do so. Therefore, developing creative ways to support these elements of change is a valuable starting point from which to create alternatives (step 4) to address the problem.

In developing the alternatives in step 4, it is important to return to the four system lenses (introduced in step 2) to ensure that all the dimensions of the problem are addressed. The task of developing the alternatives should be considered as a creative

process that draws on the rich information and knowledge developed in steps 2 to 4.

Step 5 of trade-off analysis is analyzing the alternatives using a trade-off matrix (represented previously in its generic form in Table 9.5). An important task in creating the matrix is to determine which indicators to use to evaluate each alternative. Ideally, these indicators should be developed in cooperation with stakeholders and should provide clear information on the state of the system over time. To make the analysis manageable, it is recommended that a small number of important environmental, health/safety, and monetary/financial indicators be used. The indicators can be quantitative or qualitative.

The structure of the trade-off matrix keeps the environmental, health/safety, and monetary/financial impacts in their natural units for each stakeholder group. By keeping these factors separate, it is possible to assess who benefits and who is made worse off as the result of a proposed alternative compared with the "do-nothing" scenario.* Further, the trade-offs between the costs of environmental or health improvements are made explicit if they occur. Although it has been argued that the informational burden of such an approach to decision making "tends to reduce the efficacy of political institutions" and leads to stakeholder conflict and delay (Congleton and Sweetser 1992, p. 16), hiding such information is surely inappropriate in a democratic process. Hence one benefit of using a trade-off matrix is that stakeholders have the option to become involved in the process of deciding the trade-offs. In this way, decision making becomes more open and transparent and is "based on accountability rather than accounting" (Ashford 2005, p. 5).

---

* The idea of using a form of trade-off analysis that considers utilitarian and nonutilitarian factors, as well as the consequences of alternative courses of action, was recently endorsed by the Millennium Ecosystem Assessment. See the Millennium Ecosystem Assessment report, *Ecosystems and Human Well-Being*, pp. 19–21, http://pdf.wri.org/ecosystems_human_well being.pdf (accessed May 30, 2010).

**TABLE 9.6: USING THE TRADE-OFF MATRIX FOR A COMPARATIVE ANALYSIS OF POLICY ALTERNATIVES**

| GROUP | EFFECTS AT TIME $T_1$ / $T_2$ / ... | | |
| | MONETARY/FINANCIAL | HEALTH/SAFETY | ENVIRONMENTAL |
|---|---|---|---|
| Group/region A | $\Delta C_\$$, $\Delta B_\$$ | $\Delta C_{H/S}$, $\Delta B_{H/S}$ | $\Delta C_{Env}$, $\Delta B_{Env}$ |
| Group/region B | $\Delta C_\$$, $\Delta B_\$$ | $\Delta C_{H/S}$, $\Delta B_{H/S}$ | $\Delta C_{Env}$, $\Delta B_{Env}$ |
| Group/region C | $\Delta C_\$$, $\Delta B_\$$ | $\Delta C_{H/S}$, $\Delta B_{H/S}$ | $\Delta C_{Env}$, $\Delta B_{Env}$ |
| ... | ... | ... | ... |

An additional benefit of nonaggregation is that the time period in which each effect is experienced can be revealed, and future (nonmonetary) benefits/costs need not be discounted to a present value. The impact of time can be considered by using a *time series* of trade-off matrices. These matrices can capture the changing dynamics of the system under analysis and facilitate a comparative analysis of alternatives over time. Table 9.6 shows how the generic trade-off matrix shown previously can be used in a comparative sense to present the changes in each indicator between time periods. This "back-of-the-envelope" approach to the analysis of alternatives can be relatively straightforward. It is also of particular value to decision makers, who will be able to see the likely implications of changing an existing alternative to overcome any problems that have been identified.

One challenge facing decision makers and analysts, however, is often described narrowly as how to create an alternative that arrives at an appropriate trade-off or balance between economic efficiency and equity. Given that decision making is political, not formulaic (Sagoff 1988; Swartzman 1982), arriving at a single or "right" answer is unlikely. The fact that there are likely to be multiple solutions increases the importance of transparent decision making, which makes decision makers more accountable for their actions.

In a situation where potential solutions raise unacceptable compromises in economic efficiency or equity, trade-off analysis enables the decision maker to explore more effective alternatives. In this regard, trade-off analysis resists simplistic thinking and allows decision makers to deal with difficult questions involving (1) economic efficiency/equity trade-offs and (2) alternatives analysis. In effect, uncertainties and distributive inequalities are accepted as part of the normal (real-world) decision-making process. A critical point is that trade-off analysis holds the potential for environmental, social, and monetary/financial factors to be considered on a more equal

**TABLE 9.7: A CLASSIFICATION OF APPROACHES TO DECISION MAKING AND EVALUATION**

| | IDEOLOGICALLY CLOSED | IDEOLOGICALLY OPEN |
|---|---|---|
| **Highly aggregated** | I [CBA] | II |
| **Highly disaggregated** | III | IV [Trade-off analysis] |

Source: Adapted from Söderbaum (2000, p. 80).

footing and provides a setting where alternatives can be considered that do not raise Hobson's choices.

The final step of trade-off analysis (Step 6) is identifying any potential barriers to the chosen alternative and creating strategies to circumvent them. One objective of trade-off analysis is to minimize stakeholder conflict by adjusting alternatives as potential conflicts arise. However, it is recognized that it may not be possible to address all stakeholder concerns and that disagreements occur as a normal part of the democratic process. It is the decision makers' responsibility to address any conflicts in a fair manner, recognizing that political coalition building is likely to play an important role in overcoming any barriers to change.*

Trade-off analysis has two main differences from a tool such as CBA. Whereas CBA is an aggregated and ideologically closed framework (quadrant I in Table 9.7), trade-off analysis is disaggregated and ideologically open (quadrant IV in Table 9.7). CBA is aggregated in that all factors are translated into a single monetary value, and it is ideologically closed in that neoclassical economics (or economic rationality) is the decision-making lens. Trade-off analysis is disaggregated in that environmental, social,

---

* President Obama's struggle to provide an expanded health-care system for the United States provides a vivid example of how difficult it can be to satisfy all the stakeholders in transforming a system. For that reason, asking who is standing in the way of needed progress in examining attractive alternatives is essential.

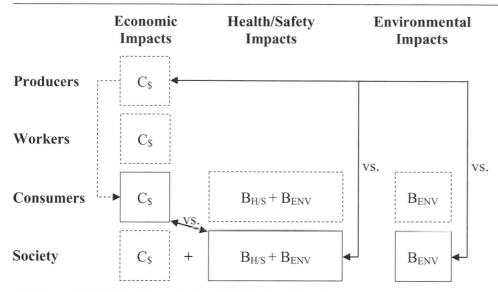

**FIGURE 9.1: TRADE-OFFS OF EPA AIR- AND WATER-POLLUTION REGULATIONS**
Source: Adapted from Ashford (1978, p. 166).

and monetary/financial factors/indicators are kept in their natural units, and it is ideologically open in that it permits evaluation of alternatives through any lens (for example, from the perspective of deep ecology, social welfare, or economic rationality).

It is helpful to consider some examples of how a trade-off matrix can be used to inform decisions. The first example explores the type of trade-offs that face the EPA when it is formulating air- and water-pollution regulations. Figure 9.1 shows how the costs of more stringent regulation are borne by all stakeholder groups (to varying degrees) and how the benefits are received primarily by customers and others (that is, society). If the EPA were to promulgate more rigorous air quality standards aimed at electricity utilities, for instance, much of the compliance costs would likely fall on consumers (assuming that the producers passed on the costs). This example demonstrates a classic externality problem where the health risks are unknowingly and involuntarily assumed by society (Ashford 1978). Thus a critical question is how much pollution abatement we are willing to pay for.

The trade-off matrix enables exploration of a range of solutions. If we adopt a polluter-pays approach, the regulation will focus on making utilities take the necessary steps for compliance.* Thus the

key trade-off is between monetary costs to the producer/consumer and environmental and health benefits to society. (Society is considered here to receive the utility for improvements in the well-being of affected species or the natural environment. An alternative approach would be to create a fifth group for species and/or the natural environment.) A different policy approach, however, would be for government to subsidize the costs of compliance, thereby passing the costs onto society. Under each regulatory scenario, a comparative analysis of the benefits, costs, and distributional effects over time can be undertaken by using a trade-off matrix (Table 9.6). In addition, the likely effects of technological change need to be considered (recall the earlier discussion of TOA), the proper treatment of uncertainty, and potential future changes to the legal environment (Ashford 1978; Driesen 2003, 2004). Each of these factors can change the outcomes in a trade-off matrix and therefore should not be excluded from the decision-making process.

---

* In this situation, a utility might decide to buy the right to pollute, adopt a more efficient technology, or search for alternative fuels or methods for producing electricity. If the focus is placed on the *availability* and *price* of electricity, the method by which it is generated becomes less of a concern to the consumer.

Therefore, adopting a polluter-pays approach might raise the price of electricity (e.g., through the introduction of a carbon tax) to a point where new ways of generating electricity that were previously too expensive become feasible. For example, households might find that it is more cost-effective to buy an array of photovoltaic cells (or hydrogen fuel cells) and produce their own electricity than pay the higher price for electricity generated by coal or gas. Interestingly, the term "polluter pays" can be confusing because it is the customer, not the producer, who will ultimately pay for the internalization of negative externalities. However, if an increase in the price of electricity results in a change in consumer behavior, the producer might "pay" in the long term if its business is disrupted by a more effective way of producing electricity.

The second example asks whether asbestos should be used in brake linings. This example is selected to demonstrate the equity problems that arise when a person is either not fully compensated for a loss or assumes a loss that others are able to avoid.

Suppose that asbestos brake linings made the most effective type of brake that saved an estimated 2,500 drivers'/pedestrians' lives a year. Suppose that it was also estimated that some 2,000 workers die each year from asbestos-related diseases as a result of manufacturing or repairing these brake linings. If we look at this scenario using CBA, one might say that the outcome is acceptable because there is a net saving of 500 lives per year. However, if the same scenario is assessed using a trade-off analysis, an inequality is revealed. The problem is that the 2,000 workers who die each year are likely to come from a certain socioeconomic class (and arguably do not represent a group actually taking on that risk voluntarily), whereas drivers/pedestrians come from all classes (and by and large represent a random group). By considering what constitutes a fair outcome, a decision maker might decide that the increase in driver fatalities that might occur from using a less effective brake-lining material is justified in fairness to the workers who are assuming a disproportionate amount of risk.

If we assume that there is a less effective but more expensive substitute for brake linings that does not harm the workers, the trade-off in Figure 9.2 arises. The monetary cost of using the new material is likely to fall on drivers (through higher vehicle prices), who might also face a small increase in rates of fatal accidents, along with other groups such as passengers and pedestrians, who are likely to face an increased risk of being killed in or by a vehicle, respectively. In this scenario, the decision maker must decide whether the costs imposed on drivers and others are outweighed by the benefits received by the workers.

It is important to recognize that a decision to improve the health of the workers at the expense of consumers and others may be defensible on the grounds of fairness. However, what happens if it is estimated that 3,000 or 4,000 drivers, passengers, and pedestrians are likely to be killed as a result of the change to the brake linings to make them safer for 2,000 workers? What is the appropriate trade-off between economic efficiency and equity? The answer to these questions is that there is no unique solution. The real decision is political, not formulaic.*

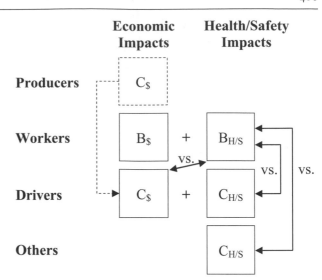

FIGURE 9.2: TRADE-OFFS OF ASBESTOS BRAKE-LINING REGULATION

The fact that the answer is not unique increases the importance of making transparent decisions, which means that decision makers become accountable for their decisions.

In summary, trade-off analysis requires decision-makers to make the difficult trade-offs among *effects*, among *actors*, and across *time periods*[†] that tend to be obscured by techniques such as CBA. As a decision-support tool, it (1) allows decision makers to avoid monetizing and aggregating nonmonetary factors over time; (2) invites the involvement of stakeholders in policy debates because there is greater transparency about who benefits and who is harmed by a particular policy; (3) enables analysts to undertake a comparative analysis of alternatives over time; (4) takes into account the important role of technological change in shaping the state and performance of a system; and (5) requires decision makers to be

---

* Nobel Prize–winning economist Kenneth Arrow (1963) was the first to highlight an inherent problem with democratic decision making: democratic voting may not lead to a clear solution, and the will of the majority might contradict itself. In situations where the collective will does not reveal a clear solution—i.e., Arrow's paradox prevails—the stalemate is likely to be resolved by political persuasion or coalition building. Thus the solution to public policy problems characterized by Arrow's paradox is political rather than formulaic.

† The recent Stern (2007) report on global climate change came under severe attack for using too small a discount rate for the benefits of preventing global warming that would accrue to some in the future. It might have been better for the effects simply to have been presented in the time period over which they occurred—with no discounting—rather than for the analysts to choose a discount rate that would engender criticism no matter what the chosen value was. See Section 1.6 in Chapter 1 for a discussion of the Stern report.

accountable for their actions. Finally, because the approach encourages the development and redesign of alternatives during the analysis to overcome difficult trade-offs, perhaps a more appropriate name for the tool might be "alternatives analysis," although one must be vigilant to ensure that alternatives analysis is not reduced to alternative cost-benefit analysis.

9.2.6.2 Trade-off Analysis in the Context of Sustainability

If achieving sustainable development is the desired objective, it is important to consider the likelihood of arriving at a more sustainable outcome when one uses trade-off analysis. Because the ideological orientations (or value systems) of decision makers and stakeholders can vary significantly, there is no guarantee that this approach will promote sustainable development. At best, keeping the environmental, social, and monetary/financial indicators in their natural units can promote a more transparent approach to considering nonmonetary indicators. But such indicators and their relative impacts can be undervalued if those engaged in the decision-making process favor (or promote) monetary/financial measures. Further, the type of indicators used in the analysis will also play a critical role. Ideally, the indicators should capture changes in the state of the system, as well as the intensity of the flows (or pressures) that change the system's state between time periods. If sustainable development is a primary concern, these indicators need to set parameters that can monitor and guide future development away from critical environmental thresholds and unsustainable activities. Again, the ideological orientations of the decision makers and stakeholders will play an important role in framing the problem and determining what is measured. Thus if sustainability is not a leading priority, it may not be adequately reflected by the indicators or the decision situation.

Therefore, there is an opportunity to consider ways to integrate a *sustainability ideology* into trade-off analysis. Because *equity* and *environmental protection* lie at the heart of sustainable development,* one way to guide decision making toward sustainability is to adopt a decision-making philosophy that is grounded on these objectives. The *revised* Rawl-

sian decision-making philosophy—developed in Section 1.2.2 in Chapter 1—is one approach that attempts to place equity and environmental protection at the forefront of decision making.

A second issue that is often left out of many analysis tools/frameworks and has a direct impact on sustainability is technological innovation. Technological change should be a central consideration in trade-off analysis, and Section 9.3 takes a closer look at how this framework can be used to consider or promote innovation.

### 9.2.7 Product Safety

9.2.7.1 General Discussion

Recent experiences in the United States with both domestic and imported contaminated food and toothpaste, and with unsafe imported toys and children's items have renewed the call for more vigorous regulation of product safety, both here and abroad. In response, in August 2008, the U.S. Congress passed the Consumer Product Safety Improvement Act, which took effect in February 2009. New features augmenting existing law are listed in Table 9.8. The agencies administering food and drugs and consumer products under existing law—the FDA and the Consumer Product Safety Commission (CPSC), respectively—have also received increased funding. In this section, we review the product-safety regime in the United States.

With the exception of manufacturers of pharmaceuticals, pesticides, and food contaminants, manufacturers of most chemical substances in consumer products are not required to do any toxicity testing before selling their products to the public (Rawlins 2009). The regulatory authority for different kinds of products is fragmented among several agencies, including the FDA (for pharmaceuticals); the EPA, the Department of Agriculture (DOA), and OSHA (for pesticides); and the FDA and the DOA (for foods). One scholar has recently opined that "our existing system [for consumer products] is deeply flawed, and this post-market chemical-by-chemical approach to regulation is a long and burdensome process, which leaves consumers unprotected in the interim" (ibid., p. 8).

The following excerpt is based on a report prepared by one of this book's authors for Health Canada (the Canadian federal government's Ministry of Health) in its exploration of adopting a General Safety Requirement (GSR) for all products in Canada.

---

* In the broader context of this book, which identifies competitiveness, the environment, and employment as the three main pillars of sustainability, equity must include both environmental justice and economic equity involving goods, services, and employment. The original formulation of trade-off analysis considers equity in this manner.

### TABLE 9.8: HIGHLIGHTS OF THE CONSUMER PRODUCT SAFETY IMPROVEMENT ACT OF 2008

| | |
|---|---|
| Mandatory standards for toy and durable nursery (e.g., cribs) products | The new law expands the number of mandatory children's safety standards enforced by the CPSC by making now voluntary industry toy standards (ASTM F-963, which includes magnet safety) and durable nursery products (e.g., cribs) standards into mandatory CPSC standards. |
| Third-party testing of all children's toys and products subject to any mandatory standards | The new law prohibits the sale or importation of any toy or children's product subject to any mandatory CPSC safety standard or rule (including the new standards above) unless it is certified by an approved third-party testing body. (This section is to be implemented on a rolling basis over time. The CPSC enforcement position has long been that products subject to standards can no longer be manufactured after implementation dates, but products in inventory can still be sold. But see lead and phthalates, below, which are subject to a different rule as banned hazardous substances.) |
| Lead paint ban strengthened | The maximum allowable amount of lead in paint decreases from the 1977 limit of 600 ppm to 90 ppm one year after enactment (August 2009). |
| Ban on lead in children's products | The new law makes lead in children's products a banned hazardous substance. The lead limits and implementation dates are as follows:<br><br>• 600 parts per million (ppm) after 180 days (February 2009)<br><br>• 300 ppm after one year (August 2009)<br><br>• 100 ppm after three years (August 2011)<br><br>The 100 ppm standard may be altered by the CPSC if it is determined to be not technologically feasible. (As banned hazardous substances, after effective dates, products exceeding these limits cannot be manufactured or sold and must be removed from shelves.) |
| Ban on toxic pthalates in toys and children's products | Child-care products and children's toys containing the phthalates DEHP, DBP, and BBP in concentrations higher than 0.1% per phthalate (1,000 ppm) are permanently banned.<br><br>Child-care products and children's toys that can be put in a child's mouth containing other phthalates: DINP, DIDP, and DnOP, in concentrations higher than 0.1% per phthalate (1,000 ppm) are provisionally banned pending results of a study committee that could rescind the ban.<br><br>Like lead, products containing phthalates exceeding these levels are banned after the effective date (February 2009). They cannot be manufactured, sold, entered into commerce, or imported and must be removed from shelves. |
| Publicly accessible database of reported potential hazards | Currently, the CPSC publishes information only on products that have already been recalled. Implementation of this new provision, modeled after similar auto and drug safety agency databases of complaints and potential hazards, is subject to funding. The database would include information reported by consumers, first responders, and doctors and hospitals, but not by manufacturers. |
| CPSC funding doubled, staffing levels increased | The last CPSC budget approved by the Bush administration was $63 million for 2007. Subject to congressional appropriations, the new law reauthorizes the CPSC for five fiscal years, with authorizations increasing annually to $136 million in 2014 and additional targeted funding to refurbish its decrepit labs. The new law also dramatically increases staffing levels, especially for inspection and import safety staff. |
| Penalty authority and recall effectiveness improved | The new law dramatically increases the civil and criminal penalty authority of the CPSC and takes numerous steps to improve recall effectiveness, including greater authority against recalcitrant manufacturers and requirements that durable items such as cribs that might be sold and resold have permanent recall information labels. |
| Other highlights | The new law also extends 1994 choke-hazard warning labels required on point-of-sale packaging to Internet and catalog sales; allows state attorneys general to enforce federal laws and retains certain state consumer laws; improves all-terrain-vehicle (ATV) safety; and provides new protections for private-sector whistleblowers. |

Source: U.S. Public Interest Research Group Education Fund, 2008. Reproduced with permission.

## Options for a Statutory General Safety Requirement (GSR): Lessons from Selected Experiences of the United States and Europe
### Nicholas A. Ashford (6 October 2006)

#### Introduction: The Legal And Policy Framework For Consumer Protection

##### Product Safety in the U.S. Legal Systems

The safety of consumer products, devices, materials, chemicals, pharmaceuticals, cosmetics, food, equipment, machinery and motor vehicles—hereafter collectively called "products"—for consumers and users is addressed in advanced economies through both common-law traditions and legislation. In the United States, common-law protection is generally provided through the case-developed state law, sometimes later codified in state statutes, [and tort liability]. . . .

Federal statutory protection for consumer products [in general] is provided by the Federal Consumer Product Safety Act and [additionally] for hazardous substances through the Federal Hazardous Substances Act, both administered by the U.S. Consumer Product Safety Commission. Excluded from both acts are pesticides, tobacco, pharmaceuticals, food, medical devices, cosmetics, motor vehicles and firearms. Harms from those categories are protected by their own particularized statutes. Other countries' jurisdictions may differ as to what is protected under general, as opposed to particularized product safety.

### Activities Relevant to Product Safety

The plethora of activities relevant to product safety include:

- Designing a safe product at the outset
- Choosing to market or use a safely-designed— or safer designed—product from readily available options (off-the-shelf)
- Establishing guidelines or mandatory standards for the safety of some aspect of a product— including product characteristics, labels, and product bans, recalls, & seizures
- Controlling the hazardous or harmful aspects of a product
- Providing meaningful warnings, instructions and antidotes
- Mitigating the harm from a dangerous product
- Monitoring and tracking the harms once the product is in commerce (data collection)
- Reporting harm/harmful incidents from a product, if known
- Recalling a product
- Compensating those harmed/injured

The first two activities—developing or adopting a safe/safer product—are pro-active or preventive in nature. Activities falling into the third activity—standards and guidelines—are preventive/proactive only to the extent that they encourage technical improvements in product safety; requirements reflecting existing technological options may foster diffusion of best practices, but are much less likely to encourage product technology innovation. Actions falling into the fourth activity include secondary prevention approaches such as cut-off electrical devices, blade shields, and the like. These approaches are acknowledged as reactive, rather than proactive; they might be described as "end-of-pipe" approaches in that they do not require changes in the functioning concept of the product or in the fundamental product design. The fifth activity shifts the avoidance of injury onto the user. The remaining activities are mitigating or minimizing damage, rather than preventing harm in the first place. In examining or developing options for government intervention, one important criterion is the extent to which a particular intervention mainly fosters primary prevention, secondary prevention, or mitigation.

Not all of these activities are backed up by statutory directives, and not all statutory directives appear in the same legislation. Statutory provisions may create an affirmative duty on the part of government or those that introduce the product into commerce—or they may simply encourage one or more of these practices. Standards may be nothing more than voluntary guidelines, or they may be requirements for voluntary commercial certification, or take the form of mandatory requirements/regulations. Adherence to, or departures from, these varying requirements have different consequences for common-law or statutory liability as to both the admissibility as evidence and as to the creation of presumptions of guilt or innocence of violations of legal duties and liabilities.

Since the 1980's in the United States, two somewhat contrary trends are visible: (1) the movement of producer responsibility from the *control* of risk to the *prevention* of possible harm and (2) the trend towards greater reliance on voluntary action, rather than on government imposition of responsibilities. In Europe, these two trends are also visible, and volunteerism characterized most early European approaches, but recently the need for stronger [interventionist] government has been recognized and the rise of the importance of [the] environment in the European Union's legal structure has caused Europe and the EU to "trade places" with regard to regulatory aggressiveness and the creation of mandatory standards in environmental, health and safety regulation.[2] Within Europe, philosophical tensions continue between some EU bureaucrats who tend to favor voluntary approaches involving all the stakeholders, characteristic of the "corporatist state," and some "northern" EU members who press for more directive, mandatory standards. In spite of these political waves, lessons relevant to [adoption of a General Safety Requirement] (GSR) can be learned from both arenas.

### Terminology

Terminology turns out to be important and in need of clarification. Regrettably, in the European realm, "standards" sometimes mean mandatory requirements and sometimes voluntary guidelines. This confusion is accelerated by the activities of the ISO and other private "standard"-setting bodies. The term "regulation" tends to be unambiguously mandatory.

Another confusion attends the label "performance." It is an adjective-label that is both attached to the term "standard" and is found in the term "performance-based approach." For our purposes, a performance standard is one that that specifies compliance with a safety aspect of a product describing its safety-relevant characteristics, e.g., "being able to withstand a pressure of 250 lbs/square inch" or "not containing phthalates." Performance standards are preferred by the CPSC. They are distinguished from "specification standards" that usually specify content/product characteristics in a positive sense—e.g., "made of chromium steel" or "wood treated with anti-fungal chemicals." (The line is not always a sharp one, e.g., is requiring a transformer to have an output of 6 volts with an operating input of 110–240 volts a performance or specification standard?) Performance standards give more leeway to the product provider or user, while specification standards tend to be more restrictive in choices. That is one reason the [former] are favored by product manufacturers and users. On the other hand, commercial actors—especially small ones or those in developing countries—are not always in a position to make informed choices and welcome [the] clarity associated with specification standards. In the context of trade, exporters from developing countries suspect that specification standards—indeed the entire ISO regime—are being used to minimize competition. WTO trade disputes are scrupulous about examining whether standards are masquerading as non-tariff trade barriers. Other standards include product bans and labels describing contents, articulating warnings, and providing instructions as to product use.

### Voluntary Versus Mandatory Approaches

So-called "performance-based approaches" to ensuring product safety are used in two different senses. One is to encourage performance standards, rather than overly-detailed specification standards. The other meaning is as a euphemism for voluntary, rather than mandatory requirements, be they performance or specification in nature.[3] The literature is unfortunately mixed on the usage. Terms such as "common-sense approaches," "regulatory reinvention," "incentive-based compliance evaluation," etc. should raise a red-flag as emphasizing voluntary approaches and the discouragement of mandatory requirements, reflecting a laissez-faire approach to product safety. Of course, a combination of mandatory and voluntary approaches might be indicated in a specific jurisdiction or system. Two different questions should be kept in mind when comparing (or choosing) approaches: (1) which approaches or combinations of approaches are favored in achieving compliance with existing guidelines? and (2) which approaches or combinations of approaches are more likely to favor "a culture of safety" that fosters inherently-safer design, marketing and use of product? These different questions suggest different evaluation criteria and philosophies.

### Incentives and Disincentives

The government, producers and consumers all have potentially important roles in advancing product safety. The government may be committed to a strong directive role if it has an emboldened sense of its responsibility under the "social contract." Otherwise, government action appears reactively in support of strong government involvement only after some social disaster such as that which followed the occurrence of asbestos-related harms, the Ford Pinto automobile injuries, BSD/mad cow disease, the VIOXX problem, and the like. Note that government does not attempt to sell voluntary programs following these kinds of disasters and events.

Producers may be motivated by cost considerations that flow directly [from] marketing unsafe products or by enlightened self-interest to avoid product recalls, withdrawals, or tort litigation, but it would be a stretch to say this latter motivation is sufficient to ensure the public safety—especially where advertising and re-branding products can mitigate the losses brought about by harm to reputation, such as with the Ford Explorer and renaming Firestone Tires. In the U.S., the tendency of courts of appeals to dramatically reduce punitive damages has taken [some of] the bite out of tort as a financial deterrent. It is true that some producers—e.g., Volvo in automobiles and Fisher-Pryce in toys—do actively market product safety, but this is a rare occurrence. Mandatory and voluntary standards do have an evidentiary role to play in tort, depending on the particular state or jurisdiction in which suit is brought or in the U.S. which state laws are followed in federal diversity cases, but since tort [liability] is generally acknowledged to be a[n uncertain] deterrent in the U.S., the differences may not be all that important. At a minimum, violation of either a mandatory or voluntary industry standard is evidence of negligence.

Consumers may be safety conscious on their own, but usually an organization—such as the Consumers Union, the National Consumers League, the National Coalition Against the Misuse of Pesticides, the Center for Auto Safety, or Ralph Nader's Health Research Group (on pharmaceuticals)—can be traced to fostering increased consumer awareness through their activities, publications, and lawsuits. Readily-available information on product-related injuries provided by either government (for example the CPSC's product injury tracking system—the National Electronic Injury Surveillance System) or NGOs is essential for fostering active participation of consumers in product safety. Some consumer groups participate in private standard-setting organizations such as the American National Standards Institute (ANSI), the American Society for Testing and Materials (ASTM), or the National Fire Protection Association (NFPA). Individuals (citizens or academics) may participate in "professional" organizations that influence worker health and safety such as the American Conference of Governmental Industrial Hygienists (ACGIH) concerned with the toxic effects of chemicals or the American Society of Safety Engineers (ASSE).

### Life-cycle Considerations and Extended Producer Responsibility

In a real sense, developing policies focusing only on the consumer safety aspects of products is out-of-date. Environmental pollution and safety risks from the extraction of materials, their transformation into feedstocks and starting materials for product manufacturing, product manufacturing, transportation, product use, and product disposal are all part of the life-cycle of products.[4] While the EU Integrated

Product Policy (discussed later) focuses mostly on environmental impact, it does pay some attention to consumer safety associated with products.

Partial attempts to integrate various stages of a product's life are reflected in the developing laws implementing extended producer responsibility, whereby producers of industrial chemicals have obligations to ensure safe use by their industrial customers, buy-back provisions are established as with used motor-oil in Germany, and the EU WEEE Initiative for electronics [see Section 10.18.2.3 in Chapter 10] establishes a complex system linking producers and users. The essential point, of course, is that these various health, safety, and environmental concerns ideally should be taken into account at the design stage, where the choice of materials, manufacturing methods, safety, and disposal consequences must be considered. The design of sustainable products is an important part of sustainable development.

In the remainder of this paper, we address important features of the U.S. and EU regulatory systems that suggest options for a GSR, the role of standards and guidelines in tort and product liability in ensuring product safety, prevention and inherent safety, technological innovation in product and process design, and compatibility of a GSR with U.S. regulatory traditions and practice.

## The Regulatory System

In this section, we review not only authorities and practices of the U.S. Consumer Product Safety Commission, we also explore the possible contributions of the authorities under (1) the "general duty" requirement to provide a safe workplace under the U.S. Occupational Safety and Health Act, (2) the "general duty" requirement to design and maintain a safe (chemical) plant under the U.S. Clean Air Act Section 112r, [and] (3) the U.S. Pollution Prevention Act [see Section 10.18.4 in Chapter 10 for a parallel discussion of the EU Integrated Pollution Prevention and Control (IPPC) Directive], the EU Seveso Directives for chemical plant safety, and the EU Integrated Product Policy (emphasizing eco-design) in support of creating an affirmative duty to design, maintain, and periodically review the safety of consumer products in a General Safety Requirement in order to promote a "culture of safety."

The interplay between the regulation of product safety and liability for harmful and/or defective products is important but very different in the United States and the EU. For an insightful treatment, see Geraint G. Howells, International Torts: A Comparative Study: The Relationship between Product Liability and Product Safety— Understanding a Necessary Element in European Product Liability Through a Comparison with the U.S. Position, Spring, 2000, 39 *Washburn L.J.* 305–346. [For a later and updated commentary, see Rawlins (2009).]

## Product Safety Regulation under the U.S. Consumer Product Safety Act (CPSA) of 1972 as Amended[*] and the Federal Hazardous Substance Act (FHSA)

The CPSA 15 U.S.C. Section 2051 et seq. states as its purposes:

(1) to protect the public against unreasonable risks of injury associated with consumer products;

(2) to assist consumers in evaluating the comparative safety of consumer products;

(3) to develop uniform safety standards for consumer products . . . ; and

(4) to promote research and investigation into the causes of product-related deaths, illnesses, and injuries.

On its face, and in regulatory practice, the term "unreasonable risks" in the first purpose anticipates a social balancing/cost-benefit approach between providing consumer protection and minimizing the burden to industry. Indeed preparation of a "regulatory analysis" is a statutory requirement precedent to establishing a consumer product safety rule [Section 9(f)(2); 15 U.S.C. Sec. 2058(f)(2)]. Predating the emergence of the "precautionary principle," the strength of evidence justifying the existence of risks before CPSC imposing regulations has varied with Administrations. . . .

In the early 1980s following the "Reagan Revolution," [much of the] CPSC authority for designating and regulating a substance (or article/product containing that substance) as a "hazardous substance" was transferred from the CPSA to the FHSA (15 U.S.C. Sections 1261–1278). [Under the CPSA, the CPSC can impose performance requirements, issue warning or instructions, or ban products, providing it first determines that the risk may not be sufficiently regulated under the FHSA or it is otherwise in the public interest to proceed under the CPSA.[5] Under the CPSA, the CPSC may ban products that create an "unreasonable risk of injury" when "no feasible consumer product safety standard" can adequately address that risk. However, a substance need not be classified as an "unreasonable risk" before it is classified as a "hazardous substance" under the FHSA.]

*Legislative Authority Relevant to Product Safety: Promulgation of Mandatory Consumer Product Safety Standards, Labeling, Recalls, Bans, Seizures, and Data Collection*

*CPSA*

*Section 7 (15 U.S.C. Sec. 2056):* CPSC "may" promulgate consumer product safety standards [but see the discussion of the FHSA limiting this authority

---

* See further changes in the authority given to the CPSC by the Consumer Product Safety Improvement Act of 2008 in Table 9.8.

below] (in accordance with the procedures set forth in section 9), which may be one or both of two types:

(a) performance requirements; or

(b) warnings or instructions.

*Section 9(d)(2) [15 U.S.C. Sec. 2058(d)(2)]:* a rule establishing a consumer product safety standard is to be promulgated according to notice-and-comment rulemaking, except that "an opportunity for the oral presentation of data, views, or arguments" is to be provided.

*Section 9(f)(3)(A) [15 U.S.C. Sec. 2058(f)(3)(A)]:* CPSC cannot promulgate a consumer product safety standard unless it finds "that the rule (including its effective date) is reasonably necessary to eliminate or reduce an unreasonable risk of injury."

However, as discussed below, there is now a preference stated in the act (Section 7) for voluntary (industry) standards over the promulgation of agency standards *(15 U.S.C. Sec. 2056b).*

*Section 8 (15 U.S.C. Sec. 2057):* CPSC "may" *ban* a consumer product where:

(a) the product presents an "unreasonable risk of injury," and

(b) a consumer product safety rule would not adequately address that risk.

CPSC must follow the procedural requirements of section 9 in promulgating such a ban.

*Section 12 (15 U.S.C. Sec. 2061):* Where there is an imminent and unreasonable risk of death, serious illness, or severe bodily injury, CPSC "may" seek appropriate relief (including seizure of the product) in the appropriate U.S. District Court. . . .

*Section 30(d) [15 U.S.C. Sec. 2079(d)]:* There is a "pass through" to the Federal Hazardous Substances Act [as well as the Poison Prevention Act (15 U.S.C. 1191 et seq.) and the Flammable Fabrics Act (Section 1191 et seq.)] for consumer products that (i) are (or contain) hazardous substances, and (ii) can be addressed adequately under that statute.

*FHSA*

*Section 2(f) [15 U.S.C. Sec. 1261(f)] states that:* The term "hazardous substance" means:

(1)(A) Any substance or mixture which is (i) toxic, (ii) corrosive, (iii) is an irritant, (iv) is a strong sensitizer, (v) is flammable or combustible, or (vi) generates pressure through decomposition, heat, or by other means, if such substance or mixture may cause substantial personal injury or substantial illness during or as a proximate result of any customary or reasonably foreseeable handling or use. . . .

(any substance or mixture that meets one of the statutory definitions, or that is designated as hazardous by CPSC under the first statutory definition.

*Exclusions:* pesticides, drugs, food, and cosmetics, containerized fuels, tobacco products, and nuclear material regulated under the Atomic Energy Act.

*Section 2(p) [15 U.S.C. Sec. 1261(p)] states that:* A "misbranded hazardous substance" is any hazardous substance "intended, or packaged in a form suitable, for use in the household or by children," which:

(i) fails to comply with an applicable labeling regulation issued by CPSC under the Poison Prevention Packaging Act; or

(ii) fails to comply with the labeling requirements set forth in this section of the statute (or with more specific labeling requirements for this substance established by CPSC under section 3 of the FHSA).

*Section 2(q)(1) states that:* A "banned hazardous substance" is

(A) any "toy, or other article intended for use by children," which is or "bears or contains" a hazardous substance that is "susceptible to access by a child" to whom it is entrusted (although items such as chemistry sets are exempted); or

(B) a hazardous substance "intended, or packaged in a form suitable, for use in the household," that the CPSC classifies as a banned hazardous substance after a finding that "notwithstanding such cautionary labeling as is or may be required under this Act for that substance, the degree or nature of the hazard involved in the presence or use of such substance in households is such that the objective of the protection of public health and safety can be adequately served only by keeping such substance, when so intended or packaged, out of the channels of interstate commerce."

*Section 3 (15 U.S.C. Sec. 1262) provides:*

(a) CPSC can, following designated Food Drug and Cosmetic Act (FDCA) procedures, declare a substance to be "hazardous" under the section 2(f)(A) definition.

(b) CPSC can, if it finds that the labeling requirements of section 2(p) "are not adequate for the protection of public health and safety" from a particular hazardous substance, promulgate more specific labeling requirements for that substance.

(c) & (d) If CPSC finds that full compliance with (some or all of) the act's labeling requirements "is impracticable or is not necessary for the protection of public health and safety," or that the substance "is adequately regulated by other provisions of the law," CPSC must (in the first case) and may (in the second case) exempt the substance from those labeling requirements.

(f), (g) & (h) impose extensive procedural requirements on CPSC's designation of a "banned" hazardous substance, give "any person" the right to propose an existing standard (or develop a voluntary standard) meant to regulate the use of the substance rather than ban it, and require CPSC to promulgate such a standard (in lieu of a ban) if it finds that the standard will be adequate. Subsection (i) prohibits CPSC from banning a substance unless it first finds that the benefits of such a ban "bear a reasonable relationship to its costs," and that the ban is "the least burdensome requirement which prevents or adequately reduces the risk."

In classifying a substance as "hazardous," or in banning a hazardous substance, CPSC must also follow certain procedures of the FDCA applicable to the establishment of a "standard of identity" for a food. These procedures give an objecting party the right to an evidentiary hearing.

*Section 4 (15 U.S.C. Sec. 1263):* The following acts are prohibited: (a) the introduction or delivery for introduction into commerce of a banned or misbranded hazardous substance; (b) the alteration, obliteration, etc., of a hazardous substance label so as to make the substance a "misbranded" hazardous substance.

. . .

[The burden of proof is on the CPSC to demonstrate, on the basis of "substantial evidence," that a substance is a known or probable carcinogen, human neurotoxin, or human developmental or reproductive toxin" (See 15 U.S.C.A §1262(a)(2) (requiring compliance with 21 U.S.C.A. §371(f)). . . .

Under the FHSA, in addition to proving toxicity, the CPSC must still show that the product may cause substantial injury as used by the consumer, including that there will sufficient "exposure."[6]]

*Voluntary Standards*[*] *and Guidelines in the CPSA Section 7b (15 U.S.C. Sec. 2056b):* CPSC "shall rely upon voluntary consumer product safety standards rather than promulgate a consumer product safety standard . . . whenever compliance with such voluntary standards would eliminate or adequately reduce the risk of injury addressed with such voluntary standards." The origin of this section lies in the 1981 changes to the CPSA during the anti-regulatory period heralded by the election of Ronald Reagan.

Howells (2000) comments on the different attitudes towards voluntary standards in the U.S. and the EU:

[There is a] different nature of [voluntary] standards in the U.S. and Europe. Whereas in the U.S. these remain very much voluntary standards, established by private actors, in Europe, at least in areas covered by "new approach directives," their use has become quasi-mandatory.

The CPSC now works on eight to fourteen mandatory standards per year and forty to fifty voluntary standards. There are numerous standards writing organizations. The three with which the CPSC works most closely are the American National Standards Institute ("ANSI"), American Society for Testing and Materials ("ASTM"), and the Underwriters Laboratories, Inc. ("UL").

Voluntary standards have no legal effect as such, although industry is often eager to develop voluntary standards and to comply with them, not only to help defend products liability claims and stave off any remaining threat of mandatory regulation, but also to use compliance as a marketing tool both at home and increasingly in the international marketplace. Also, if a producer inaccurately claims that its product conforms to a product safety standard when it does not, then it will be in breach of the truth and labeling laws administered by the Federal Trade Commission.

In the U.S., however, there is no bridge between mandatory and voluntary standards. Except in extreme cases, the U.S. system has forgone mandatory regulations and is left to rely upon freestanding voluntary standards. In contrast, in Europe, the legislatures have managed to keep a hand on the tiller of product safety regulation by developing directives, which establish a framework that integrates voluntary standards. This integration is an effort to achieve those levels of safety considered politically desirable by means with which industry is comfortable. The integration of the standards into the legal framework has also permitted greater public participation in the formation of standards [at page 308]. . . .

*Extended Producer Responsibility*

Manufacturers have no formalized responsibility under the CPSA or FHSA beyond the initial transmission of control to a buyer or recipient. However, should they become knowledgeable about a product defect or harmful product in the line of commercial/personal usage, responsibilities could "run with the product." If the product is used in an unforeseeable and unintended way, product liability may not attend, but products may none-the-less be recalled by the CPSC.

## Other Relevant U.S. Regulatory Regimes

[Both the general duty obligation of employers to provide a safe and healthful workplace in the Occupational Safety and Health Act (see Section 9.2.2.1) and the chemical safety provisions of the Clean Air Act (see Section 9.2.4) that require manufacturers to fulfil a general duty to design and maintain safe facility are relevant to product safety.] . . .

*The Pollution Prevention Act of 1990*[†]

The Pollution Prevention Act (PPA) of 1990 breaks with U.S. regulatory tradition in its proactive approach to preventing *at the source* rather than controlling

---

* See Table 9.8 for changes in the voluntary versus mandatory standards approach resulting from the Consumer Product Safety Improvement Act of 2008.

† See Section 9.2.5 in this chapter for additional details about the Pollution Prevention Act.

pollution at end-of-pipe in the hierarchy of regulatory options. [The preferred hierarchy articulated in the act over end-of-pipe pollution control is to alter the inputs or feedstocks, reformulate the final product, and/or change the production process using or producing materials and chemicals.] While never really [aggressively] implemented, the act also requires the Administrator to examine every regulation [already] issued under the media-based (air, water, waste) legislation—for both gradual pollution and sudden and accidental release of chemicals—and regulations issued under toxic substances and pesticide legislation to ensure that pollution prevention initiatives were fashioned as the preferred choice of interventions.

Taken together, the regulation of chemical safety under the Clean Air Act and the PPA impose a duty on manufacturers to *design and prevent sudden and accidental releases from chemical production, use and storage facilities.* The *design and prevent* approach is one that could be embodied in a [General Safety Requirement (GSR)] for consumer products. Commentators on U.S. and EU regulation of consumer product safety conclude that in neither jurisdiction is consumer product protection as effective as it could be [see Howells *supra*]. A design-and- prevent approach would make either system more effective.

### The Role of Tort and Product Liability in Ensuring Product Safety

An insightful comparison of product liability in encouraging product safety in the U.S. and EU treatment [is provided by] Howells (2000) [who] writes:

> The main reason for the greater impact of products liability litigation in the U.S. is the level of damages. American damage awards are considerably higher—this in itself acts as a magnet for litigants. These high awards are due to the lack of a social security system to cushion the impact of accidents, the high costs of medical treatment, the lack of public healthcare services, generous awards of pain and suffering damages, and the availability of punitive damages.
>
> . . .
>
> The role of punitive damages in the U.S. suggests that the regulatory function of litigation is important. Moreover, the threat of wide scale products liability litigation can be seen as an incentive for producers to improve the quality of their products, often with fiscal incentives from insurers. Although civil liability rules have a regulatory dimension in Europe, my impression is that products liability is more responsive to the compensatory needs of accident victims than to the regulatory aspects. Many Americans consider Europe to have a weak products liability litigation culture, but I gain the impression that there is sometimes a failure to appreciate the depth of the product safety regulatory regimes, which may explain why there is less need for products liability litigation as a means of regulatory control [at pages 307–308].

The FHSA expressly preempts any state labeling (warning) requirement for a substance that is more stringent than a labeling (warning) requirement established for that substance under the FHSA. Many courts have held that this applies to "failure to warn" tort claims for money damages as well as to state statutes and regulations. However, a state tort law claim may be based on a failure to follow the labeling requirements of the FHSA.

Violation of a mandatory standard in the majority of states is conclusive evidence of the defective nature of a product, while a minority of states regards it as a rebuttable presumption or mere evidence of negligence. [See Reimann (2003).] Similarly, compliance with a standard creates a presumption of due care, but one that can be overcome by the specifics of the case.

Violation of a voluntary standard is evidence of the defective nature of a product, but the presumption can be overcome.

### Prevention and Inherent Safety: Technological Innovation in Process and Product Design[*]

While not originally applied to product safety, the fundamental concepts of inherent safety are directly applicable and transferable to products. We have already extended the concept of pollution prevention (what the Europeans call clean technology) to products. Green products, sustainable products, and environmentally-sound products are just some of the names characterizing this extension. The EU Integrated Product Policy [discussed in Section 10.18.5 in Chapter 10] relies on the concepts of cleaner and environmentally-sound products. It is no artificial stretch to conceive of inherently-safer products that eliminate the possibility or significantly reduce the probability of harm to consumers. Of course innovation may be required. The holistic approach to health, safety and environmental improvements would be to encourage or require *the development and use of inherently-safer and environmentally-sounder products and processes.* For this to become a reality, single-purposes improvements to industrial technology have to be replaced with multi-dimensional technological change.

9.2.7.2 Prospects for Reform

A report compiled jointly by the Virginia and Washington Public Interest Research Groups (U.S. Public Interest Research Group Education Fund [USPIRG] 2008) commented on the past history of the CPSC and prospects for advancing consumer product safety protection under the Consumer Product Safety Improvement Act of 2008:

---

* Much of this discussion is taken from Ashford and Zwetsloot (1999). The concept of inherent safety in the context of process safety was discussed in Section 9.2.5 of this chapter.

B. [Historical] Neglect and Efforts to Weaken the Agency

Just over one year ago, the CPSC's budget of less than $63 million was less than half what it would have been ($145 million) had it simply been updated for inflation since its establishment in 1973. The CPSC staff in 2007, at about 400 FTEs, was again less than half its peak staffing level in 1980. For much of 2007 it operated without a legal quorum; it could conduct voluntary recalls, but do little other business. Yet the tiny agency was and is nonetheless responsible for the safety of over 15,000 separate consumer products, ranging from coffee makers and home appliances to chain saws, escalators and children's products, including toys.

C. The Solution: The Consumer Product Safety Improvement Act of 2008

In response to the Year of the Recall and the unprecedented public outcry it generated, the 110th Congress acted on a bi-partisan basis to first increase the CPSC budget significantly for both the 2008 and 2009 fiscal years while it considered broader reform legislation. Both the House and Senate then developed and passed comprehensive Consumer Product Safety Improvement Act proposals, which were reconciled in a conference committee and signed into law in August by the President. In what most analysts considered a rare consensus on the need for reform, these bills were not weakened every step of the way from introduction through passage, as is the fate of most legislation. While it is common for an introduced bill to be the high water mark with sponsors hoping to hold enough of the bill together to make it worth passing in the end, the opposite occurred in this case, thanks to the broad public support for CPSC reform and the perseverance of Congressional champions. The Senate bill, in particular, was strengthened on the Senate floor with the addition of a ban on toxic phthalates. In the conference committee, negotiations in most cases resulted in selection of the stronger of the two alternate provisions, not the weaker or a compromise."

In their 2010 25th Report updating the 2008 publication, the Alaska Public Interest Research Group (Hitchcock, Imus et al. 2010, pp. 4–5) reported that:

In April 2010, the President's Cancer Panel—a group of three distinguished experts appointed by President Bush to evaluate the nation's cancer program—raised the alarm about our ubiquitous exposure to toxic chemicals. "The American people—even before they are born—are bombarded continually," the panel wrote. In effect, our lives have become a giant, uncontrolled experiment on the relationship between toxic chemicals and our health. . . .

In 2008, Congress responded to an unprecedented wave of recalls of toys and other children's products by passing the first major overhaul of the Consumer Product Safety Commission since it was established during the Nixon Administration. By passing the landmark Consumer Product Safety Improvement Act (CPSIA) in August 2008, Congress not only expanded the agency's budget, it also gave the CPSC more tools to hold corporate wrongdoers accountable and speed recalls, moved toward limiting toxic lead and phthalates in certain toys and children's products, and greatly improved import surveillance. . . .

The Consumer Product Safety Improvement Act, together with stronger enforcement from the CPSC, has made good steps in the right direction toward reducing mechanical toy hazards like choking, and chemical hazards from lead and phthalates in certain products. However, there are tens of thousands of toxic chemicals that are still not regulated for the many uses in our children's lives.

### 9.2.8 Alternatives to Regulation

The following excerpt provides a cursory treatment of alternatives to regulation. For an extensive treatment, see Ashford and Caldart (2008, chap. 12) and Reijnders (2003).

**Alternative Forms of Government Intervention
to Promote Pollution Reduction
Nicholas A. Ashford and Charles C. Caldart**
Source: Chapter 12 in Ashford and Caldart 2008, pp. 880–881, excerpted with permission.

[Government intervention might be classified into five categories:] (1) direct controls (often called command-and-control regulation); (2) indirect controls (often called market-based approaches); (3) other policy instruments, such as information sharing, technical assistance, and government purchasing practices; (4) statutory and common-law liability for harm, and (5) encouragement of so-called voluntary initiatives. Government programs coming within this last category tend to be premised either on industry's presumed interest in meeting social demands for a cleaner environment, or on industry's desire to avoid more stringent regulation. While perhaps not strictly governmental policies, voluntary approaches of this nature often require government acquiescence and encouragement to succeed.

*Direct controls* are legal commands, imposed by a government agency, requiring firms to take some action (e.g., reduce emissions to meet environmental objectives, or provide specified information to government, the community, or the public). Firms do not have the choice of not complying with direct controls if they wish to operate within the confines of legal behavior. Noncompliance would be a violation of the law, and could subject a firm to legal sanctions, including civil (and possibly criminal) penalties. Consequently, noncompliance tends to carry with it a stigma of wrongdoing. This form of government intervention is sometimes called command-and-control regulation because it is characterized by legal compulsion.

*Indirect controls* provide incentives whose purpose is to induce firms to take some action to improve environmental quality. However, firms are not required by law to take the desired action, and normally no sense of wrongdoing accompanies a failure to do so. An emissions fee or "tax" that is imposed on firms for every unit of pollution they emit is a type of "negative" indirect control, while tax deductions and credits are types of "positive" indirect controls. Because indirect controls generally take the form of an economic charge or subsidy or some other type of financial incentive, they are often referred to as economic instruments or market-based instruments. . . .

There are other "positive" policy instruments that also are designed to indirectly stimulate industry to reduce pollution. Broadly speaking, these programs involve government provision of goods or services that private industry has been unable or unwilling to provide or develop. Examples are the creation of pollution and waste control and prevention information databases and clearinghouses, the establishment of a state office of technical assistance, the sponsoring of technical conferences, the creation of a waste recovery facility to separate out recyclable materials, government projects to demonstrate the feasibility and effectiveness of new pollution-reducing technologies, and the use of government purchasing power to promote cleaner production. Although these programs are conceptually linked to positive market-based incentives such as subsidies and tax credits, they typically involve a greater level of government involvement in the process.

*Liability statutes and common-law suits* that result in damage awards for health or environmental consequences can, under some circumstances, be incentives to reduce pollution and waste. [In the United States, the so-called Superfund statute (CERCLA)] is the most prominent of such liability statutes on the federal level. Also included in this category are financial responsibility requirements that mandate firms, or their agents, to provide collateral (such as financial bonds) to guarantee that there will be funds available to pay for future environmental damage resulting from their operations.

The types of voluntary initiatives that can be encouraged by governmental programs include so-called industrial ecology practices involving exchange of wastes and materials among commercial and industrial firms, industry self-enforcement encouraged by industry codes of practice, and voluntary programs or covenants between industry and governments to go beyond compliance.

Reijnders (2003) comments:

> Cleaner production stands to gain much by slashing subsidies and substantial eco-taxation of inputs and [pollution/waste]. Similarly, the regulatory enforcement of best available technologies, liability for waste and tradable permits may help the diffusion of cleaner production. (ibid., p. 333)
>
> Regulation has been shown to force the diffusion of new technologies and improved working practices. For instance, regulation has been very successful in forcing the widespread adoption of end-of-pipe technologies . . . especially during the 1970s and early 1980s. (ibid., p. 334)
>
> Though there has been limited use of regulation in favor of cleaner production, the scope for progress in this field is substantial. (ibid., p. 336)

### 9.2.9 U.S. and European Law Compared

Section 10.18 of the next chapter addresses the environmental regulatory system in the European Union. In a classic essay, Vogel (2003) examined the shift of creative regulatory approaches from the United States to Europe. Since then, the divergence of consumer product and environmental regulation in the two venues has become even greater, both because regulation was deliberately weakened in the United States during the ideologically antiregulatory George W. Bush administration and because it has advanced considerably in the European Union.

> From the 1960s through the mid 1980s American regulatory standards tended to be more stringent, comprehensive and innovative than in either individual European countries or in the European Union (EU). The period between the mid 1980s and 1990 was a transitional period: some important regulations were more stringent and innovative in the EU, while others were more stringent and innovative in the United States. The pattern since 1990 is the obverse of the quarter-century between 1960 and the mid 1980s: recent EU consumer and environmental regulations have typically been more stringent, comprehensive and innovative than those of the United States. . . .
>
> Regulatory issues were formerly more politically salient and civic interests more influential in the United States than in most individual European countries or the EU. More recently, this pattern has been reversed. Consequently, over the last fifteen years, the locus of policy innovation with respect to many areas of consumer and environmental regulation has passed from the United States to Europe. (Vogel 2003, pp. 557–558)

Ironically, recently the regulatory resolve of the European Union has been weakened because of intense lobbying efforts and the influence of the U.S.

chemical industry in Europe, while the election of the Obama administration in the United States has reinvigorated the role of government in environmental, consumer product, and worker safety protection. Although the government's taste for regulation in both venues seems to wax and wane with specific political leadership, the public seems increasingly committed to a strong government hand in protection.

## 9.3 STATIC VERSUS DYNAMIC EFFICIENCY AND THE IMPLICATIONS FOR PROMOTING TECHNOLOGICAL INNOVATION USING TRADE-OFF ANALYSIS

Before considering how trade-off analysis can be used to promote technological innovation, this section begins with a brief discussion of the important difference between static and dynamic efficiency (as a focus of environmental policy) and how these views can affect the analysis of technology.

It is important to emphasize the difference between achieving *static* and *dynamic* efficiency in applying technological solutions to societal problems. Having static efficiency as the mainstay of neoclassical environmental economics ignores the important role of innovation in achieving better environmental outcomes (Ashford 2001; Ashford and Caldart 2008; Driesen 2003, 2004; Jänicke, Blazejczak, et al. 2000). It assumes that the objective of decision makers is to reach an efficient state where social welfare is maximized. If the prevailing state of the world is suboptimal, a more efficient state is identified, and changes are made to move the system toward that state. In general, neoclassical economists define this efficient state by matching supply and demand in a competitive market, with the assumption that technology remains constant. In contrast, dynamic efficiency places considerable attention on instruments that will encourage transformations. Driesen observes: "Economic dynamic analysis emphasizes change over time, systematic change, and precise analysis of how incentives affect individuals and institutions" (Driesen 2004, p. 515).

The roots of dynamic efficiency must be understood in the context of institutional economics and organizational theory (Driesen 2003),* where it is important to appreciate the difficulty that a new incentive has in capturing the attention of institutions and individuals, given that their decisions are influenced by *path dependency* or *lock-in* (that is, past actions/decisions might constrain future actions/decisions) and *bounded rationality* (that is, purposes, knowledge, and habits combine to constrain the choices an institution/individual makes) (Driesen 2003, 2004).

Dynamic efficiency views technological change (with accompanying institutional, organizational, and social changes) as a central variable in the analysis of environmental policy, increasing the importance of understanding the direction of change and how technology might alter benefits/costs over an appropriate time horizon (Ashford 2002). Given that changing a sociotechnical system is likely to require a long time frame, the role of government in setting technology and environmental policy to guide innovation increases in importance. Further, whereas static efficiency focuses on the efficient state that appropriately balances competing goals, dynamic efficiency emphasizes win-win outcomes that are achieved through the co-optimization of multiple societal goals. Thus achieving dynamic efficiency focuses on the *process* of a sustainable *transformation*, while achieving static efficiency focuses on a sustainable, or more optimal, *state*. This observation highlights the implicit bias embedded in traditional analysis tools. Tools such as cost-benefit analysis, which are based on static efficiency (or optimality), move considerations of the *process* of transformations outside the analysis framework.[7] In contrast, Driesen's (2003) focus on the economic dynamics of environmental law places the *process* of transformation at the center of the analysis.

In trade-off analysis, in contrast with traditional cost-benefit analysis, the process of technological change and innovation is an explicit consideration in the analysis (Hall 2006; Hall, Ashford, et al. 2008). In addition to evaluating the multivariate impacts of different alternatives, a trade-off matrix can be used to assess the impacts of different *technology options* (Ashford 2000; Ashford, Hattis, et al. 1980). The strength of combining both kinds of impacts in a trade-off matrix is that it can be used to compare multivariate criteria—such as environmental, health/safety, and economic factors—to determine how new technology options compare with each other and with the do-nothing scenario. Further, the impacts of each technology option on different stakeholders are made explicit. The comparative analysis of different technology options in a trade-off matrix constitutes what is known as technology options analysis (TOA) (Ashford 2000; O'Brien 2000; see Section 9.2.6).

---

* See Chapter 7 on organizational innovation and learning.

The idea of TOA was first applied to the chemical industry to facilitate the consideration of technology options that could make production processes inherently safer for workers and the surrounding community. Either new technologies could be added to existing systems to mitigate risks, or a production process could be designed to remove the risk altogether (a process known as "primary prevention"). The purpose of a TOA is to inform the firm, the regulating agency, and stakeholders of the full range of technological options that can be used or developed to address a problem or achieve a desired objective.

The benefit of using TOA is that analyzing comparable factors among the technology options is easier than using techniques such as CBA that usually require monetary quantification, the aggregation of variables, and discounting to present value. Keeping the variables in their natural units within a trade-off matrix avoids unnecessary assumptions about how to translate environmental or health and safety impacts, for instance, into a dollar value. The result is a more believable, disaggregated analysis of options where the impacts of technologies are made explicit and win-win solutions can be more easily identified.

TOA can be used in both a *static* and a *dynamic* sense. When used in a *static* sense, TOA simply compares *available* (or existing) technology to decide which option should be selected. This is the approach adopted by neoclassical environmental economics (as currently practiced), which searches for optimal outcomes using static efficiency. A failure by environmental economists to take technological innovation into account means that their analysis is likely to overestimate the cost of compliance with new, more stringent environmental regulation. Setting regulation on the basis of existing technology or what is deemed feasible from a static efficiency perspective is not likely to establish an environment for system transformations toward sustainable development.

When used in a *dynamic* sense, TOA is able to compare *available* technology with technology that *could* be developed.* Using the trade-off matrix in this manner leads to a form of dynamic environmental economics that includes the consideration of technological change over time (Ashford 2001; Driesen 2003, 2004).

Achieving dynamic efficiency requires the analyst or decision maker to focus on the transformation *process*, paying special attention to *path dependency* and *bounded rationality* of institutions and stakeholders.† Given that changing a sociotechnical system is likely to require a long time frame, the role of government in setting technology and (stringent) environmental policy to guide innovation is of particular importance (see Section 8.4 in Chapter 8). Adopting an approach that *guides* technological change means that decision makers are not relying on serendipitous technological development. Instead, they are pursuing an approach where the development of technology is more likely to progress along a desired pathway. Therefore, it is the dynamic use of TOA that is likely to lead to system transformations toward sustainable development.

## 9.4 NATIONAL GOVERNMENT'S ROLE IN ACHIEVING EFFICIENCY: THE REGULATION-INDUCED-INNOVATION HYPOTHESIS

In general, classical economic analysis of regulation and competitiveness has argued that stringent regulation increases production costs, diverting resources from R&D, and consequently hinders innovation (A. Jaffe, Peterson, et al. 1995; Rennings, Kemp, et al. 2003). This assumption was challenged first in the late 1970s at MIT (Ashford, Heaton, et al. 1979) and [questioning its validity] was made popular in 1991 by the so-called Porter hypothesis.

On the basis of his research into the competitive advantage of nations (Porter 1990), Porter (1991, p. 168) claimed that "strict environmental regulations do not inevitably hinder competitive advantage against foreign rivals; indeed, they often enhance it. Tough standards trigger innovation and upgrading." He continues, "Properly constructed regulatory standards, which aim at outcomes and not methods, will encour-

---

\* One benefit that traditional cost-benefit analysis has in considering only existing technologies for the purposes of assessment is that these technologies are easy to identify and cost, although the latter usually leads to large overestimates, especially if provided by a regulated industry. By explicitly considering technological options that include innovation not yet undertaken, the assessment becomes open ended. What will the performance and cost of new technology be? Regulatory history has confirmed impressive positive results in general, justifying stringent regulatory requirements, but there will be uncertainties in any particular case. Analysts do not like open-ended assessment. Politicians may be reluctant to bank on future innovation, but

---

that is precisely what government investments in new technologies count on and what government incentives for innovation are provided for.

† The trade-off matrix enables decision makers to ask what could be done to improve the prevailing situation. Because the trade-off matrix for each technology option (existing and undeveloped) presents information in a disaggregated form, the potential political implications of setting more stringent regulation or investing in a certain type of technology become apparent. Once these factors are identified, steps can be taken to address the problems of path dependency and bounded rationality.

age companies to re-engineer their technology. The result in many cases is a process that not only pollutes less but lowers costs or improves quality. . . . Strict product regulations can also prod companies into innovating to produce less polluting or more resource-efficient products that will be highly valued internationally" (ibid.). The basic premise of Porter's hypothesis is that firms that respond to stringent regulation by developing new technologies have a "first-mover" advantage and can capture the market for their products/services. A comparison of national competitiveness with good environmental governance and private sector responsiveness showed support for the Porter hypothesis (World Economic Forum, Yale Center for Environmental Law and Policy, et al. 2002). It states that "good economic management and good environmental management are related" and that "firms which succeed in developing innovative responses to environmental challenges benefit both environmentally and economically" (ibid., p. 17).

Earlier work on this concept, along with empirical evidence, dates back some twelve years before Porter's work to research undertaken at MIT (Ashford 1993; Ashford, Ayers, et al. 1985; Ashford and Heaton 1983; Ashford, Heaton, et al. 1979). This work showed how stringent and focused regulations in the U.S. chemical-producing and using industries had the effect of stimulating fundamental product and process innovations (Ashford, Ayers, et al. 1985). The MIT studies revealed that environmental and health and safety regulation—if appropriately designed, implemented, and complemented by economic incentives—can lead to radical technological developments that can significantly reduce exposure to toxic chemicals in the natural and working environments and in consumer products (Strasser 1997).

A weakness of Porter's hypothesis is that it does not provide any detailed analysis of the process of technological innovation. More important, its focus on how incumbent firms respond to more stringent regulations ignores the important dynamics of new entrants (van de Poel 2000). Porter's focus on "innovation offsets"—the cost savings due to induced innovation that could exceed the cost of the regulation (Porter and van der Linde 1995a, 1995b)—indicate that he is mainly concerned with the costs to incumbent firms. From this insight, it is possible to differentiate between "weak" and "strong" forms of the regulation-induced-innovation hypothesis (Ashford 1999; Porter does not make this distinction). In the weak form of the hypothesis, Porter argues that firms subject to more stringent regulation respond with incremental (or sustaining) product and process innovations. Thus although environmental and worker health and safety improvements may be realized, the offending products and processes remain intact, albeit in a greener, more efficient state.

In the strong form of the regulation-induced-innovation hypothesis, Ashford argues that stringent regulation could stimulate the entrance of entirely new products and processes into the market, thereby displacing dominant technologies. In this situation, unless incumbent firms have the willingness and capability to produce and compete with the new forms of technology, they too are likely to be displaced from the market (Christensen 1997). Figure 9.3 provides a simple diagram of the likely technological responses to the strong and weak forms of the regulation-induced-innovation hypothesis. Empirically based examples were researched by Ashford and colleagues in their work. An example is the replacement of Monsanto's PCBs by transformer fluid pioneered by Dow Silicone.

Jänicke and Lindemann (2010, pp. 133–134) recently distinguished the work of Ashford and Porter:

> The potential innovation effects of regulatory instruments are traditionally considered as rather limited since innovations are allegedly confined to the prescribed emission reductions. It is assumed that the government will typically want to ensure the technological feasibility of its regulation and therefore model its standards after the BAT. This is why command and control measures are mainly perceived as instruments for the diffusion of existing technology—a claim that is indeed supported by a number of empirical studies. . . .
>
> Nonetheless, there is reason to judge the innovation potential of regulatory instruments in a more differentiated way. Ashford (2000), for instance, shows that command and control measures are typically employed in a far more flexible and innovation-oriented manner than predicted by orthodox economic theory. Also, there is evidence that firm responses to regulatory measures are very often much more innovative than expected. Ex-ante estimates of the costs to business of environmental regulation often exceed the ex-post estimates by a considerable margin, not least because the constant reduction potential of environmental innovations is typically underestimated. . . .
>
> Even more importantly, we should not overlook the scope for the innovation potential of regulatory instruments to be substantially increased by means of "technology forcing." The latter is a strategy where the regulator specifies a standard that cannot be met with existing technology and thereby forces the development of environmental innovations. In contrast to environmental standards based on BAT, its innovation effects are not confined to the diffusion phase but it also triggers technology development in the early phases of the innovation cycle. . . . "Technology

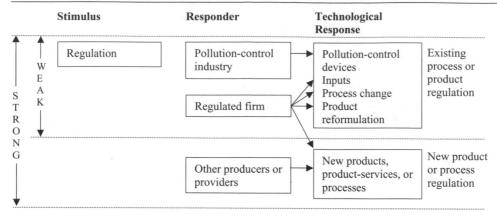

**Stimulus**      **Responder**      **Technological Response**

FIGURE 9.3: MODEL OF REGULATION-INDUCED TECHNOLOGICAL CHANGE FOR WEAK (PORTER) AND STRONG (ASHFORD/MIT) FORMS OF THE REGULATION-INDUCED-INNOVATION HYPOTHESIS
Source: Adapted from Ashford (2000, p. 90).

forcing" has been particularly present in the regulation of both stationary sources and in the American automobile sector. It has also been significant in the areas of worker protection and consumer product safety. (Ashford, Ayers, et al. 1985)

Although some economists question whether environmental regulation does generate a positive effect on innovation (A. B. Jaffe and Palmer 1997; Robinson 1995; Walley and Whitehead 1994), this type of analysis tends to miss the essence of the strong form of the regulation-induced-innovation hypothesis.*,† Although it is likely that stringent reg-

ulation will not stimulate technological innovation in most firms, some firms are likely to rise to the challenge and become technological leaders in the process. Hence the "evidence is necessarily anecdotal" (Ashford 1999, p. 3). The Schumpeterian notion of "waves of creative destruction" and the presence of Kondratieff waves of technological development describe technological development by which dominant technologies are being continually displaced as new technologies become available (see Section 3.3.1.1 in Chapter 3). The design challenge facing government is how existing, undesirable technologies can be retired (or displaced) through a combination of regulation and market incentives. These ideas thus challenge the notion that incumbent firms can reinvent themselves in a significant way and should have a major role in setting the targets for future regulation. Incumbents will not set targets they expect not to be able to meet.

By using trade-off analysis, it is possible to consider the dynamics of the impacts associated with more stringent regulation over a number of time periods (Ashford 1978; Hall 2006; Hall, Ashford, et al. 2008). Developing a series of trade-off matrices that capture how the distributed impacts adjust with improving technology might be a useful way to explain to stakeholders how their situations are likely to improve, even if at first they worsen. This approach to analysis also supports Driesen's (2003) description of the economic dynamics of environmental law. Further, the Rawlsian/utilitarian decision-making philosophy discussed in Section 1.2.2 of Chapter 1 provides the philosophical basis on which decisions for sustainable development can be made within the trade-off matrix.

---

*      For a contrasting view of the strong form of the regulation-induced-innovation hypothesis, see Gunningham and Sinclair (1999). They argue that "the most appropriate role for governmental regulation lies in nudging firms at the margin toward cleaner production, heightening their awareness of environmental issues, and encouraging the re-ordering of corporate priorities in order to reap the benefits of improved environmental performance" (ibid., p. 883). Gunningham and Sinclair (1999) disagree with the argument that more stringent regulation is the best way to encourage the development of environmental technologies, and they present a series of less intrusive policy options than regulation. Under their policy framework, the use of regulation is supported only as a last resort, when covenants between industry and government and pressure from environmental groups, for example, fail to initiate innovation and environmental improvement.

†      With regard to the weak form of the regulation-induced-innovation hypothesis, ambitious environmental policies in developed nations can lead to the formation of "lead markets" for environmental technologies (Jänicke and Jacob 2005). However, the evidence suggests that "the international diffusion of environmental innovations must be accompanied by international policy diffusion, or the adoption by other countries of the induced innovation must be economically reasonable" (Beise, Blazejczak, et al. 2003, p. 1). Both of these factors make it difficult to predict with any certainty whether an ambitious environmental policy is likely to create a lead market for the international diffusion of innovations (leading to ecological modernization). The uncertainty surrounding the likely impacts on national industries of more stringent environmental (and health and safety) regula-

tion is seen as one reason that governments hesitate to implement such policies (Blazejczak and Edler 2004).

By using trade-off analysis to assess the stringency and distributed impacts of regulation over time, along with careful consideration of the *path dependency* and *bounded rationality* of institutions and stakeholders/players, we are beginning to develop an analysis tool and way of thinking that can help formulate regulatory initiatives to nurture sustainable transformations.*

## 9.5 NATION-BASED REGULATION IN THE CONTEXT OF INDUSTRIAL GLOBALIZATION

Globalization and trade have affected the regulation of the environment, product safety, and the workplace in a number of ways: (1) increasing trade in products presents a challenge to domestic regulatory regimes because the importer of the products is generally not the manufacturer, who may actually remain unknown or unreachable under the law; (2) globalized markets are distorted by different stringency in national regulatory systems; and (3) increasing revenues from trade, as opposed to domestic consumption, change the dynamics of sector and national strategies for market competition. Recent examples of (1) are the increasing criticism and recalls of faulty imported automobile parts (Jensen 2008), toys (Phillips 2008), and food (Goldstein 2008). The following excerpt addresses the second and third concerns.

### Environmental Regulation, Globalization, and Innovation
### Nicholas A. Ashford
Source: Chapter 24 in Kevin P. Gallagher (ed.), *Handbook on Trade and the Environment*, Cheltenham: Edward Elgar, 2009.

### Introduction
[There is a ] complex relationship between environmental regulation, innovation and sustainable development in the context of an increasingly globalizing economy. . . . Health, safety and environmental regulation—herein collectively referred to as "environmental regulation"—addresses failures of the free market to internalize many of the social costs of an industrialized or industrializing economy by requiring the adoption of measures to protect the environment, workers, consumers and citizens. Regulation is criticized and resisted by many industrial firms, who argue that such measures force sometimes unnecessary "non-productive" investment that could be better directed to developing better goods and services and to

expanding markets. Further, one of the complaints made by trading firms in industrialized nations is that such measures are not required in industrializing countries that enjoy the competitive advantage of free-riding on the environment and conditions of work. [As discussed above,] a more modern view of the effects of regulation on the economy that results in competitive advantage resulting from regulation-induced innovation derives from the work of Michael Porter and Claas van der Linde (1995a; 1995b), Martin Jaenicke and Klaus Jacob (2004), Jens Hemmelskamp et al. (2000), and Ashford et al. (1979; 1985; 2000), among others, who argue that there are "first-mover" advantages to firms that comply innovatively with regulation, become pioneers in lead markets, and displace suboptimal products, processes and firms.

Globalization has indeed changed the economic landscape. It connects the national economies in new ways and denationalizes access to information, technology, knowledge, markets and financial capital. It has also opened up two distinct pathways by which a national sector or economy can compete in international markets: (1) by producing more innovative and superior technology that may or may not be first deployed in niche markets (Kemp, 1994; 1997) and (2) by adopting cost-cutting measures that involve increased economies of scale, by shedding labor, and by ignoring health, safety and environmental hazards. While some have argued that globalization also increases the demand for more protective measures worldwide (Vogel, 1995; Bhagwati, 1997), others have cautioned about a "race to the bottom" and an ever-increasing tendency to trade on environmental (and labor) externalities (Ekins et al., 1994).

Thus we see that not only are there two drivers of economic growth, technology and trade, but that trade itself can take two diametrically opposed directions, innovation-driven competition and traditional cost-cutting competition.

Health, safety and environmental regulation is the means by which industrial development is forced to become more sustainable, but the absence of strong international regulatory regimes changes the balance between industrialization and environment. . . . [We have argued] that strong national regulation can spur technological, organizational, institutional and social innovation resulting in economic and trade advantages that exceed shorter-term gains from cost-cutting and trade expansion that would otherwise weaken environmental protection, and it can result in better environmental quality as well. However, more than the "greening" of industry is needed. Creative destruction in the Schumpeterian sense is required (Schumpeter 1939; 1962). . . .

The following two chapters address environmental, health, and safety concerns in the context of regional and international regulation and international trade regimes.

---

* For further reading on stimulating dynamic transformations for environmental improvements, see Ashford (2000).

**References**

Ashford, N.A. (2000), "An innovation-based strategy for a sustainable environment," in J. Hemmelskamp, K. Rennings, and F. Leone (eds), *Innovation-Oriented Environmental Regulation: Theoretical Approach and Empirical Analysis*, ZEW Economic Studies, Heidelberg, New York: Springer Verlag, pp. 67–107.

Ashford, N.A. (2007), "The legacy of the precautionary principle in U.S. law: the rise of cost-benefit analysis and risk assessment as undermining factors in health, safety and environmental protection" in Nicolas de Sadeleer (ed), *Implementation the Precautionary Principle: Approaches from the Nordic Countries. the EU and the United States,* Earthscan: London, 2007. Available at http://hdl.handle.net/1721.1/38470 (accessed January 22, 2011).

Ashford, N.A., G.R. Heaton et al. (1979), "Environmental, health and safety regulations and technological innovation," in C.T. Hill and J.M. Utterback (eds), *Technological Innovation for a Dynamic Economy*, New York: Pergamon Press, pp. 161–221.

Ashford, N.A., C. Ayers et al. (1985), "Using regulation to change the market for innovation," *Harvard Environmental Law Review*, **9**(2), 419–66.

Bhagwati, J. (1997), "The global age: from a skeptical South to a fearful north," *The World Economy*, **20**(3), 259–283.

Ekins, P., C. Folke and R. Costanza, (1994), "Trade, environment and development: the issues in perspective," *Ecological Economics*, **9**(1), 1–12.

Hemmelskamp, J., K. Rennings, and F. Leone (eds) (2000), *Innovation-Oriented Environmental Regulation: Theoretical Approach and Empirical Analysis*, ZEW Economic Studies, Heidelberg, New York: Springer Verlag.

Jaenicke, Martin and Klaus Jacob (2004), "Lead markets for environmental innovations: a new role for the nation state," *Global Environmental Politics*, **4**(1), 29–46.

Kemp, R. (1994), "Technology and environmental sustainability: the problem of technological regime shift," *Futures*, **26**(10), 1023–1046.

Kemp, R. (1997), *Environmental Policy and Technical Change: A Comparison of the technological impact of policy instruments*, Cheltenham, UK and Lyme, USA: Edward Elgar.

Porter, Michael E. and Claas van der Linde (1995a), "Green and competitive: ending the stalemate," *Harvard Business Review*, September/October, 120–34.

Porter, Michael E. and Claas van der Linde (1995b), "Towards a new conceptualization of the environment–competitiveness relationship," *Journal of Economic Perspectives*, **9**(4), 97–118.

Schumpter, J.A. (1939), *Business Cycles: A Theoretical, Historical and Statistical Analysis of the Capitalist Process*, New York: McGraw-Hill.

Schumpeter, J.A. (1962), *Capitalism, Socialism and Democracy*, New York: Harper Torchbooks.

Vogel, David (1995), "National Regulation in the Global Economy," in *Trading Up: Consumer and Environmental Protection in a Global Economy*, Cambridge, MA: Harvard University Press, pp. 1–23.

## 9.6 NATION-BASED APPROACHES IN DEVELOPING COUNTRIES WITHOUT A STRONG REGULATORY TRADITION

Not all countries, especially developing ones, have strong regulatory traditions, either as formal law or as cultural styles and commitment. In these cases, information dissemination and technical assistance can pave the way for better health, safety, and environmental practices (see Ashford 1994b).

## 9.7 NOTES

1. For an extensive treatment of worker and community right to know, see Ashford and Caldart (2008).
2. See Vogel (2003).
3. See Coglianese and Nash (2001).
4. See Geiser (2001).
5. See Rawlins (2009, p. 26).
6. See Rawlins (2009, pp. 26–27).
7. See especially Ashford and Caldart (2008), chap. 3, "Economics and the Environment."

## 9.8 ADDITIONAL READINGS

Ashford, Nicholas A., and Charles C. Caldart (2008). *Environmental Law, Policy, and Economics: Reclaiming the Environmental Agenda.* Cambridge, MA, MIT Press.

Jänicke, M., and S. Lindemann (2010). "Governing Environmental Innovations." *Environmental Politics* **19**: 127–141.

Koch, L., and N. A. Ashford (2006). "Rethinking the Role of Information in Chemicals Policy: Implications for TSCA and REACH." *Journal of Cleaner Production* **14**(1): 31–46.

Reijnders, Lucas (2003). "Policies Influencing Cleaner Production: The Role of Prices and Regulation." *Journal of Cleaner Production* **11**: 333–338.

## 9.9 REFERENCES

Arrow, K. (1963). *Social Choice and Individual Values*, New Haven, CT, Yale University Press.

Ashford, N. A. (1978). *The Role of Risk Assessment and Cost-Benefit Analysis in Decisions Concerning Safety and the Environment*. FDA Symposium on Risk/Benefit Decisions and the Public Health, Colorado Springs, February 17. Washington, DC, Government Printing Office.

Ashford, N. A. (1993). Understanding Technological Responses of Industrial Firms to Environmental Problems: Implications for Government Policy. *Environmental Strategies for Industry: International Perspectives on Research Needs and Policy Implications*. K. Fischer and J. Schot. Washington, DC, Island Press: 277–307.

Ashford, N. A. (1994a). "Monitoring the Worker and the Community for Chemical Exposure and Disease: Legal and Ethical Considerations in the U.S.," *Clinical Chemistry*, 40/7B Supplement (July): 1426–1437. Available at http://hdl.handle.net/1721.1/1580 (accessed January 22, 2011).

Ashford, N. A. (1994b). *Government Strategies and Policies for Cleaner Production*. Paris, United Nations Environment Programme.

Ashford, N. A. (1999). "Porter Debate Stuck in 1970s." *Environmental Forum* (September/October): 3.

Ashford, N. A. (2000). An Innovation-Based Strategy for a Sustainable Environment. *Innovation-Oriented Environmental Regulation: Theoretical Approach and Empirical Analysis*. J. Hemmelskamp, K. Rennings, and F. Leone. New York, Physica-Verlag Heidelberg: 67–107.

Ashford, N. A. (2001). Innovation—The Pathway to Threefold Sustainability. *The Steilmann Report: The Wealth of People; An Intelligent Economy for the 21st Century*. F. C. Lehner, A. Bieri, S. Y. Paleocrassas, Bochum, Germany, Brainduct: 233–274.

Ashford, N. A. (2002). "Government and Environmental Innovation in Europe and North America." *American Behavioral Scientist* **45**(9): 1417–1434.

Ashford, N. A. (2004). "Major Challenges to Engineering Education for Sustainable Development: What Has to Change to Make It Creative, Effective, and Acceptable to the Established Disciplines?" *International Journal of Sustainability in Higher Education* **5**(3): 239–250.

Ashford, N. A. (2005). "Implementing the Precautionary Principle: Incorporating Science, Technology, Fairness, and Accountability in Environmental, Health, and Safety Decisions." *International Journal of Risk Assessment and Management* **5**(2/3/4): 112–124.

Ashford, N. A. (2006). "Letter to the Editor." *Issues in Science and Technology* (Winter): 22.

Ashford, N. A., C. Ayers, et al. (1985). "Using Regulation to Change the Market for Innovation." *Harvard Environmental Law Review* **9**(2): 419–466.

Ashford, N. A., and C. C. Caldart (1996). *Technology, Law, and the Working Environment*. Washington, DC, Island Press.

Ashford, N. A., and C. C. Caldart (2005). Negotiated Regulation, Implementation and Compliance in the United States. *The Handbook of Environmental Voluntary Agreements,* Environmental and Policy Series, vol. 43. E. Croci (Ed.). Dordrecht, Springer: 135–159.

Ashford, N. A., and C. C. Caldart (2008). *Environmental Law, Policy, and Economics: Reclaiming the Environmental Agenda*. Cambridge, MA, MIT Press.

Ashford, N. A., D. Hattis, et al. (1980). *Evaluating Chemical Regulations: Trade-off Analysis and Impact Assessment for Environmental Decision-Making*. Washington, DC, NTIS.

Ashford, N. A., and G. R. Heaton (1983). "Regulation and Technological Innovation in the Chemical Industry." *Law and Contemporary Problems* **46**(3): 109–157.

Ashford, N. A., G. R. Heaton, et al. (1979). Environmental, Health and Safety Regulations and Technological Innovation. *Technological Innovation for a Dynamic Economy*. C. T. Hill and J. M. Utterback. New York, Pergamon Press: 161–221.

Ashford, N. A., and G. I. J. M. Zwetsloot (1999). "Encouraging Inherently Safer Production in European Firms: A Report from the Field." Special issue, "Risk Assessment and Environmental Decision Making," *Journal of Hazardous Materials* **78**(1–3): 123–144.

Beise, M., J. Blazejczak, et al. (2003). *The Emergence of Lead Markets for Environmental Innovations*. Berlin, Forschungsstelle für Umweltpolitik (FFU).

Blazejczak, J., and D. Edler (2004). Could Too Little and Too Much Turn Out to Be Just Right? On the Relevance of Pioneering Environmental Policy. *Governance for Industrial Transformation: Proceedings of the 2003 Berlin Conference on the Human Dimensions of Global Environmental Change*. K. Jacob, M. Binder, and A. Wieczorek. Berlin, Environmental Policy Research Centre.

Carraro, C., and F. Leveque (1999). Introduction: The Rationale and Potential of Voluntary Approaches. *Voluntary Approaches in Environmental Policy*, C. Carraro and F. Leveque (Eds.). Boston, Kluwer: 1–15.

Christensen, C. M. (1997). *The Innovator's Dilemma: When New Technologies Cause Great Firms to Fail*. Cambridge, MA, Harvard Business School Press.

Coglianese, C. (1997). "Assessing Consensus: The Promise and Performance of Negotiated Rulemaking." *Duke Law Journal* **46**: 1255–1346..

Coglianese, C. and J. Nash, Eds. (2001), *Regulating from the Inside*, Washington, DC, Resources for the Future.

Congleton, R. D., and W. Sweetser (1992). "Political Deadlocks and Distributional Information: The Value of the Veil." *Public Choice* **73**: 1–19.

Driesen, D. M. (2003). *The Economic Dynamics of Environmental Law*. Cambridge, MA, MIT Press.

Driesen, D. M. (2004). "The Economic Dynamics of Environmental Law: Cost-Benefit Analysis, Emissions Trading, and Priority-Setting." *Boston College Environmental Affairs Law Review* **31**(3): 501–528.

Environmental Protection Agency (EPA) (2009). EPA's 2007 Drinking Water Infrastructure Needs Survey and Assessment. EPA 816-F-09-003. Washington, DC, EPA. Available at www.epa.gov/ogwdw/needssurvey/pdfs/2007/fs_needssurvey_2007.pdf (accessed February 13, 2011).

European Environmental Agency (EEA) (2001). *Late Lessons from Early Warnings: The Precautionary Principle, 1896–2000*. Environmental Issue Report 22. Copenhagen, EEA.

Geiser, K. (2001). *Materials Matter: Toward a Sustainable Materials Policy*. Cambridge, MA, MIT Press.

Goldstein, E. M. (2008). "Inspecting the Hands That Feed Us: Requiring U.S. Quality for All Imported Foods." *Washington University Global Studies Law Review* **7**: 137–159.

Gunningham, N., and D. Sinclair (1999). "Integrative Regulation: A Principle-Based Approach to Environmental Policy." *Law and Social Inquiry* **24**(4): 853–897.

Hall, R. P. (2006). Understanding and Applying the Concept of Sustainable Development to Transportation Planning and Decision-Making in the U.S. PhD dissertation, Engineering Systems Division. Cambridge, MA, MIT. Available at http://esd.mit.edu/students/esdphd/dissertations/hall_ralph.pdf.

Hall, R. P., N. A. Ashford, et al. (2008). Trade-off Analysis (with a Revised Rawlsian Decision-Making Philosophy) as an Alternative to Cost-Benefit Analysis (CBA) in Socio-technical Decisions. Paper presented at the COST 356 Seminar, Towards the Definition of a Measurable Environmentally Sustainable Transport, TOI, Oslo, Norway, February 20.

Hawken, P., A. Lovins, et al. (2000). *Natural Capitalism: Creating the Next Industrial Revolution*. Boston, Back Bay Books.

Hitchcock, E, B. Imus et al. (2010). *Trouble in Toyland: The 25th Annual Survey of Toy Safety,* Anchorage, The Alaska Public Interest Research and Education Fund. Available at www.akpirg.org/wp-content/uploads/2010/11/AK-toyland2010FINAL.pdf (accessed January 22, 2011).

Howells, G. G. (2000). "International Torts: A Comparative Study; The Relationship between Product Liability and Product Safety—Understanding a Necessary Element in European Product Liability through a Comparison with the U.S. Position." *Washburn Law Journal* **39**: 305–346.

Jaffe, A., S. Peterson, et al. (1995). "Environmental Regulation and the Competitiveness of U.S. Manufacturing: What Does the Evidence Tell Us?" *Journal of Economic Literature* **33**(March): 132–163.

Jaffe, A. B., and J. Palmer (1997). "Environmental Regulation and Innovation: A Panel Data Study." *Review of Economics and Statistics* **79**(4): 610–619.

Jänicke, M., J. Blazejczak, et al. (2000). Environmental Policy. *Innovation-Oriented Environmental Regulation: Theoretical Approach and Empirical Analysis*. J. Hemmelskamp, K. Rennings, and F. Leone. New York, Physica-Verlag Heidelberg: 125–152.

Jänicke, M., and K. Jacob (2005). Ecological Modernisation and the Creation of Lead Markets. *Towards Environmental Innovation Systems*. M. Weber and J. Hemmelskamp. Heidelberg, Springer: 175–193.

Jänicke, M., and S. Lindemann (2010). "Governing Environmental Innovations." *Environmental Politics* **19**(1): 127–141.

Jensen, C. (2008). "Recalls of Chinese Auto Parts Are a Mounting Concern." *New York Times*, December 19. Available at http://wheels.blogs.nytimes.com/2008/12/19/recalls-of-chinese-auto-parts-are-a-mounting-concern/?scp=1-b&sq=Recall+of+Chinese+Auto+Parts+&st=nyt (accessed January 23, 2011).

Koch, L., and N. A. Ashford (2006). "Rethinking the Role of Information in Chemicals Policy: Implications for TSCA and REACH." *Journal of Cleaner Production* **14**(1): 31–46.

O'Brien, M. (2000). *Making Better Environmental Decisions: An Alternative to Risk Assessment*. Cambridge, MA, MIT Press.

Phillips, J. A. (2008). "Does 'Made in China' Translate to 'Watch Out' for Consumers? The U.S. Congressional Response to Consumer Product Concerns." *Penn State International Law Review* **27**: 217–268.

Porter, M. E. (1990). *The Competitive Advantage of Nations*. New York, Free Press.

Porter, M. E. (1991). "America's Green Strategy." *Scientific American* **264**(4): 168.

Porter, M. E., and C. van der Linde (1995a). "Green and Competitive: Ending the Stalemate." *Harvard Business Review* **73**(September/October): 120–134.

Porter, M. E., and C. van der Linde (1995b). "Towards a New Conceptualization of the Environment-Competitiveness Relationship." *Journal of Economic Perspectives* **9**(4): 97–118.

Rawlins, R. (2009). "Teething on Toxins: In Search of Regulatory Solutions for Toys and Cosmetics." *Fordham Environmental Law Review* **20**: 1–50.

Reijnders, L. (2003). "Policies Influencing Cleaner Production: The Role of Prices and Regulation." *Journal of Cleaner Production* **11**: 333–338.

Reimann, M. (2003). "Liability for Defective Products at the Beginning of the Twenty-first Century: Emergence of a Worldwide Standard?" *American Journal of Comparative Law* **51**: 751–867.

Rennings, K., R. Kemp, et al. (2003). Blueprints for an Integration of Science, Technology and Environmental Policy (BLUEPRINT). Mannheim, Zentrum für Europäische Wirtschaftsforschung (ZEW).

Robinson, J. (1995). "The Impact of Environmental and Occupational Health Regulation on Productivity Growth in U.S. Manufacturing." *Yale Journal of Regulation* **12**: 388–434.

Sagoff, M. (1988). *The Economy of the Earth*. Cambridge, Cambridge University Press.

Söderbaum, P. (2000). *Ecological Economics: A Political Economics Approach to Environment and Development*. London, Earthscan.

Stern, N. (2007) *The Economics of Climate Change: The Stern Review* Cambridge, Cambridge University Press.

Strasser, K. A. (1997). "Cleaner Technology, Pollution Prevention and Environmental Regulation." *Fordham Environmental Law Journal* **9**(1): 1–106.

Swartzman, D. (1982). Cost-Benefit Analysis in Environmental Regulation: Sources of the Controversy. *Cost-Benefit Analysis and Environmental Regulations: Politics, Ethics, and Methods*. D. Swartzman, R. A. Liroff, and K. G. Croke. Washington, DC, Conservation Foundation: 53–85.

U.S. Public Interest Research Group Education Fund (2008). *Trouble in Toyland: The 23rd Annual Safety Survey*. Washington, DC, U.S. Public Interest Research and Education Fund. Available at www.scribd.com/doc/8613825/2008-Toy-Land-Report (accessed January 22, 2011).

van de Poel, I. R. (2000). "On the Role of Outsiders in Technical Development." *Technology Analysis and Strategic Management* **12**(3): 383–397.

Vogel, D. (2003). "The Hare and the Tortoise Revisited: The New Politics of Consumer and Environmental Regulation in Europe." *British Journal of Political Science* **33**(4): 557–580.

Walley, N., and B. Whitehead (1994). "It's Not Easy Being Green." *Harvard Business Review* **72**(3)(May/June): 46–52.

World Economic Forum, Yale Center for Environmental Law and Policy, et al. (2002). *2002 Environmental Sustainability Index: An Initiative of the Global Leaders of Tomorrow Environment Task Force, World Economic Forum*. Geneva, World Economic Forum.

Zwetsloot, G. I. J. M., and N. A. Ashford (2003). "The Feasibility of Encouraging Inherently Safer Production in Industrial Firms." *Safety Science* **41**(2–3): 219–240.

# 10

# Regional and International Regimes to Protect Health, Safety, and the Environment

## 10.1 INTRODUCTION

There are several types of environmental problems that have been exacerbated by increased industrial throughput (driven by increased consumption) of energy and materials that (1) adversely impact public health and the environment and (2) consume natural and physical resources and energy. These environmental problems are not bounded by geopolitical borders but rather have international and even global consequences that must be managed through both domestic and international legal instruments, agreements, and principles. Inherent in the concept of sustainable development is the necessity to have the fundamental tools and instruments to manage environment, health, and safety issues effectively for the well-being of both present and future generations. Chapter 9 addressed regulation of these concerns from the perspective of the nation-state, focusing on the United States as an example. This chapter explores the policy tools and instruments to improve health, safety, and the environment that function across, as opposed to within, national economies. These include efforts to harmonize national environmental legislation for nations that are members of a federated entity such as the European Union, where memberwide regional law is evolving, and for nations operating independently, but often within the context of multilateral environmental, health, and safety agreements.

This chapter on international environmental law will address the four central environmental problems of toxic pollution, climate disruption, resource depletion, and the maintenance of biodiversity and the integrity of ecosystems, as depicted in the "problems" box in Figure 0.1. In addition, concerns about environmental justice—the disparate impact of adverse effects on the environment on poorer people and nations, as well as the absence of effective ameliorating initiatives—will also be discussed, with an emphasis on the importance of stakeholder representation and participation in the governance of industrial/industrializing economies.

International aspects and dimensions of environmental, and health and safety problems are especially relevant today because of the following issues:

- Health, safety, and the environment are becoming more important in most countries.

- Continued environmental inequities have adverse social and political consequences.

- Different levels of protection can serve as subsidies or barriers to trade.

- Harmonization of legislation, regulations, implementation, monitoring, enforcement, and compliance is needed; otherwise, inequities and disparities will continue.

Underlying the concepts presented in this chapter is the necessity not only to understand the mechanisms of international environmental and health and safety law, but also to recognize the increasing importance of international cooperation as an essential element for resolving the many concerns currently plaguing global human and environmental resources. In particular, the United States bears a significant responsibility in complying with and cooperating in international law mechanisms because of its dominant position. Without its cooperation, international arrangements may be difficult to preserve and advance. Until recently, the United States has been a major obstacle to international cooperation regarding the environment and health and safety. The United States was resolutely opposed to any international arrangement that infringed on its sovereignty. The historical areas of opposition from the United States include evading commitments to the International Criminal Court, the Kyoto Protocol, many ILO conventions, the Law of the Sea Convention, and the Convention on Biological Diversity. The United States is one of only nine nations that have not ratified the last agreement. In contrast, the main sphere in which the United States is willing to cooperate is in the facilitation of international commerce. But before September 11, 2001, the Bush administration was not willing to accept OECD standards for monitoring financial transactions (the financial meltdown in the fall of 2008 may be expected to bring about significant changes in this regard). After September 11, the Bush administration was still not willing to compromise its sovereignty in waging the war on terrorism (Soros 2002).

Continued U.S. lack of cooperation would be a significant obstacle to establishing strong international regimes and mechanisms to achieve sustainable development. President Barack Obama seems dedicated to a renewed U.S. role in international cooperation and committed to changing course on environmental and energy policies.

### 10.1.1 The Increasing Importance of Health, Safety, and the Environment

With the increased globalization of the world economy, occupational and environmental health problems have taken on a multinational and international dimension. Controlling these health and environmental hazards requires both the harmonization of national legislation, standards, and practices intended to prevent waste and air and water pollution, for example, and having nations join in international agreements, with mechanisms for enforcement and verification. So-called voluntary agreements and legally enforceable codes of conduct are also important, even if they are motivated by a desire to avoid legal regulation (Ashford 1997).

One of the main challenges in achieving sustainability is that we live and trade in a world in which national autonomy compromises international agreements and where significant differences exist in environmental policies and initiatives among nations. Not only are some policy elements absent in some countries, but their scope, monitoring, enforcement, and compliance differ significantly. The concept that addresses this fragmentation is "the extent of achieving convergence." In an insightful examination of twenty-two environmental policy innovations—such as air, water, and waste regulation, national environmental policy plans, sustainable development commissions, and environmental ministries versus agencies, to name a few—Busch and Jörgens (2005) examine the extent and speed of adoption of these initiatives within central and Eastern Europe and also globally. They find "a remarkable degree of cross-national environmental policy convergence" (Busch and Jörgens 2005, p. 80). But differences really matter, especially in the context of a globalized and connected economy.

Busch and Jörgens (2005) distinguish three mechanisms favoring convergence:

1. *Harmonization*, involving the conscious modification of national policies by countries committed to international agreements or subject to supranational agreements that they had a part in formulating, such as European Union directives and regulations.

2. *Imposition*, in which countries are forced (by unilateral or multilateral conditionality) in essence to comply in order to, for example, qualify for World Bank loans.*

3. *Diffusion*, the more or less voluntary, that is, not legally imposed, adoption, mimicking, or copying of initiatives, sometimes brought about by outside or domestic pressures to conform or inspired by initiatives in other nations or by international institutions, activities, or nonbinding agreements or conventions, such as those of the OECD, WHO, or the UN Commission on Sustainable Development. Much of the nonbinding agreement and conventions is described as "soft law," which will

be discussed later in this chapter. All three mechanisms of convergence are having an impact.

Aside from activities within a nation that affect its health, safety, and domestic environment, areas of concern related to globalization include the following:

- Trade in hazardous and dangerous products
  - Pesticides, drugs, foods containing hormones
- Trade in hazardous waste
- Trade in dangerous equipment and plant
  - Export of physical plant (vinyl chloride polymerization) and export of design (Bhopal)
- Pollution of the global commons
  - Destruction of the ozone layer
  - Climate change
  - Endangered species
- Intellectual property rights
  Patents on hazardous technology, biotechnology, and pharmaceuticals
- Worker health and safety

### 10.1.2 Different Levels of Protection as Subsidies or Barriers to Trade

Different levels of health, safety, or environmental protection can act as either subsidies or barriers to trade (Plofchan 1992). Lax or nonexistent protection may relieve the producer or exporter from costly measures, in effect acting as a state subsidy through the comparative lowering of the export price of a commodity or service. Alternatively, stringent standards may prevent the importation of products or services from less compliant exporters. The implications of different levels of health, safety, or environmental protection for international trade are examined more fully in Chapter 11.

### 10.1.3 International Health, Safety, and Environmental Law Instruments and Mechanisms

In the context of today's world community of diverse interests and economic development, one must question whether global environmental law can protect the interests of all states and parties. Areas of the international commons have diminished as national jurisdiction has been extended over both living and nonliving shared resources, requiring avoidance of overexploitation or wasteful depletion. Greater involvement of states in environmental agreements, conventions, and treaties may also require increased dependency on financial, economic, and technology

---

\*    See Chapter 12, "Financing Sustainable Development."

transfer mechanisms, as well as greater public awareness of the common interest in shared resources and of the threats posed by environmental degradation. International environmental law is still at a very early stage of development and has evolved at a time when the heterogeneity of the international community has rapidly intensified. Simultaneously, economic problems have correspondingly increased, and the developmental needs and aspirations of the poorer states have become progressively more urgent. Given these problems, the progress made in developing a body of international law with an entirely environmental focus is a notable achievement despite the obstacles and hurdles that have been and still must be overcome (Birnie and Boyle 1992). In measuring the effectiveness of these international environmental law regimes, the term "effectiveness" may have multiple meanings and depends on the criteria used, for example:

- Solving the problem for which the regime was established, such as avoiding further depletion of the ozone layer

- Achieving pollution goals, such as attaining a specific reduction in sulfur dioxide emissions

- Altering behavior patterns, such as moving from use of fossil fuels to solar or wind energy production

- Enhancing national compliance with rules in international agreements, for example, those restricting trade in endangered species

Effectiveness is mainly determined by the nature of the problem and the impact of the solution. The diversity of solutions to problems is in large part due to the flexibility of international lawmaking processes, of which considerable advantage has been taken and use has been made (Birnie and Boyle 1992).

The 1972 UN Stockholm Conference on the Human Environment marked a significant point in the development of multilateral environmental treaties and accords. From 1920 to 1973, 65 multilateral environmental treaties were signed, constituting 49 percent of all recorded multilateral environmental treaties as of 1990. From 1974 to 1990, 67 treaties were concluded, or 51 percent of the total of treaties as of 1990 (Haas and Sundgren 1993). As of 2001, there were over 500 international treaties and other agreements related to the environment, of which 320 were regional. From 1972 to 2001, there was an accelerated increase in multilateral environmental agreements (MEAs); over 300 agreements were negotiated (see Appendixes 10-A and 10-B).[1]

The vast majority of environmental treaties deal with one of two types of environmental problems: (1)

protection of the physical commons *outside* national control, such as the oceans or the atmosphere, and (2) protection of assets or resources that exist *within* a country's territorial control. Both types of problems affect industrialized as well as developing nations. Commons problems dominate treaties, but few actually involve the global commons. Rather, the majority of treaties address regional commons issues regulated by adjacent states, such as regional seas. However, more recently, there has been a move toward collectively regulating global problems, such as climate change and transboundary air pollution.

Unlike the pre-1972 period, two new important clusters of MEAs have emerged: the chemicals and hazardous-wastes conventions that are primarily of a global nature, and the atmosphere-related conventions. Several of the first cluster are International Labour Organization (ILO) conventions that address occupational hazards in the workplace. Most recently, we have the adoption of the Rotterdam Convention on the Prior Informed Consent (PIC) Procedure for Certain Hazardous Chemicals and Pesticides in International Trade (1998) and the POPs (persistent organic pollutants) convention (2001). At the forefront of the atmosphere/energy-related conventions are the Vienna Convention for the Protection of the Ozone Layer (1985) and its Montreal Protocol (1987) and the United Nations Framework Convention on Climate Change (UNFCCC) (1992). MEAs for international freshwater basins are historically the most difficult to negotiate. A number of conventions and protocols have been adopted, but they are concentrated in six and four international freshwater basins in Europe and Africa, respectively.

Fundamental to international environmental law is the question of national sovereignty. Principle 21 of the Declaration of the 1972 UN Stockholm Conference states: "States have . . . the sovereign right to exploit their own resources pursuant to their own environmental policies, and the responsibility to ensure that activities within their jurisdiction or control do not cause damage to the environment of other States or of areas beyond the limits of national jurisdiction." Two elements of sovereignty are at issue here. The first is the extent to which states agree to regulate their domestic actions for the benefit of others, for example, in instances where emissions take place within territorial borders but degrade a commons through transboundary pollution. The second relates to the case in which international organizations are created in order to establish external control over national sovereignty through nongovernmental organizations (NGOs) or a body like the UN. In the second case,

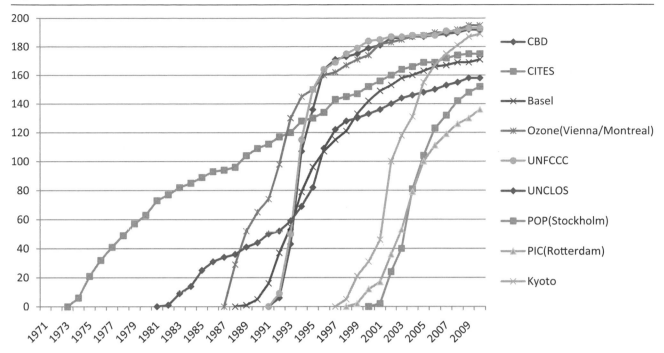

**FIGURE 10.1: GROWTH IN NUMBER OF PARTIES TO SELECTED MEAS**
Notes: CBD—The Convention on Biological Diversity; CITES—The *Convention on International Trade in Endangered Species* of Wild Fauna and Flora; Basel—The *Basel* Convention on the Control of Transboundary Movements of Hazardous Wastes and Their Disposal; Ozone—The *Montreal Protocol on Substances that Deplete the Ozone* Layer; UNFCCC—*United Nations Framework Convention on Climate Change*; and UNCLOS—The United Nations Convention on the Law of the Sea; POP—Stockholm Convention on Persistant Organic Pollutants; PIC—Rotterdam Convention; Kyoto—Kyoto Protocol
Source: Based upon UNEP (2011) GEO database.

nations demonstrate a willingness to sacrifice national sovereignty in order to submit to international obligations and to be able to monitor the cooperation or constraints of other countries also subject to an external authority (Haas and Sundgren 1993).

It is useful to classify four major categories of legal regimes for establishing international health, safety, and environment law:

- Multilateral environmental agreements (MEAs)
- Conventions of the International Labour Organization (ILO)
- Incorporation of environmental standards into trade regimes
- Incorporation of labor standards into trade regimes.

In this chapter, we explore harmonization of national health, safety, and environmental law and multilateral environmental and labor accords. The third and fourth categories in the list above will be the focus of Chapter 11, which considers trade regimes and sustainability.

Over the past few decades and into the twenty-first century, the international community has moved toward implementing multilateral environmental agreements (MEAs) as vehicles through which environmental problems requiring global cooperation are managed. MEAs can be either global or regional

agreements. However, international accords are only as effective as the parties make them. Countries may join treaties that they regard as in their interest, to make a political statement, or because of pressures from other governments. In some cases, countries may enter into MEAs without intending to modify their behavior significantly, or they may lack the capacity to do so. However, with increasing numbers of MEAs now in force, countries in both the developed and developing world are facing growing pressure for accountability to ratify these agreements.*

Appendixes 10-A and 10-B include lists of all MEAs in effect to date. The purpose of this chapter is not to review in detail all the MEAs in the United Nations Environment Programme's (UNEP's) register, but rather to analyze each problem area in terms of (1) the technologies, activities, and actors that need to be influenced, (2) the most effective approach to ameliorating the problems with current legal frameworks, and (3) identifying options for better success in the future (Ashford 1997).

Figure 10.1 and 10.2 indicate current stakeholder participation in MEAs.

---

* Although this chapter takes up many of the most important MEAs, the reader may wish to refer to UNEP (2007) for a review of these agreements.

|  | CBD (174) | CITES (145) | CMS (56) | Basel (121) | Ozone (168) | UNFCCC (176) | CCD (144) | Ramsar (114) | Heritage (156) | UNCLOS (130) |
|---|---|---|---|---|---|---|---|---|---|---|
| Africa (53) | 50 | 48 | 19 | 23 | 48 | 47 | 51 | 28 | 39 | 38 |
| Asia & Pacific (40) | 36 | 25 | 5 | 21 | 33 | 37 | 25 | 18 | 26 | 28 |
| Europe and Central Asia (54) | 47 | 35 | 25 | 39 | 48 | 48 | 29 | 41 | 51 | 28 |
| Latin America and the Caribbean (33) | 33 | 31 | 6 | 27 | 32 | 32 | 29 | 22 | 29 | 27 |
| North America (2) | 1 | 2 | 0 | 1 | 2 | 2 | 1 | 2 | 2 | 0 |
| West Asia (11) | 7 | 4 | 1 | 10 | 9 | 10 | 9 | 3 | 9 | 9 |

Key percentage of countries party to a convention

0–25%   25–50%   50–75%   75–100%

**FIGURE 10.2: PARTIES TO MAJOR ENVIRONMENTAL CONVENTIONS (AS OF MARCH 1, 1999)**
Notes:
1. Numbers in brackets below the abbreviated names of the conventions are the total number of parties to that convention.
2. Numbers in brackets after name of regions/sub-regions are the number of sovereign countries in each region/sub-region.
3. Only sovereign countries are counted. Territories of other countries and groups of countries are not considered in this table.
4. The absolute number of countries that are parties to each convention in each region/sub-region are shown in the shaded boxes.
5. Parties to a convention are states that have ratified, acceded or accepted the convention. A signatory is not considered a party to a convention until the convention has also been ratified
Key: CBD—The Convention on Biological Diversity; CITES—The *Convention on International Trade in Endangered Species* of Wild Fauna and Flora; CMS—The Convention on the Conservation of Migratory Species of Wild Animals; Basel—The *Basel* Convention on the Control of Transboundary Movements of Hazardous Wastes and Their Disposal; Ozone—The *Montreal Protocol on Substances that Deplete the Ozone* Layer; UNFCCC—*United Nations Framework Convention on Climate Change;* CCD—The *Convention* to Combat Desertification; Ramsar—The Convention on Wetlands of International Importance; Heritage—The Convention Concerning the Protection of the World Cultural and Natural Heritage; and UNCLOS—The United Nations Convention on the Law of the Sea.
Source: UNEP (2000). Available at www.unep.org/geo2000/english/i237.htm (accessed January 22, 2011).

## 10.2 THE NATURE OF INTERNATIONAL ENVIRONMENTAL LAW

International environmental law is fundamentally a specialized branch of international law.* From an environmental perspective, sources of international law essentially include the rules and principles aimed at protecting the global environment and controlling activities within national borders, including, but not restricted to, those that may affect the environment beyond national jurisdiction. In the past few decades, there has been increasing recognition of the need to provide more substantial principles and more specific rules to govern environmental issues, such as preventing marine pollution from toxic discharges, controlling emission of gases that damage the ozone layer, and regulating transboundary movement of hazardous waste. These pressing concerns have facilitated the development of international environmental law and have promoted the adoption of new concepts and principles. The framework of environmental treaties, principles, and codes that has been developed is often focused more on a so-called soft-law approach, through use of umbrella treaties or nonbinding agreements, guidelines, and principles (Birnie and Boyle 1992). This does not mean that

---

\* Although international law principles were central in the formulation and evolution of the European Union (EU), the EU is developing a regional approach to environmental policy and sustainable development that is likely to be a model for other regions. Thus EU environmental and sustainable development policies are both influenced by and influence the development of international environmental law. Therefore, EU approaches are described throughout this chapter, and selected specific EU initiatives are also described in Section 10.18.

traditional sources of law, or "hard" law, are usurped for the soft approach, but rather that there are many nuances and transformations merging both hard and soft approaches in the development of international environmental law. We begin this section by considering three sources of international environmental law: treaties, customs, and principles (Birnie 1987), while acknowledging that the writings of international law scholars are also influential in its development, for example, de Sadeleer (2002), Jans (2000), Jordan (2002), Sands (2003), and R. Winter (2000).

### 10.2.1 Treaties, Customs, and Principles as Elements of International Environmental Law

Historically, treaties and custom have traditionally been binding law. For environmental issues, treaties are a typical method of creating binding international law. They are also called conventions, protocols, covenants, pacts, and acts, and there are currently no rules prescribing their form. The 1969 Vienna Convention on the Law of Treaties provides some fundamental rules for treaties concluded after 1980 on matters such as entry into force, reservations, interpretation, termination, and invalidity. States that sign a treaty are expected, subject to ratification, not to do anything that undermines the treaty's objectives and principles. Upon ratification, the treaty becomes binding on its parties on the basis of the underlying principles of customary law. In general, treaties do not bind third-party states, although the provisions of the treaty may affect third parties or may become part of customary international law. For example, a number of general environmental principles, such as those put forward in the 1982 UN Convention on the Law of the Sea, are incorporated into regional treaties and practice. However, treaties do not always provide clear or specific rules that can be extrapolated to regional, national, or local law, but are often more a framework, outlining general guidelines in order for governments to take practical measures related to the issue at hand, such as the UNEP regional sea treaties or the 1979 Convention on Long-Range Transboundary Air Pollution. These particular treaties require states to develop appropriate measures for addressing the environmental issues related to combating oil spills, dumping of wastes, and protection of the marine habitat, as well as controlling industrial air emissions. The 1969 Vienna Convention recognized that there are certain basic "norms of international law" that no states can circumvent;

however, it does not detail what these norms entail. The obligation to preserve the environment might be one, for example, but this is not specifically addressed in the Vienna Convention (Birnie and Boyle 1992).

Treaties are the most commonly used method of international environmental law; however, some states prefer "customary lawmaking" where there is no lengthy and complicated process of ratification. Customary law may be useful for incorporating terms such as "sustainable development," "intergenerational equity," "the precautionary principle," and other commonly used environmental concepts into everyday language of national lawmaking. Conversely, it is often difficult to know whether such terms are valid and concrete parts of a law or simply descriptive terms still elusive of any binding authority. Additionally, in a world of diverse interests and cultures, new concepts and principles can be interpreted in many different ways. In this atmosphere, customary law can take some time to develop into the consciousness of a nation or place. The UN and other international bodies have primarily been responsible for representing the majority consensus of opinion on international environmental issues. However, the UN Charter gives its General Assembly power only to make recommendations; that is, the UN does not have legislative power over states, whether they are members or not. Some legal scholars continue to argue that these recommendations, or resolutions, cannot be regarded as customary law because the UN is not a lawmaking body for all nations, whereas other legal scholars taking the opposite view promote the idea that resolutions that have the consensus support of international organizations should have legal significance (Birnie and Boyle 1992). However, even if these resolutions are not enforceable, they do present principles and concepts that may be increasingly adopted by nations, and therefore they are crucial elements of international environmental law.

In addition to customary law, there now exists a significant development in the number of principles shaping international environmental law (see Section 10.4). As is the case with soft law in general, there is some controversy over whether principles are substantial elements of international environmental law. Although some principles are becoming the cornerstones of international environmental law, not all are viewed as hard law, and not all have been invoked in support of decisions related to environmental issues. This was the case in the International Court of Justice's decisions on delimitation of the continental shelf and exclusive economic or fishery zones, in which the court invoked "equitable principles" not as rules of law but as a means of facilitating an equitable solution (Birnie 1987). As more international environmental agreements are developed, it is likely that common principles—especially the polluter-pays principle and the precautionary principle (see the later discussion of both)—will start to take on a more binding nature, eventually leading to widespread acceptance of sustainable development and equitable utilization of shared resources.

## 10.2.2 "Hard" versus "Soft" Law

What distinguishes law from other social norms is that it is prescriptive and binding. Therefore, the term "soft" law seems to contradict law's authoritative power. In contrast to hard and binding laws, states often prefer nonbinding obligations as a simpler and more flexible foundation for future relations known as "soft law." The difference between hard law and soft law, therefore, "lies mainly in the parties' wish to model their relationship in a way that excludes the application of treaty" sanctions upon a breach of obligations and instead is more an approach of encouraging cooperation, dispute settlement, and conflict resolution (Hillgenberg 1999, p. 499).

However, soft-law approaches do not justify viewing such agreements as being only "political" or "moral." In each instance, it would be more appropriate to consider the extent to which the parties choose to bind themselves "voluntarily" and what legal consequences they want to attach to their agreement (Hillgenberg 1999).

Soft law is a somewhat controversial subject. However, in the case of international law, given the lack of any supreme authoritative body with lawmaking powers, it has been difficult to establish a consensus for determining binding rules. Securing agreements in an era of political, cultural, and religious diversity, even on issues of extreme importance, is particularly difficult. These constraints on the lawmaking process present problems in developing standards for environmental protection and also for worker health and safety. Treaties are useful mechanisms, but often they do not enter into force, or they do so for a limited number of parties that do not necessarily include the states whose involvement is most vital to the achievement of the treaty objectives (for example, the initial failure to get the United States to adopt the Kyoto Protocol). Treaties therefore present problems as vehicles for changing the law.

Halfway measures are increasingly being used in the lawmaking process in codes of practice, recommendations, guidelines, resolutions, declarations of principles, standards, and "framework" or "umbrella" treaties that do not fit neatly into legal categories. These elements are not binding law, but they can lead to affirmative policies. Although it is easy to be critical of soft law, it provides a vehicle for nations to express their responsibilities either in general terms—to be specified later—or in strong but nonbinding ways. Soft law often later morphs into harder law as a result of experience gained with softer initial approaches. International environmental law therefore provides numerous examples of the soft-law approach that allows states to tackle a problem collectively at a time when they may not want to restrict their actions too much. On environmental matters, this might be either because scientific evidence is not conclusive, but a precautionary approach is required (see Section 10.4.2), or because the economic costs are uncertain or overburdensome (Birnie and Boyle 1992).

Although soft law is difficult to define and may not be seen as strictly enforceable, it has an important contribution to make in establishing legal order in the development of international environmental law. The term does usefully capture an increasingly used process of moving slowly toward the formalization of obligations or of setting goals, that is, toward "harder" laws that are intended to have some authoritative status. Furthermore, soft law provides legal measures of environmental protection not only in the form of treaties but also in evolving legal concepts and principles, as will be further discussed later in this chapter.

## 10.2.3 The International Multilateral Environmental Agreement Process

International environmental agreements vary in their level of application or enforcement. Some agreements may be considered more as guidelines or criteria, whereas infringements of other more mandatory agreements may result in fines or trade restrictions (see also Chapter 11 on trade regimes). Agreements with specific provisions that are binding and set out in treaties can be considered hard law, whereby states must implement and enforce such laws in their national legal systems (Birnie 1992).

The international community's process for addressing environmental challenges begins with an effort to find common support among nations to develop new environmental policies. The process concludes with the joint implementation of the policies agreed on. As Congleton (2001, p. 6) describes, this process may pass through four stages of development:

- The *first stage* entails the recognition of the possibility of mutual advantage of joint or cooperative legal action. Without an agreement that mutual gains can be realized, there is no point to further negotiation.
- The *second stage* attempts to establish procedures by which alternative policy targets may be evaluated and chosen. Without some process of collective decision making—especially in multilateral treaties—it will be difficult, if not impossible, to proceed to the next stage.
- In the *third stage*, negotiators may attempt to agree on specific environmental targets that address the environmental problem of interest.
- Finally, after negotiators have agreed to [and formally signed on to] general principles articulated in the environmental accord and where contained, possibly more specific regulations, such as effluent limitations, each country must [ratify the treaty and then] pass appropriate domestic (i.e., national) environmental legislation to meet its treaty obligations.*

Stage four ends the strictly legal process. Actual enforcement, monitoring of compliance of the target of the legislation (for example, the industrial firm, agricultural entity, or municipal authority), and securing widespread compliance become issues of political will of the nation-state. Even in the European Union, the member states represent widely differing degrees of commitment to enforcement of the uniform EU environmental directives.†

Congleton (1995) notes that following each of the first three stages of negotiation, an environmental treaty could be signed. Treaties may represent different degrees of specificity of the nations' obligations depending on the stage at which the treaty is negotiated.

(i) Treaties negotiated after the first stage may be categorized as symbolic treaties. *Symbolic* treaties do not characterize environmental regulations, nor targets, nor even procedures by which such substantive matters might be explored. They simply express sentiments about the principles and prospects for better environmental policy.

(ii) *Procedural* treaties develop institutions, often fairly rudimentary institutions, by which substantive matters regarding environmental targets or regulations may eventually be explored or developed. Such treaties build international institutions for collective decision making on specific environmental matters but do not explicitly proscribe environmental targets or regulations. (The actual text of procedural treaties often deals fairly extensively with institutional development, and nearly always includes text on matters very similar to those of symbolic treaties.)

(iii) Agreements negotiated at the third stage allow what might called substantive treaties to be signed. *Substantive* environmental treaties specify environmental targets or regulations to be implemented via new domestic legislation by all signatory nations. (ibid.)

International conventions become binding on signatory states only after (1) their ratification by the appropriate legislative or parliamentary body and (2) their implementation/transposition into national law. Thereafter, the treaties are binding on the nation-states, and the national legislation is binding on the regulatory targets, such as firms or private individuals. Enforcement and verification of compliance at the international, national, and individual target/firm levels are crucial if harmonization is to be more than just obligations on paper.

## 10.3 FACTORS INFLUENCING COMPLIANCE WITH MULTILATERAL ENVIRONMENTAL ACCORDS

Since 1972, the number of legal instruments concerning the environment has risen significantly, and increasing attention has been given to whether the relevant actors comply with the agreements they negotiate. Compliance with international agreements is an important but neglected issue in international environmental law. States join agreements for many reasons that affect their intention and capacity to comply. For example, states may join to exercise leadership in addressing a problem, or because other states are doing so, or because states with leverage over them are pressing them to join, and states may join an agreement with no intention of complying.

International agreements evolve or change over time, as do national policies, economies, and capacities for compliance. States are the primary actors, but other actors are also essential, including intergovernmental

---

* Treaties are first signed by the executive of a nation, such as the president or prime minister. This signing must be followed by ratification by the appropriate legislature or parliamentary body and must be finalized by transposition into national law.
† The ten new accession states of the EU will be given time to adopt appropriate national legislation implementing the EU directives, a process known as "transposition of the directive(s) into national law."

organizations, secretariats to the agreements, NGOs, private industrial and commercial organizations, and individuals. All these actors interact dynamically in complex ways that change over time and that vary among the different agreements and among nations (Weiss 1999).

Evaluating a country's compliance with an international environmental agreement involves determining both whether a country adheres to the provisions of the agreement and whether the country actually takes domestic steps to implement the agreement. Compliance refers to adhering to procedural obligations, such as reporting requirements, and substantive requirements, such as obligations to cease or control activities. Effectiveness differs from compliance in that effectiveness measures an agreement's impact on behavior, whereas an ineffective agreement has little behavioral impact. In addition, developing indicators to measure effectiveness is challenging. Some of the components of assessing a treaty's effectiveness are (1) whether the treaty achieves its stated objectives; (2) whether it addresses the problems that led to the treaty; and (3) public participation (Goldschmidt 2002).* The results of a major multinational research project at the International Institute for Applied Systems Analysis indicate that efforts to open public participation in the environmental policy development process have influenced domestic policy decisions and enforcement (Jacobson and Weiss 1998).

As an example, whether the Convention on International Trade in Endangered Species of Wild Fauna and Flora (CITES) is effective in controlling international trade in endangered species might be evaluated (Weiss 1998). This evaluation involves asking whether those who export and import endangered species obtain the required permits, whether the permits provide the required information and are free from fraud, whether parties have designated scientific authorities to manage international trade, and whether parties file timely and complete reports of their trade to facilitate monitoring. A second level of inquiry addresses whether CITES, even if fully complied with, is effective in conserving biological diversity, which is the underlying purpose of the agreement. This then evaluates the effectiveness of controlling international trade in identified species as a measure to protect the species. Under CITES, a species can be consumed domestically and even eliminated domestically without violating the agree-

ment. This has led some critics to focus on the Convention on Biological Diversity and agreements that conserve habitats as potentially more effective instruments for conserving species diversity (Weiss 1999).[2]

The realities of compliance indicate the need for the different relevant actors of international environmental agreements to have available compliance strategies that can be tailored and adapted to changing circumstances of the agreements. Additionally, there are significant differences between nations in capabilities and willingness to adhere to international environmental policies and agreements. In particular, capacity building has become central to multilateral environmental accords, where developed nations are being called on to build environmental capacity for developing nations.† Many developing countries have conditioned their multilateral commitments on the provision of financial resources and technology transfer from developed nations. As a result, commitments to develop capacity are increasingly recognized as essential (Drumbl 1999). For example, the UN Framework Convention on Climate Change (UNFCCC) states that "the extent to which developing country Parties will effectively implement their commitments under the Convention will depend on the effective implementation by developed country Parties of their commitments related to financial resources and transfer of technology."‡

Although this provision arguably goes beyond what many multilateral agreements provide in regard to capacity building, perhaps the more important question is whether these commitments will actually build capacity and help developing countries adhere to the UNFCCC more than other international agreements without such provisions. In the case of climate change, the carbon dioxide emissions of developing countries are projected to equal or exceed the emissions of developed countries by 2030 (Grubb 1991). As developing nations continue to industrialize, their contribution to other forms of environmental degradation will likely increase as well. Therefore, the effectiveness of international environmental agreements will, in the long term, depend on the level of environmental policy and reg-

---

* The distinction between (1) and (2) is often described as one between an "internal" evaluation and an "external" evaluation of an initiative or program.

---

† See the later discussions of the Global Environment Facility (GEF) in Section 12.10 in Chapter 12 and the EU LIFE initiative in Section 10.18.11.

‡ See the Kyoto Protocol to the United Nations Framework Convention on Climate Change, December 10, 1997. Article 10 makes an explicit reference to capacity building. It provides that all parties "shall . . . cooperate in and promote . . . the development and implementation of education and training programmes, including the strengthening of national capacity building."

ulation capacity achieved in the developing nations (Drumbl 1999).

However, simply providing for capacity building in MEAs may not be enough to produce compliance. Rather, genuine capacity building may require a sweeping overhaul, and the state must internalize environmental performance in its politics, society, and economy, including creating domestic bureaucratic and political institutions, NGOs or other "green" interest groups, a free press, information rights, and the emergence of an "iron triangle" of cooperation among environmental organizations, government, and business (Knoepfel 1997).* It is also important to implement technology transfers that do not promote one environmental issue at the expense of another. Technological assistance that reduces dependency on fossil fuels (thereby mitigating greenhouse gas emissions and promoting compliance with the UNFCCC) but satisfies the remaining energy needs with projects that interfere with water supplies or land use should be avoided.

Public participation, particularly of NGOs, plays a crucial role in the implementation of and compliance with international environmental agreements. NGOs put pressure on governments, directly and indirectly, to release compliance information and provide the public with information about environmental, health, and safety issues. Additionally, NGOs mobilize public opinion, set political agendas, and communicate with other NGOs throughout the world. In addition, the creation of NGOs is also a very important factor in building capacity. Some developed nations, such as Germany, the Netherlands, and the United States, have long histories of very active environmental grassroots movements that have resulted in the entrenchment of effective NGOs. Their principal impact on environmental capacity building takes the form of legislative lobbying, but they also inform the general public about environmentally risky behavior through the press and can help guide consumer purchasing patterns toward more environmentally friendly products and services. In the developing world, the existence and involvement of NGOs in political decision making may be problematic because the appropriate institutional mechanisms for participation have not yet been developed, and typically, the victims of environmental degradation still have no effective formal organizations to champion their rights. This was not the case in Chile, where social forces enlivened an

environmental awareness that may have prompted the national government to solicit environmentally favorable resources and technology from abroad. In Chile, the growth of environmental grassroots organizations was facilitated by the government's interest in joining the North American Free Trade Agreement (for further details on NAFTA, see Section 10.20.6 and Chapter 11). This example is promising because it shows how the desire to participate in international trade may trigger greater national tolerance, if not demand, for democratic institutions and increased environmental capacity (Drumbl 1999).

Overall, with regard to capacity building in order to attain compliance with multilateral environmental accords, the main lesson from existing examples is that the financial and technological transfers associated with capacity building may not be effective in actually building capacity. Commitments to the UNFCCC, the Montreal Protocol, and the Biodiversity Convention may promote capacity in a narrow context. A more rigorous capacity-building mechanism would focus on the competence of governmental, nongovernmental, and private industrial relationships with enhanced availability of information and institutional relationships.

### 10.3.1 Negotiation of Environmental Accords

Over the past few decades, a great deal of effort has been devoted to obtaining written treaties or agreements pertaining to the environment; however, very few have significantly reduced pollution levels or modified consumption patterns of economic development. In negotiating these agreements, much effort has been placed on simply getting written agreements, rather than providing effective instruments by which environmentally sustainable practices may be implemented. Susskind and Ozawa (1992) point out that the typical convention-protocol approach to treaty making, which begins with years of multilateral negotiations aimed at attaining the signing of a treaty or convention and then negotiates further protocols with more specific objectives, is a lengthy process that does not often yield a desired outcome. Often the convention-protocol approach produces a lowest-common-denominator agreement designed to appeal to the largest number of signatories and impose the same requirements on all the signatories. For example, the Basel Convention includes vague language, such as calling for the disposal of hazardous waste in an "environmentally sound manner," without further defining what this may appropriately entail. Each country is left to adopt its own definition of

---

* An example of the lack of an iron triangle is Chile, in which government and business work closely together even on environmental issues, somewhat excluding NGOs.

environmentally sound practices, which may result in very little change to current and environmentally detrimental procedures. The convention-protocol approach requires hard bargaining techniques from many countries, and negotiations can become a test of wills between stakeholders without compromising. And significantly, most MEAs contain insubstantial provisions for monitoring and enforcement. Without effective monitoring and enforcement, there is little incentive for nations to implement the conditions of any agreement.

One of the other quandaries in negotiating environmental agreements, in particular, is that often there is a degree of scientific uncertainty underlying the negotiation process. If a country wishes to delay implementing pollution- or emission-reducing measures, it can reasonably argue that further study and data are necessary in order to agree to such proposals. Another obstacle, which will be discussed more fully in Chapter 11, is that environmental negotiations are conducted in isolation from other international issues, such as debt, trade, and security. The lack of environmental input into these more economic and political arenas is especially significant because environmental issues are inextricably linked to poverty, foreign debt, malnutrition, and human health, as well as trade in hazardous and toxic chemicals.

Allocation of rights over shared global environmental resources is complicated. As S. Barrett (1999, p. 136) explains, "Even if rights to such resources could be allocated (for example, the whole of an inland sea could be given to a single country), no simple rule will suffice to please all parties. Customary international law states that shared resources should be subject to 'equitable utilization,' but the law is silent on what makes for an equitable allocation."

International cooperation and the success of multilateral agreements also depend on the perceptions and aptitudes of the individuals who negotiate them, the nature of the problems or issues under discussion, and the political circumstances in which the agreements are negotiated. Often the best negotiators will encounter constraints limiting treaties to partial cooperation, and even more frequently, negotiators of these treaties have an inadequate conceptual understanding of the issues under consideration. There are also discrepancies regarding whether compliance with international treaties is the problem, and whether "sticks" are needed to deter noncompliance (S. Barrett 1999).

Regional or global public goods, or commons, problems include, among many others, harvesting of migratory tuna, polluting shared waters, protection of the ozone layer, conservation of biodiversity, and climate-change mitigation. Agreement concerning the management, use, and protection of these shared resources is a difficult and complex task. The cooperation of shared resources can be analyzed by using a "prisoner's dilemma" (PD) approach. If parties to an agreement both cooperate, they stand to gain as a result of this cooperation. However, if one party chooses to defect, this party is likely to gain more than the cheated party. If both parties defect, they will ultimately gain very little.* International environmental treaties are analogous to the PD game in that global resources may not be sustainable by a decentralized or anarchic international system. As S. Barrett (1999, p. 133) comments: "In the one-shot, single-round PD game, decentralization is fatal to the collective good. More generally, those outcomes that are welfare-superior (as compared to their anarchic counterparts) must be sustained by an enforcement mechanism of some kind. In particular, cooperation *can* be sustained for even the one-shot PD provided an agreement between the players can be enforced by a third party. However, there is no third party that can effectively enforce agreements between countries."

The challenged posed by the prisoner's dilemma is that purely rational decision makers would never cooperate. By definition, they must act in a way that is best for them whatever the other actor chooses. In reality, not all choices negotiated in environmental accords are binary (success or no success), as in the PD scenario.† In negotiating international agreements, countries cooperate through treaties with many caveats, nuances, and outcomes that affect shared global environmental resources.

In addition to the prisoner's dilemma, the free-rider problem affects the negotiation of MEAs. A free rider benefits from a public good without paying for it. The idea relates closely to Garrett Hardin's (1968) tragedy of the commons and can be a major problem for the environment. For example, if society decides to encourage people to use less of a product that harms the environment and many people actually respond to this call, the environment will improve. Although the free rider may continue using this product, he or she will benefit without changing

---

*       For a prisoner's dilemma discussion relevant to this topic, see especially Hardin (1968) and Sandler (1997).

†       For example, pollution abatement can range from 0 to 100 percent.

his or her harmful activity. If the benefits of a regulated pollution-control or some other measure are too diffuse and accrue to all nations irrespective of their behavior, nations may have very little incentive to agree to the conditions set out in the agreement (Susskind and Ozawa 1992). One of the reasons articulated by the United States in withdrawing from the Kyoto climate-change agreement (this explanation is simplified here) was concerns over the free riding of developing countries, while developed countries like the United States establish the technologies necessary to reduce greenhouse gas emissions. As the economies of developing countries such as India, China, and Brazil continue to expand, it is likely that their greenhouse gas emissions will surpass those of the United States within the next few decades.[3] Because the Kyoto agreement excluded fourteen of the top twenty emitting countries, there was a legitimate concern that some developing countries would free-ride on the emission reductions made by the United States and other industrialized nations. The climate-change discussions are just one example where the free-rider issue was brought into focus to impede progress in negotiations, but free-rider issues pervade a number of other environmental agreements and often inhibit ratification.

In addition to allocating rights in an international environmental agreement, there are also the issues of how to enforce an allocation and what to do about noncompliance with an agreement. As evidenced by the Kyoto Protocol, the negotiators of this agreement were preoccupied with negotiating targets and timetables rather than enforcement or participation mechanisms. With the omission of enforcement mechanisms, targets and timetables are eluded, participation narrows, and the agreement is at risk of not entering into force or, if it enters into force, achieving less than was anticipated. A typical approach to dealing with noncompliance is that of bad public relations. In other words, a damaged reputation resulting from noncompliance can make it difficult for a deviant to enter into future agreements, and a deviant may receive pressure from other countries to comply with the targets and timetables of the treaty. However, the same facts are open to a different interpretation. For instance, countries may sign only agreements they would be happy to comply with unilaterally, or perhaps compliance is not a problem because the obligations imposed on parties are so weak as to eliminate any incentive not to comply.

Noncompliance will be deterred only if there is a mechanism to punish the act of noncompliance. The challenge, however, is how to make the threat of punishment credible when punishing noncompliance usually also harms the countries that carry out the punishment. As S. Barrett (1999, pp. 140–144) explains:

> "Sticks" will be needed to enforce compliance, as well as to enforce participation. Indeed, there should be a natural connection between these punishments. . . . Nonparticipation in the Montreal Protocol has been deterred by the *threat* to impose trade sanctions against nonparties. Although the compliance mechanism in this treaty was left unspecified, when Russia threatened noncompliance, the parties to this remarkable treaty threatened to punish Russia by restricting trade. The threat was more implicit than explicit, but it worked all the same. . . .
>
> Trade sanctions are credible for the Montreal Protocol mainly because of the worry about "trade leakage"—that, as some countries reduce their production and consumption of ozone-depleting substances, output and usage will simply shift to nonparticipants. . . .
>
> Another reason is that for some environmental problems—climate change mitigation being the most obvious—sanctions might need to be applied very broadly. The production of all goods and services results in emission of greenhouse gases. To reduce leakage, some kind of border tax adjustment would probably be needed. But this would be impractical. It is virtually impossible to work out, for *each* traded good, the emissions resulting from its manufacture. Importantly, though the Montreal Protocol threatens to impose sanctions on trade in products made using ozone-depleting substances, such an action has not been taken and has not proven necessary. For climate change, it would seem essential, and yet the consequence may be a threat to the multilateral trading system.

There are techniques that can enhance the implementation of international agreements, including annexes or revisions of the treaties when new information or changes become available. If an annex amendment process is used, the whole process of ratification does not have to start from the beginning; instead, the changes to the treaty can be negotiated. Susskind and Ozawa (1992) offer some other solutions for enhancing the effectiveness of environmental negotiations, including the following:

- Using alliances of various countries to initiate action or forums for discussion of relevant issues

- Providing negotiation assistance to countries, especially those countries with few scientific and legal resources

- Utilizing nongovernmental organizations as independent negotiators, as well as sources of information

- Reinforcing the connection between science and politics and not using uncertain science as a political push for no action

- Appropriately linking issues such as the environment and trade or the environment and national security

- Removing the fear of competitive disadvantage, that is, not penalizing those countries that protect environmental resources in the marketplace

- Encouraging the media to provide accurate and objective information to the international community

Significant institutional reforms may be necessary in order to implement these ideas. However, it is the responsibility of the larger international powers, such as industrial powers like the United States, or the pinnacle of the international establishment, the UN, to take ownership of this process. There is additionally an important role for the International Court of Justice to play in enforcing international environmental agreements and prosecuting those who neglect their responsibilities, as well as providing decisions that act as strong incentives for those countries unwilling to ratify or otherwise cooperate with the accords. Given the substantial historical basis that now exists in negotiating these agreements, the international community should now move forward, taking heed of lessons learned in the past, and provide mechanisms for enforcing and monitoring the agreements as a monumental priority.

## 10.4 THE POLLUTER-PAYS PRINCIPLE, THE PRECAUTIONARY PRINCIPLE, AND OTHER EVOLVING PRINCIPLES OF INTERNATIONAL ENVIRONMENTAL LAW

Under the influence of international law and the civil law tradition, key concepts in international environmental law are defined in part by a set of principles that have accumulated through declarations such as the Stockholm and Rio declarations, treaties, and the practice of nations (Gaines 2002), and, increasingly, initiatives of the European Union (de Sadeleer 2002), representing a regional approach to governance. In this section, we discuss several of the key principles.

### 10.4.1 The Polluter-Pays Principle and the Coasean View

As a principle, the polluter-pays notion holds that polluting enterprises should bear the costs of controlling their polluting activities and assume the liability for correcting the consequences of these activities. In an economic sense, the polluter-pays principle seeks to avoid disruptions in trade flows that might arise if there were different degrees of subsidization of environmental controls from one country to another. In particular, there has been considerable interest in the polluter-pays principle as outlined in Principle 16 of the Rio Declaration, which states: "National authorities should endeavor to promote the internalization of environmental costs and the use of economic instruments, taking into account the approach that the polluter should, in principle, bear the cost of pollution, with due regard to the public interest and without distorting international trade and investment."[4]

The most well-known embodiment of the Polluter Pays Principle is found in the US Superfund program established in 1980 to clean up toxic-contaminated sites (see Section 9.2.3.3 in Chapter 9). The Comprehensive Environmental Response, and Compensation Act (CERCLA) includes the so-called "Superfund" trust, set up to finance the cleanup of orphaned, or abandoned" polluted sites. Under the Superfund, the Environmental Protection Agency (EPA) is responsible for cleaning up contaminated sites using money from the Superfund trust fund and then attempting to recover the costs from businesses and individuals responsible for the contamination. To finance the fund, three taxes based on the volume of chemicals produced were imposed, targeting those industries with the greatest risk of pollution—the petroleum, gas, and chemical industries. The authorization for imposing the taxes mentioned has now expired, and the states often bear the burden of cleanup to the extent that it occurs at all—see Ashford and Caldart (2008) for further discussion.

Despite the initial success of Superfund in making industry more accountable for its polluting activities, the program has been criticized by industry and some academics because site cleanup is too lengthy and costly, often requiring federal taxpayer funds to complete remediation of sites, with questionable benefits to health. As a result, the Bush administration routinely reduced the budget allocation for Superfund cleanups (Probst and Konisky 2001). Stakeholders looking to replenish Superfund's coffers by reinstating polluter-pays taxes to allow it to continue fulfilling its mission have been unsuccessful. The Superfund program has been instrumental in cleaning up the environment and protecting public health, but it has been costly. Unfortunately, much of the nation's cleanup—to the extent it occurs at all—is now undertaken outside Superfund in more community-centered and economics-driven programs such as brownfields programs, voluntary cleanups, and state programs, putting enormous financial burdens on communities and government instead the chemical-producing and using industries (Schmidt 2002).

In contrast to the U.S. Superfund scenario, a different, innovative polluter-pays policy comes from a European context, formalized recently in a new directive on environmental liability (see Section 10.12.2).[5] The chemical spill at Seveso, Italy, in 1976 and other industrial episodes of contamination established a need to ensure that the damaged environmental assets are restored, or, more ideally, that further damage to the environment is prevented through improved practices and management. The EU Directive on Environmental Liability was that response.

In contrast to the polluter-pays principle, an alternative perspective, known as the Coasean view, is advocated, especially by neoclassical economists. For example, imagine that industrial producers of a certain product freely use the air or water to dispose of a noxious substance (rather than control or treat the pollution), which imposes costs on individuals who live downstream or downwind from the site at which the noxious substance is produced. The lower cost of this method of disposal leads to the result that consumers may benefit from lower prices of the product, that firm owners may benefit from higher profits, or some combination of the two. In either case, neither suppliers nor consumers have an incentive to account for the externality costs that the production of the product imposes on persons living downstream or downwind from the site of production. In his famous, Nobel Prize–winning work "The Theory of Social Cost," Coase (1960) points out that externality problems for environmental issues can be solved by marketlike transactions involving negotiation between polluters and citizens. Coase analyzes the problem as being one in which there is a "reciprocal nature of the harm." Were it not for the polluter, there would be no problem. If the citizens did not live downstream or were willing to move, there would likewise be no problem. Coase argues that in the absence of transaction costs, it makes no sense for the government to impose a solution. Through negotiation, no matter which group initially has property rights in the air or water, the same outcome would result. The resource (air or water) would be put to its most valued use. (Of course, equity concerns are raised in terms of who ends up paying.)

Instead of the government regulating the polluter, those individuals affected by the externalities could band together and pay the firm owners to use different methods of waste disposal if they were deemed beneficial to the individuals. If not, pollution should continue because the commercial activity of the polluter is more highly valued in the marketplace. However, in assuming that transaction costs are low, Coase neglects that in reality, coordinating collective action in large groups of affected persons would require, among other things, the formation of, and agreement within, community-based organizations (Congleton 2002). Forming such organizations can be problematic. Alternatively, rather than depending on successful organizing to negotiate with polluters and consumers, those affected could pressure government to regulate or tax the harmful product or activity.*

## 10.4.2 The Precautionary Principle

The precautionary principle (or the precautionary approach, as it is called in the Rio Declaration) is more subtle and less clearly defined than the polluter-pays principle. In many cases, the timescales, uncertainties, and consequences of environmental changes are unknown and difficult to define in scientific terms, and therefore, the successful implementation of MEAs is challenged. Environmental impact from activities carried out today may not be seen for many generations and certainly may have implications beyond current political terms and agendas. In order to address uncertainties regarding environmental and health effects of anthropogenic activities more appropriately, a key concept integrated into international environmental agreements is the notion of the "precautionary principle."

---

* It bears noting that prospects for "[Coasean] solutions are also affected by a variety of government policies and may require changing those policies. The initial assignment of rights determine[s] what course of action is necessary. Within governments characterized by an aggressive tort law, those living downstream or downwind could launch a class action suit against the producers for damages imposed by the use of the air or water systems to dispose of waste products. In the absence of such legal remedies, a new organization would have to be created to collect money in order to compensate producers and consumers of X. Such organizations would require some process of collective choice to determine negotiation strategies, assign cost shares to members, and design methods for punishing those who fail to contribute.

"In the end, the [Coasean] result reflects a variety of government policies that affect organizational costs, contract enforcement, and liability under tort law. Government policies may affect such internal arrangements of such groups or special service districts insofar as its policies discourages interest group formation (as within dictatorships), is neutral toward them, or actively encourages them." R. D. Congleton, "Constitutional Design and Public Policy," Lecture 9: "Treaties as Contracts between Governments," Universiteit Leiden, Fall 2003, footnote 1, http://rdc1.net/class/constitutionaldesignclass/CONSDES9.PDF (accessed January 24, 2011).

### 10.4.2.1 The U.S. Approach to the Precautionary Principle

The precautionary approach has been applied in the United States in decisions about health, safety, and the environment for about thirty years. This is much longer than some commentaries have suggested and earlier than the appearance of the precautionary principle in European law (de Sadeleer 2000).

As discussed in Chapter 9, in the United States—depending on the particular legislation—the government often had the initial burden of showing a potential health or environmental risk. In defending environmental and health and safety regulations before the courts, the regulatory agencies were given much discretion by their enabling legislation. For example, in the late 1970s, the standards for air pollutants were required to be set to protect the public with an "adequate" or "ample margin of safety." This meant that where the data were uncertain, precautionary measures were to be taken. The courts endorsed this posture for agencies such as the Environmental Protection Agency and the Consumer Product Safety Commission. Similarly, in the face of sparse data on the toxicity of workplace chemicals, the Department of Labor was encouraged to "err on the side of caution" in protecting workers. The endorsement by the courts of a precautionary approach is the origin of the precautionary principle in U.S. environmental law in the late 1970s. Further, for certain classes of products, such as pharmaceuticals or pesticides, the manufacturer bore the initial burden of proving the adequate safety of its products. From 1980 onward, with increasingly conservative administrations, the political appointees in leadership positions in the regulatory agencies became less willing to regulate unless the evidence was strong, and the courts made it increasingly difficult for health, safety, and environmental standards to survive court review/challenge as the courts adopted an increasingly conservative tilt (Ashford and Caldart 2008).

In today's political climate, the burden of scientific proof has posed a difficult barrier to any effort to protect health, safety, and the environment in the United States. Actions to prevent harm are usually taken only after significant proof of harm is established, at which point it may be too late to prevent significant damage. Typically, hazards are addressed by industry and government agencies one at a time, in terms of a single pesticide or chemical, rather than as broader issues such as the need to promote organic agriculture and nontoxic products or to phase out whole classes of dangerous chemicals (Raffensperger and Tickner 1999).

Three factors have brought the precautionary principle into sharp political focus in the United States today: (1) the nature of scientific uncertainty is changing; (2) pressure is increasing to base governmental action on more "rational" schemes, such as cost-benefit analysis and quantitative risk assessment, the former being an embodiment of "rational choice theory" promoted by the Chicago school of law and economics; and (3) the principle has increased in importance in both European and international law. The precautionary principle has been criticized as being both too vague and too arbitrary to form a basis for rational decision making (Applegate 2000). The assumption underlying this criticism is that any scheme not based on cost-benefit analysis and risk assessment is both irrational and without secure foundation in either science or economics. In Chapter 9, we contested that view and argued that the tenets of the precautionary principle are rational within an analytical framework that is as rigorous as uncertainties permit, and one that mirrors democratic values embodied in regulatory, compensatory, and common law.

### 10.4.2.2 European and International Legal Formulation of the Precautionary Principle

The way in which the precautionary principle is formulated has important implications for environmental protection and worker health and safety. For example, Applegate (2000) seeks to make a distinction between a precautionary approach and the precautionary principle, asserting that "with rare exceptions, U.S. law balances precaution against other considerations, most importantly costs," and hence precaution is better described as a preference rather than a principle. We find this distinction superficial, if not often inaccurate, and when understood within the context of Roman- and Napoleonic-law-based European legal systems that prefer "codes" to court-based evolution of common law, a semantic rather than a real distinction. As previously mentioned, in the United States, in a series of industry challenges to regulations, courts acknowledged that even where the scientific basis for a threat to health or the environment is not compelling, regulators have the discretion to "err on the side of caution," even in the absence of a specific statutory or legal requirement to do so, although the directive to do so is often found in the enabling legislation of some regulatory regimes (see Ashford 2007).

The precautionary inclinations of the American and Anglo-Saxon jurisprudential systems, as well as codified expressions of the precautionary principle in German law, for example, have found their way into multilateral environmental agreements and international law. Principle 15 of the Rio Declaration is perhaps the best-known statement of the precautionary principle, but it uses the word "approach" rather than "principle," and considerations of cost are present in the phrases "according to their capabilities" and "cost-effective measures." Nonetheless, it is a principle, but one to be balanced in one way or another against other principles—the same situation as in U.S. law.* Curiously, this statement of the principle is expressed in the negative—that is, uncertainty should not be used to deny or delay protection—rather than mandating protection, even in the face of uncertainty (a subtle but important distinction). The latter is more positively expressed in U.S. case law (Hornstein 1992). The debate in Europe today is not whether the precautionary principle is a principle, but whether it trumps other international law, particularly the manner in which risk assessment is addressed and is relevant to trade law involving the World Trade Organization (Majone 2001).

Because the United States signed and ratified the Rio Declaration, it could be argued that it is bound to apply the precautionary principle. However, the United States currently refuses to acknowledge the obligatory nature of the principle, preferring to relegate it to a nonbinding "approach." The situation is quite different in Europe and on the international level, where the application of the principle is presently far more advanced. The precautionary principle is one of the bases for EU community policy on the environment.

In Europe, the precautionary principle had its beginnings in the German principle of *Vorsorge*, or foresight. At the core of early conceptions of this principle was the belief that society should seek to avoid environmental damage by careful forward planning, blocking the flow of potentially harmful activities. The *Vorsorgeprinzip* developed in the early 1970s into a fundamental principle of German environmental law (balanced by principles of economic viability) and has been invoked to justify the implementation of vigorous policies to tackle acid rain, global warming, and North Sea pollution. It has also led to the development of a strong environmental industry in Germany.

According to the Global Development Research Center (GDRC 1997), the precautionary principle has seven distinct elements:

- proaction: the readiness to take action in advance of scientific proof where inaction may be socially or environmentally costly;
- cost-effectiveness of action: to include in conventional cost-benefit analysis an examination of possible environmental costs and a presumption in favor of high environmental quality;
- safeguarding ecological space: leaving wide margins of tolerance in environmental capacities;
- awarding the environment intrinsic value: the grant of natural rights which may well challenge conventional views of the humans/nature relationship;
- shifting the onus of proof: imposing a duty of care on those who intend to develop the environment;
- futurity: a recognition that the future is uncertain, but that it needs to be given due weight;
- paying for ecological debt: an implication that past ecological exploitation should be compensated.

The GDRC (1997) continues that "these elements pose fundamental challenges to the conventional legal and political weight given to environmental concerns, and also to the extent to which we have come to rely on science to provide us with answers."

However, despite the challenges to conventional legal and political systems, the precautionary principle has been widely adopted in international law. Principle 15 of the Rio Declaration was the first international statement on the precautionary approach (see the Primer on Sustainable Development on the website associated with this book). The principle states that "in order to protect the environment, the precautionary approach shall be widely applied by States according to their capabilities. Where there are threats of serious or irreversible damage, lack of full scientific certainty shall not be used as a reason for postponing cost-effective measures to prevent environmental degradation."

---

* Attempts to distinguish "approaches" from "principles" by arguing that approaches are flexible, but principles are not, fail a logical test. Principles in the law are not necessarily absolute and are not without their limits. They are sometimes in direct conflict, and which of those prevail in a particular instance requires a choice or balancing of values. For example, the freedom of speech can be said to be a fundamental principle of U.S. law, but it is not absolute and may be compromised in favor of public safety: "No one has the right to yell fire in a crowded theater."

An important aspect of the principle is the emphasis placed on acting without full scientific data. The principle requires that states take a long-term perspective on environmental measures to prevent irreversible damage and adopt an anticipatory and, perhaps, a dynamic approach to environmental law that anticipates change as new information becomes available.

The GDRC (1997) notes that the adoption of the precautionary principle in particular has been motivated by the observations that

1. environmental policy is still in the early stages of its development, compared with some other policy areas;
2. as environmental issues are no respecters of national boundaries, action needs to be agreed at an international level, and so different cultures and priorities have to be reconciled;
3. the substantive policy area includes considerable scientific complexity and real uncertainties, such as climate change, requiring a much longer term commitment than most political horizons, and hence the need for agreed principles;
4. [the precautionary principle emphasizes] the need for collective action, to protect critical life-support processes such as the assimilative capacity of natural systems;
5. [there is a] . . . need to share the burden of environmental responsibility amongst nations and groups;
6. the notion of global citizenship . . . [extends] a duty of care across both space and time to existing and future generations.

The precautionary principle provides states with a legitimate approach to addressing complex problems that are characterized by uncertainty, long time horizons, and potentially irreversible environmental damage. For example, the current European Union Sixth Environmental Action Programme (from 2002 to 2012) is firmly based on a precautionary approach. The Action Programme states:[6]

> Greater focus on prevention and the implementation of the precautionary principle is required in developing an approach to protect human health and the environment. . . .

### Principles and Overall Aims

1. The Programme constitutes a framework for the Community's environmental policy . . . with the aim of ensuring a high level of protection, taking into account the principle of subsidiarity and the diversity of situations in the various regions of the Community, and of achieving a decoupling between environmental pressures and economic growth. It shall be based particularly on the polluter-pays principle, the precautionary principle and preventive action, and the principle of rectification of pollution at source. . . .

### Objectives and priority areas for action on international issues

. . .

(f) intensify efforts at the international level to arrive at consensus on methods for the evaluation of risks to health and the environment, as well as approaches of risk management including the precautionary principle; . . .

(h) further promoting a world trade system that fully recognises Multilateral or Regional Environmental Agreements and the precautionary principle, enhancing opportunities for trade in sustainable and environmentally friendly products and services.

In addition to the EU sustainability program, incorporation of the precautionary approach can be found in various other international legal instruments. For example, the 1995 Agreement on Fish Stocks adopts the precautionary approach in Article 6: states shall apply the precautionary approach widely to conservation, management, and exploitation of straddling fish stocks and highly migratory fish stocks in order to protect the living marine resources and preserve the marine environment.[7]

The precautionary approach is also included in early examples of multilateral environmental agreements, for example, in the ninth paragraph of the preamble of the Convention on Biological Diversity, in Article 3.3 of the Convention on Climate Change, and in the preamble of the Oslo and Paris (OSPAR) Convention for the Protection of the Marine Environment of the North-East Atlantic.[8] The 1996 Protocol to the London Dumping Convention states in Article 3.1: "In implementing this protocol, Contracting Parties shall apply a precautionary approach to environmental protection . . . when there is reason to believe that wastes or other matter introduced in the marine environment are likely to cause harm even when there is no conclusive evidence to prove a causal relation between inputs and their effects."

The precautionary approach is also emerging as a widely accepted fundamental concept of national environmental laws and regulations in order to protect the environment and human health. It is also increasingly applied in court decisions.[9]

## 10.4.3 Intergenerational Equity

Concern for intergenerational equity has a deep basis in international law and is one of the premises of the precautionary principle, but its importance goes well beyond that context. The United Nations Charter, the preamble to the Universal Declaration of Human Rights, and many other human rights documents prescribe a fundamental belief in the dignity of all members of human society and in an equality that extends in time. Since World War II, states have begun to express concern for the welfare of future generations in legal mechanisms. In particular, the preamble to the 1972 Stockholm Declaration on the Human Environment refers to the object of protecting the natural environment and the well-being of future generations (see the Primer on Sustainable Development found on the website associated with this book).

Although the decisions we invoke today may affect the welfare of future generations, this element is not effectively represented in the decision-making processes of international agreements. If we are to avoid and resolve likely or even possible adverse effects on future generations, a much more proactive approach to including concepts like the precautionary principle is needed not only in developing international environmental law but also in the way nations operate domestically. For example, although the U.S. National Environmental Policy Act requires environmental impact statements that consider the long-term effects of detrimental activities, they still do so from the perspective of the present generation. In other cases, including the 1992 Convention on Environmental Assessment in a Transboundary Context, the consideration of long-term effects is not explicitly required (Weiss 1993). Rather, we need to incorporate the perspective of future generations and ask what the effects of our current actions may be.* Implementing this responsibility requires raising public consciousness and also changing our institutions and political systems, which are designed to cope with short-term issues of, at most, several years' duration.

## 10.4.4 The Public's Right to Access Information and to Participate in Environmental, Health, and Safety Matters[†]

The international community is increasingly recognizing the public's right to information regarding environmental, health, and safety issues and, furthermore, the public's right to participate actively in government and business decisions. The right to participate in decision making is now considered a fundamental human right in democratic society, and although not explicitly stated in the Universal Declaration of Human Rights or other human rights documents, it is understood that the basic rights to clean water, sufficient food, and good health are directly compromised by environmental degradation.

The principle of public participation in environmental decision making was defined and endorsed by the international community at the 1992 Earth Summit, specifically in terms of three "access" rights: (1) access to the environmental information needed to understand a decision, (2) access to the decision-making process itself, and (3) access to judicial redress if a dispute arises or a decision needs to be challenged (Mock, Vanasselt, et al. 2003).

Transparency makes noncompliance more apparent to the public, NGOs, and other countries and makes it easier for international and domestic actors to take actions to encourage and enforce accountability and compliance. The availability of information to the public concerning the extent and understanding of environmental issues can affect national behavior and thus support the effectiveness of an international treaty. In addition, as the international legal system shifts away from a state-centered, hierarchical, and static model to a system of networks composed of state and nonstate actors in a nonhierarchical and dynamic framework, citizens and NGOs gain greater influence over international as well as domestic behavior (de Sadeleer 2002, pp. 192–195). Pressure from NGOs and the public is an important mechanism for promoting implementation of and compliance with treaty obligations. Furthermore, NGOs often possess specialized information that government officials use both to monitor compliance and to prosecute violations (Goldschmidt 2002).

The most progressive policy initiative toward full public access and participation is the UN's 2001

---

\*      To the extent that markets discount events far into the future, intergenerational and future equity concerns are minimized in economic-based decision processes. For this reason, among others, law and economics represent competing paradigms for fashioning policy responses. For further discussion of this, see Chapter 13.

---

†      See also the discussion of the public's right of access to information regarding the financing of economic development and sustainable development in Section 12.3.5.2 in Chapter 12.

Åarhus Convention titled "Access to Information, Public Participation, and Access to Justice in Environmental Matters," which establishes a number of rights of the public (citizens and their associations) with regard to the environment.[10] Public authorities (at the national, regional, or local level) are to contribute to allowing these rights to become effective. The convention enunciates three basic rights:[11]

- *Access to environmental information*: The right of everyone to receive environmental information that is held by public authorities. This can include information on the state of the environment, but also on policies or measures taken, or on the state of human health and safety where this can be affected by the state of the environment. Citizens are entitled to obtain this information within one month of the request and without having to say why they require it. In addition, public authorities are obliged, under the Convention, to actively disseminate environmental information in their possession.
- *Public participation in environmental decision-making*: The right to participate from an early stage in environmental decision-making. Arrangements are to be made by public authorities to enable citizens and environmental organisations to comment on proposals for projects affecting, or plans and programmes relating to, the environment. These comments to be taken into due account in decision-making, and information on the final decisions and the underlying rationale are to be provided to the public.
- *Access to justice*: The right to challenge, in a court of law, public decisions that have been made without respecting the two aforementioned rights, or in violation of environmental law in general.

Former UN secretary general Kofi Annan described the 1998 Århus convention as "*the* most ambitious venture in the area of environmental democracy" so far undertaken under the auspices of the United Nations.[12] The convention is the first multinational environmental agreement that focuses exclusively on obligations of nations to their citizens and NGOs, thus occupying the province of human rights law, as well as environmental law.[13]

As with all multilateral international conventions, the convention had to be signed and to receive the requisite number of parliamentary ratifications of the signatories to the convention. Further, the provisions of this convention were required to be transposed into individual country laws or, in the case of the EU, transposed into EU community law and subsequently transposed into individual country laws.

Although by August 2004, fifteen of the then twenty-five EU countries had signed the convention, most of the early ratifying nations were not Western European countries, but rather the Eastern European, Caucasus and Central Asia (EECCA) countries—formerly a part of the Soviet Union. All EU countries however, were signatories to the convention and participated in its subsequent development. As discussed below, the non–Western European nations were its strongest proponents, making up for prior denial of democratic institutions and avenues for participation in government.

In the EU, the initial effort to implement the Åarhus Convention came with the issuance of three EU directives, each of which corresponds to one of these three rights: 2003/04/EC, 2003/35/EC, and 2005/370/EC. A final regulation, (EC) 1367/2006, came into force on September 28, 2006.[14]

The first right is embodied in EU Directive 2003/04/EC. This directive calls for, among other things, the creation of lists and registers of environmentally relevant information (for example, legislation, environmental plans, emissions/effluents, toxicity, and exposure information), preferably using electronic databases. (This tracks the long-standing publication of laws and regulations and the more recent publication of the Toxic Release Inventory in the United States.) EC Regulation 166/2006, which also implements the Århus Convention, established as of 2007 a European Pollutant Release and Transfer Register (PRTR), harmonizing rules under which the member states are to regularly report information on pollutants to the European Union Commission.*

The convention's second right anticipates public participation in decision making in a timely manner, that is, "from the start" of plans and programs.† The convention "invites the parties to promote public participation in the preparation of environmental policies as well as standards and legislation that may have a significant effect on the environment." The EU took the first step toward the implementation of this participatory ideal with the promulgation of Directive 2003/35/EC. While this directive provides expansive access to information and decision pro-

---

\*       Article 6 of the Åarhus Convention does not require that the party seeking particular environmental information have any special interest in obtaining it. Article 7 requires public authorities to develop information systems and procedures to ensure systematic and periodic dissemination of environmental information. In other words, the convention creates not only a right of access (if requested) but also a duty to inform.

†       Article 8 of the Åarhus Convention stipulates that proposed rules be made available to the public for comment, and that those comments be considered by the public authorities.

cesses for the making of environmental laws and regulations, access to the courts specifically to facilitate review of legal decisions taken by government (that is, judicial review) is limited to those processes provided by individual Member States.

The third right—access to justice (through access to the courts and to judicial, or at least governmental, review of decision making)—met with considerable initial resistance. In many European nations with parliamentary governments, regulations, and laws are not usually challenged through review in the courts.* Nonetheless, the EU did eventually adopt this right in Directive 2005/370/EC.

There is an important caveat about this set of directives in the EU, however: particular member states may choose to limit the extent to which these participatory rights are extended to their citizens. Accordingly, executive-branch rule making may continue to operate behind closed doors, especially in parliamentary systems.

In the United States, citizens' suits are a key element of stakeholder participation and procedural rights. Under citizens' suits, an affected citizen may take legal action against a polluter by filing a complaint in federal court. One impediment to filing a citizen suit is the issue of "standing."† Citizens may sue only for ongoing polluting violations, and only if they can demonstrate that they have a personal stake in the outcome of the case. A citizen plaintiff must show that the violations injure or threaten to injure him or her in some way.

Citizens' suits are an important part of achieving environmental sustainability because they provide access to justice for persons who are injured or are likely to be injured by violations of environmental laws. Dernbach (2004, p. 503) observes:

> The law of standing requires plaintiffs to allege injury to their uses of the environment as a result of the defendant's use or misuse of the environment. It thus suggests, in rough terms, competition between sustainable uses and unsustainable uses. But the environmental laws being enforced in citizen suits

tend to be based on a damage control model of environmental protection, largely to reduce economic and social costs. In a sustainable society, by contrast, economic development could help drive both greater environmental protection and greater social well-being. Moreover, environmental protection in a sustainable society would be based on the full range of laws and policies that affect the environment, not just environmental regulation. Yet even these laws would need to include citizen suit provisions of some kind, because citizen involvement is necessary for sustainable development.

Regarding citizen access to the courts, twenty-three cases had been heard as of September 3, 2007[15] and brought mostly by EECCA countries attempting to implement unprecedented "democratic reforms." EU member states may interpret access to justice rights differently, even to the extent of making it a paper tiger.‡ Right to participation may also not be granted by a particular member state to the fullest extent expected by other signatories to the convention, and thus rule making by the executive branch of government may be exercised without effective influence from the citizenry, especially in parliamentary systems. This may contribute to a failure to ratify the convention, even among the initial signatories (Rose-Ackerman and Halpaap 2002). Not all democracies are used to operating in the sunshine.

The participatory mechanisms in the Århus Convention are the first of their kind, having failed previously to be incorporated into the Basel Convention, the Montreal Protocol, and the Kyoto Protocol, but Århus may create a precedent for future multilateral agreements.[16] Whether the lofty goals of the Århus text are realized remains to be seen and may depend on citizen and NGO pressure.

### 10.4.5 Extended Producer Responsibility

Although extended producer responsibility (EPR) for materials and products is not on entirely firm ground, it is gaining hold in international law (Tojo, Lindhqvist, et al. 2006). It has mostly been applied to various kinds of waste—especially in the EU—often with so-called buyback provisions (see the discussion of WEEE in Section 10.18.2.3). EPR is premised on "cradle-to-grave" responsibility of producers or suppliers of chemicals, materials, and

---

* The convention recognizes that national law can limit the extent of legal challenge—or require the challenging party to demonstrate a sufficient interest in the controversy or allege a sufficient impairment of a right—if national administrative law regards these as a precondition.

† In the United States, courts are increasingly eroding citizens' right to sue polluters by acting favorably on so-called slapp suits (strategic lawsuits against public participation) where violators who are not convicted of alleged violations of environmental, health, and safety laws or regulations subsequently sue citizens or NGOs for damages as a result of bringing allegedly frivolous lawsuits (Ashford and Caldart 2008, pp. 876–877).

‡ In the United States, winning plaintiffs may be awarded attorneys' fees and court costs, while winning defendants cannot recover. European courts commonly apply two-sided fee shifting, a practice that discourages citizen suits. The convention is silent on this issue (Rose-Ackerman and Halpaap 2002, p. 37).

products to ensure that individual or commercial users handle them appropriately. In the broader context of sustainability, it can be argued that the concept should be expanded to "cradle-to-cradle" responsibility to ensure recyclability and reuse (McDonough and Braungart 1998). EPR is becoming closely identified with initiatives like the EU Integrated Product Policy and the Eco-design Directive (see the discussion in Section 10.18.5).

## 10.5 HARMONIZATION OF HEALTH, SAFETY, AND ENVIRONMENTAL STANDARDS

### 10.5.1 International and European Union Efforts to Harmonize Standards and Guidelines

The many differing policies, standards, and regulations among nations sometimes cause inconsistencies in regulatory requirements and are a source of difficulty in achieving harmonization of national approaches and standards and compliance with environmental goals. Difficulties stem both from the classical free-rider problem, where noncompliant nations carry smaller burdens than compliant nations, and from a reluctance of compliant nations to do all they are capable of to reduce environmental threats.

In 1972, the OECD adopted its Recommendations on Guiding Principles Concerning the International Aspects of Environmental Policies. These incorporated the polluter-pays principle and the principle of nondiscriminatory (internationally uniform) application of national standards. It took until 1993, following the United Nations Conference on Environment and Development (UNCED) in 1992, for the OECD to follow up with its Procedural Guidelines on Integrating Trade and Environmental Policies, which address the need for transparent standards, international consultation and cooperation, and the arbitration of disputes (Altmann 1994). Harmonization of regulatory requirements, enforcement mechanisms, and actual practices remains a major problem. Nations are extremely reluctant to give up national authority (sovereignty) in health, safety, and environmental matters either to international organizations or to international tribunals for the resolution of conflicts. Even if the International Court of Justice does hear a dispute, it has no power to enforce its findings or recommendations through either injunctive or compensatory relief (Di Leva 1991). This is in sharp contrast to the trends occurring in the globalization of trade. Standardization of technologies and trade practices is more often seen as conferring a net benefit on exporting countries.

Efforts at achieving international agreement on environment and workplace health and safety have also been led by the EU, the UN (the UNEP, the UNDP, and the United Nations Industrial Development Organization [UNIDO]), WHO, the ILO, the NAFTA side agreements, and most recently the U.S.-Jordan Free Trade Agreement, addressing environmental and labor standards, and indirectly and to a lesser extent in the General Agreement on Tariffs and Trade (GATT) overseen by the World Trade Organization (WTO).

Standards may differ in different countries and theoretically may affect international trade through the imposition of different economic burdens both on products destined for export and on transnational services. The WTO is charged with harmonizing the rules of trade to create a more uniform trading environment. The WTO tends to view national environmental standards that are more stringent than international standards (including both mandatory standards and those of the international voluntary standard-setting organizations) as nontariff trade barriers under the GATT,* while others view inadequate regulation as a subsidy to production on the backs of a less regulated country's workers, or an exploited local environment (Plofchan 1992). WTO members can challenge (and have challenged) environmental standards related to product safety (especially in food, plant, and animal products) that they consider to be barriers to trade. As a result of the Uruguay round of negotiations on the GATT, process regulations that affect the final product and are more stringent than international standards may also be deemed to constitute a nontariff trade barrier. See Chapter 11 for a more detailed discussion of the differences between viewing limitations on occupational exposure to asbestos as a permissible nontariff trade barrier to protect an importer's workers or as a "technical barrier to trade" (TBT). The tendency toward adopting the least stringent or burdensome restrictions in the harmonization of environmental, health, and safety standards implicit in the GATT may be somewhat muted in North America by the NAFTA side agreements on the environment and labor, which encourage, but do not require, the harmonization of standards.

Additionally, ILO conventions on occupational health and safety and workplace initiatives contained in the EU directives are attempts to harmonize

---

*　　See especially the discussion in Chapter 11.

worker-protection regulation (see Section 10.19 on worker health and safety). Parallel efforts exist in the EU for environmental regulation (European Parliament 1995). However, compared with ILO conventions, EU directives have historically created bare-bones principles and a general framework for environmental and worker protection without mandating performance requirements for chemical exposures. In the past, the details of the members' national legislation were not really harmonized, although a common basic framework and principles did "reduce the likelihood of erratic deviations" in the national laws of EU or OECD member states (Altmann 1994, p. 177). Under general and sometimes vague EU directives, member nations are generally free to adopt specific approaches suitable to their general needs and philosophies, and enforcement of standards remains a serious limitation on achieving stated legislative goals. More recently, EU directives have been specifying performance requirements, in line with evolving and maturing EU environmental policies, such as the Integrated Pollution Prevention and Control (IPPC) Directive (see Section 10.18) and the newer emission standards to supplement air quality standards (see Section 10.18.2.1).

Although in the United States, as well as in the European Union, regulations that established testing obligations for new chemicals were implemented in the 1970s,* initially no routine tests were required for chemicals that were already on the market—the so-called existing chemicals. The problem with these regulations, however, is that the vast majority of the substances on the market are existing substances. For example, of the high-production-volume substances above 1,000 tons per year in Europe, 1,100 are existing substances, and only 3 are new substances.[17] Therefore, the different ways of data collection and risk management will be highlighted here especially with regard to existing chemicals,† although the United States and the European Union also differ in their legal framework for new chemicals. European directives have to be implemented in national legal frameworks, and as a result, there are sometimes differences in important specifics of the legal obligations established among the member states.‡

In 1993, the European Union implemented the Existing Substances Regulation (EC Regulation 793/93) to overcome the lack of knowledge with regard to the properties (hazards) and uses of existing chemicals. The regulation requires producers, manufacturers, and importers to present a base data set for existing chemicals. The time limits were one year for substances of amounts higher than 1,000 tons per year and five years for substances of amounts higher than 10 tons per year. On the basis of these data, the European Commission developed four priority lists, which include 140 existing high-volume chemicals. For each chemical, a member state was chosen to be responsible for the risk assessment, including risk-management proposals, on the basis of all available data within the firms about hazards. The proposals of the member states have to be discussed afterward at the European level and changed where required until all member states agree with them.[18] Because there were few incentives for the firms to provide risk information—and because of the extensive regulatory procedure of risk assessment—up to the end of 2002, only sixty-four risk-assessment reports had been completed (Koch and Ashford 2006).[19] Some regulatory scholars expect the situation in the EU to improve with the new REACH initiative (discussed in Section 10.18.8), but the effectiveness of this initiative has been called into question (Koch and Ashford 2006).

The OECD has made significant strides in promoting international environmental cooperation. In 1978, the OECD instituted a special Program on the

---

* These regulations refer to chemicals that were not regulated in other acts, such as pesticides, nuclear material, food additives, drugs, cosmetics, alcohol, and tobacco.
† There are several national and international programs to overcome the lack of knowledge with regard to existing chemicals—most of them voluntary—that are not considered here.
‡ The legal framework for new chemicals in the European Union requires that those substances produced before 1981

be registered in the European Inventory of Existing Commercial Chemical Substances (EINECS) without any further testing obligations. The European Chemicals Bureau (ECB) was established in 1993 by a decision of the European Commission following a proposal by the Joint Research Centre (JRC) and the European Commission's Directorate General XI (Environment, Nuclear Safety, and Civil Protection). The ECB is a unit of the Environment Institute of the JRC, located in Ispra, Italy. Work areas of the ECB include classification and labeling of dangerous substances, new chemicals, testing methods, existing chemicals, and the import and export of dangerous substances. The EINECS contains 100,106 substances. Within the implementation of a directive in Germany, authorities were given the legal authority to require tests for existing chemicals in case of supposed hazards. This legal authority was never used. Instead, a cooperative process to work up the information deficit with regard to existing chemicals was chosen (see Koch 2003). The other member states mostly abandoned work on this problem until joint regulation in 1993. The unequal treatment of new and existing chemicals is considered to have a negative impact on the innovation of new chemicals because of the testing costs for new chemicals, which increase the incentive to find new applications for existing chemicals instead of inventing and registering new (and safer) ones. See the discussion in Section 10.18.8 of the EU REACH initiative, which replaces prior directives.

Control of Chemicals under the auspices of its Environmental Program. The chemical-control program was designed to harmonize the regulatory efforts of OECD members, to prevent the creation of technical barriers to trade, and to avoid duplication of effort and cost in chemical testing among member nations. As a result, the OECD issued guidelines for (1) assessing the risks of chemicals, including encouragement of monitoring at all stages of chemical development, use, and disposal; (2) good laboratory practice; and (3) information exchange, requiring notification and consent before export of chemicals that were banned or whose use or handling was severely restricted (Shaikh and Nichols 1984). The OECD also conducts significant research into chemical safety, including risk and accident scenarios titled emission scenario documents (ESDs).

> An Emission Scenario Document (ESD) is a document that describes the sources, production processes, pathways and use patterns with the aim of quantifying the emissions (or releases) of a chemical into water, air, soil and/or solid waste. An ESD should ideally include all the following stages: (1) production, (2) formulation, (3) industrial use, (4) professional use, (5) private and consumer use, (6) service life of product/article, (7) recovery, and (8) waste disposal (incineration, landfill). ESDs are used in risk assessment of chemicals to establish the conditions on use and releases of the chemicals that are the bases for estimating the concentration of chemicals in the environment.[20]

As of February 2011, the OECD had published the following ESDs:

Guidance Document on Emission Scenario Documents ENV/JM/MONO(2000)12 (2000)

- Wood preservatives (joint project with OECD Biocides Programme) (2000)
- Plastic Additives (2004, revised 2009)
- Water Treatment Chemicals (2004)
- Photographic Industry (2004)
- Rubber Additives (2004)
- Textile Finishing (2004)
- Leather Processing (2004)
- Photoresist Use in Semiconductor Manufacturing (2004, revised January 2010)
- Lubricants and Lubricant Additives (2004)
- Automotive Spray Application (2004)
- Metal Finishing (2004)
- Antifoulants Main Document and ANNEX (2005) (joint project with OECD Biocides Programme)

- Insecticides for Stables and Manure Storage Systems (2006) (joint project with OECD Biocides Programme)
- Kraft Pulp Mills (2006)
- Non-Integrated Paper Mills (2006)
- Recovered Paper Mills (2006)
- Insecticides, Acaricides and Products to Control Other Arthropods for Household and Professional Uses (2008) (joint project with OECD Biocides Programme)
- Complementing Guideline for Writing ESDs: The Life-Cycle Step "Service-Life" (NEW, July 2009)
- Adhesive Formulation (NEW, April 2009)
- Formulation of Radiation Curable Coatings, Inks and Adhesives (2009, revised January 2010)
- Series No. 22 Coating Industry (Paints, Lacquers and Varnishes) (NEW, July 2009)
- Series No. 23 Pulp, Paper and Board Industry (NEW, July 2009)
- Series No. 24 Transport and Storage of Chemicals (NEW, July 2009)
- Series No. 25 Chemicals Used in the Electronics Industry (NEW, September 2010)
- Series No. 26 Blending of Fragrance Oils into Commerical and Consumer Products (NEW, September 2010)

Further publications are in progress for other chemical releases.

In addition to the dissemination of ESDs, the OECD also discussed the international harmonization of effluent, emission, and waste-treatment and disposal regulations/practices, but no binding instrument has yet emerged. The OECD also has responsibility for the Screening Information Data Sets (SIDS), an international voluntary testing program launched in 1989 that is aimed at developing a base set of health/environmental toxicity, exposure, and fate data on high-production-volume commercial chemicals and spreads the cost of testing among industrialized countries. The International Programme for Chemical Safety (IPCS), funded by the ILO, the UNEP, and WHO, is charged with overseeing completion of action items identified in Agenda 21 at the UN Conference on Environment and Development (the Earth Summit). Its self-description is as follows: "IPCS INCHEM is an invaluable tool for those concerned with chemical safety and the sound management of chemicals. Produced through cooperation between the International Programme on Chemical Safety (IPCS) and the Canadian Centre for Occupational Health and Safety (CCOHS), IPCS INCHEM directly responds to one of the Intergovernmental Forum on Chemical Safety (IFCS) priority actions to consolidate current, internationally peer-reviewed chemical safety-related publications and database records from international bodies, for public access."[21]

Difficulty still exists in achieving international consensus on the IPCS's Chemical Classification System for human toxicity criteria for exposures by inhalation encountered in transportation, the workplace, the environment, and consumer use. However, with increasing access to information such as the IPCS INCHEM database, progressive dialogue is taking place to resolve these differences in classification (see Section 10.19 on international efforts to improve occupational health and safety).

In an attempt to get the international community to take environmental standards and guidelines more seriously, the UN Commission on Crime Prevention and Social Justice adopted a resolution in 1998 calling for increased use of criminal law to prosecute environmental crimes. The enforceability of this convention has recently been obscured by the high-profile threats of terrorism and international security as the main priorities of the UN Commission on Crime Prevention and Social Justice. Given the inextricable link between human rights and the protection of the environment, securing a terror-free global climate is a positive outcome; however, it is also important that the commission place greater emphasis on prosecuting those who endanger both humans and the environment through their illegal and harmful activities. In 2007, the EU proposed a directive on the use of criminal law to protect the environment. The directive "defines a minimum set of serious environmental offences and obliges Member States to provide for criminal sanctions for this type of offence when committed voluntarily or through serious negligence."[22]

There are several principal international programs that are attempting to harmonize health, safety, and environmental standards. There are also many different kinds of standards, both voluntary guidelines and binding regulations (Altmann 1994). Some pertain to the safety of products that are used domestically but could also be exported. Product standards address product content, labeling, packaging, and recycling. EU directives on the classification, packaging, and labeling of dangerous substances, the marketing and use of dangerous substances, phasing out PCBs, recycling packaging waste, and road transport of hazardous materials are constantly being updated (see the discussion of the GHS system in Section 10.6). Those products that are exported and

present threats to the environment, health, and safety in the receiving countries are addressed in Section 10.6. Other standards refer more to the way products are made or used in industrial or agricultural applications, that is, process standards. These standards serve to regulate hazards from manufacturing, production, and industrial or agricultural use. Included are occupational safety and health regulations; pesticide application; and effluents, emissions, and waste from energy systems, extraction industries, manufacturing, and agriculture.

In 1994, the UNEP issued a Code of Ethics on the International Trade in Chemicals as a "voluntary" guide to standards of conduct in chemical production and management. The code's three sections address (1) a commitment to improved health, safety, and environmental protection; (2) a commitment to testing and assessment, quality assurance, classification, packaging and labeling, information exchange, education and training, and advertising and marketing; and (3) periodic monitoring and follow-up of the parties' voluntary compliance, including the UNEP's role in reporting progress on the code's implementation.

The conventional approach to chemicals policy prescribes a sequential process that includes three steps: (1) producing or collecting risk information, (2) performing a risk assessment or characterization, and (3) risk-management practices. Koch and Ashford (2006) have argued that this sequential process is too static or linear and spends too many resources on searching for or generating information about present hazards, in comparison with searching for and generating information related to safer alternatives, which include input substitution, final-product reformulation, and/or process changes. Instead, they recommend that the production of risk information necessary for risk assessment, on the one hand, and the search for safer alternatives, on the other hand, should be approached simultaneously in two parallel quests. Overcoming deficits in hazard-related information and knowledge about risk-reduction alternatives must take place in a more synchronized manner than is currently being practiced. In contrast, the European Union's efforts to reform chemicals policy and implement the REACH (Registration, Evaluation, and Authorization of Chemicals) initiative are focused on improving the production and assessment of risk information with regard to existing chemicals (see Section 10.18.8).

In summary, the many differing approaches, policies, standards, and regulations among nations sometimes cause inconsistencies in regulatory requirements and are a source of difficulty in achieving harmonization of national approaches and standards in attaining compliance with environmental goals. A more comprehensive and synchronized international system for chemical safety is necessary for effective management of the inherent risks. Some progress has been made toward meeting this need as a result of the development of a ten-year Framework of Programs on Sustainable Consumption and Production launched in 2003 following commitments made at the 2002 World Summit in Johannesburg. The UNEP is the lead agency for the so-called Marrakech Process,[23] which seeks to implement sustainable consumption and production (SCP) through[24]

- adoption and implementation of policies aimed at promoting sustainable consumption and production, including integrating SCP issues into national development strategies;
- investment in cleaner production, eco-efficiency and sustainable products and services;
- technology transfer and capacity building to increase eco-efficiency;
- awareness-raising campaigns and consumer information tools;
- promoting the collection and exchange of best practices, and know-how;
- encouraging industry to improve social and environmental performance;
- encouraging financial institutions to incorporate sustainable development considerations into their decision-making processes;
- providing training programs to small and medium-sized enterprises (SMEs); and
- promoting public procurement policies that encourage development and diffusion of environmentally-sound goods and services.

Although the United States has been slow to respond, the Marrakech Process has led to a renewed European Sustainable Development Strategy focusing on SCP as a key objective (Breukelaar and Banerjee 2007) through a green public procurement policy[25] and the Integrated Product Policy (see Section 10.18.5).

### 10.5.2 Voluntary Industry Efforts to Harmonize Practices

In contrast to the legislative approach in encouraging environmental compliance, the International Standards Organization (ISO), a private non-governmental organization, has instead been concentrating on voluntary schemes to certify companies' compliance with voluntary environmental management standards. The ISO 14000 standard includes principles,

systems, and supporting techniques an organization should consider when setting up an environmental management system (EMS). The ISO 14001 environmental management system is meant to develop a systematic management approach to the environmental concerns of an organization. The goal of this approach is continual improvement in environmental management. An ISO 14001 environmental management strategy allegedly can reduce costs, improve efficiency, and secure a competitive advantage for an organization. Section 10.18.7 gives a detailed discussion of the European Eco-Management and Audit Scheme (EMAS) and ISO 14001.*

In the United States, the Coalition for Environmentally Responsible Economies (CERES) works with environmental, investor, and advocacy groups committed to environmental principles, worker health and safety, and sustainable development with the intention of advocating that business and industry incorporate these ideas into their practices.[26] The CERES Principles include the following:

- Protection of the Biosphere
- Sustainable Use of Natural Resources
- Reduction and Disposal of Wastes
- Energy Conservation
- Risk Reduction
- Safe Products and Services
- Environmental Restoration
- Informing the Public
- Management Commitment
- Audits and Reports

By holding businesses accountable to these principles through a coalition network, CERES promotes an ethic of public accountability and continuous progress in environmental performance.

CERES is to be contrasted with the voluntary initiative of the U.S. Chemical Manufacturers Association's (now the American Chemistry Council) Responsible Care Program (originally launched in Canada in 1985) that was devised in 1988 in response to a decline in public confidence in the chemical industry and a threat of more stringent regulations. (Karkkainen 2001, p. 305) describes its explicit goal:

> To repair the chemical industry's reputation by "promoting continuous improvement in member

---

* Although ISO 14000/14001 and EMAS are "voluntary" in the sense that it is up to a firm to choose to join either, the EMAS system is actually regulated by the EU once a company has joined. See Section 10.18.7.

company environmental, health, and safety performance" and "assisting members' demonstration of improvements in performance to critical public audiences." The core idea animating Responsible Care is that by establishing a regime of peer monitoring and mutual accountability to industry "best practice" standards, the industry can regulate itself effectively but flexibly. Peer pressure would cause laggards to come up to industry-wide norms, while continuously raising the "best practice" bar through innovation, benchmarking, and inter-firm competition. As implemented to date, however, the Responsible Care regime falls short of that ideal. Responsible Care enlisted member firms to comply voluntarily with six industry written codes of best environmental management practices. But the Responsible Care codes were expressed in quite general narrative language and initially lacked mechanisms to ensure transparency and accountability.

Beyond North America, the International Council of Chemical Associations (ICCA) appears to have embarked on a more serious effort. It describes its Global Product Strategy (GPS), launched in 2006 along with its Responsible Care Global Charter, as follows:[27]

Key components of the program to improve product stewardship include:

- guidelines for product stewardship, to share best practices within the chemical industry and with customer industries;
- a tiered process for completing risk characterization and risk management actions for chemicals in commerce;
- product stewardship performance with a special focus on working directly with downstream customers of the chemical industry (the "value chain");
- exploration of a potential partnership with an intergovernmental organization to enhance global product stewardship, and,
- greater transparency, including ways to make relevant product stewardship information available to the public.

ICCA will be working with its member associations and their member companies to advance this program in the years ahead.

In Europe, the chemical industry, represented by the European Chemical Industry Council (CEFIC), is active in ICCA.[28] However, the CEFIC has been criticized as being pressured by the U.S. chemical industry to influence earlier drafts of the REACH proposal, resulting in a much weaker initiative than originally proposed (Koch and Ashford 2006).[29]

## 10.5.3 The Implications of Having Different Standards and Practices: Increased Capital Movement to Pollution Havens versus the Porter Hypothesis

For the past ten years, environmentalists and the trade policy community have engaged in an intense debate over the environmental consequences of regulation. The parties differ greatly in their trust of market forces and value the environment differently. Two essentially different views emerge:

1. Stringent regulations in developed countries shift polluting industries to the developing world, a "pollution haven" away from the controls of the regulating country.*

2. In contrast, the Porter hypothesis† suggests that environmental policy and regulation improve both

---

\* As discussed previously in Chapter 5, the rationale for trade is, in fact, to exploit differences between nations; if there were no differences, trade would be pointless. Although the comparative advantage of nations is typically based on natural resource endowments and the skills and availability of labor, it can also be extended to include differences in national environmental and labor standards (Sinden 2007). From an economic perspective, it can be argued that if the standards in each nation were *efficient*—that is, they reflected the true *preferences* of citizens—then trade that exploits a comparative advantage in lower standards would actually be welfare enhancing for all trading parties. Such an argument that favors free trade without the need to raise/harmonize standards fails to acknowledge the reality that regulations in developing (and developed) regions are often inefficient—that is, the "wealth effect" lowers the stringency of standards because there is less willingness/ability to pay for better working/environmental conditions, and there are political/market failures that lower the actual standards beyond those differences and hence contribute to inefficient standards (Gitterman 2004; Sinden 2007). The result of inefficient standards is a welfare loss in the host nation. Therefore, increasing the volume of trade would further promote a loss of welfare. Sinden (2007) argues that the solution to this problem is the upward harmonization of standards. However, harmonizing standards to the most stringent *existing* standard may not be sufficient to address many critical environmental problems and ignores changes in technology that lead to new dynamic efficiency.

† The Porter hypothesis was proposed to explain why firms would find it in their economic advantage to invest in compliance technology ahead of others in an industry (Porter and van der Linde 1995a, 1995b). In a number of MIT studies beginning in 1979, it was found that regulation could stimulate significant fundamental changes in product and process technology that benefited the industrial innovator, provided the regulations were stringent and focused (Ashford, Ayers, et al. 1985). This empirical work was published twelve years earlier (Ashford and Heaton 1983) than the emergence of the much weaker Porter hypothesis, which argued that firms on the cutting edge of developing and implementing pollution reduction would benefit economically through "innovation offsets" by being first movers to comply with regulation. Perhaps paradoxically, in Europe, where regulation was arguably less stringent and was formulated with industry consensus, regulation was not found to stimulate much significant innovation (Kemp

the environment and competitiveness. This hypothesis also suggests that stringent regulations will encourage technological innovation among polluting firms, thereby decreasing the rate at which the environment is damaged.

Porter claims that environmental regulation of businesses will actually give the businesses a competitive advantage over their counterparts in nations with less stringent regulation because it forces them to innovate,* and that by changing their production processes, the businesses will actually lower their production costs (Porter and van der Linde 1995b). If the Porter hypothesis is true, environmental regulation will increase production and environmental standards through easy legislative action. For example, China actively prefers investments in coal-fired power plants that apply clean combustion technologies. Israel has also apparently adopted EU pesticide standards in order to get increased access to European Union markets (Tietenberg 2003).

A contrasting view of the effects of stringent regulation is related to the creation of pollution havens. It is argued that stricter environmental regulations in one country will offer an incentive to businesses operating within that country to move to another country with less environmental concerns—so-called capital flight. Generally, the countries that are said to be willing to accept the polluting producers for the least amount of compensation are the third-world countries. This is no longer just an issue of relocating pollution; it is also an issue of environmental justice. The possible advantages of lower pollution-control costs might also be offset by a firm's relocating costs and reduced competitiveness because of poorer infrastructure and less skilled labor, resulting in lower productivity (Bredahl, Ballenger, et al. 1996). With some exceptions, there is scarce evidence for capital flight stimulated by lower environmental standards.

---

1997). Analysis of the U.S. situation since the earlier MIT studies reinforces the strategic usefulness of properly designed and implemented regulation complemented by economic incentives (Strasser 1997). See also Reinhardt (1999).

\* See the discussion of "first-mover" advantages of firms that respond first to new environmental requirements, articulated independently by Ashford and colleagues (Ashford, Ayres, et al. 1985; Ashford and Heaton 1983; Ashford, Heaton, et al. 1979) and Porter and van der Linde (1995a, 1995b), who argued, respectively, that there are "ancillary benefits" or "innovation offsets" to compliance costs for the firm because of the benefits of correcting production inefficiencies resulting from pollution. These may be of great economic benefit to innovating firms.

## 10.5.4 Reaching Consensus on Risk-Assessment Methodologies and Risk-Management Rationales

There has been international consensus that risk assessment and risk management are key aspects of developing international environmental, health, and safety law. Risk assessments include detailed quantitative and qualitative understandings of risk and its physical, social, economic, and environmental factors and consequences.

**Risk assessment** is the process used to evaluate the degree and probability of harm to human health and the environment from such stressors as pollution or habitat loss. The risk assessment process, as proposed by the National Academy of Sciences [NRC 1983], consists of:

- **Exposure Assessment**—describing the populations or ecosystems exposed to stressors and the magnitude, duration, and spatial extent exposure;
- **Hazard Identification**—identifying adverse effects (e.g., short-term illness, cancer) that may occur from exposure to environmental stressors;
- **Dose-Response Assessment**—determining the toxicity or potency of stressors; and
- **Risk Characterization**—using the data collected in the first three steps to estimate and describe the effects of human or ecological exposure to stressors.

**Risk Management** entails determining whether and how risks should be managed or reduced. It is based on the results of the risk assessment as well as other factors (e.g., public health, social, and economic factors). Risk management options include pollution prevention or control technologies to reduce or eliminate the pollutant or other stressor on the environment. The environmental or public health impacts resulting from risk management decisions must then be monitored so that any necessary adjustments can be made.[30]

Improvement of the methods of risk assessment has become a matter of worldwide interest in recent years, especially in terms of sharing information regarding risk-assessment practices and results. The OECD maintains a risk-assessment methodology database that includes the following information:[31]

- Types of chemicals (new industrial chemicals, existing industrial chemicals, pesticides (agricultural), biocides (nonagricultural), environmental pollutants, others)
- Areas of assessment (human health, environment)

- Human health risk-assessment components (hazard identification, dose/response, exposure assessment, risk characterization, all four components)

- Human health endpoints covered (carcinogenicity, reproductive/developmental toxicity, mutagenicity, neurotoxicity, immunotoxicity, general noncancer, other endpoints)

- Types of human health data used (human, animal, in vitro, QSAR, [Quantitative Structure Activity Relationship]

- Outcome of human health risk assessment (qualitative, quantitative, modeling)

- Human exposure covered (occupational, environmental, consumer)

- Routes of human exposure (inhalation, ingestion, dermal, multimedia)

- Types of human exposure covered (direct, indirect)

- Methods for establishing internal dose (measured, modeled, reconstructed)

- Environmental organisms covered (freshwater organisms; marine organisms; terrestrial organisms)

- Routes of environmental exposure covered (air, water, soil, biota, sewage-treatment plants)

- Scenarios/models for estimation of release/environmental exposure (fate, local models, regional models, classification)

This database provides a central bank of information for interested parties with easy and rapid access to sources of information on risk-assessment methodologies used by countries and by organizations involved in chemicals risk assessment and also aids in educating those working in hazard/risk assessment to become more familiar with the variety of hazard/risk-assessment methodologies. There are now numerous international and national databases holding valuable risk-assessment information in a wide variety of environmental, health, and safety topic areas. The U.S. EPA, one of the leaders in driving risk assessment from the 1980s to the present, has vast stores of risk information and continues to develop new initiatives to manage risk.[32]

K. Barrett and Tickner (2001, p. 5) articulate some important limitations of risk assessment:

The technique of risk assessment has evolved over the years, but the general framework for conducting risk assessments remains the same: hazard identification, dose-response assessment, exposure assessment, and risk characterization. . . . Risk assessment can be a useful tool for predicting outcomes in data rich circumstances, when the nature of the harm is specific and well-characterized and probabilities are well established. It provides a standardized, structured methodology for decision-making that has its foundations in science. It provides an aura of repeatability, objectivity, and precision.

However, over-reliance on risk assessment as the sole analytical technique in environmental and health decision-making can limit the ability of decision-makers to anticipate and prevent consumer risks. . . . Specific limitations of risk assessment include:

Risk assessments are generally used for quantifying and analyzing problems rather than trying to solve or prevent them. Quantitative risk assessments are generally used to set "safe" levels of exposure that correspond to an agency (not societally) predefined "acceptable" level of risk, and assume that a population or individual has a certain assimilative capacity.

Risk assessments tend to limit the type of information used in examining environmental and health hazards. Decision-making is often expert-driven, and does not include public perceptions and priorities, multidisciplinary perspectives, and cumulative effects. This approach tends to exclude information that is important when dealing with complex systems and interactions.

To fit models, risk assessments limit consideration of uncertainty. When uncertainty is described, it often includes only "technical uncertainties". . . . Model uncertainty, political uncertainty and indeterminacy are rarely acknowledged. Risk assessments are based on numerous—often implicit and non-scientific risk management assumptions, for example about exposures, human behavior, and chemical effects. While the process of risk assessment is considered formulaic due to these assumptions, the outcomes of risk assessments on the same problem (and using similar data sets) can differ by several orders of magnitude (Ballar and Dailer 1999). Thus, the processes of risk assessment and risk management cannot easily be separated.

Beyond risk-assessment methodologies, nations and even different regulatory regimes within a nation are likely to continue to differ in risk-management philosophies, from using cost-benefit analysis as a decision rationale to using health-based rationales with clear and convincing scientific evidence and to liberal application of the precautionary approach. Cost-benefit approaches may become standardized, but probably not regulatory approaches. Consider, for example, the U.S.-EU dispute on hormones in beef (see Section 11.2.5 in Chapter 11).

After years of criticism levied at the conduct of risk assessment, the U.S. National Academies of Sciences convened an expert panel to provide technical guidance that moves beyond the 1983 "red book" (NRC 1983) in order to advance risk assessment to a new level. The December 2008 report *Science and*

*Decisions: Advancing Risk Assessment* (NRC 2008) departs somewhat from the classic sequential approach whereby risk assessment is pursued first, followed by risk management.* A new Phase I begins the process and frames the problem by asking "What options exist for altering [the adverse environmental] conditions?" and "What risk and other technical assessments are necessary to evaluate the possible risk management options?" Although this is a good step forward, the recommendation to undertake a risk-reduction "options analysis" up front does not go far enough. The emerging analytical approach—identify existing risk-reduction options → undertake risk assessment → evaluate and implement risk management—is still sequential. Furthermore, the risk-reduction options should include not only *existing* technologies that could be *adopted*, but also *new* technologies that could be *developed*.† However, European‡ and international approaches have not adopted even this latest U.S. extension of traditional risk assessment.

### 10.5.4.1 The OECD Role in Chemical Safety and Risk Assessment

Worldwide annual chemical production was estimated to be some U.S. $1.5 trillion in 1998 and $2.2 trillion in 2004 with projections to $2.7 trillion in 2015 (approximately 75 percent of it originating in the OECD area) and to provide some 12 million jobs (OECD 2001, 2009). Within this industry, the OECD has a significant role in determining policies on chemical health and safety. The OECD Chemicals Programme, now part of the Environment, Health, and Safety (EHS) Programme, was established in 1971 to increase the OECD's capacity to foster international cooperation in order to help ensure product safety. Its work on chemicals and other topics in the fields of the environment, health, and safety is intended to assist member countries by developing harmonized policies and high-quality instruments for use in the protection of health and the environment, avoiding duplication of effort among countries,

and minimizing nontariff barriers to trade. As the OECD Environment Program (OECD 2001, p. 26) explains:

> When industry has provided public authorities with the results of the safety-testing of a chemical, the **potential risks** of its use have to be assessed and, if necessary, managed. The EHS Programme develops and **harmonises methods** to do this—on, for example, questions of environmental exposure to, or the aquatic effects of, chemicals, or the exposure of workers applying pesticides. The OECD is also assisting its Member countries in developing **risk-management approaches** such as analysis of socio-economic factors and risk communication. The OECD has developed **harmonized criteria** for classifying hazardous chemicals which will be applied globally through the United Nations. The new criteria will simplify risk communication for workers and consumers alike. The OECD is also developing harmonized criteria for the classification of chemical mixtures. The Pesticide Programme is helping OECD countries **share the work of pesticide registration** by harmonising both the way in which the industry submits data to the regulatory authorities, and the way in which regulators produce review reports. The Pesticide Programme also helps Member countries to find ways of **reducing the risks associated with pesticide use** and enables them to stay informed about other countries' activities. Work with similar objectives has started for **biocides**.
>
> The EHS Programme is also developing **harmonised methodologies for assessing the safety of the products of modern biotechnology**, such as genetically modified crops and micro-organisms, and of novel foods and feeds. There is intense public interest in these, and the OECD data is made widely available through the **"Bio-Track On-Line"** system. . . .[33] **Information** on releases into the environment of genetically modified organisms (GMOs) and the commercialization of biotechnology products is thus **easily accessible to governments, industry and the public.** The OECD also provides a forum where government and industry experts, worker representatives, international organisations and environmental interest groups can **exchange information and experience on chemical accidents**. The OECD has established guiding principles for the prevention of, preparedness for and response to chemical accidents; these principles are now also widely used outside OECD countries.

In addition to these efforts, the OECD has developed safety performance indicators that help countries measure progress in working toward safe chemical plants and warehouses. The Chemical Accident Risk Assessment Thesaurus (CARAT)—initiated by the OECD Working Group on Chemical Accidents—recognized the difficulty in communi-

---

* Actually, the traditional risk-assessment and risk-management process includes the three sequential steps of (1) producing or collecting risk-relevant information, (2) performing a risk assessment, and (3) evaluating and implementing risk-management practices.

† See the discussion in Section 9.2.6 in Chapter 9 recommending a synchronized or parallel process involving risk assessment and technology options on a *comparative* basis.

‡ Even within the European Union, let alone internationally, risk assessment procedures for the emerging challenges for risk assessment posed by endocrine-disrupting chemicals differ in different regulatory frameworks (Beronius et al. 2009).

cating among the member countries about risk assessments of hazardous installations. This difficulty was, in large part, based on the fact that certain terms have different meanings in different countries and cultures. Even different organizations within a single country sometimes use different terms to address the same concept. Unfortunately, the CARAT database was discontinued in 2005, although it can still be obtained on a CD.[34]

The OECD's effort to develop policy recommendations on the social and distributive implications of environmental policies applied in member countries is likely to contribute to better coherence and integration of economic, environmental, and social policies. Further, the impact of environmental policies—especially policies relating to climate change—on employment is becoming an area of special interest (ETUC, ISTAS, et al. 2007; OECD 2004).

## 10.6 INTERNATIONAL TRADE OF HAZARDOUS PRODUCTS

Although the United States does not have a comprehensive system for disseminating information on hazardous exports, some attempts have been made to establish notification schemes under existing laws (Ashford and Ayers 1985).* At present, seven U.S. federal statutes forbid the export of certain banned or significantly restricted substances unless the recipient country has been notified of the regulatory status of the substance in the United States. These statutes apply to toxic substances in general, pesticides, pharmaceuticals, consumer products, flammable fabrics, and waste. The United States is considering implementing the UN's Globally Harmonized System (GHS) for Classification and Labeling of Chemicals (see the discussion below).[35]

The UN's Economic Commission for Europe has launched the Globally Harmonized System (GHS) for Classification and Labeling of Chemicals,[36] including a harmonized set of classification criteria for physical, health, and environmental hazards and a comparable set of hazard-communication tools (label elements and safety data sheets for workers).[37] The GHS has been endorsed by the 1992 UN Conference on Environment and Development (UNCED) and supported by the Intergovernmental Forum on Chemical Safety (IFCS) and the 2002 World Summit on Sustainable Development (WSSD). On September 3, 2008, a large majority of the European Parlia-

ment supported a new regulation on classification, labeling, and packaging of substances and mixtures, which seeks to align existing EU legislation with the GHS. This new regulation on classification, labeling, and packaging (the CLP Regulation) will ensure that the same hazards will be described and labeled in the same way all around the world. By using internationally agreed classification criteria and labeling elements, it is expected to facilitate trade and to contribute to global efforts to protect humans and the environment from hazardous effects of chemicals. The new act will complement the REACH Regulation on the registration, evaluation, authorization, and restriction of chemicals.

The CLP Regulation will, after a transitional period, replace the current rules on classification, labeling, and packaging of substances (Directive 67/548/EEC) and mixtures (Directive 1999/45/EC). After the regulation enters into force, the deadline according to the new rules is December 1, 2010, for substance classification and June 1, 2015, for mixtures.[38]

Council Regulation 793/93/EEC, "Evaluation and Control of the Risks of Existing Substances," requires reporting to the European Chemicals Bureau by manufacturers and importers in the EU of some 3,900 high-production-volume chemicals (over 1,000 tons annually) on the EINECS inventory before June 4, 1995, and additional reports thereafter for some 10,000 substances manufactured or imported in quantities between 10 and 1,000 tons per year. The reporting is facilitated by an electronic reporting system using the Harmonized Electronic Data Set (HEDSET). Individual firm HEDSET reports are collected in the International Uniform Chemical Information Database (IUCLID). The HEDSET reporting program can also be used to submit data to the OECD Existing Chemicals Programme.

Safeguards that are based on notification systems alone assume that the recipient countries will fulfill their implied responsibility to ensure that technology is transferred with minimum risk to the health of their citizenry and the environment. This applies both to the importation of products, plant, and equipment and to blueprints for manufacturing, energy facilities, and transportation systems that might be indiscriminately used to construct systems inappropriate for the recipient country.

Going a step beyond mere notification, a panel of the UN Commission on Sustainable Development expressed a "strong sentiment" for a right-to-know policy of prior informed consent (PIC), to be required before shipments of hazardous materials could

---

\* Food safety and biotechnology products are addressed in Sections 10.14 and 10.15, respectively.

be received from exporting countries. This sentiment ripened into the 1985 International Code of Conduct on the Distribution and Use of Pesticides by the Food and Agriculture Organization (FAO) of the UN and the 1987 London Guidelines for the Exchange of Information on Chemicals in International Trade by the United Nations Environment Programme. The latter applies to all chemicals and pesticides. The former was ultimately superseded by the 1998 Rotterdam Convention on the Prior Informed Consent (PIC) Procedure for Certain Hazardous Chemicals and Pesticides in International Trade (see below). The *Codex Alimentarius* addressing banned or restricted pesticides has been supplemented by the Consolidated List of Products whose consumption and/or sale has been banned, withdrawn, severely restricted, or, in the case of pharmaceuticals, not approved by governments (Sands 2003).

Whether under notification schemes alone or with prior informed consent, in order to fulfill its responsibility to its citizens in practice, each recipient country would need to develop or have access to appropriate information systems/databases corresponding to those developed or accessed by donor countries or international organizations, which can facilitate the assessment of the efficacy, health, and environmental effects of various technologies, taking into consideration the national demographics and unique environment of the recipient country. In order to make full use of these information systems, capability in risk assessment (RA) is essential. In addition, the information systems in the recipient countries must be flexible and capable of keeping pace with rapid growth rates in developing countries. But more is needed. The undertaking of technology options analysis (TOA; see Section 9.2.6 in chapter 9) to identify alternate inputs; final products; manufacturing, industrial, and agricultural processes; and transportation and energy systems is also essential. Identifying superior technologies that could be adopted or developed, rather than doing damage control by performing assessment of existing technologies in use, is a necessary proactive approach and one not currently required by national or international regulations (UNEP 1991).

The recent The United Nations Economic Commission for Europe (UNECE) Århus Convention on access to information, public participation in decision making, and access to justice in environmental matters further promotes and ensures the role of the public in making decisions about the environment by providing it access to information (see Section 10.4.4

on public participation).[39] The implementation of the Århus Convention is of high importance for all European countries because it contributes not only to the overall effort to regulate better environmental protection but also to the process of better protection of human rights and of further democratization. If countries want to implement regulations, they should, among other things, harmonize both their legislation and their practice (of the public authorities, the judicial system, the mass media, research institutions, and other entities) with the standards set by the convention.

The Rotterdam Convention on the Prior Informed Consent (PIC) Procedure for Certain Hazardous Chemicals and Pesticides in International Trade became international law in February 2004. The convention creates legally binding obligations for the implementation of the previously voluntary prior informed consent (PIC) procedure, initiated by the UNEP and the FAO in 1989 and ending on February 24, 2006. The major provisions of the convention are as follows:[40]

> The Convention covers pesticides and industrial chemicals that have been banned or severely restricted for health or environmental reasons by Parties and which have been notified by Parties for inclusion in the PIC procedure. One notification from each of two specified regions triggers consideration of addition of a chemical to Annex III of the Convention, Severely hazardous pesticide formulations that present a hazard under conditions of use in developing countries or countries with economies in transition may also be nominated for inclusion in Annex III.
>
> There are 40 chemicals listed in Annex III of the Convention and subject to the PIC procedure, including 24 pesticides, 4 severely hazardous pesticide formulations and 11 industrial chemicals. Many more chemicals are expected to be added in the future. The Conference of the Parties decides on the inclusion of new chemicals. Once a chemical is included in Annex III, a "decision guidance document" (DGD) containing information concerning the chemical and the regulatory decisions to ban or severely restrict the chemical for health or environmental reasons, is circulated to all Parties.
>
> Parties have nine months to prepare a response concerning the future import of the chemical. The response can consist of either a final decision (to allow import of the chemical, not to allow import, or to allow import subject to specified conditions) or an interim response. Decisions by an importing country must be trade neutral (i.e., apply equally to domestic production for domestic use as well as to imports from any source).

The import decisions are circulated and exporting country Parties are obligated under the Convention to take appropriate measure to ensure that exporters within its jurisdiction comply with the decisions.

The Convention promotes the exchange of information on a very broad range of chemicals. It does so through:

- the requirement for a Party to inform other Parties of each national ban or severe restriction of a chemical;
- the possibility for a Party which is a developing country or a country in transition to inform other Parties that it is experiencing problems caused by a severely hazardous pesticide formulation under conditions of use in its territory; ROP
- the requirement for a Party that plans to export a chemical that is banned or severely restricted for use within its territory, to inform the importing Party that such export will take place, before the first shipment and annually thereafter;
- the requirement for an exporting Party, when exporting chemicals that are to be used for occupational purposes, to ensure that an up-to-date safety data sheet is sent to the importer; and
- labeling requirements for exports of chemicals included in the PIC procedure, as well as for other chemicals that are banned or severely restricted in the exporting country.

## 10.7 INTERNATIONAL TRADE OF HAZARDOUS EQUIPMENT AND PLANT

European Union Directives 89/392/EEC and 91/368/EEC restrict the free movement of machinery and personal protective equipment, respectively, that do not comply with health and safety requirements affecting workers, consumers, and animals (see the annexes to these directives, which set out the basic health and safety requirements regarding the design and construction of machinery) (European Trade Union Technical Bureau for Health and Safety 1991). These essential requirements theoretically cover all types of risks to which workers may be exposed at the various stages of the machine's life, that is, its installation, operation, adjustment, maintenance, cleaning, repairs, and transport. Conforming machinery bears the "EC" mark. For certain machines regarded as particularly dangerous, third party certification is compulsory in the absence of harmonized standards before

the machine can be marketed. Notably missing in these provisions in practice, however, are ergonomic requirements for machinery and equipment and technology-based restrictions for industrial production technology that uses or produces harmful chemicals. Although the export of nonconforming technology may be policed in the context of EU trade, it has been suggested that the importing country—especially a non-EU country—is in the best position to restrict undesirable trade through its ministries of commerce, industry, and trade (Ashford and Ayers 1985). Additionally, because equipment and machinery may be used in many ways unanticipated by the original supplier or exporting country, the importing country should exercise scrutiny (European Safety Newsletter 1996). Information on possible adverse effects from those technologies is essential for proper policing by the importing country. Following up on plans to offer guidelines that would address what information on environmental impacts the exporters of technology should provide to importers, the Advisory Committee to the UNEP Environmental Technology Assessment (EnTA) Programme has developed approaches for technology assessment leading to cleaner production where the technology involves the production or use of harmful chemicals.[41]

In order to ensure that production technologies imported into a country meet a minimum degree of environmental performance, it could be required that joint ventures or foreign-owned companies meet the same environmental controls as "at home." This is the practice already required by the OECD Council Acts for Waste Management.

## 10.8 TRANSFER OF TECHNICAL KNOW-HOW

By themselves, guidelines on the export of hazardous products, equipment, and plant are inadequate to prevent the local construction of dangerous production facilities and manufacturing of hazardous products. The Union Carbide plant in Bhopal, India, designed after a corresponding plant in Institute, West Virginia, is a notorious example. Here the transfer of technical knowledge embodied in the plant design is not easily amenable to strict control. Voluntary promises of multinational corporations that are signatories to the CERES Principles (see Section 10.5.2) and agree to operate plants according to the stricter home-based regulatory standards may help.

## 10.9 INTERNATIONAL TRADE OF HAZARDOUS WASTE

The transfer of hazardous waste is now covered by the 1989 Basel Convention on the Control of Transboundary Movement of Hazardous Wastes and Their Disposal (90/170/EEC) and by a regulation addressing its implementation (259/93/EEC). Transboundary movement and disposal of hazardous and "other" waste are prohibited unless there is written consent by all countries involved, including transit countries. Further, the exporting nation must be certain that wastes will be managed by the receiving country in an environmentally sound manner. However, the lack of enforcement and verification mechanisms, and inadequate provisions for responsibility and liability for inappropriate disposal of wastes, are major weaknesses (Hilz 1992). Only 64 of the 107 countries that have signed the 1989 convention have ratified it. Dissatisfacton with the 1989 Basel Convention lead to its amendment.

### The Basel Convention Ban Amendment

. . . At the Second Meeting of the Conference of the Parties (COP-2) in March 1994, Parties agreed to an immediate ban on the export from OECD to non-OECD countries of hazardous wastes intended for final disposal. They also agreed to ban, by 31 December 1997, the export of wastes intended for recovery and recycling (Decision II/12).

However, because Decision II/12 was not incorporated in the text of the Convention itself, the question as to whether it was legally binding or not arose. Therefore, at COP-3 in 1995, it was proposed that the Ban be formally incorporated in the Basel Convention as an amendment (Decision III/1).

### Scope of the Ban

Decision III/1 does not use the distinction OECD/ non-OECD countries. Rather, it bans hazardous wastes exports for final disposal and recycling from what are known as Annex VII countries (Basel Convention Parties that are members of the EU, OECD, Liechtenstein) to non–Annex VII countries (all other Parties to the Convention).[42]

## 10.10 TRANSBOUNDARY MIGRATION OF POLLUTION

Many (mostly industrialized) countries are expressing concern over the gases $SO_2$ and $NO_x$ that cause acid rain. Although most industrialized nations at the UN Stockholm Conference on the Human Environment in 1972 formerly endorsed the proposition that states have an obligation to control pollution that causes damage to a foreign environment (Wetstone and Rosencranz 1984), and although the OECD adopted a Council Recommendation on Transfrontier Pollution, actual controls result from national restrictions on those emissions and from many bilateral and multilateral agreements. The same is true for shared water systems, like lakes, rivers, and coastal zones.

Having problems with one's neighbors over pollution serves to provide pressure for regulatory action. This pressure is missing with pollution that disperses into the stratosphere and affects the international commons. However, in 1994, the Geneva-based UN Economic Commission for Europe renegotiated a 1985 convention on $SO_2$ that had previously had some success in forcing a reduction of emissions. There have been nine amendments to the convention, the most recent being the 1999 Gothenburg Protocol to Abate Acidification, Eutrophication, and Ground-Level Ozone. The Gothenburg Protocol "sets emission ceilings for 2010 for four pollutants: sulfur, NOx, VOCs [volatile organic compounds] and ammonia. These ceilings were negotiated on the basis of scientific assessments of pollution effects and abatement options. Parties whose emissions have a more severe environmental or health impact and whose emissions are relatively cheap to reduce will have to make the biggest cuts. Once the Protocol is fully implemented, Europe's sulfur emissions should be cut by at least 63%, its NOx emissions by 41%, its VOC emissions by 40%, and its ammonia emissions by 17% compared to 1990."[43]

Aside from $SO_2$ and $NO_x$, other transfrontier environmental problems have been recognized. The revised Seveso Directive specifically acknowledges the intercountry consequences of sudden and accidental releases of chemicals. Further, with the advent of concern about bioengineered organisms, there are European Council directives on both contained used of genetically modified microorganisms (90/219/EEC) and deliberate (field) release of genetically modified organisms (90/220/EEC). Because of the possible multiplication and migration of potentially pathogenic/ harmful organisms, neighboring countries, as well as other countries, have expressed concern.

Persistent organic pollutants (POPs) are of particular concern with regard to transboundary migration of pollution. POPs are transported across international boundaries far from their sources, even to regions where they have never been used or produced. The ecosystems and indigenous people of the Arctic are particularly at risk because of the long-range environmental transportation and biomagnification of these substances. Consequently, POPs pose a threat to the

## BOX 10.1: PERSISTENT ORGANIC POLLUTANTS (POPs)[a]

The following excerpt is from the European Commission's discussion of the Stockholm Convention on POPs:[b]

Persistent organic pollutants (POPs) are chemical substances that persist in the environment, bioaccumulate through the food web, and pose a risk of causing adverse effects to human health and the environment. This group of priority pollutants consists of pesticides (such as DDT), industrial chemicals (such as polychlorinated biphenyls, PCBs) and unintentional by-products of industrial processes (such as dioxins and furans).

Persistent Organic Pollutants are transported across international boundaries far from their sources, even to regions where they have never been used or produced. The ecosystems and indigenous people of the Arctic are particularly at risk because of the long-range environmental transportation and bio-magnification of these substances. Consequently, persistent organic pollutants pose a threat to the environment and to human health all over the globe.

### INTERNATIONAL ACTION ON POPS

The international community has called for actions to reduce and eliminate production, use and releases of these substances. To that end, two international legally binding instruments have been negotiated and concluded:
- The Protocol to the regional UNECE Convention on Long-Range Transboundary Air Pollution (CLRTAP) on POPs, opened for signatures in June 1998 and entered into force on 23 October 2003
- The global Stockholm Convention on POPs, opened for signatures in May 2001 and entered into force on 17 May 2004

These instruments establish strict international regimes for initial lists of POPs (16 in the UNECE Protocol and 12 in the Stockholm Convention). Both instruments also contain provisions for including additional chemicals into these lists. They lay down the following control measures:
- Prohibition or severe restriction of the production and use of intentionally produced POPs
- Restrictions on export and import of the intentionally produced POPs (Stockholm Convention)
- Provisions on the safe handling of stockpiles (Stockholm Convention)
- Provisions on the environmentally sound disposal of wastes containing POPs
- Provisions on the reduction of emissions of unintentionally produced POPs (e.g. dioxins and furans)

### Community ratification of the international agreements

The European Community has signed both international instruments on POPs, together with the then 15 Member States. The Community ratified the Protocol on 30 April 2004 and the Stockholm Convention on 16 November 2004.
- Council Decision 259/2004/EC of 19 February 2004 concerning the conclusion, on behalf of the European Community, of the Protocol to the 1979 Convention on Long Range Transboundary Air Pollution on Persistent Organic Pollutants
- Council Decision concerning the conclusion, on behalf of the European Community, of the Stockholm Convention on Persistent Organic Pollutants was adopted on 14 October 2004 . . .
- Stockholm Convention on Persistent Organic Pollutants

### Implementation measures

The Community is strongly committed to the effective implementation of these two environmental agreements. Based on a Commission proposal (COM (2003) 333 final), the European Parliament and the Council adopted Regulation (EC) No 850/2004 on 29 April 2004. This Regulation entered into force on 20 May 2004. The new Regulation complements the earlier Community legislation on POPs and aligns it with the provisions of the international agreements on POPs. To a certain extent the Regulation goes further than the international agreements emphasising the aim to eliminate the production and use of the internationally recognised POPs.

. . .

### European Community Implementation Plan

Each Party to the Stockholm Convention—individual states as well the European Community as a regional economic integration organisation—has to establish an Implementation Plan to show the concrete action that will be taken against the POPs listed in the Convention. The European Community Implementation Plan, which complements the national plans of the EU Member States, was adopted on 9 March 2007. . . .

### Identification of further POPs

Both international agreements on POPs include provisions for adding further substances that exhibit the characteristics of POPs to the technical Annexes. The Commission, together with the Member States, is promoting and supporting action to identify further POP candidates and initiate international action on their control.

The Commission Proposal for a COUNCIL DECISION concerning proposals, on behalf of the European Community and the Member States, for amendments to Annexes I–III of the 1998 Protocol to the 1979 Convention on Long Range Transboundary Air Pollution on Persistent Organic Pollutants and to Annexes A–C of the Stockholm Convention on Persistent Organic Pollutants COM(2004) 537 final was adopted on 4 August 2004.

---

[a] See the Stockholm Convention on Persistent Organic Pollutants (POP), http://chm.pops.int/ (accessed May 31, 2010).

[b] European Commission, POPs—Persistent Organic Pollutants, http://ec.europa.eu/environment/pops/index_en.htm (accessed May 31, 2010).

environment and to human health all over the globe. Significant action is now taking place within the international community to combat the transboundary migration of POPs, as agreed in the 2001 Stockholm Convention on POPs, which entered into force in May 2004. Box 10.1 contains more information on POPs.

## 10.11 POLLUTING THE INTERNATIONAL COMMONS

Both climate change and the destruction of stratospheric ozone are environmental effects that go beyond transfrontier pollution, resulting in the formation of acid rain, for example, or in the contamination of another nation's rivers. They are an international version of the tragedy of the commons. The Vienna Convention for the Protection of the Ozone Layer, the Montreal Protocol on Substances That Deplete the Ozone Layer (addressing chlorofluorocarbons), and the International Climate Convention address these problems, but here, as with other international attempts, enforcement and verification mechanisms are sorely lacking. The EU environment ministers agreed in 1994 to phase out hydrochlorofluorocarbons (HCFCs) and methyl bromides faster than the timetable called for in the November 1992 Copenhagen Amendments to the Montreal Protocol. The EU issued a regulation incorporating stricter controls (Regulation 3093/94/EEC, replacing Regulation 594/91/EEC, Substances That Deplete the Ozone Layer). In September 1995, representatives of the 149 countries that had ratified the 1987 Montreal Protocol drafted a series of recommendations for strengthening the protocol, and the following December, conference participants agreed to phase out methyl bromide[44] by 2010 and HCFCs by 2020. Ironically, HCFCs are less damaging to the ozone layer but present more risk for workers who handle them. Thus the implementation of environmental protection mechanisms and workplace safeguards continues to lack coordination.

Concern about the pollution of the Mediterranean Sea, the largest nonoceanic body of water, has also given rise to a number of European Council directives (77/585/EEC, 81/101/EEC, and 84/132/EEC). The Directive for the North Sea (84/358/EEC) is also relevant. The Mediterranean Action Plan brings together the Mediterranean basin countries in an attempt to address their mutual concerns.

One of the most pressing global environmental issues—and one that poses extraordinary problems for securing international consensus on action—is the impact of climate change on all aspects of human existence. Although the Framework Convention on Climate Change was initiated during the 1992 Rio Earth Summit, controversy attended the implementation of the Kyoto Protocol, the first international accord dedicated to resolving, mitigating, and adapting to the anthropogenic impact on the earth's climate. Box 10.2 outlines some of the key events of the climate-change saga over the past decade or so. After a fragile and contentious process, the Copenhagen Accord emerged at the end of 2009 (see Box 10.3).

Those who participated in or witnessed the Copenhagen event describe a chaotic, two-week negotiation process, with the potential to unravel at several junctures. Some 40,000 persons attended, including about 115 world leaders. Developed, developing, developing-island, and African nations came with very different expectations and needs and were willing to contribute in very different ways to addressing global climate change. For example, although the United States was willing to commit to a cap on emissions, China would commit only to a reduction of $CO_2$ intensity. Others were not willing to commit to any targets at the meeting, but rich countries willing to make "voluntary commitments"—that is, pledges—by 2020 were to make them known by January 31, 2010. Were it not for the EU financial and greenhouse-reduction commitments—and the presence of President Obama, who committed to helping raise $100 billion "from the world" for developing-country aid and who pressed other world leaders at the last moment—the meeting would have ended with no agreement at all. The key accomplishments were an agreed-on voluntary long-term target of a temperature increase of no more than 2°C above levels in a base year yet to be agreed on, a forest/deforestation agreement, and financial and technical aid and capacity building to developing countries. The rich countries offered 2020 targets of reductions of 14 to 18 percent from 1990 levels.

The Copenhagen meeting was followed by a second meeting in Cancun in late 2010 where the following progress was made (Vaughan 2010):

1. The pledges for greenhouse gas reductions were placed formally into UN documentation.

2. While none of the pledges were legally binding, analysis suggest the result would be a 3.2C rise, considerable above the prior goal of 2C.

3. Developing countries agreed to look into how they could cut emissions, but no specific pledges were made.

4. The establishment of a "green fund" and a "climate technology [transfer] centre" was agreed upon,

**BOX 10.2: CLIMATE CHANGE AND INTERNATIONAL ENVIRONMENTAL LAW: THE KYOTO PROTOCOL**

Despite the uncertainties surrounding the implications of global climate change, there is growing consensus on the need for international cooperation to encourage the abatement of greenhouse gas emissions. More than a decade ago, the international community agreed to the UN Framework Convention on Climate Change, "acknowledging that change in the Earth's climate and its adverse effects are a common concern of mankind."[a] Five years later, in 1997, governments took further steps to address the impact of climate change by adopting the landmark Kyoto Protocol, which contains legally binding instruments on greenhouse gas emissions and innovative mechanisms aimed at reducing the cost of emission abatement.

Although, as of January 2011, there were 193 signatories to the Kyoto Protocol (192 States and 1 regional economic integration organization), this policy instrument continued to be contentious for many nations and interests. The positions taken by the EU and the United States were of particular importance in terms of realistically reducing emissions. Before the Kyoto summit, the United States promoted the use of market-based mechanisms as policy instruments, whereas the EU favored regulatory approaches. After Kyoto, however, U.S. support declined for certain market-based mechanisms, such as an emissions-trading system, while the EU began to design and implement mechanisms such as a domestic emissions-trading system (Damro and Luaces-Mendez 2003). The protocol, which became a legally binding treaty in February 2005, required signatories to lower emissions of six greenhouse gases by about 5 percent of 1990 levels by 2012. But the United States, the world's biggest economy and then the largest emitter, failed to ratify the agreement, although it had initially been signed by President Bill Clinton.

Since 1997, EU activities have differed significantly from those of the United States.[b] After signing the protocol, the EU began designing and implementing schemes in order to achieve a 7 percent reduction in $CO_2$ emissions by 2010. $CO_2$ is not the only cause of global climate change, but it is the primary cause. Reducing $CO_2$ emissions is thought to be a necessary step to avert a potentially catastrophic future. Many countries adopted a global target of 550 parts per million (ppm), roughly a doubling of the preindustrial value, as a safe and reasonable level that can be achieved over the next century.

In October 2004, Russia ratified the Kyoto Protocol. Coming into force in February 2005, the protocol was finally ratified by developed nations that account for at least 55 percent of global greenhouse emissions. After the United States pulled out under President George W. Bush's administration, that figure could be reached only with the support of Russia, which accounts for 17 percent of world emissions.

Paul Lightfoot comments on the state of achievement as of March 28, 2008:[c]

> Overall, greenhouse gas emissions for the 40 developed countries declined by almost five percent from 1990 to 2005. While this appears encouraging, much of the decrease resulted from steep declines in the states of the former USSR and eastern Europe in the early 1990s; total emissions for all other developed countries have actually risen by about 10 percent, and since 1994 the overall trend for all 40 countries has been upward.
>
> A few Western European countries have been relatively successful in meeting their targets. Of the major sources of emissions, France, the UK and Germany achieved reductions of 7, 15 and 19 percent[, respectively]. In contrast, emissions increased by more than 50 percent in Canada, Spain and Turkey. Emissions from the USA increased by about 16 percent. While this is far from the worst performance among the developed countries, it matters hugely because the USA contributes about a third of all global emissions. . . .
>
> From a broader perspective, even if the developed countries somehow achieve the five percent emissions reduction target by 2008–2012, massive changes under way in the developing countries mean that that decline is unlikely to be enough to stabilise levels of greenhouse gases in the atmosphere. Emissions from China and India have increased substantially. One estimate suggests that total emissions rose by about 50 percent from 1990 to 2004 and that rates are increasing at the rate of 4 or 5 percent each year in each country, perhaps higher in China. China [was expected to] overtake the USA as the world's biggest source of greenhouse gases very soon.

[a] United Nations Framework Convention on Climate Change, http://unfccc.int/essential_background/convention/background/items/1350.php (accessed May 31, 2010).

[b] Damro and Luaces-Mendez (2003, p. 11) comment that "the implementation of an emissions trading system requires significant agreement on how to organize the initial allocation of emissions permits. If EU member states were allowed to buy permits on the open market and then give them to certain enterprises free of charge or without imposing conditions, it would be tantamount to state aid and would be inconsistent with EU competition rules. For this reason, the Commission decided that the allocation of quotas will be made to private companies within the same sector—mainly, energy producers or energy-intensive industries."

[c] P. Lightfoot (2008), Kyoto Protocol Achievements, The Partial Control of Greenhouse Gas Emissions, http://climate-change.suite101.com/article.cfm/kyoto_protocol_achievements (accessed May 31, 2010).

**BOX 10.3: CLIMATE CHANGE AND INTERNATIONAL ENVIRONMENTAL LAW: THE COPENHAGEN ACCORD**

UNITED NATIONS: FRAMEWORK ON CLIMATE CHANGE 18 DECEMBER 2009

**Draft decision/CP.15**
**Proposal by the President**
**Copenhagen Accord**

**The Heads of State, Heads of Government, Ministers, and other heads of delegation present at the United Nations Climate Change Conference 2009 in Copenhagen,**

*In pursuit* of the ultimate objective of the Convention as stated in its Article 2,
*Being guided* by the principles and provisions of the Convention,
*Noting* the results of work done by the two Ad hoc Working Groups,
*Endorsing* decision x/CP.15 on the Ad hoc Working Group on Long-term Cooperative Action and decision x/CMP.5 that requests the Ad hoc Working Group on Further Commitments of Annex I Parties under the Kyoto Protocol to continue its work,
*Have agreed* on this Copenhagen Accord which is operational immediately.

1. We underline that climate change is one of the greatest challenges of our time. **We emphasise our strong political will to urgently combat climate change in accordance with the principle of common but differentiated responsibilities and respective capabilities.** To achieve the ultimate objective of the Convention to stabilize greenhouse gas concentration in the atmosphere at a level that would prevent dangerous anthropogenic interference with the climate system, we shall, recognizing the scientific view that **the increase in global temperature should be below 2 degrees Celsius**, on the basis of equity and in the context of sustainable development, enhance our long-term cooperative action to combat climate change. We recognize the critical impacts of climate change and the potential impacts of response measures on countries particularly vulnerable to its adverse effects and stress the need to establish a comprehensive adaptation programme including international support.

2. We agree that deep cuts in global emissions are required according to science, and as documented by the IPCC Fourth Assessment Report with a view to reduce global emissions so as to hold the increase in global temperature below 2 degrees Celsius, and take action to meet this objective consistent with science and on the basis of equity. We should cooperate in achieving the peaking of global and national emissions as soon as possible, recognizing that **the time frame for peaking will be longer in developing countries** and bearing in mind that social and economic development and poverty eradication are the first and overriding priorities of developing countries and that a low-emission development strategy is indispensable to sustainable development.

3. Adaptation to the adverse effects of climate change and the potential impacts of response measures is a challenge faced by all countries. Enhanced action and international cooperation on adaptation is urgently required to ensure the implementation of the Convention by enabling and supporting the implementation of adaptation actions aimed at reducing vulnerability and building resilience in developing countries, especially in those that are particularly vulnerable, especially least developed countries, small island developing States and Africa. We agree that **developed countries shall provide adequate, predictable and sustainable financial resources, technology and capacity-building to support the implementation of adaptation action in developing countries.**

4. Annex I Parties commit to implement individually or jointly the quantified economy-wide emissions targets for 2020, to be submitted in the format given in Appendix I by Annex I Parties to the secretariat by 31 January 2010 for compilation in an INF [informational] document. Annex I Parties that are Party to the Kyoto Protocol will thereby further strengthen the emissions reductions initiated by the Kyoto Protocol. Delivery of reductions and financing by developed countries will be measured, reported and verified in accordance with existing and any further guidelines adopted by the Conference of the Parties, and will ensure that accounting of such targets and finance is rigorous, robust and transparent.

5. Non–Annex I Parties to the Convention will implement mitigation actions, including those to be submitted to the secretariat by non–Annex I Parties in the format given in Appendix II by 31 January 2010, for compilation in an INF document, consistent with Article 4.1 and Article 4.7 and in the context of sustainable development. Least developed countries and small island developing States may undertake actions voluntarily and on the basis of support. Mitigation actions subsequently taken and envisaged by Non–Annex I Parties, including national inventory reports, shall be communicated through national communications consistent with Article 12.1(b) every two years on the basis of guidelines to be adopted by the Conference of the Parties. Those mitigation actions in national communications or otherwise communicated to the Secretariat will be added to the list in appendix II. Mitigation actions taken by Non–Annex I Parties will be subject to their domestic measurement, reporting and verification the result of which will be reported through their national communications every two years. Non–Annex I Parties will communicate information on the implementation of their actions through National Communications, with provisions for international consultations and analysis under clearly defined guidelines that will ensure that national sovereignty is respected. **Nationally appropriate mitigation actions seeking international support will be recorded in a registry along with relevant technology, finance and capacity building support.** Those actions supported will be added to the list in appendix II. These supported nationally appropriate mitigation actions will be subject to international measurement, reporting and verification in accordance with guidelines adopted by the Conference of the Parties.

6. We recognize the crucial role of reducing emission[s] from deforestation and forest degradation [REDD] and the need to enhance removals of greenhouse gas emission by forests and agree on the need to provide positive incentives to such actions through the immediate establishment of a mechanism including REDD-plus, to enable the mobilization of financial resources from developed countries.

7. We decide to pursue various approaches, including opportunities to use markets, to enhance the cost-effectiveness of, and to promote mitigation actions. Developing countries, especially those with low emitting economies should be provided incentives to continue to develop on a low emission pathway.

8. Scaled up, new and additional, predictable and adequate funding as well as improved access shall be provided to developing countries, in accordance with the relevant provisions of the Convention, to enable and support enhanced action on mitigation, including substantial finance to reduce emissions from deforestation and forest degradation (REDD-plus), adaptation, technology development and transfer and capacity-building, for enhanced implementation of the Convention. The collective commitment by developed countries is to provide new and additional resources, including forestry and investments through international institutions, approaching USD 30 billion for the period 2010–2012 with balanced allocation between adaptation and mitigation. Funding for adaptation will be prioritized for the most vulnerable developing countries, such as the least developed countries, small island developing States and Africa. In the context of meaningful mitigation actions and transparency on implementation, developed countries commit to a goal of mobilizing jointly USD 100 billion dollars a year by 2020 to address the needs of developing countries. This funding will come from a wide variety of sources, public and private, bilateral and multilateral, including alternative sources of finance. New multilateral funding for adaptation will be delivered through effective and efficient fund arrangements, with a governance structure providing for equal representation of developed and developing countries. A significant portion of such funding should flow through the Copenhagen Green Climate Fund.

9. To this end, **a High Level Panel will be established** under the guidance of and accountable to the Conference of the Parties to study the contribution of the potential sources of revenue, including alternative sources of finance, towards meeting this goal.

10. **We decide that the Copenhagen Green Climate Fund** shall be established as an operating entity of the financial mechanism of the Convention to support projects, programme, policies and other activities in developing countries related to mitigation including REDD-plus, adaptation, capacity-building, technology development and transfer.

11. In order to enhance action on development and transfer of technology we decide to establish a **Technology Mechanism to accelerate technology development and transfer in support of action on adaptation and mitigation** that will be guided by a country-driven approach and be based on national circumstances and priorities.

12. **We call for an assessment of the implementation of this Accord to be completed by 2015**, including in light of the Convention's ultimate objective. This would include consideration of strengthening the long-term goal referencing various matters presented by the science, including in relation to temperature rises of 1.5 degrees Celsius.

Source: United Nations, Framework Convention on Climate Change, Copenhagen Accord, FCCC/CP/2009/L.7, December 18, 2009 (emphases added), http://graphics8.nytimes.com/packages/pdf/science/earth/20091218_climate_text_pdf (accessed May 6, 2011).

but specifies as to the amount of funding, location, etc.

5. Formal backing was given for the UN's deforestation scheme.

6. Decision on the future of the Kyoto protocol were deferred to the next meeting in South Africa.

Notwithstanding the absence of a legally binding international agreement and the possibility that he will be saddled with a Congress not inclined to ratify a climate-change treaty, President Obama is nonetheless committed to addressing the climate-change challenge. He announced his clear intent to use the provisions of the U.S. Clean Air Act to reduce greenhouse gas emissions from both mobile and stationary sources.[45] Conservatives in the U.S. Congress promise a spirited response.

## 10.12 LIABILITY FOR ENVIRONMENTAL DAMAGE

We are constantly confronted with cases of severe damage to the environment caused by human acts. High-profile cases capture the international community's attention briefly, such as the infamous 1989 *Exxon Valdez* oil release in Alaska's Prince William Sound and the accident with the *Erika* oil tanker in the south of Spain ten years later, and most recently in 2010 the BP oil spill in the Gulf of Mexico, three examples of cases where human activities have resulted in substantial damage to the environment. In addition to these destructive events, mankind also releases countless harmful substances to land, water, and air on a daily basis. Both the United States and the European Union responded to create liability schemes for damage to the environment, although some two decades apart. Neither scheme covers liability for personal injury or for loss of property values, leaving that to the individual fifty U.S. states and the member states of the European Union, respectively. Both schemes are described briefly below because the contrast is instructive.

### 10.12.1 U.S. Environmental Liability

The Comprehensive Environmental Response, Compensation, and Liability Act of 1980 (CERCLA) and the Superfund Amendments and Reauthorization

Act (SARA) of 1986 addressed environmental liability in the United States. CERCLA established strict liability for polluters of land and water (except for pesticide applicators, petroleum, fuels, and most nuclear materials) in sites qualifying for National Priority List (NPL) designation* and also set up a Hazardous Response Trust Fund (the Superfund) that was to be used to clean up toxic contaminants for which a financially solvent polluter could not be found.† A tax on the chemical and petroleum industries provided funding. The act imposed joint, several, and retroactive liability, which meant that if any polluter was unable to pay for the cleanup at a particular site, then the burden was imposed on other contributors, who could be said to be required to pay "more than their fair share" of the cleanup expenses. To date, billions of dollars have been spent, and not all the designated sites have been cleaned up.

Polluters are expected to report and remediate releases in excess of thresholds listed in the act for some seven hundred "hazardous substances" and for other "pollutants/contaminants." Cleanup standards are based on the most restrictive federal and applicable state standards. However, the federal water-based Maximum Contaminant Levels are presently relaxed as a result of intense industry lobbying in the past decade. Polluters are expected to remediate sites to levels indicated by those standards unless the sites qualify for "brownfield status." A brownfield designation allows sites to be cleaned up to a lesser degree for use as commercial property, partly satisfying some "environmental justice" communities with the prospects of economic development (Ashford and Rest 2001).

In addition to joint, several, and retroactive liability for contamination, the act envisioned establishing financial responsibility assurances requiring that at-risk firms set aside surety bonds or designated funds in the event that future contamination occurred from their operations. These provisions of the act were never implemented, but in May 2009, a federal district court ordered the EPA to carry out the first step of preparing and listing industries that would have to demonstrate such financial responsibility (*Sierra Club v. EPA*, N.D. Cal., No. C 08-1409, Feb. 25, 2009).

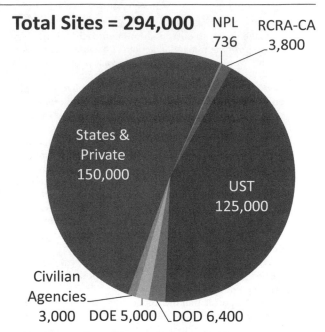

**FIGURE 10.3: ESTIMATED NUMBER OF HAZARDOUS-WASTE SITES, 2004–2033**
Note: DOD—Department of Defense; DOE—Department of Energy; NPL—National Priorities List; RCRA-CA—*Resource Conservation and Recovery Act Corrective Action Program;* and UST—Underground Storage Tank.
Source: EPA (2004b).

In December 2004, the EPA (2004a) projected that as many as 350,000 contaminated sites would require cleanup over the next thirty years, assuming that current regulations and practices remained the same. The bill for this cleanup may amount to as much as $250 billion. In its report, the EPA (2004a) provides an estimation of remaining hazardous-waste sites needing remediation efforts (Figure 10.3). The EPA explains:

> According to the report, there will be a need to address many smaller sites such as those containing Underground Storage Tanks (UST) (43% of the total sites) and various hazardous waste properties (50% of the total sites). These two site categories, however, only account for twenty two percent of the costs. The remaining seven percent of sites, including those on the National Priorities List and U.S. Department of Defense and Department of Energy sites, tend to be larger, more complex and more costly to remediate and will thus require a larger share of funding.... There is a trend toward more risk-based cleanup approaches and more attention to redevelopment of cleanedup sites in selecting and implementing remedies in most cleanup programs. Underlying these trends is the acceptance, in recent years of improved approaches to site characterization, which has been demonstrated to lead to faster, cheaper, and better cleanups.[46]

---

\*        States have the option to keep a site off the federal NPL list and address the remediation themselves. A major concern is the effect that such a designation has on property values in the contaminated community.

†        After a high of $3.8 billion in 1987, the fund has remained insolvent since 2003. Attempts to reintroduce the tax in 2009 via the Superfund Polluter Pays Act were not successful.

Although recovery for personal injury and damage to property is left to the already-existing remedies available in the fifty individual states, CERCLA/SARA did establish the Agency for Toxic Substances and Disease Registry (ATSDR), which (1) keeps a registry of exposures and diseases attributable to toxic substances, (2) constructs toxicological profiles of chemicals, and (3) performs preliminary health risk assessments at sites that are candidates for remediation. There has been enormous contention over sites and contaminated communities that have a multitude of so-called low-level exposures, no one of which has firm toxicological or epidemiological evidence of significant risk, but that suffer a myriad of health problems. The ATSDR was created because the public did not trust the EPA's assessment of risk. However, under the George W. Bush administration, the ATSDR lost the confidence of the public and did not apply the precautionary principle in its assessments.

Citizens not only have standing to intervene in government decisions (including judicial review), but also have access to the courts for injunctive relief against the government if it does not act. Exemption from liability is provided for nonmanaging lenders, some "innocent purchasers," and nonnegligent contractors. Also exempted from joint and several liability are potentially responsible parties (PRPs), who bear the burden of proving nonresponsibility (where the pollution type is identifiable and divisible) or of demonstrating that their pollution is reliably attributable in size (Liptak 2009).

### 10.12.2 European Union Environmental Liability

Taking into consideration the trials and tribulations of the U.S. Superfund model of environmental liability, the European Commission issued its *White Paper on Environmental Liability* in February 2000. The objective of the *White Paper* was to provide for strict liability for conventional and environmental damage caused by "dangerous" activities regulated by EC law, and fault liability for natural resource damage caused by nondangerous activities (Bergkamp 2000). Figure 10.4 provides a visual representation of the EU environmental liability envisioned in the *White Paper*. However, liability for "traditional damages" (personal injury and property damage) was excised from the final Directive 2005/35/EC. The *White Paper* addressed the preventive, precautionary, and polluter-pays principles and how these can best be applied to serve the aims of European Community environmental policy.

Bergkamp (2000) argued that the EC's argument in the *White Paper* was weak, and that a liability regime might not ensure further decontamination and restoration of the environment or boost the implementation of compliance because member states are already required to protect and restore damaged natural resources and mandate remediation of contaminated sites through a liability regime. In cases where environmental damage is widespread without a clear link to the activities of any individual actors (called "diffuse pollution"), the commission argued that liability is not a suitable instrument. Examples of diffuse, multisource damage include climate change due to $CO_2$ emissions, forest damage caused by acid rain, air-pollution effects from industry or traffic, and fertilizer and pesticide runoff. These shared environmental problems, as discussed elsewhere in this chapter and book, are the subject of many emerging international agreements, protocols, negotiations, and the like.

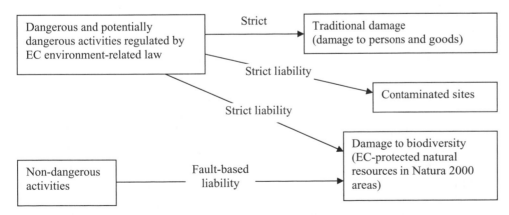

**FIGURE 10.4: SCOPE OF EC ENVIRONMENTAL LIABILITY REGIME ENVISIONED BY THE WHITE PAPER**
Note: Traditional damages were ultimately eliminated by Directive 2004/35/EC.
Source: European Commission (2000, p. 9).

However, despite criticisms of the strict and fault liability regime outlined in the *White Paper*, the EC was not discouraged by the disappointing U.S. experience with civil liability regimes for environmental harm. The EC commented:[47]

> So far, the Member States of the European Union have established national environmental liability regimes that cover damage to persons and goods, and they have introduced laws to deal with liability for, and clean up of, contaminated sites. However, until now, these national regimes have not really addressed the issue of liability for damage to nature. This is one reason why economic actors have focused on their responsibilities to other people's health or property, but have not tended to consider their responsibilities for damage to the wider environment. This has been seen traditionally as a "public good" for which society as a whole should be responsible, rather than something the individual actor who actually caused the damage should bear. The introduction of liability for damage to nature, as proposed in the White Paper, is expected to bring about a change of attitude that should result in an increased level of prevention and precaution.
>
> On adoption of the White Paper by the Commission, Environment Commissioner Margot Wallström stated: "We have now laid the foundations for an environmental liability regime for Europe. Legislation in this field will provide common rules to ensure that polluters will effectively be held responsible for environmental damage they cause. This will improve protection of the health of Europeans and our natural environment." . . .
>
> In case of environmental damage, the compensation to be paid by the polluter should be spent on the effective restoration of the damage. Furthermore, for cases concerning environmental damage, public interest groups should have a right to step into the shoes of public authorities, where these are responsible for tackling environmental damage but have not acted. Such groups should also be allowed to take action in urgent cases if there is a need to prevent damage. This is in line with the 1998 Åarhus Convention on access to information, public participation in decision-making and access to justice, a UN/ECE Convention that has been signed by the Community and all the EU Member States, as well as by other states.

In April 2004, some twenty-four years after the United States adopted CERCLA, the European Community adopted Directive 2004/35/EC on environmental liability,[48] addressing the prevention and remedying of environmental damage.[49] The directive has faced much opposition from industry, but despite this resistance, the European Community voted in favor of strict rules and called for wide financial and legal accountability of polluters. Under the new directive, the polluter-pays principle is fundamental and demonstrates that in many cases the operator who causes damage should be held liable, that is, be financially responsible. The directive aims to ensure that future (but not retroactive)* environmental damage is paid for by the polluter and preferably is prevented. The directive specifically included the issues of biodiversity and nature damage, water and land contamination, and damage from genetically modified organisms (GMOs).

Directive 2004/35/EC has been the subject of much commentary and criticism and is acknowledged to be significantly weaker than the approaches recommended in the *White Paper* (Betlem 2005; Fogelman 2006; Krämer 2005; G. Winter, Jans, et al. 2008). The following list outlines the ultimate scheme (Ashford 2009):

- Areas of Liability for Operators (private and public):
  - For Prevention and Restoration (Remediation) of Environmental Damage to water soil/land, and protected species and natural habitats:
    - Strict, joint, and several liability for damage caused after April 30, 2007 for "occupational activities" listed in Annex III reflecting IPPC permitting and 11 other Directives including the Water Directive, and directives addressing Waste Management, and Air Pollution.
  - For restoration/remediation of damage to EU directive-protected species and natural habitats arising from "other [than Annex III] activities:" at fault liability (negligence).
  - Damage is assessed relative to the (before-hand) baseline conditions.
  - Traditional damage (personal injury and damage to property) excluded.
  - Thresholds:
    - Water: *significant adverse impacts* on resource status (quality and quantity).
    - Soil: *serious potential and actual harm* to public health (soil erosion excluded).
    - Nature: *significant adverse effects* on the conservation status of the protected species and habitat.
  - Exemptions: oil spills and nuclear contamination.
- Operators (private and public):
  - have a duty to prevent, notify (report), and manage "environmental damage" to land, water, protected species, and natural habitats.
  - have a duty to prevent and remediate "environmental damage" associated with "dangerous or

---

* Not imposing retroactive liability, which was originally read into U.S. legislation by the federal courts, has left many contaminated sites in Europe without financial contribution from the original polluters. In the late 1990s, the EU countries with the greatest number of suspected sites are Germany (100,000–200,000), the Netherlands (110,000), and the United Kingdom (50,000–100,000) compared to 35,000 in the United States (Lombi et al. 1998).

potentially dangerous occupational activities" [Annex III].
— have a primary duty to act in response to any governmental order.
— have a secondary duty to bear the costs, premised on appropriate national law.
— May not always be liable for damage to species and natural habitats (if not in the EU directives).
— May not always be liable for damage to water (if not required by the Water Directive).
— May be liable for damage (contamination) to land, providing the damage creates a "significant risk" to human health. ("Significant" is undefined and creates an opportunity to impose a heavy evidentiary burden, not reflecting a precautionary approach.) Diffuse pollution damage excluded unless causal relationship established between alleged polluter(s) and damage.

- Defenses available to Operators to defeat/reduce cost-bearing:
  — Mandatory:
    ○ Operators acted in accordance with a compulsory government order.
    ○ Damage was due to the act of an unconnected third party.
  — Optional (established by each Member State):
    ○ Practices of care were based on the then-recognized potential for environmental impact by the Member State (state-of-art defense).
    ○ Operator was allowed to conduct itself in accordance with a permit issued by a Member State in accordance with legislation listed in Annex III.
- Public Authorities:
  — Must require preventive or remedial action by operators:
    ○ If damage has not yet occurred, required actions are to be determined by the appropriate Member State.
  — May, but are not obliged to, take necessary measures in the case that:
    ○ An operator is not identified, an operator doesn't meet his/her obligations, or is not required to bear the costs (as a result of available defenses).
    ○ This in effect removes an enforceable mandatory state duty to act, unless required by other EU directives, for example, the Water Directive.
  — May recover remediation/restoration costs incurred by the authority, providing the Member State required the operator to have a dedicated fund for remediation/restoration.
- Citizens/NGOs:
  — Procedural rights somewhat expanded in administrative proceedings, but not with regard to standing in courts, though there exists a right to judicial review for the decisions of authorities or their refusals to act.
  — Comments of Citizens/NGOs must be supported by evidence and their comments on preventive measures to be taken on land are allowed at the discretion of the Member State.
  — They can request public authorities to act, but Member States can sometimes restrict or delay their access to the courts, in practice.

A number of criticisms can be applied to this directive. Although there are specific targets, for example, good water quality by 2015 and favorable conservation status for birds and habitats, some benchmarks are lacking, such as specific reportable quantities of pollutants released (required under the U.S. legislation). Significant environmental damage may go unabated because public authorities, unlike those in the United States, are not required to act in many instances where polluters are not identified or insolvent.

Evidentiary burdens on citizens and NGOs are sometimes high or require too short a time to be borne, vitiating a precautionary approach. Significantly enhanced public participation promised by the Århus Convention is not achieved (see Section 10.4.4).

The prevention of pollution at the source is actually not a driver of this directive. Instead, prevention focuses on the prevention of releases or their subsequent spread.

Financial assurance mechanisms are needed, but member states are only "encouraged" to establish them. Liability will vary significantly among member states.

Although technically included, the treatment of damage relating to GMOs is inadequate.

The weakening of this directive, measured against the approaches recommended in the *White Paper*, is reminiscent of the weakening of the REACH initiative (see Section 10.18.8).

## 10.13 PRESERVING BIODIVERSITY AND ENDANGERED SPECIES

The Convention on International Trade in Endangered Species of Wild Fauna and Flora (CITES) is an international agreement to ensure that international trade in specimens of wild animals and plants does not threaten their survival. Ideas for CITES were first formed in the 1960s when international discussion of the regulation of wildlife trade for conservation purposes was something relatively new. As the website for CITES explains: "Annually, international wildlife trade is estimated to be worth billions of dollars and to include hundreds of millions of plant and animal specimens. The trade is diverse, ranging from live animals and plants to a vast array of wildlife products derived from them, including food products, exotic leather goods, wooden musical instruments, timber, tourist curios, and medicines. Levels of exploitation of some animal and plant species are high and the trade in them, together with other factors, such as habitat loss, is capable of heavily depleting their populations and even bringing some species close to extinction. Many wildlife species in trade are not endangered, but the existence of an agreement to ensure the sustainability of the trade is important in order to safeguard these resources for the future."[50]

The first conference of the parties to the convention was held in June 2007. Agreements were reached on ivory and eels, and it was agreed that trade in timber and marine species needed to be addressed.

Following the conference, the European Commission adopted a recommendation that "sets out a series of measures that Member States should implement in order to enhance their efforts to combat illegal trade. These include adopting national action plans for enforcement, imposing sufficiently high penalties for wildlife trade offences and using risk and intelligence assessments to detect illegal and smuggled wildlife products. Equally important consideration is given to raising public awareness about the negative impacts of illegal wildlife trade and ensuring greater cooperation and exchange of information within and between Member States as well as with third countries, Interpol and the World Customs Organization."[51]

## 10.14 FOOD SAFETY*

Recent problems related to global food production, processing, distribution, and preparation are creating an increasing demand for food-safety oversight in order to ensure a safer global food supply. Two international organizations are central to this goal: (1) the Codex Alimentarius Commission (CCA) and (2) the World Trade Organization (WTO). The CCA is a second-generation international organization created as a connecting organization between the UN's World Health Organization and the Food and Agriculture Organization that adopts standards on food safety (Battaglia 2006, p. 3, n. 7). Some 165 countries are represented in the CCA, whose objective "consists in defining international standard[s], codes of usage and other guidelines and regulations regarding agricultural and fish products, food products, additives and contaminants, animal feed, veterinary medicine and pesticide residues as well as labeling, methods of certification and inspection, sampling and analysis methods, codes of ethics and good agricultural procedures" (ibid.).

Two agreements related to limiting trade restrictions on the exchange of food-related items were concluded in 1994 and are administered by the WTO: the Sanitary and Phytosanitary (SPS) Agreement discussed below and the Technical Barriers to Trade (TBT) Agreement discussed in Chapter 11.

The SPS Agreement "recognizes the right of each WTO member to adopt an 'appropriate level of protection' (ALOP) of trade-restricting measures to protect human, animal, and plant life and health, but insists that such measures be based on a scientific assessment of the risks, be applied only to the extent necessary to achieve public health or environmental goals, and not discriminate between domestic and foreign products or threats. The WTO SPS Agreement is credited with increasing the transparency of countries' SPS regulations, spurring regulatory reforms, and providing a means for settling SPS-related trade disputes. The U.S. has used the SPS Agreement to challenge a number of other countries' SPS import measures in the WTO, including the EU's ban on imports of beef from cattle treated with hormones and Japan's restrictions on imported apples based on unfounded concerns over Fire blight disease."[52] (See Chapter 11 for further discussion of these trade-related food issues.)

Within the SPS agreement, there are three international standard-setting bodies: the Codex Alimentarius Commission (the food-safety standards-setting body discussed above); the Office International des Epizooties, or OIE (now the Organization for Animal Health; the animal health standard-setting body); and the International Plant Protection Convention (the plant health standard-setting body).

## 10.15 BIOTECHNOLOGY

In January 2000, the Conference of the Parties to the Convention on Biological Diversity adopted a supplementary agreement to the Convention on Biodiversity known as the Cartagena Protocol on Biosafety, which entered into force on September 11, 2003. This protocol seeks to protect biological diversity from the potential risks posed by living modified organisms resulting from modern biotechnology. It establishes an advance informed agreement (AIA) procedure for ensuring that countries are provided with the information necessary to make informed decisions before agreeing to the import of such organisms into their territory. The protocol establishes common rules for the transboundary movement of GMOs in order to ensure, on a global scale, the protection of biodiversity and of human health. The protocol refers

---

* See also Section 10.18.9 on EU policy and regulation of food safety.

to a precautionary approach and reaffirms the precaution language in Principle 15 of the Rio Declaration. Further, it establishes a Biosafety Clearing-House to facilitate the exchange of information on living modified organisms and to assist countries in the implementation of the protocol.[53]

Although this protocol is a step in the right direction, it still has many weaknesses. For example, the relationship between the protocol and the WTO is unclear. Although socioeconomic concerns are mentioned in the protocol, they are not included explicitly in the risk-assessment procedure to be used when a country has said no to an import. Thus it has been argued that with regard to finished food products, the protocol would be applicable to environmental concerns, but not to public health concerns (Redick 2007, p. 62). This remains a contentious point.

The EU is a party to the Cartagena Protocol. However, the United States, which is not a signatory to the underlying pact, was able to have great influence on the outcome via Canada, Argentina, and others that stand to gain from GMOs;[54] however, GMO products other than seeds are not covered by the advance informed agreement (whereby exporters have to inform countries of their intention to ship a GM product in advance and receive permission to do so before proceeding). Also, GMOs processed into other foods are not required to be labeled. Disputes may need to be resolved at the WTO, but it is unclear how this will take place.* The issue is becoming more and more important. By 2005, more than 8.25 million farmers around the world were growing biotech crops, and over 90 per cent of the growers resided in resource-poor developing countries (Redick 2007, p. 54). The EU has issued two traceability and labeling directives applying the precautionary principle to possible impacts of biotech crops (see Section 10.18.10). By October 5, 2006, 135 parties had ratified the protocol, and 188 parties were part of the convention (ibid., p. 58). Thus trading partners who are both parties to the protocol would seem to have to adopt similar approaches. What happens when one party is not a signatory to the protocol may throw disputes into the WTO trade dispute-resolution process, with uncertain outcomes (see Chapter 11). Worse still, there are apparent inconsistencies between the Biosafety Protocol and the Sanitary and Phytosanitary (SPS) Agreement; the latter does not embody a precautionary approach but rather requires a convincing

scientific basis (for example, a risk assessment) to justify import restrictions (see Chapter 11).

## 10.16 PHARMACEUTICAL SAFETY

Although different national jurisdictions have their own strategies and philosophies in balancing the benefits, risks, and economic costs of prescription drugs, there has been an attempt to harmonize the reporting of adverse drug reactions and safety monitoring through the International Conference on Harmonization of Technical Requirements for Registration of Pharmaceuticals (ICH) guidelines (Castle and Kelly 2008). The international requirements are fully embodied in two laws in the EU: Directive 2001/83/EC, as amended, and Regulation (EC) No. 726/2004. After a period of careless, if not scandalous, instances of the marketing of drugs in the United States that did not receive timely or sufficient government or industry response to adverse drug reactions, "industry, regulatory authorities, and consumers are now focusing on a more proactive risk management approach to drug safety monitoring . . . There has also been a realization that effective pharmacovigilance must be global" (ibid., p. 601). However, extensive harmonization between the U.S. Food and Drug Administration (whose adoption of the ICH guidelines is incomplete) and the European Medicines Agency remains elusive because of different interpretations of, and definitions used relating to, what information must be reported under the ICH guidelines, resulting in "significant differences in the information [multinational drug] companies are reporting" (ibid., p. 602). As in other areas in which harmonization of legal approaches is acknowledged to be desirable, pharmaceutical-safety reporting falls short at this time.

## 10.17 ENVIRONMENTAL LAW AND ITS ROLE IN STIMULATING TECHNOLOGICAL CHANGE

New technology is a key to achieving sustainable development, but the environment/technology nexus still remains poorly understood. Moreover, there has been little interaction between the realms of technology policy and environmental policy. Environmental policy instruments differ in their effects on innovation. *Product standards* tend to prompt incremental innovation or modifications at the margin. *Product bans* can stimulate radical innovation in the form of replacements, but they also entail disruptions and costs. *Performance standards* for industrial processes

---

*       See Section 11.2.6 in Chapter 11 for a discussion of trade disputes involving GMOs.

are technically flexible, while *technology specifications* tend to stifle innovation. *Economic instruments*, such as pollution charges and tradable permits, have more dynamic potential to stimulate innovation but have not always been set at sufficiently high levels, in the case of the former, or used extensively, in the case of the latter. Nor have *voluntary agreements* brought much pressure for technological change thus far, although newer forms of environmental compacts with industry may hold more promise. Also valuable are approaches such as extended producer responsibility, information disclosure, and environmental management systems, which can encourage the complete redesign of products and processes (OECD 1999).

Certain policy reforms could promote more environmental innovation. In general, economic instruments should be used more frequently as substitutes for, and complements to, traditional forms of regulation. Moreover, changes in implementation, as well as new approaches, could substantially improve the regulatory framework for environmental innovation. The ways in which regulations are implemented and enforced have a strong influence on industry programs to develop technologies to comply with new standards. Systems for early warning and timed introduction of new policies can reduce regulatory uncertainty for industry. Expedited government review procedures and verification and certification schemes can speed market introduction of new technologies. Shifting away from technology specifications toward end results can increase the flexibility of industry in achieving compliance. This will require an improved merger of environmental policy and technology policy and better coordination among environmental and technology agencies.

### 10.17.1 Clean Production Mechanisms

Chapter 34 of Agenda 21, endorsed by the 1992 Rio Earth Summit, called on international organizations to "promote, facilitate, and finance as appropriate, the access to and transfer of environmentally sustainable technology and corresponding know-how, in particular to developing countries" (United Nations 1993). In response to this request, several bilateral and multilateral institutions have established programs to promote cleaner technologies and techniques.

One program, the joint UNIDO/UNEP National Cleaner Production Centres (NCPC), was set up in response to Agenda 21 with the objective of promoting the widespread application of the cleaner production approach and the uptake of cleaner technologies within industry. By January 2003, the NCPC had funded twenty-five centers in developing countries on all continents in order to transfer know-how, as well as management skills, and build capacity in these countries. These centers had varying results, but although they are still reporting the outcomes of their programs, it has been concluded that cleaner production is a cost-effective approach to sustainable development and is an effective tool for identification and prioritization of technology change yielding both economic and environmental benefits (R. Luken and Navratil 2004). However, developing local capacity takes time and commitment of large international funding agencies. In addition to the NCPC program, many industrialized countries have begun their own initiatives to promote cleaner technology, including some of the programs outlined in Box 10.4.

Traditionally, producers have considered only themselves responsible for the quality of the product, but today, industries are increasingly accountable for their choice of materials through the supply chain, as well as the environmental impacts of their production processes on workers. However, more recent initiatives have placed the burden of waste management on the original producer, stimulating technological changes early by requiring producers to clean up the products they manufacture and to design them appropriately for recycling and reuse. A new practice has emerged that is referred to as extended producer responsibility (EPR) or producer takeback, requiring manufacturers to be responsible for environmentally friendly management of their product when it reaches the end of its life. EPR often incorporates the cost of waste management into the product price. It is essential for government officials and the public to be aware of EPR programs around the world where companies not only comply with regulations but also actively advocate for financial responsibility toward the environment.

In the United States, local governments currently spend an estimated $43.5 billion a year managing product waste. At the same time, state and local governments are facing considerable deficits. Given the magnitude of the deficits, state actions are likely to cut basic services, such as health care and education, or impose new tax burdens (White House Task Force 1998). Thus EPR can be viewed as one way to lower the financial burden on government. EPR initiatives could also reduce health-care costs related to health problems caused by product-related waste.

## BOX 10.4: COUNTRY PROGRAMS: CLEAN TECHNOLOGY

The following excerpts, taken from the OECD (1999) report *Technology and Environment*, provide examples of country-based initiatives to promote cleaner technology.[a]

### DENMARK

*Cleaner Technology Action Plan*. Through its Cleaner Technology Action Plan, the Danish government offers a suite of services to promote the diffusion of environmental technologies. The Plan was devised by the Danish Environmental Protection Agency (EPA) and many of its projects have been sponsored by the National Council for Recycling and Cleaner Technology. The initial Action Plan, currently in its third phase, began in 1986. The third phase, which will run through 1997, builds on initiatives launched in the first two phases. The goals of the Plan are to prevent environmental damage by promoting cleaner technology and to limit the consumption of resources. End-of-pipe technologies are not considered in the Plan, although they are acknowledged to have a continuing important role in Danish industry. Activities are directed principally toward industry decision makers and managers, but an aim of the Plan is also to educate and influence politicians, public purchasers, ordinary customers and technical and environmental staff in Danish municipalities. . . .

### IRELAND

*Clean Technology Centre*. The Clean Technology Centre (CTC) in Ireland is an independent, non-profit corporation supported by a combination of public and private sources. Specifically, 14 sponsoring companies contribute to the CTC's funding through an annual subscription fee, while additional funds are provided by the European Regional Infrastructure Development Programme (via Forbairt, the Irish State Agency for Science and Technology). Also of note is that the Centre is based at the Cork Regional Technical College and has strong links with this technical educational institute.

The mission of the CTC is to advise and assist industry, public authorities and governments on the adoption of waste minimization techniques, clean technologies and cleaner production methods. The Centre aims to help industry shift away from a focus on end-of-pipe technologies to control pollution to one based on pollution prevention. The program provides expertise and services to "once-off" clients requiring solutions to specific problems as well as ongoing environmental services to its sponsoring companies. Although the original sponsors were mostly pharmaceutical and chemical businesses in the Cork City region, the Centre currently provides industrial services to companies from a wide variety of industrial sectors throughout Ireland. It has also carried out projects for the European Commission, Forbairt, the Irish Business and Employers Confederation and the Irish Environmental Protection Agency (EPA). . . .

### THE NETHERLANDS

*Cleaner Production Programme*. An important example in the Netherlands of a program to promote diffusion of environmental technologies is the Cleaner Production Programme (CPP) initiated and funded jointly by the Ministry of Economic Affairs and the Ministry of Housing, Spatial Planning and the Environment. This program was launched in 1992 and had funding of NLG 3.6 million for an initial period of just over three years. However, the initiating ministries were so pleased with the results that they decided to extend the Programme at least through 1998. The main objective of the Cleaner Production Programme is to stimulate the utilization of clean technology in the small and medium-size business sector. The Cleaner Production Programme is executed by an integrated network of Dutch organizations, including the Netherlands Innovation Centres Network, the National Environmental Centre (NEC), 18 regional Innovation Centres (ICs) and some 20 Regional Industrial Environmental Agencies (RIEAs). The integrated nature of the Programme is one of its most interesting elements and one that other countries may find useful to emulate. The CPP is designed to reach essentially all businesses in the Netherlands, but it has identified 11 industries for special attention: the foodstuffs and stimulants industry; the wood and furniture industry; printing and allied trades; the chemical industry; the rubber and plastics processing industry; the building materials, earthenware and glass industry; the metal products industry; the engineering industry; the motor vehicle industry; the building industry; and repair shops for consumer goods. In all, there are approximately 105 000 SMEs in the Netherlands in these target groups. . . .

### UNITED KINGDOM

*Environmental Technology Best Practice Programme*. The ETBPP, which focuses on waste minimization and the use of cleaner technologies, is jointly funded by the UK Department of Trade and Industry and the UK Department of the Environment, Transport and the Regions and is managed by AEA Technology plc through the National Environmental Technology Centre and the Energy Technology Support Unit. Thus far, the Programme has targeted 11 different industrial sectors: the foundry industry, textiles, paper and board, volatile organic compounds, glass, food and drink, chemicals, printing, metals finishing, ceramics engineering, and plastics and packaging. Four distinctive program elements, three focused on providing information and one on financial assistance, comprise the bulk of the ETBPPs work: 1) the production of "good practice" guides and case studies, 2) the production of environmental performance guides, 3) the presentation of "new practice" case studies, and 4) the promotion of "future practices". . . .

### UNITED STATES

*Design for the Environment*. The Design for the Environment (DfE) program is one (of many) voluntary EPA programs related to environmental technology diffusion. Established in October 1992, the program is designed to help businesses incorporate environmental considerations, such as risk reduction, into the design and redesign of products, processes and technical and management systems. Design changes may have to do with implementing pollution prevention, energy

(continued)

> **BOX 10.4** (continued)
>
> efficiency and other resource conservation measures; making products that can be refurbished, disassembled and recycled; or keeping careful track of the environmental costs associated with each product or process. The program is focused on compiling and disseminating information needed to design for the environment and on developing new analytical tools for use by business. A typical DfE industry project includes developing a Cleaner Technologies Substitutes Assessment (CTSA) and a communication and implementation strategy. By providing detailed environmental, economic and performance information on traditional and alternative manufacturing methods and technologies CTSAs help companies compare different technologies or products and select the most environmentally-friendly alternatives. To help industry implement some of the new technologies identified in the CTSA, DfE provides a variety of outreach tools, including fact sheets, bulletins, pollution prevention case studies, software, videos and training materials. Some of the CTSAs that have been undertaken include those for printed wiring board, screen printing, lithography, flexography, garment and textile care, and metal finishing.

[a] OECD (1999), *Technology and Environment: Towards Policy Integration*, Paris, OECD.

EPR started in Europe in response to Europe's growing hazardous waste and limited landfill space and is slowly gaining momentum in some U.S. states. The OECD has also supported EPR and offers guidance on how to implement EPR policies to both OECD and non-OECD countries. The premise behind EPR is for manufacturers to take responsibility for the recycling of their own products by

- using environmentally safer materials in the production process;
- consuming fewer materials in the production process;
- designing the product to last longer and be more useful;
- creating safer recycling systems;
- being motivated to keep waste costs down; and
- no longer passing the cost of disposal to the government and taxpayers.

Many industries are proponents of the scheme, including Sony Europe, Hewlett-Packard, Braun, and Electrolux, which have set up their own individual recycling group in Europe. Japan and Europe have passed comprehensive EPR legislation for both electronic and electrical equipment (see the WEEE discussion in Section 10.18.2.3) and automobile waste. EPR has had a slower uptake in North America for a variety of reasons, but it is gaining increasing recognition, given that Americans generate 50 percent of the world's solid waste (Clean Production Action 2004).

Germany has one of the longest-running EPR programs targeting reducing consumption. The German Packaging Ordinance, starting in 1990, sometimes called the Green Dot system because licensed products carry a green dot, has resulted in an increase in reusable packaging, incorporating significant design changes in packaging, including major reductions in volume and weight by changing container shapes and sizes. There have been shifts within the plastic packaging sector away from polyvinyl chloride (PVC) to polyethylene (PE), which is easier to recycle. For comparison, between 1991 and 1995, German packaging decreased 14 percent under the German Green Dot system, while during the same period in the United States, packaging increased 13 percent (Clean Production Action 2004).

Despite slow progress toward EPR in the United States, there are successful case studies of EPR policies. In response to growing pressures from consumers and regulators, manufacturers of electronic waste, such as Hewlett-Packard, IBM, and Best Buy, have all initiated limited electronic takeback programs. Most of these programs charge the consumer a fee when the used electronic product is brought to the collection site. The Silicon Valley Toxics Coalition is working with a coalition of groups on the Computer Takeback Campaign to implement EPR for electronic waste. The campaign is particularly active in the states of Washington, Massachusetts, Maine, Texas, California, New York, Vermont, and Wisconsin.[55] In California, IBM and the television manufacturers formed a coalition that set up a government-run recycling program. The bill, SB20, which became effective in April 2004, places an advance recycling fee (ARF) on television monitors and computer displays of between $6 and $10 based on device size. The money is collected by a state-run organization and then used to pay a centralized waste-management firm. It is a traditional government-run recycling system but is financed by a fee paid by consumers. There will be no information flow between producer and recycler with the intention to encourage better product design. The scheme still has some problems to ameliorate, including the fact that taxpayers may still have to pay some of the bill for recycling because the ARFs

---

**BOX 10.5: ASEAN ENVIRONMENTAL IMPROVEMENT PROGRAM**

The following excerpt provides a more in-depth look at the key aspects of the ASEAN-EIP:[a]

In Southeast Asia, one of the world's most rapidly developing regions, concern for ensuring sustainable and environmentally acceptable economic development was the driving force behind the U.S. Agency for International Development (USAID) in 1992 to manage the ASEAN Environmental Improvement Program. The program was designed to address rising urban and industrial pollution in the then six ASEAN countries—Brunei, Indonesia, Malaysia, the Philippines, Singapore and Thailand—and to provide a region-wide programmatic framework to introduce cleaner industrial production and environmental management.

Funded by USAID and ASEAN, the monumental, six-year, $17.5-million program addressed environmental policy and institutional development, training and technology dissemination. Program tasks included analysis of the effectiveness and efficiency of existing environmental laws, regulations and institutions in each ASEAN country; introduction of market-based incentives to foster improved environmental management; encouragement of regional policies to prevent industrial pollution and raise the level of environmental awareness and concern in the region; and establishment of technical research and development centers as well as region-wide certification programs for testing laboratories.

As part of this program, environmental audits were undertaken of 15 industrial programs per year, including preparation of training courses in environmental pollution prevention practices and technologies; environmental workshops and seminars for industry; establishment of an information center to introduce state-of-the-art U.S. environmental technology to the ASEAN managers and entrepreneurs; and promotion of the export of U.S. environmental technology. In the initial phases, policy and institutional analyses were conducted in high-priority sectors in the ASEAN countries such as iron and steel, pulp and paper, metal finishing, food processing and cement industries to identify opportunities and suggest technologies that could yield significant productivity savings while reducing pollution levels. For example, discussions with iron and steel mill managers on reducing electric arc furnace dust identified the fact that no iron and steel mills in Southeast Asia were recovering metals from their metal-bearing tailings and wastes, an area in which U.S. practices are extremely advanced.

In early 1995, USAID reorganized its Asian environmental efforts, and the ASEAN program was absorbed into the larger United States–Asia Environmental Partnership (US-AEP) program, a USAID-sponsored, $100-million public-private partnership designed to encourage the transfer of American environmental management and technology skills to over 30 Asian countries. The primary focus is on the original ASEAN member countries as well as Taiwan, South Korea, Hong Kong, India and Sri Lanka. The US-AEP maintains technology representative offices in each of these countries, as well as a full-time liaison at the Asian Development Bank.

Recognizing that Asia's rapid industrial development poses one of the most significant challenges to global environmental sustainability, the US-AEP's original mission focused on pollution control, biodiversity conservation, urban environmental infrastructure development and increased energy efficiency. In 1995, the US-AEP made clean technology and environmental management (CTEM) its primary focus, while maintaining the infrastructure component and adding a new focus on public policy to encourage CTEM. Because so much of Asia's projected industrial capacity is yet to be installed, promoting CTEM now will produce significant long-term benefits. The program supports professional exchanges, technology demonstrations, seminars and workshops aimed at fostering U.S.-Asian partnerships. The US-AEP also sponsors the widely followed Environment Technology Network for Asia, which provides environmental and clean production trade leads to U.S. suppliers.

Asian environmental priorities and opportunities are identified through country assessments conducted by US-AEP staff. Following these assessments, US-AEP staff members assist interested Asian organizations in finding like-minded U.S. organizations and establishing partnerships. Mechanisms include professional exchanges, information transfer, trade and professional missions, training and encouragement of major U.S. multinational corporations to foster improved environmental management from their Asian suppliers.

[a] Louis Berger Group, ASEAN Environmental Improvemental Program, www.louisberger.com/berger/services2/16asia.php (accessed May 31, 2010).

---

may fall short of covering the full costs of collection, transportation, and recycling. In addition, some companies feel that it does not make sense economically for the burden of end-of-life management to fall on governments that do not have authority to change the design of the product to ensure that end-of-life costs are minimized (Clean Production Action 2004).

In January 2003, another scheme in Maine set an EPR precedent by holding automobile manufacturers accountable for taking back mercury switches when vehicles are scrapped. In 1993, Sweden banned the use of mercury switches in vehicles, affecting the entire European automobile market. U.S. car makers continued to use the switches through 2002. The

Maine legislation requires automakers who use mercury switches to establish a compliance plan and contract with a third party to collect switches and arrange for their recycling (Clean Production Action 2004). Automakers challenged the law in federal court, but a court opinion rejected their arguments (ibid.). The success of this initiative was the direct result of an unusual alliance between environmental organizations and auto and steel recycling associations, looking to the producer for liability, where they could make a choice to switch to substitute the mercury with a safer alternative.

Another more international endeavor toward cleaner production was the Association of Southeast

Asian Nations Environmental Improvement Program (ASEAN-EIP), which was funded by the United States Agency for International Development (USAID) in 1992 and ran for four years (Box 10.5). The program operated in six nations of the ASEAN: Thailand, Indonesia, Malaysia, Singapore, Brunei, and the Philippines. The program's objectives were to address the total production processes in these countries, including upstream and downstream consequences, with a view to mitigate these consequences through more efficient process use of inputs, better management processes, and continual improvement. The ASEAN-EIP had a significant impact on furthering the adoption of cleaner production technology in these countries but, according to some studies, fell substantially short of its potential. Program resources were stretched too thin across too many countries to make it important to the government to engage in a realistic national policy and strategy for cleaner production (Stevenson 2004). However, other initiatives can look to the trial ASEAN-EIP as a model for future strategies to incorporate cleaner production.

Cleaner technology is one fundamental basis of sustainable development. An OECD (1994) study concluded that 70 to 90 percent of current emissions can be reduced through the implementation of cleaner technology. But the pace and degree of transformation to cleaner technologies are limited: an overwhelming movement toward research, development, and deployment of cleaner technologies has not yet occurred. Nevertheless, governments and some firms in the industrial sector are increasingly expressing a clear desire for a transformation to cleaner processes and products. The system to transform to cleaner technologies requires the identification of barriers and opportunities for using a variety of appropriate policy instruments (economic, infrastructure, institutional/individual capacity, and financing mechanisms). The key is to find and implement a mix of strategic plans, goals, regulations, economic instruments, incentives, and educational programs (ibid.).

## 10.18 REGIONAL APPROACHES TO PROTECTION OF HEALTH, SAFETY, AND THE ENVIRONMENT: THE EUROPEAN UNION

### 10.18.1 Environmental Law in the European Union

Protection of the environment and the workplace is a major challenge facing Europe. In the distant past, the European Community was strongly criticized for putting trade and economic development before environmental and worker health and safety considerations. More recently, however, the European Community has recognized that sound development cannot be based on the depletion of natural resources, the deterioration of the environment and public health, and poor workplace conditions and has developed progressive environmental and labor protections in order to advance environmental and workplace goals.

Vogel (2003) has argued that the United States and the EU have actually traded places in the degree of commitment to environmental, health, and safety goals in that there has been a shift in environmental protection policies in Europe and the United States. From the 1960s to the 1980s, U.S. regulatory standards tended to be more stringent than any European standards. However, since 1990, the reverse has been true; many EU regulations are now more precautionary in their approach than the U.S. ones (ibid., p. 557).

Policy improvements in health, safety, and environmental protection, hereinafter referred to collectively as "environmental policy," would benefit from the comparative study of regulatory systems in other developed countries (Breyer and Heyvaert 2000; Brickman, Jasanoff, et al. 1985). However, this is beyond the scope of the present book. What is of more immediate importance is the study of the evolution of environmental policy in the EU, not only because more significant progress is being made there than in the United States, but also because environmental policy is on the way to becoming more fully integrated into other aspects of sustainable development.

The new politics of consumer and environmental regulation in Europe have their origins in (1) a series of regulatory failures within Europe, for example, Chernobyl, mad cow disease, and tainted blood, (2) broader and stronger political support for more stringent and comprehensive regulatory standards within Europe, and (3) the growth in the regulatory competence of EU institutions (Vogel 2003, p. 558).

In spite of the earlier history (1970–1980) of administrative advance and greater stringency in environmental instruments in the United States, such as mandatory emission and effluent standards, environmental impact assessments, and incorporation of both the precautionary principle* and the polluter-

---

\* The precautionary principle has suffered a decline in support in the United States since the Reagan revolution of 1980, with the United States denying that it is a principle and insisting

---

**BOX 10.6: ENVIRONMENTAL GOVERNANCE IN THE EUROPEAN UNION**

European environmental governance is structured as follows:

- Commission (twenty-seven commissioners)—cabinet secretaries
- Council of (twenty-seven) Ministers (different persons for different issues, for example, a council of environmental ministers)
- Parliament (members elected in scheduled national elections)
- European Court of Justice
- European Environmental Agency (Copenhagen): Information, studies, and research, but not an inspectorate

EU environmental obligations are imposed on accession countries as a condition of admission.

EU environmental law evolves through a series of treaties that further define the legal authority/policy focus of the European Community. It influences and is influenced by international environmental law, serves as a model for other/future regional environmental regimes, and requires transposition into national law and implementation.

---

pays principle into law, EU environmental law has now gone beyond U.S. approaches and even contains initiatives not present in U.S. federal law, such as eco-labeling, reduction of packaging waste, and recycling of vehicles and electronic products. The EU has also signed many multilateral environmental agreements that the United States has either not signed or not ratified, such as the Basel Convention on Hazardous Waste (discussed earlier in this chapter), the Convention on Biological Diversity, and the Biosafety Protocol (see Chapter 11 for a discussion of the last two agreements), which are now a part of EU law.

At the heart of increased demands for greater environmental protection first in Europe and again more recently in the United States is the increase in the lack of trust in either industry or the government, with a consequent demand for greater public participation. Indeed, we may be at the beginning of a more aggressive catch-up period for the United States after the complacency in the 1990s noted by Vogel (2003).

### 10.18.1.1 Background to EU Environmental Law

When the European Union was founded in 1957, it had no environmental policies or laws and was formed primarily to strengthen national economies and intergovernmental relations after World War II. Currently, however, the EU has some of the most progressive environmental, as well as worker health and safety, policies of any international regime. Throughout the 1970s and early 1980s, items of EU environmental policy were agreed by the Council of Environment Ministers.

Beginning in 1972, environmental agendas were pursued through a series of six successive environ-

mental action plans, chiefly concerned with minimum standards for air and water pollution and waste management. (Currently the EU is proceeding under its sixth environmental action plan, which is more specific and systems oriented in its approach—see the discussion below.)

In the 1980s, environmental laws and policies were enacted through an emerging trilateral arrangement of the Council of Environment Ministers, the European Commission, and the European Parliament's Environment Committee. Issues that had previously been contained in intergovernmental committees of national bureaucrats and scientists entered the political mainstream, along with increasing concerns of international nonprofit pressure groups and EU public awareness, all of which had to be accommodated in the policy-making process. The sudden change in environmental policy after the mid 1980s was also driven by greener "leader" states such as Germany, the Netherlands, and Denmark, which all influenced the EU to adopt more appropriate standards that were as high as, if not higher than, their own national standards. The European Court of Justice (ECJ) also played a critical role in raising and maintaining high environmental standards across the EU. The structure of EU governance of environmental matters is summarized in Box 10.6.*

Although EU environmental policy has progressed significantly since 1980, there are still important challenges to overcome, including how to enforce policies, such as the concept of sustainability, which calls for building alliances between different aspects of policy, as well as different actors and nations. Additionally, sustainability requires integrating an

---

instead that it is an "approach," while Europe has begun to incorporate it formally into its legal framework. See Ashford (2007).

* The Treaty of Lisbon, which was signed by the requisite number of member states on November 3, 2009, will alter the governance structure.

---

### BOX 10.7 THE SINGLE EUROPEAN ACT (1986)

The Single European Act of 1986

- included environmental measures in Title VII that went beyond mere codification of environmental law, providing for future law-making;
- required a "high level of [health, safety, and environmental] protection";
- affirmed that environmental concerns should be a part of other EC policies, especially commerce/trade within the Community;
- introduced qualified majority voting for issues affecting the "internal market";
- emphasized pollution prevention at the source;
- endorsed the polluter-pays principle;
- established the principle of subsidiarity
  — where national (member) actions would be inadequate (especially regarding transnational issues);
  — where objectives could be better achieved at the EC level; and
- authorized the EC to participate in multilateral environmental agreements.

---

### BOX 10.8: THE TREATY OF MAASTRICHT (1992)

The 1992 Treaty of Maastricht

- affirmed the environment as a fundamental EC objective;
- endorsed the development of emission standards to encourage prevention, rather than rely on environmental quality standards;
- affirmed that environmental protection was not just a component but was to be "integrated" into the definition and implementation of other EC policies;
- allowed qualified majority voting for issues affecting the environment (except for energy sources and for national water- and land-use management issues not having to do with waste-related activities);
- strengthened the role of Parliament through allowing a codecision process on "action items"; and
- provided for incorporation of the most important EC environmental acts into the law of the accession countries.

---

environmental perspective into long-term political, social, and economic priorities of the EU. Another problem is improving the implementation of policy at the national level, where not all member nations of the EU are created equal in reaching the goals of environmental policy. For example, elevating the states from the former Eastern bloc to a desired environmental standard will require significant effort while those countries are still focusing on rebuilding their capacity and economy and lowering societal barriers (Jordan 2002). In this respect, the stronger or more experienced EU states have a role to play in providing models of success for states still striving to achieve appropriate policies.

With regard to the environment, the EU has demonstrated that it is likely to perceive itself increasingly as a whole, moving closer to the "union among the peoples of Europe" called for in the preamble of the Treaty of Rome (Hildebrand 2002). Although many challenges still remain in policy implementation and enforcement, the EU is becoming the world's authority in addressing emerging environmental issues.

Through a series of three major treaties, the European Union has solidified its approach to the

environment and sustainable development (see Jans 2000, chap. 1; Jordan 2002, chaps. 3 and 4; and Sands 2003, chap. 15). The first was the Single European Act of 1986 (see Box 10.7), which did much to create a more coordinated environmental policy among EU members.

Especially notable was the endorsement of "pollution prevention at the source" as the preferred approach to reducing pollution and of the polluter-pays principle, later to be incorporated into specific liability directives. Note also the "principle of subsidiarity," whereby EU action would be indicated where separate national efforts would be inadequate or less effective than collective action at the EU level. Finally, of special significance is the replacement of negotiation of multilateral environmental agreements by individual member nations in favor of the EU representing a collective political entity in these negotiations.

The Maastricht Treaty of 1992 (Box 10.8) further raised the currency of environmental issues in the governance of the EU and required their integration into other EC matters, especially commerce, economic development, and trade. The treaty also cre-

---

**BOX 10.9: THE TREATY OF AMSTERDAM (1997)**

The 1997 Treaty of Amsterdam

- affirmed that the environment was to be "integrated" into the definition and implementation of other EC policies in order to foster "sustainable development"—a major EC goal;
- endorsed the prior emphasis of the Single European Act and the Maastricht Treaty on prevention, source reduction, polluter pays, the precautionary principle, and subsidiarity;
- added a requirement for "proportionality" of measures, commensurate with the seriousness of the problem;
- established a complex "codecision" process for developing and adopting environmental legislation that involves the Commission, the Parliament, and the Council (of Environmental Ministers) (the Council could be challenged by the Commission/Parliament in the European Court of Justice); and
- provided a "safeguard" clause by which member states could take emergency (urgent) measures if necessary.

---

ated a codecision mechanism for approving legislation between the Commission and the Parliament. Of special significance was the preference for emission standards to encourage prevention rather than reliance on environmental quality standards.

Finally, the Amsterdam Treaty of 1997 (Box 10.9) established "sustainable development" as a major EC purpose, thus integrating economic and environmental goals. In a compromise move, the treaty endorsed the principle of "proportionality." whereby the stringency (and economic impact) of environmental measures should reflect the seriousness of the environmental threat to be addressed in a balanced way. The treaty also allowed member states to establish emergency measures on their own to address local environmental threats.

The next major change to governance and procedures in the EU took form in the Lisbon Treaty. After an initial setback when Ireland rejected the treaty in a public referendum in 2008, a revised treaty was ratified by a 2–1 margin by Ireland in October 2009. The treaty was signed by the requisite number of member states on November 3, 2009.

The Lisbon Strategy (not to be confused with the Lisbon Treaty) adopted in March 2000 by the Council of the European Union established the goal of making Europe by 2010 "the most dynamic and competitive knowledge-based economy in the world capable of sustainable economic growth with more and better jobs and greater social cohesion, and respect for the environment."[56] Now superceded by Europe 2020, attempts to create a strategy for sustainable development is now dominated by economic concerns (see Section 1.5 in Chapter 1 for a fuller discussion).

Articles 174–176 (new numbering from the Amsterdam Treaty) of the Single European Act (1986) goes beyond the traditional codification of existing environmental law and provides for future environmental lawmaking. EU law imposes rights (and obligations) not only on states (members) but also on firms, NGOs, and "associations," giving them rights in national courts, and also establishes mechanisms for enforcement. In this way, it expands the narrower reach of international environmental law.

The EU Commission proposes environmental (and other) legislation. The Environment Directorate (DG XI) is responsible for administering environmental affairs. The European Environmental Agency (EEA), which became operational in 1994, is dedicated to research and information gathering and dissemination and seeks to encourage comparability in national data.[57]

The sources of EU law are the EU treaties, general principles of law, international obligations binding on the EC, and so-called secondary legislation, consisting of regulations, directives, and decisions. Regulations are directly binding in that they do not need to be implemented by the member states to be turned into national law; in contrast, directives give member states a specified time to transpose them into national law (Hall 2007).* The EU also adopts nonbinding conventions and resolutions. The EC now negotiates international environmental agreements on behalf of all EU countries.

EU environmental law prevails over national law in case of a conflict (but note the principle of subsidiarity; note also the rights of nations to go beyond EC obligations/requirements providing their measures are not arbitrary discrimination or disguised restrictions on trade).

---

\* By 2009, the EC had issued more than 220 directives dealing with the environment (Beunen, van der Knaap et al., 2009; Hall, 2007).

Directives/regulations have been issued on the following topics:

- General policy
- Air quality
- Water quality
- Biodiversity and nature
- Noise
- Chemicals and other hazardous substances
- Waste
- Radioactive substances

Other actions have been taken on the following issues:

- Environmental information (including ecolabeling and ecoaudits)
- Use of economic instruments (including a carbon tax)
- Trade and competition
- Compliance
- Liability

The EU's actual environmental programs are implemented through a series of successive EU environmental action plans. The Fifth European Community Action Programme on the Environment (1993–1997; then extended), titled "Towards Sustainability," with vertical and sectoral approaches, focused on the following issues:

- Climate change
- Acidification and air pollution
- Depletion and pollution of water resources
- Deterioration of the urban environment
- Deterioration of coastal zones
- Waste

The following sectors were targeted:

- Industry
- Energy
- Transport
- Agriculture
- Tourism

The Sixth Environmental Action Programme: Environment (2002–2012), titled "Our Future, Our Choice," focuses on the following issues:[58]

- Climate change
- Nature and biodiversity
- Environment and health (within one generation)
- Management of natural resources and waste

The Programme focuses on seven strategies:

- Air
- Waste prevention and recycling
- Marine Environment
- Soil
- Pesticides
- Natural Resources
- Urban Environment

The Programme identifies a number of priority areas for action in Article 9(2):[59]

- (a) Integrating environmental protection requirements into all the Community's external policies, including trade and development cooperation, in order to achieve sustainable development by inter alia the elaboration of guidelines; . . .
- (c) work towards strengthening international environmental governance by the gradual reinforcement of the multilateral cooperation and the institutional framework including resources;
- (d) Aiming for swift ratification and effective compliance and enforcement of international conventions where the Community is a Party;
- (e) Promoting sustainable environmental practices in foreign investments and export credits;
- Intensifying efforts to arrive at a consensus on methods for the evaluation of risks to health and the environment, as well as approaches of risk management including the precautionary principle; . . .
- (g) Achieving mutual supportiveness between trade and environmental needs, including [undertaking] . . . "sustainability impact assessments" of multilateral trade agreements;
- (h) Promoting a world trade system that fully recognizes multilateral and regional trade agreements and the precautionary principle; and
- (i) Promoting cross-border environmental cooperation with neighbouring countries and regions.

The Fifth and Sixth Action Programmes greatly influenced international environmental law, specifically EIA, the right to know, ecolabeling, EMAS, IPPC, LIFE, and REACH. The focus on sustainable development reflects the need to integrate protection of the environment into all EU policies (Article 6(3c)).

The current thrust of environmental law in the EU (through Article 174) emphasizes precaution, prevention (with a stated preference for emission limitations), reduction at the source, polluter pays, and subsidiarity—providing "a high level of protection."

### 10.18.1.2 Enforcement

The 1992 Maastricht Treaty on European Union strengthened the EC's commitment to environmental protection, including the promotion of "sustainable and non-inflationary growth respecting the environment." Environmental policy is to be based on the precautionary principle, and the existing treaty requirement that environmental protection should be integrated into other EC policies is continually enforced (Wilkinson 2002).

The Community institutions created by the EU have played a significant role in reducing the use of prior national regulations in favor of EU law subsequently transposed into national law. The European Court of Justice (ECJ) has struck down numerous national regulations that protected producers rather than workers, consumers, or the environment. It is also generally responsible for setting decisions on a wide variety of environmental, health, and safety issues, particularly where those cases that were unable to be resolved at national level were then brought into the EU community forum for greater awareness and potential adoption by other EU nation-states. Recent rulings by the ECJ concern such issues as health care and treatment, medical data protection, marketing or banning genetically modified (GM) foods if there is a suspected risk to human health, and defining a maximum weekly working time for rescue workers.[60]

Perhaps the most significant shift in European practices occurred from 1998 onward when the EU took three important steps to strengthen enforcement: (1) judicial enforcement with the threat of sanctions, (2) central coordination of inspections and monitoring, and (3) new legislation on public access to environmental information embodying the UN's Århus Convention (see Section 10.4.4) (Hall 2007). While the U.S. federal government is authorized to bring suit against states and municipalities to achieve compliance, the EU Commission's role is to oversee the adoption and implementation of environmental obligations by the member states. As a result, member states occasionally resist or delay full compliance with EU directives (ibid.).

Procedural coherence and harmonization of environmental law and practices within the EU were encouraged by the European Union Forum of Judges for the Environment, created at a meeting held at the European Court of Justice in Luxembourg on April 26, 2004. This action was a direct result of the UNEP Global Judges Symposium held in Johannesburg on the eve of the World Summit on Sustainable Development and the planning meetings held in Nairobi in January 2003 for the implementation of the outcomes of the Johannesburg Symposium.

The Forum of Judges seeks to promote contacts and exchanges of information between its members or observers and with the European Union. The purpose of the Forum is to promote, from the viewpoint of sustainable development, the implementation of national, European, and international environmental law. In particular, the Forum seeks to share experiences on judicial training in environmental law, foster the knowledge of environmental law among judges, share experience on environmental case law, and contribute to the better implementation and enforcement of international, European, and national environmental laws. These efforts will be carried out in collaboration with the UNEP.[61]

As the EU integration process goes forward, environmental laws and practices within the EU may be expected to coalesce (see Section 10.18.1.1).

## 10.18.2 Regulation of Air, Water, and Waste

There have been extensive changes in the EU's regulation of air, water, and waste over the past decade. The EU approach to air and water pollution generally parallels, and lags behind, that of the U.S. Clean Air, Clean Water, and Safe Drinking Water acts described in Chapter 9. Various directives address air pollution, the latest of which is the 2008 Directive on Air Quality and Management (2008/50/EC). A comprehensive Water Framework Directive (2000/60/EC) replaced seven older directives and now anticipates the development of water quality concentration limits and polluter discharge limitations. EU waste regulation goes beyond that of the United States in some areas, such as its Directive on Waste Electrical and Electronic Equipment (WEEE), which requires the producers of electrical and electronic products to finance the collection, treatment, recovery, and environmentally sound disposal of WEEE from households.

The following sections outline briefly the features of these media-based EU initiatives.* For a fuller treatment, consult Jans (2000), Jordan (2002), and Sands (2003), as well as the annual *Yearbook on European Environmental Law* published by Oxford University Press.

---

\*    In the area of emissions to air and water, the EU lagged behind the United States and ultimately produced legislation mirroring the U.S. approach (see Chapter 9). However, in the treatment of waste and in other areas discussed in Section 10.18, Europe has led in innovative and more comprehensive and multimedia focused approaches to reducing environmental pollution.

## 10.18.2.1 Air

EU efforts to address air pollution are now coordinated under the Air Quality Framework Directive 96/62/EC, its four daughter directives, and other directives emphasizing:

- air pollution reduction using equipment, concentration, and emission standards (phaseouts/reductions); the air framework directives 96/62/EC and 2008/50/EC, Air Quality Assessment and Management

- reduction of acidification (and reduction of ground-level ozone by two-thirds): $SO_2$, $NO_x$, VOCs, and $NH_3$ (emission ceilings by the end of 2010) (2001/81/EC)

- establishment of limit values, "alert thresholds," and monitoring requirements for $SO_2$, $NO_x$, particulate matter, and Pb (1999/30/EC); benzene and CO (2000/69/EC); polycyclic aromatic hydrocarbons (PAHs), Cd, As, Ni, and Hg (2004/107/EC)

- establishment of air quality standards and emissions limitations (on diesel engines and combustion plants)

- reduction of emissions of greenhouse gases reflecting the Kyoto Treaty and its successor agreements in Copenhagen and Cancun (constituting the EU programme on climate change)

- transboundary pollution

- reducing ozone depletion: replacement of HCFCs and methyl bromide more aggressively than the amended Montreal Protocol

- air pollution emanating from waste incineration (2000/76/EC)

- the Clean Air for Europe (CAFE) Programme (2001)

## 10.18.2.2 Water

The Water Framework Directive 2000/60/EC replaces seven older directives to provide a sufficient supply of good-quality surface water and groundwater as needed for sustainable, balanced, and equitable water use by setting concentration and discharge limits for both direct discharges (using best available techniques) and diffuse sources (using best environmental practices). The legislation is a significant driver of changes in water management for member states across Europe. The directive anticipates public participation from key stakeholders as a central feature and thus moves compliance and implementation from a purely technical undertaking to the political-social arenas (Gooch and Huitima, 2008). The directive was adopted earlier than the EU's adoption of

the Åarhus Convention into EU law.* The directive is to be integrated with the IPPC and other directives. Effluent (emission) limits on "dangerous substances" (76/464/EEC) are established through five daughter directives: mercury, cadmium, hexachlorocyclohexane, and so on. In addition to a focus on industrial chemicals, the EU requires pharmaceutical companies to analyze the *environmental* risks of new drugs, having adopted guidelines in 2006 that grew out of concerns about traces of drugs discovered in waterways and drinking water.[62]

## 10.18.2.3 Waste

EU efforts to address hazardous and solid waste emphasize:

- the Waste Framework Directive 75/442/EEC (as amended by Council Directive 91/156/EEC) has as its purposes to prevent/reduce waste production to recover waste by recycling, reuse, reclamation, or any other process and to use waste as energy. Waste-prevention approaches are to be integrated with the IPPC and REACH.

- the reduction of waste by prevention or reduction of waste production using clean technology, products designed to reduce waste, and techniques for final disposal of dangerous substances.

- distinguishing solid waste (75/442/EEC) and hazardous waste (78/319/EEC).

- disposing of hazardous waste (78/319/EEC) safely; prohibiting uncontrolled discharges; the directive requires the creation of a "competent authority" in the member states.

- adopting the End-of-life vehicles initiative.

- the WEEE Directive (see below).

- the reduction and elimination of PCBs/terphenyls/waste oils.

- establishing limits on packaging waste (94/62/EC as amended by 2004/62/EC).

- adopting landfill limitations (Directive 1999/31/EC).

The EU Directive on Waste Electrical and Electronic Equipment (WEEE) aims to reduce the amount of electrical and electronic waste disposed of in landfills and incinerators. Under the directive, producers will be responsible for taking back and recycling electrical and electronic equipment. This strategy is intended to provide incentives to design electrical and

---

* Not all EU countries have the cultural and governance traditions that are encouraging of public participation. For example, see Demetropoulou et al. (2010) for a description of the implementation of the Water Framework Directive in Greece.

electronic equipment in an environmentally more efficient way, taking waste-management aspects fully into account. To prevent the generation of hazardous wastes, Directive 2002/95/EC requires the substitution of safer alternatives for heavy metals (such as lead, mercury, cadmium, and hexavalent chromium) and brominated fire retardants (BFRs) in new electrical equipment from July 1, 2006. The WEEE Directive was published in January 2003, and member states were to bring the laws, regulations, and administrative provisions necessary to comply with the directive into force by August 2004. By August 2005, "Member States will have to set up collection systems for waste electrical and electronic equipment and take measures so that WEEE is collected separately. By December 2006, Member States have to meet a binding target of 4kg per capita/per year for the separate collection of WEEE from private households and ensure that a very high percentage of the WEEE collected will be re-used, recovered or recycled."[63]

The producers of electrical and electronic products are required to finance the collection, treatment, recovery, and environmentally sound disposal of household WEEE deposited at the collection facilities. "Concerning WEEE from business users, the text adopted foresees that producers will be directly financially responsible for the management of both new and historical WEEE. This provision has been strongly contested by industries during the last stage of the negotiations. In their view, the take-back obligation for waste equipment put on the market in the past ('historical waste') creates a retroactive liability for which no provision was made. The burden will vary depending on the volumes of equipment companies sold in the past and it will be particularly heavy for companies which have sold high volumes and whose sales [have] gone down. New companies will not bear any obligation in the treatment of historical waste."[64]

In addition, member states are to draw up a register of producers and keep information on the quantities and categories of electrical and electronic equipment placed on the market, collected, recycled, and recovered in their territory. Every three years, they must also send a report to the Commission on the implementation of this directive. The Commission is then to publish a report on the same subject within nine months after receiving the reports from the member states.

Although there are still industrial concerns about the costs of implementing and operating under the WEEE Directive, such as the implications for trade outside the EU, industries across the EU are beginning to work together in order to meet the WEEE

objectives, creating further awareness of life-cycle assessment and waste minimization of harmful contaminants on a more global scale. See also Section 10.18.5 on the EU's Integrated Product Policy and life-cycle analysis.

### 10.18.3 Prevention of Chemical Accidents

One of the most important and best-known EU directives is the EU Directive on Major Accident Hazards of Certain Industrial Activities (82/501/EEC), commonly known as the Seveso Directive. First implemented in 1982, it requires member states to ensure that all manufacturers prove to a "competent authority" that major hazards have been identified in their industrial activities, that appropriate safety measures—including emergency plans—have been adopted, and that information, training, and safety equipment have been provided to on-site employees. A revised version, the Seveso II Directive (96/82/EEC), came into effect in 1997. Seveso II introduced new concepts, such as "inherent safety,"* and extended the scope of the directive to a broader range of installations. The emphasis on inherent safety, the safety analogy to pollution prevention, as the preferred approach places the EU approach ahead of the U.S. practice, which continues to emphasize secondary prevention measures. Other updates in Seveso II include the introduction of new requirements for safety-management systems, an emphasis on emergency planning and land-use planning, and a reinforcement of the provisions on inspections to be carried out by member states.

### 10.18.4 The Integrated Pollution Prevention and Control Directive

The purpose of the European Union's Integrated Pollution Prevention and Control Directive (IPPC), adopted in 1996 and amended four times since then, was to provide a high level of environmental protection by *preventing*, wherever practicable, or otherwise reducing (controlling) emissions to air, water, and land (that is, waste) from a range of industrial and agricultural sectors and activities.[65] Its implementation is known as the Sevilla Process, named

---

* The guidelines implementing Seveso II direct that firms should adopt inherent-safety approaches as the preferred strategy over traditional safety measures, which are regarded as "secondary prevention." For a discussion of inherent safety, see Zwetsloot and Ashford (2003).

after the EU institution located in Seville, Spain, that establishes the permit conditions.

The IPPC represents a shift in focus in EU environmental law from separate emphases on pollution of air, water, and waste—usually employing end-of-pipe or secondary prevention approaches—to an integrated approach of preventing pollution (and sudden and/or accidental releases) at the source.* In this way, it parallels the U.S. approach in the 1990 Pollution Prevention Act (see the discussion in Chapter 9). Further, the IPPC Directive is anticipated to complement the adoption of environmental management systems (O'Malley 1999).

Unlike many of the very general EU directives, the IPPC places specific restrictions on member states to ensure that individual firms (in the energy industries, the production and processing of metals, the mineral industry, the chemical industry, waste management, livestock farming, and others defined in Annex I of the directive) comply with operating permits. The basic obligations defined in the permits require the regulated installation to

- use the best available pollution-prevention measures and techniques (those that produce the least waste, use the least hazardous substances, maximize the recovery and recycling of substances generated, and the like);

- prevent all large-scale pollution;

- prevent, recycle, or dispose of waste in the least polluting way possible;

- use energy efficiently;

- ensure accident prevention and damage limitation; and

- return sites to their original state when the activity is over.

In addition, the permit must contain a number of specific requirements, including the following:

- Emission-limit values for polluting substances (with the exception of greenhouse gases if an emissions-trading scheme applies)

- Any required soil-, water-, and air-protection measures

- Waste-management measures

- Measures to be taken in exceptional circumstances (for example, leaks, malfunctions, and temporary or permanent stoppages)

- Minimization of long-distance or transboundary pollution

- Release monitoring

- All other appropriate measures

Around 60,000 installations across the European Union were required to operate with IPPC permits by October 2007.[†] The permits were to be "coordinated" in addressing together all waste and pollution streams and were to be based on the concept of best available techniques (BAT) for minimizing pollution from various point sources in order to achieve a high level of protection of the environment as a whole. In many cases, BAT means radical environmental improvements within the industries, and it is expected that sometimes it may be costly for companies to adapt their plants to BAT.[‡] Identification of required performance levels achievable by BAT is undertaken by the EU Center in Seville and published in its Best Available Techniques REFerence Documents (BREFs).

In accordance with the Åarhus Convention (see Section 10.4.4) and with appropriate safeguards for commercial and industrial secrecy, this information must be made available to interested parties. Regulation (EC) 166/2006 adopted by EU law implementing the Århus Convention established as of 2007 a European Pollutant Release and Transfer Register (PRTR), harmonizing rules for the member states to report information on pollutants regularly to the Commission.

## 10.18.5 The EU Integrated Product Policy, the Environmental Technologies Action Plan, and Life-Cycle Assessment

10.18.5.1 The EU Integrated Product Policy and the Environmental Technologies Action Plan

The traditional focus in environmental policy has been on production processes and subsequent emission levels, which triggered the development of vari-

---

\* See the discussion of the Seveso Directives in Section 10.18.3.

---

† Because it was acknowledged that the implementation of these new and considerably tougher BAT rules by all existing installations in the European Union could be expensive, the directive granted the covered installations an eleven-year transition period counting from the day the directive became effective.

‡ Note that BAT in the European context can include performance requirements for technology that anticipate innovation, not just levels of control achievable by existing technology (as the use of the term "best available technology" implies in the United States). In other words, the EU's BAT requirements can be overtly technology forcing. However, considerations of economic burden may also influence the stringency of the requirements.

ous legal instruments, including permits, BAT standards and emission levels, environmental quality norms, fuel standards, and waste-related laws (Dalhammar 2007, p. 76). While the EU initiatives described in prior sections focus on the control and prevention of pollution of the environment from the perspective of facilities and installations polluting air, water, and land, the many activities associated with the production, use, and disposal of products add a different dimension to environmental degradation.

The EU Commission is developing an Integrated Policy Strategy (IPS) to strengthen product-related environmental policies with a view to promoting the development of a market for greener products. This strategy focuses mainly on environmental impacts throughout the life cycle of products and envisions the use of ecolabels both to serve as a voluntary market-focused screening mechanism (through the exercise of consumer choice) and to transmit important information about products.* It is linked to the EU New Approach (consisting of a number of directives mostly pertaining to product safety).†

Tukker and Jansen (2006, p. 159) write:

> Environmental effects of economic activities are ultimately driven by consumption, via impacts of the production, use, and waste management phases of products and services ultimately consumed. Integrated product policy (IPP) addressing the life-cycle impacts of products forms an innovative new generation of environmental policy. Yet this policy requires insight into the final consumption expenditures and related products that have the greatest life-cycle environmental impacts. . . .

Unlike most studies done in the past 25 years on similar topics, the studies reviewed [in our published work] covered a broad set of environmental impacts beyond just energy use or carbon dioxide ($CO_2$) emissions. . . . The three main priorities, housing, transport, and food, are responsible for 70% of the environmental impacts in most categories, although covering only 55% of the final expenditure in the 25 countries that currently make up the EU. At a more detailed level, priorities are car and most probably air travel within transport, meat and dairy within food, and building structures, heating, and (electrical) energy-using products within housing. Expenditures on clothing, communication, health care, and education are considerably less important.

The safety of consumer products has received attention in a number of countries (see Chapter 9), and the evidence seems to indicate that mandatory product standards (product safety and buyback) have by far been the most powerful driver for inducing ecodesign practices in industry, or in fact *the* decisive factor (Dalhammar 2007, pp. 77–78). However, "Implementation of most product-related policies and procedures has been rather ad hoc, and there has been no systematic strategy to address the environmental impacts of products over the entire life cycle" (ibid., p. 78).

In a real sense, developing policies that focus only on the consumer safety aspects of products is out-of-date. Environmental pollution and safety risks from the extraction of materials, their transformation into feedstocks and starting materials for product manufacturing, product manufacturing, transportation, product use, and product disposal are all part of the life cycle of products.[66] On the other hand, although the current EU Integrated Product Policy focuses mostly on environmental impact, it does pay some attention to consumer safety associated with products. Partial attempts to integrate various stages of a product's life are reflected in the developing laws implementing extended producer responsibility, whereby producers of industrial chemicals have obligations to ensure safe use by their industrial customers; the establishment of buyback provisions, as in the case of used motor oil in Germany; and the EU WEEE Initiative for electronics, which establishes a complex system linking producers and users. The essential point, of course, is that these various health, safety, and environmental concerns ideally should be taken into account at the design stage, where the choice of materials, manufacturing methods, safety, and disposal consequences must be considered. The

---

* The proposed strategy calls for the involvement of all parties concerned at all possible levels of action and throughout the life cycle of the products. Ecodesign must be promoted by the manufacturers so as to ensure that products on the market are more environmentally friendly. Distributors should put green products on the shelves and should inform consumers of their existence and benefits. Consumers should preferably choose green products and use them in such a way as to prolong their shelf life and reduce their impact on the environment. NGOs could play a role in identifying problems and solutions with a view to creating products that are more environmentally friendly. See Europa, Integrated Product Policy (IPP), http://ec.europa.eu/environment/ipp/ (accessed May 31, 2010).

† Consumer product safety in the EU is secured by the General Product Safety Directive (2001/95/EC) establishing a General Safety Requirement, a regulation addressing cross-border problems, a "rapid alert system," and liability for defective consumer products (85/374/EEC). See the discussion of consumer product safety in Section 9.2.7 in Chapter 9. See also the New Approach to Standardisation in the Internal Market, www.newapproach.org/ (accessed May 31, 2010).

design of sustainable products is an important part of sustainable development.

The Eco-design Directive 2005—considered the first IPP directive—does not contain many binding obligations and, in any case, may not provide first-mover advantages because the requirements are not stringent enough (Dalhammar 2007, p. 106; see the discussion of the Porter and MIT hypotheses in Chapter 9).

In commenting on the Integrated Product Policy, the European Consumers' Organization (BEUC), based in Brussels and representing a federation of national consumer organizations from the EU and other European countries, believes that "product safety is one of the key issues and BEUC wants information about chemicals used in every-day consumer products to be made available to the public."[67] Safety aspects of products, as well as environmental impact, are to be included in life-cycle analysis (see the discussion in the next section).*

One might expect much more resistance to product-based regulation than to the regulation of air and water pollution and waste in the context of facilities or installations, both because the costs of complying with those regulations have been fairly low and because products are central to a firm's domestic business and international trade. As will be discussed in the next chapter, product policies in different EU member states and among other trading partners have the potential to constitute barriers to trade, or at least trade distortions, and therefore there is a need to coordinate policies (Dalhammar 2007, p. 84).

Finally, in the EU, there is an effort to bring the IPP policies into the IPPC Directive whereby the installation permits also cover aspects of the products made, but this idea has not received enthusiastic support from industry (Dalhammar 2007, p. 107). There are also efforts to coordinate the IPP initiatives with the Environmental Technologies Action Plan (ETAP), in which

> the European Union is adopting an action plan to promote environmental technologies (technologies whose use is less environmentally harmful than relevant alternatives) in order to reduce pressures on our natural resources, improve the quality of life of European citizens and stimulate economic growth. The action plan's objectives are to remove the obstacles so as to tap the full potential of

environmental technologies, to ensure that the EU takes a leading role in applying them and to mobilise all stakeholders in support of these objectives. . . .

> This action plan in favour of environmental technologies concerns technologies to manage pollution, less polluting and less resource-intensive products and services and ways to manage resources more efficiently. These environmentally friendly technologies pervade all economic activities and sectors. They cut costs and improve competitiveness by reducing energy and resource consumption and so creating fewer emissions and less waste.[68]

The ETAP is envisioned as part of achieving green growth associated with the Lisbon Strategy. The three most important actions contemplated are the technology platforms (defining research and development priorities), the Environmental Technologies Verification System, and the development of performance targets (Callejo and Delgado 2008). The ETAP is reminiscent of the EPA's 1994 Technology Innovation Strategy. In a January 1994 report, the U.S. EPA revealed a clear evolution of thinking from a preoccupation with risk to a concern for fundamental technological change. That report's introduction stated (EPA 1994, p. 4):

> Technology innovation is indispensable to achieving our national and international environmental goals. Available technologies are inadequate to solve many present and emerging environmental problems or, in some cases, too costly to bear widespread adoption. Innovative technologies offer the promise that the demand for continuing economic growth can be reconciled with the imperative of strong environmental protection. In launching this Technology Innovation Strategy, the Environmental Protection Agency aims to inaugurate an era of unprecedented technological ingenuity in the service of environmental protection and public health. . . . This strategy signals EPA's commitment to making needed changes and reinventing the way it does its business so that the United States will have the best technological solutions needed to protect the environment.

Unfortunately, the IPP inititative did not go much beyond the announcement of the initial creation of the plan. One NGO commentator offers the following comment (Sheehan 2004, p. 3):

> IPP is an EU initiative that emerged with revolutionary flair in the late 1990s as a holistic, systems-based approach to developing and "harmonizing" policies that target the entire product life cycle. . . .

> While talk about IPP continues, the political will to advance IPP at the EU level does not appear to be present. . . .

---

* Taken together, the Integrated Product Policy, the IPPC Directive, and the Seveso Directives support inherently safer and environmentally sounder production and products. See Section 9.2.7 in Chapter 9 for a discussion of product safety in the United States.

The Commission sees IPP in the expansive sense as a dead issue; no directive is under consideration or expected.

The EU seems to be assuming a more passive stance and focusing on incremental product innovation.

What the future holds for EU product-related initiatives remains to be seen.

In the EU, manufacturers and users are concerned both with the nature of the products they are permitted to sell or use (influenced by product-safety and environmental standards, as well as labeling requirements) and with the possible damage to the environment or to persons emanating from their products (reflecting liability laws).* One paradoxical legal development in the EU is the emergence of the shift from "minimal harmonisation" to "maximal harmonisation" in the context of EU product liability laws.[69] In the federal context, this is parallel to federal preemption of state initiatives. As discussed in Section 10.18.1.1 and in previous sections presented up to this point, in most aspects of EU policies reflected in its environmental, health, and safety directives, these EU directives establish bare-bones requirements to be augmented by specific standards, regulations implementing the directives by the member states, or a performance "floor" that can be exceeded in stringency by the member states.† Recent decisions of the European Court of Justice have confirmed the maximal harmonization of the Product Liability Directive (85/374/EEC), pushing the EU toward a more complete harmonization of European product liability laws and raising the possibility that not even a "safeguard" clause would operate to protect consumers from unsafe products (Howells 2006).

10.18.5.2 Life-Cycle Assessment

Life-cycle assessment has received increasing attention in both the EU and the United States. The EU website for the IPP states: "With a view to extending eco-design across a broader range of products, steps must be taken to produce and publish information on the environmental impact of products throughout their life cycle. Life Cycle Inventories (LCIs) and Life Cycle Analyses (LCAs) are effective instruments to this end. Eco-design guidelines and a general strategy for integrating the environment in the design process could be used as instruments for the promotion of the life cycle concept within companies."[70]

The U.S. EPA has taken a proactive role in environmental life-cycle assessments and provides a framework for identifying and evaluating environmental burdens associated with the life cycles of materials and services in a "cradle-to-grave" approach. Efforts to develop LCA methodology first began in the United States in the 1970s. The EPA's website describes more recent activity:[71]

In the 1990's, the Society for Environmental Toxicology and Chemistry (SETAC) in North America and the U.S. Environmental Protection Agency (USEPA) sponsored workshops and other projects designed to develop and promote consensus on a framework for conducting life-cycle inventory analysis and impact assessment. Similar efforts have been undertaken by SETAC-Europe, other international organizations (such as the International Standards Organization, ISO), and LCA practitioners worldwide. As a result of these efforts, consensus has been achieved on an overall LCA framework and a well-defined inventory methodology.

LCA systematically identifies and evaluates opportunities for minimizing the overall environmental consequences of resource usage and environmental releases. Early research conducted by the USEPA in LCA methodology along with efforts by SETAC led to the four-part approach to LCA that is widely accepted today:

1. Specifically stating the purpose of the study and appropriately identifying the boundaries of the study (Goal and Scope Definition);
2. Quantifying the energy use and raw material inputs and environmental releases associated with each stage of the life cycle (Life Cycle Inventory, LCI);
3. Interpreting the results of the inventory to assess the impacts on human health and the environment (Life Cycle Impact Assessment, LCIA); and
4. Evaluating opportunities to reduce energy, material inputs, or environmental impacts along the life cycle (Improvement Analysis, or Interpretation).

A continuing concern is the cost and time required for LCA. Some have suggested that the LCA community has established a methodology that is beyond the reach of most potential users. Others have questioned the relevance of LCA to the actual decisions that these potential users must make. These concerns have encouraged some practitioners to investigate the possibility of simplifying the LCA approach. Other tools are being proposed that use the life-cycle concept by looking across the life-cycle

---

* See Section 10.12 for a discussion of liability for environmental damage.

† Indeed, Howells (2006, p. 3) notes that the "the very use of the instrument of a Directive, that has been implemented into national law, creates opportunities for differences to emerge [among] the Member States."

stages of a product or process system, but in shortened versions. For example, an abridged LCA approach was developed by AT&T and used by others in industry, such as Motorola. However, there is the potential that some attempts to shorten the LCA approach might result in looking at each life-cycle stage individually and might lose the ability to identify environmental trade-offs between stages.

### 10.18.6 Access to Information and Participatory Rights

The EU has implemented directives adopting the UN's Århus Convention on Access to Information and Public Participation on Decision Making and Access to Justice in Environmental Matters. See Section 10.4.4 for a discussion of these directives.

### 10.18.7 The Eco-Management and Audit Scheme and ISO 14001

For many nations, mandatory regulation is the primary instrument by which the government influences industrial compliance with environmental and worker health and safety policies. However, in the EU, it is increasingly recognized that a number of different policy instruments are useful in implementing such policies, including voluntary schemes that deal with institutional and organizational factors.

The EU's Eco-Management and Audit Scheme (EMAS) is an example of a broader category of environmental management system (EMS) standards. The EMAS was developed by the European Committee for Standardization (CEN; Comité Européen de Normalisation) and became operational in 1995. The scheme is generally regarded as the most demanding EMS standard (Gouldson and Murphy 1998b). Its main objective is to promote "continuous improvement in environmental performance" on a site-specific basis. More specifically, it requires firms to

- establish a company environmental policy;
- conduct an environmental review;
- introduce an environmental program or management system;
- carry out environmental audits; and
- prepare environmental statements to be released to the public.

The EMAS was established as an EU regulation and does not require implementing legislation at the national level. Instead, it demands that member states establish structures to promote and administer the scheme, including instituting an independent organization to accredit companies, acting like regulators by checking compliance, and providing certification. The EMAS provides a baseline for environmental performance and seeks to drive organizations beyond command-and-control requirements.

ISO 14001, in comparison with the EMAS, is the environmental management standard of the International Standards Organization. To link the two systems, EMAS II made the adoption of Chapter 4 of ISO 14001 a prerequisite of the EMAS (Kiel 2006, p. 67). The underlying principle of both EMAS and ISO 14001 is simple:[72]

> Both are environmental management system standards which define certain requirements that the particular environmental management system of a company should meet. Requirements include obligations to review the company's environmental impacts, or to design a company-specific program for improving current environmental performance. These are all procedural requirements as opposed to substantial commitments setting specified levels of environmental performance. Of course, it is expected that meeting the procedural requirements will ultimately bring about environmental improvements. Once a company meets these requirements, it can apply to external bodies (different for EMAS and ISO 14001) for certification (ISO 14001) or registration (EMAS). Certification and registration basically means being officially recognized as fulfilling the standard requirements. Once certified or registered, the company can exploit this recognition for external or internal communication purposes. A key feature of both systems is that they are voluntary, i.e., individual companies are totally free to participate or not. This creates a new challenge for the regulator in comparison with conventional policy approaches for encouraging industrial participation, since a voluntary program can only benefit the environment if at least a number of companies participate.

Although membership in the EMAS is voluntary, firms that wish to register for the scheme must agree to subject themselves to scrutiny and evaluation from an independent third body (Gouldson and Murphy 1998a). However, organizations that do become accredited by the EMAS can use this as a marketing advantage or for favorable publicity because it is voluntary and also independently certifiable. The fact that an organization has gone to the effort to receive independent accreditation may be viewed favorably by consumers and within the business environment.

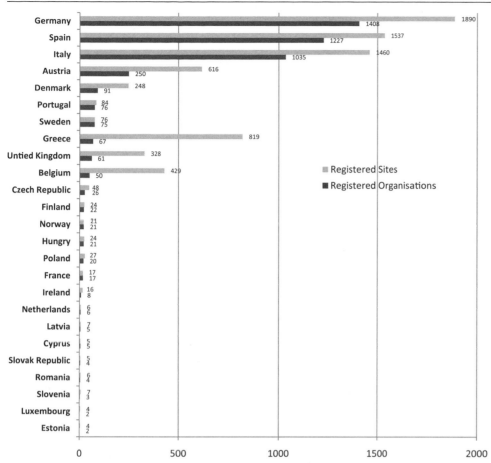

**FIGURE 10.5: EMAS ORGANIZATIONS AND SITES ACROSS THE EUROPEAN UNION**
Source: Europa (2010).

Countries across the EU vary in their firms' participation in EMAS and ISO 14001 schemes,* as shown in Figure 10.5. As of November 2004, Germany had significantly more EMAS organizations than any other EU country.† As regards EMAS, there is a striking difference between Germany and other countries, as demonstrated in Figure 10.5 and Table 10.1. While France, the Netherlands, and the United Kingdom have participation rates below 0.5 percent, 6.5 percent of German companies are EMAS registered. By contrast, participation rates in ISO 14001 are more similar, ranging from 2.2 percent in France to 9.5 percent in the Netherlands. Germany is characterized by a high EMAS participation rate and is also the only country with more EMAS than ISO 14001 participants (ISO/EMAS ratio below 1). France, the United Kingdom, and the Netherlands are characterized by an insignificant EMAS participation rate but boast higher participation in ISO 14001 (ISO/EMAS ratio above 1) (Glachant, Schucht, et al. 2002). However, there are differences within this group. The Netherlands is far more advanced in ISO 14001 registrations than France, with the United Kingdom holding an intermediate position.‡

---

\* Today there are far more ISO certificates than EMAS registrations in Europe (Kiel 2006, p. 67).

† By the beginning of 2004, 4,000 sites in 3,000 organizations were registered across Europe, mostly from the industrial sector (metals, chemicals, and food processing), but since 2001, more and more registrations have come from the service sector and local authorities (Kiel 2006, p. 64). There has been a steady decline in registered organizations (over half from German companies and organizations) since 2001, while the number of sites has held steady (ibid., p. 65).

‡ France decided to recognize the ISO 14001 standard shortly before the European Commission did, and Germany applied the Commission's decision. In the Netherlands, it was decided that the Dutch interpretation of ISO 14001 should follow the EMAS. This means that the only additional requirement of the EMAS beyond ISO 14001 is the publication of a validated environmental statement. Thus harmonization in the Netherlands made the ISO 14001 standard more demanding than in other countries (Lulofs 2000). The only case where harmonization attempts raised a problem was the United Kingdom. In 1992, the United Kingdom launched its own domestic environ-

**TABLE 10.1: EMAS AND ISO 14001 PARTICIPATION RATES IN APRIL 2000**

| | FRANCE | GERMANY | THE NETHERLANDS | UNITED KINGDOM | ALL EU MEMBER STATES |
|---|---|---|---|---|---|
| Number of registered sites or organizations | | | | | |
| EMAS | 36 | 2,432 | 26 | 73 | 3,325 |
| ISO 14001 | 550 | 1,950 | 606 | 1,014 | 7,140 |
| Ratio of Participating Companies and Potential Participants* | | | | | |
| (1) EMAS | 0.15 | 6.5 | 0.4 | 0.25 | – |
| (2) ISO 14001 | 2.2 | 5.2 | 9.5 | 3.4 | – |
| Ratio of ISO 14001 and EMAS Participation Rates | | | | | |
| (2)/(1) = SO/EMAS | 14.9 | 0.8 | 23.1 | 13.7 | – |

*As a proxy we take companies in manufacturing industry with more than twenty employees as a base for potential participants. This is only a rough measure as EMAS has so far been applied to sites (and not to complete firms) and as ISO is not restricted to industry. Source: Wätzold et al. 2001 (based on Eurostat—New Cronos Datenbank 12/98 and www.iwoe.unisg.ch/forschung/14001/weltweit.htm (16 June 2000, 10:29); own calculations.

Source: Glachant, Schucht, et al. (2002, p. 258). Reproduced with permission.

The challenge of environmental management systems is to connect the voluntary approach with binding regulations (Kiel 2006, p. 66). The benefit of ISO 14001 is seen in its worldwide acknowledgment, whereas an advantage of the EMAS is the legal character that gives it the opportunity to link the environmental management and audit scheme with European and national environmental legislation (ibid., p. 67). ISO 14001 concerns performance of environmental management systems, while the EMAS increasingly focuses on environmental performance (ibid.). Kiel (p. 96) observes: "ISO is not the driving force in the new developments of environmental management systems, offering EMAS a chance to take up this role. . . . EMAS could acquire a leading position in Europe, and even worldwide." Presently, the EMAS is limited to about 5,000 companies operating in Europe out of a total of 29 million (Nash 2009). In 2008, the EU Commission introduced a proposed regulation (COM 2008; 402/2)[73] reducing the administrative burden and increasing the visibility of participation especially to attract SMEs (Nash 2009).

mental management standard (BS 7750), which subsequently served as a basis for defining the ISO 14001 standard. Considering BS 7750 registration a stepping-stone to the EMAS, the British government hoped that the EMAS could profit from the rapid development of the domestic standard. The U.K. government quickly applied to the European Commission for BS 7750 to be recognized as equivalent to the EMAS. Because Germany blocked BS 7750 recognition in 1995, demanding prior agreement on an international standard, the British standard's recognition was delayed until February 1996, when its days seemed numbered because of the development of ISO 14001 (Eames 2000).

### 10.18.8 Chemicals Policy and REACH*

#### 10.18.8.1 The REACH Initiative

Although in the United States, as well as in the European Union, regulations creating testing obligations for new chemicals were implemented in the 1970s, no routine tests were required for chemicals that were already on the market, the so-called existing chemicals. The vast majority of the substances on the market—over 90 percent—are existing substances.

In 1993, the European Union implemented the Existing Substances Regulation (EC Regulation 93/793) to overcome the lack of knowledge about the properties (hazards) and uses of existing chemicals. The regulation required some producers, manufacturers, and importers to present a base data set for existing chemicals. The deadline for substances produced or used in amounts greater than 1,000 tons per year (t/y) was March 23, 1994; for amounts greater than 10 t/y, the deadline was June 4, 1998. On the basis of the data, the European Commission developed four priority lists that include 141 existing high-volume chemicals. For each chemical, a member state was chosen to be responsible for the risk assessment, including risk-management proposals, on the basis of all available data within the firms about hazards and exposure. Afterward, the proposals of the member states were to be discussed on the European level and changed where required, until all member states agreed with them. Because there were few incentives for the firms to provide risk information—and be-

---

\*      This section is drawn from Koch and Ashford (2006).

cause of the extensive regulatory procedure of risk assessment—only seventy risk-assessment reports had been finished after many years.

In 1999, the European Chemicals Bureau (ECB) analyzed the data it had received from industries on the properties of their high-production-volume (HPV) chemicals. This study found that (1) only 14 percent of the EU HPV chemicals had data publicly available at the level of the base set, (2) 65 percent had some data but less than the base set, and (3) 21 percent had no data. Without these data, it was impossible to assess which chemicals were a priority for further evaluation in the existing chemicals program, and it was unclear how industry was managing to carry out its other responsibilities, such as classification and labeling of chemicals and assessing risks to workers.

Because prior EU directives imposed on the regulators in the EU member states requiring their industries to provide risk assessments for existing chemicals did not produce the needed information, and in an effort to get more extensive information on the nature of the chemicals used within the EU and to lay the foundation for regulation of those chemicals, the European Commission issued a regulation in 2006 establishing what is known as the REACH (**R**egistration, **E**valuation, and **A**uthorization of **Ch**emicals) system. In essence, REACH is the European counterpart to the U.S. Toxic Substances Control Act, passed almost thirty years earlier. REACH came into force on June 1, 2007, and created the European Chemicals Agency (ECHA) in Helsinki, Finland which became fully operational a year later, to administer the European chemicals policy (see http://echa.europa.eu).

The main elements of REACH are uniform procedures (to be in place by 2012) for(1) the registration and evaluation of new and existing chemicals, (2) the transfer of responsibility for producing and assessing chemicals data to industry, (3) the expansion of the responsibilities of downstream users, and (4) the regulation of chemicals and the placing of restrictions on them through the authorization process. Chemicals of "very high concern" can be placed on the market only upon explicit authorization. It is expected that animal testing will be kept to a minimum, with reliance instead on the use of alternative testing methods.

It is estimated that there are approximately 30,000 chemicals that are of hazardous significance or that are used on a significant scale in the EU, and the requirements for their registration (to be completed over a period of eleven years) depend on the amount produced annually. Generally, the system has three tiers. By November 30, 2010 chemicals produced or imported in excess of 1000 t/yr and those considered particularly hazardous were to be registered; 4300 were in fact registered (C&ENeews 2010). The next two deadlines are June 2013 and June 2018 for chemicals produced or imported in excess of 100 t/yr, and chemicals produced or imported at a volume of 1 to 100t/yr, respectively.

All chemicals produced in amounts from 1 to 10 t/y may be initially registered upon the submission of only minimal toxicological information. A safety-assessment report is necessary for substances produced in quantities over 10 t/y (estimated to be about 15,000 substances). This report must identify the relevant chemical properties and exposure profiles and must also identify the risk-reduction measures necessary to assure the safe use of the chemical by the producer through the downstream users. Further, a safety data sheet identifying necessary risk-reduction measures must be supplied to, and if necessary modified by, all the actors in the supply chain. All substances produced in quantities greater than 100 t/y (estimated to be about 10,000 substances) and all substances produced in smaller quantities that are suspected of being hazardous (estimated to be about 5,000 substances) will be initially evaluated by the relevant authorities in the member states after registration. Different member states, selected by ECHA, will have the responsibility for evaluating different chemicals. The ECHA must approve the evaluation and will prioritize candidates for authorization and determine whether restrictions or authorization (of use or introduction into commerce) is warranted. The member states will have the responsibility for enforcing regulations issued under REACH and for establishing specific fines within their countries. As with other regulatory requirements and standards set by the central EU agency—here ECHA—member states are free to set more stringent requirements in their implementation of REACH.

In contrast to the well-defined data requirements for risk assessment, the responsibility for risk management is defined only cursorily and superficially in REACH. Manufacturers and importers must identify and apply the "appropriate" measures to "adequately control" the risks identified in the chemical safety assessment and must, where suitable, recommend them in the required safety data sheets.

If this risk-management element of REACH is to be meaningful, there must be a clear definition of "adequate control" and sanctions for noncompliance. Currently, the point of reference for adequate control appears to be the probable no-effect concentration (PNEC) for the environment and the derived no-effect level (DNEL) for human health,* but the sanctions for exceeding these levels are not clear. Moreover, the current sanctions for failing to identify risks during the registration process are very limited and often are insufficient to overcome the producer's incentive to withhold such information.

Chemicals with certain hazardous properties— known as "substances of very high concern"—must be separately authorized. These include (1) substances that can cause cancer or mutations or are toxic to reproduction (the so-called CMR substances); (2) those that are persistent, bioaccumulative, and toxic (PBT) or very persistent and very bioaccumulative (vPvB); and (3) substances that are identified on a case-by-case basis as causing probable serious effects to humans or the environment of an equivalent concern, such as endocrine disrupters.† For any of these substances, the burden of proof shifts from the authorities to the producers regardless of the amount of the substance produced. In general, an authorization of the chemical for certain uses will issue if the producer is able to prove either that the risks of those uses can be "adequately controlled" or that their socioeconomic benefits exceed their risks. If the use of the chemical cannot be "adequately controlled," an analysis of alternative substances or technologies— and an adequate substitution plan—must be provided by the firm seeking authorization. These relatively broadly worded requirements leave wide discretion to the implementing authorities.

The main motivation in revising the European chemicals policy was the past failure to mitigate the information deficit with regard to existing chemicals. Despite the planned changes of the new system, this approach basically follows the path of first solving the risk-information problem before risk management can take place. Nevertheless, because of the shift of responsibility for risk assessment to the industry, this system is argued to be more feasible than the existing regulation. Moreover, the testing demands are more flexible in comparison with the prior regulation that demands a very comprehensive risk assessment.‡ Identifying risk-reduction measures is

also integrated into the responsibility of the producers and users of chemical substances, but so far, this responsibility is described only very vaguely, in contrast to the detailed requirements of reporting data about risk information. To guarantee that the system of controlled self-responsibility of industry with regard to risk management works, it must be accompanied by adequate control mechanisms and sanctions. Otherwise, REACH will collect data about risk information without significantly forcing or encouraging risk-reduction measures.

In principle, the authorization system could establish a new form of (regulatory) risk management on the basis of the reversal of the burden of proof for substances with certain properties. The system can be seen as the embodiment of the precautionary principle because substances are to be screened for their possible potential effects and not only because risk has been scientifically validated. How this system will work depends on the form and application of this system by the authorities, but the system has come under criticism. The wide discretion within the authorization system contains the danger of not making use of the potentially available precautionary approach in REACH. As past experience shows, discretion has often weakened the application of a regulation in practice. Thus to ensure the application of the precautionary principle, it is important to strengthen its requirements in the authorization process.

### 10.18.8.2 The U.S. Toxic Substances Control Act and Lessons for REACH

In the United States, the Toxic Substances Control Act was passed in 1976 and confers on the Environmental Protection Agency (EPA) manifold rights to require testing or reporting activities for new and existing chemicals and to regulate them. The main goals of the TSCA are receiving adequate data about the negative effects of chemical substances and regulating those substances that present or will present an "unreasonable risk of injury to health or the environment."§ Negative impacts for the economy

---

*       The DNEL is equivalent to the no observed adverse effect level (NOAEL) in U.S. parlance.
†       As of June 18, 2010, there were thirty-eight substances of very high concern identified by ECHA (Cohen 2010, p. 61).
‡       One optimistic feature of REACH is that it anticipates risk evaluations that need not be based on expensive and time-consuming animal toxicity studies but rely instead on molecular structure-activity determinations (Cronin, Jaworkska, et al. 2003; Lewis, Kazantzis, et al. 2007; OECD 1993) or possibly short-term bacterial/cellular assays. However, the acceptance of these techniques to assess all toxicity concerns has been conten-

tious among both toxicologists and industry spokespersons (see Scialli 2008). However, as a result of REACH, scientists and national academies in both the US and the EU are now investing considerable effort in developing new approaches to human health risk assessment that would rely on *in vitro* assays and computer-based models; under the EU Cosmetics Directive, the cosmetics industry must eliminate the use of animals in toxicity testing by 2013 (Arnaud 2010, p. 37).
§       In the early implementation years of the TSCA (1976–1980), the EPA adopted a risk-driven approach to existing

and innovation should be avoided by using the "least burdensome [regulatory] requirements."

For new chemicals, a Premarket Manufacturing Notice (PMN) is required. Thereupon the EPA decides on a case-by-case basis if more tests are necessary, but most often no new testing is required. Existing chemicals are registered in the Inventory of Chemical Substances (ICS), the United States equivalent of the EINECS. In contrast to the European Union, where different inventories for new and existing chemicals exist, the new substances are added to the ICS after the PMN. The ICS contains some 75,000 existing substances.

Under the TSCA, testing for existing chemicals is required by the establishment of testing rules for as many as 50 chemicals per year following recommendations by the Interagency Testing Committee (ITC). On this basis, the EPA requires tests from industry or has to justify why tests from its point of view are not necessary. In practice, a relatively small number of those rules were actually promulgated. In the first fifteen years of the TSCA, the ITC proposed tests for 175 chemicals to the EPA, but the EPA thereupon required testing from industry for only 25 chemicals. For 34 other chemicals, the EPA and industry agreed on voluntary testing, and for 8 other chemicals, tests were only proposed. In contrast to the European attempts to improve the legal framework for existing chemicals, the TSCA has not changed substantially in this regard since its first implementation. However, in the late 1990s, the EPA did implement its High Production Volume (HPV) Challenge Program, under which chemical companies have begun to provide test data voluntarily on 2,800 chemicals produced in amounts greater than 1 million pounds per year, although they have not agreed to test 300 of the chemicals originally on the HPV list.

The TSCA also requires firms to deliver new information about hazards of the produced substances to EPA. The EPA has to be notified of "significant new uses" of registered chemicals as well. It is within the administrative discretion of the EPA to determine what constitutes significant new uses. Along the lines of German/European law, the EPA also has the right to require a toxicity analysis of existing chemicals if an "unreasonable risk" is supposed. The basis for risk-reduction measures in the TSCA is the existence of an unreasonable risk. It is not the intention of the TSCA to prevent any risk, but to take into account the benefits as well as the risks of a substance. In fact, only a few chemicals are restricted by the TSCA. Within the first twenty years of the passage of the TSCA, limitations were determined for only seventeen substances. As of 2005, only five chemicals or classes of chemicals were restricted or banned comprehensively: polychlorinated biphenyls, fully halogenated chlorofluoroalkanes, dioxin, asbestos,* and hexavalent chromium. In conclusion, although the opportunities for the authorities available to the EPA under the TSCA are very comprehensive, the EPA essentially did not use the variety of available options for requiring data and for minimizing risks in the past. The TSCA can truly be described as a paper tiger. Given the broad regulatory discretion of the

---

chemicals by constructing different classes of chemicals based on production volume and toxicity. This was seen as a logical necessary first step on the way to efficient regulation. This allegedly "rational" approach, which consumed most of the resources of the EPA Office of Toxic Substances, left few agency resources for actually promulgating regulations. This ultimately led to the essential failure of the TSCA to live up to expectations. A death blow was delivered in 1991 by the Fifth Circuit Court of Appeals in rejecting the EPA's attempt to ban asbestos, perhaps the most notorious and best-acknowledged carcinogenic chemical substance in commerce (see the following footnote).

*       The regulation for asbestos was vacated by the Fifth Circuit Court of Appeals (*Corrosion Proof Fittings v. EPA*, 947 F.2d 1201 (5th Cir. 1991)). The TSCA requires the EPA to consider, along with the toxic effects on human health and the environment, "the benefits of such substance[s] and mixture[s] and the *availability* of substitutes for such uses" (emphasis added). Because the EPA did not explore regulatory options other than a ban and, more seriously because, the EPA did not evaluate the toxicity (and costs) of likely substitute products in a search for "least burdensome requirements," the court vacated the proposed standard and remanded it to the EPA for further proceedings. Although arguably the court incorrectly interpreted the TSCA's requirements as mandating comparisons of substitutes' toxicity (and costs), as opposed to merely *considering the availability*, of alternatives, the EPA chose not to attempt to reinstate the asbestos ban, primarily because of the likely extensive burden on agency resources to perform extensive risk and economic assessments for substitutes. The EPA could have sought to establish a regulation for a different toxic substance that was likely to be heard in another circuit court in order to give a more favorable interpretation of TSCA's requirement vis-à-vis substitutes, but it did not. As a result, for all intents and purposes, the EPA henceforth regarded the TSCA as a "dead letter." There is a danger that REACH will suffer the same fate, with the result that regulation (authorization and restrictions) will often not be vigorously pursued. Note, as discussed earlier, that comparative assessment of risks and costs is not nearly as burdensome as conducting separate risk and cost assessments. Whether using comparative risk assessment could circumvent the hurdle the EPA needs to overcome to satisfy the requirements laid out in *Corrosion Proof Fittings* needs to be explored. Because alternatives need to be considered in formulating regulations under the TSCA, this may well be possible. In contrast, because risk assessment seems to drive the REACH process, and because the consideration of alternatives seems to come in later, whether the use of comparative analysis in the context of REACH can circumvent the need for extensive risk analyses is unclear.

EU under REACH, there is a legitimate concern that although it contains different risk-management elements, it could suffer a similar fate.

### 10.18.9 Food Safety in the EU*

A series of crises concerning human food and animal feed (for example, bovine spongiform encephalopathy [BSE] and dioxin) have exposed weaknesses in the design and application of food legislation within the EU. This has led the Commission to include the promotion of a high level of food safety among its policy priorities, emphasizing transparency, risk analysis, and prevention. The EU states that its food-safety objectives are "to protect consumer health and interests while guaranteeing the smooth operation of the single market. In order to achieve this objective, the EU ensures that control standards are established and adhered to as regards food and food product hygiene, animal health and welfare, plant health and preventing the risk of contamination from external substances. It also lays down rules on appropriate labeling for these foodstuffs and food products."[74]

Regulation EC 178/2002 of the European Parliament and the Council of January 28, 2002, laid down the general principles and requirements of food law pertaining to the entire food chain and established the European Food Safety Authority (EFSA). Member states were to have adopted the related principles and procedures by January 1, 2007. The use of the precautionary principle in the context of taking "appropriate provisional risk-management measures" where there is a lack of scientific certainty is a centerpiece of EU food law.[75] The EFSA established advisory panels on a variety of topics, including panels on food additives, contaminants in the food chain, biological hazards, and genetically modified organisms (GMOs). A "rapid alert system" was also established by which a member state can inform the EU Commission, which will in turn transmit appropriate information to other member states and order provisional emergency action as deemed necessary. Member states may take interim protective action if no EU action is taken.

The present policy decisions of the EU on food safety are influenced by its so-called white paper is-sued on January 12, 2000, setting up specific strategies for harmonization of national control systems in the member states, improvement of the legislative framework, improving risk and nutritional communication (including labeling) with consumers and other stakeholders, application of the precautionary principle, limiting contamination and pesticide residues in foods, improving the traceability of feed and food and their ingredients, and influencing international rules and policies, including those of the WTO.

Additional important commentary recited in the white paper includes the following:

> Unlike risk assessment and communication, the third element of risk analysis, namely risk management, requires legislative action and thus political decisions based not only on scientific considerations but also on a wider appreciation of the wishes and needs of society. It also requires monitoring of Member States' implementation of legislation; this function is currently carried out by the Commission in its capacity as guardian of the Treaties.
>
> The transfer of such powers of legislation and control to the [European] Food [Safety] Authority would lead to an unwarranted dilution of democratic accountability. The risk management function should therefore continue to be exercised by the European institutions rather than the [European] Food [Safety] Authority. . . .
>
> The Commission considers that a harmonised Community approach to the design of control systems would make for more consistent and better-quality controls. It therefore proposes a Community framework of national control systems comprising three core elements: definition of operational criteria set up at Community level; development of Community control guidelines; and enhanced administrative cooperation in the design and operation of control systems.
>
>> Binding labelling rules should enable consumers to make fully informed choices about the food they eat. In addition to the codification of the labeling Directive, the Commission would like to see the obligation to indicate components of foodstuffs extended to include all ingredients (and not merely those making up at least 25% of the final product).[76]

One of the major concerns about food safety is the possible contributions of food contaminants and diet to human cancer. Under Priority 5 on Food Quality and Safety of the Sixth Framework Programme for Research and Development, in May 2005 the EU established the Environmental Cancer Risk, Nutrition, and Individual Susceptibility (ECNIS) network of excellence of various research groups "to achieve improved understanding of the environmental causes of cancer, of the potential of diet to prevent cancer and

---

* See also Section 10.14 on international approaches to food-safety regulation and policy, and Chapter 11 for the EU's defense of its policy banning beef with added hormones.

---

**BOX 10.10: EU LEGAL FRAMEWORK FOR BIOTECHNOLOGY**

The excerpt below describes the main legal instruments of the revised EU legislative framework on GMOs (EC 2006 and 2007):

**Directive 2001/18/EC on the deliberate release into the environment of GMOs applying to the intentional introduction of GMOs** into the environment without specific containment measures. The Directive covers both releases of GMOs for experimental purposes (e.g. in connection with field trials) and for commercialisation (for example the cultivation, importation and processing or transformation of GMOs into industrial products).

**Regulation (EC) No 1829/2003 on genetically modified food and feed,** which regulates the placing on the market of GMOs for food and feed use, as well as food and feed containing, consisting of or produced from GMOs. If one of the uses of a GMO concerns food or feed, the applicant may file a single application for the GMO and all its uses (cultivation, processing into industrial products and feed use) under this regulation.

**Regulation (EC) No 1946/2003 on transboundary movements of genetically modified organisms** regulates unintentional trans-boundary movements of GMOs and exports of GMOs to third countries.

**Directive 90/219/EEC,** as amended by Directive 98/81/EC, **on the contained use of genetically modified microorganisms (GMMs).** This Directive regulates research and industrial work activities involving GMMs (such as genetically modified viruses or bacteria) under conditions of containment, i.e. in a closed environment (e.g., a laboratory) in which contact with the environment and the population is avoided.

**Regulation (EC) No 1830/2003 concerning the traceability and labeling of genetically modified organisms and the traceability of food and feed products produced from genetically modified organisms** and amending Directive 2001/18/EC. As regards GM food and feed, Regulation 1829/2003 lays down specific labeling requirements.

---

of the ways by which heredity can affect individual susceptibility to carcinogens."[77]

In a very controversial action, the Council of Agricultural Ministers of the EU has indicated its intent to approve the marketing of food derived from cloned animals (Harrington 2009). Applications for these "novel foods" would be sent to the EFSA for a risk assessment. However, in late October 2010, the EU Commission, following the wishes of the Council of Environmental Ministers, issued a report arguing for a five-year moratorium on these foods as well as those containing nanoparticle ingredients (European Parliament 2010). Another controversial action taken by the EFSA—like the Bush Administration's FDA—is the refusal to acknowledge the carcinogenic risk posed by the artificial sweetener aspartame, as evidenced by the Cesare Maltoni Cancer Research Center in Milan, the same laboratory that discovered that vinyl chloride was a carcinogen (Hills 2009).

### 10.18.10 Biotechnology in the EU*

The EU has been very active in the area of biotechnology oversight and regulation. The current EU legal framework fully entered into force on April 2004 and is considered to be one of the strictest in the world (EC 2006). Box 10.10 summarizes its approach and is comprised of several directives. The central directive 2001/18/EC on the deliberate release of GMOs into the environment addresses (1) the experimental release such as the conduct of field tests and (2) the cultivation, importation or transformation of GMOs into industrial products.

A considerable number of implementing measures to support operation of this framework have also been adopted by member states over the past few years. These include, among others, guidelines for risk assessment, monitoring, formats for submission of notifications, sampling and detection, and coexistence measures. For a thoughtful evaluation of the implementation of Directive 2001/18/EC on the deliberate release of GMOs into the environment, see Valve and Kaupilla (2008). Also see the discussion of legal and political conflicts among different nations regarding GMO cultivation and trade in Section 11.2.6 of Chapter 11 and Dobbs (2010) for an exploration of legal avenues under EU law, such as "safeguard measures," for allowing individual EU member states to exercise post-authorization control over GMO crops and food products in their own territories.

Traceability provides the means to trace products through the production and distribution lines. The general objectives of traceability are to facilitate

---

*    See *Questions and Answers on theRegualtion of GMOs in the European Union*, Memo/07/117, Brussels 26 March 2007, www.gmo-compass.org/pdf/documents/Questions_and_%20answers_03_07.pdf (accessed February 6, 2011). See also Section 10.15 for multilateral agreements on biotechnology.

control and verification of labeling claims; targeted monitoring of potential effects on health and the environment, where appropriate; and withdrawal of products that contain or consist of GMOs where an unforeseen risk to human health or the environment is established. The Labeling and Traceability Regulation (Regulation 1830/2003) covers all GMOs that have received EU authorization to place them on the market, namely, all products containing or consisting of GMOs, including food and feed. Examples include GM seeds and bulk quantities or shipments of whole GM grain, such as soybeans and maize. The regulation also covers food and feed derived from a GMO, such as flour produced from genetically modified maize. The traceability rules oblige the operators concerned, that is, all persons who place a product on the market or receive a product placed on the market within the EU, to be able to identify their supplier and the companies to which the products have been supplied.

A number of member states have invoked the so-called safeguard clause under Article 16 of the previous Directive 90/220/EEC. This clause is also included in Directive 2001/18/EC, which replaced Directive 90/220/EEC. The safeguard clause provides that where a member state has justifiable reasons to consider that a GMO that has been authorized to be placed on the market constitutes a risk to human health or the environment, it may provisionally restrict or prohibit the use and/or sale of that product on its territory.

The EU regulatory framework on GMOs takes account of the Cartagena Protocol on Biosafety (discussed in Section 10.15), specifically with regard to the obligations of importers of products in the EU and the obligations of exporters of products to third countries. The regulatory system for authorizing GMOs is consistent with the EU's international trade commitments and with WTO rules: it is clear, transparent, and nondiscriminatory.

The Cartagena Protocol on Biosafety is incorporated into EU legislation through the legal framework governing the use of GMOs within the European Union. As presented above, the cornerstone of this legal framework is Directive 2001/18/EC. The provisions of Directive 2001/18/EC are supplemented by the Regulation on the Transboundary Movements of GMOs (Regulation (EC) No. 1946/2003).

Regulation (EC) No. 1946/2003 was adopted in June 2003 to address specifically export obligations necessary to align the existing regulatory framework with the provisions of the Biosafety Protocol. The main features of the regulation are as follows:

- The obligation to provide notice of exports of GMOs intended for deliberate release into the environment and to secure express consent before the first transboundary movement

- The obligation to provide information to the public and to international partners on EU practices, legislation, and decisions on GMOs, as well as on accidental releases of GMOs

- A set of rules for the export of GMOs intended to be used as food or feed or for processing

- Provisions for identifying GMOs for export

### 10.18.11 Financial Assistance and LIFE

LIFE, the EU's **F**inancial **I**nstrument **f**or the **E**nvironment (*l'instrument financier pour l'environnement*), was launched in 1992 to provide cofinanced financial assistance to "all natural and legal persons" in the EU and certain other third-world or accession countries under three thematic headings: nature and biodiversity; environment policy and governance; and information and communication. Specific projects are funded for

- land-use development and planning;

- water management;

- reduction of the economic impact of economic activities;

- waste management; and

- reduction of the economic impact of products through the Integrated Product Policy.

Some 2,050 LIFE projects, including nature conservation/improvement, environmental restoration, pollution abatement, legislative infrastructure, and voluntary agreements, were supported from 1992 to 2001 at a level of hundreds of millions of euros. The program continues at a high level of funding, more than 2,000 million euros for the period 2007–2013. Of this amount, half is being earmarked for nature and biodiversity, and 889 million euros to address the thematic program on the environment and the sustainable management of natural resources, including energy.[78] The EU describes the "LIFE+" initiative as currently financing "schemes that contribute to the development, implementation and updating of Community environmental policy and environmental legislation. This financial instrument also seeks to facilitate the integration of the environment into other policies, and achieve sustainable development in the European Union. LIFE+ replaces a number of financial instruments used for environmental policy."[79]

## 10.18.12 The European Chemical Substances Information System

Supporting a variety of EU environmental directives related to chemicals is an extensive information system (see http://ecb.jrc.ec.europa.eu/esis/index.php ?pgm=ein Accessed 2 February 2011). It encompasses:

- EINECS (European Inventory of Existing Commercial chemical Substances) O.J. C 146A, 15.6.1990,

- ELINCS (European List of Notified Chemical Substances) in support of Directive 92/32/EEC, the 7th amendment to Directive 67/548/EEC,

- NLP (No-Longer Polymers),

- BPD (Biocidal Products Directive) active substances listed in Annex I or IA of Directive 98/8/EC or listed in the so-called list of non-inclusions,

- PBT (Persistent, Bioaccumulative, and Toxic) or vPvB (very Persistent and very Bioaccumulative),

- CLP/GHS (Classification, Labelling and Packaging of substances and mixtures), CLP implements the Globally Harmonized System (GHS), Regulation (EC) No. 1272/2008,

- Export and Import of Dangerous Chemicals listed in Annex I of Regulation (EC) No. 689/2008,

- HPVCs (High Production Volume Chemicals) and LPVCs (Low Production Volume Chemicals), including EU Producers/Importers lists,

- IUCLID Chemical Data Sheets, IUCLID Export Files, OECD-IUCLID Export Files, EUSES Export Files,

- Priority Lists, Risk Assessment process and tracking system in relation to Council Regulation (EEC) No. 793/93 also known as Existing Substances Regulation (ESR).

## 10.18.13 Commentary on EU Environmental Law

Elsewhere in this book we have argued that four kinds of innovation are required to bring about a sustainable transformation of industrial systems: changes in technology, institutions (government providing technical and financial assistance, incentives, and regulation/legal structure), organizations (private-sector firms with appropriate avenues to address health, safety, and environmental concerns), and society. The EU is attempting to influence sustainable development in all four realms. The IPPC Directive, the Integrated Product Policy, the Eco-design Directive, REACH, and the media-based regulatory approaches—which are *institutional* vehicles—have

the potential to directly influence *technological* innovation, while the EMAS Regulation, an *institutional* instrument, can directly influence *organizational* change. Of course, the technology and organization associated with a particular industrial activity can influence each other. However, in our view, direct incentives to change technology are more likely to affect organizational structure than the other way around. Thus faith in promoting organizational change in order to influence technology*—often through voluntary efforts—has not been empirically shown to have the impact advertised. Similarly, influencing *societal* behavioral change through labeling or the dissemination of risk information appears to have a blunt effect. The Århus Convention providing the public access to environmental information and participatory rights could change the dynamics of stakeholder influence. We argued earlier that providing the public with information about technological alternatives may be more effective than information about hazards. All this leads to the conclusion that focusing on directly encouraging/forcing technological change is central to achieving sustainability, buttressed by complementary changes in institutions, firm organization, and societal demand.† However, the last three categories of action are not sufficient by themselves.

## 10.19 WORKER HEALTH AND SAFETY

National governments employ an extensive range of legislative models and systems for occupational health and safety. Occupational health and safety laws and practices are often considered an integral aspect of a government's labor or social security policies because of a growing awareness that there are economic benefits of a healthy and productive workforce. However, despite growing awareness of the importance of health and safety legislation, there are still many burdens of injury and disease, as well as exposure to environmental hazards in the workplace. The International Labour Organization (ILO) has been active in the area of health and safety in the workplace since its creation in 1919, including the development of international treaties and other technical instruments and the development of chemical-safety information systems. The first binding international instrument directly related to a single

---

\* Recall the discussion in Chapter 7 that major advances in technological innovation are more likely to come from outside the regulated industry.

† For a recent discussion of the relevance of EU environmental directives for achieving sustainable consumption and production, see Nash (2009).

chemical was adopted in 1921, the White Lead Convention. Other conventions adopted since have addressed the hazards of benzene, asbestos, hazardous chemicals in general, and occupational cancer and the prevention of major industrial accidents (Obadia 2003).

In the United States, occupational health and safety is a federal responsibility, but twenty-three states are permitted to operate their own programs if they are as effective as the federal programs; they are monitored by federal authority.* The European Community is the main force behind the development of health and safety policies across European nations. In many European countries, such as Denmark, Italy, and the United Kingdom, as well as in Japan and some of the emerging economies of the Eastern European nations, the central government has the primary responsibility for implementing health and safety legislation (the EU member states, following EU directives and regulations). In some cases, such as Germany, responsibilities are shared: the central government makes law, and the regional governments are responsible for enforcing the regulations. With the expansion of the EU over the past few years, advances in occupational health and safety regulation have been proactive. Box 10.11 summarizes the EU directives and legal approaches. Box 10.12 describes the research institutions that are driving and disseminating information on occupational health and safety.

Governments address health and safety functions through the application of a number of policy instruments, including regulation, inspection, enforcement, consultation, technical assistance, training, education, research, certification (of materials, equipment, and processes), economic incentives (or disincentives such as fines and penalties), and criminal and civil prosecutions. Most occupational health and safety law defines the roles and responsibilities of employers and workers in general; however, employers are to ensure the health and safety of their workforce through statutory or regulatory mechanisms.

Whereas occupational health and safety standards are mandatory in the United States, the EU distinguishes mandatory obligations/standards, such as those established for carcinogens and mutagens in the Parliamentary and Council Directive 2004/37/EC, from "indicative" standards, such as the indicative Occupational Exposure Limits (OELs) in the Council Directive 2000/29/EC and Commission Directive 2006/15/EC. The individual member states implement the indicative OELs through their national laws and have the discretionary authority to make them mandatory. They can also establish more stringent levels of protection or protect workers from hazards not established by EU initiatives. The EU establishes a hierarchy for employers to reduce risk.[80] In order of preference, these include the following:

- Elimination of the need to use the substance (that is, prevention of exposure)

- Substitution by a less hazardous substance

- Technical and organizational measures to reduce contact with, or the air concentration of, a hazardous substance

- As a last resort, personal protective equipment

Although this is similar to the U.S. approach of preferring "engineering controls" to personal protective equipment, the focus on primary prevention and cleaner and inherently safer technology for worker protection has not been a hallmark of U.S. regulation.[†]

Pesticide exposure continues to be a problem for workers, consumers, and the general population. Discussions of the Framework Directive on the Sustainable Use of Pesticides started in the European Parliament and the Council in 2006. A second-reading agreement was reached in December 2008.[81] A new licensing agreement incorporating the precautionary principle could ultimately eliminate one-quarter of the pesticides currently on the European market.[82] Regulation (EC) 1107/2009 (published on November 24, 2009) replaces the prior pesticide Directive 91/414/EEC and will apply from June 14, 2011. It will continue to harmonize plant protection products across the EU as well as introduce some new requirements, such as the introduction of hazard-based criteria, assessment of cumulative and synergistic effects, comparative assessment and endocrine disruption. This regulation is part of the EU Thematic Strategy, along with the Sustainable Use Directive (2009/128/EC) and Statistics Regulation (1185/2009/EC).[83]

Workers may also have obligations, such as following the employer's health and safety policies, to take care of their own safety and to report incidents to supervisors. In general, the primary responsibility for workplace health and safety lies with the em-

---

* See Ashford and Caldart (1996) for an in-depth treatment of U.S. occupational health and safety law.

† In contrast, pollution prevention is increasingly emphasized in the environmental context in the United States. See the discussion of the U.S. Pollution Prevention Act in Chapter 9.

**BOX 10.11: SELECTED DIRECTIVES AND REGULATIONS ESTABLISHED TO PROTECT THE HEALTH AND SAFETY OF EUROPE'S WORKERS**

### DIRECTIVE 89/391—OSH "FRAMEWORK DIRECTIVE"

12 June 1989 on the introduction of measures to encourage improvements in the safety and health of workers at work. Source: http://osha.europa.eu/en/legislation/directives/the-osh-framework-directive (accessed January 15, 2011).

In 1989 some provisions of the Framework Directive brought about considerable innovation including the following: The term "working environment" was set in accordance with International Labour Organization (ILO) Convention No. 155 and defines a modern approach taking into account technical safety as well as general prevention of ill-health.

- The Directive aims to establish an equal level of safety and health for the benefit of all workers (the only exceptions are domestic workers and certain public and military services).
- The Directive obliges employers to take appropriate preventive measures to make work safer and healthier.
- The Directive introduces as a key element the principle of risk assessment and defines its main elements (e.g. hazard identification, worker participation, introduction of adequate measures with the priority of eliminating risk at source, documentation and periodical re-assessment of workplace hazards).
- The new obligation to put in place prevention measures implicitly stresses the importance of new forms of safety and health management as part of general management processes.

The Framework Directive had to be transposed into national law by the end of 1992. The repercussions of the transposition on national legal systems varied across Member States. In some Member States, the Framework Directive had considerable legal consequences due to inadequate national legislation while in others no major adjustments were necessary.

### EXPOSURE TO CHEMICAL AGENTS AND CHEMICAL SAFETY—OSH DIRECTIVES AND REGULATIONS

*Source:* http://osha.europa.eu/en/legislation/directives/exposure-to-chemical-agents-and-chemical-safety/ (accessed January 15, 2011).

Directive 2009/161/EU—indicative occupational exposure limit values of 17 December 2009 establishing a third list of indicative occupational exposure limit values in implementation of Council Directive 98/24/EC and amending Commission Directive 2000/39/EC (Text with EEA relevance)

Directive 2009/148/EC—exposure to asbestos at work of 30 November 2009 on the protection of workers from the risks related to exposure to asbestos at work (Text with EEA relevance)

Directive 2006/15/EC—indicative occupational exposure limit values of 7 February 2006 establishing a second list of indicative occupational exposure limit values in implementation of Council Directive 98/24/EC and amending Directives 91/322/EEC and 2000/39/EC

Directive 2004/37/EC—carcinogens or mutagens at work of 29 April 2004 on the protection of workers from the risks related to exposure to carcinogens or mutagens at work (Sixth individual Directive within the meaning of Article 16(1) Directive 89/391/EEC)

Directive 2000/39/EC—indicative occupational exposure limit values of 8 June 2000 establishing a first list of indicative occupational exposure limit values in implementation of Council Directive 98/24/EC on the protection of the health and safety of workers from the risks related to chemical agents at work.

Directive 98/24/EC - risks related to chemical agents at work of 7 April 1998 on the protection of the health and safety of workers from the risks related to chemical agents at work (fourteenth individual Directive within the meaning of Article 16(1) of Directive 89/391/EEC)

Directive 91/322/EEC—indicative limit values of 29 May 1991 on establishing indicative limit values by implementing Council Directive 80/1107/EEC on the protection of workers from the risks related to exposure to chemical, physical and biological agents at work.

### EXPOSURE TO CHEMICAL AGENTS AND CHEMICAL SAFETY—OSH RELATED ASPECTS

Regulation (EC) No 1272/2008—classification, labelling and packaging of substances and mixtures of the European Parliament and of the Council of 16 December 2008 on classification, labelling and packaging of substances and mixtures, amending and repealing Directives 67/548/EEC and 1999/45/EC, and amending Regulation (EC) No 1907/2006 (Text with EEA relevance)

Directive 2008/68/EC—inland transport of dangerous goods of the European Parliament and of the Council of 24 September 2008 on the inland transport of dangerous goods. This Directive replaces Council Directive 94/55/EC, Council Directive 96/49/EC and Council Directive 96/35/EC

Regulation (EC) No 1907/2006—REACH of 18 December 2006 concerning the Registration, Evaluation, Authorisation and Restriction of Chemicals (REACH) and establishing a European Chemicals Agency.

(continued)

---

**BOX 10.11** (continued)

Directive 1999/45/EC—classification, packaging and labelling of dangerous preparations of the European Parliament and of the Council of 31 May 1999 concerning the approximation of the laws, regulations and administrative provisions of the Member States relating to the classification, packaging and labelling of dangerous preparations.

Directive 96/82/EC—major-accident hazards of 9 December 1996 on the control of major-accident hazards involving dangerous substance

Directive 95/50/EC—procedures for transport of dangerous goods of 6 October 1995 on uniform procedures for checks on the transport of dangerous goods by road

Directive 91/414/EEC—plant protection products of 15 July 1991 concerning the placing of plant protection products on the market.

Directive 67/548/EEC—classification, packaging and labelling of dangerous substances of 27 June 1967 on the approximation of laws, regulations and administrative provisions relating to the classification, packaging and labelling of dangerous substances.

*EXPOSURE TO PHYSICAL HAZARDS—OSH DIRECTIVES*

*Source:* http://osha.europa.eu/en/legislation/directives/exposure-to-physical-hazards/ (accessed January 15, 2011).

Directive 2006/25/EC—artificial optical radiation on the minimum health and safety requirements regarding the exposure of the workers to risks arising from physical agents (artificial optical radiation, 19th individual directive within the meaning of Article 16(1) of Directive 89/391/EEC).

Directive 2004/40/EC—electromagnetic fields and waves of 29 April 2004 on the minimum health and safety requirements regarding the exposure of the workers to risks arising from electromagnetic fields and waves (18th individual directive within the meaning of Art. 16(1) of directive 89/391/EEC).

Directive 2003/10/EC—noise of 6 February 2003 on the minimum health and safety requirements regarding the exposure of workers to the risks arising from physical agents (noise) (Seventeenth individual Directive within the meaning of Article 16(1) of Directive 89/391/EEC).

Directive 2002/44/EC—vibration of the of 25 June 2002 on the minimum health and safety requirements regarding the exposure of workers to the risks arising from physical agents (vibration) (sixteenth individual Directive within the meaning of Article 16(1) of Directive 89/391/EEC)

Directive 96/29/Euratom—ionizing radiation of 13 May 1996 laying down basic safety standards for the protection of the health of workers and the general public against the dangers arising from ionizing radiation.

*EXPOSURE TO PHYSICAL HAZARDS—OSH RELATED ASPECTS*

Directive 2009/71/Euratom—nuclear safety of 25 June 2009 establishing a Community framework for the nuclear safety of nuclear installations

Directive 2004/108/EC—electromagnetic compatibility of the European Parliament and of the Council of 15 December 2004 on the approximation of the laws of the Member States relating to electromagnetic compatibility and repealing Directive 89/336/EEC

Directive 2003/122/Euratom—radioactive sources of 22 December 2003 on the control of high-activity sealed radioactive sources and orphan sources

Directive 2000/14/EC—noise-equipment for use outdoors of the European Parliament and of the Council of 8 May 2000 on the approximation of the laws of the Member States relating to the noise emission in the environment by equipment for use outdoors

Source: European Agency for Safety and Health at Work, http://osha.europa.eu/en/legislation/directives (accessed January 15, 2011).

ployer, who makes the decisions relating to production systems, processes, materials, practices, and conditions of work. Workers also have the right to stop or refuse dangerous work, to make proposals for improving health and safety, or to be consulted on matters relating to health and safety.

The WHO provides the following commentary on the occupational health and safety challenges faced by today's global workforce:[84]

The workplace is a hazardous environment. Occupational health and safety hazards are common in many economic sectors and affect large numbers of workers. Approximately 30–50% of workers report hazardous physical, chemical, or biological exposures or overload of unreasonably heavy physical work or ergonomic factors that may be hazardous to health and to working capacity; an equal number of working people report psychological overload at work resulting in stress symptoms. Many individuals spend one-third of their adult life in such hazardous work environments. About 120 million occupational accidents with 200,000 fatalities are estimated to occur annually and some 68–157 million new cases of occupational disease may be caused by various exposures at work.

---

**BOX 10.12: HEALTH AND SAFETY RESEARCH INSTITUTIONS ACTIVE WITHIN THE EU**

- European Agency for Safety and Health at Work—Located in Bilbao, Spain (http://osha.europa.eu/), the European Agency for Safety and Health at Work works with governments, employers, and workers to promote a risk-prevention culture; analyzes new scientific research and statistics on workplace risks; and manages the European Risk Observatory (http://osha.europa.eu/en/riskobservatory).
- European Chemicals Bureau—The European Chemicals Bureau (ECB) was established within the Environment Institute at the Joint Research Centre in Ispra, Italy. It is a division of the Institute for Health and Consumer Protection, which carries out research on chemicals.
- European Foundation for the Improvement of Living and Working Conditions—This autonomous body of the European Union carries out research to support its role to increase and disseminate knowledge to contribute to the planning and establishment of better working and living conditions.
- European Molecular Biology Laboratory—The European Molecular Biology Laboratory (EMBL) was established in 1974 and is supported by sixteen countries, including nearly all of Western Europe and Israel. The EMBL consists of five facilities: the main laboratory in Heidelberg (Germany); outstations in Hamburg (Germany), Grenoble (France), and Hinxton (the United Kingdom); and an external Research Programme in Monterotondo (Italy). The EMBL was founded with the fourfold mission to conduct basic research in molecular biology; to provide essential services to scientists in its member states; to provide high-level training to its staff, students, and visitors; and to develop new instrumentation for biological research.
- European Occupational Health and Safety Law Research Centre—The European Occupational Health and Safety Law Research Centre of the University of Salford is dedicated to the study of European occupational health and safety law. All members of the center's academic and research staff are researchers.
- European Organization for Nuclear Research—The European Organization for Nuclear Research (CERN) is the world's largest particle physics center. Founded in 1954, the laboratory was one of Europe's first joint ventures and has become a shining example of international collaboration.
- European Process Safety Centre—The European Process Safety Centre (EPSC) is an international industry-funded organization that provides an independent technical focus for process safety in Europe. Its activities are sponsored by chemical-manufacturing companies and related businesses with an interest in chemical process safety.
- European Thematic Network on Process Safety—The European Thematic Network on Process Safety has been developed to promote research in areas of process safety that has as its objective a reduction of the risk of an accident in the workplace. Its goals are to discuss safety problems, to gather new ideas from the results of the worldwide effort in safety research, to learn of new safety technologies, and to keep abreast of new legislation and standards. Its activities include a monthly electronic newsletter, the operation of a database, and the electronic publication of information on research currently under way, sources of information on standards, regulations and legislation, and process safety articles.
- European Trade Union Institute (ETUI) Health and Safety Department—The ETUI Health and Safety Department monitors the framing, national incorporation, and implementation of European legislation in the field of occupational health and safety. It is one of three departments in the ETUI. The other two departments focus on *research* relating to socio-economic issues and industrial relations and *education and training* within the European Trade Union Confederation (ETUC), respectively.
- Euroscience—Euroscience was created in 1997 with the objective of providing an open forum for debate on science and technology and research policies in Europe. Acting on behalf of the scientific community, the organization aims to provide policy-relevant scientific information and proposals to authorities at the European level.
- Major Accident Hazards Bureau—The Major Accident Hazards Bureau (MAHB) is a special unit within the Joint Research Centre's Institute of Systems, Informatics and Safety, System Analysis and Information Assessment Unit, dedicated to scientific and technical support for the actions of the European Commission in the area of the control of major industrial hazards. The overall mission of the MAHB is to assist other services of the European Commission in the successful implementation of European Union policy on the control of major hazards and the prevention and mitigation of major accidents.
- International Coordinating Group for Occupational Health Psychology—The International Coordinating Group aims to promote and facilitate the development of research, professional practice, and education in occupational health psychology (OHP, the application of psychology to occupational health and safety) within an international framework.

---

In addition to unnecessary human suffering, the costs involved in these health hazards have been estimated to amount up to several percent of some countries' gross national product (GNP).

The most important challenges for the future of occupational health are: occupational health problems linked with new information technologies and automation, new chemical substances and physical energies, health hazards associated with new biotechnologies, transfer of hazardous technologies, ageing of working populations, special problems of vulnerable and underserved groups (e.g., the chronically ill and handicapped), including migrants and the unem-

ployed, problems related to growing mobility of worker populations and occurrence of new occupational diseases of various origins.

In some regions and countries, only 5–10% of workers in developing countries and 20–50% of workers in industrialized countries (with a very few exceptions) have access to occupational health services in spite of an evident need virtually at each place of work. The need for occupational health services is particularly acute in the developing and newly industrialized countries (NICs). Furthermore, approximately eight out of 10 of the world's workers live in these countries. Such services, if organized appropriately and effectively for all workers, would contribute positively not only to workers' health, but also to overall socio-economic development, productivity, environmental health and well-being of countries, communities, families and dependants. Also the control of unnecessary costs from sickness absenteeism and work disability, as well as costs of health care and social security can be effectively managed with the help of occupational health professionals.

Rapid change of the modern working life is associated with increasing demands of learning new skills, need to adapt to new types of work, pressure of higher productivity and quality of work, time pressure and hectic jobs and with growing psychological workload and stress among the workforce. Such developments require higher priority to be given for psychological quality of work and the work environment, and more attention to psychosocial aspects of work.

Most developed countries' national policies for protecting worker health and safety have the primary aims of guaranteeing common minimum standards of protection through harmonization of the recommendations on safety and health and reducing the number of accidents at work and the number of cases of occupational diseases. All countries in the international community must take note of progressive strides to promote a safer and more healthful work environment. Policy on health and safety at work must link up with work being done by international organizations, including active collaboration with the agencies of the United Nations, WHO, and the ILO, all of which have a similar role to play in improving the level of protection of workers' health and safety.

## 10.20 THE IMPORTANCE OF INTERNATIONAL INSTITUTIONS

The 1992 United Nations Conference on Environment and Development (UNCED) in Rio represented the world's most organized response to international environmental degradation. In addition to initiating conventions on greenhouse gases and biodiversity and adopting an implementation program in Agenda 21, the conference also established a set of institutional and financial arrangements to support these changes. However, since the Rio Earth Summit, nations have become increasingly skeptical about the ability of the nation-state system to solve international environment problems (see the Primer on Sustainable Development found in the website associated with this book). States are ultimately concerned with protecting national security and maintaining economic growth, and addressing environmental issues is less of a priority. Thus stronger international institutions are needed to enforce environmental regulations. Maurice Strong, secretary general of the UNCED, has argued, "The need for international cooperation is inescapable and growing almost exponentially. This in turn has focused renewed attention on the principal instruments through which such cooperation is carried out. Most notable are the United Nations and its system of agencies, organizations, and programs. . . . These organizations provide the indispensable structure and fora on which international cooperation depends. . . . They represent not the precursors of world government, but the basic framework for a world system of governance which is imperative to the effective functioning of our global society" (Strong 1990, p. 211).

Truly effective international environmental institutions would improve the quality of the global environment. However, these institutions are still developing in their effectiveness, evolving as environmental issues evolve and scientific data change. Even given their rudimentary place in today's globalized society, institutions can be important factors in protecting the environment, as well as health and safety. The response of governments to incentives and pressures from international institutions can prevent environmental degradation and reduce negative impacts on human health. Even on environmental issues that predominantly affect developing countries, national actions are guided by international institutional pressures.

Two major classes of problems confront nations with respect to international institutions. In the first, harm is directly transmitted from one set of countries to another via a physical or biological medium, where the consequences of activities in one country are felt in another (transboundary problems) or affect a resource that is outside the jurisdiction of any one country (a commons problem). Examples of such problems are stratospheric ozone depletion, European acid rain, marine oil pollution, and overfishing. A second class of issues involves environmental problems in which direct harm is felt only within national borders, and therefore mutual restraint is felt only within national borders, such as soil erosion, lack of safe drinking water from domestic sources, and use of pesticides (particularly in the developing world). Solutions for this latter class of problems require the development of concern within the countries where they occur and the development of the domestic political and administrative capacity to implement solutions. International institutions can provide information, skills, resources, and persuasion to resolve these types of issues. Both types of problems threaten human and ecosystem survival. Commons and transboundary problems affect the long-term sustainability of the planet's ecosystems, but national problems may affect more individuals in the future, especially in the developing world (Keohane, Haas, et al. 1995).

Effective institutions can affect the political process at three key points in the sequence of environmental policy:

1. International institutions can contribute to the adoption of more appropriate agendas, reflecting the convergence of political and technical consensus about the nature and urgency of addressing environmental threats.

2. They can contribute to more comprehensive and specific international policies, agreed on through a political process whose foundation is intergovernmental negotiation.

3. They can contribute to national policy responses that directly control sources of environmental degradation, and to improving worker health and safety.

In addition, where possible, it is important that international institutions do not operate independently of each other, but resolve issues cooperatively. In light of all that has been written about jurisdictional conflicts within the United Nations system, it is heartening to discover that cooperation among agencies is more prevalent than conflict. For example, with respect to chemical pesticides, the UNEP collaborated with the FAO. Coalitions of international institutions are also evident in the UN Regional Seas Programme, also coordinated by the UNEP. However, international cooperation notwithstanding, ultimately, it is national decisions that affect environmental quality and worker health and safety, even though international measures may have been necessary to overcome initial national reluctance. Therefore, the role of international institutions in monitoring and enforcing compliance is critical in order to urge the laggards to accept and implement their commitments. Often, international institutions are required to use a combination of incentives to encourage national compliance, including a combination of binding international law and public exposure of noncompliance, persuasion, scientific argument, technical assistance, and investment (Keohane, Haas, et al. 1995).

Given that the history of international cooperation regarding environmental and worker health and safety issues is relatively short, there is as yet no standard approach to negotiating these agreements, waylaid by political, economic, and cultural implications, as will be explored in discussing the role of trade in Chapter 11. Below, we take a cursory look at the role of some major international institutions and their impact on international law in the way in which they create networks over, around, and within states that generate the means and incentives for effective cooperation.

Overall, the OECD, the ILO, the UN, the UNEP, the UNIDO, the UNDP, WHO, the WTO, the NAFTA Commission, the FAO, and nongovernmental organizations (NGOs) have all provided forums for negotiation and conflict resolution in treaties and standards. It seems likely that these organizations will increasingly seek to extend their role in environmental and worker health and safety issues.

### 10.20.1 The Organisation for Economic Co-operation and Development

The Organisation for Economic Co-operation and Development (OECD) was established in 1961 and consists of member countries committed to democratic government and the market economy. It covers economic and social issues, including macroeconomics, trade, education, development, science, and innovation. The OECD produces multilateral international agreements, decisions, and recommendations and recognizes the concept of sustainable development (even if its members do not). Its goals are to help "member countries promote economic growth, employment and improved standards of living through the coordination of policy" and to encourage "the sound and harmonious development of the world economy and improve the lot of developing countries, particularly the poorest."[85]

The OECD acts through a Council, an Executive Committee of fourteen member states, a secretariat, and committees covering the environment, energy, fisheries, and scientific and technological policy. In 1970, the OECD established an Environment Committee in which member states discuss environmental matters and make recommendations for national policy. This committee produces detailed reports on the state of the environment in member states. These reports cover, water, land, forest, and wildlife resources, in addition to the areas mentioned in the text. The OECD also analyzes the national environmental policies of its members and the economic implications of those policies. Historically, the OECD has made proposals for assessing and improving environmental quality, scrutinized health hazards presented by chemicals, evaluated the environmental implications of energy production, and addressed transboundary pollution, for which it developed the now-influential polluter-pays principle (Birnie and Boyle 1992, p. 71).

The OECD has numerous working groups and publications in the following areas:

- Chemical accidents, classification, and labeling
- Exposure assessment
- Hazard and risk assessment
- Chemical risk management
- Chemicals testing
- Climate change, energy, and transport
- Environmental impacts of production and consumption
- Environmental policies and instruments
- Trade, investment, and the environment

### 10.20.2 The International Labour Organization

The International Labour Organization (ILO) is the specialized UN agency that seeks the promotion of social justice and internationally recognized human and labor rights.[86] It was founded in 1919 and is the only surviving creation of the Treaty of Versailles, which brought the League of Nations into being; it became the first specialized agency of the UN in 1946. The ILO is primarily responsible for improving working conditions and promoting the economic and social welfare of workers by creating a code of labor standards, working through an annual International Labour Conference, a forty-eight-member Governing Body, the International Labour Office, and a secretariat. The ILO has a tripartite system of delegations that are made up of four persons, including representatives of government, employers, and workers (trade-union representatives) who vote independently on adoption of conventions (Birnie and Boyle 1992). A number of international conventions set out by the ILO impose obligations to reduce exposures to occupational health and safety hazards.[87] The United States has ratified 14 of the 185 labor conventions, compared with Germany, which has ratified 77; the United Kingdom, 86; Brazil, 90; and the Netherlands, 104.

The ILO formulates international labor standards in the form of conventions and recommendations that set minimum standards of basic labor rights: freedom of association, the right to organize, collec-

tive bargaining, abolition of forced labor, equality of opportunity and treatment, and other standards regulating conditions across the entire spectrum of work-related issues, including health and safety. It provides technical assistance primarily in the following fields:

- Vocational training and vocational rehabilitation
- Employment policy
- Labor administration
- Labor law and industrial relations
- Working conditions
- Management development
- Cooperatives
- Social security
- Labor statistics and occupational safety and health

It promotes the development of independent employers' and workers' organizations and provides training and advisory services to those organizations. Within the UN system, the ILO has a unique tripartite structure in which workers and employers participate as equal partners with governments in the work of its governing organs. Ehrenberg (2003) has recommended a merger of the ILO and the WTO, thus bringing a tripartite structure to the latter (see Chapter 13).*

### 10.20.3 The United Nations

The formation of the United Nations (UN) in 1945 changed the international system.[88] In terms of international law, under Article 102 of the Charter of the United Nations, "Every treaty and every international agreement entered into by any Member of the United Nations after the present Charter comes into force shall as soon as possible be registered with the UN and published by it." The charter includes commitments to "achieving international cooperation in solving international problems of an economic, social, cultural, or humanitarian character and in promoting and encouraging respect for human rights and for fundamental freedoms for all."[89] The United Nations has become the key force and forum for nations to negotiate international agreements related

---

* See Baccaro and Mele 2010 for a critical discussion of the shift in the ILO over the last twenty years from standard-setting to a focus on principles such as "decent work for all" and an involvement of civil society organizations (e.g., NGOs) in regulatory activities echoing a "corporatist approach" to labor issues.

all aspects of development, including environmental and humanitarian concerns.

Within the UN were established many institutions, such as the General Assembly, the Security Council, the Economic and Social Council, the Secretariat, the International Law Commission (ILC), and the International Court of Justice (ICJ). The ILC is tasked with codification and progressive development of the law. The ICJ, which sits at The Hague in the Netherlands, acts as a world court. It decides, in accordance with international law, disputes of a legal nature submitted to it by states. In addition, certain international agencies are entitled to call on it for advisory opinions.

Decisions within the UN are adopted by a voting system. Voting procedures in the UN Security Council require the affirmative vote of nine of its fifteen members but are also subject to the veto power of each of the five permanent members. Nonbinding recommendations can be adopted by a majority, which enables international bodies to influence the conduct of all states participating in the institution concerned, even if they cannot be obliged to act in a particular way, and contributes to the process of lawmaking. Since the 1972 Stockholm Conference on the Human Environment, the General Assembly has increasingly expressed recommendations and resolutions on a number of environmental issues. In addition, the role of the UN's Economic and Social Council in environmental issues is expanding, and it can make recommendations for the purpose of promoting respect for and observance of human rights and fundamental freedoms, which may be expanded to include environmental rights (Birnie and Boyle 1992).

With regard to enforceability, it is important to recognize that states are concerned with protecting their own sovereignty and may seek to restrict the independent international power of an authority such as the UN. Often at issue is whether environmental action should be taken at the international, regional, or national level. To protect their sovereignty, states may either restrict the adoption of environmental measures or inhibit their goals. The UN recently campaigned to champion issues such as climate change within its scope by designating the issue a matter of "common concern. The EC has sought to clarify this problem in its series of Action Programmes on the Environment by allocating actions to the appropriate level, with emphasis on the national level. Challenges to UN proposed actions can be referred to the ICJ's dispute-settlement procedures (Birnie and Boyle 1992). As environmental and worker health and safety issues become predominant drivers of

law—as they are likely to be, given the exacerbation of health and economic problems brought about by a history of relentlessly ignoring these matters—it is hoped that the UN will be able to provide more enforceability through adopting successful schemes, such as the Action Programmes operating in the EU or those achieving success elsewhere, to encourage increased national participation in addressing these concerns.

The following sections look more closely at three organizations within the UN system that have a direct connection with the environment and development—the UN Environment Programme (UNEP), the UN Industrial Development Organization (UNIDO), and the UN Development Program (UNDP).

### 10.20.3.1 The United Nations Environment Programme

The UN has yet to create an institution wholly responsible for the environment. Instead, the United Nations Environment Programme (UNEP) provides guidance on environmental issues rather than enforceability of resolutions. In this regard, the UNEP acts primarily as a "catalyst, advocate, educator and facilitator" for advancing the "sustainable development of the global environment."[90] It is seen as the voice for the environment within the UN system.

An example of how the UNEP plays a key role in coordinating UN environmental initiatives is the Environment Management Group (EMG), which is chaired by the UNEP's executive director.[91] Formed in 1999 by UN General Assembly Resolution 53/242, the EMG consists of all UN agencies and secretariats of multilateral environmental agreements (MEAs), the Bretton Woods institutions, and the World Trade Organization. The primary objective of the group is to share information about its members' current and future plans and activities in the area of the environment and human settlements, with the aim of creating an agreed set of priorities to which all members can contribute. It is hoped that the work of the EMG can lead to a more rational and cost-effective approach to environmental and human settlements initiatives within the UN system, which are often poorly interconnected and duplicative. Hence the extent to which interagency policy coherence and collaboration has been achieved will indicate whether the EMG's objectives are being realized.

Since its formation in 1972, the UNEP's main role has been environmental assessment, research, and monitoring, but it also played an important role in placing the link between environment and development on the international agenda (see the Primer on Sustainable Development on the website associated with this book). Attempts to address environmental concerns on a global scale reflected the increasing awareness by international organizations and states of changes in the ecosystem and the destruction of natural resources.

Although the UNEP and other UN partners have largely succeeded in promoting environmental programs within and outside the UN system (UN EMG 2006), the capability of the UNEP to manage and lead the UN's growing environmental agenda has not grown significantly since the program's formation over three decades ago. The principle reasons for this are seen to be the following: (1) the UNEP remains a program rather than a specialized agency; (2) the UNEP's governance structure has biased its focus toward the needs/demands of member states rather than advancing its overall mission; (3) the UNEP's financial structure limits its ability to finance activities for the common good; and (4) the location of the UNEP in Nairobi, away from centers of political activity, limits its ability to coordinate the initiatives of environment-related agencies (Ivanova 2005). If the UNEP is to become the principal coordinator of environmental activities within the UN system, its political influence within this system will need to be enhanced along with its financial resources, bringing it more in line with the capabilities of other UN agencies—such as the United Nations Development Programme (see Section 10.20.3.3)—that are active in the environmental arena.

Esty (2006, pp. 1555–1556) offers a mixed evaluation of the UNEP:

> UNEP has achieved a measure of success in information gathering and scientific assessments and its regional seas program is highly regarded.
>
> But in recent years, UNEP's governance activities have diminished, and it has not established itself as an independent or autonomous force in global-scale policymaking. Despite its mandate to coordinate multilateral environmental policymaking, UNEP has not been effective in setting the international environmental agenda or addressing a number of critical challenges, including climate change. Not only has UNEP failed to move toward a broader role in supranational policymaking, but its intergovernmental coordination role has also shrunk.

#### 10.20.3.2 The United Nations Industrial Development Organization

Established in 1966, the United Nations Industrial Development Organization (UNIDO) is tasked with promoting industrial development throughout the developing world.[92] To achieve this mandate, the UNIDO acts as a *global forum* for generating and disseminating knowledge relating to industrial matters and as a *technical cooperation agency* that supports the industrial development plans of its clients (which consist of governments, business associations, and individual companies).

With the emergence of the international concern for the environment during the 1960s and 1970s and for sustainable development during the 1980s and 1990s (see Chapter 2 and the Primer on Sustainable Development on the website associated with this book), UNIDO embarked on an ambitious reform process in 1990 that focused on integrating environmental considerations into the organization's technical cooperation programs (R. A. Luken 2009). This process, often referred to as the "greening of the UNIDO," led to a shift in the organization's strategic focus to strengthening industrial capacities and promoting cleaner and sustainable industrial development, particularly in least developed regions such as Africa. The UNIDO has also identified three thematic priority areas that align with industry-related aspects of sustainable development.[93] These areas focus on (1) poverty reduction through productive activities—that is, the creation of employment for the poor; (2) trade and capacity building to increase the participation of developing nations in the international economy; and (3) energy and the environment—that is, delinking the intensity of energy use from economic growth and reducing the environmental impact from energy use.

Before the Earth Summit in 1992, around 2 percent of the UNIDO's technical cooperation program was directed at environmental initiatives (R. A. Luken 2009). The primary focus of these initiatives was addressing water pollution from the leather-tanning and finishing subsector. However, by the end of 2004, the "greening of the UNIDO" meant that environmental programs and projects now constituted around 60 percent of the organization's technical delivery (ibid.). In 2007, the services offered by the UNIDO were grouped under eight modules: industrial governance and statistics; investment and technology promotion; industrial competitiveness and trade; private-sector development; agro-industry; sustainable energy and climate change; the Montreal Protocol (that is, the reduction of ozone-depleting substances); and environmental management. The majority of the UNIDO's current environmental initiatives fall under the last three service modules. Since the UNIDO's initial awakening to environmental concerns in the 1990s, some of its most notable accomplishments have included its joint effort with the UNEP, the UNDP, and the World Bank to phase out CFCs under the Montreal Protocol, the organization's creation of over thirty national cleaner production centers, and its growing number of international water and climate-related projects (R. Luken and Hesp 2006; R. Luken, Narvratil, et al. 2003). Interestingly, the experience the UNIDO gained from its reform or greening process is now being used to help the broader UN reform process.[94]

### 10.20.3.3 The United Nations Development Programme

The United Nations Development Programme (UNDP), founded in 1966, is perhaps one of the most influential organizations within the UN system for promoting sustainable development. The UNDP views itself as the UN's "global development network." Its broad mission is to advocate for change and connect "countries to knowledge, experience and resources to help people build a better life."[95] In addition to coordinating global and national efforts toward the Millennium Development Goals (MDGs), its five core focus areas—(1) crisis prevention and recovery, (2) poverty reduction, (3) HIV/AIDS, (4) democratic governance, and (5) energy and the environment—align well with the five elements of sustainable development (see the Primer on Sustainable Development on the website associated with this book).* This comprehensive focus on sustainability is further strengthened by the UNDP's promotion of human rights and empowerment of women in its general activities.

The UNDP is operational in 166 countries, where it helps governments attract and use development aid and supports national activities to formulate solutions to global and national development challenges.[96] In the first published history of the UNDP, Murphy (2006) describes a number of key aspects of the organization that support its success in the development arena. First, since its formation, the UNDP has become "the development programme of the developing countries" (ibid., p. 8). Murphy (ibid.) documents how the UNDP's responsiveness to the needs of developing nations has made it the most trusted international organization throughout the developing world. A key element of its responsiveness has been its "resident representatives" in more

than 150 country offices, whose nuanced understanding of national and regional development needs makes them welcomed partners.

Second, Murphy (2006, p. 5) argues that the UNDP has "the most extensive and most consistent presence of the entire UN system throughout the world." This international presence has meant that the UNDP's resident representatives are often responsible for coordinating the development activities of the entire UN system within a country, including the work of specialized agencies such as the ILO, the FAO, and Bretton Woods agencies. Murphy (2006) describes how the UNDP's coordination of field activities was sometimes matched by a responsibility to coordinate the development activities of organizations within the UN system.

Finally, and most impressively, the UNDP has managed to become a learning organization. To achieve this, the UNDP's founders created a fundamentally new organization. As Murphy (2006, pp. 18–19) describes, "Unlike most development agencies, UNDP (broadly understood) is *not* simply a bureaucratic hierarchy of nested roles and their related obligations. It is, instead, a decentralized complex of relatively autonomous (and creative) people and organizations involving independent experts, short-term alliances, and joint projects. It is at once public and private, international and national, bilateral and multilateral. This complex organization is held together by personal bonds, by professional norms and the external professional associations in which they are embodied, and by complex multidirectional webs of communication linking every corner of the globe. Its glue is not just messages going up and down simple chains of command, nor is it primarily money, either as an incentive to staff members or as a conditional promise to clients. . . . This, it turns out, is a kind of organization that can learn."

The UNDP's ability to learn is reflected in its influence on shaping the structure of the current UN system. Murphy (2006, p. 7) describes how approximately one-third of the ninety entities that form the UN system were once part of, funded by, or staffed by members of the UNDP. In many ways, the UNDP is a model for institutional innovation that could inform the reform of other institutions looking to become more flexible, adaptable, and responsive in a complex, dynamic, and interconnected world.

One of the most visible initiatives of the UNDP is its annual *Human Development Report* (*HDR*), which was first published in 1990. The purpose of the *HDR*s is to place "people back at the center of the development process in terms of economic debate,

---

* The five elements of sustainable development are (1) peace and security; (2) economic development; (3) social development; (4) national governance that secures peace and development; and (5) environmental protection.

policy and advocacy. The goal was both massive and simple, with far-ranging implications—going beyond income to assess the level of people's long-term well-being."[97] To measure development progress, the Human Development Index (HDI) was introduced in the first *HDR* (see Section 1.1.1 in Chapter 1). The HDI consists of three indicators: (1) life expectancy at birth, (2) educational attainment, and (3) real GDP (or income) (UNDP 1995). The index is obtained by taking a simple average of the three indicators. Today, the *HDRs* include four additional indexes to capture gender imbalances and income disparities across nations. In addition to measuring development progress, the topics of each *HDR* have been influential in opening debates on critical issues such as gender equality and cultural liberty—advancing concerns at the center of sustainable development. Further, alongside the global *HDRs*, the UNDP sponsors regional and national human development reports that reflect specific challenges facing a region or nation.

In summary, the UNDP's ability to mobilize in-country skills and resources, shape the international development debate through objective research and publications, and create and shape global development institutions makes it a significant player in international and sustainable development.

### 10.20.4 The World Health Organization

The main aim of the World Health Organization (WHO) is "the attainment by all peoples of the highest possible levels of health."[98] Because the health of the environment and working conditions affect human health, WHO has an interest in controlling environmental factors that adversely affect health, such as air pollution, polluted water and sanitation conditions, and unsafe human contact with chemicals. WHO develops and administers international health regulations and collects and disseminates information on health issues and also those related to the environment and worker health and safety. WHO is also actively promoting the Convention on Biodiversity, as well as the International Council for Exploration of the Sea (ICES), addressing the concern of marine pollution.

### 10.20.5 The World Trade Organization and the General Agreement on Tariffs and Trade

Environmental, health, and safety issues are becoming increasingly important within the World Trade Organization (WTO). The link between trade and environmental protection, consisting of both the impact of environmental policies on trade and the impact of trade on the environment, was recognized as early as 1970. In the early 1970s, there was growing international concern regarding the impact of economic growth on social development and the environment. This led to the 1972 Stockholm Conference on the Human Environment. During the preparatory phase of the Stockholm Conference, the Secretariat of the General Agreement on Tariffs and Trade (GATT) contributed a study titled *Industrial Pollution Control and International Trade*. It focused on the implications of environmental protection policies on international trade, reflecting the concern of trade officials that such policies could become obstacles to trade, as well as constitute a new form of protectionism. The GATT Secretariat and its successor, the WTO, have continually recounted their concern about potential conflicts between trade and the environment:[99]

> Between 1971 and 1991, environmental policies began to have an increasing impact on trade, and with increasing trade flows, the effects of trade on the environment had also become more widespread. . . .
>
> In 1982, a number of developing countries expressed concern that products prohibited in developed countries on the grounds of environmental hazards, health or safety reasons, continued to be exported to them. With limited information on these products, they were unable to make informed decisions regarding their import.
>
> At the 1982 GATT ministerial meeting, members decided to examine the measures needed to bring under control the export of products prohibited domestically (on the grounds of harm to human, animal or plant life or health, or the environment). This led to the creation, in 1989, of a Working Group on the Export of Domestically Prohibited Goods and Other Hazardous Substances. . . .
>
> During the Uruguay Round (1986–1994), trade-related environmental issues were once again taken up. Modifications were made to the TBT [Technical Barriers to Trade] Agreement, and certain environmental issues were addressed in the General Agreement on Trade in Services, the Agreements on Agriculture, Sanitary and Phytosanitary Measures (SPS), Subsidies and Countervailing Measures, and Trade-Related Aspects of Intellectual Property Rights (TRIPS). . . .
>
> In 1991, a dispute between Mexico and United States put the spotlight on the linkages between environmental protection policies and trade. The case concerned a US embargo on tuna imported from Mexico, caught using "purse seine" nets which caused the incidental killing of dolphins. Mexico appealed to GATT on the grounds that the embargo was inconsistent with the rules of international trade.

The panel ruled in favour of Mexico based on a number of different arguments. Although the report of the panel was not adopted, its ruling was heavily criticised by environmental groups who felt that trade rules were an obstacle to environmental protection.

In November 2001, at the Doha Ministerial Conference, an agreement was reached to begin negotiations on specific issues relating to trade and the environment (WTO 2004, p. 5): "These negotiations are conducted in a Committee established for this purpose, the Committee on Trade and Environment Special Session (CTESS). The CTE [Committee on Trade and Environment] was also requested to give particular attention to three items of its work programme. In addition, the CTE and the Committee on Trade and Development were asked to act as a forum in which the environmental and developmental aspects of the negotiations launched at Doha could be debated."

The Doha Conference provided the mandate for negotiations on a range of subjects and included further discussions of environmental, health, and safety issues, such as the following:

- Agriculture
- Trade-related aspects of intellectual property rights (TRIPS)
- Sanitary and phytosanitary (SPS) measures
- WTO rules on antidumping
- Trade and the environment
- Trade and transfer of technology
- Technical cooperation and capacity building

Despite forthcoming discussions of these issues, the WTO's role continues to be to liberalize trade, as well as to ensure that environmental policies do not act as obstacles to trade. There is still much more scope for improving international trade regimes so that trade rules do not stand in the way of adequate domestic environmental protection. Chapter 11 provides a more detailed discussion of the WTO and the evolving conflicts between trade and the environment.

### 10.20.6 The North American Free Trade Agreement

The North American Free Trade Agreement (NAFTA) was implemented on January 1, 1994. It was designed to remove tariff barriers between the United States, Canada, and Mexico over the next fifteen years. NAFTA includes two important side agreements on environmental and labor issues that extend into cooperative efforts to reconcile policies and procedures for dispute resolution between the member states.

To complement the environmental provisions in NAFTA, the North American Agreement on Environmental Cooperation (NAAEC) was created to foster the protection and improvement of the environment, improve conservation efforts, promote sustainable development, and increase cooperation on and enhanced enforcement of environmental laws and policies. The NAAEC established an international organization, the Commission for Environmental Cooperation (CEC)[100] to

- address regional environmental concerns;
- help prevent potential trade and environmental conflicts; and
- promote the effective enforcement of environmental law.[101]

One of the more progressive features of the NAAEC is that it allows a citizen of a NAFTA country to file a complaint, or a "citizen submission," with the CEC alleging that a NAFTA country is failing to enforce its domestic environmental laws effectively. To date, the NAAEC has successfully achieved one of its primary goals, that is, to promote a transparent environmental regime that emphasizes public participation in keeping with Principle 10 of the Rio Declaration on Environment and Development. Although the CEC does not have the ability to dictate domestic behavior directly through the citizen-submission process, the citizen-submission process does affect domestic environmental behavior because of its transparent effect on domestic public and private decision making and conduct and is a first step in citizen and NGO participation in international accountability in North America (Goldschmidt 2002). Box 10.13 presents a case study of a citizen submission.

The North American Agreement on Labor Cooperation (NAALC) aims at improving working conditions and living standards and fostering compliance with and effective enforcement of labor laws. The Commission for Labor Cooperation is an international organization created under the NAALC.[102] The commission is formed of a Council of Ministers, a cabinet-level body in charge of policy setting and decision making that consists of the three labor ministers or their representatives; and a trinational Secretariat that provides support to the Council and to the independent Evaluation Committees of Experts and Arbitral Panels the Council may establish under the provisions of the agreement. The commission works

## BOX 10.13: CITIZEN SUBMISSION PROCESS OF THE NAAEC

Goldschmidt (2002) provides a useful discussion of the citizen submission process in the North American Agreement on Environmental Cooperation (NAAEC).

> "Environmental law," defined in Article 45(2) of the NAAEC, includes "any statute or regulation of a Party . . . the primary purpose of which is the protection of the environment, or the prevention of danger to human life or health." Thus far, it appears that statutes that protect habitats fall within the ambit of this definition. . . . (ibid., pp. 362–363)
>
> Successful [citizen] submissions most commonly include allegations that a Party is failing to enforce its environmental laws effectively via inadequate inspection practices, failure to prosecute violations, or both. The Secretariat has rejected, however, submissions that do not involve allegations of "effective enforcement" and that merely attack the appropriateness of legislative acts. In the *Spotted Owl* submission, the Secretariat concluded that a rider modifying the implementation of the U.S. Endangered Species Act was not a failure to "effectively enforce" environmental law. The Secretariat stated that an allegation that attacked legislation on the grounds that it did not sufficiently protect the environment did not meet the threshold of "effective enforcement" because it focused on the legislation itself and not on the enforcement of that legislation. . . . Similarly, in the *Great Lakes* submission, the submitters alleged that the U.S. EPA's standards governing emissions from waste and medical incinerators in the Great Lakes region were too low and in conflict with U.S.-Canadian agreements. (ibid., p. 365)

However, statutes that protect the environment and human health from hazardous substances do qualify for citizen submissions. A case involving Mexico is illustrative. "In the *Metales y Derivados* submission, two NGOs alleged that the Mexican government failed to effectively enforce its domestic environmental laws in the case of an abandoned lead smelter that posed health risks to neighboring communities" (Goldschmidt 2002, p. 363). The Secretariat concluded in favor of the NGOs because the Mexican companies were committing environmental offenses under the Mexican Federal Criminal Code, which establishes penalties for neglecting the environment and human health.

> First, the submission alleged grave risk to the community due to toxic substances from an abandoned lead smelter. Second, the grave risk to human life and the environment from the smelter justified further study and advanced the protective goals of the NAAEC. Third, the submitters made concerted efforts to "obtain information on the situation at the site and to have the government take action;" and because the government refused to provide information or take action, it would not be reasonable to expect the submitters to do more. Finally, the Secretariat was satisfied that the submission was not based exclusively on media reports although media reports were included in the submission. In totality, these factors satisfied the requirements of Article 14(2). (ibid., p. 369)

A second informative case involves Canada:

> On April 2, 1997, the Sierra Legal Defence Fund and the Sierra Club Legal Defence (now Earthjustice) jointly filed a submission concerning Canada with the Secretariat under Article 14 of the NAAEC. . . . The NGOs alleged that the Canadian government failed to enforce Section 35(1) of the Federal Fisheries Act against the BC Hydro and Power Authority (BC Hydro), which resulted in the destruction of fish and fish habitat in British Columbia by hydroelectric dams. The submitters claimed that BC Hydro's hydroelectric dams harmed fish habitat in several different ways, including reduced flows, rapid flow fluctuation, inadequate flushing flows, altered water quality, flow diversion, and reservoir drawdown . . . in violation of Canadian law. . . . In its response, Canada stated that it was in full compliance with the NAAEC and that it effectively enforced Section 35(1) of the Act. Canada argued that under Article 5 of the NAAEC, the concept of "effective enforcement" is broad and that the submitters' definition of effective enforcement was too limited because it "equate[d] enforcement directly with legal and judicial sanctions." (Goldschmidt 2002, pp. 379–381)

In this case, the Secretariat did not make a decision without soliciting information from the interested parties and the public and seeking other scientific, technical information from other NGOs. The *BC Hydro* case is a prime example of promoting the role of transparency provided by the citizen submission process. Ultimately, the Canadian government accepted the findings of the factual record and has since been more responsive to citizen concerns.

> The more the NAFTA countries allow the participation of domestic groups and NGOs in the implementation and compliance process, the greater the probability of implementation and compliance, and thus, the effectiveness of the treaty may be realized. . . . In sum, the citizen submission provisions of the NAAEC constitute a formal and permanent instrument that enable NGOs to direct the "spotlight" on member countries that are not effectively enforcing their domestic environmental laws. This participation has influenced domestic environmental policy development, decisions, and enforcement. (Goldschmidt 2002, pp. 394–395)

in close cooperation with the national administrative offices (NAOs) created by each government within its own labor ministry to implement the NAALC.

The NAFTA side agreements on labor and on the environment have created debate over whether their principles and mechanisms are actually effective within the realm of free trade. The central focus of the debate over both agreements is whether the new measures have contributed to creation of new jobs and raising incomes in member countries while balancing this growth with the prevention of environmental degradation or compromise of health and safety. For further discussion of the side agreements and trade issues, see Chapter 11.

### 10.20.7 The Food and Agriculture Organization

The Food and Agriculture Organization (FAO), with 158 members and headquartered in Rome, is another UN specialized agency working on issues related to the environment, health, and safety. Its aims are to oppose poverty, malnutrition, and hunger, including addressing problems in agriculture, desertification, deforestation, and conservation of fisheries. In developing environmental law, the FAO's role in promoting fishery management is particularly important because it provides a substantial source of information on the activities of global and regional fisheries, although it has no mandate to change fishery law. The legal division of the FAO's secretariat also plays a significant role in collecting, analyzing, and commenting on national legislation related to the FAO's chief objectives of combating hunger and promoting sustainable land and water resources to meet this need (Birnie and Boyle 1992). The 1985 FAO Code of Conduct on the Distribution and Use of Pesticides established basic rules on pesticide management, testing, reducing health hazards, and adoption of regulatory and technical requirements, including registration and recording of import data and use, and 1989 amendments to the code established voluntary provisions on prior informed consent and information exchange (Sands 2003, p. 630). The FAO Code was ultimately superseded by the Rotterdam Convention on the Prior Informed Consent Principle for Certain Hazardous Chemicals and Pesticides in International Trade (see Section 10.6)

### 10.20.8 Nongovernmental Organizations

A number of international, national, and local organizations exist to provide scientific advice on environmental, health, and safety matters. These have generally been called nongovernmental organizations (NGOs). NGOs have an extremely important role in creating a voice for the public to force their governments, industry, and others to be accountable for policies and activities that are detrimental to the environment and to human health. NGOs also promote, encourage, and organize research and investigation of environmental, health, and safety issues and draw attention to significant shortcomings or harmful activities of governments, industries, or other organizations.

NGOs have various agendas and interests. Some NGOs are international professional bodies, often in the scientific field, such as the International Union for the Conservation of Nature (IUCN) or the International Council of Scientific Unions (ICSU). Some have educational or research purposes, such as the World Resources Institute (WRI) and the International Institute for Environment and Development (IIED). Others are campaigning organizations advocating for specific actions, such as Friends of the Earth (FOE), Greenpeace International, the Sierra Club, the National Audubon Society, and the World Wide Fund for Nature (WWF). Whatever their interest or goal, NGOs have become increasingly effective in achieving consultative status at international conferences, where their research or lobbying may influence a negotiation or legislative process. For example, in the United States, NGOs were responsible for adding the Supplemental Agreement on the Environment to NAFTA. In addition, NGOs in the United States and Europe have helped place linkages between trade and environmental policies on the agenda of the WTO (see Chapter 11). See Doh and Guay (2006) for a comparison of the role of NGOs in fostering corporate social responsibility in the United States and the EU in three areas: global warming, trade in GMOs, and pricing of antiviral pharmaceuticals in developing countries. See also Doh and Guay (2004) for NGO influence on labor and environmental codes of conduct.

### 10.20.9 The European Foundation for the Improvement of Living and Working Conditions

This nonregulatory EU research institution was set up by the European Council [Council Regulation (EEC) No. 1365/75 of May 1975] to contribute to the planning and design of better living and working conditions in Europe. Its workshops and research reports have also contributed much to the nexus between work and living policies. For example, in 2006, Eurofound held a forum questioning whether the Lisbon Strategy formulated to achieve mutual advances in competitiveness, environment, and employment was actually achievable.[103]

## 10.21 GLOBAL GOVERNANCE

Some scholars, international lawyers, and policy makers argue that enforcement of international environmental, health, and safety agreements should use coercive measures, such as sanctions, to ensure compliance. Conversely, others advocate for an approach that relies less on coercive mechanisms and more on the effects of public participation and transparency in persuading nations to comply with their international treaty obligations (Goldschmidt 2002). However, ultimately, it is likely that effective global governance will have to be a compromise of both coercion and public participation to achieve effective implementation of international environmental, health, and safety accords and agreements.

In 1970, George Kennan recommended the creation of an "International Environmental Agency" that would have great prestige and authority and would overcome resistance from individual governments and powerful interests. In the Rio Summit in 1992, governments had the forum and the opportunity to discuss environmental governance, or the idea of strengthening international environmental governance by centralizing the current system under one umbrella institution, but instead bypassed the UNEP in the new climate-change convention and created the Commission on Sustainable Development.

Global environmental governance was again raised at the 2002 Johannesburg World Summit on Sustainable Development (WSSD). Environmentalists sought an international agency that could stand up to the GATT, contending that solving the conflict of trade and the environment would necessitate not only a greening of trade rules but also a stronger organization of environmental governance. Although the multitude of public-private partnerships announced at the summit represented a positive development in international and multisector collaboration, these commitments cannot currently substitute for coordinated intergovernmental action at a global level.

Current environmental policies are inadequate to address current threats, and it has been suggested that a new Global Environmental Organization (GEO) or World Environmental Organization (WEO) be cre-

ated to consolidate the currently disconnected systems regulating the global environment. However, before one accepts too much criticism of the current regime, it should be noted that current environmental governance is not completely ineffective. The UNEP has achieved a number of successes over the years and has focused attention on global environmental problems, for example, by negotiating MEAs on biosafety, persistent organic pollutants, prior informed consent on trade in chemicals and pesticides, and liability and compensation regarding hazardous wastes, and by the introduction of the Kyoto Protocol on climate change. However, environmental governance does not function as well as it needs to, and treaties are often too weak, with missed opportunities for policy integration (Charnovitz 2002). Although the UNEP has facilitated the development of several international environmental conventions, it has not taken a proactive, hands-on approach to environmental protection (Farr 2000).

Advocates of a new WEO are not proposing full centralization, or that all environmental governance needs to be in one organizational entity, but rather that all environmental governance mechanisms that exist in each country and city in the world need to be centralized. Full centralization is impossible because no other international regulatory regime is fully centralized either. The WTO is the core of the trade regime, but many trade agencies and bodies of law lie outside it, such as the United Nations Conference on Trade and Development (UNCTAD), the World Customs Organization, the International Trade Centre, the trade directorate of the OECD, the UN Convention on Contracts for the International Sale of Goods, and other agreements on trade in food, endangered species, hazardous waste, and other items. WHO is the center of the health regime, but many health agencies and bodies of law lie outside its ambit as well.

A practical plan would centralize some but not all environmental agencies. However, the costs of reorganization are substantial, whereas the gains are speculative. In addition, the environmental regime has probably benefited from the diversity of entities that conduct environmental work. Policy makers would have to be careful not to lose the capacity for innovation in considering the implementation of such a global environmental entity.

Compared with the current arrangements, the WEO would improve environmental governance by making it more coherent, for example, by better coordination among the UNEP, MEAs, the WTO, WHO, the ILO, and the UN. However, many obstacles will have to be overcome to put such a global entity in place, including prevailing over current practical, political, economic, and logistical barriers. One major issue is that industrialized countries that have strong economies can afford to emphasize environmental protection, whereas developing countries do not have that ability when they are solving development issues. A possible model for a WEO could be WHO, which has been successful in solving problems of world health because of its stature in the international community, its broad mandate, and its fee assessment on member states. It also has a structure of regional offices that has created an atmosphere of cooperation with its members that has enabled WHO to further global health programs (Farr 2000).

## 10.22 CONCLUSIONS

International environmental, health, and safety law has made significant strides in recent decades. However, some critics argue that these laws remain predominantly "soft" in character, unsystematic, insufficiently comprehensive in scope, and weak in enforcement and implementation. Nevertheless, these skeptics overlook the significance of the broad framework for further development of the law to protect the environment that has now been established, and they fail to consider the considerable achievements of the past few decades. There is also law that has been established in a piecemeal approach in response to environmental, health, and safety disasters, such as Chernobyl or unprecedented weather-related events thought to relate to climate change. Although international law may still be striving toward basic principles and codification, there are examples of realistic and workable laws in place in many countries that are combating the environmental, health, and safety issues we face in our everyday lives. Even if in practice environmental law has not been the subject of much judicial review or elaboration or of widely accepted principles, it has exercised an influence, both in structuring the resolution of environmental disputes and as a basis for negotiation of treaty regimes. The UN General Assembly has a specific mandate to promote further development of international environmental law and to examine the feasibility of the "general rights and obligations of states, as appropriate, in the field of environment, and taking into account relevant existing international legal instruments" (Birnie and Boyle 1992, pp. 544–545).

Underlying the consensus on the principles of international environmental law is continuing political conflict between developed and developing nations, for example, in the area of climate change, because of limitations in developing countries' extent of participation. However, despite these obstacles, international treaties have been moderately successful in changing the basis and perspective of international environmental, health, and safety law, accommodating a preventive or precautionary approach. The problems of environmental lawmaking and enforcement are predominantly political and institutional. As Hurrell and Kingsbury (1992, p. 6) argue, "Collective environmental management poses a severe, and therefore, politically sensitive challenge because it involves the creation of rules and institutions that embody notions of shared responsibilities and shared duties, that impinge very heavily on the domestic structures and organization of states, that invest individuals and groups within states with rights and duties, and that seek to embody some notion of a common good for the planet as a whole."

The international control of environmental, health, and safety law requires a variety of instruments and approaches. What these problems have in common is that the solutions lie in the appropriate national and international regulation of a variety of products and practices, industries, societies, and political and economic forces, as well as consumption patterns for NAA goods and services. Commerce and trade and health, safety, and the environment are interlinked, and solutions must address those linkages. Regulation of hazardous technologies is not sufficient. Environmental, worker health and safety, development, and trade policies must be integrated wherever possible. This need will be explored further in the discussion of trade regimes in Chapter 11.

## 10.23 NOTES

1. United Nations Environment Programme (UNEP) (2001), *International Environmental Governance: Multilateral Environmental Agreements (MEAs)*, UNEP/IGM/INF/3 UNEP/IGM/1/INF/1, April 18, 2001, www.unep.org/ieg/Meetings_docs/index.asp (accessed May 31, 2010).

2. See, for example, Association of Southeast Asian Nations (ASEAN) Agreement on the Conservation of Nature and Natural Resources, July 9, 1985, reprinted in *Journal of Environmental Policy and Law* **15** (1985).

3. Elliot Derringer, *Fundamentals of Climate Change*, Pew Center on Global Climate Change, January 11, 2002, www.pewclimate.org/press-center/speeches/fundamentals-climate-change (accessed May 31, 2010).

4. UNEP (1992), Rio Declaration on Environment and Development, www.unep.org/Documents/Default.asp?DocumentID=78&ArticleID=1163 (accessed May 31, 2010).

5. See the European Commission Proposal for a Directive on Environmental Sustainability, 92FUND/A/ES.6/6, March 15,

2002, www.iopcfund-docs.org/ds/pdf/92aes6–6_e.pdf (accessed May 31, 2010).

6. European Parliament, Decision No. 1600/2002/EC of the European Parliament and of the Council of July 22, 2002 laying down the Sixth Community Environmental Action Programme, *Official Journal L 242, 10/09/2002 P. 0001–0015,* http://eur-lex.europa.eu/LexUriServ/LexUriServ.do?uri= CELEX:32002D1600:EN:HTML (accessed May 31, 2010).

7. Agreement for the Implementation of the Provisions of the United Nations Convention on the Law of the Sea, December 1982, www.un.org/Depts/los/convention_agreements/convention _overview_fish_stocks.htm (accessed May 31, 2010).

8. The 1992 OSPAR Convention, www.ospar.org/content/ content.asp?menu=00340108070000_000000_000000 (accessed May 31, 2010).

9. Global Development Research Center (GDRC), "The Rio Declaration: Principle 15—The Precautionary Approach," www .gdrc.org/u-gov/precaution-7.html (accessed May 31, 2010).

10. See the Aarhus Convention, www.unece.org/env/pp/ (accessed May 31, 2010).

11. European Commission, The Aarhus Convention, http://ec .europa.eu/environment/aarhus/index.htm (accessed February 3, 2011).

12. The Economic Commission for Europe (ECE), "The Aarhus Convention: An Implementation Guide," U.N. Doc. ECE/ CEP/72 (2000), prepared by Stephen Stec and Susan Casey-Lefkowitz, www.unece.org/env/pp/acig.pdf (accessed May 31, 2010).

13. See Kravchenko (2007).

14. European Parliament, Aarhus Convention on Access to Information, Public

Participation in Decision-making and Access to Justice in Environmental Matters to Community Institutions and Bodies, http://eur-lex.europa.eu/LexUriServ/LexUriServ.do?uri= OJ:L:2006:264:0013:0013:EN:PDF (accessed May 31, 2010).

15. Each "case" is listed and linked at Aarhus Convention, Communications from the Public, www.unece.org/env/pp/pub com.htm (accessed May 31, 2010). For an analysis of the first eighteen cases, see Kravchenko (2007).

16. See Kravchenko (2007, pp. 23, 49).

17. See Jacob (1999, p. 105).

18. See Stirba, Kowalski, et al. (2001).

19. See the *European Chemicals Bureau [ECB] Newsletter* 2002, issue 4.

20. OCED, Emission Scenario Documents, www.oecd.org/ document/46/0,3746,en_2649_34373_2412462_1_1_1_1,00&& en-USS_01DBC.html (accessed February 2, 2011).

21. International Programme on Chemical Safety, About IPCS INCHEM, www.inchem.org/pages/about.html (accessed May 31, 2010). The IPCS INCHEM database offers access to thousands of searchable full-text documents on chemical risks and the sound management of chemicals, in the following:

- Concise International Chemical Assessment Documents (CICADs)
- Environmental Health Criteria (EHC) monographs
- Health and Safety Guides (HSGs)
- International Agency for Research on Cancer (IARC)—Summaries and Evaluations
- International Chemical Safety Cards (ICSCs)
- IPCS/CEC Evaluation of Antidotes Series
- Joint Expert Committee on Food Additives (JECFA)—Monographs and evaluations
- Joint Meeting on Pesticide Residues (JMPR)—Monographs and evaluations
- Pesticide Data Sheets (PDSs)
- Poisons Information Monographs (PIMs)
- Screening Information Data Set (SIDS) for High Production Volume Chemicals

22. See Europa, Protection of the Environment through Criminal Law, http://europa.eu/legislation_summaries/envi ronment/general_provisions/l33148_en.htm (accessed May 31, 2010).

23. UNEP, The Marrakech Process, http://esa.un.org/mar rakechprocess/ (accessed May 30, 2010).

24. UNDESA and UNEP (2008), Proposed Input to CSD on a 10 Year Framework of Programmes on Sustainable Consumption and Production (10TFP on SCP), Discussion Paper for Public Consultation, http://esa.un.org/marrakechprocess/ pdf/Draft10yfpniputtoCSDv2_281008.pdf (accessed May 31, 2010).

25. See A. Ochoa and C. Erdmenger (2003), *Study Contract to Survey the State of Play of Green Public Procurement in the European Union,* Freiburg, Germany, ICLEI, http://ec.europa .eu/environment/gpp/pdf/iceisstudy.pdf (accessed May 31, 2010).

26. Coalition for Environmentally Responsible Economies (CERES), CERES Principles, www.ceres.org/Page.aspx?pid= 416 (accessed May 31, 2010).

27. International Council of Chemical Associations, The Global Product Strategy, www.icca-at-dubai.org/index.php?sec tion=2&pageId=42 (accessed May 31, 2010). See Breukelaar and Banerjee (2007) for a more in-depth description of the European chemical industry's involvement in European and international chemical policy.

28. See the European Chemical Industry Council (CEFIC), www.cefic.be/ (accessed May 31, 2010).

29. See the EurActiv network's interview with Guido Sacconi MEP on REACH, September 13, 2005, www.euractiv.com/en/ climate-environment/interview-guido-sacconi-mep-reach/ article-144196 (accessed May 31, 2010).

30. EPA, EPA Research and Development: Risk Paradigm, How ORD Is Organized around the "Risk Assessment / Risk Management Paradigm," www.epa.gov/ord/htm/risk.htm (accessed May 31, 2010).

31. OECD Database on Chemical Risk Assessment Models, www.oecd.org/linklist/0,3435,en_2649_34365_2734144_1_1_1 _1,00.html (accessed May 31, 2010).

32. For example, see the TRACI (Tool for the Reduction and Assessment of Chemical and other environmental Impacts) initiative, www.epa.gov/nrmrl/std/sab/traci/ (accessed May 31, 2010).

33. See the OECD Biosafet-BioTrack website, www.oecd .org/department/0,3355,en_2649_34385_1_1_1_1_1,00.html (accessed May 31, 2010).

34. OECD, Important Announcement about CARAT, www .oecd.org/document/57/0,3343,en_2649_34369_34512249_1_1_1 _1,00.html (accessed May 31, 2010).

35. For the status of adoption into U.S. law, see www.unece .org/trans/danger/publi/ghs/implementation_e.html#United %20States%200f%20America (accessed May 31, 2010).

36. UNCEC, Globally Harmonized System of Classification and Labelling of Chemicals (GHS), www.unece.org/ trans/danger/publi/ghs/ghs_welcome_e.html (accessed May 31, 2010).

37. See the U.S. Department of Labor, A Guide to *The Globally Harmonized System of Classification and Labeling of Chemicals* (GHS), www.osha.gov/dsg/hazcom/ghs.html (accessed May 31, 2010).

38. European Commission, GHS Legislation, CLP-Regulation: News from Co-design, http://ec.europa.eu/enterprise/reach/ghs/ legislation/index_en.htm (accessed 3 Feburary 2011).

39. See the Convention on Access to Information, Public Participation in Decision-Making and Access to Justice in Environmental Matters, www.unece.org/env/pp/documents/cep43e.pdf (accessed May 31, 2010).

40. The Rotterdam Convention, What is RC? www.pic.int/ home.php?type=t&id=5&sid=16 (accessed 3 February 2011).

41. See UNEP, Anticipating the Environmental Effects of Technology, www.unep.or.jp/ietc/publications/integrative/enta/aeet/preface.asp (accessed May 31, 2010).

42. The Basel Convention, The Basel Convention Ban Amendment, www.basel.int/pub/baselban.html (accessed February 3, 2011).

43. National Environmental Research Institute, Aarhus University, Emission Targets: Basic Information on the Gothenburg Protocol to Abate Acidification, Eutrophication and Ground-Level Ozone, www2.dmu.dk/AtmosphericEnvironment/Expost/database/docs/Gothenborg_brief.pdf (accessed February 3, 2011).

44. See Gullino, Camponogara, et al. (2003) for a discussion of the production and use phaseout schedules for methyl bromide under the EU Regulations 3093/1994 and 2037/2000.

45. See Steven V. Cook (2009), "EPA Poised to Consider Range of Mobile, Stationary Sources Emission Controls," *Environmental Reporter* 40: 2811–2813.

46. EPA, Superfund, New Report Projects Number, Cost and Nature of Contaminated Site Cleanups in the U.S. over Next 30 Years, http://ec.europa.eu/environment/legal/liability/white_paper.htm (accessed February 4, 2011). See also www.epa.gov/superfund/accomp/news/30years.htm (accessed May 31, 2010).

47. European Commission, Environmental Liability, White Paper on Environmental Liability, COM(2000) 66 final, February 9, 2000, http://ec.europa.eu/environment/legal/liability/pdf/el_full.pdf (accessed May 31, 2010).

48. Europa, Environmental Liability, Directive 2004/35/EC of the European Parliament and of the Council of 21 April 2004 on Environmental Liability with Regard to the Prevention and Remedying of Environmental Damage, http://europa.eu/legislation_summaries/enterprise/interaction_with_other_policies/l28120_en.htm (accessed May 31, 2010).

49. Europa, Environmental Liability, 79.

50. CITES, What Is CITES? www.cites.org/eng/disc/what.shtml (accessed May 31, 2010).

51. Europa, International Trade in Wildlife: European Commission Welcomes Results of CITES Conference, Adopts Recommendation on Enforcement, http://europa.eu/rapid/pressReleasesAction.do?reference=IP/07/851&format=HTML&aged=0&language=EN&guiLanguage=en (accessed May 31, 2010).

52. Office of the U.S. Trade Representative, 2010 Report on Sanitary and Phytosanitary Measures, www.ustr.gov/sites/default/files/SPS%20Report%20Final%282%29.pdf (accessed May 31, 2010).

53. See the Biosafety Clearing-House (BCH), http://bch.biodiv.org/ (accessed May 31, 2010).

54. Anup Shah (2000), Biosafety Protocol, *Global Issues* July 1, 2001, www.globalissues.org/article/175/biosafety-protocol-2000 (accessed February 7, 2011).

55. See the Electronics Takeback Coalition, www.computertakeback.com/index.htm (accessed May 31, 2010).

56. See the European Commission's website on the Lisbon Strategy, http://ec.europa.eu/growthandjobs/index_en.htm (accessed May 31, 2010).

57. See www.eea.europa.eu (accessed February 4, 2011).

58. Europa, The Sixth Environmental Action Programme of the European Community, 2002–2012, http://ec.europa.eu/environment/newprg/intro.htm (accessed May 31, 2010).

59. See Decision No. 1600/2002/EC of the European Parliament and of the Council of July 22, 2002, laying down the Sixth Community Environment Action Programme, http://eur-lex.europa.eu/LexUriServ/LexUriServ.do?uri=CELEX:32002D1600:EN:NOT (accessed February 13, 2011).

60. See the European Court of Justice (ECJ), http://curia.europa.eu/jcms/jcms/j_6/ (accessed May 31, 2010).

61. For a description of EU Forum of Judges for the Environment's activities, see www.eufje.org/ (accessed May 31, 2010).

62. See Jessica Knoblauch (2009), "Making Sure Medications Are Good for You—and for the Environment," *Scientific American News*, February 4.

63. European Commission, Sustainable Industrial Policy, Waste Management, http://ec.europa.eu/enterprise/environment/policy_aspects/waste_management/index.htm (accessed May 31, 2010).

64. Source: European Commission, Sustainable Industrial Policy, Waste Management, http://ec.europa.eu/enterprise/environment/policy_aspects/waste_management/index.htm (accessed May 31, 2010).

65. For a comparison of the differences in the implementation of the IPPC Directive in the United Kingdom and the Netherlands, see Gouldson and Murphy (1998b).

66. See Geiser (2001).

67. TNO, 2005, Making Life-Cycle Information and Interpretative Tools Available, http://ec.europa.eu/environment/ipp/pdf/study_final_clean_report.pdf (accessed May 31, 2010).

68. Europa, Action Plan in Favour of Environmental Technologies, http://europa.eu/legislation_summaries/enterprise/interaction_with_other_policies/l28143_en.htm (accessed May 31, 2010). For a detailed commentary on ETAP, see Callejo and Delgado (2008).

69. See Howells (2006).

70. Europa, Integrated Product Policy, http://europa.eu/legislation_summaries/consumers/consumer_safety/l28011_en.htm (accessed May 31, 2010).

71. U.S. EPA, Lifecycle Assessment Framework, www.epa.gov/nrmrl/std/sab/lca/lca_brief.htm (accessed May 31, 2010).

72. CERNA, Companies' Participation in EMAS: The Influence of the Public Regulator, 2000, www.cerna.ensmp.fr/Documents/MG-WP2000–2.pdf (accessed May 31, 2010).

73. See the European Commission's 2008 proposal for a regulation on the voluntary participation by organizations in a community eco-management and audit scheme (EMAS), http://ec.europa.eu/environment/emas/pdf/com_2008_402_draft.pdf (accessed February 13, 2011).

74. Europa, Food Safety, http://europa.eu/legislation_summaries/food_safety/index_en.htm (accessed May 31, 2010).

75. Europa, General Principles of Food Law—European Food Safety Authority—Procedures for Food Safety, http://europa.eu/legislation_summaries/consumers/consumer_information/f80501_en.htm (accessed May 31, 2010).

76. Europa, White Paper of Food Safety, http://europa.eu/legislation_summaries/other/l32041_en.htm (accessed May 31, 2010).

77. ECNIS, www.ecnis.org (accessed May 31, 2010).

78. European Commission, 2007 Environment Policy Review: Communication from the Commission to the Council and the European Parliament COM(2008)409, http://ec.europa.eu/environment/pdf/illust_epr.pdf (accessed May 31, 2010).

79. Europa, LIFE+: A Financial Instrument for the Environment, http://europa.eu/legislation_summaries/agriculture/environment/l28021_en.htm (accessed May 31, 2010).

80. See OSHA, Types of Occupational Exposure Limits, http://osha.europa.eu/en/topics/ds/legislation (accessed May 31, 2010).

81. See Europa, Sustainable Use of Pesticides, http://ec.europa.eu/environment/ppps/home.htm (May 31, 2010).

82. See S. Coelho (2009), "European Pesticide Rules Promote Resistance, Researchers Warn," *Science* 323: 450.

83. See the European Chemical Regulation Directorate, Regulation of Plant Protection Products in Europe, www.pesticides.gov.uk/approvals.asp?id=2310 (accessed February 5, 2011).

84. WHO, Global Strategy on Occupational Health for All: The Way to Health at Work, 1995, www.who.int/occupational_health/globstrategy/en/index1.html (accessed February 5, 2011).

85. Organization for Economic Cooperation and Development (OECD), www.oecd.org/home/ (accessed May 31, 2010).

86. See International Labour Organization (ILO), www.ilo.org/global/About_the_ILO/lang—en/index.htm (accessed May 31, 2010).

87. See ILOLEX, the Database of International Labour Standards, www.ilo.org/ilolex/english/convdisp1.htm (accessed May 31, 2010).

88. For a full account of the United Nations, see D. W. Bowett (1982), *The Law of International Institutions, (Fourth Edition)*, London, Stevens and Sons.

89. United Nations, Charter of the United Nations, www.un.org/aboutun/charter/ (accessed May 31, 2010).

90. United Nations Environment Programme, www.unep.org/ (accessed May 31, 2010).

91. United Nations Environmental Management Group, www.unemg.org/ (accessed May 31, 2010).

92. United Nations Industrial Development Organization, www.unido.org/ (accessed May 31, 2010).

93. United Nations Industrial Development Organization, UNIDO's Thematic Priorities, www.unido.org/doc/51918 (accessed May 31, 2010).

94. United Nations Industrial Development Organization, UNIDO and the UN Reform, www.unido.org/index.php?id=6400 (accessed May 31, 2010).

95. United Nations Development Programme (UNDP), www.undp.org/about/ (accessed May 31, 2010).

96. UNDP, A World of Development Experience, www.undp.org/about/ (accessed February 13, 2011).

97. UNDP, *Human Development Report*, http://hdr.undp.org/en/humandev/reports/ (accessed May 31, 2010).

98. World Health Organization, www.who.int/en/ (accessed May 31, 2010).

99. World Health Organization, Early Years: Emerging Environment Debate in GATT/WTO, www.wto.org/english/tratop_e/envir_e/hist1_e.htm (accessed May 31, 2010).

100. See Commission for Environmental Cooperation, www.cec.org/Page.asp?PageID=1115&BL_WebsiteID=1 (accessed May 31, 2010). Also see Esty (2006) for a critical evaluation of its successes. Esty (2006) argues that the CEC is more autonomous and network based than the UNEP, and that this provides it with influence over the environmental policies of NAFTA's members.

101. Commission for Environmental Cooperation, Three Countries Working Together to Protect Our Shared Environment, www.cec.org/Page.asp?PageID=1226&SiteNodeID=310&BL_ExpandID=154 (accessed May 31, 2010).

102. See Commission for Labor Cooperation, www.naalc.org/ (accessed May 31, 2010).

103. See the Eurofound forum entitled "Competitive Europe—Social Europe: Partners or Rivals?" held in Dublin, November 1–3, 2006, www.eurofound.europa.eu/events/2006/forum2006/participants.htm (accessed February 13, 2011).

## 10.24 ADDITIONAL READINGS

Dalhammar, C. (2007). "Product and Life Cycle Issues in European Environmental Law: A Review of Recent Developments." *Yearbook of European Environmental Law* **7**: 76–124.

de Sadeleer, N. (2002). *Environmental Principles: From Political Slogans to Legal Rules*. Oxford, Oxford University Press.

Gouldson, Andrew, and Joseph Murphy (1998). *Regulatory Realities: The Implementation and Impact of Industrial Environmental Regulation*. London, Earthscan.

Jordan, Andrew (Ed.) (2001). *Environmental Policy in the European Union: Actors, Institutions and Processes*. London, Earthscan.

Sands, P. (2003). *Principles of International Environmental Law*. Cambridge, Cambridge University Press.

## 10.25 REFERENCES

Altmann, J. (1994). "International Environmental Standards: Considerations on Principles and Procedures." *Intereconomics* (July/August): 176–183.

Applegate, J. (2000). "The Precautionary Preference: An American Perspective on the Precautionary Principle." *Human and Ecological Risk Assessment* **6**(3): 413–443.

Arnaud, Celia Henry (2010). Transforming Toxicology: Consortium Works to Accelerate Development of 21st-Century Toxicology." *Chemical & Engineering News* December 20, 2010, pp. 37–39.

Ashford, N. A. (1997). International Law and Control of Occupational and Environmental Health Hazards. *Issues in International and Occupational Medicine*. L. E. Fleming, J. A. Herzstein, and W. B. Bunn III. Beverly, MA, OEM Press: 47–62.

Ashford, N. A. (2007). The Legacy of the Precautionary Principle in U.S. Law: The Rise of Cost-Benefit Analysis and Risk Assessment as Undermining Factors in Health, Safety, and Environmental Protection. *Implementing the Precautionary Principle: Approaches from the Nordic Countries, the EU, and the United States*. N. de Sadeleer. London, Earthscan.

Ashford, N. A. (2009). "Reflections on Environmental Liability Schemes in the United States and European Union: Limitations and Prospects for Improvement." Presented at the Conference on Environmental Liability, Piraeus Bar Association, Piraeus, Greece, June 26–27, 2009. Available at http://hdl.handle.net/1721.1/55293 (accessed February 4, 2011).

Ashford, N. A., and C. Ayers (1985). "Policy Issues for Consideration in Transferring Technology to Developing Countries." *Ecology Law Quarterly* **12**(4): 871–905.

Ashford, N. A., C. Ayers, et al. (1985). "Using Regulation to Change the Market for Innovation." *Harvard Environmental Law Review* **9**(2): 419–466.

Ashford, N. A., and C. C. Caldart (1996). *Technology, Law, and the Working Environment*. Washington, DC, Island Press.

Ashford, N. A., and C. C. Caldart (2008). *Environmental Law, Policy, and Economics: Reclaiming the Environmental Agenda*. Cambridge, MA, MIT Press.

Ashford, N. A., and G. R. Heaton (1983). "Regulation and Technological Innovation in the Chemical Industry." *Law and Contemporary Problems* **46**(3): 109–157.

Ashford, N. A., G. R. Heaton, et al. (1979). Environmental, Health and Safety Regulations and Technological Innovation. *Technological Innovation for a Dynamic Economy*. C. T. Hill and J. M. Utterback. New York, Pergamon Press: 161–221.

Ashford, N. A., and K. M. Rest (2001). Public Participation in Contaminated Communities. Cambridge. Available at Center for Technology, Policy and Industrial

Development, Cambridge, MA, MIT. Available at http://web.mit.edu/ctpid/www/tl/ (accessed February 6, 2011).

Baccaro, Lucio and Valentina Mele (2010). "Pathology of Path Dependency? The ILO and the Challenge of 'New Governance'." Paper presented at MIT, Institute for Work and Employment Research Seminar Series, October 5, 2010. Available at http://mitsloan.mit.edu/iwer/seminar.php (accessed February 5, 2011).

Bailar, J., and A. J. Bailer (1999). Risk Assessment—The Mother of All Uncertainties: Disciplinary Perspectives on Uncertainty in Risk Assessment. *Uncertainty in the Risk Assessment of Environmental and Occupational Hazards*. J. C. Bailar and A. J. Bailer, (Eds.), Annals of the New York Academy of Sciences: 273–285.

Barrett, K., and J. Tickner (2001). Trans-Atlantic Consumer Dialogue (TACD): Briefing Paper on the Precautionary Principle. Lowell, MA, Lowell Center for Sustainable Production, www.sustainableproduction.org/downloads/TACD%20Briefing.pdf (accessed February 6, 2011).

Barrett, S. (1999). "International Environmental Agreements: Compliance and Enforcement; International Cooperation and the International Commons." *Duke Environmental Law and PolicyI* **10**: 131–145.

Battaglia, A. (2006). "Food Safety: Between European and Global Administration." *Global Jurist Advances: Global Administrative Law and Global Governance* **6**(3, Article 8): 1–14.

Bergkamp, L. (2000). *The Commission's White Paper on Environmental Liability: A Weak Case for an EC Strict Liability Regime*. Rotterdam, Erasmus University Faculty of Law.

Beronius, Anna, Christina Rudén, Annika Hanberg, and Helen Håkansson (2009). "Health Risk Assessment Procedures for Endocrine Disrupting Compounds Within Different Regulatory Frameworks in the European Union." *Regulatory Toxicology and Pharmacology* **55**: 111–122.

Betlem, G. (2005). "Scope and Defenses of the 2004 Environmental Liability Directive: Who Is Liable for What?" *ERA-Forum* **6**(3): 376–388.

Beunen, R , W, G. M. van der Knaap et al (2009). "Implementation and Integration of EU Environmental Directives: Experiences from The Netherlands." *Environmental Policy and Governance* (19): 57–69

Birnie, P. (1987). Libya-Malta Continental Shelf Case and Gulf of Maine Case. *Ocean Boundaries*. London: 15–37, 126–127.

Birnie, P. (1992). International Environmental Law: Its Adequacy for Present and Future Needs. *The International Politics of the Environment*. A. Hurrell and B. Kingsbury (Eds.). Oxford, Clarendon Press: 51–85.

Birnie, P., and A. Boyle (1992). *International Law and the Environment*. Oxford, Oxford University Press.

Bredahl, M. E., N. Ballenger, et al. (1996). *Agriculture, Trade, and the Environment*. Boulder, CO, Westview Press.

Breukelaar, J., and S. Banerjee (2007). *International Chemcals Policy Affecting the Situation in Europe*. Brussels, European Chemical Industry Council.

Breyer, S., and V. Heyvaert (2000). Institutions for Managing Risk. *Environmental Law, the Economy, and Sustainable Development*. R. Revesz, P. Sands, and R. Stewart. Cambridge, Cambridge University Press: 283–352.

Brickman, R., S. Jasanoff, et al. (1985). *Controlling Chemicals: The Politics of Regulation in Europe and the United States*. Ithaca, NY, Cornell University Press.

Busch, P.-O., and H. Jörgens (2005). "International Patterns of Environmental Policy Change and Convergence." *European Environment* **15**(2): 80–101.

Callejo, I., and L. Delgado (2008). "European Environmental Technologies Action Plan (ETAP)." *Journal of Cleaner Production* **16**(1): S181–S183.

Castle, G. H., and B. Kelly (2008). "Global Harmonization Is Not All That Global: Divergent Approaches in Drug Safety." *Food and Drug Law Journal* **63**: 601–622.

Charnovitz, S. (2002). "A World Environment Organization." *Columbia Journal of Environmental Law* **27**(2): 323–362.

Chemical & Engineering News (C&EN) (2010). "First Reach Deadline Passes Smoothly But Two More Loom" *Chemical & Engineering News* December 6, 2010, p. 11.

Clean Production Action (2004). *Extended Producer Responsibility: A Waste Management Strategy That Cuts Waste, Creates a Cleaner Environment, and Saves Taxpayers Money*. Montreal, Clean Production Action.

Coase, R. H. (1960). "The Problem of Social Cost." *Journal of Law and Economics* **3**: 1–44.

Cohen, A. (2010). "The Implementation of REACH:Initial Perspectives from Government, Industry, and Civil Society." *International Journal of Occupational and Environmental Health* **17**(1): 57–62. Available at www.ijoeh.com/index.php/ijoeh/article/view/1582/1119 (accessed January 24, 2011).

Congleton, R. D. (1995). "Toward a Transactions Cost Theory of Environmental Treaties." *Economia della Scelte Pubbliche*: 119–139.

Congleton, R. D. (2001). Governing the Global Environmental Commons: The Political Economy of International Environmental Treaties and Institutions. *Globalization and the Environment*. G. G. Schulze and H. W. Ursprung. New York, Oxford University Press.

Congleton, R. D. (2002). *Environmental Politics and Economic Development*. Fairfax, VA: 57–62.

Cronin, M. T. D., J. S. Jaworkska, et al. (2003). "Use of QSARs in International Decision-Making Frameworks to Predict Health Effects of Chemical Substances." *Environmental Health Perspectives* **111**(10): 1391–1401.

Dalhammar, C. (2007). "Product and Life Cycle Issues in European Environmental Law: A Review of Recent Developments." *Yearbook of European Environmental Law* **7**: 76–124.

Damro, C., and P. Luaces-Mendez (2003). *The Kyoto Protocol's Emissions Trading System: An EU-US Environmental Flip-Flop*. Pittsburgh, European Union Center for West European Studies, University of Pittsburgh.

Demetropoulou, Leeda, Nikolaos Nikolaidis, Vasilis Papadoulakis, Kostas Tsakiris, Theodore Koussouris, Nikolaos Kalogerakis, Kostas Koukaras, Anastasia Chatzinikolaou, and Kostas Theodoropoulos (2010) "Water Framework Directive Implementation in Greece: Introducing Particiaption in Water Governance: The

Case of the Evrotas River Basin Management Plan." *Environmental Policy and Governance* **20**: 336–349.

Dernbach, J. (2004). "Citizen Suits and Sustainability." *Widener University School of Law Review* **10**: 503–526.

de Sadeleer, N. (2000). *Two Approaches of Precaution: A Comparative Review of EU and US Theory and Practice of the Precautionary Principle.* Brussels, Centre d'étude du droit de l'environment.

de Sadeleer, N. (2002). *Environmental Principles: From Political Slogans to Legal Rules.* Oxford, Oxford University Press.

Di Leva, C. E. (1991). "Trends in International Law: A Field with Increasing Influence." *Environmental Law Reporter* **21**: 10076–10084.

Dobbs, M. (2010). "Legalising General Prohibitions on Cultivation of Genetically Modified Organisms" *German Law Journal* **11**(12): 1347–1372. Available at www.germanlawjournal.com/pdfs/Vol11-No12/PDF_Vol_11_No_12_1347-1372_Articles_Dobbs%20FINAL.pdf (accessed February 6, 2011).

Doh, J. P., and T. R. Guay (2004). "Globalization and Corporate Social Responsibility: How Non-governmental Organizations Influence Labor and Environmental Codes of Conduct." *Management International Review* **44**(2): 7–29.

Doh, J. P., and T. R. Guay (2006). "Corporate Social Responsibility, Public Policy, and NGO Activism in Europe and the United States: An Institutional-Stakeholder Perspective." *Journal of Management Studies* **43**(1): 47–73.

Drumbl, M. A. (1999). "Does Sharing Know Its Limits? Thoughts on Implementing International Environmental Agreements: A Review of National Environmental Policies, a Comparative Study of Capacity-Building." *Virginia Environmental Law Journal* **18**: 281–304.

Eames, M. (2000). Implementation of the EMAS Regulation in the United Kingdom, IMPOL Case Study Report. Brighton, SPRU.

Ehrenberg, D. S. (2003). From Intention to Action: An ILO-GATT/WTO Enforcement Regime for International Labor Rights. *Human Rights, Labor Rights, and International Trade.* L. A. Compa and S. F. Diamond. Philadelphia, University of Pennsylvania Press: 163–180.

Environmental Protection Agency (EPA) (1994). *Technology Innovation Strategy.* EPA 543-K-93 002. Washington, DC, EPA.

EPA (2004a). *Cleaning Up the Nation's Waste Sites: Markets and Technology Trends (2004 Edition).* Washington, DC, EPA.

EPA (2004b). Superfund, New Report Projects Number, Cost and Nature of Contaminated Site Cleanups in the U.S. over Next 30 Years. Washington, DC, EPA. Available at http://www.epa.gov/superfund/accomp/news/30years.htm (accessed May 31, 2010).

Esty, D. C. (2006). "Good Governance at the Supranational Scale: Globalizing Administrative Law." *Yale Law Journal* **115**: 1490–1562.

Europa (2010). EMAS Organisations and Sites: 30/06/2010. Brussels, Europa, http://ec.europa.eu/environment/emas/pictures/Stats/2010-04_EMAS_Quarterly_Graph.jpg (accessed February 13, 2011).

European Commission (EC) (2000). *White Paper on Environmental Liability.* Brussels, EC.

EC (2006). *EU Policy on Biotechnology.* Belgium, EC. Available at http://ec.europa.eu/environment/biotechnology/pdf/eu_policy_biotechnology.pdf (accessed April 8, 2007). Note: No longer available; superceded by EC (2007).

EC (2007). *Questions and Answers on the Regulation of GMOs in the European Union.* Available at www.gmo-compass.org/pdf/documents/Questions_and_%20answers_03_07.pdf (accessed February 4, 2011).

European Parliament (1995). Directory of the Most Important Community Legislative Measures in Environmental Policy, Brussels. Directorate General for Research (DG-XII), Division for Social Affairs, the Environment, Public Health and Consumer Protection.

European Parliament (2010). "MEPs Reiterate Opposition to Food From Cloned Animals." Press Release October 19, 2010. Available at www.europarl.europa.eu/en/pressroom/content/20101019IPR88128/html/MEPs-reiterate-opposition-to-food-from-cloned-animals (accessed February 5, 2011).

European Safety Newsletter (1996). "New and Used Machines—The Employer's Tasks." *European Safety Newsletter* **46**: 5–7.

European Trade Union Confederation (ETUC), Instituto Sindical de Trabajo, Ambiente y Salud (ISTAS), et al. (2007). *Climate Change and Employment: Impact on Employment in the European Union–25 of Climate Change and $CO_2$ Emission Reduction Measures by 2030.* Brussels, ETUC.

European Trade Union Technical Bureau for Health and Safety (1991). *Promoting Health and Safety in the European Community: Essential Information for Trade Unions.* Brussels, European Trade Union Technical Bureau for Health and Safety.

Farr, K. T. (2000). "A New Global Environmental Organization." *Georgia Journal of International and Comparative Law* **28**(3): 493–525.

Fogelman, V. (2006). "Liability: Enforcing the Environmental Liability Directive." *Environmental Liability* **4**: 27–146.

Gaines, S. E. (2002). "Triangulating Sustainable Development: International Trade, Environmental Protection, and Development." *Environmental Law Reporter* **32**: 10318–10347.

Geiser, K. (2001). *Materials Matter: Toward a Sustainable Materials Policy.* Cambridge, MA, MIT Press.

Gitterman, D. P. (2004). A Race to the Bottom, a Race to the Top or the March to a Minimum Floor? Economic Integration and Labor Standards in Comparative Perspective. *Dynamics of Regulatory Change: How Globalization Affects National Regulatory Policies.* D. Vogel and J. Kaiser. Berkeley, University of California Press: 331–370.

Glachant, M., S. Schucht, et al. (2002). "Companies' Participation in EMAS: The Influence of the Public Regulator." *Business Strategy and the Environment* **11**: 254–266.

Global Development Research Center (GDRC). Presentation by Prof. Elizabeth Wilson at the ISOCARP-JAPA World Planning Congress, Ogaki, Japan, September 17–

20, 1997. Available at www.gdrc.org/u-gov/precaution
.html (accessed February 2, 2011).

Goldschmidt, M. (2002). "The Role of Transparency and
Public Participation in International Environmental
Agreements: The North American Agreement on Environmental Cooperation." *Boston College Environmental Affairs Law Review* **29**: 343–398.

Gooch, G. D. and D. Huitima (2008). Participation in Water Management: Theory and Practice. *The Adaptiveness of IWRM Analysing European IWRM Research.*
J. G. Timmerman, C. Pahl-Wostl, and J. Motgen (Eds.).
London, IWA Publishing: 27–44.

Gouldson, A., and J. Murphy (1998a). Mandatory Regulation and the European Union. *Regulatory Realities. The Implementation and Impact of Industrial
Environmental Regulation.* London, Earthscan.

Gouldson, A., and J. Murphy (1998b). *Regulatory Realities: The Implementation and Impact of Industrial Environmental Regulation.* London, Earthscan.

Grubb, M. (1991). *Energy Policies and the Greenhouse
Effect: Vol. 1, Policy Appraisal.* Dartmouth, Royal Institute of International Affairs.

Gullino, M. L., A. Camponogara, et al. (2003). "Replacing Methyl Bromide for Soil Disinfestation: The Italian
Experience and Implications for Other Countries."
*Plant Disease* **87**(9): 1012–1021. Available at http://aps-
journals.apsnet.org/doi/pdf/10.1094/PDIS.2003.87.9
.1012 (accessed February 13, 2011).

Haas, P. M., and J. Sundgren (1993). Evolving International Environmental Law: Changing Practices of National Sovereignty. *Global Accords: Environmental
Challenges and International Responses.* N. Choucri.
Cambridge, MA, MIT Press: 401–427.

Hall, M. E. (2007). "Environmental Law in the European
Union: New Approaches for Enforcement." *Tulane
Environmental Law Journal* **20**: 277–302.

Hardin, G. (1968). "The Tragedy of the Commons."
*Science* **162**: 1243–1248.

Harrington, R. (2009). "New EU Regulation on Authorizing Food from Cloned Animals Sparks Heated Debate." *Food Navigator.* Available at www.foodnavigator
.com/content/view/print/251321 (accessed February 6,
2011).

Hildebrand, P. (2002). "The European Community's Environmental Policy, 1957 to 1992: From Incidental Measures to an International Regime?" *Environmental
Policy in the European Union: Actors, Institutions, and
Processes.* A. Jordan. London, Earthscan.

Hillgenberg, H. (1999). "A Fresh Look at Soft Law." *European Journal of International Law* **10**(3): 499–551.

Hills, S. (2009). "EFSA Finds No Reason to Alter Aspartame ADI." *Food Navigator.* Available at www.food
navigator.com/content/view/print/244300 (accessed February 6, 2011).

Hilz, C. (1992). *The International Toxic Waste Trade.* New
York, Van Nostrand Reinhold.

Hornstein, D. (1992). "Reclaiming Environmental Law:
A Normative Critique of Comparative Risk Analysis."
*Columbia Law Review* **92**: 562–633.

Howells, G. G. (2006). "The Rise of European Consumer
Law: Whither National Consumer Law." *Sydney Law
Review* **28**: 63–88.

Hurrell, A., and B. Kingsbury (1992). *The International
Politics of the Environment.* Oxford, Clarendon Press.

Ivanova, M. (2005). Moving Forward by Looking Back:
Learning from UNEP's History. New Haven, CT, Yale
University, Yale Center for Environmental Law and
Policy. Available at www.environmentalgovernance
.org/history/publications/Ivanova_Moving_Forward
.pdf (accessed May 12, 2010).

Jacob, K. (1999). Innovationsorientierte Chemikalienpoli-
tik. *Politische, soziale und ökonomische Faktoren des
verminderten Gebrauchs gefährlicher Stoffe.* Munich,
Herbert Utz-Verlag.

Jacobson, H., and E. B. Weiss (1998). A Framework for
Analysis. *Engaging Countries: Strengthening Compliance with International Environmental Accords.* H. Jacobson and E. B. Weiss (Eds.). Cambridge, MIT Press:
1–18.

Jans, J. (2000). *European Environmental Law.* Groningen, Europa Law Publishing.

Jordan, A., Ed. (2002). *Environmental Policy in the European Union: Actors, Institutions, and Processes.*
London, Earthscan.

Karkkainen, B. C. (2001). "Information as Environmental
Regulation: TRI and Performance Benchmarking, Precursor to a New Paradigm?" *Georgetown Law Journal*
**89**: 257–370.

Kemp, R. (1997). *Environmental Policy and Technical
Change: A Comparison of the Technological Impact of
Policy Instruments.* Cheltenham, Edward Elgar.

Keohane, R. O., P. M. Haas, et al. (1995). The Effectiveness of International Environmental Institutions. *Institutions for the Earth: Sources of Effective
International Environmental Protection.* R. O. Keohane, P. M. Haas, and M. A. Levy. Cambridge, MA,
MIT Press: 3–24.

Kiel, T. (2006). Ten Years of European Environmental
Management and Audit Scheme (EMAS): Future Perspectives. *Yearbook of European Environmental Law,*
vol. 6. Oxford, Oxford University Press: 62–96.

Knoepfel, P. (1997). The Political System's Capacity for
Environmental Policy. *National Environmental Policies: A Comparative Study of Capacity-Building.* M.
Jänicke and H. Weidner. Berlin and New York,
Springer. Available at http://74.125.155.132/scholar?q=
cache:d30pJmYkgK4J:scholar.google.com/+
%22L+Koch%22+AND+2003+AND+umweltpolitik&
hl=en&as_sdt=0,22 (accessed February 7, 2011).

Koch, L., and N. A. Ashford (2006). "Rethinking the Role
of Information in Chemicals Policy: Implications for
TSCA and REACH." *Journal of Cleaner Production*
**14**(1): 31–46.

Krämer, L. (2005). "Directive 2004/35 on Environmental
Liability and Environmental Principles." *Tijdschrift
voor Milieuaansprakelijkheid (Environmental Liability
Review)* **4**: 131–134.

Kravchenko, S. (2007). "The Aarhus Convention and Innovations in Compliance with Multilateral Environmental Agreements." *Colorado Journal of International
Environmental Law and Policy* **18**: 1–50.

Lewis, A., N. Kazantzis, et al. (2007). "Integrating Process Safety with Molecular Modeling-Based Risk Assessment of Chemicals within the REACH Regulatory

Framework: Benefits and Future Challenges." *Journal of Hazardous Materials* **142**: 592–602.

Liptak, A. (2009). "[Supreme Court] Justices Limit Liability over Toxic Spill Cases." *New York Times*, May 5.

Lombi, Enzo Walter W. Wenzel, and Domy C. Adriano (1998). "Soil Contamination, Risk Reduction and Remediation." *Land Contamination & Reclamation* **6**(4): 183–197.

Luken, R., and P. Hesp (2006). Review of Selected Industrial Environmental Initiatives of the United Nations System, Regional Development Banks and Other International Organizations. Issue paper for the United Nations Environmental Management Group. Background Paper 4. New York, United Nations Department of Economic and Social Affairs.

Luken, R., and J. Navratil (2004). "A Programmatic Review of UNIDO/UNEP National Cleaner Production Centres." *Journal of Cleaner Production* **12**: 195–205.

Luken, R., J. Narvratil, et al. (2003). "Technology Transfer and the UNIDO/UNEP National Cleaner Production Centres Program." *International Journal of Environmental Technology and Management* **3**(2): 107–117.

Luken, R. A. (2009). "Greening an International Organization: UNIDO's Strategic Responses." *Review of International Organizations* **4**(2): 159–184.

Lulofs, K. (2000). Implementation of EMAS in the Netherlands. IMPOL Case Study Report. CERNA Research Paper 2000-B-5, Paris.

Majone, G. (2001). The Precautionary Principle and Regulatory Impact Analysis. Manuscript, described as an expanded version of a paper submitted at the International Seminar on Regulatory Impact Analysis organized by Progetto AIR, Rome, June 15.

McDonough, W., and M. Braungart (1998). "The NEXT Industrial Revolution." *Atlantic Monthly* **282**(4): 82–92.

Mock, G., W. Vanasselt, et al. (2003). "Rights and Reality: Monitoring the Public's Right to Participate." *International Journal of Occupational and Environmental Health* **9**(1): 4–13.

Murphy, C. N. (2006). *The United Nations Development Programme. A Better Way?* Cambridge, Cambridge University Press.

Nash, H. A. (2009). "The European Commission's Sustainable Consumption and Production and Sustainable Industrial Policy Action Plan." *Journal of Cleaner Production* **17**: 496–498.

National Research Council (NRC) (2003). *Risk Assessment in the Federal Government: Managing the Process.* Washington, DC, National Academy Press.

NRC (2008). *Science and Decisions: Advancing Risk Assessment.* Washington, DC, National Academies Press.

Obadia, I. (2003). "ILO Activities in the Area of Chemical Safety." *Toxicology* **190**: 105–115.

O'Malley, V. (1999). "The Integrated Pollution Prevention and Control (IPPC) Directive and Its Implications for the Environment and Industrial Activities in Europe." *Sensors and Actuators B* **59**: 78–82.

Organisation for Economic Co-operation and Development (OECD) (1993). *Application of Structure-Activity Relationships to the Estimation of Properties Important in Exposure Assessment.* Environmental Monograph no. 67. Paris, OECD.

OECD (1994). *Technology and Environment: Supply Side Policies to Augment Government Support for Promoting Cleaner Technology.* Paris, OECD.

OECD (1999). *Technology and Environment: Towards Policy Integration.* Paris, OECD.

OECD (2001). *The OECD Environment Programme.* Paris, OECD.

OECD (2004). *OECD Environment Programme, 2003–2004.* Paris, OECD.

OECD (2009). *OECD Environmental Outlook for Global Chemicals Indsutry: Findings and Lessons.* Paris, OECD. Available at www.chem.unep.ch/unepsaicm/mainstreaming/Documents/GCO_SteerComm1/MichiroOI_Assessing%20the%20trends%20in%20the%20Global%20Chemicals%20Industry.pdf (accessed February 3, 2011).

Plofchan, T. K. (1992). "Recognizing and Countervailing Environmental Subsidies." *Environmental Lawyer* **26**(Fall): 763–780.

Porter, M. E., and C. van der Linde (1995a). "Green and Competitive: Ending the Stalemate." *Harvard Business Review* **73**: 120–134.

Porter, M. E., and C. van der Linde (1995b). "Towards a New Conceptualization of the Environment-Competitiveness Relationship." *Journal of Economic Perspectives* **9**(4): 97–118.

Probst, K. N., and D. M. Konisky (2001). *Superfund's Future: What Will It Cost?* Washington, DC, Resources for the Future.

Raffensperger, C., and J. A. Tickner (1999). *Protecting Public Health and the Environment: Implementing the Precautionary Principle.* Washington, DC, Island Press.

Redick, T. P. (2007). "The Cartegna Protocol on Biosafety: Precautionary Priority in Biotech Crop Approvals and Containment of Commodities Shipments." *Colorado Journal of International Environmental Law and Policy* **18**: 51–116.

Reinhardt, F. (1999). "Market Failure and the Environmental Policies of Firms: Economic Rationales for 'Beyond Compliance' Behavior." *Journal of Industrial Ecology* **3**(1): 9–21.

Rose-Ackerman, S., and A. A. Halpaap (2002). The Aarhus Convention and the Politics of Process: The Political Economy of Procedural Environmental Rights. *An Introduction to the Law and Economics of Environmental Policy: Issues in Institutional Design.* R. O. Zerbe and T. Swanson. Oxford, Elsevier Science and Technology: 27–64.

Sandler, T. (1997). *Global Challenges: An Approach to Environmental, Political, and Economic Problems.* Cambridge, Cambridge University Press.

Sands, P. (2003). *Principles of International Environmental Law.* Cambridge, Cambridge University Press.

Schmidt, C. (2002). "Not-So-Superfund: Growing Needs vs. Declining Dollars." *Environmental Health Perspectives* **111**(3): 162–165.

Scialli, A. R. (2008). "The Challenge of Reproductive and Developmental Toxicology under REACH." *Regulatory Toxicology and Pharmacology* **51**: 244–250.

Shaikh, R., and A. Nichols (1984). "The International Management of Chemicals." *Ambio* **13**: 88–92.

Sheehan, B. (2004). Environmental Policy in Europe and the United States: An NGO Perspective, manuscript,

Product Policy Institute. Available at www.productpolicy.org/ (accessed February 7, 2011).

Sinden, A. (2007). The Preference for Pollution and Other Fallacies, or Why Free Trade Isn't "Progress." *Progress in International Law*. R. A. Miller and R. M. Bratspies. Leiden, Martinus Nijhoff Press.

Soros, G. (2002). *George Soros On Globalization*. New York, Public Affairs.

Stevenson, R. (2004). "An Assessment of the Design and Effectiveness of the ASEAN Environmental Improvement Program." *Journal of Cleaner Production* **12**: 227–236.

Stirba, U., U. Kowalski, et al. (2001). *National Profile: Chemikalienmanagement in Deutschland*. Bremerhaven, Bundesanstalt für Arbeitsschutz und Arbeitsmedizin.

Strasser, K. A. (1997). "Cleaner Technology, Pollution Prevention and Environmental Regulation." *Fordham Environmental Law Journal* **9**(1): 1–106.

Strong, M. (1990). "What Place Will the Environment Have in the Next Century—and at What Price?" *International Environmental Affairs* **2**(3): 211–212.

Susskind, L., and C. Ozawa (1992). Negotiating More Effective International Environmental Agreements. *The International Politics of the Environment*. A. Hurrell and B. Kingsbury. New York, Oxford University Press: 142–165.

Tietenberg, T. (2003). *Environmental and Natural Resource Economics*. New York, Addison-Wesley.

Tojo, N., T. Lindhqvist, et al. (2006). Extended Producer Responsibility as a Driver for Product Chain Improvements. *Governance of Integrated Product Policy: In Search of Sustainable Production and Consumption*. D. Scheer and F. Rubik. Sheffield, Greenleaf Publishing.

Tukker, A., and B. Jansen (2006). "Environmental Impact of Products: A Detailed Review of Studies." *Journal of Industrial Ecology* **10**(3): 159–170.

United Nations (UN) (1993). *Earth Summit: Agenda 21, the United Nations Programme of Action from Rio*. New York, UN.

United Nations Development Programme (UNDP) (1995). *Human Development Report*. New York, Oxford University Press.

United Nations Environment Management Group (EMG) (2006). *EMG Information and Contacts Directory—2006*. New York, United Nations EMG.

United Nations Environment Programme (UNEP) (1991). *Register of International Treaties and Other Agreements in the Field of the Environment*. Nairobi, UNEP.

UNEP (2000). *Global Environmental Outlook (GEO-2000)*. Nairobi, UNEP.

UNEP (2007). *Trade-Related Measures and Multi-lateral Environment Agreements*. Geneva, UNEP.

UNEP (2011). Global Environmental Outlook (GEO) Data Portal. Nairobi, UNEP. Available at http://geodata.grid.unep.ch/ (accessed February 13, 2011).

Valve, H., and J. Kauppila (2008). "Enacting Closure in the Environmental Control of Genetically Modified Organisms." *Journal of Environmental Law* **20**(3): 339–362.

Vaughan, A. (2010). "Cancun Climate Agreements at a Glance" *The Guardian,* December 10, 2010. Available at www.guardian.co.uk/environment/2010/dec/13/cancun-climate-agreement (accessed February 4, 2011).

Vogel, D. (2003). "The Hare and the Tortoise Revisited: The New Politics of Consumer and Environmental Regulation in Europe." *British Journal of Political Science* **33**(4): 557–580.

Weiss, E. B. (1993). Intergenerational Equity: Toward an International Legal Framework. *Global Accords: Environmental Challenges and International Responses*. N. Choucri. Cambridge, MA, MIT Press: 333–353.

Weiss, E. B. (1998). The Five International Treaties: A Living History. *Engaging Countries: Strengthening Compliance with International Environmental Accords*. E. B. Weiss and H. Jacobson. Cambridge, MA, MIT Press.

Weiss, E. B. (1999). "Understanding Compliance with International Environmental Agreements: The Baker's Dozen Myths." *University of Richmond Law Review* **32**: 1555–1589.

Wetstone, G. S., and A. Rosencranz (1984). "Transboundary Air Pollution: The Search for an International Response." *Harvard Environmental Law Review* **8**: 9–13.

White House Task Force (1998). *Recycling for the Future: Consider the Benefits*. Washington, DC, Office of Environmental Executive.

Wilkinson, D. (2002). Maastricht and the Environment: The Implications for the EC's Environment Policy of the Treaty on the European Union. *Environmental Policy in the European Union: Actors, Institutions, and Processes*. A. Jordan. London, Earthscan.

Winter, G., J. H. Jans, et al. (2008). "Weighing Up the EC Environmental Liability Directive." *Journal of Environmental Law* **20**(2): 163–191.

Winter, R. (2000). "Reconciling the GATT and WTO with Multilateral Environmental Agreements: Can We Have Our Cake and Eat It Too?" *Colorado Journal of International Environmental Law and Policy* **11**: 223–255.

World Trade Organization (WTO) (2004). *Trade and Environment at the WTO*. Geneva, WTO.

Zwetsloot, G. I. J. M., and N. A. Ashford (2003). "The Feasibility of Encouraging Inherently Safer Production in Industrial Firms." *Safety Science* **41**(2–3): 219–240.

## APPENDIX 10-A: MULTILATERAL ENVIRONMENTAL AGREEMENTS IN REVERSE CHRONOLOGICAL ORDER

Table 10-A.1 provides a chronological list of the global international agreements pertaining to the environment, including some pertaining to worker health and safety, that have been adopted (or not) by nations at

varying levels over the past few decades (a more detailed list of global environmental agreements can be found at www.unep.org/DEC/index.asp, accessed May 31, 2010). Appendix 10-B lists these agreements by environmental area. In addition to these global agreements, there are a number of regional environmental agreements.

### TABLE 10-A.1: MULTILATERAL ENVIRONMENTAL AGREEMENTS

| YEAR | TITLE OF AGREEMENT |
| --- | --- |
| 2001 | Stockholm Convention on Persistent Organic Pollutants, Stockholm[1] |
| 2001 | International Treaty on Plant Genetic Resources for Food and Agriculture, Rome[2] |
| 2001 | Convention on the Protection of the Underwater Cultural Heritage, Paris[3] |
| 2000 | Cartagena Protocol on Biosafety to the Convention on Biological Diversity, Montreal[4] |
| 1999 | Agreement for the Establishment of the Regional Commission for Fisheries, Rome[5] |
| 1999 | Protocol to the 1979 Convention on Long-Range Transboundary Air Pollution to Abate Acidification, Eutrophication, and Ground Level Ozone, Gothenburg[6] |
| 1999 | [Beijing] Amendment to the Montreal Protocol on Substances That Deplete the Ozone Layer, Beijing[7] |
| 1999 | Basel Protocol on Liability and Compensation for Damage Resulting from Transboundary Movements of Hazardous Wastes and Their Disposal, Basel[8] |
| 1998 | Protocol to the 1979 Convention on Long-Range Transboundary Air Pollution on Persistent Organic Pollutants (POPs), Åarhus[9] |
| 1998 | Protocol to the 1979 Convention on Long-Range Transboundary Air Pollution on Heavy Metals, Åarhus[10] |
| 1998 | Rotterdam Convention on the Prior Informed Consent Procedure for Certain Hazardous Chemicals and Pesticides in International Trade, Rotterdam[11] |
| 1997 | Convention on the Law of Non-navigational Uses of International Watercourses, New York[12] |
| 1997 | Joint Convention on the Safety of Spent Fuel Management and on the Safety of Radioactive Wastes Management, Vienna[13] |
| 1997 | Convention on Supplementary Compensation for Nuclear Damage, Vienna[14] |
| 1997 | Protocol to Amend the Vienna Convention on Civil Liability for Nuclear Damage, Vienna[15] |
| 1997 | Montreal Amendment to the Montreal Protocol on Substances That Deplete the Ozone Layer, Montreal[16] |
| 1997 | Protocol of 1997 to Amend the International Convention for the Prevention of Pollution from Ships, 1973, as Amended by the Protocol of 1978 Relating Thereto, London[17] |
| 1997 | Kyoto Protocol to the United Nations Framework Convention on Climate Change, Kyoto (not yet in force)[18] |
| 1996 | International Convention on Liability and Compensation for Damage in Connection with the Carriage of Hazardous and Noxious Substances by Sea, London[19] |
| 1996 | Comprehensive Nuclear-Test-Ban Treaty, New York[20] |
| 1995 | Convention Concerning Safety and Health in Mines, Geneva[21] |
| 1995 | Agreement for the Implementation of the Provisions of the United Nations Convention on the Law of the Sea of 10 December 1982 Relating to the Conservation and Management of Straddling Fish Stocks and Highly Migratory Fish Stocks, New York[22] |
| 1995 | Amendment to the Basel Convention on the Control of Transboundary Movements of Hazardous Wastes and Their Disposal, Geneva[23] |
| 1994 | International Tropical Timber Agreement, 1994, Geneva[24] |
| 1994 | Protocol to the 1979 Convention on Long-Range Transboundary Air Pollution on Further Reduction of Sulphur Emissions, Oslo[25] |
| 1994 | United Nations Convention to Combat Desertification in Those Countries Experiencing Serious Drought and/or Desertification, Particularly in Africa, Paris[26] |
| 1994 | Agreement Relating to the Implementation of Part XI of the United Nations Convention on the Law of the Sea of 10 December 1982, New York[27] |
| 1994 | Convention on Nuclear Safety, Vienna[28] |
| 1994 | Energy Charter Treaty, Lisbon[29] |
| 1993 | Convention on the Prohibition of the Development, Production, Stockpiling and Use of Chemical Weapons and on Their Destruction, Paris[30] |
| 1993 | Convention Concerning the Prevention of Major Industrial Accidents, Geneva[31] |
| 1993 | Agreement to Promote Compliance with International Conservation and Management Measures by Fishing Vessels on the High Seas, Rome[32] |
| 1992 | United Nations Framework Convention on Climate Change, New York[33] |
| 1992 | Rio Declaration on Environment and Development[34] |
| 1992 | Convention on Biological Diversity, Rio de Janeiro[35] |
| 1992 | Protocol of 1992 to Amend the International Convention on Civil Liability for Oil Pollution Damage, 1969, London[36] |
| 1992 | Protocol of 1992 to Amend the International Convention on the Establishment of an International Fund for Compensation for Oil Pollution Damage, 1971, London[37] |
| 1991 | Convention on Environmental Impact Assessment in a Transboundary Context, Espoo (Note: the related Kiev Protocol on Strategic Environmental Assessment, 2003)[38] |

| YEAR | TITLE OF AGREEMENT |
|------|--------------------|
| 1991 | Protocol to the 1979 Convention on Long-Range Transboundary Air Pollution Concerning the Control of Emissions of Volatile Organic Compounds or Their Transboundary Fluxes, Geneva[39] |
| 1990 | Convention Concerning Safety in the Use of Chemicals at Work, Geneva[40] |
| 1990 | International Convention on Oil Pollution Preparedness, Response and Cooperation, London[41] |
| 1989 | Basel Convention on the Control of Transboundary Movements of Hazardous Wastes and Their Disposal, Basel[42] |
| 1989 | International Convention on Salvage, London[43] |
| 1989 | Convention on Civil Liability for Damage Caused during Carriage of Dangerous Goods by Road, Rail and Inland Navigation Vessels, Geneva[44] |
| 1988 | Protocol to the 1979 Convention on Long-Range Transboundary Air Pollution Concerning the Control of Emissions of Nitrogen Oxides or Their Transboundary Fluxes, Sofia[45] |
| 1988 | Convention Concerning Safety and Health in Construction, Geneva (ILO Convention No. 167)[46] |
| 1988 | Joint Protocol Relating to the Application of the Vienna Convention and the Paris Convention, Vienna[47] |
| 1987 | Montreal Protocol on Substances That Deplete the Ozone Layer, Montreal[48] |
| 1986 | Convention Concerning Safety in the Use of Asbestos, Geneva (ILO Convention No. 162, Asbestos Convention)[49] |
| 1986 | Convention on Early Notification of a Nuclear Accident, Vienna[50] |
| 1986 | Convention on Assistance in the Case of a Nuclear Accident or Radiological Emergency, Vienna[51] |
| 1985 | Protocol to the 1979 Convention on Long-Range Transboundary Air Pollution on the Reduction of Sulphur Emissions or Their Transboundary Fluxes by at Least 30 Per Cent, Helsinki[52] |
| 1985 | Vienna Convention for the Protection of the Ozone Layer, Vienna[53] |
| 1985 | Convention Concerning Occupational Health Services, Geneva (ILO Convention No. 161)[54] |
| 1984 | Protocol to the 1979 Convention on Long-Range Transboundary Air Pollution on Long-Term Financing of the Co-operative Programme for Monitoring and Evaluation of the Long-Range Transmission of Air Pollutants in Europe (EMEP), Geneva[55] |
| 1983 | International Tropical Timber Agreement, Geneva[56] |
| 1982 | United Nations Convention on the Law of the Sea, Montego Bay[57] |
| 1981 | Convention Concerning Occupational Safety and Health and the Working Environment, Geneva (ILO Convention No. 155)[58] |
| 1980 | Convention on the Physical Protection of Nuclear Material, Vienna and New York[59] |
| 1979 | Convention on the Conservation of Migratory Species of Wild Animals[60] |
| 1979 | Convention on Long-Range Transboundary Air Pollution[61] |
| 1978 | Protection of New Varieties of Plants (Revision of 1961 Agreement)[62] |
| 1977 | Convention Concerning the Protection of Workers against Occupational Hazards in the Working Environment Due to Air Pollution, Noise and Vibration (ILO Convention No. 148)[63] |
| 1974 | Convention for the Prevention of Marine Pollution from Land-Based Sources, Paris (revised by 1992 OSPAR Convention)[64] |
| 1974 | Agreement on an International Energy Program[65] |
| 1973 | Convention on International Trade in Endangered Species of Wild Fauna and Flora (CITES)[66] |
| 1973 | International Convention for the Prevention of Pollution from Ships, 1973, and Protocols (MARPOL 73/78) (see also 1996 Amendments and 1997 Protocol)[67] |
| 1973 | Protocol Relating to Intervention on the High Seas in Cases of Marine Pollution by Substances Other than Oil[68] |
| 1972 | Stockholm Declaration of the United Nations Conference on the Human Environment[69] |
| 1972 | Convention on the Prohibition of the Development, Production and Stockpiling of Bacteriological (Biological) and Toxin Weapons, and on Their Destruction[70] |
| 1972 | Convention for the Protection of the World Cultural and Natural Heritage[71] |
| 1972 | Convention on the Prevention of Marine Pollution by Dumping of Wastes and Other Matter (London Convention; see also 1996 Protocol)[72] |
| 1971 | Convention on Wetlands of International Importance Especially as Waterfowl Habitat (Ramsar)[73] |
| 1971 | Treaty on the Prohibition of the Emplacement of Nuclear Weapons and Other Weapons of Mass Destruction on the Sea-bed and the Ocean Floor and in the Subsoil Thereof[74] |
| 1971 | Convention Concerning Protection against Hazards of Poisoning Arising from Benzene[75] |
| 1971 | Convention Relating to Civil Liability in the Field of Maritime Carriage of Nuclear Material[76] |
| 1971 | International Convention on the Establishment of an International Fund for Compensation for Oil Pollution Damage[77] |
| 1969 | International Convention Relating to Intervention on the High Seas in Cases of Oil Pollution Casualties[78] |
| 1969 | International Convention on Civil Liability for Oil Pollution Damage (see also 1976 and 1992 Protocols)[79] |
| 1964 | Convention for the International Council for the Exploration of the Sea[80] |
| 1963 | Vienna Convention on Civil Liability for Nuclear Damage[81] |
| 1963 | Treaty Banning Nuclear Weapon Tests in the Atmosphere, in Outer Space and under Water[82] |
| 1962 | Agreement Concerning Co-operation in Marine Fishing[83] |
| 1961 | International Convention on the Protection of New Varieties of Plants[84] |
| 1960 | Convention Concerning the Protection of Workers against Ionising Radiations[85] |
| 1960 | Convention on Third Party Liability in the Field of Nuclear Energy[86] |
| 1959 | Agreement Concerning Co-operation in the Quarantine of Plants and Their Protection against Pests and Diseases[87] |
| 1958 | Convention on the Continental Shelf[88] |
| 1958 | Convention on the High Seas[89] |
| 1958 | Convention on Fishing and Conservation of the Living Resources of the High Seas[90] |
| 1958 | International Convention for the Prevention of Pollution of the Sea by Oil (OILPOL) (see also 1962 Amendment and 1969 Amendments)[91] |
| 1952 | International Convention for the High Seas Fisheries of the North Pacific Ocean (see also 1978 Protocol)[92] |
| 1951 | International Plant Protection Convention[93] |
| 1950 | International Convention for the Protection of Birds[94] |
| 1946 | International Convention for the Regulation of Whaling[95] |

(continued)

**TABLE 10-A.1** (continued)

[1] www.pops.int&sol; (accessed May 31, 2010).

[2] www.planttreaty.org&sol; (accessed May 31, 2010).

[3] http://portal.unesco.org/culture/en/ev.php-URL_ID=34114&URL_DO=DO_TOPIC&URL_SECTION=201.html (accessed May 31, 2010).

[4] www.biodiv.org/biosafety/background.asp (accessed May 31, 2010).

[5] www.fao.org/Legal/treaties/028t-e.htm (accessed May 31, 2010).

[6] www.unece.org/env/lrtap/multi_h1.htm (accessed May 31, 2010).

[7] www.unep.org/ozone/pdf/Montreal-Protocol2000.pdf (accessed May 31, 2010).

[8] www.basel.int/pub/protocol.html (accessed May 31, 2010).

[9] www.unece.org/env/lrtap/pops_h1.htm (accessed May 31, 2010).

[10] www.unece.org/env/lrtap/hm_h1.htm (accessed May 31, 2010).

[11] www.pic.int/home.php?type=s&id=77 (accessed May 31, 2010).

[12] http://untreaty.un.org/ilc/summaries/8_3.htm (accessed May 31, 2010).

[13] www.iaea.org/Publications/Documents/Conventions/index.html (accessed May 31, 2010).

[14] www.iaea.org/Publications/Documents/Conventions/index.html (accessed May 31, 2010).

[15] www.iaea.org/Publications/Documents/Infcircs/1998/infcirc566.shtml (accessed May 31, 2010).

[16] www.unep.org/ozone/pdf/Montreal-Protocol2000.pdf (accessed May 31, 2010).

[17] www.admiraltylawguide.com/conven/protomarpol1997.html (accessed May 31, 2010).

[18] www.unfccc.de/resource/convkp.html (accessed May 31, 2010).

[19] www.admiraltylawguide.com/conven/noxious1996.html (accessed May 31, 2010).

[20] www.fas.org/nuke/control/ctbt/text&sol; (accessed May 31, 2010).

[21] www.ilo.org/ilolex/cgi-lex/convde.pl?C176 (accessed May 31, 2010).

[22] www.un.org/Depts/los/convention_agreements/convention_overview_fish_stocks.htm (accessed May 31, 2010).

[23] www.basel.int/pub/baselban.html (accessed May 31, 2010).

[24] www.austlii.edu.au/au/other/dfat/treaties/1997/2.html (accessed May 31, 2010).

[25] www.unece.org/env/lrtap/fsulf_h1.htm (accessed May 31, 2010).

[26] www.unccd.int&sol; (accessed May 31, 2010).

[27] www.un.org/Depts/los/convention_agreements/convention_agreements.htm (accessed May 31, 2010).

[28] www-ns.iaea.org/conventions/nuclear-safety.htm (accessed May 31, 2010).

[29] www.encharter.org/index.jsp?psk=08&ptp=tDetail.jsp&pci=179&pti=55 (accessed May 31, 2010).

[30] www.icrc.org/ihl.nsf/0/3f233cb0f0c580f8c125641f002d42a8?OpenDocument (accessed May 31, 2010).

[31] www.ilo.org/ilolex/cgi-lex/convde.pl?C174 (accessed May 31, 2010).

[32] www.fao.org/DOCREP/MEETING/003/X3130m/X3130E00.HTM#Contents (accessed May 31, 2010).

[33] http://unfccc.int/ (accessed May 31, 2010).

[34] www.unep.org/documents/default.asp?documentid=78 (accessed May 31, 2010).

[35] www.cbd.int/convention/convention.shtml (accessed May 31, 2010).

[36] www.admiraltylawguide.com/conven/protocivilpol1992.html (accessed May 31, 2010).

[37] www.admiraltylawguide.com/conven/protooilpolfund1992.html (accessed May 31, 2010).

[38] www.unece.org/env/eia/eia.htm (accessed May 31, 2010).

[39] www.unece.org/env/lrtap/vola_h1.htm (accessed May 31, 2010).

[40] www.ilo.org/ilolex/cgi-lex/convde.pl?C170 (accessed May 31, 2010).

[41] http://fletcher.tufts.edu/multi/texts/BH981.txt (accessed May 31, 2010).

[42] www.basel.int&sol; (accessed May 31, 2010).

[43] www.admiraltylawguide.com/conven/salvage1989.html (accessed May 31, 2010).

[44] www.unece.org/trans/danger/publi/crtd/crtd_e.html (accessed May 31, 2010).

[45] http://fletcher.tufts.edu/multi/texts/BH930.txt (accessed May 31, 2010).

[46] www.ilo.org/ilolex/cgi-lex/convde.pl?C167 (accessed May 31, 2010).

[47] www.iaea.org/Publications/Documents/Infcircs/Others/inf402.shtml (accessed May 31, 2010).

[48] http://ozone.unep.org/ (accessed May 31, 2010).

[49] www.itcilo.it/actrav/actrav-english/telearn/osh/legis/c162.htm (accessed May 31, 2010).

[50] www.iaea.org/Publications/Documents/Conventions/cenna.html (accessed May 31, 2010).

[51] www.unece.org/env/lrtap/sulf_h1.htm (accessed May 31, 2010).

[52] http://sedac.ciesin.org/entri/texts/transboundary.air.pollution.protocol.sulphur.emissions.1985.html (accessed May 31, 2010).

[53] http://sedac.ciesin.org/entri/texts/vienna.ozone.layer.protection.1985.html (accessed May 31, 2010).

[54] www.ilo.org/ilolex/cgi-lex/convde.pl?C161 (accessed May 31, 2010).

[55] http://sedac.ciesin.org/entri/texts/transboundary.air.pollution.emep.protocol.1984.html (accessed May 31, 2010).

[56] http://fletcher.tufts.edu/multi/texts/BH837.txt (accessed May 31, 2010).

[57] www.un.org/Depts/los/index.htm (accessed May 31, 2010).

[58] www.ilo.org/ilolex/cgi-lex/convde.pl?C155%20 (accessed May 31, 2010).

[59] www.iaea.org/Publications/Documents/Infcircs/Others/inf274r1.shtml (accessed May 31, 2010).

[60] http://fletcher.tufts.edu/multi/texts/BH752.txt (accessed May 31, 2010).

[61] www.unece.org/env/lrtap&sol; (accessed May 31, 2010).

[62] http://fletcher.tufts.edu/multi/texts/BH425a.txt (accessed May 31, 2010).

[63] www.ilo.org/ilolex/cgi-lex/convde.pl?C148%20 (accessed May 31, 2010).

[64] http://fletcher.tufts.edu/multi/texts/BH646.txt (accessed May 31, 2010).

[65] www.iea.org/about/docs/iep.pdf (accessed May 31, 2010).

66 www.cites.org/eng/disc/text.shtml (accessed May 31, 2010).

67 http://sedac.ciesin.org/entri/texts/pollution.from.ships.1973.html (accessed May 31, 2010).

68 www.austlii.edu.au/au/other/dfat/treaties/1984/5.html (accessed May 31, 2010).

69 www.unep.org/Documents.Multilingual/Default.asp?documentid=97&articleid=1503 (accessed May 31, 2010).

70 www.unog.ch/80256EDD006B8954/%28httpAssets%29/C4048678A93B6934C1257188004848D0/$file/BWC-text-English.pdf (accessed May 31, 2010).

71 http://whc.unesco.org/en/conventiontext (accessed May 31, 2010).

72 www.imo.org/home.asp?topic_id=1488 (accessed May 31, 2010).

73 www.un-documents.net/ramsar.htm (accessed May 31, 2010).

74 www.austlii.edu.au/au/other/dfat/treaties/1973/4.html (accessed May 31, 2010).

75 www.ilo.org/ilolex/cgi-lex/convde.pl?C136 (accessed May 31, 2010).

76 www.admiraltylawguide.com/conven/carriagenuclear1971.html (accessed May 31, 2010).

77 www.admiraltylawguide.com/conven/oilpolfund1971.html (accessed May 31, 2010).

78 www.imo.org/Conventions/contents.asp?doc_id=680&topic_id=258 (accessed May 31, 2010).

79 www.imo.org/conventions/contents.asp?doc_id=660&topic_id=256 (accessed May 31, 2010).

80 www.ices.dk/aboutus/convention.asp (accessed May 31, 2010).

81 www.iaea.org/Publications/Documents/Infcircs/1996/inf500.shtml (accessed May 31, 2010).

82 http://fletcher.tufts.edu/multi/texts/BH454.txt (accessed May 31, 2010).

83 http://sedac.ciesin.org/entri/texts/cooperation.marine.fishing.1962.html (accessed May 31, 2010).

84 http://fletcher.tufts.edu/multi/texts/BH425.txt (accessed May 31, 2010).

85 www.ilo.org/ilolex/cgi-lex/convde.pl?C115 (accessed May 31, 2010).

86 www.nea.fr/html/law/nlparis_conv.html (accessed May 31, 2010).

87 http://fletcher.tufts.edu/multi/texts/tre-0260.txt (accessed May 31, 2010).

88 http://untreaty.un.org/ilc/texts/instruments/english/conventions/8_1_1958_continental_shelf.pdf (accessed May 31, 2010).

89 http://untreaty.un.org/ilc/texts/instruments/english/conventions/8_1_1958_high_seas.pdf (accessed May 31, 2010).

90 http://fletcher.tufts.edu/multi/texts/BH365.txt (accessed May 31, 2010).

91 www.admiraltylawguide.com/conven/oilpol1954.html (accessed May 31, 2010).

92 www.thecre.com/fedlaw/legal20/fisheries-north-pacific-1952.htm (accessed May 31, 2010).

93 https://www.ippc.int&sol; (accessed May 31, 2010).

94 http://fletcher.tufts.edu/multi/texts/BH255.txt (accessed May 31, 2010).

95 http://fletcher.tufts.edu/multi/texts/BH200.txt (accessed May 31, 2010).

## APPENDIX 10-B: MULTILATERAL ENVIRONMENTAL AGREEMENTS BY AREA OF THE ENVIRONMENT

The core environmental conventions and related international agreements can be divided into five clusters: the atmosphere conventions, the biodiversity-related conventions, the chemicals and hazardous-wastes conventions, the land conventions, and the regional seas conventions and related agreements (see Table 10-B.1). Although the Vienna Convention is an atmospheric agreement, its Montreal Protocol can also be considered a chemicals agreement because it deals with the phasing out of the production and consumption of selected chemicals.

The following discussion is taken from *International Environmental Governance: Multilateral Environmental Agreements (MEAs)*, UNEP/IGM/INF/3, July 18, 2001 (and a useful summary document, UNEP/IGM/1/INF/1), www.unep.org/ieg/Meetings_docs/index.asp (accessed May 31, 2010).

### B. SCOPE OF THE CORE ENVIRONMENTAL CONVENTIONS AND RELATED INTERNATIONAL AGREEMENTS

*Cluster 1: biodiversity-related conventions*

18. The scope of the biodiversity-related conventions ranges from the conservation of individual species (CITES and the Lusaka Agreement) via conservation of species, their migration routes and their habitats . . . to the protection of ecosystems. . . . The Cartagena Protocol of the CBD [Convention on Biological Diversity] specifically aims at protecting both species and ecosystems by promoting the safe transfer, handling and use of living modified organisms resulting from modern biotechnology. Five regional seas conventions . . . have protocols or annexes on specially protected areas and wildlife (SPAWs) that cover both individual species and ecosystems. While all of these agreements aim at conserving species and/or ecosystems, several also promote their sustainable use. . . . The Cartagena Protocol promotes measures related to safeguarding the sustainable use of biodiversity against adverse effects that could be caused by living modified organisms. . . .

*Cluster 2: the atmosphere conventions*

19. The Vienna Convention on the Protection of the Ozone Layer and its Montreal Protocol on Substances that Deplete the Ozone Layer and the United Nations Framework Convention on Climate Change and its Kyoto Protocol are closely associated in protecting the environment by eliminating or stabilizing anthropogenic emissions that threaten to interfere with the atmosphere. While the former focuses on the impacts that ozone depletion can have on human health, the latter addresses concerns that climate change may have on food production and economic development. The Montreal Protocol is well on its way to achieving its goal of gradually phasing out 96 listed ozone-depleting substances. Its overriding priority is to provide financial assistance through the Multilateral Fund to eligible developing countries to comply with the provisions of the Protocol and its amendments. The United Nations Framework Convention on Climate Change (UNFCCC) is in an earlier phase of implementation, with much of its future success depending on the operationalization of its Kyoto Protocol. . . .

*Cluster 4: the chemicals and hazardous wastes conventions*

21. The overarching objective of the chemicals and hazardous wastes conventions is the protection of human health and the environment from pollution by specific chemicals and hazardous substances. In the case of the Rotterdam Convention, it specifically addresses certain banned or severely restricted chemicals, as well as severely hazardous pesticide formulations, subject to international trade. The Stockholm Convention has as its priorities the phasing out of an initial list of 9 chemicals, the restriction to certain acceptable purposes the production and use of DDT, and the reduction or elimination of unintentionally produced chemicals (dioxin and furans). The Convention also has provisions to add further POPs to the treaty, and will require parties with new chemical programmes to prevent the introduction of new POPs onto the marketplace. The scope of the Basel Convention covers a broad range of hazardous wastes, including chemical wastes, subject to transboundary movements, aiming to reduce these movements to a minimum by minimizing the quantity and hazardousness of the wastes generated and by promoting the treatment and disposal of hazardous wastes and other wastes as close as possible to their source of generation. These global MEAs are complimented by regional agreements such as the Bamako Convention and the Waigani Convention, as well as the Protocol to the Barcelona Convention for the Protection of the Mediterranean Sea against Pollution from Land-Based Sources.

*Cluster 5: Regional seas conventions and related agreements*

22. By far the largest cluster of MEAs, the 17 regional seas conventions and action plans are a global mosaic of agreements with one over-arching objective: the protection and sustainable use of marine and coastal resources. In the early years shortly after the Stockholm Conference, the regional seas programmes focused on marine pollution control. In the ensuing 25 years they have evolved into multi-sectoral agreements addressing integrated coastal area management, including in several cases links to the management of contiguous freshwater basins; land-based sources of pollution; conservation and sustainable use of living marine resources; and impacts of offshore exploration and exploitation of oil and gas. The Barcelona Convention (1976), the oldest of these agreements, fostered the establishment of the Mediterranean Commission for Sustainable Development which is serviced by the Secretariat of the Convention. . . .

### C. THE LEGAL FRAMEWORK OF THE CORE MEAS

24. Of the 41 MEAs listed in Table 1, all but 6 are legally binding instruments. Sixteen are framework conventions such as UNFCCC, CBD, the Basel Conven-

tion and the Barcelona Convention that can develop protocols for addressing specific subjects requiring more detailed and specialized negotiations. Eight are self-contained conventions that work through annexes or appendices, rather than protocols, which are revised periodically through the decisions of the Conferences of the Contracting Parties (COPs) of the respective MEAs.

These include CITES, the World Heritage Convention, the Lusaka Agreement, the United Nations Convention to Combat Desertification, the Rotterdam Convention, the Stockholm Convention, the Helsinki Convention for the Protection of the Marine Environment of the Baltic Sea Area and the Convention for the Protection of the Marine Environment of the North-East Atlantic (OSPAR).

## TABLE 10-B.1: CORE ENVIRONMENTAL CONVENTIONS AND RELATED AGREEMENTS OF GLOBAL SIGNIFICANCE

| MEA | DATE ADOPTED | SECRETARIAT |
|---|---|---|
| **Atmosphere conventions** | | |
| 1. Kyoto Protocol to the United Nations Framework Convention on Climate Change | 1997 | UN |
| 2. United Nations Framework Convention on Climate Change (UNFCCC) | 1992 | UN |
| 3. Montreal Protocol on Substances That Deplete the Ozone Layer | 1987 | UNEP |
| 4. Vienna Convention for the Protection of the Ozone Layer | 1985 | UNEP |
| **Biodiversity-related conventions** | | |
| 5. Cartagena Protocol on Biosafety to the Convention on Biological Diversity | 2001 | UNEP |
| 6. Agreement on the Conservation of Cetaceans of the Black Sea, the Mediterranean Sea and Contiguous Atlantic Area (ACCOBAMS)[a] | 1996 | ACCOBAMS Sec. |
| 7. Agreement on the Conservation of African-Eurasian Migratory Waterbirds (AEWA)[a] | 1995 | UNEP |
| 8. International Coral Reef Initiative (ICRI) | 1995 | ICRI Sec. |
| 9. Lusaka Agreement on Cooperative Enforcement Operations Directed at Illegal Trade in Wild Fauna and Flora | 1994 | KWS (Kenya Wildlife Service) |
| 10. Convention on Biological Diversity | 1992 | UNEP |
| 11. Agreement on the Conservation of Bats in Europe (EUROBATS)[a] | 1991 | UNEP |
| 12. Agreement on the Conservation of Small Cetaceans of the Baltic and North Seas (ASCOBANS)[a] | 1991 | UNEP |
| 13. Agreement on the Conservation of Seals in the Wadden Sea[a] | 1990 | CWSS (Common Wadden Sea Secretariat) |
| 14. Convention on the Conservation of Migratory Species of Wild Animals CMS) | 1979 | UNEP |
| 15. Convention on International Trade in Endangered Species (CITES) | 1973 | UNEP |
| 16. World Heritage Convention | 1972 | UNESCO |
| 17. Ramsar Convention on Wetlands | 1971 | IUCN |
| **Chemicals and hazardous-wastes conventions:** | | |
| 18. Stockholm Convention on Persistent Organic Pollutants | 2001 | UNEP[b] |
| 19. Basel Protocol on Liability and Compensation | 1999 | UNEP |
| 20. Rotterdam Convention on the Prior Informed Consent Principle for Certain Hazardous Chemicals and Pesticides in International Trade | 1998 | UNEP/ FAO |
| 21. Basel Ban Amendment | 1995 | UNEP |
| 22. Basel Convention on the Control of Transboundary Movements of Hazardous Wastes and Their Disposal | 1989 | UNEP |
| **Land conventions:** | | |
| 23. United Nations Convention to Combat Desertification | 1994 | UN |
| **Regional seas conventions and related agreements[c]** | | |
| 24. Framework Convention for the Protection of the Marine Environment of the Caspian Sea[d] | 2003 | CEF (Caspian Environment Programme) |
| 25. Convention for Cooperation in the Protection and Sustainable Development of the Marine and Coastal Environment of the Northeast Pacific[d] | 2002 | UNEP[b] |
| 26. Global Programme of Action for the Protection of the Marine Environment from Land-Based Activities | 1995 | UNEP |
| 27. South Asian Seas Action Plan | 1995 | SACEP (South Asia Co-operative Environment Programme) |
| 28. The Northwest Pacific Acton Plan (NOWPAP) | 1994 | UNEP |
| 29. Convention on the Protection of the Black Sea from Pollution (Bucharest) | 1992 | BSEP[d] (Black Sea Environment Programme) |
| 30. Convention for the Protection of the Marine Environment of the Baltic Sea Area (Helsinki) | 1992 | HELCOM (The Helsinki Commission) |
| 31. Convention for the Protection of the Marine Environment of the North-east Atlantic (OSPAR convention – Oslo/Paris convention) | 1992 | OSPAR[d] |
| 32. Protection of the Arctic Marine Environment (PAME) | 1991 | PAME[e] |

(continued)

**TABLE 10-B.2** (continued)

| MEA | DATE ADOPTED | SECRETARIAT |
|---|---|---|
| 33. Convention for the Protection of the Natural Resources and Environment of the South Pacific Region (Noumea) | 1986 | SPREP (South Pacific Regional Environment Programme) |
| 34. Convention for the Protection, Management and Development of the Marine and Coastal Environment of the Eastern African Region (Nairobi) | 1985 | UNEP |
| 35. Convention for the Protection and Development of the Marine Environment of the Wider Caribbean Region (Cartagena) | 1983 | UNEP |
| 36. Regional Convention for the Conservation of the Red Sea and Gulf of Aden Environment (Jeddah) | 1982 | PERSGA (Regional Organization for the Conservation of the Environment of the Red Sea and Gulf of Aden) |
| 37. Convention for Cooperation in the Protection and Development of the Marine and Coastal Environment of the West and Central African Region (Abidjan) | 1981 | UNEP |
| 38. Convention for the Protection of the Marine Environment and Coastal Area of the South-east Pacific (Lima) | 1981 | CPPS (Permanent Commission of the South Pacific) |
| 39. The East Asian Seas Action Plan | 1981 | UNEP |
| 40. Kuwait Regional Convention for Cooperation on the Protection of the Marine Environment from Pollution | 1978 | ROPME (Regional Organization for the Protection of the Marine Environment) |
| 41. Convention for the Protection of the Mediterranean Sea against Pollution (Barcelona) | 1976 | UNEP |

[a] The seventeen regional seas conventions and action plans are a global mosaic of agreements with one overarching objective: the protection and sustainable use of marine and coastal resources. Protocols, amendments, and agreements of regional seas conventions are not listed.

[b] Non-UN regional organizations.

[c] The UNEP is providing the secretariat on an interim basis.

[d] Regional body with its own secretariat established by the Arctic Council.

[e] Although these agreements are independent treaties, they were concluded under the auspices of CMS.

Source: Adapted from "International Environmental Governance: Multilateral Environmental Agreements (MEAs)," UNEP/IGM/INF/3, July 10, 2001, www.unep.org/ieg/Meetings_docs/index.asp (accessed May 31, 2010).

# V

# International Trade and Finance

The globalization of commerce and financial capital has an increasingly large impact on most of the developed world and some of the developing world. Although there is no international department of commerce or international ministry of trade, voluntary trade regimes have sought to regularize international economic activity by establishing rules of conduct for trade and commerce, mechanisms for dispute resolution, and forums for discussion of issues of concern about the global economy.

The first of two components of Part V, Chapter 11, focuses on the legal issues related to environment and employment in the context of trade regimes. Looking ahead, we recognize four distinct approaches for coordinating, if not integrating, our threefold concern on a global scale: (1) strengthen and coordinate the existing international environmental and labor regimes and secure their ratification and implementation by all major trading partners; (2) create a world environment organization to counterbalance the ILO and the WTO, or endow the UNEP with expanded authority; (3) change the trade instruments and agreements administered by the WTO so that they explicitly accommodate concerns for the environment and employment; and (4) negotiate side agreements on the environment and trade in various (especially regional) trade regimes, such as those found in NAFTA. In Chapter 11 we explore (3) and (4). The difficulty of achieving (1) has already been addressed in Chapter 10. Approach 2 will be addressed in the final chapter of this work (Chapter 13).

At the end of the Second World War, the agreements reached at Bretton Woods attempted to establish a stabilizing architecture for the world financial system; the institutions and regulations established to do this have become unraveled with the final challenge to stability precipitated by the financial crisis of 2008 (see the discussion in Section 4.6 of Chapter 4). The second component of Part V consists of Chapter 12 on financing development, sustainably or otherwise. The chapter is divided into three main parts. Part A focuses on the main financial sources that are associated with promoting economic growth in developing regions. These include:

- Official development assistance (ODA) through loans and grants from government to government (bilateral arrangements)

- Loans from the World Bank (WB) Group to governments and firms (multilateral lending)

- Loans from private banks to firms undertaking projects in developing countries

- Foreign direct investment (FDI), mostly financed by multinational corporations for specific commercial ventures

- National-government-backed export credit agencies (ECAs) that loan or insure loans for specific projects undertaken overseas by their national firms or joint commercial ventures

- Sovereign wealth funds held by China and the energy-exporting nations, resulting in a highly distorted balance of trade

Part B takes a look at financing for environmental protection, which still remains somewhat of an afterthought when compared to financing for economic development, but is nevertheless a growing area of interest as negative environmental impacts in many developing regions continue to present challenges. The discussion in Part B focuses on strengths and weaknesses of existing financial structures for environmental protection.

Finally, Part C reviews several innovative financing solutions that hold the potential to promote more sustainable forms of development. We explore global initiatives such as George Soros's SDR proposal, Konrad von Moltke's notion of an international investment agreement, the global environment facility (GEF) partnership, and Louis Kelso's idea of binary economics, and local initiatives such as microcredit and microgrants. While several of these ideas have yet to be implemented, they are included to broaden the discussion on potential solutions to generating the necessary finance for sustainable development that existing mechanisms seem to be unable to provide.

# 11

# Trade Regimes and Sustainability

## 11.1 TRADE AGREEMENTS IN GENERAL

### 11.1.1 Introduction

Before growth in trade became important for raising sectoral or national revenues—and before globalization in its various manifestations began to influence development in individual nations (see Chapter 4), environmental policies, and employment—countries were content to focus on domestic policies affecting competitiveness (here meaning the productiveness of the economy), environment, and employment. Trade and globalization have changed this.*

Although there is no international department of commerce or international ministry of trade, voluntary trade regimes have sought to regularize international economic activity by establishing rules of conduct for trade and commerce, mechanisms for dispute resolution, and forums for discussion of issues of concern about the global economy. Other problems of globalization have been addressed in prior chapters. Chapter 5 explored the problems of globalization and trade in the context of their effects on the three pillars of sustainability. Chapter 10 explored the potential of multilateral environmental and labor agreements to harmonize environmental and labor practices and

---

\*    The effects of trade and globalization on the environment and employment have been addressed in Chapters 1 and 5;

this chapter focuses on the legal issues related to the environment and employment in the context of trade regimes.

standards through the mechanisms of international law.

The fragmentation of efforts to coordinate or integrate the components of sustainable development characterizes the international, as well as the national, economic order. In this chapter, we delve into the strengths and weaknesses of the trade regimes themselves—principally the World Trade Organization (WTO) and the North American Free Trade Agreement (NAFTA)—as vehicles for coordinating or integrating these concerns. Other regional trade regimes exist, of course, such as the Association of Southeast Asian Nations (ASEAN) and evolving regimes like MERCOSUR, involving Argentina, Brazil, Paraguay, and Uruguay, for South America. All in all, there are some 240 bilateral or regional free trade agreements (Lugard and Smart 2006); addressing them is beyond the scope of this chapter.

Looking ahead, we recognize four distinct approaches for coordinating, if not integrating, our threefold concern on a global scale: (1) strengthen and coordinate the existing international environmental and labor regimes and secure their ratification and implementation by all major trading partners; (2) create a world environment organization to counterbalance the International Labor Organization (ILO) and the WTO, or endow the United Nations Environment Programme (UNEP) with expanded authority; (3) change the trade instruments and agreements administered by the WTO so that they explicitly accommodate concerns for the environment and employment; and (4) negotiate side agreements on the environment and trade in various (especially regional) trade regimes, such as those found in NAFTA. In this chapter we explore (3) and (4). The difficulty of achieving (1) has already been addressed in Chapter 10. Approach 2 will be addressed in the final chapter of this work (Chapter 13).

## 11.1.2 Trade as a Driver of Growth*

Although modern development theory emphasizes technological innovation as the "engine of economic growth," trade also contributed to advancing industrializing nations during the nineteenth and twentieth centuries. Now trade is increasingly described as a major engine of economic growth, both for advanced economies with "excess productive capacity" and sat-

urated domestic markets and for less industrialized countries with unused natural resources increasingly needed by the industrialized economies. For both, outward-looking strategies are being fashioned for more participation in world markets.[†] The purpose of this section is to articulate why trade is seen as an important driver of development.

The rationale for trade can be traced back to David Ricardo's (1996 [1817]) theory of *comparative advantage*[‡] in the nineteenth century and more recently to Heckscher and Ohlin's *factor-endowment trade theory* (Heckscher 1949 [1919]; Ohlin 1933). The Heckscher-Ohlin model of trade suggests that countries should *specialize* in the production of commodities for which they have an advantage in resource endowments and/or productive capabilities and exchange any surplus home-produced commodities for those more easily produced by others (Todaro and Smith 2009).[§] For example, according to the neoclassical theory of supply and demand, if a country is endowed with labor, the price of labor will be relatively cheap compared with countries where labor is scarce, ceteris paribus. Therefore, the labor-endowed country is described as having a *comparative advantage* in relation to the cost of labor. From the Heckscher-Ohlin model, it follows that labor-endowed countries should focus on the production of labor-intensive commodities (such

---

[†] Schmidheiny (1992, p. 79) makes the observation that "traditionally, the industrial nations of North America and Europe have championed free trade, against the resistance of most developing nations and centrally planned economies. Today, it is the former that tend to question the benefits of liberalized trade, while developing nations and the newly emerged democracies of Eastern Europe see it as their main hope for economic development."

[‡] See Section 4.4 in Chapter 4 on trade and economic development.

[§] The early theories of comparative advantage were based on a set of *static* (endowment/core) factors—namely, labor, natural resources, land, and population size. However, comparative advantage is now understood to be more of a dynamic process (Dicken 1994). Possibly the best-known description of the factors that determine a nation's competitiveness is Porter's (1990) "diamond of competitive advantage." Porter's diamond consists of four interacting factors: *factor conditions* (such as resources, labor, and infrastructure); *demand conditions* (that is, demand from customers); *related and supporting industries*; and *industry strategy, structure, and rivalry* (that is, the factors that influence an industry's/firm's attitude toward competition and innovation). These factors can combine to generate new advanced factor endowments (such as a high-technology sector or a large pool of skilled labor) that determine a nation's *competitive* advantage. A clear omission from Porter's (1990) theory, however, is the failure to include government as a factor (Dicken 1994). Instead, government is described as having a proactive "influence" on the four endowment/core factors. See also Section 3.1.2 in Chapter 3 on factor endowments necessary for economic development.

as agricultural goods, raw materials, and minerals) and export any surplus in exchange for imports of capital-intensive commodities.

Conversely, if a country is endowed with capital, it will have a relative advantage in the production of manufactured goods (such as automobiles, trains, aircraft, and electronic equipment) that require large capital investments in technology/equipment compared with labor (Todaro and Smith 2009). Thus, in the Heckscher-Ohlin model, capital-endowed countries should focus on the production of capital-intensive commodities and export any surplus in return for imports of labor-intensive commodities. In effect, the Heckscher-Ohlin model brings the neoclassical price mechanism into the realm of (international) trade theory.

By understanding which productive factors are required to manufacture commodities and relating this information to the relative endowments and factors of production of each country, factor-endowment trade theory encourages countries to *specialize* in commodities in which they have a comparative advantage. Hence the most efficient (worldwide) allocation of resources will be achieved if all countries specialize in their relative strengths and trade their surplus for needed commodities that are more easily produced by others. This view of trade ultimately leads to the integration of regional and national markets, increasing the importance of transnational corporations and the need to transport resources and commodities between nations (Korten 2001).

Behind the majority of arguments in support of international trade is a form of "economic rationalism." Dryzek (1997)* describes an economic rationalist as someone who believes in the (free) market† and the rational pursuit of material self-interest. Advocates of pure economic rationalism believe that the free market can provide society with more of the products and services it needs and reduce the role of government in promoting a competitive economy. Thus an economic rationalist is primarily concerned with removing barriers to competition, reducing government spending, expanding the privatization of public services (such as public transportation), and the deregulation of heavily regulated markets/industries.[1] Economic rationalists, for example, might construct the problem of unsustainable development through the lens of inadequate property rights. They would argue that if property rights were reassembled in a more appropriate manner, environmental resources would be "treated as inputs to the social machine," resulting in more sustainable forms of development (ibid., p. 114).

Economic rationalists believe that governments should act in the best interests of the public, although their actions should be defined in economic rationalist terms. However, Dryzek (1997) notes that this type of economic rationalism is an inadequate mechanism to protect or enhance the environment. A major problem is that economic rationalists respond to consumer preferences and ignore citizen preferences (Sagoff 1988), thereby undermining the democratic process and the well-being of the disadvantaged. Therefore, a more moderate position tends to be adopted by those (neoclassical economists) in support of trade that recognizes the need for government to account for (that is, internalize) the environmental and social costs (or negative externalities) of the market (Driesen 2001).‡ This position aligns well with environmental and resource economics, which attempts to place appropriate market valuations on goods and services by internalizing negative externalities.§

Interestingly, those who oppose international trade recognize that the removal of trade barriers and the

---

* An approach to the concept of sustainable development that is a valuable alternative to the description of the emergence of sustainable development in Chapter 2 is found in John Dryzek's (1997) book *The Politics of the Earth: Environmental Discourses*. Instead of taking a historical approach to describe sustainable development, Dryzek uses discourses to address the concept from the full range of positions and arguments—many of which are touched on in this chapter.

† Dryzek (1997) questions the use of the term "free" market and argues that a "market is a market; so why does it need to be called a free market, especially given that markets can only operate if government supplies a supportive legal context?" (ibid., p. 114). Thus "free" market is used as a rhetorical device to represent the removal of barriers to trade in protected or insulated products and services. To many, the concept of a free market also means the elimination or minimization of "oppressive" health, safety, and environmental regulation that may hamper the free flow of goods or the conduct of commerce, or the absence of wage constraints and other restrictions on the conditions and terms of employment, characterized as a nation's industrial relations system.

The more fundamental concept traceable to both Ricardo and Adam Smith is a "competitive market," i.e., one free from the excesses of monopoly power—but not market controls—that seeks to "internalize social costs." A sleight of hand is used in confusing laissez-faire capitalism (free markets) with competitive markets.

‡ A major challenge faced by governments is that these environmental and social costs tend to have a long maturation time, which is "at odds with political democracy, which does not tend to favor long-term planning, especially if it is costly in the short-term" (Hutter 2002, p. 14).

§ Part and parcel of economic rationalism is a commitment to rational choice theory, which argues that government (like the private sector) should base its decisions on cost-benefit analysis.

integration of national economies have the *potential* to improve the well-being of humans, especially for the poor (Stiglitz 2002). Further, private enterprise, rather than government intervention, is seen as an effective mechanism for creating wealth (Soros 2002). This indicates that potential solutions to the problems raised above will lie in balancing the role of government with the benefits of the market.

Although the case that international trade can stimulate economic growth is relatively clear, the challenge is to ensure that this growth supports rather than undermines sustainable forms of development.* In Chapter 9, the argument is made that more stringent environmental regulation is likely to result in either an incremental/radical improvement in the *existing* trajectory (that is, better versions) of technology (the weak form of the regulation-induced-innovation hypothesis) or a disrupting change (the strong form of the regulation-induced-innovation hypothesis), whereby new products, product-services, and processes enter the market and displace dominant technologies. The discussion in Chapter 9 continues this line of argument by stating that if progress is to be made toward sustainable development, we need to go beyond incremental product and process innovations and search for ways to facilitate dramatic changes in products/processes, shifts to product-services, or further still, *system changes*. Two corollary questions arise: (1) how are strategies designed to encourage disrupting change likely to affect international trade? and (2) how do various trade strategies affect the nature of technological change (see the discussion of Charles and Lehner [1998] below)?

The introduction of more stringent standards (designed to facilitate dramatic and/or possibly disrupting technological change) is likely to increase production costs and might encourage industries to relocate to countries with more lenient standards.† However, in practice, it appears that environmental compliance has not yet reached a level of stringency where it influences trade flows or firm location decisions (Steininger 1994). A major concern here is that although more stringent environmental regulation regarding production is likely to improve the national environment, it might also lead to a reduction in a nation's share of international production. Steininger (1994) makes a convincing case that if countries are to implement more stringent environmental standards, the threat of competitive disadvantage must be removed. He argues that concerns for the competitiveness of national industries could be addressed if one or both of two counterbalancing measures were incorporated in trade agreements:

- the implementation of countervailing duties on countries with more lenient regulations (the lax standard could be seen as an unfair . . . subsidy), and/or
- the implementation of domestic subsidies for environmental control costs (ibid., p. 28).

Steininger (1994) argues that implementing such changes to trade laws would encourage the unilateral introduction of more stringent environmental regulations that are necessary to bring economies within

---

\*        As an interesting aside, the effectiveness of trade measures in pursuing environmental goals was a question posed by Congress to the Office of Technology Assessment (OTA) in 1992. The final report, *Trade and Environment: Conflicts and Opportunities*, concluded that "trade measures (especially import restrictions), and the threat of such measures, can potentially further environmental goals in various ways. They can help *convince* a country to join an international environmental agreement or to behave according to certain environmental norms; *deny* a country economic gain from failing to follow such norms; *prevent* a country's actions from undermining the environmental effectiveness of other countries' efforts; and *remove* the economic incentive for certain environmentally undesirable economic activity" (OTA 1992, p. 42). Examples of such measures can be found in the Convention on International Trade in Endangered Species of Wild Fauna and Flora (CITES), established to ensure that international trade in specimens of wild animals and plants does not threaten their survival, and the Basel Convention on the control of transboundary movements of hazardous waste and its disposal (see Chapter 10).

---

†        Dicken (1994) provides an insightful discussion of the complex relationship that exists between international firms and nation-states. On the one hand, the international firm "seeks to maximize its freedom to locate its production chain components in the most advantageous locations for the firm as a whole in its pursuit of global profits or global market share" (ibid., p. 117). On the other hand, the state "wishes to maximize its share of value-adding activities" (ibid.). Therefore, the outcome of firm-state interactions is predictably uneasy, one of conflict and/or collaboration. Further, firm-state interactions are also influenced by whether the international firm is based in its home country or is a guest in a host country. On the topic of regulatory structures, Dicken (1994) argues that international firms are primarily interested in access to markets and the rules of operations. What they seek would seem to be the "removal of all barriers to entry, whether to imports or to direct presence; freedom to export capital and profits from local operations; freedom to import materials, components, and corporate services; [and] freedom to operate unhindered in local labor markets" (ibid., p. 119). Dicken (1994) suggests that the variation in regulatory structures between nation-states enables firms to engage in a form of "regulatory arbitrage," whereby firms move activities in search of more profitable operations. Such activity might be construed as a race to the bottom where environmental and health and safety standards are concerned. What Dicken does not address, however, is whether more stringent regulatory structures might, in fact, provide firms with an opportunity to capture markets through the creation of advanced (possibly disrupting) technology (Oye and Foster 2002; White 1989). Porter argues that countries, as well as firms, enjoy "first-mover" advantages (Porter and van der Linde 1995); but see also see Nehrt (1998).

appropriate ecological limits. These changes, which can lead to the harmonization of environmental standards, possibly through the participation of trading nations in multilateral environmental agreements, seek to equalize environmental burdens and responsibilities.*

Correcting sustainability-driven concerns by harmonizing environmental or occupational health and safety standards is one thing, but different trade strategies themselves can affect the kinds of innovation that an economy or sector undertakes. Presumably, trade is directed toward increasing revenues in a globalized economy. Charles and Lehner (1998) compare policies that seek to maintain national competitiveness by relying on innovation-driven strategies with those that rely on cost-cutting revenue enhancement.

The challenge facing government is how to develop industrial policies that support innovation-driven strategies for competitiveness in trade. Charles and Lehner (1998) argue that identifying the appropriate role for government is a complex task that is plagued with uncertainty; however, they suggest a couple of ways in which innovation-driven strategies can be supported. First, industrial policies should be designed to incorporate differences across firms and industries. The challenge is to strike the right balance between the welfare of industries, regions, and the nation and create a regulatory framework that enables competition and cooperation. Second, new forms of state intervention are required. In particular, Charles and Lehner (1998) suggest that such intervention should support networks of innovation and play an active role in managing the dynamics of new interdependencies between the nation state, regions, and the international economy. However, a note of caution is offered: too much intervention might be self-defeating.

Finally, if it is possible to create a leading-edge economy based on environmentally focused, innovation-driven strategies that facilitate disrupting change, this outcome presents a significant opportunity to maintain/improve a nation's competitiveness while encouraging more sustainable forms of development. Although it is difficult to know how disruptive change might affect

international trade, there are likely to be improvements in the environmental performance of products and services that are traded.†

### 11.1.3 Overview of the Agreements Administered by the World Trade Organization

The WTO describes its agreements as follows:[2] "The WTO agreements cover goods, services and intellectual property. They spell out the principles of liberalization, and the permitted exceptions. They include individual countries' commitments to lower customs tariffs and other trade barriers, to minimize or eliminate subsidies, to open and keep open services markets, and to respect intellectual property. They set procedures for settling disputes. They prescribe special treatment for developing countries. They require governments to make their trade policies transparent by notifying the WTO about laws in force and measures adopted, and through regular reports by the secretariat on countries' trade policies."

The agreements are often called the WTO's trade rules, and the WTO is often described as "rules based." The "rules" are agreements that governments have negotiated, which can be renegotiated or further clarified though the resolution of trade disputes. The legal texts consist of about sixty agreements, annexes, decisions, and understandings. The main agreements fall into a simple structure with six main parts, as depicted in Table 11.1: an umbrella agreement (the Agreement Establishing the WTO); agreements for each of the three broad areas of trade that the WTO covers (goods, services, and intellectual property); dispute settlement; and reviews of governments' trade policies.

The original version of the General Agreement on Tariffs and Trade (GATT) came into existence in 1947, but it has changed considerably since its first inception. The World Trade Organization took over the administration of the GATT when it was established in 1995. Trade in merchandise in 1997 was fourteen times that of 1950. The WTO has a membership of more than 130 nations, comprising more than 90 percent of world trade; three-quarters of its members are developing or least developed countries.

A central focus of the WTO has been the discouragement of dumping (selling goods below their production cost or below their domestic sales price) and

---

* Equalizing environmental (or safety and health) performance is likely to impose similar but not entirely equal financial burdens on all producers. Pollution-control and safety equipment will cost about the same in all countries, but human resource inputs may be relatively cheaper in developing countries. On the other hand, labor standards that equalize *purchasing power* and impose lower costs on developing countries reflect an increasing concern about outsourcing labor to third-world countries by industrialized nations.

---

† Interestingly, the Obama administration has announced that it will focus on creating green jobs, encourage the greater production of automobiles produced domestically, and spur energy innovation.

## TABLE 11.1: THE WORLD TRADE ORGANIZATION (WTO)

| Umbrella | AGREEMENT ESTABLISHING THE WTO | | |
| --- | --- | --- | --- |
| Areas of trade | Goods | Services | Intellectual property |
| Basic principles | GATT | GATS | TRIPS |
| Additional details | Other goods agreements and annexes | Services annexes | |
| Market access commitments | Countries' schedules of commitments | Countries' schedules of commitments (and MFN exemptions) | |
| Dispute settlement | | | |
| Transparency | | Trade policy reviews | |

GATS = General Agreement on Trade in Services
GATT = General Agreement on Tariffs and Trade
MFN = Most favored nation
TRIPS = Trade-Related Aspects of Intellectual Property

the elimination of subsidies and tariff/nontariff trade barriers so as to facilitate fairer worldwide trade in manufactured products and eventually in agricultural products.* Victims of unfair trade practices and injured parties in trade can institute antidumping measures and antisubsidy measures and can adopt limits on imports as "safeguards" that preserve their markets. Interference by one country in another country's trade with a third country is also discouraged. In other words, the WTO/GATT seeks to facilitate unencumbered trade and encourage international commerce, giving producers and exporters assurances that foreign markets will remain open to them.

However, importing nations may have a special interest in protecting human health and the environment from hazardous imports and harmful practices of importers and are allowed to do so under the exceptions articulated in Article XX of the GATT:

### ARTICLE XX: GENERAL EXCEPTIONS

Subject to the requirement that such measures are not applied in a manner which would constitute a means of arbitrary or unjustifiable discrimination between countries where the same conditions prevail, or a disguised restriction on international trade, nothing in this Agreement shall be construed to prevent the adoption or enforcement by any contracting party of measures:

. . .

(b) necessary to protect human, animal or plant life or health; . . .

(d) necessary to secure compliance with laws or regulations which are not inconsistent with the provisions of [the GATT]; . . .

(g) in relation to conservation of exhaustible natural resources [both living and nonliving, for example, minerals].

The evolving law under the WTO and other agreements administered by the WTO (see below) addresses the tensions between the environment/public health and safety and trade. Although the exceptions may include worker health and safety, other aspects of sustainability having to do with employment, for example, wages and some conditions of work, are not clearly addressed (see the later discussion in Section 11.4.1).

In order to operationalize Article XX(b) or (g), the "measures" on imports may include bans, other import restrictions or regulations, or countervailing tariffs (taxes).† What is unclear is whether imported goods made by employing environmentally destructive practices affecting only the exporting countries

---

* Central to the goal of free(r) trade among the signatories to the GATT are nondiscrimination vis-à-vis the treatment of imports and domestically produced goods (i.e., the so-called uniformity-of-treatment requirement of the GATT) and treatment of all imported/exported goods that is the same as treatment of those of the most favored nation (MFN).

---

† Bamberger and Guzman (2008) address the increased importation of unsafe goods (e.g., drugs, foods, and toys) from abroad whose foreign-based producers are either unreachable under U.S. law or unknown. Acknowledging that a permanent ban of Chinese toys would probably not survive scrutiny as a permissible exception under Article XX(b), Cortez (2008) argues for a temporary ban to pressure China to manufacturer safer products. In contrast, rather than ineffectual regulation that might be imposed under Article XX(b), Bamberger and Guzman (2008) rely on Article XX(d) to justify the protection of domestic consumers from unsafe foreign products by imposing strict tort liability with larger penalties for importers and sellers than for their domestic counterparts. They argue that more onerous liability than is imposed on domestic producers is justified (as a necessary and least trade-restrictive approach) under XX(d) in order to create *equivalent incentives* to ensure more prevention, resulting in a safe product, and that this escapes violation of the "less favorable treatment" requirement vis-à-vis domestic products.

can be actionable.* It is also doubtful whether an importing country can give preferences to environmentally superior goods, because Article XX speaks of exceptions that are measures "necessary to protect human, animal or plant life or health," but also states that these measures must satisfy the uniformity-of-treatment and MFN requirements. In other words, what would in effect be subsidies through discounting of the prices of environmentally superior imports would not be allowed.† However, financial assistance or technical advice provided by any nation to its exporters to improve or secure its exports' heath, safety, or environmental characteristics in compliance with law or regulation is explicitly allowed by the WTO rules as "non-actionable subsidies" under the GATT.

In order to successfully avail itself of Articles XX(b) and (g), among other requirements, an importer must demonstrate that its restrictive measure falls under one of the allowable exceptions. An importing nation can unilaterally and autonomously establish the level of protection deemed necessary according to its own values, although a multilateral approach—for example, evidenced by the existence of a multilateral (or bilateral) agreement on the issue—is strongly preferred but is not a prerequisite.‡ In addition, the restrictive measure must not constitute "a means of arbitrary or unjustifiable discrimination between countries where the same conditions prevail" and must not be "a disguised restriction on international trade." Finally, the measure needs to be either *necessary* for the protection of human, animal, or plant life or health (Article XX(b)) or *in relation to* the conservation of natural resources (Article XX(g)).§

Aside from the GATT, the General Agreement on Trade in Services (GATS), and the Agreement on Trade-Related Aspects of Intellectual Property Rights TRIPS,

additional agreements relevant to health, safety, and the environment include the following:

- The Agreement on Subsidies and Countervailing Measures
- The Agreement on Technical Barriers to Trade (TBT)
- The Agreement on Sanitary and Phytosanitary Measures (SPS)

The key aspects of these agreements are found in the appendix to this chapter. After a discussion of dispute resolution in the WTO in the next section, each of these agreements is described in the remainder of this chapter.

### 11.1.4 Dispute Resolution under the WTO

The WTO has an elaborate system for resolving disputes among trading partners. The WTO describes the system as follows:[3]

#### UNDERSTANDING THE WTO: SETTLING DISPUTES

##### A unique contribution

Dispute settlement is the central pillar of the multilateral trading system, and the WTO's unique contribution to the stability of the global economy. Without a means of settling disputes, the rules-based system would be less effective because the rules could not be enforced. The WTO's procedure underscores the rule of law, and it makes the trading system more secure and predictable. The system is based on clearly-defined rules, with timetables for completing a case. First rulings are made by a panel and endorsed (or rejected) by the WTO's full membership. Appeals based on points of law are possible.

However, the point is not to pass judgment. The priority is to settle disputes, through consultations if possible. By July 2005, only about 130 of the nearly 332 cases had reached the full panel process. Most of the rest have either been notified as settled "out of court" or remain in a prolonged consultation phase, some since 1995.

Disputes in the WTO are essentially about broken promises. WTO members have agreed that if they believe fellow-members are violating trade rules, they will use the multilateral system of settling disputes instead of taking action unilaterally. That means abiding by the agreed procedures, and respecting judgments.

A dispute arises when one country adopts a trade policy measure or takes some action that one or more fellow-WTO members considers to be breaking the WTO agreements, or to be a failure to live up to obligations. A third group of countries can declare that they have an interest in the case and enjoy some rights.

---

\* This is related to the "process and production methods" (PPM) debate concerning Article XX discussed later in this chapter (see Section 11.2.1).

† Although some commentators are correct in noting that all inefficiencies due to negative externalities or positive spillovers could be "corrected" by taxes or subsidies, respectively (see LeClair and Franceschi 2006; Plofchan 1992), not all of these "inefficiency corrections" are allowed under Article XX of the GATT.

‡ Winter (2000, p. 241) comments that this is a dictum rather than a binding holding of the shrimp-turtle case discussed in Section 11.2.1.

§ The requirements articulated in this paragraph derive both from the language of Article XX and from cases following Appellate Body review of panel decisions interpreting that article that have become WTO law. See the excerpt from the panel decision on asbestos in Section 11.2.2. See also WTO (2009), "WTO Rules and Environmental Policies: GATT Exceptions," found by searching www.wto.org/ for "Article XX AND exceptions" (accessed May 18, 2010).

A procedure for settling disputes existed under the old GATT, but it had no fixed timetables, rulings were easier to block, and many cases dragged on for a long time inconclusively. The Uruguay Round agreement introduced a more structured process with more clearly defined stages in the procedure. It introduced greater discipline for the length of time a case should take to be settled, with flexible deadlines set in various stages of the procedure. The agreement emphasizes that prompt settlement is essential if the WTO is to function effectively. It sets out in considerable detail the procedures and the timetable to be followed in resolving disputes. If a case runs its full course to a first ruling, it should not normally take more than about one year—15 months if the case is appealed. The agreed time limits are flexible, and if the case is considered urgent (for example, if perishable goods are involved), it is accelerated as much as possible.

The Uruguay Round agreement also made it impossible for the country losing a case to block the adoption of the ruling. Under the previous GATT procedure, rulings could only be adopted by consensus, meaning that a single objection could block the ruling. Now, rulings are automatically adopted unless there is a consensus to reject a ruling, that is, any country wanting to block a ruling has to persuade all other WTO members (including its adversary in the case) to share its view.

Although much of the procedure does resemble a court or tribunal, the preferred solution is for the countries concerned to discuss their problems and settle the dispute by themselves. The first stage is therefore consultations between the governments concerned, and even when the case has progressed to other stages, consultation and mediation are still always possible.

### How long to settle a dispute?

These approximate periods for each stage of a dispute settlement procedure are target figures, that is, the agreement is flexible. In addition, the countries can settle their dispute themselves at any stage. Totals are also approximate.

| | |
|---|---|
| 60 days | Consultations, mediation, etc. |
| 45 days | Panel set up and panelists appointed |
| 6 months | Final panel report to parties |
| 3 weeks | Final panel report to WTO members |
| 60 days | Dispute Settlement Body adopts report (if no appeal) |
| **Total = 1 year** | **(without appeal)** |
| 60–90 days | Appeals report |
| 30 days | Dispute Settlement Body adopts appeals report |
| **Total = 1y 3m** | **(with appeal)** |

### How are disputes settled?

[See Figure 11.1 for a visual road map.]
Settling disputes is the responsibility of the Dispute Settlement Body (the General Council in another guise), which consists of all WTO members. The Dispute Settlement Body has the sole authority to establish "panels" of experts to consider the case, and to accept or reject the panels' findings or the results of an appeal. It monitors the implementation of the rulings and recommendations, and has the power to authorize retaliation when a country does not comply with a ruling.

**First stage:** consultation (up to **60 days**). Before taking any other actions the countries in dispute have to talk to each other to see if they can settle their differences by themselves. If that fails, they can also ask the WTO director-general to mediate or try to help in any other way.

**Second stage:** the panel (up to **45 days** for a panel to be appointed, plus 6 months for the panel to conclude). If consultations fail, the complaining country can ask for a panel to be appointed. The country "in the dock" can block the creation of a panel once, but when the Dispute Settlement Body meets for a second time, the appointment can no longer be blocked (unless there is a consensus against appointing the panel).

Officially, the panel is helping the Dispute Settlement Body make rulings or recommendations. But because the panel's report can only be rejected by consensus in the Dispute Settlement Body, its conclusions are difficult to overturn. The panel's findings have to be based on the agreements cited.

The panel's final report should normally be given to the parties to the dispute within six months. In cases of urgency, including those concerning perishable goods, the deadline is shortened to three months.

The agreement describes in some detail how the panels are to work. The main stages are:

- **Before the first hearing:** each side in the dispute presents its case in writing to the panel.
- **First hearing: the case for the complaining country and defense:** the complaining country (or countries), the responding country, and those that have announced they have an interest in the dispute, make their case at the panel's first hearing.
- **Rebuttals:** the countries involved submit written rebuttals and present oral arguments at the panel's second meeting.
- **Experts:** if one side raises scientific or other technical matters, the panel may consult experts or appoint an expert review group to prepare an advisory report.
- **First draft:** the panel submits the descriptive (factual and argument) sections of its report to the two sides, giving them two weeks to comment. This report does not include findings and conclusions.
- **Interim report:** The panel then submits an interim report, including its findings and conclusions, to the two sides, giving them one week to ask for a review.

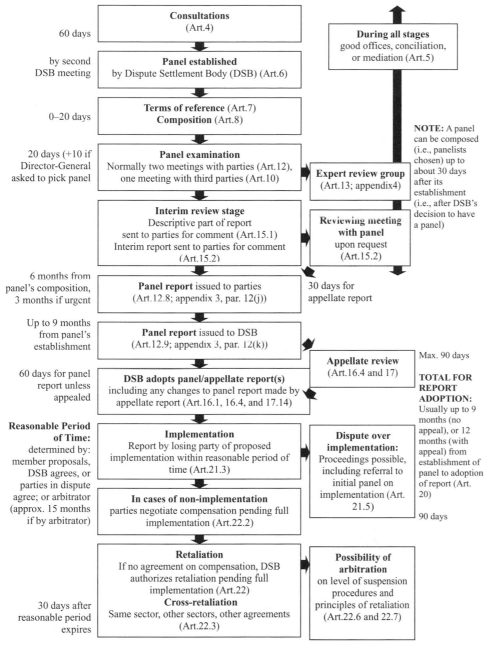

**FIGURE 11.1: SCHEMATIC OF THE WTO DISPUTE-RESOLUTION PROCESS**
Note: Some specified times are maximums, some are minimums; some are binding, some are not.
Source: Adapted from WTO (2011).

- **Review:** The period of review must not exceed two weeks. During that time, the panel may hold additional meetings with the two sides.
- **Final report:** A final report is submitted to the two sides and three weeks later, it is circulated to all WTO members. If the panel decides that the disputed trade measure does break a WTO agreement or an obligation, it recommends that the measure be made to conform with WTO rules. The panel may suggest how this could be done.
- **The report becomes a ruling:** The report becomes the Dispute Settlement Body's ruling or recommendation within 60 days unless a con-

sensus rejects it. Both sides can appeal the report (and in some cases both sides do).

*Panels*

Panels are like tribunals. But unlike in a normal tribunal, the panelists are usually chosen in consultation with the countries in dispute. Only if the two sides cannot agree does the WTO director-general appoint them.

Panels consist of three (possibly five) experts from different countries who examine the evidence and decide who is right and who is wrong. The panel's report is passed to the Dispute Settlement Body, which can only reject the report by consensus.

Panelists for each case can be chosen from a permanent list of well-qualified candidates, or from elsewhere. They serve in their individual capacities. They cannot receive instructions from any government.

### *Appeals*

Either side can appeal a panel's ruling. Sometimes both sides do so. Appeals have to be based on points of law such as legal interpretation, i.e., they cannot re-examine existing evidence or examine new issues.

Each appeal is heard by three members of a permanent seven-member Appellate Body set up by the Dispute Settlement Body and broadly representing the range of WTO membership. Members of the Appellate Body have four-year terms. They have to be individuals with recognized standing in the field of law and international trade, not affiliated with any government.

The appeal can uphold, modify or reverse the panel's legal findings and conclusions.[*] Normally appeals should not last more than 60 days, with an absolute maximum of 90 days.

The Dispute Settlement Body has to accept or reject the appeals report within 30 days and rejection is only possible by consensus.

### The case has been decided: what next?

. . .

If a country has done something wrong, it should swiftly correct its fault. And if it continues to break an agreement, it should offer compensation or suffer a suitable penalty that has some bite.

Even once the case has been decided, there is more to do before trade sanctions (the conventional form of penalty) are imposed. The priority at this stage is for the losing "defendant" to bring its policy into line with the ruling or recommendations. The dispute settlement agreement stresses that "prompt compliance with recommendations or rulings of the DSB [Dispute Settlement Body] is essential in order to ensure effective resolution of disputes to the benefit of all Members."

If the country that is the target of the complaint loses, it must follow the recommendations of the panel report or the appeals report. It must state its intention to do so at a Dispute Settlement Body meeting held within 30 days of the report's adoption. If complying with the recommendation immediately proves impractical, the member will be given a "reasonable period of time" to do so. If it fails to act within this period, it has to enter into negotiations with the complaining country (or countries) in order to determine mutually-acceptable compensation, for

instance, tariff reductions in areas of particular interest to the complaining side.

If after 20 days, no satisfactory compensation is agreed, the complaining side may ask the Dispute Settlement Body for permission to impose limited trade sanctions ("suspend concessions or obligations") against the other side.[†] The Dispute Settlement Body must grant this authorization within 30 days of the expiry of the "reasonable period of time" unless there is a consensus against the request.

In principle, the sanctions should be imposed in the same sector as the dispute. If this is not practical or if it would not be effective, the sanctions can be imposed in a different sector of the same agreement. In turn, if this is not effective or practicable and if the circumstances are serious enough, the action can be taken under another agreement. The objective is to minimize the chances of actions spilling over into unrelated sectors while at the same time allowing the actions to be effective.

In any case, the Dispute Settlement Body monitors how adopted rulings are implemented. Any outstanding case remains on its agenda until the issue is resolved.

## 11.1.5 The Prohibition against Subsidies

The Agreement on Subsidies and Countervailing Measures‡ provides prohibitions against "specific subsidies," which are "a subsidy available only to an enterprise or industry or groups of enterprises or industries within the jurisdiction of the authority granting the subsidy" in the context of export activities. The subsidies are "actionable," that is, subject to the WTO dispute machinery, if they are larger than certain minimal levels. Nonactionable subsidies are either nonspecific subsidies or "specific subsidies involving assistance to industrial research and pre-competitive developmental activity, assistance to disadvantaged regions, or certain types of assistance for adapting existing facilities to new environmental requirements imposed by law and/or regulations."

The United States used a 1984 law establishing the mechanism of foreign sales corporations to exempt a portion of income from foreign sales of its exports from

---

* Unlike U.S. courts of appeal, remanding the decision to the panel for reconsideration because of an error in law is not possible. See the later discussion in Section 11.2.4, where there was a difference of opinion between the panel and the Appellate Body regarding the appropriate trade law to apply.

† There is an argument that financial compensation (or the posting of financial bonds with a third party) is preferable to trade sanctions. Trade sanctions, while compensatory in nature, do not promote free trade unless they lead to a reduction in the offending initial tariffs or trade discrimination. Compensatory fines serve both a deterrent purpose and an efficiency benefit. Finally, some countries may not have significant market power to affect prices and hence may not be able to achieve sufficient deterrence (or gain sufficient revenues) by imposing countervailing tariffs. See Limao and Saggi (2006).

‡ See also Appendix 11-A.

tax. In 1997, the EU brought a complaint against the United States that the measures in the law constituted a prohibited subsidy under the GATT, and the dispute worked its way through a tortuous pathway provided by the WTO dispute-resolution system and remains unresolved. The United States lost the first round through the panel and appellate processes and was ordered to revise its law. The United States revised its law in 2000, but not to the satisfaction of the EU or the WTO, because some critics alleged that the prohibited subsidy remained. In 2004, the United States repealed the newer law, but the EU argued that this did not bring the U.S. tax scheme into conformity with its WTO obligations; the Appellate Body agreed and cleared the way for the EU to apply $4 billion annually in retaliatory countervailing duties on U.S. products. This case serves as a good example of the complexity and cumbersome nature of the WTO dispute-resolution system.[4] For an equally rocky process in the U.S.-EU steel wars, see Liebman and Tomlin (2008).

## 11.2 TRADE AND THE ENVIRONMENT (TRADE REGIMES AS CONSTRAINTS ON NATIONAL HEALTH, SAFETY, AND ENVIRONMENTAL POLICIES)

The relationship between trade, undertaken for economic benefit, and the environment is a complex one. Although most trade treaties do not have an overlap with environmental issues, those that do represent about 10 percent of all multilateral environmental agreements (MEAs) in force. We considered several of these in the previous chapter, where some treaties could actually be termed "environmental trade agreements." The WTO has identified fourteen agreements that include trade measures as tools to achieve health, safety, and environmental objectives.* These include treaties addressing trade in hazardous products, dangerous equipment and machinery, and hazardous waste; protection of endangered species; protection of the ozone layer; and climate change. In this chapter, we focus on those agreements that foster trade undertaken primarily for economic benefit, but that may require modification of otherwise free-trade practices for health, safety, or environmental reasons.

The WTO has long had a Committee on Trade and Environment (CTE) whose task is to make recommendations to the WTO's governing body in order to reconcile two sometimes opposing goals: economic benefit through trade and protection of health, safety, and the environment.[†] The balance of these two universally accepted goals is different in different trade agreements. Some are predominantly trade enhancing (like the GATT or the TBT), while others vary from containing a fair consideration of both to being mainly environmental (CITES). The committee has long struggled with issues that are still somewhat unresolved, such as whether a valid/actionable environmental concern of one country extends to the territory of another trading partner (extraterritoriality) and whether process and production methods (PPMs) are likewise actionable if they restrict trade.[‡] Also, a continuing point of contention is whether the precautionary principle applies to all trade agreements or just to some—that is, whether the precautionary principle is a recognized principle of international law that trumps specific trade agreements.

Aside from environmental, health, and safety provisions in the trade agreements themselves, a key issue is the legal import of MEAs for resolving trade disputes in agreements like the GATT or the TBT, for example, as dispositive or simply as relevant (and rebuttable) evidence that the health, safety, or environmental concern is a bona fide actionable concern as a matter of law. Winter (2000) argues that only if the party attempting to use one of the Article XX exceptions has signed an MEA can the MEA be used to establish the bona fide nature of the health or environmental concern, but this ignores the fact that the mere existence of an MEA is evidence that a recognized and bona fide environmental problem exists, irrespective of whether both parties or either party signed the agreement. The evidence is, of course, rebuttable, but a prima facie case will have been made in any event.

The principle of stare decisis in law requires a legal tribunal (such as those resolving disputes in the WTO)

---

\* The reader should consult UNEP (2002, 2007) for attempts to rationalize the tensions between trade and environmental goals. Also see ICTSD (2002) and WWF (2001).

---

† Unfortunately, the WTO insists that it is not in the business of environmental protection. At its website, it states: "The WTO is only competent to deal with trade. In other words, in environmental issues its only task is to study questions that arise when environmental policies have a significant impact on trade. The WTO is not an environmental agency. Its members do not want it to intervene in national or international environmental policies or to set environmental standards. Other agencies that specialize in environmental issues are better qualified to undertake those tasks." WTO, The Environment: A Specific Concern, www.wto.org/english/thewto_e/whatis_e/tif_e/bey2_e.htm (accessed May 18, 2010).

‡ The CTE did prepare a report in 1996 that it presented at the meeting in Singapore arguing the pros and cons of these issues and recommending that the WT0 resolve the opposing viewpoints, which, of course, it never has done explicitly (WTO 1996). However, this equivocal report did little more than identify the issues and did not lead to any policy actions.

to follow precedent (or depart from precedent with adequate explanation) in subsequent cases. Although this principle is not a procedural requirement under the GATT, the WTO seems to be following it (Carranza 2007–2008). Thus the evolution of cases involving the resolution of disputes should give guidance to the resolution of future disputes and the development of clear environmental policy vis-à-vis trade. The reliance on precedent reflects the practice of case-law development of law characteristic of the Anglo-Saxon legal systems originally derived from England, as opposed to the code-based Napoleonic or French legal systems used predominantly on the European Continent and francophone countries. The panel discussion in the asbestos case discussed below is replete with recitations of legal principles built on prior WTO cases. Thus, in order for one to "know what the trade law is" at any moment, one must refer to three sources: (1) the actual cases; (2) commentary and interpretation of those cases in the WTO websites and published documents; and (3) the writings of legal experts, predominantly in law-review articles, especially where issues are somewhat unresolved and not yet adjudicated in dispute resolution cases.

### 11.2.1 The Shrimp-Turtle Dispute and Article XX(g) of the GATT (Conservation of Natural Resources)

Although several environmental disputes were brought under Article XX(g), most never became full decisions of the WTO because they did not secure unanimous endorsement of the WTO members required under the so-called old rules of the GATT. The most recent and significant case brought under Article XX(g) involved the so-called shrimp-turtle dispute. Box 11.1 provides a capsule summary of the case.

This case is important on several fronts and has been the focus of much commentary. First, the Appellate Body dodged the broad question whether a country could claim an environmental "interest" even though the exporters' actions that brought about the restrictive import restrictions occurred in international waters. Thus, unlike the earlier tuna-dolphin cases, it did not address whether the "extraterritorial" nature of the objectionable consequences for nature conservancy was a reason to nullify the importer's restrictive measures.* The United States sought to have export-

ing nations agree to adopt turtle-saving devices in their own laws—in other words, to adopt U.S. law (along the lines of the Endangered Species Act) into their legal system. Because turtles found in international waters are also found in U.S. domestic waters, the Appellate Body simply found a reasonable nexus, stating that if a nexus was required, it existed under the facts of the case.[†]

Second, although the practices of the exporters involved PPMs and not the export of a harmful product per se, this did not nullify the importer's restrictions on the exporters' products. (The U.S. importer lost the case simply because the United States had not sought to negotiate the adoption of turtle-saving technology by other importers, giving rise to non-uniform treatment of ["unjustifiable discrimination" vis-à-vis] other nations.) Read in the broadest possible terms, the case brings PPM actions "under the umbrella of protection" of Article XX.

What is not decided is whether environmental damage restricted to the exporter's environment alone—as opposed to having a nexus with the international environment—is actionable. Further, if it is the exporter's workers' health that would be compromised, will this broad interpretation of the reach of Article XX(g) extend to worker and human health and safety under Article XX(a)? If this case is to have the expected precedential value in WTO case-law evolution (under the principle of stare decisis), it would seem difficult to argue against this logical extension of allowable protections. Indeed, Charnovitz (2002) has made a most persuasive case on this point.

### 11.2.2 Asbestos and Section XX(b) of the GATT (Protection of Human and Animal Life and Health)

Reproduced below is an excerpt (italicized in places to facilitate emphases for pedagogical purposes) from the Panel Opinion on Chrysotile Asbestos,[‡] perhaps

---

the catch put the activity beyond the reach of United States import sanctions, but the second case did not use this rationale as a disqualifying action on the part of the United States. Neither case ever became WTO law because under the rules at the time, the required unanimous assent of all the members of the WTO to the decisions of the dispute resolution panels was not secured.

† See Howse (2002, p. 504), who argues that "the purpose of a territorial nexus is to prevent a state that lacks legitimate concern from using a global environmental problem as a pretext for protectionist intervention." Of course, the crucial question is what constitutes a "legitimate concern."

‡ The carcinogen asbestos is acknowledged to be the most notorious example of an occupational health hazard. The product is banned in several countries and severely restricted in others.

---

* These cases involved the United States prohibition of imports of tuna caught in international waters using techniques that also snared dolphins, an endangered species. In the first tuna-dolphin case, it was decided that the extra-territorial nature of

# BOX 11.1: UNITED STATES—IMPORT PROHIBITION OF CERTAIN SHRIMP AND SHRIMP PRODUCTS

## WTO CASE NOS. 58 (AND 61). RULING ADOPTED ON 6 NOVEMBER 1998

Seven species of sea turtles have to date been identified. They are distributed around the world in subtropical and tropical areas. They spend their lives at sea, where they migrate between their foraging and nesting grounds.

Sea turtles have been adversely affected by human activity, either directly (their meat, shells and eggs have been exploited), or indirectly (incidental capture in fisheries, destruction of their habitats, pollution of the oceans).

In early 1997, India, Malaysia, Pakistan and Thailand brought a joint complaint against a ban imposed by the US on the importation of certain shrimp and shrimp products. The protection of sea turtles was at the heart of the ban.

The US Endangered Species Act of 1973 listed as endangered or threatened the five species of sea turtles that occur in US waters, and prohibited their "take" within the US, in its territorial sea and the high seas. ("Take" means harassment, hunting, capture, killing or attempting to do any of these.)

Under the act, the US required that US shrimp trawlers use "turtle excluder devices" (TEDs) in their nets when fishing in areas where there is a significant likelihood of encountering sea turtles.

Section 609 of US Public Law 101-102, enacted in 1989, dealt with imports. It said, among other things, that shrimp harvested with technology that may adversely affect certain sea turtles may not be imported into the US—unless the harvesting nation was certified to have a regulatory programme and an incidental take-rate comparable to that of the US, or that the particular fishing environment of the harvesting nation did not pose a threat to sea turtles.

In practice, countries that had any of the five species of sea turtles within their jurisdiction, and harvested shrimp with mechanical means, had to impose on their fishermen requirements comparable to those borne by US shrimpers if they wanted to be certified to export shrimp products to the US. Essentially this meant the use of TEDs at all time. . . .

In its report, the Appellate Body made clear that under WTO rules, countries have the right to take trade action to protect the environment (in particular, human, animal or plant life and health) and endangered species and exhaustible resources). The WTO does not have to "allow" them this right.

It also said measures to protect sea turtles would be legitimate under GATT Article 20 (i.e. XX) which deals with various exceptions to the WTO's trade rules, provided certain criteria such as non-discrimination were met.

The US lost the case, not because it sought to protect the environment but because it discriminated between WTO members. It provided countries in the western hemisphere—mainly in the Caribbean—technical and financial assistance and longer transition periods for their fishermen to start using turtle-excluder devices.

It did not give the same advantages, however, to the four Asian countries (India, Malaysia, Pakistan and Thailand) that filed the complaint with the WTO.

The ruling also said WTO panels may accept "amicus briefs" (friends of the court submissions) from NGOs or other interested parties.

## LEGALLY SPEAKING . . .

The Panel considered that the ban imposed by the US was inconsistent with GATT Article XI (which limits the use of import prohibitions or restrictions), and could not be justified under GATT Article XX (which deals with general exceptions to the rules, including for certain environmental reasons).

Following an appeal, the Appellate Body found that the measure at stake did qualify for provisional justification under Article XX(g), but failed to meet the requirements of the chapeau (the introductory paragraph) of Article XX (which defines when the general exceptions can be cited).

The Appellate Body therefore concluded that the US measure was not justified under Article XX of GATT (strictly speaking, "GATT 1994," i.e. the current version of the General Agreement on Tariffs and Trade as modified by the 1994 Uruguay Round agreement).

At the request of Malaysia, the original panel in this case considered the measures taken by the United States to comply with the recommendations and rulings of the Dispute Settlement Body. The panel report for this recourse was appealed by Malaysia. The Appellate Body upheld the panel's findings that the US measure was now applied in a manner that met the requirements of Article XX of the GATT 1994. . . .

## What the Appellate Body said:

185. In reaching these conclusions, we wish to underscore what we have *not* decided in this appeal. We have *not* decided that the protection and preservation of the environment is of no significance to the Members of the WTO. Clearly, it is. We have *not* decided that the sovereign nations that are Members of the WTO cannot adopt effective measures to protect endangered species, such as sea turtles. Clearly, they can and should. And we have *not* decided that sovereign states should not act together bilaterally, plurilaterally or multilaterally, either within the WTO or in other international fora, to protect endangered species or to otherwise protect the environment. Clearly, they should and do.

186. What we *have* decided in this appeal is simply this: although the measure of the United States in dispute in this appeal serves an environmental objective that is recognized as legitimate under paragraph (g) of Article

(continued)

XX of the GATT 1994, this measure has been applied by the United States in a manner which constitutes arbitrary and unjustifiable discrimination between Members of the WTO, contrary to the requirements of the chapeau of Article XX. For all of the specific reasons outlined in this Report, this measure does not qualify for the exemption that Article XX of the GATT 1994 affords to measures which serve certain recognized, legitimate environmental purposes but which, at the same time, are not applied in a manner that constitutes a means of arbitrary or unjustifiable discrimination between countries where the same conditions prevail or a disguised restriction on international trade. As we emphasized in *United States—Gasoline* [adopted 20 May 1996, WT/DS2/AB/R, p. 30], WTO Members are free to adopt their own policies aimed at protecting the environment as long as, in so doing, they fulfill their obligations and respect the rights of other Members under the *WTO Agreement*.

Source: WTO, *India etc. versus US: "Shrimp-Turtle,"* www.wto.org/english/tratop_e/envir_e/edis08_e.htm (accessed February 13, 2009).

the most important decision regarding the reach of Section XX(b) of the GATT. Note the panel's recitation of many prior decisions, such as *Thailand-Cigarettes* and *United States–Gasoline*, in the opinion, evidencing the emergence of case-based precedent in WTO lawmaking. Note also that no risk assessment or direct evidence of the carcinogenicity of *chrysotile* asbestos was performed by France, because the basis of the French ban using a Section XX(b) exception allowed a precautionary approach that relied on the well-documented carcinogenicity of *amphibole* asbestos, a closely related but not identical form of asbestos. Finally, note that the EU takes on the role of representing an EU member country in WTO proceedings rather than have the country represent itself. This practice of the EU being the relevant party having standing in international treaty negotiations and disputes is a feature of evolving EU law (see Chapter 10).

### WORLD TRADE ORGANIZATION
### WT/DS135/R 18 September 2000 (00-3353)

### EUROPEAN COMMUNITIES—MEASURES AFFECTING ASBESTOS AND ASBESTOS-CONTAINING PRODUCTS
*Report of the Panel on European Communities—Measures Affecting Asbestos and Asbestos-Containing Products.*

### 4. Applicability of Article XX of the GATT 1994

a. Arguments of the parties

8.160  The European Communities contend that the Decree falls under the exception provided in Article XX of the GATT 1994. Thus, the Decree is necessary to achieve the French Government's public health goals under Article XX(b) and is not applied in such a manner as to constitute a means of arbitrary or unjustifiable discrimination between countries where the same conditions prevail or a disguised restriction

on international trade, within the meaning of the introductory clause of Article XX.

8.161  Canada notes that, in accordance with panel and Appellate Body practice, Article XX permits a limited and conditional exception from the obligations set out in the other Articles of the GATT and must be interpreted narrowly. Although the European Communities assert that they have the right to establish the level of protection they desire, in so doing they must comply with their obligations. In this connection, *the Appellate Body has condemned abuse of rights under Article XX. Moreover, it is up to the European Communities to demonstrate that the Decree falls under Article XX(b).*

8.162  The European Communities argue that asbestos fibres and products containing them are a proven hazard for human health. The risks linked to the use of these fibres are recognized both by scientists and international organizations. By prohibiting the marketing and use of asbestos and asbestos-containing products, the Decree seeks to halt the spread of these risks, in particular for people occasionally and often unwittingly exposed to asbestos, and thereby reduce the number of deaths among the French population. It is the only measure capable of preventing the spread of the risks due to asbestos exposure. *According to the EC, the review in the light of Article XX cannot be allowed to undermine the health protection goal set by the Member concerned. Its sole purpose must be to assess whether the trade measure adopted is necessary to attain that goal. This test concerns the trade measure and not the level of protection set by the Member.*

8.163  Canada considers that the only exposures that could be affected by the Decree are exposures to chrysotile encapsulated in high-density products. In order to determine whether there is an equally effective alternative that is less restrictive for international trade and that is capable of protecting human life or health just as effectively, the health risk can and must be examined. Otherwise any country could cite the risk—real or not—in support of a prohibition measure.

8.164 Canada is of the opinion that the current uses of chrysotile do not constitute a detectable risk to human health. . . . Contrary to what the EC appear to believe, controlled use substantially reduces exposure. As a result of pre-fabrication, pre-machining, the use of fittings and compliance with work standards, workers are not subjected to high levels of exposure, as the EC claim.

8.165 Canada considers that, inasmuch as the only risk associated with asbestos is that of the past use of amphiboles and the use of friable materials, the Decree, which prohibits the contemporary uses of chrysotile, is not "necessary" to protect human life or health from the risks associated with past uses of asbestos. A ban is not "necessary" because high-density chrysotile products do not pose any detectable risk. On the other hand, controlled use indisputably constitutes an alternative to a total ban that is significantly less restrictive for international trade.

b. Approach adopted by the Panel and burden of proof
i. *Introductory remarks concerning the approach adopted by the Panel*

. . .

8.168 First of all, as regards Article XX(b), we find that the provisions of this paragraph relevant to the present case require that, subject to fulfillment of the conditions of the introductory clause of Article XX, nothing in the GATT 1994 shall be construed to prevent the adoption or enforcement by any Member of measures

"(b) necessary to protect human . . . life or health"

8.169 The Panel notes that in *United States–Gasoline*, the Panel stipulated that with respect to Article XX(b), the party invoking that provision must prove:

(a) That the policy in respect of the measures for which Article XX is invoked falls within the range of policies designed to protect human life or health; and

(b) the inconsistent measures for which the exception is invoked are necessary to fulfill the policy objective.

8.170 As regards subparagraph (a), we consider that, inasmuch as they include the notion of "protection," the words "policies designed to protect human life or health" imply the existence of a *health risk*. We must therefore determine, on the basis of the relevant rules of evidence, whether chrysotile-asbestos, in the various forms we have considered so far, poses a risk to human life or health. . . .

8.172 As regards the criterion of the *necessity* of the measure (subparagraph (b) of paragraph 8.169), we note that previous panels that had to assess the "necessity" of a measure under Article XX(b) appear to have done so solely in relation to the existence of other measures consistent or less inconsistent with the GATT in the light of the health objective pursued. Thus, in *Thailand-Cigarettes*, the Panel ruled that:

"The import restrictions imposed by Thailand could be considered to be "necessary" in terms of Article XX(b) only if there were no alternative measure consistent with the General Agreement, or less inconsistent with it, which Thailand could reasonably be expected to employ to achieve its health policy objectives."

8.173 In this particular case, the public health objectives pursued by Thailand were confirmed by a WHO expert and accepted by the parties to the dispute. In the present case, Canada does not deny that France's goal, namely to protect the health of workers and consumers, is a public health objective, but it disputes the existence of a public health problem in relation to chrysotile. Thus, Canada denies that chrysotile fibre poses a public health risk in its applications because once in place chrysotile-cement does not release any fibres and because it is possible to work with chrysotile-cement products in a safe or controlled fashion. . . .

(ii) Burden of proof

. . .

Considerations specific to the burden of proof as regards the scientific aspects

8.179 As pointed out above, three essential elements must be considered by the Panel when examining the justification of a measure in the light of Article XX(b): (a) the existence of a risk for human health; (b) the level of protection which the Member concerned wishes to achieve; and (c) the existence of other measures consistent or less inconsistent with the GATT 1994 and enabling the same objective of protecting public health to be obtained. The Panel considers that its examination of the scientific data should be exclusively concerned with points (a) and (c), inasmuch as it has long been established that Members are free to set the level of protection of their choice for their populations.

8.180 The Panel has therefore had to determine how it should assess the existence of a health risk in relation to chrysotile and, more particularly, chrysotile-cement and the necessity of the measures in question. The Panel has examined the practice in relation to Article XX of the GATT 1994, but also in the context of other WTO Agreements in which scientific studies are invoked, mainly the Agreement on Sanitary and Phytosanitary Measures. The Panel noted that the SPS Agreement contains more detailed provisions than Article XX with respect to the scientific justification of a sanitary or phytosanitary measure and that these provisions have been the subject of clarifications by panels and by the Appellate Body. However, it also noted that in the first dispute settlement proceedings initiated under the WTO Agreement concerning Article XX of the GATT 1994, the Appellate Body had not sought to extend the principles of the SPS Agreement to the examination of the measures for which Article XX(b) had been invoked or even to base itself on them, although the SPS Agreement was already in force.[5] The Panel preferred to confine itself to the provisions of the

GATT 1994 and to the criteria defined by the practice relating to the application of Article XX.

8.181 In this context, in relation to the scientific information submitted by the parties and the experts, *the Panel feels bound to point out that it is not its function to settle a scientific debate, not being composed of experts in the field of the possible human health risks posed by asbestos. Consequently, the Panel does not intend to set itself up as an arbiter of the opinions expressed by the scientific community.*

8.182 Its role, taking into account the burden of proof, is to determine whether there is sufficient scientific evidence to conclude that there exists a risk for human life or health and that the measures taken by France are necessary in relation to the objectives pursued. *The Panel therefore considers that it should base its conclusions with respect to the existence of a public health risk on the scientific evidence put forward by the parties and the comments of the experts consulted within the context of the present case. The opinions expressed by the experts we have consulted will help us to understand and evaluate the evidence submitted and the arguments advanced by the parties. The same approach will be adopted with respect to the necessity of the measure concerned.*

8.183 In proceeding with this exercise, the Panel will have to make a pragmatic assessment of the scientific situation and the measures available, as would the decision-makers responsible for the adoption of a health policy. In this connection, it notes that the determination of the existence of other measures consistent or less inconsistent with the GATT largely depends on a scientific assessment of the risk. In any event, this determination cannot be interpreted as restricting the freedom of Members to take certain measures rather than others under Article XX(b), in the absence of a measure that would be consistent or less inconsistent with the GATT 1994.

(c) Application of Article XX(b) of the GATT 1994 to the Decree
(i) "Protection of human life and health"
. . .

8.186 In principle, a policy that seeks to reduce exposure to a risk should fall within the range of policies designed to protect human life or health, insofar as a risk exists. According to the EC, the international scientific community appears to be generally of the opinion that chrysotile fibres as such are carcinogens. In this connection, we note the EC's argument that, since 1977, the International Agency for Research on Cancer (IARC) has classified chrysotile among the proven carcinogens.

8.187 Canada does not dispute that chrysotile asbestos causes lung cancer. However, Canada argues that the mechanism that could give rise to an increased risk of lung cancer has not yet been fully explained and that the link with chrysotile might only be indirect. This risk depends on the intensity and duration of the

exposure. On the other hand, according to Canada, there is a great deal of scientific evidence to support the thesis according to which chrysotile does not cause mesotheliomas. In particular, the mesotheliomas linked to asbestos could be the result of exposure to low-density products containing amphiboles. It has not been established that, in their uses, chrysotile fibres pose the same risk as amphiboles, whose chemical composition, in particular, is different.
. . .

8.189 We note, however, that Canada makes a distinction between chrysotile fibres and chrysotile encapsulated in a cement matrix. In fact, Canada challenges the Decree insofar as it prohibits, *inter alia,* the use of chrysotile-cement products. In this connection, we note that the experts consulted by the Panel agreed that the risks of fibres being dispersed due to the degradation of chrysotile-cement were limited. However, the experts acknowledged that working with non-friable products containing chrysotile might result in the dispersion of large quantities of fibres and that those fibres pose a definite health risk. The experts also noted that even though the risk might be lower than for production or processing workers, it concerned a much larger group.

8.190 In this respect, the Panel notes that the European Communities have stated that the Decree is intended, in particular, to protect categories of workers or consumers downstream of the asbestos mining or processing stage, whatever the frequency and level of their exposure. Canada considers that below a certain exposure threshold there is no detectable health risk. Accordingly, Canada believes that people only occasionally exposed are not running a detectable risk. . . .

8.193 The Panel . . . considers that the evidence before it tends to show that handling chrysotile-cement products constitutes a risk to health rather than the opposite. Accordingly, a decision-maker responsible for taking public health measures might reasonably conclude that the presence of chrysotile-cement products posed a risk because of the risks involved in working with those products.

*8.194 . . . The Panel concludes therefore that the French policy of prohibiting chrysotile asbestos falls within the range of policies designed to protect human life or health, within the meaning of Article XX(b) of the GATT 1994.*

8.195 Accordingly, the Panel will now turn to the question of whether the measure is "necessary" within the meaning of Article XX(b).
(ii) "Necessary"
The ban on chrysotile asbestos in its various forms
. . .

8.198 We note that in *Thailand-Cigarettes* the Panel defined the test of necessity applicable under Article XX(b):

> "The import restrictions imposed by Thailand could be considered to be 'necessary' in terms of Article XX(b) only if there were no alternative measure consistent with the General Agreement, or less inconsistent with it, which

Thailand could reasonably be expected to employ to achieve its health policy objectives." . . .

8.202 . . . The experts confirm the position of the European Communities according to which it has not been possible to identify any threshold below which exposure to chrysotile would have no effect. . . .

*8.203 In the light of the above, the Panel concludes that, in addition to the risk presented by low-density friable products, there is an undeniable public health risk in relation to the chrysotile contained in high-density chrysotile-cement products. This risk exists even at low or intermittent exposure levels and can affect a broad section of the population. . . .*

*8.207 We therefore find that in order to determine whether a measure is necessary it is important to assess whether consistent or less inconsistent measures are reasonably available. . . .*

*We consider that the existence of a reasonably available measure must be assessed in the light of the economic and administrative realities facing the Member concerned but also by taking into account the fact that the State must provide itself with the means of implementing its policies. . . .*

8.209 In relation to the first of these considerations, we note, first of all, that although controlled use is applied in some countries, such as the United States or Canada, and has also been applied by France, in general in certain sectors its efficacy still remains to be demonstrated. This is confirmed by a number of studies, as well as by the comments of the experts. Thus, even though it seems possible to apply controlled use successfully upstream (mining and manufacturing) or downstream (removal and destruction) of product use, it would seem to be much less easy to apply it in the building sector, which is one of the areas more particularly targeted by the measures contained in the Decree. The Panel therefore concludes that, in view of the difficulties of application of controlled use, an official in charge of public health policy might reasonably consider that controlled use did not provide protection that was adequate in relation to the policy objectives. . . .

8.214 Moreover, while controlled use may seem difficult to apply in the building sector, it is even less feasible in the case of DIY enthusiasts or undeclared workers operating outside any proper framework or system of controls. France's objective is to halt the spread of the risks associated with chrysotile. At least as far as DIY enthusiasts are concerned, controlled use is not a reasonably available option. In this context, the fact that controlled use might be reasonably available in other sectors is irrelevant. *Here, we are concerned with a product that could be installed in people's homes, not one limited to a restricted use in areas in which only professionals would be required to work.* Insofar as, once the products have been installed, it is impossible to guarantee that they will not be handled by someone who will not follow controlled use practices, it seems to us that a decision-maker responsible for adopting a

health policy might well conclude that there was still a flaw in the health protection system if only controlled use measures were applied. . . .

*8.217 We therefore conclude that the European Communities have shown that controlled use is neither effective nor reasonably available, at least in the building sector and for DIY enthusiasts. Accordingly, controlled use does not constitute a reasonable alternative to the banning of chrysotile asbestos that might be chosen by a decision-maker responsible for developing public health measures, bearing in mind the objectives pursued by France.*

*Recourse to substitute fibres and products*

. . .

8.219 The European Communities argue that the Decree does not recommend the indiscriminate use of substitute products. It leaves it to businesses to replace asbestos by whichever product they choose. In view of the procedure laid down in Article 2 of the Decree, the replacement of asbestos fibres by substitute fibres is the result of a reasonable and justified process.

8.220 The Panel notes, first of all, that the risk posed by chrysotile is recognized internationally, which in itself may justify the taking of measures to restrict its use. On the other hand, we find that the substitute fibres examined in the context of this case (PVA, cellulose and glass) are not classified by the WHO at the same level of risk as chrysotile. . . .

*Conclusion*

*8.222 In the light of France's public health objectives as presented by the European Communities, the Panel concludes that the EC has made a prima facie case for the non-existence of a reasonably available alternative to the banning of chrysotile and chrysotile-cement products and recourse to substitute products. Canada has not rebutted the presumption established by the EC. We also consider that the EC's position is confirmed by the comments of the experts consulted in the course of this proceeding.*

*8.223 At this stage, we conclude that the Decree satisfies the conditions of Article XX(b) of the GATT 1994. . . .*

(d) Application of the introductory clause (chapeau) of Article XX of the GATT 1994 to the application of the Decree
(i) "Means of arbitrary or unjustifiable discrimination between countries where the same conditions prevail"

*8.224 . . . The ban is not a means of imposing arbitrary or unjustifiable discrimination between countries where the same conditions prevail. It covers products originating in any country, including France, where the same conditions prevail. . . .*

8.227 The Panel also notes that, in *United States–Gasoline*, the Appellate Body stated that *the word "discrimination" in the introductory clause of Article XX covers both discrimination between products from different supplier countries and discrimination between domestic and imported products.* Finally, in the same case, the Appellate Body ruled that "the provisions of the chapeau [of Article XX] cannot logically refer to the same standard(s) by which a violation of a substantive rule has been determined to have occurred." In other words, we cannot conclude that discrimination exists on the basis of the violation of Article III:4 identified above. This means that the less favourable treatment of asbestos as compared with substitute fibres identified by Canada is not relevant for establishing the existence of discrimination under Article XX. The question is therefore confined to the suppliers of asbestos, whether domestic or foreign. However, we understand that another form of discrimination, for example between supplier countries, not invoked by Canada as its principal argument, could be taken into consideration under the introductory clause of Article XX. It is on this dual basis that we shall examine whether the measure is being applied in a "discriminatory" manner....

*8.230 In accordance with our approach, since discrimination has not been established in relation to the application of the Decree, there is no need to consider the question of its arbitrariness or unjustifiability.*

(ii) "Disguised restriction on international trade"

8.231 According to the EC, the Decree does not constitute a "disguised restriction on international trade."...

8.232 Canada considers that the Decree is a "disguised restriction on international trade."...

8.235 However, the remark made by the Appellate Body in *United State–Gasoline* also implies that the expression "disguised restriction on international trade" covers other requirements. In the same case, the Appellate Body mentions that "'disguised restriction' includes disguised *discrimination* in international trade."... In this respect, we note that in the above-mentioned case the Appellate Body considered that:

> "'disguised restriction,' whatever else it covers, may properly be read as embracing restrictions amounting to arbitrary or unjustifiable discrimination in international trade taken under the guise of a measure formally within the terms of an exception listed in Article XX. Put in a somewhat different manner, the kinds of considerations pertinent in deciding whether the application of a particular measure amounts to 'arbitrary or unjustifiable discrimination,' may also be taken into account in determining the presence of a 'disguised restriction' on international trade. The fundamental theme is to be found in the purpose and object of avoiding abuse or illegitimate use of the exceptions to substantive rules available in Article XX."

*8.236 ... In accordance with the approach defined in Article 31 of the Vienna Convention, we note that, as ordinarily understood, the verb "to disguise" implies an intention....*

*8.239 ... In fact, the information made available to the Panel does not suggest that the import ban has benefited the French substitute fibre industry, to the detriment of third country producers, to such an extent as to lead to the conclusion that the Decree has been so*

*applied as to constitute a disguised restriction on international trade. ...*

**5. Conclusion**

*8.241 In the light of the above, the Panel concludes that the provisions of the Decree which violate Article III:4 of the GATT 1994 are justified under Article XX(b).*

## 11.2.3 Trade and Standards under the WTO Agreements

It should be reemphasized that the GATT is a trade regime and that the governments that participate in WTO deliberations, as well as those that make up specific panels to resolve trade disputes and the Appellate Body itself, are committed first and foremost to promoting unencumbered trade. To this end, regularizing and harmonizing trade practices receive major attention. One aspect of this harmonization is the adoption of voluntary health, safety, and environmental guidelines and standards, as well as occasional binding standards (that is, regulations).* Although Section XX(b) and (g) exceptions to nontariff trade barriers clearly allow each nation to establish the degree of health, safety, and environmental protection for itself even if trade is consequently hampered,† this runs afoul of the overwhelming desire of industry, and the government trade representatives they influence, to prefer uniform minimum protection. This is evidenced in the shrimp-turtle dispute discussed earlier, where the WTO Appellate Body expressed preferences for the

---

\* The tension between voluntary guidelines and mandatory health, safety, and environmental standards in the United States is discussed in Chapter 9. For example, the American National Standards Institute (ANSI), the National Fire Protection Association (NFPA), and the American Conference of Governmental and Industrial Hygienists (ACGIH) are U.S.-based independent standards-negotiating bodies created to harmonize industrial practices, partly to promote minimum liability of the private sector for harm by establishing minimally acceptable codes of conduct. These standards are largely industry standards. However, they have often been adopted into law (see especially Section 9.2.1 on their adoption under the Occupational Safety and Health Act as minimum federal standards). But beyond these standards, the Department of Labor is expected to establish more protective standards through government regulatory processes in which the beneficiaries of those standards—i.e., workers—as well as affected industries can participate. New standards are almost always more protective and create greater burdens for industry. Independent standard-setting organizations exist at the international level as well, e.g., the International Standards Organization (ISO), known for its voluntary environmental standard ISO 14000 and its voluntary workplace standard ISO 9000.

† In addition to differences in the extent of protection preferred among nations, nations also differ in their application of a precautionary approach when there is scientific uncertainty about the nature of the harm that protection targets.

imposition of international standards instead of unilateral practices.

The tension between encouraging harmonization and allowing individual nations to adopt their own protection philosophies unilaterally also finds expression in contradictions among the various agreements under the WTO umbrella regarding the role of scientific uncertainty and the extent to which the precautionary approach is tolerated. These contradictions are particularly acute among the GATT and the TBT and SPS agreements.

The WTO states:[6]

Article 20 of the General Agreement on Tariffs and Trade (GATT) allows governments to act on trade in order to protect human, animal or plant life or health, provided they do not discriminate or use this as disguised protectionism. In addition, there are two specific WTO agreements dealing with food safety and animal and plant health and safety [the SPS agreement], and with product standards in general [the TBT agreement]. Both try to identify how to meet the need to apply standards and at the same time avoid protectionism in disguise. . . . In both cases, if a country applies international standards, it is less likely to be challenged legally in the WTO than if it sets its own standards. . . .

The *Sanitary and Phytosanitary Measures Agreement (SPS)* sets out the basic rules. It allows countries to set their own standards. But it also says regulations must be based on science. They should be applied only to the extent necessary to protect human, animal or plant life or health.[7] And they should not arbitrarily or unjustifiably discriminate between countries where identical or similar conditions prevail.

Member countries are encouraged to use international standards, guidelines and recommendations where they exist. When they do, they are unlikely to be challenged legally in a WTO dispute. However, members may use measures which result in higher standards if there is scientific justification.[*] They can also set higher standards based on appropriate assessment of risks so long as the approach is consistent, not arbitrary. And they can to some extent apply the "precautionary principle," a kind of "safety first" approach to deal with scientific uncertainty. Article 5.7 of the SPS Agreement allows temporary "precautionary" measures.[†] . . . The agreement complements that on technical barriers to trade [TBT].

Technical regulations and standards
Technical regulations and standards are important, but they vary from country to country. Having too many different standards makes life difficult for producers and exporters. If the standards are set arbitrarily, they could be used as an excuse for protectionism. Standards can become obstacles to trade. But they are also necessary for a range of reasons, from environmental protection, safety, national security to consumer information. And they can help trade. Therefore the same basic question arises again: how to ensure that standards are genuinely useful, and not arbitrary or an excuse for protectionism.

The *Technical Barriers to Trade Agreement (TBT)* [‡] tries to ensure that regulations, standards, testing and certification procedures do not create unnecessary obstacles. However, the agreement also recognizes countries' rights to adopt the standards they consider appropriate—for example, for human, animal or plant life or health, for the protection of the environment or to meet other consumer interests. Moreover, members are not prevented from taking measures necessary to ensure their standards are met. But that is counterbalanced with disciplines. A myriad of regulations can be a nightmare for manufacturers and exporters. Life can be simpler if governments apply international standards, and the agreement encourages them to do so. In any case, whatever regulations they use should not discriminate.

The agreement also sets out a code of good practice for both governments and non-governmental or industry bodies to prepare, adopt and apply voluntary standards. Over 200 standards-setting bodies apply the code.

The agreement says the procedures used to decide whether a product conforms with relevant standards have to be fair and equitable. It discourages any methods that would give domestically produced goods an unfair advantage. The agreement also encourages countries to recognize each other's procedures for assessing whether a product conforms. Without recognition, products might have to be tested twice, first by the exporting country and then by the importing country.

Manufacturers and exporters need to know what the latest standards are in their prospective markets. To help ensure that this information is made available conveniently, all WTO member governments are required to establish national enquiry points[§] and to keep each other informed through the WTO—around 900 new or changed regulations are notified each year. The Technical Barriers to Trade Committee is the major clearing house for members to share the information and the major forum to discuss concerns about the regulations and their implementation.

---

*       For a good description of the SPS and TBT agreements and a general defense of the view that standards should be based on strong science (and not the precautionary principle), see Lugard and Smart (2006); see also Fisher (2006).

†       The party that avails itself of interim precautionary protective measures is obligated to follow up by producing adequate scientific justification in a reasonable period of time.

---

‡       See also Appendix 11-A.

§       A national enquiry point is a national office that disseminates information concerning the nation's regulation of chemical products. See Menezes and de Souza Antunes (2005).

Lugard and Smart (2006, p. 70) characterize the SPS and TBT agreements as follows:

> Two examples of these specialized agreements on trade in goods are the *SPS Agreement* and the *TBT Agreement*. The *SPS Agreement*, in general terms, prohibits WTO Members from erecting trade barriers under the guise of food safety or pest control measures by requiring that such measures be based on scientific evidence and risk assessments. The *TBT Agreement* obligates each member country to not impose product standards that restrict trade more than is necessary to achieve a legitimate objective, such as environmental protection or consumer safety. As such, these agreements impose disciplines on core domestic regulations to ensure that they are based on legitimate, objective, and scientific considerations.

### 11.2.4 The Decision of the Appellate Body in the Asbestos Case and Future Uncertainty of the Availability of Articles XX(b) and (g) Exceptions

Although the Appellate Body agreed with the panel's decision (see Section 11.2.2) that France could ban Canadian asbestos under Section XX(b) of the GATT, it disagreed with the panel's conclusion of law that the ban on asbestos was not a "technical barrier to trade." The ban prohibited chrysotile asbestos as a component of a product, and the Appellate Body agreed with Canada that the ban addressed a "product characteristic"—even though it was a "negative characteristic" (a product not containing chrysotile)—and was therefore, in its view, a "technical regulation." The panel, without making extensive findings regarding Canada's claim, dismissed consideration of this contention by Canada.

No risk assessment was performed by France, because the basis for its ban was claimed to be a Section XX(b) exception that allows a nation to adopt whatever health, safety, or environmental level of protection it deems desirable and also permits a "precautionary approach" in its consideration of scientific information, but the Appellate Body said that it would have required one* had the basis for the panel's decision been based on the finding (correct in its view) that the asbestos ban was in fact a "technical regulation," and therefore the ban was a "technical barrier to trade." The Appellate Body opined that the obligations im-

posed under the TBT agreement were in addition to those imposed by the GATT, and therefore Canada's claim that the TBT agreement did apply should have been considered.

The WTO Appellate Body can reverse the panel's decision if errors of law were made, but the panel made no discernible findings on which the Appellate Body could base a judgment. Note that a peculiarity of the WTO appeal process is that the Appellate Body can reject or accept the panel's findings, but it cannot send the case back to the panel to reconsider findings of law. Thus in this case, although the Appellate Body believed that the case should have been decided under the TBT agreement, as Canada argued, it had no power to require this after the panel decision was made.† However, future panels addressing disputes in cases involving other toxic substances could very well follow the Appellate Body's preferences.

Because permanent measures have to be based on "science" for measures taken under the TBT agreement, and because there is often great uncertainty concerning the toxicity/toxicology or epidemiology of chemicals, the use of TBT instead of the escape clause of Article XX(b) or (g) could render future attempts by nations to act in a precautionary manner moot.[8]

The authors of this book argue strongly that the TBT agreement is meant to encourage the achievement of consensus regarding standards intended to harmonize safety concerns somewhat arbitrarily for commercial ease and uniformity of practice, for example, by agreeing on how much voltage variation is allowable in electrical devices. The historical origins of the TBT agreement were founded in attempts to develop voluntary consensus standards and do not reveal an intent that it was meant to be the vehicle for providing maximum protection for health, safety, and environmental hazards. The U.S. counterparts, namely, the voluntary codes of ANSI, the NFPA, and the ACGIH, similarly were not meant to provide adequate standards, although they were adopted into worker-protection standards as minimum initial protection when the OSH Act was first passed. Indeed, the original form of the TBT agreement was known as the Standards Code and came into force in 1980. The new TBT agreement came into force in 1995 with the creation of the WTO and contained more stringent obligations.[9] The inclusion of mandatory standards that are termed "technical regulations" in the new TBT agreement was most likely intended by industry to avoid aggressive health, safety, and environmental reg-

---

\* The discussion in Section 11.2.5, which follows, addresses the initial attempt of the EU to permanently ban importation of U.S. beef containing hormones, which failed precisely because the United States contested the uncertain science lacking a risk assessment that seemed to be required by the SPS agreement, like the TBT agreement.

---

† For a legal commentary disagreeing with this perspective, see Pauwelyn (2002).

ulation by governments (see the discussion of trade and standards in Section 11.2.3). What is abundantly clear is that the chemical industry and exporters of chemicals would vastly prefer to avoid the application of Articles XX(b) and (g) and instead to define their obligations around the TBT and SPS agreements, which do not accept a precautionary approach and which require scientific risk assessments. To the extent that the appointees to the Appellate Body are trade specialists and not health, safety, or environmental professionals, the future could be problematic for national safeguards.

### 11.2.5 Food Safety: Hormones in Beef and the SPS Agreement

The SPS Agreement was put to the test in *EC-Hormones* when the EU banned the import of beef treated with any of six growth hormones. This especially affected the United States, where 90 percent of cattle are given growth hormones, and in 1997 the United States filed a complaint with the WTO. After a WTO panel decision, the Appellate Body in 1998 agreed with the panel, which ruled that there was not sufficient specific scientific evidence to justify a permanent ban but agreed that a provisional ban was permitted under Section 5.7 of the agreement and urged the EU to produce more definitive scientific justification in the form of appropriate risk assessments to justify a permanent ban. Initially, the EU did not comply. Consequently, the WTO authorized the United States and Canada to place a 100 percent import duty on certain EU agricultural and manufactured goods exports to the value of U.S. $117 million and Canadian $11 million, respectively.

The EU undertook a risk assessment for oestradiol-17β, which the new panel accepted as justification of a permanent ban and ordered the United States to cease its retaliatory actions against EU product imports. On October 14, 2003, a new EU directive (2003/74/EC) was adopted based on "thorough scientific grounding" for the EU restrictions (a permanent ban on one of the hormones, oestradiol-17b, and also restrictions on the use or sale of the other five hormones) because of evidence of sufficiently "potential detrimental effects" such that application of the precautionary principle allowed these restrictions.* The EU notified the United States

of these measures in November 2003. The United States and Canada rejected the EU evidence and maintained their prior retaliatory sanctions, arguing that the proffered risk assessment did not quantify the risk and was based primarily on the fact of exposure to synthetic hormones. Two panels were subsequently created in response to the EU's November 2004 request for consultations.

A panel decision was issued on March 31, 2008, in which the panel condemned the United States and Canada for imposing the sanctions in breach of WTO rules in light of the EU's conduct of the required risk assessment(s). The panel also found that the EU directive did not comply with the SPS Agreement. The EU appealed this part of the decision—arguing that the panel did not have the jurisdiction to rule on the conformity of the directive—while the United States, which did not agree about the adequacy of the risk assessment for oestradiol-17β and the other five hormones, appealed the panel decision of March 2008 as well.

On October 16, 2008, the Appellate Body issued a decision in which it was unable to resolve the scientific dispute concerning the new risk assessments. However, it was persuaded that the panel appointees had unacceptable conflicts of interest and reversed the panel findings that the provisional bans on the other five hormones were unjustified. The Appellate Body urged the United States and the EU to settle their differences through negotiation. Parts of the decision [WT/DS320/AB/R] are reproduced below:

> 736. For the reasons set out in this Report, the Appellate Body: . . .
>
> (b) As regards the Panel's consultations with the scientific experts, finds that the Panel infringed the European Communities' due process rights, because the institutional affiliation of Drs. Boisseau and Boobis compromised their appointment and thereby the adjudicative independence and impartiality of the Panel. Accordingly, the Panel failed to comply with its duties under Article 11 of the DSU.

---

* For a strong argument in defense of the adequacy of the directive to satisfy the permanent EC restrictions under the SPS Agreement, see Chichester (2005). Chichester recommended that the United States and the EU use WTO procedures to reach an accommodation on their differences, an approach ultimately recommended by the latest Appellate Body decision

(see below). After the establishment of the directive, in 2007, the European Food Safety Authority (EFSA) issued a report in which it saw no need to revise previous risk assessments that found risks to human health from residues in meat from hormone-treated cattle. Section 5 of the SPS requires signatories to "ensure that their [SPS] measures are based on an assessment . . . of the risks to human, animal or plant life or health, taking into account risk assessment techniques developed by the relevant international organizations." The EFSA report would seem to support the assertion that the EC submission satisfies this requirement.

(c) As regards the consistency with Article 5.1 of the *SPS Agreement* of the European Communities' import ban on meat from cattle treated with oestradiol-17b for growth promotion purposes, which is applied pursuant to Directive 2003/74/EC:

(i) finds that the Panel erred in its interpretation and application of Article 5.1 in relation to risks of misuse and abuse in the administration of hormones to cattle for growth-promotion purposes;

(ii) finds that the Panel did not err in requiring the European Communities to evaluate specifically the risks arising from the presence of residues of oestradiol-17b in meat or meat products from cattle treated with the hormone for growth-promotion purposes;

(iii) finds that the Panel did not err in its interpretation of Article 5.1 and paragraph 4 of Annex A of the *SPS Agreement* as regards quantification of risk;

(iv) finds that the Panel erred in the allocation of the burden of proof in its assessment of the consistency of Directive 2003/74/EC with Article 5.1 of the *SPS Agreement*;

(v) finds that the Panel applied an incorrect standard of review in examining whether the European Communities' risk assessment satisfied the requirements of Article 5.1 and paragraph 4 of Annex A of the *SPS Agreement*, and thereby failed to comply with its duties under Article 11 of the DSU; and

(vi) reverses the Panel's finding that the provisional import ban relating to testosterone, progesterone, trenbolone acetate, zeranol, and MGA does not meet the requirements of Article 5.7 of the *SPS Agreement*; however, the Appellate Body is unable to complete the analysis and therefore makes no findings as to the consistency or inconsistency of the European Communities' provisional import ban with Article 5.7 of the *SPS Agreement*.

737. Because we have been unable to complete the analysis as to whether Directive 2003/74/EC has brought the European Communities into substantive compliance within the meaning of Article 22.8 of the DSU, the recommendations and rulings adopted by the DSB in *EC-Hormones* remain operative. In the light of the obligations arising under Article 22.8 of the DSU, we recommend that the Dispute Settlement Body request the United States and the European Communities to initiate Article 21.5 proceedings without delay in order to resolve their disagreement as to whether the European Communities has removed the measure found to be inconsistent in *EC-Hormones* and whether the application of the suspension of concessions by the United States remains legally valid.

The resolution of the conflicts in law raised by the *EC-Hormones* dispute remains cloudy. In rejecting the use of the precautionary principle, the SPS Agreement is clearly at variance not only with the specific directive in question but also with regard to environmental, health, and safety protection in the EU as a whole, which is committed to maintaining both a "high level of protection" and the precautionary principle (see Section 10.18.1 in Chapter 10). Of course, arguments over the adequacy of risk assessments have plagued environmental law disputes in U.S. tribunals (see Chapter 9), and they now cloud international environmental law as well. Furthermore, the WTO cases dealing with GATT Articles XX(b) (the shrimp-turtle case) and (g) (*EC-Asbestos*) are at variance with SPS and TBT law as it is evolving. The corruption of the panels in the hormone cases and the trade bias of the WTO Appellate Body call for serious revision and rationalization of the several WTO health, safety, and environmental agreements.* One possible avenue of at least temporary reconciliation of the beef hormones dispute was the use of labeling of hormone-fed beef, non-hormone-fed beef, or both (see Sien 2007).

However, the dispute itself has been settled, at least temporarily. On May 13, 2009, the EC and the United States signed a memorandum of understanding on a temporary solution to the hormones dispute. According to this agreement, the United States will reduce the sanctions imposed on European products. At the same time, the EC will offer better market access for high-quality beef traditionally exported by the United States and produced from cattle that have not been treated with growth-promoting hormones. The United States said that the agreement with the EC demonstrated that there was a better way forward in this dispute than pursuing further litigation.[10] Of course, the legal quagmire in WTO law discussed above remains.

## 11.2.6 Biotechnology: Genetically Modified Organisms

The application of modern biotechnology can result in genetically modified food products, such as corn and soy, or trade or transport of living modified or-

---

* Some commentators recommend incorporating the Article XX exceptions into the SPS Agreement or drafting a new set of exceptions, but not trying to solve the WTO trade conflict mechanisms (as in *EC-Hormones*) through negotiation suggested by the latest Appellate Body Decision. See Shapiro (2007).

ganisms (LMOs) in plants, vaccines, drugs, and commercial products. Either could come under the SPS Agreement or under the Cartagena Protocol on Biosafety of the Convention on Biological Diversity (CBD).* As with the difference in approaches taken in the SPS Agreement and Articles XX (b) and (g) of the GATT, the SPS Agreement and the Cartagena Protocol on Biosafety are also inconsistent in their approach to the necessity of making a strong science-based case (that is, through a risk assessment) for their application and to the use of the precautionary principle (see Cors 2001). Article 19 (paragraph 3) of the CBD anticipates the application of "advance informed consent" (AIC)—a process paralleling the prior informed consent (PIC) procedure for hazardous products and waste in other international conventions[†]—for the transboundary movement of LMOs between contracting parties. The Cartagena Protocol on Biosafety reaffirms the precautionary approach, which places it in direct conflict with the SPS Agreement.

A recent WTO challenge to the EU regulation of GMO products demonstrates the continuing tension between the SPS Agreement and multilateral environmental agreements. The following excerpt recites complex interplay between the EU and the WTO.

### Feast or Famine: The Impact of the WTO Decision Favoring the U.S. Biotechnology Industry in the EU Ban of Genetically Modified Foods

Debra M. Strauss (2008), *American Business Law Journal* 45: 775–826, excerpted with permission (footnotes omitted).

### I. Introduction

Who do we trust to control the substances in our food and to make decisions about the safety of our food supply? Should it be the regulatory agencies in each individual nation, the health agencies of the international community, or the World Trade Organization (WTO)? In the ongoing controversy on genetically modified organisms (GMOs) in food, the divergent regulatory responses to scientific uncertainty and the unknown risks have reached a crescendo in the form of an international trade dispute.

In May 2003, the United States, Argentina, and Canada filed a formal complaint with the WTO against the European Union (EU) over its five-year moratorium on approving crops engineered through

biotechnology. The EU ban effectively excluded most U.S. agricultural products because its genetically modified (GM) crops are not segregated. The United States challenged the ban on the grounds that it is an impediment to trade. In view of the high stakes, many in the industry have anxiously awaited the decision of the WTO. Consumer groups have described a preliminary ruling issued by the WTO dispute resolution panel (the Panel) on February 7, 2006 as a major step back for the democratic rights of national and local governments to set their own environmental and human health regulations when there is scientific uncertainty. On May 10, 2006, the Panel issued a final ruling that appeared to favor the U.S. biotechnology companies over the precautionary regulations of the EU by finding several trade violations in its general moratorium and failure to approve specific biotech products . . .

### II. The Context Of The Decision

. . .

#### A. *The Backdrop for the Dispute*

In examining the current trade dispute, one must recognize that the EU and United States have different regulatory approaches toward GMOs, which are in turn a reflection of the differing views and levels of concern about GM food in the face of scientific uncertainty. These differences over GM crops and food products that contain them have disrupted the agricultural trade between and among the nations.

The long-term effects of GMOs on human health and the environment are unknown. Potential risks include: toxicity, allergenicity, antibiotic resistance, negative nutritional impact, unintended health effects, insect resistance, harm to nontarget organisms, outcrossing, and damage to the balance of the ecosystem. For example, outcrossing—the spread of transgenes in the natural environment through cross-pollination—has been documented to occur even in experimental releases of a number of crops, including rice and maize, causing irreversible effects on the environment and economic loss for farmers. Long-term scientific studies in humans have not yet been done, but some initial findings in animals and several case examples suggesting hazards have caused significant concern. In view of the substantial scientific uncertainty concerning these substances, each regulatory scheme reflects the comfort level of its government and its citizens in who should bear the risk of the harms, most of which are currently unknown. U.S. consumers appear to be less aware of the potential risks and more trusting of their regulatory agencies; Europeans are more risk averse to the human health and safety issues associated with GM food products.

The concept of "substantial equivalence" as applied by the Food and Drug Administration (FDA) does not recognize any inherent risk in, or indeed any

---

* Article 2 of the CBC defines biotechnology as "any technological application that uses biological systems, living organisms, or derivatives thereof, to make or modify products, or processes for specific use." Article 8(g) of the CBC applies only to LMOs, while Article 19 (handling of biotechnology and distribution of its benefits) applies to both living and nonliving products.

† See Sections 10.6, 10.9, and 10.16 in Chapter 10.

relevance of, the source of the product. In contrast, the EU maintains a separate regulatory structure that gives close scrutiny specifically to GE processes and products. Since the development of GM foods, no federal legislation has been enacted, nor have regulatory agencies required any labeling or special approval of these substances in the United States. Instead, GMOs are handled within the regulatory framework that existed prior to their invention according to their characteristics, such as nutritional content, rather than their method of production.

In the international community, the products of biotechnology are considered to be inherently different from traditionally developed crops. In the face of insufficient scientific evidence as to the potential dangers, these riskier products must be restricted or prohibited in order to protect against future unforeseen problems. With its precautionary approach, the EU has taken a relatively proactive role in enacting strict legislation to control the spread of GMOs, including Directive 2001/18/EC that regulates and restricts the distribution of GMOs and foods containing GM ingredients. Directive 2001/18/EC sets forth measures for assessing human health and environmental risks before any GM product can be released into the environment or marketed. Most significantly, this Directive allows a temporary ban of GM products if evidence can be provided exposing risks to human health or the environment. The moratorium has been a source of friction between the United States and the EU, costing the United States an estimated $300 million in corn exports.

The strict regulatory regime restricting GMOs in the EU led to the filing of the current complaint with the WTO challenging the ban as an impediment to trade.... The U.S. government has focused its efforts on trying to break down the barriers overseas and open international markets to its GMOs, rather than to reexamine its own failure to mandate labeling and segregation practices for GM crops....

## B. The Great Stakes

...

The effects of this decision are expected to extend beyond the initial parties. Seen as a precedent for future WTO Panels, the ruling will determine how food safety, public health, and environmental health measures should be applied to international trade. It could significantly impact the regulation of other industries, as well as developing countries looking to set their own regulatory approaches.

The ruling was also looked to as a way to help build international norms about the level of substantiation necessary to justify a precautionary approach to regulation.... Some commentators had predicted that the decision would be a model for the precautionary principle.... They looked forward to a WTO decision favoring the precautionary principle as a positive development in acknowledging and supporting health

and environmental considerations in matters of international trade. However, as will be discussed below, the WTO ultimately squandered the historic opportunity to do so.

## III. The Decision Of The WTO Panel

...

On May 10, 2006, the Panel submitted its final report to the parties, substantially confirming the findings of the interim report. On September 29, 2006, the Panel reports were circulated to members. At its meeting on November 21, 2006, the Dispute Settlement Body (DSB) adopted the Panel reports.

As will be discussed in more detail below, the Panel found that the EC had applied a "general *de facto* moratorium" on the approval of biotech products, which led to "undue delays" in the completion of EC approval procedures in violation of its trade obligations. However, the Panel rejected the bulk of challenges to the EC approval process as "not inconsistent" with the relevant treaties. Indeed, it focused its criticism on the delay in the application of the EU's procedures to specific biotech products rather than on the validity of these regulations. In addition, its findings of trade violations concerned several product-specific bans by individual member states, which the Panel determined could not be justified under safeguard measures due to a lack of the requisite foundation of scientific risk assessment.

The EC decided not to appeal the ruling of the Panel, "as the current regulatory provisions are not in any way affected by the judgment." ...

## A. Analyzing its Scope and Implications

In view of the enormous stakes and great anticipation, the WTO decision is perhaps as noteworthy for what it did not decide as for what it did. The Panel expressly limited its review; in a somewhat convoluted fashion, it phrased the issue as the alleged failure of the European Communities to reach final decisions regarding the approval of biotech products from October 1998 to the time of establishment of the Panel on 29 August 2003 and the WTO-consistency of prohibitions imposed by certain EC member states with regard to specific biotech products after these products had been approved by the European Communities for Community-wide marketing.

It "did *not* examine":
— whether biotech products in general are safe or not.
— whether the biotech products at issue in this dispute are "like" their conventional counterparts ...
— whether the European Communities has a right to require the premarketing approval of biotech products ...

— whether the European Communities' approval procedures as established by Directive 90/220, Directive 2001/18 and Regulation 258/97, which provide for a product-by-product assessment requiring scientific consideration of various potential risks, are consistent with the European Communities' obligations under the WTO agreements. . . .

— the conclusions of the relevant EC scientific committees regarding the safety evaluation of specific biotech products. . . .

Thus, the Panel did not resolve the central issue in the dispute over GM food, namely, whether it is safe and whether there is scientific justification for its restriction. Nor did the Panel evaluate the past and current regulations under which the EU continues to limit GM foods, particularly its new more stringent labeling and monitoring requirements. In fact, the Panel acknowledged that both the evidence provided by the EC and the advice provided by the scientific experts indicate that some of the identified concerns, "such as those relating to the development of pesticide-resistance in target insects through exposure to pesticides (including those incorporated into biotech plants) have 'indeed been documented to occur.' " The Panel emphasized that the "right of the EC to consider these possible risks prior to giving approval for the consumption or planting of biotech plants had not been questioned by any of the parties." . . .

### 1. EC General Moratorium

. . .

The Panel found that the EC applied a "general *de facto* moratorium" on the approval of biotech products between June 1999 and August 2003, which as noted above was the only time period under consideration. The Panel further found that, by applying this moratorium, the EC had acted inconsistently with its obligations under Annex C(1)(a), first clause, and Article 8 of the Agreement on the Application of Sanitary and Phytosanitary Measures because the de facto moratorium led to "undue delays" in the completion of EC approval procedures. . . .

The Panel found that the EC had "not acted inconsistently" with its obligations under other provisions raised by the complaining parties. . . . These provisions include such requisites as: permitting SPS measures only based on "sufficient scientific evidence" (Article 2.2), prohibiting discriminations between WTO members through SPS measures (Article 2.3), requiring that SPS measures be based on risk assessments (Article 5.1), prohibiting "arbitrary or unjustifiable distinctions in the levels" of SPS measures (Article 5.5), requiring members to employ the least restrictive means to achieve the desired SPS protections (Article 5.6). . . . The complaining parties had challenged the EC approval process on each of these provisions but the Panel unequivocally found these claims to be without merit.

### 2. EC Product-Specific Measures

. . .

Several member states had declared a suspension of new GMO authorizations until the proposed new labeling and traceability rules were adopted. With regard to these product-specific EC measures, the Panel found that the EC had acted inconsistently with its obligations under . . . the SPS Agreement concerning twenty-four out of twenty-seven biotech products identified by the complaining parties because there were "undue delays" in the completion of the approval procedures for each of these products. The Panel held that the lengthy delay in approval of applications during the relevant time period was not justified by the pending revision of the EC regulations or the use of a precautionary approach in light of the evolving science. However, the Panel ruled that the moratorium was not itself an SPS measure as the United States and the other complainants had argued and thus would not require risk assessment. The Panel suggested that a member could take a precautionary approach in compliance with [the SPS Agreement] by adopting substantive rules providing provisional approvals or approvals subject to other conditions.

According to the Report, not every moratorium would necessarily violate the delay provisions; a general delay might be justifiable if new scientific evidence conflicted with available scientific evidence and affected the approval of all applications. . . .

Moreover, the Panel concluded that the EC had not acted inconsistently with its obligations under any other provisions raised by the complaining parties, including Articles 5.1, 5.5, and 2.2 of the SPS Agreement, with regard to any of the products concerned.

### 3. Member State Safeguard Measures

Most importantly, in assessing the EC member state safeguard measures,[*] the Panel found that the EC acted inconsistently with its obligations under Articles 5.1 and 2.2 of the SPS Agreement for all of the safeguard measures at issue, because the bans imposed by the individual nations . . . were not based on risk assessments satisfying the definition of the SPS Agreement and hence could be presumed to be maintained without sufficient scientific evidence. However, the Panel did not dispute the right of individual EC member states to impose SPS measures that differ from those of the EC as a whole, noting that the complaining parties had not challenged the EC approval legislation that confers this conditional right.

Specifically, the Panel concluded that, although some of the member states did provide scientific studies, they did not at the time of adoption of the

---

\*        A "safeguard measure" is a temporary measure, in the guise of an "emergency temporary action," that EU member states can take that is not part of the specific requirements imposed by an EU directive or regulation (see Section 10.18.10 in Chapter 10).

safeguard measures include an assessment of the risk "to human health and/or the environment meeting the requirements of the SPS Agreement," nor could risk assessments undertaken by the EC scientific committees supply reasonable support for prohibition of the biotech products. For each of the products, the relevant EC scientific committee had evaluated the potential risks prior to the granting of EC-wide approval and, upon reviewing the arguments and evidence submitted by the member state to justify the prohibition, did not change its earlier positive conclusions. Although the EC defended the member states' concerns based upon their higher level of risk aversion and substantial scientific uncertainty as to the risks of bioengineered products, the Panel did not follow this analysis. . . .

4. Noteworthy Rulings on Key Issues

Some of the Panel's determinations may carry significant implications in their broad potential scope. In rejecting an argument by the EC that it should consider rules of international environmental law, the Panel held that it was not necessary or appropriate to rely on these treaties in the present case. The EU had argued that these agreements needed to be taken into account because the rules of interpretation in the Vienna Convention on the Law of Treaties, Article 31(3)(c), state that "any relevant rules of international law applicable in the relations between the parties" shall be considered in interpreting a given treaty. Because the treaties–the Convention on Biological Diversity and the Cartagena Protocol on Biosafety (Biosafety Protocol)—were not binding on all member countries to the dispute, the Panel held that it was not required to take those treaties into account. In fact, the Panel even commented that "in a case where all disputing parties are parties to a convention, this fact would not necessarily render reliance on that convention appropriate." Ultimately the decision went further to give an unprecedented narrow interpretation of Article 31(3)(c) as requiring that all members of the WTO must be members of the environmental treaty in order for the Panel to need to take the treaty into account in the dispute. Under its reasoning, the phrase "the parties" refers to all the parties to the treaty, which interpretation "leads logically to the view that the rules of international law to be taken into account in interpreting the WTO agreements at issue in this dispute are those which are applicable in the relations between the WTO Members." As the International law Commission of the U.N. General Assembly critically observed, this narrow vision "makes it practically impossible ever to find a multilateral context where reference to other multilateral treaties as aids to interpretation under article 31(3)(c) would be allowed." . . .

As the only international regulatory instrument established to protect biological diversity from the risks of biotechnology, the Biosafety Protocol incorporates a precautionary approach in keeping with the language of the Rio Declaration on Environment and Development, that "[w]here there are threats of serious or irreversible damage, lack of full scientific certainty shall not be used as a reason for postponing cost-effective measures to prevent environmental degradation." The EC had contended that the precautionary principle should be taken into account because it was a "general principle of international law." In what will most likely be viewed as a major setback for the future application of the precautionary principle, the Panel declined to recognize that it was widely accepted by the member states. The Panel pointed out the absence of an "authoritative decision" by an international court declaring it to be a principle of general or customary international law and, to the contrary, referred to a 1998 statement by the Appellate Body in connection with the EU ban on beef raised with artificial growth hormones that the debate on this issue was still unsettled. As a consequence, the Panel failed to decide whether this was a principle of international law and avoided any reliance upon the precautionary principle in its Report, concluding:

> Since the legal status of the precautionary principle remains unsettled, like the Appellate Body before us, we consider that prudence suggests that we not attempt to resolve this complex issue, particularly if it is not necessary to do so. Our analysis below makes clear that for the purposes of disposing of the legal claims before us, we need not take a position on whether or not the precautionary principle is a recognized principle of general or customary international law. Therefore, we refrain from expressing a view on this issue.

The Report did appear to suggest a limited use of the precautionary principle in cases where the scientific evidence in a particular risk assessment is internally inconsistent or where there is insufficient evidence even to conduct a risk assessment as defined in Annex A(4). According to the Panel's findings, the instant case did not fit such a scenario.

Ceding to the request of the EC over the objection of the complaining parties, the Panel decided "to consult individual experts to obtain their opinion on certain scientific and/or technical issues raised in the Parties' submissions." . . .

The fact that the Panel consulted these four (and later two more) individuals designated by the Panel as "experts" indicates its recognition that there are scientific issues involved rather than simply trade; moreover, perhaps the Panel in this respect acknowledged its limitation in scientific knowledge to assess these issues. However, the selection of a small number of individuals—rather than recognized international scientific organizations like the World Health Organization who have extensively studied GM food and raised serious issues about the risks to human health and the environment—should be questioned. . . . Ultimately, this reliance on outside scientific experts highlights the shortcomings of the WTO as a forum for deciding a dispute that so critically involves science and health issues rather than the discrete trade matters for which this resolution body was designed.

5. Restrained Recommendations for Action

Consistent with the self-declared limits of the scope of its findings, the Panel seemed restrained in its recommendations, stopping short of requiring action by the EC. Despite finding a general EC moratorium, the Panel refrained from making recommendations because it found that the moratorium had already ended in the EC's approval of a biotech product in 2004. . . .

As to the specific products held in violation of the delay provision, the Panel recommended that the DSB "request" the EC "bring the relevant product-specific measures into conformity with its obligations under the SPS Agreement." This request effectively asked that the approval process be completed for any pending applications; certainly the Panel did not seek to decide whether the EC premarket approval measures comply with WTO rules or that the moratorium itself should have been based on a scientific risk assessment. It also recommended that the DSB request the EC bring the relevant member state safeguard measures into conformity with its obligations under the SPS Agreement. This could be achieved either by revoking the bans or by justifying them based on a proper risk assessment. As noted above, consistent with this decision members might still block GMO imports by justifying them with adequate risk assessments, by granting time-limited or conditional approvals pending further scientific assessment, or by delaying decisions in the event of new scientific evidence that conflicted with existing evidence.

*B. Initial Reactions to the Ruling*

The United States hailed the ruling as a victory that brings the United States "one step closer to clearing barriers . . . and expanding global use of promising advances in food production." . . .

Bold statements from the U.S. biotechnology industry and farm groups followed the ruling. "This is a good, clear signal to the world that Europe was wrong," said Leon Corzine, chairman of the National Corn Growers Association, which had claimed $300 million a year in lost corn exports as a result of the European moratorium. . . .

In contrast, consumer and environmental groups sharply criticized the WTO's ruling. Some environmental groups have further blasted the EU for not pursuing an appeal of the ruling. By failing to appeal, the EU has let stand a precedent that may have broader scope in its failure to apply multilateral environmental agreements (MEAs) to trade disputes. The environmental group Friends of the Earth insisted that this was not a victory for the United States or the biotech industry, but rather a clever public relations campaign that spun the ruling against the EU: "It's still possible to impose tough restrictions on GMOs to protect the people and the environment from genetically modified crops."

From its perspective, the EU pointed to support for its position in the WTO decision. The Panel did not rule on the safety of biotech products, nor did it criticize the regulatory framework of the EU, other than to conclude that there was "undue delay" in the way the applications were processed. In doing so, the Panel limited itself to the procedural claims, rather than adopting the more expansive U.S. view that both the general moratorium and the product-specific moratoria constitute SPS measures that violate the SPS Agreement, which would have required an examination of more critical questions such as whether the suspensions were based on a risk assessment and whether it justified special, more stringent SPS measures than the EC applies to conventional products. Thus, the WTO ruling did not question the EU's right to treat the technology differently from conventional crops or examine whether its premarket approval measures comply with WTO rules. The Panel also rejected several of the claims with respect to both the general moratorium and the product-specific measures, including the argument that the EU's procedures were discriminatory or arbitrary in their implementation.

The EU said it did not intend to change its stringent rules on approving GM foods despite the ruling. The EU described the rules that have been in effect since 2004, when the EU permitted a type of GM corn grown mainly in the United States, as in line with its WTO obligations. The approval process continued with the subsequent approval of ten biotech foods, nine of which occurred in the year immediately, preceding the final decision. Peter Power, spokesman for EU Trade Commissioner Peter Mandelson, reiterated that the complaining parties did not challenge the EU's current regulatory framework: "Nothing in this panel report will compel us to change that framework. Europe will continue to set its own rules on the import and sales of GM foods." . . .

The EU also blamed national governments for continuing to obstruct new approvals. In keeping with the ruling, the EU trade negotiator requested "a reasonable period of time" for the EU to work with its member states on their national legislation. However, widespread opposition to this technology from European consumers continues, as many Europeans are wary of buying so-called "Frankenstein" foods. For example, Austria, which has based its national ban on the absence of any long-term health safety tests and the likelihood of cross-contamination in the environment, has indicated that the WTO ruling will have no effect on its policy. . . . Given the opposition of the EU's own members, eliminating these national bans will be politically difficult to effectuate.

Meanwhile, the United States has stated that it will continue with its WTO case until it is convinced that all applications for approval are being decided on scientific rather than political grounds. . . .

## IV. New And Future Developments

The potential impact of this WTO decision is not self-evident. Biotechnology interests would like to portray the legal landscape as a fait accompli, an unequivocal endorsement of GM foods, with broad statements that "[t]he decision was never really in doubt, but its global impact could be huge." . . . However, resistance among European consumers continues and, consequently, a dramatic direct impact on the EU market appears unlikely.

The WTO can only authorize penalties for illegal trade restrictions still in force, and its recommendations do not appear to support that level of enforcement. . . .

### A. Possible Impact on European Regulatory Process

In May 2004, the EU effectively ended the moratorium by approving for human consumption a GE corn variety (Syngenta Bt-11). Since then, the EU has approved GE corn varieties (Monsanto's NK603) for humans and animals, Pioneer's 1570 corn for feed, and seventeen strains of GE corn. The Commission authorized the marketing of these products only after member state officials and ministers failed to reach a decision for or against approval. There are currently over forty-seven biotech products still awaiting EU approval, several of which have been under review for more than six years, versus an average six- to nine-month review process in Canada, Japan, and the United States. The United States reports the cessation of its corn exports to Spain, Portugal, and Italy, which had been the most significant EU importers.

Perhaps in anticipation of the final decision by the WTO, the EU had already begun to alter its regulatory process toward GMOs. On April 12, 2006, the EC approved measures aimed at improving the scientific consistency and transparency for decisions on permitting GM food and feed in the European market. As of that date, there were twelve national bans against GMOs and 172 regions that declared their wish to be GMO-free. Moreover, since the ending of the general moratorium in April 2004, no qualified majority has been reached by European ministers in favor of authorizing GMOs.

In the EU, harmonization or approximation of the laws has been a goal difficult to achieve toward which its intricate structure of directives and regulations aspire. While EU regulations have a direct effect on the states, without the necessity of passing national legislation, directives require members to bring their own laws into harmony with a standard and, politically, allow members more autonomy to implement the legislative program. The regulatory approach in the environmental area has been to proceed primarily through directives. Thus the EU and its member states seek to maintain a delicate balance between consistency of the laws and autonomy of its member states with some power to navigate their own national interests. The EU measures may, in part, be an attempt to minimize the negative impact of the WTO decision on this tenuous state of affairs.

While pressure from the United States and the WTO mounts, the member states have criticized the EU for its lack of transparency and democracy in its GM authorization process. In an attempt to please both sides, the new measures are designed to reassure these stakeholders that the EC decisions "are based on high quality scientific assessments which deliver a high level of protection of human health and the environment." The new regulations call upon the European Food Safety Authority (EFSA) to provide more detailed justification in its opinions on individual applications for permits, particularly as to overruling scientific objections raised by the national authorities; and applicants as well as the EFSA will be asked in their risk assessments to speak to potential long-term effects and biodiversity issues.

In addition, the EFSA has recently issued an opinion on GMOs that sets forth a plan for the mandatory Post Market Environmental Monitoring (PMEM) of GM plants for identifying possible unanticipated adverse effects on human health or the environment, both direct and indirect. The plan states that the EFSA is responsible for assessing the scientific quality of PMEM plans submitted with each application. The EFSA also issued a document that provides guidance for the preparation and presentation of applications submitted within the framework of Regulation (EC) 1829/2003 on GM food and feed, and Directive 2001/18/EC on the deliberate release into the environment of GMOs. This guidance further details the full risk assessment of GM plants and derived food and feed.

Thus the EU continues to augment its regulatory framework with an emphasis on transparency but with no signs of a leniency toward genetic modification. Clearly, despite pressures from the U.S. biotechnology industry, the laissez faire approach of the United States is not spreading to Europe.

### B. Developing Countries as a Target

. . .

### C. Future Attack on New EU Regulations on Labeling and Traceability

. . .

### D. Broader Implications for National Control and the Precautionary Principle

The rejection of the efforts of the member states to safeguard their food supply raises significant issues of national control. The WTO ruling has been described as a dangerous precedent because it is "a major step back for the democratic rights of national and local governments to set their own environmental and human health regulations when there is scientific uncertainty." Before the ruling, there had been calls for the EU to stop pressuring member states to lift their national bans and to stop pressing for further approvals of GM foods because there is no majority support among member states. Now, with pressure from both sides, the EU Commission's course of action will be difficult to navigate.

1. Failure to Embrace the Precautionary Principle

The ruling undermines the authority of the Biosafety Protocol, which allows its member states to take a precautionary approach to regulating GMOs when there is scientific uncertainty. . . . Thus, despite the absence of a direct finding by the Panel, the precautionary principle has been greatly diminished by its failure to give this international treaty recognition and consideration in its decision.

As a matter of law and policy, the Panel's reasoning, and in particular its prudence in relying upon an eight-year-old decision finding the issue to be unsettled, should be critically assessed. In avoiding a direct ruling, the Panel effectively held that the precautionary principle is not a general or customary principle of international law. Yet it cited ample support among academics for the contrary view that the precautionary principle currently exists as a general principle in international law, even if this was still a subject of debate. Perhaps the most significant development since the *EC-Hormones* case has been the introduction of the Biosafety Protocol, the very embodiment of the precautionary principle. In fact, the Panel noted that provisions explicitly or implicitly applying the precautionary principle have been incorporated into numerous international conventions and declarations, "although, for the most part, they are environmental conventions and declarations." Furthermore, it acknowledged that "the principle has been referred to and applied by States at the domestic level, again mostly in domestic environmental law." These qualifying references to the environmental nature of the conventions and domestic law imply that they were less worthy of weight and credibility, further undermining the legitimacy of these principles and body of law. Why was this not enough? Finding "no authoritative decision by an international court or tribunal which recognizes the precautionary principle as a principle of general or customary international law," the Panel inexplicably [b]acked away. Arguably, the time was ripe; yet the WTO dispute resolving body missed an opportunity to be the one to embrace the precautionary principle, as it was certainly empowered to do.

2. Narrow Interpretation of the Vienna Convention

International organizations and environmental groups have also criticized the WTO Panel for its narrow interpretation of the applicability of the Vienna Convention and charged that this decision would at best ignore or at worst undercut specific international environmental policies and rules relevant to WTO disputes. Under the reasoning of the Panel, multilat-

eral environmental agreements need only be taken into account in the improbable situation where all members of the WTO have ratified that particular agreement. They may be considered when the members of the dispute are also members of that particular agreement; but even this approach was at the discretion of the Panel. In light of this narrow construal, it is unlikely that the Vienna Convention will lead future WTO Panels to consider these international principles when interpreting WTO rules because, although WTO Panels legally apply only to the case they are deciding, Panels in actuality take into account earlier WTO rulings. According to the IATP [Institute for Agriculture and Trade Policy], the implications may extend well beyond the area of GMOs:

The decision says that WTO members cannot keep their commitments to multilateral environmental agreements [MEAs] if measures to do so are challenged under WTO rules. The ruling sets a terrible legal precedent that will be used to attack regulations that comply with MEA commitments.

Even more broadly, the notion that the norms of international law cannot be considered unless unanimous effectively isolates the WTO from mainstream international jurisprudence and sets it on a path that may weaken its own legitimacy. The U.N. General Assembly's International Law Commission has noted that the new standard has the ironic effect of rendering multilateral agreements as "islands" cut off from the mainstream international law as they expand, "[b]earing in mind the unlikeliness of a precise congruence in the membership of most important multilateral conventions, it would become unlikely that *any* use of conventional international law could be made in the interpretation of such conventions." As one critic has concluded,

[i]n today's interdependent world, where multiple [options] exist for creating international law, the EC-Biotech Panel's standard—that law established in a different forum must be embraced by all WTO members before it can be considered for incorporation is simply unrealistic. Behavior need not be embraced by all before it becomes custom. The same should be true of international law. Retaining the Panel's unrealistic standard will effectively isolate the WTO regime from other bodies of international law.

To avoid such fragmentation of treaties in international law, a wiser approach would be to embrace the international instruments that have set out to address specific environmental areas and have evidenced such widespread support. The WTO Panels and Appellate Body should, at the very least, mandate reference to another treaty if the parties in dispute are also parties to that other treaty. Moreover, reference to certain concepts or principles of a treaty should be permitted, even if a party to the dispute has not ratified the entire treaty, when acceptance of these principles has [reached] a level approaching customary international law.

3. Applicability of the SPS Agreement and Risk Assessment
Initial commentators had speculated that the United States was seeking a ruling, rather than a negotiated settlement in this case, in order to create a legal precedent that would hinder the use of Article 5.7 to defend domestic SPS measures. The Panel's broad interpretation of the definition of an SPS measure thereby invoked the substantial scientific justification requirements of the SPS Agreement. Yet for GMOs it is exactly this scientific uncertainty and lack of consensus that should support allowing the EU a temporary safe harbor under Article 5.7. Although the SPS requires that long-term restrictions justified on health grounds must be based upon scientific evidence, Article 5.7 does permit short-term restrictions on imports based upon lesser evidence. Thus, some experts believe that paragraph 7 provides a temporary safe harbor for EU restrictions on the production and importation of GMO products.

In addition, one must consider the possibility that "the SPS agreement is not equipped to deal with the kind of risks that GE organisms pose" and thus question the validity of "the narrow interpretation of the notion of 'risk assessment' in the panel report." Some conflict between the precautionary foundation of the Biosafety Protocol and the trade-based SPS Agreement has been observed in the past. Others have noted that, although the SPS Agreement requires countries to base such decisions to protect the health on risk assessments with sound scientific evidence, the "SPS requirement of a sound scientific basis is open to varying interpretations." In theory, the lack of full scientific certainty should not prohibit states from implementing measures to prevent serious damage; rather, some evidence—as opposed to speculation—of the risks must be shown in order to justify such measures. However, in applying the SPS Agreement, the WTO appeared to evoke more stringent risk assessment requirements to find that the national bans by EU member states violated WTO rules. But the ruling does not preclude the possibility of either [f]ollowing SPS-compatible ways of banning GE organisms or utilizing other agreements of the WTO, such as the Technical Barriers to Trade (TBT) Agreement. The TBT Agreement would be a particularly appropriate vehicle to apply in view of recent proposals [f]or the labeling of GM foods as a form of "least restrictive trade" measure.

### E. Appropriateness of the WTO in Decisions on Environment and Food

Ultimately, one must question whether the WTO is the appropriate body to be making these determinations about our food supply. . . . The WTO is a trade body with no expertise in science and the environment. Yet it has refused to accept the precautionary principle, which is a key principle in environmental governance widely recognized to allow countries to take action to protect the environment when there is scientific uncertainty. The fact that the Panel did not view the Biosafety Protocol—the only comprehensive international agreement on genetic engineering—as relevant is a "bad sign" as the WTO is currently negotiating the relationship between trade rules and global environmental agreements.

Ultimately, if the highest public policy criterion is the promotion of trade, protective measures will only be allowed if they can be proven to be "least trade restrictive." This approach risks strong disdain from the European and international community, who would view the WTO as valuing trade over their health and environment. Moreover, the WTO process lacks the institutional capacity to consider nonmarket values, such as social preferences for food and cultural attitudes about the potential risks of biotechnology. . . .

### V. Conclusion

Despite the events surrounding the biotechnology trade dispute and the anticipation of its resolution, the central questions remain unanswered. The WTO failed to assess the current regulatory system of the EU with its restrictive approach to allowing GMOs and, particularly, its stringent new labeling and traceability requirements. As emphasized by the IATP in its initial analysis, the Panel rejected the U.S. argument that there were no scientific issues to dispute in the case and, as a consequence, solicited expert opinion to assist its deliberations. The Report did not suggest insufficient evidence of risk but, rather, that there was sufficient scientific evidence to conduct a risk assessment as required under the SPS Agreement and the member states had not done so. The danger looms that this decision will be cited not for its findings but for what it did not say despite its care expressly to limit its decision. The promoters of biotechnology have already begun to spin this case as a greater victory than appears on its face, with broad words in support of GM food when no such findings were made by the Panel.

Most significantly, in failing to acknowledge and support the precautionary principle, the WTO undermined the use of this doctrine as a customary international norm. The relevance and application of environmental treaties in adjudicating disputes among nations was also seriously called into question. These critical choices may have a precedential impact on future trade disputes in agricultural biotechnology and beyond. By taking this approach in an area of such sensitivity and importance, the WTO may have further weakened its authority to make decisions affecting the human health and [the] environment and, in so doing, lessened its legitimacy in the world arena. A backlash may follow as the public realizes that its safety is ultimately in the hands of the biotechnology industry. Perhaps worse, we may be left with critical decisions about the food supply being made not by the scientists and policy makers but by isolated panels of individuals concerned primarily with the economics of international trade.

Perhaps the only saving grace of this decision is that since the EU did not appeal the decision, it did not receive Appellate Body endorsement, although it was accepted by the WTO Dispute Settlement Body. In a subsequent dispute, the Appellate Body still has a chance to bring the WTO's legal position more in line with the Biosafety Protocol and, by implication, other MEAs.*

As in the beef hormones dispute discussed earlier, without settling any of the thorny legal issues, the EU and Canada announced on July 15, 2009, that they had "settled" the case by agreeing to a continuing dialogue on agricultural biotechnology "aimed at avoiding unnecessary obstacles to trade."[11] Further, the agreement means that the "the EU is not expected to modify its current regulatory regime on biotech products, which was never subject to WTO challenge in itself." A similar agreement was reached with Argentina in March 2010.[12]

The EU Commission attempted to bypass the resolution of the deployment of bioengineered crops when it allowed Portugal to ban their use in Madeira by letting the deadline for Commission objection to pass. In July 2010, the Commission proposed a regulation that would have allowed each member state to decide for itself whether to restrict or prohibit the cultivation of GMs in its territory. However, the EU Council of Environmental Ministers, meeting on October 14, 2010, in Brussels, quashed the Commission's earlier move because it did not meet the Council's December 2008 policy of requiring and performing a socioeconomic assessment.[13] See Dobbs (2010) for an exploration of legal avenues under EU law, such as "safeguard measures," for allowing individual member states to exercise post-authorization control over GMO crops and food products in their own territories.

In a related matter, in its October 19, 2010 communication, the European Commission announced its intention to temporarily suspend animal cloning intended for food production in the EU. This declaration, which will be followed by a new regulation in 2011, nevertheless also takes into account that the descendants of cloned animals, such as embryos and eggs, could be imported into Europe under a traceability system.[14]

### 11.2.7 The General Agreement on Trade in Services[†]

In line with the general commitment to encourage global trade (open markets), uniformity in trade practices, and nondiscrimination and MFN treatment vis-à-vis national and foreign providers, the GATS promotes (but does not require) the liberalization (that is, privatization) of services, such as financial services, telecommunications, tourism, construction, and consultancies (professional services), and the elimination of disparities in the provision of services involving governments, consumers, and individuals. Movement of labor to advance the nondiscriminatory provision of services is to be encouraged, but without commitments for employment, citizenship, residence, or employment on a permanent basis.

Concerns have been raised that the GATS will encourage privatization in areas that are traditionally the province of government in some countries, such as health care and banking, and that regulatory safeguards will be challenged even where the services remain in the public sector.[‡] Pollock and Price (2003, p. 1075) observe: "There is compelling evidence to show that GATS and the WTO involve national governments in trading some of their national sovereignty for the putative economic gains of liberalization. In the process, governments lose rights to regulate and to protect non-economic values and the principles that shape provision of public services." The WTO refutes these claims and presents elaborate defenses in its website.

### 11.2.8 The Agreement on Trade-Related Aspects of Intellectual Property Rights[§]

The protection of intellectual property rights in printed materials, voice and musical recordings, design of manufactured goods, plant and animal varieties (including the results of genetic manipulation), industrial or agricultural processes, computers and software, and

---

* The lack of coordination and conflicts related to the requirements, underlying philosophies, and participatory rights of non-parties to trade treaties as among MEAs, TRIPS, and the WTO are legend (WWF 2001). Attempts to resolve these issues have yielded little results (ICTSD 2002; UNEP 2002).

† See also Appendix 11-A.

‡ This is reminiscent of the worry that there will be a race to the bottom in the efforts to harmonize environmental and consumer product protection practices. Certainly, the recent revelation of the failure of governments globally to adequately regulate the financial industry and financial transactions gives ammunition to these concerns.

§ See also Appendix 11-A.

pharmaceuticals varies considerably across the world. The TRIPS Agreement seeks to harmonize these protections to promote innovation and the transfer of technology through fair trade, and to provide a forum for dispute resolution.[15]

The recent joint report of the WTO and the WHO Secretariat (2002, p. 38) provides:

> The TRIPS Agreement requires WTO Members to establish minimum standards for protecting and enforcing intellectual property rights. Its objectives are set out in Article 7:
>
>> The protection and enforcement of intellectual property rights should contribute to the promotion of technological innovation and to the transfer and dissemination of technology, to the mutual advantage of producers and users of technological knowledge and in a manner conducive to social and economic welfare, and to a balance of rights and obligations.

Nondiscrimination vis-à-vis national treatment, MFN treatment, and balanced protection (of encouraging innovation and minimizing undue profit) are goals of the system. Unauthorized copying and use are regarded as "piracy." International recognition of patents for both products and processes in almost all fields of technology (for "at least twenty years") is envisioned. Access to technology is ensured in the TRIPS Agreement through the mechanism of compulsory licensing. International recognition of copyrights, trademarks, integrated circuit designs, and trade secrets is envisioned. Developing countries are given until 2013 to comply.

It is beyond the scope of this book to delve deeply into this important area, but one issue deserves special attention: the treatment of pharmaceuticals produced and sold "off patent" that are deemed of crucial health need for people in developing countries who cannot afford developing-country prices.* The Doha Ministerial Conference in November 2001 secured a commitment from pharmaceutical companies to extend their exemptions on patent protection for pharmaceuticals to 2016. Connected to the issue of providing access to needed pharmaceuticals is the problem of counterfeit drugs, which, of course, result in harm to unwitting consumers both in poor countries and in wealthier nations.

Yale University has proposed the creation of a governments-supported health impact fund that, in lieu of having producers charge high prices for patented drugs, would pay a tiered set of royalties to pharmaceutical producers who voluntarily provide low-priced drugs at cost.[16] The schedule of fees would be calcu-

lated by the drugs' share of positive health impacts in developing countries, and the fund thus would create incentives among producers for competition in providing better, more effective drugs for large numbers of the global poor.†

## 11.3 TRADE AND THE ENVIRONMENT (TRADE REGIMES AS TOOLS TO PROMOTE ADVANCES IN NATIONAL AND INTERNATIONAL ENVIRONMENTAL POLICIES)

### 11.3.1 Trade as a Positive Force to Improve Environmental Conditions

The GATT disputes discussed above highlight conflicts between environmental policies and trade rules. In some cases (for example, the shrimp-turtle case), these disputes centered on a deliberate application of a trade rule in the service of a national environmental policy. Some commentators who are staunch advocates of trade argue that most GATT rules generally have either no effect or a beneficial effect on national environmental standards. David Vogel is one such commentator who believes that trade agreements can actually enhance environmental goals. Excerpts from his writings are provided below.

David Vogel, "Chapter 1: National Regulation in the Global Economy," *Trading Up: Consumer and Environmental Protection in a Global Economy* (Cambridge, MA: Harvard University Press, 1995), pp. 1–23 (excerpted with permission)

#### National Regulation in the Global Economy
... A number of political scientists have explored the increasingly important role of international environmental agreements and treaties in affecting national regulatory standards. ...

The role of trade and trade agreements in promoting both the regionalization and the globalization of regulatory policy-making are much more important. ... Nations are thus increasingly importing and exporting standards as well as goods. ... Consequently, many of the conflicts over environmental and consumer regulation that formerly took place exclusively within nations are now also taking place among them.

Third, a new set of constituencies, namely, consumer and environmental organizations, have become active participants in the making of trade policy. Unlike producers or workers, these nongovernmental organizations (NGOs) are interested not in the economic impact of trade policies, but rather in the way they affect consumer health and safety and

---

* See especially the relationship between TRIPS and public health in WTO and WHO (2002, pp. 38–47).

† This seems related to the idea of trading from the bottom of the pyramid. See Hart and Milstein (1999), London and Hart (2004), and Prahalad and Hart (2002).

environmental quality in their own countries, and often in others as well. . . .

At the same time, consumer and environmental organizations are also playing a more important role in influencing the terms of particular trade agreements, attempting to make them more compatible with either the maintenance or strengthening of both domestic and international regulatory standards. . . .

### The Impact of Regulation on Trade

Since many national regulations disadvantage importers—either intentionally or unintentionally—the steady growth of protective regulations over the last three decades has made trade more difficult. Hence the growing number of trade disputes stemming from the alleged discriminatory impact of national environmental and consumer regulations on imports within the European Union and North America, and around the world. At the same time the undermining of trade liberalization by the expansion of environmental and consumer protection has also been limited by three factors: the role of international institutions, the power of internationally oriented producers, and the increasing number of international environmental agreements.

The international institutions created by the EU have played an especially important role in reducing the use of national protective regulations as trade barriers. The European Court of Justice (ECJ), the world's most powerful extra-national judicial body, has struck down numerous national regulations which protected producers rather than consumers or the environment. . . .

The removal of national regulations as obstacles to intra-Union trade remains incomplete. In some cases, the Union has simply been unable to arrive at a consensus regarding the level at which standards should be harmonized. Thus it has permitted member states to maintain their own distinctive standards, even though they interfere with the single market. . . .

### The "California Effect"

. . .

The notion that economic competition among political jurisdictions will lead to a regulatory "race to the bottom" has been labeled the "Delaware effect." . . .

However, this book demonstrates that regulatory competition can lead to a rather different outcome. A number of national patterns of health, safety, and environmental regulation illustrate the "California effect," named for the state that has been on the cutting edge of environmental regulation, both nationally and globally, for nearly three decades. The California effect refers to the critical role of powerful and wealthy "green" political jurisdictions in promoting a regulatory "race to the top" among their trading partners. . . .

The Delaware effect assumes that stricter regulatory standards represent a source of competitive disadvantage. But, in contrast to labor standards, the costs of complying with stricter consumer and environmental standards [have] not been sufficiently large to force political jurisdictions to lower their standards in order to keep domestic firms or plants competitive. On the contrary: in the case of many environmental and consumer regulations, stricter standards represent a source of competitive advantage for domestic producers, in part because it is often easier for them to comply with them. . . .

Equally significantly, when rich nations with large domestic markets such as the United States and Germany enact stricter product standards, their trading partners are forced to meet those standards in order to maintain their export markets. . . .

The impact of trade liberalization on regulatory standards is also affected by another factor: the degree of economic integration. The stronger the role of international institutions in promoting liberal trade policies, the more extensive the leverage of rich, powerful states over the regulatory powers of their trading partners. . . .

. . . But it is important not to equate stricter standards with more effective regulations. Many environmental and consumer regulations contribute little or nothing to enhancing consumer or environmental protection. To the extent that these regulations have been successfully challenged through trade agreements and treaties, public welfare has been enhanced. However, efforts to remove trade barriers to promote economic integration have at times prevented greener nations from establishing regulations as strict as [their] citizens and producers would prefer. . . .

At the same time, trade liberalization has also helped increase the leverage of NGOs and producers in greener countries over the regulatory policies of their trading partners. . . . Trade liberalization is most likely to strengthen consumer and environmental protection when a group of nations has agreed to reduce the role of regulations as trade barriers and the most powerful among them has influential domestic constituencies that support stronger regulatory standards. Thus, the stronger the commitment of nations to coordinate their regulatory policies, the more powerful is the California effect. Likewise, the weaker the institutions created by regional or international trade agreements or treaties, the weaker the California effect. . . .

### Regulations and Trade Agreements

The concept of "proportionality" has frequently been employed to assess the legitimacy or legality of a regulation which restricts trade. This approach subjects national regulations that hamper the free movement of goods, but that do serve a legitimate public purpose, to a "balancing" or minimum-means test: it requires nations to select the means of achieving their regulatory objectives that do not "disproportionately" interfere with the free movement of goods. Accordingly, the benefits of a regulation must be weighed against the burdens it imposes on international commerce. . . .

Proportionality can be regarded as the international application of cost-benefit analysis, which governments have frequently employed to assess the value or legality of domestic health, safety, and environmental laws. Both concepts seek to judge the value of a regulation by balancing its goals with its costs: cost-benefit analysis focuses on the costs of compliance to the domestic economy, proportionality on its costs to foreign producers and thus indirectly to domestic consumers as well.

Like cost-benefit analysis, however, the concept of proportionality is often difficult to apply in practice. For while the burdens imposed by a regulation on importers are readily apparent, assessing the value of a consumer or environmental regulation to the citizenry of the nation which enacted it often involves a more subjective judgment. . . .

Since there is rarely a consensus on the answers to these questions within nations, it is not surprising that there has often been substantial disagreement among the governments, firms, and citizens of different countries. . . .

David Vogel, "Chapter 4: Greening the GATT," *Trading Up: Consumer and Environmental Protection in a Global Economy* (Cambridge, MA: Harvard University Press, 1995), pp. 141–149 (excerpted with permission)

### *Conclusion*

What has been the impact of the GATT on environmental standards? . . .

There are two ways in which the GATT might have served to weaken environmental standards. One has to do with the international equivalent of the Delaware effect. By reducing tariffs in general and preventing nations from taxing imported goods produced according to laxer regulatory standards, the GATT might have prevented greener nations from enacting regulatory standards as strict as their citizens preferred. The second has to do with the role of dispute settlement panels in finding national environmental regulations to be GATT-inconsistent. In fact, neither had a significant impact.

The Delaware effect has not materialized at the global level, in part because the costs of compliance with most environmental standards [have] not been sufficiently large to force greener governments to lower them in order to maintain the international competitiveness of domestic producers. . . .

Nor have GATT restrictions on the use of regulations as non-tariff [trade] barriers to trade interfered with the steady strengthing of national, or in the case of the EU, regional environmental standards. . . . Nor do GATT rules prevent nations from acting to

preserve natural resources located outside of their borders, providing these conservation efforts are taken in conjunction with domestic restrictions on either production or consumption. Neither has the GATT prevented a steady increase in the number and scope of international environmental agreements. Thus to date, the GATT has been largely irrelevant to the steady strengthening of local, national, and international environmental standards.

While the number of trade disputes involving environmental regulations has recently increased, they still encompass only a small proportion of all trade conflicts that have come before the GATT. To date, [less than a dozen] out of the slightly more than one hundred trade disputes that have come before dispute panels have involved either environmental or consumer regulations. . . .

. . . if nations wish to strengthen one another's regulatory standards, they must do so outside the GATT framework, by signing international environmental agreements. . . . Moreover, while the EU's rules were rewritten in 1987 to facilitate the harmonization of regulatory standards by establishing a system of weighted voting, no comparable change has taken place within the global community; environment agreements still bind only the nations that sign them. . . .

The California effect does exist at the global level, as evidenced by the successful efforts of both the United States and the European Union to make access to their markets contingent upon changes in the environmental practices of their trading partners. But current GATT rules do limit its scope. . . . "Greening the GATT" does not mean making the World Trade Organization into an international environmental regulatory agency. Rather, what it would essentially mean is giving the world's greener powers wider latitude to enact regulations or trade policies that influence the environmental standards of other GATT signatories.

Beyond the GATT and the WTO, regional and bilateral trade agreements have also begun to address environmental issues.*

### 11.3.2 NAFTA and Other U.S. Bilateral Trade Regimes

In order to get labor and environmentalists' support for NAFTA, President Clinton agreed to negotiate side agreements on labor and the environment, which were not addressed in the central NAFTA agreement that came into effect in 1993. In case of any inconsistency, the agreement gave precedence to three multilateral environmental agreements: CITES, the Montreal Protocol, and the Basel Convention (discussed in Chapter 10). The salient features of the

---

* See Section 5.1.2.4 in Chapter 5 for a discussion of the adverse effects of free trade on the environment.

environment side agreement (the North American Agreement on Environmental Cooperation, NAAEC) between the United States, Canada, and Mexico were the following:

1. A commitment of all three parties to effective enforcement of their environmental laws

2. Establishment of the Commission for Environmental Cooperation (CEC), whose competence includes any environmental or natural resource issue that may arise among the three parties

3. Establishment of a citizen submission (petition) process in which any private person may raise an issue that ultimately reaches the Council (made up of government environment heads) for its attention (however, with no private right of action or private remedy for the petitioner)

4. A dispute-resolution/arbitration process by which a party may raise the allegation that one of the parties has exhibited a "persistent pattern of failure . . . to effectively enforce its environmental law"

5. Provision of means to levy an annual fee up to of $20 million for such violations, and the imposition of trade sanctions if the fee is not paid

As of early 2011, there had been no use of the dispute-resolution process. It is also noteworthy that in the NAAEC, there was no commitment to pursue the harmonization of environmental laws.

By 1997, the United States had concluded some eighteen bilateral and regional trade agreements (free trade agreements) with environment side agreements modeled on the NAAEC). In May 2007, the Bipartisan Agreement on Trade Policy called for enhanced provisions of all future U.S. bilateral and regional trade agreements on several topics, including environmental and sustainable development (see Kennedy 2009 for a full discussion). NAFTA provoked discussion from its early days (Deere and Esty 2002) and continues to generate intense criticism (Cesifo 2010; Gallagher, Peters, et al. 2009). While President Obama had indicated his intent to reexamine NAFTA and presumably other bilateral and regional trade agreements, no action has been taken. For a critical assessment of NAFTA, see Cefiso (2010) and Gantz (2011).

## 11.4 TRADE, EMPLOYMENT, AND LABOR STANDARDS

The literature on trade and labor is less developed than that on trade and the environment, but see Lee (1997), who discusses the impact of globalization on labor standards; Rodrik (1996), who provides an analysis of labor standards in North-South interests; and Caire (1994), who provides a summary of attempts

and the rationale for including a "normative content" (labor standards) in trading relationships. Also see the discussion of the work of Scott (2002) in Chapter 4, who examines the evidence for the effect of trade on U.S., Mexican, and Canadian employment.

In the formulation of the elements that make up sustainable employment as the third pillar of sustainability, we earlier listed the following as central concerns to people who work and their government:

- Wages
- Purchasing power
- Job security
- Health and safety*
- Job satisfaction
- Number of jobs

This, of course, is not an exhaustive list. Ensuring freedom from workplace discrimination, sexual harassment, and violence and providing opportunity for advancement are some other elements. The situation of unauthorized immigrant workers warrants special attention.[17]

Concerns for the welfare of citizens include labor rights, civil rights, and human rights. In one sense, human rights might correctly claim to be the larger overarching set of rights because they include the narrower categories of labor and civil rights.[†] On the other hand, these classifications are not etched in stone, nor are the lines clear. Is the right to form a labor union a civil right or a labor right? Is freedom from violence on the job a human right or a labor right? Clearly, some human rights are not labor rights, such as freedom from torture. Some labor rights may not be civil rights, such as the right to a safe and healthy workplace. Further discussion of fine distinctions is beyond the scope of this book, but here we do focus on the effects of trade and the extent to which important rights and treatment of labor can be secured or strengthened through the reach of international trade.

Not all commentators agree that incorporating labor standards into trade agreements would benefit workers in either developing or developed countries. Stern and Terrell (2003) argue that there is no evidence that "allegedly low labor standards in developing countries have a significantly adverse effect on wages in industrialized countries" and that they are

---

\* See the earlier discussion of WTO protection of worker health and safety in the context of Section XX(b) of the GATT.

† See Howse and Mutua (2000) for a discussion of labor rights as a part of the broader concept of human rights in a global economy.

a main attraction for firms in advanced countries to shift their locus of production or services, or that they cause job and wage losses in industrialized countries. Instead, they argue that imposing higher labor standards on workers in developing countries "above the market value of their productivity" would cause those workers to suffer other negative consequences. Stern and Terrell (2003) recommend the adoption of other policies to expand opportunities (for example, thorough education and transitional adjustment policies) for workers in both developed and industrialized nations. This 2003 analysis may be dated or even incorrect, given the recent large loss of Northern jobs in both manufacturing and services to Asia, as well as the experience with NAFTA (see Faux [2007] and Scott [2002], discussed in Chapter 4). Besides, the failure to find labor differentials between developing and industrialized countries does not mean that labor protections and wages have not fallen in both venues, which is likely.

The possible adverse effects of trade on employment have been addressed in prior chapters of this book.* Here we specifically address whether labor standards can alleviate those adverse effects. The easiest case for asserting that existing trade regimes encompass labor rights or unfair working conditions, as well as environmental and public health issues, can be made for health and safety. The *EC-Asbestos* case (discussed in Sections 11.2.2 and 11.2.4) addresses an avenue of protection for the receiving importer's workers using Article XX(b) or the GATT. In addition, whether the shrimp-turtle case (discussed in Section 11.2.1) can be interpreted as protecting an importer's workers by forcing an exporter to adopt superior process and production methods (PPMs)—thus eliminating the unjustified economic advantage of the exporter and reducing pressure to relax the importer's labor standards or to lower wages to compensate—and, as a result, not to harm the exporter's workers; permitting this strategic use of PPMs is, of course, by no means settled under WTO law.

However, beyond occupational health and safety, the status of employment protections through trade agreements is in doubt. Interestingly, the EU and the WTO have sharply contrasting views about the appropriateness of trade regimes incorporating employment concerns. The WTO states:[18]

> There is a clear consensus: all WTO member governments are committed to a narrower set of internationally recognized "core" standards—freedom of association, no forced labour, no child labour, and no discrimination at work (including gender discrimination). At the 1996 Singapore Ministerial Conference, members defined the WTO's role on this issue, identifying the International Labour Organization (ILO) as the competent body to negotiate labour standards. There is no work on this subject in the WTO's Councils and Committees. However the secretariats of the two organizations work together on technical issues under the banner of "coherence" in global economic policy-making. However, beyond that it is not easy for them to agree, and the question of international enforcement is a minefield.

> *Why was this brought to the WTO?*
> *What is the debate about?*
> Four broad questions have been raised inside and outside the WTO.
> - **The analytical question**: if a country has lower standards for labour rights, do its exports gain an unfair advantage? Would this force all countries to lower their standards (the "race to the bottom")?
> - **The response question**: if there is a "race to the bottom," should countries only trade with those that have similar labour standards?
> - **The question of rules**: Should WTO rules explicitly allow governments to take trade action as a means of putting pressure on other countries to comply?
> - **The institutional analytical question**: is the WTO the proper place to discuss and set rules on labour—or to enforce them, including those of the ILO?

> In addition, all these points have an underlying question: whether trade actions could be used to impose labour standards, or whether this would simply be an excuse for protectionism. Similar questions are asked about standards, i.e. sanitary and phytosanitary measures, and technical barriers to trade.

> The WTO agreements do not deal with labour standards as such.

> On the one hand, some countries would like to change this. WTO rules and disciplines, they argue, would provide a powerful incentive for member nations to improve workplace conditions and "international coherence" (the phrase used to describe efforts to ensure policies move in the same direction).

> On the other hand, many developing countries believe the issue has no place in the WTO framework. They argue that the campaign to bring labour issues into the WTO is actually a bid by industrial nations to undermine the comparative advantage of lower wage trading partners, and could undermine their ability to raise standards through economic development, particularly if it hampers their ability to trade. They also argue that proposed standards can be too high for

---

* See Section 1.1.3 in Chapter 1 and Sections 5.2 and 5.3 in Chapter 5.

them to meet at their level of development. These nations argue that efforts to bring labour standards into the arena of multilateral trade negotiations are little more than a smokescreen for protectionism.

At a more complex legal level is the question of the relationship between the International Labour Organization's standards and the WTO agreements— for example whether or how the ILO's standards can be applied in a way that is consistent with WTO rules.

*What has happened in the WTO?*

In the WTO, the debate has been hard-fought, particularly in 1996 and 1999. It was at the 1996 Singapore conference that members agreed they were committed to recognized core labour standards, but these should not be used for protectionism. The economic advantage of low-wage countries should not be questioned, but the WTO and ILO secretariats would continue their existing collaboration, the declaration said. The concluding remarks of the chairman, Singapore's trade and industry minister, Mr. Yeo Cheow Tong, added that the declaration does not put labour on the WTO's agenda. The countries concerned might continue their pressure for more work to be done in the WTO, but for the time being there are no committees or working parties dealing with the issue.

The issue was also raised at the Seattle Ministerial Conference in 1999, but with no agreement reached. The 2001 Doha Ministerial Conference reaffirmed the Singapore declaration on labour without any specific discussion.

In contrast, although the EU agrees that the ILO is the major institution for dealing with labor issues, it nonetheless states: "The Commission . . . suggests integrating core labour standards in its development policy and strengthening capacity in developing countries to apply core labour standards. It also suggests that core labour standards should have their place in bilateral agreements between Europe and third countries."[19]

The United States is also on record as favoring including core labor standards in trade agreements—at least, this was the case when it was necessary to get labor support for NAFTA.* What is interesting is that incorporating core labor standards into trade regimes is routinely opposed by third-world countries. One might think that the primary reason is that developing countries fear that they might lose the advantages that low wages provide them in international markets. This is probably not the main reason (wage advantages are largely derived from currency advantages rather than from inequalities in purchasing power that the wages provide). It is more likely that core labor standards, which include the right to form a labor union, would upset the balance of power in authoritarian regimes.[†]

The salient features of the labor side agreement (the North American Agreement on Labor Cooperation, NAALC) are very similar, with some important exceptions, to those of the environment side agreement (see Section 11.3.2), with the creation of a Commission for Labor Cooperation (CLC) and with the added commitments of the parties (1) not to lower labor standards to attract investment and (2) to provide monetary sanctions (up to $20 million) only as a final punitive measure, followed by trade sanctions only in the case of violations or lack of enforcement of worker health and safety, child labor, and minimum-wage standards, but exempting fundamental labor relations protections, such as the right to organize or strike. Significantly, freedom of association and protection of the right to organize, the right to bargain collectively, and the right to strike were exempted (see Gitterman 2002).

Complaints of violations are to go to a national administrative office (NAO), rather than to the CLC. The parties agreed to cooperate on seven objectives, including improving working conditions and living conditions and promoting eleven labor principles to protect, enhance, and enforce workers' basic rights. The parties agreed to six (voluntary) obligations that define effective enforcement and hold one another accountable through the mechanisms of consultations, evaluation, and dispute resolution. There were no commitments to harmonize labor standards. Labor disputes were to be resolved only through informal coordination, and conflicts covered by the side agreement were to be resolved through dialogue and consultation, initially at the NAO and later at the ministerial level (Gitterman 2002). Also see Gantz (2011).

Trade regimes are premised on the assumption that trade benefits humankind, but what can be done about reconciling trade with other aspects of human welfare or human rights? Howse and Mutua (2000) observe:

> There is no consensus on how trade liberalization affects human rights, nor even a well-developed methodology for determining the human impacts of

---

*    It was necessary to negotiate so-called side agreements on both labor and environment under NAFTA. Their success has been called into question. See Garvey (1995) and Section 11.3.2.

†    If people are not allowed to come together to meditate in China without being thrown into prison, is it likely that the Chinese government would tolerate the formation of an independent labor union?

trade agreements. . . . Both trade and human rights have been codified in highly-developed legal regimes, negotiated by governments since the end of World War II. These two legal regimes have developed however in splendid isolation from one another. . . . (page 2)

The correct reading of the GATT text would permit a country to impose conditions on imports related to the labour practices involved in their production. (page 6)

The authors remind us:

The Preamble to the WTO Agreement takes notice that the objectives of the system are not free trade as such but, *inter alia* "ensuring full employment and a large and steadily growing volume of real income and effective demand" and "allowing for the optimal use of the world's resources in accordance with the objective of sustainable development." (page 32)

The reader should recollect that one of the exceptions in Article XX of the GATT is section XX(d):

Article XX: General Exceptions
Subject to the requirement that such [restrictive trade] measures are not applied in a manner which would constitute a means of arbitrary or unjustifiable discrimination between countries where the same conditions prevail, or a disguised restriction on international trade, nothing in this Agreement shall be construed to prevent the adoption or enforcement by any contracting party of measures:

. . .

(d) necessary to secure compliance with laws or regulations which are not inconsistent with the provisions of [the GATT].

The UN Charter on Human Rights cites as one of its purposes to promote "higher standards of living, full employment, and conditions of economic and social progress and development" (Article 55a, UN Charter). Thus, there is an argument that human rights law trumps trade law—WTO trade law cannot be inconsistent with the UN Charter on Human Rights. This is so even if it were argued that environmental laws do not trump WTO law.

The European Union stands out for its attempt to reconcile trade policies with concerns for sustainable development, core human rights, and poverty reduction. Through an EU Council regulation, it has adopted an autonomous trade arrangement—the EC Generalised Scheme of Tariff Preferences—through which the EU provides nonreciprocal preferential access to the EU market to 176 developing countries and territories. These preferences—which take the form of duty-free access or reductions in otherwise-

applicable standard tariffs for thousands of tariff lines—act as an incentive for these developing countries to ratify and effectively implement a series of key international conventions in the fields of core human rights and labor standards, sustainable development, and good governance.[20]

## 11.5 NOTES

1. See Australian Broadcasting Corporation (ABC), *Money, Markets and the Economy*, Program 11, "The Rise of Economic Rationalism," http://abc.net.au/money/vault/programs/prog11 .htm (accessed May 18, 2010).

2. WTO, Understanding the WTO: The Agreements, Overview: A Navigational Guide, www.wto.org/english/thewto_e/ whatis_e/tif_e/agrm1_e.htm (accessed February 9, 2011).

3. WTO, Understanding the WTO: Settling Disputes, A Unique Contribution, www.wto.org/english/thewto_e/whatis_e/ tif_e/disp1_e.htm (accessed February 9, 2011).

4. See Khachuturian (2008), Levy (2007), and Ring (2008).

5. In *European Communities–Hormones,* op. cit., para. 115, the Appellate Body itself expressed its reluctance to adopt within the context of the SPS Agreement a standard of review not clearly rooted in the text of the SPS Agreement, for fear of disturbing the balance between the rights and obligations negotiated.

6. WTO, Understanding the WTO: The Agreements, Standards and Safety, www.wto.org/english/thewto_e/whatis_e/tif_e/ agrm4_e.htm (accessed February 9, 2011).

7. The SPS Agreement applies to "any measure" that is "applied to protect . . . from risks arising from additives, contaminants, toxins and disease-causing organisms in foods, beverages or foodstuffs."

8. See TUTB (2001).

9. See WTO and WHO (2002).

10. See WTO, US/EU Hormones Case Agreement Discussed at the DSB, www.wto.org/english/news_e/news09_e/dsb _19jun09_e.htm (accessed May 18, 2010).

11. Europa, EU and Canada Settle WTO Case on Genetically Modified Organisms, http://europa.eu/rapid/pressReleas- esAction.do?reference=IP/09/1142&type= (accessed February 9, 2011).

12. See European Commission, Trade, http://trade.ec.europa .eu/doclib/press/index.cfm?id=536 (accessed May 18, 2010).

13. See A. Eckstein, Environment Council: GMOS: Commission Gets Thrown against the Ropes, www.allbusiness.com/gov ernment/government-bodies-offices/15251429-1.html (accessed November 14, 2010).

14. See S. Petitjean, Foodstuffs: Executive Proposes Temporary Ban on Animal Cloning for Food, www.allbusiness.com/ science-technology/biology-biotechnology-genetic/15222719-1 .html (accessed November 14, 2010).

15. See WTO, TRIPS, www.wto.org/english/tratop_e/trips _e/trips_e.htm (accessed May 18, 2010).

16. See Incentives for Global Health, "The Health Impact Fund: Making New Medicines Accessible for All," www.yale .edu/macmillan/igh/ (accessed May 18, 2010).

17. See Lyon (2006).

18. WTO, Labour Standards: Consensus, Coherence and Controversy, www.wto.org/english/thewto_e/whatis_e/tif_e/bey5 _e.htm (accessed February 9, 2011).

19. EuropaWorld, European Commission Acts to Improve Working Conditions Worldwide, July 20, 2001, www.europa world.org/issue43/europeancommissionacts20701.htm (accessed May 18, 2010).

20. European Commission, Trade, Generalised System of Preferences (GSP), http://ec.europa.eu/trade/wider-agenda/deve

lopment/generalised-system-of-preferences/ (accessed May 18, 2010).

## 11.6 REFERENCES

Bamberger, K. A., and A. T. Guzman (2008). "Keeping Imports Safe: A Proposal for Discriminatory Regulation of International Trade." *California Law Review* **96**: 1405–1445.

Bhagwati, J. (1993). "The Case for Free Trade." *Scientific American* **269**(5): 42–49.

Borghesi, S., and A. Vercelli (2003). "Sustainable Globalisation." *Ecological Economics* **44**: 77–89.

Caire, G. (1994). Labour Standards and International Trade. *International Labour Standards and Economic Interdependence*. W. Segenberger and D. Campbell. Geneva, International Institute for Labour Studies.

Carranza, M. A. E. (2007–2008). "MEAs with Trade Measures and the WTO: Aiming toward Sustainable Development?" *Buffalo Environmental Law Journal* **15**: 43–96.

Cefiso (2010). NAFTA *CESifo Forum* **11**(4): 3–51.

Charles, T., and F. Lehner (1998). "Competitiveness and Employment: A Strategic Dilemma for Economic Policy." *Competition and Change* **3**(1/2): 207–236.

Charnovitz, S. (2002). "The Law of Environmental 'PPMs' in the WTO: Debunking the Myth of Illegality." *Yale Journal of International Law* **27**: 59–110.

Chichester, D. (2005). "Battle of the Beef, the Rematch: An Evaluation of the Latest E.C. Directive Banning Beef Produced with Growth Hormones and the U.S. Refusal to Accept the Directive as WTO Compliant." *American University International Law Review* **21**: 221–276.

Cole, M. A. (2000). *Trade Liberalisation, Economic Growth and the Environment*. Cheltenham, Edward Elgar.

Conca, K. (2002). Consumption and Environment in a Global Economy. *Confronting Consumption*. T. Princen, M. Maniates, and K. Conca. Cambridge, MA, MIT Press: 133–153.

Cors, T. A. (2001). "Biosafety and International Trade: Conflict or Convergence?" *International Journal of Global Environmental Issues* **1**(1): 87–103.

Cortez, E. (2008). "Total Recall on Chinese Imports: Pursuing an End to Unsafe Health and Safety Standards through Article XX of GATT." *American University International Law Review* **23**: 915–942.

Costanza, R., J. Cumberland, et al. (1997). *An Introduction to Ecological Economics*. Boca Raton, FL, St. Lucie Press.

Daly, H. E. (1993). "The Perils of Free Trade." *Scientific American* **269**(5): 50–54.

Deere, C., and D. C. Esty (2002). *Greening the Americas: NAFTA's Lesson for Hemispheric Trade*. Cambridge, MA, MIT Press.

Dicken, P. (1994). "The Roepke Lecture in Economic Geography: Global-Local Tensions; Firms and States in the Global Space-Economy." *Economic Geography* **70**(2): 101–128.

Driesen, M. (2001). "What Is Free Trade? The Real Issue Lurking behind the Trade and Environment Debate." *Virginia Journal of International Law* **41**(Winter): 279–369.

Dryzek, J. S. (1997). *The Politics of the Earth: Environmental Discourses*. New York, Oxford University Press.

Faux, J. (2007). Globalization That Works for Working Americans. Briefing Paper 179. Washington, DC, Economic Policy Institute.

Fisher, E. (2006). Beyond the Science/Democracy Dichotomy: The World Trade Organisation Sanitary and Phytosanitary Agreement and Administrative Constitutionalism. *Constitutionalism, Multilevel Trade Governance, and Social Regulation*. C. Joerges and E.-U. Petersmann. Oxford, Hart Publishers.

Gallagher, K. P., E. D. Peters, et al. (2009). The Future of North American Trade Policy: Lessons from NAFTA. Boston, Boston University, Frederick S. Pardee Center for the Study of the Longer-Range Future.

Gantz, D. A. (2011). Labor Rights and Environmental Protection under NAFTA and Other U.S. Free Trade Agreements. Arizona Legal Studies Discussion Paper 11–13. The University of Arizona, James E. Rogers College of Law, March. Available at http://www.ssrn.com/abstracts=1791839 (accessed May 5, 2011).

Garvey, J. I. (1995). "Dispute Resolution under the NAFTA Side Accords on Labor and the Environment." *American Journal of International Law* **89**: 439–453.

Gitterman, D. P. (2002). A Race to the Bottom, a Race to the Top or the March to a Minimum Floor? Economic Integration and Labor Standards in Comparative Perspective. *Dynamics of Regulatory Change: How Globalization Affects National Regulatory Policies*. D. Vogel and R. Kagan (Eds.). University of California International and Area Studies Digital Collection (UCIAS). Available at http://repositories.cdlib.org/uciaspubs/edit edvolumes/1/10 (accessed February 9, 2011).

Hart, S., and M. B. Milstein (1999). "Global Sustainability and the Creative Destruction of Industries." *Sloan Management Review* **41**(1): 23–33.

Heckscher, E. F. (1949 [1919]). The Effect of Foreign Trade on the Distribution of Income. *Readings in the Theory of International Trade*. H. S. Ellis and L. A. Metzler. Philadelphia, Blakiston Company: 497–512.

Held, D., and A. McGrew, Eds. (2002). *The Global Transformations Reader: An Introduction to the Globalization Debate*. Malden, MA, Polity Press.

Howse, R. (2002). "The Appellate Body Rulings in the Shrimp/Turtle Case: A New Legal Baseline for the Trade and Environment Debate." *Columbia Environmental Law Journal* **27**: 491–521.

Howse, R., and M. Mutua (2000). Protecting Human Rights in a Global Economy: Challenges for the World Trade Organization. Working Paper. Montreal, International Centre for Human Rights and Democratic Development.

Hutter, B. (2002). "Sustainable Development: Compliance and Beyond." *International Herald Tribune*, July 1, p. 14.

International Centre for Trade and Sustainable Development (ICTSD) (2002). "WTO Environment Committee Stalls on MEA Observership, TRIPs-CBD." *ICTSD Newsletter* **2**(12)(June 27): 1. Geneva, International Centre for Trade and Sustainable Development. Available at http://ictsd.org/i/news/biores/8731/ (accessed March 2, 2011).

Kennedy, K. C. (2009). International Trade: Sustainability as a Multilateral, Bilateral, and Regional Effort. *Agenda for a Sustainable America.* J. Dernbach. Washington, DC, Environmental Law Institute.

Khachuturian, A. (2008). "Reforming the United States Export Tax Policy: An Alternative to the American Trade War with the European Union." *U.C. Davis Journal of International Law and Policy* **14**: 185–203.

Korten, D. C. (2001). *When Corporations Rule the World.* San Francisco, Berrett-Koehler Publishers.

LeClair, M. S., and D. Franceschi (2006). "Externalities in International Trade: The Case for Differential Tariffs." *Ecological Economics* **58**: 462–472.

Lee, E. (1997). "Globalization and Labor Standards: A Review of the Issues." *International Labor Review* **136**: 172–189.

Levy, L. (2007). "International Trade Law—Original DSB Rulings Apply to Subsequent Remedial Measures." *Suffolk Transnational Law Review* **31**: 199–207.

Liebman, B. H., and K. M. Tomlin (2008). "Safeguards and Retaliatory Threats." *Journal of Law and Economics* **51**: 351–366.

Limao, N., and K. Saggi (2006). Tariff Retaliation versus Financial Compensation in the Enforcement of International Trade Agreements. World Bank Research Working Paper 3873, Washington, DC, April.

London, T., and S. L. Hart (2004). "Reinventing Strategies for Emerging Markets: Beyond the Transnational Model." *Journal of International Business Studies* **35**: 350–370.

Lugard, M., and M. Smart (2006). "The Role of Science in International Trade Law." *Regulatory Toxicology and Pharmacology* **44**: 69–74.

Lyon, B. (2006). New International Human Rights on Unauthorized Immigrant Worker Rights: Seizing an Opportunity to Pull Governments out of the Shadows. Working Paper 45, Villanova University School of Law.

Menezes, R. P. B., and A. M. de Souza Antunes (2005). "Using the WTO/TBT Enquiry Point to Monitor Tendencies in the Regulation of Environment, Health, and Safety Issues Affecting the Chemical Industry." *Environment International* **31**: 407–416.

Nehrt, C. (1998). "Maintainability of First Mover Advantages When Environmental Regulations Differ between Countries." *Academy of Management Review* **23**(1): 77–97.

Office of Technology Assessment (OTA) (1992). *Trade and Environment: Conflicts and Opportunities.* Washington, DC, OTA.

Ohlin, B. (1933). *Interregional and International Trade.* Cambridge, MA, Harvard University Press.

Organisation for Economic Co-operation and Development (OECD) (1994). *The Environmental Effects of Trade.* Paris, OECD.

OECD (1997). *Economic Globalization and the Environment.* Paris, OECD.

Oye, K., and J. Foster (2002). Public Environmental Regulation and Private Business Risk. Laboratory for Energy and the Environment (LFEE). Working Paper, Cambridge, MA, MIT.

Pauwelyn, J. (2002). "Cross-Agreement Complaints before the Appellate Body: A Case Study of the EC-Asbestos Dispute." *World Trade Review* **1**(1): 63–87.

Plofchan, T. K. (1992). "Recognizing and Countervailing Environmental Subsidies." *Environmental Lawyer* **26** (Fall): 763–780.

Pollock, A. M., and D. Price (2003). "The Public Health Implications of World Trade Negotiations on the General Agreement on Trade in Services and Public Services." *Lancet* **363**(9389): 1072–1075.

Porter, M. E. (1990). *The Competitive Advantage of Nations.* New York, Free Press.

Porter, M. E., and C. van der Linde (1995). "Green and Competitive: Ending the Stalemate." *Harvard Business Review* **73**:120–134.

Prahalad, C. K., and S. L. Hart (2002). "The Fortune at the Bottom of the Pyramid." *Strategy+Business* (26): 2–14.

Princen, T. (2002). Distancing: Consumption and the Severing of Feedback. *Confronting Consumption.* T. Princen, M. Maniates, and K. Conca. Cambridge, MA, MIT Press: 103–131.

Rees, W. E., and L. Westra (2003). When Consumption Does Violence: Can There be Sustainability and Environmental Justice in a Resource-Limited World? *Just Sustainabilities: Development in an Unequal World.* J. Agyeman, R. D. Bullard, and B. Evans. Cambridge, MA, MIT Press: 99–124.

Reid, D. (1995). *Sustainable Development: An Introductory Guide.* London, Earthscan.

Ricardo, D. (1996 [1817]). *The Principles of Political Economy and Taxation.* New York, Prometheus Books.

Ring, D. (2008). "What's at Stake in the Sovereignty Debate? International Tax and the Nation-State." *Virginia Journal of International Law* **49**: 155–233.

Rodrik, D. (1996). Labor Standards in International Trade: Do They Matter and What Do We Do about Them? *Emerging Agenda for Global Trade: High Stakes for Developing Countries.* R. Lawrence, D. Rodrik, and J. Whalley. Baltimore, MD, Johns Hopkins University Press.

Sagoff, M. (1988). *The Economy of the Earth.* Cambridge, Cambridge University Press.

Schmidheiny, S. (1992). *Changing Course: A Global Business Perspective on Development and the Environment.* Cambridge, MA, MIT Press.

Scott, R. (2002). Globalization and Employment. Presentation at the MIT Symposium on Exploring the Many Dimensions of Sustainable Development.

Shapiro, H. (2007). "The Rules that Swallowed the Exceptions: The WTO SPS Agreement and its Relationship to GATT Articles XX and XXI; The Threat of the EU-GMO Dispute." *International Journal of International and Comparative Law* **24**: 199–232.

Sien, I. A. R. (2007). "Beefing up the Hormones Dispute: Problems in Compliance and Viable Compromise Alternatives." *Georgetown Law Journal* **95**: 565–590.

Soros, G. (2002). *George Soros on Globalization.* New York, Public Affairs.

Speth, J. G. (2003). Two Perspectives on Globalization and the Environment. *Worlds Apart: Globalization and the Environment.* J. G. Speth. Washington, DC, Island Press: 1–18.

Steininger, K. (1994). "Reconciling Trade and Environment: Towards a Comparative Advantage for Long-Term Policy Goals." *Ecological Economics* **9**(1): 23–42.

Stern, R. M., and K. Terrell (2003). Labor Standards and the World Trade Organization. Discussion Paper 499, Gerald R. Ford School of Public Policy, University of Michigan, August.

Stiglitz, J. (2002). *Globalization and Its Discontents*. New York, W. W. Norton.

Todaro, M. P., and S. C. Smith (2009). *Economic Development*. 10th ed. Boston, Addison-Wesley.

Trade Union Technical Bureau (TUTB) (2001). "Asbestos Disputes in the WTO: Battle Won—but Not the War." *TUTB Newsletter*, Brussels, June, pp. 20–28.

United Nations Environment Programme (UNEP) (2002). *Enhancing Synergies and Mutual Supportiveness of Multilateral Environmental Agreements and the World Trade Organization: A Synthesis Report*. Geneva, UNEP.

UNEP (2007). *Trade-Related Measures and Multi-lateral Environment Agreements*. Geneva, UNEP.

White, D. L. (1989). "Shaping Antitrust Enforcement: Greater Emphasis on Barriers to Entry." *Brigham Young University Law Review* **3**: 823–851.

Winter, R. (2000). "Reconciling the GATT and WTO with Multilateral Environmental Agreements: Can We Have Our Cake and Eat It Too?" *Colorado Journal of International Environmental Law and Policy* **11**: 223–255.

World Trade Organization (WTO) (1996). *Report of the Committee on Trade and Environment*. Geneva, WTO.

WTO (2011). Dispute Settlement System Training Module: Chapter 6. The Process—Stages in a Typical WTO Dispute Settlement Case. Geneva, WTO. Available at www.wto.org/english/tratop_e/dispu_e/disp_settlement _cbt_e/c6s1p1_e.htm (accessed February 13, 2011).

WTO and World Health Organization (WHO) (2002). *WTO Agreements and Public Health: A Joint Study by the WHO and the WTO Secretariat*. Geneva, WTO and WHO.

World Wildlife Fund (WWF) (2001). "Towards Coherent Environmental and Economic Governance: Legal and Practical Approaches to MEA-WTO Linkages." Gland, Switzerland, WWF World Wide Fund for Nature. Available at www.ciel.org/Publications/Coherent_EnvirEco _Governance.pdf (accessed March 2, 2011).

## APPENDIX 11-A: SELECTED WTO AGREEMENTS

The following excerpts provide information on selected WTP agreements.

### Agreement on Subsidies and Countervailing Measures

The Agreement on Subsidies and Countervailing Measures is intended to build on the Agreement on Interpretation and Application of Articles VI, XVI and XXIII which was negotiated in the Tokyo Round.

Unlike its predecessor, the agreement contains a definition of subsidy and introduces the concept of a "specific" subsidy—for the most part, a subsidy available only to an enterprise or industry or group of enterprises or industries within the jurisdiction of the authority granting the subsidy. Only specific subsidies would be subject to the disciplines set out in the agreement.

The agreement establishes three categories of subsidies. First, it deems the following subsidies to be "prohibited": those contingent, in law or in fact, whether solely or as one of several other conditions, upon export performance; and those contingent, whether solely or as one of several other conditions, upon the use of domestic over imported goods. Prohibited subsidies are subject to new dispute settlement procedures. The main features include an expedited timetable for action by the Dispute Settlement body, and if it is found that the subsidy is indeed prohibited, it must be immediately withdrawn. If this is not done within the specified time period, the complaining member is authorized to take countermeasures. (See the section on "Dispute Settlement" for details on the procedures).

The second category is "actionable" subsidies. The agreement stipulates that no member should cause, through the use of subsidies, adverse effects to the interests of other signatories, i.e. injury to domestic industry of another signatory, nullification or impairment of benefits accruing directly or indirectly to other signatories under the General Agreement (in particular the benefits of bound tariff concessions), and serious prejudice to the interests of another member. "Serious prejudice" shall be presumed to exist for certain subsidies including when the total *ad valorem* subsidization of a product exceeds 5 per cent. In such a situation, the burden of proof is on the subsidizing member to show that the subsidies in question do not cause serious prejudice to the complaining member. Members affected by actionable subsidies may refer the matter to the Dispute Settlement body. In the event that it is determined that such adverse effects exist, the subsidizing member must withdraw the subsidy or remove the adverse effects.

The third category involves non-actionable subsidies, which could either be non-specific subsidies, or specific subsidies involving assistance to industrial research and pre-competitive development activity, assistance to disadvantaged regions, or certain type of assistance for adapting existing facilities to new environmental requirements imposed by law and/or regulations. Where another member believes that an otherwise non-actionable subsidy is resulting in serious adverse effects to a domestic industry, it may seek a determination and recommendation on the matter.

One part of the agreement concerns the use of countervailing measures on subsidized imported goods. It sets out disciplines on the initiation of countervailing cases, investigations by national authorities and rules of evidence to ensure that all interested parties can present information and argument. Certain disciplines on the calculation of the amount of a subsidy are outlined as is the basis for the determination of injury to the domestic industry. The agreement would require that all relevant economic factors be taken into account in assessing the state of the industry and that a causal link be established between the subsidized imports and the alleged injury. Countervailing investigations shall be terminated immediately in cases where the amount of a subsidy is *de minimis* (the subsidy is less than 1 per cent *ad valorem)* or where the volume of subsidized imports, actual or potential, or the injury is negligible. Except under exceptional circumstances, investigations shall be concluded within one year after their initiation and in no case more than 18 months. All countervailing duties have to be terminated within 5 years of their imposition unless the authorities determine on the basis of a review that the expiry of the duty would be likely to lead to continuation or recurrence of subsidization and injury.

The agreement recognizes that subsidies may play an important role in economic development programmes of developing countries, and in the transformation of centrally-planned economies to market economies. Least-developed countries and developing countries that have less than $1,000 per capita GNP are thus exempted from disciplines on prohibited export subsidies, and have a time-bound exemption from other prohibited subsidies. For other developing countries, the export subsidy prohibition would take effect 8 years after the entry into force of the agreement establishing the WTO, and they have a time-bound (though fewer years than for poorer developing countries) exemption from the other prohibited subsidies. Countervailing investigation of a product originating from a developing-country member would be terminated if the overall level of subsidies does not exceed 2 per cent (and from certain developing countries 3 per cent) of the value of the product, or if the volume of the subsidized imports represents less than 4 per cent of the total imports for the like product in the importing signatory. For countries in the process of transformation from a centrally-planned into a market economy, prohibited subsidies shall be phased out within a period of seven years from the date of entry into force of the agreement.

### General Agreement on Trade in Services (GATS)

The Services Agreement which forms part of the Final Act rests on three pillars. The first is a Framework Agreement containing basic obligations which apply to all member countries. The second concerns national schedules of commitments containing specific further national commitments which will be the subject of a continuing process of liberalization. The third is a number of annexes addressing the special situations of individual services sectors.

Part I of the basic agreement defines its scope—specifically, services supplied from the territory of one party to the territory of another; services supplied in the territory of one party to the consumers of any other (for example, tourism); services provided through the presence of service providing entities of one party in the territory of any other (for example, banking); and services provided by nationals of one party in the territory of any other (for example, construction projects or consultancies).

Part II sets out general obligations and disciplines. A basic most-favoured-nation (MFN) obligation states that each party "shall accord immediately and unconditionally to services and service providers of any other Party, treatment no less favourable than that it accords to like services and service providers of any other country." However, it is recognized that MFN treatment may not be possible for every service activity and, therefore, it is envisaged that parties may indicate specific MFN exemptions. Conditions for such exemptions are included as an annex and provide for reviews after five years and a normal limitation of 10 years on their duration.

Transparency requirements include publication of all relevant laws and regulations. Provisions to facilitate the increased participation of developing countries in world services trade envisage negotiated commitments on access to technology, improvements in access to distribution channels and information networks and the liberalization of market access in sectors and modes of supply of export interest. The provisions covering economic integration are analogous to those in Article XXIV of GATT, requiring arrangements to have "substantial sectoral coverage" and to "provide for the absence or elimination of substantially all discrimination" between the parties.

Since domestic regulations, not border measures, provide the most significant influence on services trade, provisions spell out that all such measures of general application should be administered in a reasonable, objective and impartial manner. There would be a requirement that parties establish the means for prompt reviews of administrative decisions relating to the supply of services.

The agreement contains obligations with respect to recognition requirements (educational background, for instance) for the purpose of securing authorizations, licenses or certification in the services area. It encourages recognition requirements achieved through harmonization and internationally-agreed criteria. Further provisions state that parties are required to ensure that monopolies and exclusive service providers do not abuse their positions. Restrictive business practices should be subject to consultations between parties with a view to their elimination.

While parties are normally obliged not to restrict international transfers and payments for current transactions relating to commitments under the agreement, there are provisions allowing limited restrictions in the event of balance-of-payments difficulties. However, where such restrictions are imposed they would be subject to conditions; including that they are non-discriminatory, that they avoid unnecessary commercial damage to other parties and that they are of a temporary nature.

The agreement contains both general exceptions and security exceptions provisions which are similar to Articles XX and XXI of the GATT. It also envisages negotiations with a view to the development of disciplines on trade-distorting subsidies in the services area.

Part III contains provisions on market access and national treatment which would not be general obligations but would be commitments made in national schedules. Thus, in the case of market access, each party "shall accord services and service providers of other Parties treatment no less favourable than that provided for under the terms, limitations and conditions agreed and specified in its schedule." The intention of the market-access provision is to progressively eliminate the following types of measures: limitations on numbers of service providers, on the total value of service transactions or on the total number of service operations or people employed. Equally, restrictions on the kind of legal entity or joint venture through which a service is provided or any foreign capital limitations relating to maximum levels of foreign participation are to be progressively eliminated.

The national-treatment provision contains the obligation to treat foreign service suppliers and domestic service suppliers in the same manner. However, it does provide the possibility of different treatment being accorded the service providers of other parties to that accorded to domestic service providers. However, in such cases the conditions of competition should not, as a result, be modified in favour of the domestic service providers.

Part IV of the agreement establishes the basis for progressive liberalization in the services area through successive rounds of negotiations and the development of national schedules. It also permits, after a period of three years, parties to withdraw or modify commitments made in their schedules. Where commitments are modified or withdrawn, negotiations should be undertaken with interested parties to agree on compensatory adjustments. Where agreement cannot be reached, compensation would be decided by arbitration.

Part V of the agreement contains institutional provisions, including consultation and dispute settlement and the establishment of a Council on Services. The responsibilities of the Council are set out in a Ministerial Decision.

The first of the annexes to the agreement concerns the movement of labour. It permits parties to negotiate specific commitments applying to the movement of people providing services under the agreement. It requires that people covered by a specific commitment shall be allowed to provide the service in accordance with the terms of the commitment. Nevertheless, the agreement would not apply to measures affecting employment, citizenship, residence or employment on a permanent basis. The annex on financial services (largely banking and insurance) lays down the right of parties, notwithstanding other provisions, to take prudential measures, including for the protection of investors, deposit holders and policy holders, and to ensure the integrity and stability of the financial system. However, a further understanding on financial services would allow those participants who choose to do so to undertake commitments on financial services through a different method. With respect to market access, the understanding contains more detailed obligations on, among other things, monopoly rights, cross-border trade (certain insurance and reinsurance policy writing as well as financial data processing and transfer), the right to establish or expand a commercial presence, and the temporary entry of personnel. The provisions on national treatment refer explicitly to access to payments and clearing systems operated by public entities and to official funding and refinancing facilities. They also relate to membership of, or participation in, self-regulatory bodies, securities or futures exchanges and clearing agencies.

The annex on telecommunications relates to measures which affect access to and use of public telecommunications services and networks. In particular, it requires that such access be accorded to another party, on reasonable and non-discriminatory terms, to permit the supply of a service included in its schedule. Conditions attached to the use of public networks should be no more than is necessary to safeguard the public service responsibilities of their operators, to protect the technical integrity of the network and to ensure that foreign service suppliers do not supply services unless permitted to do so through a specific commitment. The annex also encourages technical cooperation to assist developing countries in the strengthening of their own domestic telecommunications sectors. The annex on air-transport services excludes from the agreement's coverage traffic rights (largely bilateral air-service agreements conferring landing rights) and directly related activities which might affect the negotiation of traffic rights. Nevertheless, the annex, in its current form, also states that the agreement should apply to aircraft repair and maintenance services, the marketing of air-transport services and computer-reservation services. The operation of the annex would be reviewed at least every five years.

In the final days of the services negotiations, three Decisions were taken—on Financial Services, Professional Services and the Movement of Natural Persons. The Decision on Financial Services confirmed that commitments in this sector would be implemented on an MFN basis, and permits Members to revise and finalize their schedules of commitments and their MFN exemptions six months after the entry into force of the Agreement. Contrary to some media reports, the audio-visual and maritime sectors have not been removed from the scope of the GATS.

## Agreement on Trade Related Aspects of Intellectual Property Rights (TRIPS), Including Trade in Counterfeit Goods

The agreement recognises that widely varying standards in the protection and enforcement of intellectual property rights and the lack of a multilateral framework of principles, rules and disciplines dealing with international trade in counterfeit goods have been a growing source of tension in international economic relations. Rules and disciplines were needed to cope with these tensions. To that end, the agreement addresses the applicability of basic GATT principles and those of relevant international intellectual property agreements; the provision of adequate intellectual property rights; the provision of effective enforcement measures for those rights; multilateral dispute settlement; and transitional arrangements.

Part I of the agreement sets out general provisions and basic principles, notably a national-treatment commitment under which the nationals of other parties must be given treatment no less favourable than that accorded to a party's own nationals with regard to the protection of

intellectual property. It also contains a most-favoured-nation clause, a novelty in an international intellectual property agreement, under which any advantage a party gives to the nationals of another country must be extended immediately and unconditionally to the nationals of all other parties, even if such treatment is more favourable than that which it gives to its own nationals.

Part II addresses each intellectual property right in succession. With respect to copyright, parties are required to comply with the substantive provisions of the Berne Convention for the protection of literary and artistic works, in its latest version (Paris 1971), though they will not be obliged to protect moral rights as stipulated in Article 6bis of that Convention. It ensures that computer programs will be protected as literary works under the Berne Convention and lays down on what basis data bases should be protected by copyright. Important additions to existing international rules in the area of copyright and related rights are the provisions on rental rights. The draft requires authors of computer programmes and producers of sound recordings to be given the right to authorize or prohibit the commercial rental of their works to the public. A similar exclusive right applies to films where commercial rental has led to widespread copying which is materially impairing the right of reproduction. The draft also requires performers to be given protection from unauthorized recording and broadcast of live performances (bootlegging). The protection for performers and producers of sound recordings would be for no less than 50 years. Broadcasting organizations would have control over the use that can be made of broadcast signals without their authorization. This right would last for at least 20 years.

With respect to trademarks and service marks, the agreement defines what types of signs must be eligible for protection as a trademark or service mark and what the minimum rights conferred on their owners must be. Marks that have become well-known in a particular country shall enjoy additional protection. In addition, the agreement lays down a number of obligations with regard to the use of trademarks and service marks, their term of protection, and their licensing or assignment. For example, requirements that foreign marks be used in conjunction with local marks would, as a general rule, be prohibited.

In respect of geographical indications, the agreement lays down that all parties must provide means to prevent the use of any indication which misleads the consumer as to the origin of goods, and any use which would constitute an act of unfair competition. A higher level of protection is provided for geographical indications for wines and spirits, which are protected even where there is no danger of the public's being misled as to the true origin. Exceptions are allowed for names that have already become generic terms, but any country using such an exception must be willing to negotiate with a view to protecting the geographical indications in question. Furthermore, provision is made for further negotiations to establish a multilateral system of notification and registration of geographical indications for wines.

Industrial designs are also protected under the agreement for a period of 10 years. Owners of protected designs would be able to prevent the manufacture, sale or importation of articles bearing or embodying a design which is a copy of the protected design.

As regards patents, there is a general obligation to comply with the substantive provisions of the Paris Convention (1967). In addition, the agreement requires that 20-year patent protection be available for all inventions, whether of products or processes, in almost all fields of technology. Inventions may be excluded from patentability if their commercial exploitation is prohibited for reasons of public order or morality; otherwise, the permitted exclusions are for diagnostic, therapeutic and surgical methods, and for plants and (other than microorganisms) animals and essentially biological processes for the production of plants or animals (other than microbiological processes). Plant varieties, however, must be protectable either by patents or by a *sui generis* system (such as the breeder's rights provided in a UPOV [The Union for the Protection of New Varieties of Plants] Convention). Detailed conditions are laid down for compulsory licensing or governmental use of patents without the authorization of the patent owner. Rights conferred in respect of patents for processes must extend to the products directly obtained by the process; under certain conditions alleged infringers may be ordered by a court to prove that they have not used the patented process.

With respect to the protection of layout designs of integrated circuits, the agreement requires parties to provide protection on the basis of the Washington Treaty on Intellectual Property in Respect of Integrated Circuits which was opened for signature in May 1989, but with a number of additions: protection must be available for a minimum period of 10 years; the rights must extend to articles incorporating infringing layout designs; innocent infringers must be allowed to use or sell stock in hand or ordered before learning of the infringement against a suitable royalty: and compulsory licensing and government use is only allowed under a number of strict conditions.

Trade secrets and know-how which have commercial value must be protected against breach of confidence and other acts contrary to honest commercial practices. Test data submitted to governments in order to obtain marketing approval for pharmaceutical or agricultural chemicals must also be protected against unfair commercial use.

The final section in this part of the agreement concerns anti-competitive practices in contractual licenses. It provides for consultations between governments where there is reason to believe that licensing practices or conditions pertaining to intellectual property rights constitute an abuse of these rights and have an adverse effect on competition. Remedies against such abuses must be consistent with the other provisions of the agreement.

Part III of the agreement sets out the obligations of member governments to provide procedures and remedies under their domestic law to ensure that intellectual property rights can be effectively enforced, by foreign right holders as well as by their own nationals. Procedures should permit effective action against infringement of intellectual property rights but should be fair and equitable, not unnecessarily complicated or costly, and should not entail unreasonable time-limits or unwarranted delays. They should allow for judicial review of final administrative decisions. There is no obligation to put in place a judicial system distinct from that for the enforcement of laws in general, nor to give priority to the enforcement of intellectual property rights in the allocation of resources or staff.

The civil and administrative procedures and remedies spelled out in the text include provisions on evidence of proof, injunctions, damages and other remedies which would include the right of judicial authorities to order the disposal or destruction of infringing goods. Judicial authorities must also have the authority to order prompt and effective provisional measures, in particular where any delay is likely to cause irreparable harm to the right holder, or where evidence is likely to be destroyed. Further provisions relate to measures to be taken at the border for the suspension by customs authorities of release, into domestic circulation, of counterfeit and pirated goods. Finally, parties should provide for criminal procedures and penalties at least in cases of willful trademark counterfeiting or copyright piracy on a commercial scale. Remedies should include imprisonment and fines sufficient to act as a deterrent.

The agreement would establish a Council for Trade-Related Aspects of Intellectual Property Rights to monitor the operation of the agreement and governments' compliance with it. Dispute settlement would take place under the integrated GATT dispute-settlement procedures as revised in the Uruguay Round.

With respect to the implementation of the agreement, it envisages a one-year transition period for developed countries to bring their legislation and practices into conformity. Developing countries and countries in the process of transformation from a centrally-planned into a market economy would have a five-year transition period, and least-developed countries 11 years. Developing countries which do not at present provide product patent protection in an area of technology would have up to 10 years to introduce such protection. However, in the case of pharmaceutical and agricultural chemical products, they must accept the filing of patent applications from the beginning of the transitional period. Though the patent need not be granted until the end of this period, the novelty of the invention is preserved as of the date of filing the application. If authorization for the marketing of the relevant pharmaceutical or agricultural chemical is obtained during the transitional period, the developing country concerned must offer an exclusive marketing right for the product for five years, or until a product patent is granted, whichever is shorter.

Subject to certain exceptions, the general rule is that the obligations in the agreement would apply to existing intellectual property rights as well as to new ones.

### Agreement on Technical Barriers to Trade (TBT)

This agreement will extend and clarify the Agreement on Technical Barriers to Trade reached in the Tokyo Round. It seeks to ensure that technical negotiations and standards, as well as testing and certification procedures, do not create unnecessary obstacles to trade. However, it recognizes that countries have the right to establish protection, at levels they consider appropriate, for example for human, animal or plant life or health or the environment, and should not be prevented from taking measures necessary to ensure those levels of protection are met. The agreement therefore encourages countries to use international standards where these are appropriate, but it does not require them to change their levels of protection as a result of standardization.

Innovative features of the revised agreement are that it covers processing and production methods related to the characteristics of the product itself. The coverage of conformity assessment procedures is enlarged and the disciplines made more precise. Notification provisions applying to local government and non-governmental bodies are elaborated in more detail than in the Tokyo Round agreement. A Code of Good Practice for the Preparation, Adoption and Application of Standards by standardizing bodies, which is open to acceptance by private sector bodies as well as the public sector, is included as an annex to the agreement.

### Agreement on Sanitary and Phytosanitary Measures

This agreement concerns the application of sanitary and phytosanitary measures—in other words food safety and animal and plant health regulations. The agreement recognises that governments have the right to take sanitary and phytosanitary measures but that they should be applied only to the extent necessary to protect human, animal or plant life or health and should not arbitrarily or unjustifiably discriminate between Members where identical or similar conditions prevail.

In order to harmonize sanitary and phytosanitary measures on as wide a basis as possible, Members are encouraged to base their measures on international standards, guidelines and recommendations where they exist. However, Members may maintain or introduce measures which result in higher standards if there is scientific justification or as a consequence of consistent risk decisions based on an appropriate risk assessment. The Agreement spells out procedures and criteria for the assessment of risk and the determination of appropriate levels of sanitary or phytosanitary protection.

It is expected that Members would accept the sanitary and phytosanitary measures of others as equivalent if the exporting country demonstrates to the importing country that its measures achieve the importing country's appropriate level of health protection. The agreement includes provisions on control, inspection and approval procedures.

Source: WTO, *Overview: A Navigational Guide*, www.wto.org/english/docs_e/legal_e/ursum_e.htm (accessed May 18, 2010).

# 12

# Financing Development

## Coauthored with MARK VENEMA and ROBERT ASHFORD

## 12.1 INTRODUCTION

The international financial architecture currently still lacks an effective method of providing development aid that enables and encourages the world's poorest nations to develop and grow in a truly sustainable, efficient, and equitable way. As was expressed in the Brundtland report (WCED 1987, p. 8): "Many present efforts to guard and maintain human progress, to meet human needs, and to realize human ambitions are simply unsustainable—in both the rich and poor nations. They draw too heavily, too quickly, [on] already overdrawn environmental resource accounts to be affordable far into the future without bankrupting those accounts."

This chapter will examine the current architecture in which financing of sustainable (and unsustainable) development takes place, and it will evaluate the main drawbacks and hurdles that will have to be overcome in order to reach a truly sustainable solution in which societies will live off the dividends of our resources rather than exploit the principal (Johnston 1998).* Specifically, the aim of this chapter is to offer a holistic, integrated overview and discussion of the current debate surrounding issues of financing of sustainable development, and to demystify some of the main issues in the debate—often heavily polarized and technical—related to the financing of sustainable development.

An effective financing architecture for sustainable development not only will include sufficient *sources* of financing but also will need proper methods of *delivery*.† These two issues are highly interrelated; many countries are unwilling to contribute more money for development assistance because the achievements thus far are generally considered very unsatisfactory. This chapter will therefore discuss not only the current mechanisms through which development aid is financed but also the ways in which this money is subsequently delivered and implemented.

There are two aspects that make this chapter unique. The first is that we continue to use the concept of *threefold sustainability*, consisting of competitiveness, environmental quality, and a stable, safe, and rewarding employment economy, that was developed in Chapter 1 and has been a recurring theme throughout this book. It will become apparent in this chapter that in most discussions of financing for sustainable development, an overly narrow and inadequate definition of sustainability is adopted. Evidently, this has had a profound impact on the financing mechanisms that have been implemented thus far. As will be explained in Section 12.2, they have been overly focused on economic development, assuming that if a country prospers economically, other types of development will follow

naturally, and this will lead to economic competitiveness and the alleviation of poverty.

This error was identified and discussed at the United Nations Conference on Environment and Development (UNCED) held in Rio de Janeiro in 1992. As a consequence, definitions of sustainability were increasingly broadened and refined to incorporate environmental concerns during the 1990s (see Part B). In fact, attempts have even been made to include broader social issues such as health-care provision, education, and employment. However, the third element of the sustainability tripod—employment—has rarely been acknowledged as an important independent concern and incorporated into working definitions of sustainability. It continues to be overlooked or ignored under the assumption that if economic progress is ensured, jobs will automatically be created.‡ However, this assumption is highly questionable at best. For example, evidence on the U.S. economy shows that despite the fact that the recession following the Internet bust of 2000 officially ended in November 2001, employment fell by an additional 1 percent until 2003 (Economist 2003b). The same situation is occurring in the slow rebound from the 2008 financial crisis. If economic growth does not spur a "trickling down" of job creation in the largest developed economy in the world, why should this be expected to occur in struggling developing nations?

As will become clear in the following sections, the adoption of this threefold definition of sustainability will allow us to come to some interesting insights that will inform some important policy recommendations. But in general, it can be stated at the outset of this discussion that instead of focusing assistance on projects that are aimed primarily at fostering economic growth, as has been the case far too often in the past, unilateral and multilateral development aid organizations should strive to *co-optimize* the three factors that are fundamental to true sustainable development: economic growth, environmental quality, and employ-

---

* According to Johnston (1998, p. 2), a society that can accomplish an equitable distribution of resources while improving the security of the principal is destined to perpetuate itself. It is about "improving the quality of life, not the quantity."

† This notion is stressed by Soros (2002, p. 57) and also in a report by the World Bank (WBG, UNEP, et al. 2002). The report points out that there are two main challenges in the procurement of finance for sustainable development: attracting a greater overall *amount* of capital and ensuring that this capital is *applied* in a manner that meets sustainable development objectives (we discuss these challenges in more detail in Part C of this chapter).

‡ This is the main premise of trickle-down theory, an economic theory that states that letting businesses flourish by investing money in companies and cutting taxes is the best way to stimulate the economy, because profits will ultimately trickle down to lower-income individuals and the rest of the economy. Proponents of this theory believe that when the government helps companies, they will produce more, thereby hiring more people and increasing wages, such that the people, in turn, will have more money to spend in the economy (see Investopedia, "Trickle Down Theory," www.investopedia.com/terms/t/trickledowntheory.asp, accessed June 3, 2010). But recently, the goal to "achieve full and productive employment and decent work for all, including women and young people," was added to the UN's Millennium Development goals discussed in Appendix 12-C of this chapter.

ment concerns related to secure and meaningful jobs, with adequate purchasing power and worker health and safety (N. A. Ashford 2002). The extraordinary but unavoidable challenge that remains for the future is to strive for an orchestration of the various instruments of finance in order to reach a state of true sustainable global development.

A second important aspect of this chapter is that in its discussion of the main problems with current mechanisms and institutions for financing sustainable development, as well as in its proposal of various innovative solutions and ways to proceed, it will attempt to interweave discussions of financing of sustainability at the macro level, the meso level, and the micro level. This takes place most explicitly in Part C, where a range of innovative financing solutions for sustainable development will be introduced and analyzed.

In this chapter, we discuss the various forms of public and private finance and how they relate to sustainability goals. There are several major sources of finance:

- Official development assistance (ODA) through loans and grants from government to government (bilateral arrangements)

- Loans from the World Bank (WB) Group to governments and to firms as well (multilateral lending)

- National-government-backed export credit agencies (ECAs) that loan or insure loans for specific projects undertaken overseas by their national firms or joint commercial ventures

- Loans from private banks to firms undertaking projects in developing countries

- Foreign direct investment (FDI), mostly financed by multinational corporations for specific commercial ventures

- Sovereign wealth funds held by China and the energy-exporting nations, resulting in a highly distorted balance of trade

During the 1990s, annual ODA flows averaged between $50 billion and $60 billion, but this level of assistance had more than doubled by 2009 reaching $120 billion (OECD 2011a). The United States is the world's largest contributor of ODA in absolute terms ($28.8 billion, 2009), but one of the smallest among developed countries as a percentage of its GNI (0.21 percent in 2009).

ECAs currently finance or underwrite approximately $430 billion of business activity abroad, $55 billion of which goes toward project finance in developing countries (Wikipedia 2011). Both these fig-

ures are dwarfed by global FDI inflows that reached an astonishing $2.1 trillion in 2007, before collapsing to $1.1 trillion in 2009 (UNCTAD 2010). Inflows into developing countries are roughly 43 percent ($478 billion) of this amount (ibid.). Global inflows of FDI are predicted to rebound to $1.6–$2 trillion in 2012, but these estimates are highly uncertain due to the fragility of the global economic recovery (ibid.).

In 2011, the largest sovereign wealth funds were held primarily by energy- and product-exporting countries (amounts in billions of U.S. dollars): the United Arab Emirates (Abu Dhabi Investment Authority $627), Norway (Government Pension Fund $512), China (SAFE Investment Company $347; China Investment Corporation $332; National Social Security Fund $147; China-Africa Development Fund $5), Singapore (Singapore Investment Corporation $248; Temasek Holdings $133), Kuwait (Kuwait Investment Authority $203), and Russia (National Welfare Fund $90).[1] By comparison, in 2011 the United States held around $55 billion of foreign assets in its sovereign wealth funds. At the end of 2007, the total assets were valued at about $2.2 trillion, with the expectation that they would reach $13 trillion in a decade (Lyons 2007). In comparison, the IMF estimated that $2 to $3 trillion were held in SWFs in 2008 and expected these to reach $6 to $10 trillion by 2013 (Allen and Caruana 2008). The 2008 global economic crisis, of course, has changed these expectations.

Financing that may affect environmental sustainability consists of two dimensions. One dimension is the *type of financing supplied*. This can be broken down into (1) public finance, which is subsidized by the taxpayer to varying degrees (for example, ODA and ECAs, where the supplier of capital assumes some or all of the financing cost); and (2) private finance, which is not subsidized (that is, the borrower pays the full market price for capital, guarantees, and/or insurance). Publicly subsidized financing has been justified on humanitarian, geopolitical, and commercial risk-sharing grounds, in instances where private markets would not provide that financing or investment.

The other dimension is *the terms and conditions* that apply to various public and private finance schemes. A major effort over the past two decades has been to try to encourage suppliers of finance to take account of the environmental/social implications of the projects they finance. This first took place with the World Bank/International Finance Corporation (IFC) and has since been extended to ECAs and private banks with varying degrees of success. Table 12.1 presents the types of public- and private-sector finance avail-

**TABLE 12.1: TYPES OF PUBLIC- AND PRIVATE-SECTOR FINANCE AVAILABLE FOR DEVELOPMENT INITIATIVES**

| TYPE OF FINANCE | ENVIRONMENTAL/SOCIAL EXTERNALITIES | |
| --- | --- | --- |
| | NOT INTERNALIZED (Destructive/not sustainable) | INTERNALIZED (Sustainable) |
| **Public (subsidized):** *Multilateral lending* (loans and grants to government) | **WB/IBRD\*/IDA\*\*** (UN organizations) grants & loans before 1990 | Many **WB/IBRD/IDA** loans since 1990 (~ $59/$44/$15 billion, 2010) |
| | * mostly infrastructure loans ** health/water/social services | **UNDP** |
| | **IMF** structural adjustment loans for currency stabilization, $55 billion (2009) | |
| (loans and equity financing for private-sector projects) | | **WB/IFC**: largest multilateral source of loan and equity financing for private-sector projects in the developing world; subject to environmental/social standards |
| *Bilateral assistance* (mostly grants to government) | **USAID, JBIC** (part of); other bilateral finance | **USAID, JBIC** (part of); other bilateral finance |
| | **ODA** (target 0.7% of GNP) ~ part of $120 billion (2009) | **ODA** ~ part of $120 billion (2009) |
| | **ECA** financing ignoring OECD "common approaches" | **ECA** financing ~ $50-70 billion (2009) subject to OECD "common approaches" |
| | **SWF**—from energy profits and from manufacturing (China) | **SWF**—Norway |
| **Private (not subsidized)** (banks, venture capital) | Many energy and transport projects ~ $413 billion (net private debt flows, 2007) | Financing subject to the Equator Principles |
| **Self-financed investment** (foreign direct investment) | Business Opportunities by TNCs/MNCs ~ $616 billion (net—FDI and portfolio— private equity flows, 2007) | TNCs/MNCs signing on to the CERES Principles |

ECA = Export credit agency
IBRD = International Bank for Reconstruction and Development
IDA = International Development Agency
IFC = International Finance Corporation of the World Bank
IMF = International Monetary Fund
JBIC = Japan Bank for International Cooperation
ODA = Official development assistance
SWF = Sovereign wealth funds
TNCs/MNCs = Trans- or multinational corporations
UNDP = United Nations Development Programme
USAID = U.S. Agency for International Development
WB = World Bank Group

able for development initiatives and whether these are likely to promote unsustainable or sustainable activities. This chapter will explore these financial mechanisms in more detail.

Before turning to Part A, in which we discuss the main issues surrounding financing for economic development, we would like to mention that because of the inherently multifaceted nature of the topics addressed, this chapter will unavoidably touch on issues that have been discussed in previous chapters. In spite of this, one will find that duplication has been minimized; where it has not, it should serve to clarify linkages and to offer a more integrated and holistic view of the issues at hand through the perspective of financing sustainable development. Finally, given the number of acronyms used in this chapter, a table of acronyms is provided in Appendix 12-A.

## PART A: FINANCING OF ECONOMIC DEVELOPMENT

### 12.2 OFFICIAL DEVELOPMENT ASSISTANCE AND PRIVATE CAPITAL

This chapter begins with a discussion of financing of *economic* development. We regard this as the most appropriate topic with which to start our analysis for three specific reasons:

1. First , economic development has traditionally always been a central concern in the debate about promoting development processes.

2. Second, financing of economic development involves capital flows that are far larger than those directed toward environmental sustainability.

3. Third, this section will allow us to develop a solid understanding of the mechanisms and institutions of traditional finance. This is required for our subsequent discussion of financing for the environment because that discussion draws heavily on this understanding.

The analysis of financing of economic development consists of two main topics. First, in Section 12.3, we analyze official development assistance (ODA), because over the past few decades it has played an important but heavily debated role in promoting the development process. This will constitute the largest section of Part A. Subsequently, we will turn in Section 12.4 to an examination of the role of private capital flows in development, because these have risen so dramatically over the past fifteen years that they now far outweigh the flows of ODA. As a consequence, private capital flows have received increasing attention in the literature on development aid and sustainability. We examine this literature by surveying the main arguments that have been put forth and comparing them with the evidence that has accumulated over the past decade. We then discuss some of the most recent developments in the field of financing of economic development and the most urgent hurdles that will still have to be overcome.

### 12.3 ANALYZING OFFICIAL DEVELOPMENT ASSISTANCE

Our discussion of ODA is divided into three parts. The first subsection will provide a historical discussion of development and introduce the main concepts, mechanisms, and organizations involved.* In the second subsection, we turn to a discussion of the "aid crisis" of the 1990s, which was characterized by a strong decrease in flows of development finance and fierce criticism of the ways in which development aid was generally conducted. The third subsection discusses some of the main problems with development assistance as it has traditionally been disbursed and points out some of the major hurdles that will have to be overcome in shifting to a more productive, integrated, and equitable approach to fostering global economic and social development.† Finally, we will look at some issues beyond ODA that affect the development of the world's poorest nations in important ways. Here we discuss the development-friendliness of the foreign policies of twenty-one of the world's rich nations.

### 12.3.1 A Historical Overview of Development Aid

Development aid comes in several forms, as is explained in Appendix 12-B.‡ However, there is one type that is specifically provided by donor governments as well as multilateral agencies (like the World Bank and the International Monetary Fund) for the purpose of promoting economic development and welfare in the developing world: *official development assistance* (ODA). It is this category of financial assistance that counts as a country's "aid effort" and therefore generally dominates discussions about aid.

ODA—as well as official development finance in general—can be broadly categorized into two classes: *bilateral* aid and *multilateral* aid. Bilateral aid is direct support—either monetary or nonmonetary—given by one country to another country. It is administered by agencies of the donor country, such as the U.S. Agency for International Development (USAID) or the Japan Bank for International Cooperation. Although mechanisms of aid provision vary significantly among donor countries, bilateral aid is predominantly disbursed in the form of grants. Multilateral aid—support that is channeled through international agencies such as the World Bank or the United Nations Development Programme (UNDP)—is funded by contributions from these institutions' wealthy member nations and is offered either as grants or as loans. However, the degree of grant-making activity by multilateral organizations

---

\*         A description of the recent history and the various categories of development aid, as they have been defined by the Development Assistance Committee (DAC) of the Organisation for Economic Co-operation and Development (OECD), as well as the World Bank, is provided in Appendix 12-B of this chapter.

†         A final and integral discussion of the optimal way forward in order to promote threefold sustainability will be provided at the end of Part C.

‡         Official development *finance* consists of two parts: official development *assistance* and official *aid*. Only the former goes to developing countries, and it is ten times the amount of the latter.

is generally modest; by far most multilateral assistance is provided as a (concessional) loan. For example, the World Bank's International Development Association has a Development Grant Facility, but its budget is only $100 million. The World Bank's grant-making capacity is in fact largely limited to the profits generated by its lending activity (Soros 2002, p. 20).*

In many ways, it can be argued that the foundations for the modern international framework of multilateral aid provision were laid at the United Nations Monetary and Financial Conference, which was held at Bretton Woods, New Hampshire, in July 1944. The conference (commonly referred to as the Bretton Woods Conference) considered monetary and financial matters that were deemed vital for global peace and prosperity, in response to the financial devastation in Europe that was caused by World War II. It resulted in the creation of two of the most powerful (and, as we will see, most heavily criticized) multilateral institutions engaged in the provision of development aid today: the International Monetary Fund (IMF) and the International Bank for Reconstruction and Development (IBRD)—the original foundation of the World Bank (Army Information School 1946). From their inception, these two institutions were intended to work closely together. They share the same broad objective—to promote and sustain growth and development in their member countries—but were given different, complementary roles in pursuing this goal (Reisman 1992, p. 1). The World Bank's task was to promote development; that of the IMF was to maintain order in the international monetary system (Economist 1991).

Until the 1960s, the term "development" was interpreted by most multilateral as well as bilateral development agencies to mean economic growth. As is argued by Bradlow (1996, pp. 55–56), this notion started to evolve in response to the observation that economic growth failed to adequately address the problems of the poor. Consequently, the international development community, led by decisions of the World Bank and the IMF, began to broaden its scope of activities by focusing more directly on poverty alleviation and basic human needs.[†]

In view of the crucial role that these organizations continue to play in setting the development agenda, this section will examine their main goals and characteristics, as well as their historical development, in more detail.[‡]

### 12.3.1.1 The World Bank Group

The World Bank, founded in 1944, is a "publicly owned financial intermediary"—a bank, in fact (Economist 1991, p. 5). But it is not a bank in the common sense. It is a specialized agency of the United Nations (UN) and is made up of 187 member countries.[§] These countries are jointly responsible for how the institution is financed and how its money is spent. The original mission of the World Bank was to provide long-term capital to European countries for reconstruction of their infrastructure, which had been largely destroyed by World War II.[¶] To fulfill this mission, the World Bank raises funds mainly through the acquisition of guarantees from industrialized countries, against which it borrows in capital markets with an AAA rating. Through this ingenious financial construct, it has been able to raise the necessary funds to assist poor countries without imposing high costs on the industrialized world (Soros 2002, p. 97).[**]

---

\* There are some powerful political voices that promote expansion of these activities, arguing that the discretionary spending activities of the World Bank and other multilateral organizations are much more beneficial and have fewer adverse side effects than its lending activities. This, for instance, is the main argument of Paul O'Neill, America's former secretary of the Treasury, who argued that by lending money to poor countries, instead of giving it away in the form of grants, the World Bank has driven these countries "into a ditch." However, an obvious concern of multilateral organizations is how they will be able to sustain their funds if they scale up their grant-making activity. This would require substantial financial commitments by their members, which—given the trend in ODA observed over the past decade (see Section 12.3.2.1)—seems quite unlikely to occur.

† As an illustration, note that from the 1960s onwards, the World Bank added a variety of programs and mechanisms to its repertoire of appropriate operations, such as policy-based lending, environmental concerns, gender issues, governance, economic transformation, and private-sector development (Bradlow 1996, p. 56).

‡ A discussion that includes a wider range of international development agencies, such as the Development Assistance Committee (DAC), the United Nations Development Programme (UNDP), and the United Nations Environment Programme (UNEP), is beyond the scope of this chapter. We have, however, chosen to discuss two of the most important international agencies, the World Bank and the IMF. These organizations exert an enormous—and often heavily criticized—influence on the political economy of development aid and play a vital role in many of the issues that will be addressed in this chapter. Therefore, it is imperative that we develop a sound understanding of the main characteristics of these organizations.

§ The International Bank for Reconstruction and Development (IBRD) has 187 member countries, nearly all the countries of the world. The International Development Association (IDA) has 170 members, the International Finance Corporation (IFC) has 182 members, the Multilateral Investment Guarantee Agency (MIGA) has 175 members, and the International Centre for Settlement of Investment Disputes (ICSID) has 144 members. For complete lists, see the World Bank Group, www.worldbank.org (accessed January 27, 2011).

¶ As it turned out, the World Bank was entirely overshadowed in this role by the United States Marshall Plan (Economist 1991; Sheehy and Watkins 1996; Soros 2002).

\*\* The guarantees have never been invoked.

During the 1950s, World Bank shareholders decided that the bank would turn its attention beyond its primary mandate—postwar reconstruction of Europe—and toward the assistance of less developed countries (LDCs), many of which were newly independent from colonial rule and plagued by economic and political instability (Orr 2002). Throughout the 1950s, it concentrated its activities on providing public-sector capital, mainly for infrastructure projects such as power stations, road building, and other transport investments (Economist 1991, p. 9). Although infrastructure projects have remained an important part of its work, the World Bank has since then "sharpened its focus on poverty reduction as the overarching goal of all its work" (WBG 2003b). During the 1960s, the bank started to provide loans to support education, farming, population control, and urban development; and with the creation of the International Development Agency in 1960 (see below), it also found a way to deliver aid to the world's poorest.

The World Bank Group today consists of five closely related agencies (Orr 2002; WBG 2000a, 2003b; Weidner 2001). "World Bank" is the name that has come to be used for two of these: the International Bank for Reconstruction and Development (IBRD) and the International Development Association (IDA). The IBRD, constructed in 1945, provides loans and development assistance to middle-income and poorer nations that are deemed creditworthy. In fiscal year 2010, the combined lending of the IBRD and the IDA was $58.7 billion (WBG 2010b). The majority of lending—$44.2 billion (75 percent of the IBRD and IDA commitments)—was made by the IBRD. Latin America and the Caribbean received the largest share of IBRD-IDA lending ($14.1 billion, 24 percent of total IBRD-IDA commitments), followed by Africa ($11.7 billion, 20 percent), South Asia ($11.2 billion, 19 percent), Europe and Central Asia ($10.6 billion, 18 percent), East Asia ($7.6 billion, 13 percent), and the Middle East and North Africa ($3.5 billion, 6 percent) (ibid.). IBRD loans are funded primarily through the financial construct discussed above, which enables it to sell bonds in international capital markets (Weidner 2001). It raised $34 billion in fiscal year 2010 by issuing debt with medium- to long-term maturities in 28 currencies (WBG 2010b).

The IDA, established in 1960, remains the single largest source of donor funds for basic social services—for example, health, education, clean water, sanitation, and infrastructure—to the world's poorest countries (Orr 2002, p. 2). The IDA provides long-term interest-free loans (termed "credits") to the poorest among the developing countries. It lends to countries that have a per capita income of about $1,135 or less (2010 GNI per capita) and lack the financial ability to borrow from the World Bank's primary lending institution, the IBRD.* IDA loans constitute the remaining 30 percent of the World Bank's lending activities and are funded mainly through contributions from its wealthier member countries. These contributions are agreed on every three years in a periodic replenishment. The largest share of the $14 billion of IDA resources in 2009 was committed to Africa ($7.9 billion, 56 percent of total IDA commitments), followed by South Asia ($4.1 billion, 29 percent), and East Asia and the Pacific ($1.2 billion, 9 percent) (ibid.).†

The IDA is much more closely related to the IBRD than the three other World Bank Group affiliates. In reality, IBRD and IDA are not much more than labels that have been attached to different types of loans. Broadly, the same criteria for evaluating projects apply in each case, and both types of loans are supervised by the same managers. The main difference is that IDA loans are more "concessional" and are funded in a different way than IBRD loans.

In addition, the World Bank Group includes three other organizations: the International Finance Corporation (IFC), the Multilateral Investment Guarantee Agency (MIGA), and the International Centre for Settlement of Investment Disputes (ICSID). Founded in 1956, the IFC is the largest multilateral source of loan and equity financing for private-sector projects in the developing world. In addition, it promotes sustainable private-sector development by helping private companies in the developing world mobilize financing in international financial markets, and by providing technical assistance and advice to developing-country businesses and governments.[2]

The MIGA was set up in 1988 to help encourage foreign investment in developing countries.[3] It fulfills this mandate and contributes to development by offering political risk insurance ("guarantees") to investors and lenders against a loss that is caused by "non-commercial risks." In addition, it helps developing countries attract and retain private investment through the provision of technical assistance to help countries disseminate information to promote busi-

---

\* IDA loans carry maturities of thirty-five or forty years with a ten-year grace period on the repayment of principle. At present, seventy-nine countries, comprising over 2.5 billion people, are eligible to borrow from the IDA.

† The negotiations for the sixteenth replenishment of IDA funds resulted in $49.3 billion being made available from July 2011 to June 2014—an 18 percent increase on the previous round three years ago. See: The International Development Bank, www.worldbank.org/ida/ (accessed February 1, 2011).

ness investment opportunities. The MIGA is funded by member capital and currently has a capital stock of SDR 1 billion.*

Last, the ICSID was created in 1966 to facilitate the settlement of investment disputes—either through conciliation or arbitration—between foreign investors and their host countries, with the aim of promoting increased flows of international investment, especially from developed to developing countries.

Although the five World Bank Group agencies are formally separate, autonomous agencies, one individual serves as the president for all of them. The bank's president is, by tradition, a national of the largest shareholder, which from its inception has been the United States. Elected for a five-year renewable term, the president of the World Bank chairs meetings of the Board of Directors and is responsible for overall management of the bank. In 2005, World Bank Group approved Paul Wolfowitz, a neoconservative adviser to President George W. Bush, as its president. The World Bank is run like a cooperative, with its member countries as shareholders. The number of shares a country has is based on the amount of money it has invested in the bank. The United States is the largest single shareholder, with 16.41 percent of votes, followed by Japan (7.87 percent), Germany (4.49 percent), the United Kingdom (4.31 percent), and France (4.31 percent).[4]

Although World Bank projects have come under constant criticisms from environmentalists, the WB/IFC has adopted environmental/social standards that have acted as a filter on questionable projects (Fox and Brown 1998; Wade 1997).

### 12.3.1.2 The International Monetary Fund

As we observed above, although its approaches have evolved over the past five decades, the World Bank focuses primarily on promoting and sustaining long-term growth and development in its member countries.

The IMF works differently; it is generally concerned with short-term stabilization measures and policies.[†] The *Economist* (1991, p. 5) describes it as follows: "The IMF is not a bank, but a club. Member countries pay a subscription and agree to abide by a mutually advantageous code of economic conduct."[‡] The IMF has three main areas of activity: *surveillance*, *financial assistance*, and *technical assistance*. The surveillance process is performed through a continuous policy dialogue with each of the IMF member nations. Generally once a year, it evaluates the exchange-rate policies of its members within the overall framework of their economic policies (by means of a so-called Article IV consultation). Through the surveillance process, "the IMF provides advice to its 187 member countries, encouraging policies that foster economic stability, reduce vulnerability to economic and financial crises, and raise living standards" (IMF 2010a, p. 2).[§]

The IMF also provides financial assistance, in the form of credits and loans, to member nations with balance-of-payments problems, in order to try to reduce both the duration and the magnitude of payment imbalances. These credits and loans are often conditioned upon a county's commitment to introduce policies of structural adjustment and reform. On October 31, 2009, the IMF had credits and loans outstanding in an amount of SDR 35 billion (approximately $55 billion) (IMF 2009). The IMF makes its financial resources available to its members through a variety of financial facilities (loan programs), which are technically quite complex.[¶]

---

* In 1969, the IMF created the special drawing right (SDR) as an international reserve asset to supplement members' existing reserve assets (official holdings of gold, foreign exchange, and reserve positions in the IMF). The SDR is valued on the basis of a basket of key international currencies and serves as the unit of account of the IMF and a number of other international organizations. It is not a currency, but it offers its holders a potential claim on the usable currencies of IMF members by exchanging their SDRs for these currencies. The SDR's value as a reserve asset derives from the commitments of members to hold and accept SDRs and to honor various obligations connected with the operation of the SDR system. For more information on these special drawing rights, see IMF (2010b). We will come back to them in Section 12.8 of this chapter, where we discuss George Soros's SDR proposal.

† In fact, it is for this reason that our discussion of the goals and characteristics of the IMF will be shorter than that of the World Bank. Because its main concerns are relatively short term and not directly focused on sustainable development (even though macroeconomic stability is a crucial step in its achievement), the discussion of the IMF is kept relatively limited; a more elaborate discussion, although worthwhile, is beyond the scope of this chapter.

‡ Article I of the Articles of Agreement states that the IMF has the following purposes: it is responsible for promoting international monetary cooperation; facilitating the expansion and balanced growth of international trade; promoting exchange stability; assisting in the establishment of a multilateral system of payments; and making its resources available—under adequate safeguards—to members that are experiencing balance-of-payments difficulties. More generally, the IMF is responsible for ensuring the stability of the international financial system (see IMF 2010a).

§ In addition, the IMF also carries out multilateral surveillance. The results of this process are documented in the *World Economic Outlook* (prepared twice a year) and the *Global Financial Stability Report* (prepared once every three months).

¶ For a discussion of the various IMF loan programs, the reader is referred to the IMF website because they are beyond the scope of this discussion. The regular loan facilities are the Stand-by Arrangements; the Extended Fund Facility; the Supplemental Reserve Facility; Contingent Credit Lines; and the

Third, the IMF offers technical assistance and training in order to "help member countries strengthen their capacity to design and implement effective policies" (IMF 2010a, p. 2). Such assistance is offered in several broad areas, such as fiscal policy, monetary policy, legislative frameworks, and statistics.

To achieve a true understanding of the structure and functions of the IMF, we must go back in time and examine the original goals and tasks that it was given at its inception at the Bretton Woods Conference in 1944. This conference had set itself an extraordinarily ambitious goal. After the collapse of world trade during the Great Depression of the early 1930s and the extremely slow recovery, which was further aggravated but not solely caused by World War II, it was held with the intention to "build a new economic order, from scratch" (Economist 1991, p. 7). It chose to build this new order on a global regime of fixed but adjustable exchange rates, with parities—set in terms of gold—that could be altered only if the IMF confirmed that this was necessary in order to correct a "fundamental disequilibrium." The main task of the IMF would therefore be "to monitor the economic policies of its members, so that it could say yes or no to requests for parity changes" (ibid.). As mentioned above, this *surveillance* role basically continues to this day. However, since the early 1970s, it has been deprived of its original rationale.

The fixed-exchange-rate system that was devised at Bretton Woods seemed to work quite well; it allowed the fractured world economy to recover, and international trade flows picked up rapidly. But during the 1960s, the first inconsistencies in domestic and international policies became apparent. A lack of coordination of national monetary policies allowed differing rates of inflation to result in unbearably wide external imbalances—the United States ran a particularly large external deficit. The immediate monetary crisis that resulted in the late 1960s led to a rapid erosion of the Bretton Woods regime of fixed exchange rates and ultimately to its breakdown in the early 1970s.*

But in addition to its surveillance role, the IMF was also given a role as a lender. At Bretton Woods, its members agreed to provide the IMF with a supply of gold and currencies, which it could lend to members that were running a deficit, as long as they were behaving "responsibly."† From the 1950s onward, the IMF has greatly increased its activities as a provider of financial assistance. For example, during the 1950s, it made 43 stand-by agreements, which accounted for roughly $4 billion. In the 1960s, this had already increased to 188 agreements, worth approximately $12.5 billion.‡ During the 1970s, when the IMF increasingly realized that its surveillance of parities had become redundant, it truly seemed to have found a new role (Economist 1991, p. 9). It continued to broaden and expand its lending activities by creating various new lending facilities, and in 1976 it even started to provide loans to the world's poorest countries (subject to certain conditions). As stated above, the total amount of outstanding credit and loans on October 31, 2009, amounted to roughly $55 billion. But as the IMF did this, criticism of its activities became increasingly fierce. Indeed, as the *Economist* pointed out in 1991, it should be remembered that the IMF "is not a development institution, but a society that treats all its members alike. It stands ready to help countries that need strictly temporary assistance and can be relied upon to pay their loans back quickly" (ibid.). This difficult dilemma the IMF was facing became painfully visible during the debt crisis of the 1980s and continues to be one of the most powerful criticisms of its operations and, indeed, its very existence.§

### 12.3.2 Analysis of the Crisis in Official Development Assistance

Donor countries can have different or multiple motivations in providing bilateral financial aid, ranging from humanitarian to developmental and to geopolitical/strategic.¶ In addition, there are quasi-legal "obliga-

---

Compensatory Financing Facility. In addition, the IMF provides concessional assistance through the Poverty Reduction and Growth Facility (PRGF) and debt relief through the Heavily Indebted Poor Countries (HIPC) Initiative, an initiative launched by the World Bank and the IMF in 1996 to "provide exceptional assistance to eligible countries following sound economic policies to help them reduce their external debt burden to sustainable levels" (IMF 2001).

*      A more elaborate discussion of the problems with the Bretton Woods regime of fixed exchange rates and how it ultimately collapsed is provided in the *Economist*'s 1991 survey of the IMF and the World Bank, titled "Sisters in the Wood."

†      According to the *Economist* (1991, p. 7), it is this idea, which later evolved into the much-debated concept of *conditionality*, that continues to be used by both Bretton Woods institutions in their decisions to provide various types of loans.

‡      As discussed above, there is nowadays a wide variety of complex mechanisms through which the IMF makes its loans available. The stand-by agreement was one of the first to be devised and is still one of the most common mechanisms.

§      Interesting as it would be, we refrain from discussing the criticisms of the IMF's activities in more detail because they are tangential to the main thrust of this chapter. For some valuable information, see Carrasco (2011), Soros (2002, chap. 4), and Stiglitz (2002b).

¶      Gardner and Lugo (2009) argue that the third motivation is the most important. The geopolitical/ideological motivations" to help poor countries achieve environmental and developmental goals, stemming from "commitments" made at the UNCED in Rio, from the UN's Millennium Goals adopted in 2000, from the UN Conference on Financing Development in Monterrey, Mexico, in 2002, and more recently from promises made at the Copenhagen meeting on climate change in December 2009.* Further, Arkedis (2008) argues that although promoting development is commonly accepted as being in the donor's national security interest, achieving geopolitical goals and conferring development benefits may be quite distinct, even if they are confused rhetorically and in legal instruments. Furthermore, developmental goals vary widely, from promoting democratic institutions to addressing HIV/AIDS. These observations must be kept in mind in evaluating the effectiveness of aid programs and instruments.

Catherine Gwin (1996, p. 18) points out that over the past decade, there has been a "rising torrent of criticism of development aid—both bilateral and multilateral—which has come from all points of the political spectrum, from all parts of the world, and from both long-time friends as well as foes of foreign aid." To give but one example, Thomas Sheehy, affiliated with the Heritage Foundation, a conservative U.S. think tank, argued in a 1996 article that official development assistance has little impact except to develop the "culture of dependency" in developing countries, which is part of the problem. He states that "it is indisputable that development aid weakens thrift, industry, and self-reliance, which are the values essential for economic growth and development" (Sheehy 1996, p. 25).

Throughout the 1980s and 1990s, this criticism was directed at various institutions and mechanisms involved in the financing of both bilateral and multilateral development aid. (Actually, in the 1960s, there was earlier intense criticism of aid, but the end of the Cold War increased the imperative and geopolitical opportunity to revisit the question of aid.) Two important shifts in the global political and economic environment—the end of the Cold War and the rise in private capital flows to the developing world (see Section 12.4)—have altered the landscape for development

assistance to an extent that has led many critics to question whether there is a need for concessional financial transfers from rich to poor countries at all.[†] Although criticisms of ODA need to be taken seriously, it is also important to point out that since the 1980s, extensive reforms have been introduced in the global aid architecture, such as the incorporation of environmental/social standards (GAO 2003; Rich 2000) and subsidy/competition rules (P. C. Evans 2005; Lammersen and Owen 2001) in lending by public sources.

While acknowledging and countering the claims made by the many critics of developmental aid, Crosswell (2008), a senior economist at USAID, presents a compelling case, though admittedly "circumstantial," for the general effectiveness of bilateral aid in spurring economic growth, reducing poverty, and expanding democratic institutions over several decades.

In this section, we will examine the question whether there is a need for concessional financial transfers from rich to poor countries in more detail. This will be done in several steps. First, we will investigate the nature of the "crisis" in aid provision that took place over the course of the 1990s by examining the flows of international capital to the developing world provided by bilateral and multilateral donors. In an attempt to assess the underlying causes of this development, we subsequently take a step back and perform a critical analysis of official development aid as it has traditionally been dispensed. Because there is a vast literature on this topic, we focus on several main points of criticism that are of particular urgency and relevance to the discussion. Since the 1990s, the level of ODA to developing countries has rebounded (WBG 2008), although the global economic crisis is likely to slow this trend and perhaps reduce the level of ODA once again.

### 12.3.2.1 The Volatility of Development Aid

At the onset of the new millennium, Catherine Gwin (1996, p. 19), a leading expert in development, argued that "there seemed broader and deeper consensus on the fundamentals of development than at

---

tion behind U.S. aid is legendary, but they point out that other countries also follow suit. China uses foreign aid to Africa and Indonesia to ensure its access to natural resources. Venezuela uses foreign aid to advance its political ideology, and Japan has been providing aid to landlocked nations such as Mongolia and Mali to secure votes lifting an international whaling moratorium.
\* For a detailed discussion of the inaccuracies in the assessment of ODA assistance contributing to sustainable development—both over- and underestimates—see Gardner and Lugo (2009).

[†] As pointed out by Miller (2000), the World Bank report *Assessing Aid: What Works, What Doesn't, and Why?* discusses three main reasons for the observed downward trend in ODA: (1) fiscal problems in the industrialized countries, (2) the end of the Cold War, and (3) the strong growth in private capital flows from the North to the South (WBG 1998, p. 7). Miller identifies the last as the most dramatic and lasting development: by 1998, private capital flows amounted to over $220 billion and constituted almost 90 percent of all funds entering the developing world. The economic and environmental implications of this trend, which, as Miller points out, are heavily debated and yet to be fully understood, will be discussed in Section 12.4 on private capital flows.

any time in the past and . . . the political climate for making real development progress probably could not be better." However, by the end of the 1990s, aid levels had fallen to their lowest point in more than fifty years.

In 1968, Robert McNamara, then president of the World Bank, created the Pearson Commission—led by the former Canadian Prime Minister, Lester B. Person—to review the effectiveness of the World Bank's development assistance over the previous twenty years. A year later, the commission delivered its report *Partners in Development*, arguing that a much-increased flow of aid would be required if most developing countries were to aim for self-sustaining growth by the end of the century, and it set a specific aid target: official development aid would have to reach 0.70 percent of GNP by 1975. (The 0.70 percent of GNP figure is still widely used today, but its rationale as a target for ODA makes little sense beyond its value as a lobbying tool; see Clemens and Moss 2005.) Very few donor countries have ever reached or exceeded this target (WBG 2003c).* But throughout the 1970s and 1980s, the aggregate volume of ODA indeed increased steadily and continuously in real terms, reaching a peak at $69 billion in 1991 (expressed in 1995 U.S. dollars) (WBG 1998; see Figure 12.1). However, during the 1990s, total levels of foreign aid began to fall. For example, between 1992 and 1996, ODA from bilateral sources and multilateral agencies fell by 16 percent in real terms (Economist 2002a). Figure 12.2 shows that foreign aid flows as a percentage of gross national income (GNI) in the DAC countries fell from 0.33 percent in 1990 to 0.22 percent in 2001. However, recent trends show a rebound of ODA to around 0.31 percent of GNI (including debt relief) in 2009. In absolute terms, total ODA provided by DAC member countries was $120 billion in 2009 (OECD 2011a).

From the recipients' perspective, the picture looked equally disappointing during the 1990s. Net disbursements of official development assistance to developing countries declined from $110 billion in 1990 to $97 billion in 1995, only to return to 1990 levels during the early 2000s (see Table 12.2). On a more positive note, however, annual grant-making activities by multilateral institutions remained relatively constant during this time, at around $20 billion in real terms (constant 2005 dollars) (see Figure 12.1).

*Constant 2005 $ billions*

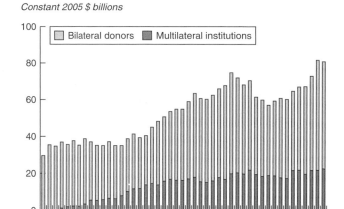

**FIGURE 12.1: NET ODA DISBURSEMENTS EXCLUDING DEBT RELIEF, 1960–2006**
Source: WBG (2008, p. 58).

### 12.3.2.2 Some Promising Signs

Despite the disappointing trends in ODA during the 1990s (described above), the seeds of some progress were planted during the first years of the twenty-first century toward increasing aid. For example, at the UN International Conference on Financing for Development that was held in Monterrey in March 2002, an important agreement was reached (the Monterrey Consensus).[†] The developed countries reaffirmed their commitment to increasing aid and making progress toward the Millennium Development Goals (see Appendix 12-C).[5] The European Union (EU) announced that it had agreed to increase its spending on development assistance to an average of 0.39 percent of GNI by 2006, up from an average of 0.33 percent (amounting to $25.4 billion) that EU members contributed in 2000 (Adesina, Graham, et al. 2005).

On the same day in March 2002, the U.S. administration announced that it would scale up its spending on foreign aid by an extra $5 billion between 2004 and 2006—a development that Nancy Birdsall, head of the Center for Global Development (CGD), called a "philosophical breakthrough" (Economist 2002a). Other DAC members also announced plans to raise aid levels. In fact, shortly after the Monterrey Consensus was reached, the DAC announced that its member nations had increased their ODA disbursements to developing countries by 4.8 percent in real terms from 2001 to 2002 (OECD 2003a).

---

* Currently, only a handful of rich countries, including Sweden, Norway, Luxembourg, the Netherlands, and Denmark, exceed this target (CGP 2009). Further, in 2007, the ODA of DAC donor countries was 0.25 percent of GNI (net of debt relief), well below the 0.33 percent level that was achieved in the early 1990s (WBG 2008).

† For more information, visit the UN website Financing for Development, www.un.org/esa/ffd/ (accessed February 1, 2011), and see the report of the UN Secretary-General on the follow-up to and implementation of the Monterrey Consensus (UN 2010).

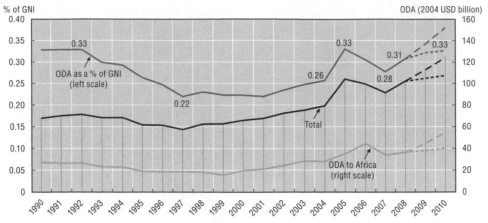

After 1980, all the three curves based on data are followed by two different estimates for the future.

– – – dashed line indicates the growth-adjusted trajectory envisaged at Gleneagles.

...... dotted line indicates estimates based on reported intentions or current 2010 budget plans made by DAC members.

...... dotted line for Africa indicates a DAC Secretariat estimate.

**FIGURE 12.2: DAC MEMBERS' NET ODA (1990–2008) AND DAC SECRETARIAT SIMULATIONS OF NET ODA (2009–2010)**
Source: OECD (2010b, p. 98).

**TABLE 12.2: NET DISBURSEMENTS OF ODA EXCLUDING DEBT RELIEF, 1990–2009 (BILLIONS OF CONSTANT 2008 DOLLARS)**

| DONOR | 1990 | 1995 | 2000 | 2005 | 2006 | 2007 | 2008 | 2009 |
|---|---|---|---|---|---|---|---|---|
| All Donors, Total | 110 | 97 | 99 | 129 | 131 | 136 | 154 | 166 |
| DAC Countries | 81 | 72 | 77 | 97 | 97 | 100 | 113 | 119 |
| Australia | 2 | 2 | 2 | 2 | 2 | 2 | 3 | 3 |
| Austria | 0 | 1 | 1 | 1 | 1 | 1 | 1 | 1 |
| Belgium | 2 | 1 | 1 | 2 | 2 | 2 | 2 | 3 |
| Canada | 3 | 3 | 3 | 4 | 4 | 4 | 5 | 4 |
| Denmark | 2 | 2 | 3 | 3 | 3 | 3 | 3 | 3 |
| Finland | 1 | 1 | 1 | 1 | 1 | 1 | 1 | 1 |
| France | 11 | 12 | 7 | 8 | 8 | 9 | 10 | 10 |
| Germany | 8 | 8 | 8 | 8 | 9 | 10 | 11 | 12 |
| Greece | .. | .. | 0 | 0 | 1 | 1 | 1 | 1 |
| Ireland | 0 | 0 | 0 | 1 | 1 | 1 | 1 | 1 |
| Italy | 5 | 2 | 2 | 4 | 2 | 4 | 4 | 3 |
| Japan | 12 | 12 | 12 | 9 | 9 | 7 | 8 | 9 |
| Korea | 0 | 0 | 0 | 1 | 0 | 1 | 1 | 1 |
| Luxembourg | 0 | 0 | 0 | 0 | 0 | 0 | 0 | 0 |
| Netherlands | 5 | 4 | 6 | 6 | 6 | 6 | 7 | 7 |
| New Zealand | 0 | 0 | 0 | 0 | 0 | 0 | 0 | 0 |
| Norway | 3 | 3 | 3 | 4 | 4 | 4 | 4 | 5 |
| Portugal | 0 | 0 | 0 | 0 | 0 | 1 | 1 | 1 |
| Spain | 2 | 2 | 3 | 3 | 4 | 5 | 7 | 7 |
| Sweden | 3 | 2 | 3 | 4 | 4 | 4 | 5 | 5 |
| Switzerland | 1 | 1 | 2 | 2 | 2 | 2 | 2 | 2 |
| United Kingdom | 4 | 5 | 6 | 8 | 9 | 9 | 11 | 13 |
| United States | 17 | 10 | 12 | 26 | 23 | 22 | 27 | 28 |
| Non-DAC Countries | 9 | 1 | 1 | 4 | 5 | 5 | 8 | 7 |
| Turkey | 0 | 0 | 0 | 1 | 1 | 1 | 1 | 1 |
| Arab countries | 8 | 1 | 1 | 1 | 2 | 2 | 5 | 3 |
| Memorandum Items | | | | | | | | |
| G7 countries | 61 | 52 | 51 | 67 | 65 | 65 | 75 | 80 |
| DAC EU members | 43 | 41 | 42 | 50 | 53 | 57 | 65 | 67 |

Note: EU = European Union; G7 = group of seven countries (Canada, France, Germany, Italy, Japan, the United Kingdom, and the United States)
Source: OECD (2011b).

Figure 12.2 indicates the increases in ODA of those early commitments.

These developments were a much-needed first step toward a stronger commitment by the developed world to a more equitable and sustainable future. As Nicholas Stern, chief economist and senior vice president of the World Bank, pointed out in his keynote address at the 2003 Annual World Conference on Development Economics, "The international community is more united in its commitment to development, as represented by the landmark Monterrey Meeting in 2002, which presented a unique opportunity to advance the MDG agenda" (Pleskovic and Stern 2003, p. 2). However, he conceded that despite the additional aid pledged at Monterrey, the total amount of foreign aid was still small relative to the financing needs of developing countries.

In 2009, ODA as a share of GNI from all DAC donors was 0.31 percent (OECD 2011a). This percentage falls below what was hoped for at Monterrey and is still just over one half the level of aid (as a share of GNI) achieved in 1960 (see Figure 12.3). Indeed, the donors present at Monterrey pledged that debt relief would not displace other ODA commitments, a pledge that seems to have been undermined by two significant Paris Club debt-relief agreements in 2005 and 2006 totaling some $32.5 billion (WBG 2008). However, there is some good news. In 2009, the DAC-EU countries had exceeded their ODA pledge (a pledge originally made by the then fifteen member countries of the EU) and were providing 0.44 percent of their GNI (amounting $67.4 billion) for ODA (OECD 2011a). Further, the level of ODA reaching sub-Saharan

Africa has increased significantly, from $11.5 billion in 2000 to $39 billion in 2006 in real terms (WBG 2008). It is also interesting to note that developing countries, such as China, Brazil, and India, are providing growing amounts of ODA to other developing nations. It is estimated that these "emerging donors" provided around $3.5 billion in concessional loans in 2006 (ibid.).

In 2009, total ODA from DAC countries was $120 billion (current prices), while net private (foreign direct and portfolio) flows were around $462 billion, a figure that was $181 billion *less* than the net private flows in 2007 that peaked at $643.2 billion (WBG 2011) (for a discussion of private capital flows, see Section 12.4). For a comparison of ODA assistance from OECD countries in 2009, see Figures 12.4 and 12.5.

Interestingly, the recent gains in ODA do not appear to be significantly affected by the global financial crisis. While ODA declined in 2006 and 2007, it increased in the following two years continuing the upward trend in OAD that began in the mid-1990s (see Figure 12.3).[6] Future levels of ODA perhaps rest less on the health of the global market and more on a nation's belief in what factors promote growth. A resurgence or continuance of a "trade, not aid" or "trade as aid" perspective (McCawley 2006; Morrissey 2006) would clearly limit the growth potential of ODA. However, there appears to be growing international interest in an "aid for trade" approach to promoting growth in developing nations that have struggled to gain from a trade-liberalization agenda (De Lombaerde and Puri 2007; Hoekman

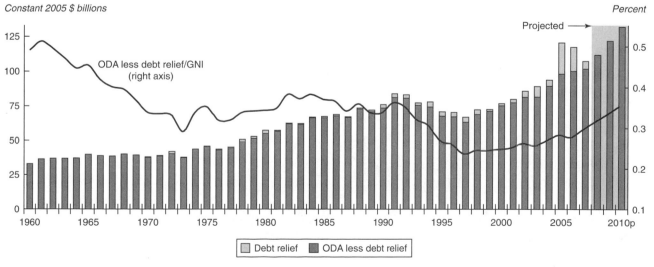

FIGURE 12.3: NET ODA DISBURSEMENTS BY DAC DONORS, 1960–2010
Note: "p" means projected.
Source: WBG (2008, p. 67).

USD billion

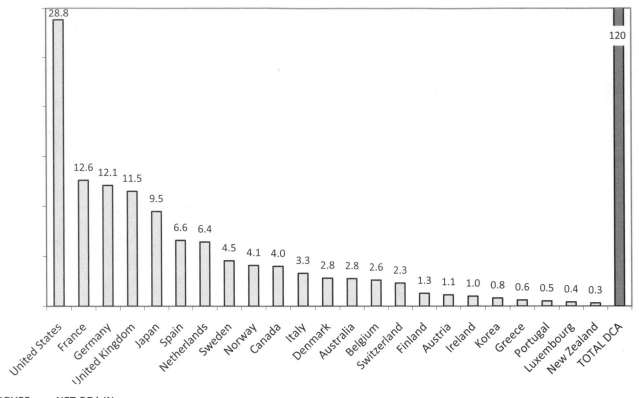

**FIGURE 12.4: NET ODA IN 2009**
Source: OECD (2011b).

As % of GNI

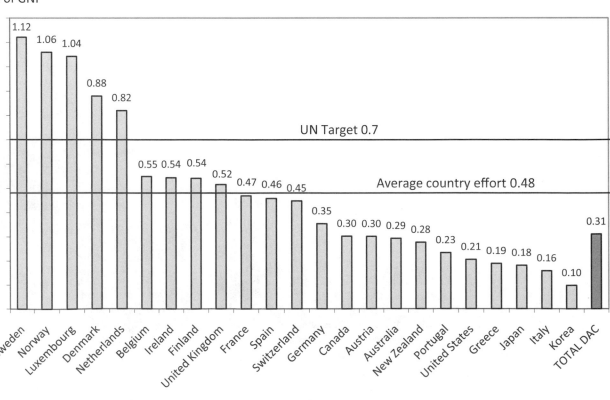

**FIGURE 12.5: NET ODA IN 2009 AS A PERCENTAGE OF GROSS NATIONAL INCOME (GNI)**
Source: OECD (2011b).

and Olarreaga 2007). Hence future ODA may find its rationale in trade-related and capacity-building efforts, designed to build human capacity and institutions to strengthen the position from which developing countries promote and protect their commercial and development interests in trade negotiations (De Lombaerde and Puri 2007). Linking aid to trade in this manner supports growth in ODA because expanding markets in developing regions present growth opportunities for the economies of donor nations.

It should be reiterated that truly dramatic progress toward a more equitable and sustainable future cannot result from increasing quantities of aid alone.* First, it is crucial that aid money be allocated in a way that ensures high effectiveness of aid. In the next subsection, the most important points of criticism of development assistance will therefore be examined in light of recent evidence, and some recommendations for ensuring higher aid effectiveness in the future will be made.

It has been argued that a new paradigm for international development assistance is in fact emerging that puts a greater emphasis on local "ownership," building indigenous and lasting capacity, and reinforcing success by stimulating those who show progress and penalizing countries that consistently fail to meet targets (Soros 2002). The World Bank's *World Development Report, 2000/2001* explores these issues and findings in more detail and includes an extensive bibliography of the relevant literature, some of which will be cited in the following sections.

Second, it must be recognized that in addition to aid, there are many other factors that are arguably much more powerful in affecting the ability of developing countries to develop and prosper. In one attempt to clarify this point, a paper by the Center for Global Development (CGD) and *Foreign Policy* magazine, which is based on this notion, will be discussed. It ranks twenty-one of the world's richest nations with respect to how effective their foreign policies are in stimulating growth and development in the world's poorer nations and is based on a holistic and integrated analysis of development-friendliness that incorporates six different categories: aid, trade, investment, migration, peacekeeping, and the environment. Subse-

quently, Section 12.4 discusses one particular factor that has gained substantial weight over the past fifteen years: private capital flows.

### 12.3.3 A Critical Assessment of Development Aid

Sadly, the heavy criticism that has been uttered with regard to development as it has been disbursed, both multilaterally and bilaterally, is not without grounds. This section is intended to provide a critical discussion of development assistance as it has been distributed over the past decades. It will evaluate several issues that are generally regarded as important defects, making use of a collection of literature and evidence gathered. While doing so, it will derive some important lessons that could improve the effectiveness and sustainability of development projects in the future.†

12.3.3.1 The Problem with Government Involvement

The first problem with foreign aid is that it is usually intergovernmental. For example, the charter of the World Bank requires that loans be guaranteed by the borrowing countries' governments (Soros 2002, p. 98; Weidner 2001). This foundation was laid in the early days of development assistance, when it seemed quite plausible that government-to-government aid was the best way to promote development. At that time, domestic markets in developing countries were virtually nonexistent. Moreover, international markets were severely damaged by the collapse of markets for goods and services as well as capital in the Great Depression of the 1930s, followed by the devastation of World War II.

As was noted in retrospect by the World Bank, the first flush of independence in many developing countries created optimism about the potential for new governments to act as agents of political, social, and economic change (WBG 1998, p. 10). This was accompanied by a strong belief that development was primarily a "money" problem that could be addressed by looking at developing countries' growth requirements and merely "filling the gaps" with ODA. Evidence that has been gathered over the years, however, has shown that these accumulationist, government-coordinated strategies often failed; one only has to

---

* It is interesting to note in this respect that there are in fact limits to the *absorptive capacity* of aid. Paul Collier and David Dollar, two World Bank economists, have gathered evidence that shows that once aid exceeds around 10 percent of a developing country's GDP, even in good policy environments the marginal cost of poverty reduction through further aid is prohibitively high (Collier and Dollar 2001, p. 5).

† In view of the scope of this chapter, the analysis provided here will inevitably be incomplete. For references to the most seminal works by various organizations, aid agencies, and academics, the reader is referred to the bibliography of the World Bank publication *Assessing Aid: What Works, What Doesn't, and Why?* (WBG 1998).

look at the developments in sub-Saharan Africa over the past fifty years to see convincing evidence of that. Zambia, for example, has received so much aid that if all of it was spent on investment, and if investment would have played the vital role in promoting development (through the so-called two-gap model), its inhabitants would have had an average income above $20,000 per annum. In reality, average income has stagnated at around only $600 (WBG 1998, p. 10).

An important drawback of intergovernmental aid is that recipient governments can exploit their role as a gatekeeper of aid inflows and use this power to divert development money to projects for which it was not originally intended (Soros 2002, p. 22; Weidner 2001). This problem not only is an important factor in the debate surrounding aid "fungibility" but also is aggravated by a lack of coordination between different donors and projects. Both these issues will be discussed below.

Another aspect that must be noted is that *donor* country governments also can often exercise a very large influence over the ways in which development aid is disbursed. This is especially true for bilateral aid projects, where many governments "tie" their aid, meaning that the recipient country must spend the aid money on goods and services from the donor country. For several years, it has been known that tying aid reduces its effectiveness—studies have shown that it reduces the value by around 25 percent (WBG 1998, p. 6)—and it has been widely acknowledged that untying aid would make it much more effective (Watkins 1996). But although there is indeed a general trend away from tied aid in the OECD countries, 2001 estimates show that approximately 40 percent of all ODA flows were still tied (CGD/FP 2003, p. 60).

Donor countries can also have a strong influence on the policies and activities of multilateral organizations. Weidner, for example, examines the strong influence that the United States has been able to exert on the lending policies and activities of the World Bank, especially during the 1990s (Weidner 2001).

In a 1996 article in *The FAO Review*, Catherine Gwin stressed that government-to-government aid was often highly ineffective. She argued that this played a major role in fueling the rising criticism of foreign aid during the early 1990s. But she holds the view that throughout the late 1980s and 1990s, many development agencies increasingly started to acknowledge the problems of overly heavy reliance on governments as the prime agent of change (Gwin 1996, p. 18). In fact, she states that since the end of the Cold War, a genuine shift has indeed taken place in the way the OECD world approaches its task of administering aid, as can especially be observed in the new emphasis that is placed on working with nongovernmental organizations (NGOs)* and building civil society.[†] Illustrative of this trend is the fact that the World Bank substantially increased its use of NGO assistance over the course of the 1990s; whereas in the period from 1987 to 1996, only 28 percent of its projects involved NGO participation in some shape or form, this figure had risen to 52 percent in 1999 (WBG 2000b) and 75 percent in 2009 (WBG 2009). In addition, it is striking to observe that over the second half of the 1990s, the grant-making activity of NGOs showed an exactly opposite trend to the declining levels of official development: NGO grants rose from a little over $6 billion in 1995 to approximately $10 billion in 2001, more than one-sixth of the total amount of ODA (WBG 2003a, p. 128).

However, three important drawbacks must be acknowledged with regard to the role of NGOs in delivering foreign assistance (Weidner 2001, p. 14). First, NGOs have no legal status with regard to governments or multilateral organizations. Therefore, these organizations are completely free in their decision to involve, or not to involve, NGOs in their activities. Although multilateral institutions such as the United Nations and the World Bank have repeatedly stressed that NGOs are of enormous value to them (Schoener 1997; WBG 2000b; Weidner 2001),[‡] it should be taken into account that NGOs may at times have difficulties in communicating their exact views because they can

---

* A more elaborate discussion of the role of NGOs from a legal perspective is provided by Schoener (1997). She describes NGOs as not-for-profit entities "whose members are citizens or associations of citizens of one or more countries and whose activities are defined by the collective will of its members in response to the needs of the members of one or more communities with which the NGO operates" (ibid., pp. 537–538). According to Schoener, NGOs have made substantial contributions in the international development policy arena in areas such as the drafting of international agreements, norm creation, and implementation of agreements (ibid., p. 538).

† The notion of fostering civil society involvement and capacity building will be discussed in a later subsection. See also chapter 3 of the World Bank publication *Assessing Aid: What Works, What Doesn't, and Why?* (WBG 1998).

‡ For example, the World Bank stated in its 1999 annual report that NGO involvement is "sought at all phases of the Bank's work—planning and design of projects, implementation, and impact evaluation—because participation improves the quality, effectiveness, and sustainability of development activities. NGOs and other civil society groups play an increasingly critical role in ensuring that Bank-supported projects are participatory in nature, through both their own involvement and their ability to reach out to other stakeholders—especially in poor and excluded communities" (WBG 2000b, p. 139).

easily be sidestepped by multilateral organizations or governments if they do not position themselves in a favorable way (Weidner 2001, p. 15).

Also, the perception that NGOs are more connected to the "grass roots" and more efficient in their use of resources is not entirely accurate—and this holds equally for Southern NGOs, which have rapidly increased in numbers over the past decades. For example, Watkins points out that in countries that receive large flows of foreign aid, many NGOs are in fact more skilled at acquiring donor funding than they are at consulting on issues with local communities (Watkins 1996, p. 32). Moreover, and in relation to the first drawback, the increased (and increasing) cooperation between Southern NGOs and their Northern counterparts and/or multilateral organizations has in some cases led to a diminished sense of control of these NGOs over project design and implementation.

Last, it should be kept in mind that the provision of aid through NGO structures that are only weakly connected to governments—which at first sight seems an appealing course of action in case of corrupt regimes and a poor policy environment—usually leads to a heavy dependence of the recipient nation on the financial and technical assistance of its donors (Watkins 1996, p. 32). This has been observed, for instance, in many African countries. This should be avoided at all costs because it undermines efforts of indigenous capacity building through the construction of a lasting favorable institutional and macroeconomic policy environment. Aid agencies must take this into account because ultimately, developing countries should learn how to mobilize their financial and human resources in order to be able to respond to the many challenges of development (CGD/FP 2003; Watkins 1996).

### 12.3.3.2  The Problem with Aid Fungibility

Especially during the first three decades after World War II, most ODA money was spent on projects that were intended to assist specific sectors, but this is still the case today (see Figure 12.6). A crucial question, therefore, is whether this targeted aid money reaches the project and sector it is intended to assist. This forms the foundation of a long-standing dilemma in the provision of aid and has been used as a line of attack against official development assistance for several decades. It is referred to as the problem of aid "fungibility."*

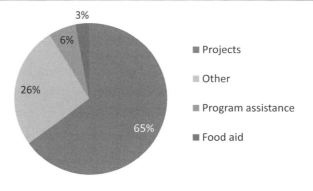

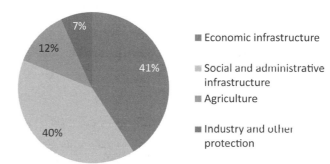

**FIGURE 12.6: DISTRIBUTION OF ODA BY PROJECT TYPE AND SECTOR**
Source: WBG (1998, p. 61).

If aid is not fungible, the overall effect of aid can readily be calculated; all one has to do is look at the aggregate of the success rates of all individual projects (usually measured by means of their rate of return). However, if aid is fungible, assessing the effects of aid is much more complex: the aid money that was intended to be spent on a carefully selected project is reallocated to other expenditures.†

The World Bank illustrated the notion of fungibility by means of a simple diagram (see Figure 12.7). Let us assume that a government spends its budget on only two goods—$R$ on roads and $S$ on schools (this is represented as point $X$ on the budget line). If a donor now comes along and makes a grant available for the financing of roads ($A$), there are two scenarios. If donor money were not at all fungible, the entire amount of aid money donated would be spent on roads. In

---

*         As is pointed out in chapter 3 of the World Bank report *Assessing Aid: What Works, What Doesn't, and Why?*, it

was emphasized as early as the 1950s that even when financing was tied to specific projects, aid money would often remain fungible. Assessments of aid in the 1960s raised the issue of fungibility (WBG 1998, p. 82, n. 1).

†         It is important to note that the fungibility argument is not based on corrupt behavior by the recipient government. It is simply a natural consequence of a sudden rise in the overall government budget.

**Schools**

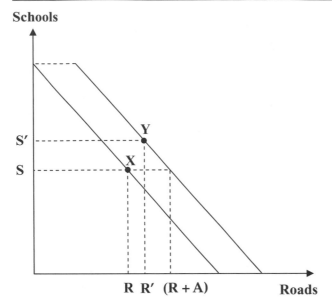

FIGURE 12.7: THE EFFECT OF FUNGIBILITY
Source: WBG (1998, p. 63).

this case, the government would now, as intended by the donor, spend $R+A$ on roads and the same amount as before on schools ($S$). However, if the money were completely fungible, the donated money would have a different effect on the net budget allocation. As long as the government spends as much money on roads as it did before it received the grant, its new budget is effectively $R+S+A$. The government will in this situation effectively divide its new budget between roads and schools in the way it sees fit, thus spending $R'$ on roads and $S'$ on schools.

This example illustrates three important points about fungibility. First, even when aid is fungible, all the aid money *is* in fact spent on roads in an administrative sense. However, the increase in the amount of money spent on roads could range anywhere from zero to the total amount of aid $A$.

Second, full fungibility does not mean that none of the donated money gets spent on roads. It means that the effect of the aid on the budget for roads is exactly the same as if the amount were provided as general budget support, to be allocated by the government as it sees fit. The practical importance of fungibility therefore depends on the extent to which the donor and recipient have common objectives.*

Third, fungibility is less likely to be a problem if the amount of aid is large relative to the recipient gov-

ernment's original budget for the specific sector that the aid is intended for. Aid agencies such as the World Bank have long used this as a defense against the fungibility argument; they reasoned that in many of the developing countries to which aid is directed, this is indeed the case (Economist 1991, p. 10). This line of reasoning seems convincing with respect to the activities of the World Bank's IDA, which operates in the world's poorest nations, but much less so for those of the IBRD. Fungibility is also less of a problem if the project to which the financing is tied is a very specific one that represents only a small fraction of the recipient's original government budget (WBG 1998, p. 63).

Over the past decades, a large body of literature on the effects of fungibility has accumulated. The most important lessons learned have been summarized in an integrated evaluation by the World Bank (WBG 1998, pp. 63–72). By far most of the evidence cited supports the view that aid is, to a large extent, fungible. For example, it has been shown that although differences are large across countries, government spending tends not to rise one-for-one with an increase in development aid. On average, some of the disbursed money is spent on tax relief or deficit reduction (ibid., p. 66).

But—as should be clear from the graphic illustration provided above—even if aid money does result in an increase in government spending, this does not mean that it is spent on development. The evidence suggests that even where aid goes mostly to government spending, the aid money is largely fungible between government "consumption" (recurrent expenditures such as administration, subsidies, and defense) and investment.

Several lessons can be learned from the observation that aid is often fungible. First, it can help explain why in some countries, such as Zambia, aid has had so little lasting effect. Aid agencies have often been too eager to look for projects to finance, even in countries where the public sector was highly distorted and inefficient and institutions and policies were in poor shape (WBG 1998, p. 80).

If, as the evidence suggests, the problem of fungibility is so widespread, why do many donors continue to deliver their aid money through specific projects? The main reason is that it is an attractive course of action for donors. Not only is it administratively attractive to provide aid in discrete and manageable "units," but it also makes it easier to create support for foreign assistance in the donor's own country by appealing to domestic single-interest coalitions (WBG 1998, p. 73).

The evidence on fungibility has shown that the preferred-project approach does not always ensure that aid money is spent usefully. Although it may create the impression of being more "controllable," it

---

\* If a donor finds it administratively convenient to provide its aid money as funding for road building but in fact wants to expand the recipient's overall government budget, then fungibility is not a problem. However, if a donor truly wants its aid money to lead to an increase in the total budget spent on roads, fungibility is a problem.

does not make an evaluation of aid effectiveness easier. If aid money is fungible, evaluations at the micro or project level cannot simply be added up to determine the macro or economy-wide effectiveness of aid.* For example, if the rate of return on a road project is a healthy 20 percent, this does not tell us anything about the overall effectiveness on development at a macro level (because the project might have been funded even in the absence of aid money). Because it is virtually impossible to assess the extent of fungibility in a recipient country during the period it receives aid funds, attempts to correct for its effects will generally be inaccurate (WBG 1998, p. 72).

The problems with fungibility, however, do not imply that project financing should be abandoned altogether. Project financing often confers other important benefits in addition to the "hard" investment. In fact, on many occasions the investment itself was not even the main priority: donors often use projects as a means to transfer new technology and knowledge, as well as to build institutional capacity (WBG 1998, p. 73). If these are the main motivations, then donor project financing can indeed be a very useful approach to foster growth and development.

In light of all this, a good approach would be for donors to accept the fact that aid is fungible and to rethink their means of aid delivery. Attempts to do this have in fact been made over the past decade; donors have tried to avoid fungibility by imposing a set of conditions that were meant to ensure that the aid funding would be *additional* to what the government would have done in any event. These attempts have generally failed because in these cases the donor was in effect financing projects that the government did not consider worth financing itself. A painful but important lesson from these experiences has been that a sense of *ownership* of projects, by governments as well as the broader community, is crucial to make them successful and lasting. This notion that ownership is crucial for sustainable progress will return many times in the following sections. One way to strive for better aid effectiveness is therefore to apply the concept of *allocative conditionality*, which will be explained below. Put simply, it means that donors channel their funds to countries with a better policy environment. Evidence discussed in the next subsection will show that this technique in general greatly increases aid effectiveness.

### 12.3.3.3 The Problem with Conditionality

A third aspect of development aid is the concept of *conditionality* (as opposed to allocative conditionality), which has been heavily criticized over the past fifteen years. It was introduced in the early 1980s, when aid agencies such as the World Bank started to notice that more and more development projects seemed to be failing than before. Upon further investigation, it seemed increasingly apparent that these projects were undermined not by defects in their design, but by adverse influences from the broader policy environment. The 1991 annual World Bank *World Development Report* analyzed the effects of the broader policy environment on development projects for the first time. It performed an analysis in which the rates of return of 1,200 projects—financed either by the IBRD or the IFC—were plotted against four policy measures: trade restrictions, exchange rates, interest rates, and the budget deficit. The results were discussed in the *Economist*'s 1991 survey of the World Bank and the IMF and were indeed remarkable (see Table 12.3). There was clear evidence that the effectiveness of aid depended to a large extent on the broader policy and institutional environment of the recipient country.[†]

A 1998 study by Burnside and Dollar, cited in the World Bank report *Assessing Aid: What Works, What Doesn't, and Why?*, investigates the direct relationship between aid and output growth.[‡] The evidence shows that there did not seem to be any simple relationship; some countries, such as Zambia, that received large quantities of ODA grew only very slowly, whereas others that received only little international assistance performed much better, such as Ghana and Botswana (WBG 1998, p. 35).

However, when countries with good management—that is, countries that have effective institutions to deliver public services and a stable macroeconomic environment, open trade regions, and protected

---

* For a helpful graphic illustration that clarifies the problem with such a calculation, see pages 72 and 73 of the World Bank report *Assessing Aid: What Works, What Doesn't, and Why?* (WBG 1998).

† For example, under high trade restrictions, the average project rate of return was 13.2 percent; under low restrictions, it was 19.0 percent. Where premiums on foreign exchanges were higher than 200 percent, the average rate of return was 8.2 percent; where they were less than 20 percent, the rate of return was 17.7 percent. The results were similar regardless of the type of project and appeared for all four policy parameters chosen. For more information, the reader is referred to the 1991 annual *World Bank World Development Report*. Also, a comprehensive summary is provided in the *Economist*'s 1991 survey of the IMF and the World Bank, titled "Sisters in the Wood" (p. 13).

‡ There is a wide body of literature on the relationship between aid, growth, and broader economic policies, only some of which can be cited here. For a more extensive overview and references to the literature, see chapter 1 of the World Bank report *Assessing Aid: What Works, What Doesn't, and Why?* (WBG 1998).

**TABLE 12.3: AVERAGE RATES OF RETURN FOR IBRD- AND IFC-FINANCED PROJECTS (1968–1989), CATEGORIZED WITH RESPECT TO FOUR MEASURES OF ECONOMIC POLICY**

| POLICY-DISTORTION INDEX | AGGREGATE OF PROJECTS |
|---|---|
| **Trade restrictiveness** | |
| High | 13.2 |
| Moderate | 15.0 |
| Low | 19.0 |
| **Foreign-exchange premium** | |
| High (> 200%) | 8.2 |
| Moderate (20–200%) | 14.4 |
| Low (> 20%) | 17.7 |
| **Real interest rate** | |
| Negative | 15.0 |
| Positive | 17.3 |
| **Fiscal deficit (% of GDP)** | |
| High (> 8%) | 13.4 |
| Moderate (4–8%) | 14.8 |
| Low (> 4%) | 17.8 |

Source: Adapted from WBG (1991b, p. 82).

property rights—were separated from those with poor management, a very different trend appeared. Burnside and Dollar (1997) showed that in low-income countries with good management, 1 percent of extra aid money increased growth by 0.5 percent (see Figure 12.8), which corresponds to a rate of return of approximately 40 percent (assuming a 10 percent annual depreciation rate).* The effects in fact go beyond growth: according to a study by Bruno, Ravallion, et al. (1998), on average a 1 percent increase in per capita income in developing countries reduces poverty by 2 percent. If we link this to the previous observation, it can be stated that in countries with sound management, an extra 1 percent of real GDP in aid results in a 0.5 percentage-point increase in growth, and hence a 1 percent decline in poverty. In countries with poor management, the expected effect of aid on poverty reduction is far less (WBG 1998, p. 39).

Even before the evidence on aid effectiveness and its links to broader policy and institutional factors began to accumulate, aid agencies had decided that lending conditions would have to expand beyond project-specific characteristics to include broader economic parameters. This formed the birth of *conditionality*: the allocation of financial assistance not simply for project implementation, but in exchange for the commitment by the recipient that certain predefined,

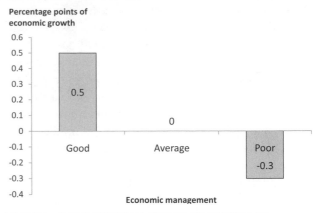

**FIGURE 12.8: THE MARGINAL IMPACT ON GROWTH OF 1 ADDITIONAL PERCENT OF GDP IN AID**
Source: Burnside and Dollar (1997), cited in WBG (1998, p. 36).

broader policy changes would be implemented (Economist 1991; Fairman and Ross 1996).[†]

The World Bank implemented the notion of conditionality as follows: instead of simply broadening its loan conditions, it developed a new type of loan, which it termed a "structural adjustment loan" (SAL). Soon after, it added "sectoral adjustment loans" (SECALs), which were intended to support reform within a particular sector, such as trade liberalization or financial deregulation (Weidner 2001, p. 5). In the provision of these types of loans, the World Bank does not provide funds for a specific project but allows the recipient government to use the aid money as it sees fit on the provision that it implements a set of key conditions and policies that are specified by the World Bank in advance. As is pointed out by Fairman and Ross, it is this notion of conditionality—also referred to as "policy-based lending" (PBL)—that has been used most widely.[‡] For example, as is published in its

---

\* The more technical details of the research cited here are explained in appendix 1 of the World Bank report *Assessing Aid: What Works, What Doesn't, and Why?* (WBG 1998).

† In the wake of the 1980s debt crisis, the IMF began to adopt conditionality policies and adjustments that went beyond its traditional short-term stabilization measures to more long-term structural adjustment programs that included reforms of the financial sector and capital markets, trade liberalization, and the privatization of public enterprises (Carrasco 2011). The IMF's structural conditionality on loans reached its peak at the 1997–1998 Asian financial crises, when Thailand, Korea, and Indonesia were subject to 73, 94, and 140 structural conditions, respectively (ibid., p. 191). Critics of the IMF's structural conditionality approach argued that the imposition of conditions on developing nations meant they had no or limited ownership of the adjustment programs, which led to significant program failures (ibid., p. 192). An independent evaluation of the IMFs efforts to reduce structural conditionality in 2007 concluded that IMF loans still include an average of seventeen structural conditions, many of which were not critical to the achievement of the intended program goals (ibid.).

‡ As will become apparent later, there is another, more effective way of implementing conditionality (Fairman and Ross 1996; WBG 1998).

1999 annual report, the World Bank in that year for the first time made more structural adjustment loans than traditional investment loans (WBG 2000b, cited in Weidner 2001, p. 5). In 2005, approximately one-third of World Bank loans supported structural adjustment programs (Clapp and Dauvergne 2005).

At first sight, this strategy is understandable because policy-based lending seems an attractive way to use development assistance to encourage policy reforms in recipient countries in a world where ODA money is scarce. However, there is a very large literature on the effects of policy-based or structural adjustment lending and its effect on policies,* and by far most of this literature suggests that policy-based lending is a frustrating and obscure technique that is usually highly ineffective and at times even counterproductive (Fairman and Ross 1996). Especially in countries that have poor policies and no movement toward reform, conditionality has more often than not been ineffective.[†]

Several broad lessons can be drawn from the evidence on conditionality as it has been implemented in the context of structural adjustment. First, there is very little evidence that structural adjustment loans actually induce recipients to implement the difficult reforms specified. For example, one study by Mosley, Harrigan, et al. (1995) shows that in Africa, structural adjustment lending from the World Bank affected the policies of recipient countries "a little, but not as much as the Bank hoped." In fact, a study by Alesina and Dollar (1998) showed that policy reform is more likely to follow after a *decrease* in aid than after an *increase* in aid. In short, the evidence does not seem to support a clear positive relationship between the amount of aid allocated and policy reforms. An important problem (and a potential cause of this) is that aid agencies are often under enormous pressure to disburse their funds. For example, the World Bank often had such strong incentives to give out its funds that it generally interpreted a country's activities as good efforts, even if only around 50 percent of the preset conditions were met (Fairman and Ross 1996; WBG 1998).[‡]

A second and related lesson is that SALs are very difficult to monitor and enforce. One of the reasons for this, as already illustrated, is that donors are often under great institutional pressure to allocate their loans, even if compliance of recipient countries does not live up to the prearranged conditions (Fairman and Ross 1996). Another problem is that conditions cannot be enforced after the loan is terminated, which makes it hard to make lasting reforms if there is no consensus.

A third and connected lesson that has been learned the hard way is that a prior commitment by the recipient government to the proposed policies is absolutely vital. A review of policy-based lending concluded: "It seems clear that the lending cum conditionality process works well only when local polities have decided, largely on their own, possibly with outside technical help, to address their reform needs, effect certain policy changes sequentially, and approach the international community for financial help in getting there" (Ranis 1995, p. 10, cited in WBG 1998, p. 52). The World Bank acknowledges that this sense of "ownership," or strong domestic support of reforms, both by government and by the broader community, is essential for adjustment lending to succeed.[§]

Fourth, even if SALs are in fact carried out effectively, this often does not have much to do with imposed donations, but more with the specific characteristics of the issues at hand (Fairman and Ross 1996, p. 33). A study by Dollar and Svensson (1998) examined a sample of adjustment loans by the World Bank (105 successful cases and 55 unsuccessful ones) and found a clear association between the success or failure of these SAL projects and several political and institutional features. When the study examined a set of "Bank effort" variables—factors under the World Bank's control (size of the adjustment loan, number of conditions, resources used to prepare the loan, and resources devoted to analytical work in the four years before the loan)—these variables turned out to be similar for successful and failed adjustment programs. An analysis of both types of variables made clear that successful reform depended primarily on a

---

* Although an extensive review is beyond our scope, some of the most important literature will be examined in the remainder of this subsection (for more literature, see WBG 1998, chap. 2). There is also literature—although much smaller and based on less experience—on the use of policy-based lending for the pursuit of noneconomic goals. The general outcome is the same: it more often fails than succeeds (Fairman and Ross 1996, p. 31).

† For instance, Paul Collier, a World Bank economist, has drawn the clear but pessimistic conclusion that "conditionality has failed" (Collier 1997, p. 57). He argues forcefully that government policy is determined by domestic political forces rather than on what the World Bank conditions its aid.

‡ Zambia, for example, received eighteen adjustment loans between 1966–1969 and 1990–1993 while its policies actually got worse over these periods (WBG 1998, p. 50, fig. 2.1).

§ As an illustration, a study has shown that until 1990, about a third of the adjustment loans failed to achieve their expected reforms. Lack of borrower ownership or commitment was a key factor in the failures (Branson and Jayarajah 1995).

country's institutional and political characteristics, whereas the World Bank's conditionality efforts had no clear and measurable influence.* As the authors put it: "We find no evidence that any of the variables under the World Bank's control affect the probability of success of an adjustment loan. It is possible of course that in exceptional cases the World Bank's effort affects reform. What this kind of econometric work identifies is what is true on average or in general. There are a number of countries—Kenya or Zambia, for example—in which the Bank had a series of mostly failed adjustment loans. Our work suggests that these were not fertile grounds for reform, that there are observable indicators that could have predicted this, and that the World Bank working harder was not going to transform Kenya or Zambia into a successful reformer" (ibid., p. 4).

With this evidence in mind, it is important to realize that in addition to policy-based lending, there is another type of conditionality, referred to by Fairman and Ross (1996) as "allocative conditionality." In this approach, aid is allocated to different recipients on the basis of their existing performance on various indicators. This second approach is fundamentally different from the first because in this mechanism donors do not attempt to bargain with recipients in order to get them to implement reforms. Instead, they simply reward the recipients that do reach effective reform.

As Dollar and Svensson (1998) point out, the evidence cited above suggests that the latter approach is likely to be a much more effective way of implementing conditionality. If we look back at the study by Burnside and Dollar (1997), it can be observed that aid is much more effective at promoting growth in a good policy environment than in a poor one. Aid agencies should thus strive to *identify* reformers, not to *create* them. The key to successful adjustment lending is therefore to find good candidates to support. Adding more conditions to loans or devoting more resources to manage them does not increase the probability of reform and has a high opportunity cost (Dollar and Svensson 1998).

Research on the effectiveness of aid by Collier and Dollar supports this notion that the emphasis in aid provision should be on identifying the right countries.

It suggests that with current policies and aid levels, poverty in sub-Saharan Africa will be reduced by 11 percent, which is far below the target of 50 percent that was set as the first Millennium Development Goal. But even if no improvements would occur in overall policy environments, a 50 percent increase in aid flows, provided it would be efficiently allocated to poor countries with good policies, could increase this reduction in poverty to 22 percent (Collier and Dollar 2001).

The trouble used to be that international assistance was rarely allocated with these points in mind. The *Economist*, for instance, cites evidence that countries with bad policies and institutions got an average of $44 a person in aid, while those with better policies got $39 (Economist 2002b). But there are some signs that aid agencies have taken this lesson on board over the past years. For example, a study by Dollar (2000) identified a clear relationship between the allocation of aid and the quality of a country's policies.† By the late 1990s, countries with better policies got $29 of aid a person, while worse countries got $16. The World Bank seems to do an even better job of alleviating poverty; its subsidized lending to the poorest countries depends more on good economic performance than that of many bilateral donors. For example, even in 1990 the World Bank spent more than twice as much per head on poor countries with good policies than on those with bad policies. In 2002, this ratio had risen further: countries that performed well received $6.50 in aid per capita, while weaker performers received $2.30. Overall, the *Economist* states that in 2002, World Bank lending to the poorest was 60 percent more effective than in 1990 (Economist 2002b).

A paper by the World Bank's International Development Association (IDA) cited evidence by Collier and Dollar (1999) that showed that its projects over the period 1996–1999—the three-year period after the eleventh IDA replenishment—had the closest link of any development assistance program to government performance on economic policy and poverty reduction (WBG 2000a). Perhaps because of this, IDA projects have on average been around

---

*        Political and economic variables successfully predicted the outcomes of 75 percent of the adjustment loans (Dollar and Svensson 1998; see also WBG 1998, appendix 2). Further, 52 percent of governments that implemented successful reforms were democratically elected, versus only 29 percent for failed programs. Governments that had been in power for a long time were less likely to implement reform successfully. Furthermore, political instability was highly correlated with failure.

---

†        Of course, one can always argue whether studies such as these, as well as aid agencies, look at the right policy indicators when they are engaging in allocative conditionality. However, although some areas continue to be fiercely debated, there does by now seem to be a broad consensus on what the important macroeconomic policies are to ensure long-term stability and encourage growth. More on this will follow in Section 12.4 on private capital flows; see also the *Economist*'s (2003a) survey of global finance.

50 percent more effective in reducing poverty than the average bilateral aid program (Collier, Devarajan, et al. 2001).

Last, one could now ask: what can we do for those countries that do not have favorable policy and institutional environments? Obviously, doing nothing is not a commendable option, but it should be clear by now that large-scale financing is also not the solution. The World Bank emphasizes the importance of "disseminating ideas, training the next generation of leaders, and stimulating policy debate in civil society" (WBG 1998, p. 54).* A crucial aspect to note, though, is that donor and recipient countries, and even donor countries among one another, often do not agree about what the right course of action toward sustainable growth and development is. Critics still remain divided about the level of involvement that aid agencies such as the World Bank should have in a country's domestic policies.†

### 12.3.3.4 Problems with Effective Coordination

Another problem with foreign aid is the lack of *coordination* that is often encountered (Fairman and Ross 1996; Soros 2002, p. 24). For example, in many developing countries, twenty-five to thirty bilateral and multilateral aid programs are usually operated at any given time. As Fairman and Ross (1996) point out, many of these countries do not have a centralized agency or process that integrates these aid programs into their government planning and budgeting or coordinates them in a centralized mechanism. Although one could argue that some level of decentralization and competition among donors may improve the efficiency of aid programs, it is commonly agreed that the costs of the lack of coordination outweigh these potential benefits. An underlying and related problem of this lack of coordination is the conflicts of interest that often exist among different donors and donor agencies, among different recipients and their agencies, and especially between donors and recipients (ibid., p. 45).

The international community has been aware of the costs of uncoordinated aid for several decades.‡ Several major problems that are caused by the lack of coordination can be highlighted.§ First, aid projects are often duplicative or even counterproductive. In some cases, aid "fads" result in disproportionate amounts of aid being allocated to particular countries or sectors. Aid projects also have a tendency to proliferate. As a result of all this, the overall effectiveness of aid is usually much lower than it could be (Fairman and Ross 1996, p. 46).

Second, donors often do not pay sufficient attention to specific national and sectoral characteristics before allocating their funding. As a result, they may provide incompatible advice or equipment for the task at hand, again resulting in losses of efficiency.

Third, because of the lack of centralized oversight in recipient countries over their aid programs, the costs of continuing to carry out these projects in the long term are often underestimated. As a result, in times of budgetary stringency, recipients often cut back operating budgets and staffing to such low levels that projects become highly inefficient (Fairman and Ross 1996, p. 46).

Fairman and Ross (1996) argue that effectively coordinating aid through regular international meetings of aid donors or by the channeling of funds through multilateral organizations could greatly improve the effectiveness of aid programs, not only by reducing duplications and trade-offs between programs, but also because it could serve as a way to curtail the political leverage of individual donors in recipient countries. But as good as this sounds in theory, it must be acknowledged that effective coordination is not easily achieved in practice. First, critics have argued that even the aid that is already channeled through multilateral organizations such as the World Bank still allows members with high voting powers, such as the United States, to exert disproportionate influence on the ways in which this aid is administered (Weidner 2001).

Second, it should be acknowledged that on many occasions, funders genuinely disagree about what aid funds should be devoted to (for either ideological or geopolitical and strategic reasons). A policy dialogue that brings donors together but does not enforce binding commitments will more often than not fail to resolve these disagreements (Fairman and Ross 1996).¶

Also, it should be noted that in spite of the obvious gains that coordination of aid could have for recipients,

---

\* It discusses these strategies in more detail in chapter 4 of its report (WBG 1998).
† See Weidner (2001) for a more detailed discussion of these issues and the obvious implications for national sovereignty and human rights.
‡ Fairman and Ross (1996, p. 46) refer to the Pearson Commission, which identified this problem as early as the late 1960s (Pearson 1969, pp. 227–228).

---

§ This section is substantially based on work by Cassen (1986, pp. 220–232), cited by Fairman and Ross (1996, pp. 45–49).
¶ The United Nations 2002 World Summit on Sustainable Development serves as a powerful illustration of this.

they may also perceive it as a threat; it provides donors with an opportunity to "gang up" on them, which reduces their ability to voice their own concerns and further their individual interests (Fairman and Ross 1996, p. 47).*

Therefore, in spite of the fact that both donors and recipients acknowledge the potential gains of improving coordination, conflicting interests will continue to pose difficult obstacles to reaching improvements.

### 12.3.3.5 The Problems with Capacity Building

The notion of *capacity building* has played an important role in the policy agenda of aid agencies for over a decade, but it has turned out to be one of the most difficult objectives to accomplish.† As the previous discussion of conditionality has indicated, it is far from easy to instigate broader institutional and policy reform; attempts to do so usually fail miserably. Fairman and Ross (1996, p. 41) cite evidence from the World Bank that has indicated that the "institutional development" component of aid programs (which includes planning, accounting, maintenance, staff training, and other forms of technical assistance) fails more than twice as often as the "hard investment" component (comprising equipment and physical infrastructure). However, it has also been found that the success of these institutional development programs varies substantially by sector, subsector, and activity (ibid.).‡

An important reason behind the low success rate of attempts to build indigenous capacity is the earlier observation of *conflicting interests*. First, donors and recipients often have very different objectives, both on what the most crucial development issues are and on what the right approach to solving them is. Because donors—especially bilateral donors—have traditionally had a strong tendency to use their obvious

power in setting the aid agenda to enforce their own interests and perceived optimal mechanisms of aid provision, without securing a sufficient level of consensus at the local government and community level, attempts to build much-needed indigenous capacity have failed altogether or have achieved only temporary success.§ Another reason is the internal conflict that exists in aid agencies themselves; their long-term goal is to foster the indigenous institutional and policy environments of aid recipients, but there is also strong political pressure to reach clear and tangible results to show to the "home base," in order to ensure that support and funding for their activities are sustained (Fairman and Ross 1996, p. 43).

A second problem is that recipient countries usually do not have sufficient *ownership* of development projects. Donors tend to rely to a substantial degree on external experts for the design and implementation of projects. As a result, the institutional components of development projects rarely remain in place after the funding is terminated, simply because the recipient does not possess the human or physical capital to sustain them (Fairman and Ross 1996, p. 43; Soros 2002, pp. 23–24).¶

During the 1990s, NGOs increasingly started to become involved in development projects in an attempt to strive for broader engagement of civil society, consensus building, and fostering indigenous institutional capacities (Fairman and Ross 1996; WBG 1998). There are many success stories, but, as was discussed above, even the widespread reliance on NGOs has its drawbacks.

In summary, it can be stated that there is a much-heightened awareness that capacity building is of crucial importance in reaching truly sustainable improvements in the growth and development of the world's poorest countries. Nevertheless, more substantial and long-term commitments by both donors and recipients will be crucial in order to make real and significant improvements.

The following section will show that many of the problems with aid highlighted here will continue to play a vital role when we examine environmental aid specifically. Before we turn to Part B, however, let us examine several other factors besides ODA that

---

\* For example, in the early 1990s, a common and powerful criticism against the World Bank and the IMF was that these institutions had started getting too involved in each other's activities. Developing countries perceived this as a threat that the developed world—and especially the United States—was using these institutions as a means to "gang up" and force its views on their economies; see Economist (1991).

† One has only to look at reports of organizations such as the World Bank (WBG 1998, chap. 4; 2003a), the United Nations (UNDP 2008), or the OECD's Development Assistance Committee (OECD 2001) to realize that capacity building is still a vital point on the political agenda for global development and sustainability.

‡ For example, the most successful programs have been encountered in telecommunications, industry, nonrural finance, and certain utilities. In the areas of agriculture, education, and rail infrastructure, programs have been much less effective; see the evidence cited by Fairman and Ross (1996, p. 42).

---

§ As will be seen in Part B of this chapter, the diverging interests of donors and recipients and the difficulties these create in building capacity and achieving sustainable progress are a vital issue in the debate over *environmental* aid as well.

¶ It must be noted that to improve ownership, reaching a consensus on what the main goals and mechanisms to reach them are is crucial as well. Without this, the long-term viability of a project is still not secure.

greatly influence the capabilities of the world's poorer countries to develop and prosper.

### 12.3.4 Bilateral Financial Transfers: Ranking Developed Countries on Their Foreign Policies

As has repeatedly been pointed out, but is still all too frequently forgotten, developed nations affect developing nations in many other ways than merely through the transfer of ODA. In fact, it can be argued that transfers of official development financing are far from being the most important way in which the world's richest countries affect their less developed counterparts.

The 2003 publication of the first annual Commitment to Development Index (CDI) attempted to incorporate this idea. The study, prepared by the Center for Global Development (CGD) and *Foreign Policy* magazine (*FP*), ranked twenty-one of the world's richest nations—Australia, Canada, Japan, New Zealand, the United States, and most of Western Europe—with respect to how effective their foreign policies are in stimulating growth and development in the world's poorer nations. The CDI ranking is based on a more holistic and integrated analysis of development-friendliness; it originally evaluated countries by assessing six different dimensions of their foreign policies: aid, trade, investment, migration, peacekeeping (later renamed security), and the environment. A technology dimension was added in 2004 and the list of nations now includes South Korea, the newest member of the OECD's Development Assistance Committee (DAC). Table 12.4 provides the 2010 CDI ranking of the twenty two countries evaluated using the index.

For each of the seven categories in Table 12.3, countries are given a score based upon certain policies that are considered to benefit the lives of people living in developing regions. The overall average determines their place in the ranking. Different scores are calculated in different ways, reflecting the particular issues involved and the availability of data.*

The *aid* score is calculated by looking at the level of ODA provided by each nation and discounting it based on certain factors such as whether the development assistant was tied to the donor nation—that is, financial assistance that requires the recipient country to spend it on goods and services provided by the donor country.

The *trade* score is devised so as to side "neither with the passionate trade critics who fear a 'race to the bottom' in environmental and labor standards nor with the equally passionate advocates who consider international commerce the prime mover of development" (CGD/FP 2003, p. 61). It is based on an overall examination of a donor country's barriers (tariffs, quotas, and domestic production subsidies) to the free movement of goods and services from developing countries and in addition directly measured and rewarded imports from the world's poorest nations.

The third category, *investment*, is based primarily on foreign direct investment (FDI). As is explained in Section 12.4, investment comes in three main forms: portfolio investment, foreign direct investment, and bank lending. The investment-related government policies of each nation are assessed using a checklist of twenty questions. For example, countries gain points "for having programs to insure nationals against political risks for investment in developing countries," but lose points "if they do not screen for and monitor environmental, labor, and human rights problems" (Roodman 2010, p. 24). The CDI focuses mainly on flows of FDI because this type is generally seen as more stable than portfolio capital and often facilitates the transfer of good management and technology. However, one out of the five groups of questions (that represents 19 percent of the investment score) does assess policies that affect portfolio flows.

The fourth category in the analysis is *migration*. It may be surprising to see that this measure has been included in the analysis of the development-friendliness of foreign policies. However, the CDI reasons that on balance, freer movement of people increases world development and therefore must be considered in an integrated assessment. The score is created from indicators such as the gross non-DAC immigrant inflow as a percentage of the receiving-country population, a measure of the movement of skilled and unskilled immigrants, and the share of foreign students that are from non-DAC countries.

The *environment* score is included to reflect the belief that the world's richer nations have special responsibilities to ensure proper management of the global environment. The score is based upon nine indicators that can be grouped into three main areas: global climate change (five indicators representing 60 percent of the total score); biodiversity and global ecosystems (two indicators representing 30 percent of the total); and fisheries (two indicators representing 10 percent of total). The nine indicators are translated into a standard scale and combined using a weighted average.

---

* See Roodman (2010) for a detailed discussion of the seven components of the CDI.

**TABLE 12.4: 2010 CDI RANKING OF TWENTY-TWO RICH COUNTRIES, BASED ON AN EXAMINATION OF SEVEN POLICY INDICATORS: AID, TRADE, INVESTMENT, MIGRATION, ENVIRONMENT, SECURITY, AND TECHNOLOGY**

| RANK | COUNTRY | AID | TRADE | INVESTMENT | MIGRATION | ENVIRONMENT | SECURITY | TECHNOLOGY | OVERALL (AVERAGE) |
|---|---|---|---|---|---|---|---|---|---|
| 1 | Sweden | 13.6 | 6.2 | 5.7 | 8.8 | 6.2 | 4.0 | 4.4 | 7.0 |
| 2 | Denmark | 13.1 | 5.9 | 4.7 | 5.7 | 6.3 | 6.2 | 5.7 | 6.8 |
| 3 | Netherlands | 12.5 | 6.4 | 6.1 | 4.6 | 6.7 | 6.0 | 4.9 | 6.7 |
| 4 | Norway | 11.4 | 1.2 | 6.5 | 7.8 | 5.7 | 6.6 | 5.3 | 6.4 |
| 5 | New Zealand | 3.8 | 8.1 | 4.7 | 6.0 | 6.7 | 8.4 | 4.9 | 6.1 |
| 6 | Finland | 6.3 | 6.3 | 5.0 | 3.4 | 7.9 | 6.0 | 5.4 | 5.8 |
| 6 | Ireland | 10.4 | 5.9 | 3.1 | 5.8 | 6.2 | 5.4 | 3.7 | 5.8 |
| 8 | Portugal | 3.5 | 6.2 | 5.4 | 4.5 | 6.3 | 5.7 | 7.3 | 5.6 |
| 9 | Canada | 5.1 | 7.1 | 6.2 | 5.9 | 3.2 | 5.4 | 5.8 | 5.5 |
| 9 | Spain | 5.7 | 6.2 | 6.0 | 5.5 | 5.8 | 2.9 | 6.5 | 5.5 |
| 11 | Australia | 4.0 | 7.5 | 6.2 | 3.9 | 4.0 | 7.2 | 5.0 | 5.4 |
| 11 | Austria | 3.3 | 6.0 | 2.8 | 10.8 | 6.0 | 4.1 | 5.0 | 5.4 |
| 11 | United States | 2.8 | 7.3 | 4.9 | 4.6 | 3.6 | 9.9 | 4.9 | 5.4 |
| 14 | Belgium | 6.7 | 6.0 | 5.6 | 3.7 | 7.0 | 1.5 | 4.8 | 5.1 |
| 14 | Germany | 3.8 | 6.1 | 6.4 | 5.4 | 6.7 | 3.2 | 4.4 | 5.1 |
| 16 | United Kingdom | 6.1 | 6.0 | 6.2 | 3.4 | 7.1 | 1.7 | 4.4 | 5.0 |
| 17 | France | 4.6 | 6.1 | 5.2 | 3.1 | 7.1 | 2.0 | 6.0 | 4.9 |
| 18 | Italy | 2.7 | 6.2 | 5.5 | 3.3 | 6.3 | 4.8 | 4.4 | 4.8 |
| 19 | Greece | 2.9 | 6.0 | 4.1 | 6.5 | 5.8 | 5.3 | 2.7 | 4.7 |
| 20 | Switzerland | 5.3 | 0.6 | 4.6 | 6.6 | 6.2 | 2.9 | 2.8 | 4.1 |
| 21 | Japan | 1.1 | 2.4 | 4.6 | 1.8 | 5.2 | 2.2 | 6.0 | 3.3 |
| 22 | South Korea | 1.1 | 3.0 | 5.8 | 1.0 | 2.7 | 1.8 | 6.5 | 3.1 |
| | Average | 5.9 | 5.6 | 5.3 | 5.1 | 5.8 | 4.7 | 5.0 | 5.3 |
| | Standard dev. | 3.7 | 1.9 | 1.0 | 2.2 | 1.3 | 2.2 | 1.1 | 1.0 |

Source: Adapted from Center for Global Development (2010, p. 6).

The *security* score is based on five indicators that measure costs (as a percentage of a rich-nation's GDP) relating to peacekeeping and humanitarian interventions. These costs include the dollar contributions to the UN peace keeping budget, the cost of maintaining and deploying personnel to support UN peacekeeping operations, and the cost of maintaining and deploying personnel to support non-UN peacekeeping and humanitarian operations that are approved by the international community.

Finally, the *technology* score is based upon two components that try to measure the generation and diffusion of innovations. The basic argument is that "people in developing countries benefit from technological advances as both producers and consumers" (Roodman 2010, p. 49). The technology score is based upon indicators that measure government support of R&D, the rate of tax subsidization of business expenditure on R&D, and policies relating to intellectual property rights that restrict the flow of innovations and technology to developing regions.

The results of the first CDI "cast traditional assumptions about the most development-friendly countries in a new, unexpected light" (CGD/FP 2003, p. 58). For instance, the United States and Japan— the two countries that provide the largest absolute amounts of ODA in 2002 to the developing world—

rank twentieth and twenty-first, respectively, in the 2003 index. The United States rank has improved since then, but Japan remains in the last two countries in the 2010 CDI, due to its low scores on aid, migration, and security. The United States finished eleventh in the 2010 CDI alongside Australia and Austria. While the United States scores well on trade and security, its poor performance on aid and the environmental prevent it from climbing higher. The top four countries in the 2010 CDI are Sweden, Denmark, the Netherlands, and Norway.

The aid provided by the United States and Japan is discounted mainly due to its classification as being tied to goods and services produced within these nations. Although the threat that tied aid poses to capacity building and ensuring sustainability of projects in the long term has long been acknowledged, many donor nations still use it as a condition for disbursing aid. In 2001 alone, approximately 40 percent of all ODA flows were tied (CGD/FP 2003, p. 60). Japan and the United States rank twentieth and twenty-first, respectively, in the aid category.

In the 2010 trade ranking, the United States finished third, behind New Zealand and Australia. Norway and Switzerland, in contrast, surprisingly rank last, mainly because they impose high tariffs on meat, dairy products, and sugar imports from devel-

Billions of Dollars

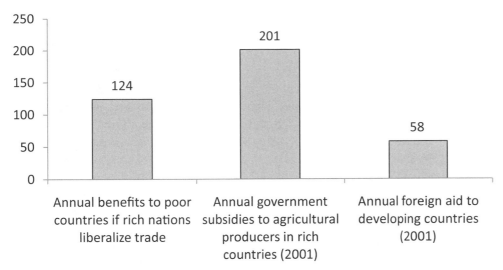

FIGURE 12.9: THE ADVERSE EFFECT OF TRADE BARRIERS ON DEVELOPMENT OF THE WORLD'S POOREST
Source: CGD/FP (2003, p. 63).

oping countries. When combined, the countries included in the CDI spend almost the same amount subsidizing their agricultural sectors as they spend on ODA—some $106 billion a year.[7] These subsidies can cause heavy losses to producers in the developing world. Protectionism in rich countries is one of the largest inhibitors of development in the world's poorest nations, especially because the most protected industries in high-income countries are precisely those where developing countries are most competitive, such as agriculture and textiles. The World Bank estimated that rich-country trade barriers cost poor and developing countries more than $100 billion annually—almost twice as much as total yearly ODA flows (see Figure 12.9). In addition, the World Bank stated that gaining unrestricted access to industrial countries' markets could improve average incomes in developing countries by up to 5 percent (WBG 2002a).*

In the investment category, the top seven countries—Norway, Germany, the U.K., Australia, Canada, the Netherlands, and Spain—all score between 6.0 and 6.5. In fact, there is less variation in this measure when compared to other measure such as aid. The high scores of these countries are due to their policies that promote investment that is considered to be good for development. In contrast, Austria ranks

last due to policies that prevent pension funds from investing in developing countries.

The migration score of the 2010 CDI shows some interesting results. Austria is ranked first due to the number of immigrants it accepts relative to its size. Switzerland, which has a reputation for being xenophobic, is ranked fourth, while the United States—a nation of immigrants—is ranked thirteenth. An important factor here is that although it is very difficult for immigrants to gain citizenship in Switzerland, obtaining legal entry for work is very straightforward. As explained above, the latter aspect is what the CDI actually measured. The U.S. score is low partly because of its large number of illegal immigrants.

In the environment category, Finland ranks highest due to its low level of per capita greenhouse gas emissions and high gasoline tax. Whereas, Australia has a low ranking due to its high level of per capita greenhouse gas emissions. The United States scores poorly since it has yet to ratify the Kyoto Protocol.

On the security measure, the United States is ranked first due to its investment in securing shipping lanes and support of approved international peace and humanitarian interventions. New Zealand, Australia, and Norway follow the United States due to their steady investments in areas experiencing or recovering from conflict.

Lastly, Portugal is ranked first in the technology score due to its high government R&D expenditures. The United States is ranked thirteenth partly due to its significant R&D investment in defense and low tax subsidies for business R&D. It is also considered

---

*       Late 2008 was a particularly difficult time in the development of international trade. The fact that Western economies were facing the severest recession since World War II not only had devastating effects on net private capital flows to emerging economies but also caused a reduction in global trade volumes for the first time since 1982 (Economist 2008).

to restrict the flow of innovations to developing countries due to its various patent policies. Ireland, Switzerland, and Greece fall at the bottom of the technology ranking due to their low investment in R&D and poor tax subsidies for business R&D.

The CDI sends two important messages. First, it indicates the hard truth that even the best performers in the ranking can and should still make substantial improvements to their foreign policies in order to make them more beneficial to the world's poorest nations and people. Sweden, which ranked highest in the 2010 CDI, was ranked fourteenth and seventeenth on the security and technology scores, respectively, indicating room for improvement.

Second, it shows that the nations that lead the world in tackling the daunting task of achieving sustainable global development are three of the world's smallest—Sweden, Denmark, and the Netherlands—while the G-7 countries, which are often characterized as the "seven leading industrial nations," do not perform well.. The first CDI publication concluded: "The G-7 nations must assume the responsibilities commensurate with their size, power, and economic might. That means reforming all their policies with an eye toward aiding development. . . . These nations' steady progress on the measures included in the CDI could inspire other rich nations to follow suit. If the richest of the rich do not lead, then no one will. But if these countries do step forward, then they will help improve the lives of millions of people who deserve better than they now have—while building a more stable world in the process" (CGD/FP 2003, p. 66).

### 12.3.5 Export Credit Agencies

Export credit agencies (ECAs) are an important class of financial institutions in the international arena. They are governmental or quasi-governmental institutions that provide government-backed loans, guarantees, and insurance to multinational enterprises based in their home country, with the aim of promoting international trade and investment.*

ECAs are now the single largest public financers of large-scale infrastructure projects (power generation, telecommunications, and transportation) in the developing and emerging economies (ECA-Watch 2003b; Rich 2000). These include large dams, coal and nuclear power plants, mining projects, roads, oil pipelines, chemical and other industrial facilities, and logging and plantation schemes. In 2002, ECAs accounted for $50 billion in support of large industrial and infrastructure projects (OECD 2003). More recent estimates put the figure somewhere between $50 billion and $70 billion annually.[8] ECAs subsidize transactions that private banks (or international lending institutions) will not support because of high financial or political risk (Rich 2000). Government-backed export credits and credit guarantees pay an important role in providing exporters with access to emerging markets in high-risk countries, especially developing and transition countries, as a kind of bank of last resort or insurer (Schaper 2009). ECAs provide twice as much money to poor countries as the total of all development aid worldwide, both bilateral and multilateral, including the UN agencies and the World Bank (Rich 2000).

In contrast to ODA lenders, ECAs are not foreign assistance agencies but domestic assistance agencies, used to boost the sales of a country's multinational corporations and undertaking activities that some call the "New Mercantilism" (Rich 2000, p. 33). ECAs are taxpayer supported, are not politically accountable, report to one ministry, and face no or very little legislative oversight. Historically, the criticisms and major policy focus directed at ECAs concerned the problem of competitive subsidization (P. C. Evans 2005; P. Evans and Oye 2001). Because of continued aversion to subsidies in international trade and the growing strength of the WTO (although the Uruguay Round of the WTO exempts these large export subsidies by major industrialized countries' ECAs from WTO reach), international efforts to rein in competitive subsidization have been largely successful. The consequence of establishing interest-rate floors and other terms and conditions has arguably been a net plus from an environmental perspective. Of course, developing countries do not like the reforms because they have raised their financing costs. However, they do mean that projects like the Yamal pipeline can no longer secure the heavy subsidization that they once did.

In recent years, ECAs have come under increasing scrutiny by civil society and policy makers because of their backing of investments that have had negative environmental, social, and human rights impacts. Of the wide range of projects that ECAs have supported—in sectors such as oil, gas, coal, and mining, but also nuclear energy, hydropower, and pulp and paper—many have had severe detrimental

---

* The U.S. Export-Import Bank offers working capital guarantees and export credit insurance to U.S. exporters and also offers direct loans and guarantees of commercial loans to foreign buyers of U.S. goods and services. In 2006, it approved $12.1 billion of this type of financial assistance while receiving a $172.5 million allocation from Congress (Nakhooda, Seymour, et al. 2009, p. 415). ECAs play a significant role in the world's poorest countries; the World Bank estimates that ECA financing currently represents 80 percent of gross capital-market financing in the seventy poorest countries of the world.

effects on the environment, social structures, and human rights.* As Norlen, Cox, et al. (2002, p. 1) describe in an ECA-Watch publication,† "Because most of these projects are high risk due to their environmental, political, social and cultural impacts, most would not come to life without the support and financial backing of ECAs. Hence, ECAs are strategic development linchpins that play an enormous part in the harmful impacts of corporate globalization."

Successful reform efforts were led in the early 1990s by the U.S. Export-Import Bank to press for the adoption of international rules under the OECD to avoid being placed at a competitive disadvantage by foreign ECAs (P. C. Evans 2005; P. Evans and Oye 2001; Schaper 2009). These efforts responded to considerable pressure and support from NGOs. In 2001, the OECD initially agreed to nonbinding guidelines, Recommendations on Common Approaches on Environment and Officially Supported Export Credits, for taking environmental and social concerns into account in lending practices of ECAs. Ultimately, as of January 1, 2004, the recommendations were accepted as binding standards for project support and requirements for ex ante transparency. However, countries could choose between World Bank/IFC standards and more lax regional bank rules, and thus the goal of harmonization was hardly achieved. In addition, transparency could be thwarted by a country's ECA invoking confidentiality or proprietary concerns (Schaper 2009).

Of course, there are significant limitations on the effectiveness of imposing higher environmental standards on ECAs. Because funds are fungible, countries can use ECA financing for "acceptable projects" while financing "dirty" projects with domestic resources and equipment (see the discussion of fungibility in Section 12.3.3.2).

### 12.3.5.1 The Functioning of ECAs

Export credits or guarantees are made available to companies working in developed and developing countries.‡ The government of the exporting country will guarantee the exporting company against nonpayment of part of the repayments that are scheduled. These guarantees are issued by the national ECA, which will usually also provide insurance against political risk. "Developing countries that accept projects financed by ECAs are in effect taking out a loan from the ECA, which then goes to the corporation providing the service. The developing-country borrower (sometimes a government, sometimes a private entity) must eventually repay the loan, not the company involved from the industrialized country. Most ECA loans to private entities in the developing world require that their governments back the loans, often turning what appears to be privately held debt into public debt" (Clapp and Dauvergne 2005, p. 212).

The rationale behind ECAs is that they can help promote capital flows to developing countries. The economic and political uncertainties from which these countries suffer often pose significant disincentives to investors considering the possibility of engaging themselves with FDI, export, or project finance in these countries. Export credits and guarantees can therefore, if used appropriately, be an important source of finance for developing countries. They can, as has been pointed out by international institutions such as the World Bank Group, act as a catalyst for private-sector activities in developing economies while at the same time promoting sustainable development. One of the continuing criticisms of ECAs is that in practice they continue to promote environmental destruction, partially through fierce international competition for funds for specific large-scale projects like dams.§

ECA loans, because of a chronic lack of public disclosure of their activities, "contradict the principles of democracy and transparency to which their parent governments aspire" (Norlen 2002). They have been under attack for spreading corruption through their projects in the developing countries in which they are investing, as well as for their involvement in the export of arms and military equipment to countries engaged in conflict.

---

* For detailed case studies in which the (mal)practices of ECAs in developing countries are analyzed, the reader is referred to the ECA-Watch publications "A Race to the Bottom" (1999) and its follow-up, "Race to the Bottom—Take II" (2003b).
† ECA-Watch is an international NGO campaign to reform export credit agencies. A wealth of information about the NGO campaign and its achievements thus far, as well as about the harmful impacts of ECAs, can be found on its website, www.eca-watch.org (accessed January 27, 2008). A significant share of the information presented in this section has been based on ECA-Watch documents and press releases.
‡ The reader is referred to case study V in ECA-Watch 1999, written by Michiel van Voorst, for a more detailed discus-

sion of the functioning of ECAs and especially the debt-creating aspects of export credits.
§ A prime example of this is the Three Gorges Dam in China. This enormous project to build the world's largest dam in the Yangtze River is expected to have disastrous consequences for the environment and the local economy. But although the World Bank and the U.S. Export-Import Bank refused to finance the project, Canadian, Swiss, and German ECAs offered to support this project in 1996. It has been troubled with corruption, cost overruns, and fierce local as well as international opposition ever since, but the Chinese government still wishes to see it completed (Norlen 2002).

Many ECAs continue to be highly resistant to change. Pascal Lamy, the former European Union trade secretary and now head of the WTO, made the following comment about this in 2000: "I too am frustrated with the ECAs' lack of progress in adopting common environmental policies. Every time any of them move forward a millimeter, they stop to see if anybody else moved."[9] However, it should be recognized that ECAs, in contrast to members of the World Bank Group, are not only more numerous and more heterogeneous, but are also a core part of each industrialized country's machinery for promoting exports. These factors greatly complicate efforts at international harmonization (P. C. Evans 2005).

### 12.3.5.2 Background on the Evolution of the OECD Common Approaches

In an attempt to raise public awareness about the above-mentioned problems and to initiate desperately needed changes, NGOs from various countries across the globe decided in 1996 to commence an international campaign calling for the reform of ECAs (ECA-Watch 2003b). The goals and demands of this campaign have been effectively captured in the Jakarta Declaration for Reform of Official Export Credit and Investment Insurance Agencies, which was first presented at an international ECA-reform strategy session in Jakarta, Indonesia, in May 2000 and was subsequently endorsed by 347 NGOs from 45 countries. This declaration focuses primarily on the impacts of ECAs in Indonesia, but it also includes a global "call for reform" that addresses the following issues (ECA-Watch 2000):

- Transparency, public access to information, and consultation with civil society

- A set of *binding* common environmental and social guidelines and standards, which are as stringent as existing guidelines and standards for international public finance institutions (such as the World Bank Group and the OECD Development Assistance Committee)

- Implementation of a set of explicit criteria to limit the adverse impact of ECA activities on human rights

- Establishment of a commitment to finance only economically productive investments

- Adoption of binding criteria and guidelines to end ECA involvement in corruption

- Adoption of ECA debt-relief schemes for poor and heavily indebted countries

After the establishment of this declaration, and with the strong support of the United States, increasing attention was given to the topics raised in the international press, among the G-8 countries, and in the OECD. As a consequence, the OECD Working Party on Export Credits (known as the Export Credit Group, or ECG)* initiated a policy discussion that in December 2001 resulted in a "Draft Recommendation for Common Approaches on Environment and Officially Supported Export Credits: Revision 6" (usually referred to as "Common Approaches Rev 6"). Despite broad consensus among ECAs, the United States—rightly—decided not to acknowledge the recommendation. It put forth two reasons for this decision. First, it considered the requirements on disclosure of project information too weak. Second, it disliked the "benchmarking" approach in which standards and guidelines for projects were set on a case-by-case basis instead of by means of a common baseline (ECA-Watch 2003b).

In spite of these objections, the other ECG members adopted Rev 6 on a voluntary basis, but NGOs have remained highly skeptical of the initiative since its adoption. ECA-Watch, in its 2003 follow-up report to its 1999 publication "A Race to the Bottom," reports through various case studies across a range of nations and industries that Rev 6 was unable to reduce the negative impacts of ECA-supported projects (ECA-Watch 2003b).

In April 2003, the chair of the ECG reopened negotiations with the aim of developing a new recommendation for "common approaches" that was to be adopted by all ECG members, including the United States. On December 18, 2003, a new common agreement on ECAs was adopted at the OECD in Paris. The new agreement was the result of a review of the 2001 Common Approaches that was conducted between September and November 2003 and involved consultations between the ECG and representatives of business, labor unions, and civil society, as well as of countries that are recipients of officially supported export credits. The new agreement took the form of an OECD recommendation, which, according to the OECD, gives the agreement a "great moral force as representing the political will of member countries and there is an expectation that member countries will do their utmost to fully implement a Recommendation" (OECD 2003b).

---

\* The following OECD countries are ECG members (in alphabetical order): Australia, Austria, Belgium, Canada, the Czech Republic, Denmark, Finland, France, Germany, Greece, Hungary, Ireland, Italy, Japan, Korea, Luxembourg, Mexico, the Netherlands, New Zealand, Norway, Poland, Portugal, the Slovak Republic, Spain, Sweden, Switzerland, Turkey, the United Kingdom, and the United States (OECD 2002).

The new agreement was improved with respect to the 2001 Common Approaches in several domains (OECD 2003):

- Projects must from now on comply with the environmental standards of the host country in all cases. Moreover, when the relevant international standards against which the project has been benchmarked are more stringent than those of the host country, these standards should be applied.*

- For the most sensitive projects, the environmental standards applied will be reported and monitored by the ECG, and exceptional deviations below international standards will have to be justified. Moreover, ECG members will seek to make environmental information—particularly environmental impact assessment reports–available to the public thirty calendar days before final commitment.

OECD secretary-general Donald J. Johnston welcomed the new agreement as "an important achievement for the OECD and a significant step for the protection of the environment that will help to foster fair competition between export credit providers" (OECD 2003). ECA-Watch, on the other hand, heavily criticized the agreement. Sébastien Godinot, member of Amis de la Terre, part of ECA-Watch in Paris, said, "The loopholes in this agreement are so huge that it hardly requires anything of ECAs" (ECA-Watch 2003a).

According to ECA-Watch, although the new agreement does make reference to international standards, it does not require ECAs to apply any specific minimum set of them to projects, but instead refers to a broad list of varying standards that ECAs can choose to apply, or not to apply, at will. Moreover, although the new agreement states that environmental information should be made publicly available thirty days before a final commitment, it still allows exceptions to this rule and does not explicitly require companies to make this information publicly accessible or consult with affected communities and stakeholders before project approval (ECA-Watch 2003a).

On June 12, 2007, the OECD issued a Revised Council Recommendation on Common Approaches on the Environment and Officially Supported Export Credits (OECD 2007). The council recommendation provided further details on how the Common Approaches are to be applied. OECD members are asked to classify projects in accordance with their potential environmental impact.† Category A projects are considered to have adverse environmental impacts that extend beyond the project site and should be submitted to an environmental impact assessment (EIA).‡ Projects that fall into this category include crude oil refineries, power stations, steel works, asbestos processing facilities, chemical installations, large infrastructure projects (for example, road and dams), and waste-processing facilities. Category B projects are considered to have less of an environmental impact than Category A projects. Category B projects can be characterized as having site-specific impacts that can be mitigated with existing technologies. The review of Category B projects is considered to vary from project to project and may or may not include an EIA. Finally, Category C projects are considered to have minimal or no environmental impacts and do not require any further review beyond their initial screening.

When evaluating the environmental impacts of a Category A or B project, countries are still required to review the project in the context of the host countries standards and to benchmark the project against relevant international standards (OECD 2007). The flexibility to select which international standards to benchmark the projects against remains a weakness of the Common Approaches methodology.

Despite the slow progress among ECAs in acknowledging the need for reforms, there have been some positive changes. The Common Approaches, despite their imperfections, represent one of these changes. Moreover, ECA-Watch points out that other countries, such as Australia, the United States, Canada, Japan, and the United Kingdom, have implemented some important reforms of ECA practices, which may lead other nations to follow suit. "Still, there remains strong resistance to change by ECAs in most leading countries, and, where change has occurred, close monitoring to ensure implementation is required" (Norlen 2002).

---

\* The relevant international standards used are those of the World Bank Group or, where applicable from a geographic viewpoint, those of regional development banks. ECG members are also allowed to adhere to higher internationally recognized environmental standards, such as those of the European Community (OECD 2002).

† OECD members are required to classify projects that are greater than SDR 10 million and all projects less than SDR 10 million are in or near environmentally sensitive areas.

‡ It is important to recognize that ECAs are likely to approach the development of an EIA differently. For example, in the United States, EIAs have been institutionalized by the National Environmental Policy Act (NEPA), which made *transparency* a critical part of the evaluation process. In contrast, in Germany the information collected as part of an EIA "is considered commercially confidential and not to be released by public agencies" (Schaper 2009, p. 205).

### 12.3.6 Private Multinational Banks and the Equator Principles

Although private multinational banks are not "public" or governmental banks, they have also been increasingly sensitive to sustainability demands. The International Finance Corporation of the World Bank has been active in attempting to influence private multinational banks, such as HSBC and Citigroup, to follow its example of using environmental/social criteria in their lending practices. The IFC launched its Sustainability Initiative in 2001 to persuade the banks that sustainable development represented an economic opportunity. In 2002, with four major multinational industrial banks expressing concern about their investments being targeted by civil society groups, the IFC convened a conference to discuss environmental and social review for projects. A year later, ten leading commercial banks adopted the Equator Principles, a voluntary code of conduct relating to environmental/social lending criteria (Wright 2005). By 2010, sixty-eight banks had adopted the principles.[10]

### 12.3.7 Sovereign Wealth Funds

Within less than a decade, governments around the world—primarily in emerging market economies—have accumulated a vast amount of capital in foreign assets (Allen and Caruana 2008; Truman 2007); their amounts are often unknown to their citizens or businesses. As with other financial institutions, transparency and accountability for the use of these funds leave a lot to be desired. The possible political use of these funds and their potential impact on the global financial system have raised some concern (ibid.). As presented in Section 12.1, the amount of money invested in several major sovereign wealth funds in 2010–2011 was approaching $2.5 trillion.

Allen and Caruana (2008, p. 5) describe SWFs as a heterogeneous group and identify five different types of SWFs that can be classified based upon their main objectives:

(i)  *stabilization funds*, where the primary objective is to insulate the budget and the economy against commodity (usually oil) price swings;

(ii)  *savings funds* for future generations, which aim to convert nonrenewable assets into a more diversified portfolio of assets . . . ;

(iii)  *reserve investment corporations*, whose assets are often still counted as reserve assets, and are established to increase the return on reserves;

(iv)  *development funds*, which typically help fund socio-economic projects or promote industrial policies that might raise a country's potential output growth; and

(v)  *contingent pension reserve funds*, which provide (from sources other than individual pension contributions) for contingent unspecified pension liabilities on the government's balance sheet.

Countries with substantial foreign assets often seek a greater return on their investments than is available from investing in domestic development and therefore are unlikely to do so. Thus these assets could be used—for better or worse—to have a significant impact in foreign venues. Norway stands out in that it has an official policy of screening the use of its funds for acquiring equity in companies having minimal adverse environmental impact and of divesting from MNEs/MNCs that violate human rights and harm the environment (Chesterman 2008). It is too early to evaluate the ultimate impact of Norway's policies because they are still emerging. Finally, in today's global financial crisis, it is hard to anticipate what impact the use of these funds by different governments might have.

## 12.4 PRIVATE CAPITAL FLOWS

Before 1990, private capital investment constituted only about half of all financial flows from North to South (Miller 2000, p. 1230). During the past two decades, however, the rapid globalization and enhanced complexity of financial markets has spurred a dramatic increase in net private capital flows to developing countries.* As a consequence, in 2006, net flows of private capital to the developing world reached an all-time high of approximately $647 billion. Given that principal repayments to official creditors exceeded disbursements by $76 billion, net private flows accounted for approximately 114 percent of total net funds entering developing countries in 2006 (WBG 2007).

As a result of this trend, private capital flows have become one of the major factors that drive the increasingly globalized world economy, with potentially profound beneficial as well as harmful effects for sustainable development. Proponents of financial globalization point out that over the past decade, tens of thousands of companies have crossed their national

---

*    As was discussed in the previous section, private capital flows now dwarf bilateral and multilateral official development assistance, which were for many years the main form of investment in the developing world.

boundaries in search of new markets, cheaper labor, and higher profits, resulting in a powerful transfer of advanced technologies, products, and managerial experience to the developing world, as well as a boost of wages, creation of jobs, and improvements in the quality of life for millions of people. Skeptics, on the other hand, point to the various adverse effects of this surge in international investment: often abominable working conditions and low wages, damage to the environment, and widespread corruption, as well as the exposure of weak economies to destructively high volatility shocks (Chesky 1998).

All these claims have strong elements of truth in them, and the economic and environmental implications of financial globalization remain highly controversial and improperly understood to this day (Miller 2000, p. 1230).* In this section, we attempt to clarify some of the main issues in the debate surrounding private capital flows and financial globalization. First, we briefly discuss the rise in private capital flows that is followed by a review of the three main types of private capital—foreign direct investment (FDI), portfolio flows, and bank lending—and the potential difficulties and drawbacks that financial liberalization may have for developing countries. We then present some recommendations on how developing countries should go about attracting favorable and sustainable funding while ensuring that their financial systems are safe from shocks and "capture" by powerful transnational corporations (TNCs). Last, we also indicate what the industrialized world can do to assist in this difficult, but much-needed, process—not just for the sake of spurring development in the poor countries, but to further their own interests as well.[†]

### 12.4.1 The Rise in Private Capital Flows

During the past two decades, rapid steps have been taken toward the emergence of a global capital market. Private-sector foreign direct investment (FDI) has grown explosively, accompanied by a rapid rise in international portfolio flows and widespread moves to privatization (WBG 2002b, 2003a, 2007, 2011). While levels of ODA (as a percentage of GNI) have remained relatively constant over this period, these trends have spurred a surge in private capital flows from the industrialized world into developing countries. In the 1970s and 1980s, official development finance from bilateral donors and multilateral institutions represented approximately 50 percent of all financial flows from the developed to the developing world (WBG 1998, p. 7). However, with private flows expanding rapidly and ODA levels faltering, in 1998 ODA constituted only a quarter of all finance available to developing countries (ibid.). By that time, annual flows of capital as a percentage of recipient-country GDP were three times as high as in the 1970s (Economist 2003a, p. 6). In 2007, combined net private debt and equity flows to developing countries increased to $1 trillion, following six years of significant growth (Figure 12.10). This figure is approximately ten times the size of ODA from DAC donor countries (see Figure 12.3 in Section 12.3.2.2).

Over the years, a variety of reasons have been given for this rapid increase in financial flows. For starters, the rise can be taken as an indicator of the private sector's eagerness to explore new global market opportunities in search of higher profits, new markets, and lower wages, as well as renewed investor interest in the emerging and transition economies (Economist 1993; WBG, UNEP, et al. 2002). The rapid privatization that occurred in many developing countries has played a role in stimulating this as well, because it has made developing countries more attractive areas in which to invest to expand markets and cut costs (Chesky 1998, p. 13). These motivations for the developed world have converged with a renewed interest and proactiveness of developing economies themselves; they increasingly seek to attract international capital not only as a means to acquire financial resources, but also to attract new technology, skills, and jobs (ibid.).

The past decade has proved that on some occasions, international capital flows can indeed be of mutual benefit to the developed and the developing world.[‡] However, the widespread optimism of the

---

* Paul Krugman argued back in 1993 that the confidence in international financial markets as drivers of development that prevailed at that time was unrealistic and could not be reconciled with economic theory or evidence from the past. This message, which was seen as extremely pessimistic, has proved to be valid in many respects. For example, as we discuss below, although financial flows surged throughout the 1990s, the world's poorest countries were unable to acquire significant amounts. Also, even if substantial inflows of foreign private capital did occur, on many occasions they did more harm than good because institutions were unprepared to properly govern and regulate the inflows and outflows and to maintain stability in a country's national financial system.

† A more detailed discussion of some of the mechanisms that could be of particular value in this process is provided in Part C of this chapter.

‡ The rapid rise in private capital flows to the developing world has led to widespread optimism about the potential for developing countries to prosper and has even led critics to ask whether there is a need for continued international aid at all. They argue that with the exception of emergencies such as a debt crisis, market forces can decide which governments are worth

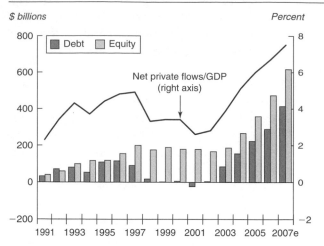

$ billions     Percent

FIGURE 12.10: NET PRIVATE DEBT AND EQUITY FLOWS TO
DEVELOPING COUNTRIES, 1991–2007
Note: "e" means estimate.
Source: WBG (2008, p. 35).

early 1990s that international capital flows would be a prime engine of growth and development, stimulating economic convergence by transferring resources from the capital-rich to the capital-poor, has broken down. Too many drawbacks of financial liberalization have become painfully apparent. As the *Economist* put it, "Even the most enthusiastic advocates of economic integration may be starting to wonder whether unimpeded flows of capital are such a blessing" (Economist 2003a, p. 3). Let us investigate the recent developments that have led to this decline in optimism and draw some important lessons that can help in reducing the costs and maximizing the benefits of financial liberalization.

### 12.4.2 Drawbacks of Financial Globalization

In this section, we will review some of the main drawbacks and problems with private capital flows as an engine of development. However, before we do so, it must be stressed that "capital flows" are a broad category. They include various types of financial transactions that are very different in nature:[11] bank

lending (short and long term); investment in public or private bonds; investment in equities; and direct investment in productive capacity. Each of these types affects an economy in its own way through its effects on economic growth, on the one hand, and exposure to capital-market risk, on the other (Economist 2003a, p. 6). Whether increases in net capital flows can be expected to have positive or negative net effects on the growth and stability of an economy therefore largely depends on what *kind* of capital is flowing in, as well as the specific sectoral or industrial targets of the investments.*

Usually, capital flows are classified into three main categories: foreign direct investment (FDI), portfolio flows, and bank lending. These three types have substantially different effects on a recipient country's economy.

#### 12.4.2.1 Foreign Direct Investment

FDI is generally seen as the "good" kind of capital. As many economists have argued, it does not only involve the transfer of financial resources, but brings with it technology, managerial skills, and market access, thereby accelerating growth and development. It may even create new jobs that might otherwise not have existed (Chesky 1998; Economist 1993; Hausmann and Fernández-Arias 2000). Moreover, FDI investments are a vote of confidence. They flow in because investors are attracted by a country's policies and institutions and its long-term growth prospects. And because private investors select the firms they are investing in, resources are channeled to their most effective use and meanwhile also put the managers of these resources under stricter discipline (Economist 1993, p. 28). In 2007, net (foreign direct and portfolio) equity inflows to developing countries reached $616 billion (see Figure 12.11) (WBG 2008). Although FDI constitutes the majority of private equity inflows, portfolio equity is growing in its share (see Section 12.4.2.3 for a discussion of portfolio flows).

FDI flows are a risk-sharing arrangement; by committing resources in the form of FDI, foreign investors are sharing much of the recipient country's risk, thereby reducing its exposure to volatility. If profits

---

lending to and which are not. This would automatically reward good policies and punish bad ones. However, there are some crucial tasks that private capital flows at present cannot and should not carry out, such as the provision of effective basic health care and education (see also Chesky 1998). Therefore, despite its drawbacks, ODA remains crucial for the achievement of sustainable and equitable global development. As will be discussed in the remainder of this section, the many financial crises and the fall in private-sector finance to developing countries that have occurred over the past five years have shown that private finance is not a panacea, and the case for the need for ODA seems to be gaining ground again.

---

\*     Another important aspect is what the targets of these inflows of finance are. This is where the painful trade-off between economic growth and environmental protection becomes apparent. As we will observe later in this section and in more detail in Part B, private capital flows—including FDI—are still much more often than not directed at projects and activities that have adverse effects on the environment.

Percent

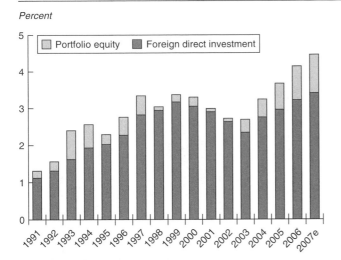

FIGURE 12.11: NET EQUITY INFLOWS TO DEVELOPING
COUNTRIES AS A SHARE OF GDP, 1991–2007
Note: "e" means estimate.
Source: WBG (2008, p. 47).

should fall, so will the returns on the investments made. Therefore, when times are hard, investments may have to be sold at a loss, if they can be sold at all. For this reason, FDI is a comparatively safe form of capital inflow: it is much harder to withdraw when economic situations worsen (Economist 1993, 2003a; Hausmann and Fernández-Arias 2000).*

However, there are some downsides to FDI flows as well. First, an important issue is FDI's cost. FDI has indeed proved to be a safer source of capital than borrowing from a bank, but in the long run it is likely to be more expensive as well. The reason for this is simple: because investors bear more risk, they also expect higher payoffs. In the end, the share of profits that FDI generates for its investors can therefore be expected to be much higher than the interest payments on a comparable bank loan (Economist 2003a, p. 9). Furthermore, although FDI generally involves the transfer of skills and technology, it may or may not be accompanied by a capital inflow. In fact, depending on the extent of constraints on expatriation of capital by MNCs, capital outflows may well occur, giving rise to the criticism that foreign investment

causes money to flow from the South to the North rather than fulfilling the promise of the reverse (Rodrik and Subramanian 2008).

Another drawback is that FDI is much more difficult to arrange. Banks specialize in bringing investors and borrowers together, minimizing transaction costs and the need for trust. In an FDI arrangement, this is not possible; it requires a much closer, long-term relationship between the investor and the company that is invested in. This makes finding investors more difficult for developing-country businesses. As stated above, this is at the same time an important advantage, for it is through this close cooperation that FDI often brings the recipient useful technical and managerial knowledge, vital contacts in world markets, and much-needed jobs. But an FDI partnership requires a big investment of time and effort, especially on the investor's side. This tends to limit FDI allocations to large projects in relatively large recipient countries, meaning that of all the developing-country businesses that could put FDI inflows to good use, only a small percentage are currently successful at acquiring it (Economist 2003a, p. 9).[†]

### 12.4.2.2 Bank Lending

At the other extreme, bank lending is the riskiest type of capital inflow—especially short-term lending. It is usually not invested on the basis of long-term considerations or with the aim of increasing the productive capacity of a business, region, or sector. Far too often, it is instead driven by speculative considerations based on interest-rate differentials and exchange-rate expectations (Hausmann and Fernández-Arias 2000, p. 2). Moreover, borrowing from a bank is not a risk-sharing activity, as is the acquisition of equity (portfolio flows or FDI). It is the first type of capital that is withdrawn in times of trouble (Hausmann and Fernández-Arias 2000, p. 2), and the risk of such outflows is fully borne by the recipient country: if, for whatever reason, the borrower's income falls, it must still service its debt requirements in spite of the fact that its capacity to do so is much lower (Economist 2003a). For this reason, bank lending inherently exposes a country to high levels of volatility. It has been held largely responsible for the many financial crises and boom-bust cycles of the 1990s (see Hausmann and Fernández-Arias 2000, p. 2). In 2007, gross cross-border bank lending to

---

* As explained in the 2003 *Global Development Finance (GDF)* report, "The benefit of FDI is not just that its returns are 'state contingent'—that is, they pay off for the investor when the country does well but absorb some of the hit when the country does badly—but that an adverse shock to the country does not typically produce a sudden rush for the exits. FDI investors generally emphasize that they are committed for the long haul and can absorb and tolerate a certain amount of near-term adversity" (WBG 2003a, p. 11).

---

† We will come back to this notion that FDI flows are highly concentrated later, where we will find that this is in fact the case for most types of private capital flows (although there are some differences across the various types).

**TABLE 12.5: CROSS-BORDER BANK LENDING TO DEVELOPING COUNTRIES BY REGION, 2000-2007 (BILLIONS OF DOLLARS)**

| INDICATOR | 2000 | 2001 | 2002 | 2003 | 2004 | 2005 | 2006 | 2007E |
|---|---|---|---|---|---|---|---|---|
| **Gross bank lending** | | | | | | | | |
| Total | 116.5 | 137.6 | 146.0 | 175.3 | 235.2 | 285.5 | 397.0 | 454.7 |
| By region | | | | | | | | |
| East Asia and Pacific | 14.9 | 20.7 | 27.3 | 37.2 | 34.8 | 43.7 | 42.4 | 65.1 |
| Europe and central Asia | 37.9 | 46.9 | 61.5 | 76.3 | 128.4 | 170.1 | 260.3 | 252.1 |
| Latin America and the Caribbean | 56.7 | 62.9 | 46.3 | 47.0 | 53.3 | 48.2 | 76.6 | 77.9 |
| Middle East and North Africa | 2.3 | 1.9 | 2.7 | 2.5 | 1.9 | 4.5 | 3.1 | 9.4 |
| South Asia | 1.5 | 3.2 | 5.6 | 8.7 | 11.8 | 11.0 | 10.7 | 32.1 |
| Sub-Saharan Africa | 3.2 | 2.1 | 2.6 | 3.7 | 4.9 | 8.0 | 3.9 | 18.1 |
| **Principal repayments** | | | | | | | | |
| Total | 120.4 | 139.6 | 147.8 | 160.1 | 184.7 | 200.1 | 224.6 | 240.0 |
| By region | | | | | | | | |
| East Asia and Pacific | 26.2 | 32.5 | 37.5 | 45.6 | 34.6 | 42.1 | 31.3 | 36.0 |
| Europe and central Asia | 28.5 | 39.6 | 45.6 | 55.8 | 81.9 | 94.1 | 120.8 | 136.2 |
| Latin America and the Caribbean | 56.1 | 57.2 | 52.3 | 48.4 | 52.4 | 49.6 | 57.0 | 50.9 |
| Middle East and North Africa | 2.1 | 2.3 | 3.2 | 3.7 | 2.6 | 3.3 | 3.9 | 4.0 |
| South Asia | 3.5 | 4.3 | 4.6 | 4.2 | 10.7 | 6.8 | 6.1 | 7.0 |
| Sub-Saharan Africa | 3.8 | 3.7 | 4.6 | 2.4 | 2.5 | 4.2 | 5.5 | 6.0 |
| **Net bank lending (gross lending less principal repayments)** | | | | | | | | |
| Total | −3.9 | −2.0 | −1.7 | 15.2 | 50.4 | 85.3 | 172.4 | 214.7 |
| By region | | | | | | | | |
| East Asia and Pacific | −11.3 | −11.8 | −10.2 | −8.4 | 0.2 | 1.6 | 11.1 | 29.1 |
| Europe and central Asia | 9.3 | 7.2 | 15.9 | 20.4 | 46.5 | 76.0 | 139.5 | 115.9 |
| Latin America and the Caribbean | 0.6 | 5.6 | −6.0 | −1.4 | 0.8 | −1.4 | 19.6 | 27.0 |
| Middle East and North Africa | 0.2 | −0.4 | −0.5 | −1.2 | −0.6 | 1.2 | −0.9 | 5.4 |
| South Asia | −2.0 | −1.1 | 1.0 | 4.4 | 1.1 | 4.1 | 4.6 | 25.2 |
| Sub-Saharan Africa | −0.7 | −1.6 | −1.9 | 1.2 | 2.4 | 3.8 | −1.5 | 12.1 |

Source: WBG (2008, p. 39).

developing countries was estimated to be $455 billion (Table 12.5).

### 12.4.2.3 Portfolio Flows

Portfolio investments (bonds, equity, securities) are situated somewhere between FDI and bank lending in terms of the risk to which they expose their recipient country.* In general, portfolio flows mitigate some risk because their value fluctuates according to the economic situation of their recipient country. Further, aside from offering valuable support to the domestic currency, portfolio inflows enhance the capitalization of stock exchanges in emerging markets and improve the financial options of local companies. The majority of portfolio flows (around three-quarters) typically go

to the BRICs (Brazil, Russia, India, and China) (see Table 12.6).

On the other hand, short-term capital is much easier to withdraw than FDI investments (WBG 2003a). This means that any threat to foreign investor confidence, which can be exogenous to the economic fundamentals of the recipient country, can cause capital flight and in turn trigger a financial crisis domestically. Critics of the proliferation of portfolio investing in developing nations argue that increased foreign capital has caused significant exchange-rate volatility among developing nations, transmitting financial shocks even in the absence of fundamental economic linkages (see Kawai, Newfarmer, et al. 2001, p. 21). Further, Shorrocks and Mavrotas (2006, p. 10) argue that even in good times, an open capital account invites short-term inflow surges that create upward pressure on exchange rates, which can have a negative effect on exports and the level of domestic investment.

Now that the basic characteristics of and differences among the three main types of capital are clear, this section will turn to some of the main drawbacks of financial liberalization for sustainable develop-

---

* During the 1990s, there was also a strong increase in portfolio flows. In theory, the main reason for this was that higher returns could be reached at lower risk in emerging markets because they did not correlate strongly with the developed ones (Economist 1993, p. 19). These flows, however, can be sensitive to herding, and the resulting volatility can be very harmful to a recipient economy's stability and long-term development (more on these problems will follow below).

**TABLE 12.6: TOP 10 PORTFOLIO DESTINATION DEVELOPING COUNTRIES, 2000–2009 (CURRENT PRICE IN BILLIONS OF DOLLARS)**

| CATEGORY | 2000 | 2001 | 2002 | 2003 | 2004 | 2005 | 2006 | 2007 | 2008 | 2009 |
|---|---|---|---|---|---|---|---|---|---|---|
| All Developing Countries | 14.0 | 6.7 | 8.3 | 26.3 | 36.9 | 67.5 | 107.7 | 133.0 | −53.1 | 108.5 |
| Top Ten Countries | | | | | | | | | | |
| Brazil | 3.1 | 2.5 | 2.0 | 3.0 | 2.1 | 6.5 | 7.7 | 26.2 | −7.6 | 37.1 |
| China | 6.9 | 0.8 | 2.2 | 7.7 | 10.9 | 20.3 | 42.9 | 18.5 | 8.7 | 28.2 |
| India | 2.5 | 2.9 | 1.1 | 8.2 | 9.1 | 12.2 | 9.5 | 32.9 | −15.0 | 21.1 |
| South Africa | 4.2 | −1.0 | −0.4 | 0.7 | 6.7 | 7.2 | 15.0 | 8.7 | -4.7 | 9.4 |
| Russian Federation | 0.2 | 0.5 | 2.6 | 0.4 | 0.3 | −0.1 | 6.5 | 18.7 | −15.0 | 3.4 |
| Turkey | 0.5 | −0.1 | 0.0 | 0.9 | 1.4 | 5.7 | 1.9 | 5.1 | 0.7 | 2.8 |
| Thailand | 0.9 | 0.4 | 0.5 | 1.8 | 1.3 | 5.1 | 5.2 | 4.3 | −3.8 | 1.3 |
| Indonesia | −1.0 | 0.4 | 0.9 | 1.1 | 2.0 | −0.2 | 1.9 | 3.6 | 0.3 | 0.8 |
| Malaysia | 0.0 | 0.0 | −0.1 | 1.3 | 4.5 | −1.2 | 2.4 | −0.7 | −10.7 | −0.4 |
| Philippines | −0.2 | 0.1 | 0.2 | 0.5 | 0.5 | 1.5 | 2.5 | 3.2 | −1.3 | −1.1 |
| Memorandum Item | | | | | | | | | | |
| BRICs | 12.6 | 6.8 | 7.9 | 19.3 | 22.3 | 38.8 | 66.6 | 96.3 | −28.9 | 89.7 |

Source: Adapted from WBG (2011, p. 2)

ment. During the remainder of this analysis, more detailed information about each of the three types of capital flows and their estimated impact on growth will be provided.

12.4.2.4 Will the Inflows Last?

The first important lesson to be learned about the high levels of private capital flows—which seemed to be grossly overlooked in the early 1990s—is that the high levels of international capital investment experienced over the past fifteen years are neither unique nor irreversible. For example, a very similar situation occurred in the late 1800s. In the last twenty-five years of the nineteenth century, the United Kingdom invested amounts of capital equivalent to 5 percent or more of host-country GDP in the United States, Canada, Australia, and Argentina. At the same time, France and Germany also exported large quantities of capital. These international capital flows collapsed at the onset of World War II, after which flows recovered shortly, only to plummet again at the end of the 1920s. From the Great Depression until the early 1970s, international flows of private capital were virtually negligible. Net flows of private capital to the developing world amounted to slightly more than 1 percent of recipient-country GDP in the 1970s—barely sufficient to finance 5 percent of all investments in most developing countries. Not until the early 1990s did these flows truly recover (Economist 2003a; Krugman 1993, pp. 19–20; von Moltke 2000).

Toward the end of the 1990s, evidence that capital flows can be volatile started to become apparent again (see Figure 12.12). For example, net private capital flows to developing countries decreased significantly after the 1997 Asian crisis and the subse-

quent slowdown of the global economy in 2001 (WBG 2008). Between 2002 and 2007, net private capital flows surged to over $1 trillion. However, in the wake of the 2008 global financial crisis they fell dramatically to $598 billion in 2009, a decline of almost 50 percent from 2007 (WBG 2011).

Regardless of what happens in the coming years, the cyclical nature of private capital flows can again induce capital withdrawal as the economic fundamentals of developed markets deteriorate (WBG 2007, 2008).

Portfolio flows have also experienced volatility. From 1990 to 1994, these flows constituted approximately $24 billion, almost half the average FDI inflows, which at that time were $52 billion. Between 1997 and 2001, however, portfolio flows into the developing economies dropped to $16 billion—only 10 percent of average annual FDI flows for that same period (WBG 2003a, p. 100). However, from 2001 to 2007, net portfolio equity flows surged from $7 billion to $135 billion, but this trend took a dramatic turnaround in 2008 as investors retreated from stock holdings in developing economies, resulting in a net outflow of $53 billion (WBG 2011). Quite remarkably, portfolio flows rebounded in 2009 to $108 billion, providing a clear indication of how quickly portfolio flows can change (ibid.).

Whereas portfolio investing has remained volatile over the past ten years, FDI has been much more stable, accounting for 2.5 percent to 3.0 percent of the GDP of developing nations (WBG 2007, p. 50). Supported by favorable policy shifts on behalf of emerging economies and boosted by increased cross-border merger and acquisition (M&A) activity in the financial services and telecommunications sectors, FDI financing has managed to keep pace with the rapid growth

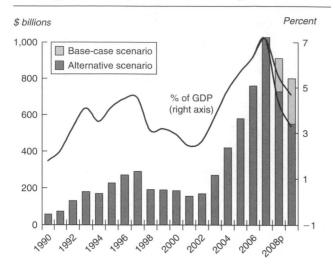

$ billions

- Base-case scenario
- Alternative scenario

% of GDP
(right axis)

Percent

**FIGURE 12.12: NET PRIVATE CAPITAL FLOWS TO DEVELOPING COUNTRIES, 1990–2009**
Note: "p" means projected.
Source: WBG (2008, p. 65).

of the largest developing economies. Even when all other types of foreign investment declined in 2001 and 2002, FDI remained relatively stable in absolute terms, between $140 to $160 billion (WBG 2003a, p. 91). Since 2003, net FDI inflows to developing countries continued to grow to $587 billion in 2008 (WBG 2011). However, these inflows declined by 40 percent in 2009 to $354 billion, the most significant drop in twenty years (ibid.). While FDI is clearly susceptible to global market forces, when compared to portfolio flows it is a more stable type of investment, and therefore more reliable for the long-term promotion of growth and development.

### 12.4.2.5 The Cost of Volatility

A second drawback of increasing financial globalization, hinted at several times already, is that the free movement of capital can cause extremely high *volatility*, leaving a country much more vulnerable to certain types of economic shocks. This downside of financial integration has long been recognized. For instance, the *Economist* (1993, p. 7) pointed out that "financial systems that work are crucial for development, but when they go wrong, nothing else is nearly so good at spreading damage."

As Soros explains, an important reason for this high volatility is that "there is a fundamental difference between financial markets and markets for physical goods and services. The latter deal with known quantities, the former with quantities that are not merely unknown but actually unknowable" (Soros 2002, p. 109). Because of this, financial markets do

not show a clear tendency toward equilibrium, as markets for goods and services usually do (although admittedly, on occasion even that remains debated).* Because of this, capital markets cannot simply be left unregulated; they must be effectively governed by monetary authorities. As we will see below, however, the evolution of the international regulatory framework has not been able to keep up with the pace of globalization of financial markets (Soros 2002; von Moltke 2000).

There is more than sufficient quantitative evidence to show that the past few decades have been marked by financial crises. In 1999, the IMF reported that sixty-four banking crises and seventy-nine currency crises had occurred since 1970.† Most of these crises were national rather than international, but international capital flows have come to play an increasingly harmful role by spreading financial breakdown across borders in times of crisis (Economist 2003a, p. 8). For example, the volatility of capital flows became painfully apparent during the financial crash in East Asia, which started with the devaluation of the Thai baht in July 1997. One senior policy adviser described the enormous outflow of portfolio investments from the region as "the great home-coming of western capital" (WBG, UNEP, et al. 2002, p. 2).

As an expanding number of studies show, the costs of these crises for economic development are substantial. Even more worrisome, they seem to be borne disproportionately by the world's poorest countries, referred to by Soros (2002, p. 113) as the "periphery of the financial system." During the 1990s, it seemed as if the developing world "went from crisis to crisis, while [the industrialized world] remained remarkably stable and prosperous" (ibid.). As a result of all this, financial markets have on average become very negative toward developing economies; the risk premium has settled at much higher levels than before, which has led to higher borrowing costs and lower returns (ibid., pp. 123–125). So although it can be argued that competitive markets ensure the *efficient* allocation of

---

* Soros takes this a step further. He argues that there is an inherent bias in financial markets because they discount a future that is itself based on how financial markets discount it at present. He calls this two-way interaction between expectations and outcomes "reflexivity." Soros argues that because of this phenomenon, when financial markets are "left to their own devices," they are liable to go to extremes and eventually break down instead of moving to an equilibrium, as market fundamentalists believe (see Soros 2002, chap. 4).

† It must be noted that these numbers include some double counting because several countries experienced both types of crisis simultaneously.

resources, recent experience has made it painfully clear that they do not ensure *equity*.

A study by Wendy Dobson and Gary Hufbauer of the Institute for International Economics* estimates the cost in lost GDP of twenty-four banking crises and thirty-six currency crises that occurred during the 1980s and 1990s. It shows that the debt crisis of the 1980s is estimated to have cost Latin America an average loss of 2.2 percent of GDP per year over that entire decade. Also, calculations showed that the financial crisis in East Asia deprived the region of 1.4 percent of its annual GDP (Dobson and Hufbauer 2002).

Another study by Hutchinson and Neuberger, reviewed in a 2001 IMF survey, looked into the output costs of currency and balance-of-payments crises as well. On the basis of a panel data set for thirty-two countries from 1975 to 1997, it concluded that financial crises reduced these countries' output over a period of two to three years by around 5 to 8 percent cumulatively (Škreb 2001, p. 259).[†]

Some countries, of course, were affected more heavily than others. Indonesia, for instance, experienced a 14 percent decline in output in 1998 alone, in contrast with an earlier trend of 7 percent annual growth—amounting to a GDP shortfall of more than 20 percent in one year (Economist 2003a, p. 8). But overall, Dobson and Hufbauer (2002) estimate that the cost of financial crises for all emerging-market economies was approximately 0.6 percent of GDP per year during the 1980s and 0.7 percent of GDP per year for the 1990s (see Table 12.7). They conclude that this loss in GDP is more than outweighed by the gains—according to their estimates, the benefits to developing countries from global access to capital markets was approximately $350 billion, amounting to an average of 5 percent of GDP. But many critics of financial globalization would challenge these estimates, especially of the reported benefits.

Surprisingly, a 2003 review of the empirical literature by the IMF—an organization that has traditionally been a great advocate of financial liberalization—supports this more critical view. It concludes that "so far, it has proven difficult to find

### TABLE 12.7: GDP LOSSES RESULTING FROM FINANCIAL CRISES

|  | 1980s | 1990s |
| --- | --- | --- |
| **GDP loss from financial crises in emerging markets, $bn** | **249** | **419** |
| Asia | 13 | 260 |
| Latin America | 207 | 123 |
| Africa | 15 | 18 |
| Europe | na | 11 |
| Middle East | 14 | 7 |
| **Average annual GDP loss in emerging markets, %** | **0.6** | **0.7** |
| Asia | 0.1 | 1.4 |
| Latin America | 2.2 | 0.7 |
| Africa | 0.5 | 0.6 |
| Europe | na | 0.1 |
| Middle East | 0.3 | 0.1 |

Source: Economist (2003a, p. 8).

robust evidence in support of the proposition that financial integration helps developing countries to improve growth and to reduce macroeconomic volatility" (Prasad, Rogoff, et al. 2003, p. 11). Of the fourteen papers it reviews, only three conclude that financial integration has a positive effect; four others find that the effects are mixed; and the remaining seven find no significant effect whatsoever (Economist 2003a, p. 8; Prasad, Rogoff, et al. 2003).[‡]

As the *Economist* points out, the fact that thus far no unambiguous relationship between financial integration and economic growth has been identified can mean two things. First, perhaps financial integration is indeed a development with both negative and positive effects, which tend to offset one another. A second possibility is that financial integration is beneficial to economic development only if certain macroeconomic and institutional foundations are in place, whereas premature liberalization of financial markets may result in failure. In both these scenarios, the net outcome tends to be difficult to identify. In fact, these two theories are not mutually exclusive (Economist 2003a, p. 8).[§]

---

\* The Institute for International Economics describes itself as a "private, nonprofit, nonpartisan research institution devoted to the study of international economic policy." See www.iie.com (accessed January 27, 2008).

† The authors observed that currency and balance-of-payments crises are typically followed by abrupt reversals in capital inflows, which require substantial real sector adjustment and output loss.

‡ As is to be expected, the IMF review argues that despite these results, there should be benefits of financial integration, and that a reason that they may not have shown up yet is that they may accrue only in the longer term. The review also investigates the relationship between other measures of economic well-being and different measures of economic openness. The evidence does indicate that trade improves economic welfare. Financial integration, however, has no significant effect (Prasad, Rogoff, et al. 2003).

§ The potential effects of financial integration, especially for developing countries, will be examined in more detail in Section 12.4.2.6.

As pointed out above, the various types of capital flows have substantially different effects on a country's economy. One such difference is the volatility to which they expose the recipient. In theory, FDI flows should be the least volatile type of capital investment, followed by portfolio investments and then bank lending.

Evidence by the World Bank has shown that FDI indeed tends to be more resilient during a financial crisis than portfolio equity or debt flows (WBG 1999a). For example, as Figure 12.13 shows, FDI flows held up well during and after the financial crises in Mexico (1994–1996), Korea (1997–1999), Thailand (1997–1999), and Turkey (1999–2001). FDI levels did drop after the crises in Argentina (2000–2002) and Indonesia (1997–1999), but both of these crises reflected more deep-rooted social and political risks than any of the others.

The above-mentioned IMF review by Prasad, Rogoff, et al. (2003, p. 20) examines the volatilities of these three types of capital in more detail and reaches a similar conclusion. It shows that even when the so-called category of least financially integrated economies is examined separately, the volatility of FDI flows is much lower than that of other types of flows.*

### 12.4.2.6 A Bias of Flows against the Poor

A third important downside of private capital flows is that they tend to flow only to a relatively small number of countries, leaving the world's poorest nations out in the cold. It is indeed true, as reported above, that total annual capital flows to the developing world, as a percentage of recipient-country GDP, had by the end of the millennium risen to a level three times as high as in the 1970s. But there are two important issues that must be kept in mind in this analysis. First, when these flows are compared with the total amount of global capital investment, they are still disappointingly low. At the end of 2001, the worldwide stock of transnational bank loans and deposits was $9 trillion, of which only around $700 billion was borrowed by developing countries. The stock of global cross-border investment in securities was around $12

trillion, of which only $600 billion flowed into the developing world (Economist 2003a, p. 6).†

Second, even the capital that is exported from rich countries to the developing world still flows into only a relatively small number of recipient countries and sectors. For example, a joint paper by the World Bank, the UNEP, and the IMF estimates that approximately 75 percent of FDI flows into the developing world have gone to just ten middle-income countries (WBG, UNEP, et al. 2002). What is more, it also shows that FDI is heavily concentrated in only a small number of sectors, the main ones being the automotive, chemicals, electronics, energy, petroleum and petrochemicals, and pharmaceuticals sectors.‡ The world's poorest countries have lost out heavily: in 1998, the forty-eight least developed countries attracted less than $3 billion in foreign capital. In the same year, the African continent received only around 1 percent of global capital flows (ibid., p. 2).§ In 2008, the top ten recipient developing countries received around 61 percent of total FDI in developing regions, an indication that FDI remains relatively concentrated in a small group of nations (WBG 2008).

Like FDI, portfolio investments also tend to be concentrated in a small number of countries. For example, the 2003 *GDF* report indicated that since 1990, the eight major recipient countries of portfo-

---

*     The IMF review also cites two other studies by Taylor and Sarno (1999) and by Hausmann and Fernández-Arias (2000), which both confirm that the volatility of FDI flows is lower than that of other types of capital investment (Prasad, Rogoff, et al. 2003, p. 20). (It also stresses an important and not-easily-resolvable dilemma that must be borne in mind in the interpretation of these results—the problem with potential misclassification of the different types of capital flows.)

†     On average, however, capital does flow from capital-rich to capital-poor countries; evidence shows that creditor countries are richer than debtor countries. But there are important exceptions even to this broad trend. For example, the U.S. economy has continued to attract enormous amounts of capital from abroad for years, while it has saved little. From 2001 to 2006, the U.S. current account deficit rose from zero to 6.5 percent of its GDP. As the economy regains momentum following the 2008 subprime mortgage crisis, policymakers will need to make important decisions on how to prevent growth in future budget deficits in the face of increasing health and social security costs (Peterson Institute for International Economics, US Current Account Deficit, www.iie.com/research/topics/hottopic.cfm?HotTopicID=9, accessed February 5, 2011).

‡     It is important to note that those sectors that receive the lion's share of FDI are among the most heavily polluting industries in the world. This again points to the difficult tensions that developing countries face in their quest to attract foreign investment to ensure economic growth while attempting to protect their natural resources and the environment. More on this will follow in Part B.

§     As Chesky (1998, p. 17) argues, "Foreign funds continue to flow mainly to areas conducive to major industry where there are concentrations of trained and trainable people, and new markets to be served, combined with appropriate natural resources and modern infrastructure." This unfortunately leaves many countries and regions out in the cold. Chesky gives the example of African governments, which during the surge in capital flows of the 1990s negotiated with foreign business "from a position of weakness, often without adequate information" (ibid., p. 15).

## Billions of U.S. Dollars

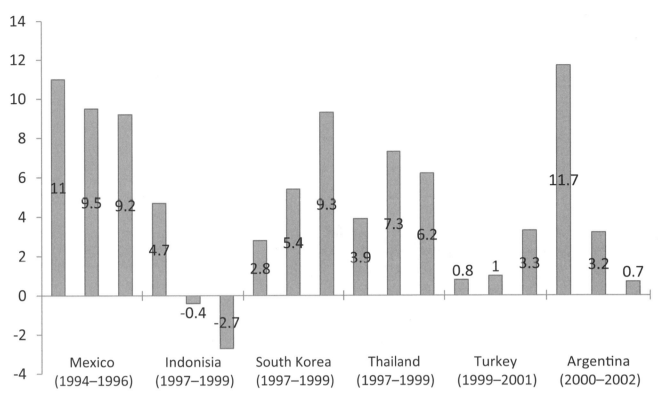

**FIGURE 12.13: FDI FLOWS DURING THE YEARS OF FINANCIAL CRISIS IN VARIOUS NATIONS**
Source: WBG (2003a, p. 89).

lio equity investment have accounted for about 85 percent of the total net flows (WBG 2003a, p. 98). As with FDI, China has historically been the largest net recipient—it has attracted 22 percent of the total since 1989 (ibid.)—although in 2008 India had attracted levels of portfolio investment comparable to those of China.* In 2008, the top ten developing-country recipients of portfolio equity received around 96 percent of all funds, with the majority (76 percent) going to the BRICs (Brazil, Russia, India, and China) (WBG 2008). Thus portfolio investments remain focused on a selected group of emerging economies.

The IMF review by Prasad, Rogoff, et al. (2003) reaches a similar conclusion. Although it argues that the dramatic increase in net private capital flows from industrial countries to eighty developing countries has been "one of the key features of global financial integration over the last decade" (ibid., p. 16), it goes on to point out that the lion's share of these high and rising global capital flows has gone to industrial nations.

To help explore some of these trends, Figure 12.14 presents the flow of private capital (FDI, portfolio equity, and commitments from private creditors—such as bonds, commercial bank loans, and other private credits) into high-income and low- and middle-income countries from 1970 to 2009. The high-income countries (sixty-nine in total) are those with a 2009 GNI per capita greater than $12,196, and low- and middle-income countries (144 in total) are those with a GNI per capita less than this amount. What is striking about Figure 12.14 is that the trends for low- and middle-income countries barely increase. It also shows how FDI and portfolio flows to high-income countries increased dramatically in the late 1990s, only to decline during the mid-2000s before resurging to historical levels around 2007. The volatility of portfolio equity to both groups of countries is also captured by their collapse in 2008 and almost complete rebound in 2009.

Figure 12.15 presents the same data separately for low- and middle-income countries. Middle-income countries (104 in total) are those with a 2009 GNI per capita between $995 and $12,196, and low-income countries (40 in total) are those with a GNI per capita of less than $995. Figure 12.15 reveals that low-income countries receive just a fraction of the private capital

---

*        Portfolio equity investments have been shown to be concentrated in another way as well. In 2002, a small number of new international equity placements accounted for a significant portion of the overall flow. Fourteen of the 115 deals that were closed in emerging markets accounted for 75 percent of the total amount of international portfolio investments (WBG 2003a, p. 98).

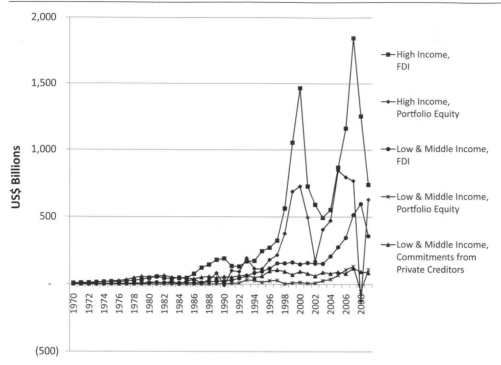

**FIGURE 12.14: PRIVATE CAPITAL FLOWS TO HIGH-INCOME ECONOMIES AND LOW- AND MIDDLE-INCOME ECONOMIES**
Notes:
High-income economies are those in which 2009 GNI per capita was $12,196 or more.
Low- and middle-income economies are those in which 2009 GNI per capita was $12,195 or less.
Foreign direct investment (FDI) is net inflows of investment to acquire a lasting interest in or management control over an enterprise operating in an economy other than that of the investor.
Portfolio equity includes net inflows from equity securities other than those recorded as direct investment and includes shares, stocks, depository receipts (American or global), and direct purchases of shares in local stock markets by foreign investors.
Commitments from private creditors is the amount of long-term loans for which contracts were signed in the year specified (data for private nonguaranteed debt are not available). It includes bonds, commercial bank loans, and other private credits. No data on the commitments from private creditors was available for high-income countries.
Source: WBG (2011).

flows to developing countries (that is, middle- and low-income countries combined). In fact, between 2000 and 2009, low-income countries received on average only 2 percent of all FDI, portfolio equity, and commitments from private creditors that entered developing countries. Figure 12.15 also reveals the importance of FDI for middle-income countries when compared to portfolio equity and commitments from private creditors. However, these latter two financial resources have also increased significantly since the mid-1990s.

While it cannot be discerned from Figure 12.15, from 1970 to the early 1990s, low-income countries were more reliant on bank lending than other sources of private capital (Prasad, Rogoff, et al. 2003). However, this changed during the 1990s when greater amounts of FDI began to enter low-income countries. From 2000 to 2009, commitments from private creditors averaged only 9 percent of FDI during this period. In parallel with this, portfolio flows

to low-income countries increased steadily from $5.2 billion in 2000 to $140.9 billion in 2008, before turning negative in 2009. With the exception of 2009, the positive trends in FDI and portfolio equity is good news for low-income countries that are less reliant on bank lending. While the level of private capital has recently declined, it is still more than double its 2003 level (WBG 2011). The effects of the above changes in the mix of capital that flows to the world's poorest countries will be discussed in Section 12.4.4.1.*

---

\* Despite the increase in capital inflows from developed countries, emerging economies still face a significant spread between long-term and short-term borrowing rates. As a result, these economies face strong incentives to borrow short term, increasing debt rollover and liquidity risk (Broner, Lorenzoni, et al. 2001). As a result of these risks, international capital seeks even higher returns from investments in developing countries, while long-term FDI investments are discouraged.

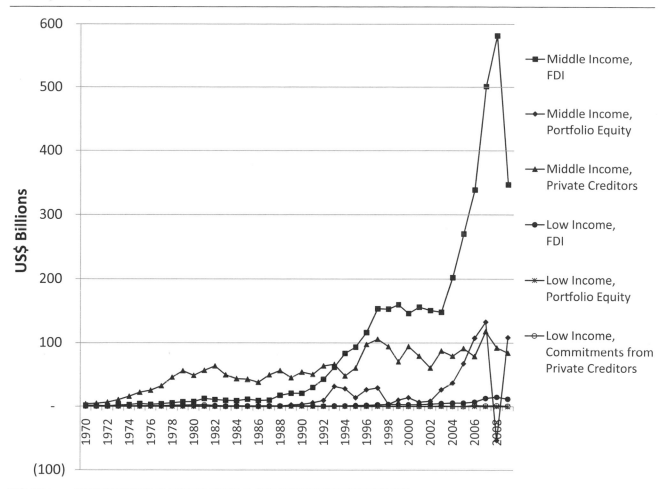

**FIGURE 12.15: PRIVATE CAPITAL FLOWS TO MIDDLE- AND LOW-INCOME ECONOMIES**

Notes:

High-income economies are those in which 2009 GNI per capita was $12,196 or more.

Middle-income economies are those in which 2009 GNI per capita was between $12,195 and $995.

Low-income economies are those in which 2009 GNI per capita was less than $995.

Foreign direct investment (FDI) is net inflows of investment to acquire a lasting interest in or management control over an enterprise operating in an economy other than that of the investor.

Portfolio equity includes net inflows from equity securities other than those recorded as direct investment and includes shares, stocks, depository receipts (American or global), and direct purchases of shares in local stock markets by foreign investors.

Commitments from private creditors is the amount of long-term loans for which contracts were signed in the year specified (data for private nonguaranteed debt are not available).

Source: WBG (2011).

The bias of capital flows against the poorer countries is not new. Paul Krugman (1993, p. 12) has argued from the onset of this renewed surge in global capital flows that it should not be interpreted as the dawn of a new era in large-scale development financing. Krugman (1993, p. 19) states that "there has never been a period in history in which capital-abundant countries have invested heavily in the development of labor-abundant countries." As noted previously, the period before World War I was characterized by especially high capital flows as a percentage of GDP as well, but very few of these large international capital movements reflected transfers from rich to poor countries. Krugman cites a study by Nurske (1954) that indicates that during this pe-

riod, capital in fact did not flow from North to South, but from East to West—from Europe to the rapidly growing "regions of settlement" in the United States, Canada, Australia, and New Zealand, which were in fact already high-income countries.* This goes to show that "during the high tide of international capital market integration, European investors were in effect willing to supply capital to meet the needs of rapidly growing, high-wage European immigrant populations overseas, but not willing to invest except

_____

* Krugman (1993) also discusses that in 1913, more than 50 percent of the United Kingdom's foreign investment was channeled to only five countries, which all had income levels comparable to or even higher than Britain itself.

to a very limited extent in low-wage economies" (Krugman 1993, p. 20).*

The natural question that now comes to mind is: why have capital transfers between the industrialized and the developed world remained so limited? One important reason, which was stressed by Krugman in 1993 and remains valid today, is that poor countries still operate on worse production functions. Therefore, the marginal product of capital in poor economies is not as high as their low capital-labor ratios would suggest. In other words, investing capital in developing countries is not as attractive as one would expect purely on the basis of these capital-labor ratios (Krugman 1993, p. 13). Put in more practical terms, this problem is related to the fact that in poor countries, the labor force is less well educated and skilled—especially in technologically intensive domains of expertise—than in the world's richer economies. Note, however, that the shift of technical service jobs, which are endemic in the information and communication technologies (ICT) sectors, to highly educated workers in developing countries such as India may be a harbinger of important changes to come.

Another important barrier to the flow of investments to the developing world is that many poor countries simply lack the economic and institutional infrastructure to maximize the returns that could theoretically be made on investments. Property rights are still insecure, the rule of law is weak and unreliable, and there are often problems of corruption and risks of political instability as well.† For these and other reasons, the theoretical argument that investing capital abroad where it is scarce offers rich-country investors the highest returns often breaks down in practice.‡

Third, it must be noted that many developing countries also consciously adhere to a set of policies that do not allow for the free movement of capital into and out of their economy. The restrictions on capital have decreased substantially over the past decades as capital markets have followed a distinct pattern of increasing liberalization, but developing economies are still significantly less integrated in their openness to international financial flows than those of the industrialized world (Prasad, Rogoff, et al. 2003).

The evidence cited in the previous discussions, however, could lead one to question whether financial liberalization is a blessing. We have observed that the adverse effects of financial liberalization can be devastating for a country's stability and growth, and we found that even the IMF has recently conceded that it is not at all clear that financial integration helps developing countries improve growth and reduce macroeconomic volatility (Prasad, Rogoff, et al. 2003; see above).

As the *Economist* points out, however, countries do not have to make an "all-or-nothing' decision with regard to integration of their capital markets. In view of the recent evidence, it may be best to follow a more moderate course. To cite but one example, it was explained previously that different types of capital flows have different advantages and disadvantages; this means that countries could go a long way in improving the ratio between risk and reward simply by altering the *mix* of capital investment that they attract. In short, countries should aim to minimize the costs of financial integration while they ensure that they do not lock themselves out of the potential benefits it could create (Economist 2003a, p. 8). As will be observed in the last part of this section, striking this balance is far from an easy task, but it is an essential one in the quest for a more sustainable and equitable future for all of the world's inhabitants.

### 12.4.2.7 Potential Hazards for Sustainable Development

The last problem of private capital flows, which is discussed in a joint report by the World Bank, the UNEP, and the IMF, is that it is very difficult for developing countries to maximize the quantity of private capital inflows they attract while at the same time ensuring that this foreign capital is invested in ways that promote—or at least do not prevent—a pathway to *sustainable* progress. In light of the fact that developing countries often bargain with foreign

---

*     In his essay, Krugman goes one step further. He makes a compelling argument that the confidence in the importance of financial integration for economic convergence and the role of capital in economic growth that dominated the international policy arena in the early 1990s is not well grounded in economic theory or empirical evidence. Basically, he argues that "capital markets as an engine of development have been oversold" (Krugman 1993, p. 12). Although a complete review of his essay is beyond the scope of this discussion, it is clear that the evidence that has accumulated over the past ten years has proved the validity of Krugman's main thesis.

†     Hellman, Jones, et al. (2002), for instance, demonstrate that corruption decreases inflows of FDI and attracts lower-quality investment in terms of governance standards.

‡     Again, the example of the United States comes to mind. It has been argued that its beneficial institutional framework and economic policies help explain why it has continued to attract such enormous quantities of foreign capital, in a manner that is completely counterintuitive to the theory (Economist 2003a, p. 5). Of course, recent revelations of corruption in U.S. equity markets and its contribution to the creation of a stock market "bubble," followed by the subsequent withdrawal of foreign

capital from the U.S. equity market, presents a sobering picture for those trying to make sense of international investment flows.

investors from the industrialized world from a position of weakness, this can be very difficult to achieve. For example, Miller (2000) explains that the developing world has borne some severe environmental and social costs in order to attract investors and acquire higher levels of private capital desperately needed for economic growth. Developing countries have for several decades now functioned as the main exporters of natural resources, with a dramatic impact not only on their environment but also on levels of human health and the incidence of many illnesses.* The recent concern about China's monopoly on the supply of rare earths provides a good example of how dependent industrialized nations are on resources outside of their borders (Hook 2010). While China does have the largest share of rare earth—estimated at 37 percent of the world's proven reserves—in 2010 it provided 95 percent of the world demand (Bradsher 2010).

A related concern—which is in fact not directly caused by the rise of private capital flows to developing countries but has become even more urgent because of it—is that there are certain domains in which private investment simply will not lead to sustainable solutions. As Chesky (1998, p. 19) points out, the provision of education and basic health care, agricultural research, and physical as well as social infrastructure cannot and should not be privatized because privatization will not allow for these essential services to be delivered effectively and in an equitable fashion.†

Third, there is the issue of ensuring a basic quality of labor standards. It has often proved difficult for the national governments of developing countries, which are often weak or corrupt, to ensure minimally decent working conditions and other protections for their communities and workers. As Chesky points out, it is imperative that national governments—as well as the international community—not only focus on the construction of a legal framework that protects the rights of responsible international investors, but also devise laws that protect communities and workers from the

potentially harmful effects of unrestrained actions by powerful firms (Chesky 1998, p. 19).‡

### 12.4.3 Maximizing the Benefits of Financial Integration

The issues raised above bring us to the goal of the last section of this part of this chapter, which is to identify strategies that could assist the developing world in reaping more of the benefits of financial integration while ensuring that the downsides are minimized. We will first look at what developing countries can do for themselves in this respect.

#### 12.4.3.1 Strategies for the Developing World

First, as was discussed above, certain kinds of capital seem better placed to assist a country in its development than others. Empirical evidence, although it is still scarce, supports the view that there are indeed such differences. As was expected on the basis of theoretical arguments, research indicates that FDI seems to be the most desirable type of capital inflow; the IMF review by Prasad, Rogoff, et al. (2003) cites research that estimates that a 1 percentage-point rise in the ratio of FDI to GDP increases host-country GDP by 0.4 percent.§ Evidence on the effect of portfolio flows on growth is even sparser, but research by Marcelo Soto, an OECD economist, suggests that it also has a positive overall effect (although bond flows seem to have a negative effect). It estimates that a 1 percentage-point increase in portfolio investments as a proportion of GDP results in a 0.2 percent rise in GDP (Economist 2003a, p. 9).¶ More recently, Ferreira and Laux (2009, pp. 290–291) found that "openness to portfolio flows is statistically conducive to growth, in that a country's

---

\* Some of the implications of these trends will be analyzed in more detail in Part B of this chapter, as well as in the final chapter of this book.

† Chesky argues that adequate public investment is crucial in these areas, not only to create an attractive private investment climate, but also to foster a basic level of human health and well-being that each individual deserves. Unfortunately, the World Bank and the IMF have in recent years shown a strong push toward privatization of even these basic services, despite mounting evidence of its ineffectiveness. At the collapsed trade talks in Cancún, Mexico, poor countries showed a clear resistance to the growing insistence on privatization in donors' loan conditions, arguing that it weakened their capacity to maintain their own public sector (Rowden 2003).

‡ It should be borne in mind here that transnational corporations (TNCs), which have become increasingly important players in developing-country industries, are often not the firms with the worst rules and regulations. In fact, Wallace (1995) shows that many TNCs apply environmental standards that exceed those required by host governments. But many of these TNCs often use subcontractors to carry out many of their activities, and subcontractors often do not uphold such high labor and environmental standards. It therefore remains crucial for governments to provide a proper set of laws to ensure that all firms adhere to a set of minimum conditions. See Section 10.5.2 in Chapter 10, for a discussion of the voluntary codes of environmental and social conduct established by the Coalition of Environmentally Responsible Economies (CERES).

§ Because ratios of FDI to GDP in developing countries on average increased from 7 percent to 21 percent during the 1990s, this suggests a growth in GDP of 5.6 percent (see Economist 2003a, p. 9).

¶ Because the ratio of portfolio capital to GDP in developing countries rose from 8 percent to 14 percent between 1990 and 2000, this suggests an average growth in GDP of 1.2 percent.

GDP grows after both positive flows of funds and also, strikingly, after some types of large negative flows of funds. . . . Overall, our results indicate that openness to flows in both directions [in and out of a country] is associated with growth, and that the portfolio flow volatility that might come with openness is not harmful for any set of countries. For less-developed countries, the results suggest that allowing for inflows of foreign capital into local equity investments, combined with the ability of locals to invest in U.S. securities, is the best recipe for future growth." While it is good news that openness to portfolio flows can support growth, it should be remembered that the volatility of portfolio flows can have significant impacts on those bearing the brunt of any substantial and rapid withdrawal of portfolio equity from a country (see Section 12.4.2.5 on the cost of volatility).

The dramatic change in the composition of capital flows to the developing world that has occurred over the past several years is encouraging. Since 2001, net equity inflows (consisting of FDI and portfolio equity) to developing countries have increased dramatically from $166 billion to $462 billion in 2009, with a peak of $643 billion in 2007 (WBG 2011). In parallel with this, net debt flows increased from $47 billion in 2001 to $136 billion in 2009, with a peak of $467 billion in 2007 (ibid.). The significant decline in net debt flows from 2007 to 2009 is due to a collapse in all three forms of long-, medium-, and short-term debt flows.

From the 1980s to the turn of the century, there was a clear shift from debt to equity flows to developing countries (WBG 2003a). While the focus on equity still holds today, debt flows have regained ground from being negative in the late 1990s, to the equivalent of one-third of the net equity inflows in 2009. There were several reasons for the general shift toward equity that occurred around the end of the 1990s. First, the preferences of foreign investors had changed. The risks of international bank lending had become painfully apparent over the course of the 1990s, especially in the East Asian crisis, while nonfinancial corporations had increasingly started to recognize the various opportunities in the so-called emerging markets of the developing world (ibid., p. 9). Moreover, the attitudes of policy makers in many developing countries had changed as well. Not only had there been a clear general trend toward financial liberalization in the developing world (see Figure 12.16), which opened up many new markets to foreign investors, but also, countries had increasingly recognized the risks of a strong dependence on external debt financing and had shifted their liabilities to more stable forms of capital, especially FDI.

On the whole, a shift from debt to equity is a positive development because it puts development finance on a more stable footing. With equity, the downsides of adverse global conditions will no longer have to be borne completely by the developing countries themselves (WBG 2003a, p. 11). But it could be helpful if developing countries knew how to accelerate this trend by altering their policies further. However, this may prove extremely difficult and should be carried out with caution (Economist 2003a). One important problem is that many borrowers in developing countries simply do not have access to FDI or equity finance. High-risk bank loans are usually the only type of capital they can acquire. Altering policies to keep out cross-border bank debt could severely limit these people's opportunities. As is often the case, this danger is greatest in the world's poorest countries; FDI and portfolio investment are safer types of capital because they ensure that the investor shares some of the financial risk.* It is highly likely that foreign investors will simply refuse to do that in the world's poorest countries. Risky as it may be, international bank lending may be the only option for such countries.

Another risk in attempting to steer the type of capital that flows into an economy is that by attempting to keep one type, such as short-term bank lending, out, one may inadvertently reduce the inflows of other, much-needed types as well. The empirical evidence, however, seems to suggest that the risks involved in keeping cross-border bank lending limited are affordable (Economist 2003a, p. 10), so cautious attempts to improve the mix of capital inflows are definitely commendable.

Besides improving the mix of capital that it attracts, there are other strategies that a developing-country government should employ in its attempts to maximize the benefits it can reap from the international private-sector capital flows it attracts into its economy. One important task is to reduce corruption. It is now widely accepted that corruption poses substantial costs for economic development. There is strong empirical evidence that higher levels of corruption are associated with lower growth and lower per capita income levels across the globe. One of the channels through which corruption hinders growth is its impact on FDI. A number of studies have shown that corruption inhibits FDI (Hellman, Jones,

---

*        As the *Economist* explains, "Legal systems may offer little or no protection against breach of contract, expropriation or outright theft. Corruption too is often an issue. In such circumstances, a western company with a reputation to lose will think twice before entering into a close economic partnership" (Economist 2003a, p. 10).

et al. 2002). In fact, they indicate that corruption has an even more profound effect on FDI levels than high corporate tax rates (Economist 2003a, p. 21).*

Rather than focusing on creating a favorable environment for FDI investors through the construction of special tax breaks and subsidies, both of which have their own drawbacks (Economist 2003a, p. 21), developing-country governments should therefore focus on reducing levels of corruption. Admittedly, this is far from easy, especially for weak governments that struggle to perform the basic functions to keep an economy going, but there are steps that can be taken. For example, better accounting standards and greater disclosure of financial information could help greatly. Also, reform of the legal system will in many cases be needed, especially with relation to strengthening property rights laws.

Evidence presented by Gelos and Wei (2002) and Prasad, Rogoff, et al. (2003) shows that faster and more accurate disclosure of information has positive effects in and of itself. It gives investors more detailed information and thereby reduces herding behavior. As a result, the problem of capital flight is less severe in countries that have more transparent economies.[†]

One last and crucial lesson for developing countries, which has been learned the hard way, is that despite their eagerness to attain higher and better flows of international capital, they should be careful not to open up their financial markets too fast. As the *Economist* argued in 1993, solid control of fiscal policies is essential, followed by reasonable trade reform. Only then can controls on capital outflows and inflows safely be reduced. Unfortunately, there were too many countries that did not take this valuable advice on board during the 1990s.

A prime example, again, is the financial crisis that struck East Asia in the summer of 1997. As previously explained, its main cause was that many countries in the region relied very heavily on extremely volatile bank loans, which exposed them to irresponsibly high levels of risk.[12] But in addition, lending standards were much too lax because of a combination of overly high eagerness and bad government policies, as well as lack of the necessary resources to uphold the needed standards in the first place.[‡]

### 12.4.3.2 What Can the Industrialized World Do?

It is important to note that sustainable, long-term solutions to the many problems of the current global financial system cannot and should not be sought only in changing the infrastructure of developing countries; they also require reform and leadership by the industrialized world. In Part C of this chapter, we will analyze several mechanisms through which the developed world can carry out this task. More specifically, we will discuss several financing innovations that could improve access to capital, especially in those nations and regions that have shockingly little of it at present.

One of these innovations, which has earned its marks over the past two decades and has become widely implemented, is the concept of *microfinance*— the deployment of capital on a very small scale in the developing world. It is meant to provide people in underdeveloped and isolated areas access to small amounts of capital in order to spur a virtuous cycle of investment, benefit, and reinvestment at the community level, which can in the medium term promote development and increase standards of living.

Another innovative suggestion to tackle many of the problems with the global financial market has been the construction of an *international investment agreement* (von Moltke 2000). Von Moltke argues that an international investment agreement is vitally needed to spur the kind of private investment that is crucial for sustainable development. It could greatly improve the trade-off between the risks and benefits of global financial integration, provided it properly accounts for the interests of the world's developing nations as well.[§] Although the concept has received strong support for several years now, the specifics of such an agreement remain fiercely debated.

The two innovations mentioned above are but a selection of subjects that will be discussed in Part C. First, however, we will turn to Part B, where we investigate the subject of financing for the *environment*.

---

*     Research discussed in the IMF review by Prasad, Rogoff, et al. (2003) shows that beside decreasing levels of FDI flowing into an economy, corruption also increases bank lending.

†     It should be noted that in these studies, transparency was measured against various corporate as well as more macroeconomic indicators.

‡     These problems are aggravated even further by the so-called contagion effect that can rapidly occur in today's global-

ized and integrated financial market, which means that financial crises can rapidly spread within and even across regions. What is more, when such contagions occur, they tend to hit the least developed financial markets hardest, which are usually those of the nations of the world that are already poorest and weakest (Soros 2002, p. 113). For more information about contagion and some empirical evidence, see Soros (2002, chap. 4).

§     The OECD in fact attempted to develop a multilateral agreement on investment (MAI) for several years. See Section 12.9 for discussion of efforts to create an international investment agreement.

## PART B: FINANCING FOR ENVIRONMENTAL PROTECTION

### 12.5 THE IMPORTANCE OF ENVIRONMENTAL FINANCING

In the second part of this chapter, we will turn our focus to a discussion of trends in *environmental* financing—a vital element of our analysis. As Wendy Franz (1996, p. 369) pointed out in the mid-1990s, financing for environmental protection has emerged as an essential component in official development assistance, both at the multilateral and the bilateral level. With environmental impacts on the rise in many developing countries, the need for environmental financing is perhaps even more important today. A wide range of development organizations—varying from multilateral institutions to national governments to NGOs—have reconsidered the goals of their programs and projects in order to respond to, and properly incorporate, the growing awareness of environmental concerns. Still, this effort to integrate environmental concerns with development assistance is relatively new, and the results to date have been far from ideal.*

The aim of this part is therefore twofold. Not only is it meant as a comprehensive overview and evaluation of the range of financing structures for environmental protection that have emerged over the past decades, but it will also highlight some of the main drawbacks from which these current structures suffer and suggest some ways in which they can be solved or minimized. This will ultimately lead to a more detailed and practical discussion of several innovative financing solutions for sustainable development in a broader sense, that is, looking beyond environmental protection, which will be provided in Part C.

### 12.6 THE EMERGENCE OF FINANCING STRUCTURES FOR THE ENVIRONMENT

#### 12.6.1 A Historical Overview of Environmental Aid: The Road to Rio

The discussion of financing for environmental protection entered the international political arena for the first time at the United Nations Conference on the Human Environment in Stockholm in 1972, which led to the establishment of the United Nations Environment Programme (UNEP). It was at this conference that a crucial friction between the North and the South first became apparent, which continues to pose one of the main barriers in the fight to protect the global environment: the developed countries wanted to protect the environment, but doing so would imply limiting the potential of the developing countries to progress economically (Redclift 1996, p. 12). According to the developing world, the environmental agenda was the agenda of the developed world.

Oddly enough, however, attention shifted away from environmental problems throughout the rest of the 1970s and most of the 1980s. The main reasons for this were the oil crises of 1973–1974 and 1978–1980, and subsequently the devastating debt crisis that paralyzed Latin America and large regions elsewhere in the developing world.[13] But during the mid-1980s, when evidence began to accumulate that the supposed economic benefits of the structural adjustment policies advocated by the Bretton Woods institutions were undermined by their adverse effects on the sustainability of natural resources and the environment, the international community started to focus its attention on the global environment in a real and more practical sense.

As examined in Chapter 2, the environmental policy debate was truly given a boost when the World Commission on Environment and Development (WCED), chaired by the then Norwegian prime minister Gro Harlem Brundtland, published its famous report titled *Our Common Future* in 1987.[†] The Brundtland report was one of the main driving forces in the process leading up to the United Nations Conference on Environment and Development (UNCED) that was to take place in Rio de Janeiro in 1992.[‡] It articulated the need for an approach to address both economic growth and the environment by arguing that "development and the environment are not separate challenges; they are inextricably linked" (WCED 1987, p. 37). For a while, it seemed that a breakthrough had been made; the poor and rich countries

---

\* The World Bank, for example, although it recruited its first environmental adviser in 1969 and established an office for environmental affairs soon after, did not bring environmental concerns into the mainstream of its operations until 1987 (Franz 1996). In 1988, the World Bank created its environment department, established four regional environmental divisions, and rapidly scaled up the number of division staff members.

† Hereafter, this report will be referred to as the "Brundtland report." As stated in Chapter 2, this report popularized the term "sustainable development," and its definition of sustainable development, despite its flaws, continues to be the most widely recognized definition today (see WCED 1987).

‡ In the year leading up to the UNCED (also referred to as the Earth Summit), public forums were held in Bangkok, Mexico City, Cairo, Buenos Aires, and Amsterdam. NGOs played a considerable role in these forums, and their consultations with governments were continued at Rio in the Global Forum that paralleled the official meetings of the various governments' representatives (Redclift 1996).

across the globe agreed with the main thrust of the report, which in turn spurred a great wave of enthusiasm about the potential for the UNCED to tackle the world's most pressing global environmental problems. Even the World Bank spoke fervently about the possibility of adopting "win-win" strategies that would help both the environment and the economy (WBG 1992).*

However, already during these preparatory discussions, a number of pressing problems arose that subsequently played an important role at the UNCED conference as well and contributed to its failure to reach any substantial practical targets. In fact, as will become apparent in the following subsection, these problems are still at the root of most of the criticism of the global environmental policy agenda today. Unfortunately, over the past decade, it has become painfully apparent that the optimism that characterized the Earth Summit was unrealistic and has not been lived up to in practice. As earlier chapters have illustrated, the progress that has been made even in the areas that UNCED highlighted as being of the most urgent environmental concern, such as climate change and loss of biodiversity, has been only modest.†

### 12.6.2 Criticism of Financing Structures for Environmental Aid: The Flaws of Rio

12.6.2.1 Conflicting Interests between North and South

One important dilemma that again started to surface during the preparations for the UNCED was that the industrialized countries and the developing world—mainly represented by the G77, a large group of developing countries that had decided to combine forces—had, and continue to have, distinctly different perspectives about what the most pressing environmental problems are. But, perhaps unsurprisingly, despite several rounds of intense dispute between the North and South, the industrialized economies largely determined the focal areas of environmental concern that were to be discussed at the Earth Summit in Rio. As a consequence, the real commitments that were made with respect to protection of the global environment, referring to climate change and biodiversity

losses in particular, principally reflect Northern concerns (Redclift 1996, p. 28).

In fact, an analysis of the documents and media coverage flowing from the UNCED would lead one to believe that the principal environmental problems for the world were confined to these two main issues: climate change and the loss of forests and biodiversity (see Chapter 2). Meanwhile, many local problems that posed much more urgent threats and fundamental questions for people's livelihoods, especially in the world's poorer countries and regions, such as how to provide clean drinking water or to reverse land degradation, received virtually no attention. As Redclift (1996, p. 28) put it, they "reflect aspects of sustainable development which were on the margins of the Rio discussions."

Although some of these more local issues have now been included in the Millennium Development Goals,‡ this discrepancy in what people from the industrialized world and the developing world regard as the most pressing environmental problems is still striking. This issue is conveyed very effectively in the *Economist*'s survey of the global environment: "Why should we care about the environment? Ask a European, and he will probably point to global warming. Ask the two little boys playing outside a newsstand in Da Shilan, a shabby neighborhood in the heart of Beijing, and they will tell you about the city's notoriously foul air: 'it's bad—like a virus!'" (Economist 2002c, p. 11).

The difference of opinion between the industrialized world and the developing world did not center merely on what the main environmental problems were; a fierce debate was also fought about who should bear the (financial) responsibility in solving them. This was illustrated, for instance, by the heated discussions between North and South over the responsibility for global climate change. The industrialized world insisted that population growth was the driving force behind this dilemma, while the developing countries pointed at "overconsumption" in the North as the main cause and argued that it was up to the industrialized world to clean up its own mess (Redclift 1996, p. 22).

12.6.2.2 The Dispute over Additionality

This dispute over responsibilities is highly relevant here because it is closely related to the vexing ques-

---

\* A prime example, which we will examine later, is taking away distorted, environmentally harmful subsidies. By doing so, one can, in theory, improve the economy and, at the same time, boost the economy.

† The *Economist*, in its 2002 survey of the global environment, argues that the progress that has been made is largely due to three main factors: more decision making and engagement at local levels ("capacity building"), the rise and better use of market forces, and technological innovation (Economist 2002c).

‡ See Appendix 12-C in this chapter. For example, in target 10 under goal 7, it has been specified that by 2015 the proportion of people without access to safe drinking water should be halved.

tion of "additionality"—one of the most contentious issues raised at the UNCED. The debate on additionality did not originate at the UNCED; it is in fact much older and has continued since then. For example, the 2009 Copenhagen Accord's call for new and additional resources to combat climate change has renewed the debate. Moreover, it is a highly complex and political issue; it has been stated that at the onset of the UNCED in 1992, "linkage politics ha[d] extended the debate to encompass other finance-related issues such as trade and debt. Additionality ha[d] thus become an umbrella term for a multitude of tightly knotted problems" (Jordan 1994, p. 16).[14] However, the main reason that it gained new political significance in the context of sustainable development resided in the aforementioned disagreement over *what* the most pressing environmental problems were, and *who* ought to carry the main responsibility for solving them.

From an early stage in the UNCED negotiations, developing countries realized that the industrialized world was primarily interested in furthering its own interests and wanted the UNCED to focus primarily on issues of *global* environmental concern. They therefore made it clear that their support for the agreements under consideration was contingent on concessions by the industrialized world that *new* aid money would be disbursed. They insisted that the financing they were to receive in order to tackle these (predominantly global) environmental problems and make a transition toward sustainable development, as outlined in Agenda 21, would have to be "new and additional" to all development aid that was already disbursed to the developing world at that time.*

A critically relevant and sensitive factor that was at the root of the debate on additionality was the longstanding dispute over the inequitable relationship between the North and the South. There was a strong and common feeling among third-world countries that the industrialized nations had in fact reaped significant benefits from a period of rapid, inefficient, and heavily polluting growth. Now that the adverse effects of this era on the global environment had become fully apparent, developing countries felt that the industrialized North was attempting to shift part of

the borne environmental costs to the developing world (Johnston 1998, p. 38).[†] Albeit grudgingly, the developing world eventually showed itself willing to accede to the focal areas of global environmental concern that were proposed by the industrialized nations, but solely on the premise that the financing necessary would be additional to the total development aid already flowing from the North to the South.[‡]

At the time of the UNCED, there was in fact a precedent for this process by which the developing countries implicitly threatened not to accede to proposed international agreements unless their interests were taken into consideration. It had been created by the international negotiations to protect the ozone layer. When the Montreal Protocol on substances that deplete the ozone layer was constructed, numerous spectators claimed that the treaty paid proper attention to the needs of developing countries, but most developing countries insisted that it was inequitable, and they fiercely negotiated with the developed countries to secure their assistance, both technically and financially, in meeting the obligations set by the Montreal Protocol.[15] In response to these requests, it was decided at the second meeting of the parties to the Montreal Protocol in London in 1990 that an International Multilateral Ozone Fund (IMOF) would be established. The fund would consist of "new and additional" money from developed-country members and was intended to pay for the incremental cost that developing countries would incur by implementing the terms of the (revised) protocol.

As Jordan (1994) explains, the decision to create the IMOF was highly contentious; it represented an important concession from the developed nations to the developing world—the commitment of additional financial and technical assistance for environmental purposes. Some developed countries, most notably the United States, were therefore very wary that the fund would create a precedent for future negotiations.[§] As the discussions at Rio illustrate, this is ex-

---

\*      Agenda 21 was the centerpiece agreement that emerged from the UNCED—the United Nations' blueprint for sustainability (see Chapter 2). The action programs and activities of Agenda 21 are organized under six themes: quality of life, efficient use of natural resources, protection of the global commons, management of human settlements, waste management, and sustainable economic growth. In most themes, both environmental and developmental concerns are addressed (see UN 1992).

†      In addition, developing countries made the convincing argument that the industrialized countries had strongly benefited from building their economies on environmentally destructive materials (such as fossil fuels), while a large share of the involved environmental costs were borne by the rest of the world (Johnston 1998, p. 38).

‡      The concept of additionality was "reiterated and reinforced" in the Beijing Declaration on Environment and Development, which was signed by forty-one of the G77 countries in June 1991. This document called for increasing financial flows to the developing world and further involvement of recipient countries in how these funds would be managed (Jordan 1994, p. 17).

§      The U.S. government in fact insisted that a clause be added to the revised Montreal Protocol that stated that the IMOF was "without prejudice to any further arrangements that

actly what happened, and the issue remains highly sensitive to this day. As DeSombre and Kauffman (1996, p. 126) put it: "Like it or not, the Fund has set a precedent for dealing with global environmental issues with North-South equity problems. It has created expectations that developing countries will be compensated for the forgone development opportunities or the added burdens required by environmental cooperation."

### 12.6.2.3 Neglecting the Tension between the Economy and the Environment

The single most important problem with the UNCED was probably that it overreached itself.* The participants at Rio "were so anxious to reach a political consensus that they agreed to the Brundtland definition of sustainable development" (Economist 2002c, p. 4). But this definition fails to be specific about what targets must be met in order to strive for the sustainable development and intergenerational equity it talks about. Its crucial flaw, also highlighted by Daniel Esty from Yale University, is that it does not properly acknowledge the difficult trade-offs between economic development and environmental protection. The Brundtland Commission was correct in pointing out that these two issues are closely coupled, and that there are many cases where economic and environmental goals are linked. However, the widespread euphoria with which this observation was interpreted initially has proved unrealistic. It has become painfully apparent that "in most cases, environmental and economic policy goals are distinct, and the actions needed to achieve them are not the same" (Daniel Esty, cited in ibid.).

Even the World Bank now acknowledges this error and accepts that its *World Development Report* of 1992 was too optimistic about the opportunity for creating "win-win" strategies. The World Bank's director for the environment, Kristalina Georgieva,

explained that she has never encountered a true win-win situation in her life. "There's always somebody, usually an elite group grabbing rents, that loses. And we've learned in the past decade that those losers fight hard to make sure that technically elegant win-win policies do not get very far" (Economist 2002c, p. 4).[†]

The profound and difficult trade-offs between economic and environmental development have become even more apparent in today's globalizing economy. One causal factor is the perverse conditions of "free trade," with subsidies and tariff schemes protecting industries in the developed world at the expense of the developing nations. The detrimental effects of these measures on the development of the world's poorest have already been pointed out in Part A, but they also have significant adverse effects on the environment because these measures force the developing world to rely on its main comparative advantage natural resources—in order to achieve economic progress.

But even irrespective of these distorted policies, there is a fundamental imperfection in the global market, explained convincingly by H. Daly and Goodland (1994), which plays a crucial role as well: the prices that operate under "free trade" do not fully internalize the social and environmental costs. As a result, "Countries that are exporting resource-based products (often among the poorest) may be subsidizing the consumption of countries that are doing the importing (often among the richest). . . . The cruel paradox we face may well be that contemporary economic development is unsustainable in poor countries because it is sustainable in rich countries" (Partha Dasgupta, cited in Economist 2002c, p. 17).[‡]

Even the World Trade Organization has openly recognized the tensions between economic develop-

---

may be developed with respect to environmental issues" (Jordan 1994, p. 18). The substitutes for ozone-destroying chlorofluorocarbons (CFCs) had already been developed by DuPont and ICI (Imperial Chemical Industries), and on introduction into world markets, these substitutes were poised to generate these U.S. and U.K. companies considerable market advantages, which is a major reason that they not only supported but also engineered the Montreal Protocol.

\* This point has been made by several expert observers (Jordan 1994; Redclift 1996); it has even been implicitly conceded by multilateral organizations such as the World Bank (WBG 1997). The criticism was reiterated in the *Economist*'s survey of the global environment, which was published in the wake of the 2002 United Nations World Summit on Sustainable Development (Economist 2002c).

---

† To the extent that both economic welfare and the environment are enhanced by cleverly designed policies, there can be a win-win outcome: both economic growth and environmental improvement can be "co-optimized" (N. A. Ashford 2000). However, this does not mean that some individual stakeholders will not lose.

‡ It should be recalled from the discussions in Chapter 5 that this is issue is linked to the main argument against trade liberalization raised by H. E. Daly (1993). A more detailed discussion of the implications of this heavily resource-intensive and "ungreen" pattern of economic development for the developing world and the global environment will be provided in Chapter 13. It is highlighted here because it is closely linked to aspects of financing environmental sustainability: as we will see later, there are strategies that can be employed to make markets more efficient, thereby not only reducing these harmful externalities but in addition freeing up additional funds for environmental protection.

ment and the global environment. In a 1999 report, it states that "economic growth is not sufficient for turning environmental degradation around.... If economic incentives facing producers and consumers do not change with higher incomes, pollution will continue to grow unabated with the growing scale of economic activity" (WTO 1999, pp. 5–6).*

### 12.6.2.4 Agenda 21: Lacking a Mandate

From the preceding discussion, it seems clear that the definition of sustainability adopted at the UNCED was too vague to be translated into workable policy measures and still allowed the various stakeholders to have distinctly different ideas about how sustainability was to be defined, and what the most pressing problems were. This lack of precision was in fact one of the main problems of the UNCED as a whole. As Redclift (1996, p. 23) commented, "by the time the UNCED was convened, the expectations for the conference far exceeded its mandate which was, as the International Institute for Environment and Development (IIED) declared, 'not . . . very workable.'" Further, Jordan (1994) argues that as obligations to address global environmental issues become more specific, the commitments related to these obligations become more ambiguous and vague. Redclift (1996, p. 28) adds to this, "It is one thing to have developed a broad consensus of opinion on the need to tackle the issues, and quite another to agree upon the formulas for funding the policy interventions that might ensue."

This vagueness becomes especially apparent upon examination of Agenda 21, the United Nations' blueprint for implementation of sustainable development across a range of economic sectors in both the developed and the developing world. It is the document that deals in most detail with sustainable development at the so-called grassroots level, and with calls for local ownership and management of resources. But, as Jordan (1994, p. 26) points out, "Agenda 21 is a statement of nonbinding principles; it does not have the force of law, and no country is under legal obligation to implement its provisions." Johnston (1998) reaches a similar verdict: "The enforcement component, as with many international agreements, is lacking (see Chapter 8 of Agenda 21). Therefore, the practical application of

principles laid out in the Rio declaration is minimal." An even harsher critique is provided by Panayotou (1994), who argues that "the pronouncements and programmes of Agenda 21, though individually reasonable and compelling, when taken together and without a reference to sources of financing, appear little more than a wish list of things good to have but beyond our reach."[16]

In particular, the finance section of the agenda—Chapter 33—is "fundamentally weak." It affirms that implementation "will require the provision . . . of substantial new and additional resources" (Jordan 1994, p. 27, n. 42), but fails to specify any quantities or to propose a concrete mechanism through which this money is to be transferred. As a consequence, the financing round that was subsequently initiated in order to ensure effective implementation of Agenda 21 failed miserably. The UNCED Secretariat estimated that implementation of Agenda 21 would require a total of roughly $125 billion in additional financing globally per year, which was quite unrealistic when compared to the level of ODA at that time. World Bank estimates were somewhat over half this figure. However, despite the range of vague promises made in Rio, the industrialized countries pledged only a disappointing $2.5 billion (Redclift 1996). When this enormous gap between what financing was required and what was made available became apparent, Agenda 21—and the UNCED with it—therefore quickly lost its credibility.

## 12.7 ISSUES OF IMPLEMENTATION IN FINANCING SUSTAINABLE DEVELOPMENT

### 12.7.1 Dilemmas and Solutions in Environmental Financing

Data on environmental financing before 1990 are very rare (Franz 1996). The reason should be clear from the previous sections: environmental financing had simply not been systematically considered part of development programs until then. The explicit articulation of the connection between sustainable development and environmental protection that was made by the Brundtland report—despite its numerous drawbacks—did serve to shift considerable attention to the environment. As Fairman and Ross (1996) explain, by bringing environmental concerns into the realm of international development assistance, it has affected strategies for sustainable development in two important ways. First, it has led to a whole range of

---

\* See the vast literature on the so-called environmental Kuznets curve, which argues that pollution initially increases with economic growth and then decreases. Although this is undoubtedly true for some pollutants, such as $SO_2$, it is not for others, such as $CO_2$ (see Scruggs 2003). See the discussion in Section 1.3.2 in Chapter 1.

new institutions, projects, and programs devoted to the protection of the environment, several of which will be analyzed in the remainder of this section. Second, it has made conventional development programs more environmentally aware, for instance, through the promotion of environmental impact statements* and the restriction of funds for environmentally harmful projects.†

The effectiveness of the various financial transfer mechanisms for environmental protection that have been put in place over the past decade, however, has been moderate at best. As is explained in a report edited by Grieg Gan, Banuri, et al. (2002) and prepared for the OECD and the UNDP, many sustainable development strategies at international, national, and local levels, such as national conservation strategies (NCSs), national environmental action plans (NEAPs), and tropical forestry action programs (TFAPs), "quickly lost momentum" because a crucial element for their long-term viability—finance—was not properly considered.‡ As the report explains:

> Strategy "finance" tasks were often limited to adding up the cost of recommended actions and proposing

increases in the government budget. While it is important to mobilize finance for a sustainable development strategy, in particular to get the formulation process started, this is not sufficient. As the concept of a sustainable development strategy has moved away from a focus on producing a plan document (often, in developing countries, containing or accompanied by a suite of proposed projects) to a more process-oriented approach, so the financial challenges have changed.†

> It is no longer simply a case of mobilizing funds for such projects or activities, with the government in the lead implementing role. A strategy is now seen as being more about setting a vision with broad directions, agreeing [on] the attributes of a path towards sustainable development, and putting in place the key mechanisms. So attention must be given also to the financial mechanisms needed to internalize environmental and social costs in order to achieve the necessary changes in direction. (Grieg-Gan, Banuri, et al. 2002, p. 288)

The World Bank acknowledged many of these drawbacks (although it neglected to link them explicitly to "flaws" of the UNCED) when it published its report titled *Five Years after Rio: Innovations in Environmental Policy*. One aspect that had become particularly apparent was that the financial resources available for environmental protection were highly insufficient to tackle the wide range of issues included in most sustainable development strategies. The report therefore emphasized that setting priorities and focusing on a limited set of problems at a time were essential for success (WBG 1997, p. 7).

As its title suggests, the report discusses much more than merely the financial aspects of environmental policy. It was intended as a "stock-taking, five years after Rio, of what has been attempted worldwide by national governments and international institutions to foster the use of economic, regulatory, and institutional instruments to better manage the environment" (WBG 1997, p. 3). The report not only analyzes these various policy instruments for environmental protection but also categorizes them in a policy matrix. It organizes all policy measures under four main headings: using markets, creating markets, using environmental regulations, and engaging the public (see Table 12.8).§

Understandably, an extensive discussion of each of these categories goes far beyond the scope of this chapter. But in the remainder of this section, it will become clear that many policy instruments that fall

---

* For example, since the World Bank introduced its Operational Directive on Environmental Assessment in 1989, it classifies all its projects into four categories on the basis of their environmental impact. Category A projects contain diverse and significant environmental impacts and thus require full, detailed environmental assessments. Category B projects have specific environmental impacts for which a more limited analysis is considered sufficient. Category C projects are likely to have no or minimal adverse environmental impacts and therefore require no environmental analysis. Last, category D projects are projects with an environmental focus, which therefore do not require a separate environmental impact. For the full details of each of these categories and the requirements for the environmental analyses to be carried out in each case, the reader is referred to the World Bank website, http://go.worldbank.org/3LBMXIFF20 (accessed February 6, 2011).

† The percentage of ODA assistance projects that have environmental protection as their primary objective significantly increased in the years after the UNCED. In addition, many environmental finance initiatives were set up that fell outside the realm of official development assistance, such as the Global Environment Facility (GEF) and many NGO activities (Franz 1996, p. 370).

‡ In the remainder of this section, some financial transfer mechanisms will be examined; however, a detailed and exhaustive discussion is beyond the scope of this chapter. (The only institution that will be analyzed at length is the Global Environment Facility, in view of its key role as an executive body of the conventions on climate change and biodiversity, its prominence at the UNCED, and its continuous controversy.) However, the book *Institutions for Environmental Aid: Pitfalls and Promise*, edited by Keohane and Levy (1996), explores the effectiveness of various financial transfer mechanisms for the environment—some global in scope (the Montreal Protocol, debt-for-nature swaps), some focused on specific regions (logging reform in the tropics, nuclear safety in Eastern Europe).

§ The policy matrix is constructed in the first part of the report. In the second part, brief case studies of many policy measures and instruments that fall in the realm of each of the four categories of the policy matrix are presented.

**TABLE 12.8: THE POLICY MATRIX**

| | POLICY INSTRUMENTS FOR SUSTAINABLE DEVELOPMENT | | | |
| THEMES | USING MARKETS | CREATING MARKETS | USING ENVIRONMENTAL REGULATIONS | ENGAGING THE PUBLIC |
| --- | --- | --- | --- | --- |
| *Resource management and pollution control* | • Subsidy reduction<br>• Environmental taxes<br>• User fees<br>• Deposit-refund systems<br>• Targeted subsidies | • Property rights/ decentralization<br>• Tradable permits/rights<br>• International offset systems | • Standards<br>• Bans<br>• Permits and quotas | • Public participation<br>• Information disclosure |

Source: WBG (1997, p. 6).

in the realm of the first two categories of the matrix—using markets and creating markets—can be used not only to improve environmental policies but also to free more financial resources or to use existing funds more effectively.

This brings us to the core concern voiced in this chapter: implementation of policies for environmental protection is greatly impeded by a lack of sufficient and adequate financial backing. (In fact, as we have seen in Part A and in previous chapters, this holds true for policies for sustainable development in a broader sense.) In the remainder of this section, we will therefore analyze several strategies that can be employed to improve this situation by ensuring a sound financial basis for environmental policy. The discussion will be structured around two main categories of strategies:*

1. Freeing up financial resources for specific activities to promote sustainable development

2. Making better use of market mechanisms to promote sustainable development

An important concern that the perceptive reader may have noticed is that the boundaries between environmental policies and broader policies for sustainable development have gradually become rather blurred. This will be the case even more in the following section, where many programs and projects that we will discuss tackle issues that extend beyond purely environmental concerns. This is in fact a positive development; as explained in Chapter 2, one of the main drawbacks of sustainable development strategies has been that they are usually too strongly focused on environmental concerns.

To highlight the trend toward further integration of environmental issues with broader questions of sustainability, the programs and projects to be discussed

in the following section will be referred to as "sustainable development strategies." Nevertheless, we have attempted to confine the discussion here to concise analyses of strategies that are at least relevant to the field of environmental management and protection. In the third and final part of this chapter, we will examine several innovative financing strategies in more detail, some of which deal with much broader issues of sustainable development or development assistance, such as the alleviation of poverty and the creation of purchasing power, and have no direct link with the environment (for example, Soros's SDR proposal).†

### 12.7.2 Freeing Up Financial Resources for Sustainable Development Activities

In 1992, the UNCED Secretariat estimated that implementing Agenda 21 in the developing countries would cost over $600 billion per year, $125 billion of which would have to be disbursed as grants or concessional finance by the international community (Grieg-Gan, Banuri, et al. 2002). We have already seen that nothing remotely close to this amount was raised in practice. Nearly two decades since Rio have shown that reliance on the mobilization of large amounts of new finance, particularly donor finance, is unrealistic.‡ For this reason, the search for new and innovative ways to secure the needed finance is unavoidable. This search will be structured along an examination of the main sources of finance: donors, governments (and other in-country sources of finance), international transfer mechanisms, national environmental funds, and trust funds.

---

\* This subsection draws many of its ideas from the chapter titled "The Financial Basis for Strategies" by Grieg-Gan, Banuri, et al. (2002).

† In fact, some of the financing innovations discussed in Part C also focus predominantly on the environment, such as the Global Environment Facility. However, the general outlook of that section will be much broader and more holistic, and the analysis of each mechanism will be more detailed.

‡ Even if the developed countries gave in to the pressures to increase their official development assistance in order to meet the target of 0.7 percent of GDP, the financing gap would still be enormous.

However, before we analyze each of these categories, two important aspects of the financial requirements of current sustainable development projects must be stressed. First, it has become clear that the disbursement of funds can no longer be confined to the implementation stage. It is equally important to ensure that adequate financial resources are available during the planning phase. It is argued that "if a strategy is to be participatory, country-led and based on comprehensive and reliable analysis . . . , then financial resources will be needed in the early stages for research, analysis, consultation, communication, and for the development and maintenance of monitoring and evaluation mechanisms. . . . The costs of these processes should not be underestimated, given the amount of time involved and the need to keep processes going" (Grieg-Gan, Banuri, et al. 2002, p. 290).

Second, it must be noted that there are two broad types of sustainable development projects. Some activities need financial support in the initial stages but have the potential to become self-financing in the longer term, such as fuel switching and the promotion of cleaner production. As we will see later, the effective use of market mechanisms can facilitate these activities, both by changing incentives and behavior and by functioning as a source of additional finance (think, for instance, of a targeted subsidy that makes cleaner fuel more attractive). However, there will always be certain activities that will require long-term funding and have limited scope to become self-financing, such as the provision of social safety nets or the protection of common areas (Grieg-Gan, Banuri, et al. 2002, p. 292). It is especially this group of activities that encounters enormous difficulties in finding sufficient and sustained funding.

### 12.7.2.1 Donor Funding

Over the past decades, most sustainable development strategies in the developing world have been closely linked to donor support; they either relied heavily on donor support from the outset or were initiated by country governments in order to meet the requirements for financial support to continue the program or start additional programs.* This brings us to one important advantage of donor support: it provides funding that is *additional* to the financing that is provided out of the recurrent budget of the recipient

country's government. This makes donor funding attractive, especially for activities that are not normally or fully funded by the government, such as techniques to ensure stakeholder participation. For example, during 2007–2008, DAC donor countries provided \$13 billion (18 percent of total bilateral sector-applicable ODA) for environmentally sound development initiatives (Table 12.9).

However, a serious drawback is that donors often set deadlines and force recipients to produce a strategy document within a rigid time frame in order to justify the support they have received or to secure future support. This can seriously affect the quality of participation. For example, the Heavily Indebted Poor Countries (HIPC) initiative provides debt relief to nations in exchange for their development of a poverty-reduction strategy (PRS). Since the initiation of the HIPC initiative in 1996, a tension has become apparent between securing quick debt relief and preparing a sound PRS that properly engages civil society (GAO 2000).[†]

Also, although developing countries have usually been able to acquire funding for the initial formulation of a sustainable development program or strategy, it has proved more difficult to secure donor financing for the ongoing processes of monitoring and review. The difficulty, as highlighted above, is to persuade donors to provide financial support for a recurrent process that has no predetermined outputs. (As we will see below, national environmental funds, or trust funds in general, can provide a solution to this dilemma.)

The third and last downside of donor financing is that donors can have very different agendas and priorities and often tend to finance distinctly different activities or types of strategies on the basis of these concerns. Sometimes these strategies even have conflicting objectives. This situation is not helped by the fact that donor priorities often change over time as a result of changes in government or trends in development or environmental aid. Properly coordinating donor-funded sustainability projects and integrating the various strategies into an overarching, effective strategy have proved extremely difficult, especially for the world's poorest nations, whose governments do not have the financial or human capital to orchestrate this process.[‡] But in spite of these drawbacks, Grieg-Gan, Banuri, et al. (2002, pp. 292–293) argue that "timely donor support, correctly provided, can be important

---

* Good examples are the hundreds of national environmental action plans (NEAPs) that were set up in the mid-1990s. For more information on these, see also the World Bank report *Five Years after Rio* (WBG 1997). The NEAPs of the Netherlands stand out as exemplary (Keijzers 2002).

† Many disadvantages and shortcomings of various bilateral donor strategies have already been discussed in Section 12.3.4.

‡ Coordination issues have been highlighted as a major problem in development aid in Part A as well (see Section 12.3.3.4).

**TABLE 12.9: AID IN SUPPORT OF THE ENVIRONMENT, 2007–2008 AVERAGE (MILLIONS OF U.S. DOLLARS)**

| | ENVIRONMENT AS A SECTOR | OTHER ACTIVITIES SCORED AS "PRINCIPAL OBJECTIVE" | ACTIVITIES SCORED AS "SIGNIFICANT OBJECTIVE" | SUB-TOTAL: ENVIRONMENT FOCUSED | NOT TARGETED | TOTAL: AID SCREENED | NOT SCREENED | MEMO: SECTOR ALLOCABLE, TOTAL |
|---|---|---|---|---|---|---|---|---|
| | | | 2007–2008 | | | | | |
| Australia | 38 | 47 | 0 | 86 | 1,085 | 1,171 | 285 | 2,657 |
| Austria | 4 | 20 | 56 | 80 | 233 | 313 | 82 | 396 |
| Belgium | 6 | 76 | 211 | 293 | 509 | 802 | 374 | 1,176 |
| Canada | 19 | 11 | 91 | 121 | 1,948 | 2,069 | 177 | 2,246 |
| Denmark | 72 | 66 | 208 | 346 | 635 | 981 | 0 | 981 |
| Finland | 36 | 75 | 88 | 199 | 336 | 534 | 0 | 534 |
| France | 502 | 251 | 713 | 1,465 | 1,670 | 3,135 | 2,734 | 5,869 |
| Germany | 267 | 915 | 1,596 | 2,778 | 2,814 | 5,593 | 1,569 | 7,161 |
| Greece | 7 | 1 | 12 | 20 | 194 | 215 | 0 | 215 |
| Ireland | .. | .. | .. | .. | .. | .. | | 561 |
| Italy | 74 | 38 | 166 | 278 | 365 | 643 | 166 | 808 |
| Japan | 484 | 2,390 | 1,414 | 4,288 | 6,372 | 10,660 | 101 | 10,761 |
| Luxembourg | .. | .. | .. | .. | .. | .. | .. | 185 |
| Netherlands | 169 | 203 | 17 | 389 | 3,020 | 3,409 | 0 | 3,409 |
| New Zealand | 1 | 3 | 32 | 37 | 159 | 196 | 0 | 196 |
| Norway | 141 | 138 | 241 | 520 | 1,827 | 2,346 | 0 | 2,346 |
| Portugal | .. | .. | .. | .. | .. | .. | .. | 262 |
| Spain | 156 | 99 | 386 | 642 | 1,710 | 2,352 | 585 | 2,936 |
| Sweden | 41 | 168 | 639 | 848 | 611 | 1,459 | 0 | 1,459 |
| Switzerland | .. | .. | .. | .. | .. | .. | .. | 864 |
| United Kingdom | 113 | 8 | 518 | 639 | 3,960 | 4,599 | 820 | 5,419 |
| United States | .. | .. | .. | .. | .. | .. | .. | 21,175 |
| Total bilateral | 2,132 | 4,509 | 6,388 | 13,029 | 27,448 | 40,477 | 6,892 | 71,617 |
| Memo: EC | 401 | 280 | 936 | 1,617 | 8,642 | 10,260 | 1,196 | 11,456 |

Note: An activity can target the environment as a "principal objective" or a "significant objective." "Principal" means that the environment was an explicit objective of the activity and fundamental in its design. "Significant" means that the environment was an important, but secondary, objective of the activity. "Not targeted" means that the activity was screened for promoting the environment but did not target it.

Source: Adapted from OECD (2010a, p. 3).

for specific issues, and can trigger the mobilization of resources several times greater than the initial amounts."

Last, it should be noted that donor finance to NGOs can be a useful mechanism to address more sustainable forms of development. While a reliance on NGO involvement can have several drawbacks (see Section 12.3.3.1), Grieg-Gan, Banuri, et al. (2002, p. 293) argue that "rather than regarding NGOs as competitors or 'environmental police,' governments can benefit by adopting a more positive approach to the contributions of NGOs, such as innovative policy proposals and sustainable development projects." Established NGOs can have strong connections with communities that can be leveraged to promote positive change in almost any area relating to sustainability.

### 12.7.2.2 Governments and Other In-Country Sources of Finance

A second source of financing for sustainability consists of the funding that national governments make

available themselves. An obvious but important difference between government financing and donor financing is that the former usually requires a *reallocation* of expenditure from other activities; the money is *not* additional. It is therefore not always easy to secure government support for programs or projects, especially in poor countries where government revenues are limited (Danish 1995, p. 151)—common challenges include the small size of the tax base and problems of tax evasion. For this reason, it is better to secure government financing for activities that may eventually become self-financing than to promote projects that will require sustained financial inputs (Grieg-Gan, Banuri, et al. 2002).

A risk of reliance on government funding for strategy formulation is that the government, and hence "ownership" and priorities of the project, may change in the course of the process. Even worse, funding may be terminated before the project has had any effect. This problem can occur even in the industrialized world. For example, Canada's Projet de Société, which started in November 1992 and was funded by Environment Canada and other government agencies, suffered a serious setback when the government changed a year later. The new government wanted to reduce the budget deficit and decided to make no further funds available for the project, even though the new environment minister was supportive of the concept (D. B. Dalal-Clayton 1996, cited in Grieg-Gan, Banuri, et al. 2002).

In many developing countries, NGOs have become an important supplement to government efforts to implement sustainable development strategies. In fact, governments often channel available donor funds to NGOs as well (if this is not done directly by the donors themselves; see above). Governments can engage NGOs in this fashion without having to use many additional financial or human resources. B. Dalal-Clayton and Bass (2002) argue that they could go further and work to strengthen social capital that eventually will help in the formulation and the implementation of a national sustainable development strategy (NSDS). This, however, would require more substantial resources.*

It should be mentioned that there are some additional in-country sources of finance, but with the exception of local NGOs that receive donor funds directly (see the previous section), these are fairly limited and will therefore not be discussed further.†

### 12.7.2.3 International Transfer Mechanisms

International transfer mechanisms constitute the third source of funding. They are transfers made by industrialized countries to assist developing countries in their activities in the realm of *global* sustainable development (such as biodiversity conservation or carbon sequestration). These financial transfers are usually made by multilateral agencies on behalf of the contributing countries. The three most important types are the Global Environment Facility (GEF), the Clean

Development Mechanism, and debt swaps. The last two will be discussed below. The GEF will be examined in a more detailed analysis in Section 12.10.

**12.7.2.3.1 The Clean Development Mechanism**[17]    The Clean Development Mechanism (CDM) is one of several "flexibility mechanisms" that was authorized in the December 1997 Kyoto Protocol to the 1992 United Nations Framework Convention on Climate Change (UNFCCC), signed at the UNCED in Rio de Janeiro. The Clean Development Mechanism allows developed countries to implement projects in developing countries if they reduce net greenhouse gas emissions. It has the additional goal of assisting developing countries to achieve sustainable development. The advantage for developed countries is that the so-called certified emission reductions (CERs) that are generated through these projects in developing countries may be used by the developed country as a contribution toward its own CER quota. Therefore, these activities make it easier for developed countries to comply with their own emission commitments. In addition, a share of the CERs generated in each of these transnational collaborative efforts will be withheld by the CDM executive in order to assist developing countries in meeting the costs of adaptation to climate change (Grieg-Gan, Banuri, et al. 2002).

The CDM seems a powerful mechanism to engage the private sector in activities to reduce net greenhouse gas emissions in the developing world. Indeed, it is attractive to become involved because it is commonly believed that there are more opportunities to reduce greenhouse gas emissions—at a lower cost—in developing countries than in the industrialized world. However, critics of the CDM have argued that these costs may in fact be lower in developing countries, not because of any difference in carbon-abatement efficiency, but because of low social and non-climate-related environmental standards (Grieg-Gan, Banuri, et al. 2002).

According to Baumert and Petkova (2000), the extent to which the CDM (and other similar carbon-offset initiatives) will be able to contribute to the achievement of sustainable development will depend largely on how it is implemented. The framework that will be put in place to assess projects according to their sustainable development impact, and the scope for stakeholder participation in project design and approval, will be of special importance in this respect (ibid.).

**12.7.2.3.2 Debt Swaps**‡    The second type of international transfer mechanism to be examined here,

---

\* Governments may therefore wish to examine ways to alter existing policies and incentives to make donations more attractive. In many developing countries, for example, donations to environmental or sustainable development objectives have not yet been recognized as eligible for tax credits, which are, in general, applicable to humanitarian aid, education, or cultural programs (Fund of the Americas 2000; cited in Grieg-Gan, Banuri, et al. 2002).

† It is important to keep in mind that the participative process of developing sustainable development strategies should recognize that some stakeholders have more financial capability than others—such as large companies and, to a lesser extent, international NGOs. However, it is not always easy to ensure that less powerful groups are not prevented from participating because of their lack of finance; financing a strategy should not mean "buying influence" (Grieg-Gan, Banuri, et al. 2002, pp. 293–294).

---

‡ A good analysis of debt swaps and their potential in achieving sustainable development is provided by Kaiser and

the debt swap, is older and more widely implemented than the first. It was introduced in the 1980s and generally works as follows: a developing country can strive to have the debt or currency claims against it canceled in exchange for that country's commitment to one or more environmental or social development programs or projects. The concept of a debt swap became financially attractive after the debt crisis, when the prices of commercial debt fell significantly (Jakobeit 1996), and has since been applied in many forms and in various regions. Until recently, the most common type was a debt-for-nature swap.[18] More recently, the HIPC initiative has linked debt relief with poverty-reduction strategies for several selected low-income countries.

As a source of finance for sustainable development, debt swaps have several main drawbacks (Grieg-Gan, Banuri, et al. 2002):

- The funds they free may not necessarily be additional, because the agencies canceling or reducing the debt may offset this by reducing other forms of aid.

- At times, they focus disproportionately on the concerns and priorities of the industrialized world. For example, this has been a main criticism of debt-for-nature swaps, particularly where these have concentrated on protected areas rather than sustainable use (see also Panayotou 1994).

- The proceeds of debt swaps are frequently larger than the financial "absorption capacity" of the recipient country and/or local NGOs involved in the project(s). This may lead to highly inefficient allocation of resources (see also Danish 1995).

Despite these persistent and difficult drawbacks, debt swaps are a policy tool that is often used. The mechanism can be useful as long as the interests of the donor country and the recipient country are properly aligned and incorporated into the proposed programs or project strategy.

### 12.7.2.4 National Environmental Funds*

A fourth type of financing for sustainable development, which emerged rapidly during the 1990s, is the concept of a national environmental fund (NEF). Grieg-Gan, Banuri, et al. (2002, p. 296) describe NEFs as funds that can "finance environmental projects through grants and soft loans. . . . Such funds have played a significant role in helping enterprises adjust to stricter environmental requirements and in accelerating environmental improvements. . . . [and] . . . could play an important role in the impementation stage of a strategy by providing temporary assistance to companies to help them make the far-reaching changes necessary to move towards sustainability, for example through giving concessional loans for clean technology."

The NEFs operating in several central and Eastern European countries, such as Poland, Bulgaria, and Slovenia, are usually controlled by autonomous government agencies and receive their money mainly through earmarked revenues from pollution charges and fines. Danish (1995), on the other hand, describes NEFs as national-level financial mechanisms that not only manage and coordinate funds but can also empower a broad cross-section of developing-country stakeholders in managing and disbursing these funds. He specifically stresses that NEFs should be distinguished from the type of environmental funds mentioned above because almost all NEFs are largely independent from their governments and can receive funds from multiple sources. Danish's definition seems more plausible, especially because the former type of environmental funds can also operate at a regional level (for example, in Poland; see Zylicz 1994) or at a municipal level (for example, in Bulgaria; see Klarer, Francis, et al. 1999).

As Danish (1995, p. 170) explains at length, NEFs are a "less centralized, more flexible, and responsive alternative" to the international institutions that have traditionally coordinated activities to protect the global environment and to achieve sustainable global development. He argues that "the NEF mechanism is an innovation that has overcome the hurdles of organizational culture and North-South politics to emerge as a promising means of financing conservation" (ibid.).

The main appeal of an NEF was initially that it could be used as a mechanism that would be able to provide long-term funding in low quantities for activities that have recurrent costs. Because of this characteristic, it can remain a stable, sustained source of money, which is especially important for the long and difficult process of capacity building. But in addition, many observers, especially those active in NGOs, over time became convinced that the value of NEFs as mechanisms to enhance participatory and

---

Lambert (1996). This report provides a very clear explanation of the practicalities of implementing a debt swap and also discusses various examples and case studies.

*        As will become clear during this subsection, the categories "national environmental fund" and "trust fund" are not mutually exclusive; many, but not all, NEFs are in fact operated as trust funds. However, in view of the importance of NEFs as a financial mechanism in striving for sustainable development, and the wide literature available, they are discussed as a separate entity.

democratic decision making in fact exceeds their more tangible, "economic" value as mechanisms for financing recurrent costs (Danish 1995).*

As a practical illustration, a study by Peltier and Ashford (1998) compares and contrasts a French environmental fund (the water agency Agence de l'Eau Rhin-Meuse) and a World Bank Cleaner Production demonstration project in China in terms of their success at implementing cleaner technologies.† The study argues that because industrial pollution is intrinsically linked to technological innovation, environmental policies—from direct regulation to economic instruments—cannot ignore the technological dimension when they strive to control or prevent industrial pollution. More specifically, the analysis is based on a three-dimensional assessment methodology developed by Ashford at MIT, which includes (1) the level of innovation, (2) the type of process targeted, and (3) a so-called process-flow-oriented categorization of technologies.

The study identifies significant differences between the two venues. Based on Foster's theory of innovation S-curves, it uses three types of interpretation to distinguish which of these differences can be attributed to intrinsic differences that exist between the various technological choices available (that is, end-of-pipe versus cleaner-production approaches), and which differences are due to other causes, such as resistance to change inside the firm or policy distortions. The analysis is rather complex, but the results suggest that the assessment methodology offers an effective way to evaluate the performance of various financial strategies to implement environmental policy. It allows for the identification of attractive technology options that should be particularly promoted, and the monitoring of the evolution of various technological choices over time (Peltier and Ashford 1998).

### 12.7.2.5 Trust Funds

The last source of finance for sustainable development addressed here is the trust fund. Most trust funds that are relevant to sustainable development have been set up for environmental purposes (see the previous section on national environmental funds), but there are some exceptions that have more "social" objectives, such as poverty reduction. Trust funds acquire their funds from various sources; usually donor funding is an important source, but debt swaps and revenues from environmental taxes or fees are also common.

Trust funds are often created and managed by private organizations or NGOs. Typically, they are governed by a board of directors drawn from the private sector, NGOs, government, and academia, while management of their assets is handed over to professional fund managers. Three types of trust funds are usually distinguished:

- *Endowment funds* are funds that spend only the income from their capital (that is, their investment income), preserving the capital itself as a permanent asset.
- *Sinking funds* disburse their entire principal and investment income over a fixed period of time (usually a relatively long period).
- *Revolving funds* are funds that receive new income on a regular basis, for instance, from special taxes or user fees, to replenish the original capital stock.

In practice, trust funds can involve a combination of these different modalities (Smith 2000). An evaluation conducted by the GEF (1999), cited in Smith (2000), found that successful environmental trust funds were the product of broad consultative processes, involved people from different sectors in their governance, and had credible and transparent procedures. It also found that active government support was necessary, even if the fund was operating beyond the government's direct control.

Trust funds are most appropriate when the issues being addressed require financing over a number of years—that is, when long-term, stable financing is required. In many poor countries, they are therefore very suitable as a mechanism for financing the development and implementation of projects and programs that have limited scope to become self-financing, such as the provision of social safety nets or the protection of common areas. Especially for this group of activities, which encounter enormous difficulties in finding sufficient and sustained funding from other sources (such as governments or donors), trust funds can be crucial in determining their success. (As observed above, the same holds true for NEFs.)

### 12.7.3 Making Better Use of Market Mechanisms to Promote Sustainable Development

The analysis will now turn to more indirect mechanisms that can be applied to free more financing for

---

\*      For a more detailed and well-documented discussion of NEFs, the reader is referred to Danish (1995). This article includes a vivid case study of the first NEF, which was launched in Bhutan in collaboration with the GEF in the early 1990s.

†      The reader is strongly advised to read this study because it provides a good illustration of the activities of environmental funds—both in the developed and the developing world—and highlights the importance of technological innovation in environmental policy.

sustainable development strategies. The most influential and attractive ways to do so fall under the heading of *utilizing market mechanisms.** For example, market mechanisms may free additional money by capturing more resources from polluters or resource users by imposing fees or taxes that internalize environmental or social externalities. However, their most important effect is not to raise funds; it is to change people's behavior and make it more sustainable. We argue that by internalizing important externalities, market mechanisms can create powerful incentives to behave more "sustainably."[19] These measures often have a more lasting effect than the provision of finance for specific sustainable development projects.[†]

We will distinguish three basic approaches to using market mechanisms:

1. *Introducing* new financial mechanisms that internalize environmental or social externalities

2. *Adapting* existing market mechanisms to promote sustainable development

3. *Removing* existing financial mechanisms that hamper sustainable development

### 12.7.3.1 Introducing New Financial Mechanisms That Internalize Environmental or Social Externalities

Mechanisms that alter the allocation of resources can contribute to sustainable development. All too often, natural resources are substantially underpriced because of a failure to internalize the costs of negative environmental or social externalities. In such cases, market prices reflect only private costs and ignore the damages inflicted on the environment and human health. One way to tackle this problem is the introduction of new market mechanisms that internalize such externalities (WBG 1997). This can be achieved in various ways. For example, market mechanisms can tax companies or individuals for their adverse environmental or social impacts. A price can be put on the use of various natural resources (user fees). A third

option is to offer a financial reward (or tax exemption) for the provision of certain environmental or social services.

Especially in developing countries, the establishment of property rights for land, water, and other natural resources, such as forests, is also a crucial step toward the creation of a properly functioning market that promotes sustainable development. Making resource users into owners provides a fundamental incentive for more sustainable management of these resources. As is painfully illustrated by the trends toward tropical deforestation and the decimation of the world's fisheries, the effects of unregulated open access to resources, without proper market forces, can be devastating (WBG 1997, pp. 11–12).[‡]

The introduction of new market mechanisms is argued to have three main advantages (Grieg-Gan, Banuri, et al. 2002; WBG 1997).

- Market mechanisms are often easier to implement than alternative, more targeted policy instruments that directly regulate behavior (often referred to as "command-and-control" approaches). These measures can therefore often achieve their objectives at significantly reduced (administrative) costs.

- Through the user fees or tax levies they bring in, market mechanisms provide a significant source of revenues. These can be invested in mechanisms aimed at achieving sustainable development (that is, earmarked funding of specific activities, a contribution to an environmental or social fund, or offsetting other taxation, for example, of labor).

- Because of their flexibility, market mechanisms provide continuing incentives for companies and individuals to innovate and improve their operations to become more in line with the objectives of the mechanism.[§]

Over the past decade, a wide range of new market mechanisms have been introduced in both developed and developing countries (see Table 12.10). The main difficulties that become apparent from an analysis of these mechanisms are the following:[¶]

---

* The literature on market mechanisms for sustainable development is extensive. As discussed above, in the World Bank report *Five Years after Rio* (WBG 1997), a policy matrix looks in detail at different market mechanisms and provides concrete examples of their implementation. The discussion here will largely be based on this report, as well as on Grieg-Gan, Banuri, et al. (2002).

† The distinction between financial mechanisms and policy instruments to achieve sustainable development can become somewhat vague and blurry in this section; market mechanisms go beyond merely freeing up financial resources. The emphasis in this section will be on policy measures that—in spite of their broader effects—can be classified as having significant financial implications.

‡ Obviously, fishing is a prime example of a "tragedy of the commons," which is encountered frequently in the area of sustainable development and environmental protection. The ocean and the fish in it are a resource that is "common" property (or at least very difficult to monitor). As a result, an individual "free rider" benefits most by catching as many fish as he can, even if this is detrimental to the long-term survival of the fleet. If property could be divided over fishermen and properly monitored, it would be in their own self-interest to fish sustainably and ensure the long-term preservation of their stock.

§ See Section 8.4 in Chapter 8 for an argument that stringent regulation is a better stimulus to innovation.

¶ It should be noted that the OECD has performed several studies that evaluate these market mechanisms in its mem-

## TABLE 12.10: MARKET MECHANISMS TO ENCOURAGE SUSTAINABLE DEVELOPMENT

Emission charges (such as effluent charges or $SO_2$ and $NO_x$ taxes) that encourage companies to reduce emissions through (preferably) process-integrated and/or end-of-pipe measures.

Waste taxes (e.g., landfill taxes) that make final waste disposal more expensive, thus promoting recycling and waste reduction.

Product taxes on, for example, energy, lubricant oils, batteries, fertilizers, pesticides, and packaging and on other products that have an environmental impact in manufacture, consumption, or disposal.

Tax differentiation that favors sustainability (e.g., for leaded and unleaded gasoline), by diverting consumption away from a more polluting product to a less polluting substitute.

User charges, such as entrance fees for natural parks.

Subsidies or preferential credits for the introduction of clean technologies or other methods of production that introduce positive environmental externalities.

Markets for environmental services (such as tradable permits for $SO_2$, carbon-offset trading, transferable development rights, or payments for watershed protection).

Deposit refund schemes (e.g., on packaging) to encourage reuse, recycling, or controlled disposal. (A deposit is made on purchase of a product and refunded when the product or, in some cases, its packaging is returned.)

Increased resource rent capture (e.g., for forest concessions) through competitive bidding and area-based taxes, and for water through abstraction charges.

Source: Adapted from Grieg-Gan, Banuri, et al. (2002, p. 301).

- Establishing the appropriate level of a charge, tax, or fee. Early schemes were introduced more with the aim of raising revenues than of changing behavior. The fees set were therefore low. Newer schemes have put more emphasis on the incentive effect.

- Enforcing payment and dealing with evasion without increasing unduly the administrative costs involved, especially where there is poor regulatory enforcement.

- Overcoming resistance from certain groups who are likely to lose as a result of the introduction of the market mechanism. International cooperation can help overcome these problems.

- Dealing with regressive impacts on the poor who are least capable of adapting to the proposed changes.*

- Ensuring that the revenue raised is used for appropriate sustainable development objectives, and providing safeguards against misappropriation. This will usually involve setting up institutional structures.†

ber countries (OECD 1997, 2001, 2006). Also see the OECD's website on scaling-up market mechanisms to promote greenhouse gas mitigation, www.oecd.org/env/cc/scalingup (accessed February 6, 2011). Also, the Economic Commission of Latin America and the Caribbean has published its first evaluation of these market mechanisms in that region (ECLAC 2002).

\* For example, the introduction of taxes on fossil fuels can have profoundly adverse impacts on the poor. Assistance, financial as well as technical, may have to be given to help them adapt to the new situation (for example, through the distribution of more energy-efficient cooking and heating equipment).

† A good example of this was mentioned in the section on national environmental funds. In Eastern Europe, these funds, which were created to disburse the earmarked finances that were raised through the various environmental charges introduced, are playing a key role in the move to address environmental problems.

### 12.7.3.2 Adapting Existing Market Mechanisms to Promote Sustainable Development

In some cases, it may be much easier to adapt existing market mechanisms or policies to align them better with certain sustainable development objectives than to introduce completely new mechanisms. There are two important reasons for this. First, adaptations of existing mechanisms are relatively easy and inexpensive to implement because, among other reasons, they require no new administrative systems for their introduction. Second, because these measures are portrayed as adaptations of existing mechanisms rather than completely new initiatives, they may encounter less opposition from groups that will be adversely affected by the scheme.

### 12.7.3.3 Removing Existing Financial Mechanisms That Hamper Sustainable Development

As the *Economist* points out, however, "Externalities are only half the battle in fixing market distortions. The other half involves scrapping environmentally harmful subsidies" (Economist 2002c, p. 16). Key productive inputs such as electricity, water, and pesticides are often priced below their market levels. There can be various reasons for this. For instance, governments may create subsidies or price controls with the aim of encouraging industrial productive activity, or to protect the interests of low-income groups, or to ensure that certain services that are considered to have public health benefits are available to everyone. In some cases, it may even be considered administratively easier to have broad instead of specifically targeted subsidies. But whatever their motivation, the effects of these subsidies are devastating, not only on the economy but also on the environment. They reduce the cost of overexploiting or polluting the environment and thereby encourage activities that rely heavily on natural resources or degrade the environment.*

The removal of distorting subsidies has a number of positive effects. First, it reduces the strain on the environment by altering incentives. But changing these incentives also improves economic efficiency. The most important effect from a financial perspective is that it frees up financial resources, which can then be deployed in activities that *promote* sustainable development. These sums can be significant (Gandhi, Gray, et al. 1997).

Even subsidies that have the aim of protecting the interests of the poor or providing public health benefits can be counterproductive for sustainable development objectives. For example, many problems in providing water and sanitation stem from inadequate cost recovery due to subsidized or free provision. At the same time, it is still the poor who are least likely to have access to these subsidized water-supply and sanitation systems (Johnstone 1997, cited in Grieg-Gan, Banuri, et al. 2002). This strongly suggests that instead of providing poor-quality water and sanitation services at subsidized rates below market levels, it would be better to charge the full rate for a service that is more reliable and pays closer attention to the needs of low-income communities (Panayotou 1994). Indeed, this approach is embodied in the emerging concept of multiple-use water services (MUS)[20] planning that provides water for both domestic (for example, drinking, cooking, washing, and bathing) and productive (for example, brick making, beer making, and water for livestock) activities. It is believed that if rural and peri-urban households were provided with an opportunity to generate income from "productive water," they would be willing to pay more for a multiple-use water system because of its potential to enhance their livelihoods.

Last, it should be noted that identifying and addressing the problems of perverse subsidies requires effective participation and collaboration of the ministry of finance (or equivalent authority) and other ministries because it may involve a radical rethinking of standard tax policies (Grieg-Gan, Banuri, et al. 2002, p. 300).

In this last section of Part B, we have examined various strategies that can be employed to improve the financial basis of activities and strategies for sustainable development, but the discussion has been limited to concise analyses of the most important types of strategies. In the third and final part of this chapter, we will examine several innovative and promising financing strategies in more detail.

## PART C: FINANCING INNOVATIONS (NEW PROPOSALS) AND COMMENTARY

In the third part of this chapter, we turn our focus to several innovative proposals to stimulate the flows of financing for sustainable development. As was pointed out by the World Bank (WBG, UNEP, et al. 2002, p. 10), the effective procurement of finance for sustainable development is in fact a twofold challenge. The first is that of attracting a greater overall amount of capital to countries and projects (*quantity*). The second is to ensure that this capital is applied in a manner that meets sustainable development objectives (*quality*). As has become clear from our observations of accumulated evidence over the past few decades, overcoming the first challenge does not mean that overcoming the second becomes easier; in fact, there seems at times to be a trade-off between the two, especially when one observes private capital flows.

This section describes a selection of financing innovations that offer solutions to either or both of the above challenges, target either the public or the private sector, and work at various levels, varying from the international to the national to the local. The innovations chosen are not an exhaustive list; they reflect the issues that the authors consider worthy of a more detailed observation. This selectivity is necessary because the number of proposals and innovations analyzed could be expanded to become a full chapter on its own.[†]

It must be noted that the innovations are at very different stages of feasibility and implementability. Some proposals are introduced by academics or professionals working in the area of development aid and are unlikely to be implemented in the short term because substantial policy and systems changes and political will, are needed. This is especially the case with the international investment agreement discussed by von Moltke, and also with George Soros's SDR

---

\* For example, it was estimated that in Poland, the removal of energy subsidies would reduce emissions of particulates and sulfur oxides by more than 30 percent between 1989 and 1995 (WBG 1992).

† In particular, we want to mention one financing innovation that is excluded here but is worth a more detailed examination by the interested reader: the Heavily Indebted Poor Country (HIPC) initiative, which has been mentioned in this chapter on several occasions. A concise and comprehensive explanation of this initiative, launched in 1996 by the World Bank and the IMF, can be found in chapter 6 of the World Bank's report *Global Development Finance* (WBG 2003a, pp. 132–135).

proposal, although support for the latter proposal is mounting. Louis Kelso's theory of binary economics also falls under this heading. Other financing innovations are at a more advanced stage; they may have already been implemented and may now be in the process of being reformed and optimized, such as the Global Environment Facility and the concept of national environmental funds. This category also includes the various microcredit and microfinance schemes that have been set up across the globe.

In the remainder of this chapter, each of the innovations mentioned above will be discussed. First, the innovations with a predominantly global outlook will be dealt with—the SDR proposal, the international investment agreement, and the GEF. Subsequently, a more nationally oriented financing proposal will be examined—the implementation of binary economics. The concepts of microcredit and microfinance will be analyzed last because these have a predominantly local or regional focus.

## 12.8 THE SDR PROPOSAL

In his book *On Globalization*, George Soros* introduces his SDR proposal, which "could make a substantial amount money available almost immediately, to finance the provision of public goods on a global scale as well as to foster economic, social, and political progress in individual countries; it is an initiative that could point the way to a large, continuous, and predictable flow of financing for development indefinitely" (Soros 2002, p. 73).[21]

As mentioned in Part A of this chapter, special drawing rights (SDRs) were introduced by the IMF as an international reserve asset for its members; they serve as a unit of account and as a means of payment. The SDR is based on the four major currencies (euro, dollar, yen, and pound) and is an interest-bearing instrument. Soros's SDR proposal is for developed countries to donate the SDRs they are allocated by the IMF, in accordance with certain rules, for the purpose of providing international development assistance. Less developed countries would benefit from such a mechanism in two important ways:

directly, because the SDR donations would increase their monetary reserves, and indirectly, from the increases in international development aid (Soros 2002, p. 181). Moreover, because SDR allocations are roughly based on the economic strength of a country, the use of SDRs as development aid would also ensure that each country contributes its share, eliminating the possibility of free riding.

The SDR proposal would be implemented in two stages. First, a special SDR issue of SDR 21.43 billion (roughly $32 billion),[†] which was authorized by the IMF in 1997, would have to be ratified by the U.S. Congress, with the condition that the developed nations donate their SDR allocations to be used for international assistance, in accordance with certain rules and regulations. Since the largest part of the allocated SDRs would flow to the richest countries, this mechanism would make almost $18 billion available for development assistance (Soros 2002, p. 74).

Soros proposes that the developed nations would be able to donate their SDRs only to a portfolio of preapproved programs that would be established by an international advisory board of experts operating under the aegis of the IMF. This board, however, would not have any authority over spending the funds; the developed nations would retain the right to make their own selections from the portfolio of projects recommended. This mechanism ensures a marketlike interaction between donors and programs—supply and demand. In the initial stage, this portfolio would be confined to four specific priority areas: public health,[‡] education,[§] information and communication technology, and judicial reform. Also, it must be noted that government-sponsored projects would not be eligible because they can be left to the existing multilateral development banks and bilateral donor programs. An independent audit commission would supervise and evaluate the chosen programs (Soros 2002, p. 182).

---

\* George Soros, having made a fortune in international capital markets as a hedge-fund manager, now heads Soros Fund Management and is the founder of a global network of Open Society foundations. As Stiglitz explains, these foundations have had enormous influence, especially in Eastern Europe, first in supporting dissidents and then in building up post-Communist institutions such as the Central European University in Budapest. According to Stiglitz, Soros's program "has been far more successful—and far more influential—than those of most governments, including that of the US" (Stiglitz 2002a, p. 24).

† The latest value of the SDR in U.S. dollars can be obtained from the International Monetary Fund's SDR Valuation website, www.imf.org/external/np/fin/data/rms_sdrv.aspx (accessed June 3, 2010). The SDR value is obtained by summing (in U.S. dollars) a basket of major exchange rates (the U.S. dollar, the euro, the Japanese yen, and the pound sterling) and is therefore subject to change with the market exchange rates of these currencies.

‡ To the extent that some environmental concerns, such as toxic chemical exposures, are directly related to public health, these environmental projects would presumably be eligible for financing. A similar argument can be made for climate-change problems that also have public health consequences, although perhaps the linkage is more tangential.

§ Educational initiatives could be directly relevant to increasing the skill level of workers and thus contribute, through increased wages, to the alleviation of poverty.

If implementation of the initial stage of the SDR proposal were successful, the second step would be to issue SDRs annually and in a broadly similar fashion. The portfolio of eligible programs could be expanded, and a limited number of government-sponsored projects could also qualify.

The SDR donation scheme would result in several advantageous developments. First, it would increase the amount of funding available for development aid at relatively low cost to the developed countries.* Furthermore, the SDR donation scheme would reduce or overcome several of the problems of development assistance as it is currently dispensed (see Part A) (Soros 2002, pp. 183–184):

1. By establishing the portfolio of eligible projects, the independent board would ensure that the interests of the recipient countries are served; the ability of donors to use aid to satisfy their own needs would thereby be greatly reduced.

2. Through the creation of a marketplace for projects, both donors and project managers would be given a sense of ownership and responsibility.

3. The frequent occurrence of intergovernmental dealings would be reduced by reducing the power of recipient governments as gatekeepers (which is all too often the case in bilateral forms of development assistance, as was discussed in Part A).

4. Coordination between donors would be enhanced by the establishment of an international board that evaluates the potential SDR project proposals.

5. In the long run, the risks/return ratio of aid projects would also be reduced as the board learned to "pick winners" and eliminate failures.

In addition to the benefits of the donation plan, the SDR proposal would, as stated earlier, also bring direct and tangible benefits to developing countries in the form of additional monetary reserves. Because international trade is growing at roughly twice the rate of global GDP, countries need to protect themselves against shocks and high volatility by maintaining a prudent ratio between their currency reserves and imports. Less developed countries have to set aside a substantial part of their export earnings to do so; SDRs could ease that burden. Moreover, SDR allocations would reduce the cost of borrowing. Because developed countries have no urgent need for SDRs, since they have ample reserves and/or easy access to international financial markets, it would make sense for these countries to donate them.

Soros points out that the notion of "linking SDRs and aid has already been discussed off and on, including during the 1980s debt crisis" (Soros 2002, p. 88). He indicates that the SDR proposal already meets all legal requirements, and he argues that the decision "whether to use [the issuance of] SDRs for international assistance is therefore clearly a political decision. I believe the time is ripe for it" (ibid., p. 89). Since Soros published his work in 2002, the world economy has experienced its worst decline since the Great Depression. It seems, therefore, that Soros's SDR proposal may not receive the political support it needs to be implemented for some time.

## 12.9 AN INTERNATIONAL INVESTMENT AGREEMENT

The second financing proposal that we will discuss is Konrad von Moltke's (2000) plea for the construction of an international investment agreement. Von Moltke argues that an international investment agreement is vitally needed to tackle many of the problems with the global financial market (see Section 12.4) and to spur the kind of private investment that is crucial for sustainable development. It could greatly improve the trade-off between the risks and benefits of global financial integration, provided it properly accounts for the interests of the world's developing nations as well. As von Moltke (2000, p. 10) explains: "Those concerned with sustainable development have a particular interest in an investment regime. Many current economic activities, in developed and developing countries alike, are known to be unsustainable. Often, alternatives are available but they require investment. In other words, without investment sustainability is unattainable. With such an urgent need for investment, the move toward sustainability requires that scarce resources be used efficiently—and that the imperatives of sustainability are respected in the investment process."

According to von Moltke, the need for an international investment agreement for sustainable development has become all the more urgent. As observed in Section 12.4, transnational investment flows have risen dramatically: at the turn of the millennium, flows of foreign direct investment (FDI) were so large that they far outweighed total official development assistance (bilateral and multilateral). For many developing countries, this has made FDI the most important source of capital inflow, overtaking both official development assistance and the funds made available by multilateral development banks. In principle, von Moltke regards this as an encouraging

---

* When fully implemented, the SDR scheme could go a long way toward meeting the United Nations Millennium Development Goals.

trend.* But the crucial problem, as we saw in Section 12.4, is that FDI is flowing only to a few favored countries. Many of the world's poorest countries are therefore left without resources—including those that most desperately need foreign capital to follow a path of sustainable development.

This trend may run contrary to the economic theory of efficient allocation of capital, which states that other things being equal, capital should be seeking the highest returns, which should be available where capital is most urgently needed—that is, in the developing world. In other words, current capital flows are counterintuitive: the largest flows still converge on the most developed countries, whereas the world's poorest receive virtually nothing. One important reason for this is that although high returns are indeed available in developing countries, the risks are also very high, which makes investment relatively unattractive.[†] One crucial task for an international investment regime is therefore to improve *efficiency* in the allocation of capital by reducing risk and uncertainty in those countries and regions that most urgently need investment. Of course, low productivity and poor output in developing countries may not immediately render such flows economically attractive. It takes time to transform a production system.

The central importance of investment for sustainable development and the value of an international agreement on investment have in fact long been recognized. The most serious effort to reach an agreement was made during the 1990s, when the OECD attempted to develop a multilateral agreement on investment (MAI). However, as von Moltke explains, it was based on the wrong premises. It focused overly strongly on the needs and concerns of the developed world and did not open up the process to participation from NGOs and developing-country governments.[‡] As a result, the MAI negotiations failed miserably and were abandoned in 1998 (Chesky 1998; von Moltke 2000).

In spite of this disappointing failure, von Moltke argues that an international investment agreement "should be a priority for those interested in the environment and sustainable development" (von Moltke 2000, p. iii). The international community seems to be asking itself the wrong question; the important question is not *whether* we need an investment agreement, but *what kind* of investment agreement we need. Von Moltke explains that "the need to strike a balance between private (investor) interests and public goods must be at the heart of any international agreement, certainly when viewed from the perspective of sustainable development" (ibid.). The MAI negotiations did not properly account for this balance, which is why they failed, and why von Moltke argues that a new international agreement must look quite different from the MAI. In fact, it must look different from any of the existing international agreements that exist today (such as the WTO's agreements).

Von Moltke's detailed study draws important lessons from the experience in building international environmental agreements and uses these to propose a new approach for devising an international investment agreement.[§] More concretely, it proposes "a framework agreement on investment combined with a number of sectoral agreements (for example, on climate change, forestry, or the provision of services for that matter), in which it becomes possible to identify the public interest being served by providing private investors with additional rights" (von Moltke 2000, p. iii).

The ultimate goal of an international investment agreement is to ensure both *equity* and *efficiency*. *Efficiency* is currently undermined, as mentioned previously, because the world's poorer countries are perceived by investors as high risk and are therefore capable of attracting investment only for projects that offer exceptionally high rates of return. Because of this, many important projects remain unfunded, and the funds that are available are often used in ways that are not optimally efficient. In addition, as explained in Part A, a lack of clear rules also creates incentives for corruption, which again serves to reduce the return on projects and investment flows, making them even less attractive.

Issues of *equity* in turn arise because of the power asymmetries and conflicting goals of the various participants in the international investment arena. First,

---

* As von Moltke explains, "Foreign direct investment [is] being undertaken by enterprises both large and small with a wide range of concerns. The option of investing in another country has become a formal part of strategic growth plans for enterprises. Individual investors are now seeking investment opportunities outside their own currency region as a matter of course. And mutual funds make these kinds of investments available to small investors" (von Moltke 2000, p. 1).

† An additional element is *perceived* risk; in some cases, the actual investment risk of a country may in fact not be very high, but investors—for various reasons—may perceive it as being much higher than it is.

‡ According to von Moltke, the MAI had such a strong focus on investor rights that it "perpetuated a polarization of the process that consistently separated investor rights from investor obligations" (von Moltke 2000, p. iii).

§ Naturally, a complete and fair explication of von Moltke's study (2000), which is eighty-eight pages long, cannot be provided here. The interested reader is therefore advised to read chapters 2–6 of the report, which is available online at www .iisd.org/pdf/investment.pdf (accessed February 6, 2011).

as von Moltke (2000, p. 2) explains, "investors from countries that are perceived as weaker will fear for the security of their investments in foreign countries." Second, some country governments are substantially weaker than some of the major corporations that are active in the global economy and may therefore find it difficult to impose their laws and regulations on them.

Investments are mostly private transactions, aimed at generating positive rates of return for the companies and investors involved. Nevertheless, "They can have far-reaching implications for the welfare of countries, including prospects for sustainable development; use and protection of natural resources; and employment, income and economic security. It is the role of government to balance these sometimes conflicting public and private interests, by promoting investment, by creating incentives to direct investment to certain activities or regions, or by maintaining a system of taxes and fees that contribute to public-policy goals" (von Moltke 2000, pp. 2–3). Of course, time horizons for investment are a crucial factor. Initially, investments may yield small short-term returns. Larger long-term investments, normally discouraged by venture-capital markets, are what are needed to achieve transformations that are sustainable in the long run.

Discussing the more practical dimensions of an international investment agreement, von Moltke goes on to explain that it must be constructed as a *dynamic* regime to ensure "flexible yet effective" implementation and allow for amendments and additions as challenges and threats change over time. This makes his proposal fundamentally different from all other attempts to address investment at the international level that have been made thus far (such as the MAI). These proposals agreed on a *fixed* system of rules that must then be applied, much as in trade regimes, by governments and reinforced through a dispute-settlement process. According to von Moltke, "This is a fundamentally static view of the investment process and its function in economic and social policy. It makes no provision for the dynamic aspects of an investment regime, nor does it reflect the complex legal and contractual relationships between investor and host country that characterize foreign direct investment. A better approach might draw some lessons from international environmental regimes, which have faced the problem of addressing issues that evolve over time and consequently demand a dynamic international regime" (von Moltke 2000, p. 69).

The approach that has over the years become well established in environmental policy is to begin with a framework agreement that establishes basic institutions and creates an organizational structure and a pathway that should be followed to achieve certain predefined aims. Because the negotiating parties do not know what measures will ultimately be required, most international environmental agreements are quite indeterminate about the appropriate institutions that will be required. But over time, as the evidence accumulates, the framework allows for additional measures to be adopted to ensure that the regime continues to move in the desired direction.

Von Moltke is of the opinion that such a framework agreement is a much more effective approach to addressing international investment policies as well. It would not require the negotiating parties to reach a fixed agreement on the entire form and features of the investment regime—something that has proved to be virtually impossible. Instead, the parties would outline a set of goals for the investment agreement and define a process to take the necessary steps toward reaching those goals. The agreement would be dynamic and fluid, that is, capable of responding to emerging needs and changing practices in the international investment arena.

For the same reason, it seems attractive to place such an agreement outside the realm of those institutions that have attempted to build an investment regime thus far: the World Bank, the WTO, the UNCTAD, and the OECD. As mentioned before, over two decades of negotiations have not brought these organizations close to reaching an agreement. Therefore, a fully independent approach that begins with modest steps and responds flexibly to new and changing challenges offers a better chance of success. But von Moltke remains realistic. He closes his study as follows: "The goal of establishing a global investment agreement is currently out of reach. On the one hand, the institutional development of international society has not progressed to the point where such a regime could be envisaged. On the other hand, public opinion in a number of key countries is strongly against a general investment agreement, making it a politically delicate undertaking. Under these circumstances a number of more modest practical steps can help to explore the real dimensions of this enterprise. A framework convention, together with investment provisions in certain sectoral agreements, is a pragmatic way to proceed" (von Moltke 2000, p. 71).

## 12.10 THE GLOBAL ENVIRONMENT FACILITY

The third financing innovation that will be analyzed here is the Global Environment Facility (GEF).[22] The establishment of the GEF has been an important development in the evolution of financing for environmental aid. It was created in 1991 as the financial mechanism for the conventions on climate change and biodiversity and also has programs addressing land degradation, ozone depletion, and persistent organic pollutants (POPs). Since its inception in 1990, it has been one of the most important financial institutions in the area of global environmental protection: from 1991 to June 1999, the GEF committed $2.5 billion in grants to over one hundred countries (Miller 2000). However, over the course of its existence, it has been subject to fierce criticism, and its form and function remain contentious to this day.

In view of the dominant role that this organization has played in the area of global environmental policy, we have chosen to provide a detailed analysis of the GEF. We will start with a brief historical review of the creation of the GEF. Next, the proposed restructuring of the GEF in the aftermath of the UNCED, and its implications for the goals and operations of the GEF, will be examined. Last, some attention will be given to more recent developments and issues that are expected to play a role in the future development of the GEF, especially engagement of the private sector.

### 12.10.1 The Establishment of the GEF

The foundations of the Global Environment Facility were laid in the aftermath of the publication of the Brundtland report, which, as discussed earlier in this section, had initiated "intense public debate on the scope, magnitude, and institutional approach to dedicated international environmental funding" (Miller 2000, p. 1233). In 1989, it was clear that there was sufficient political support for a centralized fund dedicated to global environmental issues, especially from Europe. But a difficult question remained: where would this fund be placed? Most donors agreed that any new aid should be channeled through existing organizations, although how many and which remained unclear. Developing countries, on the other hand, were in favor of the creation of a new fund because this was a way to ensure that the aid it disbursed would be "new and additional" (Jordan 1994, p. 16).

The United States had substantial arguments against the foundation of a new fund. It finally expressed its support, but on the premise that there would be a three-year pilot phase, and that the fund would limit itself to paying the *incremental* costs of *global* environmental benefits, and only to countries that "commit to appropriate environmental policies." (As will become apparent later in the analysis,

these limitations have played an important role in making the operability of the GEF highly laborious and complex.) In view of the issues that had been put on the agenda for the UNCED that was to take place in Rio in 1992, it was agreed that climate change, biodiversity, and international water resources were to be the focal areas of the new fund.

Toward the end of the 1980s, the basic elements for the new Global Environment Facility, which would start with a three-year pilot phase, were thus in place. The GEF would fund the *incremental cost* of developing countries' activities in the areas of climate change, biodiversity, and international water management. The administration of the GEF would be housed in the World Bank, but donor countries agreed that the United Nations Development Programme (UNDP) would be engaged in issues of technical implementation and institution building. Also, the United Nations Environment Programme (UNEP) would have the task of ensuring that the GEF's activities were consistent with the mandate of the conventions on climate change and biodiversity. The GEF received approximately $1 billion in funds for its three-year pilot phase. As was to be expected from the main remit of the GEF, its projects would thus focus on environmental benefits rather than development (Grieg-Gan, Banuri, et al. 2002).

### 12.10.2 The GEF after Rio

The pilot phase of the GEF began with very high hopes that it would be able to avoid the main flaws of traditional development programs: the neglect of local NGO and community participation and an overly strong focus on short-term issues. For example, upon its establishment in 1991, a GEF policy paper announced the facility's intention to involve NGOs in the "identification, design, and implementation" of its projects (WBG 1991a, p. 12). But already during the pilot phase, significant controversy over the roles and functions of the GEF became apparent. In fact, in 1992, the GEF's own Scientific and Technical Advisory Panel reported that "projects take little consideration of the involvement of local people, their expertise and their priorities," and "NGO involvement is regarded as inadequate" (GEF 1992, appendix 1).

NGOs themselves especially criticized the role carried out by the World Bank; they argued that many of the bank's projects were in fact detrimental to the environment, and that therefore its role as the administrative center of the GEF was illegitimate (Miller 2000, p. 1235; Young and Boehmer-Christiansen

1997). Moreover, they insisted on more opportunities to participate in the decision-making process of the GEF. But developing-country governments also fiercely criticized the workings of the GEF. In fact, many developing countries proposed a wide range of alternatives to the facility in the period leading up to the UNCED. They were aiming at more new funding for environmental goals and a wider scope of activities, but especially at greater political control over the environmental policy agenda than they had been given in the GEF.*

However, during the extensive discussions of the implementation of Agenda 21, it quickly became apparent that despite the various promises for more aid that had been made at the UNCED (see also above), the GEF was in effect the only real source of new funding for environmental aid. The G77 group of developing countries therefore had little choice but grudgingly to accept the GEF, but it did so on the condition that an independent evaluation of the facility's operations would be carried out and that the GEF would subsequently be restructured in line with the recommendations of this independent evaluation of the pilot phase (Young and Boehmer-Christiansen 1997, p. 195).

This evaluation came up with a number of substantial points of criticism.[†] For starters, it states that "the shaping of projects, where local participation and cooperation are essential to successful outcomes, has been particularly problematic during the pilot phase" (GEF 1994, p. 12). It therefore argued that the GEF must become much more "democratic," which practically meant that the finance and environment ministries of the G77 countries were to be given more control over its operations than had been the case until then. Also, the GEF's activities would have to become more "transparent," with documents made available to the public in several languages (Young and Boehmer-Christiansen 1997, p. 196). Third, the evaluation was highly critical of the GEF's lack of an overarching strategy and recommended that strate-

gies and programs be developed before the expenditure of new funds (Sjöberg 1999, cited in Miller 2000).[‡]

These issues were taken into consideration in the GEF's restructuring process that had been agreed on, which was carried out between December 1992 and March 1994. After sixteen months of continuous negotiation, a political compromise was reached. The restructured GEF that emerged was distinctly different in various respects. For example, although the roles of the World Bank, the UNEP, and the UNDP were preserved, formal governance of the GEF was placed in a council of thirty-two countries, which was asked to meet periodically in a so-called Participants' Assembly.[§] Day-to-day administrative functions were to be overseen by a CEO and a small secretariat—independent, but still housed in the World Bank.

After a subsequent difficult round of financial negotiations, a total of $2 billion in funds was secured for the second three-year period of the GEF. With other aid budgets shrinking (see Part A), the GEF had now become the biggest source of aid specifically directed toward the global environment (Young and Boehmer-Christiansen 1997, p. 193). The World Bank, the UNEP, and the UNDP, defined as the three implementing agencies of the GEF, were able to propose and design "country-driven" projects, which could then be carried out by virtually anyone. But, as Young and Boehmer-Christiansen (1997) explain, program and project selection was not purely a GEF task; the Conference of the Parties to the Climate Change (UNFCC) and Biodiversity (CBD) Conventions as well as the Montreal Protocol were to review the potential eligibility of projects and programs too.[¶] Furthermore, it was decided that all projects would have to be endorsed by the recipient countries (Miller 2000). Understandably, because of this wide range of structural changes, the objectives, governance, and operations of the new GEF had grown much more complex than they had been during the pilot phase (Young and Boehmer-Christiansen 1997, p. 193). Indeed, these aspects have been the

---

* As explained in Part A, the World Bank basically uses a system of "one dollar for one vote," as a result of which donor countries dominate agenda setting.

† However, it must also be acknowledged, as is stressed in the independent evaluation, that the GEF has from the outset played a leading role in the formation of partnerships with national environmental funds (NEFs; see Part B). As is explained by Danish (1995, p. 168), although "the Facility was a hesitant participant in the first national environmental fund in Bhutan, its staff now seems strongly committed to making such funds viable and effective mechanisms."

‡ This approach has since been adopted, but we will see below that it has proved to have drawbacks of its own because it makes project evaluations extremely laborious and slow.

§ This governing council is made up of representatives from fourteen donor "constituencies," with the largest contributors each having their own member; sixteen recipient constituencies; and two representatives of so-called transition countries (see Young and Boehmer-Christiansen 1997).

¶ In 2011, the GEF also served as the financial mechanism for the Stockholm Convention on Persistent Organic Pollutants (POPs) and the UN Convention to Combat Desertification (UNCCD).

root cause of many points of debate and criticism involving the GEF.[23]

As stated earlier, the GEF bases its contribution to projects on the "agreed *incremental* cost" that developing countries incur by providing *global* environmental benefits. This incremental-cost principle sounds simple in theory but has proved extremely difficult to apply in practice; it is virtually impossible to separate the local from the global benefits of a project or program and to subtract the former from the latter to identify the incremental costs (Young and Boehmer-Christiansen 1997, p. 197). This is where the emphasis on "agreed" comes from in the official formulation (Grieg-Gan, Banuri, et al. 2002, p. 294). The basic approach that the GEF has adopted is to distinguish between projects and programs that provide global benefits and those that are in the national interest of the recipient country, as defined by a national sustainable development *baseline*. It finances only the former.*

In part because of this need to establish the incremental costs of every potential funding activity, GEF projects have significant transaction costs—projects can take anywhere between nine months and four years to prepare. It has been hypothesized that this is one of the main reasons that the GEF has been so slow to disburse its funds, and also that engagement of the private sector has proved much more complicated than anticipated (Young and Boehmer-Christiansen 1997).

## 12.10.3 Recent Developments and Future Prospects

During the negotiations for a restructured GEF, it became apparent that the amount of funding available to the facility was very limited in relation to the range and magnitude of the problems it was meant to address. At the same time, private capital flows—especially FDI—emerged quickly as a critical factor in development. As a result, it was realized that the GEF would have to strive to leverage private-sector funding and "create conditions for markets to work without continued subsidy" if the GEF was to have a meaningful impact on the global environment (Miller 2000, p. 1237).

However, when a second independent review was carried out to evaluate the GEF's overall performance in 1997, before the second replenishment of the GEF, this review indicated that the facility's efforts to engage the private sector in global environmental projects had not been highly effective. Private investment in GEF projects had been only modest, and many country governments could not, or did not want to, involve the private sector in their activities. After examining the potential causes of this disappointing result, the report stated that "major barriers to increasing support from the private sector exist, particularly GEF's long and complex approval procedure and the comparatively greater risk of global environmental projects compared with normal commercial projects" (Porter, Clémençon, et al. 1998, cited in Miller 2000, p. 1239).

In May 1999, in response to the outcome of the overall performance study, the GEF approved a report that made some specific proposals to stimulate further private-sector engagement. The report highlighted three primary challenges: building awareness of the GEF in the business community; simplifying and shortening project cycles; and providing support directed more specifically toward the needs of the private sector (GEF 1999).[†] Miller (2000, p. 1240) furthermore indicates that more should be done to engage the private sector within the recipient developing countries because these local businesses play a crucial role in enabling projects to become self-sustainable after GEF financing is terminated.

The above-mentioned problems of the GEF, especially those with regard to the length and complexity of its project cycles, have long been recognized, and numerous steps have been taken in recent years in order to accelerate and simplify the process.[‡] In short, the GEF has been actively striving for further private-sector involvement in its activities, both at the level of project implementation and of strategy,

---

* If there is a gap between a county's current state and its national sustainable development baseline, it will not be able to bridge this gap using GEF funding, because the activities needed to do so are not considered incremental. The GEF takes the baseline as the zero point (Grieg-Gan, Banuri, et al. 2002, p. 294).

† Environmentally oriented businesses have in fact long been aware of the GEF and its potential, as was highlighted by the executive director of the Business Council for Sustainable Development (BCSD) back in 1994. However, thus far the scale of GEF financing has appeared to be too modest, and its various roles and goals too complicated, to justify a high level of private-sector interest (Miller 2000, p. 1240).

‡ For example, project development funds (known as PDFs) have been made available that include $25,000, $350,000, and $750,000 for PDFa, b, c project preparation grants, respectively. In addition, simplified approval procedures have been established. GEF procedures have also been aligned more closely with those of implementing agencies, and administrative steps have been eliminated wherever possible (Miller 2000; Porter, Clémençon, et al. 1998).

by using "contingent finance mechanisms," which aim to reduce investment risk (for example, for new technologies) while maintaining performance incentives for the private sector. In theory, this would not only increase the effectiveness of GEF fund use but also leverage private capital in high-risk markets and reduce the need for public subsidies in the long run (Grieg-Gan, Banuri, et al. 2002).

Last, it deserves to be mentioned that the GEF council has over the past few years been moving toward a more programmatic approach—that is, providing larger support, on more flexible terms, and over a longer time horizon, for which, in return, the recipient country becomes more closely engaged as a partner. This programmatic approach was introduced in the late 1990s, after a body of research by the World Bank and others had shown that a favorable policy environment greatly improved aid effectiveness.* Although results have thus far been modest and mixed, the theoretical underpinnings of the trend toward a more programmatic project approach suggest that it is more likely to lead to successful results: it allows for better engagement of recipient-country governments in the dialogue regarding the necessary changes in policy environment that are needed to attract private capital flows (Miller 2000).

In sum, since its inception as a pilot facility closely linked to the World Bank in 1991, the GEF has adapted and innovated substantially in response to waves of criticism and feedback, both from within and from outside. It was obvious from the outset that the GEF would be able to play only a facilitative and catalytic role in global environmental protection because its resources are not nearly sufficient to tackle the wide range of issues it is intended to address. In a new approach to solving this dilemma, the GEF has in recent years increasingly sought to engage the private sector in its struggle to protect the global environment (Miller 2000). However, a crucial dilemma that the GEF continues to face in all its activities is that it must reassure the industrialized world in order to secure and retain its funds and credibility

while at the same time ensuring that it does not completely lose the confidence of the developing world, whose approval of and participation in its activities is essential for success (Redclift 1996).

In spite of the various attempts to improve the GEF that have been made over the past decade—some successful, some less so—the rather pessimistic conclusion reached by Young and Boehmer-Christiansen (1997, p. 200) therefore unfortunately still seems valid: "In trying to deal with all demands made on it, the GEF's evolving organizational structure and role cannot but become more 'bureaucratic,' but this seems to widen the gap between public accountability and what business would like to see. The well-intentioned rhetoric of global environmental agreements: *capacity-building*, *participation*, *global environmental benefit* and, of course, *sustainable development* need to be given precise meanings in a highly political environment in which discretion is sought by some as much as others are trying to limit it."

In other words, what was stated for the field of environmental policy as a whole remains largely valid for this specific case as well: environmental funds such as the GEF can make a difference in tackling global environmental problems, but only if all major stakeholders involved are truly willing to strive to resolve their conflicts and differences and to agree to more precise, practical, and meaningful definitions of the focal problem areas, as well as the means to strive to resolve them.

In the last two subsections of Part C, we address shifts away from the focus on finance based on neoclassical economics and macroeconomics by examining binary economics and microfinance.

## 12.11 BINARY ECONOMICS†

Binary economics (also called two-factor economics and the theory of universal capitalism) is a relatively new economic theory that considers the independent productiveness of capital and the distribution of capital ownership, rather than the quantity of capital or the productivity of labor, as the central factors of economic growth (R. Ashford 2010a). The founda-

---

\* This observation was made in the 1998 World Bank report *Assessing Aid: What Works, What Doesn't, and Why?* and has been discussed extensively in Part A of this chapter. The report cites studies that show that "with sound country management, 1 percent of GDP in assistance translates into a 1 percent decline in poverty and a similar decline in infant mortality" (WBG 1998, p. 2; for more detailed information, see the references in Part A to the work of World Bank economists Collier and Dollar). A similar synergy was found between sound policies and private investment; in a good policy environment, one dollar in aid was shown to bring in roughly two dollars in private funds (WBG 1998, p. 3).

† The discussion of binary economics provided here is authored by Robert Ashford and is based on three of his essays (R. Ashford 1998, 2003, 2010a), as well as a book by R. Ashford and Shakespeare (1999). The first two references are recommended to the interested reader. Also, see Gauche (2000, p. 445), who applies the principles of binary economics to the privatization of public assets in a way that "promotes economic growth and improved standards of living." For a binary economic analysis of the classical economic perspective of Milton Friedman, see R. Ashford (2010b).

tions of the theory were first introduced by Louis Kelso (founder of the employee stock ownership plan [ESOP]) and Mortimer Adler in 1958.* Robert Ashford describes binary economics as a distinct paradigm for understanding market economics. Moreover, according to Ashford, the binary paradigm provides a theoretical foundation for structuring a private-property system that will tend more to broaden rather than concentrate capital ownership and thereby produce greater and more broadly shared prosperity and enhanced levels of sustainable growth (R. Ashford 1998, p. 26).

### 12.11.1 The Theoretical Fundamentals of Binary Economics

Binary economics can be distinguished from conventional economic theory through three fundamental and related assumptions:

1. Labor and capital† are *independently productive*.

2. Technological innovation makes capital much more productive than labor.

3. Capital has a strong, positive *distributive* relationship to growth, such that the more broadly capital is acquired, the more its productiveness increases output.

Binary economics derives its name from the premise that labor and capital are independent (or binary) factors of production. According to the binary view of production, although labor and capital may cooperate (just as people may cooperate) to do work, each factor (the human and the nonhuman) does its own work, has its own productive capacity, and demonstrates its own independent productiveness (R. Ashford 1998; 2003, p. 7). The special meaning of "independent productiveness" and the uniqueness of these premises will become clear upon closer examination of each.

The first crucial assumption underlying the theory of binary economics (the idea that capital and

labor are *independently productive*) implies that capital contributes to production and growth in a way that is *independent* of labor productivity, including the labor input necessary to employ it. This assumption is fundamentally different from the conventional view, based on Adam Smith's paradigm for growth, which assumes that capital has only an indirect effect on growth, that is, by making labor more productive and enabling the employment of more workers (R. Ashford 1998, 2003).

The binary approach is also fundamentally different from the approach of John Maynard Keynes, who in his *General Theory of Employment, Interest, and Money* distilled the operation of the macroeconomy to three fundamental variables: time, money, and labor, with labor being the only "productive" variable, and with capital being a dependent variable. In the binary approach, labor and capital are equally fundamental, independent (or binary) variables, and the productiveness, productivity, and earning capacity of capital cannot be expressed merely as a function of the productivity of labor (R. Ashford 2003, p. 5).

To comprehend fully this delicate but fundamental difference in outlook, the difference between productivity and productiveness should be well understood. *Productivity* is the ratio of the output of all factors of production divided by the input of one factor (usually labor). *Productiveness*, on the other hand, can be understood retrospectively to mean work done by each factor, and prospectively to mean productive capacity (R. Ashford 1998, p. 29; 2003, p. 8).

Let us illustrate the meaning of productiveness and its relationship to productivity by means of examples used by Robert Ashford (1996, p. 10): "Assume that in a pre-tool age, a person could dig a hole in four hours by hand. After the invention of a shovel, she can dig the same hole in one hour. In traditional economic terms, she has four times the productivity because she can perform four times as much work in the same time period. In binary economic terms, the productiveness has changed from 100% labor before the invention of the shovel, to 25% labor and 75% capital after the employment of the shovel. In terms of producing the hole, the worker contributes only one-fourth as much productive input, so her labor productiveness per hole has been reduced to only one-fourth of its former value. Seventy-five percent of the worker's former productiveness has been replaced by an equal amount of capital productiveness."

The concept of "independent factor productiveness" (that is, the concept that labor and capital are, in an important sense, *independently* productive) is perhaps more clearly revealed by the work of hauling

---

* The ESOP is the best-known practical binary economic mechanism for broadening capital ownership. It was first implemented in the United States by corporate finance attorney, investment banker, and philosopher Louis Kelso in 1956, with a company known as Peninsula Newspapers in Palo Alto, California. Since then, the ESOP has grown into one of the most widely used methods for broadening capital ownership in the United States (NCEO 1996, cited in Gauche 2000).

† As used in this theory, capital is land, animals, structures, machines, and intangibles protected as property—i.e., anything capable of being owned and producing income. It does not include financial capital or money, which are claims or bids on capital.

sacks: (1) a person can haul one sack one mile in one hour and is exhausted; (2) with a horse, five sacks can be hauled four times as far (yielding a 20-fold increase in output); and (3) with a truck, five hundred sacks can be hauled forty times as far (yielding a 20,000-fold increase in output).

In the above examples, binary economics interprets the gains in output to be primarily the result of the increased capital productiveness (achieved by the employment of capital as an independent factor in the production process). In contrast, conventional market economic theory, largely based on the works of Adam Smith, explains the increased output as a function of increased *human* productivity. It interprets the role of capital as merely facilitative; the introduction of capital increases human productivity, thereby allowing for a rise in output and the employment of more labor.

However, according to binary economics, once capital is understood to be independently productive, then it can be understood to have six powers important to production and growth. Specifically, capital can

1. replace labor (doing what was formerly done by labor);

2. vastly supplement the work of labor by employing capital to do much more of the kind of work that humans can do (such as the greatly increased hauling that can be done employing horses or trucks);

3. do work that labor can never do (for example, elevators lift tons hundreds of feet in the air; airplanes fly; scientific instruments unleash forces that create computer chips that cannot be made by hand; fruit trees make fruit, while all farmers can do is assist in the process);

4. work without labor (as in the case of washing machines, automated machines, robots, and wild fruit-bearing trees);

5. pay for itself out of its future earnings (the basic rule of business investment); and

6. distribute the income necessary to purchase its output (the logic of double-entry bookkeeping and an expression of Say's law of markets).

The first four powers concern what might be considered the "real economy" powers of capital; the last two are powers that are most clearly revealed in a private-property, market economy with a stable credit system protected by a reliable legal system. The real economy powers are most relevant to the present discussion. The last two powers will be considered in the discussion of binary growth and in Section 12.11.2, which focuses on implementing bi-

nary economics. Each of these ways of contributing to growth (including mere labor replacement, which produces the same output as before, plus leisure), is significant, but only the first directly involves the substitution of capital for labor (marginal or otherwise). Thus although some economists and policy advocates use marginal efficiency theory as the foundation of a general theory of growth, the capital/labor substitution process is only one component of growth (operating *after* the creation of greatly increased productive capacity), and its wealth-enhancing contribution to efficient pricing and resource allocation is severely limited so long as the distribution of capital acquisition remains narrow (R. Ashford 2003, pp. 10–11; R. Ashford and Shakespeare 1999, pp. 146–147).

Binary economists believe that in contributing to economic growth, capital inputs (such as the shovel, horse, truck, airplane, washing machine, and computer chip) do much more than increase the productivity of the humans who employ them; they argue that in fact these capital inputs are doing most of the extra work. As Ashford explains, when analyzing how production and productive capacity have changed since 1776, binary economists maintain that the experienced increase in production (or growth) is in fact *primarily* the result of increasing capital productiveness rather than increasing labor productivity. From a binary perspective, the economic imperative is generally to produce more with more productive capital and less labor. In other words, binary economics assumes not only that capital is productive independent of the labor input, but also that *most* economic growth occurs as a result of increasing capital productiveness rather than increasing labor productivity. This also explains the foundation of the second premise: technological innovation makes capital much more productive than labor; the greatest impact of technology is not to increase labor productivity, but rather to make capital increasingly the more productive (and important) factor of production. Although capital may be seen to concentrate higher productivity into fewer workers, as the general rule in the aggregate, the primary effect of technological advance is to replace and vastly supplement the productiveness of labor with ever-greater capital productiveness.

R. Ashford (1998) has illustrated this binary view of the labor-capital relation to growth very effectively by means of two graphs that show the trend in economic growth over time, plotted against technological innovation. Figure 12.16 depicts the conventional view, in which both labor and capital productivity increase steadily over time, so that the ratio of labor

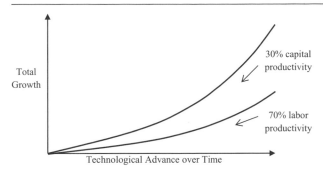

**FIGURE 12.16: ECONOMIC GROWTH—THE CONVENTIONAL VIEW OF THE LABOR-CAPITAL RELATIONSHIP**
Source: R. Ashford (1998, p. 35).

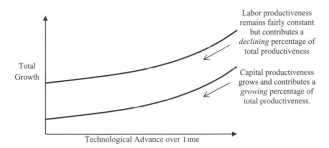

**FIGURE 12.17: ECONOMIC GROWTH — THE BINARY VIEW OF THE LABOR-CAPITAL RELATIONSHIP**
Source: R. Ashford (1998, p. 35).

to capital remains fairly constant.* Figure 12.17 shows the binary economists' view, in which labor productiveness stays roughly constant, while capital productiveness increases significantly.†

---

\* Figures 12.16 and 12.17 depict two different views of production (i.e., work done versus "productiveness"). In conventional terms, productiveness is the product of productivity (a ratio) times units of whatever is in the denominator. Figure 12.16 starts at zero because conventional economic theory considers all production and growth to be the result of human productivity, so whenever one considers humans to have begun to exist, the output per unit of human input is some quantity divided by zero (which is, of course, undefined). In contrast, binary economics recognizes that much production is the result of the nonhuman factor of production (i.e., everything that is produced beyond human work), so that whenever humans' existence is considered to have begun, there was already considerable nonhuman production.

† In truly competitive markets, therefore, the capital share of the total income of an economy would rise steadily relative to the labor share. However, available data in the United States consistently reveal that the labor share of total income is approximately 70 percent of total income; and for this reason, some economists have dismissed binary economics as contrary to fact. But this dismissal assumes that existing markets are efficiently pricing the true earning capacity of capital and labor, which runs contrary to the prevailing view among economists. In reality, every major producing nation protects its markets for labor and capital. Reliable statistics reveal that in the United States, almost all new capital is acquired with the earnings of capital, and very little is acquired with the earnings of labor. At the same time, the vast majority of people own little or no capital

Binary economists' fundamentally different view of economic growth has profound implications for how they think about the way in which people can most efficiently participate and share in this growth. Conventional economists assume that the gains for most people must come in the form of more jobs and higher wages, lower prices for goods and services, and welfare redistribution—all functions of productivity. Binary economists, on the other hand, see far greater potential for most people by way of participation in the acquisition of capital. If the effect of technological innovation is to displace and reduce the importance of labor in production while increasing the importance of capital, they argue, then we need practical mechanisms that enable all people to acquire a share of this growing capital productiveness (R. Ashford 1998, p. 34). More particularly, like people who are already well capitalized, every individual needs to be enabled to acquire capital, not merely with the earnings of labor, but also increasingly with the earnings of capital. As will be explained

---

and are thus presently excluded from the process by which capital is acquired with the earnings of capital. From a binary perspective, the market pricing of capital and labor cannot be efficient as long as most people are effectively excluded from market participation in the increased productiveness of capital. According to R. Ashford (1998, pp. 36–37), "From a binary perspective, the basic condition for market efficiency (no substantial barriers to entry) is not met in any so-called free market economy anywhere in the world because most people do not have competitive market rights to acquire capital. If those markets were efficient, then with the increase in capital productiveness that marked the industrial revolution, and continues to characterize developing high technology economies, an increasing percentage of the income derived from production would be paid for the increasing productiveness of capital while a decreasing percentage would be paid for the relatively decreasing productiveness of labor. As capital productiveness replaces labor productiveness and greatly adds to total productiveness, it may be seen to concentrate higher human productivity for doing certain tasks into relatively fewer workers while creating new productive work for others. Thus, wages might indeed increase for specified skills; more jobs may be created; and average wages (i.e., of those still working) might also rise; but in efficient markets, aggregate labor earnings will decrease as a percentage of total earnings as capital productiveness replaces labor productiveness and greatly adds to total productiveness. [Overall, employment and average wages may well go down.] Within the primary restraint imposed by productiveness, negotiations and compromises based on considerations of productivity, self-interest, equity, and politics will determine the relative compensation of capital and labor.... This decreasing labor share of total income is at the root of the social need for massive redistribution programs that have paradoxically grown in tandem with the industrialization that spawned the vast increase in the ability to produce. Because capital productiveness has the effect of concentrating productivity into relatively fewer workers per unit of output, participation by way of productivity alone leaves increasing numbers of people with lower paying jobs and welfare dependence." This effect of the redistribution of capital income to nonowners is illustrated in figure 38 of R. Ashford (1998).

below, R. Ashford and Shakespeare have advanced a system that is intended to do exactly that.

But before turning to more practical concerns, let us examine the third premise underlying the paradigm of binary economics, which states that capital has not only a productive but also an independent (and very potent) *distributive* relationship to growth.

Because capital is independently productive, it works on both sides of the production-consumption economic equation by providing vastly increased

1.  productive capacity and production and

2.  capacity to distribute income and leisure.

According to binary economists, in a private-property, market economy, it is the capacity of capital both to do much more work and to distribute much more income and leisure that explains how the distribution of its ownership has a positive impact on the employment of unutilized capacity, capital accumulation, and growth.

In this regard, consider the fifth and sixth powers of capital set forth above: capital can

5.  pay for itself out of its future earnings (the basic rule of business investment) and

6.  distribute the income necessary to purchase its output.

A broader distribution of capital acquisition, ownership, and income strengthens the promise of capital to pay for itself out of its future earnings and makes profitable the employment of more (and increasingly more productive) capital.

R. Ashford (2003, p. 6) elaborates on this point in more practical terms:

> In an economy operating at less than full capacity, a voluntary pattern of steadily broadening ownership promises more production-based consumer demand in future years and therefore more demand for capital goods in earlier years. For example, within a period of perhaps five to fourteen years, if members of the poor and middle classes are enabled to compete with existing owners for the acquisition of corporate shares representing the capital requirements of companies worthy of prime credit, these poor and middle-class people would bring to the corporate finance bargaining table a chip not possessed by existing owners: a pent up appetite for more of the necessities and simple luxuries of life that richer people enjoy. After the capital has paid for itself (repaid its acquisition debt obligations) the earnings of capital acquired by members of the poor and middle class, if paid to them, will distribute more consumer demand than if that capital had been acquired by the wealthy. Had that capital been acquired by existing owners, its income would have been courted for additional investment, but

in the context of less consumer demand. In an economy operating at less than full capacity, compared to the investment opportunities that would have existed without the availability of ownership-broadening market mechanisms, the broader market distribution of capital and income generated in a binary economy will create greater investment opportunities for existing owners as well as for the new binary owners.

The resultant binary growth is not caused by increased human productivity, capital deepening, or accelerated technological advance. It is specifically the result of the broader distribution of ownership. This distribution-based relationship to growth is not revealed by conventional classical and neoclassical analysis, which assumes that the productive input and value of capital are functions of labor productivity. Likewise, Keynesian analysis (which reduces the operation of the economy to time, money, and labor) cannot yield a conclusion that resource allocation and growth are independent functions of the productiveness of capital and the distribution of its ownership.

This premise is in fact based on another assumption, namely, that the typically wealthy capital owners have a lower marginal propensity to consume than the laboring poor. If this is the case, as binary economists believe, then a broader distribution of capital ownership would produce greater consumer spending and therefore growth. "Binary growth is a distribution-based growth that is presently impeded by the prevailing pattern of concentrated capital acquisition. Thus the binary paradigm reveals a potent distributive relationship between capital ownership and economic growth, a growth which is not comprehended by conventional economics and which is suppressed by conventional economic practices and institutions" (R. Ashford and Shakespeare 1999, p. xi).

### 12.11.1.1 Implications of Underutilized Productive Capacity

Implicit in the idea that the distribution of capital ownership has a positive relationship to growth is the idea that persistent unutilized productive capacity is a consequence of persistent concentration of capital ownership. According to binary analysis, a major reason that many prime creditworthy companies do not produce more is not that they cannot produce more at declining unit costs, but rather that normal people (that is, potential consumers) do not have access to the future earning potential of capital. This would apply not only to consumer goods but also to producer goods, so that within existing unutilized productive capacity, there is the capacity to create even more unutilized productive capacity. Thus from a binary perspective, the persistence of unutilized productive capacity and suboptimal growth are both consequences of concentrated ownership.

Mainstream economics divides into different schools on the existence, extent, and significance of unutilized productive capacity and what to do about it. In the world of perfect neoclassical efficiency, unutilized capacity (beyond need for peaks in market demand and insurance for emergencies beyond the predictable) is an anomaly that should not persist for long. Unproductive assets should be sold, even at salvage if necessary. Even before they become partially or totally unutilized, assets not earning competitive returns for their owners should be sold to those whose rate of return can be enhanced by the acquisition.

Moreover, according to neoclassical economics, as markets become more competitive, unutilized productive capacity should decrease, not increase. But to most observers, these conclusions are belied by experience. Major companies today boast that they are ready to feed, clothe, and shelter the world if there were only sufficient income to buy what can be readily produced. However true this boast was in the year 2000, it was less true in 1900 and still less true in 1800. Driven by a political ideology that confuses a neoclassical theory of marginal efficiency with an unnamed (but essentially neoclassical) macroeconomic theory of growth, so-called free-market reforms have been initiated on the national and international level, supposedly to make markets more competitive. Nevertheless, as markets have globalized and supposedly become more competitive, unutilized productive capacity of the world's major corporation has seemingly, in the eyes of many people, paradoxically increased rather than decreased. The neoclassical generic solution of simply deregulating markets without regard for remaining, embedded institutional advantages that enrich some while excluding others is therefore suspect in this context.

According to Keynesian analysis, there is indeed persistent unutilized productive capacity that belies the neoclassical assumptions of near-perfect efficiency: untapped growth potential, unutilized productive capacity, and underemployment of labor and capital persist despite classical and neoclassical economic theory to the contrary. Markets are far from perfectly competitive, and their operation results in a persistent shortfall in "effective demand." The result is an endemic underutilization of people and resources that can be at least partially corrected by government action. But in addressing unutilized productive capacity, the Keynesian analysis attaches no special significance to the distribution of capital ownership and makes no fundamental distinction between the distribution and redistribution of income and capital.*

Increasing unutilized productive capacity may well explain the driving force of the United States, Japan, and some other Northern economies to increase trade in expectation of capturing new consumers. In contrast, the European Union is actualizing "deglobalizing" as it seeks to integrate its internal market (Kleinknecht and ter Wengel 1998), and in its domestic policy design the EU concerns itself with broadening purchasing power and thus distributional and social equity. From a policy choice perspective, broadening capital ownership by democratizing access to credit presents an alternative pathway to increasing trade for decreasing unutilized capacity and reduces the imperative for increasing trade.

### 12.11.2 Implementing Binary Economics

According to Robert Ashford, the logic underlying the principle of binary growth can be understood and implemented by considering the three thousand largest corporations in the United States, which presently own over 90 percent of investable assets in the United States. Many, if not most, of these corporations exhibit the frustrating essence of unutilized productive capacity. At diminishing unit costs, they can produce much more of the goods and services people dearly need and want; but consumer spending power is lacking to render more production profitable even at greatly diminishing unit costs. If broader ownership will promote substantial growth, as binary economics contends, these corporations may have a commonly shared incentive to broaden their ownership.

Presently the ownership of this corporate wealth is highly concentrated so that approximately 1 percent

---

\* Nevertheless, although the economics of Adam Smith, Alfred Marshall, and J. M. Keynes differ in many respects, they agree on one proposition. They all implicitly or explicitly assume that the persistence of unutilized capacity has no fundamental relationship to the distribution of capital ownership (as distinguished from the distribution or redistribution of income) unless it somehow affects labor productivity. Moreover, although classical, neoclassical, and Keynesian strategies remain a central element in the workings of every major economy, unutilized productive capacity persists and is seemingly growing in the United States and most industrial economies (although we are simultaneously being told that the relevant markets are becoming more competitive). The third basic assumption of binary economics (the principle of binary growth) in effect suspends the unproven assumption of conventional economic theory that the distribution of capital has no fundamental positive relation to the persistence of unutilized productive capacity and the promotion of growth.

of people own 50 percent of this corporate wealth and 10 percent own 90 percent of this corporate wealth, leaving 90 percent of people owning little or none (Wolff 1995a, 1995b). Also through these corporations, almost all new capital is acquired with the earnings of capital, and much of it is acquired with borrowed money (Brealey and Myers 1984; Stout 1988). Thus capital returns its value at a rate reflective of its long-term (suppressed) earning capacity as it buys itself for a small minority of the population. The shortfall in effective demand that other economists see as a deficiency in productivity, wages, redistribution, and/or other government policies is seen by binary economists as a consequence of the concentration of capital acquisition.

Through the existing system of corporate finance, to acquire capital with the earnings of capital, well-capitalized people and corporations use (1) the pre-tax earnings of capital, (2) collateral, (3) credit, (4) market and insurance mechanisms to diversify and reduce risk, and (5) a monetary policy intended to protect private property.

Ashford argues that the same institutions and practices that work profitably for well-capitalized people and corporations can also work profitably for all people. The binary strategy makes this possible by extending to all people the logic of corporate finance, which enables prime creditworthy corporations to thrive while their owners generally prosper in relation to their participation (R. Ashford 1998, p. 43). The logic behind this goes as follows: "In an economy operating at less than full capacity, if capital can competitively pay for its acquisition costs out of its future earnings primarily for existing owners, it can do so even more profitably if all people are included in the acquisition process. Accordingly, to enable all people and major, prime-credit-worthy corporations to capitalize on the potent distributive relationship between voluntary ownership-broadening capital acquisition and growth, a binary economy requires only modest reforms to open the market infrastructure governing corporate finance so that all people (not merely a minority of the people) are vested with competitive capital acquisition rights to acquire capital with the earnings of capital" (R. Ashford 2003, p. 15).

A schematic overview of the binary economy, applied to the United States, is shown in Figure 12.18. The diagram represents both a single binary financing transaction and an aggregate of all binary financing transactions within an economy. It illustrates the basic institutions needed to extend to all people a competitive right to acquire capital with the earnings of capital.

Figure 12.18 shows that there are six basic categories of institutions that play a role in the operation of a binary economy:

1. Corporations
2. Constituency trusts
3. Commercial lenders (banks)
4. Private commercial capital credit insurers
5. Government capital credit reinsurers
6. The central bank

In a binary economy, in addition to the conventional closed means of corporate financing (retained earnings, corporate borrowing, and sale of shares to owners), creditworthy corporations could raise the funds to finance their capital acquisition by selling special full-dividend common shares to a constituency trust. This trust represents various groups that lack access to substantial capital acquisition (such as employees, customers, and others). The shares would be paid for with a bank loan to the trust, which is insured by a private capital credit insurer and perhaps a government reinsurer and discounted (at a rate of 99.75 percent) by the central bank. R. Ashford (2003, p. 16) explains that "once the capital acquisition loan repayment obligations are met, the full net capital earnings (net of reserves for depreciation, research and development) would be paid to the binary owners to help enable them to meet their needs and wants and to provide the basis for increased investment and production." (See Figure 12.18.)*

To cover its administrative costs of monetizing, the central bank will set a discount rate, estimated to be 0.25 percent. At this rate, the lending bank receives $99.75 for each $100 loaned to a constituency trust, which is then available for additional lending. This enables banks to increase their loan volume without the need for additional deposits or equity investment from their stockholders. Moreover, the banks are wholly insured for binary lending loss. Therefore, the bank should earn no more than the conventional "bankers' spread" for its provided service, allowing financial costs to be kept low. Ashford has estimated

---

\* For a more detailed discussion of the general binary theory, see R. Ashford (1998, pp. 44–51) or R. Ashford and Shakespeare (1999). It is beyond the scope of this analysis to explain the complete details of this voluntary system of broadening capital ownership. The aim here is to point out that binary economics offers a fundamentally new and different view of economic growth, as well as a practical means to democratize capital ownership.

## General Theory Diagram

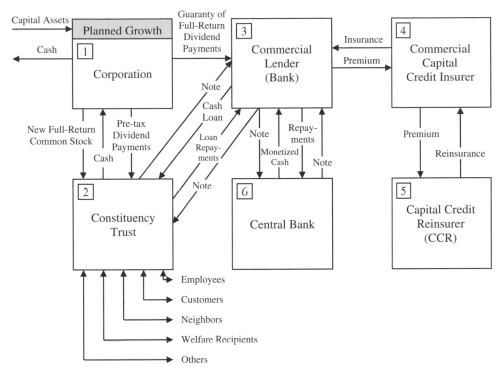

**FIGURE 12.18: THE MODEL OF BINARY ECONOMICS**
Source: R. Ashford (2010a, p. 95).

the total cost of binary financing to be around 3.25 to 4.25 percent, but he argues that even a doubling of this number would provide a competitive interest rate in many cases (R. Ashford 2003, p. 17).

If the techniques presently used to enable existing owners to acquire capital with the earnings of capital were opened competitively to all people, then, in an economy with underutilized productive capacity, the demand for investment in capital and labor would increase as its income was increasingly distributed to would-be consumers with unsatisfied needs and wants. The binary growth potential in this situation can be understood as a manifestation of the law of supply and demand within a "binary time frame"—the time expected for well-managed capital to pay for its acquisition costs (a period usually no longer than five to seven years) and then to begin earning a net income for its owners. This is a period in which capital investment is variable rather than fixed. Demand for capital goods is derivative of anticipated demand for consumer goods in a future period. The broader pattern of capital acquisition in a binary economy will structure more production-based consumer demand in the future period and therefore will provide market incentive for more capital investment in the earlier period. Admittedly, there would

be a gestation period (a period somewhat shorter than the capital-cost-recovery period, and determined by the horizon for capital investment planning) before the distributional growth effects would become noticeable; but as will be explained, their cumulative effect over time may be remarkably significant.

Binary economists argue that the distributive effect of the broader ownership of capital will lead to a steady "binary growth" of the economy. This "distributive growth-sustaining characteristic" of a binary economy is represented graphically in Figure 12.19.

For simplicity, Figure 12.19 assumes a seven-year cost-recovery period for capital investment, and it shows the number of years of annual acquisitions that will have paid for themselves over time. The figure assumes that in every year after the implementation of the binary economy, some number ($N$) of an economy's largest prime creditworthy companies have profitably utilized binary financing to acquire a percentage ($X$) of their capital investments. (These annual acquisitions are assumed to be net of any business financings that fail to repay the acquisition loans. On the basis of projection and experience, the anticipated dollar magnitude of financing failures in relation to the dollar magnitude of financing successes is assumed to determine the cost of capital credit insurance.)

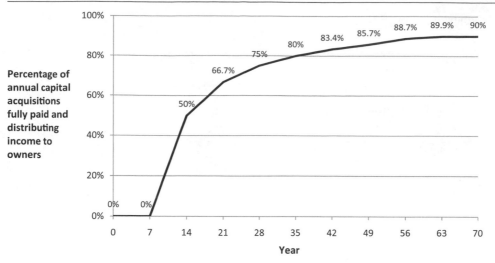

**FIGURE 12.19: PERCENTAGE OF CAPITAL ACQUISITIONS THAT LINK SUPPLY WITH DEMAND**
Source: R. Ashford (2010a, p. 97).

R. Ashford (1998, p. 50; 2003, p. 17) explains binary growth as follows: "Although beginning slowly, the broadening distribution of capital ownership and income will increase steadily and thereby provide the basis for binary growth. Each year after the initial cost recovery period of the most productive capital, more binary capital will have paid for itself and will begin distributing capital income to members of the poor and middle class."

Consistent with the conservative assumption of a seven-year capital-cost-recovery period, Figure 12.19 shows the steady growth in annual capital acquisitions. In year 8, the first annual acquisition of capital will have paid for itself and will begin paying its full return to the new binary owners. In year 14, 50 percent of the annual capital acquisitions will have paid for themselves and will have begun paying their full annual return to the new binary owners. In year 28, this will have increased to 75 percent of the acquisitions. "In the long run, the linkage between supply (in the form of the incremental productive power of capital) and demand (resulting from the widespread market distribution of capital income to consumers) approaches 100" (R. Ashford 1998, p. 51).* Note that the growth does not require anyone to work harder or smarter. "It is directly connected to the broader pattern of capital acquisition generated by the voluntary operation of the binary economy on market principles" (ibid.).

It is important to note that the additional consumer income created through the mechanism described above is not redistributionary or inflationary; it exists only if the underlying capital has produced goods or services that are sufficient first to return its cost of acquisition and then to pay net income to its binary owners.

It should also be emphasized that all binary transactions are voluntary. Extraordinary corporate transactions generally require shareholder approval. Given the decision whether to finance a portion of corporate capital acquisition through ownership-broadening capital acquisition rather than conventional capital acquisition, shareholders will consider prospects of growth and ownership distribution and their effect on their return on equity.

### 12.11.3 Some Implications of Binary Economics

If the basic premise of binary economics (that capital and labor are independently productive) and the correlative principle of binary growth (that capital has a strong positive distributive relationship to growth) are valid, they have implications that either do not follow from conventional economic analysis or may significantly vary from it. Several of these implications are discussed below.

12.11.3.1 A New Explanation of the Persistence of Pervasive Unutilized Productive Capacity and Suboptimal Growth

Binary analysis suggests a novel and elegantly simple (although not necessarily complete) explanation of the persistence of unutilized productive capacity and suboptimal growth: concentrated ownership. This analysis follows from the binary view that (1) growth

---

\* The more binary financing that is undertaken, the greater these distributional growth effects will be.

is primarily the result of increasing capital productiveness rather than increasing labor productivity, (2) almost all new capital is acquired with the earnings of capital, and (3) concentrated ownership (a) fails to distribute the earnings necessary to purchase its output and (b) therefore fails to distribute the earnings necessary to employ fully the increasing productiveness of capital. Classical, neoclassical, and Keynesian economic theories express little concern about the persistence of concentrated ownership because they place no fundamental importance on a positive relation between the distribution of ownership and the employment of unutilized capacity and the promotion of growth. Presently, the only dominant economic theory that explicitly recognizes the persistence of unutilized capacity and suboptimal growth and seeks to deal with these symptoms (that is, Keynesian economics) does not acknowledge the concentration of ownership as a cause of the persistence of unutilized capacity and suboptimal growth, but rather, in seeking to achieve fuller employment and greater growth, focuses on the distribution, redistribution, or manipulation of effective demand. In the binary analysis, the consequences of the existence of concentrated ownership (which in conventional economics are either ignored, treated as at best a secondary matter, or touted as a beneficent source for the creation of jobs or the payment of welfare redistribution) are viewed instead as a significant drag on fuller employment and a monopolistic suppression of greater growth potential.

### 12.11.3.2 A Means of Providing Greater Earning Capacity to the Economically Disadvantaged (Poor and Working People) without Redistribution

The binary economy operates in an entirely voluntary manner. No binary financing transactions are compelled. Because voluntary broader ownership carries with it the promise of greater consumer demand in a future period, it follows that with the modest changes in the market structure described in Section 12.11.2, market participants can be enabled to price the present value of the promise of broader ownership. No income is earned by binary beneficiaries (employees, consumers, or welfare recipients) unless their capital has paid for itself, and thereafter beneficiaries earn net income after all expenses of production are paid and all necessary reserves for depreciation and research and development are set aside to maintain the capital in a competitive technological condition. Thus one recurrent political objection (and, therefore, obstacle) to assisting the economically disadvantaged by conventional means (that is, that such assistance is redistributionary and therefore inefficient and a drag on growth) is eliminated if binary analysis is given credence. There is no redistribution required to enable all people to increase their earning capacity by acquiring capital with the earnings of capital, and no redistribution in binary growth.

### 12.11.3.3 A Change in the Dynamics of Globalization and Free Trade and the Arguments That Support the Various Positions on These Subjects

One rationale for free trade and the globalization of national economies is provided by the doctrine of competitive advantage, and one facilitative impetus for increasing globalization and international trade is the increasing technological capacity to operate on a global basis. Another major factor driving globalization, however, is the continuing search by producers not only for cheaper resources, labor markets, and tax systems but also for foreign consumer demand because too many indigenous consumers of national economies lack sufficient purchasing power to purchase what their economies can produce. From a binary perspective, the inadequate purchasing power of the people living within any economy is not the result of their not working hard enough, smart enough, or with capital instruments having sufficient productive power, but rather their not being able to acquire a viable-enough share of the capital that continually replaces and vastly supplements labor productiveness (which is the result of their practical inability to purchase capital with the earnings of capital, as the well-capitalized are able to do). A unique feature of a binary economy is that it is capable of enhancing the earning capacity of its people by the increasing expansion of viable capital acquisition and ownership.

According to the binary view, the growing capital-based earning capacity resulting from the voluntary operation of the binary economy may affect the incentives for globalization in several ways. First, residents of a binary economy will be better able to afford a fuller portion of what that economy can produce, thereby decreasing the need of producers to seek out and rely on foreign consumers to purchase their products. Second, with a broadening distribution of capital income, pressures for increasing wages (for many, but not all, workers) and increasing tax burdens to support welfare payments may decrease, thereby reducing the wage and tax differentials between those economies that open their capital market to binary financing and those that restrict capital acquisition essentially to the well-capitalized.

The recognition of the binary approach as a distinct voluntary alternative to conventional financing therefore has the potential to alter the debate that surrounds questions of international trade and globalization. Accordingly, the institution of binary financing may be favored or opposed in anticipation of its likely affect on the interests of those who favor the facilitation of trade and the interests of those who favor trade policies that protect domestic producers, workers, consumers, standards, and social values. Depending on those interests, the binary potential for increasing domestic capital-based consumer income may be seen to alter the incentives for international trade and to facilitate trade on a more or less viable or equitable economic foundation.

From a binary perspective, however, it should be noted that the process of finding and relying on consumer markets by way of globalization is transitory, whereas the need to broaden capital ownership so as to distribute to consumers the income to purchase what is increasingly produced by capital is ongoing and accelerating with technological advance. The processes by which local, regional, and national economies become global economies through increased trade seemingly point to a time when global differences in wages, taxes, regulatory standards, and cultural considerations may become less pronounced, but the need for every person to acquire capital with the earnings of capital (and thereby to be able to earn not only by laboring but also by owning) will increase as technology increasingly shifts production from labor to capital. In a theoretically global economy with decreasing (and eventually little or no) differences in wages, work, or production standards, regulation, and taxation, until one can expect to export to extraterrestrial economies, the imperative to distribute sufficient earning power to purchase what can be produced will remain; and the need to do so by way of a broader, more viable distribution of capital ownership will continue to increase as technology renders production increasingly capital intensive.

### 12.11.3.4 A Novel but Perhaps Indeterminate Impact on Environmental Issues and Sustainable Development

Some people have expressed concern with (or even opposition to) the implementation of a binary economy (and therefore a reluctance to teach the principles of binary economics) because of fears that binary growth will lead to increased degradation of the global environment, which is already severely threatened by developed economies such as that of the United States and developing economies in search of rapid growth strategies without concern for environmental preservation. Thus there are fears that global warming, pollution of the world's waters, soil, and air, the destruction of rain forests, and other environmental degradations may accelerate with binary growth. In attempting to evaluate this issue, it is important to bear in mind that the prospect of significant environmental degradation resulting from the implementation of binary financing is dependent on the prospect of substantial incremental binary growth beyond the growth that would occur without the implementation of binary financing. In other words, the threat of environmental degradation (if indeed it materializes as a result of binary growth) is not likely to become substantial unless the incremental capital income of presently capital-less people also becomes substantial after the institution of binary market reforms.

R. Ashford and Shakespeare (1999, pp. 379–384) have recognized the question of environmental harm resulting from binary growth and have argued that a higher portion of binary growth is more likely to be green growth rather than environmentally harmful growth:

### Conservation of the environment

Binary growth has remarkable implications for improving the environment because it offers a new way out of the quandary which seems to pit concern for the environment against immediate needs, desires, and convenience. Indeed, the promise of binary growth is a promise of green growth. It includes the promise not only of a population better able to afford more food, clothing, shelter, health care, transportation and communication around the world but also the promise of greener products, greener processes, greener activities and tastes as well as a consumer population with stronger property interests in the environment and better able to afford the greener choice.

Many difficult environmental issues (that are frequently the source of much conflict) are evidenced in the U.S.A., the U.K. and other industrial nations, where people face choices that oppose social concerns for the environment against certain needs, conveniences and preferences and where some people must choose between policies that threaten the environment or their very livelihood. Such choices (which are hard enough for members of the middle class and working poor in the industrialized economies of the world) are yet more difficult in poorer nations where people, in far greater numbers and proportions, suffer and perish for lack of necessities.

The fact has to be faced that it is difficult, and frequently impossible, to raise the "green" consciousness of people when they exist with pain, disease and poverty. Many will have trouble accepting "deep green" proposals that seemingly demand a cut in the standards of living for the millions of people who have no proper standard of living to cut in the first place. At the moment, existence for most of the world's population is a painful one in which, too often, children, partners and friends suffer and, as a result of poverty, die prematurely. Any demand, therefore, for that population to sacrifice what little wealth it has and to take a long-term view rather than a short-term one will, at best, be heard by many with incredulity or, if acknowledged, honored in the breach and not the reality.

Binary economics, however, provides a way out from the deep green dilemma, for it understands that "green" matters generally require one or more of the following:

- a change in tastes and lifestyles;
- a change to more costly processes, products, or activities;
- a discovery of greener substitute processes, products or activities;
- a tax on or a straightforward prohibition of activities;

and none of these changes, discoveries, taxes or prohibitions is practicable unless enough people and their society can afford them. Crucially, binary economics enables increasing numbers of people within any society to become better able to afford these alternatives. Any society has a theoretical power to stop people destroying something but binary economics offers people a practical power to stop environmental degradation by better enabling people to chose, discover, and accept greener ways.

For example, many of the products widely sold in the non-free market economies are manufactured in environmentally harmful ways. Greener ways are possible, but they are more expensive, and many customers cannot afford them, which means many producers cannot afford to make them. In the non-free market, all producers might be required by law to use the more expensive, greener ways, so there will be fewer producers, fewer products, and fewer people will be able to afford the products (or so that the products will be removed from the market) and other people employed in making the products will be laid off. The results in terms of i) overall wealth creation; ii) the distribution of costs and benefits among the population; and iii) the environment itself, are problematic and debatable. Moreover, the problems and debates have been divisive, often splitting families, friends and communities. Binary growth, however, offers a new possibility—as customers become better capitalized in a binary economy, they will become wealthier customers, better able to afford greener products and processes.

To take another example of the green potential of binary economics, as developing nations with binary economies become better and more broadly capitalized, their people will be better able to resist the economic pressures to destroy their environments. A well-capitalized binary nation comprised of well-capitalized citizens does not need to sell its rain forests, or its wild game, or its other precious resources in ways that threaten their renewability and viability in the long run.

The binary economy also vests more people with a property interest in the economy. It is noteworthy that in the U.S.A. and Western Europe, much activity to restrain environmental degradation came from activists eager to restrain private economic power by the use of effective political power. This involved the simultaneous effort of convincing members of the consuming public that they did not really want the products they believed they wanted, and persuading the owners and workers that they did not really need their profits, wage increases, or jobs. In the non-free market economies, the protective actions taken to preserve the environment against market forces frequently required a political effort that faced opposition from well-capitalized interests.

Yet, in communist Russia, when political will could be achieved without private capital opposition, when consumers had little say regarding products, when there was less private property interest in manufacturing profits to resist regulation, and when jobs could be eliminated or created by government fiat, there was far greater environmental degradation to the soil and air, and far greater safety risks imposed on the people, than what generally occurred during the same period in the non-free market economies of the West. In comparing environmental degradation in communist and non-free market capitalist countries, the binary paradigm reveals that:

- environmental problems are, to a significant degree, economic problems;
- with the best in green consciousness, we can have only as green an environment as we can afford; and
- a widespread, individually owned private interest in productive capital can enhance, rather than detract from, the prospects for a rich, green coexistence with other life on earth.

As another example, consider the problem of "planned obsolescence" which was once a scandal, but which now is so commonplace it receives scant mention in the media. In many instances, companies could as cheaply manufacture products that last longer, but they would fast run out of customers if they did so. In other words, the economies of more enduring (less wasteful) production cannot be supported by sufficiently widespread consumption. But with a growing portion of poor and working people steadily becoming more able to afford the basics (food, clothing, housing, health care, transportation and communication) producers will no longer be faced with as great a need to produce according to a planned obsolescence. For example, rather than produce shoes and clothes that wear out in two years for a consuming population of a certain size, and then producing an equal amount for the same people to last another two years, competitive pressures to maintain global market share and profits in a growing binary economy may induce companies to [choose] to produce shoes and clothes that last five years for a consuming population of twice the size. Thus more people may be better served with better, more durable shoes and clothes, but with relatively fewer resources consumed.

A binary economy, therefore, taking the fullest possible advantage of technology, offers to provide greater wealth and a more broadly based viable standard of living for a growing portion of the population to support both a greater voluntary market-oriented approach to improving the environment, and also, to the extent necessary, greater and more effective public investment and regulation. And with a deeper understanding of the economics of environmental issues, with a stronger market for green products, and with a stronger private property interest in the environment, there will be greater incentives for the discovery and promotion of greener ways of life.

Nevertheless, material progress and a growing population having viable standards of living may not be enough to address all pressing environmental concerns. As long as people behave as though they have almost limitless material wants (as many economists seem to assume), the prospects for the conservation of natural resources might seem dim. Indeed, to many people, the prospects appear yet dimmer if no way is found to restrain the growth in population beyond the capacity to sustainably support it. Yet binary growth holds out helpful possibilities on these matters as well.

First, in regard to population questions, . . . there is considerable evidence that stable, affordable populations are most readily achievable on a voluntary basis in stable economic circumstances characterized by a robust base of general middle-class affluence—precisely the circumstances increasingly promised with binary growth.

Second, on the question of the limitless wants of people, there is a noteworthy possibility—because poverty (with its associated suffering, fear and insecurity) promotes the desire to be as far away from poverty as possible (i.e. to have great material wealth), the increasing elimination of poverty and provision of greater material security by the binary economy will result in the diminution of perceived need with extensively benign consequences for the planet. That noteworthy possibility could turn out to be one of binary economics' greatest achievements.

In summary, the prospect of binary growth, manifested by a more efficient creation and distribution of wealth, and by a growing population with viable standards of living, offers the practical basis for:

- a deeper understanding of environmental issues;
- a voluntary turning to greener ways through market and life-style choices; and
- an economy in which it will be more practical for government to insist on solutions for protecting the environment when market choices fail to do so.

Thus, binary economics offers a just and practical way for people to make peace with technology, with one another and with the environment while enhancing rather than compromising efficiency. (R. Ashford and Shakespeare 1999, pp. 379–384, extracted with permission)

Thus in considering the environmental impact of binary growth, one must distinguish between (1) growth that might be green growth because there is a technological solution presently available or theoretically feasible, but which people presently cannot afford, and (2) growth for which there is no technological solution. The first category of growth represents yet another instance of unutilized productive capacity, which can be made more affordable as the earning capacities of people improve with broader capital ownership. The second category of growth might seemingly increase the environmental degradation feared to result, notwithstanding the increased capital income of the consumer population. But even for those products and services for which there is no immediate technological fix, it may be important to consider whether features of a binary economy would render binary growth greener, dollar for dollar, than conventional growth. For example, as Ashford and Shakespeare have suggested, in a binary economy, there may be greater political will to tax or prohibit those environmental degradations for there is no existing technological fix. Moreover, the need to practice strategies of planned obsolescence and massive advertising to promote the sale of superfluous and extravagant products and services to a relatively small population (whose basic necessities and desires for simple creature comforts are already met, but with short-lived products) may be replaced by the incentive to make longer-lasting products more consonant with a simpler lifestyle to a growing population able to afford the basic necessities and simple comforts by reason of their growing participation in capital acquisition.

In summary, therefore, the factors that suggest that binary growth may be greener growth include the following:

1. A population more able to afford greener products and processes

2. A diminished need for planned obsolescence (because producers have the option of making longer-

lasting products for sale to a growing population of people rather than shorter-lasting products for sale to a relatively smaller population of people who can afford them)

3. A diminished need for massive advertising to persuade people who have little or no substantial unsatisfied needs to satisfy manipulated appetites for unbridled materialism

4. A correlative shift in production from unneeded luxuries to basic necessities and simple creature comforts

5. In developing countries, less perceived need to sacrifice such resources as rain forests, wildlife, and other natural resources to survive

6. A growing population of people with a proper interest in the environment (compare the amount of environmental degradation in Communist countries, when there was little or no private industry, little consumer choice in product and production techniques, and little private property interest in the environment, with the amount of environmental degradation in so-called free-market economies during the same period)

7. A prospect of voluntary population control with a growing, stable middle class increasingly supported by capital earnings

8. A stronger political will to tax and prohibit those environmental degradations for which there is no existing technological fix

Robert Ashford concedes that these arguments, although plausible, are conjectural, and the net effect of binary growth on the environment may be indeterminate ex ante. Nevertheless, that indeterminacy provides no justifiable reason not to teach binary theory when the failure to teach it thereby leaves generation after generation of students with the unchallenged impression (1) that the distribution of capital ownership has no positive relationship to the employment of unutilized capacity and the promotion of growth, (2) that the only theoretical and practical means of enhancing the economic participation of poor and working people is by way of jobs and welfare, and (3) that there is no theoretical and practical way of enabling all people to acquire capital with the earnings of capital.

### 12.11.4 Commentary on the Prospects for Binary Economics

In sum, the essential effect of implementing binary economics is to open up the financial infrastructure and allow all people to have access to corporate credit on market principles, so that they can acquire capital on the net, pretax earnings of acquired capi-

tal. Binary transactions are completely voluntary; they do not involve redistributions and fully respect the private property rights of all people.

The reader must note, however, that the theory of binary economics is not a widely accepted and taught economic paradigm. Although it was first advanced by Kelso and Adler in 1958, it was not until 1996 that the first peer-reviewed journal edited by economists published an article examining binary economics as a distinct paradigm, and it was not until 1999 that the *Journal of Economic Literature* formally recognized the new binary economic paradigm.

One objection (informally raised in discussions) is a concern that the monetization of capital formation for poor and working people may or will be inflationary. R. Ashford (1998, p. 51) denies that binary financing is necessarily inflationary, particularly in the context of unutilized productive capacity. He notes that central-bank controls on the money supply remain in place in a binary economy. Nevertheless, R. Ashford (ibid., p. 55) recognizes that the economics profession has been slow to give rigorous, formal consideration to binary economics, which means that binary analysis is presently not widely accepted. Nevertheless, he notes that the potential of binary economics either is a grand illusion whose logical or practical fallacy has eluded a growing number of scholars and citizens throughout the world, or it is one of the most important concepts of the twentieth century, one that will provide a level of sustainable growth and distributive justice beyond our present dreams.

As R. Ashford (2003, p. 20) explains, the belief that broader capital ownership is good or just is by no means unique to binary economics; there are other approaches to broader ownership that are not explicitly based on binary principles. A prime example is the provision of microfinance, which brings us to the fifth and last financing innovation that will be discussed in this part of the chapter.

### 12.12 MICROFINANCE

Microfinance programs provide financial services— such as credit, savings, and insurance services—that are specifically tailored for the poor. They are powerful mechanisms to promote development; they reach out to the world's poorest, raise their income levels and living standards, and contribute to economic growth. Moreover, microfinance schemes allow for the incorporation of sustainable development criteria (such as environmental targets), thereby simultaneously promoting economic development and sustainable livelihoods (Odaga 1998).* This was affirmed in a working paper by the World Bank, the UNEP, and the IMF (WBG, UNEP, et al. 2002, p. 4): "Successful microfinance approaches can empower individuals and the informal business sector to foster sustainable livelihoods in marginalized communities worldwide. A widespread deployment of capital on a micro scale throughout the developing world could contribute in a significant way to a virtuous circle of investment, benefit, and reinvestment at the community level. Microfinance has the ability to deliver this capital, although care is needed to ensure that it is spent in ways that contribute to sustainable development."

Worldwide experience with numerous microfinance schemes and programs has led to several promising observations. First, the world's poor—who had previously been thought to be uncreditworthy—have proved to be "bankable and willing to pay a premium for quick, reliable, and convenient financial services" (Brandsma and Chaouali 1998, p. 1). Moreover, there are significant nonfinancial benefits of microfinance as well.† Third, when microfinance institutions are managed in a disciplined, businesslike fashion, they have proved to have the potential to be profitable and sustainable (Brandsma and Chaouali 1998).

In spite of these promising observations, many microfinance programs that have been set up during the past decade have failed. For example, Brandsma and Chaouali (1998) surveyed sixty microfinance programs in the Middle East and North Africa, only ten of which had achieved, or were close to achieving, financial sustainability. In the remainder of this subsection, we will therefore examine the main conditions that are required for successful microfinance. The analysis will commence with a discussion of microcredit because this is the most popular and widely implemented option. Subsequently, some alternatives

to microcredit will be discussed as well: microgrants, saving schemes, and micro-insurance.

### 12.12.1 Microcredit

Muhammad Yunus, managing director of the Grameen Bank,‡ argues, "Microfinance is a very effective instrument to empower the poor, particularly poor women, in all cultures and economies of the world. It is cost-effective, sustainable, and works in a businesslike way. It gives a poor person a chance to take destiny in his/her own hands and get out of poverty with his/her own efforts" (Yunus 2001). In an interview (Parker 2008), Yunus said "if you agree that each case of receiving microcredit is a creation of self-employment, then my argument is self-employment creates income, . . . Income is the thing which brings food. Income is the thing which creates the possibility of shelter, home. And income is the best medicine." But past experience has shown that microcredit is not always an appropriate course of action. A study by the Consultative Group to Assist the Poor (CGAP) explains that "for microcredit to be appropriate, a preexisting level of on-going economic activity, entrepreneurial capacity, and managerial talent is needed. If not, then clients may not be able to benefit from credit, and will simply be pushed into debt" (CGAP 2002, p. 2).

There are several scenarios in which microcredit is unlikely to be successful because one or more of these conditions may not hold (CGAP 2002, p. 2):

- In an immediate postemergency environment
- For the chronically impoverished unless there are preexisting efforts to reduce their vulnerability and to build basic skills, confidence, and a minimal financial foundation
- In severely disadvantaged rural areas that lack basic infrastructure, services, and/or access to markets
- In situations where severe and chronic illness prevents people from productive activities (HIV/AIDS is an extreme example of such a situation)

But even in situations where the conditions of sufficient economic activity, entrepreneurial capacity, and market opportunity are met, certain factors may

---

\* Odaga's (1998) study explores the extent to which microcredit institutions and organizations in sub-Saharan Africa have employed their lending and savings programs to promote environmental protection and sustainable development. Of the microcredit institutions examined, 32 percent incorporated environmental management into their programs. For the NGOs under examination, the results were slightly better; 50 percent of all national NGOs and 40 percent of international NGOs paid heed to environmental concerns in their activities.

† Once microfinance programs succeed in creating a "dynamic cycle of sustainable livelihoods" within a community, the collective ability of its inhabitants to pay for basic goods and services, such as clean water and secure electricity, is greatly enhanced. This leads to enormous nonfinancial benefits. For example, the improved health and time saving from clean water in turn enable greater economic opportunities and productivity and educational benefits from the ability to study during evenings (WBG, UNEP, et al. 2002, p. 4).

---

‡ The Grameen Bank can be seen as the organization that has built the reputation of microcredit. The bank, launched in 1976, popularized the idea of giving poor people small loans to launch their own businesses. In 2001, the bank had over 2.4 million borrowers, who had already paid back $3.2 billion over the past twenty-five years (Yunus 2001). In 2006, Muhammad Yunus and the Grameen Bank he founded were awarded the Nobel Peace Prize.

still cause the implementation of microfinance programs to be unsuccessful. The CGAP (2002, pp. 2–3) research note highlights the following:

- A highly dispersed population that makes it too costly to reach debtors on a regular basis

- Dependence on a single economic activity (for example, one agricultural crop), which creates "covariance" risk for the microcredit institution because of insufficient diversification

- A population with a high degree of mobility or instability, such as populations temporarily displaced because of civil conflict

- High probability of future crises such as civil violence, natural disasters, or hyperinflation

- Absence of law and order

- A distorted legal/regulatory or monitoring and enforcement environment

- A lack of social capital or societal cohesion, which undermines the viability of microcredit programs that rely not on collateral, but on peer-group monitoring*

If all the necessary conditions for an effective microcredit program are in place, there are certain *institutional* characteristics that a microcredit organization should have in order to have a high probability of being successful and profitable in the long run (Brandsma and Chaouali 1998; CGAP 2002):

1. *Permanence*: It should provide financial services on a long time scale.

2. *Scale*: It must reach a large client base of borrowers.

3. *Outreach*: It should reach the poorest (provided they fulfill the above requirements).

4. *Sustainability*: It should strive to reach full financial sustainability.

Although an increasing number of successful microfinance institutions have emerged worldwide (WBG, UNEP, et al. 2002), many microcredit organizations do not fulfill all these requirements. Moreover, those international institutions that are highly effective cannot expand everywhere.

Last, it should be emphasized that successful microcredit is crucially dependent on *discipline*—both of the *client* and the *institution*. The poor clients in

microcredit schemes should have the discipline to make on-time payments to ensure that the complete cost of the service is covered. As Grameen Bank founder Muhammad Yunus explained in a speech in 1998, this not only is crucial for the long-term viability of the microcredit program but also allows people to discover that they can determine their own future: "Credit without strict discipline is nothing but charity. Charity does not help overcome poverty. Poverty is a disease that has a paralyzing effect on mind and body. A meaningful poverty alleviation program is one that helps people gather will and strength to make cracks in the walls around them."[24]

The required institutional discipline can be summarized in a list of necessary operating procedures for building a sustainable microcredit program (CGAP 2002, p. 5). Institutions must

(a) charge interest rates that cover *all* costs (even when adjustments are made for donations and subsidies);

(b) require *full, on-time* repayment from clients and *track* repayments in a regular and frequent manner;

(c) create appropriate and efficient products and delivery techniques that *serve their clients' needs*;

(d) provide field staff with *performance incentives*;

(e) introduce sufficient *decentralization* to remain flexible and potentially expand; and

(f) *plan* for capacity, growth, and sustainability from the start.

The above-mentioned descriptions provide a tool kit that not only allows for the identification of drawbacks in existing microcredit programs but also sets the necessary conditions upon which new institutions and programs will have to be based.

For-profit banks, such as Compartamos in Mexico, have entered the microlending business and are charging enormous rates of interest.[25] As of June 2008, they had over 900,000 clients. These for-profit banks are heavily criticized by Muhammad Yunus and others for "exploiting the poor." Their defense is that they are serving a need. Clearly, if there were more banks like the Grameen Bank throughout the third world, the for-profit institutions could not compete.

In 2010, there were over one thousand micro finance institutions (MFIs) that reported to the Microfinance Information eXchange (MIX). These MFIs had total assets worth $60 billion and supported 88 million borrowers and 76 million savers (CSFI 2011). The rapid growth of these institutions over the past twenty years has captured the attention

---

*     Many microcredit institutions do not require collateral and do not directly monitor or dictate how borrowers use their loans. Instead, they often rely on a system whereby small, self-selected groups agree on a mechanism that makes them collectively responsible for the repayment of the loans. For more detailed information on this system of peer-group monitoring (which was popularized by the Grameen Bank), see Odaga (1998).

of many practitioners, analysts, regulators, and investors who are concerned that the industry has become too commercial and is losing touch with its original mission (ibid.) In 2010, the prime mister of Bangladesh, Sheik Hasina Wazed, went as far as describing microlenders as "sucking blood from the poor in the name of poverty alleviation" (Bajaj 2011, p. B3). Such sentiment has many actors in the sector asking serious questions about the future form of the industry, and whether it will evolve toward more conventional financial institutions or rediscover its roots and refocus on providing credit to a relatively limited market of lower-income groups in developing economies (CSFI 2011).

Finally, Karnani (2007) argues that employment, not microcredit, is the answer to alleviating poverty. Acknowledging that microcredit lending to women has empowered them and has yielded significant social benefits, Karnani (2007, p. 3) observes that "a significant fraction of women, in spite of having *access* to credit, do not have *control* over the loans contracted or the income generated from the microenterprises." This empowerment is not sufficient to deliver many of them out of poverty. Karnani opines that the problem is not with microcredit, but rather with the microenterprises that result; they are not competitive and do not thrive in a promising business environment. Echoing the ILO's belief that "nothing is more fundamental to poverty reduction than employment," Karnani argues instead for financing larger enterprises that can create employment and increase job-related skills.

### 12.12.2 Microgrants

As explained above, not all the poor have the entrepreneurial potential to use a loan productively. There are various reasons for this, some of which have been identified above. For people in that situation, microcredit can even erode their economic position further by putting them into debt. In these cases, microgrants may be preferable to microcredit programs.* They can enable the world's poorest to make the crucial first steps in reducing their vulnerability and move toward a stage of "economic self-sufficiency," in which they have the necessary skills and knowledge to make viable small-business plans.†
In addition, microgrants can provide a temporary safety net to people affected by crises—for example, civil conflict or natural disasters, such as earthquakes and floods—by making a one-time donation that enables them to rebuild their livelihoods and replace lost assets (CGAP 2002).‡

However, there are some important threats to the effective use of microgrants. If they are not strictly monitored, they can easily lead to abuse and long-term dependence. This can even distort the market for microcredit by leading people who are suitable for credit programs to attempt to secure grant financing. The CGAP has identified several guidelines to prevent this and to ensure that grants are a valuable complement to microcredit schemes (CGAP 2002, pp. 8–9). Microgrants

- should be carefully targeted to those who cannot be helped with microcredit (for example, the very poor and temporarily displaced persons);§

- should be a one-off payment and include a "graduation" process to market-based mechanisms such as microcredit;

- should be rigorously monitored to ensure that they are spent as intended;

- should be accompanied by proper training schemes (especially when they are intended for specific productive purposes); and

- should require the recipient to contribute at least 5 to 10 percent of the grant value to ensure commitment.

---

* Another, more sophisticated form of grant is the *termination payment*. Termination payments are an alternative to microcredit especially intended to assist people laid off from formal-sector or government employment to get into self-employment. The *pension fund* is an even more complex alternative form of termination payment, which can give a displaced worker a longer-term cushion. However, pension funds require highly sophisticated infrastructural planning and require years to implement (CGAP 2002).

† Also, the grants could be used to meet basic consumption or health needs rather than to invest in income-earning activities (as is the first step in the Bangladeshi Rural Advancement Committee's IGVGD Program mentioned below).

‡ A good example is the Income Generation for Vulnerable Groups Development (IGVGD) Program, provided by the Bangladeshi Rural Advancement Committee (BRAC). The IGVGD Program gradually helps its participants achieve economic self-sufficiency. It begins by providing people at greatest immediate risk with free food for eighteen months (with the support of the World Food Program and the government). Subsequently, it engages its participants in skills-training programs to teach them to generate their own income. Also, it helps participants learn to save for future investment and protection against future setbacks. Within two years of starting the process, roughly 80 percent of its participants had made the transition into BRAC's mainstream microfinance program as borrowers. See Imran and Hulme (2003).

§ Also, this means that they should not finance investments that generate income streams in the short run (these are better funded through a loan from a microfinance institution).

The CGAP recommends that "microfinance providers experts working in the region should first be consulted to ensure that any micro-grant program does not (at worst) compete with or undermine local microfinance institutions, and (at best) is carefully coordinated with microfinance to provide an eventual way out of grant dependence" (CGAP 2002, p. 9).

### 12.12.3 Savings and Insurance

In addition to microcredit and microgrants, the poor can also benefit substantially from access to saving and insurance schemes.

It always makes sense for people to save, no matter how poor they are. Poor households usually want to save to spread their risk and prepare for future investments.[26] Unfortunately, most poor communities still lack access to safe, accessible, and flexible saving schemes.* Currently, most NGOs and microcredit institutions do not meet the regulatory requirements to achieve this, but some are already engaged in the development of informal savings arrangements.

Last, while savings allow the poor to build a safety net for future events or emergencies, micro-insurance offers a way to manage specific risks by sharing the cost of unlikely events among many. Microfinance institutions are now paying more attention to these initiatives as well.[27]

### 12.13 CONCLUSION

As explained in the introduction, the aim of this chapter was to provide a holistic and integrated overview of the current debate about financing sustainable development. We have covered an enormous area. In Part A, the chapter opened with a discussion of financing for *economic* development, in which we examined not only the architecture—both multilateral and bilateral—in which official development aid is disbursed but also the main drawbacks encountered in its implementation. Subsequently, we examined the increasing importance of private capital flows in the international economy and their impact on sustainable development.

Part B then focused on financing structures for *environmental* protection, analyzing their emergence in the late 1980s. The role of the UNCED was extensively discussed, after which some main points of criticism were expressed about the way in which environmental policy was financed throughout the 1990s. This part concluded with two main strategies for future improvement of the financial basis of sustainable development strategies: the mobilization of finance (through various mechanisms) and the utilization of market forces.

Finally, Part C examined some promising financing innovations for sustainable development in more detail. It examined some global initiatives (George Soros's SDR proposal, Konrad von Moltke's international investment agreement, and the Global Environment Facility), one national initiative (binary economics), and a local one (microcredit and microfinance).

The aim of this extensive analysis was not to provide an exhaustive overview of all relevant topics in the field of finance for sustainable development. It was to *demystify* some of the most critical issues in the debate—often heavily polarized and technical—related to the financing of sustainable development.

We have seen that there are enormous hurdles to overcome. All too often, tensions between North and South are still preventing the highly needed cooperation that is essential to tackle problems of sustainable development. But rather than attempting to summarize the efforts made, we wish to close the chapter by reiterating the most important and valuable lesson of all, conveyed very effectively by the Economist (2002c, p. 18) in one of its surveys: "We only have one planet, now and in the future. We need to think harder about how to use it wisely."

### 12.14 NOTES

1. The SWF Institute, List of Sovereign Wealth Funds, www.swfinstitute.org/ (accessed January 31, 2011).

2. See the International Finance Corporation (IFC), www.ifc.org/about (accessed June 3, 2010).

3. See the Multilateral Investment Guarantee Agency (MIGA), www.miga.org/about/index_sv.cfm?stid=1588 (accessed June 3, 2010).

4. See the World Bank Group, About, www.worldbank.org/ (accessed June 3, 2010).

5. For a more elaborate explanation of the Millennium Development Goals, see UN (2009) and the Millennium Development Goals website, www.un.org/millenniumgoals/ (accessed June 3, 2010).

6. OECD, Net ODA disbursements from DAC countries, http://webnet.oecd.org/dcdgraphs/ODAhistory/# (accessed February 2, 2011).

7. Center for Global Development, Commitment to Development Index 2010, www.cgdev.org/section/initiatives/_active/cdi/ (access February 5, 2011).

---

* Saving schemes can best help the poorest when they are safe and accessible, and when they allow for the deposit of small amounts on a frequent basis. As the CGAP (2002) explains, to allow clients full access to their deposits, the financial institution must be well managed and have sufficient reserves to respond to periods of unusually high demand caused by natural or economic crises.

8. ECA Watch, www.eca-watch.org (accessed on February 5, 2010).

9. High Level Panel of the Trans-Atlantic Environmental Dialogue, Brussels, May 2000, www.eca-watch.org/eca/ecas_explained.html (accessed February 7, 2011).

10. See the Equator Principles, www.equator-principles.com (accessed June 3, 2010).

11. See pages 6 and 7 of the World Bank's *World Development Report, 1999/2000* (WBG 1999b). For a more detailed discussion, see the introduction of Hausmann and Fernández-Arias (2000), which provides extensive references to the literature.

12. For a comprehensive discussion of the East Asian crisis, see Soros (2002, chap. 4).

13. Michael Redclift (1996, pp. 16–17) sums up several other reasons that environmental factors were not taken into account in the development policies of the 1980s.

14. For a useful discussion of the debate over additionality, see Jordan (1994).

15. For a detailed discussion of the negotiation rounds involving the protection of the ozone layer and the establishment and performance of the International Multilateral Ozone Fund, the reader is referred to DeSombre and Kauffman (1996).

16. For a more detailed discussion of the drawbacks of Agenda 21, and the UNCED more broadly, the reader is advised to consult Jordan (1994). Also, a good analysis can be found in Panayotou (1994) and section III of Johnston (1998).

17. For more information on the Clean Development Mechanism, see http://cdm.unfccc.int/ (accessed June 3, 2010).

18. See Jakobeit (1996) for a critical review of debt-for-nature swaps.

19. See chapter 7 of the World Bank Report *Five Years after Rio* (WBG 1997).

20. See the Multiple Use water Services (MUS) Group, www.musgroup.net/ (accessed June 3, 2010).

21. For more information about SDRs, see IMF (2003a), as well as Soros (2002, pp. 76–77). For an informative and well-written review of Soros's book as a whole, see Stiglitz (2002a).

22. The analysis of the Global Environment Facility provided here is largely based on three texts: Miller (2000), Redclift (1996), and Young and Boehmer-Christiansen (1997).

23. For more information about the inherent complexities of the restructured GEF, the reader is referred to Section B of Miller (2000) and Young and Boehmer-Christiansen (1997, pp. 195–198).

24. Muhammad Yunus, managing director, Grameen Bank, "Towards Creating a Poverty-Free World," speech presented at the Club de Debate at Complutense University, Madrid, April 25, 1998 (cited in CGAP 2002, n. 2).

25. See "Doing Good by Doing Very Nicely Indeed," *Economist*, June 26, 2008.

26. See Stuart Rutherford's book *The Poor and Their Money* (2000) for a more detailed analysis of the savings strategies employed by the poor.

27. A thorough discussion is beyond the scope of this analysis. The reader is referred to the USAID website on Microenterprise Development for more information: www.usaid.gov/our_work/economic_growth_and_trade/micro/how_we_work.htm (accessed June 3, 2010).

## 12.15 REFERENCES

Adesina, J. O., Y. Graham, et al. (2005). *Africa and Development Challenges in the New Millennium: The NEPAD Debate*. London, Zed Books.

Alesina, A., and D. Dollar (1998). Who Gives Foreign Aid to Whom and Why? Working paper 6612. Cambridge, MA, National Bureau of Economic Research. Available at www.nber.org/papers/w6612.pdf (accessed February 6, 2011).

Allen, M. and J. Caruana (2008). Sovereign Wealth Funds—A Work Agenda. Washington, DC, International Monetary Fund. Available at www.imf.org/external/np/pp/eng/2008/022908.pdf (accessed February 8, 2011).

Arkedis, J. (2008). Getting to a "Grand Bargain" for Aid Reform: The Basic Framework for U.S. Assistance. Manuscript 12/05/08.

Army Information School (1946). Pamphlet 4, Pillars of Peace. Documents Pertaining to American Interest in Establishing a Lasting World Peace: January 1941–February 1946. Carlisle Barracks, PA, Book Department, Army Information School.

Ashford, N. A. (2000). An Innovation-Based Strategy for a Sustainable Environment. *Innovation-Oriented Environmental Regulation: Theoretical Approach and Empirical Analysis*. J. Hemmelskamp, K. Rennings. New York, Physica-Verlag Heidelberg: 67–107.

Ashford, N. A. (2002). "Government and Environmental Innovation in Europe and North America." *American Behavioral Scientist* **45**(9): 1417–1434.

Ashford, R. (1996). "Louis Kelso's Binary Economy." *Journal of Socio-economics* **25**(1): 1–53.

Ashford, R. (1998). "A New Market Paradigm for Sustainable Growth: Financing Broader Capital Ownership with Louis Kelso's Binary Economics." *Praxis: The Fletcher Journal of Development Studies* **14**: 25–59.

Ashford, R. (2003). Binary Economics and the Case for Broader Ownership. Available at www.globaljusticemovement.org/subpages_online_library/ashford1.pdf (accessed July 6, 2010).

Ashford, R. (2010a). "Broadening the Right to Acquire Capital with the Earnings of Capital: The Missing Link to Sustainable Economic Recovery and Growth." *Forum for Social Economics* **39**: 89–100.

Ashford, R. (2010b). "Milton Friedman's Capitalism and Freedom: A Binary Economic Critique." *Journal of Economic Issues* **44**(2): 533–542.

Ashford, R., and R. Shakespeare (1999). *Binary Economics: The New Paradigm*. Lanham, MD, University Press of America.

Bajaj, V. (2011). "Microlenders, Honored with Nobel, Are Struggling." *New York Times*, January 5, p. B3.

Baumert, K. A., and E. Petkova (2000). How Will the Clean Development Mechanism Ensure Transparency, Public Engagement and Accountability? Washington, DC, World Resources Institute Climate Notes.

Bradlow, D. D. (1996). "Social Justice and Development: Critical Issues Facing the Bretton Woods System; The World Bank, the IMF, and Human Rights." *Transnational Law and Contemporary Problems* **6**: 47–90.

Bradsher, K. (2010). After China's Rare Earth Embargo, a New Calculus. *New York Times,* October 29.

Brandsma, J. and R. Chaouali (1998). Making Microfinance Work in the Middle East and North Africa. Washington, DC, Private and Financial Sector Development Group, World Bank. Available at http://zunia.org/uploads/media/knowledge/World%20Bank.pdf (accessed February 7, 2011).

Branson, W., and C. Jayarajah (1995). Structural and Sectoral Adjustment: World Bank Experience, 1980–92. Washington, DC, World Bank.

Brealey, R. A., and S. C. Myers (1984). *Principles of Corporate Finance*. New York, McGraw-Hill.

Broner, F. A., G. Lorenzoni, et al. (2007). Why Do Emerging Economies Borrow Short Term? NBER Working Paper 13076. Available at: www.nber.org/papers/w13076 (accessed Fenruary 5, 2011).

Bruno, M., M. Ravallion, et al. (1998). Equity and Growth in Developing Countries: Old and New Perspectives on the Policy Issues. *Income Distribution and High-Quality Growth*. Cambridge, MA, MIT Press: 117 146.

Burnside, C. and D. Dollar (1997). Aid, Policies, and Growth. Policy Research Working Paper 1777. Washington, DC, Development Research Group, World Bank.

Burnside, C. and D. Dollar (1998). Aid, the Incentive Regime, and Poverty. Policy Research Working Paper 193. Washington, DC, Development Research Group, World Bank.

Carrasco, E. R. (2011). An Opening for Voice in the Global Economic Order: The Global Financial Crisis and Emerging Economies. University of Iowa Legal Studies Research Paper 11-05. Available at http://papers.ssrn.com/sol3/papers.cfm?abstract_id=1754690# (accessed March 3, 2011).

Cassen, R. (1986). *Does Aid Work? Report to an Intergovernmental Task Force*. Oxford: Clarendon Press.

Center for Global Development/Foreign Policy (CGD/FP) (2003). Ranking the Rich 2003: Who Really Helps the Poor? *Foreign Policy* **136**: 56–66.

CGD (2010). Commitment to Development Index 2010. Washington, DC, CGD.

Center for Global Prosperity (CGP) (2009). *The Index of Global Philanthropy and Remittances*. Washington, DC, Hudson Institute.

Centre for the Study of Financial Innovation (CSFI) (2011). Microfinance Banana Skins 2011: The CSFI Survey of Microfinance Risk. Losing Its Fairy Dust. New York, CSFI. Available at www.cgap.org/gm/document-1.9.49643/Microfinance_Banana_Skins_2011.pdf (accessed February 9, 2011).

Chesky, E. (1998). "International Investment." *Praxis: The Fletcher Journal of Development Studies* **14**: 5–24.

Chesterman, S. (2008). "The Turn to Ethics: Disinvestment from Multinational Corporations for Human Rights Violations; The Case of Norway's Sovereign Wealth Fund." *American University International Law Review* **23**: 577–651.

Clapp, J., and P. Dauvergne (2005). *Paths to a Green World: The Political Economy of the Global Environment*. Cambridge, MA, MIT Press.

Clemens, M. A., and T. J. Moss (2005). Ghost of 0.7%: Origins and Relevance of the International Aid Target. Working Paper 68. Washington, DC, CGD.

Collier, P. (1997). The Failure of Conditionality. *Perspectives on Aid and Development*. C. Gwin and J. Nelson. Washington, DC, Overseas Development Council: 51–77.

Collier, P., S. Devarajan, et al. (2001). *Measuring IDA's Effectiveness*. Development Research Group, World Bank, Washington, DC, http://siteresources.worldbank.org/IDA/Resources/Seminar%20PDFs/IDA%20effectiveness.pdf (accessed Febuary 2, 2011).

Collier, P., and D. Dollar (1999). *Country Assessments and IDA Allocations*. Washington, DC, World Bank.

Collier, P., and D. Dollar (2001). Can the World Cut Poverty in Half? How Policy Reform and Effective Aid Can Meet the DAC Targets. Washington, DC, Development Research Group, World Bank.

Consultative Group to Assist the Poor (CGAP) (2002). Microfinance, Grants, and Non-financing Responses to Poverty Reduction: Where Does Microfinance Fit? CGAP Focus Note 20.

Crosswell, M. (2008). The Development Record and the Effectiveness of Foreign Aid—Update. Paper presented at the 2008 Oxford Business and Economics Conference, June 22–24.

Dalal-Clayton, B., and S. Bass, Eds. (2002). *Sustainable Development Strategies: A Resource Book*. London, Earthscan.

Dalal-Clayton, D. B. (1996). *Getting to Grips with Green Plans: National-Level Experience in Industrial Countries*. London, Earthscan.

Daly, H., and R. Goodland (1994). "An Ecological-Economic Assessment of Deregulation of International Commerce under GATT (Part 1)." *Population and Environment* **15**(5): 395–427.

Daly, H. E. (1993). "The Perils of Free Trade." *Scientific American* **269**(5): 50–54.

Danish, K. W. (1995). "The Promise of National Environmental Funds in Developing Countries." *International Environmental Affairs* **7**(2): 150–175.

De Lombaerde, P., and L. Puri, Eds. (2007). *Aid for Trade: Global and Regional Perspectives; 2nd World Report on Regional Integration*. United Nations University Series on Regionalism. Dordrecht, Springer Netherlands.

DeSombre, E. R., and J. Kauffman (1996). The Montreal Protocol Multilateral Fund: Partial Success Story. *Institutions for Environmental Aid* R. O. Keohane and M. A. Levy. Cambridge, MA, MIT Press: 89–126.

Dobson, W., and G. C. Hufbauer (2002). *World Capital Markets: Challenge to the G-10*. Washington, DC, Peterson Institute for International Economics.

Dollar, D. (2000). Has Aid Efficiency Improved in the 1990s? Mimeo, Washington, DC, World Bank.

Dollar, D., and J. Svensson (1998). What Explains the Success or Failure of Structural Adjustment Programs? Policy Research Working Paper 1938. Washington, DC, World Bank, Development Research Group.

ECA-Watch (1999). "A Race to the Bottom: Creating Risk, Generating Debt and Guaranteeing Environmental Destruction." ECA-Watch. Available at www.eca-watch.org/eca/race_bottom.pdf (accessed February 5, 2011).

ECA-Watch (2000) "Jakarta Declaration for Reform of Official Export Credit and Investment Insurance Agencies." ECA-Watch. Available at www.eca-watch.org/goals/jakartadec.html (accessed February 5, 2011).

ECA-Watch (2003a) "Groups Blast Weak OECD Agreement on Environment: Loopholes Allow Export Credit Support for Harmful Projects to Continue." ECA-Watch.

Available at www.eca-watch.org/problems/fora/oecd/ECAWPR_OECD_common2003.htm (accessed February 5, 2011).

ECA-Watch (2003b) "Race to the Bottom—Take II: An Assessment of Sustainable Development Achievements of ECA-Supported Projects Two Years after OECD Common Approaches Rev 6." ECA-Watch. Available at www.fern.org/sites/fern.org/files/pubs/reports/r2b2_web_edition_sept_03.pdf (accessed February 5, 2011).

Economic Commission for Latin America and the Caribbean (ECLAC) (2002). *Annual Report on the Activities of the Economic Commission for Latin America and the Caribbean (ECLAC) in Support of the Implementation of the Plan of Action of the Third Summit of the Americas.* Santiago, United Nations. Available at www.summit-americas.org/Un-ano-de-quebec.htm (accessed February 7, 2011).

Economist (1991). "Sisters in the Wood: A Survey of the IMF and the World Bank." *Economist*, October 12.

Economist (1993). "Third-World Finance (Survey)." *Economist*, September 25.

Economist (2002a). "A Feast of Giving." *Economist*, March 21.

Economist (2002b). "Help in the Right Places." *Economist*, March 14.

Economist (2002c). "How Many Planets? A Survey of the Global Environment." *Economist*, July 6.

Economist (2003a). "A Cruel Sea of Capital: A Survey of Global Finance." *Economist*, May 1.

Economist (2003b). "The Doha Squabble." *Economist*, March 27.

Economist (2008). "Fare Well, Free Trade: With the Global Economy Facing Its Worst Recession in Decades, Protectionism Is a Growing Risk." *Economist*, December 18.

Evans, P., and K. Oye (2001). International Competition: Conflict and Cooperation in Government Export Financing. *The Ex-Im Bank in the 21st Century.* Gary Clyde Hufbauer and Rita Rodriguez (Eds.). Washington, DC, Institute for International Economics: 113–158.

Evans, P. C. (2005). "Export Finance and Sustainable Development: Do Export Credit Subsidy Rules Require Revision?" *Oil, Gas & Energy Law Intelligence* **3**(2).

Fairman, D., and M. Ross (1996). Old Fads, New Lessons: Learning from Economic Development Assistance. *Institutions for Environmental Aid.* R. O. Keohane and M. A. Levy. Cambridge, MA, MIT Press: 29–51.

Ferreira, M. A. and P. A. Laux (2009). "Portfolio flows, volatility and growth." *Journal of International Money and Finance* **28**: 271–292.

Fox, J., and D. L. Brown (1998). *The Struggle for Accountability: The World Bank, NGOs, and Grassroots Movements.* Cambridge, MA, MIT Press.

Franz, W. E. (1996). The Scope of Global Environmental Financing—Cases in Context. *Institutions for Environmental Aid.* R. O. Keohane and M. A. Levy. Cambridge, MA, MIT Press: 367–380.

Fund of the Americas (2000). *Developing a Strategy to Foment Philanthropy.* Santiago, Fondo de las Américas.

Gandhi, V., D. Gray, et al. (1997). A Comprehensive Approach to Domestic Resource Mobilization for Sustainable Development. *Finance for Sustainable Development: The Road Ahead.* J. Holst, P. Koudal and J. Vincent. New York, United Nations: 169–219.

Gardner, R. C., and E. Lugo (2009). Official Development Assistance: Toward Funding for Sustainability. *Agenda for a Sustainable America.* J. Dernbach. Washington, DC, Environmental Law Institute: 399–411.

Gauche, J. N. (2000). Binary Economic Modes for the Privatization of Public Assets. Available at www.kelsoinstitute.org/pdf/binaryeconomicmodes.pdf (accessed July 6, 2010).

Gelos, G., and S.-J. Wei (2002). Transparency and International Investor Behavior. NBER Working Paper 9260. Available at www.nber.org/papers/w9260 (accessed February 7, 2011).

General Accounting Office (GAO) (2000). Developing Countries: Debt Relief Initiative for Poor Countries Faces Challenges. GAO/NSIAD–00–161. Washington, DC, GAO. Available at www.gao.gov/new.items/ns00161.pdf (accessed February 8, 2011).

GAO (2003). Export Credit Agencies: Movement Toward Common Environmental Guidelines, but National Differences. GAO 03–1093. Washington, DC, GAO. Available at www.gao.gov/new.items/d031093.pdf (accessed February 8, 2011).

Global Environment Facility (GEF) (1992). Report by the Chairman to the Fourth Participants' Meeting. Global Environment Facility Scientific and Technical Advisory Panel, Washington, DC.

GEF (1994). *Independent Evaluation of the Pilot Phase.* Washington, DC, World Bank, UNDP, UNEP.

GEF (1999). Engaging the Private Sector in GEF Activities. GEF/C.13/Inf.5. Washington, DC, GEF. Available at www.peblds.org/files/Publications/GEF/GEF_Engaging_the_private_sector_in_GEFactivities.pdf (accessed February 8, 2011).

Grieg-Gan, M., T. Banuri, et al. (2002). The Financial Basis for Strategies. *Sustainable Development Strategies: A Resource Book.* D. B. Dalal-Clayton and S. Bass. London, Earthscan: 288–308.

Gwin, C. (1996). "A New and Improved Rationale for Aid at the 'End of History'." *Ceres. The FAO Review on Agriculture and Development* **28**:18–23.

Hausmann, R., and E. Fernández-Arias (2000). "Foreign Direct Investment: Good Cholesterol?" Working Paper 417. Research Department, Inter-American Development Bank. Available at www.iadb.org/res/publications/pubfiles/pubWP-417.pdf (accessed February 5, 2011).

Hellman, J., G. Jones, et al. (2002). Far from Home: Do Foreign Investors Import Higher Standards of Governance in Transition Economies? Working Paper, SSRN. Available at http://ssrn.com/abstract=386900 or doi:10.2139/ssrn.386900 (accessed February 5, 2011).

Hoekman, B. M., and M. Olarreaga, Eds. (2007). *Global Trade and Poor Nations: The Poverty Impacts and Policy Implications of Liberalization.* Washington, DC, Brookings Institution Press.

Hook, L. (2010). China to Cut Exports of Rare Earth Minerals. *Financial Times,* December 28.

Imran, M., and D. Hulme (2003). "Programs for the Poorest: Learning from the IGVGD Program in Bangladesh." *World Development* **31**(3): 647–665.

International Monetary Fund (IMF) (2001). Debt Relief under the Heavily Indebted Poor Countries (HIPC) Initiative—A Factsheet. Washington, DC, IMF. Available at www.mafhoum.com/press2/59E15.htm (accessed February 8, 2011).

IMF (2009). *IMF Financial Statements: Quarter Ended October 31, 2009*. Washington, DC, IMF.

IMF (2010a). The IMF at a Glance. Factsheet. Washington, DC, IMF. Available at www.imf.org/external/np/exr/facts/pdf/glance.pdf (accessed February 8, 2011).

IMF (2010b). Special Drawing Rights. Factsheet. Washington, DC, IMF. Available at www.imf.org/external/np/exr/facts/pdf/sdr.pdf (accessed February 8, 2011).

Jakobeit, K. (1996). Nonstate Actors Leading the Way: Debt-for-Nature Swaps. *Institutions for Environmental Aid*. R. O. Keohane and M. A. Levy. Cambridge, MA, MIT Press.

Johnston, T. (1998). "The Role of International Equity in a Sustainable Future: The Continuing Problem of Third World Debt and Development." *Buffalo Environmental Law Journal* **6**(1): 35–83.

Johnstone, N. (1997). Economic Inequality and the Urban Environment: The Case of Water and Sanitation. Discussion Paper DP 97-03. London, International Institute for Environment and Development. Available at http://pubs.iied.org/pdfs/8093IIED.pdf (accessed February 8, 2011).

Jordan, A. (1994). "Financing the UNCED Agenda: The Controversy over Additionality." *Environment* **36**(3): 16–20 and 26–34.

Kaiser, J., and A. Lambert (1996). *Debt Swaps for Sustainable Development: A Practical Guide for NGOs*. Washington, DC, International Union for the Conservation of Nature (IUCN).

Karnani, A. (2007). Employment, Not Microcredit, Is the Solution. Working Paper 1065, Ross School of Business Working Paper Series, University of Michigan.

Kawai, M., R. Newfarmer, et al. (2001). Crisis and Contagion in East Asia: Nine Lessons. World Bank Policy Research Working Paper 2610, SSRN. Available at http://ssrn.com/abstract=632679 (accessed February 8, 2011).

Keijzers, G. (2002). "The Transition to the Sustainable Enterprise." *Journal of Cleaner Production* **10**(4): 349–359.

Keohane, R. O. and M. A. Levy, Eds. (1996). *Institutions for Environmental Aid: Pitfalls and Promise*. Cambridge, MA, MIT Press.

Klarer, J., P. Francis, et al. (1999). Improving Environment and Economy: The Potential of Economic Incentives for Environmental Improvements and Sustainable Development in Countries with Economies in Transition. Sofia Initiative on Economic Instruments. Szentendre, Regional Environmental Center for Central and Eastern Europe. Available at http://archive.rec.org/REC/Programs/SofiaInitiatives/EcoInstruments/EcoInst.pdf (accessed February 8, 2011).

Kleinknecht, A., and J. ter Wengel (1998). "The Myth of Economic Globalisation." *Cambridge Journal of Economics* **22**: 637–647.

Krugman, P. (1993). International Finance and Economic Development. *Finance and Development: Issues and Experience*. A. Giovannini. Cambridge, Cambridge University Press: 11–23.

Lammersen, F., and A. D. Owen (2001). "The Helsinki Arrangement: Its Impact on the Provision of Tied Aid." *International Journal of Finance and Economics* **6**(1): 69–79.

Lyons, G. (2007). State Capitalism: The Rise of Sovereign Wealth Funds. Global Research at Standard Chartered. Manuscript, November 13.

McCawley, P. (2006). "Aid versus Trade: Some Considerations." *Australian Economic Review* **39**(1): 89–95.

Miller, A. S. (2000). "The Global Environment Facility and the Search for Financial Strategies to Foster Sustainable Development." *Vermont Law Review* **24**: 1229–1244.

Morrissey, O. (2006). "Aid or Trade, or Aid and Trade?" *Australian Economic Review* **39**(1): 78–88.

Mosley, P., J. Harrigan, et al. (1995). *Aid and Power*. London, Routledge.

Nakhooda, S., F. Seymour, et al. (2009). Financing Sustainable Development. *Agenda for a Sustainable America*. J. Dernbach. Washington, DC, Environmental Law Institute: 413–424.

National Center for Employee Ownership (NCEO) (1996). *A Statistical Profile of Employee Ownership*. Oakland, CA, NCEO.

Norlen, D. (2002) "Export Credit Agencies Explained." ECA-Watch, June. Available at http://alexanderhamiltoninstitute.org/lp/Hancock/Articles/2002/Export%20Credit%20Agencies%20Explained.htm (accessed February 5, 2011).

Norlen, D., R. Cox, et al. (2002). "Unusual Suspects: Unearthing the Shadowy World of Export Credit Agencies." San Francisco, Pacific Environment.

Nurkse, R. (1954). "International Investment Today in the Light of 19th Century Experience." *Economic Journal* **64**: 134–150.

Odaga, A. S. (1998). "Microcredit: A Key to Environmental Management?" *Praxis: The Fletcher Journal of Development Studies* **14**: 100–107 and 117–119.

Organisation for Economic Co-operation and Development (OECD) (1997). *Economic Globalisation and the Environment*. Paris: OECD.

OECD (2001). "Strategies for Sustainable Development: Guidance for Development Cooperation. The DAC Guidelines." Paris, OECD.

OECD (2003a). "DAC Countries Begin Recovery in Development Aid: 5% Increase in 2002." OECD, PAC/COM/NEWS(2003)15. Available at www.oecd.org/officialdocuments/publicdisplaydocumentpdf/?cote=PAC/COM/NEWS%282003%2915&docLanguage=En (accessed February 8, 2011)..

OECD (2003b). "OECD Adopts Stronger Environmental Common Approaches for Export Credits." OECD. Available at www.oecd.org/document/56/0,3746,en_2649_37431_21688824_1_1_1_37431,00.html (accessed February 5, 2011).

OECD (2006). Using Market Mechanisms to Manage Fisheries: Smoothing the Path. Paris, OECD.

OECD (2007). Revised Council Recommendation on Common Approaches on the Environment and Officially Supported Export Credits. TAD/ECG(2007)9. Paris, OECD.

OECD (2010a). *Aid in Support of Environment: Statistics Based on DAC Members' Reporting on the Environment*

*Policy Marker, 2007–2008.* Paris, OECD, OECD-DAC Secretariat.

OECD (2010b). Development Co-operation Report 2010. OECD, Development Assistance Committee (DAC), Paris.

OECD (2011a). OECD.StatExtracts. Paris, OECD. Available at http://stats.oecd.org/index.aspx (accessed February 12, 2011).

OECD (2011b). Statistical Annex of the 2011 Development Co-operation Report, Development Co-operation Directorate (DCD-DAC). Available at www.oecd.org/dac/stats/dac/dcrannex (accessed January 16, 2011).

Orr, J. C. (2002). On the World Bank's International Development Association. Statement before the International Monetary Policy and Trade Subcommittee of the House Committee on Financial Services, July 19.

Panayotou, T. (1994). Financing Mechanisms for Agenda 21 (or How to Pay for Sustainable Development). Working Paper, Harvard Institute for International Development, Cambridge, MA.

Parker, E. (2008). Subprime Lender: Interview with Muhammad Yunus, *The Weeekend Interview, Wall Street Journal,* March 1. Available at http://online.wsj.com/article/SB120432950873204335.html (accessed February 10, 2011).

Pearson, L. B. (1969). *Partners in Development.* New York, Praeger.

Peltier, N., and N. A. Ashford (1998). "Assessing and Rationalizing the Management of a Portfolio of Clean Technologies: Experience from a French Environmental Fund and a World Bank Cleaner Production Demonstration Project in China." *Journal of Cleaner Production* 6: 111–117.

Pleskovic, B. and N. Stern, Eds. (2003). *Annual World Bank Conference on Development Economics: The New Reform Agenda.* New York, Oxford University Press.

Porter, G., R. Clémençon, et al. (1998). Study of the GEF's Overall Performance. Washington, DC, Global Environment Facility. Available at http://iwlearn.net/publications/mne/ops/OPS1.pdf (accessed February 8, 2011).

Prasad, E., K. Rogoff, et al. (2003). Effects of Financial Globalization on Developing Countries: Some Empirical Evidence. Washington, DC, International Monetary Fund. Available at www.imf.org/external/np/res/docs/2003/031703.pdf (accessed February 8, 2011).

Ranis, G. (1995). On Fast-Disbursing Policy-Based Loans. Working Paper, New Haven, CT, Yale University, Economics Department.

Redclift, M. (1996). The Earth Summit. *Wasted: Counting the Costs of Global Consumption.* London, Earthscan: 11–31.

Reisman, K. (1992). "The World Bank and the IMF: At the Forefront of World Transformation." *Fordham Law Review* 60: 349–394.

Rich, B. (2000). "Exporting Destruction." *Environmental Forum* (September/October): 32–41.

Rodrik, D., and A. Subramanian (2008). Why Did Financial Globalization Disappoint? Unpublished manuscript, Cambridge, MA, Harvard University.

Roodman, D. (2010). The Commitment to Development Index: 2010 Edition. Washington, DC, CGD.

Rowden, R. (2003). "Will the World Bank's Plans Work?" September 21, 2003. London, BBC. Available at http://news.bbc.co.uk/2/hi/business/3124150.stm (accessed February 8, 2011).

Rutherford, S. (2000). *The Poor and Their Money.* New Delhi, Oxford University Press.

Schaper, M. (2009). Export Promotion, Trade and the Environment: Negotiating Environmental Standards for Export Credit Agencies across the Atlantic. *Transatlantic Environment and Energy Politics: Comparative and International Perspectives.* M. Schreurs, H. Selin and S. VanDeveer. Aldershot, Ashgate: 189–208.

Schoener, W. (1997). "Non-governmental Organizations and Global Activism: Legal and Informal Approaches." *Indiana Journal of Global Legal Studies* 4: 537–569.

Scruggs, L. (2003). *Sustaining Abundance: Environmental Performance in Industrial Democracies.* Cambridge, Cambridge University Press.

Sheehy, T. (1996). "Who Has Aid Really Helped?" *Ceres. The FAO Review on Agriculture and Development* 28: 23–26.

Shorrocks, A., and G. Mavrotas (2006). *Advancing Development: Core Themes in Global Economics.* Basingstoke, Palgrave Macmillan.

Sjöberg, H. (1999). "Restructuring the Global Environment Facility." GEF Working Paper 13. Washington, DC, Global Envirobnment Facility (GEF).

Škreb, M. (2001). "Emerging Market and Transition Economies Face Special Challenges in Globalized Economy." *IMF Survey* 30(15): 258–260.

Smith, S. (2000). What Is an Environmental Fund and When Is It the Right Tool for Conservation? *The IPG Handbook on Environmental Funds: A Resource Book for the Design and Operation of Environmental Funds.* R. A. Norris. New York, Pact Publications: 10–13.

Soros, G. (2002). *Geroge Soros on Globalization.* New York, Public Affairs.

Stiglitz, J. (2002a). "A Fair Deal for the World." *New York Review of Books* 49(9): 24–28.

Stiglitz, J. (2002b). *Globalization and Its Discontents.* New York, W. W. Norton.

Stout, L. A. (1988). "The Unimportance of Being Efficient: An Economic Analysis of Stock Market Pricing and Securities Regulation." *Michigan Law Review* 87(3): 613–709.

Taylor, M. P., and L. Sarno (1999). The Persistence of Capital Inflows and the Behaviour of Stock Prices in East Asia Emerging Markets: Some Empirical Evidence. CEPR Discussion Paper 2150, May.

Truman, E. M. (2007). Sovereign Wealth Funds: The Need for Greater Transparency and Accountability. Policy Brief PB07–6, Peterson Institute for International Economics, Washington, DC, August.

United Nations (UN) (1992). *The Rio Declaration on Environment and Development.* New York, UN.

UN (2009). *The Millennium Development Goals Report 2009.* New York, UN.

UN (2010). Follow-up to and Implementation of the Monterrey Consensus and the Doha Declaration on Financing for Development. Report of the Secretary-General. A/65/293, August 12. New York, UN.

United Nations Conference on Trade and Development (UNCTAD) (2010). World Investment Report 2010: Investing in a Low-Carbon Economy. New York, UNCTAD.

United Nations Development Programme (UNDP) (2008). Capacity Development and Aid Effectiveness: A Compendium of Needs Identified, Lessons Learnt and Good Practices. New York, UNDP.

von Moltke, K. (2000). An International Investment Regime? Issues of Sustainability. Winnipeg, International Institute for Sustainable Development. Available at www.iisd.org/pdf/investment.pdf (accessed February 6, 2011).

Wade, R. (1997). Greening the Bank: The Struggle over the Environment, 1970–1995. *The World Bank: Its First Half-Century*, vol. 2. J. P. Lewis and R. Webb. Washington, DC, Brookings Institution: 611–734.

Wallace, D. (1995). *Environmental Policy and Industrial Innovation: Strategies in Europe, the U.S. and Japan.* London, Earthscan.

Watkins, K. (1996). "Eclipsing the New Dawn of Development." *Ceres. The FAO Review on Agriculture and Development* **28**: 27–32.

Weidner, J. N. (2001). "World Bank Study." *Buffalo Human Rights Law Review* **7**: 193–226.

Wikipedia (2011). Export Credit Agencies. *Wikipedia.* Available at http://en.wikipedia.org/wiki/Export_Credit_Agencies (accessed January 31, 2011).

Wolff, E. N. (1995a). "How the Pie Is Sliced: America's Growing Concentration of Wealth." *American Prospect* **22**: 58–64.

Wolff, E. N. (1995b). *Top Heavy: A Study of Increasing Inequality in America.* New York, Twentieth Century Fund.

World Bank Group (WBG) (1991a). *Establishment of the Global Environment Facility.* Washington, DC, World Bank.

WBG (1991b). *World Development Report 1991: The Challenge of Development* New York, Oxford University Press.

WBG (1992). *World Development Report: Development and the Environment.* Oxford University Press.

WBG (1997). *Five Years after Rio: Innovations in Environmental Policy.* Washington, DC, World Bank.

WBG (1998). *Assessing Aid: What Works, What Doesn't, and Why?* Washington, DC, World Bank.

WBG (1999a). *Global Economic Prospects, 1998/99.* Washington, DC, World Bank.

WBG (1999b). *World Development Report 1999/2000: Entering the 21st Century.* Washington, DC, World Bank.

WBG (2000a). *IDA in Action: Improving Aid Effectiveness and Reaching the Poor.* Washington, DC, World Bank.

WBG (2000b). *World Bank 1999 Annual Report.* Washington, DC, World Bank.

WBG (2001). *World Development Report 2000/2001: Attacking Poverty.* New York, Oxford University Press.

WBG (2002a). *Global Economic Prospects, 2003.* Washington, DC, World Bank.

WBG (2002b). *World Development Report: Creative Financing for Sustainable Development.* Washington, DC, World Bank.

WBG (2003a). *Global Development Finance: Striving for Stability in Development Finance.* Washington, DC, World Bank.

WBG (2003b). *World Bank History.* Washington, DC, World Bank. Available at http://go.worldbank.org/2GIYUD9KB0 (accessed February 7, 2011).

WBG (2003c). *Pages from World Bank History: The Pearson Commission.* Washington, DC, World Bank. Available at http://go.worldbank.org/JYCU8GEWA0 (accessed February 7, 2011).

WBG (2007). *Global Development Finance, 2007: The Globalization of Corporate Finance in Developing Countries.* Washington, DC, World Bank.

WBG (2008). *Global Development Finance: The Role of International Banking.* Washington, DC, World Bank.

WBG (2009). *World Bank–Civil Society Engagement: Review of Fiscal Years 2007 to 2009.* Washington, DC, World Bank.

WBG (2010a) *Global Development Finance 2010: External Debt of Developing Countries.* Washington, DC, World Bank.

WBG (2010b). *The World Bank Annual Report 2010: Year in Review.* Washington, DC, World Bank.

WBG (2011). *Global Development Finance: External Debt of Developing Countries.* Washington, DC, World Bank.

WBG, United Nations Environment Programme (UNEP), et al. (2002). *Creative Financing for Sustainable Development: An Input to the World Summit on Sustainable Development.* Washington, DC, World Bank.

World Commission on Environment and Development (WCED) (1987). *Our Common Future.* Oxford, Oxford University Press.

World Trade Organization (WTO) (1999). Trade and Environment. Geneva, WTO. Available at www.wto.org/english/tratop_e/envir_e/environment.pdf (access February 6, 2001).

Wright, C. (2005). Investigating the Discursive Power of Multilateral Financial Institutions. Paper presented at the 2005 Berlin Conference on the Human Dimensions of Global Environmental Change: International Organisations and Global Environmental Governance, Berlin, Germany. Available at http://userpage.fu-berlin.de/ffu/akumwelt/bc2005/papers/wright_bc2005.pdf (accessed February 8, 2011).

Young, Z., and S. Boehmer-Christiansen (1997). "Research Note: The Global Environmental Facility; An Institutional Innovation in Need of Guidance?" *Environmental Politics* **6**(1): 193–202.

Yunus, M. (2001). "Letters to the Editor: Credit as a Human Right." *Wall Street Journal* December 12. Available at http://web01.grameen.com/wallstreetjournal/LetterToWSJEditor.html (accessed February 10, 2011).

Zylicz, T. (1994). Environmental Policy Reform in Poland. *Economic Policies for Sustainable Development.* T. Sterner. Dordrecht, Kluwer Academic Publishers: 82–112.

# APPENDIX 12-A: ACRONYMS

**TABLE 12-A.1: TABLE OF ACRONYMS**

| | |
|---|---|
| ASEAN | Association of South East Asian Nations |
| BCSD | Business Council for Sustainable Development |
| BRAC | Bangladeshi Rural Advancement Committee |
| CDF | Comprehensive development framework |
| CDI | Comprehensive Development Index |
| CDM | Clean development mechanism |
| CER | Certified emission reduction |
| CGAP | Consultative Group to Assist the Poor |
| CGD | Center for Global Development |
| DAC | Development Assistance Committee |
| ESOP | Employee stock ownership plan |
| FDI | Foreign direct investment |
| FP | Foreign Policy magazine |
| GDF | Global development finance |
| GDP | Gross domestic product |
| GEF | Global Environment Facility |
| GNI | Gross national income |
| GNP | Gross national product |
| HIPC | Heavily indebted poor countries |
| IBRD | International Bank for Reconstruction and Development |
| ICSID | International Centre for Settlement of Investment Disputes |
| IDA | International Development Association |
| IFC | International Finance Corporation |
| ILO | International Labour Organization |
| IMF | International Monetary Fund |
| LDC | Less developed country |
| LFI | Less financially integrated |
| MAI | Multilateral agreement on investment |
| MERCOSUR | Mercado común del sur (southern common market) |
| MDG | Millennium Development Goals |
| MFI | More financially integrated |
| MIGA | Multilateral Investment Guarantee Agency |
| NAFTA | North American Free Trade Agreement |
| NCS | National conservation strategy |
| NEAP | National environmental action plan |
| NEF | National environmental fund |
| NGO | Nongovernmental organization |
| NSDS | National sustainable development framework |
| ODA | Official development assistance |
| OECD | Organisation for Economic Co-operation and Development |
| PBL | Policy-based loan |
| POP | Persistent organic pollutant |
| PRS(P) | Poverty reduction strategy (paper) |
| SAL | Structural adjustment loan |
| SDR | Special drawing right |
| SECAL | Sectoral adjustment loan |
| TFAP | Tropical Forestry Action Programme |
| TNC | Transnational corporation |
| UN | United Nations |
| UNCED | United Nations Conference on Environment and Development |
| UNCTAD | United Nations Conference on Trade and Development |
| UNDP | United Nations Development Programme |
| UNEP | United Nations Environment Programme |
| UNFCCC | United Nations Framework Convention on Climate Change |
| UNIDO | United Nations Industrial Development Organization |
| WBG | World Bank Group |
| WCED | World Commission on Environment and Development |
| WHO | World Health Organization |
| WTO | World Trade Organization |

## APPENDIX 12-B: DEFINING AID

The Development Assistance Committee (DAC) of the OECD is the international forum for defining aid.* The twenty-two DAC members provided $120 billion in ODA in 2009 (OECD 2011a). (The members of the DAC are Australia, Austria, Belgium, Canada, Denmark, Finland, France, Germany, Greece, Ireland, Italy, Japan, Luxembourg, the Netherlands, New Zealand, Norway, Portugal, Spain, Sweden, Switzerland, the United Kingdom, and the United States. The DAC compiles statistics on aid and other official flows on the basis of information provided to it by bilateral and multilateral agencies (these data are available on the OECD website, www.oecd.org/dac/stats). The aid that is provided by DAC members is divided into two categories: official development assistance (ODA) and official aid (OA). These two forms of aid are similar, except that only developing countries that are listed on Part I of the DAC "List of Aid Recipients" are eligible to receive ODA. Also, only ODA may be counted by DAC countries as part of their "aid effort," the number that often appears in statistics and is defined as the donor country's aid budget relative to its GNI.

ODA is provided by donor governments and their agencies for the purpose of promoting economic development and welfare. It can comprise both loans and grants to developing countries and territories. However, if ODA is provided in the form of a loan, it must be extended on concessional financial terms, that is, with a grant element of 25 percent or more (calculated as the net present value of the future payment stream, with a discount rate of 10 percent). Countries on Part II of the DAC list (which includes countries in Eastern and central Europe, the Russian Federation, other independent republics of the former Soviet Union, and a number of high-income

---

* This appendix is based on chapter 6 of *Global Development Finance* (WBG 2003a, p. 127) and the overview in the 1998 World Bank policy research report *Assessing Aid* (WBG 1998).

countries like French Polynesia, Israel, and New Caledonia) receive OA.

In discussions of aid, one often encounters a different term as well: official development *finance*. Official development finance includes all financing that flows from developed-country governments and multilateral agencies to the developing world. ODA is therefore a subset of official development finance because it comprises only grant-making activity plus concessional loans that have a grant component of at least 25 percent.

In our analysis in Section 12.2, the focus is mainly on less developed countries (LDCs), which are listed on part I of the DAC list. When we are discussing official aid flows, we therefore mainly investigate levels of and trends in ODA. However, many of the observations and findings are relevant for the larger category of official development finance as well.

Aid flows can be represented from both the perspective of the donor and that of the recipient. Reports of aid flows *provided* by donors (see Table 12-B.1) usually include bilateral disbursements of concessional financing to developing countries, as well as concessional financing from bilateral donors to multilateral organizations (such as the International Development Association of the World Bank—see Section 12.3.1.1).

On other occasions, disbursements of aid that are *received* by recipients are reported, which may come from both bilateral and multilateral sources. This is the case, for instance, in Table 12-B.2.

The results obtained through these two measures will usually not match. There are several reasons for this. First, data on concessional flows to recipient countries do not include technical assistance. Second, it must be noted that the funds that bilateral donors make available to multilateral organizations (such as the IDA) usually do not match the distributions of funds by these organizations in that year. Third, differences also arise because high-income countries receive OA, which, as stated above, is not included in reports of a donor country's aid budgets.

**TABLE 12-B.1: TOTAL NET FLOWS FROM DAC COUNTRIES BY TYPE OF FLOW**

| | USD MILLION | | | | | | |
|---|---|---|---|---|---|---|---|
| | 1993–1994 AVERAGE | 1998–1999 AVERAGE | 2005 | 2006 | 2007 | 2008 | 2009 |
| **I. Official Development Assistance** | 57,610 | 52,910 | 107,838 | 104,814 | 104,206 | 122,359 | 120,000 |
| 1. Bilateral grants and grant-like flows | 34,365 | 33,244 | 83,750 | 79,691 | 75,677 | 88,174 | 80,800 |
| of which: Technical co-operation | 13,020 | 13,061 | 20,812 | 22,359 | 15,037 | 17,231 | 17,546 |
| Developmental food aid[a] | 1,733 | 982 | 887 | 956 | 1,056 | 1,418 | 1,484 |
| Humanitarian aid[a] | 2,323 | 2,747 | 7,147 | 6,748 | 6,464 | 8,842 | 8,633 |
| Debt forgiveness | 3,077 | 2,644 | 24,999 | 18,600 | 9,624 | 11,067 | 2,071 |
| Administrative costs | 2,582 | 2,940 | 4,135 | 4,275 | 4,650 | 5,399 | 5,295 |
| 2. Bilateral loans | 5,690 | 3,410 | −855 | −2,423 | −2,298 | −1,172 | 2,802 |
| 3. Contributions to multilateral institutions | 17,555 | 16,257 | 24,942 | 27,546 | 30,828 | 35,357 | 36,398 |
| of which: UN[b] | 4,246 | 4,043 | 5,507 | 5,287 | 5,872 | 5,870 | 6,360 |
| EU institutions[b] | 4,399 | 5,009 | 9,258 | 9,931 | 11,714 | 13,039 | 13,789 |
| IDA[b] | 4,802 | 3,537 | 4,946 | 6,787 | 5,691 | 8,150 | 7,230 |
| Regional development banks[b] | 2,558 | 1,895 | 2,222 | 2,520 | 2,418 | 3,218 | 3,114 |
| **II. Other Official Flows** | 9,836 | 14,109 | 2,151 | −9,704 | −5,433 | 113 | 9,836 |
| 1. Bilateral | 8,592 | 12,631 | 2,983 | −9,528 | −5,957 | −643 | 8,050 |
| 2. Multilateral | 1,243 | 1,479 | −832 | −177 | 524 | 756 | 1,785 |
| **III. Private Flows at market terms** | 78,480 | 114,531 | 182,885 | 202,108 | 318,626 | 129,922 | 228,407 |
| 1. Direct investment | 44,148 | 89,595 | 103,948 | 135,272 | 185,059 | 186,909 | 158,934 |
| 2. Bilateral portfolio investment | 37,178 | 26,858 | 73,335 | 60,910 | 130,122 | −53,573 | 48,185 |
| 3. Multilateral portfolio investment | −2,172 | −3,923 | 40 | 2,789 | −9,737 | −9,986 | 18,839 |
| 4. Export credits | −674 | 2,000 | 5,563 | 3,137 | 13,182 | 6,572 | 2,449 |
| **IV. Net grants by NGOs** | 5,869 | 6,173 | 14,823 | 14,749 | 18,352 | 23,787 | 22,047 |
| **TOTAL NET FLOWS** | 151,795 | 187,723 | 307,696 | 311,967 | 435,751 | 276,181 | 380,290 |
| Total net flows at 2008 prices and exchange rates[c] | 197,456 | 269,237 | 356,822 | 354,602 | 458,869 | 276,181 | 391,922 |

[a] Emergency food aid included with developmental food aid up to and including 1995.

[b] Grants and capital subscriptions, does not include concessional lending to multilateral agencies.

[c] Deflated by the total DAC deflator.

Source: OECD (2011b, table 2).

**TABLE 12-B.2: NET CAPITAL INFLOWS TO DEVELOPING COUNTRIES**

| | USD BILLION | | | | | | | |
|---|---|---|---|---|---|---|---|---|
| | 2001 | 2002 | 2003 | 2004 | 2005 | 2006 | 2007 | 2008 |
| **Current account balance** | 7.2 | 63.6 | 103.1 | 138.4 | 246.5 | 331.0 | 352.5 | 256.4 |
| *Financed by:* | | | | | | | | |
| Net private and official inflows | 224.2 | 161.0 | 262.3 | 361.4 | 501.4 | 659.0 | 1,221.6 | 780.3 |
| **Net equity inflows** | 170.9 | 160.3 | 179.8 | 254.3 | 349.9 | 469.0 | 663.8 | 536.5 |
| Net FDI inflows | 164.6 | 151.3 | 154.3 | 215.7 | 281.1 | 363.2 | 528.4 | 593.6 |
| Net portfolio equity inflows | 6.3 | 9.0 | 25.5 | 38.6 | 68.8 | 105.8 | 135.4 | −57.1 |
| **Net debt flows** | 53.3 | 0.7 | 82.5 | 107.1 | 151.5 | 190.0 | 557.8 | 243.8 |
| Official creditors | 27.3 | 6.2 | −12.4 | −26.2 | −71.9 | −72.9 | −1.9 | 28.1 |
| World Bank | 7.8 | 0.1 | −1.5 | 2.7 | 3.3 | −0.2 | 5.3 | 7.6 |
| IMF | 19.5 | 14.2 | 2.4 | −14.7 | −40.2 | −26.7 | −5.1 | 10.8 |
| Other official | 0.0 | −8.1 | −13.3 | −14.2 | −35.0 | −46.0 | −2.1 | 9.7 |
| Private creditors | 26.0 | −5.4 | 94.9 | 133.1 | 223.3 | 262.9 | 559.8 | 215.8 |
| Net medium- and long-term debt flows | 3.9 | 3.0 | 29.7 | 71.6 | 137.7 | 168.1 | 315.3 | 228.5 |
| Bonds | 12.2 | 10.6 | 22.6 | 35.8 | 56.8 | 31.6 | 87.2 | 15.0 |
| Banks and other private | −8.3 | −7.6 | 7.1 | 35.8 | 80.9 | 136.5 | 228.1 | 213.5 |
| Net short-term debt flows | 22.1 | −8.4 | 65.2 | 61.5 | 85.6 | 94.8 | 244.5 | −12.7 |
| Change in reserves (− = increase) | −80.9 | −168.7 | −292.3 | −398.5 | −393.6 | −643.5 | −1,101 | −277.1 |
| *Memorandum items* | | | | | | | | |
| Official grants excluding tech cooperation | 29.1 | 33.9 | 45.8 | 53.6 | 56.8 | 106.9 | 76.0 | 86.2 |
| Workers' remittances | 93.9 | 114.2 | 141.8 | 161.8 | 193.0 | 229.0 | 281.8 | 326.7 |

Source: WBG (2010a, p. 1).

## APPENDIX 12-C: THE MILLENNIUM DEVELOPMENT GOALS AND TARGETS

In September 2000 at the Millennium Summit, the member states of the United Nations issued the Millennium Declaration, committing themselves to a series of time-bound and quantified targets for addressing extreme poverty in its many dimensions—income poverty, hunger, disease, lack of adequate shelter, and exclusion—while promoting gender equality, education, and environmental sustainability (see Table 12-C.1).* Most of the targets are to be achieved by 2015. Known as the Millennium Development Goals (MDGs), they represent a framework for achieving human development and broadening its benefits.

---

\* The information presented in this appendix is based on the official site for the United Nations Millennium Development Indicators, http://mdgs.un.org/unsd/mdg/Host.aspx?Content=Indicators/OfficialList.htm (accessed February 7, 2011).

### TABLE 12-C.1: THE MILLENNIUM DEVELOPMENT GOALS (MDGS)

| MILLENNIUM DEVELOPMENT GOALS (MDGS) (EFFECTIVE JANUARY 15, 2008) | |
|---|---|
| Goals and Targets (From the Millennium Declaration) | Indicators for Monitoring Progress |
| **Goal 1: Eradicate extreme poverty and hunger** | |
| Target 1.A: Halve, between 1990 and 2015, the proportion of people whose income is less than one dollar a day | 1.1 Proportion of population below $1 (PPP) per day<br>1.2 Poverty gap ratio<br>1.3 Share of poorest quintile in national consumption |
| Target 1.B: Achieve full and productive employment and decent work for all, including women and young people | 1.4 Growth rate of GDP per person employed<br>1.5 Employment-to-population ratio<br>1.6 Proportion of employed people living below $1 (PPP) per day<br>1.7 Proportion of own-account and contributing family workers in total employment |
| Target 1.C: Halve, between 1990 and 2015, the proportion of people who suffer from hunger | 1.8 Prevalence of underweight children under five years of age<br>1.9 Proportion of population below minimum level of dietary energy consumption |
| **Goal 2: Achieve universal primary education** | |
| Target 2.A: Ensure that, by 2015, children everywhere, boys and girls alike, will be able to complete a full course of primary schooling | 2.1 Net enrolment ratio in primary education<br>2.2 Proportion of pupils starting grade 1 who reach last grade of primary<br>2.3 Literacy rate of fifteen–twenty-four year-olds, women and men |
| **Goal 3: Promote gender equality and empower women** | |
| Target 3.A: Eliminate gender disparity in primary and secondary education, preferably by 2005, and in all levels of education no later than 2015 | 3.1 Ratios of girls to boys in primary, secondary and tertiary education<br>3.2 Share of women in wage employment in the non-agricultural sector<br>3.3 Proportion of seats held by women in national parliament |
| **Goal 4: Reduce child mortality** | |
| Target 4.A: Reduce by two-thirds, between 1990 and 2015, the under-five mortality rate | 4.1 Under-five mortality rate<br>4.2 Infant mortality rate<br>4.3 Proportion of one year-old children immunized against measles |
| **Goal 5: Improve maternal health** | |
| Target 5.A: Reduce by three quarters, between 1990 and 2015, the maternal mortality ratio | 5.1 Maternal mortality rate<br>5.2 Proportion of births attended by skilled health personnel |
| Target 5.B: Achieve, by 2015, universal access to reproductive health | 5.3 Contraceptive prevalence rate<br>5.4 Adolescent birth rate<br>5.5 Antenatal care coverage (at least one visit and at least four visits)<br>5.6 Unmet need for family planning |
| **Goal 6: Combat HIV/AIDS, malaria and other diseases** | |
| Target 6.A: Have halted by 2015 and begun to reverse the spread of HIV/AIDS | 6.1 HIV prevalence among population aged fifteen–twenty-four years<br>6.2 Condom use at last high-risk sex<br>6.3 Proportion of population aged fifteen–twenty-four years with comprehensive correct knowledge of HIV/AIDS<br>6.4 Ratio of school attendance of orphans to school attendance of non-orphans aged ten–fourteen years |
| Target 6.B: Achieve, by 2010, universal access to treatment for HIV/AIDS for all those who need it | 6.5 Proportion of population with advanced HIV infection with access to antiretroviral drugs |
| Target 6.C: Have halted by 2015 and begun to reverse the incidence of malaria and other major diseases | 6.6 Incidence and death rates associated with malaria<br>6.7 Proportion of children under five sleeping under insecticide-treated bednets<br>6.8 Proportion of children under five with fever who are treated with appropriate anti-malarial drugs<br>6.9 Incidence, prevalence and death rates associated with tuberculosis<br>6.10 Proportion of tuberculosis cases detected and cured under directly observed treatment short course |

(continued)

**TABLE 12-C.1** (continued)

MILLENNIUM DEVELOPMENT GOALS (MDGS) (EFFECTIVE JANUARY 15, 2008)

| Goals and Targets (From the Millennium Declaration) | Indicators for Monitoring Progress |
|---|---|
| **Goal 7: Ensure environmental sustainability** | |
| Target 7.A: Integrate the principles of sustainable development into country policies and programs and reverse the loss of environmental resources | 7.1 Proportion of land area covered by forest <br> 7.2 $CO_2$ emissions, total, per capita and per \$1 GDP (PPP) <br> 7.3 Consumption of ozone-depleting substances <br> 7.4 Proportion of fish stocks within safe biological limits <br> 7.5 Proportion of total water resources used |
| Target 7.B: Reduce biodiversity loss, achieving, by 2010, a significant reduction in the rate of loss | 7.6 Proportion of terrestrial and marine areas protected <br> 7.7 Proportion of species threatened with extinction |
| Target 7.C: Halve, by 2015, the proportion of people without sustainable access to safe drinking water and basic sanitation | 7.8 Proportion of population using an improved drinking water source <br> 7.9 Proportion of population using an improved sanitation facility |
| Target 7.D: By 2020, to have achieved a significant improvement in the lives of at least 100 million slum dwellers | 7.10 Proportion of urban population living in slums |
| **Goal 8: Develop a global partnership for development** | |
| Target 8.A: Develop further an open, rule-based, predictable, non-discriminatory trading and financial system | *Some of the indicators listed below are monitored separately for the least developed countries (LDCs), Africa, landlocked developing countries and small island developing States.* |
| Includes a commitment to good governance, development and poverty reduction—both nationally and internationally | Official Development Assistance (ODA) <br> 8.1 Net ODA, total and to the least developed countries, as percentage of OECD/DAC donors' gross national income |
| Target 8.B: Address the special needs of the least developed countries <br> Includes: tariff and quota free access for the least developed countries' exports; enhanced pro-gramme of debt relief for heavily indebted poor countries (HIPC) and cancellation of official bilateral debt; and more generous ODA for countries committed to poverty reduction | 8.2 Proportion of total bilateral, sector-allocable ODA of OECD/DAC donors to basic social services (basic education, primary health care, nutrition, safe water and sanitation) <br> 8.3 Proportion of bilateral official development assistance of OECD/DAC donors that is untied <br> 8.4 ODA received in landlocked developing countries as a proportion of their gross national incomes <br> 8.5 ODA received in small island developing states as a proportion of their gross national incomes |
| Target 8.C: Address the special needs of land-locked developing countries and small island developing States (through the Programme of Action for the Sustainable Development of Small Island Developing States and the outcome of the twenty-second special session of the General Assembly) | Market Access <br> 8.6 Proportion of total developed country imports (by value and excluding arms) from developing countries and least developed countries, admitted free of duty <br> 8.7 Average tariffs imposed by developed countries on agricultural products and textiles and clothing from developing countries <br> 8.8 Agricultural support estimate for OECD countries as a percentage of their gross domestic product |
| Target 8.D: Deal comprehensively with the debt problems of developing countries through national and international measures in order to make debt sustainable in the long term | 8.9 Proportion of ODA provided to help build trade capacity <br> Debt Sustainability <br> 8.10 Total number of countries that have reached their HIPC decision points and number that have reached their HIPC completion points (cumula-tive) <br> 8.11 Debt relief committed under HIPC and MDRI Initiatives <br> 8.12 Debt service as a percentage of exports of goods and services |
| Target 8.E: In cooperation with pharmaceutical companies, provide access to affordable essential drugs in developing countries | 8.13 Proportion of population with access to affordable essential drugs on a sustainable basis |
| Target 8.F: In cooperation with the private sector, make available the benefits of new technologies, especially information and communications | 8.14 Telephone lines per 100 population <br> 8.15 Cellular subscribers per 100 population <br> 8.16 Internet users per 100 population |

Source: United Nations Statistics Division, Department of Economic and Social Affairs, Official list of MDG indicators, http://unstats.un.org/unsd/mdg/Host.aspx?Content=Indicators/OfficialList.htm (accessed January 16, 2011).

# VI

# Strategic Policy Design for Sustainable Transformations

In this last part of this book, we discuss the necessary and sufficient components of strategic policy design and implementation for sustainable transformations of the industrial state. Our focus is on the developed nations, although many aspects of the special challenges faced by nations in less advanced stages of development are also addressed. Our conviction is that developed economies must display leadership and take dramatic action to serve as a model and empirical basis for policies that might be fashioned for the developing world.

# 13

## Pathways to Sustainability: Co-optimizing Economic Development, the Environment, and Employment

## 13.1 INTRODUCTION

This book has thus far focused on the origins of the emergence of sustainability as a concept; its evolution through national and international political and legal processes; the theories of economic growth in national and global contexts; the effects of globalization and trade on sustainable development; the role of innovation and the industrial firm in achieving sustainable development; governmental industrial, employment, and regulatory policies; and financing mechanisms for growth and sustainable development. Although policy options that address various problem areas have been discussed throughout the text, it is in this final chapter that they are brought together in order to foster sustainable development in a coherent and integrated manner.

We contend that the most crucial problem in achieving sustainability is lock-in or path dependency due to (1) the failure of both government and the private sector to envision, design, and implement policies that achieve co-optimization, or the mutually reinforcing, of social goals, and (2) entrenched economic and political interests that gain from the present system and advancement of its current trends. We have argued that industrial policy, environmental law and policy, and trade initiatives must be "opened up" by expanding the practice of multi-purpose policy design and that these policies must be integrated as well. Sustainable development requires stimulating revolutionary technological innovation through environmental, health, safety, economic, and labor market regulation. Greater support for these changes must also be reinforced by "opening up the participatory and political space" to enable new voices to contribute to integrated thinking and solutions.

The scholarship on sustainable development reviewed in this work has concentrated predominantly on three issues:

1. What are the economic, environmental, and employment problems that characterize unsustainability?

2. What are the visions for a more sustainable world?

3. What combination of carrots and sticks (incentives and mandates) should be put in place to achieve greater progress toward sustainable development?

Together, getting the right answers to these questions is necessary if we are to be successful at transforming the industrial state in a beneficial way.

Interestingly, the scholarship often stops after the second question or addresses only a narrow set of policy cures, such as technological innovation, public participation, market incentives, finance, or a shift to a natural capital-based, dematerialized, and ecoefficient economic system.[1] Most often, the literature addresses only the first two of the three pillars of sustainable development: economic welfare, the environment, and employment. We anticipate that although energy and the environment will continue to command a prominent place in sustainability discussions, it is meaningful and rewarding employment with adequate purchasing power—or increasing earning capacity—that will increasingly dominate the public policy agenda over the next decade or two. It is quite possible that rather than environmental and energy concerns driving future transformations, the need to enhance the earning capacity of ordinary citizens, whether by acquiring access to capital or having meaningful, rewarding employment with adequate purchasing power—or some combination of both—may be the driver of change in the near term. This possibility makes it all the more urgent that concerns for individual earning capacity not be relegated to the back burner, while environmental and energy-related crises receive the bulk of our attention directed toward policy reforms.

Furthermore, political reality requires addressing another question that logically comes between the second and third questions above: who and what stand in the way of progress toward achieving a more sustainable future? One needs only to acknowledge the dominance of incumbent industries and firms in health care and pharmaceuticals, energy, chemicals- and material-based industries, transpor-

tation, agriculture, manufacturing, communication and information technology, retailing, banking, and the media—all of which can be characterized to some extent as profiting at the expense of society at large—to realize how important this question is. Ironically, these economic actors not only benefit from promoting the ideology of a market-based economy but also largely distort *competitive* markets to their advantage, prevent needed technological, institutional, and social innovation, and have given the term "corruption" a new meaning. For this reason, policies promoting law and social justice need to take center stage as policy interventions that replace liberalization—characterized as the "Washington Consensus" that has been until recently the dominant philosophy of the industrial and industrializing states.* We arrive at this conclusion not out of a preconceived notion or ideological commitment, but rather after a decadelong examination of the sustainable development debate. It is important to note that institutions—both governmental and academic—can be captured by private-sector interests and become their apologists by using assumptions, language, and concepts that advance those interests. Lock-in caused by the exercise of raw economic and political power also needs to be addressed by legal and institutional means, but those interventions are different from interventions focused on opening up the problem space for envisioning, designing, and implementing changes that achieve co-optimization, or the achieving of mutually reinforcing, of social goals.

Now, in the twenty-first century, it has become manifestly apparent that the various nation-states that constitute the global economy are collectively pursuing development courses that are becoming increasingly unsustainable. The purpose of this chapter is to explore a comprehensive and integrated set of policies and instruments to stimulate the kinds of technological, organizational, institutional, and social innovations necessary for the transformation of industrial societies into more sustainable ones. All economies, both developed and developing, increasingly suffer from the lack of an adequate supply of, or access to, essential goods and services for everyone, a good environment and public health, and meaningful/rewarding employment or earning ca-

---

* See especially Dernbach (2008, 2009a, 2009b). However, as a result of the banking crisis, as well as problems related to global climate change, neoliberalism is now being challenged, and a return to regulation on many fronts is being seriously considered. For example, the Obama administration has recently created a far-reaching consumer-protection finance agency.

pacity for their citizens. This state of affairs can be traced to the following major systemic problems introduced in the Overview to this book:

- The *fragmentation and inadequacy of the knowledge base*, resulting in a lack of understanding of the complex origin and interrelatedness of problems and the need for integrated solutions rather than unidisciplinarily designed, single-purpose solutions

- The *inequality of access to economic and political power* among people and nations and between individuals and corporations or business organizations

- A tendency toward *gerontocracy* whereby there is technological and political lock-in, usually, but not always, accompanied by concentration of economic and political power

- *Market imperfections* whereby prices of goods and services do not fully reflect the full and real costs of their provision (especially the environmental and social consequences)

- The *limitations of perfectly working markets* due to (1) *disparate time horizons*—whereby costs must be expended now to solve problems whose solutions yield benefits later, sometimes in generations to come, which are discounted in value in present terms, and therefore receive inadequate attention, and (2) *the delay in recognizing problems* with current industrialization and consumption (that is, the failure to perceive limits to growth), such that palliative responses come very late and are very expensive or impossible to implement; both disparate time horizons and delay in recognizing problems cause inappropriate production and consumption patterns to persist

- a *high-throughput industrial system*, driven by ever-increasing material and energy consumption

- an *addiction to growth and productivity*

- The *failure to engage individuals (citizens and workers) in society* to realize their human potential, resulting in social exclusion

- *Corruption**

Earlier in this book, we classified possible solutions to the problems of unsustainable industrial or industrializing systems into five broad areas:

- Education and human resource development

- Industry initiatives (see Chapter 7 on organizational innovation and learning)

- Government intervention/regulation (see Chapters 8 and 9 on national industrial and health, safety, and environmental policies, respectively)

- Stakeholder (firms, workers, consumers, citizens, professionals) involvement

- Financing sustainable development (see Chapter 12)

Although there are no chapters in this book specifically dedicated to education and resource development and stakeholder involvement, these are addressed throughout the text. Education and human resource development address both supply-side failings (not enough properly trained workers, professionals, and leaders to execute effective policies) and demand-side failings (a lack of understanding on the part of current society regarding what would be in its interest to demand from government and the private sector). Increasing stakeholder involvement reflects the perception that neither government nor the private sector is to be trusted, is deemed sufficiently knowledgeable, or is committed to operate in the public interest, thereby necessitating public involvement in the affairs of the state and the corporation.

Separate chapters are devoted to economic growth theory in the context of national and globalized economies (Chapters 3 and 4), the effects of globalization on sustainability (Chapter 5), regional and international governance of health, safety, and the environment (Chapter 10), and the nexus between international trade regimes and sustainability (Chapter 11).

The focus of this final chapter is on reconciling the sometimes conflicting demands on national and international resources and programs to achieve sustainable economic development, environmental protection,† and adequate employment by exploring policy options that mutually advance—that is, *co-optimize*—all three dimensions of sustainability. Sustainability is not a fixed vision of a particular (better) state of the world, but rather a world system that is markedly different from the present one, and one that maintains its capacity to adapt to change and crises in a timely, effective, and equitable way. Sus-

---

* Corruption is more than the misappropriation of funds or unjustifiably favoring a firm or person in government dealings. We argue that it includes the perversion of governmental responsibility implicit in the social contract, such as failing to enact, monitor, or enforce environmental, public health, antitrust, banking, economic, labor, social, and other regulations or laws that protect or promote the public welfare. In the United States, the financial and mortgage industry breakdown stands out as the most recent example.

---

† Although global climate change seems to dominate environmental sustainability concerns today, we are persuaded that toxic pollution, ecosystem damage, and diminishing material and energy resources deserve significant attention (see Chapter 1).

tainable employment or livelihoods* are a seriously neglected area of sustainability scholarship and policy attention.† President Obama emphasizes the creation of green jobs in his plans for economic recovery. Restructuring the economy to provide a "double dividend" of job creation and an improved environment will require deliberate and thoughtful planning. Green jobs are often created at the expense of "dirty" jobs, and it is not at all clear that net increases in employment will occur. Therefore, job-creation policies need to be devised, whether the jobs are green or not.

Specific pathways leading to more sustainable dynamics and transformations of the present state of the world involve activities that could be taken under the broad categories of solutions listed above. These activities involve both nation-based actors and institutions and those that operate at the regional or international level. Apart from the voluminous literature on problems of unsustainability,‡ an enormous amount of literature has been published on (1) a variety of visions of sustainable development, (2) specific changes that are needed to realize these visions, and (3) the role of "governance," focusing on how to change organizations, institutions, and society.§ The authors have relied on much of this literature to inform a necessarily personal blueprint or approach for achieving a more sustainable world.

One of the most important aspects of the published commentary is that most of it deals with only part of the three essentials of sustainability: sufficiency in terms of economic development; health, safety, and environmental quality; and meaningful and rewarding employment with adequate purchasing power or sustainable livelihoods. For some, sustainability is *environmental* sustainability. For others, sustainability

is the achievement of equitable economic welfare and the elimination of poverty. There is also a preoccupation with national and international peace and security. The overwhelming majority of the literature gives short shrift to at least one of the three pillars of sustainability (see Chapter 2). Framing the challenge as achieving a "balance" in the different elements is wrongheaded in that it forces unnecessary compromise among the several legitimate goals and misses opportunities to do better. *Co-optimizing* rather than balancing economic development, health, safety, and the environment, and employment invites a more creative response, even if it is more challenging.¶

Innovation is essential. Technological, organizational, institutional, and social innovations—or, together, *system* innovations—are needed to exploit the possible futures. Neither a "technological fix" nor reorganization and changes in learning routines of the firm nor new legislation and regulations nor changing societal demand *alone* will suffice. All are necessary. Failure to address and integrate all the dimensions that need to be changed can end in failure. There are many *necessary* elements for change. However, both *necessary* and *sufficient* measures have to be adopted for success.

We have argued that willingness, opportunity/ motivation, and capacity are the driving forces of a transformation to a more sustainable society. There are a number of activities reflecting different academic/professional paradigms that could potentially influence societal transformations. These include efforts to expand or elucidate the understanding of sustainability problems and possible solutions, to guide behavioral change, to transform culture and attitudes, to construct algorithms for making decisions, to change market behavior, and to alter the nature of government and governance.** It may be easier to change behavior—especially short-term behavior— than to change attitudes. However, longer-term behavioral changes must be preceded by deeper attitudinal changes, if not in individual citizens, then in those institutions and well-placed individuals that control or influence political, economic, and social outcomes. A temporal causal link might be repre-

---

*     Employment with adequate purchasing power and sustainable livelihoods are not quite the same, and neither may fully capture something more fundamental: *sufficient earning capacity*. Earning capacity might be satisfied by some combination of wages and capital ownership by people, rather than by wages alone (see R. Ashford 2009a).

†     Indeed, Speth (2010b, 2010c) identifies jobs and meaningful work as the most pressing societal imperative.

‡     Chapters 1 and 2 review this important literature, e.g., Rachel Carson's *Silent Spring*, Garrett Hardin's essay "The Tragedy of the Commons," Meadows et al.'s *Limits to Growth*, Schumacher's *Small Is Beautiful*, and more recent commentaries and calls for action. See also the Primer on Sustainable Development found in the website associated with this book.

§     Failure to ask who or what is standing in the way of the needed changes directly and early assumes, often incorrectly, that eventually good ideas will not meet sufficient resistance to be thwarted. This, of course, flies in the face of reality. Incumbent forces and prior standard approaches can lead to both technological and political lock-in, preventing progress, co-opting solutions, and subverting the outcomes of brilliantly laid plans.

¶     Alternatively, the three pillars of sustainability might not be considered separately; instead, following the perspective of ecological economics and Herman Daly, "The economy is nested within society, and society is nested within the ecological systems of the planet" (Sanders 2006, p. 339).

**     Adger and Jordan (2009, p. xvii), among others (Dernbach 1998), argue that "the crisis of unsustainability is, first and foremost, a crisis of governance" and suggest that there are three main modes of governing: markets, networks, and hierarchies (Adger and Jordan 2009, p. 13).

sented as short-term behavioral changes → attitudinal changes → longer-term behavioral changes.

The social sciences—and to some extent the economic sciences—attempt to advance the *understanding* of behavior and attitudes. Both economics and the law seek to *transform the culture and attitudes* of people, firms, organizations, and institutions, but in different ways. Economics and law also provide contrasting *rationales* for making decisions (for example, maximizing utility using cost-benefit analysis or promoting justice and fairness through the establishment of rights and imposition of responsibilities) and the *instrumentality* through which change (in both market and nonmarket behavior) is effected (for example, taxes or government fiat/mandates). Conceptual constructs—such as traditional neoclassical economics focusing on getting prices right, ecological economics (in which economic activities are carried out within the ecological limits to growth),* transition management† (a coevolutionary vision in which government guides but does not dominate directions for change), theories of governance involving more than government,‡ and new assumptions about economic growth, finance, and trade—have all contributed to the debate on how to achieve sustainability.

Perhaps the most crucial concepts differentiating these constructs are the familiar ones—faith in markets versus faith in government; *environmental* economics internalizing externalities via the price mechanism versus producing and living within ecological limits advocated by *ecological* economics; using market-based instruments versus prescriptive law; scenario building versus backcasting; revolutionary change versus evolutionary (or coevolutionary) change; pursuing win-win options rather than confronting the necessary trade-offs;§ and governance involving many stakeholders versus a strong government hand. Complicating the choice of approaches is the idiosyncratic combination of these conceptual elements. For example, ecological modernization claims

both those who are advocates for evolutionary and market-based approaches¶ and those who argue for a firm, strong government hand.[2] Ecological economics is promoted by both those who support evolutionary change driven by social actors and those who reject the North-centric market model and argue for reconceptualizing development.[3] There are also contrasting sympathies—both at the national and the supranational level—for integrating** economic, environmental, and social initiatives within one governmental or organizational sphere, as opposed to a pluralism of approaches.†† In this final chapter, our preferences are clear and are derived from arguments made throughout this book concerning the strengths and weaknesses of alternative approaches.

Much of the literature analyzes the causes and nature of unsustainability but is short on specific or practical recommendations. In contrast, on the basis of a compendium of contributions from forty-one persons (Dernbach 2009b), Dernbach (2008, pp. 97–98) groups ten recommendations for immediate steps that can be taken toward sustainability:

1. The United States should systematically reduce its ecological footprint.
2. The United States government must adopt, as soon as possible, greenhouse gas emission reduction programs that will reduce U.S. emissions to our fair share of safe global emissions.
3. The United States should create more employment opportunities in environmental protection and restoration as well as make it easier for unskilled and low-income persons to enter and remain in the workforce.
4. Sustainable development should be an organizing principle for all levels of government.
5. Nongovernmental actors should play a major role in achieving sustainability.
6. Individuals, families, and consumers should have more sustainable options in the decisions they make.

---

\* See the discussion in Section 1.3 in Chapter 1.
† The proponents of transition management argue somewhat paradoxically, that "radical" changes in sociotechnical systems can be achieved in a stepwise manner (Kemp, Loorbach, et al. 2007). See the discussion of transition management in Section 8.4.2 in Chapter 8.
‡ See Adger and Jordan (2009) and the discussion of stakeholder involvement in governance in Section 8.6 in Chapter 8.
§ The authors of this book argue that co-optimizing economic, environmental, and social improvements deserves serious attention, while others insist that this is an unrealistic diversion from confronting the necessary trade-offs—see Adger and Jordan (2009, p. 47) and Kemp, Loorbach, et al. (2007).

¶ See Beddoe, Costanza, et al. (2009). Also see Adger and Jordan (2009, p. 40) who argue that integration cannot be driven from outside; in their view, the objectives must reflect stakeholder preferences.
** It is argued that there are three kinds of integration: linking social and ecological systems; linking different actors, stakeholders, and institutions; and horizontal and vertical policy integration (Adger and Jordan 2009, pp. 36–39). Also see the prior note above.
†† One commentator argues for strengthening environmental ministries rather than integrating environmental issues into other missions (Brown 2009, p. 69), and that "policy integration is not the right way to secure environmental improvements" (ibid., p. 71).

7.  Sustainable development should become a central part of public and formal education.

8.  The United States should strengthen its laws regarding environmental and natural resources.

9.  The United States needs to play an international leadership role on behalf of sustainable development.

10. The United States needs to improve the information and data available to the public to make decisions for sustainability.

These recommendations are premised on the view that every sector of society needs to play a substantial and constructive role in a national effort to achieve sustainable development. And these recommendations are also directed at governance. They would have sustainable development become an organizing principle for all levels of government and adopt an ambitious legal program for reducing greenhouse gas emissions. They would also involve the national government working cooperatively and constructively with nongovernmental entities in a variety of ways. In other words, they would change national governance in profound ways that need to be reflected in our laws.

The last sentence is especially crucial. Dernbach (2008, p. 92) focuses on "appropriate legal tools," and in his article he devotes considerable space to exploring the options for using new and established U.S. law to implement these recommendations.* Recent European Union (EU) treaties, now incorporated into the laws of its member states have made sustainable development the main goal of the EU† and have put the EU in a leadership position. Unlike other pundits, while acknowledging complexity, Dernbach (2008, p. 100) argues for "the systematic integration of environmental [and other social concerns‡] and goals into decision making" and the adoption of a "strategic process [that] involves the development of an overall sustainability vision and objectives based on an iterative and open process; identification of the institutions and policies that will be used to achieve

those objectives; *adoption and implementation of the needed laws and policies*; and a monitoring, learning and adaptation process that informs and perhaps changes objectives, policies, and implementation" (ibid., p. 103; emphasis added).

In discussing the recommendations for limiting environmentally destructive growth, Speth (2008) observes:

Perhaps the most important prescriptions challenging unbridled growth come from outside the environmental area. . . . They include measures such as more leisure, including a shorter workweek[§] and more vacations; greater labor protections; job security, and benefits, including retirement and health benefits; restrictions on advertising; new ground rules for corporations; strong social and environmental provisions in trade agreements; rigorous consumer protection; greater income and social equality, including genuinely progressive taxation for the rich and greater income support for the poor; major spending on public sector services and environmental amenities; a huge investment in education skills, and new technology to promote both technological modernization and sharply rising labor productivity to offset smaller workforces and shorter hours. (ibid., p. 120)

Reciting the ineptitude of government, Speth (2010b, p. 4) calls for "a new politics and a new social movement . . . [involving] a fusion of those concerned about environment, social justice, and political democracy into one progressive force." Speth (2010c) also calls for a melding of environmentalism and liberalism around a "post growth" agenda.

Some of these recommendations require far-reaching social and political changes (such as changes in the laws affecting corporations,¶ social security re-

---

*  In the compendium, Dernbach (2009b, p. 479) observes that in addition to the necessary elements recognized for good governance in general, there are three additional crucial elements in the context of sustainable development: (1) a legally grounded national-level strategic sustainable development process; (2) sustainable development indicators to measure progress; and (3) public engagement and education on sustainability. The compendium focuses on the United States rather than a global context but is worth reading for the specificity and details of its recommendations.

†  See Section 10.18.1 in Chapter 10.

‡  Dernbach (2009b, p. 100) specifically mentions "production and consumption of materials and energy, climate change, and population."

---

§  See the discussion of problems in adopting a shorter workweek in the concluding commentary of this chapter.

¶  Robert Ashford (2010, p. XX) writes

Corporations are tools—legal constructs—they have no soul, mind, or conscience of their own. By way of their legal structure, corporations are able to organize the production and distribution of goods and services on a scale that can rarely if ever be achieved by individuals. Their principal advantages in their ability to produce and distribute goods and services come from limited liability, centralized management (divorced from ownership), transferability of shares, perpetual existence, and numerous tax preferences. Their productive capacity is their virtue. The purpose of corporate finance is to enable a corporation to acquire an asset before it has earned the money to pay for it. The primary individual beneficiaries of this purpose are shareholders. What corporations do is the real issue. The use or abuse of corporations is the result of the activities of certain actors (CEOs, other officers, directors, in-house and outside counsel, etc.). In the U.S., roughly 1% of the people own 50% of corporate

forms and benefits for working people and the poor, and tax reform). Others can be fashioned within existing governmental legislation and structures (such as adopting and enforcing more stringent antitrust, health, safety, and environmental regulations and changing tax and other economic incentives). Although we are totally sympathetic to the need for broader reforms and the need to confront the growth paradox through restructuring the industrial state, the recommendations articulated in the closing section of this chapter focus more on near-term achievable goals.

Although Speth (2008, pp. 192–194) endorses a variety of alternative forms of worker ownership of the means of production and wealth creation, he (along with traditional economists) neglects a fundamental difference in the meager economic opportunity of poor people and the much greater economic opportunity enjoyed by corporations and the wealthy. Existing financial regulation enables the latter, but not the former, to acquire capital with the expected future earnings of capital, a central idea in binary economics.*

According to binary economic analysis, the need to democratize ownership or wealth cannot be sustainably met without democratizing capital acquisition with the earnings of capital, a significant driver of economic growth. As long as poor people are limited to capital acquisition primarily through their labor, while wealthy people acquire capital primarily with the earnings of capital, the poor are unlikely to be able to maintain their earning capacity, because technology continually makes capital much more productive than labor.

We have argued throughout this book that key actors and institutions must have the *willingness,* the *opportunity/motivation,* and the *capacity* to change. We have emphasized the fact that too little attention has been paid to the last factor. Incumbent firms, politicians, institutions, and society generally suffer from "gerontocracy"—technological, political, attitudinal "lock-in" or "path dependency." The changes they do contemplate tend to be "boundedly rational." When one of the authors of the present work was asked years ago what might give us hope for significant change, he answered: "One or more things: (1) the emergence of a charismatic political leader who, per force of his/her personality and vision, is given the license and the trust to change the system, (2) a crisis, like an environmental,[†] public health, or economic catastrophe, or (3) a political system that has the courage to break with the past, and by its demonstrated successes, encourages emulation on a wider basis." The 2008 election of a new American president who seems to fit the hoped-for description above and the collapse of the world financial system are forcing a reexamination of time-honored assumptions to some extent. Europe has the cultural and institutional requisites of a more sustainable political system with concerns for distributional equity, but, falling victim to the same financial crisis as the United States and disillusionment (temporary, it is hoped) with the European central government, Europe may or may not be able to influence the near future sufficiently by being a role model for success.[‡]

As discussed in Chapter 3, in an interview for the MIT *Sloan Management Review,* Jay Forrester, the father of system dynamics that formed the basis of the work on limits to growth,[§] responded to the question whether crises in sustainability would lead to new opportunities for needed technological change (Hopkins 2009). Forrester argues that seeing the real opportunities in "the no-growth, no-population rise, no increase-in-industrialization areas" would require a major (perhaps fundamental) change in our culture, which assumes that "technology can solve all problems," (ibid., p. 10) that "growth is good and can go on forever," (ibid., p. 11) and that controlling population is "too treacherous a debating area" (ibid). Placing emphasis on survival[¶] rather than on long-term

---

wealth and 10% of the people own 90%. Thus in real terms, the abuse of corporations is for the primary benefit of (some of) the people who own them and the highly paid executives who do their bidding. And, of course, the loyalty of rank and file employees (essentially economic hostages in a world that denies them competitive capital acquisition) are torn between the love/hate they feel for their captors and the deep sense of the injustice regarding their own economic impotence. The problem of the corporate misconduct cannot be coherently addressed without (1) taking a more holistic approach to corporate fiduciary duties, (2) facilitating structural reform of corporate governance, (3) reforming criminal liability for individuals who act in the corporate name and (4) democratizing capital acquisition with the earnings of capital.

\*      For a discussion of binary economics, see Section 12.11 in Chapter 12.

---

†      For an analysis of expected environmental crisis-driven societal responses, see Beddoe, Costanza, et al. (2009).

‡      For an optimistic perspective, see Rifkin (2004).

§      See the discussion of limits to growth in Section 1.3 in Chapter 1. See also Kleiner (2009).

¶      For a discussion of defensive planning in reducing vulnerability to shocks (such as an industrial accident or collapse of

sustainability is shortsighted, and "efforts involving technological solutions divert attention from the real causes of our sustainability challenge" (ibid.). Although Forrester does not explicitly say so, his analysis underscores the need to engage ourselves not only in technological innovation but in organizational, institutional, and societal change as well.

Why have we been unable to make serious inroads into solving the problems of unsustainability? The list suggested by the vast sustainability literature is reminiscent of the systemic problems discussed above but includes descriptions worthy of additional commentary:

- There has been market failure due to wrong prices and monopoly power (as distinguished from the inherent failure of a perfectly working market).

- State failure and capture have led to political lock-in (is government inherently prone to bureaucratic failure, as some have argued?).

- Subsidies have distorted markets. Ideology influences policy choices in government intervention and, consequentially, the likely responses and responders.

- Technological diffusion, rather than innovation, is encouraged.

- There is often a single-purpose design for complex problems, leading to unanticipated problem shifting.

- The future agenda is dominated by incumbent firms and institutions, discouraging displacement of technologies and policies.

- Perverse incentives are maintained or extended.

- National/sectoral policies often favor expanding existing markets through trade and miss opportunities for making investment in innovative performance.

- There is no consensus on—or perhaps we are not even asking—whether we want evolution or revolution—that is, are we to change regimes or to encourage regime changes?

- Growth and environmental deterioration cannot always be decoupled.

- Consumption-side policies (demand) and production-side policies (supply) are not coordinated and are sometimes at odds.

- Change comes hard, especially in tightly coupled institutions.

We have argued that innovation is central to the needed transformations. It can be evolutionary, or it can be revolutionary. Policies, programs, and initia-

tives influencing technological, organizational, institutional, and social innovation need to be targeted toward the *determinants* of the willingness, opportunity/motivation, and capacity of the relevant actors and institutions to change. Determinants that could stimulate change *in an evolutionary way* include the following:

- Willingness
  - having the flexibility to make changes in production or services in general
  - understanding the problem
  - possessing knowledge of options or solutions (to encourage diffusion)
  - having the ability to evaluate alternatives

- Opportunity/Motivation driven by:
  - gaps in technological/scientific capability (in existing markets)
  - the possibility of economic cost savings in existing markets or new/expanded market potential (competitiveness)
  - regulatory requirements (making new markets)
  - consumer/worker/societal demand (making new markets)

- Capacity
  - understanding the problem
  - possessing knowledge of options (to encourage diffuson)
  - having the ability to evaluate alternatives
  - having resident/available skills and capabilities (necessary for innovation)
  - reaching out to outsiders (and tolerating deviants from the mainstream)

Encouragement of *revolutionary change* adds important determinants (in boldface below) to an evolutionary vision:

- Willingness
  - **Crises/tipping points/visionary leadership**
  - having the flexibility to make changes in production or services
  - understanding the problem
  - possessing knowledge of options or solutions (to encourage diffusion)
  - having the ability to evaluate alternatives

- Opportunity/motivation driven by:
  - **Crises/tipping points/visionary leadership**
  - gaps in technological/scientific capability (in existing markets)
  - possibility of economic cost savings in existing markets or new/expanded market potential (industrial competitiveness)
  - regulatory requirements (making new markets) ← **changing the rules**
  - consumer/worker/societal demand (making new markets)

---

a key supplier) and maintaining flexibility in the face of changing business environments, see Sheffi (2007).

- Capacity
  - understanding the problem
  - having knowledge of options (to encourage diffusion)
  - having the ability to evaluate alternatives
  - having resident/available skills and capabilities (innovation) ← **building new capacity**
  - reaching out to outsiders ← **new actors, innovators, institutions, political agendas**

Crises (or so-called tipping points) offer an opportunity for government, industry, firms, and society involving their planners, scientists, engineers, economists, lawyers, and others to promote new solutions.* With regard to the financial crisis, there is currently a call for new regulation (or reregulation), institutional arrangements, actors, technical capacity, and economic and political agendas. The old assumptions, rules, and arrangements are no longer deemed adequate. Similar realizations are needed regarding global climate change; other environmental, health, and safety challenges; and production, consumption, and employment concerns. Again, the key is innovation in thinking and doing (see Jansen 2003).

One caveat about *technological* innovation: although it is generally acknowledged as the historical driving force for economic growth, trade and other aspects of the globalization of the world economy are becoming increasingly important for influencing growth (specifically growth measured in economic terms). As is the case with technological innovation, the forces of trade may not always work in concert with the achievement of the threefold dimensions of sustainability. Trade may sometimes discourage the needed technological, institutional, organizational, and social innovations. Thus trade and industrial policies need to be coordinated or, even better, integrated.

As a last word in this introduction, an explanation and an apology are in order. First, an explanation. Poverty, environmental and disease devastation, and abuses of human rights continue in the developing world. More immediate pathways to sustainable development are desperately needed there. However, the technology, the finance, and the political leadership for sustainable development may need to find

their expression in the context of the developed world first, if only to be transferred then for the benefit of the developing world.[†] The apology: understanding the successes and failures of the pathways taken by Brazil, China, and India is incredibly important for fashioning suitable policies to achieve sustainable development. In a book that is already very long, we have neither the expertise nor the vision to add to the contributions of development scholars.[‡] The South needs the North to get its own house in order, and explore and experiment with different models for development that might be emulated. It is on that end that this work focuses.

## 13.2 TECHNOLOGICAL, ORGANIZATIONAL, INSTITUTIONAL, AND SOCIAL INNOVATION

Not all innovation advances all the dimensions of sustainability—or advances them sufficiently. The ideal set of policy instruments necessarily involves both those that work through markets and those that work through government intervention, especially through national and international law. Stakeholder involvement is crucial in both. In some cases, law is necessary to establish the framework or general environment in which the market can function in a better way. In other cases, the prescriptive features of law to create clear and unambiguous goals and targets and to force compliance through legal coercion are needed.

The challenge of achieving sustainability is sufficiently complex to require a complementary set of policies and instruments, without resorting to ideological preconceptions,[§] especially those that discount the potentially important role of government or adhere to the belief that all that has to be done to achieve sustainability is to "get the prices right." In addition

---

\* We argue below that the fragmentation of the knowledge base—in educational pedagogy, the ministerial organization of government, and the separate divisions in the firm—must be addressed by encouraging transdisciplinary education, research, problem analysis, and solution design and implementation. In addition, pilot or demonstration projects, sometimes on a local, state, or regional basis or over a short trial period, may be desirable in order to gain experience for continual correction and redirection of policy or programmatic elements.

---

† Alternatively, innovation originating in developing countries could very well take a different form.

‡ See especially Gilpin (2000); Kaplinsky (2005); Rodrik (2007); and Todaro and Smith (2009). Also see the discussion of growth in Chapters 3 and 4.

§ One of those ideological preconceptions is the so-called growth imperative and the conceptualization of sustainability within the neoclassical economic paradigm (see Sanders 2006). One of the ways in which we have chosen to decouple the economic paradigm from the concept of sustainability is to redefine "competitiveness" of the nation-state not in terms of market share or level of economic growth—which is how competition is measured—but rather in terms of the ability to adequately deliver *needed* goods and services to its people. It is not the "no-growth" assumption rejected by the Stockholm and Rio conferences, but rather a limited-growth goal with distribution of essential goods replacing economic growth maximization. For a treatment of the distinction between sustainable development and "sustainable degrowth," see Martinez-Alier, Pascual, et al. (2010).

to a clear understanding of the causes of unsustainability and having a vision for a sustainable transformation, what is of paramount importance is the *creation of appropriate incentives* (and removal of perverse incentives) that can transform industrial societies into sustainable ones. In the last analysis, one must be humbled by the fact that history shows us that there are many more ways to get policies wrong than to get them right. But we are compelled to try, nonetheless.

As discussed above, innovation—whether technological, organizational, institutional, or social—may be enhanced or hindered by the dynamics and culture of the society in which it might be spawned. We have argued—and hope that we have persuaded others—through this book that the rate at which nations and economies are becoming unsustainable on a global basis requires deliberate and focused visions to guide, encourage, or even force developments and changes that either would occur only slowly or would not occur at all. We are currently experiencing two tipping points—one associated with global climate change and a second related to the global financial crisis. Others are beginning to surface.* There is no time to wait for evolutionary change, although that is the ideological preference of some.

### 13.2.1 Technological Innovation

As discussed in Chapter 6, technological change is a general and imprecise term that encompasses invention, innovation, diffusion, and technology transfer. *Technological innovation* is the first commercially successful application of a new technical idea. It should be distinguished from *invention*, which is the development of a new technical idea, and from *diffusion*, which is the subsequent widespread adoption of an innovation beyond those who developed it.[†] Sometimes the innovation is embodied in hardware, devices, inputs/materials, and process technology.

Sometimes it is embodied in the skills of labor and/or the organization of production and work, and sometimes in all these factors.

### 13.2.2 Organizational Innovation[‡]

The term "organizational innovation" is usually used to refer to larger organizational features of the firm beyond the organizational characteristics of a specific product line and is concerned with changes in and among various organizational aspects of *functions* of the firm, such as R&D and product development, marketing, environmental and governmental affairs, industrial relations, worker health and safety, and customer and community relations. Discussions of "innovation networks" focus on the importance of mutual learning among the members of the "production chain" and have spawned a whole new area of attention to product-change management. It has been increasingly argued that organizational innovation within the firm, rather than technological innovation per se, is the area most in need of exploitation, especially in Europe (Coriat 1995). Certainly, changes in management attitudes, capabilities, and incentives are important determinants of the ability of a firm to change, and the idea of networks—involving actors inside and outside a company—is important. A firm participates in perhaps several networks in which mutual learning occurs involving suppliers, consultants, trade associations, geographically close industries, consumers, workers, government, and others.

### 13.2.3 Institutional Innovation

Organizational innovation in government—what might be called institutional innovation—is also a crucial and needed factor. In that sense, "institutional innovation" is defined as changes in and among various institutions/departments within a government with regard to their *functions* and *goals* and the working relationships and shared visions among them. In the literature, institutional innovation also refers to the legislation, regulations, and routines of government and governing. The use of the term is usually clear from the context. See especially Chapters 8, 9, and 10 for policies encouraging industrial, health, safety, and environmental change. Chapters 11 and 12 continue the policy discussion in the context of international trade and financial regimes.

---

\*  In our opinion, other problems in need of immediate attention include endocrine disruption affecting the reproductive health of all species (Colborn, Dumanowski, et al. 1996), pesticide and pharmaceutical resistance giving rise to virulent modified disease vectors (Pimentel, Cooperstein et al. 2007), chemically related cancer (Epstein, Ashford, et al. 2002; Sasco 2008), other threats to public health (Yach and Bettcher 1998a, 1998b), unemployment and underemployment, terrorism, tribalism, and national security threats. See also Chapters 1 and 2.

†  The distinction between innovation and diffusion is sometimes hard to draw because innovations can rarely be adopted by new users without some modification. When modifications are extensive, i.e., when adoption requires significant *adaptation*, the result may be a new innovation. See Chapter 6 for a review of innovation.

---

‡  See Chapter 7 on organizational innovation and learning.

## 13.2.4 Social Innovation

In this book, *social innovation* is intended to mean both changes in the *preferences* of consumers, citizens, and workers for the types of products, services, environmental quality, leisure activities, and work and working conditions they want and changes in the *processes* by which they influence those changes. Social innovation can alter both the demand for and the supply of what the industrial state might offer. Obviously, social innovation should not be confused with the term "social engineering," because the former rests on information, education, communication, and enlightened self-interest rather than values and conditioning imposed from outside the individual. A valid interface between social and organizational/institutional innovation is the increasingly important role of both labor and public participation in both private-sector and governmental decisions (see Section 13.4 for an expanded discussion).

More than technological, organizational, and institutional innovations is needed to change the nature of consumption. Innovations in social attitudes, communication networks, and lifestyle that affect both demand and supply are also crucial (Cohen, Brown, et al. 2010; Thøgersen and Schrader 2011). If there are limits to growth,* then there are also practical limits to social choices. (See Sagoff 1997 and commentaries on his essay by Ehrlich, Daily, et al. 1997, and Hammond 1997 for a revealing exchange of views on whether the industrialized nations consume too much. See also the later work of Mont and Lindqvist 2003 and Tukker and Jansen 2006.)

We are not arguing that government should limit social choices per se, but rather that government should expand choices into more sustainable options through technological, organizational, institutional, *and* social innovations to encourage socially responsible informed choices. The instruments available for encouraging social innovation are educational, economic, and legal or regulatory.

Education and the provision/communication of information on the desirability and availability of sustainable products and sustainable production and service systems, and about the options that could and need to be developed,† can influence consumer and worker demand for the satisfaction of basic needs, wants, and the use of leisure or saved time. Here, the "consumer" is broadly defined as including individuals and commercial and government consumers.

We treat the acquisition of employment skills as a supply-side concern and arguably within the province of *technological* innovation because physical capital, labor, and knowledge are currently considered the most important factors in production and services. Labor skills and know-how can have a profound impact on the innovativeness of a firm and a particular industrial sector.†

However, although there are great promises for the so-called knowledge-based economy, and there are certain sectors and firms for which high returns on investment in worker education and training might be expected, it is not at all clear that unfocused and large programs will be any more successful than a large increase of financial or physical capital across the board (see the discussion in Chapter 3). More targeted policies may be needed. Note that changing the capabilities and skills of workers will also alter their *demands* from the market both because it changes what workers may want and because it may augment the purchasing power of workers.

Speth (2008) and many before him speak of developing "a new consciousness" on the part of people in their choices of what they want and how they want to live. This cultural transformation could be advanced by a new narrative, by "social marketing," by social movements, by religion, and by education (ibid.). As observers of the recent unpleasant battle over health-care reform (really insurance-industry reform) in the United States, the authors of this book find it hard to imagine how cultural shifts toward real improvement can easily occur.‡ Europe may be a more receptive venue for successful cultural change, which could then be emulated if American hubris that we do everything better in the United States could be circumvented. In the meantime, educational initiatives are crucial—and may be the only practical pathway toward societal change—for

---

\* It is argued that by reducing energy and material intensity or content of products and services, limits to growth in the satisfaction of human needs might be circumvented or at least softened (Schmidt-Bleek 1998). However, given that evidence is emerging that lower and lower levels of exposure to chemicals may result in serious health and environmental consequences (N. A. Ashford and Miller 1998)—as in the case of endocrine disruption (Colborn, Dumanowski, et al. 1996)—dematerialization may not be an adequate solution in all cases.

† Vergragt and Grootveld (1994) argued that rather than forecasting, what is needed is "backcasting" in which decision makers are asked: what will we need in twenty years, and what do we need to do now to get there? The identification of options is closely related to this recommendation.

‡ Speth (2008, p. 218) quotes William Greider: "If an activist president set out with good intentions to rewire the engine of capitalism—to alter its operating values or reorganize the terms for employment and investment or tamper with other important features—the initiative would very likely be chewed to pieces by politics" because of powerful vested interests.

both increasing the capacity for critical thinking and creating change agents to conceive and apply the needed solutions.

### 13.2.5 Commentary on Innovation

The distinction between incremental and radical innovations—be they technological, organizational, institutional, or social—is not represented by points on a continuum. Incremental innovation generally involves continuous improvements—while radical innovations are discontinuous (Freeman 1987), possibly involving *displacement* of dominant firms and institutions rather than evolutionary transformations (N. A. Ashford 2000).* This book argues that more radical, rather than incremental, innovation is needed to achieve factor ten (or better) improvements in both resource productivity and pollution reduction (Schmidt-Bleek 1998). Similarly, radical interventions in employment policy may be needed to offset increasing unemployment and underemployment in the United States and Europe. Solving these problems may require instruments, policies, and targets that are very different from those that foster incremental improvements.

Further, a preoccupation with product and process innovation, to the neglect of organizational and social innovation, may shortchange the potential to advance threefold sustainability. The benefits of organizational innovation seem to be underappreciated (Andreasen, Coriat, et al. 1995), and organizational changes that ignore the potential benefits of anthropogenic or human-centered production may not achieve their intended results (see Chapter 7 on organizational innovation and learning). A focus on limited organizational change—for example, as reflected in the concept of "lean production" emphasizing the organization and selective automation of tasks—maximizes the technological and minimizes the human aspects of production, especially the extent to which problem solving is actually a significant part of the worker's involvement,[†] and repetitive,

stressful work and burnout continue to prevail (Jürgens 1995).

Finally, a simplistic call for more worker training to upgrade skills (see Reich 1992), without corresponding changes in both technological and organization innovation, may not be particularly helpful. Not all firms and sectors are in a position to use these skills either in industrialized or in developing countries.

It should be obvious that all four kinds of innovation need to receive attention in a coordinated fashion in the design of policies to promote sustainability. Moreover, there is an increasing belief that "new growth theory"—that is, the *combination* of technological, organizational, and social factors—more adequately explains growth than R&D, capital, or human investment alone.[‡] Greater investment in both physical and human capital may create positive externalities and aggregate economies-of-scale effects rather than simply augment the productiveness[§] of labor. Further, this dual investment is alleged to lead to more rapid diffusion and adoption of new production methods and techniques.

It is especially important to acknowledge the relationship of technological innovation to both the environment and employment in hopes of attaining threefold sustainability. As discussed in Chapter 6, here, it may be useful to consider the *differential* effects that product versus process innovation may have on the environment and employment. Cleff and Rennings (1999) argue that the benefits of *product* innovation may be more readily recognized and therefore pursued by industrial firms. It has been suggested that product innovations for new markets

---

\*       Kemp, Loorbach et al. (2007) argue that radical (disrupting) system innovation can be accomplished by successive step-wise changes over a period of twenty-five years or more. However, it is hard to square this assertion with the concepts of disrupting or radical innovation put forth by Christensen and Freeman. See the discussion in chapter 6 of Christensen (1997) who uses the term "disrupting innovation" rather than radical innovation, arguing that both sustaining and disrupting innovations can be either incremental or radical.

†       See Charles and Lehner (1998) for a discussion of lean production and why it imposes considerable limitations on a company's propensity to innovate.

‡       See Chapter 3 in this book. Also see the discussion of new growth theory in "Chapter 8: Technology and Economic Growth" in OECD (1992, pp. 167–174); Baldwin (1989); Easterly and Wetzel (1989); Grossman and Helpman (1994); Lucas (1988); Romer (1987, 1989, 1994); and Scott (1989). Note also the work of Ayres and Warr (2009), who argue that it is the technology of energy conversion and utilization, rather than technology in general, that drives growth.

§       We distinguish *productiveness*, which refers to the inherent contributions of labor or capital to output, from *productivity*, which is an artificial ratio of output per unit of labor or capital; the distinction is crucial. See the Overview and Section 7.6.6 in Chapter 7. Further, Tonelson and Kearnes (2010) point out that increased labor productivity metrics are greatly distorted by the fact that hours worked abroad (exacerbated by increased outsourcing) are not included in the calculations of productivity. Thus, the mere act of outsourcing mathematically improves the productivity of the industry. In those authors' view, this weakens the case for free trade. To the extent that off-shoring simply increases corporate profits at the expense of American workers, with no real gains in productivity, the national economy is not strengthened and is not as innovative, as is implied from reported productivity increases.

can result in new net employment, partly because of their greater reliance on demand-pull forces (Brouwer and Kleinknecht 1996; Matzner, Schettkat, et al. 1990), but that this is not true for all product innovations (Charles and Lehner 1998). This, of course, does not justify neglecting policies that promote process change. In fact, product innovation that is more closely linked to process innovation and in which there is more reliance on a learning-based mode than on a scientific breakthrough is argued to create more employment (ibid.). See also Chapter 7 in this work for discussion of the later work by Edquist, Hommen, et al. (2001), which provides a deep and analytic treatment of technological change and the distinction between product and process innovation in employment generation and destruction. Finally, going beyond the employment benefits of product-oriented growth, Mont and Lindqvist (2003) and Tukker and Jansen (2006) emphasize the advantages of shifting from manufacturing products to providing product-services* that could create significant opportunities for lower environmental impact and more and better job creation, upskilling, and wages.

## 13.3 GOVERNANCE OPTIONS TO ACHIEVE SUSTAINABILITY†

The problems/challenges in achieving sustainable development and solving the many problems described in this book might lead the reader to widely different conclusions. Some may believe that the situation is hopeless, citing the financial crisis, recent mine explosions, and environmental disasters such as the oil contamination of the Gulf of Mexico, as evidence of a government unwilling or unable to provide the oversight needed to prevent such crises. Others may place abiding faith in social movements‡

and national/international bottom-up democratizing approaches§ that mobilize ordinary people to drive action rather than rely on government or the private sector.

Somewhat comforting is the fact that humankind has solved some very formidable problems in the past and could rise to the sustainability challenge. However, this will require more attention to medium- and long-term initiatives, avoidance of single-purpose solutions that shift problems from one area to another, and a more holistic approach than coordinating prior fragmented initiatives. Although we acknowledge the interconnectedness of a globalized world, we side with those who believe that actions of individual nation-states are indispensable both to achieve a more sustainable future and to persuade other nation-states to cooperate in that endeavor.¶

There are four lessons that can be taken from this book: (1) everything is connected to everything; for example, global climate change, food, water, energy, pollution, and national security issues are all intertwined; (2) there are many more ways to address the problems incorrectly than correctly; (3) co-optimization** and integration rather than "balance" or compromise of various policies are needed; and (4) government intervention, although not sufficient, is a necessary component of pathways to successful transformation of the developed and developing nations.

As discussed in the Overview to this book, various commentators offer a range of strategies to improve the sustainability of the world's economies: (1) collaborative approaches among stakeholders, lo-

---

* Product-services are exemplified by a firm providing photocopying services on a leased basis rather than selling a photocopying machine. The firm takes ownership of the machine from cradle to grave, resulting in optimal design for use and resilience, energy and material content, maintenance and repair, and ultimate disposal (usually of components). Compared with the sale of machines that are ultimately disposed of entirely with large amounts of embodied energy and material (i.e., capital), leasing allows more use of higher-skilled labor to design and redesign, manufacture, maintain, and repair the machine, resulting in less adverse environmental consequence and more higher-skilled jobs with variety and job satisfaction.

† Repetition of some material discussed earlier in this book is provided here to elucidate in one place the reasoning behind recommendations made in the rest of the chapter.

‡ See especially Speth (2010b), who calls for uniting a variety of social interests into one sociopolitical force.

§ See, for example, the Great Transition Initiative (GTI) of the Boston-based Tellus Institute, which argues that a necessary element is a global citizens' movement leading to a world parliament dedicated to reforming world governance for achieving sustainability, in contrast to the state-centric political order. See www.gtinitiative.org/documents/IssuePerspectives/GTI-Perspectives-Global_Democracy.pdf and also the presentation of GTI's proponent Paul Raskin at http://environment.yale.edu/visions/ (accessed June 1, 2010).

¶ In that regard, an alternative to waiting for the developing world to commit to the reduction of greenhouse gas emissions is for the developed countries to take the lead, set the example, and provide the financing the developing world needs to acquire and invest in clean technologies without further eroding their fragile economies.

** Co-optimization has been a central theme in this book and describes the fashioning and implementation of policies and initiatives that achieve multiple goals without sacrificing one for another. Even better would be mutually reinforcing policies that act synergistically, with one policy potentiating the outcome of another. An example is the reduction of lung-sensitizing pollutants that results in less administration of counteracting medicines with attendant side effects. Reducing these pollutants and reducing the use of medicines to treat the symptoms of disease, rather than the disease itself, are two different goals.

cally, nationally, and internationally; (2) mobilization of public opinion, especially at the grassroots level, to provide pressure on government and the private sector and to shift the nature of the demand for goods and services; and (3) government intervention in areas from environmental protection to energy supply, antimonopoly action, and job creation. Government action has not been particularly popular among free-market advocates, although recent events have increased the demand for more government involvement.

Although we are strong advocates of civic engagement and participatory democracy, one needs only to examine the results of negotiated regulation in U.S. environmental and safety areas to be convinced of the inadequacy of the "collaborative approach" at the national level (N. A. Ashford and Caldart 2005).* The unimpressive commitments made at Copenhagen speak for themselves in the international climate-change debate.† Debate concerning national health-care, climate-change, and banking reform continue to be so fraught with misinformation and so influenced by vested private-sector money that the public remains confused and suspicious, especially of government. The intended outcome of these orchestrated and well-funded misinformation campaigns is to weaken the case for strong government oversight and action.

Although the recent election of a new U.S. president was accomplished by grassroots, Internet-aided communication and fund-raising, this success is now challenged by so-called grassroots rebellions in elections and town-hall meetings that are encouraged, if not funded, by an opposition exploiting an angry, uninformed, and/or manipulated polity. The facts and details of private-sector malfeasance are there to be found, but they are so overwhelmed by propaganda that hopes for public enlightenment fade quickly. The recent U.S. Supreme Court decision in *Citizens United* (*Citizens United v. Federal Election Commission*, S. Ct. 2010) establishing almost unlimited constitutional protection that "money is speech" does not bode well for the democratic process.

Although stakeholder involvement and enhancing public awareness are essential elements of a needed transformation, we believe that these vehicles alone move too slowly and ineffectively to address the challenges brought on by the tipping points immediately ahead. National health care, environmental protection, the creation of needed jobs, the saving of people's homes, and the creation of real incentives to stem financial manipulation cannot wait for enlightenment and public involvement processes. In the end, even strong leadership from the executive branch of government, in combination with public participation and increased awareness, may not come quickly enough to avoid serious consequences, but strong and deliberate executive leadership and aggressive initiatives by the administrative agencies of government already legally empowered to act are certainly necessary components worthy of resurrection in the political process. If such initiatives involve the co-optimization (or better still, integration) of economic development; health, safety, and the environment; and employment concerns, the end result (if implemented following the recommendations presented in this work) is likely to be a more streamlined (that is smaller and efficient) form of government. In our formulation, a strong interventionist government does not equate to big government (see the related discussion in Section 13.7.1.4).

## 13.4 ALTERNATIVE POSTURES OF GOVERNMENT AND THEIR IMPLICATIONS FOR SUSTAINABLE TRANSFORMATIONS

Although all stakeholders are important, government (with other stakeholder input) will have to play the leading role in setting an agenda for transformations to a more sustainable industrial system. A major and obvious reason for this is that the goal of the private sector is to maximize profit (some have even argued that this is its primary legal obligation to stockholders), and that in the process of doing this, the private sector tends to externalize the social costs of its activities or, at least, does not engage in activity that does not improve its revenues or reputation. Only government has the potential to represent all the interests of the various stakeholders—and future generations—in the sense of both effective and fair intervention. Until the recent financial crisis and the impending global climate imperative, government intervention had fallen into disfavor, spawned by the

---

* Collaboration and negotiation may well be successful at the local level, where public concern about local pollution or economic issues makes political accountability more visible and important.

† At the international level, because supranational governmental authority rarely exists, collaboration and negotiation among stakeholders may be valuable, but whether voluntary or mandatory agreements are negotiated, national governmental action must follow lest those agreements remain a paper tiger.

Reagan and Thatcher revolutions and their aftermaths. Things have changed dramatically, as we and other authors had earlier predicted. What, then, is the appropriate role of government in promoting sustainable development? There are four possible scenarios for government:

- It can *correct market failures* by regulating pollution and by addressing inadequate prices, monopoly power, uncompetitive labor markets, and lack of information. This achieves static efficiency through better-working markets.

- It can act as a *mediator or facilitator of environmental, labor, and other* disputes/conflicts among stakeholders. This achieves static efficiency through reducing transaction costs.

- It can facilitate an industrial transformation by *encouraging organizational learning and pollution prevention*, leading to win-win outcomes (ecological modernization or reflexive law). This puts faith in rational choice and evolution.

- It can move beyond markets and act as a trustee for those with unmet needs, subsequent generations, and new technologies by forcing and encouraging innovation through an integrated regulatory, industrial, employment, and trade policy. This transcends markets and replaces incumbent firms and technologies with innovative and sustainable producers and providers of services.

The first two scenarios envision minimal government intervention, relegating government actions to making markets work more efficiently with existing or slowly evolving incremental technological innovation. The first scenario establishes the legal limits of permissive behavior. The second scenario recognizes that markets can be manipulated, or they can be inefficient because of the difficulty of striking a "Coasean bargain" among actors with conflicting needs or rights.* Governments acting as referees can help facilitate agreement and build useful alliances to reach efficient outcomes, but that role as referee or facilitator of agreement should not relieve government of its responsibility to lead changes that might not otherwise emerge as a result of bargaining.† The achievement of "static efficiency" and a belief in market fundamentalism characterize these two approaches.

The third scenario recognizes that government leadership and targets are necessary, but it relegates government action to "encouraging" rather than requiring or forcing change, embodying the belief that enlightened producers and consumers will undergo a natural evolution to a more sustainable economy because it is "rational" to do so. To some extent this is correct, but once the low-hanging fruit of win-win options has been picked, no further activity is undertaken. In addition, the scenario assumes that the *incumbent* actors are *capable* of undertaking the needed innovation and changes. This neglects the Schumpeterian observation of the "winds of creative destruction" that necessitate displacement and retirement of outmoded products, firms, and, by extension, technical and political ideas. Failure to create incentives for radical change creates both technological and political lock-in.

We are left with an ambitious and risky fourth scenario that must be seriously considered if real sustainability is to be achieved. We devote Section 13.7 of this chapter to a vision for implementing this scenario. We argue that, complemented by other kinds of changes, technological and system changes are the centerpieces of this strategy. The rationale and principles behind this strategy are outlined in the next

---

* Public participation in both private-sector decisions, usually through networks involving technology providers and suppliers (Irwin, Georg, et al. 1995), and governmental decisions, through informal networks or more formal involvement through advisory panels and science shops (Sclove 1995), may have more direct and influential effects than action through the purchasing power of consumers, especially where the problems relate to material, product, and energy transfers among industrial sectors. In addition, unlike the relationship between producers and consumers, which is subject to change as consumers change allegiances and preferences for a particular product or service provider, industrialists and labor have an intricate relationship involving an explicit or implied employment contract, job health and safety, other worker safeguard legislation, and frequent, if not daily, contact. Their relationship is influenced both by a complex web of laws and by industrial custom (N. A. Ashford and Caldart 1996). Through technology bargaining between management and labor, workers could make some of their needs and wants known to management and possibly influence innovation that affects working conditions, the products or services that the firm offers to consumers and industrial customers, and the resource and environmental consequences of its activities (N. A. Ashford and Ayers 1987). In practice, management usually holds quite tenaciously to its prerogatives to make unilateral decisions concerning changes in the technology or technical trajectory of the firm. Labor and industrial relations law protects this management prerogative to various degrees, depending on the country. To the extent that decisions affecting technology are shared, what the firm produces and how the firm functions could very well change. This social innovation would require both legal/institutional and cultural changes. The codependence of workers and owners of industrial enterprises in evolving into firms that are both competitive and sustainable could become even more important with increased globalization of industrial economies. Finally, changing the nature and rewards of employment through a responsive industrial relations system could, in turn, indirectly affect the level and character of consumption that workers desire or need in their capacity as consumers.

† Of course, the government may still be needed to resolve disputes in labor arbitration and other conflicts.

section. It will be apparent that this scenario does not envision the government as picking technological winners, but rather as *creating winning forces and pathways* and providing an enabling and facilitating role for sustainable transformations.

## 13.5 REQUIREMENTS OF TRANSFORMATIONS FOR GREATER SUSTAINABILITY

Successful transformations require

- finding new ways to meet the basic needs of society;

- changing the nature of demand through cultural transformation;*

- transdisciplinary† expertise for their design and implementation;

- reconceptualizing the basis of the economy away from one preoccupied with growth toward one focusing on selective growth;

- avoiding agenda and pathway capture or lock-in by incumbent actors and ideology;

- technological displacement and substitution of new for old technology, which can include (1) new products, (2) shifts to product-services, (3) new production processes, (4) new or altered services, and (5) new systems;‡

- in some cases, displacement of not only dominant products and technologies but also incumbent firms and public institutions;

- coevolution of technological and social systems and institutions and co-optimization of complementary technological, organizational, institutional, and social innovations;[5] and

- system changes that cut across problem areas—competitiveness, the environment, and employment—and therefore also cut across sectors and firm divisions, as well as government departments and missions.

These are basic demands for transformations that are needed to achieve significant improvements in sustain-

ability. They, in turn, will influence successful strategies.

## 13.6 TECHNOLOGY-BASED STRATEGIES TO IMPROVE PRODUCTIVENESS; HEALTH, SAFETY, AND THE ENVIRONMENT; AND EMPLOYMENT

The guiding principles of a technology-based strategy for improving productiveness, health, safety, the environment, and employment are the following:

- Shift attention from problems to solutions.
  - Undertake technology options analysis,§ not merely technology/risk assessments.¶
- Design and implement comprehensive technological changes to improve productiveness;** environment, product and worker safety; and, employment.

- Expand the scope of innovation and the dimensions of the "design space."
  - The "design space" refers to the dimensions along which the designers of technical/social systems concern themselves.
  - Expanding the available sociotechnical design space includes simultaneous consideration of the determinants of competitiveness, the environment, and employment.

---

* Here, regulating commercial advertising and providing counteracting communication though government messaging are crucial.

† Costanza and Daly (1991), in advocating the approaches fundamental to ecological economics, argue that sustainability requires a transdisciplinary approach, as does Jansen (2003). See N. A. Ashford (2004) for a clear distinction between multidisciplinary thinking and transdisciplinary thinking.

‡ System innovations may be evolutionary, quasi-evolutionary (niche developments nurtured/guided by government), coevolutionary with changes in societal demand, or revolutionary (involving the setting of demanding targets, anticipating nascent future needs, and changing the rules of the game).

§ This is recommended for government in its planning processes and for the private sector. As discussed in Chapter 9, requiring industry actually to change its technology may be necessary, but in general it is likely to be resisted. One way of providing firms with the right incentives would be to exploit the opportunity to improve their technology by requiring them to identify (1) *where* in the production process changes to environmentally sounder and inherently safer inputs, processes, and final products could be made and (2) the specific better technologies that could be substituted or developed. The first analysis might be termed a "sustainability opportunity audit." The second is a technology options analysis (TOA). Unlike a hazard or risk assessment, these practices seek to identify where and what superior technologies could be adopted or developed to eliminate the possibility, or dramatically reduce the probability, of unsafe or toxic products, pollution, accidents, and accidental releases and promote a culture of real prevention. A technology or risk assessment is generally limited to an evaluation of the performance and risks associated with a firm's established products or production technology and does not include the identification or consideration of alternative technologies that could improve performance, safety, and pollution. Consequently, these assessments tend to result in incremental changes to products and existing production technology rather than encourage the exploration and development of alternatives. See the discussion in Section 9.2.6 in Chapter 9 recommending a synchronized or parallel process involving risk assessment and technology options on a *comparative* basis.

¶ See the excerpt of Koch and Ashford (2006) in Section 9.2.6 in Chapter 9.

** Repeating here a comment made earlier, we distinguish *productiveness*, which refers to the inherent contributions of labor or capital to output, from *productivity*, which is an artificial ratio of output per unit of labor or capital.

- Distinguish between "sustaining (incremental) innovation" and "disrupting (radical) innovation." (Note that the needed major product, process, product-services, and system transformations may be beyond those that the dominant industries and firms are capable of developing easily, at least by themselves.)

- Address all dimensions in which innovation and change might be encouraged: technological, organizational, institutional, and social factors.

- Influence the requisites for change: *willingness, opportunity/motivation*, and *capacity/capability*.

- Integrate, rather than merely coordinate, the various efforts and initiatives wherever possible.

## 13.7 POLICIES AND APPROACHES TO PROMOTE SUSTAINABLE DEVELOPMENT

In the Overview of this work, we contrasted the current approach to national problems with a national sustainable development agenda in a matrix (see Table 0.2). We emphasized the need for nations to integrate the various elements of sustainability, rather than have government, industry, NGOs, and professionals pursue the essential goals separately. This also needs to occur in the international context.

The remainder of this section expands on these ideas and identifies a series of specific national and international governance initiatives that, if adopted, could promote tangible progress toward sustainable development. Because they have been discussed in detail throughout the prior text, they are presented here in outline form, with occasional explanatory footnotes and references to earlier material.

Before we embark on that task, a systemic problem, discussed in Chapter 1 of this work, needs to be acknowledged. Van den Bergh (2011, p. 886) observes:

> To set in motion important systemic solutions, we need to more consistently and persistently argue against a systemic piece of misinformation, namely the GDP or aggregate income indicator and the associated pre-occupation with unconditional economic or GDP growth. GDP affects decisions in many parts and at many levels of the economy and thus acts as a systemic barrier to good policies—in the realm of the environment, social security, labor markets, income inequality and poverty, and health and leisure. The undisputed priority assigned to GDP in politics is again very well illustrated by the current media attention and public debate on the financial-economic crisis and necessary

public responses. It reflects an extreme preoccupation with getting back as soon as possible on a fast GDP growth path, more so than limiting well-being impacts due to massive unemployment. We are reminded that GDP can compete for the unflattering title "largest information failure in the world." It has more impact than many economists and environmental scientists realize. If we would manage to get GDP information out of the centre of political attention we would remove an enormous hurdle to good environmental policies.

As discussed earlier in this book, economic *growth* and economic *development* are not the same. This relates directly to the two distinctive meanings of competitiveness discussed in the Overview of this work and throughout the text.

### 13.7.1 National Governance

Who is likely to win and who is likely to lose in the transformation of the industrial state toward sustainability is a question that has to be addressed, as well as the technical policy initiatives discussed throughout this work. Persons, firms, and governments who benefit from maintaining the status quo or continuing its trends can well drive us deeper into unsustainability. They create a major source of lock-in and path dependence. Further, they stand in the way of different actors who may provide better pathways. To address these concerns requires a different focus of (mostly) legal interventions than those directed toward enhancing the *capacity* to change through a deepening and integration of interventions that "open up the problem space." Policies are needed to "open up the participatory and political space." These include using the power of legal compulsion through law and legal institutions, antitrust law, the limiting of unjustified profiteering, the cessation of rewarding excessive consumption of both materials and energy, subsidizing the wrong kind of production and provision of services, countering and punishing financial corruption and fraud, and fair employment and wage policies.* Sustainable development requires stimulating revolutionary technological innovation through environmental, health, safety, economic, and labor market regulation.

---

* See Speth (2008, 2010c) for policies to foster more democratic institutions, to minimize corruption of the social contract, and to limit the influence of corporations. These policies address campaign-finance reform; changes in the laws affecting corporations, mergers, and bankruptcy; and electoral process changes, among other issues.

Greater support for these changes must also be reinforced by enabling new voices to contribute to integrated thinking and solutions.

The different determinants of willingness, opportunity, and capacity discussed earlier offer a variety of different starting points for government policies for stimulating technological and organizational innovation to achieve a more sustainable industrial system. This represents an opportunity as well as a challenge. The opportunity is that government need not depend on a few specific instruments, but may have command of a whole variety of measures. The challenge is choosing and shaping the right instrument or instruments needed to do particular jobs. There are a variety of instruments from which to choose. These include direct performance of research and development (R&D); financial support of R&D in academia and industry through grants, subsidies, and tax incentives; removing regulatory barriers to innovation; stimulating innovation by getting the prices right for natural resources including energy; using government regulation to stimulate more environmentally-sound, inherently-safer, and employment-creating innovation; procurement and investment to develop *new* markets; advancing knowledge-transfer from universities to small and medium enterprises; implementing proactive programs for the education and training of labor for a knowledge-based economy; encouraging management and labor to bargain before technological changes are planned and implemented; and, last but not least, cultural activities to enhance openness and willingness to engage in change (Ashford 2000).

Tax policy can be particularly important. Others have called for taxing the "bads" (like pollution) and not the "goods" (like employment). But even within the present system, less bold but important changes in incentives can be fashioned. For example, if more employment is desirable, financing unemployment and workers compensation from charges on employers on a per capita (worker) basis creates disincentives to hire new workers; these could be replaced by a tax on sales or profits. Similarly, providing accelerated tax depreciation for safer and less-polluting industrial processes, rather than for end-of-pipe pollution control or injury minimizing technology, would incentivize cleaner and inherently safer technology. These require changes in law and regulation. In order for law and regulation to have its necessary stimulatory effect, it must be certain enough to change medium to long-term strategic decisions for both industry and (state and local) governmental entities. Thus, the adoption of a temporary or short-term suspension of "payroll taxes" may not lead to changes in employment. Specific initiatives involving different stakeholders are discussed below.

### 13.7.1.1 Promoting More Sustainable Industrial Production and Consumption*

#### Industry Initiatives

- Use more natural capital.[†]
- Dematerialize products and processes.[‡]
- Devote more attention to remanufacturing.[6]
- Shift to cleaner and inherently safer technology, products, processes, product-services, and services.[§]
- Use less energy in production and in the provision of products and services that themselves require less energy in their operation and use.
- Shift from selling products to selling product-services wherever possible.[¶]
- Hire scientists, environmental and public health professionals, engineers, material scientists, and energy specialists to design and work together

---

\* Technological development takes its cues from the market, and both societal/consumer demand and the regulatory environment shape the signals to which technology developers respond. This suggests that policies should be focused on influencing consumers and technology providers to adopt sustainable practices, such as dematerialization and shifts from products to to product-services and beyond require technological, organizational, institutional, and social innovation to bring about the necessary physical and material changes, changes in infrastructure, and changes in social demands and to maintain flexible and learning organizations for continuous improvement. These practices need to include but go beyond traditional models of consumer behavior and sovereignty to include government intervention (see especially Schrader and Thøgersen 2011).

† This means substituting the use of manufactured materials and making products with more natural materials and renewables as inputs and final products, as well as reducing the environmental impact of product disposal and manufacturing waste. See especially Costanza and Daly (1991), Daly (1994), Ekins, Simon, et al. (2003); Hawken (1997), McDonough and Braungart (1998).

‡ Dematerialization requires that we decrease the material content of products by a factor of ten or greater; see Schmidt-Bleek (2008).

§ See Chapter 9 and Geiser and Oldenburg (1997).

¶ See Chapter 7. Also, see especially Mont and Lindqvist (2003) and Tukker and Jansen (2006). Products in three categories, "housing, transport, and food, are responsible for 70% of the environmental impacts..., although covering only 55% of the final expenditure in the 25 countries that currently make up the EU. At a more detailed level, priorities are car and most probably air travel within transport, meat and dairy within food, and building structures, heating, and (electrical) energy-using products within housing. Expenditures on clothing, communication, health care, and education are considerably less important" (Tukker and Jansen 2006, p. 159).

to devise energy-saving, cleaner, and inherently safer products, processes, product-services, and services.

- Transform, if possible, or replace incumbent industry with innovative and sustainable producers and providers of services.

The last point deserves considerable attention. Although there is much discussion about transforming the incumbent providers of products and services through consciousness-raising and the right incentives, this book has emphasized the need to ask whether these incumbents have the capacity to change. The example that comes to mind is the oil companies that have boasted that they will become energy companies, not restricted to petroleum-based activities, but nonetheless continue their mainstream activities and promote new technology for extracting oil from shale, with minimal investment in other energy sources.

Successful management of disruptive (radical) product innovation requires initiatives and input from outsiders to produce the expansion of the design space that limits the dominant technology firms.* Especially in sectors with an important public or collective involvement, such as transportation, construction, and agriculture, this means that intelligent government policies are required to bring about necessary change.

### Education and Human Resource Development

- Educate scientists, environmental and public health professionals, engineers, material scientists, and energy specialists to design and work together to devise cleaner and inherently safer products and production processes and the provision of services.

- Educate consumers and citizens to favor energy-saving, cleaner, and inherently safer products, product-services, and services and to meet their needs with nonmaterial goods and activities wherever possible.

- Educate managers, entrepreneurs, business leaders, and workers to understand the need for more sustainable practices.

- Educate children to meet their needs with nonmaterial goods and activities wherever possible, and to recognize and want sustainable products and activities.

- Educate lawyers to develop laws to guide a transition toward sustainable development.[†]

### Government Intervention[‡] and Regulation

- Provide the physical infrastructure (for example, high-speed rail, ports, and telecommunications) and legal infrastructure (patent protection, R&D tax credits) for industrial development.

- Create and disseminate knowledge and innovative technology through experimentation and demonstration projects.

- Design legislation and regulations that create producer and consumer incentives that favor innovation in products, processes, product-services, and system changes that are energy saving, environmentally sounder, inherently safer, and employment enhancing.

- Create nascent markets for new technology through government purchasing.

- Provide favorable tax treatment for investment and for human resource development and use.

- Regulate commercial advertising[§] and provide counteracting government messaging.[¶]

### Stakeholder Involvement

- Through education and communication, encourage consumers[**] and citizens to favor energy-saving, cleaner, and inherently safer products, product-services, and services and to meet their needs (for example, for leisure or recreational activities) with nonmaterial goods and activities wherever possible.

---

played, the law does not yet address "the gamut of sustainability challenges," such as those problems that stem from excessive consumption or those that encourage unsustainable economic activity. What is needed is a restructuring of the legal system to turn "economic development laws toward greener development and green jobs" (ibid.) Dernbach sees a central role for legal education to develop laws to guide the transition to sustainable development.

‡ Sometimes government itself needs to invest in pathbreaking science and technology development for health, safety, and environmental needs and for job design. Historical examples are cancer therapies developed by the National Institutes of Health, pollution-control technology developed by the EPA, and ergonomic design in ICT developed initially by the military.

§ The need to regulate direct advertising to consumers of prescription drugs has been the subject of concern for some time in the United States (Hamburg 2009). It is widely recognized that the government cannot keep up with monitoring the commercial resources dedicated to influencing consumer demand for pharmaceuticals of dubious value or that even cause harm.

¶ In the Carter administration, Michael Pertschuk at the Federal Trade Commission tried unsuccessfully to have the FTC engage in what was called "counter-advertising" (N. A. Ashford, personal knowledge).

** Three main types of consumer need to be considered: (1) the individual *consumer* who typically purchases items available in the market; (2) the *commercial* consumer that purchases products made by industry as inputs to its manufacturing processes; and (3) the *government* that purchases military hardware and materials and equipment for infrastructure and public services. There are opportunities within each of these consumer groups to promote sustainable or green purchasing practices.

---

* See Chapter 7 and especially the work of van de Poel (2003).

† Dernbach (2009a, p. 5) notes that although he acknowledges the positive role that environmental laws have

### 13.7.1.2  Improving Health, Safety, and the Environment

#### Industry Initiatives

- Hire specialists in health, safety, environmental impact and design, and energy sources and use.

- Integrate marketing, product development, production, environmental affairs, and human resource efforts by eliminating or transcending the unnecessary divisional divides in the firm.

#### Government Intervention and Regulation

- Design legislation, regulations, and tax incentives that favor products, processes, product-services, and system changes that are energy saving, environmentally sound, inherently safer, and employment enhancing.

- Remove regulations and tax treatment that create perverse incentives.

- Tax unsustainable products and processes.

- Create nascent markets for new technology through government purchasing.

- Provide favorable tax treatment for investment and for human resource development and use.

#### Stakeholder Involvement

- Promote NGO activity to press for energy-saving, environmentally sound, and inherently safer products and production.

- Devise means to motivate consumers and citizens to press for the regulatory and educational initiatives addressed in Section 13.7.1.1.

### 13.7.1.3  Enhancing Meaningful, Rewarding, and Safer Employment and Adequate Earning Capacity*

#### Industry Initiatives

- Invest in new products, processes, product-services, and services that enhance employment.†

- Seek productivity improvements by processes that increase the *productiveness* of workers.‡

- Invest in increasing the capacity of the firm's human resources rather than replace labor with capital.

- Engage in revenue-enhancing activities and commerce through innovation and performance enhancement rather than through cost-reduction strategies involving the reduction of jobs or wages.

- Pay attention to the human-technology interface, that is, optimize matching human behavior with technological artifacts.

- Foster healthy industrial relations.

- Make changes to the social and hierarchical environment in the enterprise.§

#### Education and Human Resource Development

- Rethink educational pedagogy, focusing on the acquisition of both technical skills that engender systems and critical thinking and interpersonal skills involving the ability to communicate.

- Improve the means to enhance lifelong training and learning.

#### Government Intervention and Regulation

- Reject the liberalization of labor markets.¶

---

* We have argued earlier in this book that it is not unlikely that employment, rather than energy or the environment, will be the leading political concern in the next decade, especially because the financial-system crisis has left increasing numbers of people without sufficient purchasing power to obtain the necessary goods for a healthy and secure life. If the government wants to create jobs, it must do so with deliberation while focusing on designing specific technological changes that increase the labor content of product manufacturing, shift from products to product-services, and stimulate whole system changes. New industry creation (with new jobs) displaces existing industries (with job losses) with an unjustified optimism based on a "trickle-down" logic that these changes will result in net job gains.

The studies that have been done indicate that pollution-reduction activities will create some new jobs but destroy others with little net change in employment, although the jobs may be safer and more healthful (Getzner 2002). Similarly, activities undertaken to stem global climate change do create new jobs but destroy others with a slightly positive net gain, but the effects differ from country to country (ETUC, ISTAS, et al. 2007).

† See the analysis in Chapter 8 linking different provisions of industry for products, processes and product-services with expec-

tations whether the incumbent provider or a new entrant is likely to emerge in a new market in which sustainability is important.

‡ See the previous discussion of the important difference between *productiveness* and *productivity*.

§ See Chapter 7 on organizational innovation and learning.

¶ Kleinknecht (1998) offers a powerful argument in defense of *not* reducing wages to accommodate unemployment. Drawing on evidence from European labor markets, he maintains that although advantageous in the short run, from a Schumpeterian perspective, allowing wages to fall to accommodate less innovative firms that do not use labor or capital effectively will result in less product and process innovation in the long run. Kleinknecht (1998) argues that the process of "creative destruction" advocated by Schumpeter should be allowed to occur, lest we encourage suboptimality. Essentially, this argues for forgoing immediate gains from achieving static efficiency in order to realize a better, dynamically efficient outcome. Charles and Lehner (1995) similarly argue that labor-market liberalization can remove the pressure on firms to pursue productivity growth (most important, by using labor more effectively). Kleinknecht extends the argument of maintaining high standards not only to wages but also to other labor-protection policies, and to environmental standards as well.

Kleinknecht (1998) argues that although there has been slower growth in labor productivity in the Netherlands because of slower adoption of new *process technology*, there is likely to be a greater focus on product innovation that is expected to create more jobs and jobs of better quality if wage-flexibility measures are not adopted. Furthermore, the process of innovation will stimulate more firm-specific (tacit) knowledge, which will have a cumulative, multiplier effect on future innovativeness. In Kleinknecht's view, the longer-term contribution to the economy will more than offset the disadvantages of a longer (old) product life brought about by keeping capital stock around for a longer time. Furthermore, if the winds of creative destruction are allowed to operate, they will remove less innovative firms

- Remove disincentives to hire labor.*

- Promote incentives to use labor.†

- Support research on mechanisms for job creation (including job design) that go beyond the usual fiscal and tax incentives.

- Deliberately enhance the desirable aspects of employment and job creation through labor standards and protections (for example, for health and safety), continuing education and upskilling, tax incentives to employers, and unemployment adjustment policies, including reeducation and unemployment and income guarantees.

- Expand the opportunities for capital ownership by workers and ordinary citizens.‡

### Stakeholder Involvement

- Encourage workers to press both for more stable, more meaningful, safer, and more rewarding employment and for opportunities to acquire capital ownership.

- Educate and train workers to contribute to the adoption of more sustainable practices.§

#### 13.7.1.4 The Importance of Integration in the National Context

The areas in which government programs and initiatives are typically found, especially in industrialized nations, are depicted in Figure 13.1. The idea of integrating policy measures applies not only among the sectors and activities associated with, affected by, or affecting competitiveness and employment, but also with regard to health, safety, and the environment. The wedges in the figure relate to the different areas of sustainability concern, while the concentric circles identify areas of government authority and responsibility in the U.S. context. The figure is easily adapted

to other national systems as well. There can be three different piechart diagrams for national, regional/state, and local governmental activity. The challenge of integrating programs occurs among the different *issues*, the different *kinds of authority*, and the agencies/authorities at *different levels of government*.

At best, national governments *coordinate* but rarely *integrate* their policy planning and implementing processes, although this is precisely what is needed for success. Integration is more than coordination. Ideally, it involves (1) addressing multiple goals (for example, economic development, employment, the environment, and public health) in the same piece of legislation or at least passing a group of complementary laws in parallel fashion, (2) planning regulatory and programmatic initiatives with participants from different governmental authorities, and (3) deliberate simultaneous or staged implementation and monitoring involving different governmental authorities. Ideally, integration involves the merging of ministries or at least increasing the porosity of departmental walls, but the former is likely to be more of a hope for the future than something that can be achieved in the short run.

Integration found its first serious expression as *environmental* policy integration (EPI) as a consequence of the Brundtland report that made environmental consideration a priority to be balanced along with economic and social concerns (WCED 1987). Agenda 21, which emerged from the 1992 UN Conference on Environment and Development in Rio, endorsed the integration of economic, social, and environmental issues in the pursuit of development (UN 1993, chap. 8.4). As a principle, EPI has had mixed success. The most impressive advances have been made in some countries of the European Union (EU) (Jordan and Lenschow 2010). The EU placed the environment at the center of its recent treaties advancing the union, but it was pushed back somewhat by the adoption of the Lisbon Strategy to promote sustainable economic growth (via competitiveness) and employment while respecting the environment.[7] The importance of economic concerns slowly reemerged and has now found greater favor in the fragile balance among issues, especially after the 2008 financial crisis. Jordon and Lenschow (2010, p. 151) comment that "generally speaking, new centre-left governments have tended to push the hardest for EPI, whereas centre-right governments have held back or even dismantled EPI frameworks and instruments." They observe that "unless there is a high-level commitment to deliver greater EPI or a strong inducement, for example in the form of career enhancements,

---

from the market. In contrast, lowering wages for less innovative firms will enable those firms to remain and benefit from their short-term economic advantage. Greater latitude in firing workers would give a competitive advantage primarily to non-innovators and at the same time lower the commitment of workers to the enterprise.

\* Some suggestions have been around for decades: (1) finance health care by assessing firms not on a per capita basis (number of workers) but rather as a function of sales, and (2) similar reforms of other "per capita" payroll taxes, such as unemployment compensation, that act as a disincentive to hire additional workers.

† For example, tax credits for new hires, tax credits for providing training and upskilling, and tax credits and accelerated scheduled deductions for the employment of labor to improve the firm's health, safety, and environment.

‡ See R. Ashford (2009a, 2009b) and the discussion of binary economics in Section 12.11 in Chapter 12.

§ See Kaminski, Bertelli, et al. (1996) for case studies of the contribution of unions to the environmental performance of the firm.

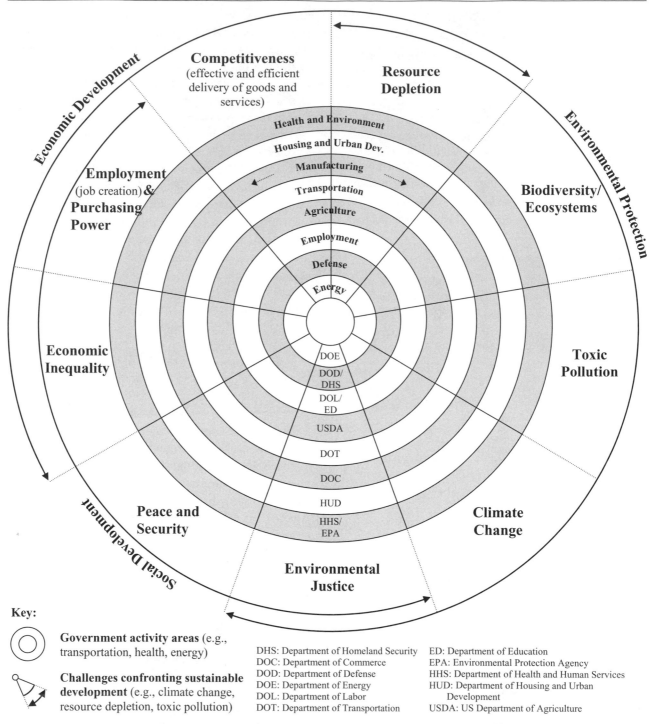

**Key:**

Government activity areas (e.g., transportation, health, energy)

Challenges confronting sustainable development (e.g., climate change, resource depletion, toxic pollution)

DHS: Department of Homeland Security
DOC: Department of Commerce
DOD: Department of Defense
DOE: Department of Energy
DOL: Department of Labor
DOT: Department of Transportation

ED: Department of Education
EPA: Environmental Protection Agency
HHS: Department of Health and Human Services
HUD: Department of Housing and Urban Development
USDA: US Department of Agriculture

**FIGURE 13.1: GOVERNMENT ACTIVITY AREAS AND CHALLENGES CONFRONTING SUSTAINABLE DEVELOPMENT**

integration simply does not happen," and that " 'learning' or a 'change of awareness' seems to take place in response to political crises (for example, accelerating climate change) rather than the combined impact of different EPA instruments" (ibid., p. 154).

In this book, we introduced the term "co-optimization," as distinguished from "balance," to describe the integration approach. Integration of goals in government (as well as private-sector) actions is indispensable for achieving major advances in sustainable development, emphasizing the view that sustainable development is a *process* rather than a particular end state. Given that the present infrastructure of government is not likely to be changed in the near to medium term, how is this integration to be accomplished?

Integration must take into account the major themes advanced in this book thus far:

1. Major technological, organizational, institutional, and social changes beyond incremental advances are necessary to achieve factor ten improvements in material and energy use; adequate reductions in exposure to toxic substances; significant opportunities for stable, rewarding, and meaningful employment with adequate purchasing power; and an adequate level and distribution of economic welfare. Such improvements require more systemic, multidimensional, and disruptive changes.

2. These changes require system changes that "open up the problem space" of the policy designer by co-optimizing advances, that is, achieving mutual gains simultaneously, in the relevant economic, environmental, and employment realms.

3. Achieving transformations to a more sustainable economic system requires stringent banking, environmental, labor-protection, and labor-market regulation, as well as the regulation of commerce, advertising, and financial transactions. Laissez-faire market approaches are inadequate.

To these should be added observations related to policy integration initiatives per se.

4. Although incremental advances are inadequate, as articulated in (1) above, major, nonincremental advances can be achieved through integration pursued deliberatively, even if piecemeal, by connecting key interventions, policies, and agency missions relevant to a specific policy domain.

For example, advancing both energy technologies and green jobs requires covisioning and implementation of industrial innovation, energy demand-side interventions, and labor-market policy integration.* Examples of policy integration in government do exist. The integration of fuel economy and emission concerns is evident in the joint efforts of the Environmental Protection Agency (EPA) and the Department of Transportation (DOT). Unfortunately, a third element of motor vehicle concern—safety—has not been optimally integrated into those efforts. In France, the French agency Afsset has merged environmental concerns with those of occupational health and safety, distinguishing itself from most countries, which separate the two concerns. In the Netherlands, there used to be one agency for environment and spatial planning; in Greece, there is a single ministry for the environment and land planning, although that ministry has been criticized for allowing land-use expansions that exacerbated the incidence of forest fires. Integration in mission titles in and of itself does not guarantee integration of all the areas in need of mutual gains.

Even in the absence of major restructuring of national governmental institutions, there are several pathways to more integrated decision making and execution of government programs:

1. The level of government at which integration is best accomplished (that is, federal/national, regional, state, urban, or local government) may depend on the specific sociotechnical goal. For example, integration of land-use planning, transportation, and housing is acknowledged to be accomplished best at the urban or local level, while integration of efforts to prevent environmental pollution and workplace exposures, and product safety might best be accomplished at the federal/national level. Integration of planning for new industry and job-creation initiatives might best be carried out at the regional level and involve state or provincial departments of commerce and labor.

2. Leadership for integration has to be emphasized at the top levels of the appropriate governmental units, and the performance of government employees has to be rewarded on the basis of multiple criteria, not only those relevant to a particular mission or agency's traditional goals.

3. The top- and midlevel managers of mission agencies, whether at the federal/national, regional, or state level, should be frequently rotated among those agencies so that fresh multifaceted expertise and interest are continually evolving. For example, the head of the federal or state departments of commerce might move to the department of labor, and then to the department of environmental protection. Slowly, this ideally will engender multidimensional thinking and planning, as well as tolerance for different missions and agencies.

4. Transdisciplinary working groups, made up of different relevant mission and agency personnel, should be constituted to work on different sociotechnical problems and should be housed together for periods of six months to two years to work together on problems involving different concerns, such as the environment, public health, and transportation.

5. Continuing education, reinforcing the related concepts relevant to interagency activities, needs to be provided to employees of different agencies in jointly held sessions and workshops.

---

* As we go to press, the latest expression of faith in a "double dividend" of environmental improvement and employment creation is found in UNEP's *Towards A Green Economy: Pathways to Sustainable Development and Poverty Eradication—A Synthesis for Policy Makers* (UNEP 2011). However, unless other deliberate structural changes are made, the economy going green presents at best a very optimistic scenario for employment enhancement.

Experiments with interagency joint action should be encouraged, and failures should be tolerated and learned from. Other initiatives should supplement the above, and a process of discovery should lead to the optimal levels and structures likely to spawn success. For all these efforts, willingness to depart from narrowly defined goals should be a starting point. The process of integration must incorporate the specific government policies discussed earlier in this section in order to achieve the desired breakthrough innovations.

Articulating policy approaches to sustainability requires more than an understanding of the *challenges* to sustainability viewed from a narrow national context. Integrated sustainability policies must use, alter, or supplant existing policies (and the institutions that administer them) in the areas of the economy, employment, the environment, *and* trade. Not only do national governments need to include trade policies in integration efforts, but, as discussed in the next section, international efforts need to integrate, for example, activities that are the traditional province of the United Nations Environment Programme and the United Nations Development Programme, the multilateral environmental secretariats, the International Labour Organization, and the World Trade Organization.

The more disparate the governmental functions, for example, economic growth, employment, and trade, the more challenging and important it is to pursue integration or suffer the consequences of unnecessary compromise.

The next section deals with governance in the international context. But because the governmental actors in international trade are nationally oriented, Figure 13.1 has omitted one additional crucial element. Policies to enhance competitiveness, the environment, and employment need to be integrated not only with one another but also with national trade policy.*

## 13.7.2 International Governance

To the four themes of this work discussed above, two more should be added:

5.  Policy integration must account for the fact that developed nations operate in a globalized market, and integration of domestic-focused policies must extend to trade policies.

For example, the U.S. promotion of hormone treatment of livestock to increase milk production and accelerate growth has run afoul of European Union trade sanctions. This has direct impacts not only on competitiveness in agricultural markets but also on trade deficits.

6.  Policy integration must occur at the international level as well.

The World Trade Organization (and other trade regimes) and the International Labour Organization address commerce and employment concerns, respectively. The multilateral environmental accords are largely neither integrated not coordinated. For example, the use of the precautionary principle differs significantly in the Sanitary and Phytosanitary Agreement and the Biosafety Protocol (see Chapter 11). It has been suggested that a world environment organization (WEO) be created to present a more uniform and coordinated environmental and public health face internationally, but this will not contribute much to integrating commerce, employment, and environmental concerns. Trade in commercial products is governed by the World Trade Organization, which depends on principles of allowable protection for environmental or public health concerns that are sometimes at variance with those in many multilateral environmental accords. Creating a world sustainability organization has been suggested in lieu of having three separate international organizations (WTO, ILO, and WEO). Whatever the eventual outcome of this proposal, national policies will need to account for the globalized nature of the major concerns. Some specific initiatives follow.

### 13.7.2.1 Promoting More Sustainable Industrial Trade

#### International Trade Regimes

*   Develop a consistent, coherent trade policy that removes the conflicts among the different trade treaties by revising the GATT, TBT, and SPS agreements.

*   Develop a more open-minded approach to respecting the right of individual nations to establish their own degree of health, safety, and environmental protection beyond minimum standards *on a precautionary basis*, reflecting their cultural preferences.

*   Recognize the importance of securing the protection of labor and human rights in all trade agreements.

*   Open up the panel process to inputs from NGOs and environmental and labor organizations.[8]

*   Consider adopting a multipartite governance structure.

*   Resolve conflicts in requirements and philosophies among MEAs, TRIPS, WTO and other trade re-

---

*        See Chapter 11 and Steininger (1994).

gimes, and national environmental and public health protection laws.

### National Governments

- Encourage national firms to trade from the "bottom of the pyramid."[9]

- Think beyond increasing revenues to the private sector, or the balance of payments, when planning trade strategies such that disadvantaged workers, citizens, and groups in need of special protection are benefited.*

### Stakeholder Participation

- Press for transparency and accountability on the part of the nation's trade representative.†

- Press for consultations of adversely affected and disadvantaged firms, workers, consumers, and citizens with the office of the trade representative.

- Press for the inclusion of both core labor standards and environmental protection in trade negotiations and agreements.

- Expand multipartite governance used in the ILO to negotiations on both multilateral environmental agreements and trade agreements.

### Financing Development and Sustainable Development

- Implement the commitment made by the richer nations at the Rio Conference to provide financial and technical assistance to the poorer nations.

- More aggressively pursue the adoption and enforcement of codes of conduct in the financing of projects in developing countries.

- Increase the transparency and accountability of the activities of export credit agencies and sovereign wealth funds.

### 13.7.2.2 Creating Incentives to Improve Health, Safety, and the Environment

#### Multilateral Environmental Agreements

- Press for the signing, ratification, implementation, and enforcement of MEAs.‡

- Open up the negotiation process to include NGOs and labor organizations.

- Either empower the UNEP as the central institution to coordinate the various MEA secretariats or create a world environment organization.[10]

### 13.7.2.3 Creating Incentives for Labor and Human Rights

- Secure the funding and aggressively pursue the nonpayment of dues by some nations to fully empower the ILO to carry out its mission.

- Begin a serious dialogue with the WTO regarding the adoption of core labor rights into the WTO agreements and machinery

- Create a multipartite governance structure in the WTO

- Advance the recognition and enforcement of human rights in international treaties/accords and relations (see the discussion in Chapters 11 and 12).

## 13.8 THE NEW ECONOMICS AND CONCLUDING COMMENTARY

### 13.8.1 The New Economics

Since the economic meltdown in 2008, economists (and others) have been trying to develop new insights into the causes of the crisis and a new theory of economics for the industrial state upon which to build future policy interventions. A variety of names are offered for the new economics: "greener growth," "selective growth," "conditioned growth," "sustainable de-growth," "post growth," and "agrowth." These are discussed in detail in the concluding section of Chapter 3 where the contributions of a number of scholars are explored.

These scholars focus on promoting environmentally and socially sustainable development through differing combinations of technological progress in dematerialization and energy-efficiency, decreased overall consumption of products and services that are environmentally destructive, reduction of the workweek, and redistribution of wealth or income through a basic income guarantee and/or the reduction of individual working time accompanied by no decrease in purchasing power, thereby retaining existing wages for current employees while adding others to the employment rolls. What they all have in common—and the way in which they differ from previous works on *environmental* sustainability—is that they deal explicitly with the immense challenge resulting from the slowdown in economic growth and the need to address the earning capacity of citizens and workers.

### 13.8.2 Monopoly Commerce, Specialization, and Vulnerability

Though not widely recognized, the possibility of monopoly or anti-trust activity was a major concern of Adam Smith. It is well understood that monopolists

---

\* Advantages to the private sector can be enjoyed at significant cost to consumers, the environment, and labor; see Chapter 5 on globalization and sustainability.

† In most countries, the trade representative is typically in the executive branch of government and often is not accountable to Congress/the Legislature and the courts.

‡ See Chapter 11 on trade regimes and sustainability.

limit the supply of a product or service in order to maximize profit by maintaining as a high a price as possible; this is often accomplished by limiting supply. Oligopolies which form cartels to fix prices, as well as quantities supplied, are of course also a concern (the economic power of domestic oil or energy companies is an example). Additional concerns have been voiced about increasing market power resulting from mergers and acquisitions. Different countries approach these issues differently (Kokkoris 2010). For example, the antitrust suit brought against Microsoft was dropped by then president George W. Bush, while the European Union successfully prosecuted Microsoft for engaging in predatory economic behavior.* Airline mergers given the "go-ahead" by the United States were stopped by the EU. When monopolistic, oligopolistic, and merger activities are treated differently by different countries, this complicates the attainment of a level playing field.

Within a given nation, concentrated economic power presents an additional problem, that of regulatory and agency capture and undue influence in the political system. Early in this text, we argued that, as a strategic and planning matter, the design space needs to be "opened up" to achieve mutually supportive social goals, co-optimizing the determinants of economic welfare, environment, consumer and public health and safety, and employment, lest one social goal be compromised by another. We also argued that the "participatory and political space" needs to be opened up to ensure that a small number of voices do not dominate (the control of the media in the hands of a small number of providers is such an example).

Limiting both the strategic space and political space leads to lock-in and path dependency. This is a major problem not only within the domestic environment, but in globalized commerce as well. The influence of international oil cartels is of course renowned, but other problems have also arisen. Interlocking directorates of corporations and international finance relationships are also legend. Most recently, China has threatened to limit to Europe and Japan the sale of "rare earths" needed for electronic components (Hook 2010; Normile 2010). China also holds an enormous amount of U.S. currency. These observations form the basis from which wars—trade or actual wars—are made. The recipient who trades

in monopoly goods becomes vulnerable to economic shocks. The provider who specializes can also be vulnerable. Forty percent of the Argentinean economy depends of genetically modified crops and agricultural products. If their safety were to become a major concern, the Argentinean economy could be wrecked. An interlocked world with global commerce has its benefits, but also has its vulnerabilities.

### 13.8.3 Concluding Commentary

The specific policies and initiatives described earlier in this chapter are all *necessary* for achieving transformations to a more sustainable industrial state. Leaving any of the major policies out of consideration could cause others to fail.† For example, shifting part of the economy from the provision of products to product-services would not succeed without significant social change influencing the desirability or acceptability of that shift. Failure to integrate initiatives in a comprehensive manner has caused many good ideas to fail to meet their potential in the past. What would translate them into necessary *and sufficient* action is that they be applied in an *integrated* fashion, such that industrial, environmental, employment, and trade policies are codesigned and coimplemented. The complexity and interrelatedness of the many forces and interests in modern society require this. A stronger government is not necessarily a bigger government. Integrating governmental functions not only connects social goals that need to be achieved in mutually supportive ways, it may also downsize the fragmented bureaucracies.

As difficult as it may be to transform industrial economies into more *environmentally* sustainable systems, the challenges facing the creation of more satisfying, rewarding, and safer jobs with improvements in purchasing power are even more daunting.‡

---

* The EU seems much more willing to pursue predatory monopoly behavior than the United States. See Kanter (2009) on action against Intel and Lohr and Kanter (2011) on action against Google.

---

† Adopting aggressive population-control or reduction policies is regarded by many as the sine qua non of policies to achieve sustainability. Although it is widely acknowledged that population growth exacerbates unsustainability, these policies have always come under criticism in democratic societies. The reduction of poverty and child/infant mortality, the emancipation of women globally, and other welfare guarantees and welfare-enhancing policies are generally more accepted in policy circles,

‡ Among sustainability commentators, it is interesting to see the increasing emphasis on the issue of jobs. For example, Speth stated in an address before the National Council for Science and the Environment that a "post-growth economy would shift resources away from consumption and into investments in long-term social and environmental needs. I put jobs and meaningful work first . . . because they are so important and unem-

Simply priming the pump to encourage economic growth is a blunt instrument for creating more employment, especially because replacing old facilities with new facilities usually results in shedding jobs, and greening the economy without attention to the redesign of jobs as well may return only a small double dividend. Therefore, many call for a reduction in hours in the standard workweek as a means for spreading out available work or even increasing the demand for work, but because workers are unlikely to be able to secure the same wages for less work, and because of the payroll tax on wages reflecting the funding of social benefits, employers, as well as current workers, are much more inclined to promote overtime than to hire new workers. Workers, on the other hand, are likely to demand higher hourly wages for a shorter workweek to maintain wage parity or seek a second job, leading to higher job turnover and net unemployment for some groups. For this reason, the French adoption of a thirty-five-hour workweek was for a while at best a temporary moderate financial success for most workers but not successful for some and it had mixed results on conditions of work and gender (Hayden 2006).* The overall level of employment was essentially unaffected (Estevão and Sá 2008). Longer-term policy, cultural, and societal changes are needed.

Developed countries (and pundits within them) are deeply divided on whether Keynesian spending to stimulate the economy in order to create jobs and lead to greater consumer purchasing is what is needed to address low economic growth and high unemployment, or whether creating more flexible work rules, allowing for wage concessions, or relaxing hiring/firing practices is needed. Germany instituted more liberal labor policies but also the "Kurzarbeit" (short work) policy by which employers were encouraged to retain workers in times of economic slowdown. When a firm needed to reduce its output, employees could either be on furlough or a shorter work schedule, with the wage shortfall made up by a government fund to which employers had contributed in better times (Kulish 2010). These employment policies supported a form of "German miracle" where an annualized growth rate of 9 percent was achieved based on 2010 second-quarter growth. This reinforces the view that direct protection of jobs, rather than indirect monetary and fiscal policies, may be a better policy direction.

Deceasing demand for the consumption of material and energy-intensive products and services may not alleviate unemployment or underemployment, but using more human rather than physical capital may yield that result. For years, capital has replaced labor in the production of goods and the provision of services. Whenever industry restructures its production systems or routinizes its provision of services through the use of menus, it seizes the opportunity to shed labor and requires less thinking (knowledge-based work) on the part of its employees. Of course, the provision of welfare for the unemployed or underemployed ultimately has to be paid from the public treasury (or the deficit has to be increased), which eventually must be supported by taxes on business, consumers, and/or workers. Reversing decades-old trends of designing labor out of production and services by redesigning the use of labor may actually be cost-effective. It will certainly use unused human capital and have social benefits as well.

Moreover, instead of a household spending its disposable income on material and energy-intensive goods and services beyond the basic necessities, it could engage persons to deliver services that employ mostly human capital, such as tutors, language teachers, music and art teachers, financial advisers, and persons engaged in providing other social services.† Also, increasing the teacher-to-student ratio in schools would be an important start.‡ The multiplier effect of employing human rather than physical or natural capital could be significant. Increasing the demand for human capital in this context would, of course, require significant medium- to long-term cul-

---

ployment is so devastating. Likely future rates of economic growth, even with further federal stimulus, are only mildly associated with declining unemployment" (Speth 2010a, p. 17).

*     Hayden (2006) provides a detailed analysis of the implementation of the shorter workweek with some wage retention that was accomplished by reducing the payroll taxes levied on employers. Thus, rather than wage parity maintained by transferring wealth from employers to workers, it was actually accomplished indirectly by transfers from the taxpayers to the workers. Even so, because of concessions in work-time flexibility of hours (including evening and weekend work) that could be demanded—on short notice—by employers of their workers in any particular week, the advantages of extra leisure time was compromised by uncertainty in time demands on workers, especially those that were lower-paid and less-skilled, as well as reductions in overtime pay.

---

†     Note that these services are above and beyond those involved in care-giving (what Dwyer 2010 calls "carework") which, while important and necessary in an aging population, will not command a high wage.

‡     Although a discussion of comprehensive educational reform is beyond the scope of this book, we regard it as essential. Basing the financing of schools on property taxes that are constrained by "proposition two-and-one-half" limitations should be eliminated in favor of federal financing of education.

tural changes,* and large corporations that have organized the current means of production driven by economies of scale and that use advertising to create artificial demand would be less likely to be interested in "selling" these services.

A comment is in order about the movement known as corporate social responsibility (CSR), involving both self-regulation and voluntary efforts on the part of business entities. Much is written about CSR, but very little is done. Firms seem to be motivated to be more environmentally responsible primarily in cases where irresponsibility adversely affects or may affect their reputation and branding. Interestingly, firms that have better industrial relations (that is, a firm's relationship with, and treatment of, its workers) also make broader commitments to environmental improvements. These go beyond reputation enhancement, giving further support for the proposition that focusing on improving the lot of people, rather than on environment pollution alone, is a long-neglected and potentially fruitful area for policy interventions. See Utting and Clapp (2010) for an especially insightful treatment of these issues.

Finally, too many critics of prior attempts to make progress toward more sustainable industrial systems may have given up too soon on the importance and potential power of government and environmental NGOs, as well as succumbing to overly romanticized expectations that cultural transformations driven by social forces and grassroots organizing† alone, without a strong government, will establish a new American narrative.[11] There are many more ways to "do things wrong" than to "do things right," but there have been plenty of successes in government, in addition to failures. It is useful to remember that since 1980, the United States has had a conservative, pro-industry government, supported by vested interests that have consistently worked against the public interest and that have made government fail through compromising Congress and/or the executive. Ours is a cumbersome political system. Actually, much social progress was made in the 1970s. President Nixon created the EPA in 1970, and under President Cart-

er's leadership, Congress passed important environmental legislation that remains the backbone of environmental and public safety protection. Had this legislation been subsequently fully implemented by successive regulations as intended, things would have been different today. The lack of political will, rather than faulty legislation or regulation, was responsible for government failure. Societal and industrial transformations are indeed needed, but establishing and enforcing clear rules of a new game through law are the key ingredients. Cultural transformations require inspirational and uncorrupted political leadership, as well as direct participation in governance by citizens. We need to ask continually what and who are standing in the way of progress toward a more sustainable future and to be prepared to challenge mainstream beliefs that limit possibilities and perpetuate the unsustainable practices and thinking of the past.

In the United States, wages and salaries make up roughly three-fourths of total family income, but that portion is even higher for the broad middle class. Policies which produce uneven and adverse impacts on various groups within a nation are not socially—or politically—sustainable, even if aggregate growth were to increase. The Economic Policy Institute produces an annual report on *The State of Working America*. Its 2009 report is a poignant reminder of the social consequences brought about by the neo-liberal policies of the Washington Consensus. The analysis by Mishel, Bernstein, et al. (2009, p. 3) reveals that:

> the most recent business cycle the 2000s—was unique: despite significant productivity growth in the overall economy, most families experienced stagnant or falling real incomes. The American workforce is working harder, smarter, and more efficiently, yet failing to share evenly in the benefits of the growth . . . It appears that the real income of a typical, middle-income family (i.e., the medium) was lower at the end of the 2000 cycle than at the beginning.

Addressing worsening mal-distributions of income, wealth, and opportunities for people in the world's nations needs to be a central focus of transformation policies.

If the authors of this work are correct in their prediction that earning capacity, purchasing power, and sustainable livelihoods of people are destined to become the major social concerns facing not only developing countries, but developed nations as well, then what are the options for addressing this concern?

---

*      Investing in better education and lifelong learning is, of course, central to cultural change and shifting demand toward the use of more human capital.

†      Ironically, leaving health-insurance reform to the states gives the insurance industry more rather than less influence. This is consistent with the conservative preference for devolving government to the states, where environmental, public health, and labor and human rights protections are generally more easily compromised.

1. Transfer wealth or income from capital owners and highly-paid workers to those under- or unemployed. *A redistribution of wealth or income.*\*

2. Engage in Keynesian spending for improving infrastructure, with government and taxpayers footing the bill. *Job creation in the face of insufficient current demand for public services, probably by deficit spending; not likely to become a successful long-term strategy.*†

3. Spread existing work out over a larger population by shortening the workweek, but without maintaining wage parity. *A redistribution of wage income from existing workers to a larger pool of potential workers, a system that involves no wealth transfer to labor as a whole.*

4. Spread out existing work over a larger population by shortening the workweek, but with the maintenance of wage parity. *More of the fruits of industrial production and services going to labor; requires a redistribution of income from either profits or the tax base.*

5. Limit the elimination of jobs, supplement most of the shortfall in paid wages from a government-administered, employer-financed fund. *Allowing a quicker recovery of fuller employment when demand—especially foreign demand—increases; used in Germany.*‡

6. Increase labor's contribution and therefore its claim on the profits from production and services by upskilling and redesigning work back into production and services. *Requires a redesign of labor's role in commercial activities that will reverse the decades-old trend in replacing labor with capital.*§

7. Meet essential human needs in a less-expensive and resource-intensive way by redesigning products, production, services, and systems. *Requires a re-conceptualized national industrial policy and restrictive trade practices.*

8. Change the nature of consumer and human-centered demand by encouraging cultural change more focused on using disposable income on services with significantly less capital and energy intensiveness and much more labor-intensiveness. *Requires a shift of demand from "stuff" to human services.*

9. Better enable poor and middle-class people to become owners. *By extending to them effective market opportunities to acquire capital with the earnings of capital, based on binary economics.*

The 2008 financial crisis, of course, has exacerbated income inequality (Eichhorst, Escudero et al. 2010). However, looking at the G20 countries, labor-market institutions (employment protection legislation, unemployment benefits, and active labor market/job creation programs) which provided strong internal flexibility in combination with relatively strict employment protection (like Germany) were able to stabilize employment, however, with the marginal workforce bearing the brunt of the crisis.

Deliberating focusing on these options, rather than on returning to a growth-based, export-led economy as we knew it, allows for creative experimentation with what is likely to become the major social concern of government, without benefiting profit-oriented, capital acquisition by the usual cast of economic actors. Such an outcome causes redistributions that exacerbate the disparity among economic winners and losers, with many people ending up as the losers. Some of these options have the potential to limit wasteful growth (6, 8) and limit underutilized human capital (4, 5, 7, 8). Some options (1, 2, 3, 4, 5, 6, 9) require other complementary policies to limit wasteful consumption as well.

The extent of unionization can be an important factor in reducing income inequality. In a detailed study of fifty Advanced, Asian, Central and Eastern

---

\* For a discussion of the redistribution of income through taxes, social transfers (social insurance, pensions, and unemployment insurance), and social expenditures (education, health, water, and other social services), see Prasad (2008). Looking over the previous fifteen years in a large number of both developed and developing countries, Prasad (2008) found that the redistributive impact of taxes and social transfers, which have become increasingly regressive over time, have thus not been able to reverse income inequality. On the other hand, as experience in Mauritius, Malaysia, Nordic countries, and for low-income people in Brazil has shown, social policy can be used more aggressively without adversely affecting growth or employment objectives. Both tax and social policy are needed to support employment objectives specifically.

† For details of options for fiscal interventions to increase economic growth and employment assembled by the U.S. Congressional Budget Office, see CBO (2010). Also see the footnote above.

‡ See Eichhorst (2010, pp. 27–29) for a detailed explanation of stable employment in Germany, even in the face of decreasing export activity.

§ Knowledge applied in an iterative way (knowledge injected periodically or continuously over time) can have a cumulative effect, with new knowledge building on past knowledge acquisition and investment. This is akin to adding financial flows to previous investments that have accumulated and appreciated

in value and is unlike investments in physical capital that depreciates in value over time because its functionality decreases due to regular utilization. Knowledge capital, even if it sometimes becomes less valuable over time, may nonetheless grow (accumulate) from using it and adding to it over time (Foray 2004). This observation has direct relevance for the choices that are made as to which factor endowments to invest in in producing a product or providing a service. Hardware deteriorates, but knowledge held by a skilled person who continues to learn can appreciate in value for many years. This calls into question the replacement of labor by physical capital as a growth strategy.

European, and Latin American countries over the period 1989–2005, Baccaro (2008) found that countries with a higher proportion of wage and salaried workers organized by trade unions and a more centralized or coordinated collective bargaining structures have produced societies which on the average are more equal (with lower income disparities) than others.* But since the 1990s this has been less the case. Much of the current increase in inequality he attributes to a mismatch between the demand and supply of skills.

As a final comment, we need to acknowledge that this book has drawn heavily on English-language writing from both America and Europe, and although the book has been largely North-centric, we see six geopolitical areas where different approaches may prevail: North America, Europe, the Middle East, Asia and the South Pacific, South America, and Africa. The United States appears to be temporarily paralyzed in addressing the critical problems ahead. Among the Northern economies, Europe may have the best chance of achieving a more sustainable agenda both because the influence of vested financial and political interests is less and because sustainability appears to be more consonant with European values of equity and social concerns. Germany, Norway, and the Netherlands certainly have successful policies that deserve careful evaluation. Other, less developed regions will be continually challenged, especially if they emulate the Northern model of development.

## 13.9 NOTES

1. See, for example, Beddoe, Costanza, et al. (2009).
2. See J. Dernbach (2009b) and Jänicke (2008).
3. See Sanders (2006) and Speth (2003, 2008).
4. See "Chapter 7: Human Resources and New Technologies in the Production System" in OECD (1992, pp. 149–166). See also OECD (1996).
5. See Butter (2002) and Butter and Montalvo (2004).
6. See Pigosso, Zanette, et al. (2010).
7. See the European Union's Lisbon Strategy, http://ec.europa.eu/archives/growthandjobs_2009/ (accessed June 17, 2010).
8. See Baker (2002).
9. See Hart and Milstein (1999), London and Hart (2004), and Prahalad and Hart (2002).
10. See Charnovitz (2002).
11. See, for example, Raskin, Banuri, et al. (2002).

## 13.10 REFERENCES

Adger, W. N., and A. Jordan, Eds. (2009). *Governing Sustainability*. Cambridge, Cambridge University Press.

Andreasen, L. E., B. Coriat, et al., Eds. (1995). *Europe's Next Step: Organisational Innovation, Competition and Employment*. London, Frank Cass and Co.

Ashford, N. A. (2000). An Innovation-Based Strategy for a Sustainable Environment. *Innovation-Oriented Environmental Regulation: Theoretical Approach and Empirical Analysis*. J. Hemmelskamp, K. Rennings, and F. Leone. New York, Physica-Verlag Heidelberg: 67–107.

Ashford, N. A. (2004). "Major Challenges to Engineering Education for Sustainable Development: What Has to Change to Make It Creative, Effective, and Acceptable to the Established Disciplines?" *International Journal of Sustainability in Higher Education* **5**(3): 239–250.

Ashford, N. A., and C. Ayers (1987). "Changes and Opportunities in the Environment for Technology Bargaining." *Notre Dame Law Review* **62**: 810–858.

Ashford, N. A., and C. C. Caldart (1996). *Technology, Law, and the Working Environment*. Washington, DC, Island Press.

Ashford, N. A., and C. C. Caldart (2005). Negotiated Regulation, Implementation and Compliance in the United States. *The Handbook of Environmental Voluntary Agreements*. E. Croci (Ed.). Dordrecht, Springer, Environmental and Policy Series, vol. 43: 135–159.

Ashford, N. A. and R. P. Hall (2011). "The Importance of Regulation-Induced Innovation for Sustainable Development." *Sustainability* **3**(1): 270–292. Available at www.mdpi.com/2071-1050/3/1/270/pdf (accessed January 20, 2011).

Ashford, N. A., and C. S. Miller (1998). *Chemical Exposures: Low Levels and High Stakes*. New York, Van Nostrand Reinhold.

Ashford, R. (2009a). "Broadening the Right to Acquire Capital with the Earnings of Capital: The Missing Link to Sustainable Economic Recovery and Growth." *Forum for Social Economics* **39**: 89–100. Available at www.springerlink.com/content/k947658040lg2n88/ (accessed January 20, 2011).

Ashford, R. (2009b). Eliminating the Underlying Cause of Poverty as a Means to Global Economic Recovery. Available at http://papers.ssrn.com/sol3/papers.cfm?abstract_id=1583653 (accessed February 12, 2011).

Ashford, R. (2010). Personal communication.

Ayres, R., and B. Warr (2009). *The Economic Growth Engine: How Energy and Work Drive Material Prosperity*. Williston, VT, Edward Elgar.

Baccaro, L. (2008). Labour, Globalization, and Inequality: Are Trade Unions Still Redistributive? Geneva, International Institute for Labour Studies, International Labour Organisation. Available at www.ilo.org/public/english/bureau/inst/publications/discussion/dp19208.pdf (accessed January 7, 2011).

Baker, J. (2002). "Trade Unions and Sustainable Development." *UNEP, Industry and Environment* (April–June): 28–31.

Baldwin, R. (1989). "On the Growth Effects of 1992." *Economic Policy* **9**: 247–282.

Beddoe, R., R. Costanza, et al. (2009). "Overcoming Systemic Roadblocks to Sustainability: The Evolutionary Design of Worldviews, Institutions, and Technologies." *Proceedings of the National Academy of Sciences* **106**(8): 2483–2489.

---

* See Section 1.1.3.1 in Chapter 1 for a review of inequality as expressed in wage and income disparities.

Brouwer, E., and A. Kleinknecht (1996). "Firm Size, Small Business Presence and Sales of Innovative Products: A Micro-econometric Analysis." *Small Business Economics* **8**(3): 189–201.

Brown, K. (2009). Human Development and Environmental Governance: A Reality Check. *Governing Sustainability*. W. N. Adger and A. Jordan. Cambridge, Cambridge University Press: 32–52.

Butter, M. (2002). A Three Layer Policy Approach for System Innovations. Paper presented at the 1st Blueprint Workshop, Environmental Innovation Systems, Brussels, January.

Butter, M., and C. Montalvo (2004). Finding Niches in Green Innovation Policy. Berlin Conference on the Human Dimensions of Global Climate Change, Greening of Policies—Interlinkages and Policy Integration, Berlin, December 3–5.

Charles, T., and F. Lehner (1998). "Competitiveness and Employment: A Strategic Dilemma for Economic Policy." *Competition and Change* **3**(1/2): 207–236.

Charnovitz, S. (2002). "A World Environment Organization." *Columbia Journal of Environmental Law* **27**(2): 323–362.

Christensen, C. M. (1997). *The Innovator's Dilemma: When New Technologies Cause Great Firms to Fail*. Cambridge, MA, Harvard Business School Press.

Cleff, T., and K. Rennings (1999). "Determinants of Environmental Product and Process Innovation." *European Environment* **9**: 191–201.

Cohen, M., H. Brown, and P. Vergragt (2010). "Individual Consumption and System Societal Transformation: Introduction to the Special Issue." *Sustainability: Science, Practice, & Policy* **6**(2): 6–12. Available at http://sspp .proquest.com (accessed March 2, 2011).

Colborn, T., D. Dumanowski, et al. (1996). *Our Stolen Future: Are We Threatening Our Own Fertility, Intelligence, and Survival? A Scientific Detective Story*. New York, Dutton Press.

Congressional Budget Office (CBO) (2010). Policies for Increasing Economic Growth and Employment in 2010 and 2011, January. Available at www.cbo.gov/ftpdocs/ 108xx/doc10803/01-14-Employment.pdf (accessed December 18, 2011). See also, CBO, Policies for Increasing Economic Growth and Employment in the Short Term, Statement of Douglas W. Elmendorf, Director, CBO, February 23. Available at www.cbo.gov/ftpdocs/112xx/ doc11255/02-23-Employment_Testimony.pdf (accessed December 18, 2011).

Coriat, B. (1995). Organisational Innovations: The Missing Link in European Competitiveness. *Europe's Next Step: Organisational Innovation, Competition and Employment*. L. E. Andreasen, B. Coriat, F. de Hertog, and R. Kaplinsky. London, Frank Cass and Co.: 3–32.

Costanza, R., and H. Daly (1991). Goals, Agenda, and Policy Recommendations for Ecological Economics. *Ecological Economics*. R. Costanza. New York, Columbia University Press: 1–20.

Daly, H. E. (1994). "Fostering Environmentally Sustainable Development: Four Parting Suggestions for the World Bank." *Ecological Economics* **10**: 183–187.

Dernbach, J. (2008). "Navigating the U.S. Transition to Sustainability: Matching National Governance Chal-

lenges with Appropriate Legal Tools." *Tulsa Law Review* **44**: 93–120.

Dernbach, J. (2009a). The Essential and Growing Role of Legal Education in Achieving Sustainability. Widener Law School Legal Studies Research Paper Series 09–20. Available at http://ssrn.com/abstract=1471344 (accessed February 12, 2011).

Dernbach, J., Ed. (2009b). *Agenda for a Sustainable America*. Washington, DC, Environmental Law Institute.

Dwyer, Rachel E. (2010) "The Care Economy? Job Polarization and Job Growth in the U.S. Labor Market." Paper presented at MIT, November 9.

Easterly, W. R., and D. L. Wetzel (1989). Policy Determinants of Growth. World Bank Working Papers, WPS 343, December.

Edquist, C., L. Hommen, et al. (2001). *Innovation and Employment: Process versus Product Innovation*. Cheltenham, Edward Elgar.

Ehrenberg, D. S. (2003). From Intention to Action: An ILO-GATT/WTO Enforcement Regime for International Labor Rights. *Human Rights, Labor Rights, and International Trade*. L. A. Compa and S. F. Diamond. Philadelphia, University of Pennsylvania Press: 163–180.

Ehrlich, P. R., G. C. Daily, et al. (1997). "No Middle Way on the Environment." *Atlantic Monthly* **280**(6): 98–104.

Eichhorst, W., V. Escudero, et al. (2010). The Impact of the Crisis on Employment and the Role of the Labour Market Institutions. Geneva, International Institute for Labour Studies, International Labour Organisation. Available at www.ilo.org/public/english/bureau/ inst/download/dp202_2010.pdf (accessed January 7, 2011).

Ekins, P., S. Simon, et al. (2003). "A Framework for the Practical Application of the Concepts of Critical Natural Capital and Strong Sustainability." *Ecological Economics* **44**(2–3): 165–185.

Epstein, S. S., N. A. Ashford, et al. (2002), "The Crisis in U.S. and International Cancer Policy." *International Journal of Health Services* **32**(4): 669–707.

Estevão, M., and F. Sá (2008). "The 35-Hour Week." *Economic Policy* **23**(55): 417–463.

European Commission (EC) (1994). *Growth, Competitiveness, Employment: The Challenges and Ways Forward into the 21st Century*. Brussels, European Commission.

European Trade Union Confederation (ETUC), Instituto Sindical de Trabajo, Ambiente y Salud (ISTAS), et al. (2007). *Climate Change and Employment: Impact on Employment in the European Union-25 of Climate Change and $CO_2$ Emission Reduction Measures by 2030*. Belgium, ETUC.

Foray, D. (2006). *The Economics of Knowledge*. Cambridge, MA, MIT Press.

Freeman, C. (1992). *The Economics of Hope*. London, Pinter.

Geiser, K., and K. Oldenburg (1997). "Pollution Prevention and . . . or Industrial Ecology?" *Journal of Cleaner Production* **5**(2): 103–108.

Getzner, M. (2002). "The Quantitative and Qualitative Impacts of Clean Technologies on Employment." *Journal of Cleaner Production* **10**(4): 305–319.

Gilpin, R. (2000). *The Challenge of Global Capitalism: The World Economy in the 21st Century.* Princeton, NJ, Princeton University Press.

Grossman, G. M., and E. Helpman (1994). "Endogenous Innovation in the Theory of Growth." *Journal of Economic Perspectives* **8**(1): 23–44.

Hamburg, M. (2009). Changing the Future of Drug Safety: FDA Initiatives to Strengthen and Transform the Drug Safety System. Washington, DC, Food and Drug Administration. Available at http://fda.gov/downloads/Safety/SafetyofSpecificProducts/UCM184046.pdf (accessed February 12, 2011).

Hammond, A. L. (1997). "Responses to Mark Sagoff." *Atlantic Monthly*, Letters, **280**(3): 4–5. Available at www.theatlantic.com/past/docs/issues/97sep/9709lett.htm#Consume (accessed February 12, 2011).

Hart, S., and M. B. Milstein (1999). "Global Sustainability and the Creative Destruction of Industries." *Sloan Management Review* **41**(1): 23–33.

Hawken, P. (1997). "Natural Capitalism." *Mother Jones* (March/April): 40–54.

Hayden, A. (2006). "France's 35-Hour Week: Attack on Business? Win-Win Reform? Or Betrayal of Disadvantaged Workers?" *Politics & Society* **34**: 503–542.

Hook, L. (2010). "China to Cut Exports of Rare Earth Minerals." *Financial Times,* December 28.

Hopkins, M. S. (2009). "The Loop You Can't Get Out Of: An Interview with Jay Forrester." *Sloan Management Review* **50**(2): 9–12. Available at http://sloanreview.mit.edu/the-magazine/files/saleable-pdfs/50201.pdf (accessed February 10, 2011).

Irwin, A., S. Georg, et al. (1995). The Social Management of Environmental Change. Manuscript.

Jänicke, M. (2008). "Ecological Modernisation: New Perspectives." *Journal of Cleaner Production* **16**: 557–565.

Jansen, L. (2003). "The Challenge of Sustainable Development." *Journal of Cleaner Production* **11**: 231–245.

Jordan, A., and A. Lenschow (2010). "Environmental Policy Integration: A State of Art Review." *Environmental Policy and Governance* **20**(3): 147–158.

Jürgens, U. (1995). Lean Production in Japan: Myth and Reality. *The New Division of Labour: Emerging Forms of Work Organisation in International Perspective.* W. Littek and T. Charles. New York, Walter de Gruyter: 349–366.

Kaminski, M., D. Bertelli, et al. (1996). *Making Change Happen: Six Cases of Companies and Unions Transforming Their Workplaces.* Washington, DC, Work and Technology Institute.

Kaplinsky, R. (2005). *Globalization, Poverty, and Inequality: Between a Rock and a Hard Place.* Cambridge, Polity Press.

Kemp, R., D. Loorbach, et al. (2007). "Transition Management as a Model for Managing Processes of Co-evolution towards Sustainable Development." *International Journal of Sustainable Development and World Ecology* **14**: 1–15.

Kanter, J. (2011). "Google Faces New Antitrust Charges in Europe" *New York Times,* February 22. Available at www.nytimes.com/2011/02/23/technology/23google

.html?sq=Google&st=nyt&scp=1&pagewanted=print (accessed March 1, 2011).

Kleiner, A. (2009). "Jay Forrester's Shock to the System." *Sloan Management Review*, February 4. Available at http://sloanreview.mit.edu/beyond-green/jay-forrester-shock-to-the-system/ (accessed February 11, 2011).

Kleinknecht, A. (1998). "Commentary: Is Labour Market Flexibility Harmful to Innovation?" *Cambridge Journal of Economics* **22**: 387–396.

Koch, L., and N. A. Ashford (2006). "Rethinking the Role of Information in Chemicals Policy: Implications for TSCA and REACH." *Journal of Cleaner Production* **14**(1): 31–46.

Kokkoris, I. (2010). Merger Control in Europe: The Gap in the ECMR and National Merger Legislation. London, Tayor And Francis Group.

Kulish, N. (2010). "Defying Others, Germany Finds Economic Success." *New York Times*, August 13.

Lohr, S. and J. Kanter (2009). "A.M.D.-Intel Settlement Won't End Their Woes." *New York Times,* November 13. Available at www.nytimes.com/2009/11/13/technology/companies/13chip.html?sq=Intel&st=nyt&scp=2&pagewanted=print (accessed March 1, 2011).

London, T., and S. L. Hart (2004). "Reinventing Strategies for Emerging Markets: Beyond the Transnational Model." *Journal of International Business Studies* **35**: 350–370.

Lucas, R. E. (1988). "On the Mechanics of Economic Development." *Journal of Monetary Economics* **22**(2): 3-42.

Martinez-Alier, J., U. Pascual, et al. (2010). "Sustainable De-growth: Mapping the Context, Criticisms, and Future Prospects of an Emergent Paradigm." *Ecological Economics* **69**: 1741–1747.

Matzner, E., R. Schettkat, et al. (1990). "Labor Market Effect of New Technology." *Futures* **22**(7): 687–709.

Mayer, J. (2010). "Reporter at Large: Covert Operations; Billionaire Brothers Who Are Waging a War against Obama." *New Yorker*, August 30. Available at www.newyorker.com/reporting/2010/08/30/100830fa_fact_mayer (accessed February 11, 2011).

McDonough, W., and M. Braungart (1998). "The NEXT Industrial Revolution." *Atlantic Monthly* **282**(4): 82–92.

Mishel, L., J. Bernstein, et al. (2009). *The State of Working America 2008/2009.* Economic Policy Institute. Ithaca, NY, Cornell University Press.

Mont, O., and T. Lindqvist (2003). "The Role of Public Policy in Advancement of Product Service Systems." *Journal of Cleaner Production* **11**: 905–914.

Normille, D. (2010). "Haunted by 'Specter of Unavailability,' Experts Huddle over Critical Materials." *Science* **330**(6011): 1598.

Organisation for Economic Co-operation and Development (OECD) (1992). *Technology and Economy: The Key Relationships.* Paris, OECD.

OECD (1996). *The Knowledge-Based Economy.* Paris, OECD.

Pigosso, D. C. A., E. T. Zanette, et al. (2010). "Ecodesign Methods Focused on Remanufacturing." *Journal of Cleaner Production* **18**(1): 21–31.

Pimentel, D., S. Cooperstein, et al. (2007). "Ecology of Increasing Diseases: Population Growth and Environmental Degradation." *Human Ecology* **35**: 653–668.

Prahalad, C. K., and S. L. Hart (2002). "The Fortune at the Bottom of the Pyramid." *Strategy+Business* (26): 2–14.

Prasad, N. (2008). Policies for Redistribution: The Uses of Taxes and Social Transfers. Geneva, International Institute for Labour Studies, International Labour Organisation. Available at www.ilo.org/public/english/bureau/inst/publications/discussion/dp19408.pdf.

Raskin, P., T. Banuri, et al. (2002). *Great Transition: The Promise and Lure of the Times Ahead.* Boston, Stockholm Environment Institute.

Reich, R. B. (1992). *The Work of Nations: Preparing Ourselves for 21st-Century Capitalism.* New York, Vintage Books.

Rifkin, J. (2004). *The European Dream: How Europe's Vision of the Future Is Quietly Eclipsing the American Dream.* New York, Tarcher/Penguin.

Rodrik, D. (2007). *One Economics, Many Recipes: Globalization, Institutions, and Economic Growth.* Princeton, NJ, Princeton University Press.

Romer, P. (1987). *Crazy Explanations for the Productivity Slowdown.* Washington, DC, Macroeconomics Annual, National Bureau of Economic Research 2: 163–210.

Romer, P. (1989). What Determines the Rate of Growth and Technological Change? World Bank Working Papers, WPS 279, September.

Romer, P. (1994). "The Origins of Endogenous Growth." *Journal of Economic Perspectives* **8**(1): 3–22.

Sagoff, M. (1997). "Do We Consume Too Much?" *Atlantic Monthly* **279**(6): 80–96.

Sanders, R. (2006). "Sustainability: Implications for Growth, Employment, and Consumption." *International Journal of Environment, Workplace, and Employment* **2**(4): 385–401.

Sasco, A. J. (2008). "Cancer and Globalization." *Biomedicine and Pharmacotherapy* **62**(2): 110–121.

Schmidt-Bleek, F. (1998). Das MIPS-Koncept. Munich, Droemer-Knaur-Verlag. See also The International Factor 10 Club (1997), Statement to Government and Business Leaders: The Carnoules Statement 1997, Wuppertal, Germany Wuppertal Institute.

Schrader, U. and J. Thøgersen (2011). *Journal of Consumer Policy* **34**(1): 3–8.

Sclove, R. E. (1995). *Democracy and Technology.* New York, Guilford Press.

Scott, J. (1989). *A New View of Economic Growth.* Oxford, Clarendon Press.

Sheffi, Y. (2007). *The Resilient Enterprise.* Cambridge, MA, MIT Press.

Speth, J. G. (2003). Two Perspectives on Globalization and the Environment. *Worlds Apart: Globalization and the Environment.* J. G. Speth. Washington, DC, Island Press: 1–18.

Speth, J. G. (2008). *The Bridge at the Edge of the World: Capitalism, the Environment, and Crossing from Crisis to Sustainability.* New Haven, CT, Yale University Press.

Speth, J. G. (2010a). A New Environmentalism and the New Economy. 10th Annual John H. Chafee Memorial Lecture, National Council for Science and the Environment, Washington, DC, January 21.

Speth, J. G. (2010b). "Towards a New Economy and a New Politics." Issue Paper 8. BC Institute of Social Ecology. Available at www.bcise.com/CurrentIssuePapers/IssuePaper8.pdf (accessed February 10, 2011).

Speth, J. G. (2010c). Letter to Liberals: Liberalism, Environemntalism, and Economic Growth. 13th Annual E. F. Schumacher Lecures, New York City, November 20.

Steininger, K. (1994). "Reconciling Trade and Environment: Towards a Comparative Advantage for Long-Term Policy Goals." *Ecological Economics* **9**(1): 23–42.

Thøgersen, J. and U. Schrader (2011). *Journal of Consumer Policy* **34**(1): 1–196. Available at www.springerlink.com/content/x81569w730v3/ (accessed March 2, 2011).

Todaro, M. P., and S. C. Smith (2009). *Economic Development.* 10th ed. Boston, Addison-Wesley.

Tonelson, A. and K. I. Kearnes (2010). Trading Away Productivity. *New York Times,* OpEd, March 6.

Tukker, A., and B. Jansen (2006). "Environmental Impact of Products: A Detailed Review of Studies." *Journal of Industrial Ecology* **10**(3): 159–170.

United Nations (UN) (1993). Earth Summit: Agenda 21. New York. Available at www.unep.org/Documents.Multilingual/Default.asp?DocumentID=52 (accessed February 12, 2011).

United Nations Envrionmental Programme (UNEP) (2011). Towards a Green Economy: Pathways to Sustainable Development and Poverty Eradication—A Synthesis for Policy Makers. Available at www.unep.org/greenconomy (accessed March 2, 2011).

Utting, P., and J. Clapp, Eds. (2010). *Corporate Accountability and Sustainable Development.* New Delhi, Oxford University Press.

van den Bergh, J. C. J. M. (2011). "Environment versus Growth: A Criticism of 'Degrowth' and a Plea for 'A-growth'." *Ecological Economics* **70**(5): 881–890.

van de Poel, I. R. (2003). "The Transformation of Technological Regimes." *Research Policy* **32**: 49–68.

Vergragt, P. J., and G. van Grootveld (1994). "Sustainable Technology Development in the Netherlands: The First Phase of the Dutch STD Programme." *Journal of Cleaner Production* **2**(3–4): 133–139.

World Commission on Environment and Development (WCED) (1987). *Our Common Future.* Oxford, Oxford University Press.

Yach, D., and D. Bettcher (1998a). "The Globalization of Public Health, I: Threats and Opportunities." *American Journal of Public Health* **88**(5): 735–738.

Yach, D., and D. Bettcher (1998b). "The Globalization of Public Health, II: The Convergence of Self-Interest and Altruism." *American Journal of Public Health* **88**(5): 738–741.

# Index

*Boxes, figures, notes, and tables are indicated by b, f, n, and t following the page number.*